Conservative Leadership Series

 Conservative Leadership Series

MW00438334

servative ership es

 Conservative Leadership Series

 Conservative Leadership Series

 Conservative Leadership Series

 Conservative Leadership Series

 Conservative Leadership Series

 Conservative Leadership Series

 Conservative Leadership Series

 Conservative Leadership Series

 Conservative Leadership Series

 Conservative Leadership Series

 Conservative Leadership Series

 Conservative Leadership Series

 Conservative Leadership Series

 Conservative Leadership Series

 Conservative Leadership Series

 Conservative Leadership Series

 Conservative Leadership Series

 Conservative Leadership Series

 Conservative Leadership Series

 Conservative Leadership Series

 Conservative Leadership Series

THE POLITICAL WRITINGS OF
JAMES MONROE

CONSERVATIVE LEADERSHIP SERIES

EAGLE PUBLISHING, INC.

Thomas L. Phillips, Chairman
Jeffery J. Carneal, President

J. Brinley Lewis, Vice President
Peter DeAngelo, Vice President
Marjory G. Ross, Vice President

Don Poudrier, Director of Operations
Fred Gearhart, Production Manager

EAGLE BOOK CLUBS, INC.

J. Brinley Lewis, General Manager

CONSERVATIVE BOOK CLUB

Jeffrey Rubin, Editor
Clay Rossi, Managing Editor
Frederick A. Ulrich, Marketing Manager
John Evans, Business Manager

REGNERY PUBLISHING, INC.

Alfred S. Regnery, President
Marjory G. Ross, Group Publisher
Harry W. Crocker III, Executive Editor

The Conservative Leadership Series is a joint project of Regnery Publishing, Inc. and Eagle Book Clubs, Inc., divisions of Eagle Publishing, Inc., to make the classics of conservative thought available in hardcover collectors' editions.

The Political Writings of James Monroe

edited with an introduction and
headnotes by
James P. Lucier

Since 1947
REGNERY
PUBLISHING, INC.
An Eagle Publishing Company • Washington, DC

ISBN 0-89526-229-0

Published in the United States by
Regnery Publishing, Inc.
An Eagle Publishing Company
One Massachusetts Avenue, NW
Washington, DC 20001

Distributed to the trade by
National Book Network
4720-A Boston Way
Lanham, MD 20706

Printed on acid-free paper
Manufactured in the United States of America

10 9 8 7 6 5 4 3 2 1

Books are available in quantity for promotional or premium use. Write to Director of Special Sales, Regnery Publishing, Inc., One Massachusetts Avenue, NW, Washington, DC 20001, for information on discounts and terms or call (202) 216-0600.

DEDICATION

To Mary Grace Lucier
Uxori carissimae et sapientissimae

Acknowledgments

In Gratitude

In the course of preparing a work such as this, every editor or author incurs a number of debts of gratitude. Such debts are owed to the following: To the James Monroe Memorial Foundation for conferring upon me the honor and opportunity to be Senior Fellow of the Foundation, and especially to the Hon. Helen Marie Taylor, President Emeritus, and G. William Thomas, President, and the members of the Board of Trustees. To the Board of Regents of the James Monroe Memorial Law Office and Library, and its Director, Mr. John Pearce. A special note of thanks is due to the distinguished constitutional scholar, Dr. James McClellan for his copious advice, and the extended loan of his rare set of the Hamilton edition of Monroe's *Writings*.

To Christopher B. Briggs, the overly patient editor of the Conservative Leadership Series for Regnery Publishing, Inc.

To Senator Claiborne Pell, former Chairman of the U.S. Senate Committee on Foreign Relations and Chairman of the Joint Committee on the Library, and to Dr. James H. Billington, the Librarian of Congress, for providing study facilities at the Library; to Dr. Daniel J. Boorstin, Emeritus Librarian of Congress, who occupied the office next to mine and offered unfailing encouragement; and to Dr. Gerard H. Gawalt, specialist in American history for the Library's Manuscript Division. To Dr. Conley Edwards, State Archivist of the Library of Virginia, and to Mr. G. William Thomas, President of the Friends of the Archives of the Library of Virginia; to Ms. Frances Pollard, Assistant Director for Library Services of the Virginia Historical Society; to Ms. Jane Sullivan, Library Manager of the Thomas Balch Library of History and Genealogy in Leesburg, Virginia, and to Mary Fishback of the Balch staff.

And most especially to my wife, Mary Grace Lucier, whose wisdom and sense of scholarship and editorial responsibility constantly reorganized muddled confusion and pruned literary excess, and whose dining room table, too long set inelegantly with Monroe files, has at last been returned to its original prandial disposition.

CONTENTS

III *Ambassador to a Revolution*
INTRODUCTION   **99**

VII *Secretary of State and Secretary of War*
   INTRODUCTION **417**

VIII *President of the United States*

INTRODUCTION

JAMES MONROE AND THE

PRINCIPLES OF 1823

T HE DATE IS June 28, 1778, and the scene is a field near Monmouth, New
Jersey.

"Sir," the twenty-year-old captain wrote to General Washington, "Upon
not receiving any answer to my first information and observing the enemy
inclining toward your right I thought it advisable to hang as close on them as
possible—I am at present within four hundred yrds. of their right—I have only
about 70 men who are now fatigued much. I have taken three prisoners—If I
had six horsemen I think if I co'd serve you in no other way I sho'd in the
course of the night procure good intelligence w'h I wo'd as soon as possible
convey you.

"I am your most ob't Serv't, James Monroe."

Now that kind of letter, scribbled in haste to his commander-in-chief, at
4:00 PM on the field at Monmouth bespeaks the practical but noble character of Monroe, who thirty-nine years later would be the fifth president of
the United States. For now he says that his men are fatigued, but he doesn't
mention anything about himself. He is only 400 yards from the enemy, and
it is his intent to hang on them as close as possible, not only now, but on
through the night. Despite danger, despite weariness, he is going to put himself totally at the service of the General because he is ready to serve whatever
the cost.

That is the kind of letter Monroe was to write day after day, month after
month throughout his life: Always on the scene of the action, always putting
his life and property on the line, always writing in the heat of battle, plunging
into treacherous diplomatic maneuvers, or fighting against dubious political
opponents for the fundamental principles of liberty and his country. Whenever
change was happening, he was in the midst of the revolution. Few leaders of
his time, or even subsequent to his time, appeared in so many theaters of action

or participated in such a variety of world-changing events. For Monroe, the devolopment of liberty was a world-wide event, and he was at every scene writing perceptive accounts of what he saw, or arguing closely defined points of history or law. Does anyone today have correspondents on the level of George Washington, John Adams, Thomas Jefferson, James Madison, John Quincy Adams, John Taylor of Caroline, Patrick Henry, Edmund Randolph, George Clinton, Thomas Paine, the Marquis de Lafayette, Andrew Jackson, and John C. Calhoun, just to name a few? And his letters are equal to the caliber of those who are addressed—letters full of substance, clear intelligence, and economical prose.

Among the writings in the present volume may be found:

- Monroe's letter to Jefferson of November 1, 1784, detailing his journey to Niagara Falls, his narrow escape from an Indian massacre, and his detailed observations of the St. Lawrence River (p. 38).

- Monroe's letter of July 12, 1788 to Jefferson giving his first-person account of the historic Virginia Convention of 1788, which provided the key ratifying vote for the U.S. Constitution (p. 50).

- Monroe's letter of August 15, 1794 as Minister to Paris giving a direct account of the fall of Robespierre, written only days after the event (p. 114).

- Monroe's journals of April-May, 1803 giving a day-by-day account of his negotiations in Paris for the Louisiana Purchase, including his dinner with Napoleon (p. 353).

- Monroe's memorandum of August 27, 1814 as Secretary of State, detailing his re-entry into Washington with President Madison after the burning of the city by the British, and his immediate deputization as Secretary of War (p. 464).

- President Monroe's correspondence of October 17, 1823 with Jefferson and Madison laying out the rationale for what came to be known as "The Principles of 1823," or the Monroe Doctrine, and his subsequent Message to Congress of December 2, 1823 (p. 632).

These materials, and the many like them, retain an immediacy of observation that was characteristic of Monroe's mind, and demonstrate a sure power of organization that holds even the modern reader to a high degree of intimacy. Monroe wasted little effort on the literary flourishes that characterize so much eighteenth and early nineteenth century prose. Instead he wrote with a direct simplicity that belies the rigorous structure of thought that supports his prose. His writing is a camera that transmits to us images of history as it unfolded. But it is also writing that constantly advocates uniform political principles of liberty, the division of powers, and the sovereignty of the people.

It is a sad comment on historical literacy in this country that no collection of the writings of James Monroe, fifth President of the United States, has been published in the past 100 years. Here and there a few documents have been published—the passages we call the Monroe Doctrine, his unfinished autobiography, his book on political theory, *The People, the Sovereigns*. But in terms of sheer output, the quantity of his writing was staggering. The prodigious efforts of the great scholar Stanislaus Murray Hamilton a century ago resulted in an edition of seven volumes, and almost 3,500 pages—a monument of scholarship which furnishes the main source of this selection. Unfortunately, they are rare volumes, since only 750 sets were printed.

Monroe's achievement is all the more interesting considering his modest background and attenuated education. His father, Spence Monroe, was highly respectable, but at the lower level of gentry. James Monroe was born on April 28, 1758 at his father's small house situated on 500 acres in Westmoreland County on Monroe's Creek, flowing into the Potomac. By comparison, the Washington family estate where George was born was not five miles from Monroe Hall and comprised 6,000 acres. Almost the whole of Monroe's education may be attributed to the Rev. Archibald Campbell's Campbelltown Academy where he pursued a traditional classical curriculum for four years. Such was the formidable reputation of the academy that the Rev. Campbell limited his students to 25. Monroe walked to school everyday with John Marshall, the future Chief Justice of the United States. But at the age of 15, Monroe's father died, and he was withdrawn from the school.

Through the influence of his mother's brother, Judge Joseph Jones, the executor of Spence Monroe's will, James was admitted at the age of 16 into the College of William and Mary at Williamsburg in 1774. William and Mary was divided into two faculties: the grammar school, teaching the ancient languages, and what was then called "natural philosophy," or science, including mathematics and astronomy, and one of "moral philosophy," which included the study of literature, logic, and rhetoric. Because he was able to demonstrate by examination that Campbelltown had already provided him with a capacity in the ancient languages, he was admitted directly into the philosophical school.

The quality of Monroe's writing strongly suggests that he obtained some benefit from the study of literature, logic and rhetoric at William and Mary. On the other hand, just down the street from the college was the Capitol, scene in 1774 and 1775 of increasingly tumultous debates about the rights of Virginia and the colonies. In between the two was the Raleigh Tavern, where the delegates met in rump session after the legislature was prorogued by Governor Dunmore. As a delegate, Judge Jones was an active participant in these debates. Presumably the young gentlemen of the College were eager spectators at these events; indeed, Monroe must have had long discussions with Judge Jones, who had become a surrogate father for him. Monroe already was no stranger to politics: At 17, he was the youngest member of the raiding party that stormed the Governor's Palace (Dunmore had taken the precaution of removing himself to a warship in the river), removed the guns that had been stored there, and restored them to the local militia.

How much time Monroe spent in the heady atmosphere of political agitation, and how much time in the sober study of literature, logic and rhetoric may be left to the imagination. In any event, the college closed in January, 1776, and Monroe, at the age of 18, enlisted as a cadet in the Third Virginia Regiment. Two years later, having in the meantime taken a rifle ball in the shoulder and nearly bleeding to death, he returned to action and was calmly sitting 400 yards from the enemy at Monmouth while coolly engaged in the practice of rhetoric in the letter to Washington quoted above.

After the war, Monroe returned briefly to William and Mary, where he read law under the tutelage of Professor Thomas Jefferson, who at that time was Governor of Virginia. Jefferson drew up for him not only a reading program for law, but one that included history, philosophy, and literature. Monroe followed this program assiduously, developing a life-long passion for books that continually added to his personal debts, but left him richer in intellect and observation. At his death, his library did not quite rival the library which Jefferson sold to the U.S. Congress (and which became the nucleus of the Library of Congress), but it was far larger than that of the typical Virginia gentleman, and, from his two stays in France, and his sojourn in England, included a wide selection of European authors that hardly would be found elsewhere in the United States.

Monroe's writing does not constitute a speculative body of work. He was a man of intellect, but not an intellectual, if by the latter term we mean one who deals in abstractions for theoretical sake. Monroe was an active man who wrote to report upon or defend the practical actions in which he was engaged. But since he acted upon a settled body of principles, his writings constitute an admirable unity of outlook, an unfolding of his vision of the American nation and its destiny in history.

MONROE'S NATIONAL VISION

In a message to Congress in 1823, Monroe, then the fifth president of the United States laid the foundation of the U.S. claim to be the leader of the free world, long before that term became associated with the Cold War of the twentieth century. But its concept was the same; that is, he believed that the United States had a unique role as the upholder of liberty against the European (including Russian) despotism. When he laid down that claim, he didn't know that he was proclaiming a "doctrine," and he certainly never thought of it as "the Monroe Doctrine." However, the "Principles of 1823," as they were then called, propelled our new republic into international prominence just as the Old World order was collapsing.

Yet that proclamation was a culmination of a lifetime of work and experience. There is a consistent line of intellectual development that goes steadily from his letter to Washington written on the battlefield of Monmouth through his multifaceted service as a Virginia legislator, governor, member of Congress before the Constitution, Senator, minister (or as we would say today, ambassador) twice to France, as well as to England and Spain, Secretary of State, Secretary of War, and President. All of his experience, all of his intellectual acuity, all of his dedication to the principles of liberty were rolled up into that declaration. That is what makes it worthwhile to study the writings which record that intellectual development.

The Monroe Doctrine is sometimes caricatured as a manifesto of imperialist aggression. It was nothing of the sort. It was a declaration of solidarity with the new republics of this hemisphere. At the time of its writing, Monroe had spent nearly 50 years in the service of his country, starting as a 19-year-old officer in the War for Independence. As president, he had unrivalled experience of the world as a soldier, legislator, and diplomat. His administration defined the concept of the United States and made us a force to be dealt with. Under Monroe, the final shape of our national geography was also fairly well defined, although certain slight details, such as Texas and California, would be filled in later. It was a product of Monroe's national vision.

It could be argued that it was in the school of diplomacy that our third, fourth, fifth, and sixth presidents were formed. Jefferson was secretary of state to Washington, Madison was secretary of state to Jefferson, Monroe was secretary of state to Madison, and John Quincy Adams was secretary of state to Monroe. The main goals of Monroe's diplomacy, which culminated in his presidency, were these:

- To force Great Britain to recognize the independence of the United States, not just in theory, but in fact;
- To further the cause of republican government;
- To develop the western frontier by securing the right of navigation on the Mississippi and the right of deposit, that is the right of export, at the port of New Orleans;
- To establish the doctrine of free ships and free ports, that is, freedom of the seas for the protection of U.S. commerce;
- To obtain the cession of East and West Florida from Spain; and
- To extend the territory of the U.S. to the Pacific.

An ambitious agenda, to be sure. Monroe began work on it in 1776 and by the time his presidency ended in 1824, it was complete.

The Development of Monroe's Career

From the outset of his political career, Monroe held to the conviction that the good of the whole nation was the paramount interest in all negotiations. In 1783, he was a member of the Congress established by the Articles of Confederation. Congress was then meeting in Annapolis, and the chief business before it was the ratification of the Treaty of Paris formally ending the War for Independence. It soon became clear to Monroe that the British had little intention to abide by its provisions, such as paying reparations for attacks on American shipping and withdrawing troops from forts on American soil. The British were confident the Americans would soon forget about independence and come running back to Mother England. Incidentally, it was at this session in Annapolis that Monroe shared lodgings with Thomas Jefferson, who brought along with him an ample selection from his library as well as his French cook. It was from this chef, M. Partout, that Monroe learned to speak French and to dream about France. Both the library and the chef were left behind for Monroe when Jefferson suddenly was chosen to be Minister to France, and departed.

Shortly after, Monroe made a journey of adventure and exploration through New York hoping to reach Detroit. It was an adventure all right; when he reached Fort Niagara, he learned that the other part of his group, which had gone on ahead, had been massacred on the shores of Lake Erie by renegade Indians.

He returned by way of the St. Lawrence. What he learned was that the British simply refused to pull out of the frontier forts, such as Fort Niagara, where he stopped. He also saw for himself the value of the forests and fur trade to Britain. He calculated that an embargo on north/south trade would force the British to withdraw making it so expensive to for Britain to maintain the colony without trade that they would give up on Canada altogether. He proposed embargo legislation in the Congress, but New England and the eastern states would have none of it. Their economy had been ruined by the War for Independence, and they wanted trade, not embargoes.

Issues Dividing Eastern and Southern States

Monroe learned in this session of Congress the extent of the phenomenon that history textbooks call "sectional rivalry." Monroe discovered two sets of interests that were fundamentally antagonistic, namely New England and the eastern states versus the southern states. Their opposing agendas even then threatened the unity of the country. After the end of the French and Indian Wars in 1763, Virginia alone was a colossus, dwarfing the eastern and New England states. Furthermore Virginia had a strong claim on the Northwest Territory, which included modern Indiana, Ohio, Michigan, Illinois, and Wisconsin; but Virginia was willing to cede those claims to the national government for the establishment of the future states. The architect of the cession was Jefferson, but when Jefferson went to France, it was Monroe who picked up where his mentor left off and proposed the concept of territorial government that later was adopted in the Northwest Ordinance of 1787. But even Virginia's offer to withdraw did not satisfy the northeastern states; they saw the potential states of the Northwest Territory as rivals draining off settlers and capital from them.

On the maps of the period, Virginia, and North Carolina extend through the Ohio Valley to the banks of the Mississippi. The remarkable thing is that in all of this huge expanse of Virginia, there is only one city, namely, the port of Norfolk. Virginia, considered the wealthiest state, had no need of cities. Jefferson in his *Notes on Virginia*, 1790, explained that it was the navigable rivers of the Commonwealth that brought commerce to everyone's own wharf, or doorstep, and cities were unnecessary. The social and economic life of Virginia was based on the model of the self-sufficient English manor-house system. The social organization of New England was quite different: It was a country of tradesmen, small farmers, shopkeepers, and artisans who prized their town meetings and interactions with each other. Increasingly it was also a society of those who made their living from the sea.

The great wealth of Virginia was derived from the land. New England grew rich from the sea. The problem for New England was that it did not hold sovereignty over the fisheries, and its carrying trade extended over the seven seas. Therefore wars, embargoes, and port restrictions could choke its economic life to death. But Virginia could go on producing from the land and find some way to get the goods to market. It didn't mind trading in English ships with English ports. The War for Independence damaged New England's economy far worse than Virginia's. By the time of the 1783 treaty, Virginia's trade had returned to normal, but New England's ports were operating at one-quarter of their former capacity.

It is sometimes said that Virginia's economy depended upon slavery, but that of New England's did not. But in the context of the 17th and 18th centuries, that assumption appears to be quite flawed.

Long before there was a New England, there was already an extensive trade between that region and Europe. By the 13th century, the codfish had become an important part of the diet of Europe. The cod, caught in huge numbers in the cold waters of the North Atlantic, could be salted, dried, shipped, and stored for long periods of time. It was the convenience food par excellence. The Norse, the Danes, the English, the French, made fortunes as purveyors of dried cod. But the Basques, operating out of Bilbao, did better than anybody else, and no one ever saw them on the regular cod fishing grounds.

When John Cabot (who was really a Genovese named Giovanni Caboto) sailed to the New World on a commission from the English King in 1497 he discovered the cod teeming teeming off the cape now known as Cape Cod and on the great banks of Newfoundland. When Jacques Cartier discovered the mouth of the St. Lawrence in 1534 and claimed it for France, he noted that there were some 1,000 Basque fishing vessels at anchor. Their secret had been discovered.

That is why when the Pilgrims came to Massachusetts, lacking training in any profession, they made directly for the great codfishing grounds and took up fishing. The Davenport Adventurers went out for the same reason, and started the Massachusetts Bay Colony. Their exports grew exponentially. The best went to Europe, but the vast bulk of it went to another market, the West Indies, where Columbus had first landed in 1492.

By the end of the seventeenth century, the West Indies had become known as the sugar islands. Sugar was a hugely profitable business. The British, French,

Dutch, and Danes established vast cane plantations in the West Indies. By the end of the 18th century, annual income from the British West Indies brought in four times the amount England obtained in trade from the rest of the world. The sugar crop from Santo Domingo, today's Haiti and Dominican Republic, provided France with an income that exceeded the value of the production of metropolitan France. But the production of sugar was labor-intensive work, and the workers were taken in bondage from Africa. Professor Philip D. Curtin, of Johns Hopkins University, in his seminal book, *The American Slave Trade*, estimates that out of some ten million Africans transported to the New World, about four million were taken to the West Indies. Nearly that same number was taken to the cane plantations in Brazil. The total taken to North America was about 400,000.

The sugar planters of the West Indies had little inclination to waste land and labor growing food for their laborers when they could buy cheap protein in the form of low-grade salt fish from New England. There was no compunction in New England about supplying food to keep the slaves in the sugar plantations alive and working. The New England economy depended on it. It wasn't until the 19th century that whaling and the China trade and the fur trade with the Pacific Northwest filled the greater part of the picture. In the 17th and 18th centuries, the fish trade was the engine of development.

The West Indian planters could trade sugar in the form of molasses for the fish without scarce specie money changing hands. The New England ships took the molasses back to supply Boston's main industry, the 63 rum distilleries operating in that city. They had another market for salt fish in the ports of Guinea in West Africa, where the British slaving ships needed easily transportable food to keep their cargoes alive for the two or three month voyages of the infamous "middle passage." New England depended on those 4 million slaves in the West Indies for its chief market, and the dependency was mutual: when Britain stopped the American trade in the third quarter of the 1700's, hunger and starvation were widespread.

All of this lucrative New England trade had been threatened by Great Britain starting with the first of the Navigation Acts in 1651. Their tax policy was to make Americans trade through British ports on British ships. The Sugar Tax and the Molasses Tax Acts were specifically aimed at the New England economy. With the closing of Boston harbor in 1774 and the imposition of a military embargo, the fisheries and the carrying trade were shut down. For a while, the New Englanders shifted to privateering under letters of marque granted by the Continental Congress. They were very good at taking prizes one-on-one, but when the British warships started showing up in convoys, the game was over.

Therefor in 1783 things seemed to be looking up for New England when Spain sent an envoy, Don Diego de Enrique Gardoqui, to negotiate a new treaty of commerce with Congress. New York and the New Englanders were delighted at the chance to have their Spanish customers back. Happy days were here again for the codfish purveyors, and perhaps some surreptitious trade with the West Indies thrown in.

But the southern states were wary. They had a different agenda. They had no objection to a treaty of commerce, but it had to include two key concessions from Spain. Spain had acquired Louisiana from France in 1763, and had closed the port of New Orleans to American shipping. She also claimed jurisdiction on both banks of the Mississippi. This put a huge obstacle in the path of the development of the west—Kentucky, the Ohio valley, the Northwest Territory—whose rivers drained into the Mississippi. The produce of that region would have to be shipped down the tributaries to the Mississippi and then to the port of New Orleans. The Southerners also looked with alarm at the Florida territories, titularly in the hands of Spain, but with virtually no governing authority in place. The land was a nest of pirates, smugglers, escaped convicts and slaves, and renegade Indian tribes given to cross-border raids. The Southerners feared that a more powerful nation might occupy it again. They had seen Britain take it from Spain at the end of the Seven Years war in 1762 and give it back in 1783 after the Treaty of Paris. At that time the term "Florida" encompassed both East and West Florida, an entity spanning the entire coast of the Gulf of Mexico, including the river ports of Pensacola, Mobile, and Pascagoula all the way to the Pearl River in present-day Louisiana. Southerners wanted defensible borders but thought it was inevitable that Florida should be ruled by the United States.

Monroe's Experience in Congress
with International Relations

Congress authorized Foreign Minister John Jay to negotiate with Gardoqui, the Spanish envoy, but gave him instructions that he was to settle only the border questions with Florida. He was specifically instructed not to agree to the closing of the Mississippi. But Jay decided that the advantages of resuming trade with Spain outweighed any issues relating to the Mississippi. It seemed reasonable to the native New Yorker to close the Mississippi, at least for a while, to get the New York and New England trade going again. He was also plotting to block the development of the new territories in the West. In short, he was fully prepared, in the idiom of a later day, to sell the interests of the South down the river.

Monroe caught wind of Jay's machinations and promptly informed Patrick Henry, then governor of Virginia. He states, "This is one of the most extraordinary transactions I have ever known, a minister negotiating expressly for the purposes of defeating the object of his instructions, and by a long train of intrigue & management seducing the representatives of the states to concur in it." Then he adds a new worry: "Certain it is that committees are held in this town [New York] of Eastern men and others of this State upon the subject of a dismemberment of the states east of the Hudson from the union & the erection of them into a separate govt. . . . In short, it is a system of policy which has for its object the keeping the weight of govt & population in this quarter, & is prepared by a set of men so flagitious, unprincipled & determined in their pursuits, as to satisfy me beyond a doubt they have adopted this as the necessary means of effecting it."

In the end, it was Monroe, through adroit parliamentary maneuvering, who stalemated the treaty proposal. But this episode set his course for his life's work in diplomacy. Within 20 years, he had secured not only the right of navigation, but the whole Louisiana Territory, and in 15 years more he had acquired East and West Florida. Nor did he neglect the New Englanders. As president, he finally established a convention with Great Britain regulating the cod fisheries on the Newfoundland Banks.

JAY'S MISSION TO LONDON AND MONROE'S FIRST MISSION TO PARIS

The election of George Washington as our first president coincided with the French Revolution in 1789. The reaction of the Washington administration was divided, and in this it reflected the ambivalent feelings of the American people. On the one hand, the people rejoiced that the principles of liberty seemingly had triumphed in Paris; but on the other, the execution of the King and his consort and the bloody purges that followed suggested that all was not well. American relations with Great Britain were also tentative. Trade with Britain had not been restored. Britain and France were at war and had both declared embargoes against neutral, that is, American ships. British ships of war were seizing American merchant vessels. There was strong sentiment in the Senate for imposing an embargo on Britain, a drastic move which was opposed by the merchant interests. So the question was: Would the United States tilt towards Great Britain or France?

These two contrary opinions stood on each side of Washington in the persons of Secretary of State Jefferson and Secretary of the Treasury Alexander Hamilton, like two admonishing angels. Jefferson, the Republican, supported peace and the revolution; Hamilton, the Federalist, wanted trade relations with England at any cost. It was said there was a British party and a French party as Congress met in Philadelphia. Monroe was now in the Senate, and he believed that Hamilton and his ilk wanted to restore the monarchy in America.

Washington sought to steer a neutral course, but before long Jefferson resigned and returned to Monticello. Meanwhile, the U.S. Minister to France was Gouverneur Morris, a staunch Federalist who was out of touch with republicanism in France. The Revolutionaries were out of touch with Morris, too; they charged him with trying to restore the royalist regime and declared him persona non grata. U.S. relations with France were at a standstill.

Then as now the rumor mill played an important role in Congress. Senator James Monroe heard that the party favoring Britain was pressing for Washington to appoint Alexander Hamilton as Minister Extraordinary to Britain to negotiate a new treaty. Monroe wrote to Washington and pointed out that the appointment of Hamilton would be "not only injurious to the public interest, but especially to your own." It was the first time that any senator had ever opposed an ambassadorial appointment before it was sent to the Senate. When the president eventually sent up his nomination for special envoy to Britain, it was none other than John Jay, Monroe's nemesis from the failed Spanish treaty. His mission was described narrowly as one of reconciliation, settling of claims, and the withdrawal of British troops from the frontier—all goals which Monroe supported.

The question of diplomatic representation to France remained. A number of names were floated, but none would be acceptable to the revolutionary government of France. Finally an offer was made to an individual so astonished that he did not know what to do. Washington asked Monroe to go to Paris, and Monroe agreed.

The contemporaneous embassies of Jay to London and Monroe to Paris were a turning point in Monroe's career. Jay, for his part, was successful in his mission to conciliate Great Britain, to get compensation for damages to U.S. shipping, and to get agreement from the British to withdraw from the frontier forts. But what was not announced was his plan to gain these concessions and reopen trade with Great Britain, even if it meant sacrificing U.S. trade with

France. France and Great Britain were in a state of war, and all of Europe was opposed to France for fear that the contagion of revolution would spread.

The mission of Monroe was brilliantly successful in overcoming the hostility of the revolutionary government and its suspicions of Jay's mission to England. Within weeks he had won over key members of the government and persuaded them to abrogate their anti-American decrees, open trade, and ameliorate the claims of American shipping. The skill of his diplomacy may be illustrated by the case of Madame Lafayette, the wife of his friend the Marquis, who had been wounded when the two young officers were at the battle of Brandywine.

When Monroe arrived in Paris he found to his distress that Lafayette had been imprisoned by the Emperor of Austria in Olmutz as a dangerous revolutionary. But Madame Lafayette was imprisoned in Paris because her husband was seen as a dangerous representative of the aristocratic order. Indeed, her mother and her grandmother had already been beheaded. Her uncle, the Marquis de Tascher, came secretly to Monroe urging him to use his influence with the government to spare her.

Yet in those first few days of turmoil in Paris, Monroe knew that the Committee on Public Safety still distrusted him; any official attempt to intervene might have the opposite effect and send Madame Lafayette to the guillotine instantly. So he developed a stratagem. His first step was to purchase with great difficulty a splendid set of horse and carriage—no mean feat, since the revolution had banished such equipage from the city, and there were none for hire. He outfitted the servants in brilliant livery. Then Elizabeth Monroe dressed in her most elegant day costume, and was driven to the gates of the prison where Madame Lafayette languished.

The keepers were astonished. Who was it? Who would dare come with such display in such volatile times? The word went out: It was the wife of the American Minister and she had come to see Madame Lafayette. The gates swung open. When the keepers went to get the prisoner, she thought that her time had come, and she was being taken to the guillotine; but instead she was brought to an iron railing where she was comforted by Mrs. Monroe.

"The scene was most affecting, the sensibility of all the beholders was deeply excited," Monroe wrote later. The account of this event quickly swept through the city, and popular opinion switched over to the side of Madame Lafayette. Monroe then was able through quiet conversations with the Committee to secure her release, and she was brought to the Minister's residence, where she stayed for several weeks. At length she was able to leave Paris with her two daughters and join her husband in Olmutz in October 1795—in prison, where she shared his misfortune and prison fare until his release several years later.

But all Monroe's achievements collapsed because of Jay's duplicity in England. His secret agenda to reestablish trade with Britain at any cost had been artfully concealed from Monroe by the written instructions given to him by Secretary of State Edmund Randolph. Rumors of the double-cross of France that Jay was engineering in London circulated in Paris, but Monroe, relying on his instructions, bravely reassured the French that all was well. At last the treaty was made public in the United States, and both France and Monroe read about it in the newspapers. It contained a clause that declared food carried in neutral ships, i.e., ships of the United States, to be contraband. In other words, Great Britain was determined to starve France out. France exploded in indignation.

Secretary Randolph had been receiving dispatches from Monroe regularly—brilliant accounts of the fall of Robespierre, the inner politics of the Jacobin society, eyewitness accounts of the Paris mobs advancing on the National Convention. But now Randolph wrote to upbraid him for failing to contain France's outrage. He was accused of exceeding his instructions by being too friendly to the revolutionary government and unnecessarily raising France's expectations. Yet everything Monroe had done had been done under the authority of the precise instructions he had received in writing. His problem was that he had been too successful for those who wanted to conciliate London, and now his enemies turned on him precisely because of his solid accomplishments. Monroe was recalled. France refused to accept his successor, the Federalist Charles Cotesworth Pinckney.

THE LOUISIANA PURCHASE AND NEGOTIATIONS FOR FLORIDA

But the affairs of men evolve. Washington's second term ended. The Federalist John Adams was succeeded by the agrarian Republican, Jefferson. In France the revolutionaries were succeeded by Napoleon Bonaparte, styled the First Consul. His armies won battle after battle, and in Spain King Ferdinand VII was forced secretly to yield to him the vast territory of Louisiana. Rumors spread throughout the Western frontier that Napoleon was about to send a military garrison to Louisiana. President Jefferson was under strong political pressure to do something. Jefferson wrote to his protégé, Monroe, and asked him to make the sacrifice of returning on a mission to France. The sacrifice went on for five years.

When Napoleon heard that Monroe was coming, he conceived a bold plan. War was brewing with England. A war with England would cost money. The undeveloped territory of Louisiana in the backwoods of North America was a liability. Napoleon would sell the whole of Louisiana to the Americans for ready cash. Virtually ignoring the permanent U.S. Minister to Paris, the ineffectual Robert R. Livingston. Napoleon waited for Monroe, who has left a day-by-day memorandum of the negotiations. It was a complicated deal, involving both the sale of the territory and French compensation to U.S. citizens for property seized in wartime. It was wrapped up in five days for 70 million francs, or $15 million.

DIPLOMACY WITH GREAT BRITAIN ON U.S. CLAIMS AND IMPRESSMENT

His finances strengthened, Napoleon was preparing to invade England. A great army was assembled at Boulogne, and a huge navy from all the nations of Europe. The Admiralty, in desperate need of sailors, was once more impressing American seamen, taking them from U.S. ships. The U.S. Minister in London, Rufus King, resigned and returned to the United States. Madison instructed Monroe to proceed to London immediately to protect American interests during the war and to seek a new treaty to guarantee the rights of neutral shipping and to end the impressment of American seamen. Monroe was presented to King George III on August 17th. Years later in his unfinished autobiography, written in the third-person, Monroe wrote:

It was impossible for Mr. Monroe to be presented to King George III without experiencing sensations of a peculiar character. From his very early youth, impressions had been made on his mind against that monarch. While at the College [of William and Mary], he had attended the debates in the General Assembly and Convention, all of which represented him as unfriendly to liberty. He had fought in our revolutionary struggle against his troops and witness in many of our states the distress to which our citizens were exposed in that unjust war. Time has essentially diminished these impressions, but it had not entirely removed them.

But the King's reception was kindly. After a change of governments in England, the new foreign minister informed Monroe that, in his opinion, Jay's 1794 treaty interdicting cargo with France was still in force. There was nothing Monroe could do.

Monroe planned next to go to Spain (via Paris) with the purchase of the Floridas topmost on his agenda. In Paris he discovered that Livingston had concocted his own scheme for obtaining the cession of the Floridas to the United States. Without any authorization from Washington, he secretly sent word to Spain that negotiations should be moved to Paris. He hinted that the U.S. would make a loan to Spain in the amount of $2 million if Spain would withdraw from West Florida. The position of Jefferson, Madison, and Monroe was that West Florida had already been conveyed to the United States with the Louisiana purchase, so that that the U.S. would be paying for land it already possessed. As a result of the confusion caused by Livingston's unauthorized actions, Monroe was again unable to get anywhere. He returned to London intending to sail home at the first opportunity.

But he found that American ships were once again being seized by the British, who, instead of blockading the French coast, chose to blockade the U.S. coast. William Pinckney of Maryland was dispatched as special envoy to be co-minister with Monroe. The two worked diligently, but it became clear that the British would never yield on the issue of greatest concern to American public opinion, the impressment of American seamen. But the two negotiators thought it best, on balance, to seek some improved relationship with Britain, and send back a treaty that did not directly address the impressment issue, except in a side letter. Jefferson rejected the treaty before he heard the explanations of Monroe and Pinckney. Under severe political attack, Monroe returned home, feeling that he had been betrayed by his two life-long friends. Shortly he found himself back in the General Assembly in Richmond; but no sooner had he been elected than the assembly chose him as governor for the second time.

Secretary of State and Secretary of War

By 1811, Britain was still struggling with Napoleon. Lord Nelson was fighting against all the ships of Europe under the Emperor's command. The British navy instituted a blockade to stand off U.S. ports. Virtually every U.S. merchant ship seeking to leave U.S. ports was seized on the grounds it might be going to France. In 1810, Congress acceded to President Madison's request for legislation authorizing the occupation of West Florida, for fear that Britain might occupy it. At this point, Madison's secretary of state resigned. Monroe was astonished to receive a letter from Madison begging him to accept this post. Assured that he would never have to support a policy contrary to his conscience, he accepted. Yet as secretary of state, his diplomacy was hampered by the weakness of the nation's defenses. The key military leaders of the Revolution had by now passed away. The second tier of leadership had been too young to gain real experience of logistics and tactics.

The ignominious surrender of Detroit by General Hull in August 1812, without firing a shot, alarmed President Madison and Secretary Monroe. The sitting Secretary of War, William Henry Eustis, was incompetent, and failed to organize the defenses. Since Monroe was the highest civilian official with real military experience, President Madison named Monroe acting Secretary of War in addition to his duties as Secretary of State. Monroe immediately began writing detailed memoranda on military strategy and materiel requirements for leaders of the Senate and House of Representatives. He gave them a grim picture of what was needed. Subsequently, General John Armstrong, Livingston's brother-in-law and bearer of the family grudges against Monroe, was named Secretary of War in order to strengthen support for the war in New York. But Armstrong turned out to be another mistake.

As the British landed in the Chesapeake and began working their way up the coast, Monroe, who was then 60 years old and whose body bore many infirmities, taking horses and a small detachment of men with him, galloped through the night until they crept up on the British fleet, counting the number of ships and estimating the number of men. We still have his intelligence dispatches to Madison written in his own hand. Meanwhile, the Secretary of War, General Armstrong, had fled to the safety of Western Maryland.

A striking memorandum written by Monroe in August 1814 vividly describes the entrance of the president and secretary of state into the smoking ruins of Washington. There was no U.S. military presence whatsoever. The inhabitants were ready to surrender. Madison deputized Monroe on the spot as secretary of war. He took charge immediately, organizing the wavering citizens for the defense of the capital, and threatening to bayonet anyone who attempted to parley with the enemy deployed at Alexandria. When Armstrong remonstrated against Monroe for supposedly usurping the duties which he had abandoned, Madison suggested that he go to New York on a vacation, and he resigned a few days later.

At first, Monroe sought to resign as Secretary of State while acting as Secretary of War, but in the end discharged both his diplomatic and military duties simultaneously. With enormous effort he rebuilt the armies—working closely with the Congress he knew so well to get enough men in the field, and conducted a highly successful military intelligence operation. When he informed General Andrew Jackson about the imminent approach of the British fleet to New Orleans, the U.S. Treasury was empty, and Jackson needed supplies and funds to pay his men. Unfortunately, the British trade embargo and the costs of the war had imposed ruin on the U.S. economy. Scores of banks had failed, and others were issuing worthless scrip. Without hesitation, Monroe pledged his private credit to a group of Washington banks, and he sent the funds to Jackson.

Despite Britain's successes in the war in America, its attention was also distracted by events in Europe. The resignation of Napoleon in 1814 changed the whole political dynamic on the continent, while American naval superiority on the Great Lakes had dimmed any chance that the British could occupy any significant portion of U.S. territory. The British foreign minister, Lord Castlereagh, offered negotiations in December 1813. As a result, Madison nominated peace commissioners, who after many detours, finally arrived at Ghent in August. The group included Albert Gallatin, John Quincy Adams, Henry Clay, J.S. Bayard, and Jonathan Russell. Months went by with no communication from Ghent, until a letter arrived saying that no peace was possible with the instructions they had been given.

With the bankruptcy of the U.S. Treasury and the desperate situation in the field, except in the Great Lakes, the Cabinet conferred. Monroe recommended that the issue of impressment be taken off the table, and the message was sent to the commissioners. Monroe refrained from commenting on the fact that the Cabinet decision restored the situation back to policy of the failed 1806 treaty.

The British commissioners, for their part, had made outrageous demands: They would not discuss the question of the Newfoundland fisheries. They would not renew the provisions of the peace treaty of 1783 ending the War for Independence. The British would remain in the forts and on the lakes. A line would be drawn from the approximate location of where Cleveland is today to the Mississippi excluding the Americans. An Indian buffer state in the Western territories would be established to block westward expansion. The British right of navigation on the Mississippi would be retained. There were suggestions that Louisiana be returned to Spain. In other words, the picture sketched was almost a reversal of the War for Independence, with the United States virtually a vassal of the motherland.

But in the United States, the situation for the British was worsening. The British were routed at the battle of Plattsburg on Lake Champlain, and when the great hero, the Duke of Wellington, was asked to take charge of military operations in America, he declined, stating, "I think you have no right, from the state of war, to demand any concession of territory from America." The other turning point was the pressure of the British merchants on their own government. Until the embargo, the United States had been a major trading partner. The desire for restoration of trade stopped the war on both sides. Neither side achieved victory; it was a question of which would collapse first. One by one, the British objections in Ghent dropped away. The Americans, for their part, gave up any insistence on the right to the fisheries, leaving the situation in all respects almost as it had been in 1811. The treaty was signed on December 24, 1814, even while Major General Andrew Jackson was clashing with the British commander, Major General Edward Pakenham, around New Orleans. On the foggy morning of January 8, not knowing the war technically was over, the British lost 2,000 men in pitched battle, while Jackson, with much smaller forces, suffered only 71 casualties. It was the most decisive battle of the war. The British withdrew to the harbor and sailed away.

FLORIDA, THE WESTERN BOUNDARIES, AND THE MONROE DOCTRINE

When the second Madison administration ended, the people of the United States looked to James Monroe as their president. Immediately he began to use his skills in diplomacy to bring together the states into one nation in spirit as well as in fact. The collapse of the Federalist Party—it did not even offer a candidate for president against Madison or Monroe—led to a migration of political leaders into the Republican Party. It was, the newspapers said, "the era of good feelings."

Monroe chose as secretary of state John Quincy Adams, who had migrated away from the Federalism of his father. Adams himself was an experienced diplomat, having served in St. Petersburg, and at the time of his appointment was minister to England. With Adams at his side, one of his first actions in 1817 was to send a diplomatic mission to South America to get first hand knowledge of the situation of the former Spanish colonies that had declared independence. At the same time, he was pursuing the leftover business of Spanish control over East and West Florida—or rather its lack of control because of the weakness and corruption of the government in Madrid. Although Spain had a garrison at St. Augustine in the east and St. Mark's and Pensacola in the west, it had little control over the actual territory, which continued to be a virtual no-man's land, a haven for hostile Indians, outlaws, and smugglers. Andrew Jackson, in a latitudinarian interpretation of his orders, chased out the Seminole Indians, then took the Spanish garrison. Monroe immediately ordered Jackson to withdraw from the fort, but not from the territory. He asserted that Jackson's actions were justifiable because the Spanish had broken the law of nations in allowing their territory to be used for lawless attacks on U.S. lands.

The Spanish protested, but eventually yielded to negotiations conducted in Washington between the Spanish minister, Juan de Onis, and Adams. On the table were not only Florida, but also the drawing of the western border of Louisiana, which had never been defined. The two diplomats fought it out, week after week. At length the lines were drawn up the Sabine River (thus excluding Texas) to the Red River, and thence to the Arkansas River—and in a breathtaking sweep across the 42nd parallel to the Pacific.

Spain was to receive payments equivalent to $5 million. The Transcontinental Treaty was signed on February 22, 1819 and approved by the Senate two days later. But it was not until 1821 that Spain finally ratified the treaty. That problem made the question of giving diplomatic recognition to the South American republics very sensitive. The mission to Latin America returned with a favorable recommendation of immediate recognition. Yet if diplomatic relations were established, would Spain be so offended that the Florida treaty would never be ratified? Once the treaties were ratified, that difficulty was resolved.

When the commissioners reported back, Monroe laid the groundwork for diplomatic recognition. An 1819 memo to Secretary of State John Quincy Adams has Monroe proposing that an agent be sent to South America. Monroe wrote: "As the [Spanish] colonies are our neighbors, and we shall of necessity have much intercourse with them, especially if they become independent, which may be presumed, and at no distant period, it is highly important that our relations be of a very amicable nature."

In 1822, Monroe sent a message to Congress calling for diplomatic recognition of the Latin American countries. He told the members, "The revolutionary movement in the Spanish Provinces in this hemisphere attracted the attention and excited the sympathy of our fellow citizens from its commencement." Only one member of Congress voted against this proposal.

Europe meanwhile was once again in turmoil. The defeat of Napoleon in 1814 let loose revolutions in Greece, Italy, and Spain. The great powers—Austria, Prussia, and Russia—united in something called the Holy Alliance to put down the revolutions and get the colonies back again.

In August 1823, George Canning, the British Foreign Minister, called in the U.S. minister, Richard Rush, to make a startling suggestion: Would the U.S. government be pleased to join with His Majesty's government in a declaration that both countries would resist any effort by the European powers to restore the colonies to Spain?

Only ten years previously, the two countries had been at war, and the U.S. capital put to the torch. But now old adversaries had common interests. Astonished, Rush could reply only that the answers to those questions exceeded his instructions.

In the summer of 1823, Monroe withdrew from Washington to his new estate in Loudoun County, Oak Hill. John Quincy Adams had fled to the cooler clime of New England. They did not see the Rush dispatches until October 9, and a few days later Monroe went to Oak Hill and wrote two extraordinary letters which, with their replies, still remain in the National Archives with their crabbed handwriting and scratched-out mistakes.

The letters were to his old friends and neighbors living at Monticello and Montpelier. "Shall we entangle ourselves at all in European politics and wars?" Monroe asked. And if it is generally a sound maxim that we should not, is not this the case, he asked, where the maxim "ought to be departed from?" Was this not an opportunity to join with Britain to take a stand "either in favor of despotism or of liberty?" Besides, Monroe added, if the European powers succeeded in an attack on the Spanish colonies, "they would extend it to us."

It was at this point, on October 24, that Jefferson responded that the question "is the most momentous which has been ever offered to my contemplation since that of independence made us a nation." And then he added, with prophetic insight, "This sets our compass and points the course which we are to steer through the ocean of time opening on us."

Madison's reply of October 30 reflected his realism: He stated his opinion that Great Britain was ready to go ahead anyway. "But this consideration ought not to divert us from what is just and proper in itself. Our co-operation is due to ourselves and to the world."

Monroe nonetheless felt a deepening concern. He decided to move ahead alone, indeed, that it was better to move alone. Furthermore, he decided that he should make a public declaration in his forthcoming message to Congress, rather than in a private diplomatic note. His draft was presented to the Cabinet on November 21, and on December 2 it was sent to Congress.

What we call the Monroe Doctrine today was not stated in abstract principles. Rather it was presented very concretely in the midst of a wide range of issues in what we would call today a State of the Union message. With regard to the settlement of Russian and British claims on the Northwest Pacific coast, Monroe stated:

"The occasion has been judged proper for asserting a principle . . . that the American continents, by the free and independent condition which they have assumed and maintain, are henceforth not be to considered as subject for future colonization by any European power . . ." Although both Russia and Great

Britain had agreed to the specific settlement in the Oregon question, neither had any idea that they were agreeing to a general principle. But at a later point in the message to Congress, Monroe went even further in attacking the Holy Alliance, issuing a warning to aggressors:

"The political system of the allied powers is essentially different from that of America . . . We . . . declare that we should consider any attempt on their part to extend the system to any portions of this Hemisphere as dangerous to our peace and safety. With the existing Colonies and dependencies of any European power, we have not interfered, and shall not interfere. But with the governments who have declared their independence, and maintained it, and whose independence we have acknowledged, we could not view any interposition for the purpose of oppressing them, or controlling in any other manner their destiny, by any European power, in any other light than as the manifestation of an unfriendly disposition towards the United States."

These words were received with calculated indifference by the European powers. What was the United States to make such a statement? How large was its navy? How rich its treasury? What standing armies would repulse the will of the Alliance? The attributes of power were pitifully small. On the other hand, Great Britain had the resources to put the Americans in their place, and Great Britain already had experienced what their own traders would say would happen if there was any interference in the U.S. trade—the United States was, after all, Britain's single largest customer. The United States had no power to enforce these principles, but, once stated, their truth became manifest to so many that they became self-enforcing.

Those lines acquired such power as an image of American conduct because they were the mature deliberation of a statesman who had spent some 48 years in public life preparing to formulate them. He was a man who still carried that British rifle ball in his shoulder from the days when he was put to the ultimate test of patriotism in the War of 1776. He was a man whose first public controversies on behalf of the nation centered on the proposed treaty with Spain in 1784. He was the patron of republican principles who, nevertheless, took hardheaded views of the insurgent mobs of Paris in 1796. He was the diplomat who actually had a personal interview with George III, had a private dinner with Napoleon Bonaparte, was in attendance at the Emperor's coronation in Notre Dame cathedral, and was presented formally to Charles IV of Spain. Moreover, he knew all of their ministers, all of their stratagems, all of their wiles. He was a man of infinite negotiations, skilled in the intricacies of international finance. As Secretary of State and Secretary of War during the War of 1812, he had brutal confrontations with invading European armies, and organized the defenses of the nation as it stood on the verge of collapse. There was nothing that he did not know about the world and its ways.

Yet he had further strengths. In formulating the Principles of 1823, he sought out the advice of two former presidents, Jefferson and Madison, not to speak of the man he chose as his Secretary of State, John Quincy Adams, son of a president, and about to be president himself. Was there ever such a parley of titans?

As the years went by, the Principles of 1823 became known as the Monroe Doctrine, and they became part of the unwritten constitution—the part that the written Constitution delegated to the president for the conduct of foreign affairs. They constituted an American doctrine, as interpreted by the American president. Nor did other nations always agree with such an interpretation. But they provided the backbone of our independence, and they can continue to provide strength and principle in an age when the growing networks of economic and political interchange seek to render obsolete the very concept of nationhood.

—JAMES P. LUCIER
Leesburg, Virginia
December 2, 2000
177th Anniversary of the Monroe Doctrine.

PART I

Revolutionary War Hero

INTRODUCTION

THE YOUTHFUL WRITINGS OF great men are seldom worth notice. But in the case of James Monroe the proclivities that shaped his life are already evident: sharp observation, keen analysis, absolute loyalty to principle, and the courage to make bold decisions. Almost the whole of James Monroe's education may be attributed to the Rev. Archibald Campbell's Campbelltown Academy where he pursued a traditional classical curriculum. But at the age of 15, his father died, and Monroe was withdrawn from the school.

Then he found a patron in his mother's brother, Judge Joseph Jones of nearby Fredericksburg, a man of parts educated in England at the Inns of Court and an influential member of the House of Burgesses. Though Jones' influence, Monroe was admitted to the College of William and Mary in Williamsburg in 1774 at the age of 16. Although he immediately advanced to a higher form because of the excellence of his studies at Campbelltown Academy, that year was not the time to get a serious education.

The Governor, Lord Dunmore, dissolved the House of Burgesses and "stole the powder" from the magazine of Williamsburg militia. The Burgesses, including Judge Jones, met in rump session at the Raleigh Tavern. It is not hard to conclude that a certain young nephew of Jones got full briefings of what was in hand. Patrick Henry marched on Williamsburg with militia members from a wide swath of Virginia counties. Dunmore retreated to a warship in the James River—and a group of 24 men under Theoderick Bland Jr. made a surprise attack on the Governor's Palace, and seized quantities of muskets and swords which were turned over to the Williamsburg fighters. The youngest member of the raiding party was 17-year-old James Monroe.

William and Mary could not hold him for long. By spring, 1776, he had dropped out again to become a cadet in the Third Virginia Infantry, and was soon commissioned a lieutenant at age 18. In midsummer, the Third Virginia marched to New York, meeting the British in engagements in Manhattan, where Monroe performed well. When Washington withdrew to New Jersey crossing the Delaware, Monroe had crossed before him as part of an advance detachment sent to guard a road crossing and prevent news of the advance from reaching the Hessian garrison at Trenton. It was in this fighting that Monroe was seriously wounded, a bullet severing an artery; but a surgeon managed to staunch the flow. Nevertheless, he was out of action for three months.

By rights, Monroe could have taken his commendation by General Washington and his promotion to captain and gone home like so many others, asserting that he had done his duty. But that was not Monroe's way. He returned as aide-de-camp to Lord Stirling, a British aristocrat who had become a patriot fighting for the American cause. At Monmouth, Monroe was an advance intelligence scout, operating within sight of the enemy forces. The first item in this collection is Monroe's letter to Gen. Washington, written on the battlefield, June 28, 1778.

Unfortunately, the victory at Monmouth was the last time Monroe saw action. After two years as a junior officer, Monroe grew bored with not being in the middle of action and resigned from Stirling's command to seek a command of his own. Despite assistance from Stirling and Washington, he was unable to find a unit in the Virginia militia that lacked a commander—and he was unable to recruit a unit of his own as the war ground down. On June 15, 1780 he wrote to his friend General Charles Lee, whose controversial actions at the battle of Monmouth had led to court martial and retirement, but who nevertheless retained wide popular approval. He applied to the Virginia assembly for a commission, but, as he wrote to Lee, "What I have to expect from this Assembly is incertain, but as they have no interest in the appointment I desire, I believe I have no probable grounds to found hopes on."

What did happen, however, was that having returned to Fredericksburg to live with Judge Jones, he began attending William and Mary at Williamsburg. Privately, he began to study law. His tutor was Thomas Jefferson, fifteen years his senior and Governor of Virginia. Besides starting him on his legal studies, Jefferson, one of the most original minds of his time, laid out a program of liberal education based on history and philosophy. Yet the war was not yet over, and with the fall of Charleston in May 1780, the very real threat of a British invasion from the south transfixed Virginians. Just as Stirling had sent Monroe to get intelligence for Washington at Monmouth, Jefferson and the Executive Council now appointed Monroe to find out whether the British armies intended to move up the coast. With characteristic energy, Monroe organized a system of relay posts to carry his dispatches back to Richmond.

His dispatch of June 26, 1778 from Cross Creek, North Carolina, is a model of analysis. In September, Monroe is writing again to Jefferson. He has a new proposal. There is talk of forming an expeditionary militia from Virginia that would drive the British back to the Charleston garrison, and thence force them to leave. He is seeking a commission in this force, and asking the Governor and the council to provide necessary supplies. It is an idea which will never come to pass, but in the course of his plea he outlines his code of service: "When we were threatened by an invasion from ye south, our prospects were so gloomy & ye. danger so imminent that I thought it ye duty of every citizen to turn out & bear a part in repelling ye invasion." Moreover, he reveals that he has never taken financial compensation for doing his duty. "My plan of taking nothing for any little service I might do ye publick in this cause did not commence with my late employment: during ye. greater part of my service in ye. army I had not my expenses borne, & as in this instance, I have only acted ye part w'ch ye opinion of ye duty I owe to ye publick dictated & . . . it is my wish not to deviate from it."

A year later, the British have invaded Virginia, and taken Richmond, to which the capital had been moved from Williamsburg. Governor Jefferson and the General Assembly had withdrawn in front of the British forces to Charlottesville; and when the British approached Charlottesville, to Staunton. Jefferson himself did not leave Monticello until British troops were coming up the hill of Monticello (he left by the back way). Monroe writes on June 18, 1781 congratulating Jefferson on his escape, but the desire to serve is still there. "I sate out to ye. Marquis' [de Lafayette] army to act in an line either himself or Council wo'd employ me in." General Weedon has asked him to carry a truce flag to Alexandria to allow supplies to be taken to prisoners of war. "So soon as I disengage myself from this affair, I shall join ye army & serve till ye enemy leave this State." But he was not to serve again. On Oct. 1, he tells Jefferson that he went to the new Governor, Thomas Nelson, to seek a commission in the militia, but "was informed ye Militia in ye field was officer's & of course . . . I co'd procure none whatsoever."

Bitterly disappointed, Monroe then sought to fulfill a long-held desire to study in France. He sold his property in Westmoreland County, realizing enough money, so he thought, to live upon the interest from the principal. He had engaged passage on a ship with a certain Col. Josiah Parker. He tells Jefferson that "I . . . have read all ye books you mention on the subject of law . . . I mean to convey to you that altho' I shall most probably be glad some time hence to acquire more by ye practice of ye law (if I have it in my power) I wo'd still wish to prosecute my studies on ye most liberal plan to qualify myself for any business I might chance to engage in. This if not profitable will be agreeable, for surely these acquirements qualify a man not only for publick office, but enable him to bear prosperity or adversity in ye capricious turns of fortune, with greater magnanimity & fortitude, by giving him resources within himself, of pleasure & content w'h otherwise he wo'd look for in vain from others."

But the European tour was not to be. On May 6, 1782 he writes to Jefferson: "Nothing but a series of disappointments in ye vessels I had appointed to sail in, depriv'd me of ye opportunity of availing myself in that instance of ye advantage it w'd have given me." But then he told Jefferson that he had taken up a new career—he had been elected to the Virginia House of Delegates. Almost immediately, he, as a House member, was appointed to the Executive Council of the Governor. It was to be the first of a long series of public offices he would occupy throughout his lifetime.

Jefferson, having withdrawn to Monticello after the debacle of the British invasion when he was governor, also appeared to have withdrawn from politics. Now it was Monroe's turn to encourage Jefferson. "How very anxiously I wish y'r. arrival & how very sincerely I join ye better part of this community in my desire that a few days more will give us y'r aid in ye House & Society to y'r friends." And on May 11, he writes a more empassioned plea: "You will readily conceive that as it furnishes those who argue on ye fundamental maxims of a republican government with ample field for declamation, the conclusion has always been, you sh'd not decline ye service of yr country." Those are words which Monroe could well have applied to himself.

Yet the dream of a military commission had not yet died. On August 15, 1782, he wrote one last formal plea to General Washington. Citing his previous military service, his studies with Jefferson, his election to the House and his appointment to the Executive Council, he placed himself at the General's disposal in grandiloquent, if indirect prose. If Fortune should put it in his power "to pay attention to or obey in any instance y'r Excellency's commands" she could do him no favor that would give him greater pleasure. But Fortune did not so smile.

MONROE'S OATH AT VALLEY FORGE

I James Monroe Aid DeCamp to Major General Lord Stirling—do acknowledge the UNITED STATES of AMERICA to be Free, Independent and Sovereign States, and declare that the people thereof owe no allegiance or obedience to George the Third, King of Great-Britain; and I renounce, refuse and abjure any allegiance or obedience to him; and I do swear that I will, to the utmost of my power, support, maintain and defend the said United States against the said King George the Third, his heirs and successors, and his or their abettors, assistants and adherents, and will serve the said United States in the office of Aid DeCamp which I now hold, with fidelity, according to the best of my skill and understanding.

Sworn before me at Valley Forge Camp May 16th 1778.

JAˢ. MONROE.
Stirling Major Ga.

TO GENERAL WASHINGTON.
June 28, 1778.

From the field of Monmouth. In General Orders, White Marsh, November 20, 1777, Monroe was appointed aide, with the rank of Major, to Lord Stirling, who commanded the left wing of the army as re-formed by Washington after he had checked the retreat of General Charles Lee. Monroe with his command had been charged with the important duty of following the enemy's movements and of reporting them to Lord Stirling and also directly to the Commander-in-chief. [HAMILTON.]

SIR,—Upon not receiving any answer to my first information and observing the enemy inclining toward your right I thought it advisable to hang as close on them as possible—I am at present within four hundred yrds. of their right— I have only about 70 men who are now fatigued much. I have taken three prisoners—If I had six horsemen I think If I co'd serve you in no other way I sho'd in the course of the night procure good intelligence w'h I wo'd as soon as possible convey you.

I am Sir your most ob't Serv't

JAˢ. MONROE.
Lᵗ. Colᵒ. Basset is with me and wishes the same. 4 o'clock.

TO GENERAL CHARLES LEE.
AYLETT'S WAREHOUSE, June 15th. (1780).

MY DEAR GEN[L].,—I am happy in accidentally meeting with a neighbor of y[rs] who tells me he lately left you well & contended with your retir'd life. I am extremely anxious for your welfare & often most sincerely lament that the temper of this continent should be such as to render it expedient for you to return to Berkley. When I left you in Phil[a]., my wish and expectation was immediately to go to Europe; on my coming to Virginia, being under age, I found it difficult to make such disposition of my property as wo[d] admit of it. I meant however to go this fall, & as I wish'd to go in the character of an officer, for that purpose I went up to H[d] Q[rs] by Phil[a] (where I wish'd much to have seen you) to require from His Excell[y] & L[d] Stirling a certificate of my good conduct. This I meant to present to the Virg[a] Assembly & from them procure an appointment. His Excellency gave the letter I co[d] have wished & Ld Stirling also treated me with gentlemanly politeness. What I have to expect from this Assembly is incertain, but as they have no interest in the appointment I desire, I believe I have no probable grounds to found hopes on. I am retiring from them to my Uncle's, M[r] Jones, near Fredericksb[g], (the Chief Justice of this State) where I propose staying perhaps this year. If it was my house, my d[r] general you sho[d] make it yours, but at present I only live in expectation of it. I may however take the liberty with my uncle to press you if you come that way to call & see me. Be so kind as write me, and direct to Fredericksb[g]. to inform me where I may wait on you. I am solicitous for y[r] interest & wish to consult you on my plan.

I am dear General with sincere esteem y[r] friend & very humble Serv[t].

JA[S]. MONROE.
The H[nble] Major Genl. LEE
Berkley Cty.

"The good figure you make flatters my vanity, as I have always asserted that you wou'd appear one of the first characters of this country, if your shyness did not prevent the display of the knowledge and talents you possess. M[r]. White tells me you have got rid of this mauvaise honte, and only retain a certain degree of recommendatory modesty. I rejoice in it with all my soul, as I really love and esteem you most sincerely and affectionately . . . General Lee's reply, July 18, 1780.

TO THE GOVERNOR OF VIRGINIA.
(THOMAS JEFFERSON.)

The want of intelligence concerning the southern movements of the enemy, and the anxieties felt on that account, necessitated the sending of a trustworthy person to observe them. Jefferson, then Governor of Virginia, entrusted this mission to Monroe. Congress expressed its appreciation by continuing this important line of communication, established by Jefferson and Monroe, from Philadelphia to Washington's headquarters. [HAMILTON.]

CROSS CREEK, June 26, 1780.

SIR,—Some few days since I arrived here & trust I have so arranged the line of communication between us, that whatever alterations the course of events may effect in my own situation, I shall have it in my power to make it subservient to my wishes. I expected I should more effectually put in execution your Excellency's orders by coming immediately here, the source from which Governor Nash at Newberry or Baron de Kalb at Hillsborough get their Intelligence, then by taking my route to either of those posts & I have had the good fortune in meeting Governor Nash here to approve my determination. The Governor was on his route to Baron de Kalb & called upon General Caswell here with a view of making himself acquainted with his force and object, in order to concert some regular & connected plan of either offensive or defensive action, as circumstances might admit, for the protection of the country. I have it not in my power to give your Excellency at present, information upon all the points you require, but an event we are informed has taken place of such importance in its probable consequences to the State of Virginia, as to make it necessary I should immediately inform you of it. We have it from authority we cannot doubt, that an embarkation has taken place at Charlestown and sailed some days since under the command of General Clinton, consisting of about 6000 men. The remainder of their army, supposed upwards of 4000, with their cavalry forming a corps of 600 under Col. Tarleton, are left behind under Lord Cornwallis. General Caswell has repeatedly had information, they had embarked, but never 'til today that they had sailed, & today I examined myself two men of Woodford's Brigade, lately escaped from Charlestown, who confirm it. A Garrison of about 800 are said to be left at Charlestown; 2500 at Camden; the cavalry are stationed about 40 miles above Camden; about 600 of the 71st regiment on the river Peedee between Long Bluff and Ansons Court House. What may be the object of those who have sailed or of those who remain is uncertain and must depend on the part the Court of France means to take this year in our favor; but if we may judge from the view which has hitherto evidently influenced their councils (if no internal event has happened to their prejudice) provided they act on a consistent plan, we must conclude they mean to land somewhere in Virginia, and by directing their armies to the same object endeavour to Conquer all these Southern States. Upon this Principle I am inclined to think their operations have of late been taken and that upon this principle they will determine. What again would induce this belief & with me it is only an inferior circumstance (for upon principles of expedience they should act thus) is the universal scarcity of all kinds of provisions, except meat, which prevails in this country. Upon this account the army under General de Kalb at Hillsborough and that under General Caswell here, are no longer able to hold those stations and are in that dilemma,that they have only the alternative of advancing shortly on the enemy or retiring to Virginia. This however will in a great degree be remedied when the harvest comes in. What plan General de Kalb may take to oppose them I cannot determine, but as that which the enemy have adopted creates a division of their force, ours also must necessarily be divided and in that case rather than hang or temporize between them, I doubt not he will take a decided part against this body, I mean I hope he will keep on their left flank and harass and retard them in all their movements as much as possible. Their forces have been pointedly directed against the Continental Troops; and to get the country and throw them down on the sea coast would necessarily be a great object. A considerable advantage, also arising from the position I have suggested, would be that the troops who oppose this army & those who oppose that which may land in Virginia might act on a common principle & when the enemy effect a junction they might join also, still keeping the command of the country. This plan has not the protection of any particular spot but is on a larger scale & has Independence for its object; acting on any other principle and taking particular positions for particular purposes, may lead the respective corps into danger & perhaps ruin.

Genl. Clinton previous to his departure issued a Proclamation discharging all who had taken them from their paroles & requiring their immediate attendance to swear allegiance and bear arms in favor of his Sovereign declaring that all who refuse to comply with these reasonable terms, who shall be found in arms hereafter in favor of the rebellion shall not be treated as soldiers & prisoners of war; but as banditti & Robbers. I have not seen the Proclamation but Govr. Nash who has, tells me this is the purpose of it. Only 1500 militia are collected here under General Caswell & about 1,100 under Brig. Rutherford, west of the enemy, who hold the position I could wish Baron de Kalb to take with the Continental Troops at least. At Charlotte, Salsbury or Chatham the country is better able to support an army & when Harvest comes in will be more so, while that near here or towards the coast is much exhausted. Between here and Halifax it is so much so (and I am told by the inhabitants on the road that want is not confined to them alone but extends considerably to the Right & left) that I could scarcely get provisions for myself & men & in many instances could not procure corn for my Horses at any rate. The Governor of this State has extensive powers & except when it affects the life—the advice of Council he knows no restraint on his will. He also seems well disposed to act with that firmness & descision in most instances which the unhappy state of his country requires, without regard to any local or personal enmity which may arise against him in the discharge of the duties of so important a trust. He is constrained to emit money constantly as occasion requires & has now ordered out 4,000 Militia in addition to those I have mentioned as already in the field. At Govr. Nash's request I shall attend him tomorrow to where Baron de Kalb may be, or if the Govr. does not go himself, shall perhaps go up on the business I have referred to & in my next shall have it in my power to inform your Excellency of the plan Baron de Kalb may take for his future operations, with the probability of success, or what effect it may have on the movements of the enemy.

I have the honor to be with the greatest respect and esteem yr. Excellencys Very humble Servt.

JA^S MONROE.

P. S. I cannot inform you where Porterfield is; but expect somewhere near the Baron. Col^o. Armand's Corps are here under command of Genl. Caswell. We have had reports a French fleet are off C. Town but not from such authority as to give assent.

TO THOMAS JEFFERSON.
RICHMOND, Sepr. 9, 1780.

DEAR SIR,—Your kindness & attention to me in this & a variety of other instances has really put me under such obligations to you that I fear I shall hardly ever have it in my power to repay them. But believe me in whatever situation of life ye chance of fortune may place me, no circumstance can happen wch. will give me such pleasure or make me so happy, at present or during my progress thro' life, as to have it in my power to convince you of ye proper impressions they have made on me. A variety of disappointments with respect to ye prospects of my private fortune previous to my acquaintance with your

Excellency, upon w'ch I had built as on ground w'ch co'd not deceive me, & w'ch fail'd in a manner w'ch co'd not have been expected, perplex'd my plan of life & expos'd me to inconveniences w'ch had nearly destroy'd me. In this situation had I not form'd a connection with you I sho'd most certainly have retir'd from society with a resolution never to have enter'd on ye stage again. I co'd never have prevail'd on myself to have taken an introduction to ye Country, or to have deriv'd any advantages or even to have remain'd in connection with one by whom I felt myself injur'd, but whose near relationship & situation in life put it in his power to serve me. In this situation you became acquainted with me & undertook ye direction of my studies & believe me I feel that whatever I am at present in ye. opinion of others or whatever I may be in future has greatly arisen from y'r friendship. My plan of life is now fix'd, has a certain object for its view & does not depend on other chance or circumstance further than ye same events may affect ye. publick at large. In ye late instance when we were threatened by an invasion from ye south, our prospects were so gloomy & ye. danger so iminent that I thought it ye duty of every citizen to turn out & bear a part in repelling ye invasion. The attention of y'r Excellency & Council paid me in calling on me to perform ye. duties of so important a trust at so critical a time if it had gone no further than intimating ye. good opinion you severally entertain'd of me, I knew did me honor & gave me more pleasure than any pecuniary compensation I cod. possibly derive from it. I was happy in undertaking ye charge with a view of performing some service to ye country & also of assuring you, that even in an affair w'ch had so distant a relation to you, how effectually you might command my small services. My plan of taking nothing for any little service I might do ye publick in this cause did not commence with my late employment: during ye. greater part of my service in ye. army I had not my expenses borne, & as in this instance, I have only acted ye part w'ch ye opinion of ye duty I owe to ye publick dictated & w'ch many worthy Republicans are now acting without even a similar compensation, it is my wish not to deviate from it. Under ye present direction my prospects are fix'd & altho' my private fortune is but small still it is sufficient for my maintenance in ye pursuit of them. Colo. Dawson waited on me ye other day & propos'd my bearing part with him in his present undertaking. I excus'd myself by every argument wch. my situation & ye nature of his plan wo'd admit of & had been happy to have evaded it altogether. I represented to him ye nature of things in that country & that ye ultimate advantage w'ch ye success of his plan co'd effect wo'd be ye driving ye enemy into Chas.town from w'ch they might advance so soon as ye militia moulder'd away. I wish'd him, as Council are making every exertion in their power for ye defence of that Country to change his view & rather form a corps within ye state or one more immediately for its defence rather than to go in search of adventures more remote w'ch promise at best but little advantage to our friends while it exhausts & weakens ourselves. But promis'd if he co'd get no one more capable or whose private circumstances wo'd better dispense with their absence than myself, if his plan succeeded I wo'd bear a part. If I can possibly avoid it I mean not to leave my study a day, but if in ye progress of things I sho'd be so circumstanc'd as in y'r opinion I ow'd it to myself or ye publick to bear a part, so far as ye publick interest will be forwarded by furnishing myself or ye troops I command with necessaries so far I shall be happy to receive them. You will forgive ye liberty I have taken in writing you a letter of this kind. Y'r kindness has really led me into it. & at ye same time it enables me to explain some part of my conduct I am happy that it gives me an opportunity of assuring you how just a sense I have of y'r good offices. I have ye honour to be, Dear Sir, with great respect & esteem y'r sincere friend & very humble serv't

JA^S. MONROE.

TO THOMAS JEFFERSON.

In May, 1781, in anticipation of an attack on Richmond, the legislature adjourned to meet in Charlottesville, May 24, and Governor Jefferson returned to his home at Monticello, in sight of Charlottesville. In the beginning of June, Colonel Tarleton, with two hundred and fifty of his legion, started on a raid on Charlottesville, in the hope of capturing the legislature and the Governor. He arrived there on the 4th of that month, to find that the birds had flown. They had received warning of his coming, a few hours before, and barely escaped. Jefferson did not leave Monticello until he was informed that the British cavalry was ascending the hill of Monticello. Then he mounted his horse, took a mountain road, and joined his family, which he had sent on before, at his estate in Bedford, about eighty miles southeast of Charlottesville. [HAMILTON.]

FREDERICKSB'G, June 18, 1781.

DEAR SIR,—I some time since address'd a letter to you from a small estate of mine in King George whither I had retir'd to avoid ye enemy from ye one I lately dispos'd of on ye Patommack river. I had then ye pleasure to congratulate you on ye safe retreat from Richmond to Charlottesville & anticipated ye joy y'r self & family must have felt on y'r arrival at Monticello from w^h. ye misfortune of ye times has long separated you. I lament y'r felicity on that head was of but short duration. I hope howe'er that neither y'rself nor Mrs. Jefferson has sustain'd injury from these obtrusions of ye enemy. In a former I advis'd you I wo'd not stay at home in ye present state of ye country & sho'd be happy to bear some part in her defence: for that purpose I sate out to join ye. Marquis' Army to act in any line either himself or Council wo'd employ me in. Being confin'd here some few days with small indisposition Gen'l Weedon has requested of me to sit out this Ev'g to manage ye British flag on its way to Alexandria. So soon as I disengage myself from this affair, I shall join ye army & serve till ye enemy leave this State. I earnestly wish to leave ye Continent & shall not alter my plan unless our publick affairs change materially. Whither you continue in your determination to retire from office I hope to see both y'rself & family in ye course of ye year. If we [*mutilated*] & in ye former instance I sho'd find you at Stanton on my way to ye Springs. Otherwise God knows where we shall be. Be so kind as to make my best respects to Mrs. Jefferson & believe me with ye greatest esteem & regard yr. friend & servant,

Jas. Monroe.

On the 7th of June, the legislature reassembled at Staunton, forty miles from Charlottesville, on the other side of the Blue Ridge. [Hamilton.]

TO THOMAS JEFFERSON.
Caroline, Oct. 1, 1781.

Dear Sir,—I propos'd to myself the pleasure of visiting y'r self & family before this at Monticello but ye prospects below & ye arrival of Gen'l Washington in ye State induc'd me to postpone ye trip of pleasure to ye less agreeable one to camp upon ye. Idea of bearing some small part in bringing about ye event we all so anxiously wish for. With this view I waited on Gov. Nelson & solicited some command in ye Militia but was inform'd ye Militia in ye field was officer'd & of course that I co'd procure none whatever. This wo'd have mortified me much had I not discover'd during my continuance with ye army that Gen'l W. had under his command 15000 regular troops, a force certainly very sufficient to reduce ye post at York. On ye contrary upon being well inform'd of our force & ye propriety of ye appointments thro' ye whole, I was ye rather surpris'd ye militia were detained at all, more especially when we take into consideration ye difficulty of supply, for surely in ye present state of things ye militia will not render sufficient service to counterbalance ye quantity of provisions they consume. I had, however, ye good fortune to effect a point w'h. since ye interruption of our civil affairs in this state I have been very desirous to accomplish & in ye expedience whereof was so happy as to have y^r. concurrence when with you last at Richm'^{d}. Colo. Josiah Parker has a ship just ready to sail to France & has been so kind as to offer me a passage in her, w^h. I have accepted. I sho'd be happy to wait on you before I sail & shall be sincerely sorry to leave ye continent without wishing y^r. self & family health & happiness in person, but as we sail ye 10th or 12th of next month from some port south of Portsmouth & I have much business to transact in these days I shall be at home, am unfortunately depriv'd of that pleasure. I have to desire of you a letter to each of our Ministers & also y^r. advice upon ye plan I had better pursue as also where I had better visit. Since my return from Richm'd I have liv'd a very sedentary life upon a small estate I have in King Georges in course of w'h time have read all ye books you mention on ye subject of law. I have made such a disposition of ye property I sold in Westmorel'd as to give me an interest nearly competent to my purpose without injuring ye principal. I mean to convey to you that altho' I shall most probably be glad some time hence to acquire more by ye practice of ye law (if I have it in my power) I wo'd still wish to prosecute my studies on ye most liberal plan to qualify myself for any business I might chance to engage in. This if not profitable will be agreeable, for surely these acquirements qualify a man not only for publick office, but enable him to bear prosperity or adversity in ye capricious turns of fortune, with greater magnanimity & fortitude, by giving him resources within himself, of pleasure & content w'h otherwise he wo'd look for in vain from others. I wish you to say whether if I am so fortunate as to sail & arrive safe you wo'd advise me to reside altogether in ye South of France or (if possible) spend a year at ye Temple in London before my return. I write you on my return home from below from M^r. Taliaferro's & as I have not a moment to lose have only time to add that whatever commands you will favor me with I shall be happy to execute & that I am with my best respects for Mr^s. Jefferson. y^r. sincere friend & very humble servant,

JA^s. MONROE.

TO THOMAS JEFFERSON.
RICHMOND, May 6, 1782.

DEAR SIR,—Mr. Short being just setting out for Monticello I am happy to take ye opportunity to assure you how sincerely I thank you for ye late instance of y^r. kindness and attention to me, w^h. I particularly value as a testimony of y^r. regard for me, & at ye same time to assure you that nothing but a series of disappointments in ye vessels I had appointed to sail in, depriv'd me of ye opportunity of availing myself in that instance of ye advantage it w'd have given me. Mr. Short will inform you of my appointm't in ye House, upon declining ye other plan, & how very anxiously I wish y'r. arrival & how very sincerely I join ye better part of this community in my desire that a few days more will give us y'r. aid in ye House & Society to y'r. friends. I have only time to desire my best respects to Mrs. Jefferson & assure I am with great respect & esteem y'r. sincere friend & servant,

JAˢ. MONROE.

TO THOMAS JEFFERSON.
RICHMOND, 11 May, 1782.

DEAR SIR,—As I so lately wrote you by Mr. Short & have since daily expected to see you here I did not propose writing you till after I sho'd have that pleasure; but as I begin to fear you will not abate that firmness & decision w'ch you have frequently shewn in ye service of y'r country even upon this occasion & as I have had an opportunity since I wrote last of being better inform'd of ye sentiments of those whom I know you put ye greatest value on, I think it my duty to make you acquainted therewith. It is publickly said here that ye people of y'r county inform'd you they had frequently elected you in times of less difficulty & danger than ye present to please you, but that now they had call'd you forth into publick office to serve themselves. This is a language w'ch has been often us'd in my presence & you will readily conceive that as it furnishes those who argue on ye fundimental maxims of a republican government with ample field for declamation, the conclusion has always been, you sho'd not decline ye service of yr country. The present is generally conceiv'd to be an important era w'ch of course makes y'r attendance particularly necessary, & as I have taken ye liberty to give you ye publick opinion & desire upon this occasion, & as I am warmly interested in whatever concerns ye publick interest or has relation to you, it will be unnecessary to add it is earnestly ye desire of, Dear Sir, y'r sincere friend & servant,

JAˢ. MONROE.

This and the preceding letter were written by Monroe for the purpose of inducing Jefferson to change the resolution he had announced of retiring from public life. The expedition of Benedict Arnold in January, 1781, resulting in the capture of Richmond and an immense destruction of public and private stores had greatly distressed the people of that

State, and they were inclined to hold Jefferson, as Governor, responsible. In fact George Nicholas, a young and impulsive delegate from Jefferson's own county, had openly charged him in the House of Delegates with neglect of duty, and demanded an inquiry into his conduct. This was promptly accepted by Jefferson's friends, and the investigation was set down for the next session. Jefferson's term of office expired June 1, 1781, and General Thomas Nelson succeeded him.

Before the legislature met again Cornwallis had surrendered at Yorktown, and discontent and despondency had given way to rejoicing and triumph. The people returned to their sense of justice, and were now anxious to right the wrong they had done their Governor. His fellow-citizens of Albemarle unanimously elected him a member of the House of Delegates, and when the time appointed for the inquiry arrived Jefferson was present and declared his readiness to answer the charges. No one appeared to prosecute them. Their author, George Nicholas, had become convinced of their injustice, and subsequently published a letter in which he frankly admitted his error. The legislature then passed the following resolution, without a dissenting voice:

"That the sincere thanks of the General Assembly be given to our former Governor, Thomas Jefferson, Esquire, for his impartial, upright, and attentive administration, whilst in office. The Assembly wish in the strongest manner to declare the high opinion which they entertain of Mr. Jefferson's ability, rectitude, and integrity, as chief magistrate of this Commonwealth, and mean by thus publicly avowing their opinion, to obviate and to remove all unmerited censure."

But this vindication did not satisfy Jefferson. He felt that he had been cruelly treated by the people whom he had spared no labor or sacrifice to serve; his sensitive spirit refused to accept the resolution of the Assembly as a compensation for the wrongs he had suffered, and he was unwilling to continue in a service which rendered him such ungrateful returns. How deeply he had taken the matter to heart is shown by his reply to Monroe.—See The Writings of Jefferson, vol. iii., p. 56.

On the 13th of June, 1781, Jefferson had been appointed a Minister Plenipotentiary, with Adams, Franklin, Jay, and Laurens as his colleagues, to negotiate a peace with Great Britain. But he was unwilling to leave the country while the charges were pending in the legislature, and declined the appointment. This appointment was renewed November 13, 1782. Meanwhile he had lost his wife, to whom he was devotedly attached, and in the hope that a change of scene might tend to mitigate his sorrow, he accepted the appointment, and made his arrangements to leave the country in a French man-of-war which had been placed at his disposal. For this purpose he proceeded to Baltimore, and waited there some time. The capes of the Chesapeake were blockaded by a British squadron, and while awaiting an opportunity to run the blockade, news arrived in this country of the negotiation of preliminary articles of peace, and Congress determined that it would be unnecessary *for him to proceed. In June, 1783, the Virginia Assembly elected him at the head of its delegation to Congress, and associated with him, as his youngest colleague, James Monroe, then twenty-five years of age.* [HAMILTON.]

TO THOMAS JEFFERSON.
RICHMOND, June 28, 1782.

DEAR SIR,—I am sorry I have had no opportunity or sho^d. have answer'd y'r. favor by ye servant sooner, indeed sho'^d. have wrote by him but was so unlucky as not to see him while in town. I have been much distress'd upon ye subject of Mrs. Jefferson & have fear'd as well from what you suggested y'r.self as what I have heard from others, that y'r. report of each succeeding day wo'd inform me she was no more. Indeed this was awhile reported & believ'd, but I flatter myself that in this instance I shall experience that common fame, who when she has propagated reports unfavorable to myself & my friends I have rarely found to be groundless, has fail'd & that it may please heaven to restore our amiable friend to health & thereby to you a friend whose loss you wo'd always lament, & to ye children a parent wh. no change of circumstance co'd ever compensate for. You will forgive this obtrusion on an affair w'h tho' greatly you are not singly interested in, & as I necessarily suppose you are entirely engaged in an attention to & discharge of those tender duties w'h her situation unhappily requires, from you & so anxious & deeply interested in ye prospect of an event w'h so materially concerns ye peace & tranquility of y'r. family, I shall forbear to trouble you with an answer to that part of y'r. letter w'h. respects y'r. retreat from publick service. This I shall postpone either till I see you or till I hear ye situation of y'r. family will leave y'r. mind more at ease & leisure to attend to a disquisition of ye kind & in ye meantime beg leave to assure you that nothing will give me so much pleasure as to hear of Mrs. Jefferson's recovery, & to be inform'd of it from yourself. I forgot in my last to inform you I had receiv'd ye parliamentary debates & annual register from Mr. Buchanan & to assure you I will keep them for ever as a testimony of your friendship & esteem. Believe me to be, Dear Sir, very sincerely your friend & servant,

JA^s. MONROE.

P.S. Your letter to Pelham I sent off instantly & receiv'd a verbal message by my servant that no answer was necessary. You have perhaps heard of my appointm'^t. in Council. Engag'd as you are in domestic duties permit me to assure you I wish, so soon as circumstances will permit you, to correspond regularly with you & to have y'r. advice upon every subject of consequence.

TO GEORGE WASHINGTON.

In 1779, Monroe, after having served two years on the staff of Lord Stirling, was anxious to obtain a position in the Continental line. Failing in this by reason of the unwillingness of the regular line officers to yield to his claims, he determined to return to Virginia and seek employment in the State service. To assist him in this, Gen. Washington gave him a letter to Col. Archibald Cary, then one of the most influential men in the State. As Chairman of the Committee of the Whole in the Virginia Convention of 1776, he had reported the resolution instructing the delegates in Congress to propose independence, and when a committee consisting of the ablest men in the Convention was appointed to prepare a declaration of rights and a plan of government for the State, Cary was placed at its head. "It was from his lips, that the words of the resolution of independence, of the declaration of rights, and of the first constitution of Virginia first fell upon the public ear." On the organization of the State government under the new Constitution, he was chosen Speaker of the Senate, and held that office at the time of his death, in 1786. His unswerving devotion to principle and his indomitable courage had won for him the sobriquet of "Old Iron." When, during the invasion of the State, there was some talk in the Assembly of declaring Patrick Henry dictator, Cary met Col. Syme, Henry's half-brother, in the lobby of the House, and thus accosted him: "Sir, I am told that your brother wishes to be dictator. Tell him from me, that the day of his appointment shall be the day of his death; for he shall find my dagger in his heart before the sunset of that day."

Washington's letter to Cary shows the high opinion the Commander-in-chief had formed of the young soldier, then just twenty-one years old. [HAMILTON.]

HEAD QUARTERS, 30 May, 1779.

DEAR SIR,—very sincerely lament that the situation of our service will not permit us to do justice to the merits of Major Monroe, who will deliver you this, by placing him in the army upon some satisfactory footing. But as he is on the point of leaving us, and expresses an intention of going to the Southward, where a new scene has opened, it is with pleasure I take occasion to express to you the high opinion I have of his worth. The zeal he discovered by entering the service at an early period, the character he supported in his regiment, and the manner in which he distinguished himself at Trenton, when he received a wound; induced me to appoint him to a Captaincy in one of the additional regiments. This regiment failing from the difficulty of recruiting, he entered into Lord Stirling's family, and has served two campaigns as a volunteer aid to his Lordship. He has, in every instance, maintained the reputation of a brave, active, and sensible officer. As we cannot introduce him into the Continental line, it were to be wished that the State could do something for him, to enable him to follow the bent of his military inclination, and render service to his country. If an event of this kind could take place, it would give me particular pleasure; as the esteem I have for him, and a regard to his merit, conspire to make me earnestly wish to see him provided for in some handsome way. I am &c

GEO. WASHINGTON.

This is the letter to which Monroe refers in his letter to General Washington above quoted, as "the introduction you gave me some time since to this State," and which, he says, he found of "essential service" to him. It secured his election to the Assembly from King George County, and his subsequent appointment by that body as a member of the Privy Council. [HAMILTON.]

RICHMOND, 15 August, 1782.

DEAR SIR,—You will pardon the liberty I take in writing you upon a subject w'ch has no relation to the publick interest when I inform you I am induc'd thereto merely from a principle of gratitude to make acknowledgment for the personal service I have rec'd from y'r Excellency. The introduction you gave me some time since to this State, for the purpose of attaining some military appointment to place me in the service of my country in a line with those worthy citizens, with whom common hardship & danger had nearly connected me, altho' it failed me in that instance has avail'd me in another line. Upon relinquishing my military pursuits, w'ch I did with reluctance, & returning to those studies in w'ch I had been engag'd previous to my joining y'r army, till of late I have been literally a recluse. Having gone thro' that course w'ch in the opinion of Mr. Jefferson to whom I submitted the direction of my studies, was sufficient to qualify me in some degree for publick business, in my application to my county in the first instance & in the subsequent appointment of the Assembly to the Executive Council of the State I have had the pleasure to experience y'r friendly letter in my fav'r of essential service to me. If, therefore, I was so fortunate in the manag'ment of my conduct more immediately under y'r eye as to gain y'r good opinion & esteem I flatter myself that in the discharge of the duties of my present office & a faithful observance & attention to the confidence repos'd in me by my country I shall take no step w'ch will entitle me to forfeit theirs or give you cause to repent y'r prepossession in my fav'r. A conscience that I had in some degree merited y'r approbation & that of the Gentlemen of the army with whom I had the honor to associate, gave me a consolation & a pleasure in my subsequent retir'ment, tho' wound'd & chagrin'd at my disappointment from the State, w'ch I co'd not have derived from any other source. If in the line of my present appointment fortune sho'd put it in my power to pay attention to or obey in any instance y'r Excellency's commands believe me she co'd not confer a fav'r on me, I sho'd receive with greater pleasure from her hands. With every sentiment of respect & esteem w'ch y'r great & unwearied service to y'r country & your kind & friendly attention to me can fill my breast I have the honor to be y'r Excellency's most obedient & most humble servant,

JAS. MONROE.

PART II
Legislator from Virginia

INTRODUCTION

A S A RESULT OF Monroe's active role as a rising young legislator in the Virginia House of Delegates, he was elected in December 1783 as a representative to the Congress organized under the Articles of Confederation, which was then meeting in Annapolis. But with the war over, the sense of unity in the new country seemed to evaporate, even though ratification of the Treaty of Paris, ending the war with Great Britain, was the key item on the agenda. Monroe took his seat in December, but the weeks dragged by, and Congress failed to assemble the nine states needed to ratify until mid-January.

But Monroe's time was not wasted. His roommate in lodgings was his mentor, Thomas Jefferson, who just happened to bring along a choice collection of books of law, history, and the philosophes. Nor was Monroe the only beneficiary of this reading; other representatives also made use of the library, foreshadowing the day many years hence when Jefferson's library at Monticello, much enhanced, would be purchased by Congress as the nucleus of the Library of Congress, now the largest library in the world. Jefferson also introduced Monroe with lavish sentiments to their fellow delegate, James Madison, whom Monroe had known only slightly. Thus began the long relationship among the three notables, a relationship that would last through the presidencies of each until their several deaths. All of them were strong-willed men, and at times the friendship of the triad was shattered. Yet at the end they had shared too much together not to be on terms of intimacy.

Jefferson also made another contribution of lasting impact on his protégé: They shared lodgings with Jefferson's French chef, Partout, who adhered to his Gallic patrimony both in food and language. By conversing with Partout, Monroe learned the rudiments of the French language, while his palate was formed to the French taste. French philosophy and French cookery made such a powerful impact on the young, would-be francophile that it shaped his political outlook, his career in diplomacy and public service, and even his artistic taste. Years later, after twice being minister, or in today's terms, ambassador, to Paris, Monroe put a French stamp on the style of the President's Mansion—the White House—that has lasted to this day, and set the course of high taste in America for generations. The remaining examples of Monroe's actual china, Monroe's furniture, and Monroe's decorative objects are the heart of the White House's décor today.

Suddenly, Jefferson was called to another duty. On May 7, he was selected to be minister plenipotentiary to France, and left immediately via Philadelphia to sail from Boston. He left behind a vacancy in Monroe's days, but he also left behind Partout. Monroe tried to keep Jefferson abreast of the news of Congress. On May 14, 1784, he wrote: "I hope before this you have safely arriv'd in Phil'a. I very sensibly feel your absence not only in the solitary situation in w'h you have left me but upon many other accounts." The letter includes a very intriguing footnote: "P.S. Partout & myself agree very well only now & then we require the aid of an interpreter. I have had one or two comfortable solitary dinners upon little more than vegetables & coffee cream"—presumably, a salad with cream dressing. The reason for the austerity no doubt was that Jefferson, now absent, had been the paymaster, for Monroe adds, showing off his fledgling French written without accents, "He says, 'comme vous dinez Monsieur tout seul il est tres necessaire pour reduire la provision and pour accommoder la depense a cette changement.'"

In the body of the letter, Monroe seeks Jefferson's advice about the problem of the British continuing to hold garrisons in the forts of the Northwest territories, a subject which will preoccupy him in the future, but which will end up saving his life, as recounted later. But for now, Monroe became a member of the committee established, according to a resolution of Congress passed while sitting at Princeton, "to repair to the lower falls of the Potomack to view the situation of the country in the vicinity of the same" and recommend whether it would be an appropriate site for the residency of Congress.

On May 20, he wrote to Jefferson, "The committee, of which I am a member, appointed to view the country around Georgetown under the Princeton engagement set out this morning upon that business. I think with you that it will be proper to effect this business before the adjournment & no time may better be spared than the present." Time was available for the journey to survey the site adjacent to Georgetown because an acrimonious dispute had broken out over whether the delegates from Rhode Island could be properly seated, their commissions having expired. As a result, all other business in

Congress was stymied. Monroe's letter to Jefferson carefully marshals the arguments on both sides of the Rhode Island issue in what was to become almost a trademark of his broad views and analytical vision. His grasp of the parliamentary maneuvering on this issue was a hallmark of his style. Monroe realized that if Rhode Island were not seated, Congress would lack a quorum to finish its business and adjourn. In the end, Monroe and the cooler heads prevailed, and the Rhode Islanders were seated.

But on May 25, he writes to Jefferson: "My letter by the last post will inform you of the occasion [i.e., the Rhode Island impasse] wh. pointed that as the favorable moment for a trip to Georgetown & of our availing ourselves of it. Yesterday evening we return'd. Our report will be in favor of the Maryland side & of a position near the town." Sectional rivalries would delay for some time approval of the Committee's recommendations, but eventually the report was approved. In 1791, Washington, president under the new Constitution, had the new capital surveyed, and on December 1, 1800, Congress moved into the new territory of Columbia. Thus, in another irony, Monroe and Washington were the only presidents to play a major role is establishing the seat of government of the United States.

On November 1, 1784, Monroe had just arrived for the new session of Congress at Trenton where delegates were slowly gathering (two months later Congress decamped to the more salubrious venue of New York). He had just completed a harrowing trip to the Great Lakes, which was really an attempt to gather intelligence about the capabilities and probabilities of the region, and the impact of trade with Canada. It was a trip that had originally been planned with Jefferson.

As the party traveled from Fort Stanwick to Niagara Falls, Monroe was separated by accident from the others, who went on ahead. Here's how Monroe told the story to Jefferson on November 1, relating "an accident which happen'd to some of the party upon Lake Erie, with whom I came from fort Stanwix [sic] to Niagara. I had separated from them by accident three days before the events. They landed near some Indian huts (a Mr. Teller from Schenactady [sic] with four men in a batteaux) and were fir'd on by those Indians. Mr. Teller & two men killed & a 4th wounded; the latter with the 5th made their escape. The Indian chiefs highly reprehended the act & were, at the earnest instigation of the gentlemen of the Brit'h garrison, endeavoring to detect & bring the villains to justice. Upon advice of this disaster Colo. Depeister, commanding at Niagara, sent an Express to me just entering upon Lake Erie advising my return, with wh. I complied. . . . My excursion hath been attended with great personal exposure

& hardship & much greater expence than I had expected. It hath, however, I hope been advantageous to me in some respects."

The rest of the letter is filled with acute observations on the wealth of Canadian timber, but the impossibility of transporting it through the rapids of the St. Lawrence, and the difficulties that the British will have in monopolizing the trade in furs. He sketches out a policy by which the United States would restrict trade from Canada, forcing the British to defend and support the colony and making it a drain on their resources. He ultimately hoped this pressure would force Britain to with draw from the garrisons from U.S. territory. Later he introduced a measure in Congress to embargo trade with Great Britain until the British garrisons withdrew to British territory.

But pressure on Great Britain was the last thing desired by New York and the New England ports. Because of Britain's restrictive measures against the American fishing and carrying trade, the economy of the northeast was in ruins. Until the blockades began, Massachusetts had been the king of cod. Since the 17th century, the fortunes of the Massachusetts Bay Colony rose and fell with the catch of this fish teeming on the Grand Banks of Newfoundland. In theory, all trade from the colonies was supposed to be carried on through British ports; but the shipments of salt and dried cod were so enormous that the British merchant marine did not have the capacity to move them. Instead, the New Englanders shipped the cod directly to markets, the principal one being the slave plantations of the West Indies.

A direct trade relationship had also established between Boston and Bilbao, where the best fish were taken and traded for Spanish wine and manufactures. But most Massachusetts cod exports were cheap, poorly processed, and of inferior quality. But it was just the kind of cheap protein that the sugar planters of the Caribbean needed to feed their exhausted workers toiling in the tropical sun. The empty American ships brought back salt from the Tortugas and molasses from the West Indies, which was turned into rum back home. Moreover, the New England ships carried all cargoes of the region on their journeys, including a sordid traffic in human beings. The New Englanders who rightly deplored the existence of slavery in the southern colonies had no compunction about basing their own economy on the provisioning of slaves, or engaging in the slave trade themselves.

Unfortunately, hard times began in the 1760s when the British began to crack down on the upstart colony, with the enforcement of the Navigation Acts, and the new taxes on "sugar," i.e., molasses, designed to kill the rum trade. Once the Revolution began, British men of war kept the American fishing vessels off the Newfoundland banks, and the West Indies ports were closed to American trading vessels, not to speak of the ports in Great Britain. The real tragedy was in the West Indies, where thousands of slaves starved because all the land was given over to the cultivation of sugar cane, and the endless supply of American cod had stopped. John Adams argued strenuously that the Treaty of 1783 ending the war should include guaranteed access to the Newfoundland banks. He lost that debate, but compromised on an agreement to continue to negotiate fishing rights after the treaty's ratification.

When Congress moved to New York, the New Englanders' desire to normalize trade at all costs soon led them to contemplate the breakup of the newly established Union. The main topic of dissension was the negotiations with Spain for a new commercial treaty. Spain sent Don Diego de Gardoqui. Spain at that time owned the Florida territories and the Louisiana territory. Diego's instructions specifically mandated him to secure the closing of the Mississippi to U.S. trade, thereby securing Spain's monopoly on the port of New Orleans, and for which he was to offer commercial concessions for trade with Spain. Congress authorized John Jay, then Minister of Foreign Affairs under the continental confederacy, to negotiate with Gardoqui. He was tasked to settle only the border questions with the Florida, and specifically instructed that he was not to agree to the closing of the Mississippi.

But despite the direct confrontation of the instructions on both sides, Jay was soon persuaded that the advantages of trade with Spain outweighed any issues relating to the Mississippi. The reasoning was based on sectional rivalry. Jay was a native of New York. With his friends, he not only wanted the north to move into trade aggressively, but he wanted to block the development of the new territories between the mountains of the East and the Mississippi. They feared that if the West, as they called this region, encompassing Tennessee, Kentucky and Virginia's Northwest territories, became highly developed, its agricultural products would rival the trade of the northeast, and politically it would be aligned with the south. But if the Mississippi were bottled up, settlers in the west would have no outlet for their trade, and the growth of the region would be discouraged. Jay was prepared to ignore the boundary question, and ignore the objections of the South and the western territories. Needless to say, the south's interests were completely the opposite.

On August 12, 1786, Monroe wrote a blistering confidential letter to Patrick Henry, then governor of Virginia, to warn him of the nefarious actions of Jay. (At that time, treaties were negotiated in secret, and discussions in Congress were considered closed as well.) Henry was no particular ally of Monroe's, since

Henry was a staunch advocate of state sovereignty, while Monroe consistently supported measure to bring closer unity to the nation. Yet on this issue they were allies. Monroe informed Henry of the particular terms of the proposed Spanish treaty, pointing out that the only commodity which would remain under restriction would be tobacco (which of course was Virginia's main export). He describes the machinations of Jay and the northeastern states to get the Congressional instructions rescinded. He states, "This is one of the most extraordinary transactions I have ever known, a minister negotiating expressly for the purposes of defeating the object of his instructions, and by a long train of intrigue & management seducing the representatives of the states to concur in it." Then he adds a new worry: "Certain it is that committees are held in this town [New York] of Eastern men and others of this State upon the subject of a dismemberment of the states east of the Hudson from the union & the erection of them into a separate govt." He is assured that "the measure is talked of in Mass: familiarly, & is supposed to have originated there."

Finally, he concludes in a prophetic postscript:

The object in the occlusion of the Mississippi on the part of these people so far as it is extended to the interest of their States (for those of a private kind gave birth to it) is to break up so far as this will do it, the settlements on the western waters, prevent any in future, and thereby keep the States southward as they now are—or if settlements will take place, that they shall be on such principles as to make it the interest of the people to separate from the Confederacy, so as effectually to exclude any new State from it. To throw the weight of population eastward & keep it there, to appreciate the vacant lands of New York & Massachusetts. In short, it is a system of policy which has for its object the keeping the weight of govt & population in this quarter, & is prepared by a set of men so flagitious, unprincipled & determined in their pursuits, as to satisfy me beyond a doubt they have adopted this as the necessary means of effecting it. In conversations at which I have been present, the Eastern people talk of a dismemberment so as to include Penna. & all the states south to the Potomack. . . .

In the end, the skilful parliamentary maneuvering of Monroe and his allies stalemated the attempt to rescind the original instructions, and the treaty attempt died. But this letter is extremely interesting for Monroe's future. Monroe's parliamentary skill in Congress stopped Jay's Spanish treaty. But shortly thereafter,

Jay was to become his nemesis. Jay was appointed minister plenipotentiary to Great Britain supposedly to negotiate questions relating to the capture of American ships. But Jay's secret intent, and probably secret instructions, was to negotiate a treaty of commerce which would be harmful to France. Within two weeks of Jay's departure, Monroe, unaware of Jay's real purpose, was unexpectedly named Minister to France. In that brilliant first mission to France, executed with such éclat in the midst of the French revolution, Monroe's position and integrity were badly undermined by Jay's secret purposes in London, leading to his recall,temporary political disgrace, and financial ruin that dogged him to his death bed.

Yet the letter to Henry is also prescient in that it takes up the themes of his second ministry to France, whereby he obtained the Louisiana Purchase from Napoleon Bonaparte, thereby opening the Mississippi and the west forever. It also looks forward to his own struggle as president to force Spain to ratify a treaty ceding the Floridas to the United States. Some may even say it presages the great struggle of 1860 when the Union was divided. But more interestingly enough, the intimate knowledge of the Jay-Gardoqui negotiations revealed in this letter was used tellingly by Patrick Henry in his opposition to Virginia's approval of the Constitution of 1789.

One happy aspect of Monroe's sojourn in New York was the acquaintance of the serious young bachelor with one Elizabeth Kortright, whom he brought back to Virginia as his devoted bride. It was to be a life-long intimacy, never shattered by attentions to another. Although reserved in talking about his family circle, Monroe in his letters to his famous friends quite frequently moves from affairs of state to touching references to his wife and children, who were frequently ill. His service to his country often brought separations from his beloved Elizabeth, but their devotion never faltered. Monroe and his bride settled into Fredericksburg at the end of 1786, a few miles from his birthplace at Monroe Hall, and where his uncle, Judge Jones, was living. Although Monroe was a man of some property, he had little ready money, and resolved to attend to the courts to make a living at the law. In 1787 he was once again elected to the General Assembly. On July 17, 1787, he wrote to Jefferson, who was still in France: "Mrs. Monroe hath added a daughter to our society who tho' noisy, contributes greatly to its amus'ment."

But in the same letter, he also worries whether his talents are being slighted by his colleagues. "The Governor [Edmund Randolph] I have reason to believe is unfriendly to me & hath shewn (If I am well inform'd) a disposition to thwart me; Madison, upon whose friendship I have calculated, whose views I have favord., and with whom I have held the most confidential correspondence since you left the continent, is in strict league with him & hath I have reason to believe concurr'd in arrangements unfavorable to me; a suspicion supported by some strong circumstances that this is the case, hath given me great uneasiness—however in this I may be disappointed & I wish it may be so."

Behind this complaint lay the circumstance that Monroe had not been chosen to participate in the Constitutional Convention in Philadelphia. Moreover, not only had he not been selected with the original group, but when Patrick Henry had refused the appointment (he was steadfastly opposed to strengthening the central government), Monroe was not chosen as the substitute. Thus neither Jefferson nor Monroe, two of the greatest minds of the time, participated in the drafting of the Constitution. Yet Monroe resolved not to allow the perceived slight to turn to rancor. In October, after the constitution had been completed, he wrote to Madison concerning the sentiment in the General Assembly:

> The report from Phila. hath presented an interesting subject to their considerations. It will perhaps agitate the minds of the people of this State more than any subject they have had in contemplation since the commencem't of the late revolution, for there will be a greater division among the people of character than then took place, provided we are well informed as to the sentiments of many of them. It is said that Mr. Henry, Genl. Nelson, Harrison & others are against it. This insures it a powerful opposition more especially when associated with that of the 2. dissenting deputies [Edmund Randolph and George Mason, who refused to sign the draft Constitution in Philadelphia]. There are in my opinion some strong objections against the project. . . . But under the predicament in wh. the Union now stands & this State in particular with respect to this business, they are over balanc'd by the arguments in its favor. . . . I believe there will be no opposition to a [ratifying] convention.

On February 7, 1788, he wrote again: "This new constitution still engages the minds of the people with some zeal among the partizans on either side. It is impossible to say which preponderates. The northern part of the State is generally for it than the southern." But then he notes that Virginia had postponed its ratifying convention, waiting to see how the other states reacted. If necessary, Virginia would lead the way in fashioning a compromise.

The Virginia Convention met on June 2, 1788. Monroe, who played a major role, nevertheless was modest in the account he sent to Jefferson in

France. But he writes a vivid account of the factions in the debate. Here is his account as a participant:

> [Edmund] Pendleton [who was elected President of the convention] tho' much impaired in health and in every respect in the decline of life shewed as much zeal to carry it, as if he had been a young man. . . . [George] Wythe acted as chairman to the committee of the whole and of course took but little part in the debate—but was for the adoption relying on subsequent amendments. The governor [Edmund Randolph] exhibited a curious spectacle to view. Having refused to sign the paper [as a delegate in Philadelphia] every body supposed him against it. But he afterwards had written a letter & having taken a part which might be calld rather vehement than active, he was constantly labouring to shew that his present conduct was consistent with the letter & the letter with his refusal to sgin. Madison took the principal share in the debate for it. In which together with the aid I have already mention'd he was somewhat assisted by Innes, Lee, [John] Marshal, [Francis] Corbin, & G[eorge]. Nicholas, as [George] Mason, [Patrick] Henry & [William] Grayson were the principal supporters of the opposition.

Although Monroe had many reservations about the draft Constitution, he eventually settled in its favor. His Observations on the Federal Government is a lawyerly section-by-section analysis. Devoid of rhetorical passion, the pamphlet rebuts the principal arguments raised against each clause. It is the work of a seasoned legal analyst tempered by practical experience. It remains an important document today to give insight to the original intent of the Founding Fathers.

During the debate on ratification, Henry cited the northern states' attempt to trade the closing of the Mississippi for Spanish trading privileges as an example of the dangers of a strong central government. As the debate on the Mississippi was known only in the secret proceedings of the congressional journal, Henry called upon former Congressmen Monroe and Grayson to reveal the details, which they were forced to do under the circumstances. Madison, whose term in Congress had not yet expired, stepped up to point out that even though the vote had been taken to repeal the instructions, they had not been implemented. In the end, the Constitution was approved contingent upon the adoption of the Bill of Rights, as demanded by Mason and others. Approval was only by a ten vote margin among the 168 delegates.

"The discussion as might have been expected where the parties were so nearly on a balance, was conducted generally with great order, propriety & respect of either party to the other—and its even was accompanied with no circumstance on the part of the victorious that was extra[ordinar]y exultation, nor of depression on the part of the unfortunate. There was no bonfire illumination . . .," he wrote to Jefferson.

Monroe's old commander also played a significant part. "The conduct of Genl. Washington upon this occasion has no doubt been right and meritorious," he wrote to Jefferson.

All parties had acknowledged defects in the federal system, and been sensible of the propriety of some material change. To forsake the honorable retreat to which he had retired & risque the reputation he had so deservedly acquired, manifested a zeal for the public interest that could after so many and illustrious servces, & at this stage of his life, scarcely have been expected from him. Having however commenc'd again on the publick theatre, the course which he takes becomes not only highly interesting to him but likewise so to us: the human character is not perfect if he partakes of those qualities which we have too much reason to believe are almost inseparable from the frail nature of our being, the people of America will perhaps be lost. Be assured his influence carried this Government; for my own part I have a boundless confidence in him nor have I any reason to believe he will ever furnish occasion for withdrawing it. More is to be apprehended if he takes a part in the public councils again, as he advances in age, from the designs of those around him than from any disposition of his own.

Monroe was never to change this estimate of Washington even though it was not to be long before the two diverged on separate political ways.

TO THOMAS JEFFERSON.

On the 7th of May Jefferson had been appointed by Congress Minister Plenipotentiary to act with John Adams and Benjamin Franklin already appointed, "for the purpose of negotiating treaties of commerce." He proceeded at once to Boston (via Philadelphia) when he sailed for France July 5th. [HAMILTON.]

ANNAPOLIS, May 14, 1784.

MY DEAR SIR,—I hope before this you have safely arriv'd in Phil'a. I very sensibly feel your absence not only in the solitary situation in w'h you have left me but upon many other accounts. What direction the delegation may take even for the short space that we shall rem^n. here, upon the few important subjects that are before us, is to me altogether incertain. The same men still act on the same principles & upon points where no personal objects are in view on either side, accommodation on the part of those gent'^{n}. is, if possible, more difficult to be attain'd. As I have not been able to finish our cypher I can only give you an acc't. of one or two measures, by the next post I will send it & before your departure give you information of whatever hath or may happen. We have appointed Colo. Humphreys secretary to the embassy or commission. The report upon taking possession of the western posts hath been before Congress. Hand moved for its postponement to take up a plan of his own, more concise, but not very explicit; his plan is to dismiss the troops at West Point & elsewhere, & enlist others for this service which he supposes may be effected in a very few weeks & in time to serve the purpose of the Indian Com'^{rs}. I wish you to inform me what posts you think troops had better be station'd at. I recollect you had thought on this subject & made some amendm't in the plan propos'd by Gen'l Washington. I am rather an advocate for the dismission of these troops for a variety of reasons which will occur to you & if the levy of others can be effected in time for the western purposes think the difficulty you had in the winter will be remov'd. I have sent your trunks by the packet to Baltimore & instructed the master of the packet to deliver them himself. I have also forwarded y^r. letter to M^r. Curson. Do you recollect anything further here that I should attend to besides those you gave me in charge? Everything relative to the negotiations are completed so that you will of course receive the instructions immediately. I think you left town before a particular clause had rec'd its negative. It was the only one which remain'd undecided on so that you will comprehend me without my particularizing it. Your letters by post I shall forward to you: the one from Mr. Hopkinson if it arrives I shall attend to & apply the contents as you desir'd me.

I am y^r. 'affec. fri^d. & servant, JA^s. MONROE.

P.S. Partout & myself agree very well only now & then we require the aid of an interpreter. I have had one or two comfortable solitary dinners upon little more than vegetables & coffee cream. He says "comme vous dinez Monsieur tout seul il est tres necessaire pour reduire la provision et pour accommoder la depense a cette changement."

Jefferson and Monroe had messed together at Annapolis and Partout was their caterer. [HAMILTON.]

TO THOMAS JEFFERSON.

Congress, while sitting at Princeton, had on October 30, 1783, appointed a committee "to repair to the lower falls of the Potomack to view the situation of the country in the vicinity of the same" and to report a proper district for the residence of Congress.

Objection had been made to the right of Messrs. Ellery and Howell, the delegates from Rhode Island, to act as members of the Congress, upon the ground that the year, for which they had been appointed, had expired. [HAMILTON]

ANNAPOLIS, MAY 20, 1784.

DEAR SIR,—I have rec^d Mr. Hopkinson's letter enclosing from the office of finance a bill containing 506 2/3 dol^{rs} which I will negotiate agreeably to your desire, pay ye Intendant the sum you owe him & transmit the balance. The committee, of which I am a member, appointed to view the country around Georgetown under the Princeton engagement set out this morning upon that business. I think with you that it will be proper to effect this business before the adjournment & no time may better be spar'd than the present. For four or 5. days past the qualification of the Delegates from R. I. hath been the only subject before us. The motion respecting them was from Mr Read. This brought forward the report of the committee which was ag^{nst} them & conformable to the principles establish'd in the case of Delanson. Upon the question shall the resolution stand? 4. States voted in the affirmative, 2. in the negative & 3. were divided. Of course it was enter'd in the journals that it was lost. The question then was, are they under this vote delegates? On the side of those in the negative the arguments are,—if 7. states were on the floor represented generally by but two members & the question was, shall a delegation retain its seat, or any particular member, the time of service having actually expir'd, y^e. vote of one member only wo'd keep him in Congress. 2. that the question is not, shall they be turn'd out? it is not an ordinary legislative act, but a judicial one & the confederation the law & to be appli'd to the case in question, it is a question of right. Does it or not exist—if it does what number of States are necessary to confirm it. That in all judicial decisions the majority of at least the sitting members is necessary to establish any right—in most or indeed all, a majority of the commission. That here it is more essentially necessary, that the majority of the U.S. in Congress assembled are competent only to the inferior duties of gov^t.: that 9. states are necessary to the most important acts: that a scrupulous attention to the object & principles of the confederation wo'd perhaps require that the number necessary to govern the States sho'^{d}. concur in the opinion of the validity of their respective credentials, but that neither the policy of the confederation nor any principle of gov'ts will admit that the consent of less than 7. States shall be necessary, that in this case there is not only a minority of the U.S. in Congress assembled in their favor but a minority of those present. On the other side, it was argued 1. that having their seats 7. States are necessary to turn them out, that the power of excluding delegations from their character & office sho^d not be committed to a less number: that if the question was shall a delegation be admitted under indisputable credentials from his State, the number present being as before stated, & only one member voted ag'nst it, it wo'd be negativ'd. that this wo^d be a dangerous engine in the hands of party men. that the resolution of the committee ag'nst them was negativ'd & of course they remain members. I submit to you the reasons on both sides as they occur to me at present but perhaps I do not recollect the whole, for being just ready to mount our horses I have not time to be so particular as I co^d. wish. Give me y^r opinion upon this aff^f. I have negotiated the aff^f. of the bill, p^d. the Intendant 7$\pounds$, 10.s & inclose you the balance except three doll'rs w'h he gave me in money & w^h. I retain not being able to send it. I inclose you a cypher which I hope you will be able to read, but upon examining it I find it incomplete & must therefore leave it with M^r. Clerici to be finish'd & sent by post. The gentlemen wait for me & have only time to add that I am y^r. affec^{te} friend & serv^t.

JA^s. MONROE.

TO THOMAS JEFFERSON.
ANNAPOLIS, [May] 25, 1784.

DEAR SIR,—I rec'^{d}. this moment yours of the 21st. My letter by the last post will inform you of the occasion w'^{h}. pointed that as the favorable moment for a trip to Georgetown & of our availing ourselves of it. Yesterday evening we return'd. Our report will be in favor of the Maryland side & of a position near the town. . . .

JA^s. MONROE

The Maryland site was finally determined upon, and is the site on which the city of Washington now stands. [HAMILTON.]

TO THOMAS JEFFERSON.

TRENTON, Nov. 1, 1784.

DEAR SIR,—Two days since I arriv'd here after performing a tour up the North river by fort Stanwix down the wood-creek, thro' ye Oneida Ontario & (by the Niagara falls) part of lake Erie, thence back by Niagara thro' ye Ontario by Coolton Island thro' the S^t. Laurence to Montreal & from Montreal over lake Champlain by Albany to N. York again. You find I have taken a route different from the one I intended, as my object was to take in my view the practicability also of a communication from Lake Erie down the Potowmack. But from this I was dissuaded by an accident w^h. happen'd to some of the party upon lake Erie, with whom I came from fort Stanwix to Niagara. I had separated from them by accident three days before the event. They landed near some Indian huts (a Mr. Teller from Schenactady with four men in a batteaux) & were fir'd on by those Indians, Mr. Teller & two men killed & a 4th. wounded; the latter with the 5th. made their escape. The indian chiefs highly reprehended the act & were, at the earnest instigation of the gentlemen of the Brit'h garrison, endeavoring to detect & bring the villains to justice. Upon advice of this disaster Colo. Depeister, commanding at Niagara, sent an Express to me just entering upon Lake Erie advising my return, with w^h I complied & took the above route to this place. My excursion hath been attended with great personal exposure & hardship & much greater expence than I had expected. It hath, however, I hope been advantageous to me in some respects. I have ascertain'd I believe with some accuracy the different degrees of difficulty from Michelemachinac down the Grand river to Montreal, thro' the Lakes to Montreal and by the North river. The preference is, at least so far, in favor of the North river. The first leisure time I have I will take the route of Fort Pitt to Lake Erie & form some estimate in that direction.

Here I find the country from Montreal much richer than I had expected although I am of opinion L'd Sheffield's expectations are visionary in his calculation that it will supply the Islands with flour & lumber. Still I think it has great resources in those articles, but the best timber is high up the river, w'^{h} together with the difficulty of getting it down the rapids & thro' the gulph of the S't Lawrence to the West Indies must make it an expensive trade to them, more expensive I am told than that from the Baltic. If I were to estimate the present or the probable future value of Canada to the Brit'^{h} dominion, consider'd in a commercial light and compare it with the expense necessarily incurr'^{d} if they keep up a military establishment in supporting it, I sho^d think Britain wo^d act a politic part in relinquishing it and the not doing it satisfies me she either has or will have other objects. Under the bounds of the U.S., by the late treaty, the principal part of the fur trade must leave it & run in some channel within the U.S. The merchants established or connected in it, the batteaux men and other dependents will take the same course. This will increase the expense of their government in supplying their upper ports in Canada as the price of hands will be higher and the means scarcer. In addition to those difficulties which nature has thrown in her way, others will exist under their government to which ours will be a stranger at present. No merchant is allowed to build vessels on the lakes, but must, if he takes the course, avail himself of those of government and this exposes them to constant and most oppressive impositions. Their peltries are subject to duties and preference passes from Lake Superior to Montreal. The duties may be taken off but the preference passes can not be prevented; while the restraints on their trade are high it will be our policy to increase them in every instance wherein they depend on us; while we give those within our bounds great indulgences we must prohibit under high penalties all commerce between the U.S. and Canada; prohibit their landing or storing their goods on our side under at least thirty per cent advalorem at the place where landed. Canada I consider as standing upon different ground with regard to us from any other part of the Dominions. A free intercourse between us and the people of Canada can, in my opinion, only be advantageous to them & will defeat any political arrangement we can adopt respecting them. By prohibiting them the participation of the advantages which we possess, we occasion them great difficulty. Their merchants might get their goods much cheaper up the North river than the S't Lawrence and until we permit them to navigate on our shore from ye commencement of the Ontario they are depriv'd of the possibility of navigating it except in vessels of considerable burden. If they take the North instead in batteaux they must go round the lake seventy miles above Niagara & down the other side before they reach it for the passage is impracticable there. I submit to you these observations that you may judge what right they sho'^{d} have in forming a treaty of commerce. The English ministry will, I am satisfied, readily agree it shall be so framed as to exclude the U.S. from a free intercourse with Canada. Their jealousy will tell them to beware how they admit it lest the sweets of those rights which we enjoy might invite them to us; but the people of Canada will be more sensible of our blessings by the restraints laid on them. They will feel their own misfortunes and envy the blessings to be attained under the protection of the federal arm. In the meantime the acquisition of Canada is not an object with us, we must make valuable what we have already acquired & at the same time take such measures as will weaken it as a British province.

As yet we have not a representation of the States but expect it in a few days. This will certainly be a very important and interesting session. In Canada I was informed that the commanding officer had received orders not to evacuate the posts and that many of the vessels laid aside under the provisional treaty had again been put in commission on the Lakes, a measure s'd to be founded upon the supposed violating of the treaty by New York and Virginia. The latter in not repealing the laws prohibiting the recovery of British debts & the former in confiscations. But if their conduct is unauthoriz'd is this the way to obtain redress? I trust that the conduct of Congress upon this occasion will be firm though temperate but indeed we are in a poor condition for war; we may lose much but can gain nothing. . . . I will write you very fully so soon as we have a Congress & by every packet & private opportunity & beg of you to do the same. I have not heard from you since you left Phil'a; perhaps your letters to me are in Virg^a if you have wrote. I reach'd New York 10 days after Mr. Short left it. I wish'^{d} to have seen him. I hope yourself & Miss Patsy are well. Where shall I address to you? I am with the greatest respect & esteem, Dear Sir, your friend & servant

JA^S. MONROE.

TO GOVERNOR PATRICK HENRY.
NEW YORK, Augt. 12, 1786.

DEAR SIR,—I have wished to communicate for sometime since to you an account of a transaction here, for your sentiments respecting it, but have declined from the want of a cypher, that of the delegation being we fear lost. The affr. however has come to such a crisis and is of such high importance to the U.S. & ours in particular, that I shall risque the communication without that cover. Jay, you know, is intrusted with the negotiation with the Sp^n. resident here for the free navigation of the Mississippi & the boundaries between Georgia and the Floridas; his instructions, altho' they authorize by implication the formation of a treaty of commerce, confine him expressly with respect to those points, & prohibit his entering into any engagement whatever wh. shall not stipulate them in our favor. Upon my arrival here in Decr. last (having been previously well acquainted with Mr. Jay) in conversation with him I found he had agreed with Gardoqui to postpone the subject of the Mississippi &c, in the first instance & to take up that of a commerce^l. treaty; that in this they had gone so far as that Mr. Jay was possessed of the principles on wh. he wo^d. agree to make it, upon condition on our part, of a forbearance of the use of the Mississippi for

25 or 30 years. I soon found in short that Mr. Jay was desirous of occluding the Mississippi and of making what he term'd advantageous terms in the treaty of commerce the means of effecting it. Whether he suppos'd I was of his opinion or not, or was endeavoring to prevail on me to be so, I cannot tell, but as I expressed no sentiment on the subject he went further & obser'd "that if the affr. was brought to the view of Congress they wo^d. most probably disagree to it, or if they sho^d. approve the project, conduct themselves so indiscreetly as to suffer it to become known to the French & Engl^h. residents here & thus defeat it. To avoid this he said it occurr'd to him expedient to propose to Congress that a Committee be appointed to controul him in the negotiation, to stand to him in the room of Congress & he to negotiate under the Committee." I then reminded him of the instructions from our State respecting the Mississippi to the delegation & of the impossibility of their concurring in any measures of the kind. Our communication on this subject ended from that time. Upon the arrival of Colo. Grayson I communicated to him all these circumstances, with my opinion on them. From that time, and I had reason to believe he had begun even before my arrival, we have known of his intriguing with the members to carry the point. On 27. of May he addressed a letter to Congress precisely in the sentiment above, stating difficulties in the negotiations & proposing that "a Committee be appointed with full power to *direct* & *instruct* him on every point relative to the proposed treaty with Spain." As we knew the object was to extricate himself from the instructions respecting the Mississippi we of course opposed it. We found he had engaged the eastern states in the intrigue, especially Mass:, that New York, Jersey & Pen^a. were in favor of it & either absolutely decided or so much so as to promise little prospect of change. The Committee propos'd by the Secretary was admitted generally to be without the powers of Congress. Since 9 states only can give an instruction for the formation of a treaty, to appoint a Committee with the power of 9 states was agreed to be a subversion of the govt. & therefore improper. The letter however was referr'd to a Committee who ultimately agreed to report that the Committee be discharged & the subject referred to a Committee of the whole & the Secr^y. ordered to attend. He did so and come forward fully with the plan of a commerc^l. treaty condition'd with the forbearance of the use of the Mississippi for 25 or 30 years, with a long written speech or report in favor of it. The project is in a few words this "I That the merch^ts. of America & Sp^n. shall enjoy, the former in the ports of Sp^n. & the Canaries, the latter in those of the U.S. the rights of native merch^ts. reciprocally. 2. That the same tonnage shall be paid on the ships of the two parties in the carriage of the productions & the manufactures of the 2 countries.

3. That the *bona fide* manufactures & productions of the United States (tobacco only excepted which shall continue under its present regulations) may be imported in American or Spanish vessels into any of his majesty's ports aforesaid in like manner as if they were the productions of *Spain*. And on the other hand that the *bona fide* manufactures & productions of his majesty's Dominions may be imported into the U.S. in Sp^n. or American vessels in like manner as if they were those of the said States, and further that all such duties and imposts as may *mutually* be thought necessary to lay on them *by either party,* shall be ascertained & regulated on principles of exact reciprocity by a tariff to be form'd by a convention for the purpose, to be negotiated & made within *one year* after the exchange of the ratification of this treaty and in the meantime that they shall severally pay in the ports of each other the duties of natives only. 4. Masts & timber shall be bought here for the royal navy, provided that upon their carriage to Spain they shall cost no more than if they were bought elsewhere. 5. That in consideration of these advantages to the U.S. they agree to forbear the use of the Mississippi for 25 or 30 years, the term for wh. the treaty shall last." This treaty independent of the sacrifice, I consider as a very disadvantageous one & such as we should not accept, since it in reality gains us nothing to very high restrictions, such as exist in none of our other treaties, altho' they are in effect bad enough. But they are to be justified especially those of France & Holland in the motives which led to them, to bring those powers into the war. The subject was referred to a Committee of the whole on Thursday last who after debate rose & reported that they have come to no decision and require leave to sit again. The delegation of Mass. moved in committee that the ultimatum in his instructions respecting the Mississippi be repealed, in which event he would have unlimited powers to act at pleasure. This they said might be carried by 7 states. We observed that without the ultimatum the instruction would be a new one, and of course 9 states necessary to it. The subject will again be taken up in a few days. It appears manifest they have 7 states & we 5, Maryland inclusive, with the southern states. Delaware is absent. It also appears that they will go on under 7 states in the business & risque the preservation of the confederacy on it. We have & shall throw every possible obstacle in the way of the measure, protest against the right of 7 either to instruct or ratify, give information of this to Mr. Jay & the Sp^n. resident so that neither may be deceived in the business. This is one of the most extraordinary transactions I have ever known, a minister negotiating expressly for the purpose of defeating the object of his instructions, and by a long train of intrigue & management seducing the representatives of the states to concur in it. It is possible some, or

perhaps one, (in which case it will be even) member may change his sentiments, but as he risqued his reputation upon carrying it, it is to be presumed he had engaged them too firmly in the business to have a possibility of their forsaking him. This however is not the only subject of consequence I have to engage your attention to. Certain it is that committees are held in this town of Eastern men and others of this State upon the subject of a dismemberment of the States east of the Hudson from the Union & the erection of them into a separate govt. To what lengths they have gone I know not, but have assurances as to the truth of the above position, with this addition to it that the measure is talked of in Mass: familiarly, & is supposed to have originated there. The plan of the govt in all its modifications has even been contemplated by them. I am persuaded these people who are in Congress from that State (at the head of the other business) mean that as a step toward the carriage of this, as it will so displease some of them as to prepare the States for this event.

I am thoroughly persuaded the govt. is practicable & with a few alterations the best that can be devised. To manage our affairs to advantage under it & remedy these defects, in my opinion, nothing is wanting but common sense & common honesty, in both of which necessary qualifications we are, it is to be lamented, very defective. I wish much your sentiments upon these important subjects. You will necessarily consider this as under an injunction of secrecy & confide with none in whom the most perfect confidence may not be reposed. If any benefit may result from it I should have no objection to your presenting it to the view of Council—of this you will judge—clearly I am of opinion it will be held connected with other objects—& perhaps with that upon which the convention will sit at Annapolis. On the part of the Delegation we can give you similar information except as to what passed between Mr. Jay & myself—will it be necessary? Of one point I have a perfect conviction & upon this the rest of the Delegation will perhaps not write you so freely as myself, which is this, that the Legislature should be convened at a time sufficiently early to elect members to take their seats precisely on the day that those of the present Delegation expire—affairs are in too critical a situation for the State to be unrepresented a day—eminent disadvantage may result from it—they did from this circumstance during the last year. Let me hear from you upon these subjects as soon as possible & believe me with great respect & esteem your friend & servant

Jaˢ. Monroe.

P. S. The object in the occlusion of the Mississippi on the part of these people so far as it is extended to the interest of their States (for those of a private kind gave birth to it) is to break up so far as this will do it, the settlements on the western waters, prevent any in future, and thereby keep the States southward as they now are—or if settlements will take place, that they shall be on such principles as to make it the interest of the people to separate from the Confederacy, so as effectually to exclude any new State from it. To throw the weight of population eastward & keep it there, to appreciate the vacand lands of New York & Massachusetts. In short, it is a system of policy which has for its object the keeping the weight of govt & population in this quarter, & is prepared by a set of men so flagitious, unprincipled & determined in their pursuits, as to satisfy me beyond a doubt they have extended their views to the dismemberment of the govt & resolved either, that sooner than fail it shall be the case, or being only desirous of that event have adopted this as the necessary means of effecting it. In conversations at which I have been present, the Eastern people talk of a dismemberment so as to include Pena. (in favor of which I believe the present delegation Petit & Bayard who are under the influence of eastern politicks would be) & sometimes all the states south to the Potomack—Altho a dismemberment should be avoided by all the states and the conduct of wise & temperate men should have in view to prevent it, yet I do consider it as necessary on our part to contemplate it as an event which may possibly happen & for which we should be guarded—a dismemberment which would throw too much strength into the Eastern Division should be prevented. It should be so managed, (if it takes place) either that it should be formed into three divisions, or if into two, that Pen^a. if not Jersey should be included in ours. Be assur'd as to all the subjects upon which I have given you information above, it hath been founded on authentic documents. I trust these intrigues are confined to a few only, but by these men I am assured are not; whatever anxiety they may give you I am persuaded it cannot be greater than that which I have felt.

J. M.

TO THOMAS JEFFERSON.
Fredericksburg, July 27, 1787.

Dear Sir,—I can scarcely venture on an apology for my silence for some time past but hope notwithstanding to be forgiven. Since I left N.Y^k. I have been employ'd in the discharge of duties entirely new to me, oftentimes embarrassing & of course highly interesting, but w^h. have sought the accomplishment of only a few objects. In Octr. last I was admitted to the bar of the C^{ts}. of Appeal & Ch'y. & the April following of the Gen! Court. In the course of the winter I mov'd my family to this town, in w^h. I have taken my residence with a view to my profession. These pursuits tho' confin'd have not been attended with the less difficulty. A considerable part of my property has consisted in debts, and to command it or any part of it, hath been no easy matter. Indeed in this respect I have fail'd almost altogether. Several considerations have induc'd me to prefer this place for the present, the principal of w^h. is the command of an house and other accomodations (the property of M^r. Jones) upon my own terms. My standing at the bar hath been so short, that I cannot judge of it in that respect, tho' am inclined to believe it, not an inelegible position for one of that profession. But I consider my residence here as temporary, merely to serve the purpose of the time, and as looking forward to an establishment somewhere on this side the mountains, and as convenient as possible to Monticello. M^r. Jones is in ill health & begins to be satisfied his existence depends in a great degree upon a similar position. I have earnestly advis'd him to move up & at least make the experiment. Mr^s. Monroe hath added a daughter to our society who tho' noisy, contributes greatly to its amus'ment. She is very sensibly impress'd with your kind attention to her, & wishes an opportunity of shewing how highly she respects & esteems you. With the political world I have had little to do since I left Congress. My anxiety however for the gen^l. welfare hath not been diminish'd. The affairs of the federal government are, I believe, in the utmost confusion. The convention is an expedient that will produce a decisive effect. It will either recover us from our present embarrassments or complete our ruin; for I do suspect that if what they recommend sho^d. be rejected this wo^d. be the case. But I trust that the presence of Genl. Washington will have great weight in the body itself so as to overawe & keep under the demon of party, & that the signature of his name to whatever act shall be the result of their deliberations will secure its passage thro' the union.

The county in w^h. I reside have plac'd me in the Legislature. I have been mortified however to accept this favor from them, at the expence of M^r. Page. I suppos'd it might be serviceable to me in the line of my profession—my services have been abroad, & the establishm^t. others have gain'd at the bar in the meantime requires every effort in my power to repair the disadvantage it hath subjected me to. The Governor, [Edmund Randolph. Ed.] I have reason to believe is unfriendly to me & hath shewn (If I am well inform'd) a disposition to thwart me; Madison, upon whose friendship I have calculated, whose views I have favor'd., and with whom I have held the most confidential correspondence since you left the continent, is in strict league with him & hath I have reason to believe concurr'd in arrangements unfavorable to me; a suspicion supported by some strong circumstances that this is the case, hath given me great uneasiness—however in this I may be disappointed & I wish it may be so. I shall I think be strongly impressed in favor of & inclined to vote for whatever they will recommend. I have heard from Beckley tho' not from himself (who accompanied the Governor up, in expectation of being appointed clerk) they had agreed upon giving the United States a negative upon the laws of the several States, if it can be done consistently with the constitution of the several States—indeed it might be well to revise them all & incorporate the fed^l. constitution in each. This I sho^d. think proper—it will if the body is well organiz'd, be the best way of introducing uniformity in their proceedings that can be devis'd, of a negative kind, or by a power to operate indirectly. But a few months will give us the result be it what it may. You mentioned in y^r last the injury you had sustain'd in y^r. wrist. How did it happen? I hope you found y^r trip to the south of advantage—y^r. Daughters I hope are well—nothing be assur'd will give me more pleasure than to hear from you frequently. If I can be of service in y^r private aff^s. in any line, or with respect to Peter Carr,[1] I beg you to command me. It will always be convenient for me to attend to anything of that kind, either in person or by a suitable messenger. I am dear sir your affectionate friend & servant.

JA^S. MONROE.

TO JAMES MADISON.
RICHMOND, Octr. 13, 1787.

The Philadelphia Convention—having framed the Constitution, and pass a resolution that it should be laid before Congress, with a recommendation that it should be submitted for ratification "to a Convention of Delegates chosen in each State by the people thereof, under the recommendation of its Legislature"—had adjourned sine die Sept. 17, 1787.

Edmund Randolph and George Mason, two of the Virginia delegates, had refused to sign the Constitution as approved by the Convention.

DEAR SIR,—I was favor'd with yours by M^r. Blair and a late one covering one from M^r. Jefferson, a few days since. I sho^d. have answer'd the former sooner but defer'd it untill my arrival here whither I was at that time on the point of setting out. Mr^s. M. accompanied me & will remain untill my return w^h. will not be untill the adjournmt. of the Assembly. The report from Phil^a . hath presented an interesting subject to their consideration. It will perhaps agi-

---

1. *Jefferson's nephew.* [HAMILTON.]

tate the minds of the people of this State more than any subject they have had in contemplation since the commencemen^t. of the late revolution, for there will be a greater division among the people of character than then took place, provided we are well informed as to the sentiments of many of them. It is said that M^r. Henry, Genl. Nelson, Harrison & others are against it. This insures it a powerful opposition more especially when associated with that of the 2. dissenting deputies. There are in my opinion some strong objections agñst the project, w^h. I will not weary you with a detail of. But under the predicament in w^h. the Union now stands & this State in particular with respect to this business, they are over balanc'd by the arguments in its favor. The Assembly will meet to morrow, & we have reason to believe we shall have an house the first or 2^d. day. We shall soon find how its pulse beats, & what direction this business will take. I believe there will be no opposition to a convention. . . .

JA^s. MONROE.

TO JAMES MADISON.
RICHMOND, Dec'r 6, 1787.

DEAR SIR,—I have had hopes of being able to give you something from the proceedings of the Assembly of an interesting nature which might also be agreeable—but perhaps yr wishes in this respect may not even yet be gratified. The resolutions respecting ye Constitution you have long since receiv'd. In those you find no provision for the pay or priviledges of the members of the Convention—those, especially the former, were thought the subject matter for an act & were separated from them. A few days since resolutions were brought in by Mr. Hopkins & supported by Mess'rs Henry & Mason for this purpose & providing funds for defraying ye expense of Deputies to attend other convention or conventions of the States, if this convention shd. think ye measure expedient, wh. were adopted by the house by a majority of abt. 15, the bill is not yet brought in—The B. [ritish] debt business hath also been another subject of usurous management—resolutions of absolute repeal pass'd the committee first by a great majority—without any apparent necessity. Mess'rs Mason & Nicholas who advocated them agreed to a clause of suspension until the other States shod. pass similar laws of repeal. When the bill was under discussion yesterday Nicholas who had been most active & zealous in the business chang'd his former ground in every instance and acceded to the proposition of Mr. Henry wh. suspended its effect until G. B. shall have complied—owning himself convinc'd by the arguments that had been us'd. This gent'n appears to have abandon'd the prospect of instalments wh. he brought forward early in the session—that of district or circuit courts seems also to be dispair'd of by those who are desirous of amending this branch of our system. A bill of Mr. Henry's for prohibiting ye importation of foreign distill'd spirits & other purposes, is among ye. orders of the day & will most probably be thrown out. It appears difficult to organize the affrs. of this & perhaps of any one state in a tolerable manner & it is doubtful, if it were done whether it cod. be executed or whether the people wod. not have it repeal'd the next assembly. The ct. of chy. breaks up tomorrow. The chancelor is yet present but in a low state of health. I doubt whether I shall stay until ye end of the session, Mrs. M. & her sister are with me. What is new with you? I think the cloud wh. hath hung over us for sometime past is not yet dispell'd or likely soon to be. Sincerely I am

Dr. Sir, yr. friend & servant

JA^s. MONROE.

Since the above the house went in committee on a bill for amending ye cty. ct. law—it terminated in 2 resolutions, 1. That the administration of justice shod. be made more equal & expeditious. 2. That under executors, property sold so low as to require some legislative provision for preventing it—afterwards in ye house a proposition for establishing district courts was agreed to; the alternative of extendg. the terms of the gen'l ct. was rejected by a great majority—the plan of instalm^{ts}. will be brot. forward, and that of altering the execut^{rs}. law so as to prevent property being sold but for 1/2 its value—the former is the favorite of Mr. N. the latter of Mr. Henry—it is not improbable but that the district bill may fail if encumber'd with either, co'd either get a decided majority in preference to the other, yt. it is possible that their division upon this point may lessen the weight of opposition to the district bill & promote its adoption.

TO JAMES MADISON.
FREDBG., Feby. 7, 1788.

DEAR SIR,—We have nothing new here—the proceedings of our assembly you are no doubt possess'd of thro' the hands of the Governor, especially that part which is connected with the U.S. I mean the revenue act & the resolutions respecting the cession. In the former as much was advanced to the U.S. as cod. be obtain'd. In the latter more moderation was observ'd than at first appearances promis'd. It was perhaps bro't forward to serve other purposes, (I mean in the extent to wh. the Chairman advocated it) but it was put in its present form without debate & by his own consent, perhaps to avoid it. The rectitude of the measure depends on the want of it in some of the Com'rs. Unless the objection against, at least one, is good, it cannot be defended. But you have the whole of the proceedings before you.

This new constitution still engages the minds of people with some zeal among the partizans on either side. It is impossible to say which preponderates. The northern part of the State is more generally for it than the southern. In this county (except in the town) they are *against* it I believe universally. I have, however, this from report only, having not been from home. My late colleague is decidedly so. Mr. Page is for it & forms an exception to the above. It is said here Georgia has adopted it, N. H. also. The object in the postponement of the meeting of our Convention to so late a day was to furnish an evidence of the disposition of the other States to that body when it sho'd be assembled. If they or many of them were *against* it our State might mediate between contending parties & lead the way to an union more palitable to all. If all were for it, let the knowledge of that circumstance have its weight in their deliberations. This I believe was the principle on wh. that measure was adopted, at least those whose sentiments I knew express'd it to be theirs. We expect you in soon & shall be happy to see you here. Sincerely I am Yr. fri'd & serv't

JA^s. MONROE.

TO THOMAS JEFFERSON.
RICHMOND, April 10, 1788.

DEAR SIR,—I must depend on your kindness to pardon my omission in not writing you oftener, for I will not pretend to justify it. I sho.^{d} have wrote you as before, and can give no satisfactory reason even to myself why I have not, for that my communications will not be of much importance I do not urge as an excuse. I will however make amends in future. The real pleasure of my life, which consists in being at home with my family, has been interrupted by an attendance at the bar & service in the legislature since I left N. Yk. Altho' neither of these employments has many allur'ments in it, yet I think the latter rather a more uncomfortable one than the former. Perhaps however I obtain'd a seat in it, at a very unfortunate period, both as to publick aff^{ts} and my own temper of mind. . . . The Convention of this State is to meet in June to take up the rep.^{t} from Phil^a. The people seem much agitated with this subject in every part of the State. The principal partizans on both sides are elected. Few men of any distinction have fail'd taking their part. Six States have adopted it, N. Hampshire the 7th that took the subject up adjourned until late in June, with a view it is presum'd, to await the decision of those States who postpon'd their meeting to the latest day as Virg.a N.Y.k & No Carolina, and from that circumstance suppos'd least friendly to it. The event of this business is altogether incertain, as to its passage thro the Union. That it will no where be rejected admits of little doubt. And that it will ultimately, perhaps in 2. or three years, terminate, in some wise and happy establishment for our country, is what we have good reason to expect. I have it not in my power at present to commit to cypher any comments on this plan but will very soon, I mean concisely as to its organization and powers: nor to give you the arrangement of characters on either side, with us. I write by Col.o Carrington & he leaves this immediately. It will give me infinite pleasure to hear from you occasionally. My country has plac'd me among those who are to decide on this question; I shall be able to give you a view of its progress that may be interesting to you.1 Can you command my services in any instance? Are you in health, how happen'd the dislocation of y.r wrist and is it well? I think I mention'd to you in my last M.rs M. had made us happy by giving us a daughter who is now 16 months old and begins to talk. I hope Miss Patsy and Polly are well. I shall write you again soon and am, affectionately, your friend & serv.t

Ja{s}. Monroe.

TO THOMAS JEFFERSON.

Monroe had been elected a delegate from Spottsylvania County to the State Convention called to ratify or reject the proposed Constitution.

The Convention met June 2, 1788.

*"The Hon. Edmund Pendleton was nominated and unanimously elected President; who, being seated in the Chair, thanked the convention for the honor conferred on him, and strongly recommended the members to use the utmost moderation and temper in their deliberations on the great and important sub*ject now before them."—Elliot's Debates, *vol. iii., p. 1.* [HAMILTON.]

Fredericksburg, July 12, 1788.

Dear Sir,—Altho' I am persuaded you will have received the proceedings of our convention upon the plan of government submitted from Phil{a}. yet as it is possible this may reach you sooner than other communications I herewith inclose a copy to you. They terminated as you will find in a ratification which must be consider'd, so far as a reservation of certain rights go, as conditional, with the recommendation of subsequent amendments. The copy will designate to you the part which different gen[m]. took upon this very interesting & important subject. The detail in the managment of the business, from your intimate knowledge of characters, you perhaps possess with great accuracy, without a formal narration of it. Pendleton tho' much impaired in health and in every respect in the decline of life shewed as much zeal to carry it, as if he had been a young man. Perhaps more than he discover'd in the commencement of the late revolution in his opposition to G. Britain. Wythe acted as chairman to the committee of the whole and of course took but little part in the debate—but was for the adoption relying on subsequent amendments. Blair said nothing, but was for it. The governor exhibited a curious spectacle to view. Having refused to sign the paper every body supposed him against it. But he afterwards had written a letter & having taken a part which might be called rather vehement than active, he was constantly labouring to shew that his present conduct was consistent with that letter & the letter with his refusal to sign. Madison took the principal share in the debate for it. In which together with the aid I have already mention'd he was somewhat assisted by Innes, Lee, Marshal, Corbin, & G. Nicholas, as Mason, Henry & Grayson were the principal supporters of the opposition. The discussion as might have been expected where the parties were so nearly on a balance, was conducted generally with great order, propriety & respect of either party to the other—and its event was accompanied with no circumstance on the part of the victorious that was extra[y]. exultation, nor of depression on the part of the unfortunate. There was no bonfire illumination &[c]. and had there been I am inclin'd to believe, the opposition wo[d]. have not only express'd no dissatisfaction, but have scarcely felt any at it, for they seemed to be gov[d]. by principles elevated highly above circumstances so trivial & transitory in their nature.

The conduct of Gen[l]. Washington upon this occasion has no doubt been right and meritorious. All parties had acknowledged defects in the federal system, and been sensible of the propriety of some material change. To forsake the honorable retreat to which he had retired & risque the reputation he had so deservedly acquir'd, manifested a zeal for the publick interest, that could after so many and illustrious services, & at this stage of his life, scarcely have been expected from him. Having however commenc'd again on the publick theatre, the course which he takes becomes not only highly interesting to him but likewise so to us: the human character is not perfect; if he partakes of those qualities which we have too much reason to believe are almost inseparable from the frail nature of our being, the people of America will perhaps be lost. Be assured his influence carried this

Government; for my own part I have a boundless confidence in him nor have I any reason to believe he will ever furnish occasion for withdrawing it. More is to be apprehended if he takes a part in the public councils again, as he advances in age, from the designs of those around him than from any disposition of his own.

In the discussion of the subject an allusion was made I believe in the first instance, by Mr. Henry to an opinion you had given on this subject, in a letter to Mr. Donald. This afterwards became the subject of much inquiry & debate in the house, as to the construction of the contents of such letter & I was happy to find the great attention & universal respect with which the opinion was treated, as well as the great regard and high estimation in which the author of it was held. It must be painful to have been thus made a party in this transaction but this must have been alleviated by a consideration of the circumstances I have mentioned.

From the first view I had of the report from Phil^a. I had some strong objections to it. But as I had no inclination to inlist myself on either side, made no communication or positive declaration of my sentiments untill after the Convention met. Being however desirous to communicate them to my constituents, I address'd the enclos'd letter to them, with intention of giving them a view thereof eight or ten days before it met, but the impression was delayed so long, & so incorrectly made, and the whole performance upon re-examination so loosely drawn that I thought it best to suppress it. There appear'd likewise to be an impropriety in interfering with the subject in that manner in that late stage of the business. I enclose it you for your perusal & comment on it.

You have, no doubt, been apprized of the remonstrance of the Judges to the proceedings of the Legislature in the passage particularly of the district court law, as likewise of its contents. The subject will be taken up in the fall. The Legislature altho' assembled for the purpose declin'd entering into it, because of the season of the year, being anxious to get home about this harvest. For this purpose they pass'd an act suspending the operation of the district court law untill some time in Decr. or Jany. next. Altho different modifications may be made of it yet I think the bill will be retained in its principal features.

I still reside here and perhaps shall continue to do so whilst I remain at the bar, especially if the district court law holds its ground. I hold a seat in the legislature & believe I shall do it for some time. The absence from my family is painful but I must indeavor to have them with me as much as possible. I hope you enjoy your health well. I have heard nothing to the contrary. I hope also that Miss Patsy & Molly are well. Short I likewise hope is in health. Remember me to them & believe me most affectionately your friend & servant.

Ja^s. Monroe.

MONROE IN THE VIRGINIA CONVENTION OF 1788.

Monroe does not, in this letter, state what part he himself took in the Convention, but it was an important one. In his first speech, on June 10th, he declared that he came "not as the partisan of this or that side of the question, but to commend where the subject appears to me to deserve commendation; to suggest my doubts where I have any; to hear with candor the explanation of others; and in the ultimate result, to act as shall appear for the best advantage of our common country."

He asserted that he was "strongly impressed with the necessity of a firm national government," but he had some decided objections to the proposed Constitution. The principal of these were:

1. The power of direct taxation vested in the Federal government.

2. The absence of a Bill of Rights, or any express provision limiting the general powers of the government.

3. The lack of responsibility on the part of the Federal legislature and Executive.

4. The re-eligibility of the President.

For the first time in his political career he found himself opposed to his friend Madison, but he had the consolation of believing that he represented the views of Mr. Jefferson, as expressed in his letter to Donald.

On the 13th of June he took a prominent part in the most interesting discussion that occurred during the sittings of the Convention.

Patrick Henry, who led the opposition, with unequalled eloquence and unsurpassed adroitness, knowing the great interest felt in Virginia, and especially by the Kentucky district, in the free navigation of the Mississippi, seized upon the repeal by Congress, in 1786, of the instructions of 1785 making it an essential condition of a treaty with Spain, as an evidence that the adoption of the Constitution would result in a government that would yield the Mississippi to Spain, and sacrifice the interest of the Southern and Western States to the commercial advantage of the Northern and Eastern States. This repeal, though not publicly announced—for it appeared only on the secret journal of Congress—was known to the leaders of both parties. Henry, resolved to make the most of it, precipitated its disclosure by calling upon those members who had been delegates in Congress to communicate the action of that body on this subject to the Convention.

In response to this call, Monroe gave a full account of the proceedings of Congress while he was a delegate, the gist of which was that, in spite of the strenuous opposition of the Southern States, the seven Easternmost States had voted to repeal the instructions which made the free navigation of the Mississippi a sine qua non of the treaty. He also declared "that the interest of the western country would not be as secure, under the proposed Constitution, as under the Confederation; because, under the latter system, the Mississippi could not be relinquished without the consent of nine States; whereas, by the former, a majority of seven States could yield it."

"The speech of Monroe was well received. It made upon the House a strong impression, which was heightened by the modesty of his demeanor, by the sincerity which was reflected from every feature of his honest face, and by the minute knowledge which he exhibited of a historical transaction of surpassing interest to the South. But if the impression was felt by the members generally, it was felt most keenly by those who were anxious about the sales of their crops and for the prosperity of their families. The members from the West were furious. They had just learned for the first time the imminent hazard to which their most valued privilege had been exposed, and they did not conceal their indignation. "—History of the Virginia Convention of 1788, *by Hugh Blair Grigsby, p. 240.*

Monroe was followed by Grayson, who confirmed his statement of facts, and reinforced his arguments. It was fortunate for the fate of the Constitution that Madison, its ablest champion in the Convention, was also a member of the current Congress, from which he had absented himself to attend the Convention. Monroe's term had expired in November, 1786, and Grayson's in November, 1787. Madison, therefore, could speak from a later date as to the temper of Congress. He was placed, however, in a delicate position. He could not deny what Monroe and Grayson had stated, and the fact was that the Congress then sitting had taken no action on the subject, and so far as the record showed, the situation there was unchanged. He himself had been and still was the most uncompromising advocate of the freedom of the Mississippi, and he could not justify or defend the repeal of 1786. He met the dilemma with the resourceful tact which distinguished him as the greatest debater of his day. He placed himself at once en rapport with the friends of the Mississippi, by declaring that neither the old Confederation nor the proposed Constitutional government cared to yield the right of its free navigation, for that would be repugnant to the law of nations. He argued that it was even more the interest of the Eastern than of the Southern States that the Mississippi should remain open, and expressed the opinion, "from the best information, that it never was the sense of the people at large, or the prevailing character of the Eastern States, to approve of the measure (of repeal)." He admitted that seven of the States had been willing to waive the right of navigation for a time, but denied that they had ever wished to yield it altogether. Of these States, he said, one, New Jersey, had since instructed its delegates not to give it up. But, he contended, if there was any such desire, it could be accomplished more easily under the Confederation than under the Constitution, while on the other hand, if the people of this country wished to secure forever the free navigation of the river, it could only be done by a strong national government that could concentrate and wield the whole power of the Union, to maintain it against all opposition. He concluded by saying: "Were I at liberty, I could develop some circumstances which would convince this House that this project will never be revived in Congress, and that, therefore, no danger is to be apprehended."

But the impression made by Monroe and Grayson was not easily overcome, and at the end of the day's discussion, the friends of the Constitution were very despondent, and Madison wrote Washington:

"Appearances at present are less favorable than at the date of my last. Our progress is slow, and every advantage is taken of the delay to work on the local prejudices of particular sets of members. British debts, the Indiana claim, and the Mississippi, are the principal topics of private discussion and intrigue, as well as public declamation. The members who have served in Congress have been dragged into communication, on the last, which could not be justified on any other occasion, if on the present. There is reason to believe that the event may depend on the Kentucky members, who seem to lean more against than in favor of the Constitution. The business is in the most ticklish state that can be imagined. The majority will certainly be small, on whatever side it may finally lie; and I dare not encourage much expectation that it will be on the favorable side. "—June 13, 1788. Madison M.S.S., Dept. of St., vol. iv., p. 40.

The friends of the Constitution, aided by the influence of Washington, finally carried its ratification, but it was by a bare majority of 10 out of 168 votes, and then only after they had agreed to submit the amendments demanded by the minority to the consideration of the first Congress under the Constitution, to be acted upon under the fifth article thereof, and to instruct the representatives of the State to urge their adoption. The principal of these were afterwards embodied in the ten amendments proposed by that body and ratified by the States. [HAMILTON.]

TO JAMES MADISON.
FREDERICKSBG, Sepr. 24, 1788.

DEAR SIR,—I was favor'd with yours of the 14—two or three days past. . . . I perfectly agree in the propriety of yielding to the majority respecting the place of residence. [i.e., the seat of government under the constitution of 1789. Monroe was on the committee of the Continental congress that surveyed and proposed the site at Georgetown, or Washington, D.C. Ed.] If a concession must be made, the minority must make it, and when the States south of us yielded all hope was at an end. I have long since desponded of Georgetown, nor are my hopes more sanguine under the new than they have been under the old government; but it has in my estimation every consideration of reason and propriety on its side, & of course every effort should be made in its favor whilst there is a prospect of success. . . .

JAS. MONROE

APPENDIX: Monroe's Paper on the Draft Constitution

OBSERVATIONS ON THE FEDERAL GOVERNMENT.

IT was discovered, soon after the peace, that the Confederation, in its present form, was wholly inadequate to the end of its creation; that of making America one State, for great national purposes. As soon as peace took place, confusion in every department of Congress, ruin of public and private credit, decay of trade, and loss of importance abroad, were the immediate consequences of the radical defects in the Confederation. During the war the fear of a powerful enemy answered all the purposes of the most energetic government. But as soon as that fear was removed, the thirteen United States began to draw different ways. Some refused to ratify the treaty of peace; others neglected to pay up their respective quotas to the public treasury; and others absolutely rejected the most salutary propositions of Congress; propositions to which the greater number of States readily assented. In vain have Congress called upon the different States to pay up their quotas in order to support the falling credit of America: In vain have they pointed out to them the necessity of establishing their public faith as a nation, by complying with their treaties: In vain have they recommended to them to forego their own immediate interests, and consider the interests of the Union. Congress might advise, or recommend measures; might approve the conduct of some States, and condemn that of others; might preach up public faith, honour, and justice: But was this sufficient to preserve a union of thirteen States, or support a national government? It had no authority, its powers expired at the peace, became a dead letter, for the fear of common danger was gone. Peace, which to other nations produces, and which under other circumstances would have produced to us, the greatest blessings, was pregnant with the greatest evil; disunion, the certain parent of internal quarrels, disorder, and blood-shed. In this situation of America, some of the best and wisest of her citizens, lamenting that the term of her glory was so short, and dreading the fatal consequences which would necessarily follow from disunion, proposed that a Convention of the States should be called for the purposes of amending the Confederation. The wisdom of the measure was instantly seen: It was approved by Congress, recommended to, and adopted by the States.

IT is on all hands agreed, that an abler or more upright Assembly never met in America, than the late Convention held at Philadelphia. The original design of their meeting was to amend the present Articles of Confederation: But upon consulting together; upon accurately investigating the Confederation, and informing each other of the real situation of their respective States, they saw so many radical defects in one, and so many alarming appearances in the other, as induced them readily and unanimously to modify the Federal Constitution: And after four months spent in painful enquiries, and diligent labour, produced the frame of government now offered to the consideration of the citizens of America. A form of government, which the President of the Convention, with the modesty peculiar to him, acknowledges to be in some respects defective; but which he likewise tells us, "was the result of a spirit of Amity, and of that mutual deference and concession, which the peculiarity of our political situation rendered indispensable."

WHEN we take a view of the respectable names who met upon this occasion, and composed this plan of government, we ought to approach it with deference and respect. Though not in such a manner as to deprive us of the power of discovering its faults; yet with such liberality as will lead us to consider it as the result of the deliberations of good and able men, actuated by just motives, and governed by pure principles. Men not swayed by selfish prospects, but urged to action by general philanthropy, and the desire of handing to posterity the best form of Federal Government, that America is capable of receiving, or perhaps that was ever offered to the consideration of mankind.

IF we read the proposed plan under these ideas, and think we discover imperfections, and faults; ought we not rather to distrust our own perceptions, than the understandings of its makers? Because it is much more probable, that a single reader, even of great capacity, should be mistaken, than that so respectable a body as the Convention, with minds equally enlightened, and more unbiased, should, after the freest and fullest investigation of this important subject, be wrong.

I CONFESS I am not one of those who would adopt without consideration, or blindly pursue a plan produced by any body of men, however eminent their characters for wisdom and virtue. "Not to pin my faith upon the sleeve of any man," was one of my earliest lessons. However, I am persuaded that the work before us, requires no blind followers: but standing upon the basis of its intrinsic merit, possesses strength sufficient to withstand the shocks of its most powerful enemies. Often have I read this work; and sometimes discovered, as I thought important defects; yet upon doubting my own judgment, and reading it again, have generally found the fault in myself, not in the Constitution. Yet I will not pretend to say that it is perfect. Did perfection ever come from the hands of man? If it were perfect, it would be illy suited to our imperfect capacities. Government in itself is not a positive good; but something introduced by societies to prevent positive evil. The best frame of government is that which is most likely to prevent the greatest sum of evil. Such I apprehend is the government now under consideration. Had the design of the Convention been to frame a Constitution for any individual State, they might perhaps have produced one, in the abstract, still nearer perfection. But far different was the purpose of their meeting! and I feel myself happy in concurring with that august body in thinking, that it is the best government which could be obtained for the thirteen States of America. Under this impression I shall attempt to explain those parts of it which are, or have been supposed to be difficult; and to answer some of the principal objections which have been made to it.

BEFORE we enter into a discussion of the different articles which compose the Constitution, it may not be improper to take into consideration the question respecting a Bill of Rights; which many, from habit and prejudices, rather than from reason, and truth, have thought necessary; and upon the want of it have founded one of their principal objections.

FEW people knew the origin of the term; still fewer have considered, without prejudice, the necessity of the thing. What is a Bill of Rights? A declaration insisted on by a free people, and recognized by their rulers, that certain principles shall be the invariable rules of their administration; because the preservation of these principles are necessary for the preservation of liberty. If this distinction be just; can there be a difference, whether these principles are established in a separate declaration, or are interwoven and made a part of the Constitution itself? Is an infringement of a Bill of Rights by the Governing powers, of more serious consequence, than an infringement of the frame of government? The question carries the answer along with it. That there is no distinction between them is a truth, an attempt to prove which would be an offence against common sense.

OF all the European governments a Bill of Rights is known, I believe, to that of England alone. The cause of this is obvious. The liberty of that country has been procured and established by gradual encroachments upon the regal powers seized by, if not yielded to, the first Prince of the Norman family. The first declaration of this sort found in the history of that government, is the Charter of Hen. the 1st, obtained in consequence of that Monarch's feeble title to the Throne. The frequent infractions of that Charter by Henry himself, as well as by subsequent Monarchs, produced the famous Magna Charta of John, which is generally considered as the foundation of English freedom. But in those ages of darkness, when scarcely a rule of descent was fixed, much less principles in politics established, Charters, or Declarations of Rights, were soon lost sight of, whenever interest induced, and circumstances offered opportunities to the English Princes, to infringe them.

THESE violations gave rise to the Charter of Hen. 3d, which was of much more importance than any of the preceding; and the discontents and confusions which led to it, in the end gave birth to the House of Commons. From this period some ideas of liberty began to prevail in the nation, but which for a long course of years was obscured by turbulant Barons, long and destructive civil wars, and the arbitrary government of an able line of Princes. The art of printing, the reformation, and the restoration of letters, at length enlightened the minds of men: Just ideas of liberty now prevailed, and the commons saw, that if the powers exercised by the Tudors were to continue in their new Sovereigns, all hope of liberty was at an end. Their restless spirit frequently shewed itself during the reign of Elizabeth; but that prudent Princess had the address to allay their fears, and the vigor to repress their spirit. A new and foreign race of Princes now ascend the Throne. The opportunity was not to be lost: Political positions were laid down in, and established by the House of Commons, which were considered by many as extraordinary, as they were true.

JAMES, without the talents, affected to reign with as high an hand as the Tudors. Charles unfortunately for himself, had been educated in the prejudices of his father. His ill advised and arbitrary measures, involved him in difficulties which produced the Petition of Right in 1628. In this was set forth the unalienable rights of English-men. New infractions produced new quarrels; which terminated in a total change of government. At the restoration all was joy and festivity. The tide of royalty ran too high, to think of Bills of Rights, or privileges of Englishmen. The conduct of James the 2d. the last King of that ill fated family, involved the nation in fresh discontents: The Prince of Orange is called to its assistance: The King quits the Kingdom: The Throne is declared vacant; and William ascended it upon terms stipulated in a Bill of Rights. It may be asked, why did the English consider a Bill of Rights necessary for the security of their liberty? The answer is, because they had no written Constitution, or form of government. For in truth the English Constitution is no more than an assemblage of certain powers in certain persons, sanctified by usage and defined by the authority of the Sovereignty; not by the people in any compact entered into between them and their rulers.

IF at the revolution the English had fully marked out the government under which they chose in future to live without contenting themselves with establishing certain principles, in a Bill of Rights, can there be a doubt, but that such frame of government would have supplied the place of, and rendered unnecessary, a Bill of Rights?

FORMER Princes had pretended to a divine right of governing: William acknowledged his to flow from the people; and previously to his ascending the

Throne entered into a contract with them, which recognized that just and salutary principle. Had the English at this time limited the regal power in definite terms, instead of satisfying themselves with a Bill of Rights, there would have been an end of prerogative; but they from habit were contented with a Bill of Rights, leaving the prerogative still inaccurately defined, to claim by implification, the exercise of all the powers not denied it by that declaration.

WHEN the United Netherlands threw off their dependence on the Crown of Spain and passed their act of Union, they thought not of any Bill of Rights; because they well knew that the States General could have no right nor pretext to pass the bounds prescribed by that celebrated act: So in the instance before us, Congress have no right, and can have no pretext, to pass the bounds prescribed them by this Federal Constitution; and the powers conceded to the Federal Government by the respective States, under this government, are as accurately defined, as they possibly could have been in a Declaration of Rights.

WHEN Independence was declared by the Americans, they had no government to controul them: Were free to chuse the form most agreeable to themselves. Six of these States have no Bill of Rights; wisely judging, that such declarations tend to abridge, rather than to preserve their liberties. They considered their Constitutions as the evidence of the social compact between the governors and the governed, and the only proof of the rights yielded to the former. In all disputes respecting the exercise of power, the Constitution or frame of government decides. If the right is given up by the Constitution, the governors exercise it; if not, the people retain it. Each of the remaining seven States has a Declaration of Rights, adopted rather from habit arising from the use in the English government, than from its being necessary to the preservation of their liberties.

PLAN OF THE FEDERAL CONSTITUTION.

WE, the People of the United States, in order to form a more perfect Union, establish Justice, insure domestic Tranquillity, provide for the Common Defence, promote the General Welfare, and secure the Blessings of Liberty to Ourselves and our Posterity, do Ordain and Establish this CONSTITUTION *for the* UNITED STATES OF AMERICA.

THE introduction, like a preamble to a law, is the Key of the Constitution. Whenever federal power is exercised, contrary to the spirit breathed by this introduction, it will be unconstitutionally exercised, and ought to be resisted by the people.

ARTICLE I.

Section 1. *All legislative powers herein granted, shall be vested in a Congress of the United States, which shall consist of a Senate and House of Representatives.*

It is necessary to observe that, Congress consists only of a Senate, and House of Representatives. The President makes no part of it; for his negative only amounts to a reconsideration of the public measures; as notwithstanding his disapprobation, a bill becomes a law, if two-thirds of each House agree to it.

Sect. 2. *The House of Representatives shall be composed of members chosen every second year by the people of the several States, and the electors in each State shall have the qualifications requisite for electors of the most numerous branch of the State Legislature.*

It will be asked by some,—Why should the Representatives to Congress be elected for two years, when in Virginia and the other States, the State Delegates are annually chosen? In answer to this question a variety of reasons occur; such as that they will have a great distance to go: That the purposes of their Legislation being purely federal, it will take them some time to become acquainted with the situation and interests of the respective States, as well as the relative situation and interest of the whole Union. That it would be difficult to get men of abilities to serve in an office, the re-election to which would be so frequent. If the election had been once in three years, it would perhaps have been an improvement. The unstable councils, the feeble laws, the relaxation of government which afflict this, and almost every State in the Union, may justly be attributed to the frequent changes which take place among the rulers in all the American governments.

Representatives and direct taxes shall be apportioned among the several States which may be included within this Union, according to their respective numbers, which shall be determined by adding to the whole number of free persons, including those bound to service for a term of years, and excluding Indians not taxed, three-fifths of all other persons. The actual enumeration shall be made within three years after the first meeting of the Congress of the United States, and within every subsequent term of ten years, in such manner as they shall by law direct. The number of Representatives shall not exceed one for every thirty thousand, but each State shall have at least one Representative: And until such enumeration shall be made, the State of New Hampshire shall be entitled to choose three; Massachusetts eight; Rhode-Island and Providence Plantations, one; Connecticut, five; New-York, six; New Jersey, four; Pennsylvania, eight; Delaware, one; Maryland, six; Virginia, ten; North-Carolina, five; South-Carolina, five; and Georgia, three.

Every free person counts one, every five slaves count three. By this regulation our consequence in the Union is increased, by an increase of numbers in the Congress. But some objectors argue that this arrangement is unjust; and that it bears hard upon the Southern States, who have been accustomed to consider their slaves merely as property; as a subject for, not as agents to taxation; and therefore by adding three fifths of our slaves to the free persons, our numbers are increased; and consequently by how much is that increase, by so much is the increase of our federal burthen. It is true, that slaves are property,—but are they not persons too? Does not their labour produce wealth? And is it not by the produce of labour, that all taxes must be paid? The Convention justly considered them in the light of persons, rather than property: But at the same time, conceiving their natural forces inferior to those of the whites; knowing that they require freemen to overlook them, and that they enfeeble the State which possesses them, they equitably considered five slaves only of equal consequence with three free persons. What rule of federal taxation so equal, and at the same time so little unfavourable to the Southern States, could the Convention have established, as that of numbers so arranged? Suppose the value of the lands in the respective States had been adopted as the measure: Let us see what then would have been the consequence. The northern States are comparatively small to the Southern, and are very populous; whilst to the southward, the inhabitants are scattered over a great extent of territory. Any given number of men in the latter States possess much greater quantities of land, than the like number in the former. It is true the lands to the northward sell for a greater price than those to the southward, but the difference in price is by no means adequate to the difference in quantity; consequently an equal number of men to the southward would have to pay a much greater federal tax than the like number to the northward.

By the 8th. Article of Confederation, the value of lands is made the measure of the federal quotas. Virginia in consequence is rated something above Massachusetts, whose number of white inhabitants is nearly double.

After all, this point is perhaps of no great consequence. The Congress probably will rarely, if ever, meddle with direct taxation, as the impost duties will in all liklihood answer all the purposes of government, or at any rate the post-office, which is daily increasing, and a tax upon instruments of writing, will supply any deficiency.

Indians are mentioned in this clause because there are nations of Indians within the limits of several of the States.

When vacancies happen in the Representation from any State, the Executive authority thereof shall issue writs of election to fill such vacancies.

THE Convention attentive to the preservation of the consequence of each State, have entrusted to the Executives thereof, the power of issuing writs of elections when vacancies happen. An additional security to the independence of the individual States.

The House of Representatives shall chuse their Speaker and other officers; and shall have the sole power of impeachment.

THE Representatives in Congress possess the sole power of impeachment: But here it may be observed, that they cannot impeach one of their own body; but have the power of expulsion, when two-thirds of their body shall agree.

Sect. 3. *The Senate of the United States shall be composed of two Senators from each State, chosen by the Legislature thereof, for six years; and each Senator shall have one vote.*

THE inequality of the representation of the Senate, has been made a great ground of objection.

WE should never forget that this is a government proposed for thirteen independent States, unequal in population, and extent of territory, and differing in a variety of other circumstances. It will not be denied that the small, have an equal right to preserve their independence with the large States; and this was their only means of preserving it. The justice of this is acknowledged by most of the objectors and amenders of the plan.

WE should here also recollect, that under the Confederation which at present exists, the small States have a vote in all respects equal to the large, even to Virginia; and it certainly was a great point gained by the large, to get their consequence increased in the House of Representatives in proportion to their numbers. In the United Provinces each of the seven States has but one vote in their Congress, and in that Confederation the disproportion between the States is much greater, than in ours; for the Province of Holland pays rather more than one half of the whole federal quota. Yet so great are the evils which would arise from a disunion, that this wealthy Province readily submits to so unequal a representation.

Immediately after they shall be assembled in consequence of the first election, they shall be divided as equally as may be, into three classes. The seats of the Senators of the first class shall be vacated at the expiration of the second year; of the second class, at the expiration of the fourth year; and of the third class, at the expiration of the sixth year; so that one third may be chosen every second year: And if vacancies happen by resignation, or otherwise, during the recess of the Legislature of any State, the Executive thereof may make temporary appointments until the next meeting of the legislature, which shall then fill such vacancies.

No person shall be a Senator who shall not have attained to the age of thirty years, and been nine years a citizen of the United States, and who shall not, when elected, be an inhabitant of that State for which he shall be chosen.

NOTWITHSTANDING the Senators are to be chosen by the Legislatures of the respective States, who surely are competent judges of those who are most capable of filling this important office: Notwithstanding one third of them are rechosen every two years: Yet the enemies to the Constitution affect to call this an aristocratic body: And endeavour to excite visionary fears in the minds of men, that they will form a distinct order in the State, and become formidable to the liberty of America. I am not gifted with the spirit of prophecy, and therefore cannot say what will happen; but this I will boldly assert, that if power cannot be trusted in the hands of men so appointed, it can be trusted no where. The different States will be well acquainted with the characters of those whom they elect to the Senate; their time of duration when elected is too short to enable them to form dangerous intrigues, or bring about important revolutions. It is a well established principal in rhetorick, that it is not fair to argue against a thing, from the abuse of it. Would you say there should be no Physicians because there are unskilful administers of medecine: No Lawyers because some are dishonest: No Courts because Judges are sometimes ignorant; nor government because power may be abused? In short, it is impossible to guard entirely against the abuse of power. Annual elections will not do it. The Delegates of Virginia are annually elected, yet it is a fact, that there has not been an Assembly since the government was framed, wherein the Bill of Rights and the Constitution have not been infringed. The instances have been of no great importance and therefore notwithstanding the danger of the principal, they have been overlooked.

The Vice-President of the United States shall be President of the Senate, but shall have no vote, unless they be equally divided.

The Senate shall choose their other officers, and also a President pro tempore, in the absence of the Vice-President, or when he shall exercise the Office of President of the United States.

THE Vice-President has been introduced from the State Government of New York. This useful, though surely inoffensive officer, has been made by some objectors the bugbear of the Constitution. It is a strong proof of want of argument in the enemies to it, when they hold up this officer as dangerous. He is elected by the same persons as the President, and in the same manner. He presides in the Senate, but has no vote except when they are divided. This is the only power incident to his office whilst he continues Vice-President; and he is obviously introduced into the government to prevent the ill-consequences which might otherwise happen from the death or removal of the President. This is the purpose for which a similar officer has been introduced into the Constitution of New-York.

The Senate shall have the sole power to try all impeachments. When sitting for that purpose, they shall be on oath or affirmation. When the President of the United States is tried, the Chief Justice shall preside: And no person shall be convicted without the concurrence of two-thirds of the members present.

Judgment in cases of impeachment shall not extend further than to removal from office, and disqualification to hold and enjoy any office of honor, trust or profit, under the United States; but the party convicted shall nevertheless be liable and subject to indictment, trial, judgment and punishment, according to law.

I CONCEIVE that the Senators are not impeachable, and therefore Governor Randolph's objection falls to the ground. I am surprised that a man of that gentleman's abilities should have fallen into this mistake. The Senators having a power over their own members, have the right of expulsion. Why then should they be impeachable? For upon impeachments, the punishment is only removal from, and incapacity to hold offices. Expulsion amounts to the same thing. Besides, the Senators are elected by the people, though mediately, as well as the House of Representatives, and therefore have not the same degree of responsibility annexed to their characters, as the officers of the government; and for this obvious reason,—the former are appointed by the people themselves to stand in their places, and they are the best judges of those who are most fit to serve them: but the latter are appointed by the servants of the people. It is a generally received maxim among writers on government, that the Judiciary and Legislative departments should be kept distinct. The position is true to a certain extent; but this like most other general rules, is liable to exceptions. In the English government, which is certainly the freest in Europe, the House of Lords not only try impeachments, but is the highest civil court in the kingdom. In that Constitution the House of Commons are the impeachers, the House of Lords the triers: But no members either of the House of Commons or House of Lords, was ever impeached as such: But whenever members of either House have been impeached, it was as great officers of State. Under the federal government this is impossible, because the members of neither House can hold any office of State.

IF this reasoning be not conclusive, the fourth section of the second article puts it out of doubt, viz. "The President, Vice-President, and all civil officers of the United States, shall be removed from office on impeachment, &c." The Senators are representatives of the people; and by no construction can be considered as civil officers of the State. If this be the case, in whose hands can this power be lodged with greater propriety, or with greater safety, than in those of the Senate? Or how can a better court be appointed? To impeach either the members of Senate or House of Representatives, would be to impeach the representatives of the people, that is the people, themselves which is an absurdity.

Sect. 4. *The times, places and manner of holding elections for Senators and Representatives, shall be prescribed in each State by the Legislature thereof; but the Congress may at any time, by law, make or alter such regulations, except as to the Places of chusing Senators.*

The Congress shall assemble at least once in every year, and such meeting shall be on the first Monday in December, unless they shall by law appoint a different day.

Sect. 5. *Each House shall be the judge of the elections, returns, and qualifications, of its own members, and a majority of each shall constitute a quorum to do business; but a smaller number may adjourn from day to day, and may be authorized to compel the Attendance of absent members, in such Manner, and under such Penalties as each House may provide.*

Each House may determine the rules of its proceedings, punish its members for disorderly behaviour, and with the concurrence of two-thirds, expel a member.

Each House shall keep a journal of its proceedings, and from time to time publish the same, excepting such parts as may in their judgment require secrecy; and the yeas and nays of the members of either House on any question, shall, at the desire of one-fifth of those present, be entered on the journal.

Neither House, during the cession of Congress, shall, without the consent of the other, adjourn for more than three days, nor to any other place than that in which the two Houses shall be sitting.

EXPERIENCE and a change of circumstances may render it necessary that the Congress should have the power of regulating the elections: But as the Senate is elected by the State Legislatures, the place of such election must be the place where they meet. Besides which, this power was necessary lest some of the States from obstinacy, or selfish views, should alter the time and place of holding the elections in such a manner, as might impede the operation of the federal government.

Sect. 6. *The Senators and Representatives shall receive a compensation for their services, to be ascertained by law, and paid out of the treasury of the United States. They shall in all cases, except treason, felony and breach of the peace, be privileged from arrest during their attendance at the session of their respective houses, and in going to and returning from the same; and for any speech or debate in either house, they shall not be questioned in any other place.*

No Senator or Representative shall, during the time for which he was elected, be appointed to any civil office under the authority of the United States, which shall have been created, or the emoluments whereof shall have been increased during such time; and no Person holding any Office under the United States, shall be a member of either House during his continuance in office.

SAY the objectors,—Why are not the salaries of the members of Congress ascertained by the Constitution? I will answer them by another question,—Why are not the salaries of every officer of the United States ascertained by it? Or rather, why should the Convention have descended into such minutia? Can it be supposed, for a moment, that in the present situation of America, when there are still left many men of talents and virtue, from amongst whom the Congress will doubtless be chosen, that they will pass a law to give themselves immoderate salaries? But even should they, what would be the mighty evil to this extensive continent from eighty or ninety persons having salaries larger than perhaps their services might merit?

IT is proper that Congress should have the regulation of this matter for another reason. It is a fact well known in the commercial world, that, from one certain cause, the quantity of specie is insensibly increasing. This of consequence lessens its value: Therefore a salary which now would be sufficient, forty years hence, would be wholly inadequate.

IN the latter part of this section there is an admirable check upon the members of both Houses; as nothing can tend in a greater degree, to preserve their independence of conduct, and prevent intriguing, than that no member shall be eligible to any office which has been created, or whose emoluments have been increased, since the time of his election, and during the time for which he has been elected.

Sect. 7. *All bills for raising revenue shall originate in the House of Representatives; but the Senate may propose or concur with amendments as on other bills.*

IN this the Constitution is an improvement upon that of England: There all money bills must not only originate but must be perfected in the House of Commons: Here though the Senate cannot originate such bills, yet they have the power of amending them, and by that means have an opportunity of communicating their ideas to the House of Representatives upon the important subject of taxation.

Every bill which shall have passed the House of Representatives and the Senate, shall, before it becomes a law, be presented to the President of the United States; If he approve he shall sign it, but if not he shall return it with his objections, to that House in which it shall have originated, who shall enter the objections at large on their journal, and proceed to reconsider it. If after such reconsideration two-thirds of that House shall agree to pass the bill, it shall be sent, together with the objections, to the other House, by which it shall likewise be reconsidered, and if approved by two-thirds of that House, it shall become a law. But in all such cases the votes of both Houses shall be determined by yeas and nays, and the names of the persons voting for and against the bill shall be entered on the journal of each House respectively. If any bill shall not be returned by the President within ten days (Sundays excepted) after it shall have been presented to him, the same shall be a law, in like manner as if he had signed it, unless the Congress by their adjournment prevent its return, in which case it shall not be a Law.

THIS power in the President is derived from the State government of Massachusetts and New-York, though in the latter the Chancellor and Chief Judges are added to the Governor. This power goes only to a reconsideration of the public measures; and the President's disapprobation, or negative, is nugatory, when two-thirds of each House concur in any measure after it has undergone his inspection. The Convention wisely judged that the President would in all probability be a man of great experience, and abilities, and as far as his powers extend, ought to be considered as representing the Union; and consequently would be well acquainted with the interests of the whole. Great utility is likely therefore to arise to Congress from his knowledge, and his reasoning upon their acts of Legislation. Farther, the experience of all ages proves that all popular assemblies are frequently governed by prejudices, passions, and partial views of the subject; nay sometimes by indecent heats and animosities. The ten days therefore given to the President for his opinion of their measures, is wisely interposed to prevent the mischiefs which might ensue from those common faults of such assemblies.

Every order, resolution, or vote to which the concurrence of the Senate and House of Representatives may be necessary (except on a question of adjournment) shall be presented to the President of the United States; and before the same shall take effect, shall be approved by him, or being disapproved by him, shall be repassed by two-thirds of the Senate and House of Representatives, according to the rules and limitations prescribed in the case of a bill.

THE reasoning upon the last clause applies also to this.

Sect. 8. *The Congress shall have power*

To lay and collect taxes, duties, imposts and excises, to pay the debts and provide for the common defence and general welfare of, the United States; but all duties, imposts, and excises, shall be uniform throughout the United States;

IT is here to be observed, that all taxes, imposts, &c., are to be applied only for the common defence and general welfare of the United States. By no possibility will the words admit of any other construction. Yet several popular declaimers have attempted to sound the alarm by their illiberal and ill-founded suggestions of peculation, bribery, and corruption, and of the probability of the public Treasury being converted to the use of the President and Congress. But how will this be possible? They will have all fixed salaries, and no perquisites. The public accounts of receipts and expenditures will be regularly kept and regularly published, for the public inspection: Besides which, the public offices will always be open for the search and inquiries of every individual. I doubt if human wisdom could devise any better mode of securing a just application of the public money.

As scarcely any article of the proposed plan has escaped censure, there are objections made to the grant of the imposts to Congress. But when we consider that the purposes for which the imposts are to be applied are merely national, and falls directly within the design of the Union, that of making all America one State for great political purposes, the objection falls; for in this view America composes but one great republic, all the citizens of which stand precisely upon the same ground, and pay only in proportion to their consumption of foreign articles. To this we may add, that those States which export the chief of the produce of their labour, and in consequence of that circumstance, import more than those which manufacture, receive a compensation for the increased import, by the exported produce being free from duties. And besides, we may fairly conclude, that the consumption of foreign articles throughout America, is nearly in proportion to the enumeration, which is the measure of the respective quotas.

To borrow money on the credit of the United States;

THIS power is lodged with the present Congress.

To regulate commerce with foreign nations, and among the several States, and with the Indian tribes;

THE power of regulating commerce gives great alarm to the enemies of the Constitution. In this, as in most other instances, they forget that this is a government for thirteen States; and think only of the immediate interests of Virginia; as if she had a right to dictate to the other twelve, and as if her interests alone were to be consulted. Be not deceived my countrymen. However important we may be in the scale of Union, there are other States which are equally so. The consequence of this power, say they, will be, that the eastern and northern States will combine together, and not only oblige the southern to export their produce in their bottoms, by prohibiting foreign bottoms; but will also lay such duties upon foreign manufactures as will amount to a prohibition, in order to supply us themselves.

UPON accurately investigating this point, we shall find the reasoning to be false, as the supposition is illiberal. It is true the eastern States can build and equip ships, upon better terms than the southern. Nay, I believe I may go father, and say, that they can upon better terms than any nation in Europe. This arises from their having all the materials for ship-building within themselves, except canvas and cordage, whilst most of the maritime powers of Europe, depend upon foreign countries, not only for these articles, but also for timber and masts. A great extent of sea coast, a cold climate, a barren soil, and above all, the fisheries, furnish an infinite number of seamen, who from necessity are willing to navigate for very moderate wages. If this be the case, is there any reason to suppose that the eastern States will not carry our produce upon as reasonable terms as any of the European powers? I believe it is a fact, that before the war, they were the principal carriers for the British West-Indies; so low were the terms upon which their vessels could be chartered. And the same causes still exists, why they should take freight upon terms equally moderate. But this is not all. The eastern States are not ignorant that the southern possess even better materials for ship-building, than they do; and therefore will take care not to excite their jealousy, nor stimulate them to build ships and become their own carriers, by exacting unreasonable freightage. But admitting that the eastern Delegates should be so dishonest as well as unwise, to combine against those of the south—I will venture to assert, that not a man in America, who is acquainted with the middle States, can suppose that they would join in such a combination. New-York is rather a country of farmers than of sailors: It possesses large tracts of fertile soil, but no fisheries, and before the war, for one ship built in that State, either for freightage or sale, there were thirty in New-England. All that she will aim at, therefore, will be ships of her own, sufficient to carry her own produce. Her interests, therefore will not induce her to enter into this formidable combination.

JERSEY, from her local situation, and a variety of peculiar circumstances, has fewer ships and seamen than even any of the southern States. Her interests, therefore, will lead her to adhere to them.

THE same reasoning applies to Pennsylvania that does to New-York; and still more emphatically; because this State is still more employed in husbandry. And as to the State of Delaware, it does not own six ships.

LET us then see how this question will stand in point of numbers. The four eastern States will have seventeen voices, which will be opposed by the nineteen voices of the middle States, and the twenty-nine of the southern.

I WILL now endeavour to answer the other objection.—The fear of a northern combination to furnish the southern States with manufactures. This I conceive, has arisen either from ignorance of the subject, or an absolute enmity to all confederation. The only manufactures which the northern States possess and with which they can furnish others, are shoes, cotton cards, nails, hats, carriages, and perhaps paper and refined sugars may be added; and should the whale-fishery be ever revived, train oil and spermacæti candles. The two first articles may be in a great measure confined to Massachusetts. Their shoes are as good and as cheap as those imported from Great-Britain, at least as the sale shoes. And as to the second article, the exportation of them from thence is prohibited by act of Parliament. Both New-York and Pennsylvania manufacture leather in all its branches, and hats; but not more than sufficient for their own consumption. Connecticut has no manufactures to export; nor has New-York, unless perhaps some refined sugar. Jersey has only domestic manufactures. Pennsylvania manufactures nails, refined sugar, cotton cards, carriages, and, of late, paper for exportation. The Delaware State has only domestic manufactures.

IF Massachusetts can furnish us with shoes, cards, train oil, and spermacæti candles; Pennsylvania with nails, white sugar, carriages, and paper, as cheap as we can procure them from beyond the Atlantic, why should not such European articles be prohibited? There is no probability that either the northern or southern States, will in many years become extensive manufacturers. The price of labour and cheapness of land, will prevent it; and the daily migrations from all the States to the western parts of America, will keep up the one, and keep down the other. I have been informed, and I believe rightly informed, that the amount of the imports from Europe, is as great or greater in the eastern or middle States, as in the southern, in proportion to their numbers.[2] This, to many, may appear

2. It is a generally received opinion in this country, that the exports of the eastern and middle States are very inconsiderable; but this is a great mistake; for when we take into consideration their wheat, flour, lumber, flax-seed, potash, fish, oyl, iron, and rum, there can be no doubt but these articles produce great sums. I am informed that the European goods annually shipped to Massachusetts, are to a greater amount than those shipped to Virginia. These goods can only be paid for by the produce of their exports.

doubtful; but I believe it, because I have good reason to think, that the domestic manufactures of the southern States, particularly of Virginia, are of greater value than the domestic manufactures of the northern and middle States, in the same proportion. This has arisen from the cultivation of cotton, which will not come to perfection to the northward; and that article is manufactured with much less labour than either flax or hemp.

IF this account be just, what have the southern States to fear? But admitting some of the eastern and middle States should enter into this illiberal, unjust, and impolitic combination: Let us see how the numbers would stand. New-Hampshire, Massachusetts, New-York, and Pennsylvania, the only manufacturing States, may combine: Their numbers will amount to twenty-five in one House, to be opposed by forty; and in the other the numbers will be eight, to be opposed by sixteen.

AFTER all, suppose these objections are founded in fact: Had we not better submit to the slight inconveniencies which might arise from this combination, than the serious evils that must necessarily follow from disunion?

To establish an uniform rule of naturalization, and uniform laws on the subject of bankruptcies throughout the United States;

To coin money, regulate the value thereof, and of foreign coin, and fix the standard of weights and measures;

To provide for the punishment of counterfeiting the securities and current coin of the United States;

To establish Post-offices and post roads;

To promote the progress of science and useful arts, by securing for limited times to authors and inventors the exclusive right to their respective writings and discoveries;

To constitute tribunals inferior to the Supreme Court;

To define and punish piracies and felonies committed on the high seas, and offences against the law of nations;

To declare war, grant letters of marque and reprisal, and make rules concerning captures on land and water;

MOST of these powers, the present Congress possess, and none of them have been objected to, except what relates to the Courts, which will be taken notice of hereafter.

To raise and support armies, but no appropriation of money to that use shall be for a longer term than two years;

BY this regulation every House of Representatives will have a share in the appropriations; and no mischief can ensue from appropriations of two years, since the proceedings of each House of Congress are to be published from time to time, as well as regular statements and accounts of the receipts and expenditures of all public money.

To provide and maintain a navy;
To make rules for the government and regulation of the land and naval forces;

THE present Congress possess the powers given by these clauses.

To provide for calling forth the militia to execute the laws of the union, suppress insur-
rections and repel invasions;
To provide for organizing, arming and disciplining, the militia, and for governing such
part of them as may be employed in the service of the United States, reserving to the States
respectively, the appointment of the officers, and the authority of training the militia
according to the discipline prescribed by Congress.

BY these clauses, the appointment of the militia officers, and training the militia, are reserved to the respective States; except that Congress have a right to direct in what manner they are to be disciplined, and the time when they are to be ordered out.

THESE clauses have been extremely misunderstood, or purposely misconstrued, by the enemies to the Constitution. Some have said, "the absolute unqualified command that Congress have over the militia may be instrumental to the destruction of all liberty, both public and private, whether of a personal, civil, or religious nature."

Is this the result of reason, or is it the dictate of resentment? How can the command of Congress over the militia be either absolute or unqualified, when its officers are appointed by the States, and consequently can by no possibility become its creatures?

THEY will generally be men of property and probity: And can any one for a moment suppose that such men will ever be so lost to a sense of liberty, the rights of their country, and their own dignity, as to become the instruments of arbitrary measures? Whenever that shall be the case, we may in vain contend for forms of government; the spirit of liberty will have taken its flight from America, and nothing but an arbitrary government will be fit for such a people, however accurately defined the powers of her Constitution may be. But so long as there shall be a militia so officered, or the majority of the people landholders, America will have little to fear for liberty. Congress have the power of organizing the militia; and can it be put into better hands? They can have no interest in destroying the personal liberty of any man, or raising his fortune in the mode of organization: They can make no law upon this, or any other subject, which will not affect themselves, their children, or their connexions.

CAN any one seriously suppose, that Congress will ever think of drawing the militia of one State out, in order to destroy the liberties of another? Of Virginia, for instance, to destroy the liberties of Pennsylvania? Or should they be so wicked, that an American militia, officered by the States, would obey so odious a mandate? The supposition is monstrous.

To exercise exclusive legislation in all cases whatsoever, over such district (not exceeding ten miles square) as may, by cession of particular States, and the acceptance of Congress, become the seat of the government of the United States, and to exercise like authority over all places purchased by the consent of the Legislature of the State in which the same shall be, for the erection of forts, magazines, arsenals, dock-yards, and other needful buildings.

SO great is the jealousy of some of our citizens, that even this clause has excited their fears. This little spot is to be the centre to which is to be attracted all the wealth and power of this extensive continent: The focus which will absorb the last remains of American liberty. Such are the visionary phantoms of the antifederalists.

THE Congress is to govern, as they shall see fit, a district not more than ten miles square. And what possible mischief can arise to the United States from hence? This district must either be purchased by Congress, or yielded to them by the inhabitants of that particular spot, which they may conceive most convenient for them to assemble at, and for which the consent of the State is necessary. If the first, there will be few or no inhabitants; they will therefore induce people to settle it, by establishing a mild government. If the second, the inhabitants of any particular district certainly have a right to submit to whatever form of government they may think agreeable, provided the State within which the district lies, consents; without giving offence to Virginia, or any other of the States. We are told that the wise Franklin has recommended to the Philadelphians to offer their city and its environs as the seat of Congress. Can it be supposed that he would recommend this measure to his favorite city were he not well assured that the government of Congress will be a good one? I have no doubt but this district will flourish; that it will increase in population and wealth: Because I have no doubt but most people would think it a happiness to live under the government of such men as will compose the Congress; or under such a government as such men will frame for that district.

And—To make all Laws which shall be necessary and proper for carrying into execution the foregoing powers, and other powers vested by this Constitution in the government of the United States, or in any department or officer thereof.

By this clause, Congress have no farther legislative authority than shall be deemed necessary to carry into execution the powers vested by this Constitution. This regulation is necessary; as without it the different States might counteract all the laws of Congress, and render the Federal Government nugatory.

Sect. 9. *The migration or importation of such persons as any of the States now existing shall think proper to admit, shall not be prohibited by the Congress prior to the year one thousand eight hundred and eight, but a tax or duty may be imposed on such importation, not exceeding ten dollars for each person.*

This clause is a proof of deference in the members of the Convention, to each other, and of concession of the northern to the southern States. There is no doubt but far the greater part of that Convention hold domestic slavery in abhorrence. But the members from South-Carolina and Georgia, thinking slaves absolutely necessary for the cultivation and melioration of their States, insisted upon this clause. But it affects not the law of Virginia which prohibits the importation of slaves.

The privilege of the writ of habeas corpus shall not be suspended, unless when in cases of rebellion or invasion the public Safety may require it.

By this clause the Congress have the right of suspending the habeas corpus in the two cases of insurrection and rebellion—a power which follows from the necessity of the thing.

No bill of attainder or ex post facto law shall be passed.

It is extraordinary that Mr. Mason should have made a part of this clause a ground of objection. 'Till that gentleman denied it, I had supposed it an universally received opinion, that ex post facto laws were dangerous in their principle, and oppressive in their execution. And with respect to bills of attainder, a very slight acquaintance with the history of that country in which alone they are used, is sufficient to discover that they have been generally made the means of oppression.

No capitation, or other direct, tax shall be laid, unless in proportion to the census or enumeration herein before directed to be taken.

This clause is a confirmation of the third clause of the second section of the first article.

No tax or duty shall be laid on articles exported from any State.

No preference shall be given by any regulation of commerce or revenue to the ports of one State over those of another: Nor shall vessels bound to, or from, one State, be obliged to enter, clear, or pay duties in another.

ALL writers upon finance hold taxes upon exports to be impolitic. Yet there are doubtless some articles which will with propriety bear an export duty; such as tobacco and perhaps indigo. But then these articles are of the growth of only five of the States; and it would be a manifest injustice that the produce of some States should be taxed for the benefit of others. The latter part of the clause provides that all Naval Officer fees and port charges shall be the same throughout the United States; and that a vessel bound to one State from another, and calling at any intermediate State, shall not be obliged to enter, clear, or pay duty, in such State. This tends to facilitate the intercourse among the States, and may produce many commercial conveniencies.

No money shall be drawn from the Treasury, but in consequence of appropriations made by law; and a regular statement and account of the receipts and expenditures of all public money, shall be published from time to time.

AS all appropriations of money are to be made by law, and regular statements thereof published, no money can be applied but to the use of the United States.

No title of nobility shall be granted by the United States:—And no person holding any office of profit or trust under them, shall, without the consent of the Congress, accept of any present, emolument, office, or title, of any kind whatever, from any King, Prince, or foreign State.

THE first part of this clause proves the Convention had no aristocratical views, nor any idea of establishing an order in the State, with rights independent of the people. The latter part of it is introduced to prevent the officers of the Federal Government being warped from their duty.

Sect. 10. *No State shall enter into any treaty, alliance, or confederation; grant letters of marque and reprisal; coin money; emit bills of credit; make anything but gold and silver coin a tender in payment of debts; pass any bill of attainder, ex post facto law, or law impairing the obligation of contracts; or grant any title of nobility.*

THE States, in their individual capacities, should be restrained from the exercise of the powers enumerated in this clause, for a variety of reasons. If any State should have a right of making treaties, granting letters of marque, and the like, America might be perpetually involved in foreign wars. By exercising the right of coinage and of emitting bills of credit, a State might, by the former, debase the currency of the United States, by mixing great quantities of alloy, and by that means defraud the Federal Treasury; and by the latter it might defraud not only its own citizens, but the citizens of other States. But this is not all. An exercise of these rights would materially interfere with the exercise of the like by the Congress; and therefore the particular, should give way to the general interest. The making anything but gold and silver a tender in payment of debts, and the impairing the obligation of contracts, is so great a political injustice, that the Constitution here requires of the States,that they will forever relinquish the exercise of a power so odious. This part of the clause would probably never have been introduced, had not some of the States afforded too frequent instances of unjust laws upon these subjects.

No State shall, without the Consent of the Congress, lay any imposts or duties on imports or exports, except what may be absolutely necessary for executing it's inspection laws; and the nett produce of all duties and imposts, laid by any State on imports or exports, shall be for the use of the Treasury of the United States; and all such laws shall be subject to the revision and controul of the Congress.

No State shall, without the consent of Congress, lay any duty of tonnage, keep troops, or ships of war in time of peace, enter into any agreement or compact with another State, or with a foreign power, or engage in war, unless actually invaded, or in such imminent danger as will not admit of delay.

IF the individual States might lay duties upon the imports, it would be counteracting the same right in Congress, and ruin the great fund out of which the present federal debts are to be paid, as well as the future federal expences defrayed. And with regard to exports, it was highly reasonable that one State should be prohibited from laying an export duty on the articles of a sister State, which may be shipped through that State.

THE exigencies of the Union may however require direct taxes. By this clause, a door is open to the States, to raise their respective quotas, in lieu of direct taxes; by laying a duty upon exports; or even duties upon imports. But as the amount of these duties are to be paid into the public Treasury, no inconvenience can, on the one hand, arise to the general welfare from them; and, on the other, the power of revision in the Congress will be the means of securing a due attention to the interests of all the States, in the mode of laying the duty, as well as in the application of it. The latter part of the clause is no more than a confirmation of principles antecedently established, and of powers before vested in the Congress, but such as are absolutely necessary for the good order, dignity, and harmony of the whole; and are such as the States have already yielded to the present Congress.[3]

3. See Article the 6th of the Confederation.

ARTICLE II.

Sect. I. *The Executive Power shall be vested in a President of the United States of America. He shall hold his office during the term of four years, and, together with the Vice-President, chosen for the same term, be elected as follows:*

Each State shall appoint, in such manner as the Legislature thereof may direct, a number of Electors, equal to the whole number of Senators and Representatives to which the State may be entitled in the Congress: But no Senator or Representative, or person holding an office of trust or profit under the United States, shall be appointed an Elector.

The Electors shall meet in their respective States, and vote by ballot, for two persons, of whom one at least shall not be an inhabitant of the same State with themselves. And they shall make a list of all the persons voted for, and of the number of votes for each; which list they shall sign and certify, and transmit, sealed to the seat of the government of the United States, directed to the President of the Senate. The President of the Senate shall, in the presence of the Senate and House of Representatives, open all the certificates, and the votes shall then be counted. The person having the greatest number of votes shall be the President, if such number be a majority of the whole number of Electors appointed; and if there be more than one who have such majority, and have an equal number of votes, then the House of Representatives shall immediately chuse, by ballot, one of them for President; and if no person have a majority, then from the five highest on the list the said House shall in like manner chuse the President. But in chusing the President, the votes shall be taken by States, the Representation from each State having one vote; a quorum for this purpose shall consist of a member or members from two thirds of the States, and a majority of all the States shall be necessary to a choice. In every case, after the choice of the President, the person having the greatest number of votes of the electors, shall be the Vice-President. But if there should remain two or more who have equal votes, the Senate shall chuse from them, by ballot the Vice-President.

It has been urged by many, that the President should be continued in office, only a given number of years, and then be rendered ineligible. To this it may be answered, were that to be the case, a good officer might be displaced, and a bad one succeed. Knowing that he could not be continued, he might be more attentive to enrich himself, should opportunities offer, than to the execution of his office. But as his continuance in office, will depend upon his discharging the duties of it with ability, and integrity, his eligibility will most probably be the best security for his conduct. The longer a man of abilities and virtue, fills an office, the better, and easier will the duties of it be discharged; The whole system of administration becomes well arranged; and every department in the government well filled. An election to this office once in every four years, is a sufficient curb upon the President. The Electors hold the reins. If he has mis-conducted himself, he will not be re-elected; if has governed with prudence, and ability, he ought to be continued.

THE Vice-President will probably be a candidate to succeed the President. The former will therefore be a perpetual centinel over the latter; will be a stimulus to keep him up to his duty, and afford an additional security for his upright conduct.

NOTWITHSTANDING these reasons, and the powerful checks opposed to the powers of the President, the enemies of the Constitution has sounded the alarm with great violence, upon the ground of his eligibility for life. Some tell us that it will be the means of his becoming the hereditary sovereign of the United States; whilst others hold up to our view the dangers of an elective monarchy.

IT is pretty certain that the President can never become the sovereign of America, but with the voluntary consent of the people. He is re-elected by them; not by any body of men over whom he may have gained an undue influence. No citizen of America has a fortune sufficiently large, to enable him to raise and support a single regiment. The President's salary will be greatly inadequate either to the purpose of gaining adherents, or of supporting a military force: He will possess no princely revenues, and his personal influence will be confined to his native State. Besides, the Constitution has provided, that no person shall be eligible to this office, who is not thirty-five years old; and in the course of nature very few fathers leave a son who has arrived to that age. The powers of the President are not kingly, any more than the ensigns of his office. He has no guards, no regalia, none of those royal trappings which would set him apart from the rest of his fellow citizens. Suppose the first President should be continued for life: What expectations can any man in the Union have to succeed him, except such as are grounded upon the popularity of his character?

NONE of its citizens possess distinct principalities, from whence money may be drawn to purchase, or armies raised to intimidate the votes. Fortunately for America, she has no neighbouring Princess to interfere in her elections, or her councils: No Empress of Russia to place the Crown upon the head of her favorite Powniotowsky.[4]

IT has also been objected, that a Council of State ought to have been assigned the President. The want of it, is, in my apprehension, a perfection rather than a blemish. What purpose would such a Council answer, but that of diminishing, or annihilating the responsibility annexed to the character of the President.

4. The present King of Poland was Stanislaus Leginski, Count Powniotowsky.

From the superiority of his talents, or the superior dignity of his place, he would probably acquire an undue influence over, and might induce a majority of them to advise measures injurious to the welfare of the States, at the same time that he would have the means of sheltering himself from impeachment, under that majority. I will here once for all observe, that descended as we are from the English, conversant as we are in the political history of that country, it is impossible not to derive both political opinions, and prejudices, from that source. The objectors probably considered, that as in the English government, the first Magistrate has a Council of State; there should be one also in the American. But they should at the same time have recollected, that the King of England is not personally responsible for his conduct; but that her Constitution looks up to his Ministers, that is, to his Council, to answer for the measures of the Sovereign. But in the American Constitution, the first Magistrate is the efficient Minister of the people, and as such, ought to be alone responsible for his conduct. Let him act pursuant to the dictates of his own judgment; let him advise with his friends; let him consult those of whom he has the highest opinion for wisdom, but let not his responsibility be diminished by giving him a Council.

The Congress may determine the time of chusing the Electors, and the day on which they shall give their votes; which day shall be the same throughout the United States.

No person, except a natural born citizen, or a citizen of the United States, at the time of the adoption of this Constitution, shall be eligible to the office of President; neither shall any person be eligible to that office who shall not have attained to the age of thirty five years, and been fourteen years a resident within the United States.

In case of the removal of the President from office, or of his death, resignation, or inability to discharge the powers and duties of the said office, the same shall devolve on the Vice-President; and the Congress may by law provide for the case of removal, death, resignation, or inability, both of the President and Vice-President, declaring what officer shall then act as President, and such officer shall act accordingly, until the disability be removed, or a President shall be elected.

The President shall, at stated times, receive for his services, a compensation, which shall neither be increased nor diminished during the Period for which he shall have been elected, and he shall not receive within that Period any other Emolument from the United States, or any of them.

Before he enters on the Execution of his Office, he shall take the following Oath or Affirmation: "I do solemnly swear (or affirm) that I will faithfully execute the Office of President of the United States, and will to the best of my ability, preserve, protect, and defend the Constitution of the United States."

THE first of these clauses is intended to prevent intrigue and tumult in chusing the Electors: And the reasons already offered, why Congress should have the right of altering "the times and manner of holding the elections for Senators," apply why they should have the power of determining the time of chusing Electors. The fifth is an additional check upon the President.

Sect. 2. *The President shall be Commander in Chief of the army and navy of the United States, and of the militia of the several States, when called into the actual service of the United States: he may require the opinion, in writing, of the principal officer in each of the Executive departments, upon any subject relating to the duties of their respective offices, and he shall have power to grant reprieves and pardons for offences against the United States, except in cases of impeachment.*

THE powers vested in the President by this and the subsequent clause, belong, from the nature of them, to the Executive branch of government; and could be placed in no other hands with propriety.

SO long as laws cannot provide for every case that may happen: So long as punishments shall continue disproportionate to crimes, the power of pardoning should somewhere exist. With whom could this power, so precious to humanity, be better entrusted, than with the President? An officer who, from his age and experience, will seldom be misled in the exercise of it; and who less liable to the influence of prejudice and passion than a popular assembly, will most probably be guided by discretion in the use of it.

WHY Govenor Randolph should wish to take from him this power, at least in cases of treason; and why he should have made a distinction between the power of pardoning before, and after conviction; I am at a loss to conceive; and shall therefore attempt no further answer to an objection which appears to me, unsupported by reason.

He shall have power, by and with the advice and consent of the Senate, to make treaties, provided two thirds of the Senators present concur; and he shall nominate, and by and with the advice and consent of the Senate, shall appoint Ambassadors, other public Ministers and Consuls, Judges of the supreme Court, and all other officers of the United States, whose appointments are not herein otherwise provided for, and which shall be established by law. But the Congress may, by law, vest the appointment of such inferior officers, as they think proper, in the President alone, in the Courts of law, or in the heads of departments.

THE Constitution has here lessened the authority of the President, by making the assent of two-thirds of the Senate necessary in the important cases of making treaties, in appointing Ambassadors, the Judges of the Supreme Court, and the great officers of State.

WRITERS upon government have established it as a maxim, that the Executive and Legislative authority should be kept separate. But the position should be taken with considerable latitude. The Executive authority here given to a branch of the Legislature, is no novelty, in free governments. In England, the Executive, or Cabinet Council, is taken indifferently from either House of Parliament. In the States of New York and Jersey, the Senate not only act as an Executive Council, but also form a part of the Court of Appeals.

THE following reasons suggest themselves in support of the propriety of vesting the President and Senate with the power of making treaties.

THE President is the Representative of the Union: The Senate the Representatives of the respective States. The objects of treaties must always be either of great national import, or such as concern the States in their individual capacities; but never can concern the individual members of the State. Secrecy and dispatch are necessary in making them: For without secrecy and dispatch, they are seldom made to purpose. Hence arises the impropriety of consulting either the Representatives of the people, or the different States. If the former were consulted, the interests of the small States might be sacrificed; if the latter, almost insurmountable obstacles would be thrown in the way of every negociation.

IN the Dutch Republic the States-General are obliged to consult their constituents, upon this, as upon every important occasion, however urgent may be the necessity. This vice in their Federal Constitution has more than once brought them to the brink of ruin.

The President shall have power to fill up all vacancies that may happen during the recess of the Senate, by granting commissions which shall expire at the end of their next session.

THIS inoffensive clause is made a ground of objection by Governor Randolph! I wish he had informed us wherefore.

Sect. 3. *He shall from time to time give to the Congress information of the state of the Union, and recommend to their consideration such measures as he shall judge necessary and expedient: He may on extraordinary occasions, convene both Houses, or either of them, and in case of disagreement between them, with respect to the time of adjournment, he may adjourn them to such time as he shall think proper; He shall receive Ambassadors and other public Ministers: He shall take care that the laws be faithfully executed; and shall commission all the officers of the United States.*

THE powers given by this section are such as in all governments, have always been, and must necessarily be, vested in the first magistrate.

Sect. 4. *The President, Vice-President and all civil officers of the United States, shall be removed from office on impeachment for, and conviction of, treason, bribery, or other high crimes and misdemeanors.*

THE persons subject to impeachment, are the President, Vice-President, and all civil officers of the United States, and no others.

ARTICLE III.

Sect. I. *The judicial Power of the United States shall be vested in one Supreme Court, and in such inferior Courts as the Congress may from time to time ordain and establish. The Judges, both of the supreme and inferior Courts, shall hold their offices during good behavior, and shall, at stated times, receive for their services, a compensation, which shall not be diminished during their continuance in office.*

Sect. 2. *The judicial power shall extend to all cases, in law and equity, arising under this Constitution, the laws of the United States, and treaties made, or which shall be made, under their authority; to all cases affecting Ambassadors, other public Ministers and Consuls; to all cases of admiralty and maritime jurisdiction; to controversies to which the United States shall be a party; to controversies between two or more States, between a State and citizens of another State, between citizens of different States, between citizens of the same State claiming lands under grants of different States, and between a State or the citizens thereof, and foreign States, citizens or subjects.*

In all cases affecting Ambassadors, other public Ministers and Consuls, and those in which a State shall be a party, the Supreme Court shall have original jurisdiction. In all the other cases before mentioned, the Supreme Court shall have appellate jurisdiction, both as to law and fact, with such exceptions, and under such regulations as the Congress shall make.

The trial of all crimes, except in cases of impeachment, shall be by jury; and such trial shall be held in the State where the said crimes shall have been committed; but when not committed within any State, the trial shall be at such place or places, as the Congress may be law have directed.

NO part of the Constitution seems to have been so little understood, or so purposely misconstrued, as this article. Its enemies have mustered all their forces against the Federal Court; and have loudly sounded the trumpet, for the benevolent purpose of alarming the good people of Virginia, with the fears of *visionary* danger and imaginary oppression. They have told them the Federal Court, like Aron's rod, would swallow up all the judiciary authority of the respective States. That a citizen of Virginia may be forced to Philadelphia for a debt of 5l.

although it was contracted with a fellow citizen: And, above all, that the trial by jury is not preserved. In a word, it is the Federal Court that is to be made the great instrument of tyranny.

THESE indeed would be serious objections were they well founded.

IT is on all hands admitted, that a Federal Court is necessary, for a variety of purposes, and under a variety of circumstances.

THE only question then is, whether the enumeration of the cases assigned to the Federal Court, by this article, is likely to produce oppression? Or if there be any ground to apprehend that Congress will not, by law, provide a remedy for all probable hardships, and render the federal jurisdiction convenient to every part of the United States?

THERE has been no objection raised to the Federal Court having original jurisdiction, in all cases respecting public Ministers, and where a State may be a party: and these are the only cases wherein it has *original jurisdiction*. In these cases, in controversies between two or more States, and between a State and citizens of another State, and between citizens of the same claiming lands under grants of different States, the present Congress have the right of determining.[5] Here the Judiciary is blended in an eminent degree with the Legislative authority; a strong reason, among many others, for new modeling that unskillfully organized body.[6]

THE Convention sensible of this defect, has wisely assigned the cognizance of these and other controversies to a proper tribunal, a Court of Law.

AMONG these controversies, there is but one possible case where a dispute between two citizens of the same State can be carried, even by appeal, to the Federal Court; and that is, when they claim the same land under grants from different States. As their title is derived through States, this case is precisely within the reason which applies to controversies wherein two States are parties.

NOTWITHSTANDING this, we are told that in the most ordinary cases, a citizen of Virginia may be dragged within the appellate jurisdiction of the Federal Court, although the transaction which gave rise to the controversy originated between fellow citizens. This, it is said, may be effected, by assigning a bond, for instance, given by one fellow citizen to another, either to a foreigner or a citizen of another State. To this I answer, that such assignment would not be attended with any such consequence; because it is a principle in law, that the

---

5. 9 Article of the Confederation.
6. Under the present Confederation, every department of government, is lodged in the same body; which alone is a sufficient reason for adopting a new federal system.

assignee stands in the place of the assignor; and is neither in a better nor a worse condition. It is likewise asserted, that if two citizens of the same State claim lands lying in a different State, that their suit may be carried to the Federal Court for final determination. This assertion is equally groundless. For this being a local action, it must be determined in the State wherein the lands lie.

AND I repeat it again, because it cannot be too often repeated, that but one possible case exists, where a controversy between citizens of the same State can be carried into the Federal Court. How then is it possible that the Federal Court can ever swallow up the State jurisdictions, or be converted to the purposes of oppression.

SEVERAL reasons occur why the Federal Court should possess an appellate jurisdiction in controversies between foreigners and citizens, and between the citizens of different States. A foreigner should have the privilege of carrying his suit to the Federal Court, as well for the sake of justice, as from political motives. Were he confined to seek redress in the tribunal of that State, wherein he received the injury, he might not obtain it, from the influence of his adversary; and by giving him this additional and certain means of obtaining justice, foreigners will be encouraged to trade with us, to give us credit, and to employ their capitals in our country. These controversies must for the most part arise from commercial transactions, by which the bulk of the people can be seldom effected. The first part of this reasoning equally applies to controversies between citizens of different States. Besides, were the jurisdiction of the Federal Court not coextensive with the government itself, as far as foreigners are concerned, a controversy between individuals might produce a national quarrel, which commencing in reprisals, would probably terminate in war. Suppose a subject of France or Great Britain should complain to the Minister residing at the seat of Congress, that it was impossible to obtain justice in a Court of Law, in Virginia, for instance. The minister represents the matter to his Court. That Court will apply to the Congress, not to the individual State, for redress. Congress replies, "we lament that it is not in our power to remedy the evil; but we have no authority over the jurisprudence of the State." Is it probable that such an answer will be satisfactory to powerful nations? Will they not say "we must take that redress by force which your feeble government denies us? We are under the necessity of seizing American property wherever we can lay our hands upon it, till the just demands of our subjects are satisfied."

THOSE objectors who are so much alarmed for the trial by jury, seem little acquainted either with the origin or use of that celebrated mode of trial.

I WILL take leave to inform them, that by our laws a variety of important causes are daily determined without the intervention of a jury, not only in the Court of Chancery, but in those of common law; and that by several of our Acts of Assembly, the General Court has a power of assessing fines as high as 500l. for inconsiderable delinquencies, without the intervention of a jury, even to find the fact.

As I have before observed, these causes will be from the nature of things, generally mercantile disputes; must be matters of account, which will be referred to commissioners, as is the practice of all common law Courts in similar cases. Whenever it may be necessary that the facts should be stated, no doubt they will be found by a jury of the State, from whence the cause is carried; and will be made a part of the record.

IN criminal cases, the trial by jury is most important. In criminal cases the Constitution has established it unequivocally. But in having only recognized this trial in criminal, it by no means follows that it takes it away in civil cases: And we may fairly presume, that by the law which the Congress will make to compleat the system of the Federal Court, it will be introduced, as far as it shall be found practicable, and applicable to such controversies as from their nature are subjects proper to be determined in that Court.

ALL civilized societies have found it necessary to punish a variety of offences, with the loss of life. The life of man is a serious forfeiture: Our law has therefore humanely and justly said, that it shall not be affected, but by the unanimous opinion of twelve men. In a political view, this mode of trial, in State prosecutions, is of still greater importance. The Chief Magistrate, or the Legislature itself, of a republic, is as liable to personal prejudice, and to passion, as any King in Europe; and might prosecute a bold writer, or any other person, who had become obnoxious to their resentment, with as much violence and rigour. What so admirable a barrier to defend the innocent, and protect the weak from the attacks of power, as the interposition of a jury? In this respect, the trial by jury may well be called the palladium of liberty.

THE framers of the Constitution viewing it in this light, although it was impossible to enter minutely into the subject of the Federal Court, and arrange it fully, took care to declare that, in criminal cases, the trial by jury should be preserved, lest we should have had some ground of uneasiness upon that important point.

I MUST farther observe, that the Federal Court has no jurisdiction over any offences except such as are against the Union: And the criminal is to be tried in the State where the fact is committed.

IT is asked, why has not the Constitution more accurately defined the jurisdiction of the Federal Court, more clearly ascertained its limits, and more fully
pointed out the modes of trial?

TO this it may be answered, that the out-lines of the piece are traced with
sufficient accuracy: That to have entered minutely into this subject, to have
filled it in all its parts, would have employed almost as much time as framing
the Constitution itself, and would have spun out the work to a tedious length.
In that case the Convention must have ascertained the number of inferior
Courts necessary, the number of Judges, and other officers, with their salaries,
the times of holding the Federal Courts, the duration of their terms; in what
cases the trial shall be by jury, in what not, with an infinite variety of circumstances, the introduction of which in a system of government, would have
made a strange appearance. They therefore properly left to the Congress the
power of organizing by law the Federal Court : Well knowing that at least
eight of the States must, from their local situation, concur in rendering it convenient to the whole.

Sect. 3. *Treason against the United States, shall consist only in levying war against
them, or in adhering to their enemies, giving them aid and comfort. No person shall be
convicted of treason unless on the testimony of two witnesses to the same overt act, or on
confession in open Court.*

*The Congress shall have power to declare the punishment of treason, but no attain-
der of treason shall work corruption of blood, or forfeiture, except during the life of the person attainted,*

THIS section is equally humane and just.

ARTICLE IV.

Sect. 1. *Full faith and credit shall be given in each State to the public acts, records, and
judicial proceedings of every other State. And the Congress may by general laws prescribe
the manner in which such acts, records, and proceeding shall be proved, and the effect thereof.*

Sect. 2. *The citizens of each State shall be entitled to all privileges and immunities
of citizens in the several States.*

*A person charged in any State with treason, felony, or other crime, who shall flee from
justice, and be found in another State, shall, on demand of the executive authority of the
State from which he fled, be delivered up to be removed to the State having jurisdiction of
the crime.*

No person held to service or labour in one State, under the laws thereof, escaping into another, shall, in consequence of any law or regulation therein, be discharged from such service or labour, but shall be delivered up on claim of the party to whom such service or labour may be due.

THE convenience, justice, and utility, of these sections, are obvious.

AT present, slaves absconding and going into some of the northern States, may thereby effect their freedom: But under the Federal Constitution they will be delivered up to the lawful proprietor.

Sect. 3. *New States may be admitted by the Congress into this Union; but no new State shall be formed or erected within the jurisdiction of any other State; nor any State be formed by the junction of two or more States, or parts of States, without the consent of the Legislatures of the States concerned as well as of the Congress.*

The Congress shall have power to dispose of and make all needful rules and regulations respecting the territory or other property belonging to the United States; and nothing in this Constitution shall be so construed as to prejudice any Claims of the United States, or of any particular State.

UPON this section I shall only observe, that illiberal and groundless prejudices against the northern States too generally prevail in this country. Hence the unwarranted jealousy of the politics of those States. But were they well founded, the powers given under this section will manifestly tend to allay our fears of a northern combination. For as the greater portion of those immense tracts of fertile land which remain uninhabited, or but thinly settled, and which are yet to be divided into new governments, lie on the south western boundary; the southern interest will be strengthened by the Representatives of the new States. Would we could forget our provincial prejudices, and consider ourselves as citizens of America![7]

Sect. 4. *The United States shall guarantee to every State in the Union a republican form of government, and shall protect each of them against invasion; and on application of the Legislature, or of the Excutive (when the Legislature cannot be convened) against domestic violence.*

THIS is an additional proof of the caution of the framers of the Constitution, and how distant their views must have been from the design of introducing and establishing an arbitrary government.

---

7. The vulgar in Massachusetts believe, that the practice of gouging in Virginia is so common, that half of its inhabitants have but one eye. This opinion is on a level with a declaration of a gentleman high in office, in this country, who declared himself against the Federal Government, because the eastern people were all rogues.

ARTICLE V.

The Congress, whenever two-thirds of both Houses shall deem it necessary, shall propose amendments to this Constitution, or, on the application of the Legislatures of two-thirds of the several States, shall call a Convention for proposing amendments, which, in either case, shall be valid to all intents and purposes, as part of this Constitution, when ratified by the Legislatures of three fourths of the several States, or by Conventions in three-fourths thereof, as the one or the other mode of ratification may be proposed by the Congress; Provided that no amendment which may be made prior to the year one thousand eight hundred and eight, shall in any manner affect the first and fourth clauses in the ninth section of the first article; and that no State, without its consent, shall be deprived of its equal suffrage in the Senate.

ALL human productions must partake of imperfection. The members of the Convention did not pretend to infallibility: They considered that experience might bring to light inconveniences which human wisdom could not foresee— And this article wisely provides for amendments, the necessity of which time may discover.

THERE is not an article of the Constitution that deserves greater praise than this. The Convention sensible that they could not foresee every contingency, and guard against every possible inconvenience: Sensible that new circumstances might arise, which would render alterations in the government necessary; have declared that whenever two-thirds of both Houses of Congress, or two-thirds of the State Legislatures, shall concur in deeming amendments necessary, a general Convention shall be appointed, the result of which, when ratified by three-fourths of the Legislatures, shall become a part of the Federal Government.

I CONFESS myself at a loss to conceive what better mode could have been adopted. If the system be reduced to practice, and experience shall discover important defects, there can be no doubt but that two-thirds of Congress will be sensible to them, and will point them out to the different Legislatures. On the other hand, it is equally certain, that if the defects be flagrant, they will be readily seen by two-thirds of the Legislatures, and a Convention will necessarily be the consequence: Nor is there any cause to apprehend, that the result of such Convention, will be rejected by one-fourth of the States: Since all the States must feel the inconvenience of important defects.

BUT, say the friends to previous amendments, friends, as many of them pretend even to an energetic Federal Government, why not amend the Constitution before it is adopted? To this it may be answered, that they should first demonstrate their objections to be well founded; and that their proposed amendments, if they can be said to have offered any, would make it better. I am inclined to think, that neither Mr. Gerry's, Mr. Mason's, nor Governor Randolph's, would. Upon this occasion I hope I shall be excused for recommending to those gentlemen, as well as to other objectors, Dr. Franklin's last speech in the Convention, which is replete with good sense, as well as a marked deference for the opinions of others. If the objections of these gentlemen be groundless, the Constitution needs no amendment: if they be not, it cannot be amended in the manner they propose. Mr. Mason, Mr. Randolph, the State of Virginia, raise objections: Mr. Gerry, and the State of Massachusetts, do the same: Every other citizen, every other State, has an equal right. A new Convention is formed, the proposed plan is amended, or a new one produced. It is again presented to the public eye. New blemishes appear; new amendments are thought necessary. That which Mr. Mason may think a perfection, another may think a fault: What would be agreeable to Massachusetts, might displease Virginia. In a word there would be no end to objections, amendments, and Conventions. All federal government falls to the ground. Anarchy ensues, and produces convulsions, which inevitably end in despotism.

ARTICLE VI.

All debts contracted and engagements entered into before the adoption of this Constitution, shall be as valid against the United States under this Constitution, as under the Confederation.

This Constitution, and the laws of the United States which shall be made in pursuance thereof, and all treaties made, or which shall be made, under the authority of the United States, shall be the supreme law of the land; and the Judges in every State shall be bound thereby, any thing in the Constitution or laws of any State, to the contrary notwithstanding.

The Senators and Representatives before mentioned, and the Members of the several State Legislatures, and all executive and judicial officers, both of the United States and of the several States, shall be bound by oath or affirmation, to support this Constitution; but no religious test shall ever be required as a qualification to any office or public trust under the United States.

THAT treaties should be the supreme law of the land is warmly opposed by the enemies of the Constitution. This power, say they, may be converted to the most arbitrary and destructive purposes.

TREATIES ought of right to be considered in the light, that the Convention has here viewed them. For why should they be made, if due obedience is not to be paid them? The negative can only be supported by those who feel it their interest, that they should be disregarded.

THE objects of government are protection and security: Many national circumstances may arise wherein these objects cannot be effected, without the observance of treaties.

WHEN we consider who it is that has the power of making treaties, the manner of his election, the checks that the Constitution has interposed to guard against his possible abuse of power, among which his liability to impeachment is not the least: When we consider the subject matter of treaties are always of national import, and cannot affect the interests of individuals, we have no reason to fear that they will be made improvidently, or converted into instruments of oppression: They may be unwise, but can never be intentionally wicked.

THIS, like every other article of the Constitution, was the subject of long and serious deliberation; and it was ultimately and rightly determined, that as the power of making treaties was necessary, it could no where so properly, or so safely be placed for the interests of the Union as in the hands of the President: And if when made they were not to have the effect of law, the power of making them would be nugatory.

THE following passage from Blackstone's Commentaries, will tend to illustrate this subject. "It is also," says that elegant commentator, "the King's prerogative to make treaties, leagues, and alliances, with foreign States and Princes. For it is by the *law of nations* essential to the goodness of a league, that it be made by the sovereign power, and that it is binding upon the whole community: And in England the sovereign power, quod hoc, is vested in the person of the King. Whatever contracts "therefore he engages in, no other person in the kingdom can legally delay, resist, or annul. And yet lest this plentitude of authority should be abused, to the detriment of the public, the Constitution (as was hinted before) has here interposed a check by means of parliamentary impeachment, for the punishment of such Ministers, as from *criminal* motives advise or conclude any treaty, which shall afterwards be judged to derogate from the honor and interest of the nation." I Bl. p. 257. I might cite all the political writers in support of the general doctrine here laid down. The Convention considered it just. They saw the necessity of entrusting the power to the President; but they also knew that in this, as in every other exercise of power, he is the Minister of the people; and that whenever in making a treaty he shall be governed by corrupt motives, he will be liable to impeachment.

HAVING thus gone through the different articles of the Constitution, I will now endeavour to answer two other objections that have been made to it. The first is, "that the liberty of the press is not secured." The second, "that it will annihilate the independence of the different States."

ON the first objection I shall only observe, that as the Congress can claim the exercise of no right which is not expressly given them by this Constitution; they will have no power to restrain the press in any of the States; and therefore it would have been improper to have taken any notice of it. The article respecting the habeus corpus act corroborates this doctrine. The Convention were sensible that a federal government would no more have the right of suspending that useless law, without the consent of the States, than that of restraining the liberty of the press: But at the same time they knew that circumstances might arise to render necessary the suspension of the habeus corpus act, and therefore they require of the States, that they will vest them with that power, whenever those circumstances shall exist. But they also knew, that no circumstances could make it necessary that the liberty of the press should be entrusted to them, and therefore they judged it impertinent to introduce the subject. But still there are fears for the district which may become the seat of Congress, and which may be ten miles square.

CAN it be for a moment supposed, that Congress will not preserve the liberty of the press in the government of that district? Or that there exist American citizens so lost to a sense of liberty, as to reside under a government where it shall be taken away.[8]

AS to the other objection, I will admit, that by this Constitution, the several States will be abridged of some of their powers: but of no more than are necessary to make a strong federal government. Sufficient still remains with the State Legislatures to preserve the quiet, liberty, and welfare, of their citizens. To them is left the whole domestic government of the States; they may still regulate the rules of property, the rights of persons, everything that relates to their internal police, and whatever effects neither foreign affairs nor the rights of the other States. Powers weighty enough to be entrusted to most men; and which good and modest men would think sufficient to be entrusted to them. Besides we should remember that every State has its proportionate share in the national government; and that the Constitution has not only guaranteed to them a republican form, but has made *their* independence necessary to *its own* existence.

---

8. It is to be observed, that the consent of the State where this district shall lie, must be obtained by the Congress: And the State may stipulate the terms of the cession.

THE adoption of this government will not only preserve our Union, and thereby secure our internal happiness; but will restore that confidence and respectability abroad, which have been lost since the days of Saratoga and York. The firm confederation of thirteen States, inhabiting a fertile soil, and growing rapidly in population and strength, will give them an importance in the world, which they can never acquire when disunited: And we are assured from the best authority, that the link of the present Union is but a thread. An energetic government will give a spring to everything. New life will be infused throughout the American system. Our credit will be restored; because the proposed Constitution at the same time that it will give us vigour, will inspire foreign nations with a confidence in us. The restoration of credit, will be the revival of commerce. The sound of the hammer will be again heard in our ports. The ocean will once more be covered with our ships, and the flag of the United States be respected by the nations.

BUT once disunited, these bright prospects immediately vanish: Our western hemisphere is clouded over; and destructive storms arise. Our inactivity and torpor produced by the relaxation of our laws will become inveterate, unless our internal quarrels shall rouse us into action; the seeds of which have been long sown, and disunion will make the harvest plentiful. Massachusetts and New-Hampshire have more than a pretext of quarrel in their pretensions to the province of Main; and their mutual interference in the fisheries will serve to increase the dispute. Connecticut and New-York may revive their old quarrel respecting boundaries. Pennsylvania will not forget that the territory of Delaware was once united to her; and will probably cast thither a longing eye. Maryland and Virginia may dispute the right to the shores of Potowmack, and the latter may readily revive with Pennsylvania, the old dispute respecting the northern boundaries: A dispute which terminated unfavourably to Virginia, and which from the peculiarity of it, was difficult to settle. When to such causes of dissention, we add the commercial regulations of the individual States, the ambitious views of their leaders, and the ill-grounded, though rooted, prejudices of the whole, have we not abundant reason to fear the most serious calamities from a disunion? Then will open a new scene in America; the sword is then drawn not against foreign foes, but against each other: The sword is then drawn never to be sheathed, till some State more powerful or more fortunate than the rest, shall subjugate the whole.

EXAMINE then, my countrymen, dispassionately the proposed plan of federal government, and you will find that so far from being full of defects, it is a system well calculated to preserve the liberty, and ensure the happiness of

America; and that it reflects additional honor on the names of a Dickenson, a Franklin, and a Washington.[9] You can not for a moment suppose that such men would deceive you! If human nature were capable of falling at once from the height of virtue to the depth of depravity; even then you were safe—for they could construct no government which would oppress you, that would not equally oppress themselves, and their posterity.

NOTE—

I INTENDED to have subjoined some observations upon Mr. Lee's letter to Governor Randolph; but finding that this manner of treating the subject has carried me farther than I expected, and that answers to most of that gentleman's objections have arisen naturally out of the different articles of the Constitution, I have declined it, for fear lest the length of the performance might become fatiguing. For however important such a subject may be to mankind; few have the art of treating political disquisitions in such a manner as to interest the majority of readers. I will however, in this place, observe, that Mr. Lee, to whose mellifluous tongue, I have often listened with pleasure, and who may be said to have grown old in politics, must have written that letter in the heat of his zeal, before he had well considered the proposed system of federal government; or he never could have talked of the rags and threads of representation, or laid himself so open to attack in every quarter. Mr. Lee, like most other enemies of the Constitution, objects without pointing out the alterations that would improve it; asserts rather than argues: An infallible mark of a bad cause. Mr. Gerry's and Mr. Mason's objections take up but a small compass: But neither of these gentlemen has deigned to give us anything like argument in support of his objections. Mr. Randolph has said much to point out the necessity of an energetic federal government; but nothing to prove that his proposed amendments are founded in reason. And Mr. Lee would have the government wholly new modelled to please himself. I suspect some of these gentlemen have upon this occasion too much resembled Dr. Franklin's French lady. I would ask Mr. Lee what advantage would result from a numerous representation in a federal Congress? If the numbers in America are not greatly exaggerated, one member for every 30,000 will make the House of Representatives to consist of an 100; which number will be increased every

---

9. I might have mentioned the names of a Madison, a Blair, a Hamilton, a Johnson, a King, a Rutledge. I acknowledge the abilities of Mr. Mason and Governor Randolph; but let it not be forgotten, that at the close of the Convention, there were but three dissenting voices.

ten years. Has not Mr.Lee's experience in public affairs taught him that even that is a number too large to transact business with facility? But let the number of that House be relatively great or small, it can in no sense be a rag or part of a representation. That House stands, as to federal purposes, in the place of the citizens of the thirteen States, and possesses all the powers conceded to it by the citizens of those States, consequently ten persons would be as much a representation as an hundred. Had Mr. Lee considered this government as intended for thirteen different States; had he considered that the powers vested in the Congress are merely national, that is such as respect America in its relative situation with foreign nations, or such as respect the relative situation of the States in their individual capacities; and that the States still retain the most important part of their rights, in as much as the right of Legislation in domestic cases, is of much greater consequence than in foreign, I think he never would have made the observation.

I CONFESS that for some time I viewed some parts of the Constitution in the light Mr. Lee and some others have done. I at first conceived that the Senators were liable to impeachment; and that some mischief might arise from treaties of peace being made the law of the land. But after mature deliberation, I was convinced that I was mistaken in the former, and that the Constitution is right in the latter.

THE foregoing little piece was intended to counteract the misrepresentations of the proposed Federal Government, which the antifederalists have most industriously disseminated in the southern counties. The writer had no idea of publishing anything upon the subject of the Constitution, till a visit he made to one of those counties, where at the desire of his friend, he was induced to write in haste the pamphlet now offered to the public. It was to have been published time enough to be dispersed before the elections, but the Printer found it impossible to deliver it in time. The primary intention being thus defeated, it would not have been published at all, had it not been put into the press at the time stipulated. The writer had neither Mr. Mason's, Mr. Gerry's, nor Mr. Lee's objections by him: This it is hoped will be a sufficient apology for its inaccuracies, as far as their objections have been taken notice of. He takes this opportunity of observing, that perhaps he, and not Governor Randolph, is mistaken as to the *impeachability* of the Senate: He acknowledges that he has never conversed with any member of the late Convention upon the subject, though he still thinks that the arguments he has used are sufficiently strong to prove that the Senators neither are nor ought to be impeachable. He does not pretend to have gone fully into the objections which have been raised to the government: His design was to obviate only the most popular, and in a manner as popular as he was able.

PART III

Ambassador to a Revolution

INTRODUCTION

HAVING BEEN CHOSEN as an U.S. Senator to the new Congress organized under the Constitution, Monroe was ardently devoted to Republican principles, that is, the principles of limited, Jeffersonian government. He accused his opponents, the Federalists, of being secret monarchists who wanted to make an alliance with George III to the exclusion of America's ally, France, which had helped the fledgling republic gain its independence. Moreover, the ideals of the French Revolution had a strong attraction to the American Republicans. The Citizen Genet affair, in which the actions of France's Minister to the United States divided Americans on attitudes towards the French Revolution, ended by solidifying the political operations of the Republicans and Federalists.

However, both Great Britain and France were behaving badly towards the United States; the two countries were at war with each other, and both accused the United States of helping their enemy. Britain acted towards U.S. shipping as though the Treaty of Paris of 1783 had never been ratified, and France had abrogated Articles 22 and 23 of the Treaty of Commerce of 1778 relating to trade, and demanded the recall of the U.S. Minister to France, Gouverneur Morris, a Federalist who was decidedly opposed to the principles of the Revolution.

George Washington had tried to steer neutral course between the two factions. He had on one side his Secretary of State, Thomas Jefferson, who was a proponent of the French; on the other side was the Secretary of the Treasury, Alexander Hamilton. But Jefferson resigned at the end of 1793, and Edmund Randolph was named in his place. Rumors flew around Congress, a situation not unlike that which often obtains today, suggesting that Washington would abandon neutrality and engage on the side of Great Britain. On March 31, 1794, Monroe wrote to Jefferson of his fears that Hamilton would be appointed as a special ambassador to Great Britain. The Republicans introduced legislation calling for an embargo on Britain. On April 8, Monroe wrote to Washington that the appointment of Hamilton would bring ruin to the United States—the first time that a senator opposed a presidential appointment before it was sent to the Senate for approval. Washington adroitly maneuvered around the Republicans, sending up the name of John Jay—Monroe's nemesis from the failed Spanish treaty—and thereby undercutting the embargo legislation.

There remained the question of who would represent the United States in France. Monroe's correspondence with Jefferson and Madison report the rumors on a day-by-day basis. No Federalist can be found to take the job; Washington has to turn to the Republicans. Monroe is supporting Aaron Burr, but in a sudden stroke, Washington sends Randolph to Monroe to ask him to take the job.

The Ministry to France was a turning point in Monroe's career, one that almost destroyed him, but paradoxically prepared him for the rest of his public service. It is important to read the written instructions which Randolph gave Monroe upon setting out, for it was upon these pro-French directives that he relied in dealing with the republican government of France. In France he met a hostile reaction. The Committee on Public Safety, which was in charge of foreign policy, wouldn't receive him. Instead he appealed directly to the President of the National Convention. His unprecedented address to the National Convention, putting before it the resolutions of the U.S. Senate and House of Representatives, revived pro-American sentiments. Within a few months he was able to remove all of the U.S. grievances against the French Republic. Trade barriers were repealed, U.S. ships were free to come to French ports, and France agreed to hear claims for seized ships and cargo.

But Monroe arrived in France at a time of turmoil: On the 6th of Thermidor, that is, the 27th of July, Robespierre was condemned and executed the next morning; Monroe arrived on August 2nd. His first official dispatch on August 15, 1794 is a vivid account of the events leading up to Robespierre's condemnation and execution. On October 15, he sends a detailed analysis of the history of the Jacobin movement, which his Federalist opponents back home think is so good they leak it to press. A year later, on October 20, 1795 he prepares a striking eyewitness account of the invasion of the Convention by armed mobs. These dispatches secure Monroe a modest reputation as an historiographer.

By any measure, Monroe's mission to France should have been accounted a great diplomatic success. Unfortunately, it was too successful for the factions in the United States that had expected him to fail. The Federalists wanted bad relations with France, not good relations. Jay's mission to Great Britain was calculated to bring that about. Monroe had been instructed by Randolph to tell the French that Jay's mission was simply to bring about conciliation with France, the withdrawal of British troops from the frontier forts in the United States, and payment of claims for past damages. In reality, Jay's real mission was to sign a treaty of commerce with Great Britain, which might be to the detriment of France. Much of Monroe's energy in Paris was spent following his instructions by reassuring the French that Jay's mandate was limited to the items of conciliation. Monroe's correspondence with Jay is instructive because it shows the extent to which Jay went to conceal his real activities in London. So when the treaty was completed, Monroe—and the French—read about it in the newspapers. From the French point of view, Jay's treaty was a betrayal of friendship: It contained a clause which defined the shipment of food to an enemy of Great Britain on neutral ships as contraband. Under the law of nations, only articles of war carried on neutral ships could be considered contraband. Randolph resigned as Secretary of State the day after the British treaty was ratified, and he was succeeded by a rabid Federalist, Timothy Pickering.

Monroe's mission to France was over. The French recalled their representative in Philadelphia. Pickering recalled Monroe and accused him of being too energetic in Paris, promising too much, and not preparing the French to accept the Jay treaty. Monroe defended his conduct to Pickering on September 10, 1796. Upon his return to Philadelphia, he further demanded a public explanation of his recall, which Pickering refused. Under widespread political attack, Monroe wrote a comprehensive defense of his mission in his book, *A View of the Conduct of the Executive, in the Foreign Affairs of the United States, Connected with the Mission to the French Republic during the Years 1774,5 & 6.* It was the first such critique of U.S. foreign policy ever to be written, and is of considerable historical significance.

Although the whole document is of considerable interest, the reader should focus attention on the concluding pages. Monroe sums up his critique with a specific list of fourteen errors committed by the administration, beginning with the appointment of Gouverneur Morris; Morris' mismanagement of the trade conflicts and the U.S. government's approval of his conduct; his own appointment in the face of his objections to the policy of Hamilton and Jay; the instructions and the Congressional resolutions he was given, implying a strong bond with the French people—and the administration's resentment that Monroe had publicized the public documents in France; the fact that the administration had praised him for ameliorating the trade issues with France; the fact that a commission was given to Jay to negotiate a trade treaty, in the midst of war, with Great Britain, while no such power was given to Monroe to negotiate with

Britain's enemy, France—which Monroe considered in itself a violation of neutrality; the withholding from Monroe of the contents of Jay's treaty, despite the embarrassment it would cause; the character of the Jay treaty itself, which "departed from the modern rule of contraband . . . and sanctioned the doctrine and practice of England . . . and yielded the principle, so important to America, that free ships shall make free goods."

As for his recall, Monroe said, it would have been "a circumstance too trivial to merit attention," were it not for the perilous state of affairs with regard to relations with France:

> Our navigation destroyed, commerce laid waste and a general bankruptcy threatening those engaged in it; the friendship of a nation lost, the most powerful on earth, who had deserved better things from us, and had offered to place us, out vessels, and commodities on the footing of its native citizens in all its dominions; war hanging over us, and that not on the side of liberty and the just affections of our people, but of the monarch and our late most deadly foe; and we are made fast, by treaty and by the spirit of those at the helm, to a nation bankrupt in its resources, and rapidly verging either to anarchy of despotism. Nor is this all. Our national honor is in the dust; we have been kicked, cuffed, and plundered all over the ocean; our reputation for faith scouted; our government and people branded as cowards, incapable of being provoked to resist, and ready to receive again those chains we had taught others to burst. Long will it be before we shall be able to forget what we are, nor will centuries suffice to raise us to the high ground from which we have fallen.

Yet despite the fact that the *View* was cogently drawn, thoroughly documented, and, if passionate in its argument, temperate in its language, the effort had little impact whatsoever. The very comprehensiveness of the documentation, including the diplomatic correspondence, made the book a fat one, long drawn-out in its journey through the press, and too expensive in its outcome for all but the most intrepid connoisseurs of controversy. Every success that it documented merely confirmed the francophobes in their opinions that Monroe was too much a francophile, and every betrayal by the Federalist administration as detailed by Monroe seemed, in their eyes, to make the American Minister look naïve and a simpleton. Naturally his friends, to whom he sent free copies of the book, took pains to assure him that just the opposite was the case.

Monroe himself never saw the criticism of the person to whom it was most particularly directed, namely, Washington himself. Long after both men were dead, the editors of Washington's papers took pains to reproduce the extensive notes which the first president had scribbled in the margins of his copy of the *View*, commenting on every paragraph that gave him offense. Against Monroe's claim of success, Washington wrote in the margin: "For this there is no better proof, than his own opinion; whilst there is abundant evidence of his being a mere tool in the hands of the French government, cajoled and led away always by unmeaning assurances. . . ." And where Monroe had written that standing well with France was in the true interest of the nation, Washington acidly objected: "But to stand well with Fr[ance] was, in other words to quit neutral gr[oun]d; and disregard every other consideration relying wholly on that nation; and this is what Monroe was aiming at."

INSTRUCTIONS FROM THE SECRETARY OF STATE TO
JAMES MONROE.

PHILADELPHIA, June 10th, 1794.

SIR,—You have been nominated as the successor of M^r. Gouverneur Morris, in the office of Minister Plenipotentiary of the United States of America to the Republic of France, from a confidence, that, while you keep steadily in view the necessity of rendering yourself acceptable to that government, you will maintain the self-respect due to our own. In doing the one and the other of these things, your own prudence and understanding must be the guides; after first possessing yourself of the real sentiments of the Executive, relative to the French nation.

The President has been an early and decided friend of the French Revolution; and whatever reason there may have been, under our ignorance of facts and policy, to suspend an opinion upon some of its important transactions; yet he is immutable in his wishes for its accomplishment; incapable of assenting to the right of any foreign prince to meddle with its interior arrangements; persuaded that success will attend their efforts; and particularly, that union among themselves is an impregnable barrier against external assaults.

How the French government, when it shall be no longer attacked by foreign arms, will ultimately settle, is a point, not yet reduced to any absolutely certain expectation. The gradation of publick opinion from the beginning of the new order of things to this day; and the fluctuation and mutual destruction of parties, forbid a minister of a foreign country to attach himself to any as such, and dictate to him not to incline to any set of men, further than they appear to go with the sense of the nation.

2. When the executive provisory council recalled Mr. Genet, they expressed a determination to render it a matter of eclat, as you have seen; and at the same time disavowed all his offensive acts. Nothing having been forwarded to us, relative to Mr. Morris, which requires a disavowal, you will, if you should be interrogated as to any particular feeling prevailing with the President upon the occasion, refer to the letter from the Secretary of State to Mr. Fauchet, as explanatory of the President's promptness to comply with their demand.

3. From Mr. Genet and Fauchet we have uniformly learned, that France did not desire us to depart from neutrality; and it would have been unwise to have asked us to do otherwise. For our ports are open to her prizes, while they are shut to those of Great Britain; and supplies of grain could not be forwarded to France with so much certainty, were we at war, as they can even now, notwithstanding the British instructions; and as they may be, if the demands to be made upon Great Britain should succeed. We have, therefore, pursued neutrality with faith-

fulness; we have paid more of our debt to France than was absolutely due; as the Secretary of the Treasury asserts; and we should have paid more, if the state of our affairs did not require us to be prepared with funds for the possible event of war. We mean to continue the same line of conduct in future; and to remove all jealousy with respect to Mr. Jay's mission to London, you may say, that he is positively forbidden to weaken the engagements between this country and France. *It is not improbable, that you will be obliged to encounter, on this head, suspicions of various kinds. But you may declare the motives of that mission to be, to obtain immediate compensation for our plundered property, and restitution of the posts.* You may intimate by way of argument, but without ascribing it to the government, *that, if war should be necessary, the affections of the people of the United States towards it, would be better secured by a manifestation, that every step had been taken to avoid it, and that the British nation would be divided, when they found that we had been forced into it.* This may be briefly touched upon as the path of prudence with respect to ourselves; and also with respect to France, since we are unable to give her aids of men or money. To this matter you cannot be too attentive, and you will be amply justified in repelling with firmness any imputation of the most distant intention to sacrifice our connection with France to any connection with England. You may back your assertions by a late determination of the President to have it signified abroad that he is averse to admit into his public room, which is free to all the world besides, any Frenchmen, who are obnoxious to the French Republic; although, perhaps, it may again happen sometimes, as many go thither, whose names and characters are utterly unknown.

It is very probable that our country will become the asylum for most of the French who expatriate themselves from their native land. Our laws have never yet made a distinction of persons, nor is such a distinction very easy. Hence some of those who are perhaps attainted in France, have thrown themselves upon the protection of the United States. This will not, as it surely ought not to be misinterpreted into any *estrangement from the French cause.* You will *explain this, whensoever it shall be necessary.*

The stories of Genet as to the Royal Medallions &c: being exhibited in the President's Room, and his giving private audiences to certain French Emigrés, are notoriously untrue. And if any insinuation should be made in regard to M. de la Fayette, so directly, as indispensably to call for an answer; it may be affirmed, that notwithstanding the warmest friendship, contracted between the President and him, in the most interesting scenes; notwithstanding the obligation of the United States to him, and the old prepossessions in his favor, the efforts of the President in his behalf have never gone further than to express a wish to the authority which held him in confinement, that he should be liberated. But even thus much need not be said without the most invincible necessity, because though what has been done is justified by every consideration, it is never well to give notice of it to those whose extreme sensibility may see impropriety where none exists.

4. If we may judge from what has been at different times uttered by Mr. Fauchet, he will represent the existence of two parties here irreconcileable to each other. One republican, and friendly to the French revolution; the other monarchical, aristocratic, Britannic, and anti-Gallican; that a majority of the House of Representatives, the people, and the President, are in the first class; and a majority of the Senate in the second. If this intelligence should be used, in order to inspire a distrust of our good will to France, you will industriously obviate such an effect:—and if a fair occasion should present itself, you may hint, that the most effectual means of obtaining from the United States what is desired by France, will be by a plain and candid application to the government, and not by those insidious operations on the people, which Genet endeavored to carry on.

5. The information which we possess of France, before and in the early stages of the revolution, must be considerably changed at this day. You will, therefore, transmit to us, as soon as possible, an account of the navy, the agriculture, and the commerce of France. It is desirable too to know, upon what footing religion really stands. These however are general objects. But we are particularly concerned to understand the true state of the different sects of politics. Are there any of the old friends to the ancient regime remaining? Are any new friends created by the course of things? Are the Brissotines extinguished? Are the Dantonists overwhelmed? Is Robespierre's party firmly fixed? Is he capable from talents and personal fortitude to direct the storm? Is his character free from imputation, as to money? Is he friendly to the United States? How is the executive power administered now? What new accession of authority may have lately accrued to the committee of public safety? What relation do the twelve commissions of administration, which have been lately established, bear to that committee? What is the true cause of the various changes, which have lately taken place, by one party rising upon the ruins of another? What assurance can be had, that any party can so long maintain itself, as to promise stability to the government? Are the people sincerely affectionate to the present government; or are they restrained by the terror of the revolutionary tribunal, or by the danger of having their country dismembered by the coalesced princes? What species of executive will probably be at last adopted? What characters bid fair to take the

helm of affairs, after the great destruction and banishment of able men? These and many other questions of the same nature ought to be solved, to enable us to see things in a true light. For without doubting the solidity of the French cause, we ought not to be unprepared for any event. If, therefore, any very momentous turn should arise in French affairs, upon which the conduct of our government may depend, you need not hesitate at the expence of an advice-boat, if no other satisfactory opportunity should occur. But it is the wish of the President, that at the end of every week, you commit to a letter the transactions of it, and embrace every proper conveyance, by duplicates, and, in great cases, even by triplicates.

6. Should you be interrogated about the treaty of commerce, you may reply that it has never been proposed to us by Mr. Fauchet. As to anything else concerning it, you will express yourself not to be instructed; it being a subject to be negociated with the government here.

7. In like manner, if a treaty of alliance, or if the execution of the guaran-tee of the French islands, by force of arms, should be propounded, you will refer the Republic of France to this side of the water. In short, it is expected, with a sure reliance on your discretion, that you will not commit the United States, by any specific declarations, except where you are particularly instructed, and except too in giving testimony of our attachment to their cause.

8. There is reason to believe, that the embargo, when it was first laid, excited some uneasy sensations in the breast of the French minister. For it so hap-pened, that at the moment before its operation, pretty considerable shipments of flour were made to the British West-Indies, and a snow, called La Camille, laden with flour, for France, was arrested near New-Castle, on the Delaware, after she had quitted the port of Philadelphia. But you know enough of the history of this business, to declare, that the embargo was levelled against Great Britain, and was made general, merely because, if it had been partial against her, it would have amounted to a cause of war; and also, that it was not continued, merely because it was reputed to be injurious to France. My letters to Mr. Fauchet will explain the case of La Camille; and all his complaints about the embargo.

Should our embargo be brought up, the way will be easy for our complaint against the embargo of Bourdeaux. At any rate, you will remonstrate against it, and urge satisfaction for the sufferers. You will receive all the papers, which have come into the department of state, relative to these matters; and you will besides open a correspondence with the captains and persons interested at Bourdeaux, in order to obtain more accurate information.

But you will go farther and insist upon compensation for the captures and spoliations of our property, and injuries to the persons of our citizens, by French cruisers. Mr. Fauchet has been applied to; and promises to co-operate for the obtaining of satisfaction.

The dilatoriness with which business is transacted in France will, if not curtailed in the adjustment of these cases, produce infinite mischief to our merchants. This must be firmly represented to the French Republic, and you may find a season for intimating, how unfortunate it would be, if so respectable a body, as that of our merchants should relax in their zeal for the French cause, from irritation at their losses. The papers on this head are a statement of French cases, Mr. Fauchet's letters to me, and the documents themselves.

9. You know the extreme distress in which the inhabitants of St. Domingo came hither after the disasters of the Cape. Private charity, and especially at Baltimore, most liberally contributed to their support. The Congress at length advanced 15,000 dollars with a view of reimbursement from France. This subject has been broken to Mr. Fauchet here, and he appears to have been roused at the idea of supporting by French money French aristocrats and democrats indiscriminately. Both he and his nation ought to be satisfied, that in the cause of humanity, oppressed by poverty, political opinions have nothing to do. Add to this, that none but the really indigent receive a farthing. It was the duty of the French Republic to relieve their colonists labouring under a penury so produced; and as it would have been too late to wait for their approbation before the payments were decreed, it will not be deemed an offensive disposal of French money that we now make a claim for repayment. If Mr. Fauchet has power upon the subject, an attempt will be made for a settlement with him here; but that being very doubtful, it will forward the retribution by discussing it in Europe.

10. You will be also charged with the demands of several American citizens for bills of exchange drawn in the French West-Indies on France. The report of a committee of them, Mr. Fauchet's letter, and the vouchers, which you will carry, leave no doubt of your success. But if there should be any difficulty, do not fail to communicate it to the Secretary of State instantaneously. The sooner, therefore, the affair is entered upon the better.

11. It is important, that no public character of the United States should be in France, which is not acceptable. You will inquire into the consuls; and inform, how they are approved, and whether they be deserving. *Although the President will avoid, as much as possible, to appoint any obnoxious person Consul, it may happen otherwise, and must be considered as accidental.* Mr. Alexander Duvernat goes for Paris in the quality of Vice-Consul, and Mr. Fauchet said that he had nothing to object to him.

Consulates are established in every port of France, where they are conceived useful. But perhaps you may find it advisable to mark out some other places for such offices.

12. It is recommended, that no business of consequence, be carried on verbally or in writing, but in your own language.

The minister of each nation has a right to use his national tongue, and few men can confide in their exactness when they do business in a foreign one. But great care is necessary in the choice of interpreters, when they are to be resorted to.

13. It is a practice of great utility to note down every conversation of consequence, which you hold, immediately after retirement; and the Executive will expect to receive copies of what shall be thus written.

14. A communication with our other ministers in Europe, under proper caution, may be advantageous.

15. Let nothing depend upon verbal communication which can be carried on in writing.

16. To conclude.—You go, Sir, to France, to strengthen our friendship with that country; and you are well acquainted with the line of freedom and ease, to which you may advance, without betraying the dignity of the United States. You will show our confidence in the French Republic, without betraying the most remote mark of undue complaisance. *You will let it be seen, that in case of war, with any nation on earth, we shall consider France as our first and natural ally.* You may dwell *upon the sense which we entertain of past services,* and for the more recent interposition in our behalf with the Dey of Algiers. Among the great events with which the world is now teeming, there may be an opening for *France to become instrumental in securing to us the free navigation of the Mississippi.* Spain may, perhaps, *negociate a peace, separate from Great Britain, with France.* If she does, *the Mississippi may be acquired through this channel,* especially if you contrive to have our mediation in any manner solicited.

With every wish for your welfare and an honourable issue to your ministry, I am, Sir, Yo. mo. ob. serv.

EDM: RANDOLPH.

TO THOMAS JEFFERSON.
BALTIMORE, June 17, 1794.

DEAR SIR,—The urgent pressure of the Executive for my immediate departure has deprived me of the pleasure of seeing you before I sailed. I sincerely regret this for many reasons but we can not control impossibilities—will you forward me a cypher, & letters for yr. friends remaining in Paris to the care of Mr. R. as soon as possible, they may probably reach Paris as soon as I shall—I beg you to add whatever occurs which may be useful where I am going to the cause in which I am engaged, or to myself in advocating it. Being well acquainted with the theatre on which I am to act, it will be much in yr. power to give me hints of that kind which may be serviceable. . . .

Yr. affectionate friend & servt.

JA^s. MONROE.

POWER OF ATTORNEY TO JAMES MADISON.

BALTIMORE, June 17, 1794.

Mr. Madison will be pleased to receive from Gen'l Wilkinson, or draw on him for the sum of three hundred doll'rs or thereabouts (due me by him) according as the Gen'l shall direct—He will likewise receive whatever is obtained from Gen'l Bradley from the sale of our Vermont property, or otherwise from the sale or upon acc't of it—He will likewise be pleased, in case he is applied to, to give advice as to the course to be taken for obtaining justice ag'nst J. Kortright and others under the will [of] L. Kortright (father of Mrs. M.) of New York—and whatever he does in the above will be satisfactory & binding on me.

JA^s. MONROE.

TO THE PRESIDENT OF THE NATIONAL CONVENTION.

[MERLIN DE DOUAI.]

PARIS, August 13, 1794.

CITIZEN PRESIDENT,—Having arrived here a few days past, commissioned by the President of the United States to represent those States in character of Minister Plenipotentiary with the French Republic, and not being acquainted with the competent department or forms of recognition prescribed by law, I have thought it expedient to make known my mission immediately to the Representatives of the people. They possess the power to affix the time and prescribe the mode by which I shall be recognized as the representative of their ally and sister Republic; and they will likewise have the goodness in case such department now exists, to cause the same to be designated to me that I may immediately present myself before it to be recognized in the character I bear. I make this communication with the greater pleasure, because it affords me an opportunity of testifying to the Representatives of the Free Citizens of France, not only my own attachment to the cause of liberty, but of assuring them at the same time and in the most decided manner of the deep concern which the Government & people of America take in the liberty, prosperity, and happiness of the French nation.

With sentiments of the highest respect

Jaˢ. Monroe.

ADDRESS TO THE NATIONAL CONVENTION.

Citizens, President and Representatives of the French People:—My admission into this Assembly, in the presence of the French Nation (for all the citizens of France are represented here) to be recognized as the Representative of the American Republic, impresses me with a degree of sensibility which I cannot express. I consider it as a new proof of that friendship and regard which the French Nation has always shewn to their ally, the United States of America.

Republics should approach near to each other. In many respects they all have the same interest. But this is more especially the case with the American and French Republics:—their governments are similar; they both cherish the same principles and rest on the same basis, the equal and unalienable rights of men. The recollection too of common dangers and difficulties will increase their harmony, and cement their union. America had her day of oppression, difficulty and war, but her sons were virtuous and brave and the storm which long clouded her political horizon has passed and left them in the enjoyment of peace, liberty and independence. France our ally and our friend and who aided in the contest, has now embarked in the same noble career; and I am happy to add that whilst the fortitude, magnanimity and heroic valor of her troops, command the admiration and applause of the astonished world, the wisdom and firmness of her councils unite equally in securing the happiest result.

America is not an unfeeling spectator of your affairs in the present crisis. I lay before you in the declarations of every department of our Government, declarations which are founded in the affection of the citizens at large, the most decided proof of her sincere attachment to the liberty, prosperity and happiness of the French Republic. Each branch of Congress, according to the course of proceedings there, has requested the president to make this known to you in its behalf; and in fulfilling the desires of those branches I am instructed to declare to you that he has expressed his own.

In discharging the duties of the office which I am now called on to execute, I promise myself the highest satisfaction; because I well know that whilst I pursue the dictates of my own heart in wishing the liberty and happiness of the

French nation, and which I most sincerely do, I speak the sentiments of my own Country; and that by doing everything in my power to preserve and perpetuate the harmony so happily subsisting at present between the two Republics, I shall promote the interest of both. To this great object therefore all my efforts will be directed. If I shall be so fortunate as to succeed in such manner as to merit the approbation of both Republics I shall deem it the happiest event of my life, and return hereafter with a consolation, which those who mean well and have served the cause of liberty alone can feel.

Along with his address Monroe delivered the official reply of the Senate and of the House of Representatives to the French Committee of Public Safety, made through the Secretary of State. In making this response Randolph wrote: "In executing this duty, which has been allotted by the President to the Department of State, the liberal succours which the United States received from the French nation, in its struggle for independence, present themselves warm to the recollection. On this basis was the friendship between the two nations founded; on this basis and the continued interchanges of regard since, has it grown; and, supported by these motives, it will remain firm and constant.

The Senate, therefore, tender to the Committee of Public Safety, their zealous wishes for the French Republic; they learn with sensibility every success which promotes the happiness of the French nation; and the full establishment of their peace and liberty will be ever esteemed by the Senate as a happiness to the United States and to humanity. And for the House of Representatives as follows: That the letter of the Committee of Public Safety of the French Republic, addressed to Congress, be transmitted to the President of the United, and that he be requested to cause the same to be answered on behalf of this House, in terms expressive of their sensibility for the friendly and affectionate manner, in which they have addressed the Congress of the United States; with an unequivocal assurance, that the Representatives of the people of the United States, have much interest in the happiness and prosperity of the French Republic.

The President of the United States has consigned this honourable and grateful function to the Department of State. In no manner can it be more properly discharged, than by seizing the occasion of declaring to the ally of the United States that the cause of liberty, in defence of which so much American blood and treasures have been lavished, is cherished by our Republic with increasing enthusiasm. That under the standard of liberty, wheresoever it shall be displayed, the affection of the United States will always rally: And that the successes of those who stand forth as her avengers will be gloried in by the United States, and will be felt as the successes of themselves and the other friends of humanity.

Yes, Representatives of our ally, your communication has been addressed to those who share in your fortunes, and who take a deep interest in the happiness and prosperity of the French Republic." [HAMILTON.]

TO THE SECRETARY OF STATE.
[EDMUND RANDOLPH.]
PARIS, August 15th, 1794.

SIR,—On the 31th ultimo I arrived at Havre, and on the second instant at this place. Mr. Morris was, upon my arrival, from town, but he came in as soon as advised of it. By him I was presented to the commissary of foreign affairs, who assured me that, as soon as the form of my reception should be settled, he would apprize me of it, but that this would unavoidably create a delay of some days, as well from the present derangement of their affairs on account of the late commotion of Robespierre, as from the necessity of making some general regulation in that respect, it being the first instance in which a minister had been addressed to the Republic. I assured him I should wait with pleasure the convenience of those whom it concerned, since which I have not seen him, but hear that the subject is under consideration of the committee of public safety, and will probably be concluded in a day or two.

I heard at Havre of the crimes and execution of Robespierre, St. Just, Couthon and others of that party, and should have written you on the subject from that port, but that I knew I could only give the current report, varying, perhaps, in every sea-port town, and which might reach you before my letter. I hastened, therefore, to Paris, in the hope of acquiring there immediately more correct information of facts, as well as of the causes which gave birth to them; but even yet, I suspect, I am on the surface only, for it will take some time to become well acquainted with the true state of things on a theatre so extensive and important.

That Robespierre and his associates merited their fate, is a position to which everyone assents. It was proclaimed by the countenances and voices of all whom I met and conversed with from Havre to Paris. In the latter place, where the oppression was heaviest, the people seem to be relieved from a burden which had become insupportable. It is generally agreed that, from the period of Danton's fall, Robespierre had amassed in his own hands all the powers of the government, and controuled every department in all its operations. It was his spirit which ruled the committee of public safety, the Convention, and the revolutionary tribunal. The Convention was soon found, after the abrogation of the constitution to be too unwieldy, and slow in its deliberations, to direct the great and complicated mass of executive business; this had given birth to two committees, the one of *salut publique,* the other of *sureté generale,* into whose hands the whole was deposited. To the former was assigned the management of foreign affairs, the direction of the armies, &c. to the latter, the interior administration, and they were respectively enjoined to render an account monthly of their transactions to the Convention. It was intended that those committees should be independent of each other, and both under the immediate controul of the Convention; but by the distribution of their powers, this design was defeated, for such an ascendancy was thereby given to the committee of public safety, that the other became its instrument, acting only under its authority. The principal members of the Convention were placed in these committees, and Robespierre, who was by far the most influential one, was assigned to the committee of public safety. It soon happened in the course of the administration, from the very extensive patronage, comparative weight of character, and immense power that this committee gained likewise an entire ascendancy in the Convention, and controuled all its measures. Nor was the organization of the revolutionary tribunal more favourable to the independence of that branch, and of course to public and personal liberty. It was equally dependant on, and the creature of, this committee. Robespierre therefore had become omnipotent. It was his spirit which dictated every movement, and particularly the unceasing operation of the guillotine. Nor did a more bloody and merciless tyrant ever wield the rod of power. His acts of cruelty and oppression are perhaps without parallel in the annals of history. It is generally conceded, that for some months before his fall the list of prisoners was shewn him every evening, by the President of the revolutionary tribunal, and that he marked those who were to be the victims of the succeeding day, and which was invariably executed. Many whole families, those under the age of sixteen excepted, were cut off upon the imputation of conspiracies, &c. but for the sole reason that some members had been more friendly to Brissot, Danton, &c. or had expressed a jealousy of his powers. His oppression had, in fact, gained to such an height, that a convulsion became unavoidable. The circumstances which immediately preceded and brought on the crisis are differently recounted. Some make him the active party and believed that he had arranged with the commune and the guards of the city, the plan of a general massacre of his enemies in the Convention. But I am of opinion, that these projects, for they were certainly contemplated, proceeded from despair, and were adopted at the moment only, as the means of defence. The time and manner of the explosion which was in the Convention support this idea. It had been intimated some days before by him or St. Just, that other conspiracies threatened the safety of the Republic and which ought to be laid open. The communication was given in such a manner as to satisfy the audience, that he meant Tallien and some other members of the house. And, in the moment of the explosion, St. Just had commenced a development of this pretended conspiracy, leading to a denunciation of these members. If the power of Robespierre remained, it was well known, that death and denunciation were hand in hand. To repel it by a counter one was the only remaining hope. It could, in no event, produce a worse effect. Tallien therefore rose and interrupted St. Just, demanding: "How long shall we be abused with denunciations of pretended conspiracies. 'Tis time to draw the veil from perfidy so flagrant." St. Just was silenced and driven from the tribune. Robespierre ascended and made many efforts to speak in vain. The whole Convention rose and cried out with one voice, "Down with the tyrant." He stood like one amazed and stupefied, staring at the Convention with a countenance equally bespeaking indignation and terror; deprived of the power of utterance, but yet afraid to descend. As soon as the convention saw its strength, he was arrested and sent a prisoner to the committee of public safety; but by this time, his immediate coadjutors had taken the alarm, and were endeavoring to excite commotions in the city in his behalf. Henriot, the commander of the guard, with a few followers, pursued and rescued him from the committee. He then took his station with the commune, heretofore the theatre of his power, and began to harangue the people, and with some effect; whilst Henriot, in the character of *general,* was busied in assembling the guards in the place before the Hall of the Convention, with intention to fire on it. There was at this moment an awful pause in the affairs of the Republic. Everything was suspended, and the public mind greatly alarmed and agitated. The situation of the Convention was truly interesting. They knew that all the appointments were conferred by Robespierre, that he had been long deemed a patriot, and still possessed, by means of affection or terror, a wonderful influence over the citizens at large; and more immediately in their presence, they saw Henriot at the head of a respectable force menacing an attack. But that body was not unmindful of its dignity or its duty upon that great occasion: On the contrary, it displayed a degree of fortitude and magnanimity, worthy of those who aspire to the exalted character of defenders of their country. It calmly entered upon the subject of defence; declared Robespierre, St. Just, Couthon, Henriot, and the commune without the protection of the law, appointed a commandant of the guard, and sent deputies to the sections to admonish them of their danger, and warm them to stand at their posts in defence of their country. A moment's reflection settled the public mind. The people beheld on the one side, the Convention labouring to save the Republic, and on the other, Robespierre and his associates in open rebellion. Hesitation was at an end. The citizens rallied immediately to the standard of their sections, and Robespierre and his associates were taken at the same time to prison, and on the next day to execution, amidst the rejoicing and acclamations of the people.

Many believe that Robespierre aimed at a despotic power, and sought to establish himself upon the throne of the Capets, in the character of protector, or some such character; and, in pursuit of this idea, say, that he counted upon the support of the armies, and particularly the army of the North, and had otherwise arranged things in such order as to favour the project. What his views of ambition and carnage were, I know not: That they had been great was certain; but that he had concerted any plan of permanent establishment for himself, or been promised such support, even where his influence was greatest, cannot be true, nor is it warranted by circumstances. If he was not promised the support, it is not probable he had such a scheme; and that it was not promised, must be obvious to those who take into view all the circumstances which merit consideration. It will be observed, by those who wish to form a just estimate of the future course and fortune of this revolution, that from its commencement, to the present time, no person ever raised himself to power but by the proof he had furnished of his attachment to the cause, by his efforts to promote it; and that from the moment doubts were entertained of the solidity and purity of his principles, did his influence begin to decline in equal degree. This was seen in the instances of La Fayette, Dumourier, Brissot, Danton, and finally, Robespierre himself; two of whom, though popular generals, were abandoned by the armies they commanded; the former compelled to seek refuge in a foreign country, and the latter in the camp of the enemy; and the others, tho' eminent in the civil department, were, upon like charges, condemned by the public voice to the same fate. In fact, the current of sentiment and principle has been such, that no character or circumstance has been able to obstruct its course; on the contrary, it has swept everything before it. Can it be presumed then, and especially at this moment, when the ardour of the nation, inflamed by conquest, is at the height, that any respectable number of citizens, of any description, would turn aside from the great object of the revolution, to countenance, in any individual, schemes of usurpation and tyranny? Did not the late event, even in Paris, disprove it, where Robespierre had most influence? There was no opposing force but what depended on public opinion, and everything tended to favour his views.

From due consideration of all circumstances, I am led to ascribe the sanguinary course of Robespierre's proceedings to a different cause. I consider the contest between him and Danton, as a contest for power between rivals, having the same political objects in view. The former was jealous of the latter, and having gained the ascendancy, and the defective organization of the government permitting it, by means of his influence in the judiciary, he cut him off. But the arrestation and condemnation were regular, according to the forms prescribed by law, and were on that account submitted to. The public, however, saw into the oppression, and disapproved of it; for at the moment when Danton was led to execution, there was a general gloom upon the countenances of the citizens. They all attended at the place in hope of hearing the explanation: They heard none and retired dissatisfied. Robespierre saw this, and in it the foreboding of his own ruin. From that moment he saw nothing but conspiracies,assassinations, and the like. He was surrounded by informers, and had spies and emissaries in every quarter. By means of severity he sought his safety, and therefore struck at all his enemies in the hope of extirpating them. But it happened in this as it always happens in like cases, every new execution increased them tenfold. It progressed thus until it could be no longer borne, and terminated as I have already stated.

It may be asked: Is there any reason to hope that the vicious operation of the guillotine will be hereafter suspended? May not factions rise again, contend with and destroy each other as heretofore? To this I can only answer, that the like is not apprehended here, at least to the same extent; that the country from Havre to Paris, and Paris itself, appears to enjoy perfect tranquility; that the same order is said to prevail in the armies, who have addressed the Convention, applauding its conduct, and rejoicing at the downfall of the late conspirators. Some circumstances, it is true, have been seen, indicating a suspicion, that all Robespierre's associates had not suffered the fate they merited, and ought not to escape; but latterly this has abated, though it is possible it may revive again. In general it may be remarked that, until peace and a well organized government shall be established, no sure calculation can be formed of what may happen in this respect. I am happy, however, to observe, that the subject of reform in the committees and revolutionary tribunals (and which was taken up immediately after the late commotion subsided) is now under discussion, and that the propositions which are depending, are calculated to preserve, as far as possible, the controul of the Convention over the former, and promote the independence, and otherwise improve the organization, of the latter.

But are not the people oppressed with taxes, worn out by continual drafts to reinforce the armies; do they discover no symptoms of increasing discontent with the reigning government, and of a desire to relapse again under their former tyranny? What will become of the army at the end of the war? Will it retire in peace, and enjoy in tranquility, that liberty it has so nobly contended for; or will it not rather turn its victorious arms against the bosom of its country? These are great and important questions, and to which my short residence here will not permit me to give satisfactory answers. Hereafter I shall be able to give you better information in these respects. At present I can only observe, that I have neither seen nor heard of any symptom of discontent shewing itself among the people at large. The oppression of Robespierre had indeed created an uneasiness, but which disappeared with the cause. I never saw in the countenances of men more apparent content with the lot they enjoy, than has been shewn everywhere since my arrival. In the course of the last year the Convention recommended it to the people, as the surest means of support for their armies, to increase the sphere of cultivation, and from what I can learn, there never was more land under cultivation, nor was any country ever blessed with a more productive harvest. Many fathers of families, and a great proportion of the young men, are sent to the frontiers, and it was feared it would be difficult to reap and secure it; but the women, the boys, and the girls, even to tender age, have supplied their places. I saw this with amazement on my route from Havre to this place, and am told 'tis generally the case. The victories of their armies are celebrated with joy and festivity in every quarter, and scarce a day has latterly passed without witnessing a deputation to the convention, and often from the poorest citizens, to throw into its coffers some voluntary contribution for the support of the war. These are not symptoms of disgust with the reigning government, and of a desire to change it!

With respect to the present disposition of the Army, or what it may be at the end of the war, I can say less as I have not seen it. At present the best understanding subsists between it and the Convention. It is possible that in the course of the service, if the war should last long, many of its members may acquire habits unfriendly to retirement; but in an army composed of the yeomanry of the country, as this is, that sentiment will be less apt to gain ground than in any other. Besides, it is not presumable, that the spirit which has raised and influenced this, will continue to produce some effect, even in its final disposition. If, however, there should still remain a considerable force on foot, which could not be prevailed on to retire; fond of conquest, of rapine, and of plunder, can it be supposed that its parent country will furnish the only and most grateful theatre to act on? Will no other portion of Europe present before it a more productive field, whereon to gratify ambition, avarice or revenge? There must always remain in the breasts of the soldiers some sentiment in favour of their relatives; and the fortunes of the wealthy will be pretty well broken and dissipated here by the course of the Revolution. The example of the Roman Empire is always before those, whose apprehensions are greatest upon this head: They see there nothing but kindred armies fighting against each other, and tearing the commonwealth in pieces: But they make no allowance for the great difference in the state of things. The armies of the Empire were raised in the conquered provinces, and composed of foreigners: They, therefore, had no attachment to Rome. The State of the Country, and the spirit of the age are likewise different. The dissentions of Rome were the convulsions of a corrupt and worn out monarchy, verging rapidly to a decline. But here the case is different; the armies are otherwise composed, and the spirit of the age, that of a rational and philosophical reform, seeking to establish the public liberty, and sweeping before it old and corrupt institutions which were no longer tolerable.

I have thus gone into this interesting subject from a desire to give the best view in my power of the late commotion, and present state of the internal affairs of this country, because I well know its importance to my own. It will be my object to improve my knowledge of it, and keep you correctly informed in every particular, and as regularly as opportunities offer.

With respect to the State of the war I can only say, in general, that the armies of France have prevailed over the combined forces every where. The commencement of the campaign was favorable to them; but the action which took place in July, near Charleroy, on the plains of Fleurus, between Cobourg, at the head of about 100,000 men, and Jourdan, with an inferior force; and which terminated after the severest conflict and great slaughter on both sides, in favour of the French arms, has evidently given them the superiority ever since. This was certainly one of the most important and bloody actions which has been fought in the course of the present war. Cobourg, unwilling to retire before the republican troops, had gathered together all his forces, with design to hazard a general action, and in the hope of regaining Charleroy. He attacked them at every point, about five in the morning, formed in the field and ready to receive him. Three times he drove them back within their entrenchments, reluctant to yield the day. But they sallied out a fourth time, with still greater impetuosity, shouting through all their ranks, *"We will retreat no more"*; and, singing the Marseillese Hymn, and other patriotic songs, advanced with an ardour which was irresistible. The attack succeeded. Cobourg, with his routed army, fled before them, leaving on the field, according to the French accounts, about 10,000 slain. The French, it is supposed, lost about 15,000 men. They have taken in the course of the present campaign, Ostend, Mons, Tournay, Namur, Tirlemont, Landrecy, Anvers, Ghent, Charleroy, Brussels, Quesnoy, Louvain, Liege, Nieuport, Cadsandt (at the mouth of the Scheldt) with some other places lying in that quarter. Cobourg at present occupies the ground in the neighbourhood of Maestricht, and endeavours to cover the frontier of Holland. It is, however, daily expected an other action will take place, which may settle the fate of the low countries. Conde and

Valenciennes, you observe, are left in the rear; they are yet possessed by the combined forces, but are invested, and it is thought will soon fall.

Their success in Spain has likewise been great. They are in possession, at present, of the whole of the province of Guypuscoa, Bilboa excepted. Many prisoners and immense parks of artillery have been taken from the Spaniards. The detail I cannot give you with any kind of accuracy, but will endeavour to comprise it in my next.

There has been but one sea action, and which was between the French and English fleets, in the course of the present summer. The French had 26 ships, and the English 28. The English, having the wind, bore down on the French and separated 7 ships from their main force. Of these they took 6 and sunk the other. It is said there never was a more bloody, or better fought action on both sides. It lasted three days. On the fourth the British filed off with the ships they had taken, and sailed into port. The French having offered to renew the combat, likewise retired afterwards to Brest, whither they conducted the merchantment convoyed from America, and which was the object of the contest, safe.

I shall write you again in a few days, and I hope to inform you of my reception. For the present therefore I shall conclude with assurance of the great respect and esteem with which I am, dear Sir, Your most obedient and very humble servant,

JAˢ. MONROE.

TO JAMES MADISON.
PARIS, Sepʳ. 2 [1794]

DEAR SIR,—Tomorrow will make one month since our arrival here, and such have been my engagements that altho. I resolved that I would begin a letter to you every succeeding day yet when the day arrived it was not in power heretofore. You will readily conceive that the variety of the objects to which I have been forced to attend, many of which requiring the utmost effort of my judgment, all delicate and interesting and you will readily admit my embarrassment when you know that I have not had a single person (Mr. Skipwith excepted and who is new in this line) with whom I could confidentially confer. I wished not to write you a superficial letter, but whether I shall be forced to hurry this is what I cannot at present determine. Between Baltimore and Paris we were 45 days. The passage was free from storms and between the soundings of each coast short, being only 29 days. We enjoyed our health; none were sick except Joseph a few days, & myself an hour or two. Mrs. M. and the child escaped it altogether. We landed at Havre and left it for this the day after, whither we arrived in three days being the [2] 3 of August. We are yet at lodgings but expect to be fixed in Mr. M's house, which I took, in less than a week. I found Mr. Morris from town but he came in, in two or three days after my arrival.

About a week before my arrival Robespierre had been executed with S^t. Just, Couthon and others so that the scene upon which I had to commence was a troubled one. The publick councils were yet somewhat agitated but tranquillity and joy upon acc^t. of that event reigned every where else. The whole community seemed to be liberated from the most pestilent scourge that ever harassed a country. I found I had better look on for some days, merely to inform myself of the course to be taken to obtaining recognition.

I found myself under difficulties from the commencement. The fall of Robespierre had thrown a cloud over all whom it was supposed he had any connection with or in whose appointment he had been in any wise instrumental. This included my fellow passenger so that it was not prudent to avail myself of his aid in presenting me or even making known my arrival to the Committee of public safety, and I was averse to taking the introduction of my predecessor for as good a reason. I did not know the ground upon which the Americans stood here, but suspected as the acquisition of wealth had been their object in coming, they must have attached themselves to some preceding party & worn out their reputations. Upon mature reflection therefore I resolved to await the arrival of my predecessor & present myself as a thing of course with him. I concluded it could do me no detriment as it was the official mode & more especially as he would have to file off at the moment I took my ground. This was done. He accompanied me to the office of foreign aff^{rs}., notified his recall & my succession. I left with the commissary a copy of my credentials & requested my recognition from the competent department as soon as possible which was promised. But my difficulties did not end here. Eight or ten days elapsed and I was not accepted, nor had I heard a syllable from the Committee or seen a member. And upon enquiry I was informed that a minister from Geneva had been here 6 weeks before me and was not yet received. Still further to increase my embarrassments I likewise heard that the Commissary to whom I was presented being of Robespierre's party was out of favor, and that probably his letter covering my credentials had not been read by the Committee. I could not longer bear with this delay. I foresaw that the impression to be expected from the arrival of a new minister might be lost, and that by the trammel of forms and collision of parties I might while away my time here forever without effect. I was therefore resolved to place myself if possible above these difficulties, by addressing myself immediately to the Convention. I knew this would attract the publick attention and if my country had any weight here produce a proportional effect not only upon that body, but upon every subordinate department. The result was as I had expected; my letter being read in the Convention was well received; taken immediately to the Committee of Publick Safety, reported on in two hours afterwards by that body & a decree passed the same day for my admission on the next, at two in the afternoon. It was at the same time intimated by a special messenger from the President that he sho^d. be glad to have a copy of what I sho^d. say an hour or two before I was presented. I had of course but little time to prepare my address. I thought it expedient to make the occasion as useful as possible in drawing the two republicks more closely together by the ties of affection by shewing them the interest which every department of our government took in their success and prosperity. With this view I laid before the Convention with suitable solemnity the declarations of the Senate and H. of R., and added a similar one for the President. The effect surpassed my expectation. My reception occupied an hour and a half, of not merely interesting but distressing sensibility, for all who beheld it. It was with difficulty that I extricated myself from the House and Committee of Public Safety and indeed the crowd which surrounded it, after the business was over. The cordial declaration of America in favor of France and of the French Revolution (for although I have not mentioned the word revolution, after the example of both houses yet after the example of both and especially the H. of R. I have strongly implied it) in the view of all Europe and at a time when they were torn in sunder by parties, was a gratification which overpowered them.

I doubt not this measure will be scanned with unfriendly eyes by many in America. They will say that it was intended that these things should have been smuggled in secretly and as secretly deposited afterwards. But they are deceived if they suppose me capable of being the instrument of such purposes. On the contrary, I have endeavoured to take the opposite ground, with a view of producing the best effect here as well as there. And I am well satisfied that it has produced here a good effect. It is certain that we had lost in a great measure the confidence of the nation. Representations from all parties had agreed (and men of different characters)

TO THE COMMITTEE OF PUBLIC SAFETY.
Paris, September 3, 1794.

Citizens,—There are some subjects to which I wish to call your attention and which I deem of equal importance to both Republics. They have grown out of the occurrences of the present war; have pressed particularly hard on the United States, and will I doubt not be immediately rectified in a manner becoming the French nation and of course satisfactory to us.

The first respects the departure on the part of France from the 23ᵈ and 24th. articles of the treaty of commerce subsisting between the two Republics.

The second the embargo of our vessels at Bordeaux and the injuries arising from it to those whom it concerns.

The third, respects the claims of some of our citizens for supplies furnished to the Government of Sᵗ. Domingo, authenticated by Bills upon the Minister of the Republic in Philadelphia, by Bills upon France, and by Mandates and other instruments usual in such cases.

By the 23ʳᵈ Article of the Treaty of Amity and Commerce it is stipulated that free ships shall make free goods, and that all goods shall be free except those which are termed contraband and that no dispute might arise as to *contraband,* all those which should be deemed *such* on the one hand, and which should be deemed *free* on the other are particularly specified in the 24th.

It is necessary for me, in bringing this subject to your view, briefly to observe, that these articles have been dispensed with on your part: that our vessels laden with merchandize, not only the property of your enemies, made free by these articles, but likewise our citizens, the latter of which was always free, have been brought into your ports, detained for a great length of time, their cargoes taken, and the captains and proprietors otherwise subjected to great embarrassments, losses and injuries. But I will not dwell upon this subject in this view, because I frankly own to you it is painful for me thus to contemplate it. I wish to reserve my free comments for the other side of the picture where I shall favorably explain the motives of the act, in communicating to my country what I hope you will enable me to communicate, the ready acquiescence with which the decree was rescinded.

It may be said that Great Britain has rendered us the same injury, and that when she shall change her conduct in that respect, France will likewise follow her example. But the case is widely different. Britain may dispute the law of nations, however clear its doctrine even with respect to contraband; but with France it is in both respects regulated by treaty. Besides we are allies, and what is more interesting, the friends of France. These considerations naturally inspire in the councils of the two countries, different sentiments in regard to us; and if Britain proves true to those which belong to her situation, shall we, on the other hand, find France reluctant to cherish such as are friendly to us, and correspondent with hers? Will she say that the injuries of Britain furnish a justificatory example for her to render us like injuries? Will our ally contend with that nation in rivalship, which shall harrass our commerce most and do us the greatest detriment? This is surely not a relation for the two Republics to bear towards each other. Other sentiments will I hope inspire their common councils; sentiments more congenial with their mutual interests and consonant to the dispositions of the citizens of both countries.

If the French Republic gained the smallest benefit from the regulation, there might be some motive for adhering to it. But this cannot, it is presumed, be the case. The most to be derived from it, is the occasional seizure of a straggling vessel destined for the ports of Spain and Portugal; for they are excluded from the ports of England, except under particular circumstances and which rarely happen. It must be obvious, if the price was higher here, this would be their destination; add to which the charges attending the seizure and conducting of vessels from their course, must be great, and will make it not only an uncertain but unprofitable mode of supply.

It may be apprehended that if this decree should be rescinded, it will open a door, through which, under the protection of our flag, the commerce of Britain may be carried on with advantage to her, and detriment to France. But a moment's reflection will demonstrate, that this apprehension cannot, in any degree, be well founded; for the navigation act of England, whose great principles have been wisely adopted here, forbids almost altogether any such commerce. By this act the manufactures of the metropolis cannot be carried to the colonies, nor can the productions of the colonies, nor the productions or manufactures of any other country, be carried in our bottoms to Great Britain. This restriction must in a great degree inhibit the use of our vessels in any but the direct trade between the two nations; for it is not probable that Great Britain will use the American vessels to export her cargoes to other countries, to any amount, if at all; since, not being able to return, they would generally be left there empty and idle. On the contrary we know that her practice, in such cases, has been not to countenance the navigation of any other country at the expense of her own; but to protect the latter by convoys. But if this were otherwise, it is to be presumed that the fortune of the present war, in the triumphant success of the French arms, will have decisively settled itself, before that could have produced any material defect.

It must be obvious that the conduct of Great Britain, and especially in regard to the articles of contraband, must depend in a great measure upon that of France in this particular. For if France decline to rescind this decree, Great Britain most probably will, unless indeed she should make a merit of receding at the expence of France; for if France should comply in the first instance, she will put Great Britain in an embarrassing dilemma; for, if she refuses afterwards, it will tend not only to cement our union with France, but combine all America in the condemnation of the conduct of Britain: And if they should then comply, to France will the credit be given of having forced her into it.

At the same time I express to you a desire that this decree be rescinded, and the parties heretofore affected by it compensated for the injuries they have received, I consider it likewise my duty to add some observations upon the state of our trade in general with the Republic. When an American vessel arrives in any port of France, it is immediately in the hands of the government. The Captain or Supercargo cannot sell the cargo to any other person, nor can he get more for it than the public agents will give, nor sail elsewhere without permission. Oftentimes it happens that great delays take place, from the necessity of communicating from the sea ports with the metropolis, and other inconveniences detrimental to the parties. A regulation of this kind, in its fullest extent, must prove very injurious to both countries, and especially to France. Trade cannot exist under it. It will soon happen that not a single adventurer will seek the French ports: no merchant will enter them but by restraint. The consequence must be, that the commerce of America so extensive and productive, and especially in those articles in greatest demand here, will be either exterminated, thrown into other channels, or forced here by public funds, and under the direction of public agents: a resource which, however productive, should not be the sole one, for many reasons; but more especially because the produce of our country, having thus become the property of France, will be liable, by the law of nations, equally in yours and in our vessels, to seizure and condemnation by your enemies; and because if we succeed in securing the respect which is due to our flag by other nations, and which would enable our citizens in their own bottoms to supply in abundance your markets (and in which I trust we shall succeed) it would be of no use to you; and lastly, because the competition of private adventurers would thus be destroyed, a competition which, with suitable encouragement, would not only supply the defect of these agents and satisfy the demand of the market; but by making known constantly and regularly the prices in America, form a check on their conduct and furnish the best test of their integrity.

You will observe I do not complain that the public are the sole purchasers and regulate at pleasure what shall be exported, provided the vendors are paid for their cargoes in some commodity or specie, at their option; or that agents of the public are appointed in the United States, and as many as may be thought necessary, to purchase our productions on public account and send them here. These are subjects which the legislators of the Republic will regulate according as public exigencies may in their judgment require. What I wish is that the ports of France may be opened freely to the enterprizes of my countrymen, and which will be the case provided they be permitted to leave them immediately if they do not like the market, and despatched without delay in case they do. To accomplish the first point a general order only will be requisite to the officers of the customs or other persons in authority in the several ports; and the latter, a regulation of the prices to be immediately given by these officers upon all occasions, when a vessel should arrive, and which might be furnished as often as any change should be deemed necessary. This would, I am satisfied, banish every cause of complaint, greatly increase the competition and of course the supply of the market, and at a much less expense.

Upon the second subject, the Bordeaux Embargo, I find the Committee has already passed an Arret which secures to the persons interested an indemnity for the delay and other injuries sustained; it only remains, therefore, to adjust the amount of the claims and pay the parties entitled to it.

The third which respects the claims for supplies rendered by our citizens to the government of St. Domingo, is likewise a matter of account, and which it is earnestly hoped will be immediately adjusted and paid. A person authorized will appear in support of the claims, with the evidence, before any board or tribunal which shall be appointed for that purpose.

I have to observe that I shall be happy to give every paid aid in my power to facilitate the adjustment and subsequent payment of these several classes of claims. So far as they are well founded I doubt not they will be allowed by the French Republic, and where this is not the case they will not be supported by me. Is the aggregate view they respect the great mass of American merchants. It is of importance for France to cultivate that interest, and the present is, for many reasons, a critical moment to make an impression on it. I hope, therefore, it will not be neglected.

It is my duty to observe to you that I am under no instruction to complain of, or request the repeal of, the decree authorizing a departure from the 23ᵈ. and 24th. articles of the Treaty of Amity and Commerce; on the contrary I well know that if, upon consideration, after the experiment made, you should be of opinion that it produces any solid benefit to the Republic, the American government and my countrymen in general will not only bear the departure with patience but with pleasure. It is from the confidence alone which I entertain that this departure cannot be materially beneficial to you, and that the repeal would produce the happiest effect, in removing every possible cause of uneasiness and concilliating still more and more toward each other the affections of the citizens of both Republics, and thereby cementing more closely their union, that I have taken the liberty, as connected with the other concerns, to bring the subject before you. To cement that union in other situations has long been the object of my efforts; for I have been well satisfied that the closer and more intimate it was, the happier it would be for both countries. America and France thus united, the one the greatest power in the European World and the other rapidly repairing the wastes of war, and rising to the first rank in the scale of nations, both bounding by and measuring an immense space along the Atlantic, abundant in productions, suiting the demand of each other, and above all, both Republics, have nothing to fear from foreign danger, and everything to hope from the happiest and most beneficial domestic intercourse. By a generous and liberal policy, France has it at the present moment much in her power to promote this more intimate union, and in the hope she will avail herself of it I have thought proper thus to develope the subjects which I have submitted to your consideration.

JAS. MONROE.

TO THOMAS JEFFERSON.
PARIS, Sepr. 7, 1794.

DEAR SIR,—I have been here rather more than a month and so much engaged with the duties which devolved on me immediately that I have not yet been able to send a single private letter to America. It happened that I took my station a few days after Robespierre had left his in the Convention by means of the guillotine, so that everything was in commotion, as was natural upon such an event; but it was the agitation of universal joy occasioned by a deliverance from a terrible oppression & which had pervaded every part of the Republick. After encountering some serious difficulties growing out of the existing state of things, I was presented to the Convention and recognized in the manner the enclosed paper will shew you. Many incidents have since turned up to shew the pleasure with which the organized departments and the people generally have received a mission immediately from our Republick to theirs, and I have every reason to believe that it will not only remove any previous existing solicitude,but tend to encrease permanently the harmony between the two countries.

After Robespierre's exit there seemed to be an end of divisions and altercations for some time in the Convention. Even those of his own party were most probably happy in the event, for in the progress of his power a connection with him had already been of little service, and it was to be apprehended that it would prove of less hereafter. It was not only necessary to be devoted to him, but to be unpopular with the community also. The list of his oppressions and the acts of cruelty committed by means of his influence, in the Convention & in consequence the revolutionary tribunal, would amaze you. He was believed by the people at large to be the foe to Kings, nobles, Priests, etc., the friend of republican govt. regardless of mercy & in fact devoted to their cause. Under this impression he perpetrated acts, which without perceiving the cause, had gradually spread a gloom over the whole republick. But as soon as they saw him in opposition to the Convention, the cause was known, his atrocities were understood, and the people abandoned him with demonstrations of joy rarely seen.

But it seemed improbable he sho'd. have been able to carry every thing in the committee of p: safety & by means of it in the Convention &c. with out more associates than St. Just & Couthon, who were executed with him or rather this was the opinion of others, for I can readily conceive that a man may gain an influence in society powerful enough to control every one & every thing. As soon, therefore, as the preternatural calm subsided, which the liberation from him had universally created, a spirit of enquiry began to shew itself, as to other accomplices. It terminated in the denunciation of Barrere, Collot d' Herbois, & some others. The Convention gave a hearing to the charges, rejected them, & pass'd a censure upon the author as seeking to disturb the publick repose. Thus, therefore, that business rests, and I declare to you that I not only think hereafter they will be more free from parties of the turbulent kind heretofore known, but if they sho'd. not, that I am persuaded their revolution rests perfectly secure in the unanimity & affections of the people. Greater proofs of patriotism and personal sacrifice were never seen in any country than are daily shewn in this, and in acts of heroism they have thrown a shade over the ancient and modern world. The spirit of the combination is absolutely broken. In the neighbourhood of Charleroy a decisive action was fought in July between Jourdan & Cob[1]: & in which the former gained the victory with the loss of abt. 1500 men, & at the expense to the latter of abt. 10,000 slain on the field. This has eventually driven the troops of the combined powers to Mastrecht and the neighbourhood of the Rhine, & of course out of all their possessions, not only in France [including Condé & Valenciennes] but likewise their proper territory in the low countries. 'Tis

---

1. *The Prince of Coburg.* [HAMILTON.]

thought they are abt. to hazard another great action, but they do it with hazard for they fight dispirited troops against those who are flushed with victory, superior numbers, & resolved to conquer, & sure in case of misfortune of immediate succour. If France succeeds and which I am led to believe from every thing I can hear & very dispassionately, the combination in the ordinary course of war will be at an end, and the several powers composing it entirely at the mercy of France, except the Islands in her neighbourhood whose safety will depend altogether on the superiority at sea, if preserved there. 'Tis said that these powers (the Islanders excepted & who probably prompted the others with a view of taking advantage in case of success) sounded this govt. last winter upon the subject of peace, but without effect: that on the contrary they were treated with the utmost contempt, and I have reason to believe they will never treat with them under the govts. at present existing in each, to press the war till no force shews itself against them & in case the people sho'd. rise in any one & organize themselves, treat such organiz'd body as the only legitimate gov't. & aid it in crushing the ancient one. If France succeeds in the battle contemplated this will soon be the state of things: indeed it must be so immediately after.

That Mr. Jay sho'd. easily obtain the object of his errand in Engl'd. will be readily inferred. The successful battles of France have plead our cause with great effect in the councils of that humane Cabinet. He will however arrogate to himself much merit for address in negotiation, and the concession of the court will be a theme for high panegyric to many in our country. They will deem it a proof of that sincere attachment to us which has already been shewn in that quarter.

The spirit of liberty begins to shew itself in other regions. Geneva has undergone revolution—the people have taken the gov't. into their hands, apprehended the aristocrats, & executed seven of the most wicked. And in Poland under the direction of Kosciusko who acted with us in America, a formidable head has been raised against Prussia & Russia. I have hopes that our trade, by mere negotiation, will be plac'd on a very safe & good footing shortly: and that France will rescind the decree respecting the seizure of our vessels laden with provisions &c. as heretofore. Indeed I think she will go back to the ground of the commercial treaty. I have hinted the good effect such a measure wo'd. have in America, without positively requesting it to be done.

I rely upon yr. self & Mr. Jones in planning the many little tho' very important matters for me, abt. my farm. Such as fixing the place for my house orchards & the like. It will not be very long before we join you—we are all well—Mrs. M. is with her child a pupil to a professor in the French language. They desire to be affectionately remembered to yr. self & family taking it for granted you have Mrs. Randolph & both yr. daughters with you.

    I am, Dear Sir,

      Yr. affectionate friend & servant

J^A^. Monroe.

It is to be remembered that the report that Jay's negotiations contained stipulations unfriendly and injurious to the interests of the French nation did not reach Paris until December; and that Monroe's only understanding of the purpose of Jay's mission at this time was based on the language of Randolph's instructions. [Hamilton.]

TO THE PRESIDENT OF THE NATIONAL CONVENTION.
Paris, September 9, 1794.

Citizen,—The Convention having decreed, that the flag of the American and French Republics should be united together and suspended in its own hall, in testimony of eternal union and friendship between the two people; I have thought I could not better evince the impression this act has made on my mind, or the grateful sense of my constituents, than by presenting in their behalf, that of the United States to the representatives of the French people. Having caused it, therefore, to be executed, according to the modes prescribed by a late act of Congress, I now commit it to the care of Captain Barney, an officer of merit in our own revolution, and who will attend for the purpose of depositing it wherever you will be pleased to direct. I pray you therefore to accept it, as a proof of the sensibility with which my country receives every act of friendship from our ally, and of the pleasure with which it cherishes every incident which tends to cement and consolidate the union between the two nations.

TO THE SECRETARY OF STATE.
[Edmund Randolph.]
Paris, Octr. 16th. 1794.

Sir,—I gave you in my last a sketch of the embarrassments under which our commerce laboured in the ports of this Republic, and of my efforts to emancipate it, as shewn by my letter to the Committee of Public Safety, a copy of which was likewise forwarded. To this I have as yet received no answer although I have requested it more than once. To my applications, however, which were informal I was informally answered, that the subject was under consideration, and would be decided on as soon as possible.

But as these propositions were of extensive import, and connected with the system of commerce and supply, which had been adopted here, 'tis probable I shall not be favoured with an answer until the subject is generally reviewed. Nor shall I be surprized to find extraordinary efforts to protract a decision, and even defeat the object in view. But as the opposition will not be warranted by the interest, so I am well satisfied it will not be supported by the sense of the French nation, when the object is well understood. To make it so will be the object of my future, and I trust not ineffectual endeavours.

You were, I doubt not, surprised to hear that the whole commerce of France, to the absolute exclusion of individuals, was carried on by the government itself. An institution of this kind would be deemed extraordinary, even in a small state; but when applied to the French Republic it must appear infinitely more so. Nor were the circumstances which gave birth to it, more a proof of the calamities with which the society was inwardly convulsed than of the zeal and energy with which it pursued its object. Through the channel of trade it was found, or suspected, that the principles of the revolution were chiefly impaired; that through it, not only the property of the emigrants and the wealth of the country were exported, but that foreign money was likewise thrown in, whereby the internal dissensions were fomented, and in other respects the intrigues of the coalesced powers promoted. For a considerable time it was believed that most of the evils to which France was a prey, proceeded from this source. Many remedies were in consequence applied, but still the disease continued. Finally an effort was made to eradicate the cause by exterminating private trade altogether, and taking the whole commerce of the country into the hands of the government. A decree to this effect accordingly passed on the day of October 1793, and which has since continued in force.

But now many circumstances incline to a change of this system. The act itself was considered as a consummation of those measures which completed the ruin of the Girondine party, whose principal leaders had already fallen under the guillotine. By it, the commercial interest, as distinct from the landed, and dividing in certain respects with opposite views, the councils of the country, was totally destroyed. All private mercantile intercourse with foreign nations was cut off, and so severe were the measures, and great the odium on the mercantile character that none were pleased to have it attached to them. But when the apprehension of danger from that source was done away, the motive for the act itself was greatly diminished. Accordingly the public mind was soon seen vibrating back to its former station; and in which it was greatly aided by the fortune of the late dominant party, whose principal leaders had now likewise in their turn settled their account with the Republic at the receipt of the guillotine. Thus we find, and especially in great commotions, that extraordinary measures not only bear in general the strong character of their author, but frequently share his fate. The fall of the Brissotine party extirpated private trade; the fall of Robespierre's may probably soon restore it.

At present many symptoms indicate that a change is not distant, though none seem willing so prominently to take the lead, as to make themselves responsible for the consequences. The only active interest that I can perceive against it, consists of those who have managed the public trade and been entrusted with the public monies for that purpose. They readily foresee that a change will not only take from them the public cash but likewise lead to an adjustment of their accounts for past transactions. 'Tis however generally the fortune of an opposition of this kind, to precipitate the adoption of the measure it wishes to avert; for as every one suspects that its motive is not found, and which is proportionally increased by the degree of zeal shewn, so every one feels an interest in defeating it.

I have endeavoured in my propositions to confine them entirely to external objects, by suggesting such remedies as might be adopted without any interference with the interior general system of France. By so doing I hoped that the injuries of which we complain might be sooner redressed and not made dependant on the great events which happen here.

I soon found that the extraordinary expedient to which this Republic had had recourse, of excluding individuals from trade and conducting it themselves, would require in a great measure, a correspondent regulation on our part: For if the conduct of the public servants, on the one side, was not in some measure supervised, and which it could not be, but by public agents on the other, the impositions which might be practised on our improvident countrymen would be endless. In every contest between a public officer here, and the citizens of another country in the purchase of supplies for the Republic or execution of a contract, the bias of the government and of the people would be in favour of the former. The consulate, under the superintendance of the minister, forms their natural bulwark in the commercial line against impositions of every kind. Indeed it is the only one which can be provided for them. But to guard them against those proceeding from the source above described, it should be organized with peculiar care. I was sorry, therefore, upon inspecting into our establishment, to find that whatever might be its merits in other situations, it was by no means in general endowed with sufficient strength or vigour for the present crisis. American citizens alone can furnish an adequate protection to their countrymen. In the hands of a Frenchman or other foreigner, the consular functions lie dormant. In every litigated case the former shrinks into the citizen and trembles before the authority of his country; and the latter, especially if the subject of one of the coalesced powers, finds our commission only of sufficient force to exempt him from the decree which would otherwise doom him to a prison. . . .

In the movements of the present day, the Jacobin Society has, as heretofore, borne its part. The history of this Society, from its origin to the present time, is of importance to mankind and especially that, portion upon which Providence has bestowed the blessing of free government. It furnishes a lesson equally instructive to public functionaries and to private citizens. I am not yet fully possessed of the details, although I have endeavoured to acquire them; but the outline I think I now understand. In its history, as in that of the revolution itself, there are obviously two great eras. The first commenced with the revolution and ended with the deposition of the King. The second fills the space between that event and the present day. The former of these is still further divisible into two parts, upon each of which distinct characters are marked. The first commenced with the revolution and ended with the constituent assembly, or adoption of the constitution. The second comprises the administration under the constitution. During the first of these, the Jacobin Society was composed of almost all the enemies to the ancient despotism; for in general those who were friends of the public liberty, and wished its establishment under any possible modification, became at this time members, and attended the debates of this Society. But with the adoption of the constitution many were satisfied and kept it. After this and during the second part of this era, it was composed only of the enemies to hereditary monarchy, comprising the members of the three succeeding parties, of Brissot, Danton, and Robespierre. During the whole of the first era, therefore, or until the deposition of the King, this society may be considered as the cradle of the revolution, for most certainly the Republic would not have been established without it. It was the organ of the public sentiment and, by means of discussion and free criticism upon men and measures, contributed greatly to forward that important event.

But from that period and through the whole of the second era, this Society has acted a different part and merited a different character. The clergy, the nobility and royalty were gone; the whole government was in the hands of the people, and its whole force exerted against the enemy. There was, in short, nothing existing in that line which merited reprehension, or with which the popular sentiment could take offence. But it had already gained a weight in the government, and which it had now neither sufficient virtue nor inclination to abandon. From this period, therefore, its movements were counted Revolutionary, and we behold the same Society which was heretofore so formidable to the despotism, now brandishing the same weapon against the legitimate representation of the people.

Its subsequent story is neither complicated nor various. As the revolution was complete so far as depended on the interior order of things, it had no service of that kind to render, nor pretext to colour its movements. It was reduced to the alternative of either withdrawing from the stage, or taking part in the ordinary internal administration, and which it could not do otherwise than becoming an instrument in the hands of some one of the parties against the other. This station, therefore, it at once occupied, and has since held it to the present time. It became the creature of Robespierre and under his direction the principal agent in all those atrocities which have stained this stage of the revolution. It was by means of this society that he succeeded in cutting off the members of the two succeeding parties of Brissot and Danton, and had finally well nigh ruined the Republic itself.

It is an interesting fact and very deserving of attention, that in the more early and latter stages of this society, the best men of France were seeking an admittance into it, but from very different motives. In the commencement and until the establishment of the Republic, it was resorted to by them for the purpose of promoting that great event. But in the latter stage and until the fall of Robespierre, it was resorted to by them merely as a shelter from danger. Virtue and talents, with every other great and noble endowment, were odious in the sight of that monster, and were of course the object of his persecution. Nor was any man of independent spirit, possessing them, secure from his wrath. The Jacobin Society could alone furnish any kind of protection, and to this circumstance it was owing that many deserving characters were seen there, apparently countenancing measures which in their souls they abhorred. It is therefore only justice that the present preponderating party in France, and the world at large, should now look with indulgence, and indeed with forgiveness, upon the conduct of many of those who seemed at the time to abet his enormities. Unfortunately for them and for their country, their presence secured only a personal exemption from danger: the preponderating influence had long been in the hands of those of a different description.

In the last scene which was acted by Robespierre, and in which he placed himself at the Commune in open rebellion against the Convention, 'tis said that this Society arranged itself under his banner against that assembly. But after his fall, and which was instantaneous, it immediately endeavoured to repair the error of this step, by charging it upon some who were admitted to be bad members, and others who were said to have forced themselves, at that tumultuous moment, unlicensed into the society, and who were not members at all. It even went into high crimination of Robespierre himself. But the principles of the controversy were too deeply rooted in the minds of all to be so suddenly eradicated. It was obvious that a crisis had arrived which must eventually settle the point, whether the Convention or this Society should govern France, and equally so, that the public mind was, and perhaps long had been, decisively settled in favor of the former. As the catastrophe was approaching, this Society, as heretofore, used, at one time, an elevated or commanding tone, and at others, an humiliating one. But the Convention acted with equal dignity throughout. Whether it contemplated to strike at its existence, by an overt act, or to seek its overthrow by contrasting the wisdom, the justice and magnanimity of its own present conduct, with the past and recent enormities of this Society is uncertain. The leading members of the preponderating party seemed doubtful upon this point. But finally the rash and outrageous extremities of the Society, which was secretly exciting commotions through the country forced the convention into more decisive measures. By its order the Secretary of the Society at Paris was arrested, and all the deputies from those associated with it through France, and who had arrived to deliberate upon the state of their affairs, were driven from the city, under a decree which exempted none, not inhabitants of Paris, except our countrymen. Of all France, Marseilles was the only district, in which its efforts produced any effect. A small commotion, excited there, was immediately quelled by the ordinary police, and who after making an example of the leaders, reported it to the Convention.

What further measures may be adopted by the Convention, in regard to this Society is uncertain. The subject is now under discussion, and, I shall, I presume, be able in my next to give you the result.

The same success continues to attend the arms of the Republic, and in every quarter. They have taken, since my last, in the north, Juliers, Aix-la-Chapelle, Cologne and Bois-le-duc, and in the south, Bellegarde, with immense stores of cannon, provision, &c. in each, and particularly in Juliers and Bois-le-duc, at both of which latter places, a general action was hazarded by the opposite generals, and in which they were routed with great loss. It is said, indeed, that the action which atchieved Juliers, was among the most important of the present campaign, since they consider it as deciding, eventually, the fate of Maestricht, Bergen-op-Zoom, and of Holland itself. Maestricht is now closely invested and must fall in the course of a few weeks, since the Austrian general has obviously abandoned it to its fate. Holland must fall immediately afterwards; for there is, in truth, nothing to prevent it. Indeed I think it probable they will previously detach twenty or thirty thousand men to take possession of it; for it is generally believed it may be easily accomplished.

What effect these events may produce in England it is difficult for me to say. That Austria, Prussia and Spain have been for some time past wearied with the war, and have wished to withdraw from it is certain. That they will withdraw from it soon is more than probable, and upon the best terms they can get. England, therefore, will have to maintain the contest alone; for Holland will be conquered and subject to the will of the conquerors. This, however, is not the only danger which impends over her. Denmark and Sweden, offended at the unlawful restraints imposed by her on their trade, in the arbitrary rule of contraband, have for near three months past, united their fleet to the amount of about thirty sail, for the purpose of vindicating their rights; and Spain, equally unfriendly, and irritated with that power, has, I have reason to believe, serious thoughts, not only of abandoning the war but of acceding to this combination. The lapse of a few weeks, however, will, no doubt, unfold these subjects more fully to view.

I have the honor to be, dear Sir, with great respect and esteem,

Your most obedient and very humble servant,

Ja^s. MONROE.

Monroe's history of the Jacobins arrived very seasonably for Washington in his denunciation of the "Democratic" societies in our own country. Randolph in acknowledging it wrote "Your history of the Jacobin societies was so appropriate to the present times in our own country, that it was conceived proper to furnish the public with those useful lessons, and extracts were published, as from a letter of a gentleman in Paris to his friend in this city." Madison wrote to Monroe under date of March 11, 1795. "I have not yet rec^d. a single-line from you except yours of Septr. 2 long since acknowledged. Your last letters of the official kind were duplicates of October 16, Nov. 7 & 20. You will perceive in the newspapers that the parts of them relating to the Jacobin Societies have been extracted and printed. In New York they have been republished with your name prefixed. The question agitated in consequence of the President's denunciation of the Democratic Societies will account for this use of your observations. In New York where party contests are running high in the choice of a successor to Clinton who declines, I perceive the use of them is extended by adroit comments to that subject also. It is proper you should be apprised of these circumstances that your own judgment may be the better exercised as to the latitude or reserve of your communications." [HAMILTON.]

TO EDMUND RANDOLPH.
PARIS, Decr. 18th. 1794

DEAR SIR,—Within a few days past English papers have been received here stating that M^r. Jay had adjusted the points in controversy between that country and the United States: in some of those papers it is stated that Canada is to be ceded with the ports, that privileges are to be given in the West Indies and other stipulations which imply an alliance offensive & defensive as likewise a commercial treaty. As this government has always felt uneasiness upon the subject of his mission, and which was greatly mitigated but not entirely done away by the solemn declarations I had made upon the authority of my instructions, that he had no power other than to demand the surrender of the ports & compensation for injuries, this recent intelligence has excited a kind of horror in the minds of those acquainted with it. And as it will probably get into the papers I fear the same sensation will be universal for a while. As it is that this accomodating disposition in the Cabinet of S^t. James, if it really exists, is owing to the successes of the French arms, the good understanding between the United States and this Republick, and the decisive temper of our government as shewn in the movements and letters of Wayne, and which were previously published in the opposition papers here, it might perhaps be expected from a just and generous people that we would pursue the adjustment of our controversy with that country in concert with this: in any event that we would not bind up ourselves in relation to the present war, in any manner to prevent us from fulfilling existing stipulations if called on to execute them, or rendering other service to our ally which a recollection of past and recent good offices might incline us to render. But to take advantage of the success of the French arms, of the good understanding subsisting between this Republick and our own, and which was created by the dismission of a minister odious to all France, and the frank declarations which I made in obedience to my instructions in the presence of the Convention and in the view of Europe, of our attachment to their welfare and sollicitude for their success, to part the two countries and draw us into the bosom of our mortal foe, would be an act of perfidy the example of which was perhaps never seen before.

As yet I have not been spoken to upon this subject by the Committee nor do I expect to be, for *reserve* is the peculiar characteristic of that department, and from which it never deviates except in cases when the person in whose favor the deviation is, possesses their entire confidence. Notwithstanding the harmony of opinion which prevailed among all their parties here, in respect to my political principles and attachment to their nation for services in our revolution, yet this impenetrable cloak was for some time after my arrival, assumed even towards myself. It was laid aside by degrees only and upon their own experience of the verity of these reports: for so common are the cases of political depravity in the Courts of the European world, that they act as if nothing else were to be found any where. If then this report should be entirely discredited, or if it should be credited, I think I shall not be spoken to. In the former instance they will not offend me, by letting it be seen that they had even noticed it. And in the latter as they will be mortified for having given me a rank in their estimation more elevated than that of other political agents whom they class generally or in the mass as rascals, and will consider themselves as duped they will endeavour to hide it from me. So that in either case 'tis probable I shall not be spoken to on the subject. If credited it will be seen only by their relapse into the former state of reserve and which the first interview will decide.

On my part I entirely disbelieve it. I can readily conceive that the British administration under the pressure of the French Arms, and the decisive tone of our government will yield the ports and pay us for our losses, or rather it would be the endeavour of that administration to make us pay for it if possible by betraying us into some stipulation which would weaken our connection with France and stain our national character, for they know too well the temper of the publick mind to think it possible to connect us with them. And I can also readily conceive that our agent there would be well disposed to harmonize with that administration in an effort to weaken that connection, and that in the pursuit of this object he would not be over nice or scrupulous as to the means. But I rest with unshaken confidence in the integrity of the President and in the veracity of the instructions given me to declare that he had no such power. When I contemplate the fixed and steady character of the President, cautious in his measures, but immoveable after he has adopted them, jealous of his honor & regardful of his fame, the precious acquirement of great services and of a long and venerable life, I cannot hesitate for a moment in pronouncing that in placing me here he meant what he said, and that I should be the organ of an honest and not a double and perfidious policy. Upon this point I am perfectly at ease. The only point therefore upon which I feel any concern, is the apprehension of the dish which may be prepared for the palate of those who have particular interests with us & which 'tis possible may be contrived with great art by Messr^s. Pitt & Jay, the latter of whom would be useful in giving information how such interests might be acted on so as to make it irresistible. And what increases this apprehension is the report that several of the stipulations are provisional, to be executed hereafter whereby the hostage remains in the hands of Great Britain, it being only a project (and of course no violation of instructions in form tho' absolutely so in fact) to be offered for the approbation of the President and the Senate. By this he would keep his ground in England, harmonize with the administration, and aid it in the means of attacking the integrity of our Councils. Upon this point I have my fears for I knew him play the same game upon the subject of the Mississippi. He was instructed to enter into no *stipulation* which did not open that river and fix the boundaries according to our treaty with Great Britain. He should therefore not have heard a proposition on that subject: on the contrary he absolutely entered into a stipulation which shut the river up, or according to his own language *forbore the use of it,* and left the boundaries to be settled by Commissaries to be appointed by both countries, as I understand is the case with some of the litigated points in the present case. The analogy in the project reported to be now depending with that I have here recited (and which I have often wished the President would peruse from beginning to the end) together with my own perfect knowledge of the principles and crooked policy of the man disguised under the appearance of great sanctity and decorum, induce me to pay more attention to those papers than I otherwise should do.

If any thing of this kind should have taken place I know the dilemma into which you will be all thrown. *The western ports are offered you—compensation for losses*—free *trade* to the *Islands*—under the protection of the all *powerful British flag—Canada is* or *will be* given up, whereby the fisheries become more accessible—Eng^d. will no longer support Spain in favor of the *Mississippi* &c. This will be resounded in the public papers and the impudence of the British faction become intolerable. But will it not be perceived that whatever is offered cannot be deemed the amicable concession of England but is already your own, attained by the illustrious atchievments & prosperous fortunes of your ally, & the decisive of your own councils? Will you take therefore in breach of plighted faith, and expense of our national character, and of an amicable concession of England what may be obtained without loss, and is in truth due to the merits of our ally? I will candidly own that I do not think it in the power of Messrs Pitt. and Jay to succeed in any project they can contrive whereby to weaken our connection with France & put us again under the influence of England, for such would be the case provided that connection was weakened.

I have written you freely upon this subject as well to state the report and explain the light in which such an adjustment would be received here, as to put you on your guard in relation to transactions in England, a country which will never smile upon but to deceive you. Tis impossible to be closely connected with both these countries if no other considerations prevented from the animosity, and frequent wars that will take place between them, and which must terminate from the superior strength of this in the ruin at least to a certain degree of the other: unless indeed we should now abandon our ally to prop the declining fortunes of hers and our adversary. I write to you in confidence that you will make no improper use of this & that from the necessity of retaining a copy you will excuse its being dressed in the character of a friend. With great respect and esteem I am dear Sir very sincerely yours

Jaˢ. MONROE.

TO THE COMMITTEE OF PUBLIC SAFETY.
PARIS, December 27th., 1794.

CITIZENS,—I was favoured this morning with yours of yesterday, intimating that the report of a treaty, said to have been concluded by Mr. Jay, envoy of the United States of America to England, with that nation, derogatory to the treaties of alliance between those States and this Republic, had given you some disquietude and requesting information from me upon that point. I obey the invitation with pleasure because I well know that a candid policy is that alone which becomes Republics, and because it is likewise most correspondent with the wishes of the American government and my own feelings.

Having already communicated to you the limited object of Mr. Jays mission, it only remains for me to inform you what I know of the result. All that I know upon this subject is comprized in a letter received yesterday from Mr. Jay of November 25th., in which he says that he had fulfilled the principal object of his mission, by concluding a treaty, signed on the 19th. of the same month, which contains a declaration. "That it should not be construed, nor operate, contrary to our existing treaties, and that, therefore, our engagements with other nations were not affected by it." He adds that as the treaty is not yet ratified, it would be improper to publish it. I am altogether ignorant of the particular stipulations of the treaty, but I beg leave to assure you that as soon as I shall be informed thereof, I will communicate the same to you.

I take it, however, for granted, that the report is without foundation; for I cannot believe that an American minister would ever forget the connections between the United States and France, which every day's experience demonstrates to be the interest of both Republics still further to cement.

Jaˢ. MONROE.

TO JAMES MONROE.
London, November 28th. 1794.

Sir,—Within this week past I have written to you two letters to inform you that on the 19th. instant a treaty between the United States and his Britannic Majesty was signed. The design of this letter is chiefly to introduce to you Mr. Pleasants of Philadelphia, whose connections there are respectable, I have not the pleasure of being personally acquainted with this gentleman, but as a fellow citizen I wish to do him friendly offices; and I am persuaded that a similar disposition on your part will insure to him such a degree of attention as circumstances may render proper.

As Mr. Pinckney has a cypher with our other ministers in Europe, either he or I will shortly use it in communicating to you the principal heads of the Treaty *confidentially.* You need not hesitate in the mean time to say explicitly that it contains nothing repugnant to our engagements with any other nation. With the best wishes for your health and prosperity I have the honor to be, Sir, your most ob.t and h.ble servant.

John Jay.

TO JOHN JAY.
Paris, January 17, 1795.

Sir,—Early in December last, English papers were received here, containing such accounts of your adjustment with the British administration, as excited much uneasiness in the councils of this government, and I had it in contemplation to dispatch a confidential person to you, for such information of what had been done, as would enable me to remove it. At that moment, however, I was favoured with yours of the 25th., November, intimating, that the contents of the treaty could not be made known until it was ratified; but that it contained nothing derogatory to our existing treaties with other powers. Thus advised I thought it improper to make the application; because I concluded the arrangement was mutual and not to be departed from. I proceeded, therefore, to make the best use in my power of the information already given.

To day, however, I was favoured with yours of the 28th of the same month, by which I find you consider yourself at liberty to communicate to me the contents of the treaty, and as it is of great importance to our affairs here, to remove all doubt upon this point, I have thought it proper to resume my original plan of sending a person to you for the necessary information, and have in consequence dispatched the bearer, Mr. John Purviance for that purpose. I have been the more induced to this from the further consideration that in case I should be favoured with the communication promised in cypher, it would be impossible for me to comprehend it, as Mr. Morris took it with him. Mr. Purviance is from Maryland, a gentleman of integrity and merit, and to whom you may commit whatever you may think proper to confide with perfect safety. It is necessary, however, to observe, that as nothing will satisfy this government but a copy of the instrument itself, and which, as our ally, it thinks itself entitled to so it will be useless for me to make to it any new communication short of that. I mention this that you may know precisely the state of my engagements here, and how I deem it my duty to act under them in relation to this object. I beg leave to refer you to Mr. Purviance for whatever other information you may wish on this subject, or the affairs more generally of this Republic. I have the honor to be with great respect your most obedient servant.

JA^s. MONROE.

PHILADELPHIA, December 2, 1794

SIR—With the frankness of friendship, I must discharge the obligation of my office, by communicating to you the opinions which we entertain here concerning the speech which you made on your introduction into the National Convention.

When you left us, we all supposed, that your reception, as the minister of the United States, would take place in the private chamber of some Committee. Your letter of credence contained the degree of profession which the government was desirous of making; and though the language of it would not have been cooled, even if its subsequent publicity had been foreseen; still it was natural to expect that the remarks with which you might accompany its delivery would be merely oral and therefore not exposed to the rancorous criticism of nations at war with France.

It seems that upon your arrival the downfall of Robespierre, and the suspension of the usual routine of business, combined perhaps with an anxiety to demonstrate an affection for the United States, had shut up for a time the diplomatic cabinet, and rendered the hall of the national convention the theatre of diplomatic civilities. We should have supposed that an introduction there would have brought to mind these ideas. 'The United States are neutral: the allied powers jealous: with England we are now in treaty: By England we have been impeached for breaches of faith in favor of France: Our citizens are notoriously Gallican in their hearts: It will be wise to hazard as little as possible on the score of good humour: And therefore, in the disclosure of my feelings something is due to the possibility of fostering new suspicions.' Under the influence of these sentiments we should have hoped that your address to the national Convention would have been so framed as to leave heart-burnings nowhere. If private affection and opinions had been the only points to be consulted, it would have been immaterial where or how they were delivered. But the range of a public minister's mind will go to all the relations of our country with the whole world. We do not perceive that your instructions have imposed upon you the extreme glow of some parts of your address; and my letter in behalf of the House of Representatives which has been considered by some gentlemen as too strong, was not to be viewed in any other light than as executing the task assigned by that body.

After these remarks which are never to be interpreted into any dereliction of the French cause I must observe to you that they are made principally to recommend caution; lest we should be obliged at some time or other, to explain away or disavow an excess of fervor, so as to reduce it down to the cool system of neutrality. You have it still in charge to cultivate the French Republic with zeal but without any unnecessary eclat; besides the dictates of sincerity do not demand that we should render notorious all our feelings in favor of that nation."

EDM: RANDOLPH.

TO THE SECRETARY OF STATE.
[EDM. RANDOLPH.]
PARIS, February 12, 1795.

SIR,—I was honored with yours of the 2nd. December, three days since, and by which I find that my third letter only had then reached you, although the two preceding, with duplicates, were forwarded according to their respective dates, and by opportunities which promised security and dispatch.

I read, with equal surprize and concern, the strictures you deemed it necessary to make upon some particulars of my conduct here; because I think it did not merit them, and trust upon a further view of all circumstances, you will entertain the same opinion. Of these, by this time, you will possess a general view: A more particular detail, however, I think proper now to communicate.

It is objected that I addressed the Convention with a glow of sentiment not warranted by my instructions. Secondly; that I made public what was intended and policy dictated, should be kept private. And thirdly, that I compromitted the government, by saying, that it was willing to tolerate injuries, which it was not disposed to tolerate; whereby an important interest to our country was slighted or given up.

Whether my address contains a single sentiment or expression different from what my instructions and the declarations of the legislative branches contain, is to be determined by comparing the one with the other. I had them before me at the time and drew it by them; of course I thought it did not, and I now think so. The force, however of this objection is, I presume, comprized in the second; for if the communication had been in private and not in public, the objection most probably would not have been made. Upon this point, therefore, a more thorough explanation is necessary, and for this purpose a full view of the circumstances and motives which influenced my conduct equally so.

Upon my arrival here, I found our affairs, as it was known they were before I sailed, in the worst possible situation. The treaty between the two Republics was violated: Our commerce was harrassed in every quarter, and in every article, even that of tobacco not excepted. Our seamen taken on board our vessels were often abused, generally imprisoned and treated in other respects like the subjects of the powers at war with them: Our former minister was not only without the confidence of the government, but an object of particular jealousy and distrust: In addition to which it was suspected, that we were about to abandon them for a connection with England, and for which purpose *principally,* it was believed that Mr. Jay had been sent there. The popular prepossession too in our favor had abated, and was in some measure at a stand; for the officers of the fleets from America had brought unfavourable accounts of our disposition towards them. Thus the connection between the two countries hung, as it were, upon a thread; and I am convinced, that if some person possessing their confidence had not been sent, it would have been broken.

My first reception was marked with circumstances which fully demonstrated these facts, and shewed how critical the ground was on which we stood; for it is unquestionably true, that notwithstanding my political principles were subscribed to, the Committee, or the governing party in it, were disposed to delay my reception, throw me entirely out of view, and destroy altogether the effect of my mission. It was said that as my principles were with them, I ought on that account to be the more dreaded; for if they confided in me, I should only lull them asleep as to their true interest, in regard to the movements on foot; and under this impression I was viewed with a jealous eye, and kept at the most awful distance. This deportment towards me was so observable, that it attracted the attention of the representatives of the other powers here, and was most probably communicated elsewhere.

Into what consequences this policy, which was hostile to us, might lead, I could not readily perceive; but I was alarmed on that head; for I well knew that an avowed enmity by this government, against our executive administration, and in which shape it threatened to break out, pursued with passion as I had reason to apprehend it would be, would not only injure our national character, but likewise disturb our internal tranquility, and perhaps involve us in war. The interval between such a step and the existing state of things was small, and in the tide of their fortunes which were prosperous, I was fearful it would be taken. Thus circumstanced what course did policy dictate that I should pursue? Did it become me to look on as a tranquil spectator of machinations that portended so much mischief to my country; or was it more wise, more consistent with the obligations of the trust I had accepted to make a decisive effort to defeat them? And, in adopting the latter counsel, in what line should that effort be directed, or by what means enabled to succeed? The doors of the Committee, as already mentioned, were closed against me: And had it been otherwise, knowing as I did the disposition of that body towards us, would it have been prudent to have deposited those documents under its care, since they furnished the only means by which I could counteract its views? Or was it to be presumed, that the declarations of friendship which they contained, would produce in the councils of that body any change of sentiment, advised as it had been, and armed as it was, with a series of contrary evidence, and in which it would place a greater confidence? I can assure you and with great sincerity, that after taking in my mind, so far as I was able, and with perfect calmness (for the imputations against me were not of a nature to inspire zeal) that range of our affairs in their general relation to those of other powers, and in which you deem my conduct defective,—that the measure I adopted appeared to me not only the most eligible one; but that in the then juncture of affairs, I thought it my indispensable duty to adopt it. Nor was I disappointed in any of the consequences upon which I had calculated; for by this public demonstration of our regard for this nation and its *revolution* (though indeed the word was not used) the people at large were settled on the right side. The abettors of a contrary doctrine were in a great measure confounded; and as soon as the impression upon the public mind had time to react back upon the public councils, aided by the little incidents I caught at to inspire confidence, together with a change of the members of the Committee, was the object, even in that body, though slowly, yet finally, completely accomplished.

But you intimate that I ought to have shunned this publicity, from the fear it might injure our depending negociations with Britain and Spain. Had I seen cause to apprehend that consequence, I should certainly have been more averse to the measure: But there was none; on the contrary that it would produce the opposite effect, was in my opinion certain. In demonstrating this, permit me to develope, according to my idea of it, the object of Mr. Jay's mission, and the contingencies upon which his success depended. This will shew the relation which mine had to his, and more satisfactorily than I can otherwise do, the motives in that respect of my conduct.

I understood that the sole object of Mr. Jay's mission was to demand the surrender of the posts, and compensation for injuries, and was persuaded that his success would depend upon two primary considerations; the success of the French arms and the continuance of a most perfect good understanding between the two Republics. If we were disappointed in either of these events, I concluded that his mission would fail; for we knew that a long and able negociation for the first object had already proved abortive, and we saw that in the preceding year, when Toulon, was taken and fortune seemed to frown upon the arms of this Republic, that an order was issued for those spoliations of which we so justly complain. We likewise saw afterwards when the spirit of this nation was roused and victory attended its efforts, that that order was rescinded and some respect was shewn to the United States. Thus it appeared that our fortune, at least so far as depended upon Britain, and of course the success of Mr. Jay's mission, depended upon that of France.

But the success of France could not redound to our advantage, and especially in the negociation with Britain, without a good understanding and concert with the French government: For without that, we could neither count upon success in negociation, nor in case it failed, upon the fortunate issue of arms, if war should be appealed to. By negociation we could not hope with success otherwise than from the apprehension in the British cabinet, than if we were not accommodated, we would join in the war against them: We could not accept it at the price of an equivalent, and thus pay again for what was already our due: Nor could we expect it from the affection, the justice or the liberality of that court; for we well knew that if it had possessed those virtues, we should have had no cause of complaint. But we could not join in the war, nor even avail ourselves of that argument in negociation, without a concert with France; for without such concert, we might commence at the moment she was about to conclude; whereby we should be left alone to contend with that power; who would probably be supported by Spain. If then our good understanding with France was broken, or the necessary concert between us incomplete, Britain would only have to amuse us 'till the crisis had passed, and then defy us.

If this doctrine is true, and it is admitted, that the success of Mr. Jay's mission depended upon a good understanding with the French Republic, it follows, that the more cordial it was, and the more generally known, the happier the effect would be; and of course, that by exhibiting this public proof of it, instead of retarding, I forwarded essentially the object of that negociation: And such, indeed, was my idea at the time; for I knew that the movement would be so understood on the other side of the channel; and in consequence, believed it would produce a good effect, and in which I was the more confirmed by the information of several of my countrymen, who were in England when the embargo was imposed, and who assured me that if it had been continued, Mr. Jay's success would have been immediate.

That the English administration would complain of this movement, and of me, was what I expected; but I knew that I was sent here not to subserve the views of that administration, and trusted that whilst I rested on my instructions, and performed my duty with integrity, although my judgment might occasionally err, as those of most men sometimes do, that no concession would be made to my discredit, in favour of that administration: On the contrary, that I should be firmly supported against its attacks by those who sent me here. I trust that this has been the case in the present instance, and upon which point I am more anxious, upon public than upon private considerations; because I well know, that if any such concession has been made, it was immediately communicated by its instruments here, and for the purpose of weakening the confidence of this government in our own; a practice systematically pursued heretofore, and with the hope of separating, or at least of preventing any kind of concert between the two countries.

Had the fortunes of France been unprosperous upon my arrival, the motive for greater caution would have been stronger. But the case was in every respect otherwise. Her fortunes were at the height of prosperity, and those of her enemies decisively on the decline. It was obvious that nothing was wanting to preserve tranquillity at home, and to ensure success in our foreign negociations, but the good wishes and the good offices of this Republic towards us. By the measure therefore, I thought that every thing was to be gained and nothing to be lost.

Upon the third point little need be said. I have some time since transmitted to you a decree which carried the treaty into effect, and yielded the point in question. Satisfied I am, too, it was greatly forwarded if not absolutely obtained, by the manner in which it was urged: For a generous policy is better calculated to produce to good effect here, than a strict one: And other than in that light my declaration cannot be considered. Surely I did not concede the point, nor intimate an indifference upon it: On the contrary, I laboured, with the greatest force of which I was capable to demonstrate the interest we had in it as well as themselves: Nor did I condescend in that or any other transaction. In general I know I am more apt to err on the other side; and I am persuaded, that in the present instance you will find, upon a reperusal of the paper in question, that although it contains expressions of friendship, it certainly betrays none of condescendsion.

I have thus answered the objections contained in your strictures upon my conduct, by stating the circumstances under which I acted, with my motives of action; and I presume satisfied you that I did not merit them. But I cannot dismiss the subject without observing; that, when I review the scenes through which I have passed, recollect the difficulties I had to encounter, the source from whence they proceeded, and my efforts to inspire confidence here in our administration, and without which nothing could be done, and much mischief was to be apprehended,—I cannot but feel mortified to find that, for this very service, I am censured by that administration.

You have already seen by the course of my correspondence, that however difficult it was to succeed, yet at certain times, we were completely possessed of the confidence of this government; and that, at those times, I had the good fortune to accomplish some objects of importance to us. But it is likewise my duty to inform you, that I was at the same time enabled to penetrate more accurately into what would most probably be its policy towards us, in case we continued to possess that confidence unimpaired: And I now declare that I am of opinion, if we stood firmly upon that ground there is no service within the power of this Republic to render, that it would not render us, and upon the slightest intimation. In the interval between the period of those communications which were made by me to the committee, explanatory of our situation with Britain Spain, &c., and the arrival of the intelligence of Mr. Jay's treaty, the indications of this disposition were extremely strong: for at that time I had reason to believe, that it contemplated to take under its care, and to provide for our protection against Algiers; for the expulsion of the British from the western posts and the establishment of our right with Spain to the free navigation of the Mississippi, to be executed in the mode we should prefer, and upon terms perfectly easy to us; terms, in short which sought only the aid of our credit to obtain a loan from our own Banks for an inconsiderable sum, to be laid out in the purchase of provisions, within our own country, and to be reimbursed, if possible by themselves. But by *that* intelligence, this disposition was checked, but not changed; for it is with the course of opinions as with that of bodies, and which are not easily to be forced in an opposite direction, after they have decisively taken a particular one. I mention this for your information, not indeed in relation to the past, but the future measures of the Executive; for I am still inclined to believe that if the arrangement with England, or the negociation with Spain should fail, it is possible, provided a suitable attempt be made here before a peace is closed with those powers respectively, to accomplish the whole through the means of this government, and upon terms which would perhaps require on our part no offensive movement, or other act which would rightfully subject us to the imputation of a breach of neutrality. Well satisfied I am that the full weight of its fortunes might be thrown with decision into our scale and in a manner that would enable us to turn those fortunes to the best account in negociation.

I am happy to inform you that Mrs. Lafayette was lately set at liberty; and although I could not make a formal application in her favour, yet it was done in accommodation with that which was informally made. She attended immediately at my house, to declare the obligations she owed to our country, and of which she manifested the highest sensibility. Unfortunately she is, and has been for some time past, destitute of resource, and in consequence required aid not only for present support, but to discharge the debts that were already due, and for which she applied to me and was accordingly furnished with a sum in assignats equivalent to about one thousand dollars in specie. I made this advance upon the principle it was my duty to make it, as the representative of the United States, and in the expectation, that the like sum which should be paid to my order by our Bankers in Amsterdam, would be taken from the fund appropriated to the use of her husband by the Congress in the course of the last year. Is this approved, and may I upon that fund make future advances adequate to her support, and for which the interest will perhaps suffice?

A treaty of peace or rather of Amity with Tuscany with the progress of a revolution in Holland, and which has been more rapid than I expected it would be, are the only events worthy notice, that have taken place since my last, and for more particular details respecting which I beg leave to refer you to Mr. Adet, to whose care the present is committed.

With great respect and esteem, I have the honor to be, dear Sir, Your. most ob^t. servant.

JA^s. MONROE.

TO JAMES MADISON.
PARIS, Feb. 18, 1795.

DEAR SIR,—I was yesterday favored with yours of the 4th of Dec'r the only one yet rec'd. I had perfectly anticipated the secret causes & motives of the western business [The Whiskey Rebellion.] and was extremely happy to find that the patriotism of the people in every quarter, left to its own voluntary impulse and without any information that was calculated to stimulate it, was sufficient to triumph over the schemes of wicked and designing men. I have been always convinced that this was a resource to be counted on with certainty upon any emergency, & that the more frequent these were, the sooner wo'd the possibility of success in such schemes be destroyed, & our gov't assume a secure and solid form. I likewise perfectly comprehended the motive and tendency of the discussion upon the subject of the societies, but was persuaded that the conduct of the societies themselves upon that occasion, together with the knowledge diffused every where of the principle upon which they were formed, would give that business likewise a happy termination. This was the case in *one* house and will I doubt not likewise be so in the publick mind if the discussion sho'd be provoked. The fact is, such societies cannot exist in an enlightened country, unless there is some cause for them: their continuance depends upon that cause, for whenever you test them by the exigence and it is found inadequate they will fall: and if there is one an attack upon them will encrease it, for they are not even to be put down by law. I was fearful the conduct of the Jacobin society here would injure the cause of republicanism every where by discrediting popular complaints and inclining men on the side of government however great its oppressions might be. But that society was different from those that ever existed before; it was in fact the government of France, and the principal means of retarding the revolution itself; by it all those atrocities which now stain & always will stain certain stages of the revolution were committed, and it had obviously become the last pivot upon which the hopes of the coalesced powers depended. This society was therefore the greatest enemy of the revolution, and so clear was this that all France called for its overthrow by some act of violence. It is easy for designing men to turn the vices of one society, somewhat similar in its origin, and which became such only in the course of events by degenerating and losing sight of the object which gave birth to them, ag'nst all others, altho' the parallel may go no further than that stage in which they all had merit. As the conduct of the Jacobin society made such an impression upon Aff'rs here it became my duty to notice it in my official despatches: I accordingly did so by giving an historic view of its origin, progress, & decline, truly & of course under the above impression, & which I think will be found marked upon the statement to an observant reader: for in one stage viz. from the deposition of the king I say that the danger was from confusion alone, since the old government was overset & the new one intirely in the hands & exerted virtuously for the sole benefit of the people, and it is intimated in the close that however enormous the vices may be, provided treasonable practices be not discovered, that its overthrow must be left to publick opinion only. It became my duty to notice this subject & I think I have done it with propriety, however examine it & write me what you think of it.

I rec'd some days past a letter from Mr. Randolph containing a severe criticism upon my address to the convention & the publication of the papers committed to my care, and which justified that address & makes its defense ag'nst the attacks of that party with you. I was hurt at the criticism & equally surprised, for I did not expect it would be avowed that it was wished I sho'd make a secret use of them, giving them weight by any opinion which might be entertained of my own political principles, or in other words that I would become the instrument of that party here, thereby putting in its hands my own reputation to be impeached hereafter in the course of events. They were deceived if they supposed I was such a person. On the contrary I was happy in the opportunity furnish'd not only on acc't of the good effects I knew it would produce in other respects, but likewise as it furnished me with one of presenting to the eyes of the world the covenant which subsisted between them and me: by the publication they are bound to the French nation & to me to observe a particular line of conduct. If they deviate from it, they are censurable and the judicious part of our countrymen as well as posterity will reward them accordingly. The fact is I would not upon my own authority make those declarations of their sentiments, & therefore I was glad to embrace the opportunity to let them speak for themselves. I felt some concern for M^r. Randolph because I feared it would expose him to some attacks but I concluded he would despise them: for in truth I do not apply to him the above comments. I have answered those criticisms with suitable respect but as becomes a free and independent citizen whose pride is to do his duty but who will not yield where he is undeservedly attacked. I have reviewed the state of things upon my arrival & showed the necessity of some bold measure to retrieve it. What I have stated in my reply is true, I have many documents to prove it in each particular. 'T is possible this business may end here, for I have since rec'd a letter in answer to my 2 first, which were not then rec'd by M^r. Randolph, in a different style; and to which latter I shall likewise write a suitable answer: but it is also possible it may not. I have therefore tho't proper to transmit to you a copy of it, that you may perfectly comprehend the state of this business with the ground upon which I rest. Perhaps it may be proper for you to show it in confidence to others but this is entirely submitted to you. I wish it seen by Mr. Jefferson & Mr. Jones. . . .

I think upon the whole y'r prospects independent of foreign causes are much better than heretofore: the elections have been favorable: but with the aid of foreigners they are infinitely so. We are well—our child is at school in a French family & already speaks the language tolerably well. Joe is also at school & rather in a line of improvement. I have little leisure & of course am but little improved in the language. We desire to be affec'y remembered to y'r lady whose esteem we shall certainly cultivate by all the means in our powers. If a loan is obtained can it be laid out to advantage? inform on this head—remember me to Mr. Beckley, to Tazewell, Mason & all my friends & believe me sincerely y'rs.

JAᔆ. MONROE.

P. S. Pinckney is ab't sitting out for Sp'n—suppose the peace with France is made before his arrival, what success will he have?

TO JAMES MONROE.
PHILADELPHIA, December 5th. 1794.

SIR,—Since my letter of the 30th. ultimo, which will be conveyed by the same vessel with this, I have had the honor of receiving your very interesting letters of August 15th and 25th. They are the more acceptable, as affording an earnest of your attention to the kind of intelligence which is to us very important.

We are fully sensible of the importance of the friendship of the French Republic. Cultivate it with zeal, proportioned to the value we set upon it. Remember to remove every suspicion of our preferring a connection with Great Britain or in any manner weakening our old attachment to France. The caution suggested in my letter of the 30th. ultimo arises solely from an honorable wish to sustain our character of neutrality, in a style which may be a pattern for the morality of nations. The Republic, while they approve of the purity of your conduct, cannot but be persuaded of the purity of our affection.

The President approves your conduct as to the national house, offered for your residence. Your interpretation of the Constitution is correct. But you are charged to make known his sense of this evidence of respect.

The affair of the Consul is noticed in my letter of the 30th. ultimo.

I am &c. EDM. RANDOLPH, *Secretary of State.*

TO THE SECRETARY OF STATE.
[EDMUND RANDOLPH.]
PARIS, February 18, 1795.

SIR,—I have just been honored with your favor of the 5th. of December, and am much gratified by its contents. The preceding one of the 2nd. had given me great uneasiness but this has removed it. I sincerely wish my two first letters had reached you in the order they were written, as they would have prevented yours of the 2nd. of December by preventing the impression which gave birth to it.

Be assured, I shall continue to forward by all the means in my power, the objects of my mission, and I am persuaded with the success which might be expected from those efforts, addressed to the Councils of a nation well disposed favourably to receive them. The object of this is to acknowledge the receipt of your last letter, and in the expectation that it will accompany, under the care of Mr. Adet, my last dispatch which was in answer to the preceding one.

With great respect and esteem, I have the honor to be your most obt. and very humble servant.

JA^S. MONROE.

TO THE SECRETARY OF STATE.
[EDMUND RANDOLPH.]
PARIS, June 14th, 1795.

SIR,—It seemed probable, after the movement of the 12th Germinal (2nd of April) and which terminated in the banishment or rather deportation (for the hand of government was never withdrawn from them) of Barrere, Billaud de Varennes and Collot d'Herbois, and the arrestation of several of the leading members in the mountain party, that the convention would be left at liberty to pursue for the future the great object of the revolution, and without further molestation; and the calm which ensued, for a considerable time, that movement, although the scarcity of bread continued, gave strength to this presumption. But a late event has shewn that the victory which was gained upon that occasion by the convention, over the enemies of the present system, was not so decisive as there was reason to presume it would be; for within a few days after my last, which was of the 17th of May, another attempt was made upon that body, and which menaced for a while at least, in respect to the personal safety of the members, the most alarming consequences. I am happy, however, to be able now to assure you that this has likewise failed, and without producing, according to present prospects, and in regard to the main course of the revolution, any material effect.

The circumstances which characterize this latter movement were in general the same with those of that which preceded it; except that it was attended with greater violence and its views were more completely unfolded. On the 20th of May, a party from the Faubourgs of St. Antoine and St. Marceau, armed, and consisting of several thousands, approached the convention early in the morning, having previously circulated a paper that their object was a redress of grievances; of which the scarcity of bread was the principal, and which could only be accomplished by the establishment of the constitution of 1793, and the recall of Barrere and his colleagues; or, in other words, the revival of the reign of terror. As these measures could not be carried into immediate effect, without the overthrow of the preponderating party, so the movement appeared to be directed unequivocally to that object. The centinels of the convention were forced upon the first approach, and in an instant the party, preceded by a legion of women,entered and spread itself throughout the hall of that assembly. The sitting was broken and every thing in the utmost confusion. In a contest which took place between Ferraud, one of the deputies, (a gallant and estimable young man) and some of the party, for the protection of the chair and person of the President, which were threatened with violation,—the former was slain, and soon afterward his head, severed from his body, was borne on a pike by the perpetrators of this atrocious crime, in triumph, into the bosom of the convention itself. It really seemed for some time, as if that body, or at least the leading members in the preponderating party, were doomed to destruction, or safety to be secured only by disguise and flight. During this conflict, however, the whole assembly behaved with the utmost magnanimity: No symptoms of fear were betrayed: No disposition to yield or otherwise dishonor the great theatre on which they stood; and Boissy d'Anglas, who happened to preside, not only kept his seat, but observed in his deportment a calmness and composure which became the dignified and important station which he filled. This state of confusion lasted until about twelve at night; when it was terminated by the decisive effort of a body gathered from the neighbouring sections, planned by the united committees of public safety, sureté generale and militaire, and led on by several deputies, among whom were most distinguished, Kervelegan, Anguis, Mathieu, Delmas, Freron and Legendre. They entered precipitately the hall, attacked the intruders, sabre and bayonet in hand; nor did they cease the charge until they had rescued it from the profanation. A little after twelve the convention was re-established, and proceeded, as upon the former occasion, to a review of what had passed, in the course of the day.

Whilst the insurgents were in possession of the reins of government, and after Boissy d'Anglas had retired, they placed the President Vernier, in the chair by force, and began an organization upon the principles that were first avowed. They repealed in a mass all the laws that were passed since the 9th Thermidor; recalled Barrere, Billaud de Varennes and Collot d'Herbois; took possession of the tocsin and the telegraph; ordered the barriers of the city to be closed, and were upon the point of arresting all the members of the committee of the executive branch, having appointed a commission of four deputies, to take their places and with full power to act in their stead; so that in truth the reign of terror was nearly revived, and with accumulated force. At this moment, however, the plan of the committees, who had continued their sitting, was ripe for execution and fortunately the stroke was given before the system was completed.

But the commotion was not ended by the expulsion of the insurgents from the hall of the Convention itself. They retreated back to the faubourgs to which they belonged, and where, for a while, they opposed its authority. In the course, however, of the succeeding day, a considerable force was collected, under the authority of the Convention, from those sections who voluntarily offered their service, amounting, perhaps, to 20 thousand; and which being marched against them in different directions, surrounding, in a great measure, both faubourgs, reduced them immediately to order, and without the effusion of blood.

On the same day an insurrection took place at Toulon of the same kind, and with the same objects in view, and which for several days wrested that port and its dependencies, the fleet excepted, from the authority of the government. Upon that theatre too, some outrages were committed, and fatal consequences in other respects were apprehended. But this was likewise lately suppressed by the efforts of good citizens, drawn by the representatives in mission there, from Marseilles and the neighbouring country; a report to that effect being yesterday presented to the convention by the committee of public safety: So that order may be considered as completely established, the authority of the convention being triumphant every where.

As soon as the Convention resumed its deliberations, the punishment of those who had offended in the course of the commotion was the first object which engaged its attention. Whilst the insurgents were in possession of the hall, and enacting their short but comprehensive code of legislation, several members of the mountain party not only retained their seats, but joined in the work. Four were appointed to the commission, which was designed to supercede the executive administration, and who accepted the trust. These circumstances, with many others which occurred, created a belief that the movement was in harmony with that party. It was therefore concluded, that more decisive measures ought to be taken with those members, and with the party generally, than had been heretofore adopted; and in consequence, about 30 of them were arrested on that and the succeeding days, within the course of a week, and who are to be tried according to a late decree, in common with others charged with offences, said to be committed in the course of the commotion,—by a military commission appointed at the time, and invested with full power for that purpose.

It is to be observed, that the character of this movement was decisively anti-monarchical. Its success, if it had succeeded, would have revived the reign of terror, and most probably carried all the aristocrats, with the leading members of the preponderating party, to the scaffold. *Bread and the Constitution of* 1793, were written upon the hats of many of the insurgents; and whilst the hall and its vicinity resounded in favor of the patriots, meaning Barrere, &c. the feeble voice of one solitary aristocrat only was heard in favor of the constitution of 1789. Indeed the aristocrats, who had before the 12th Germinal contributed much to foment the discontents which broke out on that day, in the hope that if a commotion took place and the Convention was overthrown, the standard of Royalty would be erected, and the monarchy re-established,—and who were in the interval, from the dubious character of that movement, which was crushed before it had fully unfolded itself, of neither side, for, nor against the Convention,—were observed in the commencement of this, to remain in the same state of inactivity, greatly agitated, but taking no part. As soon, however, as the object of this latter movement was understood, and it became obvious, that in case it succeeded, terrorism, and not royalty, would be reestablished, the disposition of this party towards the Convention changed. It no longer shewed an indifference to its welfare; on the contrary, it became active in its support. But in truth, the force of this party in this City, and especially upon the late emergencies, did not appear to be great. The most gallant of its members are either upon the frontiers, at war against the republic, or have fallen already in the cause of royalty. These, too, consist of those who were of sufficient age to take their part in the commencement; for the young men of Paris, who are descended from it, or from others of the more wealthy inhabitants of the city, and who have attained their maturity during the revolution, or are now growing up, have imbibed the spirit which it was natural to expect such splendid examples of patriotism would create upon young and generous minds, and are in general on the side of the revolution.

That there should be a party of any force within the republic, or rather of sufficient force to disturb the government in the manner we have seen, disposed to subvert the present system, and establish that of terror, must excite your surprise. You will naturally be inclined to ask of what character of citizens is it composed; what their numbers and ultimate views; since it is to be presumed that a system of terror, as a permanent system of government, cannot be wished by any one? You have seen that the movements in question proceeded principally from the two faubourgs of St. Antoine and St. Marceau; the enquiry, therefore, will be satisfied by exposing the character of those two sections. In general, I am told, they are artisans, and among the most industrious in Paris. Many of them are said to be foreigners, Germans, and which explains the motive of their partiality for the constitution of 1793, which naturalizes them. That they are opposed to monarchy is certain, for such has been their character from the epoch of the destruction of the Bastille, in which they had a principal hand, to the present time. Indeed, upon this point, the late movements speak with peculiar force; for if those movements were spontaneous, and commenced by the people themselves, it follows, as they cannot be suspected of any deep political finesse, and of aiming at royalty through the medium of terrorism, that the latter, and not the former, was the object. And if they were set on by foreign influence, as is believed by many, the conclusion must be the same; for as royalty is unquestionably the object of those persons who are suspected of such interference, it is to be presumed, that, if practicable, they would have taken a more direct course to promote it, by an immediate declaration in its favour, since thereby they would rally under its standard all those who were the friends of that system: Whereas, by declaring in favour of terrorism, the opposite effect was produced; for the royalists themselves were thereby driven into the expedient of using their utmost endeavours to save the Convention, as the only means whereby they could save themselves. In every view, therefore, they must be deemed enemies to royalty, and as such it is natural to expect they will feel a great sensibility upon all those questions, which, in their judgment, have a tendency to promote it. Whether any such have been agitated or contemplated is, perhaps, doubtful: I have thought otherwise, and still think so. But that many circumstances have presented themselves, in the course of the collision of parties, that were sufficient to create a suspicion with persons of that portion of discernment, which laborious artizans usually possess, that the leading members of the preponderating party were prepared to abandon the republican scale, and incline towards monarchy, is certain. The inhabitants of these faubourgs having sided always with the mountain party, have of course, brought upon themselves the particular enmity of the royalists. They have, therefore, or rather their leaders have been, in their turn, persecuted by the royalists. But they have likewise thought themselves persecuted by the present preponderating party, with whom they were engaged in uninterrupted warfare, before and since the time of Robespierre. In this respect, therefore, they saw the present preponderating party and the royalists acting apparently in harmony together, and concluded that the former were likewise royalists. They have likewise seen, under the administration of this party, the royalists enlarged from prison, and other measures of that kind adopted, which have probably fortified them in this belief. A report, too, which has been circulated through the city, that under the name of organic laws, it is contemplated by the committee of eleven, to introduce some important changes in the constitution of 1793, has, no doubt, tended in a great measure to increase their disquietude. In an attempt to explain the cause of these movements, the above circumstances have appeared to me to merit attention, and, with that view, I have presented them.

But that there was no real harmony of political views between the present preponderating party and the royalists, even with respect to the terrorists, is a fact of which I have no doubt. The reign of terror continued until it could last no longer: It was necessary to suppress it, and it was suppressed. That the royalists wished this event, and gave it all the aid they could, is certain; but that their efforts were of any service in that respect is doubtful: Indeed, I was persuaded that for some time they produced the opposite effect, and for reasons that are obvious: For as the preponderating party sought the establishment of the Republic, and knew that the mountain party had the same object in view, it was reasonable to expect, that after the former had gained the ascendency it would be disposed to exercise towards the latter some degree of moderation and humanity; and equally so to presume, that the same spirit of magnanimity which inculcated this disposition towards its antagonist, chiefly from a respect for its political principles, would dispose it to reject with disdain the aid of the royalists who were enemies to both. This sentiment I think is to be traced through all the measures of the convention, from the 9th of Thermidor to the 1st of Prairial; for we behold, through that interval, the preponderating party rescuing from the guillotine and prison, the royalists, whilst they reprobated their principles, and terminating in other respects the reign of terror; whilst they avoided, as far as was possible, the punishment of those who had been the principal authors and agents under that reign. Indeed this party has appeared to me to be, and so I have often represented it to you, as equally the enemy of the opposite extremes of royalty and anarchy; as resting upon the interest and the wishes of the great mass of the French people, and who I have concluded, and from those data the revolution itself has furnished, as well as from my own observations since my arrival (the latter of which, it is true, has been confined to a small circle) are desirous of a free republican government; one which should be so organized as to guard them against the pernicious consequences that always attend a degeneracy into either of these extremes.

You will likewise ask; what effect have these movements had upon the public mind, in regard to the present system? Is it not probable they have already wearied the people out, and in consequence inclined them to royalty merely from a desire of repose? That they are all wearied is most certain, and what may be the course of events, in the progress of time, I do not pretend to determine: These lie beyond my reach, and indeed beyond the reach of all men. I only undertake to deduce immediate consequences from the facts which I witness; and when I see that these movements have produced upon the royalists themselves the opposite effect, and forced them, at least for the present, to renounce their creed and cling to the convention for their safety, I cannot presume that the moderatists, who are republicans, will quit the safe ground on which they rest, their own ground too, and become royalists. Royalty, therefore, I consider at present as altogether out of the question. But that these convulsive shocks, and which proceed from the opposite extreme, may produce some effect, is probable. In my opinion they will produce a good one; for I am persuaded they will occasion, and upon the report of the committee of eleven, some very important changes in the constitution of 1793; such as a division of the legislature into two branches, with an organization of the executive and judiciary upon more independent principles than that constitution admits of: Upon those principles indeed which exist in the American constitutions, and are well understood there. Should this be the case, the republican system will have a fair experiment here; and that it may be the case, must be the wish of all those who are the friends of humanity every where.

On the day that this late commotion commenced, Mr. Pinckney arrived here on his way to Madrid, and was a spectator of the great scene it exhibited to the close: A few days after which he pursued his route, by the way of Bourdeaux, where before this he is probably arrived. Whilst here, I presented to his view what had passed between this government and myself, upon the subject of his mission, assuring him from what I had heard and seen, that I was of opinion, that in case he would explain himself to the committee upon that subject, and express a wish they would give what aid they conveniently could, in support of his negociation; satisfying them, at the same time, that they were not injured by Mr. Jay's treaty, they would do it. I likewise shewed him a letter I had just received from Mr. Short, written at the instance of the Duke de la Alcudia; to request that I would promote, by certain communications to this government, a negociation between Spain and this Republic; he having previously and positively assured Mr. Short, that our demands should be yielded and adjusted at the same time. Mr. Pinckney was sensible of the benefit which the aid of this Republic could yield in his negociation, and wished it; but, upon mature consideration, was of opinion he could not request such aid without having previously exposed to its view Mr. Jay's treaty, and which he did not chuse to do, for considerations delicacy forbade me to enquire into. It was, however, equally his and my wish, that his journey through the country should be marked with all those circumstances of reciprocal civility between the government and himself, which are always due, and generally paid, when the minister of a friendly power passes through the territory of another; and in consequence I announced his arrival to the committee, and obtained for him an amicable interview with the members of its diplomatic section, and by whom he was received with the most perfect attention.

You have already seen that England and Spain are each, and without the knowledge of the other, seeking a separate peace with this republic. What the motive for such secrecy on the part of the former is remains to be hereafter unfolded: But what it is on the part of the latter is easily understood; for, as she apprehends, in case a peace is made with France, a declaration of war from England, and, of course, in case the attempt to obtain a peace is known, some new pressure from that power,—it follows, that she must wish the arrangement to be complete, to guard her against the ill consequences which might otherwise attend such an event, before any thing upon that head transpires. As soon, however, as it is known to Spain, that England seeks a separate peace, her jealousy of the views of England will be increased; as, likewise, will be the motive for an immediate accommodation with this Republic. The period, therefore, when a good understanding, embracing, perhaps, the ancient connection between the two nations, will be revived cannot be considered as remote. Whether our claims upon Spain will be attended to, under existing circumstances, in that adjustment, is a point upon which it is impossible for me to determine: for, as I was not possessed of Mr. Jay's treaty, and could give no other information on that head, than I had before given, I have latterly forborne all further communication with the committee upon that subject. Mr. Pinckney will be able, soon after his arrival at Madrid, to ascertain the temper of the Spanish court in regard to our demands, and the means by which his negociation may be forwarded; and, as he likewise knows the state of things here, he will be able also to point out the line in which, if in any, I may be serviceable; and, in the interim, I shall not only be prepared to co-operate with him in whatever movement he may suggest; but to obey, with promptitude, any instructions you may be pleased to give me in this, or any other, respect.

Since my last, the treaty with the United Provinces has been concluded and ratified, of which I send you a copy, and the garrison of Luxembourg, consisting of 12,000 men, with an immense amount in military stores, cannon, &c. has surrendered. The achievement of this post, one of the strongest in Europe, has opened the campaign on the part of France with great brilliancy: As it was taken, too, after a long siege, and when all possible efforts to raise it had proved abortive, it not only demonstrates the superiority of the French arms in the present stage of the war, but furnishes satisfactory ground whereon to calculate, according to the ordinary course of events, its ultimate issue.

You will, perhaps, have heard before this, that the British have recommenced the seizure of our vessels laden with provisions, destined for the ports of this republic. An American, just from Hamburg, charged with other articles, informed me the other day, that he was boarded on his way by two frigates, whose officers informed him, they were ordered to take in all vessels thus laden.

Within a few days past, the son of the late king departed this life. A minute report will be published by the government of his decline, having lingered for some time past, and of the care that was taken to preserve him. They are aware of the criticisms to which this event may expose them, and suffer, on that account, an additional mortification. His concession to Spain, as was contemplated, made his life, with the government, an object of interest; since it would have forwarded, in some respects, its views in the depending negociation.

I have just been honored with yours of April 7th, and shall pay due attention to its contents.

I have the honor to be, Sir, with great respect and esteem your very humble serv^t.

JA^S. MONROE

TO THE SECRETARY OF STATE.
[EDMUND RANDOLPH.]
PARIS, June 26th, 1795.

SIR,—Since my last, it is reduced to a certainty, that the British government has revived its order of the 6th of November, 1793, and commenced, on this side of the Atlantic, the same system of warfare and pillage upon our commerce, that was practised on it by that government, at that very calamitous æra. Between 30 and 40 sail destined for the ports of this Republic, charged with provisions, have been already taken from their destination, and carried into those of that Island: and: as the period has arrived, when the invitation which the distresses of this country gave to our merchants *here* and at *home,* to embark their fortunes in this supply, is likely to produce its effect, it is more than probable that other vessels, and to a great amount, will share the like fate. Among those of our merchants who are here, this measure has created a kind of panic; for they think they see in its consequences little less than the ruin of their trade; and under which impression many are about to abandon it for the present, and send their vessels home in ballast.

What effect this measure will produce upon this government, under existing circumstances, I cannot pretend to determine. Formerly it adopted the same measure, for the purpose of counteracting its enemy; but the impolicy of that procedure was afterwards discussed and demonstrated, and the measure itself, in consequence, abandoned. At present, the distress of the country is great, and the government will, no doubt, be mortified to find, that, whilst our flag gives no protection to *its* goods, nor even to *our* goods, destined for the ports of this Republic, the whole of which become the spoil of its enemy; that it does protect not only *our* goods destined for the English ports, but likewise British goods destined equally for those, and the ports of other countries. The measure has obviously excited a kind of ferment in their councils; but which, I presume, will be directed against their enemies only. Be assured I shall do every thing in my power to give it that direction, and to enforce those arguments which were used upon the former occasion: But, should they fail in producing the desired effect, and a less amicable policy be adopted, which, however, I think will not be the case, I shall deem it my duty immediately to advise you of it, by a vessel (in case none other offers) to be despatched for the purpose.

It will obviously attract your attention, that this measure was so timed by the British cabinet, that it might have no influence in the decision of the senate upon the treaty of Mr. Jay; nor can the motive for such an accommodation be less doubtful; for in case it be rejected, they will deem the stroke a lucky one; since thereby, they will say, they had fortunately gained so much time; and if it be adopted, they will probably presume, that so much time will be consumed in convening the Congress, should that measure be deemed expedient, that the course of events here may render it impossible for our efforts to produce a favorable effect; and which consideration, they will likewise infer, will be an argument against convening the Congress. This kind of policy, however, shews not only the profligacy, but the desperation of that government, and will probably precipitate the crisis, which, notwithstanding all its follies and enormities, might yet have been postponed for some time to come. I think the measure will give new vigor to the French councils, and will probably bring immediately upon its authors, Denmark and Sweden: Upon this latter point, however, I am authorized to say nothing; for, as I was not instructed to confer with the representatives of those powers here, I have carefully avoided several conferences, that were sought of me by Baron Stahl from Sweden, soon after his arrival; because

I knew nothing could result from them, and was fearful, as I presumed the result would be known to the committee, it might produce an ill effect there.

Your measures will, no doubt, be greatly influenced by the probability of the early termination or continuance of the war with this Republic, and upon which some information will of course be expected from me. You will, however, perceive the disadvantage under which I must give any opinion upon that point, and estimate it accordingly; for as I am authorized to say nothing to this government of what we will probably do, in case the war continues (for the revival of the order of the 6th November could not be foreseen) you will of course conclude it is impossible for me to sound it upon that topic. Indeed I was fearful that, by my former communications upon a similar occasion, slight and informal as they were, I might embarrass you, and was therefore extremely uneasy on that account, after I heard of Mr. Jay's treaty, and until I had obtained a conference with the committee on the subject. My judgment must, therefore, be formed upon general and external circumstances, and by which I perceive no prospect of an early accommodation of the war between France and England. On the contrary, the preparations on both sides seem to go on with all possible activity, for its continuance. The fleet of England is said to be raised to a height beyond what it ever attained before, and efforts are still making to keep it there, if not to increase it: And France is exerting her utmost endeavours to increase hers. . . .

I have the pleasure to inform you, that the committee of 11. have at length reported a plan of Government, of which I herewith inclose you a copy. The discussion upon the merits will commence in a few days, and as soon as the question is finally decided I will transmit to you the result.

With great respect and esteem I have the honour to be, Sir, your very h^{ble}. and ob^t. ser^t.

JA^s. MONROE.

TO THOMAS JEFFERSON.
PARIS, June 27, 1795.

DEAR SIR,—Of the above hasty view I have sent a copy to one or two other friends. Since it was written the Committee of II have reported a plan of govt. as suggested of 2 branches, the one to be called a council of 500, consisting of so many members, the other of 250, called the council of ancients. The age of the Ist to be 30 & of the 2d 40. They are to be chosen each for 2 years but to be supplied annually by halves. The Executive to be composed of 5 members to be elected for 5 years, but so arranged that only one withdraws annually. Each member is to have a salary of abt. ,5000 sterg. pr. ann. the object whereof to receive & entertain foreign ministers &c. The council of ancients cannot originate a bill. If possible I will procure & send you a copy of the plan—

The British have recommenc'd the seizure of our vessels as formerly under the order of the 6th of Novr. 1793, near 40 being carried in by our last & which were the first accts. This has produced an extreme ferment here, & it will be difficult under the irritation existing in consequence of Jay's treaty, to prevent a revival of the same practice on the part of France. And if we do nothing when it is known in America, but abuse the English and drink toasts to the success of the French revolution, I do not know what step they will take in regard to us. My situation since the report of Mr. Jay's treaty has been painful beyond any thing ever experienc'd before, and for reasons you can readily conceive—I have, however, done everything in my power to keep things where they shod. be, but how long this will be practicable under existing circumstances I know not. Denmark & Sweden will I think be active.

TO THE SECRETARY OF STATE.
[TIMOTHY PICKERING, ACTING.]
PARIS, October 20th, 1795.

SIR,—The breach which I lately intimated to you had taken place between several of the Sections of this city, and the Convention, respecting two decrees of the 5th and 13th Fructidor, and whose object was to transfer from the Convention so many of its members, as would constitute two thirds of the legislature of the new government, continued daily to widen afterwards till at length all hope of amicable compromise was gone. A final appeal, therefore, was made to arms; and which took place on the 5th instant (13th Vendemiaire) and in which the Convention prevailed. The details of this contest, though very interesting, are not lengthy. In the morning of the 5th, a force was marshalled out by the revolting sections upon their respective parades, in concert, and under officers already engaged, and who led it on by different avenues towards the national palace; so that by four in the evening the Convention was nearly invested on every side. Within the garden of the Thuilleries and around the national palace were collected the troops destined for the defence of the Convention; and which were advantageously posted with cannon to guard the several avenues by which approaches might be made. The members remained within the hall, prepared to await the issue of the day. The disposition, therefore, was that of besiegers against besieged, and which grew out of the disparity of numbers on each side; for on that of the Convention, taking the whole together, there were not more than 6,000; whilst on the side of the sections, there were in activity at least 10,000, and a still greater body in arms, which was supposed to be on the same side, or at least neutral. The countenance too of the parties bespoke a strong sympathy for their respective situations; that of those without exhibited an air of cheerfulness and alacrity, and which nothing but the confidence of success could inspire, whilst that of those within was dejected and melancholy. The action commenced a little after five in the evening by the advance of the troops of the sections, and ended about ten by their retreat. Wherever they approached they were repulsed by heavy discharges of artillery and musketry, which ranged and cleared the streets of their columns, as soon as presented. For some time, towards the close, the contest was sustained on the part of the sections, from the windows of the neighbouring houses; and from whence, perhaps, more of the troops were slain than from any other quarter. The loss on either side is unknown, and perhaps will continue so, and the reports are so various and contradictory, that they furnish but little data whereon to found a conjecture. Judging, however, from what I saw of the disposition of the troops who were presented at the corner of streets, or when advancing by the head of the column only, and of the time and nature of the action, which was by intervals, I cannot think that more than 500 were killed and wounded on both sides; though some of the reports make it as many thousands. It was generally understood by the assailants, that little or no opposition would be made, and that two of the regular regiments, in particular, were on their side, and that they would so declare themselves when the crisis approached. But in this they were mistaken; for all those troops behaved with great bravery and intrepidity, acquiting themselves as they had done before on the Rhine; having been drawn from the army of the north. Indeed, the probability is, the report was only circulated to inspire the troops of the sections with confidence, and to produce a suitable impression on the citizens of Paris in general. Many circumstances occurred in the course of the commotion, to countenance this opinion, of which the strongest is that, although it lasted until about 10 at night, yet by the citizens generally it was abandoned or feebly supported after the first onset, and repulse which immediately followed; and after which it was sustained principally by those who were really and truly the parties to it; for as such the great bulk of those who were in the rank ought not to be considered. This opinion is likewise countenanced by a train of incidents which attended this movement, from 10 at night to its close, and which was about 12 the next day. The troops of the Convention kept their ground all night, being unwilling to press as far as they might have done, the advantage gained; since it appeared, that by such pressure they might slay more of their countrymen, but not gain a more complete victory. On the other hand, the troops of the sections filed off gradually in small parties, as the darkness of the night or other circumstances favoured; till finally none were left, except those who were not properly of that description. By the morn every thing was tranquil, as if nothing had passed. At the entrance of every street you saw the pavement taken up, and waggons and other impediments obstructing the passage; but not a centinel was to be seen. The only armed force, remaining in opposition to the Convention, was of the section of Lepelletier, consisting of a few hundred only, and which had in part retired and was retiring to its commune as a place of retreat, rather than of defence. But now the scene began to change and exhibit to view precisely the reverse of what was seen the day before,—the besieged becoming the besiegers; for by this time the troops of the Convention were advancing towards the commune of this section, under the command of Barras, who had commanded formerly on the great epoch of the 9th Thermidor, and of Berruyer, who made regular approaches and by different routes, till finally this corps was completely surrounded. A peremptory summons was then sent to it to surrender, and which was immediately obeyed, by laying down their arms and submitting to the will of the conquerors; and thus was this movement crushed; the authority of the Convention vindicated, and Paris restored to complete tranquillity, and within less than 24 hours after the action commenced.

Such was the order, and such the issue of this contest: A contest, in many respects, the most interesting and critical that I have yet witnessed, and which promised, had the assailants succeeded, not perhaps essentially to impede or vary the direct course of the revolution; but, most probably, to involve the nation in a civil war; open a new scene of carnage more frightful than any yet seen, and deluge the country by kindred arms with kindred blood. In this view the character and object of the movement, on the part of the insurgents, merit some attention.

You have already seen that the decrees above mentioned were the ostensible, if not the real, cause of this controversy, and these you have. But to enable you to form a just estimate of its merits in other respects, and thereby of the probable views of the insurgents, it will be necessary for me to state other facts, and which preceded the final appeal to arms. These decrees, as you likewise know, were submitted with the constitution to the people, and according to a report of the convention by them adopted. But the verity of this report, of which I herewith send you a copy, was denied by the sections. By the report, however, you will perceive that the names of the departments voting for and against the decrees, were published some time since, and to which it may be added, that no department or commune has since complained; that the statement given of its vote was untrue. Still a doubt arises upon it, admitting that a majority of those who voted, was in favour of the decrees, whether those who did vote for them constituted a majority of French citizens entitled to vote, and upon which I cannot yet positively decide. The sections affirm the contrary, and likewise contend, that all who did not vote ought to be counted against the decrees. It is probable that some of the communes, foreseeing a storm gathering from that source, did not choose to vote for or against them, and therefore evaded the question by design, and it is certain that in others, it was understood by the people, that the question was taken upon the constitution and the decrees together; for latterly this was notified to the convention by several who had voted for the decrees, and particularly Nantes, to prevent a misapprehension of what their real intention was. I send you, however, the several papers which illustrate this point, and by which you will be enabled to form as correct an opinion on it, as present lights will admit: Observing further, that the report made by the convention respecting the decrees, was made, as you will perceive, at the same time with that upon the constitution; and that another report, containing a complete detail of the proceedings of every commune, is making out for the satisfaction of the community at large, and which was commenced by order of the Convention, immediately after the first one was rendered. It is to be wished that this had been some time since published; but when it is recollected that the publication must contain the proceedings of upwards of 7000 primary assemblies, many of which are perhaps, lengthy; impartial people will perceive, that it could not be soon done, especially when it is also recollected, that the whole of the interval since the order was given, has been a time of unusual fermentation and trouble.

Under these circumstances, the electoral assemblies were to meet, and the day of meeting was not distant. The decrees, and the evidence of their adoption were before France, and would, of course, be before these assemblies: Nor were the electors bound by any legal penalty to regard them, if they thought they were not adopted, or even disapproved them. The presumption, therefore, was (and especially if they discredited the report of the convention) that every assembly, whose constituents voted against the decrees, would disregard them; and, rejecting the two thirds of the present Convention, vote for whom they pleased; leaving it to those who were elected, by the several departments, to the legislature of the new government, whether they were entirely new men, or partly such, and partly of the Convention,—according to the mode that each department might adopt, to settle the point among themselves, and with the Convention, who should constitute the legislature of that government; or whether the whole proceeding should be declared void, and a new election called for; and which, in that event, would most probably have been the case. But the party opposed to the Convention, preferred a different series of measures, whereby to forward its views; the details whereof, so far as I have any knowledge of them, I will now communicate.

The primary assemblies were by law, to meet on the 10th of Fructidor, and dissolve on the 15th. In general, however, those of Paris prolonged their sitting beyond the term appointed; and many of them declared their sessions permanent, and exhibited, in other respects, a tone of defiance and great animosity towards the existing government. Finally, however, the primary assemblies were dissolved; and after which the sections of Paris, to whom the same spirit was now communicated, became the channel, or rather the instruments, of the same policy; many of whom likewise declared their sessions permanent, and assumed, in other respects a tone equally unfriendly and menacing towards the Convention. The section of Lepelletier in particular, which is in the centre of Paris, and which always was, and still is, the theatre of its greatest gaiety and dissipation, took the lead in these councils. At one time it presented an address to the Convention, copiously descanting upon the horrors of terrorism, demanding that those who were called terrorists, should not only be inhibited the right of voting, but forthwith punished; and that the troops in the neighborhood of Paris should be stationed further off, although there were then in the neighborhood not more than 3,000 foot, and 600 horse, and which were there for six months before. At another time it placed, by its own arrêté, under the safeguard of the primary assemblies, all those who had delivered their opinions in those assemblies, and invited the other sections of Paris to form a meeting of 48 commissioners, to declare to all France the sentiments of this commune upon the state of affairs in the present juncture. On the 10th of Vendémiaire, this section resolved that a meeting of the electoral corps should be held at the Theatre Français on the next day, and admonished the other sections to a like concurrence; as likewise to escort the electors to the place of rendezvous, and protect the assembly whilst sitting, with an armed force, if necessary. A partial meeting was in consequence held there, and which continued its sitting for some time after a proclamation was issued by the Convention, ordering the electors to disperse. Indeed it was not without great difficulty that this proclamation was read before the door of that assembly. An armed force was then ordered out under

General Menou, the commandant of the guard, to support the proclamation; but they were gone before he arrived. On the 12th, this section issued other inflammatory arrêtés; and on the night of the 12th, another fruitless attempt was made by the government to surround the commune of this section, and secure its members; for which failure, Genl. Menou, who withdrew the troops after he had surrounded it, was degraded, and the command transferred to Barras. On the 13th, the catastrophe took place and ended as I have already stated.

That the party in question meant to subvert the revolution, and restore the ancient monarchy, and that the destruction of the Convention was the first step in the train of those measures, which were deemed necessary to accomplish it, cannot be doubted. A slight attention only to the above facts sufficiently demonstrates the truth of the assertion in all its parts. Even in the primary assemblies, a ground was taken incompatible with the present system: Some free latitude, it is true, the people have a right to take in those assemblies, however limited or special the object may be, upon which they are convened to decide. But as soon as the sections took the same ground, acting in harmony with the electoral corps, in contempt of the law, and in defiance of the convention, the case was altered. From that moment rebellion was announced in form, and the sword of civil war was completely unsheathed; nor could it be restored whilst the convention survived, or without a counter-revolution, otherwise than by reducing the revolted sections to order. Fortunately the latter was the issue, and in consequence whereof every thing has since progressed as the friends of the revolution have wished. The revolted sections were immediately afterwards disarmed, and without opposition, and the electoral corps is now legally convened (those of it who have not, in dread of punishment, made their escape) and with a disposition to be more observant of the decrees, and accommodating to the existing government.

But, if this party had succeeded in its attack upon the convention, what would have followed? Would it likewise have succeeded in the other object, to which this was only a step? A conjectural answer can only be given to a suppositious case. My opinion then is, that although the impression would have been a deep one, yet the ultimate issue would have been the same. It is said, and perhaps with truth, that in case the attack succeeded, it was intended the electoral corps should immediately assemble, and place itself, in some measure, at the head of France. The overthrow of the Convention would have left the nation without a government or head, to influence public measures; and in which case, this corps, being a legal one, and at the head of this great City, would have had stronger pretensions to the public attention, than any whatever. 'Tis not, however, to be presumed, that it would have assumed the reins of government; but it would have doubtless undertaken to admonish, and the probability is, that in such a state of things, its admonition would have been regarded. With this view, it is believed that the crisis was brought on, at that precise point of time, before the meeting of the electoral assemblies, to admit, in the interval, the communication of the event (in case it were perpetrated) to all France, without allowing to the people sufficient time to recover from the dismay and confusion into which they would be thereby thrown. In such a state of things this corps might have made a great impression upon the whole nation, supported as it would appear to be, by all Paris; and as it really would be, at least to that stage, by a considerable portion. At the head of this corps was already placed the old ci-devant Duke of Nivernois,—a man not without some literary merit, and whose character had been so free from enormity, and his temper so dormant, that, although imprisoned, and in the list of those who are deemed, under what is called the reign of Robespierre, a fit subject for the guillotine, yet he survived that reign, and received his life as a boon from those who were now threatened with destruction. It was said he declined the presidency; but it is also believed, that his modest disqualification was more the effect of an accurate calculation of chances, in the great game they were playing, than of principle; and of course, that if the blow succeeded, he might be prevailed on to serve. A majority of the corps, many of whom were likewise ci-devant nobles, was believed to be of the same principles. The nation would therefore have beheld, on the one side, the Convention overthrown, perhaps massacred, and whose members were, in general, known to be attached to the revolution; and on the other, the electoral corps, with this person at its head, and which it would, of course, conclude was decidedly of opposite political principles; the latter advanced forward upon the ruin of the former, and in some sort possessed of the reins of government. Surely no opportunity more favourable to the views of the royalists could have been sought, than this would have presented. How they meant to improve it, had fortune placed them in that situation, is not known, nor is it probable it will be; for it is to be presumed, that whatever the plan was, admitting there was one already formed for such an event, it had been concerted by the leaders only, and was not to be unfolded, until after the sections were thus far plunged into the same atrocity with themselves. There were two ways by which this opportunity might have been improved; the first, by an immediate declamation in favour of royalty; the second, by electing their own deputies, and inviting the other departments to do the same, for the purpose of putting the constitution in motion. Had the first been adopted, the nation would have, doubtless, have been greatly confounded, and in the moment of dismay, the royalists would, most probably, have come forward, and the patriots lain quiet. Soon, however, in Paris herself, symptoms of discontent would have been seen, and perhaps even in some of those sections which were foremost in the late revolt; many of whose citizens had joined the opposition from principle, in respect to the right of suffrage; some because they had been persecuted, or censured as terrorists, and only because they were patriots; and others because they doubted the political integrity of the present house, and wished it changed. All of these would have been struck with consternation, when they heard that a king was proclaimed, and would have looked back with horror at the scene through which they had passed.

By this time too, some one of the armies would have been seen advancing towards Paris, and which would most probably have had little to do: For I am persuaded, that as soon as the citizens recovered from the extravagance into which they had been betrayed, they would be among the first to fall upon their betrayers. Had the second been adopted, it is probable it would have secured the elections in favour of the royalists; the decrees would have been of course rejected; nor would any of the present members have been re-elected. Soon, however, this would have been seen by the people, and being seen, half the danger would have been provided against. In the memory of those who were friendly to the revolution, (and the catalogue of its friends must be a long one, counting those only whose fathers and sons were slaughtered in its defence on the frontiers,) the destruction of the Convention, under whose banners they had bled, would form a moral cause that would hang heavy on the shoulders of the subsequent administration. The manner of the suffrage, though in form free, would be deemed an usurpation, and the slightest deviation afterwards become a signal for revolt. If they used their power with violence, the same effect would be produced as if a king were immediately proclaimed, and if they used it with moderation they might perhaps prevent the calamity of another crisis; and whiling away in office the time allotted by the Constitution, be enabled in the interim, so far to efface the memory of what had passed, as to secure to themselves afterwards a retreat which would exempt them from punishment. But in neither case would they be able to restore the ancient monarchy. You will observe that my reasoning is founded upon a belief that the army is sound; that the great bulk of the citizens of Paris are so likewise; and that the farmers or cultivators in general, if not decidedly in favor of the revolution, though in my opinion they are, are at least, not against it; and which belief, though perhaps erroneous, is the result of an attentive observation to such facts and circumstances as have appeared to me to merit attention.

But you will ask, if Paris is on the side of the revolution, how happened that such a force was formed there against the Convention, whilst so small a one was marshalled on its side? Let us first establish facts and then reason from them. Paris consists of 48 sections; and of 8 only were actually in arms against the Convention, three for it, and the others neutral. Of those too, who were sent by the eight sections, it is presumable from the peremptory manner of their retreat, and the ease with which they were afterwards disarmed, as likewise by their uniform declarations, at the time and since,—that the greater number did not expect to be led against the Convention, or if they did, that they went with reluctance; so that, the real force which marched out for the purpose of actual hostility was in my opinion, inconsiderable: And this too, it is said, was in part composed of adventurers from other quarters, and in some instances even of foreigners. Still however, there was an actual revolt by those sections, and at best a neutrality on the part of the others; the three who declared themselves for the Convention excepted. How account for this? That the royalists had gained the preponderance in some few of the sections, and particularly that of Lepelletier, is certain. But that this was not the case with many is presumable. It is well known that the inhabitants of Paris in general, wished to get rid of their present deputies, and for reasons heretofore explained. The opposition to the decrees, therefore, may be thus accounted for; and with the greater propriety, because it is certain they were opposed and even by the royalists, upon republican principles; the unalienable right of suffrage, &c. and by which an impression was made in the primary assemblies upon the audience, and thence gradually extended throughout the city. In the primary assemblies too every person was allowed to speak; and it happened, that among the royalists there were some good speakers, and who by taking popular ground, engrossed for the time the public attention; by means whereof they were enabled to practise more extensively upon the credulity of the less enlightened of their countrymen, than they were aware of. It often happens when a collision takes place between friends, and even upon a trivial cause, that one act of irritation begets another, till finally the parties become irreconcilable. How much more easy was it then for artful men, at the present moment, to prevail over the ignorant, and seduce them into error; especially when it is known that the latter already wished a change; that they thought they had a right to make it, and of which right they could not be deprived without the sacrifice of their liberty, in whose cause they had already so long contended, and so greatly suffered.

How explain the extraordinary phenomenon, why the very sections, who on the 4th of Prairial were on opposite sides, should now shift their ground,—

so as that those who then supported the convention, should now be against it, and those who opposed should now be for it? Taking the convention as the standard, it remains only in any case to explain the motive of such party as wanders from it; for *that* circumstance alone creates doubt, and of course alone requires explanation. No one will ask why such a party supports the convention, because there can be no motive for such an enquiry. In some cases a party yielding such support may have less honourable motives for it than another party had. I think I have seen such myself: But in no case can the object be a counter-revolutionary one. To this enquiry, then, in this view, I have already given a satisfactory answer, at least so far as I am able to do it; for I have already explained what I deemed in general the cause of the aberration of the sections upon the present occasion, as I did upon the former one; that of the Faubourg St. Antoine and whose present conducts warrants the opinion then given upon that head.

But how happened it, that so many of the disaffected were chosen into the electoral corps, as to give the royalists a preponderance there? How could a people attached to the revolution commit the care of it to those who were its foes, especially to such as, by their station and character, were universally known to be such? This touches a subject extremely interesting; for it leads to facts over which a veil has yet been thrown, but to which history will doubtless do justice; and in which case it will present to view a scene of horror, in some respects, not perhaps less frightful than that which was exhibited under the reign of terror. Behind the curtain, as it were, for it has made but little noise in several of the departments, the terrible scourge of terror has shifted hands, and latterly been wielded by the royalists; who, beginning with the subaltern, and perhaps wicked agents of the former reign, had persecuted and murdered many of the soundest patriots, and best of men. To such a height has this evil risen, and so general was the imputation of terrorism, that in certain quarters the patriots in general were not only discouraged, but in a great measure depressed. It is affirmed to be a fact, by those who ought to know, and who merit belief, that in some of those quarters, and even where the preponderance in point of numbers was greatly in their favour, none attended the primary assemblies; and that in others a few only attended, and who took no part in the proceedings. This, therefore, will account why the royalists took the lead in those assemblies, and why so many of them were chosen into the electoral corps.

But by what strange vicissitude of affairs was this effect produced? How could it happen under an administration unfriendly to royalty? In truth, the explanation is distinctly marked by preceding events, and has been in part unfolded, in preceding communications. Terrorism, or what was then called so, the persecution of the royalists, had gone to such a length, that it became indispensably necessary to end it. To this object, therefore, the whole force of the government was directed, and with effect, for it was accomplished. But in striking at terrorism, perhaps by the unguarded manner of the blow, perhaps by those consequences which are inseparable from such vibrations, and which I deem the most likely,—an elevation was given for a while to the opposite extreme. The terrorism of that day was the excess of the passion for liberty, but it was countenanced by those in office, as necessary in their judgment, to bring about the revolution; nor were its acts displayed in private assassination. On the contrary, they were sanctified by public judgments and public executions. The most culpable, therefore, were those who expiated for their crimes on the 9th Thermidor. But with others in general, and even where the excess was criminal, the intention was otherwise. At that point, therefore, which discriminated between the vicious extravagancies of the moment, and the spirit of patriotism itself, should the scale have been suspended. And there by the law it was suspended; for I do not recollect any act of the Convention which passed beyond it. Special outrages were, it is true, specially corrected; but even in these cases I do not know an instance where the correction was disproportioned to the offence. But so nice was the subject upon which they had to act, and so delicate is the nerve of human sensibility, that it was perhaps impossible for the government under existing circumstances, to moderate its rigour towards the royalists, without giving, to a certain degree, an encouragement to royalty. In this view, therefore, it is to be presumed the late event will produce a beneficial effect; for as the views of the royalists were completely unmasked, and defeated, and which were always denied to exist, until they were thus unmasked,—it cannot otherwise than tend to open the eyes of the community in that respect, and in the degree to repress the arrogant spirit of royalty. To your judgment, however, these facts and observations, in respect to the late movement, are respectfully submitted.

I have lately been honoured with your several favours of May 29th, June the 1st and 7th, and of July the 2d, 8th, 14th, 21st, 29th and 30th; all of which came to hand almost at the same time, and generally by the route of England; and to which I will certainly pay the utmost attention. As, however, this letter has already gone to an unreasonable length, and especially as I wish you to be correctly informed of the character and fate of the movement in question, I think it best to despatch this immediately, reserving a more particular reply to those favours for a future communication. For the present, however, permit me to add, that as yet no complaint has been made to me against the treaty; nor have

I heard any thing from the committee on the subject, since the application requesting information, in what light they were to view the reports respecting it; and which was made soon after the treaty was concluded. If any thing is intended to be said, I think it will not be said until after the new government is organized; nor then, until after it is known that the treaty is ratified; and in which case I have reason to apprehend I shall hear from them on the subject. I trust, however, let the event in that respect, or the opinion which the Committee may entertain of that event, be what it may, I shall find that the same amicable and dispassionate councils still prevail towards us, that have been shewn for some time past. To inculcate which disposition, not only by the documents and lights derived from you, but by such others as my own imperfect experience, and often too wandering judgment, have supplied has been, and be assured will continue to be, equally the object of my most earnest wishes, and undeviating efforts.

With great respect and esteem I have the honour to be, Sir, your very obedient and humble servant,

JA^s. MONROE.

P.S. October 25th. As the vessel by which this will be forwarded will not sail until a gentleman, who is now here, arrives at Havre, I have kept the letter with me for the purpose of adding to it what might immediately happen before his departure. On the day after to-morrow, the new government is to convene, and the prospect is now favourable that it will then convene, and precisely on the ground stated in the preceeding letter. Some symptoms were latterly seen which gave cause for apprehension, that the expiring moments of the convention would be moments of great agony and convulsion. Some denunciations and counter-denunciations were made, proceeding from causes connected with the late movement; but happily they are over, without producing any serious effect. A commission of 5 was appointed to make a supplemental report, respecting that movement, and it was expected by many it would end in a proposal to annul the proceedings of several of the departments, whose primary assemblies were said to be under constraint by the royalists, and probably also in the arrestation of several deputies; but that commission has freed every one from uneasiness on that account, by a report just made; and which proposes only some new provisions for the trial of offenders in that movement, and others in several of the departments, who have committed atrocities of various kinds, under the pretext of punishing the terrorists. Every moment must be deemed critical, in the existing circumstances of this country; being at the eve of a great revolution, a transition from one government to another; and especially when it is known, that there is a party, not despicable in point of numbers, and less so in activity and talents, always ready to seize every incident that occurs to throw things into confusion; and which party is connected, not only with the emigrants abroad, but with the surrounding powers, by whom the necessary means are furnished for the purpose. But yet it seems as if the Convention would retain its strength to the last moment of its existence, and transmit its powers unimpaired to its successors. The decrees are said to be universally observed, and the leading members of both sides of the house are in general re-elected; these are to elect the others, so as to make up the two-thirds of the new government.

Lately Jourdan received a check on the other side of the Rhine, and which occasioned his falling back to the Rhine, upon which river both his and the army of Pichegru are posted. The cause of this is not distinctly known; but certain it is, that the deputy of the military section of the Committee of public safety has been since arrested, upon a suspicion of treachery; as are three others, upon a charge of treasonable correspondence with their enemies; but with what propriety I do not pretend to determine. 'Tis worthy of remark, that it was known in England and in Basle before it happened, that there would be a movement here at the time it happened; at which time too, the count d'Artois landed from England upon the Isle Dieu, near the French coast, opposite the Vendée, where he still is.

A report was yesterday made to the Convention, of an important advantage gained in a rencounter in the Mediterranean, in which the French took a ship of the line and damaged greatly two others; and likewise took 14 merchant ships richly laden and estimated at an enormous sum. Two other advantages in other quarters are spoken of, still more signal than this, but not by authority.

Moneron is returned, but whether by order of the French government (as I suspect, and in consequence of the fortunate issue of the late movement) or the failure of his mission, be it what it might, is uncertain. Be assured if Mr. Jay's treaty is ratified, it will excite great discontent here. Of this, however, I shall be able to speak with more certainty, after the new government is organized.

TO JAMES MADISON.
PARIS, July 5, 1796.

DEAR SIR,—Yesterday the Fourth of July was celebrated here by the Americans. I intended to have done it, but having given them an entertainment last year they returned the compliment this. You will observe by the copy sent in, that [in the toast] to the American government the term "executive" is used and not "president." The course of the business was as follows: The project [of the celebration] began first with the friends of the British treaty, and fell through, and was then [taken] up by its enemies, and after which the others came in. But the first party had appointed a committee (or rather the second in order) and who conducted the business, the majority of whom were for giving "the Congress" only, or drinking no toasts. I told them if they would give the "executive," I supposed all would be satisfied and I would attend and which I could not otherwise do. The first party however in order were not consulted or disliked what was done and when the toasts [were] gone through, one of them ro[se] and proposed a volunteer in favor of G[en] Washington &c. and which was [opposed] by some of the others. This made a noise here and perhaps will with you and as some slander may in consequence be leveled at me, I therefore give you the facts. The Minister of France and the foreign ministers were present.

I trouble you with another incident of the same kind: Paine having resolved to continue in Europe some time longer and knowing it was inconvenient for me to keep him longer in my family and wishing also to treat on our politics which he could not well do in my house, left me some time since. He thinks the President winked at his imprisonment and wished he might die in goal, and bears him resentment for it; also he is preparing an attack upon him of the most virulent kind. Through a third person[2] I have endeavoured to divert him from it without effect. It may be said I have instigated him but the above is the truth.

But to come to a subject of more importance.—I think myself ill treated here by the administration and doubt how to act in consequence of it so as to advance the public interests without injuring my own character. The following is a literal extract from my instructions, [with] professions testifying the President's attachment to the French revolution "and to remove all jealousy with respect to the mission to London,—You may say that he [Jay] is positively forbidden to make the engagements between this country and France. It is not improbable that you will be obliged to encounter on this head suspicions of various kinds; but you must declare the motives of that mission to be to obtain immediate compensation for our plundered property and restitution of the ports"—with much more in the same spirit. An equivocation may be taken on the word *motives* but the counter sense is a declaration that he had no other business there and which was otherwise.

The object I presume was to lay a good basis here by means of my mission and taking advantage of which and of the success of France which would cost

2. *Dr. Enoch Edwards.* [HAMILTON.]

us the respect of the English Court; make a barter for commercial stipulation of a faith and alliance with France and which probably would have succeeded had I not blown them up by discourse in the Convention and by their own documents by means whereof that Court lost all confidence in them, thinking their professions insincere and of course *that* what it gave was given for *nothing,* or had the negociator possessed as capable a head as he did a corrupt heart.

Since the ratification of the treaty by the President I have received but three letters from the Department of State and which were from Timothy Pickering and the last now six months—April, and these were not of a very conciliatory kind. After denying that this government had any right to complain of the treaty, he adds that the article respecting contraband inserted the old list by way of admonition to our people to avoid danger: that the provisional article was useful to us as it paid for contraband and, in respect to other seizures that we were the only judges whether we would go to war for cause or otherwise accommodate the difficulty and would never consult any other power on that head; and with many professions of regard for this country or explanation of further views breaks off the subject and thus ends it.[3]

This tone may proceed either from a desire to court a rupture with this country or be the effect of wounded pride and it would be natural to ascribe it to the last cause if the President had not owned that the ratification of the treaty hazarded a war here and if policy did not dictate, as the way to avoid it a more conciliatory one; or if he was not conciliating, through Gouverneur Morris, at the same moment the Court in England or if the gasconades business of the flag[4] had not been a desperate movement calculated to deceive the people of America while it gave disgust here or if a different tone had not been assured in my instructions before the issue of the treaty with England was known and whilst appearances here were necessary to obtain a favourable issue. These considerations make the nature of this conduct more doubtful than it otherwise would be.

It is however the interest of America to avoid a rupture here and I have in consequence done all in my power to prevent it and I think and without vanity with some effect. If things stand as they do here and our admistration changes everything will come right. A new treaty may be formed of a different stamp from that with England and which will not only tie the two republics closer together than they were ever before and by ties of interest, but by contrasting

---

3. *The original letter is practically entirely in cipher. Some difficulty has been experienced in deciphering it, as many of the characters are indistinct and others not correctly given (according to the key) by the writer.* [HAMILTON.]
4. *Article XVIII. of Jay's treaty, "Contraband Goods."* [HAMILTON.]

its credit and advantage with the distress of the other by reviewing the friendship and harmony with this country which was nearly gone, and which is desired by our citizens, completely relieve us of our present dangers and difficulties and ruin the aristocratic faction.

But if we do not change the administration [through] timid influences with the republican party, who will always be branded as anarchists, and the present administration continuing and the interest of the two nations requiring it and surmounting all obstacles, a new treaty will be formed here under its auspices and which though less favorable than might otherwise be obtained will serve as a colouring whereby to deceive posterity as to the nature of the crisis we have passed as well as many of the present day with respect to the merits of the contending parties: still however I consider it as the effect of passion for Washington is an honest man.

I have suffered much personal mortification here and for reasons that are obvious; and should demand my recall, did I not think that my continuance for some time longer was somewhat necessary in the views above suggested and did I not wish rather to be recalled than to demand it for in the last case I am to defend my character to my country and which I would do by a publication of my whole correspondence and instructions and the like and which I could not otherwise well do. How long I shall be able to bear my situation I cannot say. I will bear it however till I hear from you in reply to this or until the ensuing election shall confirm in office the present tenants.

I should like much to make a new treaty with this government after things are settled on both sides because I think a good one might be made for both countries; and in my opinion here is the place to make it. Let the trust be committed to a minister in Philadelphia and his own credit is the object; but appeal to the fulfillment itself and a different merit may be found. And having borne the storm whilst my efforts were employed only to prevent disunion I should like to have an opportunity to promote union. However this is of no consequence.

I most earnestly hope that Mr. Jefferson will be elected and that he will serve. If he is elected every thing will most probably be right here from that moment and afterwards on the other side of the channel. And in my opinion there never was such an opportunity offered for the acquisition of fame in the restoration of national credit abroad and at home as is now present presented, independent of the gratification an honest mind will always feel in rendering useful service to his country. He will be able at the same time that he secures the preponderating republican councils and gives stability to republican government, to conciliate the well meaning of the other party and thus give peace to his country.

In a few words I give you the state of the war. All Italy is in truth subjugated and peace made with all the powers (either by definitive treaties or by provisional agreements), Naples excepted, and who has an Envoy now on the road to treat also. They have all paid or agreed to pay considerable sums, given up pictures, the most celebrated pieces of art and in truth accepted their authorities from this government. The representative of St. Peter has agreed to pay 21 millions of livres for the provisional suspension of arms, to give up 100 pictures & 300 manuscripts; to exclude the British from his ports etc., etc. The French have entered the territory of the Grand Duke and put a garrison in Leghorn, upon the principle that the English held it and had violated against France the neutrality of Tuscany. In entering they laid hold of [manuscript effaced] tapistry they could find which they say was worth 7 or 8 millions of livres. And upon the Rhine the same good fortune has attended the French arms. In several engagements the French have prevailed; and seem now to have gained a complete preponderance. In short their success seems complete, so much so however as to threaten ruin to the Emperor if he does not make peace and which is therefore in all probability now at hand. England will be reserved for the last and against whom the resentment of this country if not increased by its tyde of good fortune is certainly not diminished. Projects are spoken of in regard to that country which never seemed to merit attention before but which now and especially if a peace is made with the Emperor, assume a more serious aspect. You will conjecture these and therefore I will not mention them.

July 31.—This is the third copy I have sent you of the above, or rather this is the original of the two already forwarded. Since the above the scene has varied but little in any respect. The French continue to hold their superiority on the Rhine, but press forward with great circumspection, the Austrians retiring to strong positions, and protecting their retreat by strong fortifications. Frankfort is taken by the French and upon which city and imposition was laid of 35 million florins but which it is thought cannot be paid.

This will be committed to Dr. Edwards and who will hasten home as fast as circumstances will permit. He is possessed of very extensive and correct information of affairs here as well as in regard to those which concern this republic and the war in general, as our own affairs, and to him therefore I refer you for such details as are not here communicated.

[5] From what I learn from the bearer of this and notwithstanding my efforts to prevent it Paine will probably compromise me by publishing some things

---

5. *The cipher was again had recourse to for this last paragraph.* [HAMILTON.]

which he picked up while in my house. It was natural unaided as I have been [here] or rather harassed from every possible quarter that I talked with this man, but it was not so to expect that he would commit such a breach of confidence as well as of ingratitude. Perhaps it may appear to proceed from other sources. If so my name will not be involved and that is greatly to be wished. But otherwise the above is the state of the facts. Upon no point but in my relations with either government am I personally uneasy, let what may happen and this is a thing of a personal delicacy more than anything else.

TO GEORGE CLINTON.[6]
PARIS, July 25, 1796.

DEAR SIR,—I have just heard that some benevolent minded people in Phila. have circulated a report that I am engaged in speculations in this country in land &c. & with Mr. Skipwith: and that I omitted to forward or neglected, the remittance hence of a sum of money committed to me by draft of Swan upon the H. of Dallardt & Swan here to be remitted to Holland to our bankers. I enclose you the affidavit of Mr. Skipwith to disprove the first calumny, & the correspondence with this govt., our bankers in Holland &c to disprove the 2d. In truth I have bought nothing here but the house & lot on wh. I live, the furniture which I use—my books & a few other trifling articles wh. I intend to carry with me when I return home such as a few glasses &c. The house I mean to keep till I set out home—having bought it to live in, in a retired & pleasant part of the town from a man who sold it to pay his debts, (often the case here & elsewhere) an architect, & who is now my neighbour. I have never bought another foot of ground in this country or any other article not above mentioned. I might it is true embark in speculations here, & purchase rich seats for two years purchase, & presume I might procure the money to do it: for national domains sell at that rate: but I declare to you solemnly that I have not, nor shall I embark in such a business: not that I think it so culpable to do it, as to buy the claims of our soldiers before a provision was made for their payment, & then make the provision; or to buy up the debts of individual states before they were assumed & then assume the payment of them as many profligate men in office with us were known to have done. But because I will have nothing to do with a traffic dishonorable in some situations and commendable in few. With respect to the purchase of the house in which I live, I see no greater impropriety in the measure than in renting it. A house I must have over my head, and I think it more creditable to own it than to rent it, & so far as it applies to the confidence of this govt., a thing of some importance, it was certainly calculated to produce a good effect.

Upon the other point, the correspondence I enclose (the originals of wh. I have) will give you such full satisfaction that I need add nothing upon it. You will perceive by it, how much trouble I had with that contest—how anxious I was to conduct it to the best advantage of the U. States—and how little ground there is for censure. You will observe too that this item in my duties here (for comparatively with others then pressing it was a very trifling one) was at a moment when I had little leisure for it, & will therefore I think be surpris'd that I got thro. it so well, or kept up such a regular chain of correspondence. I think you will also be surprised that I bore with such patience the unbecoming stile of the bankers letters to me, & wh. in truth upon now reading them over I am surprised at myself—but I recollect my motive was to avoid anything wh. by giving offense might diminish the zeal of others, labouring always by getting rid of the money to rid myself at the same time of their unpleasant & disgusting correspondence.

I defy the malice of my enemies to impeach the ground on wh. I stand & wh. is correctly as above stated. Perhaps I may be near them before they are aware & then may discuss these things personally. I prefer much that mode & shall reserve myself the right of so doing on my return if worth my notice. In the meantime I enclose for your inspection & afterwards to be forwarded to Mr. Madison the within papers on these topics. If you have heard of these calumnies or others have heard of them, you are at liberty taking extracts from these papers to shew the papers before forwarding them to Govr. Clinton, Chr. Livinston, M. Smith, Mr. Gelston or any few others of yours & my friends— particularly Mr. Governeur & Mr. Knox. I shall in that case thank you or indeed in any case if you think fit, to explain the above, or shew such papers as you think fit to my friend Mrs. Montgomery who always takes an interest in what concerns my honor & welfare to whom & whose family as to the above mentioned friends I beg you to make my affectionate regards.

TO JAMES MADISON.
Paris, Sept. 1st, 1796.[7]

Dear Sir,—This government has at last and against my most [earnest] efforts to prevent it sent an order to their minister to withdraw, giving for reason our treaty with England and declaring that the customary relations between

---

7. *In cipher.* [Hamilton.]

the two nations shall cease. I have no official communication and can not be more particular. After deliberating about seven months, they resolved that the honour of their country would be tarnished in their hands if they acted otherwise. I have detained them seven months from doing what they ought to have done at once. It is impossible to for see the consequences of this measure which I sincerely regret, but here no change can be expected and of course if the same councils prevail in America the alliance is at an end not to count the other injuries we shall receive from the loss of this nation so preponderant as it is with such valuable possessions in our seas. I do not know whether my functions are suspended. In any event I must wait the orders of our government. At this moment I receive a letter from Timothy [Pickering] in reply to my first on this subject addressed as from an overseer on the farm to one of his gang ascribing (if not absolutely the existenence of any complaint to me) yet that it is altogether owing to my misconduct that it broke out since I had acknowledged [a letter] from him three months before which he says proved they had no right to complain. Hence he concludes that I suppressed that luminous work to this [government]. I have yet given no answer nor do I at present propose it. It will occur to you that I could not defend the treaty until there was a charge brought against it and to prevent which was always the object of my efforts. Delay was therefore always favorable. This letter [from Pickering] corresponds so much with the publication in the New York paper[8] that it tends to create a suspicion they were written by the same hand, but these little Connecticut Jockey tricks are too easily seen through now a days to produce any effect. Poor Washington. Into what hands has he fallen!

TO THE SECRETARY OF STATE.
PARIS, September 10, 1796.

SIR,—I have been just favored with yours of the 13th of June; the only one received from the Department of State, since that of the 7th of January last, a note from Mr. Taylor [Chief Clerk of the Department of State.] of the 13th of May excepted.

---

8. *"The 'Minerva' of N.Y. lately announced, with an affected emphasis, a letter from Paris to N.Y., intimating that influential persons in the U.S. were urging measures on France which might force this country to chuse agnst. England as the only alternative for war against France. It is probable that categorical steps on the part of France towards us are anticipated as the consequence of what has been effected by the British party here, and that much artifice will be practised by it to charge them in some unpopular form on its Republican opponents."—Madison to Jefferson, May 22, 1796.* [HAMILTON.]

You charge me in this letter with a neglect of duty, in omitting, as you state, to dissipate by a timely and suitable application of the lights in my possession the discontents of this government, on account of our late treaty with England; and you support this charge by a reference to certain passages in my own correspondence, which state that this discontent broke out in February last, four months after I had received a letter from yourself and Mr. Randolph, upon the subject of that treaty; and whence you infer, and on account of the delay or interval which took place between the one and the other event, that I was inattentive to that important concern of my country, and urge the previous and strong symptoms of discontent which I witnessed and communicated, as an additional proof of my neglect.

Permit me to remark that this charge is not more unjust and unexpected, than the testimony by which you support it is inapplicable and inconclusive: Indeed it were easy to shew, that the circumstances on which you rely, if they prove any thing, prove directly the reverse of what you deduce from them.

If such discontent existed and the formal declaration of it, or commencement of measures in consequence of it was delayed (and the greater the discontent, and the longer the delay, the stronger the argument) and any inference applicable to me was drawn from the circumstance, I should suppose it would be precisely the opposite one from that which you draw. Where a discontent exists, it is natural and usual for the party feeling it, to endeavour to remove it, or express its sense of it; but the pursuit of an opposite conduct for a great length of time, and especially a time of revolution, and when a different and more peremptory one was observed to all the other powers, is no proof, without other documents of negligence in me.

But why did this discontent not break out before these letters were received? You saw by my communications, as early as December 1794, and which were frequently repeated afterwards, that it existed, was felt upon our affairs here, and was likely to produce the most serious ill consequences, if the cause continued to exist. If these accounts were correct, why did this government take no steps under its first impressions, and particularly in August 1795, when Paris was starving, and our vessels destined for the ports of France were seized and carried into England? Was not this a crisis difficult for me to sustain here; when the eyes of France were fixed upon me, as the representative of the nation upon whose friendship they had counted; as the man who had just before been the organ of declarations the most friendly? Why leave us afterwards, and until the last stage, to our unbiased deliberations upon that subject, and without an effort to impede their free course? Do difficulties like these, with the result which followed, give cause to suspect that I was idle or negligent at my post? That I was at any time a calm or indifferent spectator of a storm which was known to be rising, and which threatened injury to my country? Or that I withheld any light which came to my aid, and which might be useful in dissipating it?

I do not wish to be understood as assuming to myself the merit of this delay; because I know, thinking and feeling as the government did on this subject, that the strong bias of affection which this nation entertained for us, was the true cause of it. But I well know, that I have done every thing in my power, and from the moment of my arrival to the present time, to promote harmony between the two republics, and to prevent this from taking any step which might possibly disturb it, and which I have done as well from a sincere attachment to both, as from a persuasion, let the merit of the points in discussion be what they might, that a continual, temperate, and friendly conduct towards us was the wisest policy which this government could adopt, and would produce the best effect upon that union, which it is, I presume, equally its wish and its interest to preserve, and of course leave to its councils less cause hereafter for self reproach. It is from the sincerity of these motives and the knowledge this government has of it, that I have incessantly made efforts to preserve that harmony, and been heard in friendly communication, and often in remonstrance upon the topics connected with it, in a manner I could not otherwise have expected.

But you urge, that as I knew this discontent existed, I ought to have encountered and removed it. I do not distinctly comprehend the extent of this position, or what it was your wish, under existing circumstances, I should have done. Till the 15th of February, no complaint was made to me by this government against that treaty; nor did I know before that period that any would be; for from the moment of its organization till then, the utmost reserve was observed to me by it on that subject. The intimations which I witnessed, were written before the establishment of the present government, and drawn of course from circumstances which preceded it. Of the probable views therefore of the present government in that respect, I spoke only by conjecture. Was it then your wish, that because I suspected this government would be or was discontented with that treaty, that I should step forward, invite the discussion, and provoke the attack? Would it have been politic or safe for me to do it; and especially upon a subject so delicate, and important as that was! And had I done it, would I not have been justly censured for my rashness and indiscretion? And might not even different motives have been assigned for my conduct? To me, I own, it always appeared most suitable, as well as most wise, to stand on the defensive; and to answer objections only when they were made; upon the fair and reasonable presumption, till they were made, that none would be; and upon the principle, if none were made, that our object was obtained; and if there were, that then there would be sufficient time to answer them, and in a regular and official manner. By this however I do not wish to be understood, as having declined at any time informal friendly communications, on this or other subjects, when suitable occasions occurred; for the contrary was the case, as is already observed.

What the circumstances were, upon which I founded my opinion of the probable ill consequences of that treaty, in case it were ratified, were in general communicated, as they occurred. There was however one other, and which was particularly impressive at the time, omitted then, but which I now think proper to add, because it was that upon which I founded the intimation given you, in my letter of the 20th of October on that head. Calling one day, upon the subject of our Algerine affairs, informally, upon Jean de Brie, who had, in the committee of public safety, the American branch under his care, I found him engaged upon that treaty, with a copy of it before him, and other papers on the same subject. I began with the object of my visit, and from which he soon digressed upon the other topic, and with great asperity; adding that he was preparing a letter for me on that subject, to be submitted to the committee. I answered his charges in the manner which appeared to me most suitable, and finally asked him, if he had received the correspondence which took place on that subject between Mr. Adet and Mr. Randolph; and to which he replied that he had not. I then informed him I had that correspondence, which was an interesting one; and requested he would permit me to give him a copy of it; and further that he would delay his report to the committee, until after he had perused and fully weighed it, which he promised; and in consequence I immediately afterwards gave him a copy of that correspondence. This incident took place just before the movement of Vendemiaire, by which the execution of the project *contemplated* was probably prevented. I omitted this before, because I hoped it would never be revived; and because I did not wish to give more pain on this subject, and especially as I soon afterwards found that the treaty was ratified, than could be avoided. And I now mention it, as well to shew the strong ground upon which that intimation was given; as to prove that none of the lights furnished me, in that respect, were withheld.

So much I have thought proper to say in reply to your favor of the 13th of June; and now it remains for me to proceed with a detail of the further progress of this business here, since my last; at least so far as I am acquainted with it.

I sought immediately after my last was written, and obtained as soon as I possibly could obtain it, an informal conference with some members of the directoire, upon the subject of my last: beginning by expressing my concern to hear they were still dissatisfied with us, and proposed taking some step in consequence thereof; and which I sincerely regretted because I had concluded the contrary was the case, after the explanation I had given to their several complaints; and because I thought any measure which had an unfriendly aspect towards us, would be equally detrimental to theirs and our interest. They severally replied, they were dissatisfied with us, on account of our treaty with England, and thought that the honor of their country would be sullied in their hands, if they did not say so. I endeavoured to lead them into conversation upon the points to which they objected; but soon found they were averse to it, and were of the opinion that too much time had already been bestowed on that subject. One of the members however observed, that the abandonment of the principle that *free ships made free goods,* in favor of England, was an injury of a very serious kind to France; and which could not be passed by unnoticed. I told him, that in this nothing was abandoned, since by the law of nations, such was the case before; and of course that this article only delineated what the existing law was, as I had fully proved in my note to the minister of foreign affairs; that we were not bound to impose the new principle on other nations. He replied, if we could not carry that principle with England, nor protect our flag against her outrages, that that was always a reason why France should not complain; that they never asked us to go to war, nor intended so to do; but that the abandonment of that principle formally by treaty, at the time and under the circumstances we did it, in favor of that power, was quite a different thing. Finding that a further pressure at the time might produce an ill effect, and would certainly not produce a good one, I proceeded next to the other points, and to hint what I had heard of their intention with respect to Canada and Louisiana, and to which it was replied, that in regard to Canada, they had no object for themselves; and in regard to Louisiana, none which ought to disquiet us; that they sincerely wished us well, and hoped matters might be amicably adjusted, since they were disposed to meet suitable propositions to that effect with pleasure; adding in the close, that the minister of foreign affairs was instructed to communicate to me the arrêté they had passed; but in a manner to impress me with a belief it was done rather for the purpose of enabling me to transmit it to you, than address them at present further on the subject. Through other channels I have since heard, that this arrêté is withheld from me, and will be, until the dispatch is gone; and with a view of securing themselves against further interruption from me, in the present stage, upon the measure adopted.

From what information I can collect of the contents of this arrêté from other sources (for from the above none was collected) it is to suspend Adet's functions; instructing him to declare the motive of it; and which, I presume, will correspond with what was declared here, leaving him there for the present: But what he is farther to do is not suggested, nor can I form a conjecture of it, until I receive the communication promised by the minister of foreign affairs; and which I shall endeavour to procure, as soon as possible.

I herewith enclose you a copy of a communication from the minister of foreign affairs, with my reply to it; and by which it appears that a truce is obtained by our agent from the Regencies of Tunis and Tripoli, and with the aid of France.

I have the honor to be, Sir, your most ob.^t humble serv.^t

JA^s. MONROE.

TO THE SECRETARY OF STATE.
PHILADELPHIA, July 6, 1797.

SIR,—It was my wish, after the receipt of your letter of the 22^d of Aug. last announcing my recall, to repair home without delay, But as I did not receive the letter until some time in November, nor obtain my audience for taking leave of the French government till the first of Jany following, it was impossible for me to sail before the Spring without hazarding a winters passage, & to which I did not wish to expose my family. This explains the cause why I did not render myself here at a much earlier period.

I postponed my reply to that letter till my arrival, because I deemed it more suitable for many reasons to answer it in my own country than from a foreign one. I think proper however now to call your attention to the subject of that letter, with a view to justify myself against any imputations that have been or were intended to be raised against me, by the measures it announced. I observe by that letter that although you found this measure, principally on the ground taken in that of the 13th of June preceeding, yet you intimate there were other concurring circumstances which had weight inducing the Executive in its favor. The object of this therefore is, to request of you a statement of what those circumstances were, that correctly knowing I may distinctly answer them. To the suggestions contained in yours of the 13. of June I shall likewise make such further reply as appears now to be necessary.

I request this statement as a matter of right and upon the principle that altho the Executive possesses the power to censure & remove a public minister, yet it is a power which ought to be exercised according to the rules of Justice: which only are too well defined, by the Principles of our government, to require illustration here. I make this request therefore in a confidence that you will comply with it as soon as you can with convenience.

With due respect, I am Sir your most obedient Servant

JAS. MONROE.

TO THE SECRETARY OF STATE.
PHILA., July 8, 1797.

SIR,—Upon leaving Paris I committed my letter books to the care of Mr Prevost, & after his departure to the care of Mr Skipwith, sealed up for Genl Pinckney in case he arrived whilst either of those gentlemen was there, to furnish him with such light, upon our affairs as he could not have derived from your department when he left this. I had previously given to Genl. Pinckney, copies of some papers which he found necessary upon his first arrival, so that in any possible case I trust that your wish was fulfilled in possessing him with such documents as have been or may be necessary for some time to come. I think proper however to suggest the propriety of such a complete copy being furnished from your office as you seem to deem necessary for our representative at Paris, since when I arrived there no paper whatever was furnished to me by my predecessor, either of his own correspondence, of Mr. Jefferson's or Dr. Franklins.

I have thought it my duty to state to you how I found & left this business, to enable you to make such disposition therein according to the rules of your department, as is thought suitable.

I shall be absent from this city till Thursday next at which time I shall be happy to receive an answer to the letter I had the pleasure to write you yesterday.

TO THE SECRETARY OF STATE.
PHILA., July 19, 1797.

SIR,—I have been favored with yours of the 17th inst. and answer it without delay. If you supposed that I would submit in silence to the injurious imputations that were raised against me by the administration you were mistaken. I put too high a value upon the blessing of an honest fame, & have too long enjoyed that blessing, in the estimation of my countrymen, to suffer myself to be robbed of it by any description of persons, and under any pretence whatever.

Nor can I express my astonishment which the present conduct of the administration excites in my mind; for I could not believe till it was verified by the event, after having denounced me to my countrymen as a person who had committed some great act of misconduct, & censured me for such supposed act by deprivation from office, that when I called upon you for a statement of the charge against me, with the facts by which you support it, I should find you disposed to evade my demand & shrink from the inquiry. Upon what principle does the administration take this ground, and what are its motives for it?

Do you suppose or contend that the power committed to the Executive by the Constitution, to remove and censure a public minister, or any other public servant, has authorized it so to do, without a sufficient cause? Or that the Executive is not accountable to the publick & the party injured for such an act, in like manner as it is accountable for any and every other act, it may perform by virtue of the Constitution? Upon what principle is a discrimination founded, which presumes restraints in certain cases, against the abuse of Executive power, and leaves that power without restraint in all other cases? And how do you designate, or where draw the line between these two species of power, so opposite in their nature & character? This doctrine is against the spirit of our Constitution which provides a remedy for every injury. It is against the spirit of elective government, which considers every public functionary as a public servant. It becomes the meridian of those countries only, where the monarch inherits the territory as his patrimony, and the people who inhabit it as his slaves.

That the right to censure and remove a public officer was delegated to the Executive with peculiar confidence, is a motive why it should be exercised with peculiar care; for the more confidential the trust which is committed to a public functionary, in a responsible station, the greater circumspection should he use in the discharge of it. It was not intended thereby to dispense with the principles of justice or the unalienable rights of freemen, in favor of Executive *pleasure*. On the contrary it was expected that that *pleasure* would be exercised with discretion, & that those principles & rights would be invariably observed. It is an incompetent recompense to a person who has been injured by the Executive, to be told that the Constitution permits the injury, if the power intrusted was hereby abused and the principles of the Constitution violated. And it is an unbecoming measure in the administration to defend by the argument of power, what it cannot justify at the tribunal of reason and justice.

I have been injured by the Administration and I have a right to redress. Imputations of misconduct have been by it raised against me, and I have a right to vindicate myself against them. I have invited you to state and substantiate your charges if you have any, & I repeat again the invitation.

You suggest that you have facts & information which warrant this procedure. Let me know them, as likewise your *informers,* that I may be able to place this act of the Executive, and my own conduct in the light which they respectively merit to stand.

The situation of the United States has become in many respects a very critical one, & it is of importance that the true cause of this crisis be distinctly known. You have endeavoured to impress the public with a belief that it proceeded in some respects from me. Why then do you evade the inquiry? Is it because you know that the imputation was unjust & wish to avoid the demonstration of a truth you are unwilling to acknowledge? Or that you fear a discussion which may throw light upon a topic heretofore too little understood.

I am with due resp^t y^r. ob^t. serv^t.

JAS. MONROE.

TO JAMES MONROE.

Philadelphia, July 25, 1797:—Sir,—It has been deemed improper, for the reasons assigned in my official letters to attempt an official explanation of the reasons and motives which influenced the late President, in terminating your functions as minister plenipotentiary of the United States to the French Republic. This I shall not venture to do in any capacity. But it is in my power, as an individual citizen, to communicate the considerations which induced me last summer when called upon by the President in the line of my office to advise that this measure should be taken. If, in this form, my sentiments will give you any satisfaction and you desire to receive them, they shall be furnished.

I have conversed with Mr. McHenry & Mr. Lee on this subject, and in the like form you may receive their sentiments respectively. Mr. Walcott being absent, I can say nothing in respect to him. I am, with due respect, Sir, your ob^t. Servant.

TIMOTHY PICKERING.

TO TIMOTHY PICKERING.
July 31, 1797.

Mr. Monroe requests Col. Pickering to inform his colleagues, that the evident impropriety of his having any communication with the administration otherwise than with the administration itself upon an act for which he holds the administration responsible, precludes his receiving from them as individual citizens any information whatever respecting the motives which governed them in the case referred to. He declines this with the greater pleasure because the course he finds it necessary to adopt for the examination & development of this subject generally, offers to those gentlemen as individual citizens an opportunity to communicate the motives of their conduct in that case to the community at large thro' which channel only can he attend to them.

TO JAMES MADISON.
ALBERMARLE, Septr 24, 1797.

DEAR SIR,—Since my return I have devoted all the leisure time I have had in preparing my narrative for Mr. Bache but yet it is not finished. I suppose I have yet about a 3^d to do which I hope to complete this week. The whole when completed will make a pamphlet of between thirty and forty pages. It has cost me much trouble on account of the necessity of observing great accuracy in facts, dates etc. Of the correspondence I have about 250 pages from Bache who is going on with the residue of the work at the rate of about 40 per week. The whole will I presume make a volume of near 400 pages. I wish you to come up in the course of the week when most convenient to you. We beg you also to make our best respects to Mrs. Madison and request her to accompany you. We will be very happy to see her provided she can submit to our accommodation of which you can give an account having an upper room in one of our offices, there being no additional room as you supposed. But we will do all in our power to make it tolerable. Our best respects to your father and family. Sincerely I am your friend and servant.

JA^S. MONROE.

TO THOMAS JEFFERSON.
(Probably Oct. 15, 1797.)

DEAR SIR,—I shall send Mr. Bache to-morrow about two thirds of my narrative and the residue by the next post. I have nothing from him by the last wch. gives cause to apprehend either that his people or himself are sick of the yellow fever. It becomes necessary that I give the publication a title, and therefore I wish yr. opinion upon that point. I subjoin one wch. is subject to your correction. You mentioned some time since the propriety of my discussing the question whether a minister was that of his country or the admn. It is a plain one, but yet I will thank you to put on paper what occurs to you on it, any time within a day or two & send it me.

There are letters of the secry. of State wch. are omitted, such for example as that wch. I send, being rather a document accompanying one, than a letter. You will perceive it is lengthy and not applicable to the object of my publication. As also another respecting Mr. Fenwick containing a charge against him of wch.

some notice is taken in one of mine by way of reply. It was omitted as a personal thing from motives of delicacy to him—wod. you publish both or either of these in the appendix? Skipwith's report to me is omitted also: wod. you instruct Bache to publish it in the appendix the one I refer to is that published by Pickering with Mr. Adams's message to the last Session of Congress.

Yours respectfully,

JAS. MONROE.

Sunday—Octr. 1797.

"A View of the conduct of the admn. in the management of our foreign affairs for the year 1794, 5 and 6 by an appeal to the official instructions & correspondence of James Monroe, late minister p: of the U. States to the French republick; to wch. is prefix'd an introductory narrative by the sd. James M."

or

"A view of the conduct of the Executive of the U. States in the management of the affrs. of those States with foreign powers for the years 1794 &c." as above.

TO THOMAS JEFFERSON.
(Nov. qu. 97.)

DEAR SIR,—I have a letter from Mr. Bache with the printed documents complete all but a page or two & 12 pages of "the view &c." I enclose a note to correct by way of erratum an important omission of almost a line in the latter. He tells me the late expln. at Paris has produced a wonderful effect on our rascals at home, who he thinks were in harmony with those there. I have no doubt that the stronger the attack upon them is, hinting a belief of bribery (I mean by the members in debate) the better: for yet the republican cause has never had a chance. Be assured the people are ready to back those who go most forward. I repeat my best wishes for yr. happiness. Remember us to Mr. M. & Lady. Mr. Barnes has paid the money. If I can place funds I shall begin soon to trouble you abt. windows, &c. as my cabin castle goes on—

[not signed]

TO THOMAS JEFFERSON.
ALBEMARLE, Dec. 25, 1797.

DEAR SIR,—I have your favor of the 14, the only one since you left the State. Your other was I hope of no consequence, as it has probably undergone the inspection of those for whom not designed. In truth there is no confidence to be reposed in the fidelity of the post office.

I have two accounts to settle with the Department of State. The first respects my own salary, the second a remittance made of 6,000 dollars for the family of Fayette.

I had no other money entrusted to me for foreign officers: nor for any other purpose except a remittance of 120,000 dollars by a draft of Swan upon his house in favor of the Secretary of the Treasury to be remitted to our bankers in Holland. Upon this latter point an attempt was made to injure me in my absence, but abandoned when it was found that I could not be assailed. Still some injury was perhaps done me in the beginning in whispers. It therefore merits attention whether I ought not to take the subject up openly & pursue Mr. Wolcott, either to an explicit disavowal of calumnies, or to a conviction of being guilty of them, as I have the most ample proof of the rectitude & propriety of my own conduct in that respect. This is for your opinion.

I must request you will be so kind as settle for me the two first accounts viz: of my salary & that of the remittance for the family of La Fayette. I enclose you a note of both: as also of my advance for our government as mentioned in my note to the bankers; which forms a third item or what may be called a 3^d account.

Upon the account for salary a question may arise when my service ended. I have stated it to be on the first of January 1797, when I took my leave of the French Government, because till then I could not leave Paris, being ordered to take a formal leave, was at expense, & in some sort in public service. It may be urged it ought to end sooner, for example when I presented Mr. Pinckney to the Minister of Foreign Affairs on the 9th of December. I think otherwise but leave the affair to your judgment whether in case T. P. decides narrowly it is worth while to mention the affair to the President as from yourself. If my idea is allowed a balance will be due me on this head of between five and 600 dollars.

The next item is the remittance of 6000 dollars for the family of La Fayette— of whose application I add a particular statement. I will thank you to give it in to the Secretary or a copy of it as he prefers. If he settles it, you will be able if necessary to prove M^{dme}. La Fayette's handwriting by Mr. Noailles her brother-in-law in Paris; as also Massons, tho' I presume the comparison with that in Paris's certificate will establish it. I am indifferent how he settles it, as I want to have nothing to do with the government or rather administration. But in case he makes me pay anything, & disallows any point, viz. either the proper depreciation—2^d. the 3000 $ or 3^d the payments to Moubourg, I think it ought to be so arranged that upon producing the proof he deems satisfactory I be repaid & likewise indemnified against the 9000 $.

The 3ᵈ item respects my advances to the government for books, instruments,—to the cannon founder &c. Of this I have heretofore sent an account to the department of war requesting that so much might be credited me with the Department of State. This is a delicate point. Full power was given me by T. P. when in the Department of War to purchase what was proper & reference made to Colo. Vincent a respectable Engineer who built the fort on Governors Island New York. Together we made a most extensive & valuable collection of which there are but few like it in France—none here—I procured also a most reliable & skillful cannon founder with great difficulty—and my bill in favor of Mr. Jones, for the first part was paid with difficulty & myself not answered. The articles were got at 1/3ᵈ their value; & if the Department complains or does not acknowledge the service gratefully I would take the whole on myself. I refer you to the account rendered that Department for the amount,lest that which I annex should be incorrect, since the former was made out in my office when all the vouchers were before the gentleman who made it.

I hope you will be able to understand these memoranda; it will be best for you to get a copy of what was sent the Department & get Mr. Beckly to make out a regular account for me.

I entered the 3ᵈ Virginia regiment & served the campaign of 1776 in it. Was then appointed to Lᵈ Stirlings family where I served 1777. & 1778. I was known by all the officers to have served those three years: by Mr McHenry himself.

I trouble you much with my concerns—but you have the consolation to reflect that these are all. They are of infinite importance to me and therefore I beg your very particular attention to them. Believe me sincerely your friend & Servant

Jaˢ Monroe.

A VIEW OF THE CONDUCT OF THE EXECUTIVE, *in the Foreign Affairs of the United States, connected with the mission to the French Republic, during the years 1794, 5, & 6.—By James Monroe, Late Minister Plenipotentiary to the said Republic— Illustrated by his Instructions and Correspondence and other authentic documents.* Philadelphia: Printed by and for Benj. Franklin Bache, and to be had at the office of the Aurora, No. 112 Market Street. M,DCCXCVII.

From the original manuscripts in the Department of State the following are extracts: August 9, 1797, Pickering wrote to General Washington: "Mr. Monroe has anticipated me in

furnishing you by his publication in the newspapers, the correspondence between us on the subject of his demanding the reasons of his recall. After such a solemn demand, so zealously maintained and after such professions of candour—I did not imagine he would have the folly to avow, as in his last letter that he in fact wanted no information on this point: proving, what I supposed was the real object at first, that he made the demand in order to be denied.—I kept a table ready for him in my office during a week, while I expected him to review his correspondence with the Department; but he has never called, although he stated this as necessary for his information in his intended vindication." Monroe did, however, review, at some time after the date of this letter, his correspondence with the Secretary of State, as the records bear indications of his having done so. Washington replied: "*Colonel Monroe passed through Alexandria last week, but did not honor me by a call.—If what he has promised the public does him no more credit than what he has given to it, in his last exhibition, his friends must be apprehensive of a recoil.*" On January 20, 1798, Pickering wrote to Washington: "*I send in the mail, with this letter, Monroe's book and Fauchet's pamphlet. . . Monroe's publication, like Randolph's vindication, is considered by every one whom I have heard speak of it as his condemnation or as some have expressed themselves, his death warrant. A writer in Fenno's paper, under the signature of Scipio, has undertaken the examination of it and clearly convicted Monroe from his own written documents. I believe the writer of Scipio is Mr. Tracy. The pieces are written with uncommon perspicuity. If you do not get Fenno's paper, and will permit me I will send you the whole series. Eleven numbers have already appeared, and I suppose the writer is near the conclusion.*" [HAMILTON.]

In the month of May, 1794, I was invited by the President of the United States, through the Secretary of State, to accept the office of Minister Plenipotentiary to the French republic. The proposition was plain and direct, announcing to me, for the first time, that the executive thought of me for that office; and certain it is, I did not solicit, desire or even think of it for myself. The secretary observed that Mr. Morris was to be recalled, and it being necessary to appoint a successor, the President had requested him to inform me, he should be glad I would take his place. I received the communication with a due degree of sensibility; but yet the proposal was so new and unexpected, that it was, from a variety of considerations, impossible for me to give an immediate answer to it. I requested some days to deliberate on the subject, which were granted.

I was at this time a member of the Senate of the United States, for the State of Virginia, which station I had held for several years before. It had been too my fortune, in the course of my service, to differ from the administration, upon many of our most important public measures. It is not necessary to specify here the several instances in which this variance in political sentiment took place between the administration and myself: I think proper however to notice two examples of it, since they serve essentially to illustrate the principles upon which that variance was founded, and the light in which I was known to the administration and my country before this proposal was made to me. The first took place when Mr. Morris was nominated minister plenipotentiary to the French republic; which nomination I opposed, because I was persuaded from Mr. Morris's known political character and principles, that his appointment, and especially at a period when the French nation was in a course of revolution, from an arbitrary to a free government, would tend to discountenance the republican cause there and at home, and otherwise weaken, and greatly to our prejudice, the connection subsisting between the two countries. The second took place when Mr. Jay was nominated to Great Britain; which nomination too I opposed, because under all the well known circumstances of the moment, I was of opinion we could not adopt such a measure, consistently either with propriety, or any reasonable prospect of adequate success; since being a measure without *tone,* and one which secured to that power *time,* which of all things it wished to secure, it seemed better calculated to answer its purpose than ours; moreover, because I was of opinion, in the then state of European affairs, it would be made by the enemies of the two republics the means of embroiling us with France, the other party to the European war; and because I thought it was unconstitutional to appoint a member of the judiciary into an executive office: And lastly,because I also thought, from a variety of considerations, it would be difficult to find within the limits of the United States, a person who was more likely to improve, to the greatest possible extent, the mischief to which the measure naturally exposed us. This last example took place only a few weeks before my own appointment, which was on the 28th of May 1794.

When I considered these circumstances, I was surprised that this proposal should be made me by the administration, and intimated the same to the Secretary of State; who replied, that my political principles, which were known to favor the French revolution and to cherish a friendly connection with France, were a strong motive with the President for offering me the mission, since he wished to satisfy the French government what his own sentiments were upon those points. He added, that in his opinion, the President was as sincere a friend to the French revolution and our alliance with France, as I could be, and of course that nothing would be required of me inconsistent with my own principles; on the contrary that I should be placed on a theatre where I might gratify my feelings in those respects, and at the same time render a most useful and acceptable service to my country; for that our affairs with France had fallen into great derangement, and required an immediate and decisive effort to retrieve them. Thus advised I submitted the proposition to my friends, who were of opinion I ought to accept it, and whereupon I did accept it.

My instructions were drawn in strict conformity with these sentiments, as will appear by a perusal of them. They enjoined it on me, to use my utmost endeavours to inspire the French government, with perfect confidence in the solicitude which the President felt *for the success of the French revolution; of his preference for France to all other nations as the friend and ally of the United States; of the grateful sense which we still retained for the important services that were rendered us by France, in the course of our revolution;* and to declare in explicit terms that although neutrality was the lot we preferred, yet in case we *embarked in the war it would be on her side and against her enemies, be they who they might.* Several incidents which had occurred in the course of our affairs of a nature to create in France doubts of a contrary disposition in our councils, were expressly adverted to, for the purpose of enabling me to dissipate those doubts, by such explanations as might be most successful. The mission of Mr. Jay to London was particularly noticed; because it was, I presume, deemed most likely to produce or foster such doubts. Upon this point my instructions were as follows: "It is not improbable you will be obliged to encounter on this head suspicions of various kinds. But you may declare the motives of that mission to be, *to obtain immediate compensation for our plundered property and restitution of the posts.*"

Another incident was taken advantage of by the administration, with a view to satisfy the government of France that its professions were in all respects sincere. The Senate and House of Representatives had each passed a resolution, expressive of the interest they took, respectively, in the welfare of the French republic, with a request by each to the executive, to transmit the same in its behalf to the French government. In fulfilling this duty the executive availed itself of the opportunity furnished, to declare its own sentiments on the same subject, which it did in terms the most strong and emphatic that could be used. In communicating the resolution of the Senate it was observed by the Secretary of State (through whose department the communication passed) "that in executing this duty, the liberal succours which the United States received from the French nation, in their struggle for independence, present themselves warm to the recollection. On this basis was the friendship between the two nations founded: On this basis and the continued interchange of regard since has it grown; and supported by these motives it will remain firm and constant. The Senate therefore tender to the committee of public safety, their zealous wishes for the French republic; they learn with sensibility every success which promotes the happiness of the French nation; and the full establishment of their peace and liberty will be ever esteemed by the Senate as a happiness to the United States and to humanity." And in communicating that of the House of Representatives, it was further added; "that in no manner could this honorable and grateful function be more properly discharged than by seizing the occasion of declaring to the ally of the United States, that the cause of liberty, in the defence of which so much American blood and treasures have been lavished, is cherished by our republic with increasing enthusiasm; that under the standard of liberty wheresoever it shall be displayed, the affection of the United States will always rally; and that the successes of those who stand forth as her avengers will be gloried in by the United States, and will be felt as the successes of themselves and the other friends of humanity. Yes, representatives of our ally, your communication has been addressed to those who share in your fortunes, and who take a deep interest in the happiness and prosperity of the French republic."

These resolutions were public, being printed and published on the journal of each house; whence it was reasonable to infer, that the communication of the executive, which announced them to the French government, was likewise of a public nature, especially when it was considered that the committee of public safety might publish the whole, if it thought fit. No intimation was given me by the administration that it was its wish they should be kept secret; I therefore concluded that the publication thereof, was a circumstance, that must have been contemplated by the executive.

Upon this basis my mission was laid; a basis which satisfied me, that whatever might be the success of our extraordinary mission to England, its objects were so few, and its powers so strictly limited and well defined, that nothing could possibly result from it, that would lessen the confidence of France in the friendship and affection professed towards her, or call in question the purity of my motives in accepting, under the administration, this mission to the French republic. The prospect before me therefore every way was an eligible one. My connection with the administration was formed upon my own principles; or rather our principles appeared to be the same in all the points in question; and the duties it was enjoined upon me to perform, were those in which of all others I wished to succeed: for nothing could be more delightful to me, than by labouring to inspire the French government, upon terms safe and honorable to myself, with a confidence in the fair and friendly views of our own, to contribute to reclaim to the bonds of a close amity, two countries whose friendship was contracted in the war of our revolution, and which ought to be eternal; but who were now unhappily diverging from each other, and in danger of being thrown wholly apart; and, as I presumed, equally against the interest and inclination of both. Nor could any thing be more delightful to me, than to be able, by means of that confidence, to recover to our citizens a full indemnity for the injuries they had already sustained by the loss of it: And these were the particular duties it was enjoined upon me to perform. I embarked therefore immediately with a view to commence and pursue them with zeal.

Upon my arrival in Paris, which was on the 2d of August 1794, I found that the work of alienation and disunion had been carried further than I had before even suspected. The harassment of our commerce had commenced, and gone to some extent; and a coolness and distrust of our policy were marked strongly in their proceedings. In short it was apparent that things were in train for an entire separation of the two countries, as may be seen by reference to the documents which exhibit a correct view of the then state of our affairs.[9]

I presented my credentials to the commissary of foreign affairs, soon after my arrival; but more than a week had elapsed, and I had obtained no answer, when or whether I should be received. A delay beyond a few days surprised me, because I could discern no adequate or rational motive for it. The state of things occasioned by the fall of Robespierre, which took place just before my arrival, might protract it for that term, but not a longer one. Soon however intimations were given me, that it proceeded from a very different cause; one too which materially affected the honor of our administration as well as my own. It was intimated to me that the committee, or several at least of its members, had imbibed an opinion that Mr. Jay was sent to England with views unfriendly to France, and that my mission to France was adopted for the purpose of covering and supporting his to England; that the one was a measure of substantial import, contemplating on our part a close union with England; and that the other was an act of policy, intended to amuse and deceive. It was added that this impression not only caused the delay of my reception, but that the committee being unwilling to become the dupes of that policy was devising how to defeat it, and in consequence that it was impossible to say when I should be received. I was equally disgusted and disquieted with this intelligence, because I thought the

9. See a summary in letter of February 12, 1795 to the Secretary of State; also my notes to the committee of public safety of September 3, 1794, and letter to the same of October 18, 1794.—As also Mr. Skipwith's report to me heretofore printed by order of the House of Representatives.

impression the committee had taken of the views of our administration was unfounded; and because I foresaw if it influenced their councils it would produce effects very injurious to our affairs. And on my own part I felt a degree of resentment towards the committee, for suspecting that I would become the instrument of a policy so opposite to my own principles; or in other words that I would in list under the administration for the purpose of promoting the views, that were ascribed to it, by betraying those republican principles which were near to my heart, and to the advancement whereof my past life and services had been dedicated. Upon consideration of these circumstances, and especially as I conceived myself strong in the ground upon which I stood, in respect to the views of the administration as well as my own, I was resolved to take the subject from the committee, and present it before another tribunal. With this view I addressed a letter to the convention on the 14th of that month, notifying it of my late arrival, and asking to what department of the government I should present myself for recognition; and I was happy to find that this expedient produced immediately its desired effect, for I was in consequence thereof received and recognized by the convention itself on the day following.[10]

When I delivered my address to the convention, I thought proper likewise to lay before it, the resolutions of the Senate and House of Representatives, as communicated by the administration, and with design to place the views of the administration as well as my own, in respect to France and the French revolution upon clear, just, and honorable ground. I thought I perceived distinctly that not only the temper which had been shewn by the committee, but the general

10. Note of Mr. Skipwith—SIR, In answer to your request of my stating to you such incidents as concerned and preceeded your recognition by the national convention, I am enabled to say, from a most perfect remembrance of the fact, that from the many days' silence of the committee of public safety, who had the sole control of diplomatic relations, some doubts had began to circulate of the ultimate issue of your reception; and I well recollect that upon an interview during that period with a certain French gentleman, who had before for many years filled, and who does now fill, a respectable station under this government, he gave me to understand, that there might be in the committee of public safety an indisposition or some opposition to your being recognized, and therefore strongly recommended the expediency and propriety of your addressing yourself directly to the convention. The substance of this conversation was more than once repeated to me by said gentleman, and with the particular desire of my communicating it to you. You may also recollect, as I think I do, that another person at that time holding an office which gave him the best possible means of information, did make to both you and myself like intimations. Indeed, the delay of the committee of public safety after you had announced your mission in causing you to be recognized, was enough to inspire, and did inspire, very serious doubts of its final issue. With very sincere esteem, I am dear Sir, your most obedient servant,

FULWAR SKIPWITH.

derangement of our affairs with France, proceeded in a great measure, if not altogether, from the same cause, a suspicion that we were unfriendly to them; hence feeling no motive to discriminate between us and the other neutral powers, which were royal powers, and secretly hostile to the revolution, they had comprized us in their regulations with respect to them. *This* therefore appeared to me to be the most suitable time to make an effort to remove that suspicion, and *that* measure the most likely to accomplish it. Upon this principle then that step was taken, and I was happy to find that it produced immediately in the convention, and throughout France, the favorable effect I had expected from it. With the committee however it did not produce an effect so immediate, nor ever in the same degree.

Being recognized, I now applied myself to the ordinary duties of my office, and with all the zeal of which I was capable. The first object to which I turned my attention was the deranged state of our commerce, and the first application I made to the committee of public safety was for a restoration of the ancient and legitimate order of things, with reparation to our citizens for the injuries they had sustained by a departure from it. My first note to the committee of public safety on this subject, bears date on the 3d of September, 1794; in which I discussed and combated copiously, and as ably as I could, the conduct of France in thus harassing our commerce, against the stipulations of certain articles in our treaty with her; and urged earnestly the immediate repeal of the decrees which authorized that proceeding. I had closed my note with this demand, when further reflection, strengthened by the apparent temper of the committee, suggested a doubt whether I had not transcended my instructions, and might not by such a demand, under such circumstances, and upon my own responsibility, bring on my country the embarrassment of demands on the other part, under another article of the treaty. I examined again and again my instructions, and was finally of opinion they did not contemplate the demand. But yet I was unwilling to suffer the impression which the manner of my reception by the convention had made upon the community at large, to pass off, without an effort to improve it to advantage; and was persuaded from what I witnessed of the general temper of the public councils, that the way to turn that impression to the best account, was to make a liberal and generous appeal, on our part, to like motives on theirs. Upon this principle, therefore, and upon due consideration of the above circumstances, the last clause in that note was drawn. By this however I do not wish to be understood as having been guided by political motives only in expressing the sentiments contained in that clause; on the contrary I admit they were strictly my own; affirming at the same time that they would never have been thus expressed, had I not been satisfied, they were such, as it was honourable for the United States to express, and were likely also to promote their interest.

The passage in my instructions applicable to this subject was as follows. After speaking of the Bordeaux embargo it adds: "But you will go farther and insist upon compensation for the captures and spoliations of our property, and injuries to the persons of our citizens, by French cruisers." There appeared to me to be a material difference between a power to demand compensation for captures and spoliations already made, or which might afterwards be made, and that of calling specifically on the French government, to execute certain articles of the treaty between the United States and France, which it was known before I left America were set aside, and the reasons for so doing explained. I concluded if it had been intended to demand an execution of those articles of the treaty, I should have been specially instructed so to do, since the object appeared to me to be too particularly important to have escaped the attention of the administration; or, being attended to, to have been meant to be comprized in the above article of instruction. And the circumstance which suggested caution on my part, lest I should expose my country to injury and myself to censure, was the stipulation in our treaty of alliance with France of 1778, by which we bound ourselves, in return for her guarantee of our independence, to guarantee to her forever, her possessions in the West Indies. I was fearful if we pressed her to fulfill strictly those articles in our treaty of commerce, which were favorable to us, it might induce her to call upon us to fulfill the article above mentioned in our treaty of alliance.

My note was now before the committee, and my efforts to obtain an early and full compliance with its several objects, earnest and unceasing. Six weeks, however, elapsed and I had made no progress at all. On the 18th of October I sent in a second note in support of the former and with like effect. From the committee itself I could obtain no answer, and to my informal applications to some of its members, I found that the difficulty of allowing our vessels to protect the property of English subjects, whilst they gave none to that of French citizens, against the English cruisers, with that of distinguishing in our favor from the case of Denmark and Sweden, in which we were now involved, were objections of great weight with the committee. But yet I thought I could discern another motive which though withheld, or rather not avowed, was likewise a powerful one. I thought I perceived, still remaining in the councils of that body, a strong portion of that suspicion of our views, in regard to our mission to England, so impressive upon my arrival; but which I had hoped was eradicated; and the more earnestly I pressed an accommodation with my demands the more obviously did this motive present itself to my view. Thus our affairs were at a stand and the prospect of making any progress in them at best a gloomy one. In the interim too our commerce was harassed, and the same system continued in other respects, which I was labouring to change. Possessing then, as I thought I did, the specific remedy, I was resolved to apply it to the disease. For this purpose therefore I sought and obtained an interview with the diplomatic members of the committee, commencing a conversation with design to lead them to that point, that I might explain in a suitable manner the objects of Mr. Jay's mission to England, and in which I easily succeeded.[11]

The subject was introduced by Mr. Monroe's observing on the necessity that all powers at war must feel to bring their disputes to a close—That this was often effected by the interposition or mediation of a third power—That, on the present occasion, the United States, actuated by the warmest wishes for the tranquility and happiness of the republic, would cheerfully contribute their good offices towards bringing about a pacification with the allied powers, if their *entremise* would prove acceptable or useful to the Republic; at the same time, declaring explicitly, they were by no means disposed to listen to any overtures that might be made them by the other powers at war, for conciliating their mediation.

To this it was replied, that the government received those offers as a distinguished mark of the friendly disposition of the United States towards the Republic, and would not lose sight of them:—But that her enemies, if they felt a necessity for peace, must make direct application for it; and, that the dignity of the Republic, supported as it was by the successful progress of its arms, rendered this mode of treating only admissible.

It was asked; if Mr. Monroe was in correspondence with Mr. Jay? To which he replied, he was not.—And it was then further asked; if Mr. Jay was expected soon in Paris?

Some conversation led to Mr. Monroe's observing, that the object of Mr. Jay's mission to England was confined solely to the procuring compensation for the depredations committed on our trade, and obtaining the surrender of the western posts.

By the diplomatic members, it was mentioned, that it was understood, the United States had declined acceding to some proposals made them by Sweden

---

11. Memorandum of a conversation that passed some time in November, in an interview between Mr. Monroe and two Diplomatic members of the committee of *Salut Public;* at which, by his desire, I was present.

and Denmark, for joining their armed neutrality—to which Mr. Monroe observed, that he was unacquainted with such proposals, but admitting they were made, the result could not be known, until after the opening of the session of congress.

The offer of the mediation of the United States, made by Mr. Monroe, appeared to me to be received with coolness, though the expressions acknowledging their sense of it were perfectly polite; and in the questions relative to Mr. Jay, above cited, with others of more indifferent nature, there appeared to be couched a degree of jealousy and suspicion of the object of his mission.

Paris, January 16th, 1795.   JOHN H. PURVIANCE.

The Gazettes had teemed with reports for some time before this, that Mr. Jay was about to pass over to France, to propose a mediation of peace, on the part of America, at the instance of England, which reports had, as I understood (impressed as the committee was with his political character) contributed to keep alive, if not increase, the suspicion above referred to. I began therefore by making a kind of offer of our services to the republic to promote peace, by way of mediation, according to an article in my instructions; but in a manner to create a belief that we neither wished nor would undertake that office unless by solicitation; nor then except at the instance of our ally: adding that I wanted no immediate answer to this communication, having made it only to inform them of the amicable views of our administration towards France. So far my chief object was to discredit that report without noticing it. The members however adverted directly to it, asking me whether it was true, and to which I replied, that it could not be true, since Mr. Jay was sent to England upon special business only, "to demand compensation for the depredations on our trade and the surrender of the western posts,"[12] to which his authority was strictly limited. The members acknowledged, in terms sufficiently polite, the attention which was shewn upon that occasion, by the administration, to the interest of France, as well in the offer of service to the French republic by the United

---

12. See Mr. Purviance's note of the conference, which may be relied on as accurate; because he interpreted between the members and myself, upon that occasion; since at that time I could not so much rely on my knowledge of the French language, as to depend on myself in that respect. By his note I am also reminded, that other topics were touched on by these members, and in particular, that I was asked, whether I corresponded with Mr. Jay? and replied, that I did not (as was the fact at the time) on political topics, which was doubtless the object of the enquiry. I recollect too, that when the question was propounded, it was done in a manner to impress me with a belief it was suspected I made the proposition at the instance of Mr. Jay, and in harmony with the British government.

States, as in the confidential communication I had made upon the subject of our own affairs, and thus the conference ended.

About this time I was applied to by Mr. Gardoqui, minister of finance in Spain, to obtain for him of the French government permission to enter France, ostensibly to attend certain baths on account of ill health; but, as I supposed, to open a negociation for peace with the French republic. At first I was averse to comply with his demand; because I was persuaded, from what I saw of the jealous temper of the committee towards us, that an agency in the affairs of the enemies of France, however friendly the motive for it in regard to France might be, was more likely to encrease than diminish their distrust, and by means thereof injure our own affairs; and because I did not like to repeat overtures of friendly offices, when it was possible the motive for so doing might be misinterpreted. The demand however being reiterated, and passing by trumpet through the Spanish and French armies, I could not well avoid presenting it to the view of the French government. I resolved however, in so doing, to express myself in such terms as to shew my independence, equally of Spain and France; upon which principle my note to the committee of public safety of the 13th of November 1794, inclosing copies of Mr. Gardoqui's letters to me, was drawn; for by the manner in which I delivered my sentiments of Mr. Gardoqui's views in writing those letters to me, it must have been obvious, that there was no political concert between him and me; and by the manner in which I addressed the committee upon that occasion, it must have been equally so, that although I wished success to the French republic, yet I had too high a respect for the United States, and knew too well what was due to myself, to weary that body with professions or overtures of friendly offices, which were not solicited. This incident I am satisfied produced a good effect in our favor, by drawing towards me the confidence of the French government, and of course to the communications which I made it on the part of our own.[13]

Just after this, I was asked by the diplomatic members of the committee of public safety, whether I thought they could obtain by loan, of the United States, or within the United States, some money to aid the French government in its operations. I understood, about four or five millions of dollars were wanted, to be laid out in the purchase of provisions and other supplies in the United States. The inquiry was rather an embarrassing one, for many reasons. Upon a full view however of all circumstances, I thought it best to refer the committee for an answer to the administration; availing myself of the occasion it furnished, to

13. See letter of November 13, 1794, to committee of public safety.

unfold more fully the then subsisting relations of the United States with Britain and Spain respectively, with a view not only to dissipate all remaining doubt on those points, but to engage France to assist us in our claims upon those powers in case it should eventually be necessary so to do. Shortly after this I was informed by the diplomatic members of the committee of public safety, that their minister then about to depart for the United States would be instructed to propose to our government an arrangement, whereby France should engage to secure the attainment of all our claims upon those powers, when she made her own treaties with them, as likewise to protect our commerce against the Algerines.

By these several communications and explanations, on my part, which were much aided by the movements of General Wayne on the Frontiers, shewing that if we were not in a state of actual war with Great Britain, so neither were we in that of actual peace; as likewise, by some changes in the committee itself, it was soon to be seen, that the doubts which that body had heretofore entertained of the sincerity of our professions, and rectitude of our views began to wear away; for, from this period, may be dated a change in its policy towards the United States; a change which soon became so visible afterwards.

About this time, it is important to be remarked, that I received a letter from the Secretary of State, of the 25th September, 1794, which assured me, that in his judgment our negociation with England was likely to fail in all its objects, and that *that* with Spain was at a stand; the courts of Madrid and London being cordial in their hatred of the United States, and a determination to harass them through the Indians. By this letter too, I was advised of the efforts made by the French Minister, Mr. Fauchet, through his Secretary Mr. Le Blanc, to inspire the French government with a belief, that *certain members in our own had a British tendency;* and admonished of the means I had to confront that idea, *since I knew how Mr. Jay was restricted;* an object to which my attention was now particularly called, since, under existing circumstances, it was deemed *indispensable for us to stand well with the French Republic.* Thus advised, I not only felt myself fortified in the measures I had already taken to cultivate a good understanding with the French government, as above stated; but stimulated to pursue the same object by like means, with new zeal.

By this time I had become personally acquainted with many of the members of the committee, the reserve heretofore shewn me being in a great measure thrown off; nor did I ever fail to avail myself of the opportunities thereby furnished, to urge as a *man,* what I had so often before pressed as a public minister; nor can it be doubted, that the effect thereby produced, in regard to the objects in view, was a salutary one.

On the 18th of November 1794, the committees of public safety, commerce and supplies united, passed an arreté, by which the commissary of marine was ordered to adjust the amount due to our citizens on account of the Bourdeaux embargo; as likewise for supplies rendered to the government of St. Domingo. By it, too, the embarrassments which impeded our direct commerce with France, as also those which impeded it with other countries, by the arbitrary rule of contraband, in respect to provisions destined for those countries, were done away. Free passage, in our vessels, was likewise allowed to the subjects of the powers at war with France, other than soldiers and sailors in the actual service of such powers. In short, all the objects to which my note of the 3d of September extended, were yielded; except that of allowing our vessels to protect enemies' goods, which point was declared to be withheld, until such powers should agree, that the merchandise of French citizens, in neutral vessels, should likewise be free.

Thus the business of reform in our affairs with the French Republic was happily commenced. By the above arreté an important change was actually produced in the general temper and conduct towards us; for by it many practices, very injurious to us, and heretofore legal and even commendable, were now prohibited and made criminal. And much likewise was done by the mitigation, which this change in the public councils, now become general in our favour, produced in the execution of that which was yet tolerated; for after this I do not recollect an instance, especially in France, where a vessel of ours was brought in upon the suspicion of having enemies' goods on board.

But the business of reform did not end here; on the contrary it was only commenced; for not long after this it was proposed by the above named committees, united with that of legislation, in a report to the convention, as the part of a general system, to put in execution likewise that article of our treaty, which stipulates, that free ships shall make free goods, which proposition was adopted on the 3d of January, 1795, and announced to me by the committee of public safety immediately afterwards. Thus the ancient harmony between the two countries was completely restored by a repeal of the several decrees and arretés which had disturbed it.

It is a circumstance worthy of attention, that as, upon a former occasion, the United States followed the fortune of the other neutral powers, such as Denmark, Sweden, &c. when the decrees restrictive of their commerce passed, so upon the present one those powers followed the fortune of the United States, by participating with them in the benefit of the repeal of those decrees. In the former stage, the United States had not sufficient weight to separate themselves from the condition of those powers, which were royal powers, and unfriendly to the French revolution; in the latter they had acquired sufficient weight to recover the ground they had lost, and even to impart the advantages of it to those powers also; for having been heretofore connected, it was now difficult for the French government to distinguish, in that respect, between those states and those other powers.

Our affairs with France were now in a prosperous state. By the repeal of the decrees under which our trade was harrassed, there was an end put to complaints from that cause; and, as orders were issued for the adjustment of the accounts of such of our citizens as had claims upon the French Republic, with a view to their payment, the prospect of retribution for past losses was likewise a good one. Soon too our commerce flourished beyond what was ever known before; for by virtue of our treaty with France of 1778, whose stipulations were now respected in every article, we were becoming, and actually became, not only the carriers of our own bulky and valuable materials to England and her allies (with the exception, in their case, of the strict contraband of war only) and of course to every port of the sea, which gave us a friendly welcome; but were likewise, on account of the protection which our vessels gave to the property of the enemies of France, becoming also the carriers of England and her allies in the war. Such, too, was the friendly bias of the people of France towards us, that notwithstanding our vessels gave no protection to French property against English cruizers, nor in certain cases to the productions of the French islands become American property, yet we were become likewise the principal carriers of France. Even the privilege of American citizenship was an object of great value to the owner (I mean in a mercantile view) for an American citizen could neutralize vessels, funds, &c. and thus profit, in many ways, by the condition of his country. Nor did France invite us to the war, or manifest a wish that we should engage in it; whilst she was disposed to assist us in securing our claims upon those powers, against whom we complained of injuries. In short, such was our situation with the French Republic, and with other powers, so far as depended on the French Republic, that there was but one point upon which we had cause to feel or express any solicitude, which was that it might not vary.

But unhappily this state of things, so correspondent with our ancient relations with that country, so congenial with the public sentiment, and necessary to the public welfare, was not doomed to be a permanent one; for even whilst the proposition, last above-mentioned, was depending before the convention, accounts were received from England, that Mr. Jay had concluded a treaty with that power, of very different import from what I had been taught by my instructions to expect, and had likewise taught the French government to expect would result from his mission. Hitherto I had understood, and had so stated, that his powers were limited to the adjustment of the particular points in controversy between the two countries; but by these accounts it appeared, that a treaty was formed, upon very different principles, whereby our connection with France was essentially weakened, by a new and very close one with England. Here then began a new era in our affairs, which will be perhaps forever memorable in the annals of our country, the incidents attending which I will proceed to relate.

It will readily occur to every dispassionate mind, that this report, though merely a report, must have subjected me to some embarrassment, which would continue 'till I was enabled completely to disprove it. But I will not dwell on this circumstance. I will proceed to narrate facts which shew how we lost the ground we had gained as above, and ultimately reached the point where we now are.

As soon as this report reached Paris, it was obvious that it produced in the committee a very disagreeable sensation in regard to us; for immediately afterwards, I was applied to by that body in a letter, which stated what they had heard of the contents of that treaty, and asking in what light they were to consider it. It happened, that I had received on the same day a letter from Mr. Jay, of the 25th of November, informing me, that he had concluded on the 19th of the same month, a treaty with Great Britain, which contained a declaration "that it should not be construed, or operate, contrary to our existing treaties;" but, "as it was not ratified, it would be improper to *publish* it." I therefore made his letter the basis of my reply to the committee, inserting verbatim so much of it as applied; adding, that although I was ignorant of the particular stipulations of the treaty (which, however, for the removal of all possible anxiety on that subject, I would communicate as soon as I knew them) yet I took it for granted, the report was altogether without foundation. My answer was so far satisfactory to the committee as to prevent, at the time, any change in the policy recently adopted towards us; for the decree, which proposed to put into full execution our treaty of commerce with France, then depending, as already observed, before the convention, was passed without opposition.

In promising to communicate to the committee the contents of this treaty as soon as I knew them, I did so in the expectation of fulfilling my promise, when I received a copy of the treaty from the Department of State, and not before; for I expected no further information upon that subject from Mr. Jay. I concluded, as he had already communicated to me a part of the treaty, and withheld the residue, that he had done so upon mature deliberation, and meant to communicate to me no more of it; and in this opinion I was the more confirmed, from that passage in his letter, which stated, that as the treaty was not ratified, it would be improper to *publish* it; since I could not understand that passage, otherwise than as an intimation, he should withhold from me the other parts of the treaty. And in making that promise to the committee, I did it with a view to preserve the same spirit of candour in my communications with that body, *now that the treaty was concluded,* that I had done whilst the *negociation was depending,* a departure from which would doubtless have been immediately noticed. To the Department of State therefore alone I now looked for such information respecting that transaction, as the public interest required I should possess; always presuming it would place the result, upon a footing correspondent with its previous communications to me, and mine to the French government, with which they were sufficiently acquainted.

On the 16th January, 1795, I received another letter from Mr. Jay of the 28th of November preceding, informing me that he proposed soon to communicate to me, in cypher, the *principal heads* of the treaty *confidentially.* This information surprised and embarrassed me. It surprised me, because it promised a result different from what I had expected from his preceding letters; and it embarrassed me because, although it was for many reasons an object of great importance with me to possess the treaty, in case it were of the kind I had understood it would be, yet I was now very averse to receive it, in case it were otherwise, on account of the promise I had already made to the committee, to communicate to it the contents, as soon as I knew them, as above stated. Thus circumstanced I resolved to write to Mr. Jay, by a confidential person, and inform him of my engagement with the committee, requesting a copy of the treaty to enable me to comply with it; urging as a motive for his sending one and truly, the good effect it would produce upon our affairs there; in the expectation of obtaining one, only in case the treaty was of a particular import, in which case I could see no motive why he should refuse that mark of confidence to the committee; and of preventing its being sent, in case it was otherwise, or in case Mr. Jay did not wish its contents to be known to the French government; for in either of those cases, and especially if clogged with any condition whatever, I did not wish to possess it. I committed this letter to the care of Mr. Purviance, a very respectable and deserving citizen of Baltimore, who departed with it a few days after the receipt of Mr. Jay's letter above mentioned, and returned with his answer, bearing date on the 5th of February, sometime early in March following. In his reply he refused to send me a copy of the treaty as I had requested; urging as a motive for his refusal, that we were an *independent* nation, *&c. had a right to form treaties, &c.* with other sound maxims which were never questioned.

Here again I concluded and hoped that the business between Mr. Jay and myself was at an end, and of course, that I should hear nothing further from him upon the subject of his treaty. But here again I was disappointed; for sometime in March I received another letter from him of the 19th of February, by Colonel Trumbull; in which he informed me, he had authorised that gentleman, to communicate to me the contents of that treaty, in *perfect confidence,* to be imparted to no other person. This last letter was still more extraordinary than any which preceded it: For as he had refused to send me a copy of the treaty, according to my request, by Mr. Purviance, and omitted, not to say refused (though indeed I understood his omission in the light of a refusal) otherwise to inform me of its contents, by that very safe opportunity, I did not see how the correspondence could be continued on that subject, on his part. Nor was my surprise otherwise than greatly increased, after having informed him, that the only acceptable mode by which the contents of the treaty could be conveyed was by the transmission of a copy of the instrument itself, at the proposition which he now made, to communicate them to me *verbally,* upon a presumption that it would be *more satisfactory* to me, to receive them *thus,* than by written *extracts from the treaty,* and upon condition that I would communicate them to *no other person whatever.* This proposition being altogether inadmissible, was of course rejected.

Soon after this, Colonel Trumbull made a communication, upon the subject of this treaty, to Mr. Hichborn of Boston, with design that he should communicate the same to me unconditionally; and of course, in the expectation that I would communicate it to the French government. In consequence I received this communication in *writing* from Mr. Hichborn, with the attention which was due, to those two gentlemen, whom I personally respected; and made of it, afterwards, all the use which a paper so informal would admit of: And thus was executed Mr. Jay's promise to communicate to me the contents of his treaty with the English government; upon which topic I will now make a few observations only, and then dismiss it.

My promise to communicate to the committee the contents of Mr. Jay's treaty, as soon as I knew them, sufficiently explains the motive of that intimation to him; but why demand a copy of the instrument for that purpose? Why not make my representations to that body, upon the faith of Mr. Jay's to me, without further proof? Ought this to be expected under like circumstances by any one? Or, ought any person who refuses to repose confidence in another, as was the case in the present instance, by withholding the document in question, to expect that *that other* would confide in him? Is not the very circumstance of withholding a document, whilst the party possessing it labours to impress you with a belief that *such* are its contents, calculated to create at least a suspicion that the fact is otherwise; and that the solicitude shewn proceeds from a desire to deceive? And if such would be the effect of such conduct on the part of a man indifferent or unknown to you, what ought to be expected from it when practised by one in whose political morality you had no confidence, and of whose obnoxious political principles and views you were already forewarned, by a long acquaintance with them? These considerations will, I presume, likewise sufficiently explain why I would make no representation to the French government of the contents of that treaty, for which I became personally responsible, upon the mere authority of Mr. Jay, or otherwise than upon a copy of the instrument itself.

But I had another reason of great weight in my mind for requiring a copy of the treaty from Mr. Jay, or preventing further communication with him on that subject, in case he would not send one. My object, as already stated, was by fair and honest means, to remove the suspicions which the French government entertained upon that subject; and with a view to promote the interest of my country. If then, Mr. Jay enabled me to accomplish the object, by a copy of the treaty, he seconded my views. But if he did not, every communication from him short of that, only tended to weaken the ground upon which I stood; whilst it personally embarrassed me. It will be remembered, that by my instructions I stood upon strong ground; since by their authority I could declare what I believed the treaty was, as I had before done what I believed it would be. But this I could not do in the case of a difference of the treaty from my instructions, unless I remained absolutely ignorant of its contents: Nor would the French government believe me in case I did, unless the declaration was supported by circumstances the most satisfactory, of which would be a belief, that there was no confidential understanding between Mr. Jay and myself; for knowing, as was to be presumed, the footing upon which we stood before we left America, as well as the administration knew it, or even we ourselves, and suspecting (as the committee always did) the object of his mission to England, which suspicion was now revived, perhaps much increased,—it would not fail to construe such intimacy into a proof of my apostacy, and his and my mission, on the part of the administration, into an act of political intrigue, directed against the cause of liberty, of which France was to be alike the dupe and the victim; an imputation

I not only did not merit, but to which I was resolved to give no countenance or sanction whatever, by any part of my conduct. This consideration, therefore, likewise fortified me in the resolution I had already taken, to request a copy of the treaty as the only document that could be useful to me, and neither to accept from him that or any other, otherwise than unconditionally.

Such was my conduct upon the above occasion, and such the motives of it. Such was, likewise, Mr. Jay's conduct upon that occasion, on whose motives I shall forbear to comment. What they were throughout, it is submitted to others to determine, upon a view of the facts and circumstances presented; which cannot otherwise than furnish to the impartial a satisfactory guide. Henceforward, therefore, I looked to the department of state, for all further information respecting the contents of that treaty, and in the interim, upon the faith of my instructions and the clause sent me by Mr. Jay, continued to assure the committee, that, in my opinion, it contained nothing which ought to give them just cause of uneasiness; but if it did, that it would be disapproved in America: Which assurance was, most certainly, not without effect; since, by means thereof, the committee was preserved, if not in a state of perfect confidence, yet in one of perfect tranquillity.

Heretofore, the few letters I had received from the Secretary of State were written before he was apprized of my arrival in France; and, of course, referred to a state of things which preceded that event: But about this period, being the beginning of February 1795, I received a letter from him of the 2d of December 1794, which was written after he knew of my arrival, and upon the receipt of my third letter (of the 15th of September, of the same year) the two preceding letters having not yet reached him. In this he notices my address to the convention; as also my letter to the committee of public safety of the third of September following; both of which acts he censures in the most unreserved and harsh manner. In the first he charges me with having expressed a solicitude for the welfare of the French Republic, in a stile too warm and affectionate; much more so than my instructions warranted; which too he deemed the more reprehensible, from the consideration, that it was presented to the convention *in public and before the world,* and not to *a committee in a private chamber;* since thereby, he adds, we were likely to give offence to other countries, *particularly England, with whom we were in treaty;* and since, also, the dictates *of sincerity do not require that we should publish to the world all our feelings in favor of France.* For the future he instructs me, to cultivate the French Republic with *zeal,* but without any unnecessary *eclat,* and by my letter to the committee, demanding an indemnity for spoliations, and a repeal of the decrees suspending the execution of certain articles of our treaty of commerce with France, he objects that I had yielded an interest it was my duty to secure. To support this charge, he selects out the last clause in that letter, and without entering into the spirit of the paper, or its probable effect upon the committee, reasons upon it as if it stood alone, and contained an absolute and formal surrender of the right in question; for which act of indiscretion, or rather misconduct, he intimates in pretty strong terms, that the administration think a mere reprimand inadequate.

To this letter I replied immediately, in one of the 12th of February, in which I answered, explicitly, his several charges, and, I presume, proved they were unfounded in every instance. Upon this occasion I thought proper in reply to his first charge, to lay open more fully than I had before done, some truths, at which, indeed, I had before only glanced; particularly the light in which our administration was viewed by the committee upon my arrival;[14] a circumstance which had subjected me to so many and painful embarrassments at that period, and for some considerable time afterwards, and so much to the injury of our affairs; details I would never have given, had I not thus been called on to do it in my own defence: For, in truth, as I thought after those embarrassments were surmounted, that complete harmony was perpetually re-established between the two countries, it was my wish as well from public considerations, as from motives of personal delicacy towards the parties interested, to bury them in oblivion. And in reply to his second charge, I answered by informing him, that some time before the receipt of his letter I had transmitted him a copy of a decree which carried into full execution the violated articles of our treaty of commerce with France; whereby the very object was obtained (as in my judgment it had been much forwarded by the mode in which it was pressed) the abandonment whereof he had laid to my charge.

14. To convey an idea of the rise and progress of the discontent and distrust of the French government, it would be necessary to go back to a period antecedent to my mission,—to the appointment of a man of the political principles and character which were known to belong to Mr. Morris, my predecessor; to his conduct during the early stage of the French revolution, and whilst in office; which by constantly favoring the royal party, in opposition to the republican course of things, rendered him odious to the French government; to his being continued in place, notwithstanding all this, till his recall was absolutely demanded by the French government; and lastly, to the discovery made by that government, that ours was not dissatisfied with his conduct; since to its demand, and not to a disapprobation of any part of Mr. Morris's conduct was his recall owing; which discovery was made by an intercepted letter from the Secretary of State, to Mr. Morris, expressly assuring him that such was the case. It would be painful to go into details on this subject; but the circumstances here hinted will make it easy to conceive the unfavorable inferences that must have been drawn respecting the temper and views of our administration.

I likewise thought proper, upon this occasion, to explain fully the light in which I had understood my mission, as stated in my instructions; with the relation it bore to that of Mr. Jay; all doubts respecting which, in the French government, I was instructed to remove, by making explanations the most explicit, and upon those points upon which such doubts were most likely to arise. In discussing this subject, and stating how I had acted, I plainly told our administration within what limits I expected the result of that mission would be found; intimating, that I had a character not to be sacrificed. To this view I was led by the general tone of the Secretary's letter; which created a doubt, whether the ground upon which I was placed by the administration was a solid one; for I could not conceive, if Mr. Jay's mission was limited to the objects specified in my instructions, and was otherwise of the character I was taught to believe it was, why such sensibility, or rather such dissatisfaction, should be shewn on account of my presenting to the convention, publicly, those documents which tended to prove how strong the feelings of the administration *were in favor of the French nation*. To express sentiments in private, which it was wished should not become public, appeared to me a strange doctrine to be avowed by the administration of a free people; especially as it was known that the sentiments, thus expressed, were in harmony with those of the people, and with those publicly and formally expressed by the representatives of the people. Nor could I reconcile such a solicitude for privacy to any idea of consistent or rational policy, in regard to the object of the mission to England: For if the object of that mission was to press that government into a compliance with our just demands, as I understood it to be, I could not conceive how that pressure could be weakened by a knowledge, that we were upon a good footing with the French Republic. On the contrary, I did suppose, that a knowledge of that fact would produce the opposite effect, by giving us a more advantageous attitude in the negociation. These considerations, therefore, suggested a train of reflection which gave me much disquietude, from a fear that the administration had dealt uncandidly with me from the commencement.

Scarcely, however, had I dispatched this letter, when I received another from the administration of the 5th December 1794 (three days later only than the former one) but of a very different import from the former one. In this last letter, my two first of the 11th and 25th of August 1794, were acknowledged and approved, and a kind of apology made for the harsh language used in the preceding one. In this also was renewed, in general but very strong terms, the injunction formerly laid on me, "to cultivate with the utmost zeal the friendship of the French Republic, taking care to remove every suspicion of our preferring a connection with Great Britain or weakening our old attachment to France." To this letter I likewise gave an immediate answer, in which I assured the Secretary that it had removed the disquietude his former one had occasioned, and that thus instructed I should continue to use my utmost efforts to forward the objects of my mission, as I had done before.

It will be remembered that before the accounts of Mr. Jay's treaty arrived I had availed myself of some incidents that occurred, to explain to the committee the actual situation of the United States in regard to Britain and Spain; with a view, among other objects, to obtain the aid of France in our depending negociations with each, in case it were deemed necessary by our Executive; and that the French government proposed instructing its minister, then about to depart for America, to make some proposition to our administration upon that subject. But as soon as those accounts were received, that project was of course abandoned; for it was entertained only at a time, when it was supposed the mission to England would fail. Still however I wished most earnestly to embark the committee in support of our claims upon Spain; since *they* formed a distinct interest, as yet unprovided for, and now much exposed to danger by the appearance of an approaching peace between France and Spain; for I thought it probable, if they were not then adjusted, much time might elapse before they would be. Nor did I doubt, it would be easy to accomplish the object, especially if I could satisfy the committee, beyond all controversy, that the interest of France was not injured by our Treaty with England, without which indeed I felt a reluctance to ask that aid; and in order to enable me to do which, by an act of confidence and candour (in case I found it necessary) and not to satisfy any unwarrantable demands of the French government, for none such were made, was a strong motive why I had requested of Mr. Jay a copy of his treaty as above related.

Upon due consideration therefore of these circumstances (although Mr. Purviance, to whom I intrusted my letter for Mr. Jay had not yet returned) I addressed the committee upon that subject, in a letter of the 25th of January 1795, in which I explained, more fully than I had before done, the nature of our claims upon Spain; and likewise endeavoured to prove that independent of the motive of rendering an useful and acceptable service to the United States, which I presumed was a strong one, since it would always draw after it its own reward, from a just and a generous people,—there were other considerations of interest, growing out of the relation which the territory, to be benefited by the security of those rights, had with the French islands, which in themselves were sufficient to prompt the French government to yield us the aid. To this letter I received an answer from the committee, of the 8th of February following, addressed in very polite terms, promising to examine with profound attention the observations I had submitted to it, and to give me the result without delay.

Thus this affair rested till sometime in the beginning of March following, when I was informed by Mr. Pelet of the diplomatic section of the committee of public safety, and afterwards by Mr. Cambaceres, likewise of that section, that in reliance that our treaty with England contained nothing injurious to France, they had expressly instructed their agent, then negociating with Spain, to use his utmost endeavours to secure for the United States the points in controversy with that power. And shortly afterwards, as their negociation advanced, I was asked, as well as I remember by those members, as likewise by Boissy D'Anglas, whether we wished to possess the Floridas, since it was intimated it would be easy for France to obtain them; but which she would not do otherwise than with a view to cede them to the United States. I replied I had no power to answer such an interrogatory; but was well persuaded we did not wish an extention of our territory. Well satisfied I am, that France declined taking them in her treaty with Spain, which soon followed, from a fear it might weaken her connection with the United States.[15]

It merits attention, that the part which the French government now took, with a view to secure the claims of the United States against Spain, in its own treaty with that power, was taken merely from motives of friendship for those States, without any claim to, or demand of retribution of, any kind whatever. It equally merits attention, that it was taken at a time when the contents of the English treaty were unknown to the French government, and not unsuspected by many to be of a nature injurious to France. Had that treaty then never passed, and had we also otherwise preserved the ground upon which we stood with that nation, in the commencement of its revolution, what might we not have expected from its friendship?

About the middle of May I received a letter from Mr. Short at Madrid, written by the desire of the duke of Alcudia, chief minister of Spain, to request that I would, as minister of the United States, endeavour to open a new and more

---

15. I did not mention the intimation about the Floridas to the administration, because I thought it a subject with which I had nothing to do, seeking only to open the Mississippi and settle the boundary, according to my instructions; and because, had the case been otherwise, that state of things was too transitory to admit anything being done to it. I find, however, afterwards, when the French government began to change its policy towards us, and were supposed to be treating for that territory with Spain, that in communicating what I heard of the depending negociations, I mentioned also, its former disposition in that respect, as a proof of the change.

active negociation between that power and France, he having previously assured Mr. Short, that the claims of the United States should be adjusted to their satisfaction. The prospect therefore of success in that important concern was now as fair as it could be.

Shortly after this Mr. Pinckney, who was commissioned to negociate and adjust our interfering claims with Spain, arrived in Paris on his way to Madrid. I informed him of what had passed between the committee of public safety and myself upon that subject; assuring him I was of opinion, if he would explain the object of his mission to the committee and ask its friendly cooperation, satisfying it at the same time, that the interests of France were not injured by our treaty with England, that such aid would be granted. Mr. Pinckney was aware of the benefit which would be derived from such aid; but yet did not consider himself at liberty to obtain it, by shewing a copy of Mr. Jay's treaty, which I intimated might be necessary completely to remove the doubts that were entertained in that respect, and therefore deemed it most suitable to say nothing to the committee upon the subject of his mission. I obtained for him, however, an interview with the diplomatic members of the committee, by whom he was received with respectful attention; after which he proceeded on his route to Spain. From this period I never mentioned to the committee the subject of our dispute with Spain; because all agency in that business seemed now to be completely withdrawn from it, and because I could not well do it, under existing circumstances, without violating equally the rules of decorum to both governments. By the committee indeed, a further pressure on my part for its aid, would most probably have been deemed an act of extreme impropriety; and by our administration it might have been deemed an indelicate and ill-timed interference with its measures. Had the committee, however, secured for us those objects in its own treaty, without regarding our mission to Spain, it would have exhibited a novel spectacle to the world; that of one government pursuing another with good offices, apparently against its wishes; nor would the surprise, which that spectacle must have occasioned, have been diminished by a knowledge of the interior details which produced it. It would at least have greatly embarrassed the administration to explain the cause of such a phenomenon to its credit; notwithstanding the advantage thereby gained to the public.

Such was the state of things when Mr. Pinckney arrived in Spain; who very wisely and very fortunately pushed his negociation to a close, whilst that state lasted.

Sometime in the beginning of May 1795, I received a letter of the 8th March, from the Secretary of State, and shortly afterwards two others; one of the 15th February and the other of the 7th of April following. In that of the 15th February, the Secretary informed me he had not then received Mr. Jay's treaty, but observes, "it is probable our commercial intercourse has also been regulated: Say, if you please, that a treaty has been concluded for commerce also, &c." He adds, "that in the principal heads of the negociation, the surrender of the posts, the vexations and spoliations of our commerce, and the payment of the British debts, France can have no possible concern;" that by our treaty with her, she enjoys all the advantages of the most favoured nation, &c. and by that of the 8th of March, he acknowledged the receipt of the British treaty on the 7th, but says it will remain undivulged by the Executive till the 8th of June, when the Senate would convene to deliberate on it. In this he notices the uneasiness of the French Minister on account of that treaty, upon which point he makes some general observations declaratory of our right to regulate, by treaty, our affairs with England, in regard to the posts, spoliations and commerce, as we pleased, adding, that "so far as a cursory perusal of the treaty enabled him to speak, he discovered no reasonable ground for dissatisfaction in the French republic." And in that of the 7th of April, the same sentiments in general were expressed, with a remark, "that the confining of the contents of the treaty to the President and Secretary of State, was not from any thing sinister towards France, but from the usages in such cases; not from an unwillingness that the executive conduct should be canvassed, but from a certain fitness and expectation arising from such a diplomatic act." He adds also, "that the invariable policy of the President is, to be as independent as possible of every nation upon earth, &c."

By these letters it appeared that Mr. Jay had concluded a treaty upon other principles than those to which his powers were restricted, as inferred from my instructions, and of course, that the nature and object of his mission to England had been misrepresented, through me, to the French government. This circumstance subjected me to a degree of embarrassment which may be easily conceived; nor was it lessened by the intimation of the Secretary, that he saw no *reasonable* ground for dissatisfaction in the French republic, especially as he admitted the uneasiness of its Minister, and likewise withheld from me the contents of the treaty; a reserve I could not account for upon any consistent principle on the part of the administration; nor otherwise, but upon its belief that the treaty would be deemed injurious to France by the French government. The more, therefore, I reflected upon this subject, the more uneasiness it gave me. I was aware of the reproach to which I was personally exposed, let the commercial part of the treaty be what it might. But this was not the only consideration which gave me pain; I was also fearful that this transaction would bring on a crisis in our affairs, which might be productive, in many respects, of much harm. Soon, however, I resolved upon the line of conduct, which, in the then juncture of affairs, it became me to pursue. That the administration had injured me, was a point upon which I had no doubt; that it had likewise compromised its own credit, and with it that of the United States, was also a truth equally obvious to my mind. But the regard due to these considerations was the point to be determined. What did the honor and interest of my country require from me in the actual state of affairs? What was my object in accepting the mission to the French republic, and how, under existing circumstances, could that object be best promoted? These were considerations of primary importance which presented themselves, and claimed a more early and dispassionate decision. Upon mature reflection, therefore, it appeared that I had but one alternative, which was to remain where I was, and proceed in the functions of my office, notwithstanding the embarrassments to to which I might be personally subjected, or to retire, and in retiring, to do it tranquilly, without explaining my motives for it; or by explaining them, denounce the administration to the public. But by withdrawing tranquilly, I should not only have admitted the misconduct of the administration, which I did not then wish to admit, but likewise my own, since it would have exposed me to the suspicion of having accepted the trust to serve a particular purpose, and withdrawing after that was accomplished. Besides, it seemed probable that my retreat at that moment, in either mode, might have some influence in inducing the French government to adopt a system of policy towards us, which it was equally my duty and my wish to prevent. I resolved, therefore, to stand firm at my post, and let occurrences be what they might, to continue as I had done before, to use my utmost endeavours to preserve harmony between the two countries; since that being an object invariable in my mind, I did not see how I could abandon it at a moment when it was menaced by a new danger, from whatever cause or quarter proceeding. To this resolution too I was the more inclined, from the consideration that it was now probable, in case the treaty with England was in other respects of a different import from what I had been taught to expect it would be, and should likewise be ratified—that I should be recalled by the administration; which compulsory mode of retreat I preferred to a voluntary one, upon the principle, if the administration took that measure without shewing a sufficient cause for it, consistent too with its previous declarations, that it would not only furnish to the world a new datum, whereby the better to estimate its general policy; but likewise leave me completely at liberty to explain, in every particular, the motives of my own conduct.

Having then resolved to stand at my post, or rather not desert it by a voluntary retreat, the path before me, though likely to be difficult, was nevertheless a direct one. On the one hand it was my duty, let the treaty be what it might, to endeavour by all suitable means to reconcile the French government to it. And on the other, to state faithfully to our own such facts and circumstances as occurred, tending to shew the impression which the treaty made on the French government; so that the administration, being correctly advised, might act accordingly. Upon this principle, therefore, I replied to the Secretary, in answer to his letters above mentioned, that I regretted the decision of the administration to keep the treaty secret for the term specified; since, as I had explained to the French government the object of Mr. Jay's mission whilst its issue was uncertain, it was thought strange the result should now be withheld; a circumstance too, I added, which, by keeping alive the suspicions that were at first imbibed of its contents, would not fail to prove hurtful to our affairs in the interim. I assured him, however, that I should continue to endeavour to inspire the French government with a confidence, either that the treaty contained nothing improper, or would not be ratified in case it did.

About the last of June or beginning of July 1795, Colonel Humphreys, then resident minister of the United States at Lisbon, arrived at Paris with a view to obtain of the French government its aid, in support of our negociations with the Barbary powers. He brought no letter from the administration to the French government, to authorize his treating with it in person, and of course it became my duty to apply in his behalf for the aid that was desired. Accordingly I addressed a letter to the committee of public safety on the 5th of July 1795, opening the subject to its view generally, and requesting its aid in such mode as should be agreed between us. I own I made this application with reluctance, because under existing circumstances I did not think it could be made without compromitting in some degree the credit of the United States; for between governments as between individuals I deem it undignified, however friendly their antecedent relation may have been, to solicit good offices, at a time when the friendship of the soliciting party is doubted, as was the case in the present instance. But I own also that my reluctance was diminished by the knowledge that the administration possessed the treaty with England, whilst Colonel Humphreys was in America, and the presumption thence arising, that this objection was weighed and overruled before his departure. Having however made the application I was resolved to pursue the object of it with the utmost possible zeal. In consequence I sought and had many conferences with the members of the diplomatic section of the committee of public safety, and the commissary of foreign affairs upon the subject, in which I was assured the aid desired should be given in the most efficacious manner that it could be. After some delays too, attributable at one time to us, on account of the situation of our funds, and at another, to the committee then much occupied with their own affairs, arrangements were taken for pursuing those negociations under the care of Joel Barlow, and with the full aid of France. At the moment however when Mr. Barlow was upon the point of embarking with our presents, &c. intelligence was received that a Mr. Donaldson, whom Colonel Humphreys had left at Alicante with a conditional power, but in the expectation that he would not proceed in the business till he heard further from him, had passed over to Algiers and concluded a treaty with that regency, and of course without the aid of France; and thus ended our application to the French government for its aid in support of our negociations with those powers, and nearly in the same manner as that did, which I made for its aid in support of our negociation with Spain. But as Mr. Barlow was likewise impowered by Colonel Humphreys to treat with Tunis and Tripoli, and the real state of the business with Algiers was unknown; it was still thought advisable that he should proceed thither, in the hope by concentring in his hands our general concerns with those regencies, that not only any error which had been committed, if such were the case, might be corrected, but that by his observations upon the character and circumstances of those powers, such light might also be obtained, as would prove useful in the guidance of our affairs with them for the future. Accordingly Mr. Barlow departed soon after this in the discharge of the duties of the trust reposed in him, and to whose very important and extraordinary services to his country, in the course of his mission, I with pleasure add here my testimony to that of all those who are acquainted with his conduct in it.

From this period I had but one object to attend to, the preservation of our actual footing with France, which was, as already shewn, as favorable as we could wish it to be. Nor was there any cause to apprehend a change for the worse, unless it was produced by the English treaty. But the contents of that treaty were unknown and of course there could be no fair ground for a change of policy towards us on the part of France. And upon the subject of it, but little was now said, either by the committee or myself, in our occasional interviews. By the committee indeed it was never mentioned even informally, except when some occurrence brought to view the subsisting relations between the United States and France, such for example as the arrival of Colonel Trumbull, Mr. Jay's secretary, of Mr. Pinckney on his route to Spain, and of Colonel Humphreys, as above stated; or upon some pressure for the settlement of the claims of individuals, upon which occasions it was easy to perceive, it was a subject not lost sight of. And by me it was never introduced, for as I had no new communication to make to the committee upon it, whereby to remove the suspicions that were entertained of its contents, and any allusion to it in that state could of course only serve to revive unpleasant sensations to our disadvantage, I thought it most eligible to keep it out of view. I continued however to look with anxious expectation to the administration, in the hope of receiving from it soon such information, respecting that treaty, and of the future views of our government towards France, as might at least preserve the subsisting harmony between the two nations.

Early in June 1795 accounts were received in Paris that the British government had revived its order for the seizure of provision vessels destined for France. At that period Paris, and many other parts of France, were in the greatest distress for provisions, in consequence whereof the attention of the government was directed with great solicitude to those quarters whence supplies were expected, particularly to the United States of America, where great sums had been expended in the purchase of them. Unfortunately however but few of those vessels reached their destination, for in general they were taken into port by the British cruisers. It was soon obvious that this aggression of Great Britain upon the rights of neutral nations, being made with the intent to increase the distress of famine which was then raging at Paris, and thereby promote the disorders which were in part attributable to that cause, excited a ferment in the French councils which was not pointed against Great Britain alone. The neutral powers were likewise animadverted upon, particularly the United States, to whom the attention of the committee was, as I had reason to believe, in a more especial manner drawn, by the report of one of its secret agents from England, who stated that he was advised there through a channel to be relied on, that the English administration had intimated the measure would not be offensive to our government, since it was a case provided for between the two governments. I was however happy to find that this report, which I treated with contempt, was at the time not much attended to by the committee; for it was deemed impossible, that our government should give a sanction to the system of kings for starving France. Nevertheless after the treaty appeared, I thought it my duty to communicate the purport of that report to the administration, with the comments that were made on that part of the treaty, which was supposed to authorize the British seizures; in the hope that such a conduct would be observed in regard to that proceeding of the English government, as would exempt us from the imputation of countenancing it.

About the middle of August 1795, American gazettes were received at Paris containing copies of the English treaty, whereby its contents were made known to the committee of public safety without my aid. From this period therefore all mystery upon that subject was at an end. The possession of the treaty enabled the French government to judge for itself upon all the points which it involved. Nor was the effect which it produced an equivocal one; for there did not appear to me to be a description of persons, not in the interest of the coalesced powers who did not openly and severely censure it. True it is, it made its appearance at a time when it was likely to produce the worst effect, being when Paris and many other parts of France were, as above mentioned, in the utmost distress for provisions, and when the British were likewise seizing our provision vessels destined for their relief.

It will readily occur, from a variety of considerations, that my situation was now truly an embarrassing one. I had, however, long before this settled in my mind the part it became me to act during this crisis of our affairs; which was to do everything in my power, consistent with propriety, to reconcile the French government to that treaty. I had therefore *now* no new decision to make, but simply to pursue *that* which I had already made. But as yet it was not known that the treaty was ratified, nor certain that it would be, for the spontaneous and almost universal disapprobation that was bestowed upon it throughout the United States, as soon as it was seen, was sufficient at least to inspire a doubt on that point: Nor had I any letter from the Department of State of a late date, to intimate the course our administration was likely to take. At this period, therefore, comprehending the months of August and September, 1795, I did not know how to act; for admitting that neither my previous well known political principles, nor the communications I had made to the French government, which were in opposition to the result now before it, imposed upon me any restraint, tho' doubtless in strict propriety they ought so to have done, yet until our government took a part, it was impossible for me to take one. Had I for example, turned out in that stage as a partizan of the treaty, and provoked a discussion of its merits with the French government, and a month afterwards received advice from the administration that it was rejected, I should not only have exposed myself to contempt, but likewise have deprived the United States of the merit which the rejection would have entitled them to with the French nation. Besides, what advantage was to be gained by such a course of proceeding in any stage? Was it not always in time to discuss the merits of that treaty, when the French government resolved to do it? and was it not my duty, seeking to preserve harmony between the two countries, to labour rather to prevent a discussion throughout, than to promote one? A certain portion of reserve, therefore, on my part, was now particularly necessary; and such was the conduct which I observed. At the same time I affirm, that it was my invariable practice to avail myself of every opportunity that occurred, to inculcate by all the means in my power, as well by obviating such objections as were made to the treaty, in the best way I could, as by urging considerations of a more general nature, the propriety and policy of preserving the subsisting harmony between the two countries, and with what effect will be seen by the documents which follow.

At this period I witnessed a very extraordinary political phenomenon. The appearance of the treaty excited the general disgust of France against the American government, which was now diminished by the opposition which the American people made to the treaty: for as soon as France saw that the Americans took up the cause as their own, and were indignant at a measure which they thought arranged them on the side of Britain and of kings, against France and public liberty; from that moment did a friendly sentiment discover itself in her councils and throughout the community towards us, which by moderating the temper of the French government promoted of course the views of the administration. The contrary effect was charged upon that display of the public sentiment in America; but the charge was dictated, more in the spirit of party than of true philosophy; for it was not warranted at the time by the principles of the human heart nor did it correspond with the fact.

But near the middle of September had now arrived and I had heard nothing from the administration of its decision on the British treaty, or its views in that respect, and in the interim had the mortification to see that we daily lost ground which it would not be easy to recover. In short it was obvious not only that the French government no longer confided in the amicable professions of our own, but that this treaty had otherwise produced an effect so unfavorable in the public councils towards us, as to give cause to apprehend in case it were ratified consequences of a very serious nature.

By my original instruction it appeared that in case our negociation with England failed and measures of some tone were in consequence taken towards her, that much reliance would be put on France. It was in fact the plain import of those instructions; that if war was resorted to, which in that case seemed to be contemplated by the administration, that we should be arranged again on the same side with France, *our first and natural ally* (to use the words of the administration) since I was expressly instructed to *let that be seen by the French government*. And by subsequent letters, particularly that of the 25th of September 1794, this idea was reiterated and inforced. It was upon this principle that I touched upon that topic, in my communications with the committee of public safety at a certain period, the result whereof was always made known to the administration immediately afterwards. Nor can it be doubted, in case that negociation had failed, or the treaty been rejected, that such would have been the policy of our administration. Having then at that period intimated the reliance, which in that case might be placed on France, it became my duty, now that it appeared probable the treaty would be rejected, and myself in consequence called on to verify the intimations I had given of the disposition of France to support our claims against that power, to state the arrangements it would be necessary for us to adopt to secure that support. Accordingly I informed the administration explicitly, that if the treaty was rejected, and it was wished to command with effect the fortunes of France in any further negociation with England we, *remaining at peace and relying on France for the support of those claims against that power without any effort of our own, that under existing circumstances* it would not only be necessary for the administration to avail itself of some well known pronounced character in regard to the great question which now agitates the world, to whose care the negociation should be committed, but that in other respects extraordinary circumspection should be used in the prosecution of the negociation itself:—For otherwise it would not command the confidence of France, nor could her support without it be counted on as sure or effectual. If this was done I repeated to the administration my assurance that I was satisfied the full aid of France might be obtained to support our claims upon that power, and upon terms fair and honorable to us: Nor have I a doubt that such support wisely managed in negociation would have been effectual.

About the last of September, or first of October 1795, I received several letters from the Secretary of State, of which those of June 1st July 2d, 14th and 21st alone merit attention: All of which came to hand at or about the same time, and generally by the route of England; the vessels by which they were sent being taken into port there, under the order of the British government which issued in the spring for seizing all vessels laden with provisions destined for France.

The letter of June 1st contained a justification of the conduct of the administration in forming a commercial treaty with Great Britain at that period; and likewise a vindication of the administration against the charge of a want of candor (which seemed to be apprehended) in the explanations that were given by it of the motives of that mission; in which the idea of a commercial power was always withheld. The letter of July 2d contained advice, that the treaty was not ratified, and that the President was undecided upon the point of ratification; which uncertainty too as to the ratification was encreased by those of the 14th and 21st. A copy of the treaty accompanied the letter of July 2d, and a copy of the correspondence with Mr. Adet, upon the subject of the treaty, that of July 14th.

It was inferred from these letters, that, when that of June 1st was written, the executive had resolved to ratify the treaty in case the Senate approved it, and that the hesitation which afterwards took place proceeded more from the shock which the general disapprobation of the treaty by the people gave the administration, than from any disinclination on its own part to the ratification. It was likewise inferred that that *letter* was written with a view to lay the foundation for such an event, in the expectation the ratification would probably embroil us with France. In one particular the contents of this letter affected me personally, by affirming that my instructions had not warranted the construction I had given them, in explaining as I had done the motives of Mr. Jay's mission to London. In this was opened a subject for discussion between the executive and myself of a very delicate nature. It was however still my hope that our affairs with the French republic would be so managed, as to prevent any controversy whatever, or even discussion of an unfriendly kind between the two governments, and, in any event, my firm resolution to engage in none of a personal nature, with either of them, if to be avoided. Upon this principle I answered the above letters of the Secretary, simply by an acknowledgment of their receipt; repeating to him at the same time my assurance that I had done and should continue to do every thing in my power, not only by a proper use of the documents and lights derived from him, but of such others as my own imperfect experience and erring judgment had supplied, to preserve harmony between the two countries.

It happened that a few days after the receipt of the correspondence between the Secretary of State and Mr. Adet, which accompanied the letter of the 14th of July above noticed, I had occasion to use and accordingly did use it. I had called upon Mr. Jean Debry, the member of the committee of public safety who was charged with American affairs, to procure the passports, dispatches, &c. which were promised by the French government for Mr. Barlow, who was upon the point of departing for Algiers to pursue the negociation of our treaties with the Barbary powers. Scarcely however was this topic closed, when my attention was drawn by this member to another, that of our treaty with England, which he said was considered by the committee as injurious to France. He added that he was then preparing a letter in behalf of the committee, and by its order, to me upon that subject. We discussed this point some time, till at length I asked him if the committee had received the correspondence of our Secretary of State and Mr. Adet's upon it, to which he replied in the negative.—I then asked permission to put into his hands a copy of that correspondence; requesting further that the letter spoken of might be deferred until the committee had examined and weighed it, to which he readily assented: A copy of the correspondence was in consequence sent him on the next day, or very soon afterwards.[16] It was upon this ground that I intimated in my letter of the 20th of October my opinion, that if the treaty was ratified, I should hear from the French government upon the subject of it: Of the symptoms of discontent which I witnessed, I had before given frequent intimations.

The conversation digressing from the above topic to others, turned on that of the treaty concluded between the United States and England, a copy of which, with the news of its ratification by the Senate, accompanied by certain comments or strictures thereon by a French citizen, Jean Debry said had been just received by the committee, and if I recollect right he immediately after hinted at the dissatisfaction excited by this treaty in the mind of the government.

Being asked by Mr. Monroe if they had received the correspondence which had passed between their minister, Mr. Adet, and our government on the subject, he replied they had not;—whereupon he was promised by Mr. Monroe a copy of that correspondence, and it was accordingly delivered to him the next day, or in a very few days after.

Upon his intimating to Mr. Monroe the intention of the committee to address him a letter upon the subject of the treaty, it was requested this letter might be deferred until the correspondence just spoken of had been examined and weighed by the committee.—In this proposition he acquiesced, and presumed they would likewise.—The topic being pursued, Mr. Monroe took occasion to represent the great importance of cool and dispassionate measures on the part of the French government in their relation with the United States, assuring J. Debry, that the pursuit of such measures could not fail to produce the happiest effects, while from a different policy might flow consequences highly gratifying to the enemies of both republics.

16. See Mr. Purviance's note—About the end of September, or perhaps the beginning of October last, 1795, I accompanied Mr. Monroe at a conference he had with the representative, Jean Debry, then a member of the committee of *Salut Public,* and charged with the department of American affairs.

This conference was for the purpose of engaging the good offices of the French government in aid of our negociations then pending with Algiers, &c. Applications on the same subject had some time before been made to the committee, and assurances returned, that measures would be taken to promote our wishes.

Some particular expression used by Mr. Monroe, in urging this point, provoked on the part of J. Debry a reply, in which he dwelt at some length, and with some warmth too, upon the perfect competency of the French government to discern and decide upon what measures were proper to be taken by it under particular circumstances; upon its uniform friendly disposition towards the United States and upon the evil effects that must result from a final adoption of the treaty with Britain.

Some hints too were given by J. Debry of a project which had been sketched for either extending or strengthening the existing connections between the two republics, which from its not being sufficiently matured, and owing to the other great labours of the committee had not been hitherto intimated to Mr. Monroe.

J. H. PURVIANCE.

Paris, Aug. 1796.

On the 27th of October, 1795, the convention closed its career, by transferring its powers to the present government of France, founded in a constitution which had been regularly submitted to the people, and adopted by them. To this new government was likewise transferred the subsisting relations between France and other powers, comprehending, of course, those with the United States of America.

Just before this change of government in France, Mr. Fauchet arrived from the United States with an account, that the treaty was ratified; of whose arrival, dissatisfaction with the treaty, and apparent favorable reception by the committee of public safety I informed our administration in my letter of the 5th of November, which immediately followed.

In the beginning of December, 1795, I received two letters from Mr. Pickering, who had been called by the President provisionally to the Department of State, upon the resignation of Mr. Randolph; the first of which bore date on the 12th, and the second on the 14th of September of the same year. By that of the 12th I was informed officially, and for the first time, that the treaty was ratified, although near a month had elapsed since the ratification. And by that of the 14th I was advised of an attempt made by the Captain of a British frigate, to seize Mr. Fauchet, the late French minister, within the limits of the United States, on his return home, as likewise of the measures taken by our administration to obtain of the British government adequate satisfaction to the United States for that violation of their rights.

The letter of the 12th of September, first above mentioned, which announced the ratification of the treaty, was written expressly for the purpose of designating to me the conduct I was to observe for the future, and in consequence of the ratification, in my deportment towards the French republic. It will therefore be proper to present here, concisely, the substance of that letter.

Mr. Pickering begins by observing, that as the treaty with Great Britain was ratified, and likely to become a compact between the two nations, it was proper I should become possessed of the opinions of our government, especially as it *appeared probable from my letters and the movements of disaffected persons in the United States,* that unfavorable impressions upon the government and people of France were to be apprehended. He adds, that from motives of friendship, and with a view to produce tranquillity and satisfaction, the administration had acted with the utmost candor towards the French government in every stage of the negociation; of which he gives the explanations that were made it of the motives of Mr. Jay's mission to London, whilst the negociation was depending, and the communication of the treaty to Mr. Adet, after the advice of the Senate, and before the ratification by the President, as distinguished examples: affirming that by the treaty itself the rights of France, whether founded in the laws of nations or treaties with the United States, remained unviolated and unimpaired. He then adverts to the late seizures by order of the British government, of provision vessels destined to France, as a circumstance likely to create inquietude, with a view to explain the 18th article; which he says had been misrepresented in America, as being unfriendly to France. The first paragraph of that article, he admits, had departed from the spirit of modern treaties, in allowing certain articles of merchandize, made free by such treaties, to be deemed contraband of war; but yet, he says, we have not departed from the spirit of the old law of nations, by admitting any article to be contraband which by that law was not. Britain he said would not relax; and therefore the best that could be done in that case was to recite in the treaty the list of contraband designated by the old law *by way of advertisement to our maritime and commercial people, to admonish them of a risk which existed.* And by the second paragraph of that article, which refers to the doctrine insisted on by England, that provisions may be contraband when destined to places not blockaded or invested, he says that without acknowledging her doctrine, we have guarded against its ill effects, by stipulating that when provisions and other articles, not generally contraband, shall become such, and for that reason be seized, they shall not be confiscated but paid for: A stipulation, he adds, it was evidently expedient for the United States to obtain, since by it our commerce is no longer left a prey *to future spoliations without any definite means of liquidation or redress:* That, *whether it was best to oppose this pretention of England by force was a question which pertained to the proper authorities of the United*

States to decide, who alone had a right to determine in what manner it was best to obviate *an evil,* and when it was proper *to repel an injury:* That as an independent nation we were the exclusive judges, and competent guardians of whatever concerned our interest, policy and honor; upon which subjects we would never ask the advice, or be governed by the councils, of any foreign nation whatever. He then proceeds to animadvert upon the impolicy of going to war with England; since thereby, he says, our commerce would be ruined, and thousands of our citizens be shut up or die in jails and prison-ships; our landed interest would suffer; agriculture decline; the sources of revenue fail, and other thousands of our citizens dependent on it, be involved in ruin; whence would follow the calamity of a direct tax to support the war, and happy should we be if our misfortunes ended there, or if we could contemplate only a foreign war, in which all hands and hearts might unite. He adds that by going to war, we should even hurt France, since our ports would be blocked up and our commerce at an end. That *a fruitless diversion* on the side of Canada would nearly bound our efforts; whereas, whilst we remained neutral, the aid we give her was immense; for as, by the clause in question, payment was stipulated for our provisions destined to France, when taken, being contraband, it was presumed our merchants would find therein a new stimulus for pushing their enterprizes to that country. He affirms however, that the late order for seizing did not proceed from that clause in the treaty; because the British had seized, before the treaty, and because also the order applied to other neutral powers with whom there was no similar stipulation. Finally he proceeds to lay down certain positions to which, he says, I may give the solemnity of truths; such as, that the late negociation did not proceed from any predilection in our government towards England; that the remembrance of the last war, from which we just began to recover, made us deprecate whatever even seemed to look like a renewal of it; that there were many causes of difference between the United States and Great Britain, the adjustment whereof could not longer be delayed; that the commercial part of the treaty, though important, was a subordinate one, and not a new measure; that the government of the United States was sincerely friendly to the French nation.

My wish was to conciliate the French government towards the treaty which was now ratified, and most anxiously had I looked to the administration for the means of doing it: But no person will, I am persuaded, be able to point out any trait in the above letter that was likely to produce that effect. The eulogium bestowed by it, in the beginning, upon the candor of the administration, which it says was shewn towards the French government in every stage of the negociation, and whilst the treaty was depending, if admitted by that government, was not a thing for me to dwell on. Acts of candor when performed, if acknowledged by the party to whom they are said to be rendered, ought not to be boasted of by those who perform them. But if they are not acknowledged, and especially if the act upon which the pretension is founded is viewed in a different light, as there was reason to presume was the case in the present instance, then the pretension, if urged, is likely to produce an ill effect. This, therefore, was not a topic for me to open to the French government; nor did the commentary on the treaty which the letter contained, furnish one better adapted to the purpose. Indeed it professes to notice, and in fact notices only one article, the 18th, and in so doing, admits in effect all the objections that were urged against it: For it agrees that we had thereby not only yielded the modern rule of contraband, with respect to general kinds of merchandize, which by special treaties were made articles of free trade; but that we had also made an arrangement with England, whereby she was permitted to seize our provision vessels destined to France, whenever a crisis arrived which made it eligible for her so to do, upon the condition of paying us for the provisions thus seized a reasonable mercantile profit, including freight and the expenses incident to detention. The explanation given of the second clause which respects provisions is, it is true, at first view, somewhat ambiguous, yet the true import of that explanation is as above. Indeed the disguise is so thin as to make it doubtful whether it was intended as a disguise; or rather whether the explanation was not given with a view to let it be seen, that such was the real object of that stipulation. An *evil*, it says, was thereby *remedied*, which it was deemed better *thus to adjust than to repel by force.* Of what nature then was that evil? Did it consist in the seizure of provision vessels destined to a blockaded port? Did any one ever complain of such a seizure as an injury? Or did the administration contemplate war in case that point was not yielded to us? Besides, a mode was adopted, whereby the means of *liquidation* and *redress* were provided against future *spoliations;* what spoliations? Such seizures as were made of provisions destined to a blockaded port? Are such to be called spoliations? What was the point in controversy between the two countries, which it is said was thus adjusted? Was it not simply whether the pretensions of England, who claimed a right to seize provisions, as contraband, at pleasure, with a view to starve France, should be allowed? And were not those the *spoliations* for whose *liquidation* and *redress, definite means* were said to be provided? Or would the administration, in a demand of payment for those seizures, which took place after the treaty was concluded, distinguish the cases, and confine that demand to such vessels as were taken in their route to a blockaded port, saying, for these only we will be paid, but for the others, comprehending perhaps 99 out of 100, we will not—and thus revive the controversy which it was said was thus amicably closed? This, it is presumed, would not be done. This, therefore, was not a ground to conciliate upon, nor did the other parts of the letter furnish one that was more so; for the picture of the horrors of war which it presented, a picture common to all wars, was either altogether inapplicable, or if applicable, was so only by furnishing a reply to objections, which it was apprehended would be raised against the conduct of the administration; as was the declaration which the letter contained, that the late seizures were not made in consequence of that treaty; and as was likewise the argument it furnished, that the stipulation in the 18th article, which secured payment in case of seizure, would, by encouraging the enterprizes of our merchants to France, be for her benefit. These two latter topics were indeed delicate ones for me to touch on, especially as it was known that the other neutral powers complained that we had slighted, if not injured, them; and as it was likewise known by the example of the seizures in the spring, which ensued after the treaty was concluded, that if the practice was permitted, let the encouragement be what it might, Britain, preponderating at sea, might take almost every vessel that attempted to enter the French ports. And with respect to the declaration, that we were an *independent people* and had a *right to decide for ourselves,* &c. so often repeated, I did not perceive how it applied at the time: there had been no question on that point that I knew of. France had attempted to impose on us no conditions; had asked of us no favours; on the contrary had shewn a disposition to render us many; under which circumstances we had made a treaty with Britain, which it was expected by the administration would produce an ill effect in France, but of which she had not yet complained: to prevent which and reconcile her to that treaty was the object, and to accomplish which required on our part wise and temperate councils. It became us with that view to convince her judgment, and to avail ourselves of her antient and friendly disposition towards us, not to provoke and irritate her passions. So that upon the whole, I did not perceive a single trait in this letter, which was written after long delay, and doubtless with mature deliberation, to designate the course I was to pursue in consequence of the ratification of the treaty, which breathed a spirit of conciliation; not even in that part which contained what was called positions to which I was instructed to give the solemnity of truths; for they also were calculated only to meet objections, and were otherwise expressed in such a tone of moderation, in point of friendly regard, as to have been well adapted to a communication in a like case to Russia, Turkey, or any other power with whom we had no political connection. On the contrary, that letter appeared to me, in its general tenor, to be dictated in a spirit of hostility, and more with a view to promote a rupture than prevent one.

To reconcile France to that treaty, I expected to have been authorised to explain to her government how long the commercial part was to remain in force; to state to it formally, that we were ready to enter into a new commercial treaty with her, and upon what principles, to be commenced either in Paris or Philadelphia: In which expectation, and with a view to the event of a ratification, I had told the administration, when I advised it of the ill-effect the treaty, whose contents were then known, had produced, that I should await its orders without any, the slightest, compromitment either of it or myself.[17] But nothing of this kind was to be found in that letter, nor in any which preceded or followed it. For all that the letters contained or attempted, which touched that subject, *was a justification of the administration, against the charge which was either raised or expected, of having evaded the overtures of France to treat on commerce, at a time when it was admitted that an advance was made by the administration to treat on that subject, and a commercial treaty actually concluded by it, with Great Britain.* Still, however, my object was the same, which was to conciliate and prevent, if possible, a rupture between the two countries; and I was resolved, if I could derive no aid from the administration to promote that end, at least not to become its instrument in defeating it, if such was its view, which now seemed probable.

But it was my duty to answer this letter, which I did without a comment; for it was improper for me to censure and useless to advise. I simply acknowledged its receipt with an assurance that due attention should be paid to it, as occasion required; to which I likewise added the fact, that symptoms of discontent were still seen, but whether they would assume an aspect more unfavorable I knew not: If they did I would immediately communicate it.

There was however one trait in that letter to which a more explicit answer became necessary. It had been intimated to me in that of June the 1st, that my instructions had not warranted the explanation I had given of the object of Mr. Jay's mission to London; which intimation was here repeated, in a manner it is true, not so direct, but yet in a tone not less positive. I had avoided answering that passage in the former letter, from the consideration that, in the then state of our affairs, the interest of our country required cool and united councils, to extricate us from the difficult situation into which we were thrown. But by reviving and pressing this point upon me, it seemed as if the administration expected an answer, with design to ground on it some measure it was much

17. *See letter of August 17, 1795, to the Secretary of State.* [HAMILTON.]

bent on, in which view it was my duty to give one. I therefore answered that passage by observing, that my former communications had shewn that I had understood and acted on that part of my instructions differently from what it appeared by these letters, it was intended I should understand and act on it; whereby I was placed, by the course of events, in a very delicate and embarrassing dilemma, from which indeed I was not then perhaps relieved, though I hoped and thought I was. In my answer I stated the fact correctly, and left it to the administration to pursue its policy.

The tone of the new government was cool and reserved towards me. But my conduct was the same, because my object was the same. I shewed, it is true, no mark of undue condescention to that government, but yet I certainly omitted no opportunity that occurred to conciliate its good will towards us. Unhappily however a very different spirit now displayed itself in our administration, whose measures obviously tended to promote a rupture.

Soon after the new government was organized I received a letter from the minister of foreign affairs, complaining of the misconduct of Mr. Parish, American consul at Hamburgh, in granting passports to English subjects as American citizens, and in being the agent of England for the equipment of the emigrants, desiring that I would communicate his note to our government with a request that Mr. Parish be removed. Some considerable time before this I had earnestly recommended this measure to our administration, urging many considerations, suggested as well by some particulars of his own conduct, as by the circumstance of his being a British subject, why it was of importance to our interest and character as a separate and neutral people, that his commission should be revoked and committed to an American citizen. Those considerations appeared to me to be so strong and pressing, that I concluded, as soon as they were brought to the view of the administration, he would be removed, and of course that the measure was already taken: In which expectation I answered the minister politely, intimating that I should communicate to our government the request of his in that respect, not doubting that it would be readily complied with. I should have stated, that I had anticipated the demand sometime before, and recommended the measure of my own accord; but I wished, now that it was asked by the French government, that it might appear to be granted at its request; an accommodation which I was persuaded would produce a good effect at the time. But I was soon advised by Mr. Pickering that this British subject should not be compelled to yield his post to an American citizen, at my request, supported as it was by such weighty reasons. And the subsequent management of the affair upon the application of the French government shewed that the

incident became rather a cause of irritation, than of conciliation with that government; notwithstanding the evident impolicy of such a procedure at the time,
on account of the crisis to which we were brought: For although the administration (not being able to resist the objections to his continuance) did remove
him, yet it was done in a manner so as to shew the French government, it was
not done in compliance with its request.

In January 1796, Mr. Randolph's pamphlet was received in Paris, which
contained several of the President's letters, in some of which the French republic was spoken of in terms by no means respectful, and the friends of the French
revolution in the United States reproached with being the friends "of war and
confusion;" and shortly after this, was received also, the President's address
to congress, upon the opening of the session, which in treating of the flourishing
condition of the United States, contrasted *it* with the miserable, famished, and
disorganized state of other powers. Much too was said in that address of the
advantage of our accommodation with Britain, as likewise of the favourable disposition of that power towards us, without the slightest attention being shewn
to the French republic; unless indeed it was referred to in the picture of distress
above noticed, as was inferred by the French government, as I understood from
good authority, at the time.

In the course of the year 1795, the French government had repealed, as
already shewn, all the decrees which were passed during the mission of Mr.
Morris, under which our trade had been harrassed, and had also, notwithstanding its suspicion of the contents of the British treaty, shewn a disposition to assist
us in other cases, and had actually taken measures to assist us in those of Spain
and the Barbary powers; yet none of those acts or of the disposition which produced them were even glanced at in the President's address to congress,
although it was to be inferred, such notice would have produced a good effect,
and although it was then as just as it was politic to notice them. This conduct
in the administration was the more extraordinary, from the consideration that
those decrees, by whose authority our trade was harrassed, with the harrassment
itself, had been announced in former communications to the congress, when
the British depredations were announced. It seemed natural therefore, now that
so much was said upon the subject of our accommodation with England, that
something should also be said of the repeal of those decrees by the French government, as of the proofs of friendship it had shewn us in other respects. But
this was not done.

Under such circumstances it was impossible for me to succeed in conciliating the French government towards the British treaty, since my efforts were

not only not seconded in that respect, by our administration, but absolutely counteracted by it. Nevertheless I continued to pursue the same line of conduct that I had done before, being resolved not to relax in my efforts, however unsuccessful I might be.

The sequel of my mission exhibits an interesting but painful spectacle, the distinguishing characteristics whereof are; the avowed decision of the French government to take some measure towards us in consequence of our treaty with England, as illustrated by many examples; with my efforts to prevent any such measure taking effect; and the attack made on me by our administration, upon pretexts equally unjust, frivolous and absurd. This part therefore I shall reduce to as small a compass as possible.

On the 15th of February 1796, I called on the minister of foreign affairs to state to him the distress of many of our citizens, merchants at Paris, on account of their claims upon the French government, with a view to engage his aid for their relief; but was immediately diverted from that object by information which he gave me, that the directory had at length made up its mind how to act in regard to our treaty with England; which it considered as having annulled our treaty of alliance with France, from the period of its ratification; and had appointed or intended to appoint an envoy extraordinary, to repair to Philadelphia to remonstrate against it; adding that he was ordered to send me an official note upon the subject, which he should accordingly do. I expressed to him my great surprise and concern at the communication, and was disposed to enter immediately fully upon the subject, but was prevented by observing that he was upon the point of going out, whereupon I left him for the time.

I attended him again on the day following, and remonstrated most earnestly against the measure, urging every argument that I could avail myself of to divert the government from it; offering to enter with him, whenever he thought fit, into a discussion of his objections to our treaty, or any other act of our government; assuring him that I should not only be always ready to enter with him into such explanations, but in the present instance should do it with pleasure, since by being possessed of our view of the subject, they would be better able to decide whether the complaint was well or ill founded, and of course how far it merited to be considered in that light. Upon this occasion, as upon the preceding one, the minister declined stating any specific objections to the treaty, or any other act of our government, and therefore I could make no specific defence. He admitted however that the objections I had urged to the measure had weight, and promised to communicate them to the directory, from whom, he doubted not, they would receive the attention they merited.

Thus I continued without intermission my efforts to break this measure, repeating in my conferences with the minister of foreign affairs, who always heard me with attention, all the objections that I could urge against it; assuring him that it was not admitted by our government, that any deviation was made by our treaty with England, from those with France; and renewing my proposition to enter with him into a discussion of that point. Finally upon hearing from him that the subject was still before the directory, and fearing the communication promised me might be deferred, till it would be too late for me to produce an effect upon the measure itself (if indeed it were possible in any case) I asked and obtained an audience of the directory on the 8th of March, with a view at least to attempt it. The result of this audience was a promise by the directory, that the order for sending an envoy extraordinary to the United States should be rescinded, and the minister of foreign affairs be instructed, to furnish me a copy, and discuss with me its several complaints against the conduct of our government, and that no measure should be taken upon the subject of those complaints, till after my answer was received and fully weighed.

Accordingly a summary of those complaints was presented me by the minister of foreign affairs in a paper bearing date on the 19th of March 1795. (19th of Ventose by the French calendar) to which I replied in one of the 15th of the same month. Copies of these communications were transmitted to the Department of State in my letter of the 2d of May following.

About the 20th of April I received from the Department of State a letter of the 7th of January, transmitting the correspondence which took place between the President and the minister of France, when the flag of the French republic was presented by the former to the government of the United States. I received at the same time, from the Secretary of State, a letter to the directory of France, from the President of the United States, upon the same subject; which I was instructed to take the earliest opportunity to deliver. Accordingly I delivered that letter to the minister of foreign affairs on the next day, with a request that he would present the same to the directory as soon as possible. A few days after this I received from the minister a short note, informing me that he had submitted to the directory the dispatch which was addressed to it, by the President of the United States, in the name of the Congress; and that the French government could not but receive with satisfaction whatever tended to confirm the bonds of friendship between the two nations.

From the period of my audience by the directory, and more especially after my communication with the minister of foreign affairs was handed in, I had frequent conferences with several of the members of the directory, in which

I labored to promote the same object, and at one time, as I thought, with complete success; being informed by a member, upon one of those occasions, that the directory had done nothing towards us in regard to its complaints, and he presumed would not. The purport of this communication was immediately made known to the Department of State in my next letter of the 12th of June 1796.

But this prospect was soon changed; for on the 25th of the same month I received a letter from the minister of foreign affairs requesting information, whether the intelligence which the gazettes announced, of the House of Representatives having agreed to carry the treaty into effect, was to be relied on, and in case it was, asking further in what light they were to view that event, before he called the attention of the directory to those consequences resulting from it, which specially interested the French republic. I replied to the minister, that with respect to his first interrogatory, whether the House of Representatives had passed a law to carry the treaty into effect, I could give him no authentic information, having no official advice upon it. And with respect to the second, that as I had already answered, and as I supposed to his satisfaction, his several objections to that treaty, to which I had received no reply, it was impossible for me to enter again, under such circumstances, into that subject. But if there were any points in the communication I had made him, upon which he thought I had not been sufficiently explicit, and he would be pleased to state them to me, that I would immediately notice them more particularly than I had done, and I hoped satisfactorily.

On the 7th of July following I received another note from the minister, stating certain objections to the British treaty, to which I made a reply on the 14th of the same month.

In the beginning of August 1796, the directory recalled Mr. Adet and appointed a gentleman to take his place, with the grade of chargé des affaires; who, I concluded from particular considerations, could not be well received by our government. As soon therefore as I heard of this appointment, I remonstrated strenuously against it, with the French government, and with success; for it was revoked.

In the beginning of August, I saw in the gazettes a communication from the minister of foreign affairs to Mr. Barthelemy, the ambassador of France to the Swiss Cantons; announcing an arreté of the directory, by which it was determined to act towards the commerce of neutral powers in the same manner as those powers permitted the English government to act towards them. In consequence I applied also to the minister for information relative to that arreté;

from whom I received a general answer only, corresponding in sentiment with his letter above mentioned, to the ambassador of the republic at Basle.

About the last of August, I heard that Mr. Adet (who had heretofore been reinstated when the arretés for appointing an envoy extraordinary, and chargé des affaires were respectively revoked) was now recalled and no successor appointed to him. I was advised, at the same time, that any further application from me to the French government would be improper; since it would not only prove fruitless, but most probably produce an ill effect.

Near seven months had now elapsed since the minister of foreign affairs communicated to me the discontent of the directory, on account of our treaty with England, and its decision to make the same known to our government, by an envoy extraordinary, to be dispatched to the United States; in the course of which time I had not received a single line from the Department of State (a letter of the 7th of January excepted, which applied to another subject) although I had regularly informed it of every incident that occurred; and although the crisis was a very important one, requiring the profound attention of the administration. In the course of this time, therefore, I was left alone by the administration, to oppose the discontent of France, not only unaided, but likewise under circumstances otherwise the most unfavourable. At this period, however, which was in the beginning of September, 1796, I received a letter from the Secretary of State of the 13th of June preceding, communicating to me the high dissatisfaction of the President on account of my conduct respecting the British treaty. To that letter I returned an answer of the 10th of the same month.

On the 12th of Oct. following I received a letter from the minister of foreign affairs, announcing the recall of Mr. Adet, with the motive of it. To that letter I replied in one of the 12th of October.

In the beginning of November 1796, I received a letter from the Secretary of State of the 22d of August, announcing my recall by the President of the United States. In this letter the Secretary refers me for the motives of that measure, to his former letter of the 12th of June. He adds, however, in *this* that the President was further confirmed in the propriety of that measure by other concurring circumstances, but of which he gave no detail. To this letter I made no reply until after my return to Philadelphia, in July 1797.

About the 10th of November 1796, General Pinckney arrived in Paris with my letters of recall, by which my mission to the French republic was terminated. I presented him immediately to the minister of foreign affairs for recognition, and at the same time, delivered to the minister a copy of my letters of recall, requesting that I might have a day assigned me for taking leave of the French government as soon as convenient.

It gives me pleasure to remark here, that the conduct of General Pinckney, upon that occasion, which was one of peculiar delicacy to me, was in every respect candid, manly, and honorable.

On the first of January 1797, I took leave of the executive directory of France, in an audience specially assigned me for the purpose, and sailed with my family for the United States, as soon as the season would permit.

Upon leaving France I committed my letter-book and other public documents to the care of Mr. Prevost who had acted with me in the character of Secretary of Legation, a young man of merit and talents, well qualified to serve his country in a more important trust.

The above is a plain narrative of the facts and incidents attending my mission, from its commencement to the close; upon which I will make a few comments.

The present situation of America is understood by every one, because almost every one is some way or other affected by it. And what it has been in every preceding stage of this European war, is equally well known, for the same reason. The picture she has exhibited is an uniform one. Its characters are strong, but yet not diversified. In her foreign relations nothing is to be seen but the waste and pillage of her commerce, sometimes by several powers, always by some one power; and little less than anarchy at home; for the seeds of discontent, jealousy and disunion have been scattered throughout these States, in the course of a few years past, with a wasteful hand. By what means then was this state of things produced, and why was it produced?

It is well known, that the executive administration has heretofore guided all our measures; pursuing, in many instances, a course of policy equally contrary to the public feeling, and the public judgment: And it was natural to expect that that administration would now be held highly responsible for the embarrassments it has thus brought upon our country. But by this attack on me, a new topic has been raised for discussion, which has drawn the public attention from the conduct of the administration itself; for in consequence the only question now before the public seems to be, whether I have merited the censure thus pronounced upon me, by the administration, or have been dealt hardly by. But this was a mere political manouvre, intended doubtless to produce that effect.

Whether I have performed my duty to my country, as I ought to have done, in the various, contradictory, and embarrassing situations, in which I was placed by the administration, is a point upon which my country will determine, by the facts and documents submitted to it. Upon this point I fear not the result, because I have the utmost confidence in the wisdom and rectitude of a public decision, when facts are before the public; and because, knowing what my conduct was, I can always find a consolation in my own breast, if the contrary should be the case. But whether the administration has performed its duty to the public, by a proper discharge of the great trust reposed in it, during this awful crisis of human affairs, is a question of much greater importance; which ought to be well understood. I am happy however in reflecting that these two points are altogether unconnected with, and, independent of each other; since the establishment of misconduct on *its* or *my part,* is no proof of the good conduct of the other party. To each a separate duty was allotted, and the question is entirely a distinct one, how each performed that duty, in its appropriate sphere.

Nor should I, in respect to myself, add a word to the light which those documents contain, being willing so far as the propriety of my own conduct is involved, to submit the point to the judgment of my countrymen, upon the documents alone. But the administration has attempted by this attack on me, to shield itself from the censure it justly apprehended, in the hope of throwing the blame on others; a finesse which ought not to succeed. It is proper therefore to strip the administration of a mantle thus artfully drawn over it: With which view I propose to examine briefly the charge alledged against me by the administration, with the evidence by which it supports it: Not for the sake of shewing, I repeat again, that my conduct did not merit the attack, but that the administration knew it, at the time it made the attack.

The charge which the administration alledged against me is to be found in a letter from the Secretary of State, referred to above, of the 13th of June 1796; the purport of which is, that I withheld certain documents from the knowledge of the French government, illustrative of the views of ours, respecting the British treaty, although I knew the French government was dissatisfied with that treaty, and had likewise acknowledged the receipt of those documents: and the testimony adduced to support this charge consists of the three following circumstances: First the importance of the documents themselves, which were deemed conclusive, and sufficient to have silenced the French government had they been thus applied: The second, the delay of that government to express its discontent, for sometime after I was possessed of those documents; notwithstanding such discontent was known to exist on account of the British treaty, and was likewise much aggravated by other causes; and the third, the success which attended my efforts to remove that discontent, after the 15th of February 1796, when *it* was announced to me by the minister of foreign affairs, as heretofore shewn; whence it was inferred, that had I begun in time, the affair would have been smothered in embrio.

This is the charge, and this the testimony by which it is supported. The Secretary adds, it is true, in his letter of the 22d of August following, that there were other concurring circumstances which confirmed the President in the propriety of the measure he had taken towards me; but these he did not *then* communicate, nor has he *since,* though called on to do it; nor has he communicated other testimony to support the charge already raised. To that charge therefore with the testimony adduced, I shall confine my comments.

It is proper to observe here that the documents, the withholding which the Secretary lays to my charge, were two letters, one from Mr. Randolph of the 14th of July, 1795, communicating his correspondence with Mr. Adet, upon the subject of the treaty, received about the beginning of October following, and one from Mr. Pickering of the 12th of Sept. received sometime about the last of November, or beginning of December, of the same year; for these were the only letters which I received from the Department of State on that subject, after the treaty was submitted to the Senate; or indeed before, except such as shewed the fluctuating state of the executive mind respecting the ratification; which letters could not be referred to as explaining the views of the executive, since then it had none. To these two letters therefore the charge solely applied.

It is also proper to observe here, that the first of these letters was (as heretofore stated) put into the hands of the committee of public safety, as soon as it was received, a suitable occasion permitting it; that the second was not then received, and of course could not be thus applied; though indeed had it been then received, I do not think I should have thus applied it, for reasons heretofore given. It will however be seen by a perusal of my discussion with the minister of foreign affairs, that I omitted nothing which either of those papers contained, which could be turned to any account. The first of these facts, it is true, was not then known to the Secretary; for as the object, at that time contemplated by the committee, was not pursued, on account I presume of the change of government which took place immediately afterwards in France, and might possibly never be revived, I declined mentioning it to our administration, from motives of delicacy to both governments; wishing, if to be avoided, that no such evidence of the discontent of France, should appear in my correspondence. The omission however to communicate it to the administration, was no ground whereon to charge me with a contrary line of conduct, against the force of so many other facts and circumstances as were at the time in its possession. The other fact could not then be known, because the decision respecting me was hurried, before a copy of that discussion was received. The cause of such precipitation, at that precise time, and under the then existing circumstances, the administration ought to explain.

But I will proceed to examine the Secretary's charge with the testimony by which he supports it; the first item of which is, the importance of the documents in question; which he says were sufficient to have silenced the French government, had they been thus applied, whence he infers that they were not thus applied. In noticing this piece of testimony, I do not wish to be understood as derogating from the merit of those documents: I will admit, at least for argument-sake, that the letters referred to are well written. But I deny that the conclusion drawn from that circumstance is a just one; or in other words that the continuance of the discontent of the French government, after I received those documents, is a proof that the light they contained was withheld. It is well known, that every free government *is the proper guardian of whatever concerns its interest, policy, or honor, upon which subjects it takes its own counsel, and pursues its own measures;* nor does it often happen, that such government regards the counsel of any foreign nation whatever. I believe no instance can be adduced, by the administration, of any counsel being asked or attention shewn on its part to the counsels of the French nation, from the commencement of the administration to the present day, nor to the counsels of a minister of that nation; one instance only excepted, in which his counsel was asked, but immediately rejected. Why it was asked it will be easy to explain, as it likewise will be to shew, that it was determined to reject it before it was asked. This sentiment then, which is a just one, ought to be admitted as reciprocal; but although the Secretary is firm and peremptory, when he applies it in our favor, yet he denies its existence as applicable to the French republic. He supposes after those letters were written, that the affair with France was settled; that we were to hear no more of her discontent about the British treaty, or if we did, that I was to be responsible for it. In short he seems to have concluded, from the moment those letters were forwarded to me, that he had put that nation under my care, and if I did not keep *it* in order, that I merited censure. This indeed were an easy way to settle our controversies with foreign powers, and fortunate should we be if we could thus adjust them. But how happens it, that none of our controversies have been thus adjusted? Many letters have been written; much labour bestowed in that line by the Secretary himself, and still we are involved in many controversies; none of which, even of the old ones, seem yet to be finally settled, though the opportunity for it was a most favourable one; whilst others are accumulated. I think therefore it must be admitted, that

the continuance of the discontent of the French government, after those documents were received, however important they might be, was no proof that
any light they contained was withheld by me.

And with respect to the second circumstance relied on;—the delay of the
French government to bring forward its complaints, for sometime after I
received the documents in question, notwithstanding its discontent, &c. I cannot conceive how that can be urged in support of the charge. If that argument
was sound, it would follow that if that government had brought forward its
complaints sooner, my conduct would have been correct; whilst on the other
hand, if it had never complained, there would have been a complete demonstration of the charge. It is impossible to reason on an argument so absurd. I shall
only observe upon it, that had I been called on for a proof of my activity and
zeal, to preserve tranquillity between the two countries, I should have urged the
delay of the French government to complain, discontented as it was, as a most
satisfactory one. Indeed I do not know, before the government did complain,
how I could produce any other.

And the third circumstance relied on, to prove misconduct in me, seems to be
equally absurd. I believe it is the first time that the success of exertions was ever
urged as a proof that none were made, or that they were not made in due time.
Such success, where the object was a desirable one, is generally received by the
party for whom, or under whose auspices, it is rendered, with pleasure; and
obtains for the party rendering it, some degree of acknowledgment. But that it
should be adduced as a proof of previous misconduct, and treated as such, is an
act of which I think there is no example. Ardent must have been the pursuit of
some political object thereby counteracted, or keen and violent the passions which
otherwise hurried the administration on, or surely it would not have used such an
argument. I will ask, and the question ought to be attended to, whether those
efforts whose details were then before the administration, contained the evidence
of a mind indifferent to the object in view? Whether the success which attended
them, whereby the course of the French government was actually checked and
suspended, for about seven months, was a proof that that government thought me
insincere, or that the counsel I gave was unworthy its attention?

I might observe, that for this argument to have weight, my success ought
to have been complete. But unfortunately this was not the case as is too well
known. My efforts produced an effect for a certain term only: A sufficient one
however to have permitted the administration to interpose, and assist me. It
did interpose, it is true, but it was not for that purpose. Had my success been
complete we should have witnessed an extraordinary political phenomenon,

that of a public minister furnishing, by successful services to his country, testimony to an administration hostile to him, to prove that he had rendered none, and was a delinquent. Such an argument is too absurd to be dwelt on. It requires only to be understood, to be despised.

Whether I pursued the wisest course that could have been pursued, to prevent the complaints of that government and to reconcile it to our treaty with England, I will not pretend to say. The course which I pursued was a plain one: It was to prevent, by informal explanations, &c. the necessity of an official discussion; a practice I had been long in the habit of, as was well known to the administration. As soon however as the French government took up the subject officially, I was likewise prepared in that line to oppose and did oppose, its measures; nor did I relax in my efforts, till they were evidently fruitless.

From the period when the treaty was concluded in Nov. 1794 till February 1796, when the French government first took up the subject as above stated, fourteen months had elapsed; and from that period to the time when the first act respecting the commerce of the neutral powers was passed, near seven months more had elapsed; forming in the whole about twenty one months, before any step was taken: Nor did it take a single step until after the treaty was ratified by the President and Senate, and the House of Representatives had likewise given its sanction, by the passage of a law to carry it into effect. Yet it was known that the French government was jealous of the object of the mission which produced that treaty from the period of its nomination; that it suspected the treaty was founded upon principles injurious to France before its contents were seen; and that those suspicious were confirmed when they were seen.

Whether I contributed in any degree to divert the French government from opposing the ratification of that treaty, or taking its measures after the treaty was ratified, I will not pretend to say. This is submitted for others to determine. If I did, I am not boastful of it; since as our administration did not take advantage of that delay to heal the breach in time, it was of no real service to my country. Well however do I know, after the French government had rejected my counsel, and taken a different course, that I was viewed by that government for sometime in a questionable light: Nor were the motives of my conduct justly appreciated by it, until after I was censured by our own.

Such were the facts and documents in possession of the administration, when it pronounced a censure on my conduct. Can any one then believe, that the motive assigned for it was the true one? And if it was not, what was the true one?

To determine this latter point some attention is due to the conduct of the administration through every stage of this European controversy; for the whole of its conduct forms a system, which ought to be taken together, to judge correctly of its motives in any particular case. To do justice to the subject, in this view, would require more time and attention than I am now able to bestow on it. I will however notice some facts and circumstances, which being duly appreciated, cannot otherwise than facilitate the labors of others, in making a more accurate research.

The first is, the appointment of a person as minister plenipotentiary to France, in the commencement of the French revolution, who was known to be an enemy to that revolution, and a partizan of royalty; whereby the name and weight of America (no inconsiderable thing at that time in that respect) was thrown into the scale of kings, against that of the people and of liberty.

Second, the continuance of that person in office, till every misfortune predicted of his mission, by those who opposed it in the Senate, and disapproved it throughout the community at large (which latter description was a very numerous one) was nearly verified; the connection between the two countries having gradually diminished, as the French revolution advanced, till at the time of his recall it was reduced to a slight bond indeed: In the course of which time the embargo at Bordeaux was imposed, and continued, till removed upon the application of Mr. Fenwick, consul at that port; for our minister was not attended to: Sundry articles of our treaty of commerce were likewise set aside by formal decrees and many spoliations in consequence made upon it.

Third, the final removal of that person, not from a regard to the public interest which was known thus to suffer, but because it was demanded by the French government. Upon which occasion it was intimated to him, that his removal was attributable to that cause only; which intimation became known to the French government.

Fourth, my appointment to the French republic with the circumstances attending it: It being known that, with other members of the Senate, I had opposed in many instances the measures of the administration, particularly in that of the mission of Mr. Morris to France, and of Mr. Jay to London; from the apprehension those missions would produce, in our foreign relations, precisely the ill effect they did produce.

Fifth, the instructions that were given me to explain to the French government the motives of Mr. Jay's mission to London, not as an act of condescension on our part, at the demand of the French government, put of policy, *to produce tranquility, and give satisfaction,* whilst the negociation was depending; by which instructions, if the existence of a power to form a commercial treaty was not positively denied, yet *it* was withheld, and the contrary evidently implied.

Sixth, the strong documents that were put in my possession at that period, by the administration, of its attachment to France and the French revolution; so different from anything before expressed.

Seventh, the resentment shown by the administration on account of the publication of those documents; it having been intended they should *produce* their effect, *at the same time,* and yet be kept *secret.*

Eighth, the approbation bestowed on me by the administration when I made vehement pressures on the French government for a repeal of its decrees, under which our commerce was harrassed, exhibiting a picture of its spoliations, &c. and the profound silence and inattention of the administration when those decrees were repealed, and a disposition shown by that government to assist us in other cases.

Ninth, the power given to Mr. Jay to form a commercial treaty with England, in the midst of a war, by a special mission, at a time when no such advance was made to treat on that subject with France, and her advances at best coolly received.

Tenth, the withholding from me the contents of that treaty until after the meeting of the Senate; notwithstanding the embarrassment to which I was, in the interim, personally exposed, in consequence of the explanations I had before given to the French government, by order of the administration, of the motives of the mission which produced it; which deportment proves clearly that the administration did not deal fairly with me from the commencement.

Eleventh, the submission of the treaty to Mr. Adet after the advice of the Senate, before the ratification of the President; at a time when, as it appears by satisfactory documents, it was resolved to ratify it, which submission therefore was probably not made to obtain the aid of Mr. Adet's counsel, in which light it would have been improper, especially as it had been withheld from his government; but to repel an objection to the candor of the administration, in its conduct in preceding stages.

Twelfth, the character of the treaty itself by which (according to the administration) we have departed from the modern rule of contraband, with respect to many articles made free by modern treaties; have also made an arrangement, by which, whilst it professes not to have sacrificed the right, has actually and avowedly sanctioned the doctrine and practice of England, in seizing provisions at pleasure, as contraband of war; and have likewise yielded the principle, so important to America, that free ships shall make free goods.

Thirteenth, the conduct of the administration after the ratification of the treaty, being in all cases irritable towards France; although it was apprehended the ratification would embroil us with that power; and although at a moment, when it was proposed to decline the ratification, a most soothing and humiliating apology was drawn, to be presented to the English government, for declining so to do.

Fourteenth, I should not notice my recall, being in itself a circumstance too *trivial* to merit attention, if it were not for the state in which our affairs were in my hands, when my recall was decided; being at a period when it appeared I had succeeded in quieting the French government for the time, and was likely to do it effectually. To be left there to that precise time, and then withdrawn and censured, seems to authorise a presumption, that I was left there in the first instance in the expectation I would not defend that treaty, and in consequence whereof a rupture would ensue, and recalled afterwards, when it was known I had done my duty, and was likely to prevent a rupture.

Due attention to the above facts and circumstances in connection with others that will readily occur, will, I am persuaded, contribute essentially to explain the views and policy of the administration, through the whole of this European war; the effects whereof have been so injurious to our national character, as likewise to the agricultural and commercial interests of these States.

I have omitted to comprize in the above enumeration, the nature of this great crisis itself, because *that* being a general topic, will be embraced in the mind of every one, who examines with care the incidents attending it, in its relation to every country. It is known to have been produced by a war undertaken on the part of all the kings of Europe against France, with a view to prevent the success of a revolution in that country, in favor of liberty. Whether the nature of this crisis contributed in any degree to influence our measures, by repelling us from France and attracting us towards England, is submitted for others to determine. That it ought to have done so, will I presume not be avowed *publicly* by any one.

Whether the motives which governed the administration in its policy through this crisis are justifiable, is a point upon which the public and posterity will decide. I am happy however to observe, that no imputation can be raised against the administration, against which it may not vindicate itself, if its conduct admits of vindication.

Be this however as it may, it is nevertheless obvious, that the policy itself, was, at best, shortsighted and bad. To stand well with France through the whole of this European war, was the true interest of America; since great advantage was to be derived from it in many views, and no injury in any. What would have been the condition of these States had France been conquered, and the coalesced powers triumphed, it is easy to perceive. Had the duke of Brunswick, for example, reached Paris, and the kings of Europe, after distributing among themselves such portions of that flourishing country as suited each, dictated to the residue such form of government as they pleased (if indeed they had not annihilated the name of France as they have done that of Poland) was it to be presumed that America, who, as the parent of liberty, was likewise the parent of the French revolution, would have escaped their notice? Or was it likely, that by a variance with France, preserving as we do, and I trust always shall preserve, our free elective government, that we should have stood well with them, hated as we know we are by one of the parties, who cannot view us in any other light than that of rebels? Fortunately the successes of France permitted us to have only a glimpse of the danger which menaced us. But the existence of such a danger, or even the probability that it existed, was a sufficient motive why we should preserve a good understanding with the power, by whose successes it was sure to be averted.

In many other views too, it was of importance for us to stand well with France. We had claims to adjust with other powers, the favourable adjustment whereof depended much on her success: For if she was conquered, it did not seem likely that we should accomplish any of our objects with those powers; nor could we profit of her success otherwise than by preserving a good understanding with her.

Besides our footing with France was in itself highly advantageous to us. By our treaty of 1778, we enjoyed the privilege of the modern law of nations in our intercourse with her enemies. By it our ships gave protection to the goods of her enemies, and to all kind of merchandize in our trade with her enemies, strict contraband of war only excepted. The beneficial effects too of this stipulation which was respected by France at the time that treaty passed, was most sensibly felt upon our navigation and commerce; for in consequence of it, we were then become the principal carriers of the enemies of France. It was therefore of importance to us to continue this stipulation in force, and the obligation upon the administration, to be attentive to the means of preserving it, was the stronger from the consideration, that by the misconduct of the administration, it had been already once lost in the course of the present war; as from the further one, that as Britain did not recognize the same principle, the observance of it by France could not otherwise than be hurtful to her.

And in contemplation of future and more beneficial commercial arrangements, it was of great importance for us to stand well with France. The fertility and extent of her colonial possessions, with the amount and value of their productions, surpassing by far those of any other European power, (to say nothing of the importance of the commerce of France herself) are facts well understood by our commercial people. It was highly for the interest of America to improve our footing in that commerce, and easy was it to have done so, had due attention been paid to the necessary means of improving it.

These were considerations which ought to have been attended to, and would have been attended to by the administration, if some more powerful motive had not interposed to prevent it.

Nor was it difficult to stand well with France through the whole of this crisis, and profit of her fortunes, without the smallest possible loss or even hazard. The demonstration of this position is complete; for we know that although our ground was once lost by the administration, in the course of the present war, it was nevertheless afterwards recovered; although it is much easier to preserve a friendship, whilst at the height, than to recover it after it is gone. And how was it recovered? Not by any address on my part, for I pretend to none: But simply by presenting to the French government the documents that were committed to my care for that purpose; illustrative of the good wishes of our administration for the French nation, and its revolution; and likewise by supporting those documents by my own conduct; by which however I was known, as a spectator only, not as a partizan in their affairs; for I do not recollect that I gave an opinion upon a single point, with which I had no concern, whilst I was there;nor did I ever associate with their parties, or with any description of persons as a party. All Frenchmen were kindly received at my house: In short I did nothing but mind my own business in a plain and simple way; which thousands of my countrymen might have done equally well, perhaps much better. And of her disposition to extend to us the aid of her fortunes, in every line where they could aid us, sufficient proof was likewise given.

Nor did we hazard any thing in any view by standing well with France, whilst much was to be gained. The administration admits she did not wish us to embark in the war. Perhaps this was admitted to preclude the claim of merit for not wishing it. But the fact in my opinion was so. I speak with confidence of the views of the French government, in that respect, after I got there; especially whilst our footing was most cordial. Of the motive I say nothing; but I think it not only due to candor, but sound policy, to admit in all cases the motive to be good, when the effect was salutary.

Such was the situation of America in the commencement of this war! Such our standing with the French nation, so advantageous in itself, so easy to preserve! And yet all these advantages have been thrown away, and instead of that secure and tranquil state which we might have enjoyed throughout, we have been likewise plunged, so far as the administration could plunge us, into a war with our ancient ally, and on the side of the kings of Europe contending against her for the subversion of liberty!

Had France been conquered, to what objects that administration would have aspired, has fortunately, by her victories, been left a subject for conjecture only. Of its zeal to push things to a dangerous extremity we have many proofs: Of its moderation, none.

We have heard much of intrigues, between the people of these States and the government of France. But free people seldom intrigue together; because there is no motive for it. Between the leaders however of a free people, and the neighbouring monarchs, such intrigues have often taken place, and always will take place, whilst liberty is odious to monarchs, and men can be found base enough to betray her. If we read the history of the ancient Grecian republics, we shall see many examples of intrigues between the kings of Persia and the leaders of those republics; whilst none are to be seen of combinations between the people of any of those republics and the free governments of another, except of the purpose of overthrowing their tyrants. But in America we have no tyrant except that of prejudice, which time and information alone will overthrow.

The contrast between the situation we might have held, through the whole of this war, and that which we have held, is a striking one. We might have stood well with France, avoiding all the losses we have sustained from her; enjoying the benefits of the principles of free trade, and even appeared as an advocate for those principles, and without going to any extremity: We might have preserved our ancient renown; bought at a great expense of blood and treasure, in a long war, in a contest for liberty, and even appeared as a defender of liberty, and without fighting for her: We might too, in my opinion, have commanded a better fortune in our negociation with Britain, and only by availing ourselves, in a suitable manner, of the fortunes of France. And instead of a situation so advantageous, so honorable, so satisfactory to our country, what is that into which our government has conducted us? Our navigation destroyed, commerce laid waste and a general bankruptcy threatening those engaged in it; the friendship of a nation lost, the most powerful on earth, who had deserved better things from us, and had offered to place us, our vessels, and commodities on the footing of its native citizens in all its dominions; war hanging over us, and that not on the side of liberty and the just affections of our people, but of monarchy and our late most deadly foe; and we are made fast, by treaty and by the spirit of those at the helm, to a nation bankcrupt in its resources, and rapidly verging either to anarchy or despotism. Nor is this all. Our national honor is in the dust; we have been kicked, cuffed, and plundered all over the ocean; our reputation for faith scouted; our government and people branded as cowards, incapable of being provoked to resist, and ready to receive again those chains we had taught others to burst. Long will it be before we shall be able to forget what we are, nor will centuries suffice to raise us to the high ground from which we have fallen.

APPENDIX: Monroe is offered Minister of Paris

EVENTS LEADING UP TO MONROE'S PARIS POST
TO THOMAS JEFFERSON.
Mutilated in the original. [HAMILTON.]

PHILA., March 31, 1794.

DEAR SIR,—The embargo passed two days since. . .of some moment in the character . . . of this city was discovered . . . had opposed the embargo on Friday—and on Monday introduced the proposition himself. It contained a proviso wch. implied a right that those vessels wch. had already obtained clearances shod. be exempt from the operation—but this was amended in the Senate. A vessel of his was caught near the capes by a French Frigate & sent up with a British passport, w'ch had cleared out on Saturday. Propositions for sequestration & organizing the militia are dependent—an Envoy Extry. is spoken of for Britn.—& Hamilton, Jay, & King are those urged by that party. It will probably be one of them unless there shod. be found a vote for their rejection in the Senate wch. is not presumable. Either will answer to bind the aristocracy of this country stronger & closer to that of the other. Yrs. affecy.

JAS. MONROE.

TO GEORGE WASHINGTON.

This letter seems to have raised, for the first time, the question as to the right of a Senator to criticise the nomination of a public officer before its presentation to the Senate. Washington submitted the matter to the Secretary of State, for his opinion. Randolph's opinion was "that the Secretary of State inform Col. Monroe verbally, that his station entitles his communications to attention; that it is presumed, that he has considered and made up his mind as to the kind of interference, which a senator ought to make in a nomination beforehand; that upon this idea the President will be ready to afford an interview at a given time." Washington did not accord in this opinion, and wrote Monroe, the next day, ignoring his suggestion of a personal interview, but at the same time requesting that if he was "possessed of any facts or information which would disqualify Colonel Hamilton for the mission," that he would "communicate them in writing." Monroe was not alone in his opposition to Hamilton. Washington received other protests. John Nicholas wrote to Washington: "I confess myself astonished to hear the nomination which is made for this office, at a time when perhaps more than half America have determined it to be unsafe to trust power in the hands of this person however remotely it is connected with many of the odious traits in his character—at a time when at least one half the Legislature are afraid to exert themselves in the most trying situation of their country, lest his present powers should enable him to wrest them to purposes which he is supposed by them to entertain & which they dread more than the open attack of Great Britain—at a time when this person is the avowed friend of Great Britain in the most infamous contest, when all his measures have tended to throw this country into her arms & many entertain suspicion with some grounds that the present hostility of that country to this is partly intended to aid his well known attachment to it—to appoint him to an office in which he cound immediately and successfully advance his purposes would be to stake the American happiness on the justice of one of two opinions when both are advocated by equal numbers. Every man in a republic is a centinel on public safety and the warnings of danger should be listened to rather than the assurances of safety from the importance of the consequences which may follow." [HAMILTON.]

PHILADA., April 8, 1794.

SIR,—Having casually heard that it was requested by many of Colo. Hamilton's political associates, that you would nominate him as Envoy to the Court of Great Britain, and as I should deem such a measure not only injurious to the publick interest, but also especially so to your own, I have taken the liberty to express that sentiment to you & likewise to observe farther, that in case it is your wish I should explain to you more at large my reason for this opinion, I will wait on you at any hour you may appoint for that purpose.

With great respect & esteem

I am, Sir, Your most humble servt.

JAS. MONROE.

TO THOMAS JEFFERSON.
PHILA., May 4, 1794.

DEAR SIR,—Yours of April 24th. reached me yesterday. Since my last the proposition of Mr. Clarke for prohibiting the importation of British goods until the posts shall be surrendered & compensation made for the depredation on our trade, was rejected in the Senate. Upon the question on the first section wh.

determined the fate of the bill, Jackson and Bradley withdrew which left us 11. only against 14.: in consequence of w^h. every sect. was negatived, yet a question was notwithstanding taken whether the bill sho^d. be read a 3^d. time and in favor of which these gent^n. voted, & Ross the successor of Gallatin taking into his head now to withdraw, the house was equally divided & the casting vote given by V. President agñst it. Thus the bill was lost, the most mature and likely to succeed of all the propositions respecting G. Britn. w^h. have been presented before the legislature during the session. Its fate may be ascribed to an executive manouvre; for whilst it was depending in the Rep^l. branch & obviously a great majority in its favor, the nomination of M^r. Jay was introduc'd, as Envoy Extr^y. for the British court. From that moment it was manifest the measure wo^d. be lost, and altho' it passed the other branch & perhaps with greater vote than would have been the case, had not the sense of the Senate been clearly indicated by the approbation of the nomination, yet it was plain the prospect of success was desperate. An Extr^y. mission was a measure of conciliation, it was urged; prohibitory regulations were of a different character & wo^d. defeat its object. Thus you find nothing has been carried agñst that nation, but on the contrary the most submissive measure adopted that co^d. be devised, to court her favor & degrade our character.

Tis said that the Envoy will be armed with extr^y. powers, & that authority to form a commer^{cl}. treaty will likewise be comprized in his instructions. Under a similiar power upon a former occasion, granted too by implication only, this person had well nigh bartered away the Mississippi. What then may we not expect from him upon the present crisis, when the power is expressly granted and the fortune of the party whose agent he is, may be considered as hazarded in the success of his mission? After degrading our Country by shewing to the world, that they were more willing to confide in retribution &^{c}. from their justice & favor, than from the strength of our union & the decision of our councils, will this man return baffled in the enterprize, & seek to atone for himself & those who sent him, to the community, by owning his and their folly which had exposed us to such humiliation? And when it is considered that Britain contemplates the conquest of the French & perhaps afterwards of the Sp^h. Islands, & the downfall of the Sp^h. power in this region of the world—a course of policy which will part her not only from Sp^h. but perhaps from the present combination of powers, is it not probable she will be disposed to seek an alliance here as well for the purpose of aiding her in these projects as detaching us from France? Some symptoms of discontent have already appeared in the Sp^h. cabinet, and these it is probable will be increased when the conquest of Brit[n]. in the Islands is attended to, and her views become further developed. The circumstance of sending an envoy to negotiate with Engl[d]. at the time that the Minister of France, on the ground & cloathed with similar powers, is only amused with acts of civility, shews that a connection with the former power is the real object of the Executive.

The present French minister expressed lately the wish of his country that G. Morris sho[d]. be recalled & in consequence arrangm[ts]. are making for that purpose. Being forced to send a republican character the adm[n]. was reduc'd to the dilemna of selecting from among its enemies or rather those of opposite principles, a person who wo[d]. be acceptable to that nation. The offer of the station has been presented to Ch[lr]. Livingston as I hear in a letter written by the President. Tis tho[t]. he will accept it. Burr's name was mentioned to Randolph but with the success that was previously expected, indeed it was not urged in preference to the other, but only noted for consideration. I thank you for the intelligence respecting my farm near you. I think we shall adjourn in ab[t]. 3 weeks after w[h]. I shall immediately proceed home. M[rs]. M. joins in best wishes for y[r]. health & that of y[r]. family. Sincerely, I am, Dear Sir, your friend & servant

JA[s]. MONROE.

"My objects are, to prevent a war, if justice can be obtained by fair and strong representations (to be made by a special envoy) of the injuries which this country has sustained from Great Britain in various ways; to put it into a complete state of military defence; and to provide eventually for such measures as seem to be now pending in Congress for execution, if negotiation in a reasonable time proves unsuccessful."—Washington to Edmund Randolph, on Jay's nomination. Ford's Writings of George Washington, *vol, xii., p. 419.*

cf. Washington's letter to Robert R. Livingston, April 29, 1794: "PRIVATE. Circumstances have rendered it expedient to recall Mr. Gouv[r]. Morris from his mission to the Republic of France. Would it be convenient and agreeable to you to supply his place? An affirmative answer would induce an immediate nomination of you, for this appointment to the Senate; and the signification of your sentiments relative thereto, as soon as your determination is formed, would oblige me particularly, as it is not expected that that body will remain much longer in session." *May 10th, Livingston replied to Washington, placing his reluctance to accept the appointment on the difficulty of making immediate arrangements for a permanent residence abroad. Washington's wish was to accommodate Livingston, as far as the public service would permit. May 14th, Washington had not decided, as he was awaiting Livingston's answer to his question:* "What would be the shortest possible time necessary for his preparations." [HAMILTON.]

TO THOMAS JEFFERSON.

"The intelligence which has been received this morning is, if true, hostility itself. The President of the United States has understood, through channels of real confidence, that Governor Simcoe has gone to the foot of the rapids of the Miami, followed by three companies of a British regiment, in order to build a fort there."—The Secretary of State to Mr. Hammond, May 20, 1794. Am. State Papers—Foreign Relations, vol. i., p. 461. [HAMILTON.]

PHILA, May 26, 1794.

DEAR SIR,—The session begins to draw to a close. The 3d. of June is agreed on by both houses as the day on which it shall end, and I believe the agreement will be executed. The inclosed paper will shew you the state of things with Engl'd. This incursion into our country has no pretext to be call'd or considered otherwise than an actual invasion; and as such I presume it will be treated by the President whose powers are competent by the existing law to its repulsion. The Govr. of Pennsyla. has a small force within 16 miles of Presque Isle, & intends taking possession of the latter post. Within a few days past however it has been notified to him by some Indians that it will be opposed, and in consequence thereof he has ordered out 1000 of the western militia to secure the lodgment. I suspect however these movements were dictated in Nov'r. last and sho'd not be considered as an indication of the temper of the Engl'h. Ct. at present. They may even be disavowed if a change in circumstances requires it. The incident has been seized, you will observe, as a ground for pressing an increase of the military force, in consequence of which a proposition was immediately introduced into the Senate for authorizing the President to raise 10,000 additional troops under provisions more popular than those rejected in the Rep's. and of course more likely to succeed even there. In the Senate it will pass immediately, for the republican party is entirely broken in that branch. Thus it results that thro' the influence of the Executive aided by the personal weight of the President, the republican party notwithstanding its systematic & laborious efforts has been able to accomplish nothing which might vindicate the honor or advance the prosperity of the country. I believe I intimated to you in my last that the President had offered to Mr. Livingston, after the refusal of Mr. Madison, the legation to France in the place of Gr. Morris who would be recalled. That Colo. Burr had been a competitor. Since that time Livingston has declined and Burr has continued, under auspices very favorable to his success, sole candidate. Present appearances authorize the belief he will be appointed. Of course he goes as a republican and I am inclined to think the President supposes he lays that party under obligations to him for the nomination, for I am persuaded in addition to other considerations he really surmounts some objections of a personal nature in making it. But when it is known that the Jersey members, Judge Patterson &c. have promoted his interest, our confidence in the steadiness of his political tenets will not be increased. We shall be with you as soon as possible after the adjournment. Sincerely I am yr. friend & servt.

JAS. MONROE.

As Mr. M. gives you the paper containing the correspondence referred to, and the others contain nothing, I send none.

The Secretary of State to Washington, May 22d: "E. Randolph has the honor of returning to the President, the list which was yesterday put into his hands; and at the same time incloses a letter from Mr. Frelinghuysen as to Mr. Burr. In a conversation with Mr. Madison, his opinion appears to be decided, that the Constitution does not incapacitate Mr. Burr; and that he is a proper person. An objection seems to be ready in the mouth of some for young Adams; as being the author of some pieces, signed Publicola, about two years ago.—Fauchet did not appear to know Franklin, nor his character; nor yet to feel any attachment to him." [HAMILTON.]

TO JAMES MADISON.

PHILA., May 26, 1794.

DEAR SIR,—I have been with Mr. Randolph & have given him no final answer. The fact appears to be that the message to me was directly from the President, so that a decision settles it—He has also had an interview with Mr. Dayton.

May I request of you to go to Mr. Randolph, & settle the matter with him. I promised him you wo'd in the course of 1/2 an hour. If it has not the approbation of my few friends & yourself in particular, I certainly will decline it.—Weigh, therefore, all circumstances & paying as little regard to private considerations as sho'd be, tell him for me what answer to give—I write in haste in the Senate, being engaged on the balance bill—Y'r friend & servt,

JAS. MONROE.

An answer must be given the President immediately.

TO THOMAS JEFFERSON.
PHILA., May 27, 1794.

DEAR SIR,—Early yesterday morning & immediately after my last was written I was called on by Mr. R. to answer the question "whether I wod. accept the legation to France?" The proposition as you will readily conceive surprised me, for I really thought I was among the last men to whom it wod. be made, & so observed. He said the President was resolved to send a republican character to that nation; that Mr. Madison & Ch^r. Livingston had refused, that he wod. not appoint Colo. Burr, lest it shod. seem as if he sought persons from that state only, & probably it would not have been offered to L. but on acct. of his having been in the department of foreign affairs & under these circumstances & considerations he was desired by the President to call on me & ascertain whether I wod. act. As I had espoused B. I told Mr. R. I could not even think on the subject whilst there was a prospect of his success. He assured me he was out of the question, & if I declined, it wod. probably be offered to Govr. Paca of Maryld. or some person not yet thot. of. That he would satisfy the friends of Colo. Burr on this head. Before I wod. consult my friends I requested that this be done—& in consequence the above assurance was given some of them, & I presume they were satisfied. This point of delicacy being removed, I then desired Mr. Madison in conference with a few of our friends to determine what answer shod. be given to the proposition. The result was that I sho'd. accept upon the necessity of cultivating France; & the uncertainty of the person upon whom it might otherwise fall. An answer was accordingly given last evening to the President to that effect, & the nomination sent in today. I have not attended nor shall I till after that body shall be pleased to decide upon it. If approved, it is wished that I embark immediately for France. I am however extremely anxious to visit Albemarle before I set out taking Mr. Jones in my way. But whether I shall be able to visit either of you is uncertain, & will depend in a great measure upon the practicability of getting a vessel about to sail, in a term short of the time, it will take me to perform the journey— upon this head however I can say nothing until the nomination is decided on, nor can I say how the decision will be, for my services in the Senate have given me but little claim to the personal regards of the reigning party there. I suspect the nomination created as great a surprise in that house as the proposition to me did, yesterday morning. As yet I have not seen the President—I shall write you more fully in my next—With great respect & esteem I am

Yr. affectionate friend & servant

JA^S. MONROE.

TO GEORGE WASHINGTON.
PHILADELPHIA, June 1, 1794.

I was presented yesterday by Mr Randolph with the commission of Minister for the French Republic, which you were pleased, with the approbation of the Senate, to confer on me. As I had previously intimated to him my willingness to accept that trust, I have only now to request that you will consider me as ready to embark in the discharge of its duties as soon as I shall be honored with your commands and a suitable passage can be secured for myself & family to that country.

In accepting this very distinguished mark of your confidence, I should do injustice to my own feelings if I did not express to you the particular obligation it has conferred on me, and assure you of the zeal with which I shall endeavour to discharge the duties of so high a trust in a manner that may justify the Executive in committing it to me. On that zeal but principally on the councils which will direct my conduct I rely, as the resources which are to supply the inadequacy of my abilities to a station at all times important and at the present crisis peculiarly arduous and delicate. Be assured however it will be my study & give me the highest gratification to have it in my power to promote by my mission the interest of my country & the honor & credit of your administration which I deem inseparably connected with it.

TO THOMAS JEFFERSON.
PHILA, June 6, 1794.

DEAR SIR,—Since my appointment I have been extremely occupied in a variety of respects—I had likewise flatter'd myself with the hope I shod. see you before my departure till within a day or two past—but of this I now begin to despair. I shall sail from Baltimore, for which place I set out in 4 days hence. 'Tis possible the vessel may not be ready altho' I am advised she is. I feel extremely anxious upon the subject of a cypher—our former one is in a small writing desk at my house. Can you get it & send it after me in case I do not see you before I sail? Danton has been executed,—the charge the plunder of publick money—the King of Prussia withdrawn—& the British driven from Corsica—I will write by the several succeeding posts whilst I stay

I am yr. affectionate friend & servt.

JAS. MONROE.

PART IV

Relations with the Marquis de Lafayette and Thomas Paine

INTRODUCTION

ONE SIDE STORY TO MONROE'S MISSION to France was the opportunities it gave to provide dramatic assistance to those heroes of the American Revolution, the Marquis de Lafayette and Thomas Paine. The friendship and sympathy with Lafayette was lifelong, continuing to the twilight years of both those doyens of history. Paine proved to be an obnoxious braggart who returned Monroe's kindness by nearly derailing his mission.

As a young officer, he had met Lafayette in Lord Stirling's camp in 1778, where the circle of his friends included Alexander Hamilton, John Marshall, Aaron Burr and John Mercer, his old roommate from William and Mary. Although Lafayette was a general, he was but a few years older than Captain Monroe, and the two formed an attachment despite the differences in rank. At the battle of Brandywine, Lafayette was standing next to Lord Stirling surveying the battlefield when a rifle ball struck Lafayette in the shin. This circumstance gave the two wounded fighters for liberty something else in common. When Lafayette returned to France, he demonstrated his continuing affection for the United States in 1782 by convincing the government to open the chief ports of France to the United States.

When Monroe arrived in Paris he found to his distress that Lafayette had been imprisoned by the Emperor of Austria in Olmutz as a dangerous revolutionary. But Madame Lafayette was imprisoned in Paris because her husband was seen as a dangerous representative of the aristocratic order. Indeed, her mother and her grandmother had already been beheaded. Her uncle, the Marquis de Tascher came secretly to Monroe urging him to use his influence with the government to spare her.

Yet in those first few days of turmoil in Paris, Monroe knew that the Committee on Public Safety still distrusted him; any official attempt to intervene might have the opposite effect and send Madame Lafayette to the guillotine instantly. So he developed a stratagem. His first step was to purchase with great difficulty a splendid set of horse and carriage—no mean feat, since the revolution had banished such equipage from the city, and there were none for hire. He outfitted the servants in brilliant livery. Then Elizabeth Monroe dressed in her most elegant day costume, and was driven to the gates of the prison where Madame Lafayette languished.

The keepers were astonished. Who was it? Who would dare come with such display in such volatile times? The word went out: It was the wife of the American Minister and she had come to see Madame Lafayette. The gates swung open. When the keepers went to get the prisoner, she thought that her time had come, and she was being taken to the guillotine; but instead she was brought to an iron railing where she was comforted by Mrs. Monroe.

"The scene was most affecting, the sensibility of all the beholders was deeply excited," Monroe wrote later. The account of this event quickly swept through the city, and popular opinion switched over to the side of Madame Lafayette. Monroe then was able through quiet conversations with the Committee to secure her release, and she was brought to the Minister's residence, where she stayed for several weeks. At length she was able to leave Paris with her two daughters and join her husband in Olmutz in October 1795—in prison, where she shared his misfortune and prison fare until his release several years later.

Finding that Lafayette was without funds as a result of the revolution, and in distress, Congress made a grant of $20,000 for his services to the American Revolution, plus a grant of western lands. Such a grant was the prerogative of any officer of his rank who had served, but Lafayette had never sought financial recompense for serving the cause of freedom. Monroe used the certificate authenticating the ownership of the American property as a rationale to the Committee of Public Safety for granting Madame Lafayette a passport to leave France, and loaned her $2,000 to enable her to travel, all of which he duly reported to President Washington in a letter of January 3, 1795.

When Monroe returned to Paris in 1803 for the negotiations on Louisiana, he discovered his friend Lafayette in bed with a broken hip after a fall on the ice, and his financial circumstances likewise broken. He had sold his lands in France to pay his debts, but the continental bankers would not lend him money secured by the American property. Monroe was able to put in his hands the papers authenticating ownership, then when he went to London, he acted as a middleman with the British firm Baring Brothers. The banking house, which stood to make millions from buying the U.S. paper issued for the purchase of Louisiana, was only too happy to accommodate America's French hero, lending him

100,000 pounds with the U.S. property as security. Monroe announced the happy news to Lafayette in a letter of March 16, 1806. "Economise your expences without expecting anything further from that source for a few years," he warned. On March 18, he wrote to Baring Brothers, "I shall immediately communicate to my government this strong proof of your disposition to befriend a family in whose welfare the U. States take a deep interest."

In 1824, while Monroe was President, Congress invited the veteran hero to visit the United States, even making the offer of a ship of war to convey him. Lafayette declined the offer of the war ship, but arrived in August and toured the country for a year. Monroe, in his eighth message to Congress on December 7, 1824, gave an account of the visit: "At every designated point of rendezvous the whole population of the neighboring country has been assembled to greet him, among whom it has excited in a peculiar manner the sensibility of all to behold the surviving members of our Revolutionary contest, civil and military, who had shared with him in the toils and dangers of the war, many of them in a decrepit state." Monroe did not see him until October, when he arrived at Washington, having taken a leisurely tour meeting the people before going to the seat of government, as Monroe reported to Madison and Jefferson in separate letters on October 18. "Time has produced less waste of his form, since you last saw him, than it does on most men, and none on his mind," he told Jefferson. Lafayette made his way to Albemarle county to visit with the two former presidents, but even though Monroe was spending a few days at his Albemarle property, Ashlawn-Highland, near Monticello, the press of business in Washington took him away before Lafayette's arrival.

Monroe's farewell to his friend took place in August 1825 after he had retired to his Loudoun County home, Oak Hill. President John Quincy Adams came up 30 miles from Washington, the New Englander complaining about the Virginia August heat. The group went with military honor guard to the county seat, Leesburg, about six miles away. Ten thousand people had gathered in that dusty little town to see the Revolutionary hero and the two presidents. Speeches, displays of precision military marching, and martial music filled the air. By nightfall, there were illuminations, and entertainment at nearby plantation houses. Even now, Leesburg historians will point out the old inn where a new wing was built in 1825 just to hold the ball for Lafayette. It is still an inn today.

After that last meeting, Lafayette returned directly to France. Monroe continued to correspond. On May 2, 1829—less than two years before his death— he wrote a deeply poignant letter to Lafayette filled with the premonition that the shades were closing in. "My dear Friend," he wrote, using an unusual salutation that seldom appears elsewhere in his letters, "It is some time since I wrote to you, in answer to your affectionate letters, altho' I have long intended to do so. . . . So many interesting circumstances have occurred between us, to which we have been parties, and others of which we have been spectators, in both countries, since the battle of Brandywine, that I never can review them without peculiar interest and sensibility. . . . If I was ever to visit France your house would be my home, but we are both too far advanced in years to think of such a voyage. We must content ourselves with writing to each other, which I shall do hereafter more frequently." If he did so, those letters are lost.

The story with Paine, the author of the celebrated tract in the American Revolution, *Common Sense*, was quite different. Although Paine was a citizen of the United States he went to France during the revolution with the intention of assisting in the formation of the government. He held a seat in the National Convention, became a member of the Brissot faction, and when that worthy gentleman fell, was cast into cellars of the Luxembourg Palace. There he languished for eight months. Gouveurneur Morris, the previous American minister, Federalist that he was, considered Paine an unstable radical, a French citizen because of his role in the Convention, and not worth helping. Although today the Luxembourg is a splendid building and the Luxembourg Gardens are one of the jewels of central Paris, for Paine it was a grim fortress, from whence he might be led to execution if he didn't die first in the squalid dampness of the basement.

A week after hearing of the American Minister's arrival, he sent a pitiful letter by a trusted friend, even though, in prison, he did not even know Monroe's name. He claimed he had no knowledge of why he had been imprisoned, except that he was a foreigner. But as in the case of Madame Lafayette, Monroe knew that it would take skilful handling of the situation so as not to precipitate action against the prisoner. He knew that Paine had allowed himself to become involved in the dangerous politics of the revolution and a false step could provoke an overreaction. Whereas he knew that Madame Lafayette was innocent of any crime, he could not be sure that Paine had not transgressed the changeable and unwritten rules of revolutionary conduct.

Nevertheless, Paine was ill, an American citizen, and needed help. Monroe's cautious but informal discussions with the Committee of Public Safety and the Sûreté General dragged on—too slowly for the frightened and impatient Paine. "The room where I am lodged is a ground floor level with the earth in the garden, and floored with brick, and so wet after every rain that I cannot guard against taking colds that continually check my recovery," he wrote in a second letter. At length, on September 18th, Monroe sent a formal letter directly to Paine, who had been complaining that the minister wasn't paying enough attention to his case. It was a very blunt letter: "You mention that you have been informed, that you are not considered an American citizen by the Americans; and that you have likewise Heard, I had no instructions respecting you by the government. . . . the most anyone could say is that you had become, likewise, a French citizen, which, by no means, deprives you of an American one. . . . It becomes my duty, however, to declare to you, that I consider you an American citizen, and that you are considered, universally, in that character, by the people of America. As such, you are entitled to my attention. . . ."

He then conveyed the best wishes of President Washington, although there is nothing on record to suggest to that the President thought highly of Tom Paine. But he also told Paine that he was in no danger, and that he would have to wait until things could be worked out. "To liberate you will be the object of my endeavours, and as soon as possible. But you must, until that event shall be accomplished, bear your situation with patience and fortitude. You will likewise have the justice to recollect, that I am placed here upon a difficult theatre; many important objects to attend to, with few to consult. It becomes me, in pursuit of them, so to regulate my conduct in respect to each, as to the manner and the time, as will, in my judgement, be best calculated to accomplish the whole."

By October, Monroe had worked out a plan. He would ask the government either to put Paine on trial, or release him on the grounds that there were no charges against him. On the first of November, he wrote to the Committee of General Surety, stating that any American citizen who transgressed the laws of France should, in full respect of France's sovereignty, be tried before a French tribunal, and that he had full confidence in the judicial system of France. In this case, however, he noted that "The citizens of the United States can never look back to the area of their own revolution, without remembering, with those of other distinguished Patriots, the name of Thomas Paine. The services which he rendered them in their struggle for liberty have made an impression of gratitude which will never be erased." But in spite of this, he asked only that "you will hasten his trial in case there be any charge against him, and if there be none, that you will cause him to be set at liberty."

Paine was set at liberty, because by this time Monroe had established himself as reliable friend of the revolution. But no doubt there were many moments when Monroe wished Paine back in the Luxembourg. With his usual generosity, Monroe took Paine, whom he had not known at all, into his own house, where he was nursed back to health. But with health, his hot-headed nature re-emerged.

Paine nursed a grievance against Washington because the president had not instructed Morris to get him out of prison, and it was not long before Monroe discovered him sitting at a desk in his house in the act of writing a pamphlet against Washington's policies in general.

On January 20, 1796, Monroe wrote to Madison about the troubles he was having with Paine: "I had occasion soon after Mr. Paine's enlargement [i.e., being set at large by the French authorities] to intimate to him a wish that whilst in my house, he would write nothing for the publick, either of Europe or America, upon the subject of our affairs, which I found even before his enlargement he did not entertain a very favorable opinion of." He told Paine that his demand rested upon "the injury such essays would do me, let them be written by whom they might & whether I ever saw them or not, if they proceeded from my house."

Paine did not take the hint; he said "that he was accustomed to write upon public subjects & upon those of America in particular, to which he now wished to turn his attention, being able to depart thither & reside there for the future." After a heated argument, Paine appeared to acquiesce, but not because he believed there was any merit to Monroe's argument. Shortly thereafter, while Charles Pinckney, the Minister to Spain, was visiting he revealed that Paine had asked him to take a sealed package to his publisher in England. Upon Monroe's advice, Pinckney declined to take the package, but Monroe continued to fear that Paine would find some way to get his manuscripts either to England or America. The unwelcome guest remained in Monroe's house for a year and a half until Monroe himself departed for home. Monroe had spent about $2500 in loans and accommodations for Paine, not a penny of which was ever paid back.

CORRESPONDENCE BETWEEN MR. MONROE AND MR. PAINE.

When Mr. Monroe arrived in France, in August, 1794, Mr. Paine was imprisoned in the Luxemburg, on which occasion the following correspondence took place between them. Mr. Paine had been arrested with Brissot and other members of that party, most of whom had been guillotined. This correspondence is very voluminous, but it is deemed unnecessary to publish more of it than the following extracts, which give a just view of his situation at that time. Mr. Monroe, though very anxious to obtain Mr. Paine's discharge, considered it his duty, in the then state of affairs, to be very circumspect in taking any measures in his favour. He had many interviews with members of the two great committees of the government, of "Salut Publique" and "Sûreté Generale," before he made an official application for his release, and it was after the affair was thus informally arranged, that he addressed a note to the latter committee on the subject, a copy of which was enclosed to the Secretary of State, with his letter of Nov. 7th, 1794. The two committees met immediately, and passed an order for his release, which was sent to Mr. Monroe, at daylight the next morning. Mr. Monroe sent his secretary with it, to the Luxemburg, in obedience to which Mr. Paine was immediately discharged, and brought by his secretary to the house. Mr. Paine was destitute of everything, and in ill health, and Mr. Monroe took him to his house and accommodated him with lodging, money, clothes, etc. He lived with Mr. Monroe a year and a half, and when Mr. Monroe left France, Mr. Paine was indebted to him for money loaned, besides the other accommodations and expenses incurred on his account, about 250 louis, of which no part was ever paid. [HAMILTON.]

LUXEMBURG, 29th Thermidor.

MY DEAR SIR:—As I believe none of the public papers have announced your name right, I am unable to address you by it—but a new Minister from America is joy to me, and will be so to every American in France.

Eight months I have been imprisoned, and I know not for what, except that the order says that I am a foreigner. The illness I have suffered in this, and from which I am but just recovering, had nearly put an end to my existence; but life is of little value to me in this situation, though I have borne it with a firmness of patience and fortitude.

I enclose to you a copy of a letter, as well the translation as the original, which I sent to the convention, after the fall of the monster Robespierre; for I was determined not to write a line during the existence of his detestable influence. I sent also a copy to the Committee of Public Safety, but I have not heard anything respecting it.

I have now no expectation of delivery, but by your means. The gentleman who will present you this has been very friendly to me. Wishing you happiness in your appointment, I am, sir, yours affectionately,

THOMAS PAINE.

4th Year.

DEAR SIR:—I need not mention to you the happiness I received from the information you sent me by Mr. Beresford. I easily guess the persons you have conversed with, on the subject of my liberation: but matters, and even promises, that pass in conversation, are not quite so strictly attended to here, as in the country you came from.

I am not, my dear sir, impatient from anything in my disposition; but the state of my health requires liberty and a better air; and, besides this, the rules of the prison do not permit me, though I have all the indulgence the *concierge* can give, to procure the things necessary to my recovery, which is slow as to health. The room where I am lodged, is a ground floor level with the earth in the garden, and floored with brick, and so wet after every rain, that I cannot guard against taking colds, that continually check my recovery. If you could, without interfering with, or deranging the mode proposed for my liberation, inform the committee, that the state of my health requires liberty and air, it would be a good ground to hasten my liberation. I leave it entirely to you to arrange this matter.

Yours affectionately,

THOMAS PAINE.

PARIS, September 18th, 1794.

DEAR SIR:—I was favoured, soon after my arrival here, with several letters from you, and more recently with one in the character of a memorial, upon the subject of your confinement, and should have answered them at the time they were respectively written, had I not concluded you would have calculated, with certainty, on the deep interest I take in your welfare, and the pleasure with which I shall embrace every opportunity to serve you. I should still pursue the same course, and for reasons which must obviously occur, did I not find that you are disquieted with apprehensions, upon interesting points, and which justice to you and our country, equally forbid you should entertain. You mention, that you have been informed, that you are not considered an American citizen by the Americans: and that you have likewise heard, I had no instructions respecting you by the government. I doubt not, that the person who gave you the information meant well; but I suspect he did not even convey, accurately, his own ideas on the first point; for I presume the most anyone could say is, that you had become, likewise, a French citizen, which, by no means, deprives you of the rights of an American one. Even this, however, may be doubted—I mean the acquisition of citizenship here. I confess that you have said much, to shew that it has not been made. I really suspect this was all that gentleman who wrote you, and those Americans he heard speak on the subject meant. It becomes my duty, however, to declare to you, that I consider you an American citizen, and that you are considered, universally, in that character, by the people of America. As such, you are entitled to my attention; and so far as it can be given, consistently with those obligations which are mutual between every government, and even a transient passenger, you shall receive it.

The Congress have never decided upon the subject of citizenship, in a manner to regard the present case. By being with us through the revolution, you are of our country, as absolutely as if you had been born there; and you are no more of England, than every native of America is. This is the true doctrine in the present case, so far as it becomes complicated with any other consideration. I have mentioned it, to make you easy upon the only point which could give you any disquietude.

It is necessary for me to tell you, how much all your countrymen, I speak of the great mass of the people, are interested in your welfare? They have not forgotten the history of their own revolution, and the difficult scenes through which they have passed—nor do they review its several stages, without reviving in their bosoms, a due sensibility of the merits of those who served them in that great and arduous conflict. The crime of ingratitude has not yet stained, and, I trust, will never stain, our national character. You are considered by them, not only as having rendered important services in our own revolution, but as being, upon a more extensive scale, the friend of human rights, and a distinguished and able advocate, in favour of the public liberty. To the welfare of Thomas Paine, the Americans are not, nor can they be, indifferent.

Of the sense which the President has always entertained of your merits, and of his friendly dispositions towards you, you are too well assured, to require any declaration of it from me. That I forward his wishes in seeking your safety, is what I well know; and this will form an additional obligation on me, to perform what I should otherwise consider my duty.

You are, in my opinion, at present, menaced by no kind of danger. To liberate you will be the object of my endeavours, and as soon as possible. But you must, until that event shall be accomplished, bear your situation with patience and fortitude. You will likewise have the justice to recollect, that I am placed here upon a difficult theatre; many important objects to attend to, with few to consult. It becomes me, in pursuit of them, so to regulate my conduct in respect to each, as to the manner and the time, as will, in my judgment, be best calculated to accomplish the whole. With respect and esteem, consider me, personally, your friend,

JAMES MONROE.

THOMAS PAINE.
LUXEMBURG, 14th Vendémiaire, Oct'r 4th.

DEAR SIR:—I thank you for your very friendly and affectionate letter of the 18th of September, which I did not receive till this morning. It has relieved my mind from a load of disquietude. You will easily suppose, that if the information I received had been exact, my situation was without hope. I had, in that case, neither section, department, nor country to reclaim me—But this is not all; I felt a poignancy of grief, in having the least reason to suppose, that America had so soon forgotten me, who had never forgotten her.

Mr. Sabonidière directed me, in a note of yesterday, to write to the Convention. As I suppose this measure has been taken in concert with you, I have requested him to show you the letter, of which he will make a translation, to accompany the original.

If the letter I have written, be not covered with better authority than my own, it will have no effect; for they already know all that I can say. On what ground do they pretend to deprive America of the service of one of her citizens, without assigning a cause, or only the flimsy one of my being born in England? Gates, were he here, might be arrested on the same pretence, and he and Burgoyne be confounded together. I conclude, with thanking you again for your very friendly and affectionate letter.

I am, with great regard, yours,

THOMAS PAINE.

TO THE COMMITTEE OF GENERAL SURETY.
PARIS, November 1st, 1794.

CITIZENS,—In all cases where the citizens of the United States commit themselves to the jurisdiction of the French Republic, it is their duty to obey the law, in consideration of the protection which it gives, or otherwise submit to its penalty. This principle is unquestionable; it belongs to the nature of sovereignty, it can never be separated from it. All that my countrymen thus circumstanced have a right to claim of me as their representative, is to see that they have justice rendered them, according to the nature of the charge, and their offence, if they have committed any, by the tribunals whose duty it is to take cognizance of it.

I hope that few cases will ever happen where the conduct of an American citizen will become the subject of discussion here before a criminal tribunal. In those cases which may happen, if any do, I shall repose entire confidence in the justice of the tribunal, being well satisfied, that if any bias existed in the bosom of the judge, it would be in favor of my countrymen. To hasten their trial before the judge, where one was deemed necessary is I am persuaded, the only point upon which I shall ever feel or express any solicitude.

I should not at the present crisis, call your attention to any case of the kind, if I were not impelled by considerations of peculiar weight. Considerations which I know you will respect; because every succeeding day more fully demonstrates how thoroughly the whole French nation is devoted to the cause which gave birth to them. The great efforts which it has already made and is now making in favor of the public liberty, sufficiently shows how highly it estimates that blessing, and gratitude to those who have served that cause is deemed by you inseparable from a veneration for the cause itself.

The citizens of the United States can never look back to the æra of their own revolution, without remembering, with those of other distinguished Patriots, the name of Thomas Paine. The services which he rendered them in their struggle for liberty have made an impression of gratitude which will never be erased, whilst they continue to merit the character of a just and generous people. He is now in prison, languishing under a disease, and which must be increased by his confinement. Permit me then, to call your attention to his situation, and to require that you will hasten his trial in case there be any charge against him, and if there be none, that you will cause him to be set at liberty.[1]

JA^S. MONROE.

---

1. *Paine was liberated by the Committee of General Surety in consequence of Monroe's assertion of his American citizenship, and demand for his release; but he had suffered an imprisonment of ten months and nine days before Monroe's generous and manly aid reached him.* [HAMILTON.]

TO THE SECRETARY OF STATE.
[EDMUND RANDOLPH.]
PARIS, November 7th, 1794.

I was extremely concerned, upon my arrival here, to find that our country-man Mr. Paine, as likewise Madame La Fayette were in prison; the former of whom had been confined near nine months and the latter about two. I was immediately entreated by both to endeavour to obtain their enlargement. I assured them of the interest which America had in their welfare; of the regard entertained for them by the President, and of the pleasure with which I should embrace every opportunity to serve them; but observed at the same time that they must be sensible it would be difficult for me to take any step officially, in behalf of either, and altogether impossible in behalf of Madame La Fayette. This was admitted by her friend, who assured me, her only wish was that I would have her situation in view, and render her, informally, what services I might be able, without compromitting the credit of our government with this. I assured him she might confide in this with certainty, and further, that in case any extremity was threatened, that I would go beyond that line and do everything in my power, let the consequence be what it might to myself to save her; with this he was satisfied. She still continues confined, nor do I think it probable she will be soon released. I have assured her that I would supply her with money and with whatever she wanted; but as yet, none has been accepted, though I think she will soon be compelled to avail herself of this resource.

The case was different with Mr. Paine. He was actually a citizen of the United States, and of the United States only; for the revolution, which parted us from Great Britain, broke the allegiance, which was before due to the crown, of all those who took our side. He was, of course, not a British subject, nor was he strictly a citizen of France; for he came by invitation, for the temporary pur-pose of assisting in the formation of their government only, and meant to with-draw to America when that should be completed: And what confirms this, is the act of convention itself arresting him, by which he is declared to be a for-eigner. Mr. Paine pressed my interference. I told him I had hopes of getting him enlarged without it; but if I did interfere, it could only be by requesting that he be tried in case there was any charge against him, and liberated in case there was none. This was admitted. His correspondence with me is lengthy and interest-ing, and I may probably be able hereafter to send you a copy of it. After some time had elapsed without producing any change in his favour, as he was press-ing and in ill health, I finally resolved to address the Committee of general surety in his behalf, resting my application on the above principle. My letter was delivered by my secretary, in the Committee to the President, who assured him he would Communicate its contents immediately to the Committee of public safety and give me an answer as soon as possible. The conference took place accordingly between the two Committees and as I presume, on that night, or the succeeding day; for on the morning of the day after, which was yesterday, I was presented by the Secretary of the Committee of general surety, with an order for his enlargement. I forwarded it immediately to the Luxembourg and had it carried into effect, and have the pleasure now to add that he is not only restored to the enjoyment of his liberty, but in good spirits. I send you a copy of my letter to the Committee of general surety, and of their reply.

Since my last the French have taken Coblentz, and some other post in its neighborhood; they have likewise taken Pampeluna, and broken the whole of the Spanish line through a considerable extent of country. About twenty standards, taken from the routed Spaniards, were presented to the Convention a few days past.

I likewise send in the enclosed papers, a decree respecting the Jacobins by which all correspondence between the different societies is prohibited, as likewise is the presenting a petition to the Convention in their character as such, with some other restraints I do not at present recollect.

With great respect and esteem, I am, Dear Sir, your most ob^t. & very Humble Servant,

Ja^s. Monroe.

TO THE PRESIDENT.
[George Washington.]
Paris, Jan'y 3, 1795.

Dear Sir,—Your favor of the 5 of June did not reach me till a few days past or it sho'd have been sooner answered. I am happy now to answer it because I am able to give you details of the lady in question which will be very agreeable to you. I had advanced her near 2000 dol'rs when I was advised here by Jacob Van Staphorst that you had plac'd in the hands of his brother for Madame La Fayette the sum of two thousand, three hundred & ten guilders & which had never been rec'd. At this time she was soliciting permission to leave France with a view of visiting & partaking with her husband the fortune to which he was exposed. I had given her a certificate that her husband had lands in America & that the Congress had appropriated to his use upwards of 20,000 dol'rs, the am't w'h was due for his services in our revolution, & upon which basis her application was founded &

granted. I made known to her the fund you had appropriated for her use & which she readily & with pleasure accepted, & which served to defray the expense of her journey. She pursued her route by Dunkirk & Hamburg to which places I gave & procured letters of recommendation, & at the former of which she was rec'd in the house & entertained by our consul Mr. Coffyn. I assured her when she left France there was no service within my power to render her & her husband & family that I would not with pleasure render them. To count upon my utmost efforts & command them in their favor. That it was your wish & the wish of America that I should do so. To consult her husband as to the mode & measure & apprize me of his opinions thereon. She departed grateful to you & our country & since which I have not heard from her. She had thoughts of visiting in person the Emperor & endeavoring to obtain the release of her husband; but whether she did or not I cannot tell. It was reported sometime since he was released & afterwards that she was admitted with her family into the same state of confinement with him: the latter of which I believe to be true.[2] Before she left this I became responsible in her favor for 9000^{l}. upon a month's notice (in specie) the object of w'h was to free a considerable estate from some encumbrance & which was effected upon my surety, as yet I have not been called on to pay it. As soon, therefore, as I rec'd the draft on Holland for six thousand dol'rs in her behalf, I wrote her by two different routes to assure her that I had funds for her & her husband's support & upon which she might for the present draw to the am't of £250. ster'g, & afterwards as occasion might require & to which I have rec'd no ans'r.

What may be the ultimate disposition of France towards Mr. Lafayette it is impossible now to say. His integrity so far as I can find remains unimpeached, & when that is the case the errors of the head are pardoned as the passions subside. It is more than probable I may be able to serve him with those by whom he is confined, & that I may do this without injury to the U. States here; acting with candor and avowing the motive, since it is impossible that motive can be otherwise than approved, especially if the step be taken when their aff'rs are in great prosperity. For this, however, I shall be happy to have y'r approbation, since if I do any thing with the Emperor it must be done in y'r name, if not explicitly yet in a manner to make known to him the interest you take in the welfare of Mr. Lafayette. Young Lafayette is I presume now under y'r auspices.

---

2. Madame de Lafayette, with her two daughters, joined her husband in the prison of Olmutz in October, 1795.—SPARKS. [HAMILTON.]

Within a few days past a truce or armistice was concluded between Pichegru & Jourdan on the one side & Clairfayt & Wurmser on the other as it is said for three months: this was of course subject to approbation or rejection of the gov't on each side. I hear that it was rejected on the side of France, orders being sent by the directoire to pursue the war without cessation. Both armies are in the neighborhood of Mayence where the country is almost entirely devastated. In Italy the Austrians are completely routed & their whole army nearly demolished. 'Tis said that 8000 prisoners are brought to one of the French villages. Mrs. Monroe desires her best respects to be presented to yourself & Mrs. Washington, who we hope enjoy good health. If there is anything in which I can be servicable to you here, any article of curiosity or taste you wish to possess & which can be procured, I beg of you to make it known to me that I may procure it for you. With great & sincere respect and esteem I am, Dear Sir, your most ob't & very humble servant,

Ja^s. Monroe.

P. S. There are many articles of tapestry the most beautiful that can be conceived, & w'h are intended for the walls of rooms, for chair bottoms &ca., some of which perhaps wo'd be acceptible to the Com'rs of the federal town, & which if permitted by you or them I wo'd immediately procure & forward.

TO JAMES MADISON.
Paris, Jany. 20, 1796.

Dear Sir,—I think I mentioned to you sometime since that M^r. Paine was with me. Upon my arrival I found him in Prison, & as soon as I saw my application in his behalf would be attended to, I asked his release & obtained it. But he was in extreme ill health, without resources, & (affairs being unsettled) not without apprehensions of personal danger, & therefore anxious to avail himself as much as possible of such protection as I co^d. give him. From motives that will readily occur to you I invited him to take a room in my house, & which he accepted. It was his intention at that time, sometime in Octr. 94, to depart for America in the Spring, with which view in feb^y. following, I asked permission of the Com: of p: safety for him to depart, charged with my despatches for the Department of State, a motive w^h. I presumed wo^d. authorize them to grant the permission asked: but was answer'd it co^d. not be granted to a deputy; tho' indeed he co^d. scarcely be considered as such, having been excluded the Convention as a foreigner, & liberated upon my application as an American citizen. His disease continued & of course he continued in my house, & will continue in it, till his death or departure for America, however remote either the one or the other event may be. I had occasion soon after M[r]. Paines' enlargement to intimate to him a wish, that whilst in my house, he would write nothing for the publick, either of Europe or America, upon the subject of our affairs, which I found even before his enlargement he did not entertain a very favorable opinion of. I told him I did not rest my demand upon the merit or demerit of our conduct, of which the world had a right to form & wo[d]. form its opinion, but upon the injury such essays wo[d]. do me, let them be written by whom they might & whether I ever saw them or not, if they proceeded from my house. He denied the principle, intimating that no one wo[d]. suppose his writings which were consistent, were influenced by anyone: that he was accustomed to write upon publick subjects & upon those of America in particular, to which he now wished to turn his attention, being ab[t]. to depart thither & reside there for the future. But as I insisted that I owed it to the delicacy of my publick & private character to guard myself even by erroneous inferences, agñst any improper imputation or compromittment whatever & especially as I did not wish any impression to be entertained of me which I did not create myself, being the arbiter of my own measures & the guardian of my own name, & which I knew wo[d]. be affected thro. that door if it were opened, with many if not generally & therefore entreated him to desist. He then accommodated, more however from an apparent spirit of accommodation, than of conviction that my demand was reasonable or my argument sound. Thus the matter ended and I flattered myself I shoud, for the future, enjoy the pleasure of extending to Mr. Paine, whilst he remained here, the rights of hospitality & without exposing myself to the inconvenience I so much dreaded and laboured to avert. Latterly however an incident has turned up which has again disquieted me on the same subject. He had committed to M[r]. Pinckney when here the other day on his return from Spain a letter from his bookseller in London, upon the propriety of carrying & delivering which unsealed M[r]. Pinckney asked my opinion. I frankly told him, in his place I wo[d]. carry nothing I did not see & approve of & as he was of the same opinion he desired me to communicate it to Mr. Paine & which I did. M[r]. Paine owned that his letter contained an extract of one he was writing or had written to Frederick Muhlenburg in Philad[a]. [in cypher. Ed.] upon eng[h]. & american affairs & which he intended sho[d]. be published with his name. M[r]. Pinckney returned the letter, not chusing to be the bearer of it. Upon this occasion I revived with M[r]. Paine the argument I had used before, expressing my extreme concern that he pursued a conduct which, under existing circumstances, gave me so much pain, & to which he made little other reply than to observe, he was surprised. I continued of the same opinion I formerly was upon this subject. Whether he will send the one or the other letter I know not. I shall certainly prevent it in both cases if in my power. That to Engl^d. is not sent as yet. 'Tis possible the one for America has gone or will be sent. Let me entreat you therefore to confer with the gentl^m. to whom it is addressed & request him in my behalf if he receives such an one, to suppress it. In any event I have thought it necessary to possess you with these facts that you may use them as occasion may require to guard me agñst unmerited slander.

Your China will go from hence in the course of a few days when I will send you an invoice of it. It is a plain neat service, sufficient in number & cheap. If you will permit me I will procure for you in the course of the present year furniture for a drawing room, consisting of the following articles. 1. Chairs, suppose 12. or 18.—2^d. two tables or three after the taste which we prefer—3^d. a sofa, perhaps 2. These all of tapestry & to suit, if to be had, the curtains we sent you, either one or the other sett. 4th. a clock to stand on the chimney piece, & which chimney piece I will send also, of marble, if you wish it. I wish you to send me a list of what other things you want & especially of books, & I will provide & send or bring them with me when I return home. I will procure every thing as cheap as possible, & adjust the amount when I have occasion for it. Mr. Jefferson proposes to have a house built for me on my plantation near him & to w^h. I have agreed under conditions that will make the burden as light as possible upon him. For this purpose I am about to send 2 plans to him submitting both to his judgment, & contemplate accepting the offer of a skilful mason here who wishes to emigrate & settle with us, to execute the work. I wish yrself & M^r. Jones to see the plans & council with Mr. Jefferson on the subject.

TO THOMAS JEFFERSON.
RICHMOND, March 14, 1802.

DEAR SIR,—I found your favor of the 28th. ult°. communicating an extract of a letter from Dupont de Nemours relative to the claim of the artist Houdon to be paid the sum which he lost by the depreciation of the assignats in the last instalment which he rec^d. for the statue of Genl. Washington. I postponed an answer untill I had taken the advice of council by which I am authorised to inform you that whatever sum you state to be due shall be paid on y^r. certificate of the same. I send you a letter of yours to Govr. Brooke, one of Houdon to the Govr. of Virg^a. and a copy of one from the banker Grand to Houdon certified by the latter, which shew that the contract was in specie, that the assignats were accepted by him with the approbation of M^r. Morris on the principle and in the expectation that they sho^d. be sealed. I hope and presume that M^r. Morris will be able to establish the facts not known to you, necessary to adjust the account, to your satisfaction, so that we may be enabled to pay the artist what is justly his due. We do not think ourselves authorised to purchase the bust of Franklin, without the sanction of the legislature. We are persuaded its sanction might be had at the next session, tho' [we?] are not authorised to commence a treaty or make any stipulation relative to it.

The repeal of the judiciary law of the last session forms an interesting epoch in our affr^s. We shall soon see whether the party which created it are disposed and able to convulse the country on pretext of the repeal. I sho^d. not be surprised to [see] the court of app^{ls}. advancing with a bold stride to effect the object. But I trust its efforts will be fruitless. Sincerely I am yr. friend & servant.

TO THE MARQUIS DE LA FAYETTE.
London, March 16, 1806.

My Dear Sir,—I had the pleasure to receive your two letters sometime since which obtained the attention which any communication from you or in which your family is interested will never fail to command. The object in which you desired my co-operation is happily accomplished. The house of Baring has agreed to advance you on loan the sum of one hundred thousand livres in addition to what you have already rec^d. I asked it of them in a manner to let it be understood that the accomodation would be felt by my government, who never ceased to take a deep interest in your welfare on account of the important services which you had rendered to the U. States. By their reply, a copy of which is enclosed you will find, that they have yielded the accomodation in a manner which is equally flattering to you & respectful to the U. States. You will also receive within a letter to our friend M^r. Parker w^h. contains an order in his favor for that sum to be applied to your use. I most earnestly hope that this sum will put you at ease, and profiting of the experience which you have had you will make such an arrangement of your affairs by means of it, as will protect you from all future anxiety much less embarrassment on that head. The land granted to you by Congress must be pledged for the reimbursement of this money with the interest. Œconomise your expences without expecting any thing further from that source for a few years: in that time it is hoped that your friends in America may be able to make it the means of replacing this money & furnishing an additional income for your support. You will know that they will pay all the attention which you could desire. M^r. Parker will I am satisfied take as much pleasure in executing this trust, as you can possibly derive from it.

My family have been in delicate health since our return to Eng^ld. They will probably not recover their health till we get back to our own country, w^h. we intend doing in the course of this spring or summer. We intended to have gone long since, but circumstances of an imperious nature prevented it. They desire their best regards to Mdme. La Fayette & your daughters, to which you will be so good as to add mine & to be assured of my constant & sincere friendship.

P. S. I inclose this to General Armstrong & commit it to D^r. Morris a respectable young American, who will probably deliver it to you in person. Should he be the bearer I beg your kind attention to him.

TO BARING BROS. & CO.
LOW LAYTON, March 18, 1806.

GENTLEMEN,—I have rec^d. your letter of the 14th. & transmitted yesterday to General La Fayette by an American gentleman going to Paris, the order which it communicated for the sum he had requested of y^r. house on loan on the credit of the land which had been granted him by Congress. I shall immediately communicate to my government this strong proof of your disposition to befriend a family in whose welfare the U. States take a deep interest, and have no doubt that your reimbursement by means of the funds relied on so far as depends on it will form a particular object of its care.

Major Thos. Sumter lives in Statesborough, a town in the upper part of S^o. Carolina. He is the son of General Sumter of the U. States service. I send you a letter to accompany the draft, which I wish to be forwarded without delay. I am gent^n. with great respect &c.

TO JAMES MADISON.
WASHINGTON, October 18, 1824.

DEAR SIR,—I returned to the city lately to receive our old friend Genl La Fayette, who, after remaining here a few days, set out on Saturday for Yorktown. He has I presume reached that port by this time. He is in good health & spirits, and less altered in his form than I expected, and not at all in his mind, unless by improvement. He appears to me to have a profound knowledge of mankind, & of the present state of Europe, & of this hemisphere. He did well by commencing with our constituents, & coming from them to the government. It shows that the sentiment in favor of our republican principles is universal, & that he is respected & beloved by all for his devotion to those principles, of which he has been the victim. Showing him all possible kindness and attention here, the object has been to let the public demonstrations be those of our constituents only. By this the gov^t. is less compromitted with the holy alliance, with whom also the effect will be more imposing.

I have long wished to visit Albemarle, & to pass some hours at least with you. I must be here the beginning of next month to prepare for the meeting of Congress. If I can go, I shall set out in a few days.

Our accounts from Russia are favorable, & the late treaty relating to the Northwest coast, & the Pacific, all that we could desire. Our best regards to Mrs. Madison. Mrs. Monroe would be happy to come with me, but it will be impossible. Her state of health forbids it.

With very sincere regard I am your friend—

TO THOMAS JEFFERSON.
WASHINGTON, October 18, 1824.

DEAR SIR,—General La Fayette left this for York, on Saturday, and is I presume, now near his post of destination, whether he will proceed thence, by Richmond, to your house, or directly, to Charlestown, & Savannah, & return by your residence, he had not decided, when he left us. Time, has produced less waste of his form, since you last saw him, than it does on most men, and none on his mind. His mov'ment since his arrival in the U. States, has been well directed. Had he visited this city in the first instance, the compromitment of the gov^t., with the holy Alliance, would have been much greater, than by going directly to our fellow citizens, & from them to the gov^t. By this course, the nation has the credit. The holy Alliance, & all the gov^t. of Europe, must therefore look to us, as an united people, devoted to the principles of our revolution & of free republican government. My hope is, that the nation will provide for him, in a way, to put him at ease, the remainder of his days, and to indemnify his family, for the losses, which the principles which he imbibed in our great strength, & of which he has been the victim, subjected them to.

It is my earnest desire to visit Albemarle, & to pass a day, with you, and one with M^r. Madison, before the commenc'ment of the Session. If I do, it must be soon, as I must be back, early in the next month, to prepare for that event. My present impression is, that I will go, & set out in the course of this week.

All our accounts from Russia are favorable. The treaty lately concluded, respecting the N°. West Coast, & the Pacific is, I think, all that we could have asked.

TO THOMAS JEFFERSON.
HIGHLAND, Octr. 31, 1824.

DEAR SIR,—Finding that Genl. La Fayette will not arrive till Thursday, and that the dinner will not be given, on that day, and may be deferred some days longer, I regret that it will be utterly out of my power to remain in the county to unite with you and other friends, in those demonstrations of regard for him, to which he is so justly entitled, & we all so sincerely feel. I have resolv'd therefore to set out, on my return to the city, early in the morning, wishing you to be so kind as to make the necessary explanations to him of the cause, in aid of those which are hastily suggested in the enclos'd letter, which you will be so good as to deliver to him, on his arrival at your house. The meeting of Congress, is so near at hand, that I have not a moment to lose, in making the preparations which will be necessary, for my communications to that body. The collection & arrangement of the documents, will require time, as will the digest of the subject matter, to be communicated. I shall be heartily rejoiced when the term of my service expires, & I may return home in peace with my family, on whom, and especially on M^rs. Monroe, the burdens & cares of my long public service, have borne too heavily. With great respect, etc.]

FROM EIGHTH ANNUAL MESSAGE.
WASHINGTON, December 7, 1824.

Fellow-Citizens of the Senate and of the House of Representatives:
    In conformity with a resolution of Congress of the last session, an invitation was given to General Lafayette to visit the United States, with an assurance that a ship of war should attend at any port of France which he might designate, to receive and convey him across the Atlantic, whenever it might be convenient for him to sail. He declined the offer of the public ship from motives of delicacy, but assured me that he had long intended and would certainly visit our Union in the course of the present year. In August last he arrived at New York, where he was received with the warmth of affection and gratitude to which his very important and disinterested services and sacrifices in our Revolutionary struggle so eminently entitled him. A corresponding sentiment has since been manifested in his favor throughout every portion of our Union, and affectionate

invitations have been given him to extend his visits to them. To these he has yielded all the accommodation in his power. At every designated point of rendezvous the whole population of the neighboring country has been assembled to greet him, among whom it has excited in a peculiar manner the sensibility of all to behold the surviving members of our Revolutionary contest, civil and military, who had shared with him in the toils and dangers of the war, many of them in a decrepit state. A more interesting spectacle, it is believed, was never witnessed, because none could be founded on purer principles, none proceed from higher or more disinterested motives. That the feelings of those who had fought and bled with him in a common cause should have been much excited was natural. There are, however, circumstances attending these interviews which pervaded the whole community and touched the breasts of every age, even the youngest among us. There was not an individual present who had not some relative who had not partaken in those scenes, nor an infant who had not heard the relation of them. But the circumstance which was most sensibly felt, and which his presence brought forcibly to the recollection of all, was the great cause in which we were engaged and the blessings which we have derived from our success in it. The struggle was for independence and liberty, public and personal, and in this we succeeded. The meeting with one who had borne so distinguished a part in that great struggle, and from such lofty and disinterested motives, could not fail to affect profoundly every individual and of every age. It is natural that we should all take a deep interest in his future wellfare, as we do. His high claims on our Union are felt, and the sentiment universal that they should be met in a generous spirit. Under these impressions I invite your attention to the subject with a view that, regarding his very important services, losses, and sacrifices, a provision may be made and tendered to him which shall correspond with the sentiments and be worthy the character of the American people.

TO GENERAL LAFAYETTE.
OAK HILL, May 2, 1829.

MY DEAR FRIEND,—It is some time since I wrote to you, in answer to your affectionate letters, altho' I have long intended to do it, and to acknowledge that particularly in which you enclosed me one to Mr. Graham, but the feeling which it excited has, in truth, been the cause of the delay. So many interesting circumstances have occurred between us, to which we have been parties, and others of which we have been spectators, in both countries, since the battle of Brandywine, that I never can review them without peculiar interest and sensibility. The letter referred to brought them to my recollection with great force. But, my dear friend, I can never take anything from you, nor from your family.[3] I have known and seen too much of yours, and their sufferings to commit such an outrage to my feelings. Your claims are too strong on me personally, on my country, and on the friends of liberty everywhere, for me to do it. I sent your letter to Mr. Graham, with instruction not to think of the measure, or rather, to take no step in the execution of it, and with which he has complied. If I was ever to visit France your house would be my home, but we are both too far advanced in years to think of such a voyage. We must content ourselves with writing to each other, which I shall do hereafter more frequently.

With my ill state of health, and the accident from which it proceeded in the first instance, you have been acquainted, I have suffered much thro' the winter, but am now so far recovered as to be able to take my usual exercise on horseback, and which I do daily, when the weather will permit.

The legislature of this State have called a convention, to be held in October next, to amend the Constitution. It was the first formed in the Union, & has managed affairs successfully; but it is generally admitted to have defects which require amendment. Mr. Madison has been invited by his district to become a member, and to which he has consented, and will be elected. A like invitation has been given to me in this. I hesitated on account of ill health, but have at length expressed a willingness to serve, if they desire it. I am personally little known in the district, and can therefore form no estimate of the result.

My pursuits at home are interesting. My mind is not inactive, and in the employment given to it, a review of past occurrences in which I have acted, and of which I have been a witness, occupies a large portion of my time. I do not know that anything will appear to the public during my life, but whenever it does, should it be deemed worthy notice, a just regard will be shewn to your services, and claims on our countries, as well as to the friendly relation which has existed between us and our families.

Mrs. Monroe, & my whole family, take a deep interest in the welfare & happiness of yours, as well as in your own. All the details which you give us respecting them are gratifying. Your own health, we are happy to hear, is quite restored, & good. We hope that that of your son & daughter likewise is, & of their offspring.

I sent to Mr. Gouverneur the papers you forwarded to me, from the physicians in Paris, expressive of their opinion respecting the infirmity of his son, &

3. Referring to Lafayette's generous offer of pecuniary assistance. [HAMILTON.]

of your desire to receive, & render him any service in your power, & for which he is most grateful. The boy is at a school near the city of New York, in which those thus afflicted are educated, and his improvement is a cause of surprise, as well as of consolation to all the family. Should he ever visit France he will avail himself most willingly of your good offices.

I shall write you again soon. I have received Mr. Marbois' book, relative to Louisiana. He speaks of me with kindness & does justice to me, in many interesting circumstances, and, as I believe, to the full extent of his knowledge. There are some facts, however, with which I am satisfied he was unacquainted. He states, for example, that he had commenced with Mr. Livingston before my arrival in Paris, in April 1803, and that he had done it in compliance with the instruction of Bonaparte, the First Consul. You will observe that the interview stated by Mr. Marbois, between the First Consul and his two ministers, took place on the tenth of April; on which day it was known to Mr. Livingston, & of course to the govt., that I had arrived at Havre, and was on the route to Paris. The conference referred to is stated in page 285. Mr. Livingston's letter in reply to mine announcing my arrival, bears date likewise on the 10th, of which you will see a translation in page 468. If it was known to Mr. Livingston on the 10th. that I had arrived, it must have been known to the First Consul. It was known to all at Havre, as a salute was fired from the battery, and a guard of 50 men sent to the hotel where I stopped, whom I dismissed. That the First Consul should have delayed his conference till that day is a proof of this fact, for otherwise why did it not happen a day or a week before, or after? He stated in the conference that, coming 2000 leagues, I must have more extensive powers, which shews that he waited for my arrival—page 267. He knew that nothing could be done till that event occurred. That he gave the instruction, as stated by Mr. Marbois, to proceed forthwith I have no doubt, but that he gave it with a knowledge of the above facts, and with intention only to put the affair in train, I am equally confident.

In this circumstance I think that Mr. Marbois is mistaken, as already observed, that he had commenced with Mr. Livingston before my arrival. The day after my arrival I dined with Mr. Livingston, having Col. Mercer and Mr. Skipwith with me, which was on the 12th or 13th of April, and while at dinner, Mr. Marbois arrived, & being informed that the family were at dinner, he walked in the garden until we arose from dinner. Mr. Livingston had not then read his instructions, which was an additional motive for wishing to accompany him, in the interview, to guard against his compromitment of himself. Many other circumstances of a like kind, in support of what is above noticed, occurred, and of which I have proofs, which have never been stated, or published to promote any object, on my part, either of advancement, or fame, altho' they have been called for by misrepresentation here. It is admitted that a war with England menaced, but it appears, by Mr. Marbois' statement, that that war was considered ascertain, as early as January, and was deemed inevitable soon afterwards, if not before. Mr. Marbois states, in page 275, that before the message of the King of England, of the 8th of March, 1803, the First Consul had considered the war inevitable. Mr. Tallyrand's letter to Mr. Livingston, of the 24th of March, declaring that he should wait my arrival, is a faithful proof that the First Consul knew the fact, and gave his instructions to Mr. Marbois in consequence thereof. The order to Bernadotte, which you communicated to me, to leave Paris the day I entered it, shews that he was acquainted with it, & intended to prevent an interview between him & me.

If you see no impropriety in it, I have no objection to your shewing to Mr. Marbois what I have stated above. I wish nothing but the truth, in which I am satisfied he concurs. A communication took place between him & me, on this subject, before my retirement, in which I stated to him, at his request, some facts, particularly the letter of Mr. Tallyrand to Mr. Livingston of 24th of March, & Mr. Livingston's letter to me of the 10th of April, which he has published.

I have entered further into this subject than I intended, but I have done it from a knowledge of the interest which you take in what relates to my welfare & character. Retired now from public life, with no desire ever to enter it again, I can have no [other] object, in what relates to the past, than a strict regard to justice.

Let me hear from you as soon as convenient, and give us all the details mentioned respecting your family, as well as yourself. Our affectionate regards to you and them.

PART V

Governor of Virginia and Gabriel's Uprising

INTRODUCTION

D ESPITE THE MASSIVE ATTACK of the Federalists on Monroe's reputation, the Virginia Republicans rallied to his support. Jefferson and Madison wanted him to enter the U.S. House of Representatives, but Monroe realized that he would be the constant butt of attack from his Federalist colleagues, and the debate would be about his actions rather than his policies. Instead in 1799 the Virginian Republicans decided to elect him governor of the commonwealth, which at that time was a duty of the legislature. The vote was two to one in his favor.

Although the powers of the governor were limited under the state constitution—Virginians still remembered the autocratic governors of colonial times—Monroe set out to reform the organs of government by working through the legislature and the Governor's Council, where the real powers lay. The other major power that the governor had was that of commander of the militia.

Within a few months his skill as a military commander was put to the test. On the afternoon of August 30, 1800, the governor received alarming news that slaves in Henrico, south of Richmond, planned to rise during the night, slay their masters while they were sleeping, and march on Richmond. The bloody uprisings in Santo Domingo in 1789 were still fresh in the minds of the planters, and they realized that the fractures in an untenable social structure could burst into upheaval at any time.

The calculation of the number of slaves exported in the slave trade is highly controversial. But Philip D. Curtin, in *The American Slave Trade*, perhaps has provided the most credible estimates based on meticulous calculations. According to Curtin, about ten million Africans were taken out of Africa in bondage. 427,000 were taken to North America, but more than four million were taken to the West Indies. Close to four million were taken to Brazil, where a less successful attempt to produce sugar was underway.

So of the ten million Africans transported to the new world, about four percent were taken to the future territory of the United States. The extent of slavery in the United States nevertheless was more widespread than generally recognized. The first U.S. Census in 1790 shows 293,000 slaves in Virginia, or about 40 percent of the population there; 107,000 in South Carolina; 100,000 in North Carolina; 103,000 in Maryland; 29,000 in Georgia; 21,193 in New York; 12,400 in Kentucky; 11,400 in New Jersey; 8,900 in Delaware; 3,700 in Pennsylvania; 2,650 in Connecticut; 958 in Rhode Island; and 157 in New Hampshire; Although there were exceptions, most slave-holding families had less than ten slaves.

The 1790 census shows no slaves in Maine, Vermont, or Massachusetts, but that was because slavery had been outlawed in Massachusetts in 1788. The small-scale agriculture of New England had no need of slaves, but slavery had long been legal in the Bay Colony and provided house servants to anyone with pretensions of wealth. As Samuel Eliot Morison wrote in *The Maritime History of Massachusetts* in 1922, "Most Boston merchants owned slaves as house servants and bought and sold them like other merchandise."

In a series of letters, dispatches, and orders, reproduced here—which convey the sense of crisis—Monroe left an exact record of swift and decisive action to fortify the city. These measures, augmented by a fortuitous heavy downpour of rain, led to the failure of the uprising, which secretly had been planned to encompass five counties, as well as the capital itself. Led by a slave named Gabriel, the ringleaders were rounded up and condemned to death. Yet Monroe was deeply troubled by the need to execute the rebels. In his limited authority, he had no power to stay the sentence. He won reprieves for some from the governor's council, but the councilors could not be persuaded to delay the sentence until the legislature could be brought back into session.

Nothing more illustrates the ambivalence of Virginians towards slavery than Monroe's letter to Madison on August 14, 1800 where he inquires "whether you had heard of the overseer you promised to endeavor to engage for me." Monroe had about 30 slaves on his Albemarle property. This was only two weeks before Gabriel's uprising. Yet at the same time, there was a recognition that there was something fundamentally wrong with the practice of enslaving human beings. Monroe's correspondence with Jefferson on June 15, 1801, February 13, 1802 and June 11, 1802 shows them discussing efforts to recolonize slaves in Africa— at first as a means of resettling rebels and felons, but with the dawning realization that only freed men could return. He proposes a gradual process of emancipation, with the slaves working off the costs of transportation back to Africa:

Might not those who are sent (hereafter to be emancipated) be bound to service for a few years, as the means of raising a fund to defray the charge of transportation? The ancestors of the present negroes were brought from Africa and sold here as slaves, they and their descendants forever. If we send back any of the race subject to a temporary servitude with liberty to their descendants will not the policy be mild and benevolent? . . . I do not know that such an arrangement would be practicable in any country, but it would certainly be very fortunate attainment if we could make these people instrumental to their own emancipation, by a process gradual and certain, on principles consistent with humanity. . . .

Later on as President, Monroe would become a supporter of the American Colonization Society, with the result that Monrovia, the capital of Liberia, was named after him. After Congress outlawed the slave trade in 1819, he used the power of his office as President to capture American ships illegally in the slave trade and free the captives aboard. On July 24, 1820, he wrote to then Secretary of State John Quincy Adams, "I had supposed that it would be the duty of any of our ships of war, which might seize any of our private vessels engaged in the slave trade, either to bring the people of color to the United States States or land them in Africa; but I presume that the course taken, in the case mentioned . . . that is, the delivery of them to the Consul at the Cape de Verde Islands, is admissible. . . . I hope that the offenders will be made an example of."

In another case, he writes to Adams on August 3, 1820,

I return you Mr. Habersham's letter respecting the capture made by the revenue cutter Dallas, Captn. Jackson, of a brig with the Artigan flag with about 270 Africans on board. The Dist. Attorneys order to the Captn. To deliver the negroes to the Marshall was I think in strict conformity with the act of 1819. Taking into view the provisions of that act with those of the act of the 25th of May last, I am inclined to think that all those concerned in the business who were American citizens whether in foreign or American vessels will be considered by the Court as pirates. There will be no security for the safekeeping of these Africans if permitted to go out of the hands of the Marshall, nor for the suppression of this nefarious practice without a rigorous execution of the law.

Furthermore, he adds, "I do not think that any foreigner can sustain a claim against an African brought directly from Africa as a slave, in our Courts, but that when brought within our jurisdiction he must be free."

However, Monroe realized that his authority extended only to American ships for slavery had not been outlawed by the law of nations. In writing to Daniel Brent, a clerk at the State Department, he notes on September 17, 1821:

"I have examined carefully the law of March 3rd, 1819. . . . The President is authorized by it to employ any of our armed vessels to cruise on the coasts of the U States, or on the coast of Africa, & to instruct their commanders to seize & bring into port all ships or vessels of the U States, wheresoever found, which may have taken on board, or be intended for the purpose of taking on board, or of transporting or may have transported any negro, mulatto, or person of color. . . . This act give authority to the President to cause to be seized . . . all ships of the U States, & of the U States only."

Then he goes on: "There is no question of the law of nations in this case, for the slave trade is not prohibited by that law. It is an abominable practice, against which nations are now combining, & and may be presumed that the combination will soon become universal." And indeed, Monroe was already pursuing negotiations with Great Britain, Spain, Portugal, and the Netherlands for an international convention for the suppression of the slave trade.

Of these countries, only Great Britain responded. Monroe instructed the U.S. minister in London, Richard Rush to negotiate with George Canning, the British Foreign Minister. A convention was drafted using the American laws as a model, declaring those engaged in the slave trade to be pirates punishable under the laws against piracy. Monroe sent the treaty to the Senate on May 21, 1824 with a strong message urging ratification. But there the convention ran into opposition, principally from the northern states where the carrying trade was concentrated. The treaty included the right to stop and search vessels for contraband slaves.

The memory of Britain's high-handed history of stopping American vessels, seizing cargoes and impressing U.S. sailors into British service was too strong. Even John Quincy Adams, who was already beginning to line up support for his presidential bid, worried that the search provisions would depart from the American doctrine of neutrality, and would cost him support in his home territory. Monroe told the Congress that if the convention were adopted, "there is every reason to believe that it will be the commencement of a system destined to accomplish the entire abolition of the slave trade." If the convention were rejected, "it would place the Executive Administration under embarrassment, and subject it, the Congress, and the nation to the charge of insincerely respecting the great result of the final suppression of the slave trade." The convention was approved by the Senate— but with crippling amendments. As a result, Canning rejected the amended treaty and the anti-slavery convention was dead because of the New England objections.

Yet despite Monroe's passion for the suppression of the international slave trade, despite his sympathetic support for the African colonizers, he never put forward any program for the emancipation of slaves who had been brought to America before the importation of slaves was forbidden by the U.S. Constitution. Like many Americans of that period, both in the north and the south, he seemed to have a blind spot that prevented him from seeing people of color as fully human. Ever since Europeans had encountered Africans and Indians in the sixteenth and seventeenth centuries, many suspected that forest peoples, living in semi-permanent villages, were not capable of the organization and abstraction that characterized Western civilization. Since the dawn of history, weaker nations had been enslaved and exploited by all races and all cultures. Only in Europe itself, under the influence of Christianity, had slavery died out. But the rules taken for granted in Europe didn't seem to apply to other continents. It would have taken a leap of the moral imagination to look upon primitive societies as fellow man.

Today such a view is so odious that it is difficult to understand how the same thinkers who could draft the lofty aspirations of the Declaration of Independence, the U.S. Constitution, and the Bill of Rights could at the same time be so obtuse about the moral dilemma presented by slavery. Yet even the 20th century has presented us with like spectacles of ethical blindness. How could western nations stand by while Hitler was engaged in the Holocaust? How could a country of freedom and justice such as the United States make common cause in World War II with a mass murderer like Josef Stalin? Can the principles of a just war be applied to the use of nuclear weapons? Can the dignity of the individual human being be reconciled with the totalitarianism of a centrally controlled economy? Is capital punishment an offense against life, or is it a recognition of the consummate value of the life taken by the murderer? Is abortion an expression of a woman's right to choose, or is it a judgment that some human beings, already complete in all the elements of their distinct, personal DNA, are somehow less than human?

Monroe retired from the presidency burdened with debts occurred in a life-long defense of liberty and the liberation of humanity. He was a man who had devoted a substantial part of his public service to the suppression of the international slave trade. His country—the Congress—refused to reimburse him for the expenses of his service to the nation, and in 1828, he was forced by creditors to sell his property in Albemarle county. On March 28, he wrote to Madison: "I have sold my slaves in that county to Col. White of Florida, who will take them in families to that territory. He gives me for them (with the exception of a few sold there) five thousand dollars."

TO JAMES MADISON.

ALBEMARLE, Aug. 14, 1800.

DEAR SIR,—I wrote you two days since & sent the letter to Charlottesville. It is only this moment that I recollect I omitted to enquire whether you had heard of the overseer you promised to endeavor to engage for me. I shall take no step relying on him till I hear from you. Perhaps he wo^d. be satisfied with £50. as it is in a healthy country, and the entire command of the plantation in his hands. But you will do the best you can; since my last my child has had no relapse of his former complaints, but I have rec^d. a notice which shows I ought to be at Richm^d. I wish I had more command of my time, that I might be with you some days before I go down. Our best respects to M^rs. Madison & family. Sincerely I am y^r. friend & serv^t.

TO THE MAYOR OF PETERSBURG.

RICHMOND, August 30th, 1800.

SIR,—Some information has been received of a proposed insurrection of the slaves in this city and its neighbourhood of a nature to merit attention. It is said it is to take place tonight and as it is probable from a communication received not long since from your city if there be any foundation whatever for the report it may be connected with a like movement there, I have thought proper to apprise you of it. By being on your guard no injury can be done and mischief may be prevented. With great respect I am Sir &c.

TO THE MAYOR OF RICHMOND.

RICHMOND, September 1st, 1800.

SIR,—I deemed it necessary to continue the measures for defence of the city last night that were adopted the preceding one against the supposed projected insurrection. Some additional circumstances that were communicated to me increased the probability that a partial movement at least was contemplated, and there was no reason to suppose it was abandoned, especially as the execution of it might have been prevented by the badness of the night. It seems to me proper that the cause of this alarm should be examined into, that we may know whether anything of the kind imputed was really intended, and to what extent. Perhaps the best course will be to lay hold of the informers, and the suspected, and extort from them what can be obtained. By apprehending the informers they will be secure against the suspicion of being such. This can only be done by the civil authority, on which account I suggest the above to you. As the negroes of the country are said to be a party in the affair it will be well that a magistrate or two be appointed with a like number of the town to make the enquiry that process be issued at the same time against all who are accused or suspected of being concerned in the affair. Some more recent information makes it necessary this commission should be organized without delay. You will observe I only suggest this measure for your consideration. With respect I am Sir &c.

TO COLONEL DAVID LAMBERT.
RICHMOND, September 2ᵈ, 1800.

SIR,—It is expedient that a Guard of sixty men to be commanded by a Captain and suitable number of subalterns and non-commissioned officers be stationed every night in this city for its defence till further order. I have to request you will furnish these from your regiment, twenty-five to be stationed at the Penitentiary, fifteen at the Magazine, ten at the Capitol, and ten at the Gaol. Let them commence duty at six in the evening and remain until sunrise next morning. They will receive their arms at the Penitentiary, and each guard will deliver them over to the succeeding one. With respect I am Sir &c.

TO JAMES MADISON.
RICHMOND, Sept. 9, 1800.

DEAR SIR,—I have yʳ. favor of the 27. (last) in wʰ. you inform me of yʳ. engagement with Mʳ. Macgee to overlook my business in Albermarle, with which I am much gratified. I believe the one on the mountain will remain, but whether he does or not I shall put great confidence in Macgee, and altho' in case he stays and in consequence Macgee's attention be confined to the lower place, I shall if you advise raise his wages to £60. and allow him to possess a horse. I very much hope under Mʳ. Macgee's auspices to encourage considerably the product of plantation, of wʰ. I am satisfied it is capable. I was surprised to hear nothing of the papers sent & letter I wrote you from Albemarle, as I am not to have recᵈ. the letter you mention to have written me the mail before that wʰ. broᵗ. this. My letter convey'd one from Mʳ. Mason having reference to you, of wʰ. we confer'd before, as also mine to Colº. Smith, both of wʰ. ought be seen by yʳ.self only. I hope you have them, & will keep them till we meet. The latter subject ought to be viewed with great favor to the party interested from the footing between him & me, in addition to wʰ. I think he had a discretionary power over what concerned me in every emergency. There has been an alarm here of an insurrection of the blacks w^h. has not entirely subsided. It seems to be evident that something of the kind was contemplated. Ab^t. 25 of this neighborhood are committed who are to be tried next week. It is said they intended to seize the publick arms that were at the penitentiary, burn the city, &c. The evidence of its comprising many of the negroes of Henrico part of Hanov^r. & Chesterfield is satisfactory; but it is at our end of it it was contemplated. M^rs. M. is gone on a visit to my sister Buckner in Carolina and writes me she and Eliza are well & the child much improved. By moving him ab^t. he will I hope get the better soon of those diseases of childhood, & recover his strength. This alarm has kept me much occupied & I write this in haste. We have nothing new from abroad. Our com^rs. and gov^t. keep their secrets to themselves. Of the state of the publick mind we have no positive proof, but cause to think it is changing for the better. Our best wishes to M^rs. Madison & family. Sincerely I am your friend & serv^t.

TO THOMAS JEFFERSON.
RICHMOND, Sept. 9, 1800.

DEAR SIR,—There has been great alarm here of late at the project of an insurrection of the negroes in this city and its neighbourhood wch. was discovered on the day when it was to have taken effect. Abt. 30 are in prison who are to be tried on Thursday, and others are daily discovered and apprehended in the vicinity of the city. I have no doubt the plan was formed and of tolerably extensive combination, but I hope the danger is passed. The trial will commence on Thursday, and it is the opinion of the magistrates who examined those committed, that the whole, very few excepted, will be condemned. The trial may lead to further discoveries of wch. I will inform you. We have nothing new from abroad. Very sincerely I am yr. friend and servt.

GENERAL ORDERS
RICHMOND, September 10th, 1800.

The Governor as Commander in Chief of the Militia, directs that the Commandant of the 19th. Regiment place, of that Regiment, fifty men well officered at the Penitentiary for the guard of the arms and prisoners there. That he place sentinels so as to command the access to that post and the town from the river to the mouth of the lane just above the Penitentiary leading to it from the main road. He will also place two sentinels on the Richmond side so as to observe any approach from the quarter next Mr. Rutherford's. He will establish a guard at the Capitol of a subaltern and twenty-five men with sentinels properly posted to observe any approach from any direction. He will also place a guard of fifty men at the Jail under a Captain who will cause patrols to be constantly moving up the valley, on Richmond hill, and to Rocketts to observe any movement from any quarter. He will place a guard of twenty-five men in the rear of the town whose business it shall be to watch any approach from that quarter. In case of alarm the sentinel will discharge his piece, the guard to which he belongs will form and defend it's post and never yield it. The residue of the regiment will retire to their houses for the night, ready to attend on the first alarm, those living on the Shockoe side of the creek to the Capitol square on the side next Colonel Goodall's tavern. Those living on the Richmond side to the Market house. The Commandant will appoint an officer at each place whose business it shall be to form the men at those places. When formed they will wait the order of the Commander in Chief. It is hoped the citizens exempted by law on each side of the creek who are able and willing to yield their assistance on such an occasion will arrange themselves in like manner. The discharge of muskets at either post, the discharge of a cannon or ringing of the Capitol bell will be considered as an alarm. It is expected the whole Regiment will parade at nine o'clock in the morning at the Capitol square for the purpose of relieving the Guards. By the Commander in Chief.

Attest: SAM. COLEMAN D^y Adj^t. Genl.

GENERAL ORDERS.
RICHMOND, September 15th. 1800 P.M.

The Chief Magistrate is happy to announce that the late combination of slaves in this city and its neighbourhood for the purpose of an insurrection appears to be so completely broken as to authorize him to make arrangements which will contribute greatly to the convenience of the citizens. He is of opinion the force in service may be considerably diminished without hazard to the city or any other of the very important objects for which it was embodied: He therefore directs that of the 19th. Regiment only one hundred and fifty men be kept in service for the protection of the city to be stationed as heretofore; of the 23^d. Regiment thirty men for protection of the arms at Manchester; and of the 33^d. Regiment twenty five men to be stationed near Prosser's tavern. All beyond this number will be forthwith discharged. The Chief Magistrate returns his very sincere thanks to the officers and men composing these several corps, as also to the officers and soldiers of the cavalry who have been called into service on this occasion for the promptitude and alacrity with which they obeyed the summons, and for the good order and discipline observed by them while in service. The trials which have been held of the slaves who were apprehended, with their conviction and execution, is a solemn and incontrovertible proof that a serious conspiracy against the lives and property of the good people of this Commonwealth has existed. Nor can it be doubted that it's danger has been in a great measure averted by the patriotism and good conduct of the citizens, who were called into service on the present occasion. Checked by the extraordinary torrent of rain which fell and warned that we were on our guard prepared to receive them, they trembled in contemplation of the enterprise they had undertaken. They saw by the preparation which was made and the decision which was shewn that their effort would be in vain, and therefore recoiled from it. The slave who discovered this conspiracy has merited well of the community. On account of which discovery and the interference of Providence which has been so conspicuously displayed on this important occasion, our most grateful acknowledgments are forever due to the great disposer of events. Occasional patrols may yet be necessary from Captain Austin's troop of Horse, of which he will have due notice. And the detachment from Captain Myers's company of Artillery will continue in service till further orders. By the Commander in Chief

Attest: SAM. COLEMAN Dᵞ. Adjᵗ. Gᵉⁿˡ.

TO THOMAS JEFFERSON.
RICHMOND, Sept. 15, 1800.

DEAR SIR,—We have had much trouble with the negroes here. The plan of an insurrection has been clearly proved, & appears to have been of considerable extent. 10 have been condemned & executed, and there are at least twenty, perhaps 40. more to be tried, of whose guilt no doubt is entertained. It is unquestionably the most serious and formidable conspiracy we have ever known of the kind; tho' indeed to call it so is to give no idea of the thing itself. While it was possible to keep it secret, wʰ. it was till we saw the extent of it, we did so. But when it became indispensably necessary to resort to strong measures with a view to protect the town, the publick arms, the Treasury and the Jail, wʰ. were all threatened, the opposite course was in part taken. We then made a display of our force and measures of defence with a view to intimidate those people. When to arrest the hand of the Executioner, is a question of great importance. It is hardly to be presumed, a rebel who avows it was his intention to assassinate his master &ᶜ. if pardoned will ever become a useful servant. And we have no power to transport him abroad, nor is it less difficult to say whether mercy or severity is the better policy in this case, tho' when there is cause for doubt it is best to incline to the former council. I shall be happy to hear y^r. opinion on these points. Y^r. friend & servant.

TO THOMAS JEFFERSON.
RICHMOND, Sept. 22, 1800.

DEAR SIR,—This will be delivered you by Mr. Peters with whom you are acquainted. He was presented to me in a very favourable light by Mr. Buckly. Unfortunately my situation as he pass'd thro' lately to Norfolk put it out of my power to profit of his acquaintance and the dangerous indisposition of my child deprives now of that pleasure. Our Infant is in the utmost danger & I begin to fear that we shall want that consolation wch. I was abt. to offer to the afflicted Mr. & Mrs. Carr. This business of the insurrection encreases my anxiety. The danger has doubtless passed but yet it wod. be unwise to make no provision agnst. possibilities. The subject too presses in the points of view on wch. you have been so kind as favor me with some remarks. 15 have been executed. Several others stand reprieved for a fortnight so that shod. anything occur in the interim will thank you to communicate it. I will attend Darrelle whenever invited so to do. Yr. affectionate friend & servt.

Callender to Jefferson, dated Richmond Jail, September 29, 1800. [Jeff. Ms. 2nd. Ser., Vol. 18, No. 59.] "I have not been able to get any more of the Prospect; but next week I shall be able to send either the whole, or nearly so. I beg leave to enclose a copy of a letter to Mr. Duane on the negro business. It contains some trifles which may amuse. Governor Monroe has, last night, lost his only son." [HAMILTON.]

GENERAL ORDERS.
RICHMOND, September 25th, 1800.

The Chief Magistrate has heard with concern of the misconduct of Patrick Donnally and Richard Bennett jun. two of the citizens called into service on the present occasion. He finds the former guilty of disobedience of orders, drunkenness and disorderly conduct while on duty, and sentenced by a court martial to receive thirty-nine lashes as a punishment due to his offences; and the latter of being drunk while on duty, and sleeping on his post as a Centinel, for which offences he is adjudged by a Court Martial to receive twenty lashes. The Chief Magistrate laments that *citizens,* called in to service for the defence of their country, should dishonor that *title*. They ought to shew themselves worthy of the exalted condition of *freemen* in every situation in which they are placed, especially in the character of *soldiers,* where the eye of the observer is sure to criticise their conduct. It requires time to give them the exact discipline of regular troops, but the practice of morality, good order and sobriety belong to private life and ought to be displayed conspicuously when called into military service. A citizen who fails in any of these virtues dishonors himself and the society to which he belongs. The Chief Magistrate hears however with pleasure that the said Patrick Donnally and Richard Bennett junior repent of their said misconduct and promise a complete reformation in their deportment. He is also highly gratified to learn that these are the first reprehensible acts with which they have been charged. On consideration of which circumstances he hereby revokes the said sentences of the said court martial and remits the punishment. He directs however that the Captain Commandant reprimand the said Patrick Donnally and Richard Bennett junior on the ground in presence of the whole Guard and make it known that they are pardoned of the said offences in the expectation that they will never commit the like again.

By Order of the Commander in Chief.
Attest: SAMUEL COLEMAN D^y. Ad^t. G^r.

TO THE MEMBERS OF COUNCIL.
RICHMOND, September 28th, 1800.

GENTLEMEN,—The cause which prevented my meeting you at your last sitting still exists, and deprives me of that pleasure today. You are apprized of the motive of your summons, the apprehension and delivery of Gabriel at the Penitentiary. I send you the papers which appertain to that transaction. It will be proper that advice be given to whom and in what proportions the reward be paid, and by whom his confession, which it appears is promised, shall be taken: and whether in any degree, and on any conditions the faith of the Government shall be compromitted. This slave was brought to my house yesterday about four in the afternoon, and a great crowd of blacks as well as whites gathered round him. I requested Captain Giles who was present to form a guard of fifteen or twenty of the citizens he could collect on the ground and take him under its care to the Penitentiary and continue to guard him there with that number of men, in a separate cell till further orders: holding no conversation with him on any subject, or permitting any other person to do so. The Council will advise whether this additional guard be dismissed or continued for any term.

Mr. Johnston says the arms are arrived. Under the first reply given him the Executive would not decide on the sample. He wishes to know whether they shall be sent to the Penitentiary as a place of safety, at publick expense. Major Quarles's account is also submitted to your consideration.

Colonel Preston has sent waggons for the arms of his and some other counties under a mistake of the purport of the letter I wrote him, which letter will be before you. By a report from Major Coleman it appears those arms are not prepared. You will advise whether this case admits of any remedy by sending other arms hence or from the Point of Fork. With great respect I am Gentlemen &c.

TO THE COMMANDANTS OF THE 12TH AND 38TH REGIMENTS—EACH
RICHMOND, October 3d, 1800.

SIR,—On a presumption the defeat of the late meditated insurrection of the slaves has in a great measure subdued their spirit, it is thought expedient to dismiss the Militia that were called into service for defence of the Arsenal at the Point of Fork. I have instructed the officer commanding there to this effect, and presume by the time you receive this, those respectable citizens will be at liberty to retire to their respective homes. I offer to those of your regiment, through you, my acknowledgment for their good conduct on this occasion. Should any emergency arise hereafter to endanger that post, I have directed the officer to call on you again for suitable aid for it's defence, and have to request you will comply with such application. The dismission of this force however, makes it an object of great importance that you keep out strong patrols, with orders to visit all suspected places. If this is done the country may be considered in a state of safety; but should it be neglected and a relaxation be observed, there is no security that the spirit of insurrection which was lately so bold and daring will not again be revived, with projects equally nefarious, with those that were lately discomfited. With great respect I am Sir &c.

TO COLONEL THOMAS NEWTON.
RICHMOND, October 5th, 1800.

SIR,—I lately received your letter of the 24th. ultimo respecting Gabriel, the slave for whose apprehension a reward was offered by the Government, on account of the part he had in the late meditated insurrection of the negroes. This slave will be tried tomorrow, and as his guilt is well established there can be no doubt of his fate. By your letter it appeared he had promised a full confession, but on his arrival here he declined making it. From what he said to me, he seemed to have made up his mind to die, and to have resolved to say but little on the subject of the conspiracy. This affair may be considered as crushed, at least for the present. The militia, that were called into service, are all dismissed except a guard of seventy-five in this city for the defence of the arms, the Capitol and Jail. I should be glad to know if any symptom of a like spirit has been observed, of late, in Norfolk, or the counties contiguous to it. It will give me great pleasure to hear, the fever, with which you have been afflicted, is at an end. As soon as you are at liberty to communicate this agreeable intelligence, the intercourse will be put on its former footing. I should have answered your several letters of late more regularly, had not my time been greatly engrossed, by the commotion excited by the negroes, and the sickness of a child which unhappily terminated in his loss. With great respect, I am &c.

TO JAMES MADISON.
RICHMOND, Octr. 8, 1800.

DEAR SIR,—I ought to have answered y^r. last favor sooner relative to an advance made me at Fredbg. but many interesting concerns have prevented it. That advance was I presume made to M^r. Jones, as I recollect writing by him to request ab^t. that sum to be applied to my use there. I think too you advanced him the cash as he paid the debt w^h. I owed on his arrival at Fredbg; tho' I rather think it was in Septr. the year before on his way to the district court. I have seen an interesting paper in several of the gazettes taken from a Paris paper respecting the state of our negotiation with France. By this it appears to be suspended on a strange pretext of our Com^{rs}. that we have no right to put France on a footing with Engl^d.; a pretext worthy the head of a little lawyer but unworthy a diplomatic agent. The insurrectional spirit in the negroes seems to be crushed, tho' it certainly existed and had gone to some extent. 15 have been executed, and 10 or 12 more will be on Friday next. I have submitted the question to the council whether those less criminal in comparison with others, sho^d. be reprieved that their case might be submitted in all the lights in w^h. it may be contemplated to legislative consideration; the council was divided & having no vote those not recommended to mercy by the court will be executed. Our best regards to y^r. lady & family. Your friend &c.

TO WILLIAM PRENTIS.

SIR,—Many interesting concerns have prevented my answering your last letter sooner. A man named Samuel Bird, a free mulatto of Hanover town, was

arrested on suspicion of being concerned in the conspiracy of the negroes; he was
sent here, committed to Jail, and finally discharged for want of evidence, it being
decided that people of his own colour, in slavery, could not give testimony against
him. His son, a slave, was condemned, and executed yesterday. I have sent your
letter to the examining Magistrates here, and requested they would be so obliging as communicate to you, any thing that occurred interesting to Petersburg; or
to me, in which case I shall not fail to transmit to you. The ill success of the project here has suppressed it I presume every where, at least for the present. There
is strong evidence that such a project existed being known in many and some distant parts of the State, by the negroes, but yet it is difficult to decide how extensive the combination was. On that point the evidence is less satisfactory; though
it is presumable had they made any impression here, even momentarily, we should
have beheld a frightful scene in the country. With great respect, I am &c.

TO JOHN DRAYTON.
[LIEUTENANT-GOVERNOR OF SOUTH CAROLINA.]
RICHMOND, October 21st, 1800.

SIR,—I have been honored with your letter of the 27th. ultimo, relative to
the late conspiracy of the Negroes in this State, and with pleasure give you the
information you desire on that interesting subject. The Court, by whom those
who were apprehended were tried, has nearly completed the business, so that
it is presumable we have all the light we shall ever obtain from that source. The
conspiracy was, in some respects, a formidable one to this State, but we have no
reason to think it extended to any State south of us. Had any circumstance
occurred to make that event presumable I should have communicated it to you
with the utmost dispatch. The conspiracy commenced here, since its chiefs were
of this city and neighbourhood. The first attempt was to have been made here,
in which had they succeeded, it is probable a frightful scene would have been
exhibited for a while through the country, which might have extended to you.
Fortunately the plot was discovered, about two o'clock in the afternoon of the
day on which the stroke was to have been given, in consequence of which measures were taken to avert the danger. Much embarrassment too was occasioned
to the authors of the conspiracy, by a rain which fell about the time appointed
for the rendezvous of the different parties, which prevented the meeting of
many who were engaged in it. Being thus checked the Government had time
to act with effect, which it did, for from that period it had the entire command
of the affair. All who were most active, were apprehended, and those most

guilty have suffered the punishment prescribed by the law for so great a crime. Twenty-five have been executed, and a few more probably will be, making in the whole about thirty. According to our present information the conspiracy was quite a domestic one, conceived and carried to the stage at which it was disclosed, by some bold adventurers among the slaves, who were willing to hazard their lives on the experiment, and who counted more on the favorable consequences likely to result from the first effort, which they thought would be successful, than on any very extensive preconcerted combination. If white men were engaged in it, it is a fact of which we have no proof. Should anything occur more fully to illustrate this very distressing incident, I shall hasten to apprize you of it, for I consider the subject to which it refers, in many lights in which it may be viewed, as one in which all the Southern States are equally and deeply interested, and on which their respective Governments, especially in emergencies of this kind ought to be full and regular in their communications to each other. With great respect I have the honor to be &c.

TO THE SPEAKERS OF THE GENERAL ASSEMBLY.
RICHMOND, December 5th, 1800.

SIRS,—An important incident has occurred since your last session, which I consider it my duty to submit fully and accurately, in all its details to the wisdom of the General Assembly. On the 30th. of August, about two in the afternoon, Mr. Moseby Shephard a respectable citizen of this country called and informed me he had just received advice from two slaves that the negroes in the neighborhood of Thomas H. Prosser intended to rise that night, kill their masters, and, proceed to Richmond, where they would be joined by the negroes of the city; that they would then take possession of the arms, ammunition, and the town. He added he had long known these two slaves and had no doubt of the truth of the information they gave him, and that he communicated it to me that the proposed insurrection might be defeated if possible. This communication was very interesting, and the source from whence derived, calculated to inspire a belief it was true. The day was far advanced when I received it, so that if any provision was to be made to avert the danger, not a moment was to be lost. I immediately called in the officers commanding the regiment of Militia & troop of Cavalry in town, and made the best disposition for such an emergency the time would allow. A guard of a Captain and thirty men was placed at the Penitentiary where the publick arms were deposited, twenty at the Magazine, and fifteen at the Capitol, and the Horse was ordered to patrol the several routes leading to the city from

Mr. Prosser's estate, and to apprize me without delay, if anything like a movement of the negroes was seen, or other circumstance creating a suspicion such was contemplated. The close of the day was marked by one of the most extraordinary falls of rain ever known in our country. Every animal sought shelter from it. Nothing occurred in the night, of the kind suspected, to disturb the tranquility of the city, and in the morning the officer commanding the Horse reported he had seen but one circumstance unusual in the neighborhood, which was, that all the negroes he passed on the road, in the intervals of the storm, were going from the town, whereas it was their custom to visit it every Saturday night. This circumstance was not otherwise important than as it was said the first rendezvous of the negroes was to be in the country. The same precautions were observed the next night against the threatened insurrection and the same report made the next day by the officers on duty, so that I was on the point of concluding there was no foundation for the alarm, when I was informed by Major Mosby and other gentlemen of character from his neighborhood, they were satisfied a project of insurrection, such as above described, did exist, and that the parties to it meant still to carry it into effect. These gentlemen stated facts and gave details, which left no doubt in my mind of the existence of such a project. From this period the affair assumed a more important aspect. It did not seem probable the slaves in this city and neighbourhood would undertake so bold an enterprise without support from the slaves in other quarters of the State. It was more reasonable to presume an extensive combination had been formed among them for that purpose. Heretofore I had endeavored to give the affair as little importance as the measures necessary for defence would permit. I had hoped it would even pass unnoticed by the community. But as soon as I was satisfied a conspiracy existed it became my duty to estimate the crisis according to its magnitude, and to take regular and systematic measures to avert the danger. In consequence I issued a summons to convene the Council at ten the next day, and in the interim advised the gentlemen who gave me the information, to apprehend and commit to prison without delay all the slaves in the county whose guilt they had good cause to suspect. I also gave a like intimation to the Mayor of the city, which advice was duly attended to. When the Council convened (on the 2^d. of September) I laid before it the evidence I had received of the meditated insurrection of the slaves, and asked its advice as to the measures necessary to be taken in such an emergency. The Council concurred in opinion that such a project existed and ought to be guarded against with peculiar care. But as the extent of the danger was not yet known, it was thought sufficient at the time to confine our measures of defence to those objects which it was understood were to be first assailed, the Penitentiary, the

Capitol, and the Magazine in this city; and the Arsenal at the Point of Fork. It was natural to conclude the attention of the insurgents would be directed in the outset to these objects; and this presentiment was confirmed by every one who knew and communicated to us any thing of their designs. Accordingly guards were established at those places in this city, and an additional force of fifty men ordered to the Point of Fork. At the same time letters were written to the Commandants of every regiment in the Commonwealth, admonishing them of the existing danger, and requesting that vigilant attention be paid to the police of the country, by ordering out suitable and active patrols in every county. In the evening of the same day about twenty of the conspirators were brought to town from Mr. Prosser's and the neighbouring estates, and as the jail could not contain them, they were lodged in the Penitentiary. The chiefs were not to be found. Some of the arms which they had prepared for the occasion, formed of scythe blades, well calculated for execution were likewise brought with them. By the information now received as by former communications, it appeared that the inhabitants of that neighbourhood were in a particular degree, exposed to danger: the conspiracy commenced with their slaves, and they were to be its first victims. It was therefore deemed proper, with a view to their safety, by advice of Council, to order from the thirty third Regiment a guard of a Captain and sixty men to take post near Watson's tavern in the centre of that neighbourhood. By like advice the troop of the city was at the same time subjected to such duty as should be required of it. Every day now threw new light on this affair, and increased the idea of its importance. On the 6th. by advice of Council, an order was issued for the removal of the powder from the Magazine to the Penitentiary; the distribution of the arms which were stamped and prepared for the several counties according to a law of the last session, was suspended; the whole militia of the city was armed, its guard increased from sixty to a hundred men, and a power vested in the Chief Magistrate to call out such proportions of the militia of Henrico, Chesterfield and the city of Richmond, as in his judgment the emergency might require. The trials had now commenced whereby the nature and extent of the conspiracy became better understood. It was satisfactorily proven that a general insurrection of the slaves was contemplated by those who took the lead in the affair. A species of organization had taken place among them. At a meeting held for the purpose, they had appointed a commander, to whom they gave the title of General, and had also appointed some other officers. They contemplated a force of cavalry as well as infantry and had formed a plan of attack on the city which was to commence by setting fire to the lower end of the town where the houses consisted chiefly of wood, in expectation of drawing the people to that quarter, while they assailed the Penitentiary, Magazine and Capitol, intending after achieving these, and getting possession of the arms, to meet the people unarmed on their return. The accounts of the number of those who were to commence the movement varied. Some made it considerable, others less so. It was distinctly seen that it embraced most of the slaves in this city and neighbourhood, and that the combination extended to several of the adjacent counties, Hanover, Caroline, Louisa, Chesterfield, and to the neighbourhood of the Point of Fork; and there was good cause to believe that the knowledge of such a project pervaded other parts, if not the whole of the State. At this time there was no reason to believe if such a project was ever conceived, that it was abandoned. Those who gave the earliest information and were best informed on the subject, thought otherwise. It was understood that the leaders in the conspiracy, who had absconded, were concealed in the neighborhood. And as several of the parties to it were confined in the Jail condemned to suffer death, and many others in the Penitentiary, likely to experience the same fate, it was probable sympathy for their associates might drive them to despair, and prompt them to make a bolder effort for their relief. The opposite effect was expected from the measures pursued by the Government, but yet the result was uncertain. Other considerations presented themselves to view, in weighing the part it was then incumbent on me to take. The number of slaves in this city and its neighbourhood, comprising those at work on the publick buildings, the canal, and the coal pits, was considerable. These might be assembled in a few hours, and could only be opposed by a respectable force, which force if the city was surprised, could not be collected in a short time. The probability was if their first effort succeeded, we should see the town in flames, its inhabitants butchered, and a scene of horror extending through the country. This spectacle it is true, would be momentary only, for as soon as a body of militia could be formed the insurrection would be suppressed. The superiority in point of numbers, in the knowledge and use of arms, and indeed every other species of knowledge which the whites have over the blacks in this Commonwealth is so decisive, that the latter could only sustain themselves for a moment in a rebellion against the former. Still it was a crisis to be avoided so far as prudent precautions could accomplish it. There was one other consideration which engaged the mind in the commencement of this affair from which it was not easy to withdraw it. It seemed strange that the slaves should embark in this novel and unexampled enterprise of their own accord. Their treatment has been more favorable since the revolution, and as the importation was prohibited among the first acts of our independence, their number has not increased in proportion with that of the whites. It was natural to suspect they were prompted to it by others who were invisible, but whose agency might be powerful. And if this was the case it became proportionally more difficult to estimate the extent of the combination, and the consequent real importance of the crisis. On consideration of all these circumstances it was deemed necessary to call out such a force as might be fully adequate to the emergency; such an one as would be likely to over-awe and keep down the spirit of insurrection, or sufficient to suppress it in case it broke out. On that principle I called into service on the 9th. the 19th. and 23d. regiments, and a detachment of fifty men, additional, from the 33d.; which detachment with the whole of the 19th. regiment and one hundred men of the 23d., were ordered to take post in this city. The residue of the 23d. were stationed in the town of Manchester. While there was a hope the report of this conspiracy was unfounded, or a possibility of controlling it in silence, that object was pursued with zeal. But as its existence had become known to the publick, it only remained to make the incident as harmless in other respects as circumstances would permit. Having with a view to the publick safety, called out a respectable force, I was resolved to derive from it all the aid it could yield in reference to the objects contemplated. It was paraded daily on the Capitol square, and trained as well that it might be prepared for action if occasion required, as that our strength might be known to the conspirators. The effect which this measure produced was easily and soon perceived. It was evident that the collection and display of this force inspired the citizens with confidence, and depressed the spirits of the slaves. The former saw in it a security from the danger which menaced them; the latter a defeat of their nefarious projects. On the 12th. of September, five, and on the fifteenth following, five others were executed. On those occasions the whole force in service in the city (infantry and horse) attended the execution. On the 27th Gabriel, one of the chiefs of the conspiracy, for whom a reward had been offered, and who had been apprehended at Norfolk, was delivered up and committed to Jail. As these executions were carried into effect without any movement of the slaves, and their chief apprehended, it was fair to presume the danger of the crisis had passed. It became from that period the object of the Executive to diminish the force with a view to lessen the expense; which object was pursued with undeviating attention. On the 13th. it was reduced to 650 men, including those at the Point of Fork. On the 16th. to 225; occasional reductions were afterwards made, as circumstances permitted, till finally on the 18th. of October, it was reduced to a Serjeant and twelve men at the Penitentiary, and a Corporal and six at the Jail, at which point it now stands. You will receive herewith a copy of the documents which illustrate the transaction, with a report from the Auditor of the expenses attending it: to which is added a letter from the Treasurer, communicating an opinion of the Attorney General respecting payment for some of the slaves who were executed. I cannot too much commend the conduct of the Militia on this occasion. They were obedient to order, exact in their discipline, and prompt in their execution of every duty that was enjoined on them. Their improvement was rapid and far exceeded anything I had ever witnessed. Nor can it be doubted, had a crisis occurred, they would have proved as firm and decisive in action, as they were patient and persevering in the discharge of every other duty. Their example teaches a useful lesson to our country. It tends to confirm the favorable idea before entertained of their competence to every purpose of publick safety. It belongs to the Legislature to weigh with profound attention, this unpleasant incident in our history. What has happened may occur again at any time, with more fatal consequences, unless suitable measures be taken to prevent it. Unhappily while this class of people exists among us we can never count with certainty on its tranquil submission. The fortunate issue of the late attempt should not lull us into repose. It ought rather to stimulate us to the adoption of a system, which if it does not prevent the like in future, may secure the country from any calamitous consequences. With great respect I have the honor to be, Your most obed. Servant.

TO THE MAYOR OF THE CITY OF RICHMOND.
RICHMOND, December 27th, 1800.

SIR,—Since I saw you I have taken every possible precaution in my power to prevent a movement of the negroes, and defeat its object should one take place by giving suitable instructions to the Commandant of the Militia in town, and the Superintendant of the Penitentiary. But it appears to me that some important regulations are wanting to which the Corporation alone is competent. It is represented that many negroes were yesterday and still are in town from the country, perhaps from the coal pits, who acting in a body at their ordinary labour, are more capable of forming and executing any plan, than such as are dispersed on estates. I should suppose it would have a good effect to expel those negroes from the town, and prohibiting their entering except in the day, to be admitted at a certain hour and depart in such time. For this purpose it would be necessary to enregister all the negroes of the town, and pass a law that each should have a passport or certificate from his master, shewing he belonged to the town, to enable the constables or watch to execute the restriction on those from the country. The negroes from the country have no business in town, but to attend at market; that being ended they ought to depart. The constables or watch should act by day as well as night. Eight men as constables or watchmen would be sufficient, to supervise the police of the town. They should be always in pay, precluded any other occupation, have their duty strictly defined, and held to rigorous account by the Corporation for the faithful performance of it. I flatter myself the funds of the Corporation will be adequate to this expense, since the men being engaged for a term of some months or a year might be had at a moderate price. Being persuaded that we ought not to consider ourselves exempt from danger, from the source referred to, I have thought it my duty to submit the subject to your consideration, in hope the Corporation will make such arrangement as it may deem proper. I shall unquestionably continue to pay all the attention in my power to the police of the city, and to contribute to its safety by a proper application of any means which are or may be committed to the Executive for that purpose. But these can never extend to regulations of the kind above referred to. With great respect I am Sir &c.

TO COLONEL THOMAS NEWTON.
RICHMOND, 11th. February, 1801.

SIR,—I have your letter of the 4th. instant. Captain Barron's conduct in seizing an American vessel engaged in the Slave trade, was proper and commendable. That trade is prohibited not only between Africa and the United States respectively, by their respective Legislatures, but between that country and foreign ports, by American citizens, by a law of the United States. I hope the example which will be made of this defaulter, will deter other citizens from being concerned in so disgraceful a traffic. From a view of the laws of our own State, I am inclined to think the negroes ought not to be admitted into it. The law which seems to be particularly applicable to the case, bears date on the 12th. of December 1793, which I beg to recommend to your attention. By the 4th. section of that law, if they were introduced it would be the duty of a magistrate to remove them. I do not suggest this with a view to prevent their being landed temporarily if humanity requires, or Captain Barron finds it necessary for his convenience. However I will write you again on this subject in the course of a few days. With great respect I am Sir &c.

TO MRS. SHEPHARD.
RICHMOND, 23d. February, 1801.

MADAM,—Being authorized to purchase the negro man, Tom, one of those who gave information of the late conspiracy of the slaves, for the purpose of liberating him, I shall thank you to inform me the lowest price you are willing to take for him. I doubt not you will take an interest in an event which is intended to benefit a servant, who I understand has at all times been faithful to you, and will meet the disposition of the General Assembly to reward him for an act of signal merit, with a spirit equally just and benevolent on your part. With great respect I am, Madam, Your very obed^t. servant.

TO THOMAS JEFFERSON.
RICHMOND, June 15th, 1801.

SIR,—I enclose you a resolution of the General Assembly of this Commonwealth, of the last Session, by which it is made my duty to correspond with you on the subject of obtaining by purchase lands without the limits of this State, to which persons obnoxious to the laws or dangerous to the peace of society may be removed. This resolution was produced by the conspiracy of the slaves which took place in this city and neighbourhood last year, and is applicable to that description of persons only. The idea of such an acquisition was suggested by motives of humanity, it being intended by means thereof to provide an alternate mode of punishment for those described by the resolution, who under the existing law might be doomed to suffer death. It was deemed more humane, and it is hoped would be found in practice not less expedient, to transport such offenders beyond the limits of the State.

It seems to be the more obvious intention of the Legislature, as inferred from the resolution, to make the proposed acquisition of land, in the vacant western territory of the United States, but it does not appear to me to preclude one without the limits of the Union. If a friendly power would designate a tract of country within its jurisdiction, either on this Continent or a neighbouring Island, to which we might send such persons, it is not improbable the Legislature might prefer. In any event an alternative could not otherwise than be desirable, since after maturely weighing the conditions and advantages of each position the Legislature might still prefer that which appeared to it most eligible.

It is proper to remark that the latter part of the resolution which proposes the removal of such persons as are dangerous to the peace of society, may be understood as comprizing many to whom the preceding member does not apply. Whether the Legislature intended to give it a more extensive import, or rather whether it contemplated removing from the Country any but Culprits who were condemned to suffer death, I will not undertake to decide. But if the more enlarged construction of the resolution is deemed the true one, it furnishes in my opinion, a strong additional motive, why the Legislature, in disposing of this great concern should command an alternative of places. As soon as the mind emerges, in contemplating the subject, beyond the contracted scale of providing a mode of punishment for offenders, vast and interesting objects present themselves to view. It is impossible not to revolve in it, the condition of those people, the embarrassment they have already occasioned us, and are still likely to subject us to. We perceive an existing evil which commenced under our Colonial System, with which we are not properly chargeable, or if at all not in the present degree, and we acknowledge the extreme difficulty of remedying it. At this point the mind rests with suspense, and surveys with anxiety obstacles which become more serious as we approach them. It is in vain for the Legislature to deliberate on the subject, in the extent of which it is capable, with a view to adopt the system of policy which appears to it most wise and just, if it has not the means of executing it. To lead to a sound decision and make the result a happy one, it is necessary that the field of practicable expedients be opened to its election, on the widest possible scale.

Under this view of the subject I shall be happy to be advised by you whether a tract of land in the Western territory of the United States can be procured for this purpose, in what quarter, and on what terms? And also whether any friendly power will permit us to remove such persons within its limits, with like precision as to the place and conditions? It is possible a friendly power may be disposed to promote a population of the kind referred to, and willing to facilitate the measure by co-operating with us in the accomplishment of it. It may be convenient for you to sound such persons especially those more immediately in your neighborhood, on the subject, in all the views which may appear to you to be suitable.

You will perceive that I invite your attention to a subject of great delicacy and importance, one which in a peculiar degree involves the future peace, tranquility and happiness of the good people of this Commonwealth. I do it, however, in a confidence, you will take that interest in it, which we are taught to expect from your conduct through life, which gives you so many high claims to our regard. With great respect I have the honor to be your most obt. servant.

TO THOMAS JEFFERSON.
RICHMOND, February 13th, 1802.

SIR,—I enclose you some resolutions of the General Assembly of this Commonwealth, passed at its last session explanatory of a resolution of the preceding session authorizing a correspondence with you relative to the purchase of lands without the limits of the State, to which persons obnoxious to the laws or dangerous to the peace of society might be removed. You will recollect that as the precise import of the first resolution was not clearly understood, it was thought proper to submit our communication on it to the General Assembly, that its object and policy might be more accurately defined. The resolutions which I have now the pleasure to communicate to you have removed all doubt on that subject, by confining the attention in procuring the asylum sought to the accommodation of negroes only, and by specifying for what causes, under what circumstances, and (in the case of felons) to what countries it is wished to send them. You will be pleased to observe that there are two descriptions of negroes embraced by these resolutions, the first comprizes those who being slaves may commit certain enumerated crimes. For *such* an asylum is preferred on the continent of Africa or the Spanish or Portuguese settlements in South America. The second respects free negroes and mulattoes, including those who may hereafter be emancipated and sent, or choose to remove to such place as may be acquired. For *these* a preference is not expressed in favor of any partic-ular region or country, nor is the right of sovereignty over such place desired. In removing these people without our limits, no restraint is imposed to preclude the attainment of an asylum anywhere, whereby the object of the State might be defeated, or to prevent that attention to their interests in case an alternative of places is presented, by inhibiting a preference for *that* which may be deemed best adapted to their constitution, genius, and character.

TO JOHN COWPER.

RICHMOND, May 25th, 1802.

SIR,—After the most mature consideration it is resolved to let the law take its course, in the case of Jeremiah at the expiration of the reprieve whose benefit he now enjoys. The circumstances which have been communicated, are too slight to induce the Executive to suspend for a longer term, in favor of a person other-wise of bad character, the judgment of the Court founded on testimony satisfac-tory to it, which convicts him of a crime the most atrocious. Very deliberate attention has been paid to the subject; an attention which was due to the nature of the case, and the benevolent motives of those who communicated to the Executive some circumstances which occurred after the trial, the result whereof is to leave him to the fate to which he is doomed by the judgment of the Court. It is hoped that his example will prove an useful admonition to the slaves, his accomplices, and totally suppress the spirit of insurrection in that quarter of the

State. In the case of Ned some mitigating circumstances appear which were thought worthy of attention. He is represented to be almost an idiot, little capable of acting for himself, inoffensive and so far as any indication of intellect is discernible to give any trait to his character, that that was heretofore of the mild and peaceable cast. If such is the case it may be proper to mitigate his punishment by transportation. To obtain full information on that point a further reprieve is granted in his favor. I shall therefore be glad to hear from you on this subject and to receive such light respecting him as you possess. I am Sir, with great respect &c.

TO THOMAS JEFFERSON.
RICHMOND, June 11th, 1802.

SIR,—I find by your letter of the 3d. that you think Sierra Leone, on the coast of Africa, a suitable place for the establishment of our insurgent slaves, that it may also become so for those who are or may hereafter be emancipated, and that you are disposed to obtain the assent of the company to such a measure through our minister in London, while your attention will be directed in the interim to such other quarters as may enable us to submit a more enlarged field to the option of our Assembly. By the information of Mr. Thornton, the British chargé des affaires, which you have been so kind as to communicate, it appears that slavery is prohibited in that settlement, hence it follows that we cannot expect permission to send any who are not free to it. In directing our attention to Africa for an Asylum for insurgents it is strongly implied that the Legislature intended they should be free when landed there, as it is not known that there exists any market on that coast for the purchase of slaves from other countries. Still I am persuaded that such was not the intention of the Legislature, as it would put culprits in a better condition than the deserving part of those people. This opinion is further supported by a law still in force which authorizes the Executive to sell, subject to transportation, all slaves who are guilty of that crime. I submit this idea to your consideration not with a view to prevent your application to the company for its assent to the settlement within its limits, but as a motive in case you concur with me in the above construction of the resolution, why you should more particularly seek an establishment for them in the Portuguese, Dutch or Spanish settlements in America. In obtaining permission to send our negroes to that settlement we may avail ourselves of it on the principles of the company as far as it suits our interest and policy.

If the Legislature intends that insurgents shall enjoy their liberty on landing there, the accommodation would be general; but if they are excluded and the door is opened on favorable conditions to such only as are or may hereafter become free, it will nevertheless be important as it will give the Legislature an opportunity to deliberate on and perhaps provide a remedy for an evil which has already become a serious one. I cannot otherwise than highly approve the idea of endeavoring to lighten the charge of transportation to the publick, wheresoever they may be sent. A permission to send certain articles of merchandize, which would be sure to command a profit, if that could be relied on, would contribute much to that end. Perhaps other means not incompatible with the charter of the company might be devised. Do their regulations permit temporary servitude? If they do, might not those who are sent (hereafter to be emancipated) be bound to service for a few years, as the means of raising a fund to defray the charge of transportation? The ancestors of the present negroes were brought from Africa and sold here as slaves, they and their descendants for ever. If we send back any of the race subject to a temporary servitude with liberty to their descendants will not the policy be mild and benevolent?

May not the same idea be held in view in reference to any other place in which an establishment is sought for them? I do not know that such an arrangement would be practicable in any country, but it would certainly be a very fortunate attainment if we could make these people instrumental to their own emancipation, by a process gradual and certain, on principles consistent with humanity, without expense or inconvenience to ourselves.

TO JOHN QUINCY ADAMS.
HIGHLAND, July 24, 1820.

DEAR SIR,—I have your letter of the 18th., with all the papers mentioned in it.

I had supposed that it would be the duty of any of our ships of war, which might seize any of our private vessels engaged in the slave trade, either to bring the people of color to the United States or land them in Africa; but I presume that the course taken, in the case mentioned in yours, that is, the delivery of them to the Consul at the Cape de Verde Islands, is admissible, & think that you acted properly in accepting his bill. I hope that the offenders will be made an example of.

The answer of the Governor of Teneriffe to Mr. O'Sullivan, is in a very conciliatory spirit and should I think be satisfactory.

In the case of Richard Hull condemned in Alexandria to suffer death, I had, in a paper forwarded to you some time since, as well as I remember authorized his reprieve for a certain term. If you think it a case meriting pardon I am willing that an order to that effect should issue. I now return the papers.

The heat has been excessive till of late & Mrs. Monroe's indisposition continuing, I have omitted to return some communications from you as yet. Her health is now improving with a change in the temperature of the weather so that I hope to return you all now remaining by me by next mail. With great respect and esteem.

TO JOHN QUINCY ADAMS.
August 3, 1820.

The instructions to Mr. Forbes, a copy of which I received with your letter of the 28th will in connection with those to Commodore Perry fully meet every object. I have retained the copy on the presumption that occasional references to it may be necessary. I return you Mr. Habersham's letter respecting the capture made by the revenue cutter *Dallas,* Captn. Jackson, of a brig under the Artigan flag with about 270 Africans on board. The Dist. Attorneys order to the Captn to deliver the negroes to the Marshall was I think in strict conformity with the act of 1819. Taking into view the provisions of that act with those of the act of the 15 of May last, page 102, I am inclined to think that all those concerned in the business who were American citizens whether in foreign or American vessels will be considered by the Court as pirates. There will be no security for the safe keeping of these Africans if permitted to go out of the hands of the Marshall nor for the suppression of this nefarious practice without a rigorous execution of the law. The expense of keeping them by the Marshall must be borne. A few strong examples will terminate it with the trade. I think that it will be advisable for you to send Mr. Habersham's letter to the Attorney General & request him to give the District Attorney the necessary instructions for the further prosecution of the business. (Instruct the D. Attorney to pursue the affair in its several relations with the utmost attention;—first, to contend for the complete liberation of every African against every claimant, Portuguese, Spaniard or others; and secondly, for the punishment of all concerned in taking them who are exposed to it under our laws. I do not think that any foreigner can sustain a claim against an African brought directly from Africa as a slave, in our Courts, but that when brought within our jurisdiction he must be free. I think that this is in the spirit of our laws, if not more explicitly provided for by them. In any case of doubt it will be proper to take the opinion of the Attorney General who has examined the subject professionally with great care.)

The disposition of Colonel Trumbull's pictures in the Senate chamber is I believe the best that can be made of them for the present. Of this be so good as to inform Col. Lane or Mr. Bullfinch that the necessary preparation may be made for their reception.

As I presume that Mr. Graham's salary will cease while at home, Mr. Appleton takes of course the grade of a Chargé des Affaires with its compensation in his absence.

For the present we had better make no new appointment to Pernambuco. The delay will give Mr. Ray the opportunity he requests to vindicate the character of his brother which may be gratifying altho. he may not be reinstated. Mr. Graham will be able to give you further information on this subject.

I intimated in my last that I thought you had acted properly in accepting the bill of Mr. Hodge Consul at the Cape de Verde Islands, for the sum agreed to be given by him for the transportation of certain persons engaged in the slave trade taken by Captain Trenchard & delivered by him to the Consul. . . .

TO DANIEL BRENT.

OAKHILL, Sep^t. 17th. 1821.

DEAR SIR,—I have examined carefully the law of March 3^d. 1819 entitled an act in addition to the acts prohibiting the slave trade, and it appears to me to correspond with the view I took of it in my preceding letter to you. The President is authorized by it to employ any of our armed vessels to cruise on the coasts of the U States, or on the coast of Africa, & to instruct their commanders to seize & bring into port all ships or vessels of the U States, wheresoever found, which may have taken on board, or be intended for the purpose of taking on board, or of transporting, or may have transported any negro, mulatto, or person of colour, in violation of any of the provisions of the act, &c. This act gives authority to the President to cause to be seized, &c. all ships of the U States, & of the U States only. If a ship is seen at sea, or elsewhere, under foreign colours, the presumption is that she is of the nation whose flag she bears, & not of the U States. If she be seized, & it appears that she was not American, but foreign, we commit an offense to that power, if the practice be persevered in the *excuse of mistake* might not be satisfactory.

There is no question of the law of nations in this case, for the slave trade is not prohibited by that law. It is an abominable practice, against which nations are now combining, & it may be presumed that the combination will soon become universal. If it does the traffic must cease, if it does not it will still be carried on, unless the nations favorable to the suppression unite to crush it, under flags whose powers tolerate it, which would in effect be to make war on those powers.

We should be guarded, in the pursuit of this object, to give no countenance by any act of ours to the right of search, which may be applied to other purposes. For the ship of one nation to elude the pursuit of a ship of war of that nation by hoisting the flag of another is an odious fraud, which deserves severe punishment in itself. It may happen in respect to us, but it may happen also in respect to others. It is therefore an evil in the suppression of which all nations opposed to the trade are equally interested. If they see that this fraud is practiced they will doubtless agree that the commander of a ship of any nation in pursuit of vessels of that nation, having satisfactory proof that any particular vessel thereof had assumed another flag to avoid seizure, may nevertheless take her. A power of this kind ought to be guarded to prevent abuse, & probably will be by treaties.

Whether it will be proper, where our citizens fit out ships in foreign countries, & navigate them under foreign flags by American citizens, to authorize the seizure of such vessels appears far from certain. This might give some countenance to the practice of impressment, and the vessel being equipped, tho' even originally American, in a foreign port, & protected by a foreign flag, ought not, I presume, to be touched.

I wish what I have written above, with my former remarks, to be communicated to Mr. Adams, & to the heads of Departments in Washington, & to the Attorney General.

TO JOHN C. CALHOUN.
Highland near Milton, Sept. 24, 1821.

Dear Sir,—I received yours of the 21st. and am happy to hear that you have in a great measure recovered your health. I hope that the use of the Bladensburg water, with the exercise you take in going there, will soon remove all disease, if it has not already done it. I came here to look into my affairs, which required it, & likewise to take exercise, by a ride along our so. west mountain, which I trust will be beneficial, tho' indeed my health has been remarkably good of late.

Your view of requiring inspection of the papers is perfectly satisfactory to me, indeed my own did not preclude it, tho in guarding against a violation of our own principles respecting search &c, and against a quarrel with France & other foreign powers, the idea did not occur to me. There is a clear distinction between the practice of search, under the right as claimed, & a call for the papers, & I should suppose, if on such call being made, it should appear, that the flag had been fraudulently assumed; that the papers, for example of France, could not be shown by a vessel which had hoisted her flag, that her gov^t. would be gratified at her seizure, it being done, more especially, on the belief, & satisfactory proof that she was American. In the case of the *Jeune Eugene*, I am informed that her papers were French, the equipment, having been from one of the Islands of France. A general order, to the effect stated, would I presume not include, that case. I think that such an instruction should be given, to our public ships, sailing on the African coast, and elsewhere, to suppress the slave trade. What shall be done with the *Jeune Eugene* who sailed under the French flag, & according to my recollection, French papers? Had we not better surrender her to the French consul, according to the request of the French Minister, altho' she might have been navigated by American citizens, and owned by them also? He proposes to send the vessel to France for trial. A generous & liberal conduct, on our part, to that gov^t, in strict accord with our principles, might obtain us their favor, a stronger support from it, & be useful in other respects. Communicate on this subject with Mr. Thompson.

TO CONGRESS—REMOVAL OF INDIANS.
WASHINGTON, March 30, 1824.

To the Senate and House of Representatives of the United States:
    I transmit to Congress certain papers enumerated in a report from the Secretary of War, relating to the compact between the United States and the State of Georgia entered into in 1802, whereby the latter ceded to the former a portion of the territory then within its limits on the conditions therein specified. By the fourth article of that compact it was stipulated that the United States should at their own expense extinguish for the use of Georgia the Indian title to all the lands within the State as soon as it might be done *peaceably* and on *reasonable* conditions. These papers show the measures adopted by the Executive of the United States in fulfilment of the several conditions of the compact from its date to the present time, and particularly the negotiations and treaties with the Indian tribes for the extinguishment of their title, with an estimate of the number of acres purchased and sums paid for lands they acquired. They show also the state in which this interesting concern now rests with the Cherokees, one of the tribes within the State, and the inability of the Executive to make any further movement with this tribe without the special sanction of Congress.
    I have full confidence that my predecessors exerted their best endeavors to execute this compact in all its parts, of which, indeed, the sums paid and the

lands acquired during their respective terms in fulfillment of its several stipulations are a full proof. I have also been animated since I came into this office with the same zeal, from an anxious desire to meet the wishes of the State, and in the hope that by the establishment of these tribes beyond the Mississippi their improvement in civilization, their security and happiness would be promoted. By the paper bearing date on the 30th of January last, which was communicated to the chiefs of the Cherokee Nation in this city, who came to protest against any further appropriations of money for holding treaties with them, the obligation imposed on the United States by the compact with Georgia to extinguish the Indian title to the right of soil within the State, and the incompatibility with our system of their existence as a distinct community within any State, were pressed with the utmost earnestness. It was proposed to them at the same time to procure and convey to them territory beyond the Mississippi in exchange for that which they hold within the limits of Georgia, or to pay them for it its value in money. To this proposal their answer, which bears date 11th of February following, gives an unqualified refusal. By this it is manifest that at the present time and in their present temper they can be removed only by force, to which, should it be deemed proper, the power of the Executive is incompetent.

I have no hesitation, however, to declare it as my opinion that the Indian title was not affected in the slightest circumstance by the compact with Georgia, and that there is no obligation on the United States to remove the Indians by force. The express stipulation of the compact that their title should be extinguished at the expense of the United States when it may be done *peaceably* and on *reasonable* conditions is a full proof that it was the clear and distinct understanding of both parties to it that the Indians had a right to the territory, in the disposal of which they were to be regarded as free agents. An attempt to remove them by force would, in my opinion, be unjust. In the future measures to be adopted in regard to the Indians within our limits, and, in consequence, within the limits of any State, the United States have duties to perform and a character to sustain to which they ought not to be indifferent. At an early period their improvement in the arts of civilized life was made an object with the Government, and that has since been persevered in. This policy was dictated by motives of humanity to the aborigines of the country, and under a firm conviction that the right to adopt and pursue it was equally applicable to all the tribes within our limits.

My impression is equally strong that it would promote essentially the security and happiness of the tribes within our limits if they could be prevailed on to retire west and north of our States and Territories on lands to be procured for them by the United States, in exchange for those on which they now reside. Surrounded as they are, and pressed as they will be, on every side by the white population, it will be difficult if not impossible for them, with their kind of government, to sustain order among them. Their interior will be exposed to frequent disturbances, to remedy which the interposition of the United States will be indispensable, and thus their government will gradually lose its authority until it is annihilated. In this process the moral character of the tribes will also be lost, since the change will be too rapid to admit their improvement in civilization to enable them to institute and sustain a government founded on our principles, if such a change were compatible either with the compact with Georgia or with our general system, or to become members of a State, should any State be willing to adopt them in such numbers, regarding the good order, peace, and tranquillity of such State. But all these evils may be avoided if these tribes will consent to remove beyond the limits of our present States and Territories. Lands equally good, and perhaps more fertile, may be procured for them in those quarters. The relations between the United States and such Indians would still be the same.

Considerations of humanity and benevolence, which have now great weight, would operate in that event with an augmented force, since we should feel sensibly the obligation imposed on us by the accommodation which they thereby afforded us. Placed at ease, as the United States would then be, the improvement of those tribes in civilization and in all the arts and usages of civilized life would become the part of a general system which might be adopted on great consideration, and in which every portion of our Union would then take an equal interest. These views have steadily been pursued by the Executive, and the moneys which have been placed at its disposal have been so applied in the manner best calculated, according to its judgment, to produce this desirable result, as will appear by the documents which accompany the report of the Secretary of War.

I submit this subject to the consideration of Congress under a high sense of its importance and of the propriety of an early decision on it. This compact gives a claim to the State which ought to be executed in all its conditions with perfect good faith. In doing this, however, it is the duty of the United States to regard its strict import, and to make no sacrifice of their interest not called for by the compact nor contemplated by either of the parties when it was entered into, nor to commit any breach of right or of humanity in regard to the Indians repugnant to the judgment and revolting to the feelings of the whole American people. I submit the subject to your consideration, in full confidence that you will duly weigh the obligations of the compact with Georgia, its import in all its parts, and the extent to which the United States are bound to go under it. I submit it with equal confidence that you will also weigh the nature of the Indian title to the territory within the limits of any State, with the stipulations in the several treaties with this tribe respecting territory held by it within the State of Georgia, and decide whether any measure on the part of Congress is called for at the present time, and what such measure shall be if any is deemed expedient.

TO THOMAS JEFFERSON.
WASHINGTON, April—1824.

DEAR SIR,—The claim of the State, for the allowance of interest, on monies borrowed & applied to the payment of the militia in the late war, has been consider'd by the administration, in a full meeting, at the instance of the Senators, & of Mr. Cabell, & the result has been, that the allowance, could not be made by the Executive, the uniform decision in such cases, having been against it. The claim will be brought before Congress, and either by one, or the members, as may be deem'd most adviseable. If presented by one, as there are many states having similar claims, it is thought that I should, take it up on general principles, applicable to all, & it was urg'd in the adm^n. & apparently acquiesced in, that if a State had money in hand, as was the case with Maryland, & paid it to the militia as called for, that the State is entitled to interest, on the principles of justice, in equal degree, as if she had borrowed the money, & paid the interest on it. It was urg'd that if there was anything peculiar, in the circumstances, of the claim of Virg^a. more favorable, than of the other States, it might be urg'd with greater advantage, if brought forward, by the members, than by one. I shall make myself master of the subject, and take any course safe & proper in itself, which may be most agreeable to our members, & in accord with the views of the Adm^n. Should you have form'd any opinion on this head, it will give me pleasure to be made acquainted with it. My solicitude is the greater, from the reliance on this fund, in aid of our University, on which the State, & indeed our whole system of gov^t., so essentially depend.

You are acquainted with all the circumstances, relating to the compact with Georgia, enter'd into in 1802, for the extinguishment of the Indian title to land, within the State, on the condition specified. During your term, & that of M^r. Madison, much land was acquir'd, as there has been since I held this office. I was also going on, to press the object, with much zeal, & as I thought in harmony, with the delegation from the State, looking to the claims of humanity as well as of right on the part of the Indians, when on an earnest remonstrance from a deputation of the Cherokee nation here, against farther cessions or appropriations of money to obtain cessions, which was communicated to the members from the State, they addressed to me a letter replete with the most bitter reproaches, expressed in the harshest language, against the conduct of the Executive in the execution of that article of the compact, from its date. I take this however to myself, for whom it was I presume principally intended. Being satisfied that M[r]. Crawford knew nothing of the measure, I communicated the papers to him, with an intimation that if the members asked to withdraw their paper, I would permit it. He disapprov'd their conduct, intimated through one, to the others, his wish that they would withdraw it. They met, & decided that they would not withdraw it, nor communicate with him on the subject. Finding it necessary to bring the wishes of the State before Congress, I sent in this paper, with others, with a message, some few days since. I will forward to you a copy of the message & documents as soon as printed.

I send you a copy of the message & documents relating to the Massachusetts claim, for militia services in the late war. On the great consideration of the subject, & communication with the most enlightened of the republicans of that section, I was satisfied, that the measure, especially should it be supported, by the republicans to the South wo[d]. give great aid to the republican party, to the Eastward, & in consequence to our system of gov[t].

TO THE SENATE—SLAVE TRADE CONVENTION WITH GREAT BRITAIN.

WASHINGTON, May 21, 1824.

To the Senate of the United States:

Apprehending from the delay in the decision that some difficulty exists with the Senate respecting the ratification of the convention lately concluded with the British Government for the suppression of the slave trade by making it piratical, I deem it proper to communicate for your consideration such views as appear to me to merit attention. Charged as the Executive is, and as I have long been, with maintaining the political relations between the United States and other nations, I consider it my duty, in submitting for your advice and consent as to the ratification any treaty or convention which has been agreed on with another power, to explain, when the occasion requires it, all the reasons which induced the measure. It is by such full and frank explanation only that the Senate can be enabled to discharge the high trust reposed in them with advantage to their country. Having the instrument before them, with the views which guided the Executive in forming it, the Senate will possess all the light necessary to a sound decision.

By an act of Congress of 15th of May, 1820, the slave trade, as described by that act, was made piratical, and all such of our citizens as might be found engaged in that trade were subjected, on conviction thereof by the circuit courts of the United States, to capital punishment. To communicate more distinctly the import of that act, I refer to its fourth and fifth sections, which are in the following words:

"Sec. 4. *And be it further enacted,* That if any citizen of the United States, being of the crew or ship's company of any foreign ship or vessel engaged in the slave trade, or any person whatever, being of the crew or ship's company of any ship or vessel owned in the whole or part or navigated for or in behalf of any citizen or citizens of the United States, shall land from any such ship or vessel, and on any foreign shore seize any negro or mulatto not held to service or labor by the laws of either of the States or Territories of the United States, with intent to make such negro or mulatto a slave, or shall decoy or forcibly bring or carry, or shall receive, such negro or mulatto on board any such ship or vessel, with intent as aforesaid, such citizen or person shall be adjudged a pirate, and on conviction thereof before the circuit court of the United States for the district wherein he may be brought or found shall suffer death.

"Sec. 5. *And be it further enacted,* That if any citizen of the United States, being of the crew or ship's company of any foreign ship or vessel engaged in the slave trade, or any person whatever, being of the crew or ship's company of any ship or vessel owned wholly or in part, or navigated for or in behalf of, any citizen or citizens of the United States, shall forcibly confine or detain, or aid and abet in forcibly confining or detaining, on board such ship or vessel any negro or mulatto not held to service by the laws of either of the States or Territories of the United States, with intent to make such negro or mulatto a slave, or shall on board any such ship or vessel offer or attempt to sell as a slave any negro or mulatto not held to service as aforesaid, or shall on the high seas or anywhere on tide water transfer or deliver over to any other ship or vessel any negro or mulatto not held to service as aforesaid, with intent to make such negro or mulatto a slave, or shall land or deliver on shore from on board any such ship or vessel any such negro or mulatto, with intent to make sale of, or having previously sold such negro or mulatto as a slave, such citizen or person shall be adjudged a pirate, and on conviction thereof before the circuit court of the United States for the district wherein he may be brought or found shall suffer death."

And on the 28th February, 1823, the House of Representatives, by a majority of 131 to 9, passed a resolution to the following effect:

"*Resolved,* That the President of the United States be requested to enter upon and prosecute from time to time such negotiations with the several maritime powers of Europe and America as he may deem expedient for the effectual abolition of the African slave trade, and its ultimate denunciation as piracy under the law of nations, by the consent of the civilized world."

By the act of Congress referred to, whereby the most effectual means that could be devised were adopted for the extirpation of the slave trade, the wish of the United States was explicitly declared, that all nations might concur in a similar polity. It could only be by such concurrence that the great object could be accomplished, and it was by negotiation and treaty alone that such concurrence could be obtained, commencing with one power and extending it to others. The course, therefore, which the Executive, who had concurred in the act, had to pursue was distinctly marked out for it. Had there, however, been any doubt respecting it, the resolution of the House of Representatives, the branch which might with strict propriety express its opinion, could not fail to have removed it.

By the tenth article of the treaty of peace between the United States and Great Britain, concluded at Ghent, it was stipulated that both parties should use their best endeavors to accomplish the abolition of the African slave trade. This object has been accordingly pursued by both Governments with great earnestness, by separate acts of legislation, and by negotiation almost uninterrupted, with the purpose of establishing a concert between them in some measure which might secure its accomplishment.

Great Britain in her negotiations with other powers had concluded treaties with Spain, Portugal, and the Netherlands, in which, without constituting the crime as piracy or classing it with crimes of that denomination, the parties had conceded to the naval officers of each other the right of search and capture of the vessels of either that might be engaged in the slave trade, and had instituted courts consisting of judges, subjects of both parties, for the trial of the vessels so captured.

In the negotiations with the United States Great Britain had earnestly and repeatedly pressed on them the adoption of similar provisions. They had been resisted by the Executive on two grounds: One, that the constitution of mixed tribunals was incompatible with their Constitution; and the other, that the concession of the right of search in time of peace for an offense not piratical would be repugnant to the feelings of the nation and a dangerous tendency. The right of search is the right of war of the belligerent toward the neutral. To extend it in time of peace to any object whatever might establish a precedent which might lead to others with some powers, and which, even if confined to the instance specified, might be subject to great abuse.

Animated by an ardent desire to suppress this trade, the United States took stronger ground by making it, by the act above referred to, piratical, a measure more adequate to the end and free from many of the objects applicable to the plan which had been proposed to them. It is this alternative which the Executive, under the sanction and injunctions above stated, offered to the British Government, and which that government has accepted. By making the crime piracy the right of search attaches to the crime, and which when adopted by all nations will be common to all; and that it will be so adopted may fairly be presumed if steadily persevered in by the parties to the present convention. In the meantime, and with a view to a fair experiment, the obvious course seems to be to carry into effect with every power such treaty as may be made with each in succession.

In presenting this alternative to the British Government it was made an indispensable condition that the trade should be made piratical by act of Parliament, as it had been by an act of Congress. This was provided for in the convention, and has since been complied with. In this respect, therefore, the nations rest on the same ground. Suitable provisions have also been adopted to protect each party from abuse of the power granted to the public ships of the other. Instead of subjecting the persons detected in the slave to trial by the courts of the captors, as would be the case if such trade was piracy by the laws of nations, it is stipulated that until that event they shall be tried by the courts of their own country only. Hence there could be no motive for an abuse of the right of search, since such abuse could not fail to terminate to the injury of the captor.

Should this convention be adopted, there is every reason to believe that it will be the commencement of a system destined to accomplish the entire abolition of the slave trade. Great Britain, by making it her own, confessedly adopted at the suggestion of the United States, and being pledged to propose and urge its adoption by other nations in concert with the United States, will find it for her interest to abandon the less-effective system of her previous treaties with Spain, Portugal, and the Netherlands, and to urge on those and other powers their accession to this. The crime will then be universally proscribed as piracy, and the traffic be suppressed forever.

Other considerations of high importance urge the adoption of this convention. We have at this moment pending with Great Britain sundry other negotiations intimately connected with the welfare and even the peace of our Union. In one of them nearly a third part of the territory of the State of Maine is in contestation. In another the navigation of the St. Lawrence, the admission of consuls into the British islands, and a system of commercial intercourse between the United States and all the British possessions in this hemisphere are subjects of discussion. In a third our territorial and other rights upon the northwest coast are to be adjusted, while a negotiation on the same interest is opened with Russia. In a fourth all the most important controvertible points of maritime law in time of war are brought under consideration, and in the fifth the whole system of South American concerns, connected with a general recognition of South American independence, may again from hour to hour become, as it has already been, an object of concerted operations of the highest interest to both nations and to the peace of the world.

It can not be disguised that the rejection of this convention can not fail to have a very injurious influence on the good understanding between the two Governments on these points. That it would place the Executive Administration under embarrassment, and subject it, the Congress, and the nation to the charge of insincerity respecting the great result of the final suppression of the slave trade, and that its first and indispensable consequence will be to constrain the Executive to suspend all further negotiation with every European and American power to which overtures have been made in compliance with the resolution of the House of Representatives of 28th February, 1823, must be obvious. To invite all nations, with the statute of piracy in our hands, to adopt its principles as the law of nations and yet to deny to all the common right of search for the pirate, whom it would impossible to detect without entering and searching the vessel, would expose us not simply to the charge of inconsistency.

It must be obvious that the restriction of search for pirates to the African coast is incompatible with the idea of such a crime. It is not doubted also if the convention is adopted that no example of the commission of that crime by the citizens or subjects of either power will ever occur again. It is believed, therefore, that this right as applicable to piracy would not only extirpate the trade, but prove altogether innocent in its operation.

In further illustration of the views of Congress on this subject, I transmit to the Senate extracts from two resolutions of the House of Representatives, one of the 9th February, 1821, the other of 12th April, 1822. I transmit also a letter from the charge d'affaires of the British Government which shows the deep interest which the Government takes in the ratification of the treaty.

This Treaty, embodying the administration's efforts for the suppression of the African slave trade, signed at London, March 13, 1824, was not ratified. Mr. Adams records the President's solicitude for its fate and gives details regarding this message and the proceedings in the Senate on the Treaty. [HAMILTON.]

TO JAMES MADISON.
OAK HILL, Sept. 23, 1827.

DEAR SIR,—For some time after my return home from your house my health was affected, & that of Mrs. M. very delicate, but that of both has improved somewhat of late, and that of the rest of the family is in a favorable state. The sale of my slaves, &c., in Albemarle, it is expected will take place in Nov^r., so that it will be very painful for me to attend there at the next meeting. You shall however hear from me on the subject. The best regards of my whole family to you & Mrs. Madison, and your mother.

TO JAMES MADISON.
OAK HILL, March 28, 1828.

DEAR SIR,—I have had the pleasure to receive yours of the 20th. by yesterday's mail. The letter from the Governor, communicating our re-appointment as visitors of the University, and requiring a meeting of the board on the first Monday in the next month, I had receiv'd, as I had one from Mr. Cabell, apprizing me that it was a mere measure of form, in complyance with the law, & there would be no necessity for the meeting. I was very glad to receive the latter communication, as it would have been impossible for me to have attended on account of the continued indisposition of Mrs. Monroe. Her attack has been more severe than any she had before experienced. She is now however so far recovered as to move about her room, & we hope, when quite restored, that it will be to better health than she has enjoyed for several years.

I send you a copy of my memoirs, which has been reprinted in a pamphlet, under the direction of my friends in Albemarle. I have sold my slaves in that county to Col. White of Florida, who will take them in families to that territory. He gives me for them (with the exception of a few sold there) five thousand doll^rs., which are paid by obtaining for me a return in that amount from J. J. Orton, for a loan obtained of him in the late war, offer'd by himself, on hearing that I was pressed for money.

The best regards of my family to Mrs. Madison & your mother—

PART VI

The Louisiana Purchase: Minister to France, Spain, and Great Britain

INTRODUCTION

WHEN WASHINGTON'S SECOND TERM ended in 1797, the Federalist John Adams was elected by a margin of four electoral votes over Jefferson, the agrarian Republican. But in 1801 when Jefferson and Aaron Burr both received 73 votes in a tie, Adams came in third with 65. The election was decided in Jefferson's favor after a bitter battle in the House of Representatives.

Meanwhile, in France, the revolutionaries had been succeeded in 1795 by the Directory, men who were frequently at Monroe's dinner table before he returned to the United States in quasi-disgrace. On October 20, 1795, Monroe had written his famous detailed account of the events of October 5, when Parisian mobs marched upon the National Convention meeting in the Tuileries. Monroe dutifully noted that the defense of the National Convention had been directed by Vicomte Paul de Barras who had been given the powers of dictator. But he failed to mention that the actual military operations against the mob were performed by the man Barras had put second in command, a young officer named Napoleon Bonaparte. Napoleon was made commander in chief in March 1796, about a year before Monroe returned home.

Napoleon began leading France's armies across Europe, reducing Austria, Sardinia, Malta, Nice and Savoy, ultimately obtaining the Netherlands and Lombardy, and pushed the boundaries of France to the Rhine. And in 1799, the Directory itself was toppled by a Bonapartist putsch. The General now styled himself the First Consul, the first of three. His armies continued to win battle after battle; Egypt alone resisted his prowess. Only Great Britain remained at war, but in 1802 at the Peace of Amiens, the Germans and the British acquiesced to his sway over Europe.

In Spain, the decaying monarchy was not able to resist Napoleon either. In 1795, Spain at last had signed a treaty with the United States guaranteeing the right of deposit for Americans at the Port of New Orleans. Charles IV became an ally of France. In 1800 Napoleon secretly convinced him to yield the vast territory of Louisiana—surrendered with the stipulation that it would never be transferred to another country. Now a greater project was forming in his mind: The defeat of Britain's navy and the invasion of Great Britain itself.

As knowledge of the secret retrocession to France reached the United States, rumors spread throughout the Western frontier that Napoleon was about to send a military garrison to Louisiana. President Jefferson was under strong political pressure from the inhabitants of the frontier territories to head off threats from that quarter. Hotheads in the Federalist party were urging the United States to take New Orleans by force, hoping that a war would give them a chance to be authorized for privateering. The U.S. Minister to France, Robert R. Livingston had been ineffectual in his efforts to get Napoleon to guarantee the right of deposit in New Orleans.

On January 10, 1803, Jefferson wrote to his protégé Monroe: "I have but a moment to inform you, that the fever into which the Western mind is thrown by the affair at New Orleans, stimulated by the mercantile and generally the federal interest, threatens to overbear our peace. In this situation, we are obliged to call on you for a temporary sacrifice of yourself, to prevent this greatest of evils in the present prosperous tide of our affairs. I shall tomorrow nominate you to the Senate for an extraordinary mission to France, and the circumstance are such, as to render it impossible to decline."

Two days later, Jefferson wrote again: "All eyes are now fixed on you; and, were you to decline, the chagrin would be great, and would shake under your feet the high ground on which you stand with the public. Indeed I know nothing which would produce such a shock; for on the event of this mission depend the future destinies of this Republic." With the offer stated in these terms, Monroe could not decline. The "temporary sacrifice" lasted five years.

When the First Consul heard from his ministers that Monroe was coming, there was little need to talk to the ineffectual Livingston. He knew the stature of Monroe, and Monroe's relationship with President Jefferson. He had a bold plan to finance his coming invasion of England, confided to his minister only on the day Monroe set foot in France. War was brewing with England. The pretext was that Britain would not leave Malta as she had agreed to do at Amiens; but in reality both countries were spoiling to settle the question of hegemony of the seas. A war with England would take money. Napoleon saw that, with this greater project unfolding before him, the undeveloped territory of Louisiana was suddenly a liability in the backwoods of North America. It was not just the port of

New Orleans that would be put in play. He would sell the whole of Louisiana to the Americans for ready cash. Therefore the Foreign Minister, Talleyrand informed Livingston that he would wait for Monroe's arrival. Napoleon was convinced, correctly, that Monroe had direct authority from the president and could act upon the proposal he had just sprung upon his cabinet. Napoleon's pressing need for money was evident when it was not Talleyrand who began the discussions, but the Minister of Finance, François Barbé-Marbois. A few days after Monroe arrived, Marbois opened the whole matter: the First Consul was offering the whole, uncharted territory of Louisiana. Would President Jefferson accept?

Monroe has left a day-by-day memorandum of the negotiations entitled *Journal or Memoranda—Louisiana.* It was a complicated deal, involving both the sale of the territory and French compensation to U.S. citizens for property seized in wartime. Marbois started by demanding 100 million francs from the U.S. government for the territory, and offering 4 million for U.S. claims. In the end Monroe whittled the price down to 50 million francs, plus 20 million in claims due to Americans, or 70 million francs total, amounting to $15 million. The United States would pay France in what at that time were called stocks, but we would call bonds, paying six percent per annum, which France could then discount to bankers for ready cash. The distinguished English banking houses of Baring Brothers and Hope and Co. just happened to have representatives in Paris to confirm their readiness to buy the bonds. The United States would be obliged to make redemption payments every month. Within five days, it was all wrapped up.

Meanwhile, Monroe was invited to dine with the First Consul. So what does one say when one meets the most powerful man on earth? Monroe's account of the conversation goes like this:

> When the Consul came round to me. . . [he] observed that he was glad to see me. "You have been here 15 days?" I told him I had. "You speak French?" I replied, "A little." "You had a good voyage?" "Yes. "You came in a frigate?" No in a merchant vessel charged for the purpose. . . .
>
> We dined with him. After dinner when we retired into the saloon, the first Consul came up to me and asked whether the federal city grew much. I told him it did. "How many inhabitants has it?" It is just commencing, there are two cities near it, one above, the other below, on the great river Potomack, which two cities if counted with the federal city would make a respectable town; in itself it contains only two or three thousand inhabitants. "Well; Mr. Jefferson, how old is he?" About sixty. "Is he married or single?" He is not married. "Then he is a garçon." No,

he is a widower. "Has he children?" Yes, two daughters who are married. "Does he reside always at the federal city?" Generally. "Are the publick buildings there commodious, those for the Congress and President especially? They are. "You the Americans did brilliant things in your war with England, you will do the same again." We shall, I am persuaded, always behave well when it shall be our lot to be in war. "You may probably be in war with then again." I replied I did not know—that was an important question to decide when there would be an occasion for it.

Those who may have dreamed of having a private conversation with the then most powerful man in the world might expected something more dazzling.

The only drawback to this episode was the deep resentment which Livingston felt towards Monroe's success. Monroe himself never attempted to push Livingston aside, attributing the outcome to the dispositions of the French and the instructions he had been given by Jefferson. Livingston spread rumors that the sale of the whole of Louisiana had been decided before Monroe arrived. He even tried to alter the dates in his record book of dispatches already sent to Washington. Monroe set the record straight by publishing the correspondence from Tallyrand and from Livingston itself, proving otherwise. Livingston's jealousy manifested itself when he stalled on agreeing to an advance payment to France of $2 million from a discretionary fund entrusted to the two ministers, which led the French to threaten to add new conditions.

But even worse was yet to come. Jefferson had given Monroe an additional mission before he left: to secure the purchase of the Floridas from Spain. Monroe had obtained a promise from Talleyrand to help the United States achieve this object.

On May 18, he wrote to Madison, who was then Secretary of State that he didn't know whether to proceed to Madrid directly or not. "We have already stipulated for a much greater sum [for Louisiana] than it was contemplated we should give for the object of my mission. To go further might embarrass our treasury . . . The result is that I am of opinion that its is more in conformity to the spirit of my instructions, and to the interest of my country, that I should proceed immediately to Madrid to endeavour to obtain the Floridas. . . . The purchase of the whole of Louisiana, tho' not contemplated is nevertheless a measure founded on the principles and justified by the policy of our instructions, provided it be thought a good bargain."

But other events intervened. Napoleon had been putting together a fleet of 2,000 ships, and had concentrated his troops at Boulogne. The British Admiralty, in desperate need of sailors, was once more impressing American seamen by taking them from U.S. ships. The U.S. Minister in London, Rufus King, resigned and returned to the United States. Madison instructed Monroe to proceed to London immediately to protect American interests during the war and to seek a new treaty to guarantee the rights of neutral shipping and to end the impressment of American seamen.

Monroe arrived in London and at length was presented to King George III on August 17th. He makes reference to this event in his letter to Madison of August 31, 1802. It was a remarkable occasion. Years later in his third-person autobiography, Monroe wrote more openly of his feelings on that occasion:

> It was impossible for Mr. Monroe to be presented to King George III without experiencing sensations of a peculiar character. From his very early youth, impressions had been made on his mind against that monarch. While at the College [of William and Mary], he had attended the debates in the General Assembly and Convention, all of which represented him as unfriendly to liberty. He had fought in our revolutionary struggle against his troops and witnessed in many of our states the distress to which our citizens were exposed in that unjust war. Time had essentially diminished these impressions, but it had not entirely removed them.

But the King's reception was kindly.

When Monroe arrived at the Court of St. James's, the war with France had begun. George III had chosen Henry Addington to form the government in 1801, and it was Addington who formed the treaty of Amiens with Napoleon in 1802. When it became clear that Napoleon was not pacified, Addington's stock fell when he did not seem to be able to cope with the coming crisis. With England in a war mode once more, the portions of the Jay treaty of 1794 which referred to the previous war with France had expired. Monroe dutifully sent a memorandum to Addington's Foreign Minister, Lord Hawkesbury, protesting against the continuing impressment of American seamen.

But Hawkesbury took no action. The government of Addington was losing authority every day and would give way in a few months to the second ministry of William Pitt the Younger. Under Pitt's regime, the new Foreign Minister, Lord Harrowby, took a distant view of Monroe and U.S. shipping interests. Discussions for a new commercial treaty bogged down when Harrowby casually informed Monroe that, in his opinion, Jay's 1794 treaty interdicting cargo with France was still in force, or ought to be, in as much as there had been no actual peace with France. Monroe had no opening for further discussions.

Stymied by events in England, the time was ripe for Monroe to go to Spain with the purchase of the Floridas very much on his agenda. He passed through Paris at the end of October, where he found himself in a dilemma. Napoleon had set November 2 as the date for his coronation as Emperor. Monroe was not in awe of the putative Emperor. He saw clearly that Napoleon, although he had begun as president of the Jacobin society and depended upon the support of the revolutionary party against the aristocrats, had abandoned all republican principles. He was an autocrat. Yet the American minister needed the French government's promised support in his proposed negotiations with Spain. He was afraid that if he left before the coronation, his absence would be interpreted negatively. Dining with Marbois the night before, he mentioned that he had no ticket of admission, whereupon the finance minister immediately wrote a note to the master of ceremonies of the event. The next day he found himself sitting across the aisle from Talleyrand, whom he acknowledged with a "salutation."

But the diplomatic gesture was of no use. Monroe discovered in Paris that Livingston, who was about to be replaced as minister by his brother-in-law, John Armstrong, had had concocted his own scheme for obtaining the cession of the Floridas to the United States. Without any authority from Washington, he secretly had sent word to Spain, backed up by France, which now thoroughly dominated Spain, that the negotiations should be moved to Paris. He intimated that the United States would make a loan to Spain of $2 million if Spain would withdraw from West Florida. The position of Jefferson, Madison and Monroe was that West Florida, from the Pearl River near the present boundary of Louisiana to the Perdido River near Pensacola was part of Spain's cession of Louisiana to France, and had been conveyed to the United States with the Louisiana purchase. Livingston's unauthorized proposal would have the United States paying for rights it believed it already possessed. To Monroe's chagrin, he found that Talleyrand now supported Spain's claim to West Florida. This was the gamesmanship of the wily French diplomat: Monroe noted that if the United States made the so-called loan to Spain, then Spain could pay its military debts to France. He was furious.

Nevertheless, Monroe set out for Madrid. On December 16, his journey was halted for a time in Bordeaux, giving him time to send a dispatch to Madison. It gives the reader in the year 2000 some idea of what the life of an ambassador was like in 1804:

It is necessary to write forward two days to Bayonne to make arrangements for the mules which are to take me to Madrid. The intermediate country of the greater part of it is said to be almost a desert. There are but few taverns on the route, and those furnish neither beds, provision or other accommodations than that of shelter; in addition to which there is danger of being attacked by robbers, especially to publick characters who travel slowly with a guard. . . . Hence it becomes necessary to adopt precautions against all these evils. With a relay of mules the journey may be made, without halting . . . in five or six days. With the [one] set [of mules] it requires 12 or 15."

In Madrid, he found that Charles Pinckney of North Carolina, the permanent U.S. minister to Spain and his designated co-negotiator, had fallen out of favor with the Spanish court and wanted to return home. Monroe was presented to Charles IV, and opened discussions for Florida. But the Spaniards sent to Paris for instructions, and Talleyrand continued to support the Spanish position on West Florida. As a result of the confusion caused by Livingston's unauthorized actions, Monroe's position was hopeless. By July 1805, he had returned to London, intending to sail for the United States at the first opportunity.

In London he encountered a new crisis. He found that American ships were once again being seized by the British for cargoes that supposedly violated Britain's interpretation of neutrality. No instructions arrived from Madison, although apparently some letters had been sent but not received. Then William Pinkney, a Baltimore attorney who had been a commissioner adjusting claims in London under the Jay treaty of 1794, arrived with instructions from Madison to negotiate a new treaty of commerce. The succeeding months in London were not successful ones. Britain was preoccupied with the war with France and was ready to take any action, including a hostile containment of American shipping, to win. The fall of Addington, the unexpected death of Prime Minister William Pitt the Younger on January 23 1806 in his second ministry, and the sudden death of Lord Grenville's Foreign Secretary, Charles James Fox, on September 13, 1806, dissipated the American efforts. The British would not yield on the key issue demanded by Jefferson and Madison, an end to impressment. The two diplomats judged that, to prevent a war with England, they would sign a treaty on commerce without the abolition of impressment and accept a side letter expressing Britain's good intentions.

But Jefferson decided that he could not even send such a treaty to the Senate, certain that it would be defeated. Monroe returned to the United States bitterly disappointed that, without even waiting for his explanations, the treaty was deemed unacceptable. He became deeply estranged from his two friends, especially convinced that Madison was sacrificing their friendship to his presidential ambitions.

WASHINGTON, Jan. 10, 1803.

GOVERNOR MONROE:—

DEAR SIR:—I have but a moment to inform you, that the fever into which the Western mind is thrown by the affair at New Orleans, stimulated by the mercantile and generally the federal interest, threatens to overbear our peace. In this situation, we are obliged to call on you for a temporary sacrifice of yourself, to prevent this greatest of evils, in the present prosperous tide of our affairs. I shall to-morrow nominate you to the Senate, for an extraordinary mission to France, and the circumstances are such, as to render it impossible to decline; because the whole public hope will be rested on you. I wish you to be either in Richmond or Albemarle, till you receive another letter from me which will be within two days hence, if the Senate decide immediately; or later, according to the time they take to decide. In the meantime, pray work night and day, to arrange your affairs for a temporary absence—perhaps for a long one. Accept affectionate salutations.

TH. JEFFERSON.

COPY OF A LETTER FROM MR. JEFFERSON TO COL. MONROE.
WASHINGTON, January 13th, 1803.

DEAR SIR,—I dropped you a line on the 10th, informing you of a nomination I had made of you to the Senate, and yesterday I enclosed you their approbation, not having then time to write. The agitation of the public mind on occasion of the late suspension of our right of deposit at New Orleans, is extreme. This in the Western country is natural, and grounded on operative motives. Remonstrances, memorials, &c., are now circulating through the whole of that country, and being signed by the body of the people. The measures which we have been pursuing, being invisible, do not satisfy their minds; something sensible, therefore, has become necessary, and indeed our object of purchasing New Orleans and the Floridas, is a measure likely to assume so many shapes, that no instructions could be squared to fit them. It was essential, then, to send a Minister Extraordinary to be joined with the ordinary one, with discretionary power, first however, well impressed with all our views, and therefore qualified to meet and modify to these every form of proposition which could come from the other party. This could be done only in frequent and full oral communication. Having determined on this, there could not be two opinions as to the person. You possessed the unlimited confidence of the administration, and of the Western people, and were you to refuse to go, no other man can be found who does this. All eyes are now fixed on you; and, were you to decline, the chagrin would be great, and would shake under your feet the high ground on which you stand with the public. Indeed I know nothing which would produce such a shock; for on the event of this mission depend the future destinies of this Republic. If we cannot, by a purchase of the country, ensure to ourselves a course of perpetual peace and friendship with all nations, then, as war cannot be far distant, it behoves us immediately to be preparing for that course, without however hastening it, and it may be necessary (on your failure on the continent) to cross the ground. We shall get entangled in European politics, and figuring more, be much less happy and prosperous. This can only be prevented by a successful issue to your present mission. I am sensible, after the measures you have taken for getting into a different line of business, that it will be a great sacrifice on your part, and presents, from the season, and other circumstances, serious difficulties. But some men are born for the public. Nature, by fitting them for the service of the human race on a broad scale, has stamped them with the evidences of her destination and their duty.

COPY OF A LETTER FROM MR. TALLEYRAND
TO MR. LIVINGSTON.
Paris, 1 Germinal, 11 year (24th March, 1803).

Sir:—I see with pleasure by the last letters, of the French Legation to the United States, that the species of fermentation raised there on account of Louisiana, has been carried back, by the wisdom of your government, and the just confidence which it inspires, to that state of tranquility which is alone suited to discussions, and which, in the relations of sentiment and interest existing between the two people, cannot but conduct them to understand themselves, upon the simple difficulties of circumstances, and to bind more and more the bonds of their mutual union. I ought to own to you, sir, that, in the eclat which has been so lately given there to the affairs relating to Louisiana, it has been difficult to discover the ancient sentiments of attachment and confidence with which France has always endeavoured to inspire the people of the United States, and who, from the first moment of their existence as an independent and sovereign nation, have always held their political relations with France above all other political relations.

How could the neighbourhood of France affect unfavourably the American people, either their commercial or political relations? Has the French Republic ever shown a desire to impede the prosperity of the United States, to lessen their influence, to weaken the means of their security, or oppose any obstacle to the progress of their commerce? Your government, sir, ought to be well persuaded that the First Consul bears to the American nation the same affection with which France has been at all times animated, and that he considers the new means which the possession of Louisiana affords to him of convincing the government and people of the United States of his friendly disposition towards them, in the number of advantages which ought to derive from its acquisition.

I shall, for the present moment, confine myself to this declaration, which ought to remove the inquietudes which you have expressed in your last letters. The subject is not established upon information sufficiently extensive to authorize a detailed explanation. In announcing to me, moreover, the approaching departure of Mr. Monroe, appointed Minister Extraordinary to discuss this subject, you give me to conclude that your government desires that this Minister be waited for and heard, that every matter, susceptible of contradiction, be completely and definitely discussed? In the meantime, sir, the First Consul charges me to assure your government, that, far from thinking that our new position in Louisiana could be an object of solicitude, or cause the least injury to the United States, he will receive the Minister Extraordinary whom the President sends to him, with the greatest pleasure, and that he hopes that his mission will terminate to the satisfaction of both nations.

CH. M. TALLEYRAND.

TO THOMAS JEFFERSON.
NEW YORK, March 7, 1803.

DEAR SIR,—I rec^d. yours of the 25. ulto. with one to M^r. Cepeda this morning, when I also rec^d. my instructions from the department of State, with all the other documents connected with my mission to France & Sp^n. The ship, Richmond, of ab^t. 400 tons burden, whose cabbin I have taken, cleared at the custom house on Saturday, my baggage was put on board, in expectation of sailing yesterday as M^r. Madison informed me my instructions ought to arrive by 8 in the morning; but it being Sunday, they were delayed till to-day. We are now detained by a snow storm and contrary wind, but I shall sail as soon as it clears up, & the wind shifts.

The resolutions of M^r. Ross [Requiring the President to at once take New Orleans by an armed force.—*Annals of Congress*—"The Mississippi Question"—February 15, 1803. S.M.H.] prove that the federal party will stick at nothing to embarrass the adm^n., and recover its lost power. They nevertheless produce a great effect on the publick mind and I presume more especially in the western country. The unanimity in the publick councils respecting our right to the free navigation of the river, and its importance to every part of the U States, the dissatisfaction at the interference of Sp^n. which will not be appeased while the power of a similar one exists, are calculated to inspire the hope of a result which may put us at ease forever on those points. If the negotiation secures all the objects sought, or a deposit with the sovereignty over it, the federalists will be overwhelmed completely: the union of the western with the Eastern people will be consolidated, republican principles confirmed, and a fair prospect of peace and happiness presented to our country. But if the negotiation compromises short of that, and leaves the management of our great concerns in that river, which comprize everything appertaining to the western parts of the U States, in the hands of a foreign power, may we not expect that the publick will be disappointed and disapprove of the result. So far as I can judge, I think much would be hazarded by any adjustment which did not put us in complete security for the future. It is doubtful whether an adjustment short of that would be approved in any part of the union; I am thoroughly persuaded it would not to the westward. If they were discontented, there would grow up an union of councils and measures between them and the Eastern people which might lead to other measures & be perverted to bad purposes. The Eastern towns, which govern the country wish war for the sake of privateering: the western would not dislike it especially if they were withheld from a just right, or the enjoyment of a privilege necessary to their welfare, the pursuit of which by force would create a vast expenditure of money among them. Their confidence is now reposed in the adm^m. from the best of motives,—a knowledge that it is sincerely friendly to their interests: it is strengthened by a distrust of these new *friends*; but an inquietude has been created by the late event, an inquiry has taken place which has shown that every part of the union especially the Eastern, is deeply interested in opening the river; that the attempt to occlude it on a former occasion was a base perhaps a corrupt intrigue of a few; their hopes and expectations have been raised, and it is probable they expect from the mission by a peaceful course everything which their enemies promised by war. The consequences of a disappointment are not easily calculated. If it restored the federal party to power and involved us in war, the result might be fatal. It therefore highly merits consideration whether we should not take that ground as the ultimatum in the negotiation which must in every possible event preserve the confidence & affection of the western people. While we stand well with them we shall prosper.

We shall be most apt to avoid war, taking ten years ensuing together; and if we are driven by necessity into it, it is much better that it be under the auspices of a republican than a monarchial adm^n. These ideas are expressed in haste for y^r. consideration for I have not time to give them method or form. I shall most certainly labour to obtain the best terms possible, but it is for you to say, what are the least favorable we must accept. You will have time to weigh the subject & feel the publick pulse on it before anything conclusive may be done. I hope the French gov^t. will have wisdom enough to see that we will never suffer France or any other power to tamper with our interior; if that is not the object there can be no reason for declining an accommodation to the whole of our demands.

I accept my appointment with gratitude and enter on its duties with an ardent zeal to accomplish its objects. I derive much satisfaction from a knowledge that I am in the hands of those whose views are sound, are attached to justice, and will view my conduct with candour and liberality, under these circumstances I embark with confidence & am fearless of the result as it respects myself personally. I shall take the liberty to write you occasionally and shall at all times be most happy to hear from you and receive your commands.

Your private objects were attended to as I came here. I have the book for M^r. Volney & left the bottle of wine in a train to reach its destination. Will you be so kind as forward the enclosed to M^{rs}. Trist & Major Lewis. That to Major Randolph you will I hope be able to present, as it respects a private object in which I am interested. Our best regards to our friends in Albemarle. It was cause of much regret that we could not see them before our departure, but the cause you can explain. I am dear Sir very sincerely affectionately y^r. friend & servt.

9th. Eight o'clock in the morning, the wind has shifted and we expect to be on board in an hour.

COPY OF A LETTER FROM ROBERT R. LIVINGSTON TO MR. MONROE.

PARIS, 10th April, 1803.

DEAR SIR:—I congratulate you on your safe arrival. We have long and anxiously wished for you. God grant that your mission may answer yours and the public expectation. War may do something for us, nothing else would. I have paved the way for you, and if you would add to my memoirs an assurance that we were now in possession of New Orleans, we should do well; but I detain Mr. Bentalou, who is impatient to fly to the arms of his wife. I have apprised the Minister of your arrival, and told him you would be here on Tuesday or

Wednesday. Present my compliments and Mrs. L's to Mrs. Monroe, and believe, dear sir,

Your friend, and humble servant,

ROBT. R. LIVINGSTON.
To His Excellency JAS. MONROE.

A COPY OF THE EXTRACTS FROM
COL. JOHN MERCER'S JOURNAL.

"Extracts from my journal, commencing on the 8th of March, 1803, the day on which I sailed from New York for France.

"April 8th, we arrived off Havre about two o'clock in the morning, twenty-nine days from Sandy Hook; two French pilots came on board at three.

"About one in the afternoon Mr. Monroe was received with very particular and marked attention. A salute was fired from the fort soon after his being at the hotel. In the course of the day he was waited upon by the General commanding at Havre, attended by officers, who expressed their satisfaction at his safe arrival. In the evening a guard of fifty soldiers was paraded before the hotel, and ordered to receive Mr. Monroe's directions; but upon his requesting that only two might be permitted to remain, which he should consider equally respectful, the others were marched off, and the two regularly relieved.

"8th. Finding it inconvenient on account of our baggage, &c. to proceed immediately to Paris, we remained at Havre this day. In the evening the officers of the Navy waited upon Mr. Monroe to pay their respects to him, as did several Americans who were in this town.

"10th. We left Havre at ten o'clock in the morning, and arrived at St. Germain, within ten or twelve miles of Paris, at ten in the evening.

"12th. I arrived in Paris about one o'clock P.M. with Mr. Monroe, he leaving his family at St. Germain. Mr. Monroe immediately wrote a note to Mr. Livingston, the American Minister, informing him of his arrival, and of his intention to wait upon him in the evening if Mr. Livingston would be at home, and without company, as he, Mr. M., was much fatigued with his journey, and a little indisposed. In Mr. Livingston's answer, he congratulated Mr. M. upon his arrival—informed him he would be without company in the evening, and would be glad to see him, but if Mr. M. was too much indisposed to go out, he would do himself the pleasure of waiting upon him. Having letters for Mr. Livingston, Jr. from his friend Mr. Cutting, at New York, I accompanied Mr. Monroe in the evening, to the Minister's. None but the family were present. We were received in a friendly and polite manner. We had been seated only a few minutes when the conversation turned upon the state of things in America at our departure. In the course of it, Mr. Livingston asked 'What had become of Mr. Ross's resolutions?' Being answered by Mr. M. that they were superceded by others of a more pacific character, he said, 'I am sorry for it. I wish they had been adopted. Only force can give New Orleans to us"; and farther declared, that he believed nothing but the actual possession of the country by the Americans would give success to the mission in which he was associated with Mr. M. To this Mr. M. made no reply. Upon leaving Mr. L's I expressed my surprise at the opinion entertained by this gentleman and regretted that the prospect of peaceable result to the negotiation appeared to him so gloomy."

JOHN MERCER.

TO ROBERT R. LIVINGSTON.
April 13, 1803

DEAR SIR,—I think you intimated your intention to present me this evening to the minister of foreign affairs, which I presume must be at his house informally at a party. On consideration I beg to suggest whether it would not be better for you to write him a note informing him of my arrival in town & requesting him to appoint an hour for you to present me to him. My anxiety for you to make this communication without delay is the motive for my writing to you to that effect before I have the pleasure to see you today at 11 o'clock, at which hour I am to call on you. The idea is however only submitted to you^r. judgment. With great respect &c.

TO JAMES MADISON.
PARIS, April 15, 1803

DEAR SIR,—It is proper for me to mention to you in confidence some circumstances which I wish not to include in an official letter. I was informed on my arrival here by Mr. Skipwith that Mr. Livingston mortified at my appointment had done everything in his power to turn the occurrences in America, and even my mission to his account, by pressing the Government on every point with a view to show that he had accomplished what was wished without my aid: and perhaps also that my mission had put in hazard what might otherwise have been easily obtained. His official correspondence will show what occurred prior to my arrival & sufficiently proves that he did not abstain even on hearing that

I was on my way, from the topics intrusted to us jointly. Col. Mercer who was present says this information was given next morning at the second interview. When I called on him he told me that this government had resolved to sell Louisiana &c but that the resolution had grown out of the state of things in Europe, & the danger of a war with England: that that point would be decided in a fortnight, perhaps immediately on the return of a courrier from Russia who was expected in less time: that he had been with Tallyrand that day, advised him that I was on the way from Havre & pressed him on the subject of my mission, & ultimately on being asked what we would give had actually offered terms. On the next day dined with Mr. Livingston; while at dinner Mr. Marbois came there, withdrew and returned after we arose from dinner; they had a private conference and it was agreed, there being company with him, that Mr. Livingston should call on him after the company despersed at his (Mr. Marbois') house to confer relative to the purchase of Louisiana. He told me he was going there & the object, and in a private conference with Mr. Skipwith who dined with him on the same day, after repeating the above, he regretted his misfortune in my arrival, since it took from him the credit of having brought everything to a proper conclusion without my aid. You will perceive the dilemma into which I have been & am still placed by this course of proceeding, since I have not only to negotiate with the French Government, especially its ministers, but my colleagues also. There is a plausible pretext for not presenting me to the Consul till the monthly audience, & in strict propriety I ought to hold no communication or sanction one with this government till I am presented: tho' my colleague considers my reception by the minister, his official notes relative to it, the terms in which he spoke of me on the part of the Consul, & the information he gave us that a person would be designated to treat with us, with whom we might hold informal communications in the interim as placing me on the ground of a person recognized. If I held back on the rule of strict etiquette & permitted no communication at all in case our negotiation failed I exposed myself & our government to the charge of having lost, by the measure taken, a brilliant opportunity of securing all our objects here & myself particularly of sacrificing everything thro' selfish motives. It is well known that the crisis pressed here and still does, that the Consul had resolved to sell, that Marbois was a minister & entitled to credit, that my colleague was one also already recognized & jointly associated with me in the trust. He was also possessed with the views of our government as well as myself, & might speak without my approbation with whom he pleased. I could not withhold confidential communications with him. Under these circumstances I have been driven by necessity, in private communications with him, signing nothing or authorizing it on his part, to permit him to state to Mr. Marbois that I would assent to the purchase of Louisiana at the price we were willing to give for the territory to the left of the river, France relinquishing all pretensions to the Floridas, & engaging to support with her influence our negotiation with Spain for them. By so doing I disarm those who might wish it of charging on me or our government the fault of future events, should they be unpropitious, and am not aware that I substantially hazard anything. All this attention to my colleague &c may be an intrigue tho' on the part of Marbois. I put confidence in the facts he states. It may be wished to inspire jealousy and distrust between my colleague & myself; the minister may suppose he will be less reserved, tho' it is certain till my appointment was known that he often treated him with great neglect & even disrespect. The opinion entertained of the character of the Consul for promptitude & decision, that if he liked the terms he would conclude at once, & if he was disgusted would perhaps not soon return to the subject induced me with the consideration mentioned to assent to the above. My Colleague has now promised me in the most explicit terms to hold no further communication with Mr. Marbois or any other person, till I am recognized, & a person regularly appointed to treat with us. I do not know that any real injury will occur to the object of the mission by what has passed.

JOURNAL OR MEMORANDA—LOUISIANA.
April 27.

M^r. Marbois came to my lodgings by appointment of M^r. Livingston, at two o'clock and I being indisposed it was agreed that I might repose as it suited me. M^r. Marbois opened the conversation by presenting us with a project of a treaty given him by the gov^t. to be proposed to us, which he admitted he thought hard and unreasonable; he presented at the same time another project which he called his own, which had not been seen by the gov^t., but to which he presumed the first consul would assent, as he had told him he would not insist on the terms contained in the first, and would only ask or propose such as he had drawn in the second; but to which he declared that the first consul had not assented explicitly. M^r. Marbois thought himself however at liberty to propose his own project as the basis of our negotiation. That project claimed one hundred millions & the debts due our citizens estimated at 20. more. His own reduced that demand to 80, including the debt. There were some other differences between them, his going more into detail, in the form of a publick act. M^r. Livingston observed that the debt was a thing to be provided for in an especial manner; that the consul had said to him it should be paid; that we ought to begin from points agreed & proceed to difficulties—that the points agreed were the debts that were due and our right of deposit. M^r. Marbois said that if we made a treaty on the general & great subject of the Louisiana, he would include in it a provision for the debts; that if he did not make a treaty of that kind he would have nothing to do with the debts. M^r. Livingston repeated the promise of the Consul &c. for the payment of them, to which M^r. Marbois replied that he did not mean to impair the force of our claim founded on the treaty & the promise of the gov^t.—what he meant to say was, that if our negotiation succeeded in the object of it, the debts would be comprized in it & provided for, and if it did not succeed he would leave them where he found them; the claim would still be supported by the treaty & any assurance M^r. Livingston may have received from the gov^t. since. M^r. Livingston still pressing the high ground on which the claim to the payment of the debt rested, M^r. Marbois observed that in the promise referred to no time was fixed or sum specified, & intimated that the Consul did not contemplate a greater sum than 3 or 4 millions of livres. I then observed that I thought we were all of the same opinion respecting the debts that the ground on which they stood could not be impaired by the failure of this negotiation; that a provision might be made for the payment of them by it; that we had better go on to the other object & with that view to examine & discuss the project presented by M^r. Marbois. One of the articles contained in M^r. Marbois's project, proposed that the payment to our citizens & the French gov^t. should proceed in equal degree regarding the amount to be paid to each party, by the month, that is that neither should have a priority or preference, to the other as to time or proportion. M^r. Livingston insisted that the payment to our citizens should be prompt & full, which he supposed we might make, without rendering ourselves unable to meet the views of the French gov^t. in any sum we might stipulate to give in point of time: to that M^r. Marbois seemed to have no objection.

My colleague took M^r. Marbois's project with him & brought one very loosely drawn founded on it, which with our communications together on the subject & the modifications we gave it, will be noted hereafter.

We called on M^r. Marbois the 29th. and gave him our project which we read to him & discussed. We proposed to offer 50. millions to France & 20. on acc^t. of her debt to the citizens of the U States, making 70. in the whole. On reading that article he declared that he would not proceed in the negotiation on a less sum than 80. Millions, since it would be useless as the Consul had been sufficiently explicit on that point; Indeed he assured us that his government had never positively instructed him to take that sum, but that as he had told the

Consul it was enough, that he would ask no more, and to which he understood the Consul as giving his assent, he M^r. Marbois had thought himself authorized to accept & propose it to us, but that he could not proceed unless we agreed to give it. On this frank & explicit declaration on his part & after explaining to him the motive which led us to offer that sum we agreed to accede to his idea & give 80. millions. He asked us if we could not advance something immediately, we replied, we did so in discharge of their debt to our citizens; that they had suffered and it was for the interest of France as well as the U States, that they should be promptly paid, or as soon as possible. To the payment in stock he did not object, nor did he say anything respecting the loss to be sustained by it; he asked what effect the protracting the redemption of the stock for 15 years would have on its value; we told him to raise its price.

On the proviso to the commercial stipulation he seemed to entertain a doubt, but on our shewing the abuse of which the article was capable without it, being not simply to give a preference for 12 years to French vessels & manufactures over those of other countries in the ports of the ceded territory, but to enable France to monopolize the carriage of the exports from the Mississippi, and prevent a single article raised there being brought from the other States, such as tobacco, rice, &c. He admitted that such a power was not sought on their part.

He seemed desirous to secure by some strong provision the incorporation of the inhabitants of the ceded country with our union; we told him that we would try to modify the article to meet his ideas as fairly as we could—we left our project with him, in expectation of hearing from him soon the result, as he said he should see the Consul next morning on the subject. He informed me that M^r. Tallyrand had asked him whether I was in health to be presented to the first Consul, & on my answering in the affirmative; advised me to let him know it. My colleague promised as we returned home to inform the minister next day that I had recovered my health. To guard against accidents however I wrote the minister to that effect next morning, and a note to my colleague to request him to call for me as he went to the house of the minister. Just as I was ready to visit the minister my colleague returned from him & informed me that it was arranged that I should be presented next day, that is on the first of May.

May 1st. 1803 Sunday

I accompanied my colleague to the Palace of the Louvre, where I was presented by him to the Consul. While standing in the circle I received a communication by the prefect of the palace, from the minister, stating that he was indisposed, but that I must present the Consul my letter of credence, & that the Consul desired I would dine with him.

When the Consul came round to me, M^r. Livingston presented me to him, on which the Consul observed that he was glad to see me. "Je suis bien aise de le voir." "You have been here 15 days?" I told him I had. "You speak French?" I replied "A little." "You had a good voyage?" Yes. "You came in a frigate?" No in a merchant vessel charged for the purpose. Col: Mercer was presented; says he "He is Secretary of legation?" No but my friend. He then made enquiries of M^r. Livingston & his secretary how their families were, and then turned to M^r. Livingston & myself & observed that our affairs should be settled.

We dined with him. After dinner when we retired into the saloon, the first Consul came up to me and asked whether the federal city grew much, I told him it did. "How many inhabitants has it?" It is just commencing, there are two cities near it, one above, the other below, on the great river Potomack, which two cities if counted with the federal city would make a respectable town, in itself it contains only two or three thousand inhabitants. "Well; M^r. Jefferson, how old is he?" Ab^t. sixty. "Is he married or single?" He is not married. "Then he is a *garçon*." No he is a widower. "Has he children?" Yes two daughters who are married. "Does he reside always at the federal city?" Generally. "Are the publick buildings there commodious, those for the Congress and President especially?" They are. "You the Americans did brilliant things in your war with England, you will do the same again." We shall I am persuaded always behave well when it shall be our lot to be in war. "You may probably be in war with them again." I replied I did not know, that that was an important question to decide when there would be an occasion for it.

At 1/2 after eight we met M^r. Marbois at his own house, in conformity to an appointment which we made with him at the Consuls, and entered on the subject of our proposed treaty. He objected to the first article as being long & containing superfluities, & shewed us a remark to that effect on it by the department of foreign affairs, as being an act more suited to a private transaction before a notary publick. He objected also to any guarantee against France or Spain, as against France as useless, since the cession was as strong a guarantee against her as she could make, and against Spain as improper & useless since it would be an ungracious act to her from France, & we had nothing to fear from Spain. He had no objection to inserting the art: of the treaty of Il defonso by which France acquired the territory, in our treaty, & would make her good offices with Spain in support of our negotiation for the Floridas. From the 2^d. art: he agreed to strike out whatever restricted the application of publick buildings to the same use hereafter; & to be contented with the security of property to individuals; and also to omit the obligation to transfer the archives &c. to the local authorities. The articles at the close of our project which respected the cession & transfer of the territory, he proposed to put together in the commencement, which we examined & modified somewhat by consent. That which respected the commercial privilege, he said was objected to in the proviso; he admitted however that it was not wished or contemplated to enjoy more than an exemption from foreign duties in favor of French productions, manufactures & tonage in the transportation of the same into the ports of the Mississippi but not to affect the terms on which our produce should be carried from it, since he readily foresaw that such a power might be greatly abused. I proposed an amendment which was in sentiment agreed to. To the payment to be made them in stock, and the mode by which we proposed to ascertain the amount and persons entitled to the debt which they owed our citizens, he said objections were entertained. They wish the payment to be made here of 5. millions of livres the month, which we told him was impossible—He believed it was. He wished the term for which the stock was irredeemable to be omitted & adjusted afterwards between ourselves, intimating that on that point difficulties existed with his gov^t. which proceeded from want of time to examine it, but that we must agree [on] something, indeed seemed to assent explicitly to our ideas on the subject. On our explaining the reasons why some check on the liquidation of the debt due our citizens was necessary, since otherwise the sum destined to them might be absorbed, by liquidations in favor of Americans not entitled, or even not Americans, he admitted the propriety of the check we proposed. He said he would see the Consul next morning, fix the points in question, & come prepared sometime in the course of that day to conclude & sign the treaty as of yesterday, being Saturday.

May 2^d. We actually signed the treaty and convention for the sixty millions of Francs to France in the French language, but our copies in English not being made out we could not sign in our language. They were however prepared and signed two or three days afterwards. The convention respecting American claims took more time & was not signed till about the 8. or 9th. A more minute view of this business as promised in the third page will be annexed hereafter.

We nominated provisionally Col: John Mercer, J. C. Barnett & W^m. M^c. Clure to examine the claims of Americans on the French gov^t. and perform the duties assigned to our board by the convention respecting that subject.

As soon as we had dispatched the treaty &c. by M^r. Hughes, with duplicates & triplicates I resolved to go to Spain in pursuit of my instructions, which M^r. L.

approved of and strongly urged. With that view I wrote a note to the minister of foreign affairs asking the good offices of his gov^t. with Spain as had been promised by M^r. Marbois intimating that I wished to set out in a few days for Madrid. On the Sunday following I dined with the Consul Cambacérès, who arrived late from the council at St. Cloud. The party was not large; I sat next him; he observed "you must not go to Spain at present." I asked his reason. He replied "it is not the time, you had better defer it." I revived the subject repeatedly but he declined going more into it. After dinner when we were in the saloon, he came up to me, and on my telling him that he had given me some concern by what he had said, he replied "it was only his opinion, but you will talk on the subject with the minister of the publick treasury." (M^r. Marbois) which I promised. I went immediately to M^r. Marbois's but he was not at home. Reflecting on the hint from the Consul it occurred it would be proper to call on the ambassador of Spain & confer with him on the subject, as I had always intended before I sate out for Spain. I found him at home with two Spanish gentlemen, one the husband of the daughter of Don Galvez who was also present. I told him that I intended going to Spain to treat for Florida with the ministers of his Catholic Majesty, & asked what he thought of it. He replied with great candor that he wished the affair amicably settled between our gov^{ts}., and that two days before he had written to his Court by an extraordinary courier at the desire of M^r. Livingston to propose to it the question whether it would make the cession to the U States and as I understood to authorize him to treat here for it. As M^r. Livingston had never spoken to me on the subject, as he had pressed my going to Spain, or at least given his decided opinion that I ought to go there, this information surprised me much, especially when I recollected that he not only had no power to treat on the subject, but knew that it was committed to others. I asked when he expected an answer to his letter? He said if it was sent by an extr^y. courier it might be in 12 days, as it required 7 to go and as many to return; & it had been sent 2 already: that if it came by the ordinary post it would take a much longer time as it required 12 days to convey a letter from Paris to Madrid in that mode. I told him that I thought I should go to Madrid & then explained to him something of the nature of the commission which existed for treating with his government, it being thought by *ours* more respectful to *his* to treat at Madrid than here, but without giving cause to infer that I disapproved the measure taken by M^r. Livingston or indeed that I was ignorant of it.

Next day M^r. Livingston and myself called on M^r. Marbois on some question relative to the treaty &c. On our return he asked me when I should set out to Spain? I told him that I had called on the Marquis D'Azara to confer with him on the subject, the night before, and of the step he had taken at his request to draw the subject here; that under those circumstances it would be an idle errand for me to go there, at least till the Marquis got an answer to his letter; that the affair ought not to play between the two countries; He said that what had passed between him and the Marquis had happened casually at the minister of foreign affairs: that the Marquis had sent the Extr^y. courier to announce our treaty, & hearing him say he intended to send one, he had suggested the idea of his proposing to his court to make the cession, but not to obtain the authority to treat here for it. I told him that after the arrangement made by our gov^t. with respect to Spain, the affair ought to have its course in the train in which it was placed by it: that I could not see any benefit to be derived from an application of the Ambassador of Spain to his court in the manner stated by M^r. Livingston, especially if I was to go there.

ADDENDA: JOURNAL OR MEMORANDUM—LOUISIANA.

I objected to the commerc^t. priviledge, as being calculated to embarrass our revenue system, create irregularities between one part and another, give offence to foreign powers, fix a badge of degradation on that part of the Union, & actually defeat the policy of France in inclining us to Engl^d.—He seemed to think that being the condition of the cession it was not liable to all the objections stated—both my colleague and myself observed that that idea had not been communicated by him to either of us in our former conversations, w^h. he admitted on our word, but observed that it was an omission on his part, his gov^t. having always contemplated it—that it imported the honor of the govt., to furnish a publick motive for the cession distinct from money—I then objected to the perpetuity of the stipulation to which he assented—12 years were proposed to which he agreed.

At the same time that we presented to Mr. Marbois our project we gave him a paper drawn by my colleague on the subject, translated in French, w^h. being long, it was deemed then unnecessary to read it, but proposed by my colleague that Mr. Marbois sho^d. keep & read it himself & shew it to the consul, w^h. he promised. This paper was given me by my colleague some days before, but it being lengthy & I being much engaged in the arrangement of our project had paid but little attention to it—when my colleague called on me on his way to Mr. Marbois he asked me for it; I gave it to him, he asked me to sign it—I told him there were passages I did not like, particularly the admission that the formation of our adm^{ns} depended on the conduct of foreign powers: that that was not the fact, that that idea was degrading to our country, that the application of the term sovereign to the first consul was improper, that of Ch: Magistrate was the correct one—I also did not like the terms used relative to the debts due by France—tho' I wished & wod. secure them in our treaty—he said that the paper contained mere cursory observations,—that the first idea w^h. I objected to wo^d. have weight here, since this gov^t. did not wish a change of adm^n. in the U. States so that he thought the paper might have use. On the intimation that he considered the paper as containing cursory observations, by which I understood that he meant it as informal, I signed it—I did this on the principle that the negotiation had reached a stage which prevented this paper from doing harm, and to put it out of my colleague's power to say that I prevented his doing good. I never heard of the paper afterwards, tho' my colleague told me next day on leaving the first consul's that Mr. Marbois had informed him that the first consul had approved it—I had conferred with Mr. Marbois just before my colleague did & arranged our meeting that night at his home, in w^h. he said nothing of that paper. I therefore inferred that what he did say was in consequence of the enquiry of my colleague, & on perusing that he felt some interest respecting it.

TO JAMES MADISON.

PARIS, May 18, 1803.

SIR,—Since the conclusion of the treaty with France for the purchase of Louisiana, which was forwarded to you on the 13th. by M^r. Hughes, with a joint letter from my colleague and myself, I feel myself much at a loss what part to take respecting the Floridas. There are some considerations in favor of an immediate pursuit of that object with Spain which have great weight on my mind. The cession of Louisiana by France to the U. States must lessen the value of the Floridas to Spain, and she will be apt to feel that effect more sensibly immediately after she hears it than at any other time. France too who has promised her aid in the negotiation with Spain, would probably take more interest in it, at this moment, while the obligation to yield it, is in a manner personal, than she might do hereafter. At this crisis of affairs between France and England which comprizes Spain in an equal degree, there is reason to believe that we should derive much aid from a pressure on Spain, from that cause. It is equally presumable that England even in case of war would not interfere with our pursuit, much less break with us for obtaining the Floridas. The exclusion of her manufactures from the Continent of Europe, is a principle cause of her present unquiet and distressed situation. It is her interest to cherish the U. States and Russia, as her best markets; a policy which I believe she understands and pursues with sincerity. To be involved in a war with us at this epoch would prove a great calamity to her. I have no doubt that at this time she is either indifferent respecting our acquisition of Louisiana, and that which we propose to make of the Floridas, or in no situation to oppose it. Indeed it is not improbable that she may wish it, as it weakens these powers, in that quarter and promises to open new markets to her manufactures. Should we not however acquire this territory of Spain at this period, there is danger of its falling into the hands of some other power hereafter; a circumstance which might give us much trouble, as it commands the mouths of several of our rivers, and gives a right to the navigation of the Mississippi. There are also considerations against my pursuing the object at present of great weight. We have already stipulated for a much greater sum than it was contemplated we should give for the object of my mission. To go further might embarrass our treasury. It may be advisable to exchange a portion of Louisiana next Mexico for the Floridas, and I have no power to make such an arrangement. I have weighed these considerations with the attention they merit, and the result is that I am of opinion that it is more in conformity to the spirit of my instructions, and to the interest of my country, that I should proceed immediately to Madrid to endeavour to obtain the Floridas than remain inactive and suffer the favorable occasion which is now presented to be lost. The acquisition of the Floridas is an important object with our government, as is sufficiently shewn by our instructions. The purchase of the whole of Louisiana, tho' not contemplated is nevertheless a measure founded on the principles and justified by the policy of our instructions, provided it be thought a good bargain. The only difference between the acquisition we have made, and that which we were instructed to make in that respect, is, that a favorable occasion presenting itself which indeed was not anticipated by the administration, in the measures which led to that event and laid the foundation for it, we have gone further than we were instructed to do. But the extent of that acquisition does not destroy the motive which existed before of acquiring the Floridas, nor essentially diminish it. In our instructions the idea entertained by the President of the value of that country is defined. It is to be presumed that under existing circumstances it may be had at a cheaper rate, since its importance to Spain is much diminished. And altho' the sum to be paid for Louisiana is considerable, yet the period at which that portion which is applicable to the government of France is to be paid, is so remote, and such delays are incident to that which will be received by our citizens, that it is to be presumed the payment of what it would be proper to stipulate for the Floridas, would subject our treasury to no embarrassment. I am the more confident in this opinion, from the belief that it would be easy to raise on the land alone, retaining to our government the jurisdiction, a sum which would be sufficient to discharge the greater part of what it is probable Spain would ask for it. The bias of my mind therefore is to pursue this object by repairing immediately to Madrid and endeavouring to obtain by treaty the territory in question thereby extirpating the last remaining source of controversy or indeed jealousy with these powers. If I proceed it will be in a week from this time, within which term every arrangement incident to the treaty and convention we have formed with this republick will probably be compleated, and the little provision necessary for my journey to Spain likewise made. On this subject I shall write you again soon, let the decision which I take be what it may. In case I go I shall leave my family at St. Germain till my return, which I shall expect to do in a few months. I am with great respect & esteem y^r. ob^t. servant.

TO VIRGINIA SENATORS.

PARIS, May 25, 1803

[Endorsed "To Genl Mason. Col. W. C. Nicholas & John Breckenridge—private—enclosed to Mr. M."]

GENTLEMEN,—We have as you will find concluded a treaty & two conventions with this Government for the cession of the whole of Louisiana. I flatter myself that the terms will be thought reasonable when compared with the immense advantages resulting from the acquisition. The subject however will be before you, & it belongs to the suitable authorities to decide whether we have acquitted ourselves with propriety in the trust reposed in us. I consider this transaction as resulting from the wise & firm tho' moderate measures of the Executive and Congress during the last session. Without these measures we should not have acquired Louisiana. The pressure of the crisis here, but an approaching rupture with England, assisted in producing the result, but had our country not formed a character, or rather a prominent feature in the transactions of the day, it would not have taken place. Nor could it have succeeded so promptly or advantageously, by taking any other attitude than that which was taken. Had we broken the pacific relations subsisting between these countries & the United States, or indeed had not a respect for this Government, and a desire to preserve peace with it, been clearly marked in our measures I do not think that we should have brought it to the issue we have. It is proper that you should possess a correct knowledge of the facts here which led to this result. I arrived at Havre on the 8th of April, which fact was known here on the 9th. On the 10th this Government resolved to offer us by sale the whole of Louisiana, at a certain price, which was diminished by the negotiation. On the 12. I arrived in town, on the 14th was received by the minister, recognized by him, by order of the First Consul &

informed that altho I might not be presented to the Consul till the audience day according to usage, that a person would be appointed to treat with us with whom we might proceed in the interim. This was accordingly done, Mr. Marbois was appointed, the negotiations immediately commenced, & brought to as speedy a conclusion as possible. The decision to offer us the territory by sale was not the effect of any management of mine, for it took place before I reached Paris; nor of my colleague or it would have taken place sooner: Being postponed until my arrival in France or indeed till the mission was known, is a full proof that it was the result of the causes above mentioned & of those only. I enclose you a copy of a letter from Mr. Livingston bearing date on the 10th of April, in answer to one from me of the 8th announcing my arrival, which establishes the above facts. I communicate this letter to you as a measure of precaution, that you may not only know that the above facts exist but the nature of the evidence which supports them. Had the measures of our government, of which my mission was only a sub-altern part, failed, whether the failure might be attributed to their impolicy, or to such a delay on my part as suffered the crisis with England to pass, all the responsibility would have been on the government & myself. It is equally just in reference to the result that facts should be correctly known to guard against misrepresentation. Personally I pretend to nothing but zeal & industry after I got here, a merit which is equally due to my colleague. If my mission produced any effect it was owing altogether to the motive which induced the President to nominate me, that is, the pronounced character which I had in reference to the object in question, & a belief that I would bring the affair promptly to an issue. It is to be presumed that the transaction will rest on its true ground in the United States, but as the contrary may be the case & it is impossible to foresee what misrepresentations may be given of it, or the ends that may be intended to subserve, I think it not only justifiable but a duty to make to you this communication. You will consider the letter itself as strictly confidential since altho' it is proper to communicate it to a few from whom it is my custom to withhold nothing, yet it would be otherwise if it should go further, for reasons that will readily occur. It is proper to add that I expect no misrepresentation from my colleague & that I am happy to have it in my power to bear testimony in the most explicit manner in favor of his zealous, sincere & diligent co-operation thro' the whole of this business.

TO THE SECRETARY OF STATE.
PARIS, 8th of June, 1803.

SIR,—Since my letter of yesterday I have had an interesting communication with the Minister of foreign affairs. Our letter had been restored to M^r. Livingston by M^r. Marbois in a casual interview who also shewed him the order to M^r. Pinchon, which was substituted for it. To see that order and receive one to him for the surrender of the country to the United States, I called yesterday evening by appointment on the Minister, where I found M^r. Marbois also. They had expected M^r. Livingston and myself together, but on my observing that we had not so understood it, he having already seen the paper. The Minister read the order to me and asked how I liked it, I replied that it was not for us to say, it being the act of his government only, but says he, comparatively which do you prefer, this mode or the other? I replied this without doubt. He said it was on the idea it would be more agreeable to us and our government that it was adopted, since suppressing our letter it became, as it ought to be, entirely the act of [the] government and in his opinion strictly a justifiable one, the Consul having a right to annex a condition to the ratification in the spirit of the treaty at any time before the exchange. I told him that having discussed the subject already, I had only to repeat that I preferred much this mode to the other. He added that he hoped no difficulty would take place hereafter; that we had sufficient time to perform what we had stipulated, and that he sincerely wished we might do it in due time, as his government had much at heart the future harmony of the two nations. I replied that similar sentiments animated the government of the United States; that I was persuaded the treaty would be ratified; that even before the creation of the stock I was confident that the President far from delaying the payment of what was stipulated, would if [in] his power after the ratification promote aid which might be useful to them in the United States to evince his desire of a prompt execution of the treaty; that on our part and on our own responsibility if it was desired we would prevail on the house of Baring and Hope to advance the first payment, that is six millions of livres, before we heard from our government, in confidence that our conduct would be approved. I told him I thought my colleague would unite in this sentiment. He expressed himself highly gratified with the communication, which he considered as a strong proof of the friendship of the government of the United States for the nation and government of France. [He] declared that as it was made after everything was concluded it was the more honorable to us, and would affect in a greater degree the sensibility of the First Consul, to whom he would make it known, tho' he knew that he would accept nothing but as it became due in strict conformity to the treaty. I should deem it fortunate for the United States if the payment was made as being an act of liberality on our part, and in the degree a prompt execution of the treaty. It would bind this government more completely to the execution of it on its part. I am happy however that the offer was refused, since while it cannot fail to produce a good effect, it avoids all responsibility on our part, or that of the President, tho' indeed in the payment here the responsibility would be entirely on us. It is proper to inform you that the treaty and conventions bear date from the period when [every] thing was agreed on, the thirtieth of April, but as it [was necessary] to reduce them to writing the treaty was signed on the second of May, and the convention concerning the claims of our citizens the ninth or tenth which will explain why they were not sooner despatched from Paris. I am Sir with great respect & esteem y^r. obt^t. serv^t.

TO THE SECRETARY OF STATE.
PARIS, June 19, 1803.

SIR,—We have rec^d. y^r. communications of the 18. and 20. of April & after due consideration deem it most advisable that I sho^d. proceed immediately to England. The departure of M^r. King from that country at the commencement of a war between it & France, without nominating a *charge des affaires* may expose our commercial concerns to much embarrassment if there is no one there soon to take charge of them. The arrangement however proposed by the President will probably obviate any inconvenience since the place will be occupied in a fortnight from this date. I am happy to have it in my power to add that the state in which our affairs are here admits a complyance with this arrangement without inconvenience to any interest of a publick nature. Since the despatch of the ratifications of the treaty &c, there is nothing to be done here till the question is decided by our government, nor even then in case of ratification, as the instruments will be given by you to the Minister of France to be forwarded to his government here. It is only in case of difficulty from some cause or other, that the commission will have to act again in this affair, & then it will be in your power, if a joint agency is deemed necessary to avail y^r.self of it, by suitable instructions to the members who compose it. In regard to Spain it is not likely that any injury can result from the delay which becomes inevitable by this measure. It was never a very clear point that I ought to pursue the object with that power, after what was done here, until I heard from you. The motive which inclined me to it at first diminished daily by my detention here, so that your late instructions arrived in good time to relieve me from further suspense. My visit to England will not I think be attributed by this gov^t. to an improper motive. It seems to have a just view of the policy of our government in regard to both powers, which is to cultivate their friendship by fair & honorable means while it pays a scrupulous attention & maintains with firmness the respect which is due to our national character rights & interests. My position in England will not prevent my attention in due time to the object with Spain, if the President should be of opinion that it might be useful. I have suggested to this government the probability of my being instructed by him to pursue that object with that power, after the decision on our treaty &c. with France, in which case I informed the Minister that I sho^d., according to the promise made to M^r. Livingston and myself by M^r. Marbois, expect the good offices of his government with its ally, and of which he gave me the most positive & satisfactory assurance. On this subject as on what concerns us more generally I shall write you here after more fully. I shall only add at present that in the communications which have passed between this government & myself since my last, to which this incident has in part given the occasion, much has occurred to inspire me with confidence in its friendly disposition towards our gov^t. & country and in a mode that could not otherwise than be peculiarly grateful to me. I am with great respect & esteem y^r. most ob^t. servant.

P.S. I have sent you two copies of the view I have taken of the question whether W. Florida is comprized in the cession of Louisiana, which I think too clear to admit of a doubt. I have many reasons for believing that the gov^t. of Spain entertains the same opinion on that point. I doubt not if it is taken possession of as a part of Louisiana, that the measure will be acquiesced in by that gov^t., or at least that it will not be taken ill by it, or impede an amicable and favorable adjustment relative to the territory of Spain Eastward of the Mississippi.

The ratifications of the treaty &c. have been sent by way of Havre, as have duplicates by another vessel. The former under the care of M^r. Jay.

OPINION RESPECTING WEST FLORIDA.

Inclosed in official despatch to Madison of June 19, 1803. . . . (Three copies were sent; one is with the original of the Louisiana treaty, the other in the Jefferson Papers 2d. Ser., Vol. 57, No. 124, and this one in the Monroe Papers. [HAMILTON.]

I^st. October 1800. Treaty Between France & Spain of S^r. Ildephonso.

His Catholic Majesty promises and engages on his part to cede back to the French Republick, six months after the full and entire execution of the conditions and stipulations above mentioned, relative to his Royal Highness the Duke of Parma "the Colony or Province of Louisiana, with the same extent that it actually has *in* the hands of Spain, that it had when France possessed it, and such as it ought to be after the Treaties passed between Spain and other States."

30 April 1803. France ceded to the United States all the Territory which she had thus acquired of Spain. Of what extent is the acquisition? The question is

suggested by a doubt whether it comprizes the territory which was called by the British W. Florida: to decide it a view must be taken of the facts & principles on which it depends.

When France possessed Louisiana formerly, that is prior to the year 1762, its eastern boundary extended to the River Perdigo. All the Country which she possessed in that quarter was called & known by the name of Louisiana, & it is a well established fact that it extended eastward to that limit. *Vide charts, authorities, &*[ca].

By a Secret Convention, bearing date the 3rd. of November 1762, between France & Spain, the former ceded to the latter the Island of New Orleans and the West bank of the Mississipi, that is all that part of Louisiana which lies westward of what was called by the British W. Florida. This Convention has not been published that I know of, for I have not been able to get a Copy of it.

On the 21 April 1764, the King of France gave an Order to his Governor, Mons[r]. d' Abbadia, at N. Orleans, to surrender the said Territory to such Officer as the King of Spain might appoint to receive it. The surrender did not take place till some years afterwards, according to an account which I have seen, the 18 of August 1769.

10 Feb[y]. 1763. In a Treaty to which France, Britain, Spain & Portugal were parties, France ceded to Britain the Territory lying eastward of the Island of New Orleans, that is the territory called afterwards by the British W. Florida, & Spain ceded to Britain, in the same treaty Florida, that is the territory which Britain afterwards called East Florida. It was after Britain had thus become possessed of this territory, that she laid off that portion of Louisiana which lies between the Island of N. Orleans & the river Perdigo, into a separate province & called it W. Florida; calling the other East.

The Preliminary Articles of this Treaty bear date on the 3rd. November 1762, the same day with the secret Convention. *See Martin's Coll. Vol. 1. p. 17.*

3 Sept. 1783. In a Treaty between Britain & Spain, the former cedes to the latter East & West Floridas.

27 Oct. 1795. In a Treaty between the United States and Spain, the latter stipulates in favor of the former the free navigation of the Mississippi—, with the right of deposit at N. Orleans.

The above are all the parts which belong to the question, on which it remains to decide whether W. Florida is comprized in the cession of Louisiana, lately made by Spain to France, & by the latter to the United States.

The intention of the parties is to govern in all Treaties as in other contracts; to ascertain that intention in the present Case, it is necessary to take into view the whole article, & construe it so as to give to each part its fair and obvious import.

The article consists of three distinct parts or members; the first stipulates that the cession shall comprize Louisiana in the same extent that it actually has in the hands of Spain; 2dly. that it had when France possessed it; 3dly. as it ought to be after the Treaties subsequently passed between Spain & other powers.

The import of the first member of the article seems to be clear and distinct, & to depend on a single fact, what Louisiana was in the hands of Spain, at the time this Treaty was made. To establish that fact, it seems to be necessary only to ascertain what the limits of the Province then were, by the regulations of Spain respecting it, which it is presumed may be easily done. Has Spain considered W. Florida, since her Treaty with G. Britain, in 1783, as a part of Louisiana? What is the extent of the jurisdiction of the Governor established at New-Orleans? Does it go to the river Perdigo, or is it confined to the Island of New-Orleans, and western bank of the river Mississippi? What is the extent of the jurisdiction of the Governor at S^{t}. Augustine? Does it comprize East-Florida only, or both the Floridas? I am informed by good authorities that since the Treaty of 1783, between Britain & Spain, by which the latter became possessed of the whole of Louisiana, & also of East-Florida, that she has governed it as it was governed by France, comprizing W. Florida as a part of Louisiana, or in other words that the distinction between E. & W. Florida, which was created by and known only to the British ceased.

The import of the second member of the article "that Louisiana shall comprize the same extent that it had when France possessed it," is also obvious. That also depends on a fact which it is presumed is not controverted. We are however led to inquire why were two Clauses, which are supposed to mean the same thing introduced into the article? To this question a very satisfactory solution may be given, one which tends more fully to shew the intention of the parties, as to the territory ceded to France by this Treaty. That Spain should cede the Province of Louisiana as she held it is not strange; her motive for inserting a clause to that effect is therefore too obvious to require explanation. But why insert the other? Had the cession of that part to Britain, which was by her afterwards called W. Florida, & the subsequent transfer or cession of it by Britain to Spain, created any doubt of what was meant by the Province of Louisiana, or was it likely to create any? The apprehension that such a doubt might exist suggested the propriety of the second Clause, to reduce to certainty what might otherwise be uncertain. With that view it was thought expedient to go back to an anterior state of things, to a period which, by preceding the possession of G. Britain, would preclude all reference to that power or her regulations relative to the territory. This was done by stipulating that the limits or extent of Louisiana should be ascertained by reference to what they were, when France possessed the Province; and that was the motive for introducing the Clause.

It is a sound doctrine in the construction of Treaties, which is equally applicable or indeed more so to a single article, that where there are two passages having in view the same object, the one of equivocal & doubtful import, the other clear & explicit, the latter should prevail. Indeed this is the obvious dictate of common sense; there can be no motive for introducing a second passage in a treaty, or an article of a treaty, on the same subject, for the same purpose, but to explain what was doubtful in the first: that the second member was introduced into this article with this view, & for the reason above stated is obvious. It would be absurd to attempt to construe an intelligible passage in a treaty by an unintelligible & doubtful one. This doctrine is fully illustrated by writers on the law of nations, particularly by Vattel, page 235–6.

Thus it appears clear by the obvious import of the two first members of the article referred to, that W. Florida is comprized in the Cession made by Spain of Louisiana to France, & by the latter to the United States. Is then the import of those Clauses detracted from or changed by the 3^d. and last one which stipulates that "it shall be such as it ought to be after the treaties passed subsequently between Spain and other powers"? Let us examine the Treaties referred to, and their effect on the point in question.

The only Treaties which Spain formed after the Secret Convention with France, of 3rd. Nov. 1862, relative to Louisiana or any part of it, were that of 1783, with G. Britain, whereby that portion called by her W. Florida was ceded to Spain, and that of 1795, with the U. States, whereby the free navigation of the river Mississippi, & the right of deposit at N. Orleans were stipulated in favor of the latter. The term *subsequently* is relative & refers to the possession of France, prior to that treaty or secret Convention. These therefore were the Treaties contemplated by the parties in this member of the article.

If either of these treaties is relied on as exempting W. Florida from the said Cession of Louisiana, it must be the British Treaty, since that alone can be considered as having any reference to the subject. But how can that Treaty justify such a pretention, a Treaty which did not sever W. Florida from, but united it to Louisiana in the hands of Spain? By it the two first clauses of the article referred to, are made to have their due effect, since by it Spain became possessed of Louisiana in the same extent that France held it, except what portion the U. States had lawfully acquired by their independence. Had that Treaty not been formed, the contrary would have been the case; the description given in the most important and ruling clause in the article would have been inapplicable.

Does not this then prove that the two first Clauses, especially the second, were introduced into the article, on due consideration, and for a definite object: that the British Treaty was referred to in the 3^d., on account of the cession of the W. Florida made by it to Spain, and with a view to comprize it in the Cession of Louisiana then made to France.

If the Treaty between Spain & England had dismembered Louisiana, by separating W. Florida from it for ever, the pretention would be well founded, because Spain could not cede Louisiana otherwise than as she held it, after the Treaties passed between her & other powers. In that case there might be some pretext to the Claim, even had W. Florida afterwards been returned to Spain, by another Treaty, tho' in my opinion not a solid argument in its favor, against the obvious intention of the parties, as expressed in the two first clauses. But that treaty, as already mentioned, did not separate W. Florida from, but united it to Louisiana in the hands of Spain.

Let us suppose this clause standing alone and unconnected with any other, what would its import be? Spain cedes to France Louisiana, "such as it ought to be after the treaties passed subsequently between Spain & other Powers"? Could the Treaty with Britain, which enlarged the limits of the Province in her hands, be construed as lessening the extent of the cession? No part of Louisiana was hers by discovery; she acquired it of France and Britain, making the last acquisition of the latter nation; the treaty making which, with that with the U. States, which imposed on the territory certain conditions, the observance of which it was proper to stipulate in their favor, were the Treaties referred to in the last member of the article.

When a Cession is made of a tract of Country and territory, comprehended under a certain description or name, which conveys an idea of definite limits, from which cession it is intended to except a certain portion of said territory, the restrictive clause should be made explicit, as well to shew the intention of the party ceding to make the exception, as the part he intends to except. Such exemption can never be made by inference against the positive terms of the Cession. In the present case, there is not the slightest ground to infer that an exemption was contemplated, while the terms of the Cession are general, clear, and positive. Is it presumable, if Spain had intended to exempt W. Florida from the Cession of Louisiana, that she would have use[d] the terms adopted in the article to accomplish it, terms that would fail of the object, if they stood alone in a treaty? Is it not more presumable that she would have restricted the Cession in express terms to that portion of the territory, which she had received from

France? Or as that Cession was made in a treaty to which those powers alone were parties, it was natural to expect that in a subsequent Treaty between them on the same subject, they would confine themselves to the Treaty & Cession formerly made, if such had been their intention. It was the more to be expected, as by so doing it was the readiest mode of expressing in the clearest manner what their present intention was. If Spain had intended to make the exception and to rely on the British distinction, as the rule & limit of it, would she not have mentioned it in express terms, by reserving W. Florida by name from the Cession? Lastly, would she have used terms which instead of detracting from or exempting any portion of the Territory from the Cession, tended essentially to illustrate the construction, and confirm the import contended for in the preceding Clauses?

It remains to examine whether France had so dismembered Louisiana, while she possessed it, that the reference to the state in which it was, in her hands, applied to a part and not the whole of the Province. By the Treaties above referred to, by which she ceded it to Spain & Britain, the first bearing date on the 3rd. November 1762, the second on the 10th. Feby 1663. I was led to apprehend that some doubt might exist on that point; but fortunately there is room for none, since the preliminary articles of the Treaty of 1763 were entered into and dated on the 3d. of Novr. 1762, the same day with the secret Convention. France therefore parted with the whole territory at the same time. The Treaties which transferred dismembered it, but that was in the hands of the other powers, not in those of France. It was known in her possession as the entire province of Louisiana and not otherwise.

TO ROBERT R. LIVINGSTON.
PARIS, June 23, 1803.

DEAR SIR,—I intended calling on you this morning but on my return home last night found a note from the Minister of Foreign Affairs inviting me to his house at 12. to proceed to St Cloud to be presented by him at one to the First Consul for the purpose of taking leave of him. This puts it out of my power to see you this morning. I have however signed the Commissions for two of our board & the agent which are sent you.

In addition to the papers promised me, permit me to request you will be so obliging as let me have copies of our letter to Mr. Marbois & his answer relative to the aid promised us by his government in the negotiations with Spain for Florida: also of his letter to us & our answer relative to the treaty after its conclusion: & lastly Mr. Kings letter to us & our answer to him, & respecting the treaty we have formed with this Republic. Your Secretary may not be able to make copies of all these papers, if you will be so kind let Col: Mercer have the originals, we will make them here. I am dear Sir &c.

TO ROBERT R. LIVINGSTON
[No date.]

DEAR SIR,—I have received your letter of the 23. expressing your idea of the extent of the acquisition we have made by the late treaty with France, which I have read with attention. I thank you for the communication, as it tends to throw light on that interesting topic.

Before however I proceed to make any remark on that subject permit me to observe that I am sorry I cannot agree with you in the last sentiment expressed in your letter, that it is not necessary to probe this business to the bottom nor until future circumstances should render it proper. Had I thought so I should not have asked of you your ideas on paper on the subject. My opinion has been from the moment that our treaty with France was concluded, that it was my first duty to ascertain correctly the extent of that acquisition, by reference to all the authentic documents to which access could be had, & such other sources of information as might illustrate it. There are a variety of considerations which imposed this duty on me; I will however only mention that which grows out of the transaction itself, the propriety of communicating to our government, such information as we possess & such opinion as we have formed of the extent of the acquisition. This consideration is much strengthened by the advice which you propose to give to our government to take possession of W. Florida as a part of Louisiana. We ought not to give such advice till we had probed the question to the bottom, and seen that it was founded in principles of Justice such as could be demonstrated to the impartial world, even to Spain herself. Nor can I agree with you that my motive for asking your ideas on that subject on paper, was because I had not leisure to examine it myself. The fact is I was at the time engaged in the examination of it, as I have been ever since, and with the greatest attention that other duties would permit, as indeed I think I mentioned to you at the time. My object in making the request was that we might examine the question separately, compare our ideas together and after forming our opinions, take the course which in reference to our respective duties might appear to be proper. I have made these observations solely for the purpose of explaining to you the motive which induced me to make the above mentioned request, which I have been sorry to find you had misunderstood.

Having also examined the question with some attention and committed my ideas to paper I shall have the pleasure to communicate them to you at our first interview. I shall only observe at present that we perfectly agree in the opinion that Louisiana, as it was in the hands of France prior to the year 1763, extended to the River Perdigo, & that it was restored to her by Spain, in the treaty of Il Dephonso, precisely in the same extent: that the reservation contained in the last member of the article, which respects the subject, is in favor of the United States only, intended to secure their rights under their treaty with Spain in 1795. I also think with you that the communications of the Spanish Minister at Madrid to Mr. Pinckney tend to confirm this doctrine. But in tracing this subject under the several treaties which respect it, I had a difficulty on a point which appeared to me to be of importance. Did France dismember the Country while she was possessed of it? it is not material to how many powers she granted it provided it was at one & the same time, that is that it did not remain her property in a dismembered state. At first I was led to fear that a strong argument might be drawn against us from this source. The secret treaty by which New Orleans & the Western bank of Louisiana was ceded to Spain bears date on the 3ʳᵈ Nov. 1762; the order of the King to his governor for the surrender of it on the 21 April 1764 and the actual surrender did not take place till some years afterwards, according to one of the papers which I have seen, not till 18 Augt 1769. The treaty between France, Great Britain, Spain &c by which the part since called W. Florida was ceded to Great Britain bears date on the 10th Feby 1763. I presume that the cession of a country takes its date from the treaty making the cession, not from the surrender: but in the present case whether we date the cession referred to, under the secret treaty of '62, to Spain from the one or the other epoch, the effect would be the same. If these were the only facts in the case, it might be said that there was a dismemberment of Louisiana in the hands of France. Happily these are not the only facts existing; by a note in one of the books I have obtained, it appears that the preliminary articles of the treaty of 1763 were actually signed on the same day with the secret convention above mentioned, & of course that the transfer or cession of the whole country by France was made on the same day. I presume that this note may be relied on, & verified by reference to authentic documents, to which access may be had. I communicate its contents with pleasure, because it seems to place beyond all controversy our right to West Florida under the treaty we have lately formed with France.

N.B.—As the joint commission for Mʳ. Pinckney and myself could be of no use until the farther orders of the President it has not been forwarded.

TO THE SECRETARY OF STATE.
LONDON, 26 July, 1803.

SIR,—On the 20th. Ul[to]. I wrote Lord Hawkesbury by M[r]. Sumter and apprized him of my arrival in town in the character of Minister Plenipotentiary from the United States to his Britannic Majesty, & requested that he would be pleased to appoint a time when I might have the honor to wait on him with my letters of credence. His Lordship answered that he would receive me the next day at one o'clock at his office if that hour was convenient to me. I called there at that hour with M[r]. Sumter & was received by him. I gave him a copy of my letters of credence & expressed a desire to be presented to their Majesties as soon as it might be convenient. He regretted that I had not arrived a few days sooner, as in that case I might have been presented at the last levee, but added that it should be soon done. I asked him in what mode I should proceed, whether I should call on him again for information? He replied that Sir Stephen Cotterel would present me by whom I should be informed of the time. Not much conversation took place on political subjects in the interview. He observed that all the points in which there had been heretofore any collision between the two Nations were now happily arranged, such as the debts, spoliations and boundaries; the latter of which he had adjusted by treaty with M[r]. King just before he sailed. I assured him in general terms, that it was the wish of our Government to be on the most friendly footing with great Britain. He then congratulated me on the conclusion of our treaty with France which he said I had found in good train on my arrival there & had been lucky enough to arrange to my satisfaction. I replied that I hoped it was concluded on terms that would be found advantageous to our Country & be approved by our Government: that we had been careful in forming the treaty not to interfere with the rights of any other friendly power. The conversation was not otherwise sufficiently interesting to be reported. As such interviews are formal, especially when the parties are entirely strangers to each other, as we were, they are I believe generally short. As soon therefore as it appeared that the object of the interview was fully answered I withdrew.

The next levee is early in the next month at which time I hope to be presented to his Majesty, and in the interim I shall endeavor to make myself acquainted with the state of our affairs in this country with which we have so many relations that are so highly interesting to us, and which I shall endeavor to preserve and if possible improve.

You will observe that I expressed myself, in my replies to Lord Hawkesbury's remarks, in general rather than precise terms, and from your knowledge of facts you will I am persuaded be sensible that it was impossible for me to do otherwise. As I knew nothing of the treaty lately concluded with this Government by M^r. King I could of course say nothing about it; nor could I reply otherwise to his allusion to the state in which I found the negotiation on my arrival in Paris. His Lordship did not state the pretentions of any party to agency or service in that transaction which I knew to be unfounded, and it was therefore unnecessary & impolitic to presume that such was his intention. Still as his allusion might be construed into a countenance of such pretentions, I thought it my duty to express myself in a manner which while it manifested a disposition to conciliate, should nevertheless give them no sanction. It would be matter of regret if such pretensions existed, since every transaction should appear in its true character and be attributed to its proper causes. Justice and candor require this in all cases in reference to the parties concerned. In the present one it is peculiarly important that this correct maxim should be strictly observed. This affair is not yet concluded, tho' I hope it is in a good train and will soon be put beyond the reach of fortune.

Our government ought to know to the minutest detail the motives which induced the government of France to adopt this measure, to enable it to do justice to those motives & bring the affair itself to a happy conclusion. The extrication of ourselves from a dangerous, perhaps a disastrous, war, by the acquisition of an important territory which gives such vast relief and comfort to so many of our people, is an event which if the causes which produced it are well understood, may serve as a monitory lesson to influence if not prescribe the course to be pursued in our future controversies with the European powers, if any should occur. America certainly bears a very distinct relation to Europe, from what the several powers of the latter bear to each other, which it is equally important for her to understand & to have understood by the latter. Of this truth the event referred to is a striking example as it is a very satisfactory illustration. I should weary you if I pursued this subject. I have touched it to remark that for these and other obvious reasons I have considered it my duty to communicate to you every fact belonging to this transaction with which I was acquainted that it might be seen by the President in its true light. To these I shall at present take the liberty to add a few observations.

You saw by M^r. Livingstons and my joint letter which bore date a day or two before I left Paris about the 11th. Ulto^{mo}. that the English government had no agency in this affair: that it never had made a question of Louisiana in its discussions with the government of France, at any period since the French possessed it. This information was obtained of Lord Whitworth on the application of M^r. Livingston on his & my part at a time when we deemed it important to know what interest that power had taken in the affair if any. Lord Whitworth's answer was as I understand frank and explicit to that effect. It therefore proves fully that the Cession of Louisiana did not proceed from any interference of G. Britain respecting it.

The proof is in other respects positive and conclusive that it was produced by the measures of our Government and that the decision to make the cession was intended to meet them in the spirit in which they were taken. It is a well established fact that before those measures were well known in France the First Consul had manifested no inclination to make the Cession. For some time after they were known his disposition to retain the territory remained unshaken, tho' it was evident he had become more conciliatory in his deportment towards our country. As late as the 10. of March he announced his resolution not even to discuss the subject in any light until after he had sent a Minister to the U.S. and received from him such information as he deemed necessary for the purpose. On the 22^d. of March he manifested his desire to retain the country to be as strong as ever, intimated that he had always considered the possession of it as furnishing him with the means of giving new proofs of his friendship for the U. States, by which he meant, as is presumed, the opening of the river to our Citizens, on more favorable terms than had yet been enjoyed by them, he absolutely refused to treat at that time, tho' he acknowledged his sensibility to the conduct of the President in the conjuncture which had produced an extraordinary mission, and declared that he would receive the Envoy with pleasure & hoped that his mission would terminate to the satisfaction of both powers. The decision to make the cession was taken on the 10th. of April after the arrival of that Envoy at Hâvre (which was on the 8th.) was known at Paris, and with a view to lay the foundation for the negotiation which was so soon to commence. For the proof of these facts I refer you to the official notes of M^r. Tallyrand to M^r. Livingston of the 10th. and 22nd. of March, which I presume are in your possession, and to such other information as you have heretofore received of the latter. The demonstration which they furnish of what I have above stated, is too strong to be resisted by any one whose mind is not sealed by prejudice against the clearest result. Had the disposition of the first Consul to make the cession been produced by any but the measures of our government and country taken together, but more especially by the firm & dignified yet conciliatory conduct of the President, he would not have postponed the discussion of the subject till he was apprized of those measures, nor would he, after he knew of them, have delayed the avowal of his disposition to the period that he did, or have assigned the motive which he gave in the letter of March 22^d. for the delay.

It was impossible, had we possessed the requisite power, after our negotiation commenced to have opened any communication with this government without great hazard to our interest & credit, while it was impossible to derive any advantage from it. A proposition to Britain for her agency in the affair, could not have been expected to succeed without our paying some equivalent for it, which must have been by making common cause with her in her own controversy and perhaps also by giving her some portion of the territory or rights in the navigation of the river. Had we stipulated either of these considerations we should most probably have been carried into the war with her, the result of which is very uncertain. By making any stipulation in favor of G. Britain we should have tied up our hands in the degree from doing anything for ourselves, while we bound ourselves to her fortunes. Had we made any overture for such an arrangement we hazarded its being made known, with a view to her own interest, to the government of France, with whom it could not fail to have produced an ill effect in regard to ours. Perfect freedom to take such part as our interest required was the happiest situation, in which we could be placed in the negotiation, & it equally comforted with honor & policy not only to remain so in reality, but to preserve also the appearance of it, while there was a prospect of success. Had we erred in the present case our folly and disposition for intrigue must have been extreme, since from the commencement there was great probability of success, which continued to increase till the object was accomplished.

It cannot be doubted that there were a variety of causes, which contributed to produce a change, in the mind of the first Consul relative to Louisiana, & to facilitate the cession which I flatter myself our government has been fortunate in obtaining. Among these may be calculated the failure of the Expedition to S^t. Domingo, the pressure of the crisis in Europe &c. There are occasions which it is fair and honorable for every government to take advantage of & which none fail to do, when those at their head have discernment enough to see them. They are such as our distance from Europe, & fortunate situation in other respects, will I hope always furnish us, when they may be necessary. I affirm however, with perfect confidence in the opinion, that notwithstanding these favorable circumstances, we should not have succeeded had the amiable relations between America & France been broken, or had the President have taken an attitude of menace towards that power, or any other than precisely that which he did take.

I have been happy to take advantage of M^r. Sumter's services who lives in the neighborhood of London, which his friendship and disposition to be useful have induced him to render me. As he will embark in a month or six weeks for the U.S. I shall experience some embarrassment when he leaves me unless

M^r. Purviance arrives in the mean time. If he has not yet sailed I beg of you to prevail on him to do so as soon as possible.—I am with great respect & esteem your very hum^{ble}. Ser^t.

TO THE GOVERNOR OF VIRGINIA.
[JOHN PAGE]
August 12, 1803.

I hope that my friends in Virginia have given me the proof which I have so often experienced from them of indulgence for failing to write them as I wished to have done since I left Richmond. The truth is, I have been engaged in a course of laborious duty, not in the best health at times, and further restrained by the fear that my communications might be interrupted on the way. At present I have only to remind you and my other friends that I have not, and shall not, forget them, and also to transmit you a receipt[1] from the artists Houdon, at Paris, for the amount of his claim of a balance due him on account of the Statue of the late Genl Washington which I have paid him. You will recollect, or rather several of our estimable friends in the Council will, that it was decided that the artist should not loos by the depreciation of the paper in which the payment of the balance claimed was only delayed to have been correctly ascertained by Mr. Jefferson.

On my arrival in Paris, this poor man applied to me for justice, and I thought it best to pay him. It did not suit the character of the State or the transaction, that a just claim should be delayed on account of that Statue. I had the account

1. The undersigned, Commerical agent of the United States at Paris, having by desire of James Monroe, Envoy Extraordinary, &c., to the French Republic, examined the several papers exhibited by Mr. Houdon in the support of his claim against the State of Virginia for the loss by depreciation on the sum of nine thousand Livres paid him in assignats by the late Bankers of the United States, Messrs. Grande & Co., on the 29th of November, 1792, on account of the Statue of General Washington, made by him for the State of Virginia, does hereby certify that by the scale of depreciation established by law in this country, it appears that on the aforesaid 29th of November, 1792, the sum of nine thousand Livres in assignats was worth six thousand two hundred Livres specie, and that therefore that the said Houdon did sustain a loss thereon of two thousand eight hundred Livres.

In witness thereof I have hereunto signed my name and affixed my seal of office to this duplicate certificate this 10th day of June, 1803, at Paris.

        (seal)   Fulwar Skipwith.

[The receipt of M. Houdon in French, through Mr. James Monroe, at Paris on the 16th of June, 1803, of Two Thousand eight hundred Livres in full of balance found due him by Fulwar Skipwith for the execution of the Statue of General Washington, is on file.—Note by Editor of *Va. State Papers*.]

examined and settled by Mr. Skipwith, who has, I am persuaded, done ample justice to the parties. If what I have done is approved of, I have to request that you will be pleased to pay the amount to my friend, Mr. Tyler, of the Council, who will apply it as I shall desire in a letter I shall write to him in a day or two by N. York. I beg you to present my most friendly regards to the gentlemen of the Council, as also to Major Coleman and Mr. Hylton. I should impose too great a burden on you in requesting the like attention to my other friends in Richmond and elsewhere, to many of whom, I hope to be able occasionally to write. I am & c.

TO THE SECRETARY OF STATE.
LONDON, August 15, 1803

SIR,—I wrote you lately by M^r. Baring since which nothing material has occurred here, except that I was called on yesterday by Sir Stephen Cotterel & notified that I should be presented to the King on Wednesday next. After the presentation I shall give you the result.

The enclosed which I received last night from Paris by an American gentleman, containing important information, is therefore transmitted to you. I intimated to you by M^r. Baring that the power over the two millions of dollars subjected to our disposition by the act of Congress and order of the President, would also so far as depended on me, be applied to a guaranty of the stipulations of the treaty. This measure is nothing more than a faithful performance of what was promised in the course of the negotiation, & throughout the early stages of the business, or in other words, than a guaranty to the extent, in obedience to powers committed to us for the purpose of the execution of the treaty itself. I flatter myself that M^r. Livingston will concur with me in the object, since I am persuaded that he must see the importance of it in the present state of affairs. I shall give you a more correct view of this business in my next.

I consider the present moment an all important one in our history, and that much, perhaps everything, depends on what is done by our government in its several branches. If the treaty is ratified, so that the President is left free to carry it into effect, the most prompt and decisive measures appear to me to be necessary on his part. My advice is that he order the troops down immediately to take post at New Orleans. In a mild and friendly manner the Spaniards should see that he expects they will surrender the territory promptly. Perhaps they will give it up without delay or equivocation. If they do not & our government does not take an imposing attitude the favorable moment may pass & everything be lost. If the affair is whiled away by negotiation, France may assume the character of mediation between us, and a year hence a bargain be made up by compromise much to our injury. But if the President pushes the affair with decision and promptitude, the First Consul will find himself bound by honor & interest to take a part in it which must be in the present juncture in favor of the United States. He must interpose so as to compel Spain to yield & put us in possession of the territory we have bought and paid France for. Should the Spaniards delay, the incident may probably furnish another occasion for the President to give a new proof of the energy of his character, and the happy effects of his administration. I am persuaded that a tone of decision, should the occasion require it, would give great effect to the proposed negotiation with Spain for Florida & the debts, while it made immediately a very favorable impression, with the powers in this quarter. I would not hesitate on the arrival of the troops at New Orleans to consider the jurisdiction of Spain as terminated, to open the ports under the authority of the United States and exercise all the rights of sovereignty. By giving them time to remove the troops according to the treaty, or rather longer if necessary, every accommodation will be given them that they have a right to expect, & the interest and character of the United States at the present moment will permit.—I am with great respect Sir, your M^r. ob^t. Ser^t.

TO R. R. LIVINGSTON.
LONDON, August 20th, 1803.

DEAR SIR,—I have received your letter of . . . by M^r. Baring and avail myself of the earliest opportunity to answer it. I perceive that you have misconceived my powers & instructions in what concerns our transactions with France. Our instructions unite us, our commission does so, as does the act which gives us power over a certain sum of money to be applied promptly to the object of the negotiation, by the two latter instruments which would control the former, if there was a variance between them, neither of us has power to act singly, but in case of the death of the other. You will know that this construction prevailed thro' the whole of what has passed; on what principle then is it now supposed to be altered? I can conceive some reasons why if it is, the power should be considered as vested exclusively in you, not one, why exclusively in me. The truth is it remains in reference to any act to be performed under the commission precisely where it did at first, that is in both of us. Had I possessed the power exclusively, I should most certainly have exercised it by making a prompt payment to the Government of France of the sum in question in obedience to our instructions, with a view to secure more effectually a compliance with our treaties. Such prompt payment would have formed the basis of every consultation & conference with the Minister of France on the subject. It was owing to the circumstance of our power being joined to your desire to apply that money to the payment of the debts and to the pressure of other important considerations at the moment that that payment was not made. I am persuaded, had it been done then we should have avoided the anxiety which we afterwards felt, the details of which were communicated in our joint letter of June 7th. to the Secretary of State; that we should in fact place beyond all hazard the final execution of the treaties—a result of primary importance to the creditors since on it alone could we be justified in assuming the payment of their debts by our Goverm^r. which they so much desired. It was to remedy that error on an experience of its ill effects that I suggested to the Ministers Tallyrand or Marbois the idea of a guarantee to Hope & Co. so far as depended on me of the sum subjected to our disposition with a view to promote on the principle of our treaty & the contract of that company with the French Government a prompt payment of the amount by the company to the Government. I made this suggestion to those Ministers on the evening of the 7th. of June, the day on which I called to see the order of their Government to M^r. Pichon for the delivery of the ratification & surrender of the territory, a period it is true when our anxiety for the consequences was more excited. I remember on stating to you immediately afterwards what had passed there you did not hesitate to approve it, tho' you expressed some satisfaction that the offer was not accepted, as I had supposed was the case. In what I stated I spoke for myself not for you observing that our authority was joint, a fact however with which they were well acquainted otherwise. When this subject was revived afterwards in conversation with M^r. Marbois at the Consul Lebruns, & he intimated his willingness to receive the guarantee since he saw that it might be done with advantage to the completion of the transaction between the two nations, & I assured him that my disposition was the same, I nevertheless repeated the remark that our power was joint, but promised to confer with you on the subject & apprise him of the result. I did confer with you, & finding you indisposed to the object & he being out of town left the affair in that state.

I am still of opinion that the guarantee of the sum proposed is an expedient and suitable measure, & shall therefore execute it so far as my act can have that effect. All human events are subject to uncertainty. Accidents may happen which may put it out of the power of our Goverm^t. to ratify the treaties or create the stock within the terms specified. It appears to me to be proper to prevent the possibility of any discussion in such cases by increasing the disposition as well as the obligation of the French Govern^t. to execute them notwithstanding & from what I have seen of the integrity & fair dealing of the First Consul

& the Ministers in this transaction I am satisfied that the acceptance of the guarantee & payment of the money which the bankers will make in consequence of it would produce that effect. I trust that this disposition exists without it. I am persuaded it does. But this would be a fair & honorable mode of acting with them, which by binding us as well as themselves might make the result more secure, nor can I discern any solid objection to the measure, since it is not an advance of money by the United States as you insinuate, but simply a guarantee of the treaty which we have lately formed to the amount of the sum committed to our care for the purpose on which the bankers will pay the same to the French Government on the principle of their contract with it. It will not injure our citizens who are creditors of France but make the payment of their debts more secure, or at least more steady. Being deeply impressed with this view of the subject, I have annexed such an act to the instrument giving us power over the sum in question with my signature as appeared to me to be proper for the purpose, which I forward you herewith. If you approve you will sign it & not otherwise.

As the apprehension of delay in the ratification of the treaties &, the creation of the stock by our Government which might be produced by various causes, was given as the motive of the anxiety which was expressed by the First Consul after he had ratified them & this guarantee will give him the command of a considerable portion of the sum stipulated, it will I doubt not be deemed so strong a proof of the fair intentions of our Government as will satisfy him that there is no cause for such apprehension. Under such circumstances it is reasonable to expect a declaration on his part thro' M^r. Marbois addressed to us that he will take no advantage of such delays as are accidental or such as a sincere desire to execute all the stipulations of the treaties by our Government according to the principles of good faith will not prevent. I think it more than probable that our Gov^t. will perform every stipulation within the terms specified in the treaties & that such a stipulation by the First Consul, or declaration for the term is not material, would prove of no effect. As the contrary however might be the case it seems reasonable for us to expect it, especially at the present time when there are several considerations which make it desirable. I have no doubt that the First Consul will readily accede to the measure on its being suggested to him, since he will perceive that it is an act in itself just, & that will do him honor; nor have I any doubt that M^r. Marbois & M^r. Tallyrand will suggest it to him, since it is in the spirit of the whole transaction which has been fair & honorable in the highest degree.

I wish this affair, if you approve, concluded immediately that it may produce the good effect that is contemplated by it. You will of course see M^r. Marbois

& make the communications & arrangements with him that are suited to either event.

Nothing is more uncertain than whether Spain will preserve her neutrality in the present war. Her Minister is here still nor is any reason to suppose that he will not remain—too much caution cannot be observed in our communications on European occurrences to which you will attribute my not going further into the topic. Happily we are at present but little interested in them, & I hope we shall continue to be so.

I wish you to forward the Memorial respecting M^r. Beaumarchais' claim to the Secretary of State; we omitted doing it according to our promise to Genl. Dumas. I have forwarded the letters I brought over for you to our Gov^t., as I did those delivered me by M^r. Baring. I shall pay like attention to any others you may send.—I am Dear Sir with Great esteem Your very ob^t. serv^t.

TO THE SECRETARY OF STATE.
LONDON, August 31st, 1803.

SIR,—I was presented by Lord Hawkesbury to the King on Wednesday the 17 ins^t., who received me with attention. The audience, according to usage, was private, no other person being present. I endeavored in a short address which the occasion invites, is always expected & I believe made, to do justice to the amiable policy of our government to Great Britain. I informed his Majesty that I was instructed, when I should have the honor of being presented to him, to express in strong terms the desire of the President to maintain the best understanding between the two nations, & his intention to cultivate it, by a conduct the most just, fair and honorable on his part. I adverted to the motives of interest that are felt and acknowledged in favor of that policy by the United States, which I observed we presumed & hoped were however well provided for by the Constitution, becomes vain and useless if the people in general are not competent judges, in the course of the administration, of all the questions which it involves. If it was wise, manly and patriotic in us to establish a free Government, it is equally incumbent on us to attend to the necessary means of its preservation. The money thus raised, might form the commencement of a system, which under favorable auspices, especially the humane patronage of the Legislature, might be matured hereafter and extended throughout the Commonwealth. You will excuse the liberty I have taken to make this suggestion, and be assured that it will give me great and sincere pleasure to have it in my power while I remain abroad to render service to my country and my friends in this or any other mode in which they will be pleased to command me. Be so kind as to present my most friendly regards to the gentlemen at your Board, and believe me to be, dear sir, with great respect and esteem, Affectionately yours, &c.

TO THE SECRETARY OF STATE.
LONDON, December 15th, 1803.

SIR,—I have just received your circular letter of October 22d. with a copy of the President's message to the Congress at the commencement of the Session. It is with the highest satisfaction I learn that the treaty and conventions with France are ratified by the President with the advice of the Senate; that the ratifications are exchanged; and that the ceded territory will be taken possession of immediately by our troops. These events are of incalculable advantage to our country, as they secure to us the great object on which its happiness is so dependent. By taking possession of the territory the business may be considered as essentially concluded. It is impossible that we should ever be disturbed in the enjoyment of it. Spain would never be able to molest us, if she should have the inclination; nor can any other power be so disposed if it had the ability. The promptitude and decision with which the object is pursued, will I am persuaded reflect much honor on our councils, while it produces the happiest effect in our concerns with every European power. Had the President hesitated to take possession of the country, other powers might have been prompted thereby to intermeddle in the affair. Good offices might have been offered us by some to pursue the object, while she might have been encouraged by others to oppose us in it. But by taking immediate possession, all political calculation or speculation respecting either party is at an end. We want no aid of any power to secure us in it, and certainly none will be offered her to turn us out of it. Our title under our treaty with France is as good to Louisiana, as it is under our revolution and charter to any portion of the old States, and I would as soon submit to the negotiation a question relative to the one as the other.

The President's message to Congress has I think produced a good effect here. It has been published in all the papers and criticised in one only, which is enclosed. A principal ground of objection in that is, the application of the term "enlightened" to the government of France, which the writer tortures into an expression of an opinion on the merits of the controversy between these powers. The sentiment has not been adopted by any other editor, nor have I heard it expressed in conversation. All impartial persons seem aware that the phrase is applicable only to the great transaction between the two countries, to which it specially refers, and tho' a handsome, was nevertheless a fair and candid comment on the motives which governed the councils of France in the part which she acted in it. The strong manner in which it announces a resolution to observe an impartial neutrality, in the present war, and to cultivate the friendship of the parties to it, by fair and honorable means, appears to give satisfaction to all.

I have lately presented a note to this government on the impressment of our seamen, of which I send you a copy. It is founded as you will see on a report of M^r. Erving, which, being drawn on due consideration, and appearing well adapted to the object, I did not enlarge on it. I expect soon to get a satisfactory answer to it: though as it goes to an object, in detail, of great importance to them, especially at this moment, it is natural to infer that it will be referred to the Admiralty and be a subject of much deliberation in their councils. In conversations with the ministers, which were frequent before the note was presented, I had assurances that any communications I might find necessary to make them on the subject would be duly attended to. I thought it better to present a note than to rely on informal conversations alone, since, altho' by the latter mode occasional accommodations in special cases may be obtained, yet by the former only can any useful principles or regulations be established for the common interest and harmony of the two countries. You will, I am persuaded, find by the communication, that, altho' our rights and views are sufficiently explained and vindicated, yet no specific point is positively insisted on. If this government accedes to what we have a just right to claim, its conduct will be the more deserving of our esteem, since, by the mode of application, it will be the more voluntary than under a stronger pressure. By the mode nothing is conceded on our part, so that I have it in my power to take the course which you shall instruct on a view of all the circumstances which merit attention, in the present juncture of affairs.

Whether Russia or any other power will take part in the war seems to be quite uncertain. Great reliance has been placed on Russia here of late, but not on ground sufficiently satisfactory that I have seen tho' it is possible that others may be better informed on that head. All the powers on the Continent, especially those in the neighbourhood of France, were so exhausted by the late war, that I am persuaded they will not embark in it unless some very favorable occasion should invite them, or urgency in other respects make it inevitable. Much may depend on the issue of the projected invasion, whether it succeeds, fails, or is declined: and as much must depend also in either case on the circumstances attending it, it would be in vain to hazard any conjecture on events so contingent. I see no symptom which indicates any immediate change being likely to

take place in the ministry, nor is there anything more doubtful of what characters it would be composed should one take place. The respective parties at
whose head are M^r. Pitt and M^r. Fox, have opposite views. The first seems to
be friendly to a vigorous prosecution of the war, and a support of the high prerogative of the crown; the second to peace and a reform. The ministry seems to
have compromitted itself with neither as yet, while by pursuing the war it has
the support in a certain degree, of the first, and by its moderation and amiable
deportment in a degree also, of the other; so that any conjectures on this point
would likewise be equally vague. I am happy to observe that I see no reason to
suppose, that there would be any alteration in the conduct of this government
towards us under any change which might possibly take place in the ministry.
I am, Sir, with great respect & esteem &c.

TO JAMES MADISON.
LONDON, Decr. 17, 1803

DEAR SIR,—The opposition of Spain to our treaty with France, by her minister in the U States, attracts some attention here, and is the subject of speculation in certain circles as to the causes & probable effects. Some suspect France
at the bottom of it, others ascribe it to the measures of this gov^t.: but I am far
from suspecting either of any agency in the affair. I see no reason to doubt the
good faith of France in the transaction. Her interest is as strong or rather more
so, to execute as to form the treaty; her conduct seems to be direct to the object:
and the reproach which would follow a conduct so opprobrious renders it quite
improbable, especially as it would be sure to be discovered soon. It was natural
to presume that the President would take immediate possession of the country
on the exchange of ratifications, in which case France would be called on to fulfill any engagement she might have entered into with Spain to prevent it. It is
equally improbable that this gov^t. sho^d. have given Spain any encouragement of
the kind. It wo^d. be in the face of her uniform assurances to us on the subject,
and equally in opposition to her interest, since if called on to execute any
engagement in support of the pretensions of Spain, she must either fail to do it,
or by complying embark in a war against the U States & France. That co^d. not
be to her interest at present, if it ever might be. How far it may be agreeable to
either of the parties to see us & Spain engaged in a quarrel separately I cannot
say. Be that as it may, I do not think that either wo^d. promote it, or that if they
did that the council of either would be much regarded by Spain, where it was
not to be supported by other more efficient aid.

TO WILSON CARY NICHOLAS.
LONDON, Jany 22, 1804.

DEAR SIR,—Accept my acknowledgment for the communication contained in yours on a publick subject, to which I am happy to give the following explanation: The sum which the first consul had resolved to ask for Louisiana was 100 millions of livres, clear of the debt to our citizens w^h. we were to pay. He agreed to reduce it, under the deliberations of his council to 80. including the debt which was estimated at 20. The latter was the proposition made to us in the first formal interview which we had with Mr. Marbois; not as a thing decided on, but one to which it was thought that the first consul would accede, if we were willing to give it. The expectation, however, was that we should pay the whole in one year in Paris by equal monthly instalments. He finally agreed to take stock instead of cash, as you have seen by the treaties, on a belief that by possessing the stock he could command, at a moderate sacrifice, the whole sum at once. He seemed to have fixed his mind to 80. millions of livres, including the debt as the least sum that he would take from us, and I had good reason to believe that he would not have assented to a diminution of it, under any accommodation in payment which it was in our power to propose. Indeed I was inclined to think that we should hazard much by sending any such proposition to him. We requested Mr. Marbois to offer him 70. millions, to which he replied that by our desire he would do so, but that in his opinion it would most certainly be rejected, and probably hazard more than we were aware of. There is something in all transactions to be taken from the spirit which is manifested by those with whom you treat, which merits the attention of those to whom the opposite interest is intrusted. From what had occurred in this, I did not hesitate a moment longer to abandon the idea of attempting any diminution of the sum below 80. millions; I^st. because I considered the terms as very advantageous to our country and the object too important to be hazarded by attempts not likely to succeed to obtain better. 2^d. because I had reason to think that M^r. Marbois had already compromitted himself with his government in laboring to reduce them to that sum. 3^d. because we were pressed for time, the rupture with England menacing to take place daily & it being important that we sho^d. close before that event. Had it been practicable to reduce the sum on an engagement to pay specie instead of stock, there were difficulties attending it of a serious nature. The sum to be paid must have been regulated by the supposed value of eighty millions of livres, or rather 60. the am^t. which was to be paid directly to France. It would have been dishonorable to have fixed it at a price, by depreciating our credit, by which we were to make a profit & likely also to do us more harm than that profit would compensate. We had not the money in the treasury and must have raised it, by the creation & sale of stock, in America or Europe. Such a map thrown on the market in the U States was likely to sink the price, and the remittance of the amount by bills, to expose our government to a loss by its effect on the exchange, while it did a great and general injury to our commercial interest. Had the stock been exposed to sale in Europe the price must also have fall'n, for it was reasonable to expect a combination among the great bankers or many of them, to depreciate it, with a view to make better bargains. After the war which was to be expected, it was not [an] advisable thing for our gov^t. to be engaged in the sale of stock here, the proceeds whereof were to be remitted to France. It was likely to expose us to the jealousy & resentment of this gov^t., perhaps its interference to prevent the operation; the apprehension of which, compelled as we should have been, to raise money to make punctual payments in France, would have created a dependence of our gov^t. on this which would not have comported with its character or the publick interest. A failure to place the money punctually in France might have endangered the treaties; especially if her gov^t. sho^d. be disposed to get rid of them. But by creating stock, and paying the debt by a transfer of it to France all these inconveniences are avoided. We fulfil the stipulations of the treaty without wounding or exposing to injury an essential interest of our country; without being under the necessity of asking or receiving favors of either power or any way responsible for the place or price at which the stock is sold. Our relations & duties in that respect cease to be foreign; they become entirely domestic; all that we have to do is to provide for the payment of the interest annually, and the principal at the end of 15 years, which will I trust be no difficult thing.

The provision and arrangement for the payment of the debt due our citizens, I hoped would be well received. Being all that was made payable in cash, it seemed probable that the amount would create no embarrassment in the treasury; as there was a considerable portion of the money in hand & the balance likely to come in, before the debts could be liquidated & the payment called for. Should that however not be the case, it might even be better to borrow of one of our banks the deficiency, reimbursible at pleasure, than create stock to be redeemed at the end of several years. It was important to prevent debts being imposed on us, not American, and prevent the payment of any money till the territory was surrendered to our gov^t., which were provided for.

The principle which I understood was adopted in the contract between the gov^t. of France & the bankers to whom the stock was sold, in fixing the price, was by reference to the then current price at this market, supposing they had been imployed for that purpose, & something as an indemnity against the probable depreciation, which such an increase of our debt might possibly create. Before the French gov^r. concluded a bargain with the purchasers, I have reason to believe that propositions were invited from all the bankers at Paris, and that none offered as much for the stock, while the prospect of complyance with any contract they might make was much more uncertain. It was understood that these latter, in general, calculated on raising the money to enable them to fulfill their engagements, had they entered into any by sales of the stock to others; an operation which might have sunk its credit, injured France, & ruined the bankers. From the immense capital of the houses who bought the stock it was anticipated, that no such forced sales would be necessary, or consequences to be dreaded. It is to that immense capital I presume it is owing that the houses will make a considerable profit by the bargain.

It gives me pleasure to assure you that I am perfectly satisfied that the individuals concerned in the transaction on the part of France did not make one cent by it. From motives of delicacy we did not even pay M^r. Marbois's clerk who copied the instrument several times, in consequence of the amendments they rec^d., anything for the service. In important transactions of confidence between individuals he would probably have rec^d. two hundred guineas for the same service. Nor do I believe that one cent was made by them in the sale of the stock to the purchasers. M^r. Marbois's conduct through the whole was open, delicate, and honorable, evincing feelings & an elevation of mind which plac'd him far above the suspicion of the influence of any corrupt or sordid motive. He is in my opinion one of those who would rather eat the bread of poverty, with an approving conscience, than enjoy the most unbounded wealth exposed to its censure.

I have so far endeavored to answer such objections of my friends as I have heard of, because they are reasonable and proceed from honest motives. . . .

With great respect & esteem I am dear Sir very sincerely yours.

TO BARBÉ MARBOIS
LONDON, Feby 14th, 1804.

DEAR SIR,—My last letter from the Secretary of State of Decr. 26th. mentions that Louisiana was surrendered to the perfect of France the latter end of Novr. who was to transfer it to the com^{rs}. of the U States on their arrival at N. Orleans wch. was expected in a day or two from that date. M^r. Madison adds that he considers all difficulties on that subject as happily terminated. M^r. B. is expected here daily with every thing belonging to a complete execution of this transaction. In the meantime I am persuaded that the house in Holland will consider it as concluded and act accordingly. It gives me pleasure to observe that the prompt & unconditional exchange of ratifications by y^r. chargé des aff^{rs}. at Washington, & his correct conduct in promoting the transfer of the territory to the U States, in obedience to the orders of his gov^t. are unequivocal proofs of the good faith with which the treaties were formed. The manner in wch. the President expressed himself in his message to Congress of the enlarged liberal & friendly policy wch. gov^d. the first Consul in the transaction shews in strong terms the sense wch. he entertains of it. May it seal forever the friendship of the two nations. To have been in any degree instrumental to that important result, is one of the circumstances of my life wch. will always give me the highest satisfaction. In society with my respectable colleague, to have met an old friend on the occasion who had experienc'd as well as myself some vicissitudes in the extry. movements of the epoch, in wch. we live is an incident wch. adds not a little to the gratification which I derive from the event.

TO M. TALLEYRAND.
PARIS, November 8—1804.

SIR,—Before the conclusion of the late treaty between the U States & France, your Excellency will recollect that it was an object of the President, to acquire of Spain by amicable arrangement, Florida, it being a portion of her territory which she held Eastward of the Mississippi. It was also his object after the conclusion of that treaty, not that it was pressed by such imperious considerations as before, but that it would contribute to remove all cause of uneasiness & jealousy between the two powers, they might adopt & harmonize in future, in such a system of policy as might secure to them peace, and give additional protection to their possessions in that quarter especially to those of Spain. In the conferences which produc'd the treaty above mentioned, the good offices of his Imperial Majesty were engaged to the U States in any negotiation which the President might commence with the Catholick king for the acquisition of Florida. The same assurance was renewed after the conclusion of the treaty, tho' it was intimated that that was not a suitable time for the commenc'ment of such a negotiation. It was on that intimation, as your Excellency will also recollect, at a moment when I was about to set out for Spain in pursuit of the object, (the then recent orders of the President permitting it) that I postponed my journey thither, and took a different position. The proposed negotiation with Spain was in consequence, and has since remained suspended, and it is in obedience to late orders from my government that I am now so far on my way to Madrid on that subject and that M^r. Livingston has requested the good offices of the Emperor in support of it. It is proper here to remark that since the epoch referred to, the treaty then just concluded between the U States & France, has been carried into effect in its great points with that scrupulous attention to good faith which does to both parties the highest honor. Their conduct in that transaction gives to each a pledge for the integrity which is to prevail in their future intercourse. I may be permitted to add that as I declined my visit to Spain at that epoch the more readily, to give an opportunity for the complete execution of that treaty, so now that it is carried into effect, I undertake it with the greater pleasure, since it confirms me in the confidence before mentioned, of the support which wo^d. be given in it by his Imperial Majesty.

The President has been induc'd to adopt this measure at this time by considerations the most urgent. As these are inseparably connected with the proposed negotiation, indeed form in part the object of it, it is due to the friendship subsisting between our governments, and to the candour which the President will never fail to observe in his transactions with the Emperor, to give you a distinct idea of them. They will I doubt not satisfy you that the President has heretofore shewn a sincere desire to cultivate the friendship of the Catholick king, and that the attempt which he now makes to preserve that relation is a new and signal proof of that disposition.

Since the treaty between the U States and France whereby Louisiana was ceded to the former, a question has arisen between those States & Spain relative to the boundaries of the ceded territory. It is understood that the government of Spain entertains an idea that that cession comprizes only that portion of Louisiana which was ceded to it by France in 1762; that it does not comprize the portion also which was ceded by her at the same time to G. Britain, distinguished while in her possession by the name of W. Florida. This pretention of the court of Spain cannot, it is presumed, be supported by even the colour of an argument. Had that been the intention of the parties in the treaty of S^t. Ildephonso it would have been easy to have provided for it. The idea was a simple one which a few plain words would have expressed. But the language of the article referr'd to conveys a very different sentiment. We find in it nothing which countenances a presumption that the Emperor meant to retake from Spain only a portion of Louisiana; or to refer to it in a dismembered state. It was natural to suppose, in accepting a retrocession of that province from a power possessed of the whole, that he would take it entire, such as it was when France possessed it. Accordingly we find that the terms of the article making the cession are as full and explicit to that object, as it was possible to use. It is not stipulated that Spain sho^d. cede to France that portion of Louisiana only which she had rec^d. from France; or that W. Florida should be excepted from the cession. It is on the contrary stipulated that she shall cede it "such as it was when France possessed it," that is such as it was before it was dismembered by the cessions afterwards made to Spain & G. Britain. That she sho^d. cede it "with the same extent which it became by the treaty of 1783 whereby W. Florida was ceded by G. Britain to Spain": "such as it is according to subsequent treaties between Spain & other powers," a stipulation which does honor to his Catholick Majesty since it proves that in making the cession to France he intended to cede only what he had a right to cede; that he recollected the treaty which he had concluded with the U States in 1795; knew the extent of its obligations and was resolved to execute them with good faith. Your Excellency will receive within a paper containing an examination of the boundaries of Louisiana which it is presumed proves incontestably the doctrine above advanc'd, as also that the river Perdido is the antient and of course present boundary of that province to the East and the Rio Bravo to the West.

The U States have other causes of complaint against Spain of a serious import. In the course of the last war many aggressions were committed under the authority of the government of Spain but as is presumed without its sanction on the commerce of the U States. Her ships of war and privateers took many of their vessels in Europe & America carried them into her ports, detained & condemned them under pretexts which cannot be justified. The injury sustained by this proceeding was great and extensive, for which it is the duty of the President to obtain for the sufferers an adequate reparation. A convention was entered into at Madrid about two years since between the two powers which provided a partial remedy for the injuries. The greater object however was left open for future arrangement. It was owing to that consideration and to a knowledge that the principal cause of variance was unprovided for, that the negotiation was in truth unfinished, that neither government took any interest in ratifying or executing that convention. The whole subject therefore now lies open for discussion, and it is very much desir'd to conclude it on such fair principles, as may be satisfactory to his Catholick Majesty, while it enables the President to vindicate the character of his administration, in obtaining for American claimants the justice to which they are entitled.

The occlusion of the river Mississippi about two years past contrary not only to the spirit but the express stipulations of the treaty of 1795 between the U States & Spain was an act which exposed to essential injury the interest of the western Inhabitants of those States, while it could not be considered otherwise than as an high indignity to their government. His Catholick Majesty did not hesitate to disavow the act when complained of by the American Minister at Madrid. This disavowal made some attonement to the violated honor of the government, but no reparation for the injury which had been sustained by individuals. A reasonable but adequate reparation is still due on that acc^t. and it is expected that his Catholick Majesty will see the justice and propriety of making it.

These circumstances have produced an interesting crisis in the political relation of the U States and Spain which it is the sincere desire of the President to remove by fair and amicable arrangement. If the negotiation which is about to be commenc'd by his order, does not terminate in that result, it will be owing altogether to the gov^t. of Spain. The measure which is now adopted, the negotiation which is invited is a convincing proof of the sincerity and good faith with which the President seeks to preserve the relations of friendship between the two powers. In the pursuit of its objects no unreasonable pretention is entertained, no unjust demand will be made. On the subject of boundaries, altho the Congress on a thorough conviction of its rights authorises the taking immediate possession of Louisiana according to its antient limits, and of course to the river Perdido to the East, yet the President from motives of respect to the Catholick King, postponed the execution of the measure to give time for amicable explanations with his government, in full confidence that they will produce their desir'd effect. In respect to aggressions on our commerce, and other injuries, it cannot be doubted that a suitable indemnity will be made for them. The cession of Florida is a question which rests on different ground. The policy of that measure and the conditions of it, in case the policy is admitted are points to be decided by each gov^t. for itself, from a view of its interest and other circumstances. Should the cession be made and the other points be adjusted there is no reason why the peace and friendship of the two nations should not be perpetual. There would remain no cause of jealousy between them; no points of collision. Possessed of ample territory to satisfy their growing population for ages to come, the States would be left at liberty to pursue their interior arrangements without apprehending the interference, or having the disposition to interfere with their neighbours. Such a system of policy on their part would contribute in a very eminent degree to the security of the vast dominions of Spain to the south of us. To Spain it is presumed that the territory is of but little importance. In itself it is of none as it is a barren tract. If she retains it, it must be as a post for troops to be plac'd there in opposition to us; a measure which tends to provoke hostility & lead to war. The Havanna is a post which answers more effectually every object which she could contemplate from this, while it is free from all the objections that are applicable to the latter. Being an Island it is less assailable by a foreign power; situated in the gulph of Mexico it furnishes the means of giving all the protection to her other possessions that she could desire; and by uniting her whole force at one point encreases her means of defence against attack as of annoying her enemies in time of war. It is earnestly hoped that the Catholick King will take a dispassionate view of these circumstances and of the relative situation of the two powers and meet the President in a suitable provision for their future friendship. Should he however be disposed to pursue a different policy, on him will the responsibility rest for the consequences.

The relation which has subsisted invariably between his Imperial Majesty & the government which I have the honor to represent, has been of the most friendly character. If it is on the knowledge of that fact and the satisfactory evidence which it furnishes that the Emperor takes an interest in the welfare of the U States; it is on the promise above adverted to, made on his part to support with his good offices any negotiation which the President might commence with the court of Spain for the acquisition of Florida, as also on the firm belief that the attainment of that object, with the amicable adjustment of all subsisting differences between the U States and Spain, must be advantageous to France, that his good offices have been and are now requested in support of that negotiation.

My mission to Spain being extraordinary is also temporary. As soon as its objects are accomplished it is my duty to return to London, which I shall do thro this metropolis, where I hope to have the honor & pleasure of being presented again to his Imperial Majesty & of acknowledging in person his friendly aid to my government and country in a transaction of high importance to its interest, which the President has thought fit to commit in part to my agency. I beg your Excellency to accept the assurances of my high consideration.

TO ROBERT R. LIVINGSTON.
PLACE VENDOME, 13 Nov^r, 1804.

DEAR SIR,—I received your letter yesterday with one to M^r. Tallyrand, in support of mine to him, on the subject of the proposed negociation with Spain, for Florida. Your letter to him is quite satisfactory to me, indeed such an one as

I wished you to write him. It appears to me to be very proper for you to remind him of his assurances renewed to you to support that negociation; and that you have done it in unexceptionable terms.

I sent the communication to M. Tallyrand this morning, being fully satisfied of the propriety of the measure. As you had communicated to me on my first arrival very fully everything that had passed between you and this Government on the subject, I thought myself as completely possessed of it as it was possible to make me, especially as it was one with which I was in other respects acquainted. As we were together every day, conferred freely on it, were to move in concert, I meant to do nothing without consulting you. I really thought that to read the details was more a matter of form than anything else. Nevertheless I always meant to read them, and to request of you copies of the several papers, before I set out for Spain, where recurrence to you being impossible, they may be useful and perhaps indispensible. The circumstance of my having repeated in my letter to M. Tallyrand what you have already urged is no objection to it. It only shews that we think alike on the same subject & adopt the same means to promote it. On the policy of the measure itself, I have so often and fully expressed my ideas to you, that I will not trouble you with a lengthy repetition of them, I will only observe that in consideration of the engagement of this government to support our negociation with Spain, for the acquisition of Florida, of the moral obligation it is under to support our claim to boundaries, in their just extent, of the inseparable connection which a negociation for those objects has with the others which claim our attention, of the influence which France may have in the negociation & probably will have, of the change of opinion which you have reason to think has taken place here, and of the crisis to which our affairs with Spain have gone, it would have been highly improper for me to have proceeded to Spain without the subject having been brought in the extent it has been before this government. I am decidedly of opinion that the step taken in the present state of affairs is the strongest proof that we can give of the candor of our government and of its sincere desire to perpetuate the friendship subsisting between the United States and France. By possessing her government with a just view of our claims, & the danger of the crisis existing, we enable it freely to take that part, which its honor and interest may dictate, which might be more difficult in any stage of the business. If the Emperor is disposed to assist us in the negociation, in which I repose much confidence, I hope and think that the communication made will tend to confirm him in that disposition. In any event, it may enable us to say something with certainty to our government on that point, and it to decide on a full view of all circumstances at the present time, the course which it is most consistent with the public honor and interest for it to take. Whether my judgment is correct in these respects I will not pretend to say. I am happy however in knowing that altho' we differ in the mode to be pursued at this moment, we are united in the objects, and that the step being taken, I shall have all the aid which you may be able to give to insure success to the negociation.

TO THE SECRETARY OF STATE.[2]
BORDEAUX, December 16, 1804.

SIR,—I arrived here last night in seven days from Paris which I left on the 8th. It is necessary to write forward two days to Bayonne to make arrangements for the mules which are to take me to Madrid. The intermediate country or the greater part of it is said to be almost a desert. There are but few taverns on the route and those furnish neither beds, provisions or other accommodations than that of shelter; in addition to which there is danger of being attacked by robbers, especially to publick characters who travel slowly without a guard, of which an example lately occurred in the case of the Ambassador of Portugal who was attacked and plundered of everything he had with him. Hence it becomes necessary to adopt precautions against all these evils. With a relay of mules the journey may be made, without halting as I presume a moment, in five or six days. With the same set it requires 12 or 15. I have requested M[r]. Lee in harmony with an acquaintance of his here, a respectable merchant to whom I was addressed from Paris, to write to Bayonne to have the necessary arrangement made for my immediate departure on my arrival there for Madrid, to proceed with the greatest dispatch, under an injunction however to dispense with the relay, in case on a comparison of the difference in the time incident to each mode, it appeared to be less an object than I had understood it was. This gives me two days at this place and the opportunity of communicating what it is material to add to my letter of the 27th. ult[o].[3]

On the day of my arrival at Paris M[r]. Livingston informed me, after having stated what had occurred respecting the disposition of the French government on the points depending between us and Spain, that he had a plan for the adjustment of our differences with Spain which he thought would be effectual and we might adopt with advantage. His project was that Spain should put us in possession of the disputed territory and that we should create a stock of about sev-

---

2. *From Letter-book, Library of Congress.* [HAMILTON.]
3. *Monroe's Letter-book, New York Public Library.* [HAMILTON.]

enty millions of livres which should be transferred to Spain of which ten millions should be reimbursible annually, and that provision should be made for
settling amicably in the interim the question of boundaries between the two
countries. He informed me that he had communicated his plan to you for the
consideration of the President. I observed that I was persuaded that the adoption of such a plan could not fail to terminate in our paying twice for the same
thing, since it was not presumable that we should ever get back any of the
money which might thus be advanced, or that the boundary would be settled
otherwise than it now is without our sacrificing the stock thus transferred; that
his plan was further objectionable as it did not secure us East-Florida, the only
point which we admitted to be in question, or the payment of the sums due to
our citizens. He replied, on the contrary, that by his plan we should get the
country without paying a farthing for it, as the reimbursement might be secured
by drafts on Mexico, and that East-Florida might be comprized in it and likewise put in our possession. I have since understood of Gen[l]. Armstrong, that
such a disposition of East-Florida formed a part of the plan, and it is proper to
observe that I understood of M[r]. Livingston that the transfer of the stock to
Spain was to be considered in the light of a loan. As however the project has
been communicated to you, it is unnecessary to go further into that subject than
to state the light in which it appeared to me by his own representation. As it
was obviously incompatible with your instructions to me, and with every idea
which I entertained of our rights and interests in the points to which it referred,
after stating the objections above mentioned in as delicate terms as I could, tho'
distinctly, I declined a further discussion of the project from a sensibility to his
own feelings, which I was fearful I might hurt by pushing it further. I asked him
to be so good as to present me to the government which he promised and complied with. When he presented me to M. Tallyrand he said nothing of my being
on my way to Spain, or of the motive which brought me to Paris: he observed
the same conduct when he presented me to the Emperor. I could not help
observing the circumstance in the first instance; however when I recollected
that he had before informed me that he had apprized M. Tallyrand of my arrival
in Holland, my destination, &c., I considered it as a casual omission to which I
attached no consequence, and perhaps it merits to be viewed in that light. He
obligingly asked an audience of the Arch-Chancellor Cambaceres and Arch-
Treasurer Le Brun to which he accompanied me as he had done in a visit to
M. Marbois and in two afternoon visits to M. Tallyrand in neither of which did
we find him at home. When I was presented to M. Tallyrand, he received me
with great kindness, and told me that he should be glad to see me often, with

other expressions of the same kind. After some few remarks relative to the time of my departure from England, my journey, &c. he asked me if I would stay some time in Paris? I replied that I should, but that I was on my way to Madrid, he paused and seeming to collect himself added, "Aye, I understand you. You will have much difficulty to succeed there."

I observed, that, I hoped not, with the aid of his good offices. He smiled, but made no reply passing on to others. The other gentlemen above mentioned treated me with the friendly regard they had always done.

After these forms were gone through I asked M^r. Livingston if he could do any thing more to forward the business which had brought me to Paris, to which he replied "that he could not." I then asked if he had any objection to my entering into communication with the Ministers of the government and doing everything in my power to forward it? He said that he had none, on the contrary he thought it was very proper that I should do so. On very mature reflection I resolved to take the course which is detailed to you in my letter of the 27th. and accordingly immediately set to work to prepare the paper which accompanies it. I was the more prompted to this from what escaped M. Marbois in a conversation three days after my arrival in Paris, in which I communicated very fully the object of my visit to Spain, of passing thro' Paris on the route and of the expectation which I entertained of aid from his government. He observed, that such was the situation of Spain at this time, that if we would make her suitable pecuniary accommodations we might succeed. I availed myself of the occasion which the remark furnished to shew the impossibility of such accommodations being made, while it was admitted that we treated on a footing of equality, and paid any regards to the rights and interests of our fellow-citizens. He observed that our claims were unsettled, and that it was a very important object to the U. States to extinguish the right of Spain to any territory within our limits: I had by accident unfortunately left with M^r. Purviance my copy of the paper entitled "an examination into the boundaries of Louisiana": M^r. Livingston had committed his copy of the same document to M. Marbois, with a view to promote its doctrines some time before my arrival, to whom he had referred me for it. On delivering me the paper M. Marbois observed, that in my communication with M. Tallyrand which I had intimated I intended to have, it would be proper to have my note prepared, and after conversing freely with him on the subject to deliver it in person, asking of him at the same time another interview. In conversation with M. Hauterive at M. Tallyrand's some days after this, on the same subject, he expressed to me the same sentiment that M. Marbois had done, as the principle on which our differences with Spain must be adjusted. He observed that both parties must make sacrifices; that Spain must cede territory, and that the U. States must pay money. I made the same objections to this remark that I made to M. Marbois', tho' less in detail as the opportunity was less favorable. From all these circumstances I was the more confirmed in the opinion that a paper containing a general view of our differences with Spain, should be presented to the French government, which should in the clearest manner possible prove, that in no event could any money be paid to Spain in consideration of the proposed adjustment.

M^r. Livingston happening to call on me soon after I commenced the paper which I contemplated to present to M. Tallyrand, I shewed him what I had written and asked him what he thought of the plan, of which what he saw might enable him to form some opinion. He noticed that part which respected the debts due by Spain to our citizens and seemed to think that it was improper for me to advert to it in a communication with the French government. I told him that my motive was to preclude the idea of our paying to Spain any money by virtue of the proposed treaty. He said no more from which I concluded that he saw the propriety of the measure. Two days afterwards he called and asked if I had received any new instructions from you relative to our differences with Spain. I replied that I had not of a late date. He said that he meant more especially the part to be taken with the French government. I gave the same answer. He then observed that it was in his opinion improper for me to hold any direct communication with the French government: that none ought to be made but by himself or his successor, in his name and of course such as he approved. He hinted that such an interference had the appearance of an intrigue, tended to undermine the minister, and as we might think differently on the subject, might embarrass him in his course with this government in promoting an adjustment with Spain, especially if the contents of the communication were not known to him. These remarks were so singular and unexpected that they utterly astonished me. They led us into a conversation of some length and earnestness, the substance of which is as follows. He further observed that as I was a mere passenger not accredited to the French government, he doubted whether the minister would answer my note: that the object which I sought had been already obtained of it, by instructions to Genl. Bournonville,[4] and that my application might produce a revocation of those instructions and draw a decisive answer from the government against our pretentions and thereby do essential mischief: that he had told me on my first arrival what had passed between him and this

---

4. *Pierre de Ruel Beurnonville, French Ambassador at Madrid.* [HAMILTON.]

government on the subject, and offered to shew me the correspondence which
I had declined reading. To these objections, after expressing my surprize, I
replied that till then I had supposed that we were acting together; and that the
course I was pursuing had had his entire approbation; he had informed me on
my arrival that he had apprized M. Tallyrand of my being on the route, my destination and the object of it; had presented me to the government, declined acting farther, as he said, on the occasion, on account of the arrival of his successor
at the port, and expressly sanctioned the measure I was about to take, which
seemed to be the more necessary as Genl. Armstrong had not when I commenced the paper arrived, was not then received and might not be for some
time: that I did not think that my agency merited to be viewed in the light in
which he seemed to place it; that I was not interfering in concerns with which
I had nothing to do, and undermining the minister to whom it belonged; that
I had been formerly accredited to the French government on this very subject,
had had communications with it on it, and had left the affair in such a state,
when I took my leave of the First Consul & went to England, with him, and all
the chief officers of the government, as excited the expectation that I would
renew them on my return; that as I was a minister of our government proceeding thro' Paris with its approbation and for the express purpose of doing
everything in my power to promote the object of the mission to Spain, I did
think that I had a right to communicate with the French government in the
manner I proposed, nor could I suppose that my note would remain unanswered; that it was not likely I should take a view of the subject, different
from his, as I acted under instructions which I should obey strictly; it would be
strange indeed if I who was charged (in association with M^r. Pinckney) with the
business, by our government, who possessed all its views on the subject, should
embarras the minister there whose duty it was only to obtain the aid of the
French government in support of the negotiation: that I could not imagine what
had suggested the idea of secrecy on my part in respect to him, since no act of
mine justified it; I had already shown him what I was about when I had drawn
only a few paragraphs of the paper, which proved not only that I withheld nothing from him, but that I meant to consult him on what I did: that the object
which I sought was not obtained, since from what he told me of the actual disposition of the French government, it was manifest that without new instructions to Genl. Bournonville I could not rely on his aid; that the former were
probably revoked, but if they were not, it could not be doubted that they would
be as soon as I proceeded on to Madrid, unless some new impression was made
on his government to prevent it; that so far from considering the object as being

obtained, by the instructions which were given to Gen[l]. Bournonville a year past, I sincerely regretted that any application had ever been made to his government for them until the negotiation was about to commence, as by frequently calling its attention to the subject out of season, the idea of its importance was likely to be magnified and thereby essential injury done: that by our commission and instructions neither M[r]. Pinckney or myself could commence the negotiation in the absence of the other except in case of his death: that I had always intended to read his correspondence with this government on the subject, and had declined it on the night of my arrival only because I was fatigued and there was company present. This is I think a correct view of what passed between us. In adverting to it some days afterwards, he seemed to have taken some of my remarks, in a light different from what I had intended to place them; for example that I was better acquainted with the subject than himself, and would be concerned in no negotiation I did not controul. I very well remember that the idea which I meant to convey was, that I was better acquainted with my instructions than he could be; unless a copy had been sent to him, which I did not suppose was the case, since there could be no object for it, and the multiplication of such documents was always to be avoided when possible, and that I ought to be the judge how far an insight into my instructions, on the general object of the proposed negotiation with Spain, should be opened to the French government, and that I had a right to expect of the minister there an accommodation with my wishes in that respect. You will observe that by the nature of the subject it is not likely that I could have been drawn by any degree of provocation, into the expression of a different sentiment, was my character in other respects open to the imputation belonging to that attributed to me. It was not the great question of Louisiana, its boundaries &c. that we were discussing. On these points there did not occur between us any difference of opinion, and with regard to any negotiation none was to be carried on with the French government. The object simply was to gain the aid of France in support of a negotiation with Spain. He said also that by my doctrine which precluded his agency in it, till I left England, it was improper for him to oppose the measures of the Admiral Gravina; I reminded him that in our conversation that circumstance had been noticed by him and that in my reply I had expressed a different sentiment; that I had made a distinction between his being prepared at all times and taking suitable measures when necessary to prevent mischief, and interfering in the manner he had done out of season to ask the aid of the French government in support of a negotiation which did not exist. I told him that had I not been advised by him that the French government had intimated its willingness to assist our negotiations with

Spain, before I left England I should have remained there till I did receive such information: that under such circumstances I should have written him as soon as I received your instructions to enter on that business, to request him to communicate the same to that government, and ask its aid as has been promised us; that except to prevent mischief, that was the time to ask it, and not sooner. I might mention other things, which he said, tending to irritate, if it was proper to enter further into the subject in that view. These however I pretermit, as I wish only to give you a correct idea of the occurrence, not to recite the remarks which perhaps were made in the warmth of discussion and regretted afterwards. One circumstance however it is proper to mention, because it is connected with the present topick, somewhat in character with it, tho' it happened on a former occasion. In the course of the conversation he reminded me of a difference which took place between us last year on a question to which the Chevalier d'Azara was in some respects a party, the substance of which he said he had communicated to you. I told him that I had never mentioned that incident to you from motives of delicacy to him and was surprized that he had done so. He intimated that he did not know what I had done in that respect and had thought it proper (as he never withheld anything from his government) to communicate what had occurred; that he had however done it in a manner that would be satisfactory to me. The circumstances of that incident are as follows. After we had concluded the treaty with France and been promised and were in daily expectation of receiving the ratification of the French government, I had decided as you know to proceed to Spain, of which I had apprized the minister of foreign affairs. M^r. Livingston had urged the propriety of my so doing, and pressed my departure. At that moment I was advised by the Consul Cambaceres not to go, with an assurance that that was not a favorable time, an advice which was given afterwards by the Consul Le Brun and others, and finally confirmed by the First Consul himself. When the first intimation was given to that effect by the Consul Cambaceres he referred me to M^r. Marbois for more precise details. I went immediately to M^r. Marbois's but not finding him at home thought proper to call on M. d'Azara, in the hope of getting some information from him on the subject. I had apprized him that I had intended to go to Spain, the object of the visit, and been promised letters by him. As soon as I mentioned the subject to M. d'Azara, he told me that he had written to his court a few days before by an extraordinary courier, at the request of M^r. Livingston, to propose to it, to cede Florida to the United States, and to submit to it the propriety of treating for it at Paris. I asked when he expected an answer to his proposition? He said if it was sent by an extraordinary courier it would be in 20—days from the time his left

Paris, but if by the post, a much longer time. Of this step M^r. Livingston had given me no information, and it was by accident that I discovered it, to my utter astonishment, as he was actually pressing me at the time to set out for Madrid, in obedience to my instructions, to commence a negotiation there, even against the advice which I had received from the second and third Consuls as above mentioned. I saw M^r. Livingston the day after I had received this information from M. d'Azara, for the incident was so extraordinary and unexpected to me that I declined calling on him in the evening, when he asked me again, when I should set out to Madrid. I replied that a new difficulty had occurred in the business & then recounted to him the above. He spoke of it as a mere casual conversation with the Chev^r. d'Azara. I observed, that it appeared that the Chev^r. had viewed it in a very different light, by having submitted it to his court by an extraordinary courier: that under such circumstances it would be very absurd for me to proceed to Spain, at a time when a power to treat on the subject which carried me there, might be so soon expected at Paris. I reminded him that if the power had arrived, even while I was there, no negotiation could be commenced by us, as it was entrusted to M^r. Pinckney and me; much less could be carried on by him alone in the absence of M^r. P. and myself. We went together by accord to the Chev^r. d'Azara, when he requested the Chev^r. to announce to his government that I was about to proceed to Madrid for the purpose &c. and to consider what he had said as of no consequence. I never mentioned this subject to you for the reason above suggested, and the more especially as by the manner in which it terminated, there seemed to be no necessity for it. At that time and since M^r. Livingston has spoken of the subject in different lights. At one time he has represented it as a casual and jocular occurrence between him and the Spanish Ambassador, which meant nothing. At another, as having been an eligible expedient which would most probably have succeeded, had it been pursued. If it is to be considered in the manner first mentioned, no harm could be done by putting an end to it. On the contrary some good might be, as important concerns ought not to be trifled with. If it is to be viewed otherwise, the proceeding is open to the severest criticism, in respect to his conduct in it, while the demonstration is complete that no harm was done by putting an end to it. Without relying on the important fact that he had no power to treat, it was sufficiently evident by subsequent events, that no negotiation carried on at Paris or Madrid could have succeeded. Before we parted I renewed to M^r. Livingston the assurance that as I had never contemplated taking any step in the business on which we conferred, without the knowledge of Genl. Armstrong and himself, so he might be perfectly satisfied that I should adhere to that resolution.

As I had adopted the plan of presenting a correct view of our differences with Spain to the French government, on reflection, so I resolved notwithstanding the above occurrence to pursue it. It was incumbent on me however for many reasons that now occurred to act with great circumspection. As soon as I had finished my note I called on General Armstrong who was not yet presented to the Emperor, read it to him and observed that it contained the view which I wished to be presented to the French government relative to our business with Spain; that since what had passed with Mr. Livingston, with which he was acquainted, I should be better satisfied that the substance should be communicated in his name or that of M^r. Livingston than mine. He told me that he saw no objection to its being presented in mine: that as he was not yet received by the Emperor, he could not do it, and wished no delay. I then called on M^r. Livingston and made the same proposal to him. He read the paper and approved it with some modifications, which were of no great importance, to which I readily assented. He said that he had no objection to my presenting it as an informal note, or if I preferred that he would enclose it to M. Tallyrand and ask him to give me an interview on the subject, tho' he intimated that that would take time. I suggested the idea of himself, Genl. Armstrong and myself going together to the minister, and presenting him the paper, to which he seemed to be averse. I then said that I would call in person and present it myself, to which he assented. In an interview however with Genl. Armstrong the same day, I expressed a desire that he would accompany me, to give the paper more weight, to which he readily agreed, tho' he said it would be better that we all three went, and promised to confer with and endeavour to prevail on M^r. Livingston to accompany us. I saw Genl. Armstrong next morning and heard that his endeavours had not been successful. As M^r. Livingston was unwilling to accompany us, the General seemed averse to go without him, especially as he was not presented. In consequence I went immediately to M^r. Tallyrand's office, and was informed by the porter that it was a day of audience for the foreign ambassadors, whom alone he was ordered to admit; that as I was not one he could not admit me without the special license of the minister, which he would apply for if I desired it. As I saw his Courtyard full of carriages, and concluded that I could do nothing if admitted, I resolved not to ask it, and returned home to reflect further on the course to be taken. My final decision was to take no step on my own ground alone. I was aware that I was pursuing a course and pressing a point which was not well relished by those or some of them with whom I had to deal, and was therefore resolved to keep within strict rule and etiquette in every movement which I made. Of this decision I apprized Genl. Armstrong & M^r. Livingston without delay; of the latter I requested a letter to the minister, introductory of mine which he promised and complied with. I send you a copy of his letter which was perfectly satisfactory to me. He wrote me however at the same time a letter to dissuade me from the measure, which I answered in one which acknowledged my satisfaction with his to the Minister, and justified the measure I had taken. Of these I should send you copies had I not unfortunately left them at Paris, among papers which were deemed useless at Madrid. Some days after our letters were sent to the Minister M^r. Livingston received from him a short note which promised an answer to the communication, as soon as the sense of the Emperor could be taken on it, which however was not given when I came off. From an informal but authentick source I was assured that a report had been made on the whole communication by the department to be submitted to the Emperor, the substance of which was to declare, that West Florida was not comprized by the terms of the treaty or intention of the parties in the cession of Louisiana by Spain to France, or by the latter to the United States; and also that the claim on Spain by the United States for vessels condemned then taken by French privateers was precluded by our treaty with France of 1800. The first of these doctrines was said to be supported by a correspondence which took place at the time of the negotiation between France and Spain. I asked this gentleman why was this correspondence withheld from M^r. Livingston and myself during our negotiation at Paris? Was it to enhance the price to be given for the territory? Why bring it forward now, to benefit Spain at our expence? Could such a course of conduct be deemed compatible with the honor of the French government? Would such a correspondence affect our claim under a purchase made without a knowledge of its contents? When I left Paris the report had not been submitted to the Emperor owing to the nature and urgency of the business in which the government was engaged. I did not hesitate in many informal communications, the substance of which I was persuaded were made known to those in power, to declare most solemnly that I would sanction no measure which contemplated a payment of money to Spain, in any transaction we might have with her, in the affair: that neither the state of things between the parties, the example of France in a similar case, or my instructions permitted it. These conversations were with a person who possessed the confidence of certain persons in power as well as my own, tho' they were not of a nature to compromit either party. That circumstance enabled me to speak with the utmost freedom, and perhaps to say things which it might have been difficult to press directly in the same manner to the parties themselves. From the sums due France by Spain it was to be supposed that whatever the latter got of us would be paid to the former. I did not omit to press that fact in all the views of

which it was susceptible. When I found that it was expected that we should pay
a considerable sum of money to adjust the business with Spain, I declined seeking any conversation with the minister on the subject until I could send my note
in, to prevent his compromitting himself till he saw our views. After my note
was sent in, I preferred the informal communications above adverted to for
the same reason, especially as I had cause to think that they were preferred
on the other side. When I came off my note had not been answered. General
Armstrong apprized the Minister that I was to set out immediately for Spain, of
whom he asked my passport, and I called to take leave of him with intention not
to avoid a conversation on the subject if the opportunity permitted, but he was
from home, so that I did not see him on my departure, which was precisely what
I wished. The affair stands thus; they have our views of the subject; know our
determination not to give one cent, and that we are resolved to push the point,
and I think must see that they cannot take part against our claims without discredit and injury. General Armstrong intended some few days after I left Paris to
call and tell the minister that I calculated with confidence on the good offices of
the Emperor in the affair, and is prepared to discuss the merits of any answer
which may be received unfavorable to our pretentions, tho' it is not improbable
that none will be given, as I left Paris without one. You will perceive that I staid
long enough to obtain one and could not justify remaining longer under existing circumstances between Spain & Britain. Indeed I wished none of the kind
I thought it probable would be given while there: at the same time it is not
improbable that this government will not be satisfied with a pretext for withholding one. You will see by the above how the affair stands and what prospects
there is of success under the present powers. I had reason to think, indeed I was
so assured, that France would have the negotiation transferred to Paris to secure
the controul of it in respect to Spain, and that some propositions would be
made in that state of it. I shall hope to be able to prevent this. But in balancing
the great interests of our country, and the course which this affair may possibly take, the President will decide whether any new powers may be necessary
to the commission, or modification of it. I am personally willing to act in any
situation, or place, or association, tho' it is proper to remark that the situation
of M^r. Pinckney having demanded and obtained his passport, as I am informed,
may create some difficulty in the business; none however which I shall not
endeavour to remove.

I have had as you see by the above details, much vexation, and trouble, in
this affair. So far as it respects M^r. Livingston, it is at an end. We had no rupture, tho' some warm discussion. We parted as heretofore. In respect to this

government, I have had to press things very disagreeable to some in power, the effect of which I thought I felt, in my relation to them. To balance between evils, without the hope of any profit to France, it has not been used to, and it takes it ill, of anyone, to expose it to that dilemma. Should the President deem it proper, to make a provisional arrangement, to meet all possible contingencies, the communication ought to be forwarded by a special messenger, without delay. I hope however that the existing one will prove adequate. I shall endeavour all in my power to make it so. I am with great respect and esteem, your very obedient Servant,

TO THOMAS JEFFERSON.
BAYONNE, Decr. 21, 1804.

DEAR SIR,—I am so far on my way to Madrid and on the point of recommencing my journey this morning. My letters to M^r. Madison have been so full that it is unnecessary to enter into the same topicks here even had I time, tho I have not as I set out in an hour. It is possible that y^r. attention may be directed to the fortification of our ports, since the establishment of certain fortifications on the coasts as places of security for our vessels to retreat to in wars to which we are not a party, independent of the great object of protecting our cities from the insult of cruisers &c may make it advisable to take the subject up. My mind has been long made upon that point, and that an attention to the object as soon as others were arranged wo^d. add much to the weight of our gov^t. My attention however has been drawn to it at this moment by meeting here a most able & respectable engineer Col: Vincent who made some important [original mutilated] at New York, & was introduced to me when formerly in France by a letter from Govr. Clinton. It was Col: Vincent who assisted in (or rather did it himself) in procuring that most valuable library which I sent to the department of war, which was most unfortunately destroyed at Washington by fire. I do presume that the aid of some very skilful engineers would be found useful in such a business when undertaken and that these must be procured from abroad. It is not improbable that this gentleman might be prevailed on to engage in this service, as he is very much attached to our government & country. He is a Colonel of long service in France of great experience, and of the fairest character. If he was engaged he might take others with him, three or four and who would not only accomplish the great object proposed, but lay the foundation of a military school. It is not impossible that Carnot who is his friend might accompany him. I only give you these hints for consideration. Sho^d. you wish anything of the kind, an authority to me or General Armstrong mentioning these men would be necessary. The approbation of their gov^t. I presume might easily be obtained & would be indispensable. I am dear Sir with very great & sincere regard y^r. friend & servant.

TO JOHN ARMSTRONG.[5]
ARANJUEZ, July 2, 1805.

DEAR SIR,—I did not receive yours of the 6th ult^o. till within these few days past. I thank you for it and the papers inclosed. On the pressure of M^r. Pinckney some months since to obtain the ratification of the treaty of Augt. 1802, an attempt was made by this gov^t. thro its minister at Washington, to prevail on ours to accept it with the exclusion of French spoliations which was peremptorily rejected. The Marquis [blank] was then informed by the Secretary of State in a letter of Octr. 25th "that the whole business was referr'd to the diplomatick agency of the U States at Madrid, and notwithstanding what had occurr'd that the mission extraordinary which had been provided for the general object would not be interrupted." By a letter of the 26th of the same month to me, of which a copy was sent to London on the presumption that I might not have set out for this place, I was instructed so to do: and as M^r. Pinckney had asked his recall and intimated, that relying on its being granted, he might sail leaving a chargé des aff^{fs}. in his place, a new and separate commission was granted me authorising me to act alone. On my arrival here M^r. Pinckney and myself were associated in the same commission, we were so in the letter of credence w^h. I presented to the King, nevertheless he observed to me that as the discussions which had taken place between him and the Spanish government, might have excited in him some prejudice against him, which might be injurious to the proposed negotiation in case he acted in it, that he was perfectly willing to withdraw & leave the conferences to me, but would sign whatever might be agreed on to give it effect. When he presented me to M^r. Cevallos he gave the same intimation to him as he also did to the prince of peace on a like occasion: the former replied that he should be happy to treat with whomever the President authorised for the purpose: the latter seemed to take no notice of the intimation, but behaved very politely to M^r. Pinckney. On a consideration of these circumstances as also of what had passed between him & the Spanish government, on the public questions depending between the two governments in

5. *From* Bulletin of the New York Public Library, *Vol. IV., No. 2, February, 1900.* [HAMILTON.]

which he appeared to me to have acted with firmness and ability, I saw no reason after the receit of the letter of Octr. 26 and the new commission why he should withdraw from the negotiation. At my request therefore he continues in it. The business has been open'd fully to this government but nothing has yet occurr'd to justify a satisfactory opinion of the result.

It is probable that it will be insisted on that French spoliations are provided for by our treaty with France: that W. Florida is no part of Louisiana & that an attempt will also be made to refer us generally to France for a demarkation of boundaries, and even refuse to cede E. Florida. Their object probably will be to interpose the gov^t. of France between them and us; but that gov^t. will have too perfect a recollection of the stipulation of the treaty between the U States & it, & too much regard for its faith and interest to be drawn into such a dilemma. After declining all demark^n. of boundaries in the cession w^h. is made to us of Louisiana, it is I think plain to be inferr'd from M^r. Talleyrand's answer that the Emperor is not disposed to make himself a party to our differences with Spain: on the contrary that he wishes to promote an adjustment of them. Still it becomes us to do justice to the interests of our country, and the already pronounc'd views of our gov^t. By pushing our own cause we shall have less occasion for the good offices of others, w^h. in a case of such delicacy to France as the present one between the U States & Spain it is painful to ask because it wo^d. embarrass her to render them. In many views it may be proper that it be distinctly known at Paris, as it is here, that the business is not transferr'd to America & will not be; that the power to settle it definitely is vested here, & that on the report from this place of the result will the ulterior measures of our government be taken.

P.S. I have just rec^d. dispatches from our gov^t. by a special messenger Captn. Dutton as late as the 3^d. w^h. are strong on the above and every pt already known to us.

TO JAMES MADISON.[6]
PARIS, July 6, 1805.

DEAR SIR,—Since my letter of the 30th. ult^o. some facts have come to my knowledge which it may be of advantage to you to know. I have been told that M^r. Tallyrand has replied when pressed in the winter to aid the negotiation at Madrid, that it could not be expected of him as a project of a very different

---

6. *From* Bulletin of the New York Public Library, *Vol. IV., No. 2, February, 1900.* [HAMILTON.]

character countenanced by our agents meaning M^r. L. was before our gov^t. This fact is unquestionable as I have it from authority too direct and deserving of confidence, in every view to be doubted. Thus it appears by the clearest demonstration, that the failure of that negotiation is entirely owing to the misconduct of that individual. Many facts go to prove that the many acts of his misconduct while here, are not attributable to folly alone. I have heretofore thought him entitled to that apology: but I am far from thinking so at present: indeed there is much reason to suspect him of the grossest iniquity. I give you this hint to put you on your guard. Be assured that he will poison what he touches. His object is to obtain some appointment of the President, to Eng^ld. if possible. Counting on it, he has proposed a change to Genl. Armstrong here, to get back to this place to pursue the same game that he has heretofore done. I sho^d. not be surprised if this gov^t. on seeing the stand made here & at Madrid, agnst the project submitted by him, to our gov^t., apprehending its failure, in that extent, had charged him, with some other more reasonable, in the hope of better success. If he is admitted, in the least degree, into confidence, or if cause is given him, to infer that sacrifices wo^d. be made for peace, or that our councils balance, and are not decided, he will communicate the same here. In short he is the man of all others whom you sh^d. avoid, as most deserving the execrations of his country. These ideas were never expressed before, because some of the facts, which inspire them were not known, even when I wrote you last. I write you, in haste, to take advantage of a private conveyance to Bordeaux. Genl. Armstrong & myself have united in a letter to M^r. Pinckney for M^r. Bowdoin to advise, that he decline treating with the gov^t. of Spain, sho^d. his powers authorise it (w^h. however we presume cannot be the case) till he hears from you, after the rec^t. of the result of the negotiation at Madrid. I shall leave this on Wednesday next, by the way of Antwerp, for London. The above is of course confidential, being intended only for the purpose of putting you on y^r. guard.

TO THE SECRETARY OF STATE.

LONDON, August 6th, 1805.

SIR,—I left Madrid on the 26 of May & arrived here on the 23^d. ult^o. by the route of Paris & Holland. I reached Paris on the 20th. June & left on the 17th. of July. I should have remained there longer had I seen reasonable cause to presume that any advantage might have been derived from it in respect to our business with Spain. But none such occurred, & of course there was no motive for delaying longer my journey here. The French govern^t. had been invited as I passed thro' Paris to aid our negotiation with Spain according to its engagement on a former occasion; it was apprized in the progress of what occurred in it, knew the time of its conclusion & that I should return thro' Paris, so that had it been disposed even in that state to interpose its good offices to promote an adjustment of our differences with that power, on such terms as we could accept, it might have done it with effect. I had flattered myself that it would have interposed at that period, & with a view to draw its attention in an especial manner to the object, had made such a communication to General Bournonville its ambassador at Madrid, as seemed most likely to secure it. Of this & all other documents relative to the subject a copy was sent you from Madrid by Capt Dalton. It is proper to add that when I delivered that communication to General Bournonville which I did in person, I intimated to him verbally that as I should take Paris on my return, the opportunity for such friendly interference on the part of his government would again be presented to it: that I had a power to act singly & if a like one should be given to the Spanish Ambassador there, we might renew the business & conclude it. General Bournonville transmitted immediately this communication to his government then at Milan by a courier, so that it must have been received in a week after I left Madrid, & as I was more than three weeks on the route from Madrid to Paris, the French government had sufficient time to make an arrangement for the purpose even before my arrival at Paris. While there I was attentive to every circumstance from which an inference could be drawn of the disposition of the French government on that head, & as I was frequently in society with some of the members of the government who were left behind, especially the arch-chancellor who is considered as its head in the absence of the Emperor, the opportunity to make a correct estimate was a very favorable one. But nothing occurred to authorise an inference that it intended to make me any proposition on the subject. On the contrary I had sufficient reason to believe that the French government still indulged the expectation that the proposition which M^r. Livingston had submitted to you before I set out from this country to Spain would finally be accepted. As this fact had been avowed by the Minister of foreign affairs it could not be questioned. Having done everything in my power to expose the fallacy of this expectation in obedience to my instructions while at Paris in my way to Spain & in Spain I was surprised that the idea should still be entertained & the more so as Genl. Armstrong had equally labored to remove it.

Under these circumstances it seemed highly improper to present again any application to the French government for its aid in that business. It was sure to fail of success & therefore to be avoided. But that was not the only objection to it. It seemed likely by weakening the force of the part which had been taken at

Madrid to diminish the good effect which we flattered ourselves might [have] reasonably been expected from it. It was even probable in relation to what had passed, that it might be considered as betraying a want of just sensibility to what was due to the character of our government & country, & lessen the effect of such measures as our government might think proper to adopt on a view of the result & whole proceedings at Madrid. On full consideration therefore of all circumstances I deemed it most consistent with the publick honor & interest, after waiting about three weeks at Paris & furnishing the opportunity & drawing the conclusion above stated of the disposition of the French gov^t. to interfere in a suitable manner in our business with Spain, to proceed on my journey here, without making any application for it, which I did accordingly.

COPY OF A LETTER FROM COL. JAMES LEWIS.
ALBEMARLE, NEAR CHARLOTTESVILLE, October 12, 1826.

SIR:—In compliance with your request, that I would communicate the reasons which induced you to sell your land above Charlottesville, while you were in Europe, in your mission to France, I readily make you the following statement, which you will find substantially correct, and will correspond with the report which I formerly made to you: but as my papers are in Tennesse, and having only my memory to assist me, I cannot go so minutely into the details as I could wish; but should you deem it necessary, on my return, I will be able to give you an exact account of the quantity of land sold, the price it sold for, with every other information you may want, relative to the business I transacted for you, during your absence in Europe.

As soon as you were appointed, you informed me of it, and that you must sail immediately, and requested me to come to Richmond, as you intended to give me the charge of your estate in Albermarle during your absence. I complied with your request, and proceeded forthwith to Richmond, which, as well as my memory serves me, was in January or February, 1803. You appointed me your agent, with instructions and a power of attorney to act for you during your absence, with a power to sell a portion of your property to discharge your debts, should I at any time find it necessary to do so. You stated to me that you only could advance me a trifle, and actually did not advance me more than one hundred dollars, if so much, and assigned as a reason that the government had not made you such an allowance as would enable you to do it; that you would be exposed to great expense in your mission, and would require all the money you could obtain to bear it. You expressed great concern at being compelled to depart in such haste, that you could not settle your private affairs, not make provision for any debts you might owe, but that you would not allow any person to whom you might be indebted, to suffer in your absence. I took charge of your estate, and was able to avoid a sale for about two years, within which time you were expected home; but as you still continued abroad, and the proceeds of the farm not being able to meet all the demands, and it being uncertain at what time you might return, and some of your creditors being themselves pressed for money, I thought it best to advertise some of your property for sale. I accordingly advertised your large tract of land in Kentucky, and your land in this county that lay above Charlottesville. Not being able to get a bid for the Kentucky land, I was obliged to sell the tract of land above Charlottesville, which contained, as well as my memory serves me, something like nine hundred and fifty acres, on which the University now stands, and which I sold for five or six dollars the acre. The amount, I am confident, did not exceed six dollars. At the time I sold that land, I conceived it to be worth more; but being obliged to have a part in cash, for the payment of one of your debts, I could at that time do no better, and was acting, at the same time, agreeably to your instructions; to make a sacrifice rather than let your creditors suffer. Had you been able, at that time, to have advanced me the sum of two thousand dollars, I am confident I could have made the creditors easy, and not been obliged to sell the land; and perhaps a less sum than that would have been sufficient.

You also wish to know of me the difference in the price of the land that I sold, whereon the university is now fixed—that is, the difference in the present prices. Having not been here for some time, I can only state the present prices from information. I am told that an acre of land, which I sold to Wm. G. Garner, on the road near the Rotunda, would sell at this time for seven or eight hundred dollars, and perhaps more. I am also informed that John M. Perry sold to Col. Wm. Garth one hundred acres at one hundred dollars per acre; that there have been sold other parts of the land, formerly yours, at eighty dollars per acre; and the remotest parts of the tract have been sold, or would now command, forty dollars per acre. But, as to the present price of the land, you can get the most correct information from the people of Charlottesville and its vicinity.

I remain, with sentiments of respect, yours, &c.

JAS. LEWIS.

P.S. Should it be necessary, I am willing to qualify to the correctness of the above. My address is Franklin county, Winchester, Tennessee.

TO COL. JAMES MONROE:—ALBEMARLE.

PART VII

Secretary of State and Secretary of War

INTRODUCTION

LTHOUGH MONROE SLOWLY ACCEPTED Jefferson's explanations, relations with Madison remained cold. In an uncharacteristic fit of pique, he allowed his name to be placed against Madison for the Republican nomination by the faction of so-called Old Republicans, led by John Randolph of Roanoke, in the election of 1808. In words that sometimes have emitted from candidates over the years, he stated he would take no part in the nominating process, but if nominated he would run. It was a futile gesture. The Republicans put forward Madison, who easily won election. Monroe turned back to the Virginia General Assembly in Richmond; but no sooner had he been elected than the Assembly chose him as Governor—for the second time. In the letters of Chapman Johnson to Monroe and his reply (January 12, and January 14,1811), Monroe's reluctance to be seen as seeking the position is painful. In subsequent letters to Jefferson, John Taylor, and John Randolph over the next two weeks he continues the need to explain his motives.

After Monroe had been but three months as Governor of Virginia, when the situation of the United States became yet more grave. Although Britain had warded off the threat of Napoleonic invasion by Nelson's victories at Cadiz and Trafalgar in 1805, the Emperor had turned his armies from the site at Boulogne for the jump-off of invasion across the Channel, and pushed them to the Danube entering Vienna and crushing the Austrians and Russians at Austerlitz. Napoleon dethroned the Bourbons in the Kingdom of Naples, and installed his brother Joseph on the throne. In 1808, Charles IV of Spain sought to abdicate in favor of his son, Ferdinand VII; but Napoleon forced them both to abdicate and placed Joseph on the Spanish thrown. With all continental Europe under his sway, he issued an interdict against the importation of British products in all the ports of Europe. In his famous phrase, he was about to starve out "the nation of shopkeepers."

The British retaliated with a counter-embargo, proclaiming once more the principle that neutral vessels, i.e., American ships, could not carry supplies to French ports. The British instituted a blockade. But the fleet was not sent to stand off the French ports; it was sent to stand off U.S. ports. One U.S. merchant ship after another seeking to leave U.S. waters was seized on the grounds that it might be going to France; in the end, the total of ships seized was close to 1,000. The two nations were edging towards war.

In 1810, Congress, recognizing the danger that Britain might seize the disputed territory of West Florida, had acceded to Madison's request, based on the legal interpretation Monroe had carefully worked out in a memorandum in 1803, for legislation authorizing the occupation of West Florida. When Madison's Secretary of State resigned the next year, Monroe was astonished to receive a letter from his erstwhile friend begging him to accept the post of Secretary of State. For after all, who better knew the British ministers than Monroe?

The correspondence between Daniel Brent, the clerk of the State Department, Monroe, and Madison is one of extreme delicacy. Monroe, with some justification, felt a difficulty in resigning so soon from the post of governor, saying he could withdraw only if there were some "higher necessity." Behind that embarrassment was the question of whether he would be able to support the principles of Madison's administration. He felt that, had the principles he had followed in the failed negotiations for the treaty of commerce been accepted by Madison in 1807 as Secretary of State, the nation would not find itself in its present danger. In the end he accepted, after Madison most generously assured him he would never have to support any policy which was contrary to his conscience.

This assurance gave Monroe as Secretary of State room to pursue in supporting the cause of republican revolution, but he found that the brewing war overshadowed other interests. His diplomacy was hampered by the weakness of the nation's defenses. The key military leaders of the Revolution by now had passed away. The second tier of leadership had been too young to gain real experience of logistics and tactics. The ignominious surrender of Detroit by General Hull in August 1812, without firing a shot, alarmed Madison and Monroe. His letters to Jefferson, John Taylor, Henry Clay, and Gen. Henry Dearborn chronicle his disgust. The Secretary of War, William Henry Eustis, a New Englander, chosen to appease the eastern states, was incompetent, and had failed to organize efficient defenses.

When Eustis resigned, Madison named Monroe Acting Secretary of War, even though he continued as Secretary of State. It was a shrewd move on Madison's part; Monroe was the highest civilian official with real military experience. He knew just what to do: He immediately began writing detailed memoranda on military strategy and materiel requirements which were supplied to the leaders of the U.S. Senate and House of Representatives, giving a grim picture of what was necessary. Then General John Armstrong, Livingston's brother-in-law, and bearer of the family grudges against Monroe, was named Secretary of War in order to strengthen support for the war in New York.

In 1814, the British landed in the Chesapeake and began working their way up the coast. Monroe, who was then 60 years old and whose body bore numerous infirmities, took horses and a small detachment of men with him, galloping through the night until they crept up on the British fleet, counting the number of ships and estimating the number of men. We still have his intelligence dispatches to Madison written in his own hand. The Secretary of War, General Armstrong, meanwhile, had fled to the safety of western Maryland.

A striking memorandum written by Monroe in August, 1814 vividly describes the entrance of the President and the Secretary of State into the smoking ruins of Washington. There was no U.S. military presence whatsoever. The inhabitants were ready to surrender. Madison deputized Monroe on the spot as Secretary of War. He took charge immediately, organizing the wavering citizens for the defense of the capital, and threatening to bayonet anyone who attempted to parley with the enemy deployed at Alexandria. When Armstrong, he remonstrated against Monroe for supposedly usurping the duties which he had abandoned. Madison suggested that he go to New York on a vacation, and he resigned a few days later.

One consequence of the burning of the U.S. Capitol was the loss of its library, and the need to replace it. Monroe knew that one of most magnificent private libraries in the United States was that of Thomas Jefferson at Monticello, and that his old friend was in dire financial straits. On October 10, hardly more than six weeks after the fire, he wrote to Jefferson suggesting the library become the patrimony of the nation. Thus Jefferson's library became the core of the Library of Congress, which today has grown to become the largest collection in the world.

At first, Monroe sought to resign as Secretary of State while acting as Secretary of War, but in the end discharged both his diplomatic and military duties simultaneously. With enormous effort he rebuilt the armies—working closely with the Congress he knew so well to get enough men in the field, and conducted a highly successful military intelligence operation. When he informed Gen. Andrew Jackson about the imminent approach of the British fleet to New Orleans, the U.S. Treasury was empty, and Jackson needed supplies and funds to pay his men. Unfortunately, the British trade embargo and the costs of the war had imposed ruin on the U.S. economy. Scores of banks failed, and others were issuing worthless script. Without hesitation, Monroe pledged his private credit to a group of Washington banks, and sent the funds to Jackson.

Despite Britain's successes in the war in America, its attention was also distracted by events in Europe. Napoleon's retreat from Moscow in November 1812, his retreat from Leipzig a year later, and his abdication in 1814 changed the whole dynamic on the continent, while American naval superiority on the Great Lakes had dimmed any chance that the British could occupy any significant portion of U.S. territory. The British foreign minister, Lord Castlereagh, offered negotiations to the United States in December 1813. As a result, Madison nominated peace commissioners who after many detours, finally arrived at Ghent, in August. The group included Albert Gallatin, John Quincy Adams, Henry Clay, J. A. Bayard and Jonathan Russell. Months went by with no communication from Ghent, until a letter arrived saying that no peace was possible with the instructions they had been given. With the bankruptcy of the U.S. Treasury and the desperate situation in the field, except in the Lakes, the Cabinet conferred. Monroe recommended that the issue of impressment be taken off the table, and so the message was sent to the peace commissioners. Monroe refrained from commenting on the fact that the situation was back to the failed 1806 treaty.

The British commissioners, for their part, had made outrageous demands: They would not discuss the question of the Newfoundland fisheries. They would not renew the provisions of the peace treaty of 1783 ending the War of Independence. The British would remain in the forts and on the lakes. A line would be drawn from the approximate location of Cleveland today to the Mississippi excluding the Americans. An Indian buffer state in the Western territories would be established to block westward expansion, the British right of navigation on the Mississippi would be retained. There were suggestions that Louisiana be returned to Spain. In other words, the picture sketched was almost a reversal of the War for Independence, with the United States virtually a vassal of the Motherland.

But the situation was worsening for British forces in the United States. In September, the British were routed at the battle of Plattsburg on Lake Champlain. "14,000 British myrmidons were defeated and put to flight by 5,000 Yankees and Green-Mountain Boys," a broadside of the time gleefully reported. And when the great British hero, the Duke of Wellington, was asked to take charge of military operations in America, he declined, stating "I think you have no right, from the state of war, to demand any concession of territory from America."

The other turning point was the pressure of the new economy in Britain fueled by industrial production. The two-hundred year old sway of the mercantilists, based on trade monopoly, was declining; the industrialists wanted a policy based on exports and free trade. Until the embargo, the United States had been a major trading partner. The desire for the restoration of trade stopped the war on both sides. Neither side achieved victory; it was a question of which would collapse first.

One by one the British objections in Ghent dropped away. The Americans, for their part, gave up any insistence on the right to the fisheries, leaving the situation in all respects almost as it had been in 1811. The treaty was signed on December 24, 1814, yet unbeknownst to Madison and Monroe in Washington. Nor was it known to Major General Andrew Jackson who on that day was clashing with the British commander, Major General Edward Pakenham around New Orleans. On the foggy morning of January 8, 1815 the British lost 2,000 men in pitched battle, while Jackson, with much smaller forces, suffered only 71 casualties. The British withdrew to the harbor and sailed away, not realizing that they had lost the decisive military battle of the war after the peace treaty had been signed.

TO JAMES MONROE.

RICHMOND, January 12ʰ, 1811.

DEAR SIR,—You have been informed that it is the wish of many of your old friends and of the friends of the Administration, that you should fill the vacancy, in the Office of Governor of this Commonwealth, which is anticipated, from the appointment of Mr. Tyler, to the bench of the Federal Court. You already know that it would give me great satisfaction to promote your election. You are assured, too, I hope, that I feel the greatest confidence in your political principles, and in the sincerity of your disposition to promote the interests of the Republican cause. This confidence will be my justification, to the Republicans for using my exertions to effect a general concert amongst the friends of the Administration in your favor. But I find that there are amongst them, gentlemen who hesitate in giving you their support, and hesitate only from an apprehension, that in doing so they will afford the public reason to believe that they distrust the Administration in which they have confidence, and countenance an opposition which they disapprove. Though these are not my fears, yet I have no hesitation in thinking, that they are honestly the fear of others, and that in acting under their influence, they feel that they are obeying an impulse of duty to their Cause and Country. It is for the purpose of being enabled to remove these fears, that I trouble you with this letter.

If your own sense of propriety will permit, I should be pleased, that you would authorize me to say, whether, if elected, you would carry into the Government, a disposition to cooperate with the Administration and to encourage union and harmony, for the purpose of ensuring success to their measures.

CHAPMAN JOHNSON.

RICHMOND, Janʸ. 14ᵗʰ, 1811.

DEAR SIR,—Your letter of the 12ᵗʰ. instant has afforded me great: satisfaction, because it manifests a spirit of amity and conciliation which ought always to characterise the conduct of those who are attached to the same principles, and engaged in support of the same great cause. It is evidently your object to correct errors in the minds of others, not to impose conditions on me.

My support of the republican cause has been the result of feeling, and of my own best judgment. It commenced at a very early period, and has been continued in every situation in which I have been placed. The same principle will animate and guide me thro' life.

I cannot conceive on what ground an idea is entertained that I should carry into the government of this Commonwealth a disposition unfriendly to the administration, and a desire to embarrass its measures. Such a suspicion is entirely destitute of foundation. Whatever difference of opinion there may have been on certain points of policy, respecting our foreign relations, I never failed when apprized of the views of my gov^t., to use my best efforts to carry them into effect. A difference of opinion on a point of policy wo^d. never excite in me a disposition to oppose or counteract any measure of the government, or to impeach its claims to the respect and confidence of the people—

As I believe the Executive to be attached to free government, the natural bias of my mind and feelings is in its favor. I wish the administration success, because its success will promote that of the republican cause, and the general prosperity of my country. I add with pleasure that there is nothing of a personal nature, in the relation which subsists between the chief magistrate and myself, that can possibly impair the force of this sentiment.

I cannot presume that any one of the gentlemen who entertain the apprehensions to which you allude, feel disposed to approve without examination and conviction every measure of any administration. Such a disposition cannot be indulged and acted on, without a surrender of the first principles of free government: those principles which our constitution was instituted to preserve, and which the administration must and no doubt does revere. All that any administration can desire of a free and independent people, is a rational and manly support of its conduct when it bears the test of impartial investigation by the standard of the constitution, and by its tendency to promote the publick welfare. In any situation in which I may be placed, I shall expect the support of my fellow citizens on no other condition. On the same condition I shall not fail to afford it to the government of the U. States.

JA^s. MONROE

TO THOMAS JEFFERSON.
RICHMOND, Jany. 21, 1811.

DEAR SIR,—I have the pleasure to return you your correspondence with the directors of the Rivanna Company which I lately rec^d. from you. I had submitted it to the perusal of a few friends only, in confidence, and had determin'd for the present, at least, not to publish it, from a fear that the publication might lead to some unpleasant discussion.

You will have seen by the news papers that I have been placed in a situation of which I had no anticipation when I left home, nor indeed desire. I was induc'd to accede to it only, by the manifestation of a general sentiment among the republicans, that I should do so, and the hope that it may be useful in uniting the party more closely together for general purposes, and more especially for the support of the cause. I am aware that my private affairs will suffer by it, as the salary is insufficient, and I shall not be able to pay due attention to those at home. It is my intention to return immediately after the rising of the Assembly, when I shall have the pleasure to see you. In the meantime I beg you to command me in all things in which I may be useful, being with great respect, etc.

TO COLONEL JOHN TAYLOR.
RICHMOND, Jany. 23ᵈ, 1811.

DEAR SIR,—I have intended for some time past to write you, but the many very interesting and pressing duties which devolved on me in my legislative character prevented it. In entering on these duties I found myself quite ignorant of forms, and equally a stranger to the more difficult task of publick discussion. I did not however shrink from them in any instance, but performed them as well as I could, calculating on reasonable allowance for deficiencies by their being imputed to the proper cause.

By a vote of the Genˡ. Assembly I have been placed in a new situation, as you will probably hear before you receive this. I had been pressed to allow myself to be nominated for the Senate, to which I gave an explicit dissent. My attention having been called to that object before the meeting of the Assembly, by several communications, I had made up my mind on it, which could not be altered. In fact I thought that the acceptance of such a trust woᵈ. be ruinous to me, and therefore declined the nomination. The vacancy in the govᵗ. of the State occurring, and being pressed on me with still greater earnestness, I consented to be brought forward. Among those who urged me to this measure were some who had been much opposed to me on a late occasion, and who expressed a desire to avail themselves of the opportunity to give such a proof of their confidence. I replied that if the whole republican party would unite & place me where they had done 10 or 12 years ago, that I woᵈ. accept the trust, &with much satisfaction: a satisfaction which I shoᵈ. not feel if such an union did not take place, altho' I might be elevated, as my election coᵈ. not be productive, in certain respects, of the useful effects which I might hope from it, I mean in the way of conciliation. Thus the affair commenced. These friends asked information on certain points which had been topics of misrepresentation & popular clamour against me on other occasions. I professed my willingness to give it on the principle that the enquiry was a reasonable one, the constituent having a right to know, on great questions especially, the sentiments of the person he was about to vote for. I was the more willing to give it because it was asked by those friends, not to remove doubts of their own, but to enable them to do me justice against the misrepresentations of others. The questions in which most interest was taken related to the disposition which I might entertain towards the adm^n., and the republican minority that was opposed to it. It was represented by some that I sho^d. carry into the government a disposition unfriendly to the adm^n., & a desire to embarrass its measures. These persons were favorable to the election of Mr. Barbour, to promote which they were desirous of reviving the animosities of the late presidential controversy, & to turn them to his account. At one time I had reason to think that it was contemplated to bring into the legislature resolutions approving the conduct of the gov^t. in all its measures, & of course in which I had differed from it, & censuring the minority in those in w^h. I had agreed with it. I gave it to be understood that I wo^d. be at my post and do my duty: that if such resolutions were presented I wo^d. open the whole subject, so as to place my own conduct in a just light, shewing wherein I had agreed or disagreed with each party, and contrasting, of course, the system of policy w^h. I had advised, with that which had been pursued. I afterwards heard that such resolutions wo^d. not be introduced, but that the same effect wo^d. be attempted in the nomination to be made which would necessarily happen in my absence. Impelled by the motive above stated, & by the necessity of enabling my friends to do me justice in any case of attack, I thought it proper to give them full information on those subjects. For this purpose I recurred to certain documents which I had brought with me (it having been hinted to me before I left home that I sh^d. be put to the test while here) and I also took the liberty to read, to those friends, my letters to you. As those letters contained a distinct analysis, and comprehensive view of all the circumstances relating to those transactions, it was easier to impart the information which I wished to give by reading them than in any other mode. You are not at all compromitted in those letters. They only refer to questions stated by you without the expression of your opinion in either of them. Your letters to me have not been shown to any person whatever, tho' there is nothing in them to give offence to any one. I hope therefore that you will see no impropriety in my having read my letters to you to a few friends, under the circumstances stated.

You will have seen in the newspapers a communication between Mr. Chapman Johnson & myself on the topics alluded to, the object of which on his part is explained in his letter. I the more readily consented to answer it, to prevent misrepresentations of what might pass in private conversations. The correspondence will be regarded, as it is intended to be, an exposition of all that did pass. His object was quite a friendly one. I think you will find that I have conceded nothing, in my answer, from the ground on which I have heretofore stood. I am no enemy of the adm^n., nor am I disposed to embarrass its measures. On the contrary I wish them success for reasons stated in my answer. I have shewn, I think, perfect delicacy towards the minority, against whom the invitation was given to express a censure. In asserting my own independence, in the passage which relates to that point, I assert it equally in favor of every other person.

I have felt that I acted with the utmost delicacy towards the minority. As the question relating to it, was that alone, about which any solicitude was felt, it would have been more satisfactory to the parties feeling it, that I should have settled the relation which I had always borne to it only, without saying anything of that which I had borne to the adm^n. But I would not state my relation to the minority, without stating at the same time my relation to the administration. I would not permit those with whom I communicated to say that in any point I had differed from the minority, without making it their duty to say at the same time that the adm^n. and I had also differed on important points of policy. My object has been to do strict justice to both parties, as well as to myself. I have stood on distinct ground from each, and I have wished to shew in what that difference consisted.

It would be strange if we who have been at home, who have never been consulted on any important question; who knew not how any party would act till we were apprized of it by the newspapers, sho^d. be considered as belonging to either party. This would deprive us of the independence, in point of principle as well as of character, which it is highly important to preserve.

The truth is that on points of policy there has been great difference of opinion between the adm^n. & me. My letters to you shew that fact. This applies to the rejection of the treaty, and to the measures that have resulted from it. There can be no doubt that if I had had any weight in the publick councils our course would have been a different one. My views of policy have not altered, nor has anything escaped me to countenance such an idea. There is certainly nothing in my letters to you to countenance it. They, on the contrary, have presented in a more distinct light than I had done before, even to you, what my views were. I am persuaded that the adm^n. would not be much gratified by the view of past transactions which those letters give. With respect to the future I am under no pledge other than you are. My opinion however of the course which ought to be pursued, in the case of a difference of opinion in the republican party, has not altered since I wrote you, nor is it probable that it ever will, as it was not lately formed, nor on light consideration.

It happened that Mr. Randolph arrived here while this business was depending, and hearing, as I presume he did, statements of what had passed in the part which related to the minority, and, from the excitement existing at the moment, most probably, with great exaggeration, he felt, as I understood, much hurt at it. I was astonished and hurt to find that this was the case. From my knowledge of Mr. Randolph I had always believed that he would have seized with pleasure any favorable opportunity to do me justice against the charge alluded to which had been alledged against me, as it impeached my character in the most delicate points, as far especially as it related to my conduct while abroad, the period at which his difference with the adm^n. commenced. In doing me that justice, and placing me on independent & honorable ground, he would not impair his own standing with the publick. He would on the contrary essentially improve it. I am persuaded that Mr. Randolph's impression was momentary. I expect also from his justice, such a representation of my conduct, whenever it may be necessary to my character, as is strictly due to it.

I have wished to communicate to you everything that has passed here in the late occurrence, or that was any way connected with it. I wish also to receive your unreserved sentiments on the whole subject.

TO JOHN RANDOLPH.
RICHMOND, Feby. 13, 1811.

DEAR SIR,—As I have believed that the communications which you made to me when here were the effect of excitement, produced by misrepresentation, I shall write to you in the same spirit as if they had not been made. In doing so I assure you that I gratify my feelings.

Having deemed it proper to state to Col: Taylor all the circumstances attending the late occurrence, I cannot better convey to you the same information, than by transmitting to you a copy of my letter to him. My motive for it is increased by the consideration that I took the liberty to mention you in that letter. You will be so good as to return it to me, at your leisure, after perusing it.

My previous letters to Col: Taylor, which were submitted to your view when here, were intended when written for his inspection, and for that of a few others, friends only, among whom you were included. Having had occasion to write to him on some of the topics treated in these letters, I was led by the interest which the subject naturally excited, and by the connection of its parts, to enter more fully into it than I had at first intended. I was the more readily induced to do so by a personal consideration which had much weight on my mind. The incidents of my late mission to Europe, tho' not involving an official answer on me, had affected sensibly my character among my fellow citizens. Under another adm^n., and under other circumstances, I sho^d. have vindicated my conduct before the publick, but I declined it in this instance for reasons which appeared to me to be conclusive. I was however anxious to prepare and possess a document which might serve to vindicate my character hereafter against the many imputations that had been raised against it, should it ever stand in need of such a vindication. This then was one of my objects in making so full a communication to an old friend. It was the effect of accident only that I read these letters to any person without the circle described. They were however read to no one whose mind was not already made up to support me; nor do I think they wo^d. have produced that disposition in any of the bigotted friends of the adm^n.; or in others who were not independent and able to speak & act for themselves. My motive for reading them at all is fully explained in the inclosed paper.

The facts stated in these letters are, I presume, in every circumstance correct. It was far from being my intention to make them otherwise, and if it sho^d. appear that any error had been committed, I would most willingly correct it. As to the policy of the measures to which I have objected, my mind has experienced no change in that respect. It has on the contrary been confirmed by events in the opinions which I had formed by anticipation. And as to the propriety of conciliation (by which I do not mean a sacrifice of principle or even of opinion) in the members of the republican party who differ on certain measures of policy from the adm^n., and from the majority, I am equally confident of the solidity of the opinion expressed in these letters, whether the object be to promote success in the special questions depending, or in those of a more general nature. Emergencies may arise in which the preservation of the cause itself may depend on the united efforts of the whole party. Conciliation may contribute by its salutary effect in many ways to prevent those emergencies, as union may do, if they occur, to save the country & the cause. I have acted on this principle, on considerations which are fully explained in these letters, in every step I took thro' the whole period alluded to. I very much fear that a crisis is approaching which will enforce, by the circumstances likely to attend it, the justice of the reasoning contained in these letters on this topic. Should it unfortunately arrive it is much to be desired that the sentiments of those in the republican party who have differed from the adm^n. in the course which has been pursued sho^d. have the weight, with the majority, and with the publick, which they may merit.

I have thought that I owed it to the friendship which has subsisted between us, & to the opinion which I have entertained of your talents and worth, to make this communication to you. Whatever may be our future relation, which must depend on you, my best wishes for your welfare will always attend you.

An indisposition for more than a week past has in a great measure disqualified me for the ordinary duties of the station I hold. It is owing to that cause that I have not written to you sooner.

TO L. W. TAZEWELL.
RICHMOND, Feby. 25, 1811.

DEAR SIR,—I have read with great interest and satisfaction your letter of the 13. instant, and am happy to find that the part which I acted in the late election obtains your approbation. It was not premeditated, or planned by anticipation, but grew out of circumstances which were not foreseen. When it was first proposed to bring me into the Executive it was supposed by those who proposed it, some of whom were among my former opponents, that there wo^d. be no opposition to me. The opposition was an experimental one. It was managed with some address, and abandoned only when it was seen that it could not succeed. The precaution which I took to enable my friends to vindicate me against certain misrepresentations in the house & elsewhere, sho^d. they be made in my absence, was suggested by the nature of the attack. You are mistaken in the idea that any of those who now supported me, who were among my former opponents, were prompted by the leaders of that opposition. They acted independently, without the knowledge of those leaders, and against the wishes of such of their friends who were present in the legislature, or resided, or happened to be here at the time. The discovery of the change of these persons in my favor astonished such of their former associates in whom a similar disposition did not exist & who were resolved to oppose me. You have mistaken another fact, anterior in date, which is equally proper that you sho^d. have a just idea of. My opponents in Albemarle on a former occasion were not my friends in the election which took place last Spring. It was by the sentiment of the country that I was brought into the Assembly. It is not improbable, had it been understood that my election might have been prevented, that these persons would have been active against me. They took no part in the election, and voted for me after it was evident that my election was secure. The principal character [Jefferson] was in Bedford at the time attending to his private concerns. I mention these things to satisfy you that the movement in both instances was independent: that it was neither prompted by a particular interest, nor made in concert with it, and that the ground gained has been gained, as far as an estimate may be formed, from circumstances of a strong character against that interest.

Had resolutions been brought forward to approve the measures of the adm[n]. in the rejection of the British treaty, embargo, &c., and censure the minority in those cases, I wo[d]. have opposed them, & shewn distinctly what my conduct had been in our foreign transactions, what the policy was which I had advised with every power, and how far that policy merited consideration in a comparison with that which was pursued, enlightened as we now are by events. This was understood at the time by those unfriendly to me. In the informal communications which I made to some friends the same view was taken of the whole subject. They already saw wherein I had agreed or disagreed with the adm[n]. or the minority.

That nothing has been gained, or thought to be gained, against me in favor of the measures in which the adm[n]. and I differed is shewn by the silence of all the ministerial prints on the subject of the late election. None of them boast of it as an event propitious to the system of national policy which has been pursued, nor do they think that their strength as a party is increased by it. The contrary is undoubtedly the fact, and nothing can prevent [it] being universal, unless it is counteracted by the improper sensibilities and indiscretion of some of our friends in the minority.

To the latter part of your letter it is not in my power to give a full answer in this. I intended to have written to you on the subject treated in it, in reply to your former letter, when I came here last year, but was prevented by your indisposition. On my return home I received a communication from Col. Taylor involving considerations of a similar nature to which I prepared a reply, which I retained in my hands sometime for the purpose of shewing it to you. I had indulged the hope of seeing you in Albemarle after your recovery, which was strengthened by a letter from W[ms]burg from a friend who had heard that such was your intention. I shall send you by a private hand a copy of this paper, on which I shall be happy to receive the result of your examination and reflection. You will find that I have discussed the subject at some length in it, and particularly that portion which relates to parties. I do not think that there is any difference between us except on one point, & am inclined to think that on that it is not irreconcilable. You wish to see a third party distinctly formed & announced to the country. In this, to the extent to which your idea seems to lead, I do not concur, & I am persuaded that there never can be more than two efficient parties in the country. The measure of this opinion is fully explained in the paper alluded to. There may be, & there are, at this moment, men, who belonging to the republican party, differ from the majority of that party as to certain important measures of policy. Men of this description constitute in reality a party, capable, while they remain in all great constitutional topics connected with the present majority, of affording every benefit w^h. could be expected from the establishment of another party, distinctly announced as such, without doing any injury to the cause which they, as well as the majority, profess that they mean to support. I have supposed too that the discrimination in policy between the adm^n. and these men was already sufficiently marked to enable the publick to determine between them & that as the destiny of free gov^t. must finally depend, in an eminent degree at least, on the efforts of the republican party, nothing should be done by the minority which may tend, when the crisis comes on, to prevent the majority from joining the minority. In other words, that nothing sho^d. be done which sho^d. in that stage prevent the union and cooperation of the whole party, supported, as it probably would be when its councils took a new course, by the great body of the federalists, who I am satisfied are good republicans. As I shall expect to hear from you very soon after you have read the paper alluded to I shall say nothing more to you on this subject at present.

I have made an arrangement by which the amount which I owe you will be remitted to you by Mr. Hay by the 4th. of March. For your great kindness, continued under circumstances which exposed you to much trouble, I need not repeat to you my very sincere acknowledgement.

I expect to leave this for Albemarle to-morrow, to be absent about a fortnight. You will not write me sooner than the 10th. of next month, unless it be by a private conveyance, addressed to the care of Mr. Hay. With my best respects to Col: Nevison, & your family, I am, dear Sir, sincerely your friend.

TO JAMES MONROE.

MY DEAR SIR,—Your last letters have been unanswered in consequence of the badness of my health and it is with difficulty that I now hold a pen. You must therefore excuse my present brevity. I shall write you in full so soon as my health will permit. In the mean time I have to inform you that your business has not been neglected by me. I wish you immediately on the receipt of this, to write me that I [am] authorised to say that you will accept the appointment of Secretary of State. I am not expressly authorised to say that this appointment will be offered to you but I have no doubt but it will in a few days after you shall have authorised me to say that you will accept the appointment. When consulted whether, in the event of such a proposition being made, it was my opinion you would act, I have expressed a belief that the thing was not to be doubted of. I express this confidence, from a conviction of what ought to be your line of conduct on this occasion. My dear Sir, the situation of the Country is such, as to make your services, on this occasion indispensable. I, therefore, will not permit myself to entertain one moments doubt as to the line of conduct you will, on this occasion pursue. Write to me immediately and direct to Dumfries. With great sincerity and affection, I am my dear Sir your friend & ob. serv^t. RICHARD BRENT.

TO RICHARD BRENT.
RICHMOND, March 18, 1811.

DEAR SIR,—When your letter reached this place I was in Albermarle, so that I had not the pleasure to receive it until after my return on the 14th. instant. Its contents gave me much concern, which has not been removed by the reflection which I have been able since to bestow on the subject. I have great sensibility to the proposition which seems to be made to me thro' you, as a mutual friend, to come into the Department of State, and many strong motives prompt me to accede to it, but the appointment which I now hold presents a most serious obstacle. I feel that I owe to this State the utmost gratitude for this recent and strong proof of its confidence, and I fear that I should be thought to fail in that delicate and important duty if I relinquished the station in which it has placed me. I shall be glad to receive your further sentiments on this subject. Do you think it possible for me to withdraw from the Executive of this State without exposing myself to this painful imputation, and even lessening the weight which I might otherwise bring into the government?

You intimate that the situation of our country is such as to leave me no alternative. I am aware that our publick affairs are far from being in a tranquil & secure state, I may add that there is much reason to fear that a crisis is approaching of a very dangerous tendency, one which menaces the overthrow of the whole republican party. Is the administration impressed with this sentiment & prepared to act on it? Are things in such a state as to allow the adm^n. to take the whole subject into consideration, and to provide for the safety of the country & of free government, by such measures as circumstances may require, and a comprehensive view of them suggest? Or are we pledged by what is already done to remain spectators of the interior movement, in the expectation of some change abroad as the ground on which we are to act? I have no doubt from my knowledge of the President & Mr. Gallatin, with the former of whom I have been long and intimately connected in friendship, and for both of whom, in great &leading points of character, I have the highest consideration and respect, that if I come into the government the utmost cordiality would subsist between us, and that any opinions which I might entertain and express respecting our publick affairs would receive, so far as circumstances would permit, all the attention to which they might be entitled, but if our course is fixed, and the destiny of our country is dependant on arrangements already made, on measures already taken, I do not perceive how it would be possible for me to render any service, at this time, in the general government. My impression is that no consideration would justify my withdrawing from the Executive of this State unless it had sufficient force to make it a matter of duty, the obligation of which would not be felt by myself alone, but be distinctly understood by the publick. Having however never failed to accept a trust to which my duty called me, I should not hesitate to accept that proposed if I perceived that the obligation to do so was paramount to that which I owe to the State under my present appointment. Should there be any objection to communicate with me in this mode on these topics, and a personal interview be preferred, I would with pleasure attend at Washington for the purpose on receiving such an intimation.

I am very sincerely your friend & servant.

TO JAMES MONROE.
Private & confidential.
WASHINGTON, Mar. 20, 1811.

DEAR SIR,—I may perhaps consult too much my own wishes public & personal, and too little a proper estimate of yours, in intimating the near approach of a vacancy in the Department of State, which will present to your comparison, as far as lies with me, that sphere for your patriotic services, with the one in which they are now rendered. Should such a transfer of them be inadmissible or ineligible, on whatever considerations, this communication will I am sure be viewed in the light, to which its motives entitle it, and may rest in confidence between us. In a contrary result, be so good as to let me have your agreeable determination as soon as possible. Permit me to add that even in this result, it will be best for reasons reserved for personal explanation, that the precise time of the communication, may be confidential.

I am the more anxious to hear from you as soon as possible, since besides the more obvious calls for it, the business of that Dep^t. is rendered by the present conjuncture, peculiarly urgent as well as important. It would be of the greatest advantage, if it could be in the hands which are to dispose of it, in about two weeks from this date, and receive a close attention for a short period thence ensuing. It is probable that an interval of relaxation would thereby be rendered consistent with the public interest. Accept assurances of my great esteem and sincere friendship. JAMES MADISON.

TO JAMES MADISON.
RICHMOND, March 23^d. 1811.

DEAR SIR,—Your letter of the 20th. instant reached me yesterday morning. The subject which it presents to my view is highly interesting, and has received all the consideration which so short a time has enabled me to bestow on it. My wish to give you an early answer, in compliance with your request, has induced me to use all the despatch which the delicacy and importance of the subject would permit.

The proof of your confidence which the proposition communicated by your letter affords is very gratifying to me, and will always be remembered with great satisfaction.

I have no hesitation in saying that I have every disposition to accept your invitation to enter into the Department of State. But in deciding this question, on your part as well as on mine, some considerations occur which claim attention from us both, and which candour requires to be brought into view, and weighed at this time.

My views of policy towards the European powers are not unknown. They were adopted on great consideration, and are founded in the utmost devotion to the publick welfare. I was sincerely of opinion, after the failure of the negotiation with Spain, or rather France, that it was for the interest of our country, to make an accommodation with England, the great maritime power, even on moderate terms, rather than hazard war, or any other alternative. On that opinion I acted afterwards, while I remained in office, and I own that I have since seen no cause to doubt its soundness. Circumstances have in some respects changed, but still my general views of policy are the same.

If I come into the government my object will be to render to my country, and to you, all the service in my power, according to the light, such as it is, of my knowledge and experience, faithfully, and without reserve. It would not become me to accept a station, and to act a part in it, which my judgment and conscience did not approve, and which I did not believe would promote the publick welfare & happiness. I could not do this, nor would you wish me to do it.

If you are disposed to accept my services under these circumstances, and with this explanation, I shall be ready to render them, whenever it may suit you to require them. In that event a circumstance of importance & delicacy will require attention from you as well as from me. It relates to the office which I now hold. I feel much difficulty in withdrawing from it, nor could I do so, but on considerations which it is fair to presume would be satisfactory to my constituents. I am persuaded that my fellow citizens would have no objection to my leaving this station to go into the general government at a crisis so important to the publick welfare, and to the republican cause, from an opinion, as the security of these great interests depends in the present conjunction more on the councils and measures of the general than of the State government, that I might be able to render more service there than here. They would I am satisfied be reconciled to the act, if I received an invitation from you, suggesting a motive for it arising out of the present state of publick affairs, which I might lay before the Council when I communicated to it my acceptance of an appointment under the general government.

TO JAMES MADISON.
RICHMOND, March 29, 1811.

DEAR SIR,—I have received your letter of the 26. instant. Its contents are very satisfactory to me. The just principles on which you have invited me into the department of State have removed every difficulty which had occurred to me to the measure, they afford also a strong ground for hope that the joint counsels & labours of those who are thus associated in the government will promote the best interests of our country. To succeed in that most desirable object my utmost exertions will be made. I add with pleasure that I shall carry into the government, a sincere desire to harmonize in the measures necessary to that end on the fair and liberal principles expressed in your letter.

I shall be prepared to set out for Washington on Tuesday next, provided I receive your letter, & the commission which is to accompany it, on or before Sunday. One day's detention here after Sunday, for the purpose of taking my leave of the Council, in case these documents are previously received, is all that I shall require. Every preparatory arrangement of a publick and private nature will be by that time compleated.

I am with great respect and esteem your friend & servant.

TO THOMAS JEFFERSON.
RICHMOND, April 3, 1811.

DEAR SIR,—An unexpected change has taken place in my situation since I had last the pleasure to see you. An invitation from the President to enter into the department of state will take me to Washington. Having accepted the office, I set out tomorrow in the stage to commence its duties. This appointment subjected me, in the first intimation, to great concern, from a doubt of the propriety of resigning that so lately conferr'd on me by the Gen¹. Assembly. But all those friends with whom I had an opportunity to confer, having concurr'd in favor of it, I have been taught to believe that that difficulty had not the weight, which I had supposed. I accept the office in part hope that some good effect will result from it, in promoting harmony at least in the republican party. The manner in which the proposition was made to me, was liberal and manly, so that every other difficulty was immediately at an end. I shall always be happy to hear from you and to receive your opinions on publick measures. I am, etc.

Monroe arrived in Washington on Friday, April 5th, and the next day entered on the duties of his office. [HAMILTON.]

TO JOEL BARLOW.
DEPARTMENT OF STATE,
February 24, 1812.

SIR,—No intelligence is yet received of a change of policy in England, nor is there any certainty of such a change, even after the Prince Regent is invested with the full power of the Crown, although it be by the demise of his father. It is to be presumed therefore that our affairs will go forward in an uniform direction, to the result to which they point, and to which they are invited by accumulated injuries. Great exertions will be made to bring into activity the force provided for by law with the least possible delay. Some months, however, must elapse before it can be raised. In the interval the door is open to propositions of accommodation from Great Britain and it is hoped that a more just and enlightened view of her interests, and of our rights, will be taken by her Government before it is too late.

The French Government must not suppose that the attitude now taken by the United States towards Great Britain has changed their sentiments or their expectation of redress, for the various injuries received from French Decrees enumerated in your instructions. The impulse which this Nation has received proceeds from a strong sense of injury from both the Belligerants. A fair discrimination has been made in favor of France in the particular circumstances in which her conduct has merited it. But on every other ground of complaint the sensibility and opinion of this Government are the same. Nor will the pressure on France be diminished by any change which may take place in our relations with England to whatever extent it may be carried.

TO COL. JOHN TAYLOR.
WASHINGTON, June 13, 1812.

DEAR SIR,—I have been afraid to write you for some time past because I knew that you expected better things from me than I have been able to perform. You thought that I might contribute to promote a compromise with Great Britain, and thereby prevent a war between that country and the United States: that we might also get rid of our restrictive system. I own to you that I had some hope, tho' less than some of my friends entertained, that I might aid in promoting that desirable result. This hope has been disappointed. It is most certain however that I did everything in my power to promote it, consistent with the rights and interests of this country. My communications were conciliatory; on the ground of blockade nearly of accord; and no other interest was pressed to increase the difficulty of adjusting that respecting the orders in Council. Everything too was said, in an informal way, which could be said, with propriety, to bring about an accommodation. Nothing would satisfy the present Ministry of England short of unconditional submission, which it was impossible to make. This fact being completely ascertained the only remaining alternative was to get ready for fighting, and to begin as soon as we were ready. This was the plan of the administration when Congress met in December last; the President's message announced it; and every step taken by the administration since has led to it. The delay, it was hoped, would give to Great Britain an opportunity to reflect further on the subject, and to change her policy. But the misfortune is that we have been so long dealing in the small way of embargoes, non-intercourse, and non-importation, with menaces of war, &c., that the British government has not believed us. Thus the argument of war, with its consequences, has not had its due weight with that government. We must actually get to war before the intention to make it will be credited either here or abroad. The habitual opponents of the government, and some who have lately become so by particular causes, more violent than the old federalists, expected when the Congress met, that the administration would recommend the bolstering up the non-importation act as the sure means of bringing the British government to reason: that it would propose some new and more efficient plan for preventing smuggling, and catching smugglers. They came here, as there is good cause to believe, prepared to treat with vast asperity and contempt such an inefficient expedient. When they found that they had misconceived the views of the administration they were rather at a loss how to proceed. To oppose war would be inconsistent with their past conduct, I mean the malcontents; to join in with the views of the administration very inconsistent with their present plan. It required time to digest a system of conduct suited to present emergencies. The committees of foreign relations in the two Houses, and of war, apparently united, and sincerely so, as most of the members were, in resisting the foreign aggressions, consulted the administration as to the force that would be necessary for the purpose. The object of the administration was not to starve the cause. In case of war it might be necessary to invade Canada, not as an object of the war but as a means to bring it to a satisfactory conclusion. The estimate of the force had relation to that measure. In raising a force equal to it, it was sought not to go beyond it for two reasons, that the standing army should not be greater than was absolutely necessary, and secondly that no taxes ought to be imposed which could be avoided. The administration thought that 20,000 men (regulars) with volunteers and militia would be adequate to every object. The old establishment was 10,000, which it was proposed to complete, to be enlisted for five years; the other 10,000 to be enlisted for a shorter term. As soon as this estimate was known the persons alluded to separated themselves immediately from the government, taking what was called strong ground, and introducing a bill for 25,000 additional troops, making in the whole 35,000, all for five years. By this they attempted to gain credit, as being great advocates for war, and to throw discredit on the administration by implying on account of the moderation of its views that it was not in earnest, and really did not contemplate war. By enlisting the whole for *five years,* a difficult thing in this country, the means of making war were put at a distance; and by the volunteer plan (which was not intended to be by the administration the revival of M^r. Adams measure, but a regular body, under a popular name, for short enlistment) by keeping the appointment of the officers out of the hands of the President, that force was rendered nugatory. And as it seemed to be substituted to the militia, on the idea that the latter could not be marched without the limit of the United States, the arms of the government were in fact tied up till the regular force for five years should be raised, or as many of it as would be necessary for efficient measures. The system of revenue by internal taxation, of course, as that on trade was impaired by the restrictive regulations, was to be adopted to this great establishment of 25,000 men. The latter seemed to be a necessary incident to the former, indeed grew out of it; and satisfied I am that the report of these taxes from the Treasury was forced on that Department to shew how the war was to be maintained, which it had proposed (on a very different scale however) rather as the means of defeating the measures of the government, and breaking it down, than to give effect to that war.

The government has gone on and made its preparations, in which it has succeeded better than was expected; and finally, after proposing an embargo, which was prolonged to connect it in character with the former one, has brought distinctly the subject of war before the legislature as the only possible means of giving effect to the just claims of the country on foreign powers. This proposition passed rapidly through the House of Representatives, but has hung in the Senate.

Mark the conduct of certain individuals in the latter body where every pestilent scheme has been contrived and managed since the commencement of the session. It is here, and not so much by the federalists as by men heretofore the strong advocates of war, who promoted embargoes &c., that the plan of 25,000 men was set on foot. These men have unceasingly circulated the report that the Executive did not intend to make war, and thereby deceived the people, and deceived the British government, depriving our country of the effect which that argument might have had in the British Cabinet. These men being now brought to the issue, by the proposition for war, are those who create all the embarrassments in the way of it. They ask a statement of the military force, expecting that their dilatory measures would have had less success than has actually attended them, how many troops (regular) are in all our towns, and along our coast, our frontiers, &c., as a motive for delay. The government has met these calls by fair statements, and is willing to take great responsibility on itself in every thing that it recommends. I have no doubt that the measure will finally pass, and perhaps by the votes of those very men, who, finding that their inconsistency and improper views are seen thro', and perhaps that they cannot defeat it, will join in to mask their real conduct & views from the public eye.

In the commencement of this European war the United States had the alternative either to leave our commerce to itself, or to yield it all the protection in their power. I am convinced if the former plan had been adopted that the republican party would have been overset long since, if the Union itself had not been dissolved. The Eastern people would have complained that their rights and interests were sacrificed by those in power, who were planters & negro holders, who cared for the sale of their wheat, corn, and tob°. only. The other plan was preferred, of yielding to it what protection we could. In pursuing this plan I have always thought that a fair and reasonable arrangement with the great maritime power was the true interest of this country. On this principle I signed the treaty with England, which was rejected, & its rejection has been followed with the restrictive system of embargo, non-intercourse, &c., which failed in their object. In coming here I found my country in the same controversy with the same powers, & at issue particularly with G. Britain, & the question after the failure of the negotiation with Mr. Foster, if it may be so called, whether we shall submit, or maintain our rights against that power; on that point I could have no doubt. My letter from Richmond did not propose a surrender of those rights. It explained the treaty which had been rejected according to our understanding of it. It did not even say that it ought to have been adopted. It expressed a confidence in the patriotism and wisdom of the adm^n., & a wish to aid it in asserting our rights under the restrictive system, aided, no doubt, by other causes, particularly a desire in those out of power to get into power, a desire in many to change our system of gov^t., in others to separate the Union. A strange revolution has been produced, considering the interests of the different parts of the U. States as to the supporters & opponents of present measures. It is strange to see Southern people supporting neutral & maritime rights, who have comparatively so small an interest in their support, against Eastern people, whose prosperity depends on the support of those rights. The truth is the restrictive system contributed much to produce this effect. The government had it in its power to make a compromise in this point with its opponents by retiring from the contest with G. Britain, repeating the non-importation act, & leaving our commerce to be regulated by her gov^t.. The opponents of the gov^t., federalists & others, invited this course, & had it been taken their opposition must have ceased. But where would it have left the U. States? & what effect would it have had on the character & destiny of our republican system of gov^t.? My idea was that such a step would have put it in great danger, if it had not subverted it eventually. The gov^t. thought it important to the best interests of our country to go forward, & push the controversy with decision, since it could not be avoided.

My candid opinion is that we shall succeed in obtaining what it is important to obtain, and that we shall experience little annoyance or embarrassment in the effort. I have great hope that decision here will at an early day rid the British nation of its present ministry, and that an accommodation will soon follow the change. Should the war however be prolonged I do not apprehend either invasion, the desolation of our coast, the battering our towns, or even any greater injury to our commerce than has existed since 1807, the period of the first embargo. I am persuaded, on the contrary, that it would be more flourishing in war than it has been since 1807, taking the whole term of five years together. Spain & Portugal must have provisions; Britain herself wants, & must have them, as do her Islands. If war does not procure immediate accommodation her gov^t. will afford vast facilities to our trade. It will find its way to hungry mouths.

Nor do I apprehend any dismemberment of the Union, or opposition to the gov^t. These are idle fears. They serve to excite alarm, to aid the cause of opposition, but if we open our ports & *trade* & *fight*, & *fight* & *trade*, & let all the embarrassments proceed from the enemy, & none from our own gov^t., I think we shall soon have much internal quiet.

War was declared by Act of Congress June 18th, and the same proclaimed by the President June 19th. [HAMILTON.]

TO HENRY CLAY.
WASHINGTON, August 28, 1812.

MY DEAR SIR,—Yours of the 29th ultimo and 12th instant have been received. The former should have been answered sooner, had I not been absent in Virginia, where I had gone to take my family for the advantage of the mountain air.

We have just heard with equal astonishment and concern, that General Hull has surrendered, by capitulation, the army under his command at Detroit, to the British force opposed to him. The circumstances attending this most mortifying and humiliating event are not known; but so far as we are informed on the subject, there appears to be no justification of it. I cannot suspect his integrity; I rather suppose that a panic had seized the whole force, and that he and they became victims of his want of energy, promptitude of decision, and those resources, the characteristics of great minds in difficult emergencies. We understand that, after passing the river, he suffered his communication to be cut off with the States of Ohio and Kentucky, and without making any active movement in front to strike terror into the enemy, he remained tranquil, thereby evincing a want of confidence in his own means, and giving time to collect his forces together. No intelligence justifies the belief that he gave battle in a single instance. It appears that he surrendered on a summons from Fort Sandwich, on the opposite side of the river, after firing of some cannon or mortars, which did no great mischief.

Before this disastrous event was known, the force now, I presume, on its march, was ordered from Kentucky, and the appointment of brigadier had been conferred on Governor Harrison. Your letters had produced all the effect on those subjects, which their solidity justly merited.

I most sincerely wish that the President could dispose of me at this juncture, in the military line. If circumstances would permit, and it should be thought that I could render any service, I would, in a very few days, join our forces assembling beyond the Ohio, and endeavor to recover the ground which we have lost. He left this to-day for Virginia, as did Mr. Gallatin for New York, but expresses being sent for them, they will probably both return to-morrow.

TO GENERAL DEARBORN.
WASHINGTON, Augt. 28, 1812.

DEAR SIR.—We have just rec^d. an account of the surrender of Genl. Hull, with the forces under his command, to the British general in that quarter. I cannot express to you the astonishment, and mortification which this most extraordinary event has produc'd here, and indeed everywhere; the severest imputations are levelled against him, but for my part, I do not entertain a doubt of his integrity. I think that he wanted a mind equal to the difficulties of his situation and that he sunk under them. He does not appear, from what has reached us, to have made a single effort, of that high character that was expected from him, to save himself & his army. He suffer'd the communication between him & the state of Ohio, to be cut off, and without making any effort in front, retired to Detroit, where it is said he surrender'd, on a summons from fort Sandwich. No official dispatch is rec^d. from him, but a copy of his capitulation is rec^d. from the state of Ohio, from Judge Pease and others. The intelligence seems to be too well authenticated to admit any reasonable doubt of its truth. The whole western frontier of the U. States is in commotion. I wish most sincerely that the President could find employment for me, in so interesting a crisis, in the military line. I do not know that I could render any service, but I well know that neither in the disposition or zeal, should I be deficient.

It was owing to my absence from this place, on a visit to my plantation in Virg^a. that an earlier answer was not given to your favor of the 30 ult^o. I write you in haste to give you most distressing intelligence. The President left town this morning for Virg^a. as did Mr. Gallatin for New York, but expresses are sent to acquaint both of them of this disaster, so that it is probable that both will return.

I am, dear Sir, with great regard, Sincerely yours.

TO THOMAS JEFFERSON.
WASHINGTON, Augt. 31s^t. 1812.

DEAR SIR,—We have heard with great astonishment and concern that Genl. Hull has surrendered the Army under his command to the British force opposed to him in upper Canada. No letter has been yet rec^d. from him, but communications from the gov^r. of Ohio, & others in that State leaves no doubt of the fact. Till his report is made, it is impossible to form a just opinion of his conduct; but from every thing that is known, it appears to have been beyond example, weak, indecisive, and pusilanimous. When he passed the river he had 3 or 4 times the force of the enemy; yet he remained inactive, by reasons which if good at all, were equally good against passing the river, by which, he gave the enemy time, to collect its force, recover its spirits, and assume the offensive; in which time too, the hesitating mind of the Indians and Canadians became fixed, that of the former to cling to their antient ally, and of the latter to risk nothing on an event so precarious. After pausing a longtime without doing any thing, he retired to Detroit, where he surrendered on a summons from the other side of the river, after a short cannonade. It is possible that in this shape it might have been impossible to maintain his ground at Detroit, but why he did not retreat I cannot imagine; nor can it be conceived why, he suffer'd his communication to have been previously cut off, with the forces of Ohio & Kentucky. For if he was not in a situation to attack Malden, he surely had the means of securing the country opposite to it.

This most disgraceful event may produce good. It will rouse the nation. We must efface the stain before we make peace, & that may give us Canada. Very sincerely.

TO HENRY CLAY.
WASHINGTON, September 17, 1812.

MY DEAR SIR,—I have had the pleasure to receive several letters from you in relation to our affairs to the westward, and I hope that one which I wrote you on the receipt of the first, has long since reached its destination. Every effort has been made by the government to remedy the shameful and disastrous loss of the army and fort at Detroit, and I hope the best effect will result from them. In aid of the force which has so generously volunteered its service from Kentucky and Ohio, fifteen hundred are ordered from Pennsylvania, and a like number from Virginia, so that I think you will have on the borders of Lake Erie, early in the next month, eight thousand or ten thousand men, well equipped, prepared to march on to recover the ground lost, and resume the conquest of Upper Canada. I have the utmost confidence in the success of the expedition which is set on foot, because the spirit of the people appears to be roused to that state which is best adapted to manly and heroic achievements. I am willing to trust to their sense of honor and to their patriotism, to efface the stigma which has been fixed on our national character. I hope they will exhibit a noble contrast to that degenerate spirit which has of late and continues to exhibit itself to the eastward, in the dominant party there. The command of this force is committed to Governor Harrison, who, it is believed, will justify the favorable expectation entertained of him by those who are best acquainted with his merit. You and our other friends in Kentucky will find that the utmost attention has been paid to your opinions and wishes on all these subjects.

A large park of heavy artillery is sent on to Pittsburg, to be forwarded thence toward Cleveland, for the use of the army, whose duty it will be to retake Detroit, and expel the British from Malden and Upper Canada. In short, every arrangement is made to give effect to our operations in that quarter that has appeared to be necessary.

On the intelligence of the surrender of Detroit, the President expressed a desire to avail himself of my services in that quarter, and had partly decided so to do. He proposed that I should go in the character of a volunteer, with the rank of major general, to take command of the forces. I expressed my willingness to obey the summons, although it was sudden and unexpected, as indeed the event which suggested the idea was. On mature reflection, however, he concluded that it would not be proper for me to leave my present station at the present juncture. I had no opinion on the subject, but was prepared to act in any situation in which it might be thought I might be most useful.

From the northern army we have nothing which inspires a confident hope of any brilliant success. The disaffection in that quarter has paralyzed every effort of the government, and rendered inoperative every law of Congress; I speak comparatively with what might have been expected. On the public mind, however, a salutary effect is produced even there, by the events which have occurred. Misfortune and success have alike diminished the influence of foreign attachments and party animosities, and contributed to draw the people closer together. The surrender of our army excited a general grief, and the naval victory a general joy. Inveterate Toryism itself was compelled, in both instances, to disguise its character and hide its feelings, by appearing to sympathize with those of the Nation. If Great Britain does not come forward soon and propose honorable conditions, I am convinced that the war will become a national one, and will terminate in the expulsion of her force and power from the continent.

Should you see my old and venerable friend, General Scott, I beg you to present my best regards to him.

TO GENERAL DEARBORN.

WASHINGTON, Sep[r]. 17, 1812.

DEAR SIR,—The surrender of the post and army at Detroit, has put us in a certain degree on the defensive in that quarter, and indeed in every other. But every possible effort has been made to repair the injury. The public spirit too has favor'd the object, for the greatest zeal & enthusiasm prevailed throughout the whole of the western country. It is expected that from Kentuckey, Ohio, Penn[a]. & Virg[a]. there will be on the borders of lake Erie, early next month, about 10,000 troops, militia & volunteers, with a few hundred regulars, moving towards Detroit, to recover the ground lost, & pursue the conquest of Upper Canada. A park of heavy artillery is already on its way from this place to Fort Pitt, to be carried thence to Chastaud, for Detroit; every supply is order'd and provided for, so that I hope our operations will soon take an active & imposing character there, and be felt at Niagara & below it. Gov[r]. Harrison is appointed to command these troops & will, I trust, do well, as he appears to be popular with the western people, especially those of Kentuckey.

On the first intelligence of the surrender of Detroit, the President expressed a desire of giving my services a direction to that quarter, & had in part so decided. He proposed that I sho[d]. act as a volunteer & with the com[n]. of Major Gen[l]. take the command of the expedition. I assur'd him that I was ready to obey his call, tho' it was sudden, as the event was which suggested the idea. On mature reflection he concluded that it would be improper at the present juncture for me to leave my present station. I had no opinion on the subject, and I may add, no wish, being willing to serve in any station where it might be thought I might be most useful.

I feel great anxiety for the fate of our aff[rs]. in your quarter. The disaffection which has prevailed in the Eastern States has paralized every mov'ment, & it has checked the recruiting business, prevented volunteers from tendering their service, & injured the loan. Still I have hoped that, with the aid of what you drew from the middle states, you would get together a strong force, so as to make an impression on lower Canada. The great object seems to me to be a pressure on all the posts at the same time, as it will keep their force divided. If Niagara is under no apprehension of attack, & you approach St. John's & Montreal, the force will be drawn from that quarter to meet you. The same remark is applicable to the other posts. The force will be drawn from the posts not pressed or menac'd to those which are, and having command of the water, its mov'ment will be rapid. Whereas the force which we might bear on Niagara or Kingston, being militia, could not well be carried elsewhere, and if moved, would move slowly. These are reasons for pressing all the points at once and with the greatest force that could be collected.

In general I would make no attack which had not great probability of success, for we had better remain inactive than be repulsed. If, however, our force was strong, so as that we might lose men & have them replac'd soon; a thing which the enemy could not do; for the loss of every man of the regular corps would be in that degree an annihilation of their power, there would [be] less reason for so much caution. I would call into service from Vermont, & wherever I could get them, an overwhelming force, for in our main attack we must if possible succeed, & that we cannot expect to do, unless the force is greatly superior to theirs. I mean there will be no certainty of it. I think that in moving towards Lake Champlain, or taking post within striking distance of the enemy, I wo^d. do it with a force sufficient to maintain the ground; otherwise you will invite attack before you are prepared to receive it.

Before you receive this you will have seen Col. Cass's statement of the causes which produced the surrender of the army under Genl. Hull, or rather the circumstances attending it. I cannot see on what grounds he can attempt to palliate, much less justify his conduct.

You have seen Mr. Gallatin & conferred fully with him on the state of our affairs, with you, as well as elsewhere. I hope your interview will prove useful to the public. It would give me great pleasure to be able to visit you, but it is not now in my power. Your interview with Mr. Gallatin will make it of less importance. I set out for Virg^a. to morrow to bring Mrs. Monroe back here, which I expect to do in ten or 12 days. I am dear Sir with great respect & esteem sincerely yours.

TO THOMAS JEFFERSON.
WASHINGTON, Novr. 11th, 1812.

DEAR SIR,—M^r. Russell has arrived at New York & is expected here in a day or two. He made the second proposition to the British gov^t. authorized by his instructions, which you have seen published, which was also rejected, & in terms rather acrimonious, imparting to it a character which it did not merit. This gov^t. has been sincerely desirous of an accommodation but it appears that the British gov^t. will not even treat on the subject of impressment, as a condition of, or connected with measures leading to, peace. Put down our arms, and they will receive our communications on that subject, & pay to them the same favorable attention that they have heretofore done.

The Massach: elections are terminating unfavorably, as will probably those of N. Hampshire.

TO WILLIAM H. CRAWFORD.
December 3, 1812.

DEAR SIR,—I wish to confer with you and M[r]. [mutilated] early in the morning, before 10., if in your power, on an interesting subject, and to avoid attention should prefer meeting you rather here than at the office, or at your lodgings. M[r]. Eustis (I mention it in confidence) sent his resignation to the President to-day, & it is not improbable that the place will be offered to me. I wish to converse with you both on all the circumstances connected with this event, not as it may relate to me, but the public also. This is the time when the arrangements that are to insure success to the republican party & to free government for our country, are to be made, or which will lay the foundation of their overthrow.

EXPLANATORY OBSERVATIONS, Submitted to Hon. George W. Campbell, chairman of the Military Committee of the Senate [Ed.].

To make this war effectual as to its first objects so much of the physical force of the Country must be brought into activity as will be adequate. The force exists in an abundant degree, and it is only necessary to call it forth, and make a proper use of it. This force must be employed alike in defensive and offensive operations. The exposed parts of our own country claim a primary attention, after providing for their defence, all the remaining force may be employed in offensive operations. I will begin with that part which requires protection.

DEFENSE OF THE COAST.

The whole coast from our northern limits to St. Mary's should be divided into military districts.

Boston, including New Hampshire and Massachusetts, to constitute one.

New Port, including Rhode Island and Connecticut, another.—New York, including the State of New York and Jersey, a third.—Philadelphia, including Pennsylvania and Delaware, a fourth.—Norfolk, including Maryland and Virginia, a fifth.—Charleston, including North & South Carolina and Georgia, a sixth.

At Boston, and at each of the other posts, let a Company of Artillery, or more than one according to circumstances, of the Regular Army, and a small portion of its Infantry, be stationed. Let them be placed under the command of a Brigadier in the following manner, and let him have attached to him an Engineer. This force will constitute the nucleus of a little army, to be formed, in case of an invasion, of the Militia, Volunteers, or such other local force as may be specially organized for the purpose. This apportionment is intended to give an idea. It would be carried into detail by the Executive.

At Boston, including a suitable proportion of Artillery, and at Eastport, and other posts eastwards	600
At Newport, with a Company of Artillery	350
At New York, with a suitable proportion of Artillery	1,000
At Philadelphia, with a Company of Artillery	200
Norfolk, with a Company of Artillery at Annapolis	300
North Carolina, one Company of Artillery	100
Charleston, with a Company of Artillery	300

By placing a general officer of the Regular Army of some experience in command at each of these stations, charged with the protection of the country to his right and left, to a certain extent suitable provision will be made for the whole. The country will have confidence, and by degrees a system of defence, suited to any emergency, may be prepared for the whole coast. This may be done by the local force with economy, and, what is also of great importance, without drawing at any time for greater aid on the regular force of the nation, which may be employed in offensive operations elsewhere. There should be some flying Artillery at each station, ready mounted, and prepared to move in any direction which may be necessary. An Engineer will be useful to plan and execute any works which may appear proper for the defense of the principal station, or any other within each military district.

It may be said that it is not probable that the enemy will attempt an invasion of any part of the coast described with a view to retain it, and less so for the purpose of desolation. It is nevertheless possible, and being so provision ought to be made against the danger. An unprotected coast may invite attacks which would not otherwise be thought of. It is believed that the arrangement proposed will be adequate, and that none can be devised to be so which would prove more economical.

For Savannah and East Florida special provision must be made, whether East Florida is left in possession of Spain, or taken immediate possession of by the United States. In either case it menaces the United States with danger to their vital interests. While it is held by Spain it will be used as a British province for annoying us in every mode which may be made instrumental to that end. The ascendancy which the British government has over the Spanish Regency secures to Great Britain that advantage while the war lasts. We find that at present the Creek Indians are excited against us, and an asylum afforded to the Southern slaves who seek it there. To guard the United States against the attempts of the British government in that vulnerable quarter, the province remaining in the hands of the Spanish authorities, a force of about two thousand regular troops will be requisite. It will require no more to hold it should possession be taken by the United States.

For New Orleans and Natchitoches, including the Mobile and West Florida, about two thousand five hundred men will be necessary. A local force may be organized in that quarter in aid of it, which it is believed will be adequate to any emergency.

The next object is Detroit and Malden, including the protection of the whole of our Western frontier. For these it is believed that two thousand regular troops, with such aids as may be drawn from the States of Kentucky and Ohio will be amply sufficient.

The following then is the regular force requisite for the defence of those places.

Boston	600	Charleston	300
New Port, R. I.	350	Savannah & E. Florida	2000
New York	1000	New Orleans	
Philadelphia	200	Mobile &c	2500
Norfolk	300	Detroit, Malden &c	2000
North Carolina	100		9350

This leaves a force of about twenty-six thousand regular troops, consisting of Infantry, Artillery, & Cavalry, provided the whole force contemplated by law is raised and kept in the field, to be employed in offensive operations against Niagara, Kingston, Montreal and all lower Canada, and likewise against Halifax. This whole force, however, even if raised, cannot be counted on as effective. The difference between the force on the muster rolls and the effective force in the field through a campaign, is generally estimated at a deficiency in the latter of one fourth, with troops who have already seen service. With young troops it may be placed at one third. Take from the nominal force ten thousand, and it would leave about sixteen thousand for these latter purposes.

Will this force be sufficient? This will depend, of course, on the number of the British force which may be opposed to us. It is believed that the British force at Niagara, & its neighborhood, at Kingston, Montreal, Quebec, and in all lower Canada, ought to be estimated at twelve thousand regulars, and several thousand militia, say in all sixteen or eighteen thousand, and at Halifax at three thousand.

To demolish the British force from Niagara to Quebec would require, to make the thing secure, an efficient regular army of twenty thousand men, with an army of reserve of ten thousand. The Commander ought to have power to dispose of them as he thought fit. The movement against Niagara, & lower Canada ought to be in concert, and of course under the control of the same Commander, who alone could be a competent judge of the suitable time and manner. A corps of reserve is indispensible to guard against casualties, especially with raw troops. Nothing should be left to hazard. The Expedition should be of a character to inspire a certainty of success, from which the best consequences would result. Our troops would be more undaunted, and those of the enemy proportionately more dismayed. In the interior on both sides the effect would be equally salutary, with us it would aid in filling our ranks with regular troops, and drawing to the field, such others as occasion might require. With the enemy the effect would be equally in our favor. It would soon drive from the field the Canadian Militia, and by depressing the spirits of the people, interrupt and lessen the supplies to the British army.

If the conquest of Canada should prove to be easy, a part of this force might be directed against Halifax, but for that purpose a force should be specially provided, to consist of not less than six thousand men. Before this time next year the honor & interest of the United States require that the British forces be driven into Quebec and Halifax, and be taken there if possible. They must at all events be excluded from every foot of territory beyond the reach of their cannon. This may be done if timely and suitable measures are adopted for the purpose, and they be executed with vigor and skill.

If the government could raise, and keep in the field, thirty five thousand regular troops, the legal complement of the present establishment, the deficiency to be supplied, even to authorise an expedition against Halifax would be inconsiderable. Ten thousand men would be amply sufficient. But there is danger of not being able to raise that force, and to keep it at that standard. The estimate therefore of the force to be raised for the next campaign, in addition to the legal complement, should cover any probable deficiency in it, as well as the addition which ought to be made to it. My idea is that provision ought to be made for raising twenty thousand men in addition to the present establishment. How shall these men be raised? Shall new regiments be added to the standing army to constitute a part of it, the volunteer Acts to be relied on, or any other expedient be adopted?

The first question to be answered is, can more than the force contemplated by the present military Establishment be raised in time for the next campaign, and that force be kept in the field by new recruits, to supply losses produced by the casualties of war? Will the state of our population, the character & circumstances of the people who compose it, justify a reliance on such a resource alone? The experiments heretofore made, even under the additional encouragement given by the Acts passed at the last session of Congress, and the excitement produced by the war, tho' great, forbit it. Abundant & noble proofs of patriotism have been exhibited by our citizens in those quarters where the approach and pressure of the enemy have been most felt. Thousands have rallied to the standard of their country, but it has been to render voluntary service, and that for short terms. The encrease of the regular army has been slow, and the amount raised, compared with the number sought, inconsiderable. Additional encouragement may produce a more important result, but still there is cause to fear that it will not be in the degree called for by the present emergency. If then there is cause to doubt success, that doubt is a sufficient motive for the Legislature to act on, and to appeal, in aid of the existing resource, to another not likely to fail.

In rejecting a reliance on the regular military Establishment alone, for the force necessary to give effect to the next campaign, the alternative is too obvious to be mistaken by any one. The occurrences of the present year designate it in the most satisfactory manner. The additional force must be raised for a short term, under every encouragement to the patriotism of the people which can be given consistently with the circumstances of the country, and without interfering with enlistments into the old corps. The volunteer Acts of the last session may be the basis on which this additional force may be raised, but these Acts must be radically altered to enable the President to raise the force. Experience has not been less instructive on this very important point. Altho' whole sections of our country, and among them many of our most distinguished & estimable citizens, have risen in arms and volunteered their services, & marched in the ranks, it has not been done under the volunteer Acts. Those Acts contemplate a beginning at the wrong end, & require too long an engagement to produce the desired effect. They contemplate a movement in no particular quarter, and by no particular person—they require that the people shall take the affair up of their own accord, enroll themselves into companies, and then recommend their officers to the President; and that the President shall not appoint the field officers until a sufficient number of companies are formed to constitute a regiment. Thus it may happen that companies from different States, all strangers to each other, may be thrown into a regiment, & that the field officers appointed to command them may be strangers alike to all the company, officers & men. They contemplate also an enrolment for three years, with a service only of one. Conditions which in themselves could not fail to defeat the object, as they enlist on their side not one motive to action. The patriot citizen who really wished to serve his country would spurn the restraint imposed on him of two years of inactivity out of three, and enter the regular army, where he would find active employment for the whole term of his enlistment. And the farmer, the merchant, and the artist, willing to make a sacrifice of a certain portion of their time to the urgent calls of their country, would find a check to their impulse by the obligation they must enter into for so long a term. And by allowing no bounty, no pecuniary inducement, no aid to enable a man to leave home, is offered. It is impossible that such a project should succeed on an extensive scale. The ardent patriotism of a few, in detached circles of our country, may surmount these obstacles, but such examples will be rare.

To give effect to such a measure the President alone should have the appointment of all the officers under the rank of Colonel, and it should be made in the following manner: He should first select such prominent men as bad merited and acquired by a virtuous conduct the confidence of their fellow citizens, and confer on them, with the advice & consent of the Senate, the rank of Colonel, & then confide to them the selection & recommendation of all their officers, to be approved by the President. These men would go to their homes, look around the country where they are known, and where they know every one, select the prominent men there, such as enjoyed the esteem & confidence of their fellow citizens, & recommend them, according to their respective pretensions, as field officers, captains, & subalterns under them. Thus the service would be truly voluntary, as every man would act under officers to whose appointment he had essentially contributed. The several corps would consist of neighbors, friends, & brothers. Example would animate to action. Generous motives would be excited, patriotism roused, and the ties of kindred would unite with the love of country, and of free government, to call our young men to the field.

The first object is to complete the regular Establishment to its legal complement, & to keep it there. The pay of the soldiers has already been raised during the present session of Congress; but this, it is feared, will not afford a sufficient inducement to fill the ranks within the requisite time. Let the bounty be raised to the sum of forty dollars to each recruit, and let the officers receive the sum of five dollars per man for all whom they may recruit. These additional encouragements will, it is presumed, secure the desired success. When filled, how keep the regiment full? The presence of all the officers will be necessary, in that State, for their command. None could be spared to recruit. Different expedients have occurred to supply supernumerary officers for the recruiting business. It has, for example, been proposed to add a certain number of regiments, from fifteen to twenty, to the present military Establishment, but this would be to rely on that Enstablishment alone, which, as is presumed, it would be highly improper to do. This plan is farther objectionable on account of the expense attending it, and likewise as it would create delay in the organization of the corps, and appointment of the officers. The same objections are applicable to the addition of a company to each battalion, not to mention others. On much consideration the following expedient has occurred as most eligible. Let one field officer, a major, be added to each regiment, and a third lieutenant to each company. This will allow a field officer and ten company officers from each regiment for the recruiting service, which would be sufficient.

The additional force proposed for one year is intended to supply the probable deficiencies in the present military Establishment. This force to be raised for a shorter term, and for a special purpose, it is presumed that much aid may be drawn from that source, and with great despatch, for the purposes of the next campaign. It is probable also that it may be done without essentially interfering with enlistments into the old corps, as most of the men who may enter into this might not be willing to engage in them.

If a lingering war is maintained the annual disbursements will be enormous. Economy requires that it be brought to a termination with the least possible delay. If a strong army is led to the field early in the Spring the British power on this Continent must sink before it, and when once broken down it will never rise again. The reconquest of Canada will become, in the opinion of all enlightened men, and of the whole British nation, a chimerical attempt. It will therefore be abandoned. But if delay takes place reinforcements may be expected, and the war prolonged. It is to save the public money, and the lives of our people, and the honor of the nation, that high bounties & premiums, and the most vigorous exertions in other respects are advised. The prolongation of the war for a single campaign would exceed these expenditures more than tenfold.

NOTES ON IDEA OF A PLAN OF CAMPAIGN FOR THE YEAR 1813.

The plan of campaign must be formed by the general who commands the expedition. He alone can best decide at what points to make attacks and where to make feints, if any ought to be made. The plan of campaign must depend on circumstances, & may be altered just before it commences.

Some steps however should be taken by the Department of War preparatory to the Commencement of the campaign, for on these will its success depend. Supplies of every kind should be provided without delay, and placed at such stations in advance, as may best favor the intended operations. These should consist of provisions, or subsistence, for the troops, of ordnance, munitions of war, and every other article necessary for the service. They may be procured & collected without entering essentially into the plan of the campaign, or the number of divisions into which the army may be formed. We know that the enemy are posted along the S^t. Lawrence, from Niagara to Quebec, at different stations, at considerable distance from each other, and that it is on that river or near it, at some or at all of these stations, that we must attack them. The disposition of the supplies should be such, as to leave the commander perfectly at liberty to form his plan of attack & to conduct his military operations as he thought fit. There are two principal routes by which lower Canada may be entered; one by the Onandaga river into Lake Ontario, by the east side of that Lake to the S^t. Lawrence and down the S^t. Lawrence to Montreal; the other by Lake Champlain. The supplies necessary for the campaign should be collected on both routes & as near the enemy's lines as may be done with safety. This would secure to the commander as wide a range as he could desire for his operations & without loss to the public, even with respect to the article of supplies. By whatever route he entered Canada, he might avail himself of them. To facilitate the transportation of these supplies a sufficient number of boats should be provided for the purpose on each route. Everything should be prepared to move with the utmost rapidity, when the occasion called for it.

Of heavy ordnance there will be no occasion, until our Army lays siege to Quebec. It is the only fortified town in all Canada & of course the only one against which heavy ordnance can be of any use. The bayonet is the arm which will be principally relied on, in all the encounters that may be expected before we reach that city. It will be well however to be provided with a proper train of light artillery, as opportunities may offer for using it with advantage. The same remark is applicable to Cavalry. The main army especially should consist of a due proportion of that force. The heavy ordnance must be taken to Canada by Lake Champlain; to each division of the army light artillery in sufficient number must be attached as it may be equally useful in attacking the posts along the S^t. Lawrence, in descending the river from Ontario to Montreal, as in approaching that city by Lake Champlain.

When the supplies are secured, the force collected, and everything prepared, the commander will put his columns in motion and will himself direct the movement. Congress having passed a law authorizing the President to raise an additional force of about 20,000 men for one year it remains to be decided what portion of that force shall be raised & how much of it shall be applied to the invasion of Canada from Niagara to Quebec.

[INDORSED] "WAR PAPERS—NOTES—CERTAIN REPORTS— JESSUP GRAHAM, &C."

Can an expedition be set on foot against Canada this winter & if so at what time?

What force would be adequate? At what point should it be directed?

What preparation would be necessary in ordnance, sleighs, clothing & camp equipage?

If by Champlain, what portion of regular troops could be brought to act in the expedition?

If such an expedition is deemed impracticable during the winter what is the earliest season at which it may be undertaken in the Spring?

What the force necessary for it? At what points should we enter? What the equipment in ordnance and every other article?

If different columns are led by different routes the force composing each should be considered & the ordnance, transportation & every other preparation be adapted to it. How pass the river etc.?

What number of regular troops aided by militia will be adequate to the conquest of Canada in the Spring? The regular force will be required for the van & to head the columns, & to be interpersed in other parts of the army, to give an example to the militia. Of militia any number may be obtained, which may be thought necessary.

Where should camps be formed with a view to the proposed invasion, whether to be made by regular troops only or with the aid of militia: What the preparation in either instance?

The risk seems to be great, and the loss attending it, may be that of the whole force. If we are repulsed again in our own country, that is by land, the effect may be easily anticipated. If we lose our army, by a hazardous measure, where there was no adequate motive for the risk, it may be difficult to trace its consequences. It is safe to put veteran troops in situations of imminent danger, because their courage being tried & mechanical, may be relied on, but the mere circumstance of the danger is apt to overwhelm young troops, even before the reality appears. Altho' our troops have been brave, yet we have seen in many instances, ever since the present war, the justice of this remark. While our army has the enemy in front, & our own country & people in its rear, it will have confidence, & be safe.

If we contemplate offensive operations there are three points of attack—

One by lake Champlain—

Another on Kingston—

A third on Niagara.

The first is supposed to be impossible at the present time, & with our present force.

The second seems to be declined for one principal reason, that we have not the command of the lake, & may not have it; tho' it is not said that our land force is in a state to push the war in that quarter if we had the command of the lake.

The last seems to be that only which is offer'd for consideration. One objection to the mode proposed is that, altho' a measure exposed to much danger, it is rather a defensive than an offensive mov'ment. It merits consideration, at least, if an attack on the strait of Niagara is contemplated, it may not be arranged in a manner, more free from danger, as to the force to be employed in it, and with a better prospect of success, in regard to the corps of the enemy intended to be taken by it.

If a position at Burlington might be deemed important for any distinct purposes may not the object be accomplished without marching our whole force there? One thousand picked men, commanded by a gallant officer, might hold it against any force likely to be brought against it. The British force on the Strait would not be apt to move to attack it with the reminder of our army in its rear, and the force at Sacketts Harbour might keep in check the British force at Kingston, while it might be necessary to sustain the position at Burlington Heights—

5000 men at Burlington Heights—

500 at Matchadash—

a road of 50 miles between them.

The enemy holding 2000 at Forts George, Niagara, Erie, &c—

The enemy commanding the Lake at this time, & thro' this month—The command likely to be ours, thro' July, & the first weeks of August. The command afterwards theirs, without a battle, & victory on our side.

Arguments in favour of this position.

1. It secures to us the peninsula between that line & Detroit, & may check their communication with the upper lakes—

2. It enables us to cut off the force at Fort George and Niagara in case we have the command of the lake, and they be not withdrawn before we get the command.

3. May proceed thence, in case there be an object, on the north side of the lake, to Kingston.

4. A position secure against attacks—high on all sides, & rocky & inaccessible on the side of the lake.

Examination of these arguments.

1. No Indians, in the peninsula—the possession of Detroit, Sandwich & the upper lakes, which we now have, protects us against all the Indians against whom we should be protected (or nearly all) by the positions at Burlington Heights and Matchadash. It is indispensable to retain the posts of Detroit and Sandwich, and the command of the upper lakes, altho' we take the positions proposed at Burlington Heights & Matchadash. In this view therefore no material advantage can be derived from the latter positions, while without lessening the expence of the natural barrier behind, vast expence will be incurred by that to be taken in advance.

2. A force posted at Burlington Heights can afford aid in cutting off the force at forts George & Niagara only in case of its retreat and in that direction. If our force placed there is to be useful elsewhere, it must move to the place where it must act. If the British force is to be taken where it is, it must be invested there, and all retreat cut off. While our force is so distant from it, a squadron may take it off without any check from us. The mov'ment of the squadron up the lake, making a feint towards Burlington Heights, would alarm our troops there, & put them on the defensive. Wheeling round, it might pass the mouth of the strait, &

take off the troops, before ours knew its project. A closer investment taken at the proper time, perhaps that contemplated for the other position, might as effectually cut off its retreat by land, while it embarrassed, if it did not prevent it, by water. The British force must be withdrawn by water, while the enemy has command of the lake, or not at all. It will probably not be withdrawn now in the expectation of losing that command. The presumption therefore is that it will not be withdrawn at all by water. Should it however be attempted to withdraw it by water a close investment would give us all the advantage that circumstances would admit of for annoying it, with the certainty of preventing its retreat by land.

3. No attack is contemplated against Kingston without the command of the lake, as is understood. If that command is not obtained there will be no occasion for these troops to move down to Kingston—If it is they may be mov'd sooner, and at less expence, by water.

4. To this argument no remark is thought necessary. The idea is supposed to be correct.

The above remarks make it probable that all the advantages expected from the proposed positions may not be realized, while the following positive objections have occurred to them.

1. It puts our whole stake in that quarter, in the enemy's country, at a distance from supplies, and from aid in case of danger, however imminent, by our militia or other force. If the enemy commands the lake it will cut off all but the first supplies by water; and the troops on the strait may do the same by land, unless they be sent round by Matchadash. The enemy will also have an opportunity of attacking this force with advantage. It may send up by water all the force from below which it can spare, to co-operate with that at the strait, both of which may be brought to bear on it, without our being able to afford it much assistance, if any. By what route, in that event, would it retreat.

2. By taking that position in the enemy's country it leaves our own country open to the incursions of the enemy, unless we have a sufficient force to prevent it, in the neighborhood of the strait, which we have not.

3. It takes a position distant from the enemy, menacing no vital interest, leaving it optional with the enemy when to attack it if ever, but under no absolute necessity to attack it at all. In itself it makes no attacks on the enemy, and is a force, put, as it were, in that respect *hors de Countrie*.

4. It is a good rule to make no hazardous experiments. War is, it is true, a game of risk, but yet the risk should in all cases be made as little as possible, care be taken that the losses attending it be made as small as possible.

TO THOMAS JEFFERSON.

WASHINGTON, June 16th, 1813—

DEAR SIR,—At the commencement of the war I was decidedly of your opinion, that the best disposition which could be made of our little navy, would be to keep it in a body in a safe port, from which it might sally only, on some important occasion, to render essential service. Its safety, in itself appeared to be an important object, as while safe, it formed a check on the enemy in all its operations along our coast, and encreased proportionally its expence, in the force to be kept up, as well to annoy our commerce, as to protect its own. The reasoning against it, in which all our naval officers have agreed, is that if station'd together, in a port, New York for example, the British would immediately block it up thus, by a force rather superior, and then harrass our coast and commerce without restraint, and with any force however small: in that case, a single frigate might, by cruizing along the coast and plundering & menacing occasionally, at different points, keep great bodies of our Militia in motion: that while our frigates are at sea, the expectation that they may be together, will compel the British to keep in a body, whenever they institute a blockade, or cruize, a force, equal at least to our whole force: that being the best sailors, they hazarded little by cruizing separately, or together occasionally, as they might bring on an action or avoid one, whenever they thought fit: that in that measure they would annoy the enemy's commerce wherever they went, excite alarm in the W Indies & elsewhere, and even give protection to our own trade, by drawing at times the enemy's squadron off from our own coast: that by cruizing, our commanders would become more skilful, have an opportunity to acquire glory, and if successful, keep alive the public spirit. The reasoning in favor of each plan is so nearly equal, that it is hard to say, which is best. I have no doubt at some future day, that a fortification will be erected on the bank in the middle of the bay, and so connected in the manner you propose with a naval force in Lynhaven bay, for the protection of Norfolk, and all the country dependant on the Chesapeake. In time of war it will be difficult to accomplish so extensive an object.

The nomination of ministers, for Russia is still before the Senate. M^r. Giles & Genl. Smith, uniting with M^r. King, & others, against M^r. Gallatin have so far succeeded in preventing its confirmation. They appointed a committee, the object of which was, to communicate with the President, on the subject, & give him to understand that if he would supply his place in the Treasury, they would confirm the nomination to Russia. The President, had before answer'd a call of the Senate, that the appointment to Russia did not vacate the commiss^n. in the dep^t. of the Treasury & that the Secretary of the Navy did the business in M^r. G's absence. To the chairman, who asked & obtained a personal interview, he communicated his objections, to a conference with the committee, on the ground, that the resolution under which they were appointed, did not authorize it, even could any advantage result from it, which however was improbable, as neither party would be apt to change its opinion, and on the principle of compromise that nothing could be done, or ought to be done. Various resolutions tending to embarrass the nomination, divide the republican party in the Senate, & perpetuate that division, by irritating its members towards each other, have been introduced & are still depending. Among them is one, intended to express the sense of the house, against the compatability of the two offices. The delay has done harm & doubtless was intended to have that effect. The result is yet uncertain.

With great respect, etc.

The President is indisposed, with a bilious attack, apparently slight.

TO THOMAS JEFFERSON.
Octr. 1st. 1813.

DEAR SIR,—I have read with great interest & satisfaction your remark s on finance, which I return by the bearer. We are now at the mercy of monied institutions, who have got the circulating medium into their hands, & in that degree the command of the country, by the adventurers in them, who without much capital are making fortunes out of the public and individuals. Many of these institutions are hostile to the gov^t., and the others have already gone far in loans made to it. Hamilton's plan, was a reliance on monied institutions, aided by taxes, at the head of which he had plac'd a national bank, since extinct; and Gallatins has been the same, in respect to a national bank, having proposed to reinstate it, & in respect to any species of taxes. Yours appears to me to be more simple, more consistent with original principles & with those of the Constitution, much more economical, and certain of success, in both its parts, if it could be got into operation. I fear however that has become difficult if not impracticable, by the ascendancy gain'd by the existing institutions, and the opposition they would be sure to make, to its introduction in the radical form proposed, on which its success would principally depend. That corporate bodies would make a great struggle, before they would surrender either their power, or the profit they are making by the use of it. Something however ought to be done to relieve the nation from the burthen & danger inseparable from the present plan.

The fatiguing process of my concerns here has kept me constantly at home and engaged. We will have the pleasure to dine with you to-morrow if the weather permits, and Mr Hay who join'd us last night, indisposed, will accompany us, if his health should improve.

With great respect, etc.

TO JAMES MADISON.
WASHINGTON, December 1813.

DEAR SIR,—The following communication from the Secretary of the Navy is the cause of this letter. Just before I left the office he came into it and informed me that Genl. Armstrong had adopted the idea of a conscription, and was engaged in communicating with members of Congress in which he endeavored to reconcile them to it. I believe that the militia could not be relied on & regular troops could not be enlisted. Mr. Jones was fearful should such an idea get into circulation, that it would go far, with other circumstances to ruin the Administration. He told me that he had his information from Genl. Jacock, and he authorised me to communicate it to you. I suspect that many other members have already been sounded on it, as Mr. Roberts remarked to me yesterday that Genl. Armstrong had returned & had many projects prepared for them.

Other circumstances which have come to my knowledge ought to be known to you. Mr. Dawson called on me yesterday-week & informed me that Mr. Fisk of New York intended to move on the next day a resolution calling on you to state by what authority Genl. Armstrong had commanded the Northern Army during the late campaign—who had discharged the duties of his office in his absence, and for other information relating particularly to his issuing commissions & exercising all the duties of Secretary at War on the frontiers. I satisfied Mr. Dawson that an attack on the Secretary on those grounds would be an attack on you, & that we must all support him against it, to support you. He assured me that he should represent it in that light to Mr. Fisk & endeavor to prevail on him to decline the measure. I presume he did so.

Genl. K. whom I have seen, informed me that this gentln. was engaged in the seduction of the officers of the army, particularly the young men of talents; promising to one, the rank of Brigadier, to another that of Major General, as he presumed without your knowledge, teaching them to look to him & not to you for preferment and exciting their resentment against you if it did not take effect. He says that the most corrupting system is carrying on, throughout the State of New York, particularly in the Q^r. M^s. dept., by placing in office his tools and the sons of influential men under them as clerks etc. I did not go into detail. Other remarks of his I will take another opportunity of communicating to you.

It is painful to me to make this communication to you nor should I do it if I did not most conscienciously believe that this man if continued in office will ruin not you and the administration only, but the whole republican party & cause. He has already gone far to do it and it is my opinion, if he is not promptly removed, he will soon accomplish it. Without repeating other objections to him & if the above facts are true none others need be urged, he wants a head fit for his station &, indolent except for improper purposes, he is incapable of that combination & activity which the times require. My advice to you therefore is to remove him at once. The mere project of a conscription adopted & acted on without your approbation and knowledge, is a sufficient reason—the burning of Newark if done by his order is another—the failure to place troops at Fort George another. In short there are abundant reasons for it. His removal for either of the three, would revive the hopes of our party now desponding &give a stimulus to measures. I do not however wish you to act on my advice—Consult any in whom you have confidence. He has as you well know few friends & some of them cling to him as I suspect either from improper motives or on a presumption that you support him.

This communication is of course confidential, because I see no reason why it should be considered otherwise. Either of the persons above mentioned will if asked support the facts stated on his authority & their truth is the only material point in question.

TO GENERAL ARMSTRONG.
WASHINGTON, Aug. 18 1814.

DEAR SIR,—The movement of the enemy menaces this place among others, and this, I conceive, in a more imminent degree than any other.

In aid of the measures of the Government I should be happy to proceed with a troop of horse to the coast opposite the enemy, from which point I will advise you of their force & objects so far as I may be able to collect them, & should they land, retire before them. It would be agreeable to me to set out this evening. Should you approve the suggestion, I will thank you to give an order to Genl. Van Ness to supply the force necessary. With great respect & esteem yours &c.

TO THE PRESIDENT.
HORSE ROAD, 21ˢᵗ. August, 1814.

DEAR SIR,—I quartered last night near Charlotte Hall, and took a vie w this morning at 8 oclock, from a commanding height, below Benedict creek, of all the enemy's shipping near the town, and down the river to the distance at least of 8 or 10 miles. I counted 23 sq: rigged vessels. Few others were to be seen, & very few barges. I inferred from the latter circumstance that the enemy had moved up the river, either against Com: Barry's flotilla at Nottingham, confining their views to that object, or taking that in their way & aiming at the city, in combination with the force on Powtowmac, of which I have correct information. I had, when I left Aquosco Mills last night, intended to have passed over to the Powtowmac, after giving you an account of the vessels from the height below Benedict: but on observing the very tranquil scene which I have mentioned, I was led by the inference I draw from it to hasten back to take a view of the enemy's movements in this quarter, which it might be more important to the govt. to be made acquainted with. I am now on the main road from Washington to Benedict, 12 miles from the latter, & find that no troops have passed in this direction. The reports make it probable that a force by land and water has been sent against the flotilla. I shall proceed with Capt. Thos. Trist immediately to Nottingham, and write you thence whatever may be deserving notice.

The enemy have plundered the country to the distance of 3 or 4 miles of all their stock &c.

The intelligence of the enemy's force in the Potowmack varies here as much as in Washington. I have had no means of forming a correct estimate of it.

"J. M'S NOTES RESPECTING THE BURNING CITY IN 1814."

The President, secretary of state, and attorney general returned to the city of Washington on Saturday, the 27th of August, at which time the enemy's squadron were battering the fort below Alexandria, whose unprotected inhabitants were in consternation, as were those of the city and of Georgetown, and indeed of all the neighboring country. After the affair of the 24th General Winder rallied the principal part of the militia engaged in it at Montgomery Court-House, where he remained on the 25th and part of the 26th, preparing for a new movement, the necessity of which he anticipated. The secretary of state joined him; a portion of the forces from Baltimore at Montgomery Court-House on the 25th had returned to that city. About midday on the 26th the general having received intelligence that the enemy were in motion towards

Bladensburg, probably with intention to visit Baltimore, formed his troops without delay, and commenced his march towards Ellicott's Mills, with intention to hang on the enemy's left flank in case Baltimore was their object, and of meeting them at the mills if they took that route. Late in the evening of that day he resolved to proceed in person to Baltimore, to prepare that city for the attack with which it was menaced. As commander of the military district, it was his duty to look to every part and to make the necessary preparation for its defense, and none appeared then to be in greater danger or to have a stronger claim to his attention than the city of Baltimore. He announced this, his resolution, to Generals Stansbury and Smith, instructing them to watch the movements of the enemy, and to act with the force under their command as circumstances might require, and departed about 7 P.M. The secretary of state remained with Generals Stansbury and Smith.

The President crossed the Potomac on the evening of the 24th, accompanied by the attorney-general and General Mason, and remained on the south side of the river a few miles above the lower falls, on the 25th. On the 26th he recrossed the Potomac, and went to Brookville, in the neighborhood of Montgomery Court-House, with intention to join General Winder.

On the 27th the secretary of state, having heard that the enemy had evacuated the city, notified it, by express, to the President, and advised immediate return to the city for the purpose of reestablishing. He joined the President on the same day at Brookville, and he, accompanied by the secretary of state and attorney-general, set out immediately for Washington, where they arrived at five in the afternoon. The enemy's squadron was then battering Fort Washington, which was evacuated and blown up by the commander, on that evening, without the least resistance. The unprotected inhabitants of Alexandria in consternation capitulated, and those of Georgetown and the city were preparing to follow the example. Such was the state of affairs when the President entered the city on the evening of the 27th. There was no force organized for its defense. The secretary of war was at Fredericktown, and General Winder at Baltimore. The effect of the late disaster on the whole Union and the world was anticipated. Prompt measures were indispensable. Under these circumstances, the President requested Mr. Monroe to take charge of the Department of War, and command of the District *ad interim,* with which he immediately complied. On the 28th in the morning, the President, with Mr. Monroe and the attorney-general, visited the navy yard, the arsenal at Greenleaf's Point, and passing along the shore of the Potomac, up towards Georgetown, Mr. Monroe, as secretary of war and military commander, adopted measures, under sanction of the President, for the defense of the city and of

Georgetown. As they passed near the capitol he was informed that the citizens of Washington were preparing to send a deputation to the British commander for the purpose of capitulating.

He forbade the measure. It was then remarked that the situation of the inhabitants was deplorable; there being no force prepared for their defense, their houses might be burnt down. Mr. Monroe then observed that he had been charged by the President with authority to take measures for the defense of the city, and that it should be defended; that if any deputation moved towards the enemy it should be repelled by the bayonet. He took immediate measures for mounting a battery at Greenleaf's Point, another near the bridge, a third at the wind milpoint, and sent an order to Colonel Winder, who was in charge of some cannon, on the opposite shore above the ferry landing, to move three of the pieces to the lower end of Mason's Island, and the others some distance below that point on the Virginia shore, to co-operate with the batteries on the Maryland side. Colonel Winder refused to obey the order, on which Mr. Monroe passed the river, and riding to the colonel gave the order in person. The colonel replied that he did not know Mr. Monroe as secretary of war or commanding general. Mr. Monroe then stated that he acted under the authority of the President, and that he must either obey the order or leave the field. The colonel preferred the latter.

TO THE PRESIDENT.
Sep. 3, 1814.

DEAR SIR,—It is necessary that I should distinctly understand my own situation to give it the greatest effect.

In the absence of the Secretary of War, on your arrival here, and of Gen[l]. Winder the duties of both devolved on me. It was your wish that I should act in both places, and the desire of the officers and citizens concurred. The duties of the military commander was undertaken, not on the principle that I might exercise them as Secretary at War, but common consent founded on and growing out of the actual emergency.

In discharge of those duties I have acted on those principles, and I think that affairs are in such a train as to promise a happy result, not only here but at Baltimore & elsewhere, provided I have adequate support.

Since my return I understand that Genl. Winder has acted in my absence as commander of the District, in directing a guard to you, and perhaps in other things. This of course tends to deprive me of all military command. You may recollect that before he came here I offered to you to resign the momentary power which I had assumed to him, and repeated the same to him after his arrival, which you forbade, and he declined. Unless I am strongly supported I had better decline at once. There can be no interfering command or authority, and I am far from wishing to embarrass others. I prefer to aid them as a volunteer, tho' I am not unwilling to take any ground, with the responsibility attached to it, which you may think proper to support me in.

Your friend

[Endorsement] To the President.—He called on me and stated that he would give me a commission P. T., of Secretary at War, & that I should command by consent.

TO THE PRESIDENT.
25 Sepr. 1814.

DEAR SIR,—I have thought much on the state of the Departments at this time, and of the persons whom it may be proper to place in them, and have concluded, that whatever may be the arrangement with regard to other Departments, that the Department of War ought to be immediately filled. I think also, that I ought to take charge of it.

I have been twice brought into it by circumstances, by temporary arrangement, in consequence, I presume, of a prevailing opinion, that I might discharge its duties to the satisfaction of the public. I made the arrangements for the campaign 1813, and had I continued in the Dept., would have conducted it, on different principles from those observed by General Armstrong. I must now lay the foundation for the next campaign, and if another takes the Dept. there is no certainty that he will follow the plan which will be in contemplation.

By taking charge of the Dept. twice, and withdrawing from it a second time, it may be inferred that I shrink from the responsibility, from a fear of injuring my reputation; and this may countenance the idea, that the removal of the other was an affair of intrigue, in which I partook, especially in the latter instance, from selfish and improper motives; and did not proceed from his incompetency or misconduct. It seems due therefore to my own reputation, to go thro' with the undertaking, by accepting permanently a trust, which I have not sought, never wished, and is attended with great responsibility and hazard. By taking the place all clamour will be silenced. It is known here at least that I was put into it, when the other could no longer hold it; those who wished it in the first instance will be satisfied, and I shall go on with your support, and a favorable expectation of the public, that I shall discharge to advantage its duties.

If the office is given to another some weeks must expire before he can take it, and be able to act. For the interim it will be as if it was vacant. No one will be responsible for the safety of this place against another attack. Preparations for another year will go on heavily. In short I think that great injury to the adm^n., to the country, and its cause will arise, from suffering things to remain in that state a single week, and that every day does injury.

If the War Dept. is filled, you may take some days to fill that of the State. Its duties may be discharged in two days that are pressing, which I can do, without interference with those of the other Dept., and would wish to do, as the letters to be now written to our ministers abroad will form a kind of termination to that highly interesting branch of our affairs, and of course to my agency to them.

TO GENERAL JACKSON.

WAR DEPARTMENT, Sept. 27th, 1814.

SIR,—I have had the honour to receive your letter of the 10th. August by Mr. Capida, and subsequent letters of August 23^d. 24th. 25th. and 27th. by mail.

By these communications, which are strongly supported by others from various quarters, there is great cause to believe that the enemy has set on foot an expedition against Louisiana, thro' the Mobile, in the expectation, that while so strong a pressure was made from Canada, and in this quarter, whereby the force of the country, and attention of the government, would be much engaged, a favorable opportunity would be afforded them to take possession of the lower parts of that State, and of all the country along the Mobile.

In this, as in all their other disorganizing and visionary projects, they will be defeated, by the virtue and gallantry of our people. The European governments, reasoning from examples of their own, are always led into false conclusions of the consequences to be expected from attacks on our Union, and the distress of our citizens. This war will give them useful lessons in every quarter of the U. States where the experiment may be made.

By your last letters it seems probable that a considerable British force had been landed at Pensacola, with the connivance of the Spanish authorities there, and at Havana; and by other intelligence it may be presumed that a pressure, or at least a menace, will be made on the Western side of the Mississippi by Nacagdoches and Natchitoches, which latter will probably be by Spanish troops, and for the purpose of menace only.

You have had at your command all the regular force in the District, with the detailed militia in Louisiana & Mississippi Territory, and Tennessee. And you have also had authority to engage on our side the warriors of the Choctaw, Chickesaw & Creek Nations, or so many of them as you might think proper to employ, having it in view, at the same time, to secure the affection and neutrality of all the members of those tribes. It is known that the regular troops are distributed into many posts, and that the militia of Louisiana will be less efficient for general purposes from the dread of domestic insurrection, so that on the militia of Tennessee your principal reliance must be.

The President, taking all circumstances into consideration, has thought proper to order five thousand additional troops from Tennessee to march to your aid as soon as possible, in the most direct and convenient routes, unless before they set out on their march they shall receive countermanding orders from you. He has likewise requested the Governor of Georgia to hold in readiness, subject to your order, twenty five thousand men, on the presumption that a cooperating force from that quarter may possibly be necessary. I send you a copy of my letter to the Governor of Tennessee, to whom you will hasten to communicate your views and wishes. Full confidence is entertained in your judgment in the discharge of this discretionary power vested in you.

Measures are taken for procuring in the neighboring towns, and forwarding to your order, blankets, and some other presents, for the Creeks, Choctaws, and other friendly Indians. These will be sent by wagons direct to. . . . Apprehending much difficulty in the prosecution of your campaign, which it may not be in your power to remove without money, I have transmitted to Governor Blount one hundred thousand dollars in Treasury notes to be applied to the necessary expenses of the campaign, in discharging Indian claims, and supplying their wants, an object to be attended to at the present time, equally from motives of policy and humanity. You will therefore draw on him for the necessary funds. Should it be found more convenient, you are authorized to draw on this Department for such expenditures, at sixty or thirty days sight.

I have the honor to be

TO THOMAS JEFFERSON.
WASHINGTON, Octr. 4, 1814.

DEAR SIR,—I have had the pleasure to receive your favor of the 24th. of Sep^r., to which I shall pay particular attention, and on which I will write you again soon.

Nothing but the disasters here, and the duties which have devolved on me, in consequence, the most burthensome that I have ever encountered, would have prevented my writing you long since, as well as more recently. I have devoted this morning to a full communication to you, but have been pressed by committees, on military topics, till the period has passed. You shall hear from me again in a few days.

With great respect, etc.

TO THOMAS JEFFERSON.
WASHINGTON, Octr. 10th, 1814.

DEAR SIR,—The suspension of payments in specie by the banks is undoubtedly a species of insolvancy. At this time, the foundation of their credit with the public, in a principal degree at least, is the stock of the U. States in their possession. On it they issue their paper, for which they obtain an interest of about 7 p^r. cent. The U. States pay them that interest on advances, on the credit of their own funds. The demonstration is complete, that having better credit than any bank, or than all the banks together the gov^t. might issue a paper, which would circulate without their aid, throughout the U. States, and on much better terms to the public. Your letters I shall take the liberty of shewing to M^r. Dallas, who is expected here in a day or two. They were put up with my papers on the late occurrence, and are not yet unpacked, being sent to Kirby.

I shall be happy to promote the disposition of your library in the manner you propose, tho' I regret that you are to be deprived of such a resource & consolation in your retirement.

TO THOMAS JEFFERSON.
WASHINGTON, Decr. 21, 1814.

DEAR SIR,— On inquiry I found that Major Armstead had been regularly appointed principal assessor for our district by the advice of the Senate & been furnished with his commission. It had been intended, as I understood, to app^t. M^r. Minor, but the office of Collector, having been disposed of in our county, it was decided on the distributive principle to confer the other office on some person in another county. The functions of the Assessor having hitherto been suspended led to the mistake that the office had not been disposed.

I have never been in a situation of as much difficulty & embarrassment as that in which I find myself. I came into it not as a volunteer. This city might have been sav'd, had the measures proposed by the President to the heads of dep^{ts}. on the 1st. of July, and advised by them, and order'd by him, been carried into effect. For this there was full time before the attack was made. Whatever may be the merits of General Winder, who is undoubtedly intelligent & brave, an infatuation seemed to have taken possession of Genl. Armstrong, relative to the danger of this place. He could never be made to believe that it was in any danger. The representatives of corporate bodies, committees of citizens &^{c}. were slighted & divided both before & after the first of July. As late as the 23. of Augt. when the enemy were within 10 miles, by a direct route & marching against it, he treated he idea with contempt altho there was no serious impediment in their way, for the force intended for its defense, was then to be collected at the places of rendevouz & formed into an army. The battle of the next day gave the city to the enemy. The consternation attending in Alex^a. & the neighboring country need not be describ'd. The President, M^r. Rush & I return'd on the 27th. The squadron of the enemy was then before fort Washington. Alex^a. had capitulated; this city was prepar'd to surrender a second time, & Georgetown, was ready to capitulate. The infection ran along the coast. Baltimore totter'd, as did other places, all of which were unprepar'd to resist an immediate attack. Armstrong was at Frederick town & Winder at Baltimore. No time could be spar'd. The President requested me to act in their stead, which I did as well as I could. The citizens cooperated with me. In two or three days the Secr^y. of war return'd, but all confidence in him was gone. I observ'd to the President that the Secry. having return'd my functions must cease; that the delicate relations subsisting between the heads of dept^s. rendered it improper for me to act while he was here, without his knowledge & consent. The President saw the justice of the remark. He had an immediate interview with the Secry., the consequence of which was the departure for his home the next morning. Such was the state of affairs, and the evident tendency, that no time could be spar'd for corresponding with any one at a distance to take the office. The pressure on Alex^a., and approaching attack on Bal: with other dangers and in many quarters allowed not a moment of respite for the dep^t. 24 hours of inaction was sure to produce serious mischief. These considerations induc'd me to retain the office & to incur a labour, & expose myself to a responsibility, the nature & extent of which I well understood, & whose weight has already almost borne me down.

Our finances are in a deplorable state. With a country consisting of the best materials in the world, whose people are patriotic & virtuous, & willing to support the war; whose resources are greater than those of any other country; & whose means have scarcely yet been touch'd, we have neither money in the treasury or credit. My opinion always was that a paper medium supported by taxes, to be funded at proper times would answer the public exigencies, with a great saving to the Treasury. Your plan with some modifications, appear to me to be admirably well adapted to the object. M^r. Dallas had decided on another, which he reported to the committee immediately after his arrival. As soon as I obtain'd my papers from Freds'burg, I put your remarks on the subject into his hands. He spoke highly of them, but adhered to his own plan, & such is the pressure of difficulties, and the danger attending it, that I have been willing to adopt almost any plan, rather than encounter the risk, of the overthrow of our whole system, which has been so obvious & imminent. Mr. Dallas is still in possession of your remarks, but I will obtain & send them to you in a few days.

Of the Hartford convention we have yet no intelligence. These gentry, will I suspect, find that they have over acted their part. They cannot dismember the union, or league with the enemy, as I trust & believe, & they cannot now retreat without disgrace. I hope that the leaders, will soon take rank in society with Burr & others of that stamp.

With great respect, etc.

TO PETER S. DUPONCEAU.
[June 27, 1816.]

DEAR SIR,—I took charge of the Dep^t. of War on the 30 of Augt 1814. All the letters of which copies have been sent you were written by me. The first to Genl. Jackson bears date on the 5th of Sepr. To prevent a mistake as to persons my name had better be signed to each.

The most laborious effort of my life was certainly made in the dep^t. of war. When I took charge of it the enemy were menacing, with an immense force from Europe, every part of our Union. This city was still smoking, its public buildings in ruin: Alexandria had capitulated to a squadron which lay before it: Georgetown was preparing to follow the example: Baltimore, & in fact the whole coast, was agitated with the impending danger. The dep^t. of war was vacant. It had become so by the voluntary act of the late incumbent. I had no desire to supply the vacant office.

I have now the pleasure to forward to you copies of all the documents not lately transmitted, & which have not heretofore been published, relating to Genl. Jackson's campaign, which appear to be of the slightest importance. Of those already published, such as are not in the memoir will be found in Niles' Register. You will arrange them in the manner you think best, & should you find anything deficient, I shall be happy to supply on y^r. pointing it out.

TO GENERAL ANDREW JACKSON.

WASHINGTON, December 14, 1816.

DEAR SIR,—I have since my last to you had the pleasure of receiving two letters from you, the last of the 12. of Nov[r]. The advantage of the late treaties with the Indians is incalculable. One of the benefits consists in putting an end to all dissatisfaction on the part of Tennessee, proceeding from the former treaty. This has been done on very moderate terms. Another consists in enabling the government to bring to market a large body of valuable land, whereby the public debt may be considerably diminished. A third in extending our settlements along the Mississippi, and towards the Mobile, whereby great strength will be added to our Union in quarters where it is most wanted. As soon as our population gains a decided preponderance in those regions East Florida will hardly be considered by Spain as a part of her dominions, and no other power would accept it from her as a gift. Our attitude will daily become more imposing on all the Spanish dominions, and indeed on those of other powers in the neighbouring Islands. If it keeps them in good order in our relations with them, that alone will be an important consequence. I have communicated what you suggested, respecting Gen[l]. Coffee and Lieut. Gadsden, to the President, who is, I am satisfied, well disposed to promote their views.

It is very gratifying to me to receive your opinions on all subjects on which you will have the goodness to communicate them, because I have the utmost confidence in the soundness of your judgment, and purity of your intentions. I will give you my sentiments on the interesting subject in question likewise without reserve. I agree with you decidedly in the principle that the Chief Magistrate of the Country ought not to be the head of a party, but of the nation itself. I am also of opinion that the members of the federal party who left it in the late war, and gallantly served their Country in the field, have given proofs of patriotism and attachment to free government that entitle them to the highest confidence. In deciding however how a new administration ought to be formed, admitting the result to correspond with the wishes of my friends, many considerations claim attention, as on a proper estimate of them much may depend the success of that administration, and even of the republican cause. We have heretofore been divided into two great parties. That some of the leaders of the federal party entertained principles unfriendly to our system of government I have been thoroughly convinced; and that they meant to work a change in it, by taking advantage of favorable circumstances, I am equally satisfied. It happened that I was a Member of Congress under the Confederation just before the change made by the adoption of the present Constitution, and afterwards of the Senate, beginning shortly after its adoption. In the former I served three years, and in the latter rather a longer term. In these stations I saw indications of the kind suggested. It was an epoch at which the views of men were most likely to unfold themselves, as, if anything favorable to a higher toned government was to be obtained, that was the time. The movement in France tended also to test the opinions and principles of men, which were disclosed in a manner to leave no doubt on my mind of what I have suggested. No daring attempt was ever made, because there was no opportunity for it. I thought that Washington was opposed to their schemes, and not being able to take him with them that they were forced to work, in regard to him, underhanded, using his name, and standing with the nation, as far as circumstances permitted, to serve their purposes. The opposition, which was carried on with great firmness, checked the career of this party, and kept it within moderate limits. Many of the circumstances on which my opinion is founded took place in debate, and in society, and therefore find no place in any public document. I am satisfied however that sufficient proof exists, founded on facts, and opinions of distinguished individuals, which became public, to justify that which I had formed.

The contest between the parties never ceased, from its commencement to the present time, nor do I think that it can be said now to have ceased. You saw the height to which the opposition was carried in the late war; the embarrassment it gave to the government, the aid it gave to the enemy. The victory at New Orleans, for which we owe so much to you, and to the gallant free men who fought under you, and the honorable peace which took place at that time have checked the opposition, if they have not overwhelmed it. I may add that the daring measure of the Hartford Convention, which unfolded views which had been long before entertained, but never so fully understood, contributed also in an eminent degree to reduce the opposition to its present state. It is under such circumstances that the election of a successor to Mr. Madison has taken place, and that a new administration is to commence its service. The election has been made by the republican party, supposing that it has succeeded, and of a person known to be devoted to that cause. How shall he act? How organize the administration, so far as dependent on him, when in that station? How fill the vacancies existing at the time?

My candid opinion is that the dangerous purposes which I have adverted to were never adopted, if they were known, especially in their full extent, by any large portion of the federal party; but were confined to certain leaders and they principally to the eastward. The manly and patriotic conduct of a great proportion of that party in the other States, I might perhaps say of all who had an opportunity of displaying it, is a convincing proof of this fact. But still, southern and eastern federalists have been connected together as a party, have acted together heretofore, and altho' their conduct has been different, of late especially, yet the distinction between republicans and federalists, even in the Southern and Middle and Western States, has not been fully done away. To give effect to free government, and secure it from future danger, ought not its decided friends, who stood firm in the day of trial, to be principally relied on? Would not the association of any of their opponents in the Administration itself wound their feelings, or, at least, of very many of them, to the injury of the republican cause? Might it not be considered by the other party as an offer of compromise with them, which would lessen the ignominy due to the councils which produced the Hartford convention, and thereby have a tendency to revive that party on its former principles? My impression is that the Administration should rest strongly on the republican party, indulging towards the other a spirit of moderation, and evincing a desire to discriminate between its members, and to bring the whole into the republican fold as quick as possible. Many men very distinguished for their talents are of the opinion that the existence of the federal party is necessary to keep union and order in the republican ranks, that is that free government cannot exist without parties. This is not my opinion. That the ancient republics were always divided into parties; that the English government is maintained by an opposition, that is by the existence of a party in opposition to the Ministry, I well know. But I think that the cause of these divisions is to be found in certain defects of those governments, rather than in human nature; and that we have happily avoided those defects in our system. The first object is to save the cause, which can be done by those who are devoted to it only, and of course by keeping them together; or, in other words, by not disgusting them by too hasty an act of liberality to the other party, thereby breaking the generous spirit of the republican party, and keeping alive that of the federal. The second is, to prevent the reorganization and revival of the federal party, which, if my hypothesis is true, that the existence of parties is not necessary to free government, and the other opinion which I have advanced is well founded, that the great body of the federal party are republican, will not be found impracticable. To accomplish both objects, and thereby exterminate all party divisions in our country, and give new strength and stability to our government, is a great undertaking, not easily executed. I am nevertheless decidedly of opinion that it may be done, and should the experiment fail, I shall conclude that its failure was imputable more to the want of a correct knowledge of all circumstances claiming attention, and of sound judgment in the measures adopted, than to any other cause. I agree, I think, perfectly with you in the great object, that moderation should be shewn to the federal party, and even a generous policy adopted towards it; the only difference between us seems to be how far shall that spirit be indulged in the outset, and it is to make you thoroughly acquainted with my views on this highly important subject that I have written to you so fully on it. Of the gentleman of whom you have spoken I think as you do, of which I gave him proof when in the Dept. of War, by placing him in the board of officers for digesting and reporting a system of discipline for the army, and afterwards by other tokens of confidence, and I add with pleasure that I should be gratified, regarding the feelings and claims above stated, to find an opportunity, at a proper time hereafter, (should the event in contemplation occur) to add other proofs of my good opinion and high respect for him.

In the formation of an Administration it appears to me that the representation principle ought to be respected, in a certain degree at least, and that a head of a Department (there being four) should be taken from the four sections of the Union, the East, the Middle, the South and the West. This principle should not be always adhered to. Great emergencies and transcendant talents would always justify a departure from it. But it would produce a good effect to attend to it when practicable. Each part of the Union would be gratified by it, and the knowledge of local details and means, which would be thereby brought into the Cabinet, would be useful. I am nowise compromitted in respect to anyone, but free to act, should I have to act, according to my own judgment, in which I am thankful for the opinions of my friends, and particularly for yours.

On the subject of fortifications, or works, for the defence of the coast and frontiers, an arrangement has lately been made by the President with which I wish you to be well acquainted. You have, I presume, heretofore been apprized that General Bernard, of the French corps of engineers, under the recommendation of Gen¹. La Fayette, and many others of great distinction in France, had offer'd his services to the U. States, and that the President had been authorized by a resolution of Congress to accept them, confining his rank to the grade of the chief of our Corps. This resolution being communicated to Gen¹. Bernard by the late Secretary of War, to whom he was known, he came over, in compliance with the invitation which accompanied it. From Mr. Gallatin he brought letters stating that he was the 7th. in rank in the Corps, and inferior to none in reputation and talents, if not first. It required much delicacy in the arrangement, to take advantage of his knowledge and experience in a manner acceptable to himself, without wounding the feelings of the officers of our own Corps, who had rendered such useful services, and were entitled to the confidence and protection of their country. The arrangement adopted will I think accomplish fully both objects. The President has instituted a board of officers, to consist of five members, two of high rank in the Corps, Genl. Bernard, the Engineer at each station (of young Gadsden, for example, at New Orleans) and the naval officer commanding there, whose duty it is made to examine the whole coast, and report such works as are necessary for its defence to the chief Engineer, who shall report the same to the Secretary of War, with his remarks, to be laid before the President. Mc Rae and Totten are spoken of for the two first, who, with General Bernard, will continue 'till the service is performed; the two latter will change with the station. The General commanding each division will be officially apprized of this arrangement that he maybe present when he pleases, and give such aid as he may think fit. The attention of the Board will be directed to the Inland Frontiers likewise. In this way it is thought that the feelings of no one can be hurt. We shall have four of our officers in every consultation against our foreigner, so that if the opinion of the latter becomes of any essential use it must be by his convincing his colleagues, where they differ, that he has reason on his side. I have seen Genl. Bernard, and find him a modest unassuming man, who preferred our country, in the present state of France, to any in Europe, in some of which he was offered employment, and in any of which he might probably have found it. He understands that he is never to have the Command of the Corps, but always will rank second in it.

This letter you will perceive is highly confidential, a relation which I wish always to exist between us. Write me without reserve, as you have done, and the more so the more gratifying your communications will be.

With great respect and sincere regard yours,

MR. RINGGOLD'S DEPOSITION.
WASHINGTON, February 14, 1826.

When Mr. Monroe was appointed Secretary of the Department of War, in September, 1814, he appointed and selected me as the clerk in that department to take charge, under him, of all the money transactions thereof. Upon entering on these duties, it was found that a large amount of drafts, which had been accepted by the late Secretary of War, were lying over under protest; and that drafts for immense amounts were hourly appearing, for the payment of which the Treasury was totally unable to furnish funds, except in depreciated Treasury notes. Mr. Campbell had resigned the office of Secretary of the Treasury, and Mr. Dallas had not been appointed to succeed him. The only alternative left for Mr. Monroe, in this disastrous state of the finances of the government, was loans, to be obtained by the Department of War, under the sanction of the President, if possible. By authority of Mr. Madison, the President, loans amounting to about five millions, were negotiated by Mr. Monroe, as Secretary of War, as will appear, reference being had to his correspondence, now on file in the Department of War, commencing with his letters of the 5th September, 1814, to General Bloomfield, and ending with a letter to Governor Shelby, dated 30th January, 1815.

In addition to these loans, Mr. Monroe borrowed large sums from the Banks of this District, simply by pledging the faith of the government to pay them, with legal interest, so soon as the Treasury was in a situation to furnish the funds. I do not at present recollect the amount of these last mentioned loans; they were upwards of a million of dollars; and thus the government saved 20 per cent. on these loans, that being the difference between the *par* and the depreciated value of the government securities, at that gloomy period of the war.

In the winter of 1814–15 (January, 1815), I think the Paymaster General received information, that his deputies had no funds in their hands to pay the troops of General Jackson, defending New Orleans. I made application to Mr. Dallas, by order of Mr. Monroe, for funds to be transmitted to New Orleans, to pay this army. It was totally out of Mr. Dallas's power to furnish a dollar. Application was then made to our District Banks, which we had before exhausted by loans: and refusals were received from all, with the exception of the Bank of the Metropolis, and the Farmer's Bank of Georgetown. The presidents of these institutions furnished Mr. Monroe with $125,000 each; and Captain Knight, a deputy paymaster, was instantly dispatched with $250,000: and I have been informed, arrived in time to relieve the pressing wants of Jackson's gallant army, by paying the notes of these two little Banks *at par;* when the depreciated Treasury Notes of the government were refused throughout the country, by the creditors of the United States. And this loan was made on the bare word of Mr. Monroe, that the banks should be honourably paid, whenever the state of the Treasury would permit.

Another transaction of Mr. Monroe's, while Secretary of War, ought to be mentioned by me, as it places his disinterested patriotism in such colours, that to withhold it would be sheer injustice. In the year 1814, the Paymaster General was presented with a draft, from one of his deputies in the Northwestern army for $50,000, belonging (as my present recollection serves me) to the Miami Exporting Company, who had advanced the money in Ohio, for the amount thereof. Orders were given to William Whann, the cashier of the Bank of Columbia, to whom the draft was sent for collection, to protest and send it back instantly, if it was not promptly paid; and as Mr. Brent had no funds to meet it, except *depreciated Treasury Notes,* Whann was on the point of sending it back. Mr. Monroe, however, prevailed on him to write to the holders, that the draft had been paid, on Mr. Monroe's accepting, in his *private capacity,* a draft, drawn on him on short date, for $50,000, by the Paymaster General, and pledging his word that it should be paid when at maturity. I have, within a few days, endeavoured to find this draft in the War Department, but am informed it cannot now be found; but the bill-book now in the Department, records the draft accepted by Mr. Monroe. A short time after, another draft was presented under similar circumstances and with similar orders, and Mr. Monroe accepted under like responsibility in his private capacity. Mr. Whann is dead, but I have been informed that Mr. William Stewart, a clerk in the office of the Second Auditor, has heard him relate the facts, as above stated by me.

All which is respectfully submitted to the Committee on the claims of Mr. Monroe, in conformity to the letter of its chairman, dated February, 1816, requesting any information in possession, in relation to loans made by James Monroe, in 1814, 1815.

TENCH RINGGOLD.

PART VIII

President of the United States

INTRODUCTION

WHEN THE SECOND MADISON administration was over, the people of the United States almost naturally looked to James Monroe as their President. He was elected with an unprecedented 183 electoral votes to 34 for the Federalist Rufus King of New York. The Federalist party had collapsed. (For his second term in 1820, Monroe received 231 votes, with only one vote against—and that was for John Quincy Adams).

In his Inaugural Address on March 4, 1817, he laid out his philosophy:

> From the commencement of our revolution to the present day, almost forty years have elapsed and from the establishment of this Constitution, twenty-eight. Through this whole term the Government has been what may emphatically be called self-government; and what has been the effect? To whatever object we turn our attention, whether it relates to our foreign or our domestic concerns, we find abundant cause to felicitate ourselves in the excellence of our institutions. During a period fraught with difficulties and marked by very extraordinary events, the United States have flourished beyond example. Their citizens, individually, have been happy and the Nation prosperous.

For Monroe this was not simply empty rhetoric; it was part of his vision. He immediately began to use his skills in diplomacy to bring together the states into one nation in spirit as well as fact. The collapse of the Federalists led to a migration of political leaders into the Republican party. It was, the newspapers said, "The Era of Good Feeling." In that mode, he wrote to John Quincy Adams, then serving as Minister to London on March 6, 1817, only two days after his inauguration, to offer him the post of Secretary of State. He had no doubts whatsoever about this New Englander who had migrated away from the Federalism of his father.

In late spring he set out on a tour of the United States, with the intention of encouraging every state to think of its place in the nation. At first he had hoped to travel with little circumstance to confer with local leaders; but at every stop those same leaders organized mass welcoming rallies, banquets, speeches and illuminations. On July 27, he wrote to Jefferson describing the reception he had had. Addressing the legislature of Massachusetts in Boston, he laid out his philosophy of government.

In October he submitted a memorandum to his cabinet on whether or not to send a diplomatic mission to South America to get first hand knowledge of the situation of the former Spanish colonies that had declared independence. The commissioners were sent.

At the same time he was pursuing the left-over business of Spanish control over East and West Florida—or rather its lack of control because of the weakness and corruption of the government at Madrid. The question was brought to a head by the precipitate action of Gen. Andrew Jackson, the hero of New Orleans.

Although the Spain had a garrison at St. Augustine in East Florida and another St. Mark's West Florida, the Spanish had little control over the actual territory, which became a no-man's land, a haven for hostile Indians, outlaws, and smugglers. Andrew Jackson, in a latitudinarian interpretation of his orders, chased out the Seminole Indians, then took the Spanish garrison at St. Marks. Monroe immediately ordered Jackson to withdraw from the fort, but not from the territory, telling Jackson that hot pursuit of raiders was justifiable. He asserted in letters to Madison and Jefferson that Jackson's actions were reasonable because the Spanish had broken the law of nations in allowing their territory to be used for lawless attacks on U.S. lands. In his Second Message to Congress on November 16, 1818, Monroe reviewed the entire Spanish question in length detail.

The Spanish protested Jackson's action, but eventually yielded to negotiations conducted in Washington between the Spanish Minister, Juan de Onis, and Adams. On the table was not only Florida, but also the drawing of the western border of Louisiana, which had never been defined. The two diplomats fought it out, week after week. At length the lines were drawn, up the Sabine River (thus excluding Texas) to the Red River, and thence to the Arkansas River—and in a breathtaking sweep, across the 42nd parallel to the Pacific. Thus Monroe was to complete his vision of the United States as a continental power, from sea to sea, a program which had begun with the Gardoqui negotiations in 1783, been pursued through the negotiations for Louisiana, and now would be complete with Florida and the West. Spain was to receive payments equivalent to $5 million. The Transcontinental Treaty was signed on February 22, 1819 and approved by the Senate two days later.

But it was to be until 1821 that Spain finally ratified the treaty. The restoration of Ferdinand VII in 1814 after Joseph Bonaparte fled to Paris resulted in eddies and cross currents in Spanish politics, compounded by corruption and ambition in the court. Favorites had been exiled by the suspicious king, and new favorites arose from nowhere. Even Juan de Onis was afraid to return home immediately after the treaty was signed. Some voices in Congress urged the U.S. government simply to occupy the lands granted in the unratified treaty. In 1820, Monroe sent a special message to Congress on the Spanish question, urging caution. "Is this the time to make the pressure?" he asked. "If the United States were governed by views of ambition and aggrandizement, many strong reasons might be given in its favor; but they have no objects of that kind to accomplish, none of which are not founded in justice and which can be injured by forbearance. Great hope is entertained that this change will promote the happiness of the Spanish Nation. The good order, moderation and humanity which have characterized the movement are the best guarantees of its success." Monroe made sure that the fiery Jackson got a copy of that message, as well as a long letter of May 23rd explaining that the problem was not just problems in Spain, not just the territory in question, but also the jealousy of the eastern states.

That problem made the question of giving diplomatic recognition to the South American republics very sensitive. The mission to Latin America returned with a favorable recommendation of immediate recognition. Yet if diplomatic relations were established, would Spain be so offended that the Florida treaty would never be ratified? At length Monroe was able to write to Jefferson on February 17 that Spain had ratified the treaty unconditionally.

In his Second Inaugural Address, Monroe stated:

To the acquisition of Florida too much importance cannot be attached. It secures to the United States a territory important in itself, and whose importance is much increased by its bearing on many of the highest interests of the Union. It opens to several of the neighboring states a free passage to the ocean, through the Province ceded, by several rivers having their sources higher up within their limits. It secures us against all future annoyance from powerful Indian tribes. It gives us several excellent harbors in the Gulf of Mexico for ships of war of the largest size. It covers by its position in the Gulf the Mississippi and other great waters within our extended limits, and thereby enables the United States to afford complete protection to the vast and very valuable productions of our whole Western country, which find a marked through those streams.

Jackson was appointed as the first governor of Florida in May, given elaborate instructions; but he resigned at the end of 1821.

In his eighth and final message to Congress, Monroe noted with satisfaction the revolutionary governments in Greece and Turkey. He described the measures he had taken for a strong national defense, including the construction of fortifications at strategic points. Perhaps the best example of this legacy is Fort Monroe, which may still be visited at Old Point Comfort on the Chesapeake Bay, in Norfolk, Virginia.

INAUGURAL ADDRESS.
MARCH 4, 1817.

Under the auspices of a delightful day, yesterday took place the interesting ceremony attendant on the entrance of the President elect of the United States, on the duties of his arduous station. The ceremony and the spectacle were simple, but grand, animating and impressive. . . . The principles developed in his Inaugural Speech are such as adhered to will triumphly bear him through. They are those of the honest Republican, and at the same time of the practical statesman. They afford us the highest presage of an upright and unsophisticated administration of the public affairs, on the solid principles of the constitution, regulated by reason, and tempered by the wisdom of experience.—National Intelligencer, *March 5.* [HAMILTON.].

I should be destitute of feeling, if I was not deeply affected by the strong proof which my fellow citizens have given me of their confidence, in calling me to the high office, whose functions I am about to assume. As the expression of their good opinion of my conduct in the public service, I derive from it a gratification, which those who are conscious of having done all that they could to merit it, can alone feel. My sensibility is increased by a just estimate of the importance of the trust and of the nature and extent of its duties; with the proper discharge of which, the highest interests of a great and free people are intimately connected. Conscious of my own deficiency, I cannot enter on these duties without great anxiety for the result. From a just responsibility I will never shrink; calculating with confidence that in my best efforts to promote the public welfare, my motives will always be duly appreciated and my conduct be viewed with that candour and indulgence which I have experienced in other stations.

In commencing the duties of the chief executive office, it has been the practice of the distinguished men who have gone before me, to explain the principles which would govern them in their respective administrations. In following their venerated example, my attention is naturally drawn to the great causes which have contributed, in a principal degree, to produce the present happy condition of the United States. They will best explain the nature of our duties, and shed much light on the policy which ought to be pursued in future.

From the commencement of our revolution to the present day, almost forty years have elapsed and from the establishment of this Constitution, twenty-eight. Through this whole term the Government has been what may emphatically be called self-government; and what has been the effect? To whatever object we turn our attention, whether it relates to our foreign or our domestic concerns, we find abundant cause to felicitate ourselves in the excellence of our institutions. During a period fraught with difficulties and marked by very extra-ordinary events, the United States have flourished beyond example. Their cit-izens, individually, have been happy and the Nation prosperous.

Under this Constitution our commerce has been wisely regulated with for-eign nations and between the States; new States have been admitted into our Union; our territory has been enlarged, by fair and honorable treaty, and with great advantage to the original States; the States, respectively, protected by the National Government, under a mild parental system, against foreign dangers and enjoying within their separate spheres, by a wise partition of power, a just proportion of the sovereignty, have improved their police, extended their set-tlements, and attained a strength and maturity which are the best proofs of wholesome laws well administered. And if we look to the condition of indi-viduals, what a proud spectacle does it exhibit. On whom has oppression fallen in any quarter of the Union? What has been deprived of any right of person or property? Who restrained from offering his vows, in the mode which he prefers, to the Divine Author of his being? It is well known that all these blessings have been enjoyed in their fullest extent; and I add, with peculiar satisfaction, that there has been no example of a capital punishment being inflicted on any one for the crime of high treason.

Some, who might admit the competency of our Government to these benef-icent duties, might doubt it in trials which put to the test its strength and effi-ciency as a member of the great community of nations. Here, too, experience has afforded us the most satisfactory proof in its favour. Just as this Constitution was put into action, several of the principal States of Europe had become much agitated, and some of them seriously convulsed. Destructive wars ensued, which have of late only been terminated. In the course of these conflicts the United States received great injury from several of the parties. It was their interest to stand aloof from the contest; to demand justice from the party committing the injury; and to cultivate by a fair and honorable conduct, the friendship of all. War became at length inevitable and the result has shown that our Government is equal to that, the greatest of trials, under the most unfavorable circumstances. Of the virtue of the people, and of the heroic exploits of the army, the navy, and the militia I need not speak.

Such, then, is the happy Government under which we live; a Government adequate to every purpose for which the social compact is formed; a Gov-ernment elective in all its branches, under which every citizen may, by his merit, obtain the highest trust recognized by the Constitution; which contains within it no cause of discord; none to put at variance one portion of the community with another; a Government which protects every citizen in the full enjoyment of his rights and is able to protect the Nation against injustice from foreign Powers.

Other considerations of the highest importance admonish us to cherish our Union, and to cling to the Government which supports it. Fortunate as we are, in our political institutions, we have not been less so in other circumstances on which our prosperity and happiness essentially depend. Situated within the temperate zone and extending through many degrees of latitude along the Atlantic, the United States enjoy all the varieties of climate and every production incident to that portion of the globe. Penetrating internally to the great lakes and beyond the sources of the great rivers which communicate through our whole interior, no country was ever happier with respect to its domain. Blessed, too, with a fertile soil, our produce has always been very abundant, leaving, even in years the least favorable, a surplus for the wants of our fellow men in other countries. Such is our peculiar felicity, that there is not a part of our Union that is not particularly interested in preserving it. The great agricultural interest of the Nation prospers under its protection. Local interests are not less fostered by it. Our fellow citizens of the north, engaged in navigation, find great encouragement in being made the favored carriers of the vast productions of the other portions of the United States; while the inhabitants of these are amply recompensed in their turn, by the nursery for seamen and naval force thus formed and reared up for the support of our common rights. Our manufacturers find a generous encouragement by the policy which patronizes domestic industry, and the surplus of our produce a steady and profitable market, by local wants in less favored parts, at home.

Such, then, being the highly favored condition of our country it is the interest of every citizen to maintain it. What are the dangers which menace us? If any exist they ought to be ascertained and guarded against.

In explaining my sentiments on this subject, it may be asked, what raised us to the present happy state? How did we accomplish the revolution? How remedy the defects of the first instrument of our Union, by diffusing into the National Government sufficient power for national purposes, without impairing the just rights of the States or affecting those of individuals? How sustain and pass with glory through the late war?

The Government has been in the hands of the People. To the People, therefore, and to the faithful and able depositories of their trust, is the credit due. Had the people of the United States been educated in different principles; had they been less intelligent, less independent, or less virtuous, can it be believed that we should have maintained the same steady and consistent career, or been blessed with the same success? While, then, the constituent body retains its present sound and healthful state, everything will be safe. They will choose competent and faithful representatives for every department. It is only when the People become ignorant and corrupt, when they degenerate into a populace, that they are incapable of exercising the sovereignty. Usurpation is then an easy attainment and an usurper soon found. The People themselves become the willing instruments of their own debasement and ruin. Let us then look to the great cause and endeavor to preserve it in full force. Let us, by all wise and constitutional measures, promote intelligence among the People, as the best means of preserving our liberties.

Dangers from abroad are not less deserving of attention. Experiencing the fortune of other nations, the United States may be again involved in war, and it may, in that event be the object of the adverse party to overset our Government, to break our Union and demolish us as a Nation. Our distance from Europe, and the just, moderate and pacific policy of our Government, may form some security against those dangers; but they ought to be anticipated and guarded against. Many of our citizens are engaged in commerce and navigation, and all of them are, in a certain degree, dependant on their prosperous state. Many are engaged in the fisheries. These interests are exposed to invasion in the wars between other Powers, and we should disregard the faithful admonition of experience if we did not expect it. We must support our rights or lose our character, and with it perhaps our liberties. A people who fail to do it can scarcely be said to hold a place among independent nations. National honor is National property of the highest value. This sentiment in the mind of every citizen is National strength; it ought, therefore, to be cherished.

To secure us against these dangers, our coast and inland frontiers should be fortified; our army and navy, regulated upon just principles as to the force of each, be kept in perfect order; and our militia be placed on the best practicable footing. To put our extensive coast in such a state of defence as to secure our cities and interior from invasion will be attended with expense, but the work when finished, will be permanent; and it is fair to presume that a single campaign of invasion, by a naval force superior to our own, aided by a few thousand land troops, would expose us to greater expense, without taking into the estimate the loss of property and distress of our citizens, than would be sufficient for this great work. Our land and naval forces should be moderate, but adequate to the necessary purposes: the former to garrison and preserve our fortifications, and to meet the first invasions of a foreign foe, and, while constituting the elements of a greater force, to preserve the science as well as all the necessary implements of war in a state to be brought into activity in the event of war; the latter, retained within the limits proper in a state of peace, might aid in maintaining the neutrality of the United States with dignity in the wars of other Powers, and in saving the property of our citizens from spoliation. In time of war, with the enlargement of which the great naval resources of the country render it susceptible, and which should be duly fostered in time of peace, it would contribute essentially, both as an auxiliary of defence and as a powerful engine of annoyance, to diminish the calamities of war, and to bring the war to a speedy and honorable termination.

But it ought always to be held prominently in view that the safety of these States and of every thing dear to a free people, must depend in an eminent degree on the militia. Invasions may be made too formidable to be resisted by any land and naval force which it would comport either with the principles of our Government or the circumstances of the United States to maintain. In such cases recourse must be had to the great body of the People and in a manner to produce the best effect. It is of the highest importance, therefore, that they be so organized and trained as to be prepared for any emergency. The arrangement should be such as to put at the command of the Government the ardent patriotism and youthful vigor of the country. If formed on equal and just principles, it cannot be oppressive. It is the crisis which makes the pressure, and not the laws, which provide a remedy for it. This arrangement should be formed, too, in time of peace to be the better prepared for war. With such an organization of such a people the United States have nothing to dread from foreign invasion. At its approach, an overwhelming force of gallant men might always be put in motion.

Other interests of high importance will claim attention; among which the improvement of our country by roads and canals, proceeding always with a constitutional sanction, holds a distinguished place. By thus facilitating the intercourse between the States we shall add much to the convenience and comfort of our fellow citizens; much to the ornament of the country; and what is of greater importance, we shall shorten distances, and by making each part more accessible to and dependant on the other, we shall bind the Union more closely together. Nature has done so much for us by intersecting the country with so many great rivers, bays and lakes, approaching from distant points so near to each other, that the inducement to complete the work seems to be peculiarly strong. A more interesting spectacle was perhaps never seen than is exhibited within the limits of the United States—a territory so vast and advantageously situated, containing objects so grand, so useful, so happily connected in all their parts.

Our manufacturers will likewise require the systematic and fostering care of the Government. Possessing, as we do, all the raw materials, the fruit of our own soil and industry, we ought not to depend in the degree we have done, on supplies from other countries. While we are thus dependant, the sudden event of war, unsought and unexpected cannot fail to plunge us into the most serious difficulties. It is important, too, that the capital which nourishes our manufacturers should be domestic, as its influence in that case, instead of exhausting, as it may do in foreign hands, would be felt advantageously on agriculture and every other branch of industry. Equally important is it to provide at home a market for our raw materials, as, by extending the competition, it will enhance the price, and protect the cultivation against the casualties incident to foreign markets.

With the Indian tribes it is our duty to cultivate friendly relations and to act with kindness and liberality in all our transactions. Equally proper is it to persevere in our efforts to extend to them the advantages of civilization.

The great amount of our revenue, and the flourishing state of the Treasury are a full proof of the competency of the National resources for any emergency, as they are of the willingness of our fellow citizens to bear the burdens which the public necessities require. The vast amount of vacant lands, the value of which daily augments forms an additional resource of great extent and duration. These resources, besides accomplishing every other necessary purpose, put it completely in the power of the United States to discharge the National debt at an early period. Peace is the best time for improvement and preparation of every kind; it is in peace that our commerce flourishes most, that taxes are most easily paid, and that the revenue is most productive.

The Executive is charged, officially, in the departments under it, with the disbursement of the public money and is responsible for the faithful application of it to the purposes for which it is raised. The Legislature is the watchful guardian over the Public purse. It is its duty to see that the disbursement has been honestly made. To meet the requisite responsibility, every facility should be afforded to the Executive to enable it to bring the public agents intrusted with the public money strictly and promptly to account. Nothing should be presumed against them; but if, with the requisite facilities, the public money is suffered to lie long and uselessly in their hands, they will not be the only defaulters, nor will the demoralizing effect be confined to them. It will evince a relaxation and want of tone in the administration, which will be felt by the whole community. I shall do all I can to secure economy and fidelity in this important branch of the administration, and I doubt not that the Legislature will perform its duty with equal zeal. A thorough examination should be regularly made, and I will promote it.

It is particularly gratifying to me to enter on the discharge of these duties at a time when the United States are blessed with peace. It is a state most consistent with their prosperity and happiness. It will be my sincere desire to preserve it, so far as depends on the Executive, on just principles with all nations—claiming nothing unreasonable of any and rendering to each what is its due.

Equally gratifying is it to witness the increased harmony of opinion which pervades our Union. Discord does not belong to our system. Union is recommended, as well by the free and benign principles of our Government, extending its blessings to every individual, as by the other eminent advantages attending it. The American People have encountered great dangers, and sustained severe trials with success. They constitute one great family with a common interest. Experience has enlightened us on some questions of essential importance to the country. The progress has been slow, dictated by a just reflection, and a faithful regard to every interest connected with us. To promote this harmony, in accord with the principles of our Republican Government, and in a manner to give them the most complete effect, and to advance in all other respects the best interests of our Union, will be the object of my constant and zealous attentions.

Never did a Government commence under auspices so favorable, nor ever was success so complete. If we look to the history of other Nations, ancient or modern, we find no example of a growth so rapid—so gigantic; of a people so prosperous and happy. In contemplating what we have still to perform, the heart of every citizen must expand with joy, when he reflects how near our Government has approached to perfection; that, in respect to it, we have no essential improvement to make; that the great object is to preserve it in the essential principles and features which characterize it, and that that is to be done by preserving the virtue and enlightening the minds of the people; and, as a security against foreign dangers, to adopt such arrangements as are indispensable to the support of our independence, our rights and liberties. If we persevere in the career in which we have advanced so far, and in the path already traced, we cannot fail, under the favor of a gracious Providence, to attain the high destiny which seems to await us.

In the administrations of the illustrious men who have preceded me in this high station, with some of whom I have been connected by the closest ties from early life, examples are presented which will always be found highly instructive and useful to their successors. From these I shall endeavor to derive all the advantages which they may afford. Of my immediate predecessor, under whom so important a portion of this great and successful experiment has been made, I shall be pardoned for expressing my earnest wishes that he may long enjoy, in his retirement, the affections of a grateful country—the best reward of exalted talents and the most faithful and meritorious services. Relying on the aid to be derived from the other departments of the Government, I enter on the trust to which I have been called by the suffrages of my fellow citizens, with my fervent prayers to the Almighty that he will be graciously pleased to continue to us that protection which He has already so conspicuously displayed in our favor.

TO JOHN QUINCY ADAMS.
WASHINGTON, March 6, 1817.

DEAR SIR,—Respect for your talents and patriotic services has induced me to commit to your care, with the sanction of the Senate, the Department of State. I have done this in confidence that it will be agreeable to you to accept it, which I can assure you will be very gratifying to me. I shall communicate your appointment by several conveyances to multiply the chances of your obtaining early knowledge of it, that, in case you accept it, you may be enabled to return to the U States, and enter on the duties of the office, with the least delay possible.[1] This letter is delivered to Mr. Cook, a respectable young man from Kentucky, who is employed as a special messenger for the purpose.

TO THEODORE LYMAN, JR.
April—1817

I have rec[d] your letter of the 12th of April, [Asking for an explanation of certain parts of the London treaty of 1806, not yet communicated to the public.] and, far from seeing any impropriety in your calling on me for any information which I may possess respecting our transactions with foreign powers in which I have been engaged, I am very sensible of your attention in making such a call. Nothing can be more important than a correct knowledge of our conduct in those transactions in all their circumstances, & of the consequences resulting from the policy which was pursued, & it is very proper for you to obtain it, and to present to the public a corresponding view therewith, as far as you may be able.

It fell to my lot to be employed a long time, and at the most difficult periods, in missions to foreign powers. My first mission was to the French Republic

---

1. Mr. Adams arrived in Washington on Saturday, September 20th, and on Monday, the 22d, the oath of office and the oath to support the Constitution were administered to him by Robert Brent, a justice of the peace for the District of Columbia.—*Memoirs of John Quincy Adams.* [HAMILTON.]

in 1794, from which I returned in 1797. The second was in 1803, to France and Spain, & also to G. B., in which I was engaged nearly five years. In the first the French Revolution was at its height, & its bearing on us by the cause of the war, the views of the coalesced powers, and the ill digested & indiscreet policy of those at the head of the French gov^t., was very interesting. From this mission I was recalled & censured, and in vindication of my conduct in it I published a book entitled, *A view of the conduct of the adm^n. &c.,* with my correspondence with both gov^{ts}., & all the documents connected therewith.

The epoch on the second mission was likewise very interesting. The affairs of France & of Europe were still unsettled, & the cause which produc'd my mission, independent of others which arose, after the war in Europe was renewed, showed that we had very important rights as well as a character to sustain in it. In that portion of this mission which related to G. B. I was associated with Mr. Pinkney in a negotiation with the British gov^t., in which we concluded a treaty in 1806, which was rejected by our gov^t., & is that respecting w^h. you request information from me.

As we were instructed to renew the negotiation with the British gov^t., in the hope of obtaining better conditions than we had done in the treaty, & did renew it, Mr. P. & I thought it improper to say anything in vindication, or explanation of our conduct in that occurrence while the renewed negotiation was depending. As soon as it was finish'd, & my correspondence with the British gov^t., respecting the attack on the Chesapeake, was terminated, I retired from that office, & return'd home. I then thought myself at liberty to give the explanation w^h. the case requir'd, which I did in a letter from Richmond, bearing date on the 28th. of Feby. 1808. In that letter the whole subject is reviewed, and the considerations which induced us to sign the treaty fully explained. We were positively instructed to conclude no treaty with the British gov^t. which sho^d. not provide against the impressment of our seamen. We did conclude one without obtaining such provision, & for that reason more especially the treaty was rejected. Mr. Madison, then Sec^{ry}. of State, explains the ground of the rejection in his letter by Mr. Purviance, who brought the treaty to our gov^t. & took it back, and my letter above mentioned contains a reply to his, with a full explanation of all the considerations which induced us to take the part we did. We gave notice to the British Commiss^{rs}., who acted with great candour in the whole affair, when we signed the treaty that we did it on our own responsibility, in direct violation of our instructions, & that our gov^t. would not be bound to ratify it. Among our motives for signing it, you will observe that it is stated in my letter from Richmond above noticed, that we considered that treaty the alternative to war, & for which we did not think we were then prepared. By that letter, with other documents which have since been published, every fact & view of the subject which involve the merits [of] the question, in regard to the public, as to the policy pursued, or to ourselves, are fully stated. A war ensued in which [we] acquired glory, and which terminated with honor to our country. It was a necessary tho' bold experiment. It has I am satisfied strengthened our Union.

In addition to the documents referr'd to, it may not be improper to mention the memoir, documents, &c. which I published in Novr. last, & which illustrate certain incidents in reference to each mission. I have no idea that your view will enter into such details, or even touch the causes which produce them, the perusal of them may, however, give you views which may be useful in the more general work which you contemplate. Should there [be] any fact within my knowledge on which you may desire information, & apprize me of it, I will most cheerfully communicate it to you.

TO THOMAS JEFFERSON.
PLATTSBURG, July 27, 1817.

DEAR SIR,—I arriv'd here the day before yesterday on my way to Sacketts harbour, & thence to the westward, in completion of the tour, which I advis'd you, that I had in contemplation, before I left Washington. I have been, eastward, as far as Portland, and after returning to Dover in N. Hampshire, have come here, by Concord & Hanover in that State, & Windsor, Montpelier, & Burlington, in Vermont. Yesterday, I visited Rouse's point, within two hundred yards of the boundary line, where we are engaged in erecting a work of some importance; as it is supposed, to command the entrance into the lake from Canada. Genl. Brown met me here. To-morrow I proceed, with him, by Ogdensb^g. to Sacketts harbour, & thence to Detroit, unless I should be compelled, on reaching Erie, to cling to the south-eastern side of that lake, & seek my way home, through the State of Ohio, by circumstances I may not be able to controul.

When I undertook this tour, I expected to have executed it, as I might have done, in an inferior station, and even of a private citizen, but I found, at Baltimore that it would be impracticable for me to do it. I had, therefore, the alternative, of either returning home, or complying with the opinion of the public, & immediately, I took the latter course, relying on them, to put me forward as fast as possible, which has been done. I have been exposed to excessive fatigue

& labour, in my tour, by the pressure of a very crowded population, which has sought to manifest its respect, for our Union, & republican institutions, in every step I took, and in modes w^h. made a trial of my strength, as well physically as mentally. In the principal towns, the whole population, has been in motion, and in a manner, to produce the greatest degree of excit'ment possible. In the Eastern States of our Union, I have seen, distinctly, that the great cause, which brought the people forward, was a conviction, that they had suffer'd in their character, by their conduct in the late war, and a desire to show, that unfavorable opinions, and as they thought, unjust, had been form'd in regard to their views and principles. They say'd the opportunity, which the casual incident of my tour presented to them, of making a strong exertion, to restore themselves to the confidence and ground which they had formerly held, in the affections of their brethren, in other quarters. I have seen enough to satisfy me, that the great mass of our fellow-citizens, in the Eastern States are as firmly attached to the union and to republican gov^t. as I have always believ'd or could desire them to be.

In all the towns thro' which I passed, there was an union between the parties, except in the case of Boston. I had supposed that that union, was particularly to be desir'd by the republican party, since as it would be founded, exclusively on their own principles, everything would be gain'd by them. Some of our old, and honest friends at Boston, were, however, unwilling to amalgamate with their former opponents, even on our own ground, and in consequence presented an address of their own. This formed the principal difficulty, that I have had to meet, to guard against any injury arising from the step taken to the republican cause, to the republican party, or the persons individually. You will have seen their address, & my reply & be enabled to judge of the probable result.

I hope to see you the latter end of next month, when we will enter into details, which the few minutes I now enjoy do not admit, however glad I should be to do it. I most ardently wish to get home, to meet my family & friends & to enjoy in peace some moments of repose to which I have been an utter stranger since I left Washington.

THE ERA OF GOOD FEELING.

Referring to the address of the Minority of the Legislature of Massachusetts, the President's reply was: "I have received, with great satisfaction, the very friendly welcome which you have given me, on the part of some of the members of the legislature of Massachusetts, and of others, citizens of Boston, who had deputed you to offer me their congratulations on my arrival in this metropolis. Conscious of having exerted my best faculties with unwearied zeal, to support the rights, and advance the prosperity of my fellow citizens, in the various important trusts with which I have been honored by my country, the approbation which you have expressed of my conduct is very gratifying to me. It has been my undeviating effort, in every situation in which I have been placed, to promote to the utmost of my abilities, the success of our republican government. I have pursued this policy from a thorough conviction that the prosperity and happiness of the whole American people depended on the success of the great experiment which they have been called upon to make. All impartial persons now bear testimony to the extraordinary blessings with which we have been favored. Well satisfied I am that these blessings are to be imputed to the excellence of our government, and to the wisdom and purity with which it has been administered.

"Believing that there is not a section of our Union, nor a citizen who is not interested in the success of our government, I indulge a strong hope that they will all unite, in future, in the measures necessary to secure it. From this very important change I consider the circumstances of the present epoch peculiarly favorable. The success and unexampled prosperity with which we have hitherto been blessed, must have dispelled the doubts of all who had before honestly entertained any, of the practicability of our system, and from these a firm and honorable cooperation may fairly be expected. Our Union has also of late acquired much strength. The proofs which have been afforded of the great advantages communicated by it to every foreign part, and of the ruin which would inevitably and promptly overwhelm even the parts most favored, if it should be broken, seem to have carried conviction home to the bosoms of the most unbelieving. On the means necessary to secure success and to advance with increased rapidity, the growth and prosperity of our country, there seems now to be but little, if any, difference of opinion.

"It is on these grounds that I indulge a strong hope, and even entertain great confidence, that our principal dangers and difficulties have passed, and that the character of our deliberations, and the course of the government itself, will become more harmonious and happy than it has heretofore been.

"Satisfied as I am, that the union of the whole community, in support of our republican government, by all wise and proper measures, will effectually secure it from danger, that union is an object to which I look with the utmost solicitude. I consider it my duty to promote it on the principles, and for the purposes stated, and highly gratified shall I be if it can be obtained. In frankly avowing this motive, I owe it to the integrity of my views to state, that as the support of our republican government is my sole object, and in which I consider the whole community equally interested, my conduct will be invariably directed

to that end. In seeking to accomplish so great an object, I shall be careful to avoid such measures as may by any possibility sacrifice it." [HAMILTON.].

[MEMORANDUM BY James Monroe, OCTOBER 1817, Ed.]
TO THE MEMBERS OF THE CABINET.

Has the Executive power to acknowledge the independence of new States whose independence has not been acknowledged by the parent country, and between which parties a war actually exists on that account?

Will the sending, or receiving a minister to a new State under such circumstances be considered an acknowledgement of its independence?

Is such acknowledgement a justifiable cause of war to the parent country? Is it a just cause of complaint to any other power?

Is it expedient for the U States, at this time, to acknowledge the independence of Buenos Ayres, or of any other part of the Spanish dominions in America now in a state of revolt?

What ought to be the future conduct of the U States towards Spain, considering the evasions practiced by her gov^t., in procrastinating negotiations, amounting to a refusal to make reparation for injuries?

Is it expedient to break up the establishments at Amelia Island, & Galveston, it being evident that they were made for smuggling, if not for piratical purposes, & already preverted to very mischievous purposes to the U States?

Is it expedient to pursue the measure which was decided in May last, but suspended by circumstances, of sending a public ship along the Southern coast, particularly that of the Spanish Colonies, with three citizens of distinguished abilities and high character, to examine the state of those colonies, the progress of the revolution, & the probability of its success, and to make a report accordingly?

Is it expedient to publish the communication of the French Minister' of a projected movement of the French emigrants for the establishment of Joseph Bonaparte in Mexico, and of the correspondence with him?

TO JAMES MADISON.
WASHINGTON, November 24th, 1817.

DEAR SIR,—I have been, since my return here, so incessantly engaged in the most interesting business, that I have not had a moment to say anything to you. I am now engaged in preparing the message to Congress, whose meeting is so near at hand, that I shall, I fear, be badly prepared. The question respecting canals & roads is full of difficulty, growing out of what has passed on it. After all the consideration I have given it, I am fixed in the opinion, that the right is not in Congress and that it would be improper in me, after your negative, to allow them to discuss the subject & bring a bill for me to sign, in the expectation that I would do it. I have therefore decided to communicate my opinion in the message & to recommend the procuring an amendment from the States, so as to vest the right in Congress in a manner to comprise in it a power also to institute seminaries of learning. The period is perhaps favorable to such a course.

The establishments at Amelia Island & Galvestown have done us great injury, in smuggling of every kind & particularly in introducing africans as slaves into the United States. The Southern States have complained also at their being made a receptacle for runaway slaves, particularly the former. We have resolved to break them up for which measures are taking. Mr. Rodney, Mr. Graham and Judge Bland are to go in the *Congress* along the coast to Buenos Ayres for the purpose known to you. I have appointed Calhoun Secretary of War and Mr. Wirt Attorney General. The receipts into the Treasury have been very good, perhaps twenty millions, instead of twelve, & Mr. Crawford is of opinion that I ought to recommend the repeal of the internal revenues, which I shall probably do. We are in pretty good health & all my family desire their best regards to you and Mrs. Madison.

Memoranda for Cabinet meeting, December 1817 [HAMILTON.]

1. policy of resorting to loans in time of peace unjustifiable & inexpedient. only justifiable to meet debts previously incurred, or necessary expenditures, on a sudden temporary reduction of the revenue, to avoid unnecessary imposition of taxes, or change of system of policy adopted on great deliberation, deemed necessary for public security & prosperity.

2. That it is the constitutional duty of this gov^t. to take efficient measures for redemption of the public debt, & to provide for the public defense.

3. That it is believed that the revenue to be derived from imports, tonage and the sales of public lands, is sufficient, without a resort to internal taxes, to meet all the objects above stated, by adherence to a proper system of removing & making such retrenchment in expenditures, & by reducing all such salaries as may appear to be too high, as may be done consistently with the public interest, & especially where such change, by the establishment of a system necessary to carry it into effect, wo^d. create in itself an annual expenditure nearly exact to the sum required.

4. that the Tariff sho^d. be so modified as to give the greatest protection to manufactures, encouragement to agriculture, & commerce, & revenue.

5. that this being the only republic as yet fully established, & resting solely on the sovereignty of the people, it is due to the best interests of the people, & required in [the] present state of the world, to adopt in peace all the measures necessary to the defence of the country.

resolv^d. that the time of peace is the time to prepare for war, it being the time when the expences can best be met, & best be borne by the people—preparations best made.

TO JAMES MADISON.
WASHINGTON, Dec. 22, 1817.

DEAR SIR,—You know so much of the nature of the pressure to which I am subjected at this time, that you will excuse my not giving an earlier answer to your letter of the 9th. The documents relating to Galveston and Amelia Island, published in this days paper will reach you with this. They shew the reasons which operated with the Executive in taking the measures noted in your letter. They appeared to be conclusive, as being mere piratical establishments, probably unauthorised by any of the Colonies, but forfeiting all claim to consideration by their conduct, if authorised, & that in putting them down, especially if disavowed by the Colonies, we should advance their cause, in the opinion of the civilized world. It is hoped that the object will be attained without the use of force. Orders to that effect are given, the resort to force being authorised in case of necessity only. . . .

The National Intelligencer, under date of Monday, December 22d (issued the 23d), publishing selections of the documents transmitted to the House of Representatives by the President, with editorial note:—"We present to our readers a selection of the most interesting of the documents transmitted to the House of Representatives from the Department of State in relation to Galveston and Amelia Island.

*"In regard to the first-named rendez-vous, (of the many conspicuous characters and notorious offenders against our laws) the propriety of the seizure of which has been most questioned, the facts now disclosed are so strong as to place the correctness, we may say the unavoidable necessity, of the measure beyond all doubt. With regard to Amelia Island so much was already known to the public from its immediate proximity to our settled borders, that little remained to be told. On this point, therefore, the additional information imparted by the documents, is of minor interest, compared with that relating to the former place." [*HAMILTON.*]

TO JAMES MADISON.

LITTLE RIVER, LOUDOUN COUNTY, NEAR ALDIE, July 10, 1818.

DEAR SIR,—I had the pleasure to see Mr. Todd, just before I came here, and requested him to inform you that some delay would necessarily occur, before I could leave the city for the Summer. That I should remain here 'till we heard from Genl. Jackson, on which I should return to the city, then back here & then proceed by your house to Albemarle.

In truth, besides this motive for delay, to avail myself of the aid of the heads of departments, in regard to General Jackson's report of his proceedings in Florida, on the reply to be given the Spanish Minister & instructions to Mr. Erving. There were others, particularly the daily expected return of our Commissioners from Buenos Ayres, & the instructions to Mr. Rush relative to the formation of a new commercial treaty with England, which required my presence in this quarter. General Jackson's report is received in consequence of which I shall return to Washington on Monday next, the 13th.—He imputes the whole Seminole war to the interference & excitement, by the Spanish authorities in the Floridas, of the Indians, together with that of foreign adventurers imposing themselves on those people for the agents of foreign powers. I have no doubt that his opinion is correct, though he has not made his case as strong as I am satisfied he might have done. There are serious difficulties in this business, on which ever side we view it. The motive for pressing Spain in the present state of affairs, having the Mississippi, Florida, &c. founded on the interest of the country, is not urgent, but the sense of injury from her & of insult, together with the desire of aiding the Colonies by pressing her, strong.

Our Commissioners have left Buenos Ayres on their return home; that is Mr. Rodney & Graham, Mr. Bland having taken a trip to Chili. We have no intelligence from them of interest. From Mr. Prevost of Valparaiso, we have letters, very satisfactory as to his reception, & effect of the *Ontario* in that sea. His account of the victory of the Patriots represents the Royal Army as destroyed.

TO GENERAL JACKSON.

WASHINGTON, July 19th, 1818.

DEAR SIR,—I received, lately, your letter of June 2nd, by Mr. Hambly, at my farm in Loudoun, to which I had retired to await your report, and the return of our Commissioners from Buenos Ayres. In reply to your letter I shall express myself with freedom and candor which I have invariably used in my communications with you. I shall withold nothing in regard to your attack of the Spanish posts, and occupancy of them, particularly Pensacola, which you ought to know; it being an occurrence of the most delicate and interesting nature, and which without a circumspect and cautious policy, looking to all the objects which claim attention, may produce the most serious and unfavorable consequences. It is by a knowledge of all the circumstances and a comprehensive view of the whole subject that the danger to which this measure is exposed may be avoided and all the good which you have contemplated by it, as I trust, be fully realized.

In calling you into active service against the Seminoles, and communicating to you the orders which had been given just before to General Gaines, the views and intentions of the Government were fully disclosed in respect to the operations in Florida. In transcending the limit prescribed by those orders you acted on your own responsibility, on facts and circumstances which were unknown to the Government when the orders were given, many of which, indeed, occurred afterward, and which you thought imposed on you the measure, as an act of patriotism, essential to the honor and interests of your country.

The United States stand justified in ordering their troops into Florida in pursuit of their enemy. They have this right by the law of nations, if the Seminoles were inhabitants of another country and had entered Florida to elude pursuit. Being inhabitants of Florida with a sovereignty over that part of the territory, and a right to the soil, our right to give such an order is the most complete and unquestionable. It is not an act of hostility to Spain. It is the less so, because her government is bound by treaty to restrain, by force of arms if necessary, the Indians there from committing hostilities against the United States.

But an order by the government to attack a Spanish post would assume another character. It would authorize war, to which, by the principles of our Constitution, the Executive is incompetent. Congress alone possesses the power. I am aware that cases may occur where the commanding general, acting on his own responsibility, may with safety pass this limit, and with essential advantage to his country. The officers and troops of the neutral power forget the obligations incident to their neutral character; they stimulate the enemy to make war; they furnish them with arms and munitions of war to carry it on; they take an active part in their favor; they afford them an asylum in their retreat. The general obtaining victory pursues them to their post, the gates of which are shut against him; he attacks and carries it, and rests on those acts for his justification. The affair is then brought before his government by the power whose post has been thus attacked and carried. If the government whose officer made the attack had given an order for it, the officer would have no merit in it. He exercised no discretion, nor did he act on his own responsibility. The merit of the service, if there be any in it, would not be his. This is the ground on which the occurrence rests, as to his part. I will now look to the future.

The foreign government demands:—was this your act? or did you authorize it? I did not: it was the act of the general. He performed it for reasons deemed sufficient himself, and on his own responsibility. I demand, then, the surrender of the post, and his punishment. The evidence justifying the conduct of the American general, and proving the misconduct of those officers, will be embodied to be laid before the Sovereign, as the ground on which their punishment will be expected.

If the Executive refused to evacuate the posts, especially Pensacola, it would amount to a declaration of war, to which it is incompetent. It would be accused of usurping the authority of Congress, and giving a deep and fatal wound to the Constitution. By charging the offence on the officers of Spain, we take the ground which you have presented, and we look to you to support it. You must aid in procuring the documents necessary for this purpose. Those which you sent by Mr. Hambly were prepared in too much haste, and do not I am satisfied, do justice to the cause. This must be attended to without delay.

Should we hold the posts, it is impossible to calculate all the consequences likely to result from it. It is not improbable that war would immediately follow. Spain would be stimulated to declare it; and, once declared, the adventurers of Britain and other countries, would under the Spanish flag, privateer on our commerce. The immense revenue which we now receive would be much diminished, as would be the profits of our valuable productions. The war would probably soon become general; and we do not foresee that we should have a single power in Europe on our side. Why risk these consequences? The events which have occurred in both the Floridas show the incompetency of Spain to maintain her authority; and the progress of the revolutions in South America will require all her forces there. There is much reason to presume that this act will furnish a strong inducement to Spain to cede the territory, provided we do not wound too deeply her pride by holding it. If we hold the posts, her government cannot treat with honor, which, by withdrawing the troops, we afford her an opportunity to do. The manner in which we propose to act will exculpate you from censure, and promises to obtain all the advantages which you contemplated from the measure, and possibly very soon. From a different course no advantage would be likely to result, and there would be great danger of extensive and serious injuries.

I shall communicate to you, in the confidence in which I write this letter, a copy of the answer which will be given to the Spanish Minister, that you may see distinctly the ground on which we rest, in the expectation that you will give it all the support in your power. The answer will be drawn on a view and with attention to the general interests of our country, and its relations with other powers.

A charge, no doubt, will be made of a breach of the Constitution, and to such a charge the public feeling will be alive. It will be said that you have taken all the power into your hands, not from the Executive alone but likewise from Congress. The distinction which I have made above between the act of the government refutes that charge. This act, as to the General, will be right if the facts on which he rests made it a measure of necessity, and they be well proved. There is no war, or breach of the Constitution, unless the government should refuse to give up the posts, in which event should Spain embargo our vessels, and war follow, the charge of such breach would be laid against the government with great force. The last imputation to which I would consent justly to expose myself is that of infringing a Constitution to the support of which, on pure principles, my public life has been devoted. In this sentiment, I am satisfied, you fully concur.

Your letters to the Department were written in haste, under the pressure of fatigue and infirmity, in a spirit of conscious rectitude, and, in consequence with less attention to some parts of their contents than would otherwise have been bestowed on them. The passage to which I particularly allude, from memory, for I have not the letter before me is that in which you speak of the incompetency of an imaginary boundary to protect us against the enemy—the ground on which you bottom all your measures. This is liable to the imputation that you took the Spanish posts for that reason, as a measure of expediency, and not on account of the misconduct of the Spanish officers. The effect of this and such passages, besides other objections to them, would be to invalidate the ground on which you stand and furnish weapons to adversaries who would be glad to seize them. If you think proper to authorize the Secretary or myself to correct those passages, it will be done with care, though, should you have copies, as I presume you have, you had better do it yourself.

The policy of Europe respecting South America is not yet settled. A Congress of the allied powers is to be held this year (November is spoken of) to decide the question. England proposes to restore the Colonies to Spain with free trade and colonial governments. Russia is less favorable, as are all the others. We have a Russian document written by order of the Emperor, as the basis of instructions to his ministers at the several Courts, speaking of the British proposition favorably, but stating that it must be considered and decided on by the allies and the result published to produce a moral effect on the Colonies, on the failure of which force is spoken of. The settlement of the dispute between Spain and Portugal is made a preliminary. We partake in no councils whose object is not their complete independence. Intimations have been given us that Spain is not unwilling, and is even preparing for war with the United States, in the hope of making it general, and uniting Europe against us and her colonies, on the principle that she has no hope of saving them. Her pertinacious refusal to cede the Floridas to us heretofore, though evidently her interest to do it, gives some coloring to the suggestions. If we engage in a war, it is of the greatest importance that our people be united, and, with that view, that Spain commence it; and, above all, that the government be free from the charge of committing a breach of the Constitution.

I hope you have recovered your health. You see that the state of the world is unsettled, and that any future movement is likely to be directed against us. There may be very important occasions for your services, which will be relied on. You must have the object in view, and be prepared to render them.

TO JAMES MADISON.
WASHINGTON, July 20, 1818.

DEAR SIR,—I have this moment received yours of the 17th., & shall do everything in my power to reach your house by the day mentioned. We have met every day, one excepted, since my arrival here, on the business of the Spanish posts taken in Florida by General Jackson. Onis has demanded whether they were taken by order of the Government. If not, that they be surrendered and General Jackson punished. We have yet given no answer, but as the fact is that General Jackson was not authorised to take them, & did it on his own responsibility, and the holding them would amount to a declaration of war, or come so near it, that in case war followed, it would be so considered, it appears to be proper to surrender them. Jackson charges the Governor of Pensacola with a breach of neutrality in stimulating the Indians to war, furnishing the means of carrying it on &c. This affords an opportunity to charge him—the gov^r.—with the aggression & those under him as the ground of a demand of their punishment of the King. I shall write you more fully on this subject before I leave this, which you will communicate in equal confidence to Mr. Jefferson as I wish you to do the Russian paper already in your possession.

TO THOMAS JEFFERSON.
WASHINGTON, July 22, 1818.

DEAR SIR,—I expected long before this to have had the pleasure of seeing you in Albemarle, but the necessity of being here, on the receipt of Genl. Jackson's report of his operations in Florida, & in the expectation of the return of our Commiss^{rs}. from Buenos Ayres, whom I wished to meet, detain'd me in Loudoun till lately, when on the occasion of both events I return'd to the city.

The occurrence at Pensacola, has been full of difficulty, but without incurring the charge of committing a breach of the Constitution, or of giving to Spain just cause of war, we have endeavour'd to turn it to the best account of our country, & credit of the Commanding General. We shall tell the Spanish Minister, that the posts will be deliver'd up, but that their attack, was owing to the misconduct of the Spanish officers, whose punishment wo^d. be demanded of his gov^t. and that his gov^t. must keep a strong force in Florida, to enable it to comply with the stipulation of the treaty of 1795, which would be vigorously exacted. The proof of misconduct in the Spanish officers, in stimulating the Indians to make war, furnishing them with munitions of war to carry it on &c. is very strong. It has appear'd to be altogether improper, to hold the posts, as that would amount to a decided act of hostility, and might be considered an usurpation of the powers of Congress. To go to the other extreme has appear'd to be equally improper, that is, to bring Genl. Jackson to trial, for disobedience of orders, as he acted on facts which were unknown to the gov^t. when his orders were given, many of which indeed occasion'd afterwards; & as his trial, unless he should ask it himself, would be the triumph of Spain, & confirm her in the disposition not to cede Florida.

I lately transmitted to M^r. Madison a copy of a paper, written at Moscow, by order of the Emperor, as the basis of his instructions to his Ministers at the Allied Courts, relative to the difference between Spain and her Colonies, and likewise a copy of a letter which I have written to Genl. Jackson, on the subject mention'd above, for your joint information. Those papers will give you full information, on both subjects. I shall leave this today or tomorrow for Loudoun; whence I shall proceed without delay with my family for Albemarle, where I hope to find you in good health.

TO JOHN QUINCY ADAMS.
ALBEMARLE, August 17th, 1818.

DEAR SIR,—I have your letter of the 13th with the papers mentioned in, but omitted to be sent, with that of the 12th.

It does not appear to me to be necessary or proper to say anything more to M^r. Onis in reply to his note respecting occurrences in Florida than that an order has been given to the American commander to deliver up Pensacola &c. to the

Spanish officers and troops who may be duly authorized to receive possession thereof. I shall write to Mr. Calhoun to issue such an order, and it will be proper that your answer should bear date after the order. If you mention S^t. Marks you will of course preserve the distinction taken between it and Pensacola in your former letter, & recited in his. I would take the opportunity, presented in the latter part of his letter, of expressing a strong hope that he would be enabled at an early day to settle all differences between the two countries on such conditions as will ensure their peace and friendship, it being an object which the United States have always had in view, and have acted on.

Your answer to Mr. Aguirre, informing him that he could not be protected against arrest for the reasons stated, was very correct. He ought to have known the fact, and not mentioned it, but in truth his whole proceeding here, has manifested his utter incapacity for his trust, or that, misguided by others, he has believed that he could, by taking advantage of the public feeling in favor of the colonies, force the government into measures forbidden by our laws, disgraceful to the character, and repugnant to the national interest. M^r. Guall acted on the same principle, as have also the latter agents of the Colonies.

Our law, in allowing vessels of any size to be built in the country and sent out of it, provided they be not armed, or, if armed provided the intent is not made to appear that they are to be employed against a power with whom we are at peace, as is the case according to my understanding of it, is as favorable to the Colonies as it can be to be consistent with our neutrality. I should suppose that he ought to have known that it was improper to communicate any plan of his to contravene that law to the Dep^t. of State. Ignorance of the law is no justification of his conduct, for he ought to have made himself acquainted with it before he spoke to Mr. Rush, or you, on the subject. In entering the vessels built in the names of his captains he exposed himself to the consequences that have followed, from which he cannot escape, at least by Executive agency. . . .

TO GENERAL JACKSON.

WASHINGTON, October 20, 1818.

DEAR SIR,—I received your letter of the 19th. of August while I was at home, on my farm in Albemarle; and there appearing to be no necessity for giving it an immediate answer, I delayed it until my return here.

I was sorry to find that you understood your instructions relative to operations in Florida differently from what we intended. I was satisfied however, that you had good reason for your conduct, and have acted in all things on that principle. By supposing that you understood them as we did, I concluded that you proceeded on your own responsibility alone, in which, knowing the purity of your motives I have done all I could to justify the measure. I well knew, also, the misconduct of the Spanish authorities in that quarter, not of recent date only.

Finding that you had a different view of your power, it remains only to do justice to you on that ground. Nothing can be further from my intention than to expose you to a responsibility, in any sense, which you did not contemplate.

The best course to be pursued seems to me for you to write a letter to the Department, in which you will state that, having reason to think that a difference of opinion existed between you and the Executive, relative to the extent of your powers, you thought it due to yourself to state your view of them, and on which you acted. This will be answered, so as to explain ours, in a friendly manner by Mr. Calhoun, who has very just and liberal sentiments on the subject. This will be necessary in the case of a call for papers by Congress, as may be. Thus we shall all stand on the ground of honor, each doing justice to the other, which is the ground on which we wish to place each other.

I hope that your health is improved, and Mrs. Monroe unites in her best respects to Mrs. Jackson.

SECOND ANNUAL MESSAGE.
November 16, 1818.

Fellow Citizens of the Senate and of the House of Representatives:

The auspicious circumstances under which you will commence the duties of the present session will lighten the burdens inseparable from the high trust committed to you. The fruits of the earth have been unusually abundant, commerce has flourished, the revenue has exceeded the most favorable anticipation, and peace and amity are preserved with foreign nations on conditions just and honorable to our country. For these inestimable blessings we can not but be grateful to that Providence which watches over the destiny of nations.

Our relations with Spain remain nearly in the same state in which they were at the close of the last session. The convention of 1802 providing for the adjustment of a certain portion of the claim of our citizens for injuries sustained by spoliation, and so long suspended by the Spanish Government, has at length been ratified by it, but no arrangement has yet been made for the payment of another class of like claims, not less extensive or well founded, or for other classes of claims, or for the settlement of boundaries. These subjects have again been brought under consideration in both countries, but no agreement has been entered into respecting them. In the meantime events have occurred which clearly prove the ill effect of the policy which that Government has so long pursued on the friendly relations of the two countries, which it is presumed is at least of as much importance to Spain as to the United States to maintain. A state of things has existed in the Floridas, the tendency of which has been obvious to all who have paid the slightest attention to the progress of affairs in that quarter. Throughout the whole of those provinces to which the Spanish title extends the government of Spain has scarcely been felt. Its authority has been confined almost exclusively to the walls of Pensacola and St. Augustine, within which only small garrisons have been maintained. Adventurers from every country, fugitives from justice, and absconding slaves have found an asylum there. Several tribes of Indians, strong in the numbers of their warriors, remarkable for their ferocity, and whose settlements extend to our limits, inhabit those provinces. These different hordes of people, connected together, disregarding on the one side the authority of Spain, and protected on the other by an imaginary line which separates Florida from the United States, have violated our laws prohibiting the introduction of slaves, have practiced various frauds on our revenue, and committed every kind of outrage on our peacable citizens which their proximity to us enabled them to perpetrate. The invasion of Amelia Island last year by a small band of adventurers, not exceeding 150 in number, who wrested it from the inconsiderable Spanish force stationed there and held it several months, during which a single feeble effort only was made to recover it, which failed, clearly proves how completely extinct the Spanish authority has become, as the conduct of those adventurers while in possession of the island distinctly shows the pernicious purposes for which their combination had been formed.

This country had, in fact, become the theatre of every species of lawless adventure. With little population of its own, the Spanish authority almost extinct, and the Colonial governments in a state of revolution, having no pretension to it, and sufficintly employed in their own concerns, it was in a great measure derelict, and the object of cupidity to every adventurer. A system of buccaneering was rapidly organizing over it which menaced in its consequences the lawful commerce of every nation, and particularly of the United States, while it presented a temptation to every people, on whose seduction its success principally depended. In regard to the United States, the pernicious effect of this unlawful combination was not confined to the ocean; the Indian tribes have constituted the effective force in Florida. With these tribes these adventurers had formed at one period a connection with a view to avail themselves of that force to promote their own projects of accumulation and aggrandizement. It is to the interference of some of these adventurers, in misrepresenting the claims and titles of the Indians to land and in practicing on their savage propensities, that the Seminole war is principally to be traced. Men who thus connect themselves with savage communities and stimulate them to war, which is always attended with acts of barbarity the most shocking, deserve to be viewed in a worse light than the savages. They would certainly have no claim to an immunity from the punishment which, according to the rules of warfare practiced by the savages, might justly be inflicted on the savages themselves.

If the embarrassments of Spain prevented her from making an indemnity to our citizens for so long a time from her treasury for their losses by spoliation and otherwise, it was always in her power to have provided it by the cession of this territory. Of this her government has been repeatedly apprised and the cession was the more to have been anticipated as Spain must have known that in ceding it she would in effect cede what had become of little value to her, and would likewise relieve herself from the important obligation secured by the treaty of 1795 and all other compromitments respecting it. If the United States, from consideration of these embarrassments, declined pressing their claims in a spirit of hostility, the motive ought at least to have been duly appreciated by the Government of Spain. It is well known to her Government that other powers have made to the United States an indemnity for like losses sustained by their citizens at a like epoch.

There is nevertheless a limit beyond which this spirit of amity and forbearance can in no instance be justified. If it was proper to rely on amicable negotiation for an indemnity for losses, it would not have been so to have permitted the inability of Spain to fulfill her engagements and to sustain her authority in the Floridas to be perverted by foreign adventurers and savages to purposes so destructive to the lives of our fellow citizens and the highest interests of the United States. The right of self defense never ceases. It is among the most sacred, and alike necessary to nations and to individuals, and whether the attack be made by Spain herself or by those who abuse her power, its obligation is not the less strong. The invaders of Amelia Island had assumed a popular and respected title under which they might approach and wound us. As their object was distinctly seen, and the duty imposed on the Executive by an existing law, was profoundly felt, the mask was not permitted to protect them. It was thought incumbent on the United States to suppress the establishment and it was accordingly done. The combination in Florida for the unlawful purposes stated, the acts perpetrated by that combination, and, above all, the incitement of the Indians to massacre our fellow citizens of every age and of both sexes, merited a like treatment and received it. In pursuing these savages to an imaginary line in the woods it would have been the height of folly to have suffered that line to protect them. Had that been done the war would never cease. Even if the territory had been exclusively that of Spain and her power complete over it, we had a right by the law of nations to follow the enemy on it and to subdue him there. But the territory belonged, in a certain sense at least, to the savage enemy who inhabited it; the power of Spain had ceased to exist over it, and protection was sought under her title by those who had committed on our citizens hostilities which she was bound by treaty to have prevented, but had not the power to prevent. To have stopped at that line would have given new encouragement to those savages and new vigor to the whole combination existing there in the prosecution of all its pernicious purposes.

In suppressing the establishment at Amelia Island no unfriendliness was manifested toward Spain, because the post was taken from a force which had wrested it from her. The measure it is true was not adopted in concert with the Spanish Government or those in authority under it, because in transactions connected with the war in which Spain and the Colonies are engaged it was thought proper in doing justice to the United States to maintain a strict impartiality toward both the belligerent parties without consulting or acting in concert with either. It gives me pleasure to state that the Governments of Buenos Ayres and Venezuela, whose names were assumed, have explicitly disclaimed all participation in those measures, and even the knowledge of them until communicated by this Government, and have also expressed their satisfaction that a course of proceedings had been suppressed which if justly imputable to them would dishonor their cause.

In authorizing Major-General Jackson to enter Florida in pursuit of the Seminoles care was taken not to encroach on the rights of Spain. I regret to have to add that in executing this order facts were disclosed respecting the conduct of the officers of Spain in authority there in encouraging the war, furnishing munitions of war and other supplies to carry it on, and in other acts not less marked which evinced their participation in the hostile purposes of that combination and justified the confidence with which it inspired the savages that by those officers they would be protected. A conduct so incompatible with the friendly relations existing between the two countries, particularly with the positive obligation of the 5th Article of the Treaty of 1795, by which Spain was bound to restrain, even by force, those savages from acts of hostility against the United States, could not fail to excite surprise. The commanding general was convinced that he should fail in his object, that he should in effect accomplish nothing, if he did not deprive those savages of the resource on which they had calculated and of the protection on which they had relied in making the war.

As all the documents relating to this occurrence will be laid before Congress, it is not necessary to enter into further detail respecting it.

Although the reasons which induced Major-General Jackson to take those posts were duly appreciated, there was nevertheless no hesitation in deciding on the course which it became the Government to pursue. As there was reason to believe that the commanders of these posts had violated their instructions, there was no disposition to impute to their Government a conduct so unprovoked and hostile. An order was in consequence issued to the general in command there to deliver the posts—Pensacola unconditionally to any person duly authorized to receive it—and St. Marks, which is in the heart of the Indian Country, on the arrival of a force competent to defend it against those savages and their associates.

In entering Florida to suppress this combination no idea was entertained of hostility to Spain, and however justifiable the commanding general was, in consequence of the misconduct of the Spanish officers, in entering St. Marks and Pensacola to terminate it by proving to the savages and their associates that they should not be protected even there, yet the amicable relations existing between the United States and Spain could not be altered by that act alone. By ordering the restitution of the posts those relations were preserved. To a change of them, the power of the Executive is deemed incompetent; it is vested in Congress only.

By this measure, so promptly taken, due respect was shown to the Government of Spain. The misconduct of her officers has not been imputed to her. She was enabled to review with candor her relations with the United States and her own situation, particularly in respect to the territory in question, with the dangers inseparable from it, and regarding the losses we have sustained for which indemnity has been so long withheld, and the injuries we have suffered through that territory, and her means of redress, she was likewise enabled to take with honor the Course best calculated to do justice to the United States and to promote her own welfare.

Copies of the instructions to the commanding general, of his correspondence with the Secretary of war, explaining his motives and justifying his conduct, with a copy of the proceedings of the Courts-Martial in the trial of Arbuthnot and Ambristie, and of the correspondence between the Secretary of State and the Minister plenipotentiary of Spain near this Government, and of the Minister plenipotentiary of the United States at Madrid with the Government of Spain will be laid before Congress.

The civil war which has so long prevailed between Spain and the Provinces in South America still continues, without any prospect of its speedy termination. The information respecting the condition of those countries which has been collected by the Commissioners recently returned from thence will be laid before Congress in copies of their reports, with such other information as has been received from other agents of the United States.

It appears from these communications that the government at Buenos Ayres declared itself independent in July 1816, having previously exercised the power of an independent government, though in the name of the King of Spain, from the year 1810; that the Banda Oriental, Entre Riof, and Paraguay, with the city of Santa Fee, all of which are also independent, are unconnected with the present government of Buenos Ayres; that Chili has declared itself independent and is closely connected with Buenos Ayres; that Venezuela has also declared itself independent, and now maintains the conflict with various success; and that the remaining parts of South America, except Monte Video and such other portions of the eastern bank of the La Plata as are held by Portugal, are still in the possession of Spain or in a certain degree under her influence.

By a circular note addressed by the ministers of Spain to the allied powers, with whom they are respectively credited, it appears that the allies have undertaken to mediate between Spain and the South American Provinces, and that the manner and extent of their interposition would be settled by a Congress which was to have met at Aix-la-Chapelle in September last. From the general policy and course of proceeding observed by the allied powers in regard to this contest it is inferred that they will confine their interposition to the expression of their sentiments, abstaining from the application of force. I state this impression that force will not be applied with the greater satisfaction because it is a course more consistent with justice and likewise authorizes a hope that the calamities of war will be confined to the parties only and will be of shorter duration.

From the view taken of this subject, founded on all the information that we have been able to obtain, there is good cause to be satisfied with the course heretofore pursued by the United States in regard to this contest, and to conclude that it is proper to adhere to it, especially in the present state of affairs.

I communicate with great satisfaction the accession of another State (Illinois) to our Union, because I perceive from the proof afforded by the additions already made the regular progress and sure consummation of a policy of which history affords no example and of which the good effect can not be too highly estimated. By extending our Government on the principles of our Constitution over the vast territory within our limits, on the Lakes and the Mississippi and its numerous streams, new life and vigor are infused into every part of our system. By increasing the number of the States the confidence of the State governments in their own security is increased and their jealousy of the National Government proportionally diminished. The impracticability of one consolidated government for this great and growing nation will be more apparent and will be universally admitted. Incapable of exercising local authority except for general purposes, the general government will no longer be dreaded. In those cases of a local nature and for all the great purposes for which it was instituted its authority will be cherished. Each government will acquire new force and a greater freedom of action within its proper sphere. Other inestimable advantages will follow. Our produce will be augmented to an incalculable amount in articles of the greatest value for domestic use and foreign commerce. Our navigation will in like degree be increased, and as the shipping of the Atlantic States will be employed in the transportation of the vast produce of the Western country, even those parts of the United States which are the most remote from each other will be further bound together by the strongest ties which mutual interest can create.

The situation of this District, it is thought, requires the attention of Congress. By the Constitution the power of legislation is exclusively vested in the Congress of the United States. In the exercise of this power, in which the people have no participation, Congress legislate in all cases directly on the local concerns of the District. As this is a departure, for a special purpose, from the general principles of our system, it may merit consideration whether an arrangement better adapted to the principles of our government and to the particular interests of the people may not be devised which will neither infringe the Constitution nor effect the object which the provision in question was intended to secure. The growing population, already considerable, and the increasing business of the District, which it is believed already interferes with the deliberations of Congress on great national concerns, furnish additional motives for recommending this subject to your consideration.

When we view the great blessings with which our country has been favored, those which we now enjoy, and the means which we possess of handing them down unimpaired to our latest posterity, our attention is irresistibly drawn to the sources from whence they flow. Let us, then, unite in offering our most grateful acknowledgements for these blessings to the Divine Author of All Good.

TO GENERAL JACKSON.
WASHINGTON, December 21, 1818.

DEAR SIR,—I received your letter of November 13 some time past, and should have answered it sooner but for the great pressure of business on me, proceeding from duties connected with the measures of Congress. The step suggested in mine to you of October 20 will, I am inclined to believe, be unnecessary. My sole object in it was to enable you to place your view of the authority under which you acted in Florida on the strongest ground possible, so as to do complete justice to yourself. I was persuaded that you had not done yourself justice in that respect, in your correspondence with the Department, and thought that it would be better that the explanation should commence with you than be invited by the Department. It appeared to me that that would be the most delicate course in regard to yourself. There is, it is true, nothing in the Department to indicate a difference of opinion between you and the Executive, respecting the import of your instructions, and for that reason, that it would have been difficult to have expressed that sentiment without implying by it a censure of your conduct, than which nothing could be more remote from our disposition or intention.

On reviewing your communication by Captain Gadsden, there were three subjects preëminently in view: the first, to preserve the Constitution from injury; the second, to deprive Spain and the allied powers of any just cause of war; and the third, to improve the occurrence to the best advantage of the country, and of the honor of those engaged in it. In every step which I have since taken I have pursued those objects with the utmost zeal and according to my best judgment. In what concerns you personally I have omitted nothing in my power to do you justice, nor shall I in the sequel.

The decision in the three great points above stated, respecting the course to be pursued by the administration, was unanimously concurred in; and I have good reason to believe that it has been maintained since, in every particular, by all, with perfect integrity. It will be gratifying to you to know that a letter of instructions has been drawn by the Secretary of State to our Minister at Madrid, in reply to a letter of Mr. Pizarro, which has been published, in which all the proceedings in Florida, and in regard to it, have been freely reviewed, and placed in a light which will, I think, be satisfactory to all. This letter will be reported to Congress in a few days, and published of course.

TO THOMAS JEFFERSON.

WASHINGTON, Feby. 7, 1820—

DEAR SIR,—I send you by this days mail, the documents of greatest interest, which have been presented to Congress during the present Session. On our concerns with Spain we have nothing new, & little reason to expect a Minister here from that country, during the Session, M^r. Vivas, said to have been appointed some months ago, being under quarantine, within a few leagues of Madrid, in consequence of passing on his way thither, through some town infected with disease. The Missouri question, absorbs by its importance, & the excit'ment it has produc'd, every other & there is little prospect, from present appearances of its being soon settled. The object of those, who brought it forward, was undoubtedly to acquire power, & the expedient well adapted to the end, as it enlisted in their service, the best feelings, of all that portion of our Union, in which slavery does not exist, & who are unacquainted with the condition of their Southern brethren. The same men, in some instances, who were parties to the project in 1786, for closing the mouth of the Mississippi for 25 years, may be consider'd as the Authors of this. The dismemberment of the Union by the Allegheny Mountains, was then believ'd to be their object; and altho' a new arrangement of powers, is more particularly sought on this occasion, yet it is believ'd, that the anticipation, of even that result, would not deter its Authors from the pursuit of it. I am satisfied that the bond of Union, is too strong for them, and that the better their views are understood, throughout the whole Union, the more certain will be their defeat in every part. It requires, however, great moderation, firmness, & wisdom, on the part of those opposed to the restriction, to secure a just result. These great & good qualities, will I trust, not be wanting.

Your letters in favor of the gentlemen, mention'd in them, were receiv'd with the best disposition, to promote your wishes, but it is impossible for me to say what can be done in any instance. Wherever territory is to be sold, within a *State,* the Senators oppose, the appointment of the officers intrusted with it, of persons from other States, an opposition which is now extended even to Indian agencies. The number of applicants too, for every office, is so great, & the pressure from the quarter interested, so earnest, that, it is difficult in any case to be resisted. With my best wishes, etc.

TO THOMAS JEFFERSON.
WASHINGTON, Febr^y. 19, 1820.

DEAR SIR,—I forward to you by this days Mail a copy of the Journal of the Convention which formed the Constitution of the U States. By the Act of Congress providing for the distribution of them, one is allowed to you, & likewise to M^r. Madison & to Mr. Adams.

The *Intelligencer* will communicate to you some account of the proceedings of Congress on the Missouri Question, & particularly of the late votes taken on different propositions in the Senate. It seems, that a resolution was adopted on the 17th., which establishes a line, to commence, from the western boundary of

Missouri, in Lat: 36. 30. & run westward indefinitely, north of which slavery should be prohibited; but permitted South of it. Missouri & Arkansas, as is presum'd, to be admitted, without restraint. By the terms applied to the restriction "for ever" it is inferr'd that it is intended, that the restraint should apply to territories, after they become States, as well as before. This will increase the difficulty incident to an arrangement of this subject, otherwise sufficiently great, in any form, in which it can be presented. Many think that the right exists in one instance & not in the other. I have never known a question so menacing to the tranquility and even the continuance of our Union as the present one. All other subjects have given way to it, & appear to be almost forgotten. As however there is a vast portion of intelligence & virtue in the body of the people, & the bond of Union has heretofore prov'd sufficiently strong to triumph over all attempts against it, I have great confidence that this effort will not be less unavailing.

TO JOHN ADAMS.
[February 20, 1820.]

DEAR SIR,—I have the pleasure to forward to you by the mail of this day a copy of the Journal of the Convention which formed the constitution of the U States.

This instrument having secured to us, & to our latest posterity, as I trust and believe, the great blessings of the revolution, I always look with profound respect & regard to those who contributed as much as you three have done to the accomplishment of that great event.

Congress having appropriated a copy for you, & one for Mr. Jefferson, & likewise for Mr. Madison, I have charged myself with the ex^n. of so much of the resolution as relates to each of you.

I avail myself of this opportunity to acknowledge y^r. kind attentions on former occasions, & to assure you of the great interest which I take in the preservation of your health & happiness, being with the greatest respect & regard very sincerely yours.

TO THOMAS JEFFERSON.
WASHINGTON, May 3– 1820.

DEAR SIR,—We are still destin'd to have further trouble with Spain. It was hoped, that the Minister lately arriv'd, would have terminated every difficulty, but it appears that he has come to act the part of his predecessor, to make complaints, demand explanations & report them to his government, who may take as many years to conclude another treaty, as they did the last. This Minister admits, that there is no cause for his gov^t., to decline the ratification of the treaty, but insists that it shall be made dependant, not on the conditions contain'd in it, but a stipulation, that the U States will form no relations with the S°. A: Colonies, especially of recognition, untill they be recognized by other Colonies. I shall lay the correspondence before Congress, the latter end of this week.

I hope that your health is good, & that I shall be able to visit Albemarle, soon after the adjournment of Congress, & to find you then. The contiguity of my farm in Loudoun, to this place, together with a desire to attend to its improv'-ment, with a view to its sale, when good land will sell for anything, to place me finally out of debt, with a moderate subsistence in Albemarle, will induce me to divide my time between the two places. Very sincerely, etc.

TO THOMAS JEFFERSON.
WASHINGTON, May 20, 1820.

DEAR SIR,—I have receiv'd your letter of the 14, containing a very interesting view of the late treaty with Spain, and of the proceedings respecting it here. If the occurrence involv'd in it nothing more, than a question between the U States & Spain, or between them & the Colonies, I should entirely concur in your view of the subject. I am satisfied, that we might, regulate it, in every circumstance, as we thought just, & without war, that we might take Florida as an indemnity, and Texas for some trifle as an equivalent. Spain must soon be expelled from this Continent, and with any new gov^t. which may be form'd in Mexico, it would be easy to arrange the boundary in the wilderness, so as to include as much territory on our side as we might desire. No European power could prevent this, if so disposed. But the difficulty does not proceed from these sources. It is altogether internal, and of the most distressing nature and dangerous tendency. You were apprized by me, on your return from Europe, of the true character, of the negotiation, which took place in 1785–6. with the Minister of Spain, for shutting up the mouth of the Mississippi, a knowledge of which might have been deriv'd in part from the secret journal of Congress, which then came into your hands. That, was not a question with Spain, in reality, but one among ourselves, in which her pretentions were brought forward, in aid of the policy, of the party at the head of that project. It was an effort to give such a shape to our Union, as would secure the dominion over it, to its eastern section. It was expected that dismemberment by the Allegheny Mountains, would follow the occlusion of the river, if it was not desir'd, tho' the latter was then & still is my opinion. The Union then consisted of eight navigating and commercial States, with five productive, holding slaves; and had the river been shut up, and dismemberment insured, the division would always have been the same. At that time Boston ruled the four New England States, and a popular orator in Fanuel hall, ruled Boston. Jays object was to make N. York a New England State, which he avowed on his return from Europe, to the dissatisfaction of many in that State, whose prejudices had been excited in the revolutionary war by the contest between N. York and those States respecting interfering grants in Vermont. It was foreseen by these persons, that if the Mississippi should be open'd, and new States be established on its waters, the population would be drawn thither, the number of productive States be proportionally encreased, & their hope of dominion, on that contracted sectional scale, be destroyed. It was to prevent this that that project was formed. Happily it failed, & since then, our career, in an opposite direction, has been rapid & wonderful. The river has been open'd, & all the territory dependant on it acquir'd, eight states have already been admitted into the Union, in that quarter; a 9th. is on the point of entering, & a 10th. provided for, exclusive of Florida. This march to greatness has been seen with profound regret, by them, in the policy suggested, but it has been impelled by causes over which they have had no control. Several attempts have been made to impede it, among which, the Harford Convention in the late war, and the proposition for restricting Missouri, are the most distinguished. The latter measure contemplated, an arrangement on the distinction solely, between slave holding and non-slave holding States, presuming that on that basis only, such a division might be formed, as would destroy, by perpetual excit'ment, the usual effects proceeding from difference in climate, the produce of the soil, the pursuits & circumstances of the people, & marshall the States, differing in that circumstance, in unceasing opposition & hostility with each other.

To what account, this project, had it succeeded, to the extent contemplated, might have been turn'd, I cannot say. Certain however it is, that since 1786, I have not seen, so violent & persevering a struggle, and on the part of some of the leaders in the project, for a purpose so unmasked & dangerous. They did not hesitate to avow that it was a contest for power only, disclaiming the pretext of liberty, humanity, &c. It was also manifested, that they were willing to risk the Union, on the measure, if indeed, as in that relating to the Mississippi, dismemberment was not the principal object. You know how this affair terminated, as I presume you likewise do, that complete success, was prevented, by the patriotic devotion of several members in the non slave holding States, who preferr'd the sacrifice of themselves at home, to a violation, of the obvious principles of the Constitution, & the risk of the Union. I am satisfied that the arrangement made, was most auspicious for the Union, since had the conflict been pursued, there is reason to believe that the worst consequences would have followed. The excitement would have been kept up, during which it seemed probable, that the slave holding States would have lost ground daily. By putting a stop to the proceeding, time has been given for the passions to subside, & for calm discussion & reflection, which have never failed to produce their proper effect in our country. Such too was the nature of the controversy, that it seem'd to be hazardous, for either party to gain a complete triumph. I never doubted the right of Congress, to make such a regulation in [the] territories, tho' I did not expect that it would ever have been exercised.

From this view, it is evident, that the further acquisition, of territory, to the West & South, involves difficulties, of an internal nature, which menace the Union itself. We ought therefore to be cautious in making the attempt. Having secur'd the Mississippi, and all its waters, with a slight exception only, and erected States there, ought we not to be satisfied, so far at least as to take no step in that direction, which is not approved, by all the members, or at least a majority of those who accomplished our revolution. I could go into further details had I time. I have thought that these might afford you some satisfaction. When we meet in Albemarle we will communicate further on the subject.

MESSAGE—SPAIN.
WASHINGTON, May 9, 1820.

To the Senate and House of Representatives of the United States:

I communicate to Congress a correspondence which has taken place between the Secretary of State and the Envoy Extraordinary and Minister Plenipotentiary of His Catholic Majesty since the message of the 27th March last, respecting the treaty which was concluded between the United States and Spain on the 22nd, February, 1819.

After the failure of His Catholic Majesty for so long a time to ratify the treaty, it was expected that His Minister would have brought with him the ratification, or that he would have been authorized to give an order for the delivery of the Territory ceded by it to the United States. It appears, however, that the treaty is still unratified and that the Minister has no authority to surrender the territory. The object of his mission has been to make complaints and to demand explanations respecting an imputed system of hostility on the part of citizens of the United States against the subjects and dominions of Spain, and an unfriendly policy in their Government, and to obtain new stipulations against these alleged injuries as the condition on which the treaty should be ratified.

Unexpected as such complaints and such a demand were under existing circumstances, it was thought proper, without compromitting the Government as to the course to be pursued, to meet them promptly and to give the explanations that were desired on every subject with the utmost candor. The result has proved what was sufficiently well known before, that the charge of a systematic hostility being adopted and pursued by citizens of the United States against the dominions and subjects of Spain is utterly destitute of foundation, and that their Government in all its branches has maintained with the utmost rigor that neutrality in the Civil war between Spain and the Colonies which they were the first to declare. No force has been collected nor incursions made from within the United States against the Dominion of Spain, nor have any naval equipments been permitted in favor of either party against the other. Their citizens have been warned of the obligations incident to the neutral condition of their country; their public officers have been instructed to see that the laws were faithfully executed, and severe examples have been made of some who violated them.

In regard to the stipulation proposed as the condition of the ratification of the treaty, that the United States shall abandon the right to recognize the revolutionary Colonies in South America or to form other relations with them when in their judgment it may be just and expedient so to do, it is manifestly so repugnant to the honor and even to the independence of the United States that it has been impossible to discuss it. In making this proposal it is perceived that His Catholic Majesty has entirely misconceived the principles on which this Government has acted in being a party to a negotiation so long protracted for claims so well founded and reasonable, as he likewise has the sacrifices which the United States have made, comparatively, with Spain in the treaty to which it is proposed to annex so extraordinary and improper a condition.

Had the Minister of Spain offered an unqualified pledge that the treaty should be ratified by his Sovereign on being made acquainted with the explanations which had been given by this Government, there would have been a strong motive for accepting and submitting it to the Senate for their advice and consent, rather than to resort to other measures for redress, however justifiable and proper; but he gives no such pledge; on the contrary, he declares explicitly that the refusal of this Government to relinquish the right of judging and acting for itself hereafter, according to circumstances, in regard to the Spanish

Colonies, a right common to all nations, has rendered it impossible for him under his instructions to make such engagement. He thinks that his Sovereign will be induced by his communications to ratify the treaty, but still he leaves him free either to adopt that measure or to decline it. He admits that the other objections are essentially removed and will not in themselves prevent the ratification, provided the difficulty on the third point is surmounted. The result, therefore, is that the treaty is declared to have no obligation whatever; that its ratification is made to depend not on the considerations which led to its adoption and the conditions which it contains, but on a new article unconnected with it, respecting which a new negotiation must be opened, of indefinite duration and doubtful issue.

Under this view of the subject the course to be pursued would appear to be direct and obvious if the affairs of Spain had remained in the state in which they were when this minister sailed. But it is known that an important change has since taken place in the Government of that country which cannot fail to be sensibly felt in its intercourse with other Nations. The Minister of Spain has essentially declared his inability to act in consequence of that change. With him, however, under his present powers, nothing could be done. The attitude of the United States must now be assumed on full consideration of what is due to their rights, their interest and honor, without regard to the powers or incidents of the late mission. We may at pleasure occupy the territory which was intended and provided by the late treaty as an indemnity for losses so long since sustained by our citizens; but still, nothing could be settled definitely without a treaty between the two nations. Is this the time to make the pressure? If the United States were governed by views of ambition and aggrandizement, many strong reasons might be given in its favor; but they have no objects of that kind to accomplish, none which are not founded in justice and which can be injured by forbearance. Great hope is entertained that this change will promote the happiness of the Spanish Nation. The good order, moderation and humanity which have characterized the movement are the best guarantees of its success.

The United States would not be justified in their own estimation should they take any step to disturb its harmony. When the Spanish Government is completely organized on the principles of this change as it is expected it soon will be, there is just ground to presume that our differences with Spain will be speedily and satisfactorily settled.

With these remarks I submit it to the wisdom of Congress whether it will not still be advisable to postpone any decision on this subject until the next session.

TO GENERAL JACKSON.
WASHINGTON, May 23ᵈ. 1820.

DEAR SIR,—I sent you lately a copy of the last message to Congress on the subject of Spanish affairs, and I now seize the first moment of leisure to acknowledge the receipt of yours of the 15th of April last. I have long known your wish for retirement, and that you have looked to the adjustment of our differences with Spain as the period when it should take place. It is painful to me to oppose any obstacle to your wish, but still candour requires that I should state to you such facts as you ought to take into view in making your decision on the subject. Our differences with Spain are not settled, nor is it certain that they will be by the Cortes on its first meeting. And should that not take place it is difficult to say at what time they will be settled. The change of government in Spain, some progress being made in favor of a better system, made delay, after it was known, expedient and proper. A movement against Florida then would have been represented as against the Cortes. The Missouri question has also excited feelings & raised difficulties, of an internal nature, which did not exist before. Some parts of our Union became less anxious even for the acquisition of Florida, while others, not content with that, were desirous of taking possession also of Texas. Many disliked any movement for a territory which we might take when we pleased, lest it might produce hostilities, and the injury of our commerce, & revenue. On full consideration therefore of all circumstances, and particularly of the change in Spain, further delay was recommended, as you have seen, by the message.

Having long known the repugnance with which the eastern portion of our Union, or rather some of those who have enjoyed its confidence (for I do not think that the people themselves have any interest or wish of that kind) have seen its aggrandizement to the west and south, I have been decidedly of opinion that we ought to be content with Florida for the present, and until the public opinion in that quarter shall be reconciled to any future change. In 1785 & 6 an attempt was made to shut up the mouth of the Mississippi to prevent our progress in that direction. When we reflect how gigantic our growth has since been there; that we have acquired the Mississippi, and both its banks; have erected eight States in that quarter, and made provision for more, I think we ought to pause before we push matters to a dangerous extremity. I mention these circumstances to shew you that our difficulties are not with Spain alone, but are likewise internal, proceeding from various causes which certain men are prompt to seize, and turn to the account of their own ambitious views.

Most of the governments of Europe are unsettled. The movement has assumed a more marked character in Spain, but a like spirit exists in Great Britain, France, Russia, and many parts of Germany, and in Italy. Where this will terminate, or what will be its immediate course, is uncertain, as it likewise is what effect it will produce on the contest between Spain and the Colonies. The policy here hath been to throw the moral weight of the U. States in the scale of the Colonies without so deep a compromitment as to make ourselves a party to the war. We have thought that we even rendered them more service in that way than we should have done by taking side with them in the war, while we secured our own peace and prosperity. Our ports were open to them for every article they wanted; our good offices are extended to them, with every power in Europe, and with great effect. Europe has remained tranquil spectators of the conflict, whereas had we joined the Colonies, it is presumable that several powers would have united with Spain. The effort however of the Colonies has been to draw us into the contest, in which they have been supported by a party among ourselves, not, as I confidently believe, to benefit them, but to make an impression unfavorable to the administration. It is obvious that a recognition of any of the Colonies, if it did not make us a party to the war, as the recognition of the U. States by France made her, would have no effect, but be a dead letter; and if it made us a party, it would, as I already observed, do more harm than good. Should any event force us into the war, which we of course wish to prevent, the whole energies of the nation might be called into action, in which case your aid would be of the highest importance. A respectable attitude in land and naval force, and in fortifications along the coast, during this troubled state of the world, is the best expedient to prevent war, and to carry us with safety & honor through it in case it should be inevitable. I have seen with some surprise propositions made tending to involve us in the war, and others to reduce the army, & by the same persons, than which nothing can be more inconsistent.

Such being the state of affairs, I leave it entirely to yourself to decide whether to remain in the service, or to retire at this time. I well know that wherever you may be you will always be ready to obey the call of your country in any extremity. But whether your being in service may not have a tendency to prevent such extremity, and have a happy effect on other important interests of our country, especially in preserving order along our frontiers, is to be decided. Whatever your decision may be, be assured that my entire confidence, & affectionate regards, will always attend you, as will those of Mrs. Monroe, and my daughters, for Mrs. Jackson.

TO THOMAS JEFFERSON.
WASHINGTON, Feby. 17, 1821.

DEAR SIR,—I regret to have to inform you of the death of M^r. W. Burwell which took place on yesterday after a long & distressing illness. All possible care was taken of him. He was a most virtuous man & estimable member of the H. of Rep^s.

The treaty with Spain has been ratified by her gov^t., unconditionally, & the grants annulled in the instrument of ratification. It is before the Senate, on the question, whether it shall be accepted, the time stipulated for the ratification, having expir'd. It is presum'd that little if any opposition, will be made to it.

There is also some hope that Missouri will be admitted into the Union, on a patriotic effort from the Senators & other members from Pennsyl^a. Hope is also entertain'd that our commercial difference with France will be adjusted.

SECOND INAUGURAL ADDRESS.

Fellow Citizens:

I shall not attempt to describe the grateful emotions which the new and very distinguished proof of the confidence of my fellow-citizen, evinced by my re-election to this high trust, has excited in my bosom. The approbation which it announces of my conduct in the preceding term affords me a consolation which I shall profoundly feel through life. The general accord with which it has been expressed adds to the great and never ceasing obligations which it imposes. To merit the continuance of this good opinion, and to carry it with me into my retirement as the solace of advancing years, will be the object of my most zealous and unceasing efforts.

Having no pretensions to the high and commanding claims of my predecessors, whose names are so much more conspicuously identified with our Revolution, and who contributed so pre-eminently to promote its success, I consider myself rather as the instrument than the cause of the union which has prevailed in the late election. In surmounting, in favor of my humble pretensions, the difficulties which so often produce division in like occurences, it is obvious that other powerful causes, indicating the great strength and stability of our Union, have essentially contributed to draw you together. That these powerful causes exist, and that they are permanent is my fixed opinion; that they may produce a like accord in all questions touching, however remotely, the liberty, prosperity, and happiness of our country will always be the object of my most fervent prayers to the Supreme Author of All Good.

In a government which is founded by the people, who possess exclusively the sovereignty, it seems proper that the person who may be placed by their suffrages in this high trust should declare on commencing its duties the principles on which he intends to conduct the administration. If the person thus elected has served the preceding term, an opportunity is afforded him to review its principal occurrences and to give such further explanation respecting them as in his judgment may be useful to his constituents. The events of one year have influence on those of another, and, in like manner of a preceding on the succeeding administration. The movements of a great nation are connected in all their parts. If errors have been committed they ought to be corrected; if the policy is sound it ought to be supported. It is by a thorough knowledge of the whole subject that our fellow citizens are enabled to judge correctly of the past and to give a proper direction to the future.

Just before the commencement of the last term the United States had concluded a war with a very powerful nation on conditions equal and honorable to both parties. The events of that war are too recent and too deeply impressed on the memory of all to require a development from me. Our commerce had been in a great measure driven from the sea; our Atlantic and inland frontiers were invaded in almost every part; the waste of life along our coast and on some parts of our inland frontiers, to the defense of which our gallant and patriotic citizens were called, was immense, in addition to which not less than $120,000,000 were added at its end to the public debt.

As soon as the war had terminated, the nation, admonished by its events, resolved to place itself in a situation which should be better calculated to prevent the recurrence of a like evil, and, in case it should recur, to mitigate its calamities. With this view, after reducing our land force to the basis of a peace establishment, which has been further modified since, provision was made for the construction of fortifications at proper points through the whole extent of our coast and such an augmentation of our naval force as should be well adapted to both purposes. The laws making this provision were passed in 1815 and 1816, and it has been since the constant effort of the Executive to carry them into effect.

The advantage of these fortifications and of an augmented naval force in the extent contemplated, in a point of economy, has been fully illustrated by a report of the Board of Engineers and Naval Commissioners lately communicated to Congress, by which it appears that in an invasion by 20,000 men, with a correspondent naval force, in a campaign of six months only, the whole expense of the construction of the works would be defrayed by the difference in the sum necessary to maintain the force which would be adequate to our defense with the aid of those works and that which would be incurred without them. The reason of this difference is obvious. If fortifications are judiciously placed on our great inlets, as distant from our cities as circumstances will permit, they will form the only points of attack, and the enemy will be detained there by a small regular force a sufficient time to enable our militia to collect and repair to that on which the attack is made. A force adequate to the enemy, collected at that single point, with suitable preparation for such others as might be menaced, is all that would be requisite. But if there were no fortifications, then the enemy might go where he pleased, and, changing his position and sailing from place to place, our force must be called out and spread in vast numbers along the whole coast and on both sides of every bay and river as high up in each as it might be navigable for ships of war. By these fortifications, supported by our Navy, to which they would afford like support, we should present to other powers an armed front from St. Croix to the Sabine, which would protect in the event of war our whole coast and interior from invasion; and even in the wars of other powers, in which we were neutral, they would be found eminently useful, as, by keeping their public ships at a distance from our cities, peace and order in them would be preserved and the Government be protected from insult.

It need scarcely be remarked that these measures have not been resorted to in a spirit of hostility to other powers. Such a disposition does not exist toward any power. Peace and good will have been, and will hereafter be, cultivated with all, and by the most faithful regard to justice. They have been dictated by a love of peace, of economy, and an earnest desire to save the lives of our fellow-citizens from that destruction and our country from that devastation which are inseparable from war when it finds us unprepared for it. It is believed, and experience has shown, that such a preparation is the best expedient that can be resorted to prevent war. I add with much pleasure that considerable progress has already been made in these measures of defense, and that they will be completed in a few years, considering the great extent and importance of the object, if the plan be zealously and steadily persevered in.

The conduct of the Government in what relates to foreign powers is always an object of the highest importance to the nation. Its agriculture, commerce, manufactures, fisheries, revenue, in short, its peace, may all be affected by it. Attention is therefore due to this subject.

At the period adverted to, the powers of Europe, after having been engaged in long and destructive wars with each other, had concluded a peace, which happily still exists. Our peace with the power with whom we had been engaged had also been concluded. The war between Spain and the colonies in South America, which had commenced many years before, was then the only conflict that remained unsettled. This being a contest between different parts of the same community, in which other powers had not interfered, was not affected by their accommodations.

This contest was considered at an early stage by my predecessor a civil war in which the parties were entitled to equal rights in our ports. This decision, the first made by any power, being formed on great consideration of the comparative strength and resources of the parties, the length of time, and successful opposition made by the colonies, and of all other circumstances on which it ought to depend, was in strict accord with the law of nations. Congress has invariably acted on this principle, having made no change in our relations with either party. Our attitude has therefore been that of neutrality between them, which has been maintained by the Government with the strictest impartiality. No aid has been afforded to either, nor has any privilege been enjoyed by the one which has not been equally open to the other party, and every exertion has been made in its power to enforce the execution of the laws prohibiting illegal equipments with equal rigor against both.

By this equality between the parties their public vessels have been received in our ports on the same footing; they have enjoyed an equal right to purchase and export arms, munitions of war, and every other supply, the exportation of all articles whatever being permitted under laws which were passed long before the commencement of the contest; our citizens have traded equally with both, and their commerce with each has been alike protected by the Government.

Respecting the attitude which it may be proper for the United States to maintain hereafter between the parties, I have no hesitation in stating it as my opinion that the neutrality heretofore observed should still be adhered to. From the change in the Government of Spain and the negotiation now depending, invited by the Cortes and accepted by the colonies, it may be presumed that their differences will be settled on the terms proposed by the colonies. Should the war be continued, the United States, regarding its occurrences, will always have it in their power to adopt such measures respecting it as their honor and interest may require.

Shortly after the general peace a band of adventurers took advantage of this conflict and of the facility which it afforded to establish a system of buccaneering in the neighboring seas, to the great annoyance of the commerce of the United States, and, as was represented, of that of other powers. Of this spirit and of its injurious bearing on the United States strong proofs were afforded by the establishment at Amelia Island, and the purposes to which it was made instrumental by this band in 1817, and by the occurrences which took place in other parts of Florida in 1818, the details of which in both instances are too well known to require to be now recited. I am satisfied had a less decisive course been adopted that the worst consequences would have resulted from it. We have seen that these checks, decisive as they were, were not sufficient to crush that piratical spirit. Many culprits brought within our limits have been condemned to suffer death, the punishment due to that atrocious crime. The decisions of upright and enlightened tribunals fall equally on all whose crimes subject them, by a fair interpretation of the law, to its censure. It belongs to the Executive not to suffer the executions under these decisions to transcend the great purpose for which punishment is necessary. The full benefit of example being secured, policy as well as humanity equally forbids that they should be carried further. I have acted on this principle, pardoning those who appear to have been led astray by ignorance of the criminality of the acts they had committed, and suffering the law to take effect on those only in whose favor no extenuating circumstances could be urged.

Great confidence is entertained that the late treaty with Spain, which has been ratified by both the parties, and the ratifications whereof have been exchanged, has placed the relations of the two countries on a basis of permanent friendship. The provision made by it for such of our citizens as have claims on Spain of the character described will, it is presumed, be very satisfactory to them, and the boundary which is established between the territories of the parties westward of the Mississippi, heretofore in dispute, has, it is thought, been settled on conditions just and advantageous to both. But to the acquisition of Florida too much importance can not be attached. It secures to the United States a territory important in itself, and whose importance is much increased by its bearing on many of the highest interests of the Union. It opens to several of the neighboring States a free passage to the ocean, through the Province ceded, by several rivers having their sources high up within their limits. It secures us against all future annoyance from powerful Indian tribes. It gives us several excellent harbors in the Gulf of Mexico for ships of war of the largest size. It covers by its position in the Gulf, the Mississippi and other great waters within our extended limits, and thereby enables the United States to afford complete protection to the vast and very valuable productions of our whole Western country, which find a market through those streams.

By a treaty with the British Government, bearing date on the 20th of October, 1818, the convention regulating the commerce between the United States and

Great Britain, concluded on the 3d of July, 1815, which was about expiring, was revived and continued for the term of ten years from the time of its expiration. By that treaty, also, the differences which had arisen under the treaty of Ghent respecting the right claimed by the United States for her citizens to take and cure fish on the coast of His Britannic Majesty's dominions in America, with other differences on important interests, were adjusted to the satisfaction of both parties. No agreement has yet been entered into respecting the commerce between the United States and the British dominions in the West Indies and on this continent. The restraints imposed on that commerce by Great Britain, and reciprocated by the United States on a principle of defense, continue still in force.

The negotiation with France for the regulation of the commercial relations between the two countries, which in the course of the last summer had been commenced at Paris, has since been transferred to this city, and will be pursued on the part of the United States in the spirit of conciliation, and with an earnest desire that it may terminate in an arrangement satisfactory to both parties.

Our relations with the Barbary Powers are preserved in the same state and by the same means that were employed when I came into this office. As early as 1801 it was found necessary to send a squadron into the Mediterranean for the protection of our commerce, and no period has intervened, a short term excepted, when it was thought advisable to withdraw it. The great interests which the United States have in the Pacific, in commerce and in the fisheries, have also made it necessary to maintain a naval force there. In disposing of this force in both instances the most effectual measures in our power have been taken, without interfering with its other duties, for the suppression of the slave trade and of piracy in the neighboring seas.

The situation of the United States in regard to their resources, the extent of their revenue, and the facility with which it is raised affords a most gratifying spectacle. The payment of nearly $67,000,000 of the public debt, with the great progress made in measures of defense and in other improvements of various kinds since the late war, are conclusive proofs of this extraordinary prosperity, especially when it is recollected that these expenditures have been defrayed without a burthen on the people, the direct tax and excise having been repealed soon after the conclusion of the late war, and the revenue applied to these great objects having been raised in a manner not to be felt. Our great resources therefore remain untouched for any purpose which may affect the vital interests of the nation. For all such purposes they are inexhaustible. They are more especially to be found in the virtue, patriotism, and intelligence of our fellow-citizens, and in the devotion with which they would yield up by any just measure of taxation all their property in support of the rights and honor of their country.

Under the present depression of prices, affecting all the productions of the country and every branch of industry, proceeding from causes explained on a former occasion, the revenue has considerably diminished, the effect of which has been to compel Congress either to abandon these great measures of defense or to resort to loans or internal taxes to supply the deficiency. On the presumption that this depression and the deficiency in the revenue arising from it would be temporary, loans were authorized for the demands of the last and present year. Anxious to relieve my fellow-citizens in 1817 from every burthen which could be dispensed with, and the state of the Treasury permitting it, I recommended the repeal of the internal taxes, knowing that such relief was then peculiarly necessary in consequence of the great exertions made in the late war. I made that recommendation under a pledge that should the public exigencies require a recurrence to them at any time while I remained in this trust, I would with equal promptitude perform the duty which would then be alike incumbent on me. By the experiment now making it will be seen by the next session of Congress whether the revenue shall have been so augmented as to be adequate to all these necessary purposes. Should the deficiency still continue, and especially should it be probable that it would be permanent, the course to be pursued appears to me to be obvious. I am satisfied that under certain circumstances loans may be resorted to with great advantage. I am equally well satisfied, as a general rule, that the demands of the current year, especially in time of peace, should be provided for by the revenue of that year.

I have never dreaded, nor have I ever shunned, in any situation in which I have been placed, making appeals to the virtue and patriotism of my fellow-citizens, well knowing that they could never be made in vain, especially in times of great emergency or for purposes of high national importance. Independently of the exigency of the case, many considerations of great weight urge a policy having in view a provision of revenue to meet to a certain extent the demands of the nation, without relying altogether on the precarious resource of foreign commerce. I am satisfied that internal duties and excises, with corresponding imposts on foreign articles of the same kind, would, without imposing any serious burdens on the people, enhance the price of produce, promote our manufactures, and augment the revenue, at the same time that they made it more secure and permanent.

The care of the Indian tribes within our limits has long been an essential part of our system, but, unfortunately, it has not been executed in a manner to accomplish all the objects intended by it. We have treated them as independent nations, without their having any substantial pretensions to that rank. The distinction has flattered their pride, retarded their improvement, and in many instances paved the way to their destruction. The progress of our settlements westward, supported as they are by a dense population, has constantly driven them back, with almost the total sacrifice of the lands which they have been compelled to abandon. They have claims on the magnanimity and, I may add, on the justice of this nation which we must all feel. We should become their real benefactors; we should perform the office of their Great Father, the endearing title which they emphatically give to the Chief Magistrate of our Union. Their sovereignty over vast territories should cease, in lieu of which the right of soil should be secured to each individual and his posterity in competent portions; and for the territory thus ceded by each tribe some reasonable equivalent should be granted, to be vested in permanent funds for the support of civil government over them and for the education of their children, for their instruction in the arts of husbandry, and to provide sustenance for them until they could provide it for themselves. My earnest hope is that Congress will digest some plan, founded on these principles, with such improvements as their wisdom may suggest, and carry it into effect as soon as it may be practicable.

Europe is again unsettled and the prospect of war increasing. Should the flame light up in any quarter, how far it may extend it is impossible to foresee. It is our peculiar felicity to be altogether unconnected with the causes which produce this menacing aspect elsewhere. With every power we are in perfect amity, and it is our interest to remain so if it be practicable on just conditions. I see no reasonable cause to apprehend variance with any power, unless it proceed from a violation of our maritime rights. In these contests, should they occur, and to whatever extent they may be carried, we shall be neutral; but as a neutral power we have rights which it is our duty to maintain. For like injuries it will be incumbent on us to seek redress in a spirit of amity, in full confidence that, injuring none, none would knowingly injure us. For more imminent dangers we should be prepared, and it should always be recollected that such preparation adapted to the circumstances and sanctioned by the judgment and wishes of our constituents can not fail to have a good effect in averting dangers of every kind. We should recollect also that the season of peace is best adapted to these preparations.

If we turn our attention, fellow-citizens, more immediately to the internal concerns of our country, and more especially to those on which its future welfare depends, we have every reason to anticipate the happiest results. It is now rather more than forty-four years since we declared our independence, and thirty-seven since it was acknowledged. The talents and virtues which were displayed in that great struggle were a sure presage of all that has since followed. A people who were able to surmount in their infant state such great perils would be more competent as they rose into manhood to repel any which they might meet in their progress. Their physical strength would be more adequate to foreign danger, and the practice of self-government, aided by the light of experience, could not fail to produce an effect equally salutary on all those questions connected with the internal organization. These favorable anticipations have been realized.

In our whole system, National and State, we have shunned all the defects which unceasingly preyed on the vitals and destroyed the ancient Republics. In them there were distinct orders, a nobility and a people, or the people governed in one assembly. Thus, in the one instance there was a perpetual conflict between the orders in society for the ascendency, in which the victory of either terminated in the overthrow of the government and the ruin of the state; in the other, in which the people governed in a body, and whose dominions seldom exceeded the dimensions of a county in one of our States, a tumultuous and disorderly movement permitted only a transitory existence. In this great nation there is but one order, that of the people, whose power, by a peculiarly happy improvement of the representative principle, is transferred from them, without impairing in the slightest degree their sovereignty, to bodies of their own creation, and to persons elected by themselves, in the full extent necessary for all the purposes of free, enlightened, and efficient government. The whole system is elective, the complete sovereignty being in the people, and every officer in every department deriving his authority from and being responsible to them for his conduct.

Our career has corresponded with this great outline. Perfection in our organization could not have been expected in the outset either in the National or State Governments or in tracing the line between their respective powers. But no serious conflict has arisen, nor any contest but such as are managed by argument and by a fair appeal to the good sense of the people, and many of the defects which experience had clearly demonstrated in both Governments have been remedied. By steadily pursuing this course in this spirit there is every reason to believe that our system will soon attain the highest degree of perfection of which human institutions are capable, and that the movement in all its branches will exhibit such a degree of order and harmony as to command the admiration and respect of the civilized world.

Our physical attainments have not been less eminent. Twenty-five years ago the river Mississippi was shut up and our Western brethren had no outlet for their commerce. What has been the progress since that time? The river has not only become the property of the United States from its source to the ocean, with all its tributary streams (with the exception of the upper part of the Red River only), but Louisiana, with a fair and liberal boundary on the western side and the Floridas on the eastern, have been ceded to us. The United States now enjoy the complete and uninterrupted sovereignty over the whole territory from St. Croix to the Sabine. New States, settled from among ourselves in this and in other parts, have been admitted into our Union in equal participation in the national sovereignty with the original States. Our population has augmented in an astonishing degree and extended in every direction. We now, fellow-citizens, comprise within our limits the dimensions and faculties of a great power under a Government possessing all the energies of any government ever known to the Old World, with an utter incapacity to oppress the people.

Entering with these views the office which I have just solemnly sworn to execute with fidelity and to the utmost of my ability, I derive great satisfaction from a knowledge that I shall be assisted in the several Departments by the very enlightened and upright citizens from whom I have received so much aid in the preceding term. With full confidence in the continuance of that candor and generous indulgence from my fellow-citizens at large which I have heretofore experienced, and with a firm reliance on the protection of Almighty God, I shall forthwith commence the duties of the high trust to which you have called me.

MARCH 5, 1821.
TO JAMES MADISON.
WASHINGTON, March 31, 1821.

DEAR SIR,—Since I have been in this office many newspapers have been sent to me, from every part of the Union, unsought, which having neither time nor curiosity to read, are in effect thrown away. I should have stopped the practice, but from delicacy to the Editors, & expecting also that they would subject me to no charge. Lately I have been informed that the same practice took place in your time, & had been tolerated till you retired, when the Editors sent you bills for the amount of the subscription to their papers, for the eight years, making an enormous sum. Be so kind as to inform me whether this was the fact, as in case it was I may write to the Editors (a few excepted & very few) not to send them.

The law for executing the Florida treaty has subjected me to great trouble and embarrassment. The organizing a gov^t. in Florida & appointing of officers there, is in itself a serious duty. I have as yet appointed the gov^r. only, who is

Genl. Jackson. The institution of a board of Commissioners for the settlement of claims on Spain, is attended with still greater difficulty. In general the persons best qualified live in the great towns, especially to the Eastward. In those towns also the claimants live. If I appoint a Commiss^r. in one only, & not in the others, all the latter will complain; and it is impossible to appoint them in all, the number not admitting of it. I have therefore thought it best to avoid the great towns, & propose to appoint Govr. King of Maine, Judge Green of Fredericksburg & Judge White of Knoxville, Tenn.; two lawyers & one merchant. They are all able & upright men unconnected with the claims or claimants. I may make some change, the Comm^n. not having issued & therefore wish you not to mention it. . . .

TO GENERAL JACKSON.
WASHINGTON, May 23, 1821.

DEAR SIR,—This letter, with such further communications from the Secretaries of State & War as the arrangements in Florida may require, will be forwarded to Milledgeville by mail, and thence by a special messenger to you at Pensacola, or elsewhere, to whatever place you may be at.

The arrangements under the treaty being committed to me by a concise law, expressed in general terms, I have bestowed on the subject all the consideration which its high importance required, and used my best exertions to give effect to every object contemplated by it, in a manner to satisfy the just claims of my country. Several duties, distinct in their nature, were enjoined on me by the law. The territory ceded was to be taken possession of, & the Spanish officers & soldiers were to be transferred to Cuba: A temporary government was to be organized over the Floridas, for the protection of the inhabitants in the free enjoyment of their liberty, property, and religion, for which purposes the military, civil, and religious powers, heretofore exercised by the authorities of Spain, should be vested in proper officers of the United States, and exercised in such manner as should be designated. The laws of the United States relating to revenue and slave trade were declared to be in force in the said territories, and it was enjoined on me to establish such districts for the collection of the revenue, and to appoint such officers, whose commissions should expire at the next session of Congress, to enforce the said laws as might be deemed expedient. The establishment of the boundary between the United States and Spain, westward of the Mississippi, was another object, and the institution of a Board of Commissioners, to consist of three persons for the settlement of the claims of such of our citizens as had been plundered at sea and elsewhere, was a third. As incident to the last was the distribution of 5 millions of dollars, should the claims amount to that sum, by a proportionate reduction of each, so as to render to every one justice, giving him his due and no more, and in so doing, sustain the character of the government & nation for integrity and impartiality.

Altho' these duties were distinct, and to be performed at places very distant from each other, yet in providing for their execution it was necessary for me to take a combined view of the whole, and in the appointment of officers especially to look to the nation: distributing them among the States, so far as it might be practicable, without neglecting other objects equally important.

In executing that portion of the trust relating to the Floridas, I have gratified in a high degree my feelings in committing the chief power to you, who have rendered such important services, and have such just claims to the gratitude of your country. It must be agreeable to you, for many considerations which will occur, to take possession of the Floridas, and cause the Spanish authorities and troops to be removed to Cuba. It must be equally so to establish the government of the United States, and to administer it in their behalf, in those territories. I have every reason to believe that the nation generally have beheld with profound interest and satisfaction your appointment, considering it a just tribute of respect to your extraordinary services and merit, and having the fullest confidence that its duties will be discharged with the utmost ability and integrity.

As the territory had been divided into two provinces under Spain, and still retained that form, notwithstanding all that part of W. Florida west of the Perdido had been taken from it, and more especially as Pensacola & St. Augustine were separated at such a distance, and by a wilderness, it was thought advisable, for the present, to adapt the arrangement, in some of its parts, to that circumstance. In regard to your office, both provinces will form but one territory. Your powers will be the same over the whole, but as your residence will be fixed at one only, and, as I presume, at Pensacola, I have thought it proper to appoint two secretaries, one for Pensacola, and the other for St. Augustine, both equally under your control. I have divided the territory, with a view to revenue, into three districts, that portion which lies between the St. Marys and Cape Florida into one, St. Augustine being its port of entry and delivery; that between the cape and the Appalachicola into another, St. Marys being its port, and that lying between the Appalachicola and the Perdido into a third, Pensacola being its port. I have established two Judicial districts, one Judge in each, Pensacola to be the residence of one, and St. Augustine of the other. I have appointed Mr. Fromentin Judge at the former, and Mr. Duval at the latter. Both these gentlemen I presume you are acquainted with, the one having served in the Senate, from Louisiana, and the other in the House of Representatives, from Kentucky. Mr. Walton of Georgia is Secretary at Pensacola, the descendant and representative of the Member of Congress of that name who voted for, and signed, the Declaration of Independence; Mr. Worthington of Maryland is Secretary at St. Augustine, a person who acted as political agent of the U States some years at Buenos Ayres & Chili.

Mr. Alexander Scott, of Maryland, is appointed to the Collector of the Customs, Mr. Steuben Smith, of New York, Naval officer, Mr. Hackley, of Virginia, Surveyor, and Mr. Baker, of this place, Inspector at Pensacola. The first mentioned is a man of considerable literary acquirements & strict integrity, well connected in his State. The second is the son of Col. W^m. Smith, who was Aid de Camp to General Washington in the revolutionary war, and afterwards Secretary of Legation at London, where he married the daughter of Mr. Adams, former President. He is the nephew of the present Secretary of State, and his wife is the sister of Mr. Adams. Of Mr. Hackley you may have heard in Spain, his wife is the sister of Governor Randolph of Virginia, and Mr. Madison, and others, our friends, have strongly recommended him to me. As these persons are, I believe, literally poor, as is indeed Mr. Baker, who was formerly Consul in Spain & Italy, and in whose favor Mr. Jefferson takes an interest, I wish you to place them, if possible, in some of the public buildings, of which I presume there are some not necessary for your own accommodation. It is I believe customary for the revenue officers to be thus provided, wherever it is practicable, and in no instances can such provision be more important, or indispensable to the parties than the present. Mr. Rodman of New York is appointed Collector at St. Augustine, and Mr. Mark Hardin, of N°. Carolina, at St. Marks. Young Anderson of Tennessee is appointed District Attorney.

To the Board of Commissioners Judge White of Tennessee, Gov. King, of Maine, and Mr. Tazewell, of Virginia are appointed. As the claimants reside in the great towns along the coast, it was thought best to select the Commissioners from other quarters, in, the belief that as they would be, not only disinterested, but unprejudiced; being equally unacquainted with the parties of their claims, a Board thus composed would inspire greater confidence in the nation, if its decisions might not be more correct.

Col. Butler, lately of your staff, is appointed Colonel of the 4th. regiment of infantry, and Major Call retains his rank of captain in the line. It would have given me pleasure to have placed the latter near you, but, on great consideration, I thought it better for you, as well as myself, to pursue the course I have done. Mr. Walton was strongly supported by the two Senators from Georgia, Mr. Walker and Mr. Elliott, both estimable men. I could do nothing else for him, and Mr. Call was already provided for.

You go, and take M^rs. Jackson with you, into a new climate, as is represented, and we believe, a very healthy one. Take care of yourself, and of her, for we wish to meet you both again.

I have full confidence that your appointment will be immediately and most beneficially felt. Smugglers & slave traders will hide their heads, pirates will disappear, and the Seminoles cease to give us trouble. So effectual will the impression be that I think the recollection of your past services will smooth your way as to the future. Past experience shows that neither of us are without enemies. If you still have any, as may be presumed, they will watch your movements, hoping to find some inadvertent circumstance to turn against you. Be therefore on your guard. Your country indulges no such feeling. From it you will find a liberal confidence, and a generous support. With my best wishes for your welfare, and the best regards of my family for M^rs. Jackson, I am dear Sir, Your friend and servant

TO GENERAL ANDREW JACKSON.
WASHINGTON, December 31, 1821.

DEAR SIR,—I received some time since your resignation, and should have answered it sooner had I not wished to retain you in the service of your country until a temporary government should be organized over the Floridas, and an opportunity be afforded me to appoint your successor. On great consideration, especially as I know that it is your fixed purpose to withdraw, I have at length determined to accept it, in which light you will view this letter. The same sentiments which I have heretofore entertained of your integrity, ability, & eminently useful services are still cherished towards you. That you may long live in health & in the affections of your country is my most earnest desire. With high respect & sincere regard,

TO JAMES MADISON.
WASHINGTON, August 2, 1824.

DEAR SIR,—I intended soon after the adjournment of Congress to have visited Albermarle, & to have passed some time with you, but there have been so many objects to attend to here, of one kind or other, that it has been impossible for me to execute a purpose which I had much at heart. A fortnight ago I took my family to Loudon, where they now are. My return here was produced by the arrival of Genl. Clark, with upwards of 20 chiefs from the different tribes, inhabiting the country between our settlements & the Rocky Mountains, & by the necessity of having a consultation on some points relating to the new gov^ts. to the South, and also on the convention lately concluded with Russia for the adjustment of differences respecting the Northwest coast. I shall remain a few days only, & then join my family. Whether I shall be able to see you this summer is uncertain. I do not think that Mrs. Monroe could go with me, & doubt whether I can go without her. Her health is much impair'd by many causes, particularly by our long service, & the heavy burdens & cares to which she has been subjected, and to which the strength of her constitution has not been equal. If the retirement to the country, & change of air should relieve her, and other circumstances should permit, I will certainly see you as soon as I may be able.

Mr. Salazar, the Minister from Columbia, stated lately, by order of his gov^t., that a French agent was expected at Bogota, having already arrived at the port, with power to treat with his gov^t. respecting its independence. He observed that his gov^t. had been advised, from an authentic source, that the gov^t. of France would acknowledge its independence on one condition, the establishment of monarchy, and leave the person to be placed in that station to the people of Columbia. That Bolivar would not be objected to if preferred by them. He asked, should the proposition be rejected, and France become hostile in consequence, what part the U States would take in that event? What aid might they expect from us? The subject will of course be weighed thoroughly in giving the answer. The Executive has no right to compromit the nation in any question of war, nor ought we to presume that the people of Columbia will hesitate as to the answer to be given to any proposition which touches so vitally their liberties.

The convention with Russia will, I presume, be very satisfactory to the nation. It consists of 6 articles. By the 1st it is stipulated that the citizens and subjects of the two parties shall not be disturb'd in navigating the great Pacific ocean, nor in landing on the coast (at points which are not already occupied) for the purpose of commerce with the nations, under the following restrictions. Art: 2^d. that the citizens of the U States shall not land at any point where there is a Russian establishment without permission from the Governor, or Commandant—reciprocated as to Russians in our favor. 3^d. no establishment shall be formed by citizens of the U S., nor under their authority, on the N^o.west coast of Am.; nor in the adjacent Islands, north of 50°. 40′. north Latitude; nor by Russians south of that Latitude. 4th. For 10 years from the signature of the treaty the vessels of the two powers, & of their citizens & subjects may reciprocally frequent, without impediment, the interior seas, gulphs, harbours & creeks on the coast to fish, and trade with the natives. 5ᵗʰ. From this priviledge of trade are excepted spirituous liquors, arms, swords, powder & munitions of war of every kind. Both powers agree to give effect to this provision, it being stipulated that the vessels of neither shall visit, or detain the vessels of the other, by the seizure of merchandize, or any measure of force, which may be engaged in this commerce; the high contracting powers reserving to themselves the right to fix and inflict the penalties on any breaches of the article. The 6ᵗʰ. requires that the ratifications be exchanged in 10 months from its signature.

By this convention the claim to the "mare clausum" is given up, a very high northern lat: is established for our boundary with Russia, and our trade with the Indians placed for 10 years on a perfectly free footing, and after that term left open for negotiation. The British govᵗ. had, at our suggestion, agreed to treat in concert with us on both topics, the navigation, & boundaries, including the trade with the Indians, but on seeing that passage in the message which discountenanced the idea of further colonization on this continent, declined it, on the presumption that it would give offense to Russia, a reason which was communicated by Mr. Bagot to the Russian govᵗ., & also to Mr. Middleton. By entering into the negotiation with us singly, & conceding to us these points, especially that relating to navigation, the Emperor has shewn great respect for the U States. England will, of course, have a similar stipulation, in favor of the free navigation of the Pacifick, but we shall have the credit of having taken the lead in the affair. I think also that the event derives additional importance from the consideration that the treaty has been concluded since the receipt at Petersburg of the message at the opening of the last Session of Congress, which expressed sentiments in regard to our principles & hemisphere adverse to those entertained by the holy alliance.

Our best regards to Mrs. Madison and your mother—very sincerely I am, dear Sir, your friend & servant—

FROM EIGHTH ANNUAL MESSAGE.
WASHINGTON, December 7, 1824.

Fellow Citizens of the Senate and of the House of Representatives

In turning our attention to the condition of the civilized world, in which the United States have always taken a deep interest, it is gratifying to see how large a portion of it is blessed with peace. The only wars which now exist within that limit are those between Turkey and Greece, in Europe, and between Spain and the new Governments, our neighbors, in this hemisphere. In both these wars the cause of independence, of liberty and humanity, continues to prevail. The success of Greece, when the relative population of the contending parties is considered, commands our admiration and applause, and that it has had a similar effect with the neighboring powers is obvious. The feeling of the whole civilized world is excited in a high degree in their favor. May we not hope that these sentiments, winning on the hearts of their respective Governments, may lead to a more decisive result; that they may produce an accord among them to replace Greece on the ground which she formerly held, and to which her heroic exertions at this day so eminently entitle her?

With respect to the contest to which our neighbors are a party, it is evident that Spain as a power is scarcely felt in it. These new States had completely achieved their independence before it was acknowledged by the United States, and they have since maintained it with little foreign pressure. The disturbances which have appeared in certain portions of that vast territory have proceeded from internal causes, which had their origin in their former Governments and have not yet been thoroughly removed. It is manifest that these causes are daily losing their effect, and that these new States are settling down under Governments elective and representative in every branch, similar to our own. In this course we ardently wish them to persevere, under a firm conviction that it will promote their happiness. In this, their career, however, we have not interfered, believing that every people have a right to institute for themselves the government which, in their judgment, may suit them best. Our example is before them, of the good effect of which, being our neighbors, they are competent judges, and to their judgment we leave it, in the expectation that other powers will pursue the same policy. The deep interest which we take in their independence, which we have acknowledged, and in their enjoyment of all the rights incident thereto, especially in the very important one of instituting their own Governments, has been declared, and is known to the world. Separated as we are from Europe by the great Atlantic Ocean, we can have no concern in the wars of the European Governments no in the caurses which produce them. The balance of power between them, into whichever scale it may turn in its various vibrations, cannot affect us. It is the interest of the United States to preserve the most friendly relations with every power and on conditions fair, equal, and applicable to all. But in regard to our neighbors our situation is different. It is impossible for the European Governments to interfere in their concerns, especially in those alluded to, which are vital, without affecting us; indeed, the motive which might induce such interference in the present state of the war between the parties, if a war it may be called, would appear to be equally applicable to us. It is gratifying to know that some of the powers with whom we enjoy a very friendly intercourse, and to whom these views have been communicated, have appeared to acquiesce in them.

From the view above presented it is manifest that the situation of the United States is in the highest degree prosperous and happy. There is no object which as a people we can desire which we do not possess or which is not within our reach. Blessed with governments the happiest which the world ever knew, with no distinct orders in society or divided interests in any portion of the vast territory over which their dominion extends, we have every motive to cling together which can animate a virtuous and enlightened people. The great object is to preserve these blessings, and to hand them down to the latest posterity. Our experience ought to satisfy us that our progress under the most correct and provident policy will not be exempt from danger. Our institutions form an important epoch in the history of the civilized world. On their preservation and in their utmost purity everything will depend. Extending as our interests do to every part of the inhabited globe and to every sea to which our citizens are carried by their industry and enterprise, to which they are invited by the wants of others, and have a right to go, we must either protect them in the enjoyment of their rights or abandon them in certain events to waste and desolation. Our attitude is highly interesting as relates to other powers, and particularly to our southern neighbors. We have duties to perform with respect to all to which we must be faithful. To every kind of danger we should pay the most vigilant and unceasing attention, remove the cause where it may be practicable, and be prepared to meet it when inevitable.

Against foreign danger the policy of the Government seems to be already settled. The events of the late war admonished us to make our maritime frontier impregnable by a well-digested chain of fortifications, and to give efficient protection to our commerce by augmenting our Navy to a certain extent, which has been steadily pursued, and which it is incumbent upon us to complete as soon as circumstances will permit. In the event of war it is on the maritime frontier that we shall be assailed. It is in that quarter, therefore, that we should be prepared to meet the attack. It is there that our whole force will be called into action to prevent the destruction of our towns and the desolation and pillage of the interior. To give full effect to this policy great improvements will be indispensable. Access to those works by every practicable communication should be made easy and in every direction. The intercourse between every part of our Union should also be promoted and facilitated by the exercise of those powers which may comport with a faithful regard to the great principles of our Constitution. With respect to internal causes, those great principles point out with equal certainty the policy to be pursued. Resting on the people as our Governments do, State and National, with well-defined powers, it is of the highest importance that they severally keep within the limits prescribed to them. Fulfilling that sacred duty, it is of equal importance that the movement between them be harmonious, and in the case of any disagreement, should any such occur, a calm appeal be made to the people, and that their voice be heard and promptly obeyed. Both Governments being instituted for the common good, we can not fail to prosper while those who made them are attentive to the conduct of their representatives and control their measures. In the pursuit of these great objects let a generous spirit and national views and feelings be indulged, and let every part recollect that by cherishing that spirit and improving the condition of the others in what relates to their welfare the general interest will not only be promoted, but the local advantage be reciprocated by all. . . .

PART IX

Veto Message on
Internal Improvements

INTRODUCTION

THE VETO POWER IS an inherent part of the President's Constitutional office. The number of bills which have been vetoed since 1789 cannot be ascertained. The veto power is not only a prerogative, but also an exercise of political acumen. It is seldom that a President will veto a bill that is extremely popular, and that fits in with his own idea of the national good.

In 1822, President Monroe vetoed the Cumberland Road Bill, even though he recognized that the Cumberland Road would be beneficial to westward expansion. He vetoed it because the Constitution did not provide authority to the Federal government for the construction of internal improvements. He urged that, since the purpose was a good one, a constitutional amendment be adopted to make it possible.

The modern reader may be surprised that any one could ever doubt that the Federal government had the power to build highways. But even as late as the administration of President Dwight D. Eisenhower, the construction of the first interstate highway system, so soon after World War II, was justified on the grounds of national defense. That argument was raised in favor of the Cumberland Road also, but Monroe took pains to deflate that kind of puffery in 1822.

Monroe begins his legal analysis not with the text of the Constitution, as do so many modern scholars, but with the charters of the several colonies as independent, unconnected entities. "Before the Revolution, the present States, then colonies, were separate communities: unconnected with each other except in their common relation to the Crown. Their governments were instituted by grants from the Crown, which operated, according to the conditions of each grant, in the nature of a compact between the settlers in each colony and the Crown."

He then proceeds to discuss the status of each colony and the powers that each held after independence, and then under the Articles of Confederation. He examines the deficiencies of Congress under the Confederation. Next he moves on to the Constitution itself, and the circumstances under which it arose, all under the power of the people. "Had the people of the several States thought proper to incorporate themselves into one community, under one government, they might have done it. They had the power, and there was nothing then nor is there anything now, should they be so disposed, to prevent it. They wisely stopped, however, at a certain point, extending the incorporation to that point, making the National Government thus far a consolidated Government, and preserving the State governments without that limit perfectly sovereign and independent of the National Government."

For Monroe, these were not abstract, theoretical theories. He had struggled through all these phases. He had heard all the arguments since the time he was 16 in Williamsburg, listening to the debates in Raleigh Tavern. It was Monroe who, in the Congress of the Confederation, had argued in 1783 that the Articles be amended so that there could be a common policy for commerce among the states; it was his proposal, never adopted then, that became the basis of the interstate commerce clause in the Constitution. But he refused to use interstate commerce or the common defense as powers under which the national government could claim the right to build roads across the territory of the states. "Commerce between independent powers is universally regulated by duties and imposts," he wrote. "It was so regulated by the States before the adoption of this Constitution equally in respect to each other and to foreign powers. The goods and vessels employed in the trade are the only subjects of legislation. It can act on none other. A power, then, to impose such duties and imposts in regard to foreign nations and to prevent any on the trade between the States was the only power granted."

So the document which began as a veto message on the Cumberland Road became a lengthy treatise on Constitutional law, its origins, and its function, written by a man with nearly 50 years of direct experience of the issues and debates which shaped it. It becomes then a precious resource for understanding the Constitution and its purpose. As Monroe wrote,

> The establishment of our institutions forms the most important epoch that history hath recorded. They extend unexampled felicity to the whole body of our fellow-citizens, and are the admiration of other nations. To preserve and hand them down in their utmost purity to the remotest ages will require the existence and practice of virtues and talents equal to those which were displayed in acquiring them. It is to be ardently hoped and confidently believed that these will not be wanting.

VIEWS ON THE SUBJECT OF INTERNAL IMPROVEMENTS.

It may be presumed that the proposition relating to internal improvements by roads and canals, which has been several times before Congress, will be taken into consideration again either for the purpose of recommending to the States the adoption of an amendment to the Constitution to vest the necessary power in the General Government or to carry the system into effect on the principle that the power has already been granted. It seems to be the prevailing opinion that great advantage would be derived from the exercise of such a power by Congress. Respecting the right there is much diversity of sentiment. It is of the highest importance that this question should be settled. If the right exist, it ought forthwith to be exercised. If it does not exist surely those who are friends to the power ought to unite in recommending an amendment to the Constitution to obtain it. I propose to examine this question.

The inquiry confined to its proper objects and within the most limited is extensive. Our Government is unlike other governments both in its origin and form. In analyzing it the differences in certain respects between it and those of other nations, ancient and modern, necessarily come into view. I propose to notice these differences so far as they are connected with the object of inquiry, and the consequences likely to result from them, varying in equal degree from those which have attended other governments. The digression, if it may be so called, will in every instance be short and the transition to the main object immediate and direct.

To do justice to the subject it will be necessary to mount to the source of power in these States and to pursue this power in its gradations and distribution among the several departments in which it is now vested. The great division is between the State governments and the General Government. If there was a perfect accord in every instance as to the precise extent of the powers granted to the General Government, we should then know with equal certainty what were the powers which remained to the State governments, since it would follow that those which were not granted to the one would remain to the other. But it is on this point, and particularly respecting the construction of these powers and their incidents, that a difference of opinion exists, and hence it is necessary to trace distinctly the origin of each government, the purposes intended by it, and the means adopted to accomplish them. By having the interior of both governments fully before us we shall have all the means which can be afforded to enable us to form a correct opinion of the endowments of each.

Before the Revolution, the present States, then colonies, were separate communities, unconnected with each other except in their common relation to the

Crown. Their governments were instituted by grants from the Crown, which operated, according to the conditions of each grant, in the nature of a compact between the settlers in each colony and the Crown. All power not retained in the Crown was vested exclusively in the colonies, each having a government consisting of an executive, a judiciary, and a legislative assembly, one branch of which was in every instance elected by the people. No office was hereditary, nor did any title under the Crown give rank or office in any of the colonies. In resisting the encroachments of the parent country and abrogating the power of the Crown, the authority which had been held by it vested exclusively in the people of the colonies. By them was a Congress appointed, composed of delegates from each colony, who managed the war, declared independence, treated with foreign powers, and acted in all things according to the sense of their constituents. The declaration of independence confirmed in form what had existed before in substance. It announced to the world new States, possessing and exercising complete sovereignty, which they were resolved to maintain. They were soon after recognized by France and other powers and finally by Great Britain herself in 1783.

Soon after the power of the Crown was annulled the people of each colony established a constitution or frame of government for themselves, in which these separate branches—legislative, executive, and judiciary—were instituted, each independent of the others. To these branches, each having its appropriate portion, the whole power of the people not delegated to Congress was communicated, to be exercised for their advantage on the representative principle by persons of their appointment or otherwise deriving their authority immediately from them, and holding their offices for stated terms. All the powers necessary for useful purposes held by any of the strongest governments of the Old World not vested in Congress were imparted to these State governments without other checks than such as are necessary to prevent abuse, in the form of fundamental declarations or bills of right. The great difference between our governments and those of the Old World consists in this, that the former, being representative, the persons who exercise their powers do it not for themselves or in their own right, but for the people, and therefore while they are in the highest degree efficient they can never become oppressive. It is this transfer of the power of the people to representative and responsible bodies in every branch which constitutes the great improvement in the science of government and forms the boast of our system. It combines all the advantages of every known government without any of their disadvantages. It retains the sovereignty in the people, while it avoids the tumult and disorder incident to the exercise of that power by the people themselves. It possesses all the energy and efficiency of the most despotic governments, while it avoids all the oppressions and abuses inseparable from those governments.

In every stage of the conflict from its commencement until March 1781, the powers of Congress were undefined, but of vast extent. The assemblies or conventions of the several colonies being formed by representatives from every county in each colony and the Congress by delegates from each colonial assembly, the powers of the latter for general purposes resembled those of the former for local. They rested on the same basis, the people, and were complete for all the purposes contemplated. Never was a movement so spontaneous, so patriotic, so efficient. The nation exerted its whole faculties in support of its rights, and of its independence after the contest took that direction and it succeeded. It was, however, seen at a very early stage that although the patriotism of the country might be relied on in the struggle for its independence, a well digested compact would be necessary to preserve it after obtained. A plan of confederation was in consequence proposed and taken into consideration by Congress even at the moment when the other great act which severed them from Great Britain and declared their independence was proclaimed to the world. This compact was ratified on the 21st March 1781, by the last State, and thereupon carried into immediate effect.

The following powers were vested in the United States by the Articles of Confederation. As this, the first bond of Union, was in operation nearly eight years, during which time a practical construction was given to many of its powers, all of which were adopted in the Constitution with important additions, it is thought that a correct view of those powers and of the manner in which they are executed may shed light on the subject under consideration. It may fairly be presumed where certain powers were transferred from one instrument to the other and in the same terms, or terms descriptive only of the same powers, that it was intended that they should be construed in the same sense in the latter that they were in the former.

[The Articles of Confederation are here set forth.]

This bond of union was soon found to be utterly incompetent to the purposes intended by it. It was defective in its powers; it was defective also in the means of executing the powers actually granted by it. Being a league of sovereign and independent States, its acts, like those of all other leagues, required the interposition of the States composing it to give them effect within their respective jurisdictions. The acts of Congress without the aid of the State laws to enforce them were altogether nugatory. The refusal or omission of one State to pass such laws was urged as a reason to justify like conduct in others, and thus the Government was soon at a stand.

The experience of a few years demonstrated that the Confederation could not be relied on for the security of the blessings which had been derived from the Revolution. The interests of the nation required a more efficient Government, which the good sense and virtue of the people provided by the adoption of the present Constitution.

The Constitution of the United States was formed by a convention of delegates from the several States, who met in Philadelphia, duly authorized for the purpose, and it was ratified by a Convention in each State which was especially called to consider and decide the same. In this progress the State governments were never suspended in their functions. On the contrary they took the lead in it. Conscious of their incompetency to secure to the Union the blessings of the Revolution, they promoted the diminution of their own powers and the enlargement of those of the General Government in the way in which they might be most adequate and efficient. It is believed that no other example can be found of a Government exerting its influence to lessen its own powers; of a policy so enlightened; of a patriotism so pure and disinterested. The credit, however, is more especially due to the people of each State, in obedience to whose will and under whose control the State governments acted.

The Constitution of the United States, being ratified by the people of the several States, became of necessity to the extent of its powers the paramount authority of the Union. On sound principles it can be viewed in no other light. The people, the highest authority known to our system, from whom all our institutions spring and on whom they depend, formed it. Had the people of the several States thought proper to incorporate themselves into one community, under one government, they might have done it. They had the power, and there was nothing then nor is there anything now, should they be so disposed, to prevent it. They wisely stopped, however, at a certain point, extending the incorporation to that point, making the National Government thus far a consolidated Government, and preserving the State governments without that limit perfectly sovereign and independent of the National Government. Had the people of the several States incorporated themselves into one community, they must have remained such, their Constitution becoming then, like the constitution of the several States, incapable of change until ordered by the will of the majority. In the institution of a State government by the citizens of a State a compact is formed to which all and every citizen are equal parties. They are also the sole parties and may amend it at pleasure. In the institution of the Government of the United States by the citizens of every State a compact was formed between the whole American people which has the same force and partakes of all the qualities to the extent of its powers as a compact between the citizens of a State in the formation of their own Constitution. It cannot be altered except by those who formed it or in the mode prescribed by the parties to the compact itself.

This Constitution was adopted for the purpose of remedying all defects of the Confederation, and in this it has succeeded beyond any calculation that could have been formed of any human institution. By binding the States together the Constitution performs the great office of the Confederation; but it is in that sense only that it has any of the properties of that compact; and in that it is more effectual to the purpose, as it holds them together by a much stronger bond; and in all other respects in which the Confederation failed the Constitution has been blessed with complete success. The Confederation was a compact between separate and independent States, the execution of whose articles in the powers which operated internally depended on the State governments. But the great office of the Constitution, by incorporating the people of the several States to the extent of its powers into one community and enabling it to act directly on the people, was to annul the powers of the State governments to that extent, except in cases where they were concurrent, and to preclude their agency in giving effect to those of the General Government. The Government of the United States relies on its own means for the execution of its powers, as the State governments do for the execution of theirs, both governments having a common origin or sovereign, the people—the State governments the people of each State, the National Government the people of every State—and being amenable to the power which created it. It is by executing its functions as a Government thus originating and thus acting that the Constitution of the United States holds the States together and performs the office of a league. It is owing to the nature of its powers and the high source from whence they are derived—the people— that it performs that office better than the Confederation or any league which ever existed, being a compact which the State governments did not form, to which they are not parties and which executes its own powers independently of them.

There were two separate and independent governments established over our Union, one for local purposes over each State by the people of the State, the other for national purposes over all the States by the people of the United States. The whole power of the people, on the representative principle, is divided between them. The State governments are independent of each other, and to the extent of their powers are complete sovereignties. The National Government begins where the State governments terminate, except in some instances where there is a concurrent jurisdiction between them. This Government is also, according to the extent of its powers, a complete sovereignty. I speak here, as repeatedly mentioned before, altogether of representative sovereignties, for the real sovereignty is in the people alone.

The history of the world affords no such example of two separate and independent governments established over the same people, nor can it exist except in governments founded on the sovereignty of the people. In monarchies and other governments not representative there can be no such division of power. The government is inherent in the possessor; it is his and cannot be taken from him without a revolution. In such governments alliances and leagues alone are practicable. But with us individuals count for nothing in the offices which they hold; that is, they have no right to them. They hold them as representatives, by appointment from the people, in whom the sovereignty is exclusively vested. It is impossible to speak too highly of this system taken in its twofold character and in all its great principles of two governments, completely distinct from and independent of each other, each constitutional, founded by and acting directly on the people, each competent to all its purposes, administering all the blessings for which it was instituted, without even the most remote danger of exercising any of its powers in a way to oppress the people. A system capable of expansion over a vast territory not only without weakening either government, but enjoying the peculiar advantage of adding thereby new strength and vigor to the faculties of both; possessing also this additional advantage, that while the several States enjoy all the rights reserved to them of separate and independent governments, and each is secured by the nature of the Federal Government, which acts directly on the people, against the failure of the others to bear their equal share of the public burdens, and thereby enjoys in a more perfect degree all the advantages of a league, it holds them together by a bond altogether different and much stronger than the late Confederation or any league that was ever known before—a bond beyond their control, and which cannot even be amended except in the mode prescribed by it. So great an effort in favor of human happiness was never made before; but it became those who made it. Established in the new hemisphere, descended from the same ancestors, speaking the same language, having the same religion and universal toleration, born equal and educated in the same principles of free government, made independent by a common struggle and menaced by the same dangers, ties existed between them which never applied before to separate communities. They had every motive to bind them together which could operate on the interests and affections of a generous, enlightened, and virtuous people, and it affords inexpressible consolation to find that these motives had their merited influence.

In thus tracing our institutions to their origin and pursuing them in their progress and modifications down to the adoption of this Constitution two important facts have been disclosed, on which it may not be improper in this stage to make a few observations. The first is that in wresting the power, or what is called the sovereignty, from the Crown it passed directly to the people. The second, that it passed directly to the people of each Colony and not to the people of all the Colonies in the aggregate; to thirteen distinct communities and not to one. To these two facts, each contributing its equal proportion, I am inclined to think that we are in an eminent degree indebted for the success of our Revolution. By passing to the people it vested in a community every individual of which had equal rights and a common interest. There was no family dethroned among us, no banished pretender in a foreign country looking back to his connections and adherents here in the hope of a recall; no order of nobility whose hereditary rights in the Government had been violated; no hierarchy which had been degraded and oppressed. There was but one order, that of the people, by whom everything was gained by the change. I mention it also as a circumstance of peculiar felicity that the great body of the people had been born and educated under these equal and original institutions. Their habits, their principles, and their prejudices were therefore all on the side of the Revolution and of free republican government.

Had distinct orders existed, our fortune might and probably would have been different. It would scarcely have been possible to have united so completely the whole force of the country against a common enemy. A contest would probably have arisen in the outset between the orders for the control. Had the aristocracy prevailed, the people would have been heartless. Had the people prevailed, the nobility would probably have left the country, or, remaining behind, internal divisions would have taken place in every State and a civil war broken out more destructive even than the foreign, which might have defeated the whole movement. Ancient and modern history is replete with examples proceeding from conflicts between distinct orders, of revolutions attempted which proved abortive, republics which have terminated in despotism. It is owing to the simplicity of the elements of which our system is composed that the attraction of all the parts has been to a common center, that every change has tended to cement the Union, and, in short, that we have been blessed with such glorious and happy success.

And that the power wrested from the British Crown passed to the people of each Colony the whole history of our political movement from the emigration of our ancestors to the present day clearly demonstrates. What produced the Revolution? The violation of our rights. What rights? Our chartered rights. To whom were the charters granted, to the people of each Colony or to the people of all the Colonies as a single community? We know that no such community as the aggregate existed and of course that no such rights could be violated. It may be added that the nature of the powers which were given to the delegates by each Colony and the manner in which they were executed show that the sovereignty was in the people of each and not in the aggregate. They respectively presented credentials such as are usual between ministers of separate powers, which were examined and approved before they entered on the discharge of the important duties committed to them. They voted also by Colonies and not individually, all the members from one Colony being entitled to one vote only. This fact alone, the first of our political association and at the period of our greatest peril, fixes beyond all controversy the source from whence the power which has directed and secured success to all our measures has succeeded.

Had the sovereignty passed to the aggregate, consequences might have ensued, admitting the success of our Revolution, which might even yet seriously affect our system. By passing to the people of each Colony, the opposition to Great Britain, the prosecution of the war, the Declaration of Independence, the adoption of the Confederation and of this Constitution are all imputable to them. Had it passed to the aggregate, every measure would be traced to that source; even the State governments might be said to have emanated from it, and amendments of their constitutions on that principle be proposed by the same authority. In short it is not easy to perceive all the consequences into which such a doctrine might lead. It is obvious that the people in mass would have had much less agency in all the great measures of the Revolution and in those which followed than they actually had, and proportionably less credit for their patriotism and services than they are now entitled to and enjoy. By passing to the people of each Colony the whole body in each were kept in constant and active deliberation on subjects of the highest national importance and in the supervision of the conduct of all the public servants in the discharge of their respective duties. Thus the most effectual guards were provided against abuses and dangers of every kind which human ingenuity could devise, and the whole people rendered more competent to the self-government which by an heroic exertion they had acquired.

I will now proceed to examine the powers of the General Government, which, like the governments of the several States, is divided into three branches—

a legislative, executive, and judiciary—each having its appropriate share. Of these the legislative, from the nature of its powers, all laws proceeding from it, and the manner of its appointment, its members being elected immediately by the people, is by far the most important. The whole system of the National Government may be said to rest essentially on the powers granted to this branch. They mark the limit within which, with few exceptions, all the branches must move in the discharge of their respective functions. It will be proper, therefore, to take a full and correct view of the powers granted to it.

[Provisions of the Constitution relating to the powers of Congress, the Executive and Judiciary, fully quoted.]

Having presented above a full view of all the powers granted to the United States, it will be proper to look to those remaining to the States. It was by fixing the great powers which are admitted to belong to each government that we may hope to come to a right conclusion respecting those in controversy between them. In regard to the National Government, this task was easy because its powers were to be found in specific grants in the Constitution; but it is more difficult to give a detail of the powers of the State governments, as their constitutions, containing all powers granted by the people not specifically taken from them by grants to the United States, can not well be enumerated. Fortunately a precise detail of all the powers remaining to the State governments is not necessary in the present instance. A knowledge of their great powers only will answer every purpose contemplated, and respecting these there can be no diversity in opinion. They are sufficiently recognized and established by the Constitution of the United States itself. In designating the important powers of the State governments it is proper to observe, first, that the territory contemplated by the Constitution belongs to each State in its separate character and not to the United States in their aggregate character. Each State holds territory according to its original charter, except in cases where cessions have been made to the United States by individual States. The United States had none when the Constitution was adopted which had not been thus ceded to them and which they held on the conditions on which such cession had been made. Within the individual States it is believed that they held not a single acre; but if they did it was as citizens held it, merely as private property. The territory acquired by cession lying without the individual States rests on a different principle, and is provided for by a separate and distinct part of the Constitution. It is the territory within the individual States to which the Constitution in its great principles applies, and it applies to such territory as the territory of the State and not as that of the United States. The next circumstance to be attended to is that the people composing this Union are the people of the several States and not of the United States in the full sense of a consolidated government. The militia are the militia of the several States; lands are held under the laws of the States; descents, contracts and all the concerns of private property, the administration of justice, and the whole criminal code, except in the cases of breaches of the laws of the United States made under and in conformity with the powers vested in Congress and of the laws of nations, are regulated by State laws. This enumeration shows the great extent of the powers of the State governments. The territory and the people form the basis on which all governments are founded. The militia constitute their effective force. The regulation and protection of property and of personal liberty are also among the highest attributes of sovereignty. This, without other evidence, is sufficient to show that the great office of the Constitution of the United States is to unite the States together under a government enowed with powers adequate to the purposes of its institution, relating, directly or indirectly, to foreign concerns, to the discharge of which a National Government thus formed alone could be competent.

This view of the exclusive jurisdiction of the several States over the territory within their respective limits except in cases otherwise especially provided for, is supported by the obvious intent of the several powers granted to Congress, to which a more particular attention is now due. Of these the right to declare war is perhaps the most important, as well by the consequences attending war as by the other powers granted in aid of it. The right to lay taxes, duties, imposts and excises, though necessary for the support of the civil government, is equally necessary to sustain the charges of war; the right to raise and support armies and a navy and to call forth and govern the militia in the service of the United States are altogether of the latter kind. They are granted in aid of the power to make war and intended to give effect to it. These several powers are of great force and extent and operate more directly within the limits and upon the resources of the States than any other powers. But still they are means only for given ends. War is declared and must be maintained, an army and a navy must be raised; fortifications must be erected for the common defense, debts must be paid. For these purposes duties, imposts, and excises are levied, taxes are laid, the lands, merchandise and other property of the citizens are liable for them; if the money is not paid, seizures are made and the lands are sold. The transaction is terminated; the lands pass into other hands, as the former proprietors did, under the laws of the individual States. They were means only to certain ends; the United States have nothing to do with them. The same view is applicable to the power of the General Government over persons. The militia is called into the service of the

United States; the service is performed; the corps returns to the State to which it belongs; it is the militia of such State and not of the United States. Soldiers are required for the Army, who may be obtained by voluntary enlistment or by some other process founded in the principles of equality. In either case, the citizen after the tour of duty is performed is restored to his former station in society, with his equal share in the common sovereignty of the nation. In all these cases which are the strongest which can be given, we see the right of the General Government is nothing more than what it is called in the Constitution, a power to perform certain acts and that the subject on which it operates is a means only to that end; that is was both before and after that act under the protection and subject to the laws of the individual State within which it was.

To the other powers of the General Government the same remarks are applicable and with greater force. The right to regulate commerce with foreign powers was necessary as well to enable Congress to lay and collect duties and imposts as to support the rights of the nation in the intercourse with foreign powers. It is executed at the ports of the several States and operates almost altogether externally. The right to borrow and coin money and to fix its value and that of foreign coin are important to the establishment of a National Government, and particularly necessary in support of the right to declare war, as, indeed, may be considered the right to punish piracy and felonies on the high seas and offenses against the laws of nations. The right to establish an uniform rule of naturalization and uniform laws respecting bankruptcies seems to be essentially connected with the right to regulate commerce. The first branch of it relates to foreigners entering the Country; the second to merchants who have failed. The right to promote the progress of useful arts and sciences may be executed without touching any of the individual States. It is accomplished by granting patents to inventors and preserving models, which may be done exclusively within the Federal district. The right to constitute courts inferior to the Supreme Court was a necessary consequence of the judiciary existing as a separate branch of the General Government. Without such inferior court in every State it would be difficult and might even be impossible to carry into effect the laws of the General Government. The right to establish post-offices and post-roads is essentially of the same character. For political, commercial and social purposes it was important that it should be vested in the General Government. As a mere matter of regulation and nothing more, I presume, was intended by it, it is a power easily executive and involving little authority within the States individually. The right to exercise exclusive legislation in all cases whatsoever over the Federal district and over forts, magazines, arsenals, dockyards, and other needful buildings with the consent of the State within which the same may be is a power of a peculiar character and is sufficient in itself to confirm what has been said of all the other powers of the General Government. Of this particular grant further notice will hereafter be taken.

I shall conclude my remarks on this part of the subject by observing that the view which has been presented of the powers and character of the two Governments is supported by the marked difference which is observable in the manner of their endowment. The State governments are divided into three branches—a legislative, executive, and judiciary, and the appropriate duties of each assigned to it without any limitation of power except such as is necessary to guard against abuse in the forms of bills of right. But in instituting the National Government an entirely different principle was adopted and pursued. The Government itself is organized, like the State Governments, into three branches, but its powers are enumerated and defined in the most precise form. The subject has been already too fully explained to require illustration by a general view of the whole Constitution, every part of which affords proof of what is here advanced. It will be sufficient to advert to the eighth section of the first article, being that more particularly which defines the powers and fixes the character of the Government of the United States. By this section it is declared that Congress shall have power, first to lay and collect taxes, duties, imposts, and excises, etc.

Having shown the origin of the State governments and their endowments when first formed; having also shown the origin of the National Government and the powers vested in it, and having shown, lastly, the powers which are admitted to have remained to the State governments after those which were taken from them by the National Government, I will now proceed to examine whether the power to adopt and execute a system of internal improvement by roads and canals has been vested in the United States.

Before we can determine whether this power has been granted to the General Government it will be necessary to ascertain distinctly the value and extent of the power requisite to make such improvements. When that is done we shall be able to decide whether such power is invested in the National Government.

If the power existed it would, it is presumed, be executed by a board of skillful engineers, on a view of the whole Union, on a plan which would secure complete effect to all the great purposes of our Constitution. It is not my intention, however, to take up the subject here on this scale. I shall state a case for the purpose of illustration only. Let it be supposed that Congress intended to run a road from the city of Washington to Baltimore and to connect the Chesapeake Bay with the Delaware and the Delaware with the Raritan by a canal. What must be done to carry the project into effect? I make here no question of the existing power. I speak only of the power necessary for the purpose. Commissioners would be appointed to trace a route in the most direct line, paying due regard to heights, water courses, and other obstacles, and to acquire the right to the ground over which the road and canal would pass with sufficient breadth for each. This must be done by voluntary grants, or by purchases from individuals, or, in case they would not sell, or should ask an exorbitant price, by condemning the property and fixing its value by a jury of the vicinage. The next object to be attended to after the road and canal are laid out and made is to keep them in repair. We know that there are people in every community capable of committing voluntary injuries, of pulling down walls that are made to sustain the road, of breaking the bridges over water courses, and breaking the road itself. Some living near it might be disappointed that it did not pass through their lands and commit these acts of violence and waste from revenge or in the hope of giving it that direction, though for a short time. Injuries of this kind have been committed and are still complained of on the road from Cumberland to the Ohio. To accomplish this object Congress should have a right to pass laws to punish offenders wherever they may be found. Jurisdiction over the road would not be sufficient, though it were exclusive. It would seldom happen that the parties would be detected in the act. They would generally commit it in the night and fly far off before the sun appeared. The power to punish these culprits must therefore reach them wherever they go. They must also be amenable to competent tribunals, Federal or State. The power must likewise extend to another object not less essential or important than those already mentioned. Experience has shown that the establishment of turnpikes, with gates and tolls and persons to collect the tolls, is the best expedient that can be adopted to defray the expense of these improvements and the repairs which they necessarily require. Congress must therefore have power to make such an establishment and to support it by such regulations, with fines and penalties in the case of injuries as may be competent to the purpose. The right must extend to all those objects, or it will be utterly incompetent. It is possessed and exercised by the States individually, and it must be possessed by the United States or the pretension must be abandoned.

Let it be further supposed that Congress, believing that they do possess the power, have passed an act for those purposes, under which commissioners have been appointed, who have begun the work. They are met at the first farm on which they enter by the owner, who forbids them to trespass on his land. They offer to buy it at a fair price or at twice or thrice its value. He persists in his refusal. Can they, on the principle recognized and acted on by all the State governments that in cases of this kind the obstinacy and perverseness of an individual must yield to the public welfare, summon a jury of upright and discreet men to condemn the land, value it and compel the owner to receive the amount and to deliver it up to them? I believe that very few would concur in the opinion that such a power exists.

The next object is to preserve these objects from injury. The locks of the canal are broken, the walls which restrained the road are pulled down, the bridges are broken, the road itself is plowed up, toll is refused to be paid, the gates of the canal or turnpike are forced. The offenders are pursued, caught and brought to trial. Can they be punished? The question of right must be decided on principle. The culprits will avail themselves of every barrier that may serve to screen them from punishment. They will plead that the law under which they stand arraigned is unconstitutional, and that question must be decided by the Court, whether Federal or State, on a fair investigation of the powers vested in the General Government by the Constitution. If the judges find that these powers have not been granted to Congress, the prisoners must be acquitted, and by their acquittal all claim to the right to establish such a system is at an end.

I have supposed an opposition to be made to the right in Congress by the owner of the land and other individuals charged with breaches of laws made to protect the works from injury, because it is the mildest form in which it can present itself. It is not, however, the only one. A State, also, may contest the right, and then the controversy assumes another character. Government might contend against Government, for to a certain extent both the Governments are sovereign and independent of each other, and in that form it is possible, though not probable, that opposition might be made. To each limitations are prescribed, and should a contest rise between them respecting their rights and the people sustain it with anything like an equal division of numbers, the worst consequences might ensue.

It may be urged that the opposition suggested by the owner of the land or by the States individually may be avoided by a satisfactory arrangement with the parties. But a suppression of opposition in that way is no proof of a right in Congress, nor could it, if confined to that limit, remove all the impediments to the exercise of the power. It is not sufficient that Congress may by the command and application of the public revenue purchase the soil, and thus silence that class of individuals, or by the accommodation afforded to individual States put down opposition on their part. Congress must be able rightfully to control all opposition or they cannot carry the system into effect. Cases would inevitably occur to put the right to the test. The work must be preserved from injury, tolls must be collected, offenders must be punished. With these culprits no bargain can be made. When brought to trial they must deny the validity of the law, and that plea being sustained all claim to the right ceases.

If the United States possess this power, it must be either because it has been specifically granted or that it is incidental and necessary to carry into effect some specific grant. The advocates for the power derive it from the following sources: First, the right to establish post-offices and post-roads; second, to declare war; third, to regulate commerce among the several States; fourth, from the power to pay the debts and provide for the common defense and general welfare of the United States; fifth, from the power to make all laws necessary and proper for carrying into execution all the powers vested by the Constitution in the Government of the United States or in any department or office thereof; sixth, and lastly, from the power to dispose of and make all needful rules and regulations respecting the territory and other property of the United States. It is to be observed that there is but little accord among the advocates for this power as to the particular source from whence it is derived. They all agree, however, in ascribing it to some one or more of those above mentioned. I will examine the ground of the claim in each instance.

The first of these grants is in the following words: "Congress shall have power to establish post-offices and post-roads." What is the just import of these words and the extent of the grant? The word "establish" is the ruling term; "post-offices and post-roads" are the subjects on which it acts. The question therefore is, What power is granted by that word? The sense in which words are commonly used is that in which they are to be understood in all transactions between public bodies and individuals. The intention of the parties is to prevail and there is no better way of ascertaining it than by giving to the terms used their ordinary import. If we were to ask any number of our most enlightened citizens, who had no connection with public affairs and whose minds were unprejudiced, what was the import of the word "establish" and the extent of the grant which it controls, we do not think there would be any difference of opinion among them. We are satisfied that all of them would answer that a power was thereby given to Congress to fix on the towns, court-houses, and other places throughout our Union at which there should be post-offices, the routes by which the mails should be carried from one post-office to another, so as to diffuse intelligence as extensively and to make the institution as useful as possible, to fix the postage to be paid on every letter and packet thus carried, to support the establishment, and to protect the post-office and mails from robbery by punishing those who should commit the offense. The idea of the right to lay off the roads of the United States on a general scale of improvement, to take the soil from the proprietor by force, to establish turnpikes and tolls, and to punish offenders in the manner stated above would never occur to any such person. The use of the existing road by the stage, mail carrier, or postboy in passing over it as others do is all that would be thought of, the jurisdiction and soil remaining to the State, with a right in the State or those authorized by its legislature to change the road at pleasure.

The intention of the parties is supported by other proof which ought to place it beyond all doubt. In the former act of Government, the Confederation, we find a grant for the same purpose expressed in the following words: "The United States in Congress assembled shall have the sole and exclusive right and power of establishing and regulating post-offices from one State to another throughout all the United States, and exacting such postage on the papers passing through the same as may be requisite to defray the expenses of the said office." The term "establish" was likewise the ruling one in that instrument and was evidently intended and understood to give a power simply and solely to fix where there should be post-offices. By transferring this term from the Confederation into the Constitution it was doubtless intended that it should be understood in the same sense in the latter that it was in the former instrument, and to be applied alike to post-offices and post-roads. In whatever sense it is applied to post-offices, it must be applied in the same sense to post-roads. But it may be asked if such was the intention, why were not all the other terms of the grant transferred with it? The reason is obvious. The Confederation being a bond of Union between independent States, it was necessary in granting the powers which were to be exercised over them to be very explicit and minute in defining the powers granted. But the Constitution to the extent of its powers having incorporated the States into one Government like the government of the States individually, fewer words in defining the powers granted by it were not only adequate, but perhaps better adapted to the purpose. We find that brevity is a characteristic of the instrument. Had it been intended to convey a more enlarged power in the Constitution than had been granted in the Confederation, surely the same controlling term would not have been used, or other words would have been added, to show such intention and to mark the extent to which the power should be carried. It is a liberal construction of the powers granted in the Constitution by this term to include in it all the powers that were granted in the Confederation by terms which specifically defined and, as was supposed, extended their limits. It would be absurd to say that by omitting from the Constitution any portion of the phraseology which was deemed important in the Confederation the import of that term was enlarged, and with it the powers of the Constitution, in a proportional degree beyond what they were in the Confederation. The right to exact postage and to protect the post-offices and mails from robbery by punishing the offenders may fairly be considered as incidents to the grant, since without it the object of the grant might be defeated. Whatever is absolutely necessary to the accomplishment of the object of the grant, though not specified, may fairly be considered as included in it. Beyond this the doctrine of incidental can not be carried.

If we go back to the origin of our settlements and institutions and trace their progress down to the Revolution, we shall see that it was in this sense, and in none other, that the power was exercised by all our colonial governments. Post-offices were made for the country and not the country for them. They are the offspring of improvements; they never go before it. Settlements are first made, after which the progress is uniform and simple, extending to objects in regular order most necessary to the comfort of man—schools, places of public worship, court houses, and markets; post-offices follow. Roads may, indeed, be said to be coeval with settlements; they lead to all the places mentioned, and to every other which the various and complicated interests of society require.

It is believed that not one example can be given, from the first settlement of our country to the adoption of this Constitution of a post-office being established without a view to existing roads or of a single road having been made by pavement, turnpike, etc., for the sole purpose of accommodating a post-office. Such too is the uniform progress of all societies. In granting, then, this power to the United States it was undoubtedly intended by the framers and ratifiers of the Constitution to convey it in the sense and extent only in which it had been understood and exercised by the previous authorities of the country.

This conclusion is confirmed by the object of the grant and the manner of its execution. The object is the transportation of the mail throughout the United States, which may be done on horseback, and was so done until lately, since the establishment of stages. Between the great towns and in other places where the population is dense stages are preferred because they afford an additional opportunity to make a profit from passengers; but where the population is sparse and on crossroads it is generally carried on horseback. Unconnected with passengers and other objects, it cannot be doubted that the mail itself may be carried in every part of our Union with nearly as much economy and greater despatch on horseback than in a stage, and in many parts with much greater. In every part of the Union in which stages can be preferred the roads are sufficiently good provided those which serve for every other purpose will accommodate. In every other part where horses alone are used if other people pass them on horseback surely the mail carrier can. For an object so simple and so easy in its execution it would doubtless excite surprise if it should be thought proper to appoint commissioners to lay off the country on a great scheme of improvement, with the power to shorten distances, reduce heights, level mountains, and pave surfaces.

If the United States possessed the power contended for under this grant, might they not in adopting the roads of the individual States for the carriage of the mail, as has been done, assume jurisdiction over them and preclude a right to interfere with or alter them? Might they not establish turnpikes and exercise all the other acts of sovereignty above stated over such roads necessary to protect them from injury and defray the expense of repairing? Surely if the right exists these consequences necessarily followed as soon as the road was established. The absurdity of such a pretension must be apparent to all who examine it. In this way a large portion of the territory of every State might be taken from it, for there is scarcely a road in any State which will not be used for the transportation of the mail. A new field for legislation and internal government would thus be opened.

From this view of the subject I think we may fairly conclude that the right to adopt and execute a system of internal improvement, or any part of it, has not been granted to Congress, under the power to establish post-offices and post-roads; that the common roads of the country only were contemplated by that grant and are fully competent to all its purposes.

The next object of inquiry is whether the right to declare war includes the right to adopt and execute this system of improvement. The objections to it are, I presume, not less conclusive than those which are applicable to the grant which we have just examined.

Under the last mentioned grant a claim has been set up to as much of that system as relates to roads. Under this it extends alike to roads and canals.

We must examine this grant by the same rules of construction that were applied to the preceding one. The object was to take this power from the individual States and to vest it in the General Government. This has been done in clear and explicit terms, first by granting the power to Congress, and secondly by prohibiting the exercise of it by the States. "Congress shall have a right to declare war." This is the language of the grant. If the right to adopt and execute this system of improvement is included in it, it must be by way of incident only, since there is nothing in the grant itself which bears any relation to roads and canals. The following considerations, it is presumed, prove incontestably that this power has not been granted in that or any other manner.

The United States are exposed to invasion through the whole extent of their Atlantic coast by any European power with which we might be engaged in war—on the northern and northwestern frontier on the side of Canada by Great Britain, and on the southern by Spain or any power in alliance with her. If internal improvements are to be carried to the full extent to which they may be useful for military purposes, the power as it exists must apply to all the roads of the Union, there being no limitation to it. Wherever such improvements may facilitate the march of troops, the transportation of cannon, or otherwise aid the operations or mitigate the calamities of war, along the coast or in any part of the interior, they would be useful for military purposes, and might therefore be made. The power following as an incident to another power can be measured as to its extent by reference only to the obvious extent of the power to which it is incidental. So great a scope was, it is believed, never given to incidental power.

If it had been intended that the right to declare war should include all the powers necessary to maintain war, it would follow that nothing would have been done to impair the right or to restrain Congress from the exercise of any power which the exigencies of the war might require. The nature and extent of this exigency would mark the extent of the power granted, which should always be construed liberally, so as to be adequate to the end. A right to raise money by taxes, duties, excises, and by loan, to raise and support armies and a navy, to provide for calling forth, arming, disciplining, and governing the militia when in the service of the United States, establishing fortifications and governing the troops stationed in them independently of the State authorities, and to perform many other acts is indispensable to the maintenance of war—no war with any great power can be prosecuted with success without the command of the resources of the Union in all these respects. These powers, then, would of necessity and by common consent have fallen within the right to declare war had it been intended to convey by way of incident to that right the necessary powers to maintain war. But these powers have all been granted specifically with many others, in great detail, which experience had shown were necessary for the purposes of war. By specifically granting, then, these powers it is manifest that every power was thus granted which it was intended to grant for military purposes, and that it was also intended that no important power should be included in this grant by way of incident, however useful it might be for some of the purposes of the grant.

By the sixteenth of the enumerated powers, Article 1, section 8, Congress are authorized to exercise exclusive legislation in all cases whatever over such district as may by cession of particular States and the acceptance of Congress, not exceeding 10 miles square, become the seat of Government of the United States, and to exercise like authority over all places purchased by the consent of the legislature of the State in which the same shall be, for the erection of forts, magazines, arsenals, dockyards, and other useful buildings. If any doubt existed on a view of other parts of the Constitution respecting the decision which ought to be formed on the question under consideration, I should suppose that this clause would completely remove it. It has been shown after the most liberal construction of all the enumerated powers of the General Government that the territory within the limits of the respective States belonged to them; that the United States had no right under the powers granted to them, with the exception specified in this grant, to any the smallest portion of territory within a State, all those powers operating on a different principle and having their full effect without impairing in the slightest degree this right in the States; that those powers were in every instance means to ends, which being accomplished left the subject—that is, the property, in which light only land could be regarded—where it was before, under the jurisdiction and subject to the laws of the State governments.

The second number of the clause, which is applicable to military and naval purposes alone, claims particular attention here. It fully confirms the view taken of the other enumerated powers, for had it been intended to include in the right to declare war, by way of incident, any right of jurisdiction or legislation over territory within a State, it would have been done as to fortifications, magazines, arsenals, dockyards, and other needful-buildings. By specifically granting the right as to such small portions of territory as might be necessary for these purposes and on certain conditions, minutely and well defined, it is manifest that it was not intended to grant it as to any other portion on any condition for any purpose or in any manner whatsoever.

It may be said that although the authority to exercise exclusive legislation in certain cases within the States with their consent may be considered as a prohibitive to Congress to exercise like exclusive legislation in any other case, although their consent should be granted, it does not prohibit the exercise of such jurisdiction or power within a State as would be competent to all the purposes of internal improvement. I can conceive no ground on which the idea of such a power over any part of the territory of a State can be inferred from the power to declare war. There never can be an occasion for jurisdiction for mil-

itary purposes except in fortifications, dockyards and the like places. If the soldiers are in the field, or are quartered in garrisons without the fortifications, the
civil authority must prevail where they are. The government of the troops by
martial law is not affected by it. In war, when the forces are increased, and the
movement is on a greater scale, consequences follow which are inseparable from
the exigencies of the State. More freedom of action and a wider range of power
in the military commanders, to be exercised on their own responsibility, may
be necessary to the public safety; but even here the civil authority of the State
never ceases to operate. It is also exclusive for all civil purposes.

Whether any power short of that stated would be adequate to the purposes
of internal improvement is denied. In the case of territory, one government
must prevail for all the purposes intended by the grant. The jurisdiction of the
United States might be modified in such manner as to admit that of the State in
all cases and for all purposes not necessary to the execution of the proposed
power; but the right of the General Government must be complete for all the
purposes above stated. It must extend to the seizure and condemnation of the
property, if necessary; to the punishment of offenders for injuries to the roads
and canals; to the establishment and enforcement of tolls, etc. It must be a complete right to the extent above stated or it will be of no avail. That right does
not exist.

The reasons which operate in favor of the right of exclusive legislation in
forts, dockyards, etc., do not apply to other places. The safety of such works and
of the cities which they are intended to defend, and even of whole communities, may sometimes depend on it. If spies are admitted within them in time of
war, they might communicate intelligence to the enemy which might be fatal.
All nations surround such works with high walls and keep their gates shut. Even
here, however, three important conditions are indispensable to such exclusive
legislation: First, the ground must be requisite for and be applied to those purposes; second, it must be purchased; third, it must be purchased by the consent
of the State in which it may be. When we find that so much care has been taken
to protect the sovereignty of the States over the territory within their respective limits, admitting that of the United States over such small portions and for
such special and important purposes only, the conclusion is irresistible not only
that the power necessary for internal improvements has not been granted, but
that it has been clearly prohibited.

I come next to the right to regulate commerce, the third source from
whence the right to make internal improvements is claimed. It is expressed in
the following words: "Congress shall have power to regulate commerce with

foreign nations and among the several States and with the Indian tribes." The reasoning applicable to the preceding claims is equally so to this. The mischief complained of was that this power could not be exercised with advantage over the individual State, and the object was to transfer it to the United States. The sense in which the power was understood and exercised by the States was doubtless that in which it was transferred to the United States. The policy was the same as to three branches of this grant and it is scarcely possible to separate the two first from each other in any view which may be taken of the subject. The last, relating to the Indian tribes, is of a nature distinct from the others for reasons too well known to require explanation. Commerce between independent powers is universally regulated by duties and imposts. It was so regulated by the States before the adoption of this Constitution equally in respect to each other and to foreign powers. The goods and vessels employed in the trade are the only subjects of legislation. It can act on none other. A power, then, to impose such duties and imposts in regard to foreign nations and to prevent any on the trade between the States was the only power granted.

If we recur to the causes which produced the adoption of this Constitution, we shall find that injuries resulting from the regulation of trade by the States respectively and the advantages anticipated from the transfer of the power to Congress were among those which had the most weight. Instead of acting as a nation in regard to foreign powers, the States individually had commenced a system of restraint on each other whereby the interests of foreign powers were promoted at their expense. If one State imposed high duties on the goods or vessels of a foreign power to countervail the regulations of such power, the next adjoining States imposed lighter duties to invite those articles into their ports, that they might be transferred thence into the other States, securing the duties to themselves. This contracted policy in some of the States was soon counteracted by others. Restraints were immediately laid on such commerce by the suffering States, and thus had grown up a state of affairs disorderly and unnatural, the tendency of which was to destroy the Union itself and with it all hope of realizing those blessings which we had anticipated from the glorious Revolution which had been so recently achieved. From this deplorable dilemma, or, rather, certain ruin, we were happily rescued by the adoption of the Constitution.

Among the first and most important effects of this great Revolution was the complete abolition of this pernicious policy. The States were brought together by the Constitution as to commerce into one community equally in regard to foreign nations and each other. The regulations that were adopted regarded us in both respects as one people. The duties and imposts that were laid on the vessels and merchandise of foreign nations were all uniform throughout the United States, and in the intercourse between the States themselves no duties of any kind were imposed, other than between different ports and counties within the same State.

This view is supported by a series of measures, all of a marked character, preceding the adoption of the Constitution. As early as the year 1781 Congress recommended it to the States to vest in the United States a power to levy a duty of 5 per cent on all goods imported from foreign countries into the United States for the term of fifteen years. In 1783 this recommendation with alterations as to the kind of duties and an extension of this term to twenty-five years, was repeated and more earnestly urged. In 1784 it was recommended to the States to authorize Congress to prohibit under certain modifications, the importation of goods from foreign powers into the United States for fifteen years. In 1785 the consideration of the subject was resumed, and a proposition presented in a new form, with an address to the States, explaining fully the principles on which a grant of the power to regulate trade was deemed indispensable. In 1786 a meeting took place at Annapolis of delegates from several of the States on this subject, and on their report a convention was formed at Philadelphia the ensuing year from all the States, to whose deliberations we are indebted for the present Constitution.

In none of these measures was the subject of internal improvement mentioned or even glanced at. Those of 1784, 1785, 1786 and 1787 leading step by step to the adoption of the Constitution, had in view only the obtaining of a power to enable Congress to regulate trade with foreign powers. It is manifest that the regulation of trade with the several States was altogether a secondary object, suggested by and adopted in connection with the other. If the power necessary to this system of improvement is included under either branch of this grant, I should suppose that it was the first rather than the second. The pretension to it, however, under that branch has never been set up. In support of the claim under the second no reason has been assigned which appears to have the least weight.

The fourth claim is found on the right of Congress to "pay the debts and provide for the common defense and general welfare" of the United States. This claim has less reason on its side than either of those which we have already examined. The power of which this forms a part is expressed in the following words: "Congress shall have power to lay and collect taxes, duties, imposts and excises; to pay the debts and provide for the common defense and general welfare of the United States; but all duties, imposts, and excises shall be uniform throughout the United States."

That the second part of this grant gives a right to appropriate the public money and nothing more, is evident from the following considerations: First. If the right of appropriation is not given by this clause, it is not given at all, there being no other grant in the Constitution which gives it directly or which has any bearing on the subject, even by implication, except the two following: First, the prohibition, which is contained in the elements of the enumerated powers, not to appropriate money for the support of armies for a longer term than two years; and, second, the declaration of the sixth member or clause of the ninth section of the first article that no money shall be drawn from the Treasury but in consequence of appropriations made by law. Second. This part of the grant has none of the characteristics of a distinct and original power. It is manifestly incidental to the great objects of the first part of the grant which authorizes Congress to lay and collect taxes, duties, imposts and excises, a power of vast extent, not granted by the Confederation, the grant of which formed one of the principal inducements to the adoption of this Constitution. If both parts of the grants are taken together (as they must be, for the one follows immediately after the other in the same sentence), it seems to be impossible to give to the latter any other construction than that contended for. Congress shall have power to lay and collect taxes, duties, imposts, and excises. For what purpose? To pay the debts and provide for the common defense and general welfare of the United States, an arrangement and phraseology which clearly show that the latter part of the clause was intended to enumerate the purposes to which the money thus raised might be appropriated. Third. If this is not the real object and fair construction of the second part of this grant, it follows either that it has no import or operation whatever or one of much greater extent than the first part. This presumption is evidently groundless in both instances. In the first, because no part of the Constitution can be considered useless; no sentence or clause in it without a meaning. In the second, because such a construction as made the second part of the clause an original grant, embracing the same object with the first, but with much greater power than it, would be in the highest degree absurd. The order generally observed in grants, an order founded in common sense, since it promotes a clear understanding of their import, is to grant the power intended to be conveyed in the most full and explicit manner, and then to explain or qualify it, if explanation or qualification should be necessary. This order has, it is believed, been invariably observed in all the grants contained in the Constitution. In the second, because if the clause in question is not construed merely as an authority to appropriate the public money, it must be obvious that it conveys a power of indefinite and unlimited extent; that there would have been no use for the special powers to raise and support armies and a navy, to regulate commerce, to call forth the militia or even to lay and collect taxes, duties, imposts and excises. An unqualified power to pay the debts and provide for the common defense and general welfare, as the second part of this clause would be if considered as a distinct and separate grant, would extend to every object in which the public could be interested. A power to provide for the common defense would give to Congress the command of the whole force and of all the resources of the Union; but a right to provide for the general welfare would go much further. It would, in effect, break down all the barriers between the States and the General Government and consolidate the whole under the latter.

The powers specifically granted to Congress are what are called the enumerated powers, and are numbered in the order in which they stand, among which that contained in the first clause holds the first place in point of importance. If the power created by the latter part of the clause is considered an original grant, unconnected with and independent of the first, as in that case it must be, then the first part is entirely done away, as are all the other grants in the Constitution, being completely absorbed in the transcendent power granted in the latter part; but if the clause be constructed in the sense contended for, then every part has an important meaning and effect; not a line, a word, in it is superfluous. A power to lay and collect taxes, duties, imposts and excises subjects to the call of Congress every branch of the public revenue, internal and external, and the addition to pay the debts and provide for the common defense and general welfare gives the right of applying the money raised—that is of appropriating it to the purposes specified according to a proper construction of the terms. Hence it follows that it is the first part of the clause only which gives a power which affects in any manner the power remaining to the States, as the power to raise money from the people, whether it be by taxes, duties, imposts, or excises, though concurrent in the States as to taxes and excises, must necessarily do. But the use or application of the money after it is raised is a power altogether of a different character. It imposes no burden on the people, nor can it act on them in a sense to take power from the States or in any sense in which power can be controverted, or become a question between the two Governments. The application of money raised under a lawful power is a right or grant which may be abused. It may be applied partially among the States, or to improper uses in our foreign and domestic concerns; but still it is a power not felt in the sense of other power, since the only complaint which any State can make of such partiality and abuse is that some other State or States have obtained greater benefit from the application than by a just rule of apportionment they were entitled to. The right of appropriation is therefore from its nature secondary and incidental to the right of raising money, and it was proper to place it in the same grant and same clause with that right. By finding them, then, in that order we see a new proof of the sense in which the grant was made, corresponding with the view herein taken of it.

The last part of this grant which provides that all duties, imposts, and excises shall be uniform throughout the United States, furnishes another strong proof that it was not intended that the second part should constitute a distinct grant in the sense above stated, or convey any other right than that of appropriation. This provision operates exclusively on the power granted in the first part of the clause. It recites three branches of that power—duties, imposts and excises—those only on which it could operate, the rule by which the fourth—that is taxes—should be laid being already provided for in another part of the Constitution. The object of this provision is to secure a just equality among the States in the exercise of that power by Congress. By placing it after both the grants—that is, after that to raise and that to appropriate the public money—and making it apply to the first only it shows that it was not intended that the power granted in the second should be paramount to and destroy that granted in the first. It shows also that no such formidable power as that suggested had been granted in the second, or any power against the abuse of which it was thought necessary specially to provide. Surely if it was deemed proper to guard a specific power of limited extent and well known import against injustice and abuse, it would have been much more so to have guarded against the abuse of a power of such vast extent and so indefinite as would have been granted by the second part of the clause if considered as a distinct and original grant.

With this construction all the other enumerated grants, and, indeed, all the grants of power contained in the Constitution, have their full operation and effect. They all stand well together, fulfilling the great purposes intended by them. Under it we behold a great scheme, consistent in all its parts, a Government instituted for national purposes, vested with adequate powers for those purposes, commencing with the most important of all, that of the revenue, and proceeding in regular order to the others with which it was deemed proper to endow it, all, too, drawn with the utmost circumspection and care. How much more consistent is this construction with the great objects of the institution and with the high character of the enlightened and patriotic citizens who framed it, as well as of those who ratified it, than one which subverts every sound principle and rule of construction and throws everything into confusion.

I have dwelt long on this part of the subject from an earnest desire to fix in a clear and satisfactory manner the import of the second part of this grant, well knowing from the generality of the terms used their tendency to lead into error. I indulge a strong hope that the view herein presented will not be without effect, but will tend to satisfy the unprejudiced and impartial that nothing more was granted by that part than a power to *appropriate* the public money raised under the other part. To what extent that power may be carried will be the next object of inquiry.

It is contended on the one side that as the National Government is a government of limited powers it has no right to expend money except in the performance of acts authorized by the other specific grants according to a strict construction of their powers; that this grant in neither of its branches gives to Congress discretionary power of any kind, but is a mere instrument in its hands to carry into effect the powers contained in the other grants. To this construction I was inclined in the more early stage of our government; but on further reflection and observation my mind has undergone a change, for reasons which I will frankly unfold.

The grant consists, as heretofore observed, of a twofold power—the first to raise, the second to appropriate, the public money—and the terms used in both instances are general and unqualified. Each branch was obviously drawn with a view to the other, and the import of each tends to illustrate that of the other. The grant to raise money gives a power over every other subject from which revenue may be drawn, and is made in the same manner with the grants to declare war, to raise and support armies, and a navy, to regulate commerce, to establish post-offices and post-roads, and with all the other specific grants to the General Government. In the discharge of the powers contained in any of these grants there is no other check than that which is to be found in the great principles of our system, the responsibility of the representative to his constituents. If war, for example, is necessary, and Congress declare it for good cause, their constituents will support them in it. A like support will be given them for the faithful discharge of their duties under any and every other power vested in the United States. It affords to the friends of our free governments the most heartfelt consolation to know—and from the best evidence, our own experience—that in great emergencies the boldest measures, such as form the strongest appeals to the virtue and patriotism of the people, are sure to obtain the most decided approbation. But should the representative act corruptly and betray his trust, or otherwise prove that he was unworthy of the confidence of his constituents, he would be equally sure to lose it and to be removed and otherwise censured, according to his deserts.

The power to raise money by taxes, duties, imposts, and excises is alike unqualified, nor do I see any check on the exercise of it other than that which applies to the other powers above recited, the responsibility of the representative to his constituents. Congress know the extent of the public engagements and the sums necessary to meet them; they know how much may be derived from each branch of revenue without pressing it too far; and, paying due regard to the interests of the people, they likewise know which branch ought to be resorted to in the first instance. From the commencement of the government two branches of this power, duties and imposts, have been in constant operation, the revenue from which has supported the government in its various branches and met its other ordinary engagements. In great emergencies the other two, taxes and excises, have likewise been resorted to, and neither was the right or the policy called in question.

If we look to the second branch of this power, that which authorizes the appropriation of the money thus raised, we find that it is not less general and unqualified than the power to raise it. More comprehensive terms than to "pay the debts and provide for the common defense and general welfare" could not have been used. So intimately connected with and dependent on each other are these two branches of power that had either been limited the limitation would have had the like effect on the other. Had the power to raise money been conditional or restricted to special purposes, the appropriation must have corresponded with it, for none but the money raised could be appropriated, nor could it be appropriated to other purposes than those which were permitted. On the other hand, if the right of appropriation had been restricted to certain purposes, it would be useless and improper to raise more than would be adequate to those purposes. It may fairly be inferred these restraints or checks have been carefully and intentionally avoided. The power in each branch is alike broad and unqualified, and each is drawn with peculiar fitness to the other, the latter requiring terms of great extent and force to accommodate the former, which have been adopted, and both placed in the same clause and sentence. Can it be presumed that all these circumstances were so nicely adjusted by mere accident? Is it not more just to conclude that they were the result of due deliberation and design? Had it been intended that Congress should be restricted in the appropriation of the public money to such expenditures as were authorized by a rigid construction of the other specific grants, how easy would it have been to have provided for it by a declaration to that effect. The omission of such declaration is therefore an additional proof that it was not intended that the grant should be so construed.

It was evidently impossible to have subjected this grant in either branch to such restriction without exposing the Government to very serious embarrassment. How carry it into effect? If the grant had been made in any degree dependent upon the States, the government would have experienced the fate of the Confederation. Like it, it would have withered and soon perished. Had the Supreme Court been authorized, or should any other tribunal distinct from the government be authorized to impose its veto, and to say that more money had been raised under either branch of this power—that is, by taxes, duties, imposts, or excises—than was necessary, that such a tax or duty was useless, that the appropriation to this or that purpose was unconstitutional, the movement might have been suspended and the whole system disorganized. It was impossible to have created a power within the government or any other power distinct from Congress and the Executive which should control the movement of the government in this respect and not destroy it. Had it been declared by a clause in the Constitution that the expenditures under this grant should be restricted to the construction which might be given of the other grants, such restraint, though the most innocent, could not have failed to have had an injurious effect on the vital principles of the government and often on its most important measures. Those who might wish to defeat a measure proposed might construe the power relied on in support of it in a narrow and contracted manner, and in that way fix a precedent inconsistent with the true import of the grant. At other times those who favored a measure might give to the power relied on a forced or strained construction, and, succeeding in the object, fix a precedent in the opposite extreme. Thus it is manifest that if the right of appropriation be confined to that limit, measures may oftentimes be carried or defeated by considerations and motives altogether independent of and unconnected with their merits, and the several powers of Congress receive constructions equally inconsistent with their true import. No such declaration, however, has been made, and from the fair import of the grant, and, indeed, its positive terms, the inference that such was intended seems to be precluded.

Many considerations of great weight operate in favor of this construction, while I do not perceive any serious objections to it. If it be established, it follows that the words "to provide for the common defense and general welfare" have a definite, safe, and useful meaning. The idea of their forming an original grant, with unlimited power, superseding every other grant, is abandoned. They will be considered simply as conveying a right of appropriation, a right indispensable to that of raising a revenue and necessary to expenditures under every grant. By it, as already observed, no new power will be taken from the States, the money to be appropriated being raised under a power already granted to Congress. By it, too, the motive for giving a forced or strained construction to any of the other specific grants will in most instances be diminished and in many utterly destroyed. The importance of this consideration can not be too highly estimated, since, in addition to the examples already given, it ought particularly to be recollected that to whatever extent any specified power may be carried the right of jurisdiction goes with it, pursuing it through all its incidents. The very important agency which this grant has in carrying into effect every other grant is a wrong argument in favor of the construction contended for. All the other grants are limited by the nature of the offices which they have severally to perform, each conveying a power to do a certain thing, and that only, whereas this is coextensive with the great scheme of the government itself. It is the lever which raises and puts the whole machinery in motion and continues the movement. Should either of the other grants fail in consequence of any condition or limitation attached to it or misconstruction of its powers, much injury might follow, but still it would be the failure of one branch of power, of one item in the system only. All the others might move on. But should the right to raise and appropriate the public money be improperly restricted, the whole system might be sensibly affected, if not disorganized. Each of the other grants is limited by the nature of the grant itself; this, by the nature of the government only. Hence it became necessary that, like the power to declare war, this power should be commensurate with the great scheme of the government and with all its purposes.

If, then, the right to raise and appropriate the public money is not restricted to the expenditures under the other specific grants according to a strict construction of their powers, respectively, is there no limitation to it? Have Congress the right to raise and appropriate the money to any and to every purpose according to their will and pleasure? They certainly have not. The Government of the United States is a limited government, instituted for great national purposes, and for those only. Other interests are committed to the States, whose duty it is to provide for them. Each government should look to the great and essential purposes for which it was instituted and confine itself to those purposes. A State government will rarely if ever apply money to national purposes without making it a charge to the nation. The people of the State would not permit it. Nor will Congress be apt to apply money in aid of the State administrations for purposes strictly local in which the nation at large has no interest, although the State should desire it. The people of the other States would condemn it. They would declare that Congress had no right to tax them for such a purpose, and dismiss at the next election such of their representatives as had voted for the measure, especially if it should be severely felt. I do not think that in offices of this kind there is much danger of the two governments mistaking their interests or their duties. I rather expect that they would soon have a clear and distinct understanding of them and move on in great harmony.

Good roads and canals will promote many very important national purposes. They will facilitate the operations of war, the movements of troops, the transportation of cannon, of provisions, and every warlike store, much to our advantage and to the disadvantage of the enemy in time of war. Good roads will facilitate the transportation of the mail, and thereby promote the purposes of commerce and political intelligence among the people. They will by being properly directed to these objects enhance the value of our vacant lands, a treasure of vast resource to the nation. To the appropriation of public money to improvements having these objects in view and carried to a certain extent I do not see any well founded constitutional objection.

In regard to our foreign concerns, provided they are managed with integrity and ability, great liberality is allowable in the application of the public money. In the management of these concerns no State interests can be affected, no State rights violated. The complete and exclusive control over them is vested in Congress. The power to form treaties of alliance and commerce with foreign powers, to regulate by law our commerce with them, to determine on peace or war, to raise armies and a navy, to call forth the militia and direct their operations belongs to the General Government. These great powers, embracing the whole scope of our foreign relations, being granted, on what principle can it be said that the minor are withheld? Are not the latter clearly and evidently comprised in the former? Nations are sometimes called upon to perform to each other acts of humanity and kindness, of which we see so many illustrious examples between individuals in private life. Great calamities make appeals to the benevolence of mankind which ought not to be resisted. Good offices in such emergencies exalt the character of the party rendering them. By exciting grateful feelings they soften the intercourse between nations and tend to prevent war. Surely if the United States have a right to make war they have a right to prevent it. How was it possible to grant to Congress a power for such minor purposes other than in general terms, comprising it within the scope and policy of that which conveyed it for the greater?

The right of appropriation is nothing more than a right to apply the public money to this or that purpose. It has no incidental power, nor does it draw after it any consequences of that kind. All that Congress could do under it in the case of internal improvements would be to appropriate the money necessary to make them. For every act requiring legislative sanction or support the State authority must be relied on. The condemnation of the land, if the proprietors should refuse to sell it, the establishment of turnpikes and tolls and the protection of the work when finished must be done by the State. To these purposes the powers of the General Government are believed to be utterly incompetent.

To the objection that the United States have no power in any instance which is not complete to all the purposes to which it may be made instrumental, and in consequence that they have no right to appropriate any portion of the public money to internal improvements because they have not the right of sovereignty and jurisdiction over them when made, a full answer has, it is presumed, been already given. It may, however, be proper to add that if this objection was well founded it would not be confined to the simple case of internal improvements, but would apply to others of high importance. Congress have a right to regulate commerce. To give effect to this power it becomes necessary to establish custom-houses in every State along the coast and in many parts of the interior. The vast amount of goods imported and the duties to be performed to accommodate the merchants and secure the revenue make it necessary that spacious buildings should be erected, especially in the great towns for their reception. This, it is manifest, could best be performed under the direction of the General Government. Have Congress the right to seize the property of individuals if they should refuse to sell it, in quarters best adapted to the purpose, to have it valued, and to take it at the valuation? Have they a right to exercise jurisdiction within those buildings? Neither of these claims has ever been set up, nor could it, as is presumed, be sustained. They have invariably either rented houses where such as were suitable could be obtained, or, where they could not, purchased the ground of individuals, erected the buildings and held them under the laws of the State. Under the power to establish post offices and post roads houses are also requisite for the reception of the mails and the transaction of the business of the several offices. These have always been rented or purchased and held under the laws of the State in the same manner as if they had been taken by a citizen. The United States have a right to establish tribunals inferior to the Supreme Court, and such have been established in every State in the Union. It is believed that the houses for these inferior courts have invariably been rented. No right of jurisdiction in them has ever been claimed, nor other right than that of privilege, and that only while the court is in session. A still stronger case may be urged. Should Congress be compelled by invasion or other cause to remove the government to some town within one of the States, would they have a right of jurisdiction over such town, or hold even the house in which they held their session under other authority than the laws of such State? It is believed they would not. If they have a right to appropriate money for any of these purposes, to be laid out under the protection of the laws of the State, surely they have a right to do it for the purposes of internal improvements.

It is believed there is not a corporation in the Union which does not exercise great discretion in the application of the money raised by it to the purposes of its institution. It would be strange if the Government of the United States, which was instituted for such important purposes and endowed with such extensive powers, should not be allowed at least equal discretion and authority. The evil to be particularly avoided is the violation of State rights. Shunning that, it seems to be reasonable and proper that the powers of Congress should be so construed as that the General Government in its intercourse with other nations and in our internal concerns should be able to adopt all such measures lying within the fair scope and intended to facilitate the direct objects of its powers as the public welfare may require and a sound and provident policy dictate.

The measures of Congress have been in strict accord with the view taken of the right of appropriation both as to its extent and limitation, as will be shown by a reference to the laws, commencing at a very early period. Many roads have been opened, of which the following are the principal: The first from Cumberland, at the head waters of the Potomac, in the State of Maryland, through Pennsylvania and Virginia to the State of Ohio (March 29, 1806, see Vol. iv., p. 13, of the late edition of the laws). The second from the frontiers of Georgia, on the route from Athens to New Orleans, to its intersection with the thirty-first degree of north latitude (April 31, 1806, p. 58). The third from the Mississippi at a point and by a route described to the Ohio (same act). The fourth from Nashville, in Tennessee, to Natchez (same act). The fifth from the thirty-first degree of north latitude, on the route from Athens to New Orleans, under such regulations as might be agreed on between the Executive and the Spanish Government (March 3, 1807, p. 117). The sixth from the foot of the rapids of the river Miami, of Lake Erie, to the Western line of the Connecticut Reserve (December 12, 1811). The seventh from the Lower Sandusky to the boundary line established by the treaty of Greenville (same act). The eighth from a point where the United States road leading from Vincennes to the Indian boundary line, established by the treaty of Greenville, strikes the said line, to the North Bend, in the State of Ohio (January 8, 1812). The ninth for repairing and keeping in repair the road between Columbia on the Duck River, in Tennessee, and Madisonville, in Louisiana, and also the road between Fort Hawkins, in Georgia, and Fort Stoddard (April 27, 1816). The tenth from the Shawneetown, on the Ohio River, to the Sabine, and to Kaskaskias, in Illinois (April 27, 1816). The eleventh from Reynaldsburg, on Tennessee River, in the State of Tennessee, through the Chickasaw Nation, to intersect the Natchez road near the Chickasaw old town (March 3, 1817). The twelfth: By this act authority was given to the President to appoint three commissioners for the purpose of examining the country and laying out a road from the termination of the Cumberland road, at Wheeling, on the Ohio, through the States of Ohio, Indiana, and Illinois, to a point to be chosen by them, on the left bank of the Mississippi, between St. Louis and the mouth of the Illinois River, and to report an accurate plan of the said road, with an estimate of the expense of making it. It is, however, declared by the act that nothing was thereby intended to imply an obligation on the part of the United States to make or defray the expense of making the said road or any part thereof.

In the late war, two other roads were made by the troops for military purposes—one from the Upper Sandusky, in the State of Ohio, through the black Swamp, toward Detroit, and another from Plattsburg, on Lake Champlain, through the Chatauga woods towards Sacketts Harbor, which have since been repaired and improved by the troops. Of these latter there is no notice in the laws. The extra pay to the soldiers for repairing and improving those roads was advanced in the first instance from the appropriation to the Quartermasters' Department and afterwards provided for by a specific appropriation by Congress. The necessity of keeping those roads open and in good repair, being on the frontier, to facilitate a communication between our ports, is apparent.

All of these roads except the first were formed merely by cutting down the trees and throwing logs across, so as to make causeways over such parts as were otherwise impassable. The execution was of the coarsest kind. The Cumberland road is the only regular work which has been undertaken by the General Government or which could give rise to any question between the two governments respecting its powers. It is a great work, over the highest mountains in our Union, connecting from the seat of the General Government the Eastern with the Western Waters, and more intimately the Atlantic with the Western States, in the formation of which $1,800,000 have been expended. The measures pursued in this case require to be particularly noticed as fixing the opinion of the parties, and particularly of Congress, on the important question of the right. Passing through Maryland, Pennsylvania, and Virginia, it was thought necessary and proper to bring the subject before their respective legislatures to obtain their sanction, which was granted by each State by a legislative act, approving the route and providing for the purchase and condemnation of the land. This road was founded on an article of compact between the United States and the State of Ohio, under which that State came into the Union, and by which the expense attending it was to be defrayed by the application of a certain portion of the money arising from the sale of the public lands within that State. In this instance which is by far the strongest in respect to the expense, extent and nature of the work done, the United States have exercised no act of jurisdiction or sovereignty within either of the States by taking the land from the proprietors by force, by passing acts for the protection of the road, or to raise a revenue from it by the establishment of turnpikes and tolls, or any act founded on the principle of jurisdiction or right. Whatever they have done has, on the contrary, been founded on the opposite principle, on the voluntary and unqualified admission that the sovereignty belonged to the State and not the United States, and that they could perform no act which should tend to weaken the power of the State or to assume any to themselves. All that they have done has been to appropriate the public money to the construction of this road and to cause it to be constructed, for I presume that no distinction can be taken between the appropriation of money raised by the sale of the public lands and of that which arises from taxes, duties, imposts and excises; nor can I believe that the power to appropriate derives any sanction from a provision to that effect having been made by an article of compact between the United States and the people of the then Territory of Ohio.

By an act of April 30, 1802, entitled "An act to enable the people of the eastern division of the territory northwest of the river Ohio to form a constitution and State government, and for the admission of such State into the Union on an equal footing with the original States, and for other purposes," after describing the limits of the proposed new State and authorizing the people thereof to elect a convention to form a constitution, the three following propositions were made to the convention, to be obligatory on the United States if accepted by it: First, that section No. 16 of every township, or, where such section had been sold, other lands equivalent thereto should be granted to the inhabitants for the use of free schools. Second, that the 6 miles reservation, including the Salt Springs commonly called the Sciota Salt Springs, the salt springs near the Muskingum River and in the military tract with the sections which include the same, should be granted to the said State for the use of the people thereof, under such regulations as the legislature of the State should prescribe: *Provided,* That it should never sell or lease the same for more than ten years. Third, that one-twentieth part of the proceeds of the public lands lying within the said State which might be sold by Congress from and after the 30th. June ensuing should be applied to the lying out and making public roads from the navigable waters emptying into the Atlantic, to the Ohio, and through the State of Ohio, such roads to be laid out under the authority of Congress, with the consent of the several States through which they should pass.

These three propositions were made on the condition that the convention of the State should provide by an ordinance, irrevocable without the consent of the United States, that every tract of land sold by Congress after the 30th. of June ensuing should remain for the term of five years after sale exempt from every species of tax whatsoever.

It is impossible to read the ordinance of the 23rd. of April, 1784, or the provisions of the act of April 30, 1802, which are founded on it, without being profoundly impressed with the enlightened and magnanimous policy which dictated them. Anticipating that the new States would be settled by the inhabitants of the original States and their offspring, no narrow or contracted jealousy was entertained of their admission into the Union in equal participation in the national sovereignty with the original States. It was foreseen at the early period at which that ordinance passed that the expansion of our Union to the Lakes and to the Mississippi and all its waters would not only make us a greater power, but cement the Union itself. These three propositions were well calculated to promote these great results. A grant of land to each township for free schools, and of the salt springs which were within its limits to the State, for the use of its citizens, with 5 per cent. of the money to be raised from the sale of lands within the State for the construction of roads between the original States and the new State, and of other roads within the State, indicated a spirit not to be mistaken, nor could it fail to produce a corresponding effect in the bosoms of those to whom it was addressed. For these considerations the sole return required of the convention was that the new State should not tax the public lands which might be sold by the United States within it for the term of five years after they should be sold. As the value of these lands would be enhanced by this exemption from taxes for that term, and from which the new State would derive its proportional benefit, and as it would also promote the rapid sale of those lands, and with it the augmentation of its own population, it cannot be doubted, had this exemption been suggested unaccompanied by any propositions of particular advantage, that the convention would, in consideration of the relation which had before existed between the parties, and which was about to be so much improved, most willingly have acceded to it and without regarding it as an onerous condition.

Since, then, it appears that the whole of the money to be employed in making this road was to be raised from the sale of the public lands, and which would still belong to the United States, although no mention had been made of them in the compact, it follows that the application of the money to that purpose stands upon the same ground as if such compact had not been made, and in consequence that the example in favor of the right of appropriation is in no manner affected by it.

The same rule of construction of the right of appropriation has been observed and the same liberal policy pursued toward the other new States, with certain modifications adapted to the situation of each, which were adopted with the State of Ohio. As, however, the reasoning which is applicable to the compact with Ohio in relation to the right of appropriation, in which light only I have adverted to it, is equally applicable to the several compacts with the other new States, I deem it unnecessary to take a particular notice of them.

It is proper to observe that the money which was employed in the construction of all the other roads was taken directly from the treasury. This fact affords an additional proof that in the contemplation of Congress no difference existed in the application of money to those roads between that which was raised by the sale of lands and that which was derived from taxes, duties, imposts and excises.

So far I have confined my remarks to the acts of Congress respecting the right of appropriation to such measures only as operate internally and affect the territory of the individual States. In adverting to those which operate externally and relate to foreign powers I find only two which appear to merit particular attention. These were gratuitous grants of money for the relief of foreigners in distress—the first in 1794 to the inhabitants of St. Domingo, who sought an asylum on our coast from the convulsions and calamities of the island; the second in 1812 to the people of Caracas reduced to misery by an earthquake. The considerations which were applicable to these grants have already been noticed and need not be repeated.

In this examination of the right of appropriation I thought it proper to present to view also the practice of the government under it, and to explore the ground on which each example rested, that the precise nature and extent of the construction thereby given of the right might be clearly understood. The right to raise money would have given, as is presumed, the right to use it, although nothing had been said to that effect in the Constitution; and where the right to raise it is granted without special limitation, we must look for such limitation to other causes. Our attention is first drawn to the right to appropriate, and not finding it there we must then look to the general powers of the government as designated by the specific grants and to the purposes contemplated by them, allowing to this (the right to raise money), the first and most important of the enumerated powers, a scope which will be competent to those purposes. The practice of the government as illustrated by numerous and strong examples directly applicable, ought surely to have great weight in fixing the construction of each grant. It ought, I presume, to settle it, especially where it is acquiesced in by the nation and produces a manifest and positive good. A practical construction, thus supported, shows that it has reason on its side and is called for by the interests of the Union. Hence, too, the presumption that it will be persevered in. It will surely be better to admit that the construction given by these examples has been just and proper than to deny that construction and still to practice on it—to say one thing and to do another.

Wherein consists the danger of giving a liberal construction to the right of Congress to raise and appropriate the public money? It has been shown that its obvious effect is to secure the rights of the States from encroachment and greater harmony in the political movement between the two governments, while it enlarges to a certain extent, in the most harmless way, the useful agency of the General Government for all the purposes of its institution. Is not the responsibility of the representative to his constituent in every branch of the General Government equally strong and as sensibly felt as in the State governments, and is not the security against abuse as effectual in the one as in the other government? The history of the General Government in all its measures fully demonstrates that Congress will never venture to impose unnecessary burdens on the people or any that can be avoided. Duties and imposts have always been light, not greater, perhaps, than would have been imposed for the encouragement of our manufacturers had there been no occasion for the revenue arising from them; and taxes and excises have never been laid except in cases of necessity, and repealed as soon as the necessity ceased. Under this mild process and the sale of some hundreds of millions of acres of good land the government will be possessed of money which may be applied with great advantage to national purposes. Within the States only will it be applied, and, of course, for their benefit, it not being presumable that such appeals as were made to the benevolence of the country in the instances of the inhabitants of St. Domingo and Caracas will often occur. How, then, shall this revenue be applied? Should it be idle in the Treasury? That our resources will be equal to such useful purposes I have no doubt, especially if by completing our fortifications and raising and maintaining our navy at the point provided for immediately after the war we sustain our present attitude and preserve by means thereof for any length of time the peace of the Union.

When we hear charges raised against other governments of breaches of their constitutions, or rather of their charters, we always anticipate the most serious consequences—communities deprived of privileges which they have long enjoyed, and individuals oppressed and punished in violation of the ordinary forms and guards of trials to which they were accustomed and entitled. How different is the situation of the United States! Nor can anything mark more strongly the great characteristics of that difference than the grounds on which like charges are raised against this government. It is not alleged that any portion of the community or any individual has been oppressed or that money has been raised under a doubtful title! The principal charges are that a work of great utility to the Union and affecting immediately and with like advantage many of the States has been constructed; that pensions to the surviving patriots of our Revolution, to patriots who fought the battles and promoted the independence of their country, have been granted, by money, too, raised not only without oppression, but almost without being felt, and under an acknowledged constitutional power.

From this view of the right to appropriate and of the practice under it, I think that I am authorized to conclude that the right to make internal improvements has not been granted by the power "to pay the debts and provide for the common defence and general welfare," included in the first of the enumerated powers; that that grant conveys nothing more than a right to appropriate the public money, and stands on the same ground with the right to lay and collect taxes, duties, imposts and excises, conveyed by the first branch of that power; that the government itself being limited, both branches of the power to raise and appropriate the public money are also limited, the extent of the government as designated by the specific grants marking the extent of the power in both branches, extending, however, to every object embraced by the fair scope of those grants and not confined to a strict construction of their respective powers, it being safer to aid the purposes of those grants by the appropriation of money than to extend by a forced construction the grant itself; that although the right to appropriate the public money to such improvements affords a resource indispensably necessary to such a scheme, it is nevertheless deficient as a power in the great characteristics on which its execution depends.

The substance of what has been urged on this subject may be expressed in a few words. My idea is that Congress have an unlimited power to raise money, and that in its appropriation they have a discretionary power, restricted only by the duty to appropriate it to purposes of common defense and of general, not local, national, not State, benefit.

I will now proceed to the fifth source from which the power is said to be derived, viz, the power to make all laws which shall be necessary and proper for carrying into execution all the powers vested by the Constitution in the

Government of the United States or in any department or office thereof. This is the seventeenth and last of the enumerated powers granted to Congress.

I have always considered this power as having been granted on a principle of greater caution to secure the complete execution of all the powers which had been vested in the General Government. It contains no distinct and specific power, as every other grant does, such as to lay and collect taxes, to declare war, to regulate commerce, and the like. Looking to the whole scheme of the General Government, it gives to Congress authority to make all laws which should be deemed necessary and proper for carrying all its powers into effect. My impression has been invariably that this power would have existed substantially if this grant had not been made; for why is any power granted unless it be to be executed when required, and how can it be executed under our Government unless it be by laws necessary and proper for the purpose—that is, well adapted to the end? It is a principle universally admitted that a grant of a power conveys as a necessary consequence or incident to it the means of carrying it into effect by a fair construction of its import. In the formation, however, of the Constitution, which was to act directly upon the people and be paramount to the extent of its powers to the constitutions of the States, it was wise in its framers to leave nothing to implication which might be reduced to certainty. It is known that all power which rests solely on that ground has been systematically and zealously opposed under all governments with which we have any acquaintance; and it was reasonable to presume that under our system, where was a division of the sovereignty between the two independent governments, the measures of the General Government would excite equal jealousy and produce an opposition not less systematic, though, perhaps, less violent. Hence the policy by the framers of our government of securing by a fundamental declaration in the Constitution a principle which in all other governments had been left to implication only. The terms "necessary" and "proper" secure to the powers of all the grants to which the authority given in this is applicable a fair and sound construction, which is equally binding as a rule on both governments and on all their departments.

In examining the right of the General Government to adopt and execute under this grant a system of internal improvement the sole question to be decided is whether the power has been granted under any of the other grants. If it has, this power is applicable to it to the extent stated. If it has not, it does not exist at all, for it has not been hereby granted. I have already examined all the other grants (one only excepted which will next claim attention) and shown, as I presume, on the most liberal construction of their powers, that the right has not been granted by any of them; hence it follows that in regard to them it has not been granted by this.

I come now to the last source from which this power is said to be derived, viz, the power to dispose of and make all needful rules and regulations respecting the territory or other property of the United States, which is contained in the second clause of the third section of the fourth article of the Constitution.

To form a just opinion of the nature and extent of this power it will be necessary to bring into view the provisions contained in the first clause of the section of the article referred to, which makes an essential part of the policy in question. By this it is declared that new States shall be admitted into the Union, but that no new States shall be formed or erected within the jurisdiction of any other State, nor any States be formed by the junction of two or more States or parts of States, without the consent of the legislatures of the States concerned as well as of the United States.

If we recur to the condition of our country at the commencement of the Revolution, we shall see the origin and cause of these provisions. By the charters of the several Colonies limits by latitude and other descriptions were assigned to each. In commencing the Revolution, the colonies, as has already been observed, claimed by those limits, although their population extended in many instances to a small portion of the territory lying within them. It was contended by some of the States after the declaration of independence that the vacant lands lying within any of the States should become the property of the Union, as by a common exertion they would be acquired. This claim was resisted by the others on the principle that all the States entered into the contest in the full extent of their chartered rights, and that they ought to have the full benefit of those rights in the event of success. Happily this controversy was settled, as all interfering claims and pretensions between the members of our Union and between the General Government and any of these members have been, in the most amicable manner and to the satisfaction of all parties. On the recommendation of Congress the individual States having such territory within their chartered limits ceded large portions thereof to the United States on condition that it should be laid off into districts of proper dimensions, the lands to be sold for the benefit of the United States, and that the districts be admitted into the Union when they should obtain such a population as might be thought proper and reasonable to prescribe. This is the territory and this the property referred to in the second clause of the fourth article of the Constitution.

All of the States which had made cessions of vacant territory except Georgia had made them before the adoption of the Constitution and that State had made a proposition to Congress to that effect which was under consideration at the time the Constitution was adopted. The cession was completed after the adoption of the Constitution. It was made on the same principle and on similar conditions with those which had been already made by the other States. As differences might arise respecting the right or the policy in Congress to admit new States into the Union under the new government, or to make regulations for the government of the territory ceded in the intermediate state, or for the improvement and sale of the public lands, or to accept other cessions, it was thought proper to make special provisions for these objects, which was accordingly done by the above recited clause in the Constitution.

Thus the power of Congress over the ceded territory was not only limited to these special objects, but was also temporary. As soon as the territory became a State the jurisdiction over it as it had before existed ceased. It extended afterwards only to the unsold lands, and as soon as the whole were sold it ceased in that sense also altogether. From that moment the United States have no jurisdiction or power in the new States other than in the old, nor can it be obtained except by an amendment of the Constitution.

Since, then, it is manifest that the power granted to Congress to dispose of and make all needful regulations respecting the territory and other property of the United States relates solely to the territory and property which have been ceded by individual States, and which after such cession lay without their respective limits, and for which special provision was deemed necessary, the main power of the Constitution operating internally, not being applicable or adequate thereto, it follows that this power gives no authority, and has even no bearing on the question of internal improvement. The authority to admit new States, and to dispose of the property and regulate the territory is not among the enumerated powers granted to Congress, because the duties to be performed under it are not among the ordinary duties of that body, like the imposition of taxes, the regulation of commerce and the like. They are objects in their nature special, and for which special provision was more suitable and proper.

Having now examined all the powers of Congress under which the right to adopt and execute a system of internal improvement is claimed and the reasons in support of it in each instance, I think that it may fairly be concluded that such a right has not been granted. It appears and is admitted that much may be done in aid of such a system by the right which is derived from several of the existing grants, and more especially from that to appropriate the public money. But still it is manifest that as a system for the United States it can never be carried into effect under that grant nor under all of them united, the great and essential power being deficient, consisting of a right to take up the subject on principle; to cause our Union to be examined by men of science, with a view to such improvements; to authorize commissioners to lay off the roads and canals in all proper directions; to take the land at a valuation if necessary, and to construct the works; to pass laws with suitable penalties for their protection; and to raise revenue from them, to keep them in repair, and make further improvement by the establishment of turnpikes and tolls, with gates to be placed at the proper distances.

It need scarcely be remarked that this power will operate, like many others now existing, without affecting the sovereignty of the States except in the particular offices to be performed. The jurisdiction of the several States may still exist over the roads and canals within their respective limits, extending alike to persons and property, as if the right to make and protect such improvements had not been vested in Congress. The right, being made commensurate simply with the purposes indispensable to the system, may be strictly confined to them. The right of Congress to protect the works by laws imposing penalties would operate on the same principles as the right to protect the mail. The act being punishable only, a jurisdiction over the place would be altogether unnecessary and even absurd.

In the preceding inquiry little has been said of the advantages which would attend the exercise of such a power by the General Government. I have made the inquiry under a deep conviction that they are almost incalculable, and that there was a general concurrence of opinion among our fellow citizens to that effect. Still, it may not be improper for me to state the grounds upon which my own impression is founded. If it sheds no additional light on this interesting part of the subject, it will at least show that I have had more than one powerful motive for making the inquiry. A general idea is all that I shall attempt.

The advantages of such a system must depend upon the interests to be affected by it and the extent to which they may be affected, and those must depend on the capacity of our country for improvement and the means at its command applicable to that object.

I think that I may venture to affirm that there is no part of our globe comprehending so many degrees of latitude on the main ocean and so many degrees of longitude into the interior that admits of such great improvement and at so little expense. The Atlantic on the one side, and the Lakes, forming almost inland seas, on the other, separated by high mountains, which rise in the valley of the St. Lawrence and determine in that of the Mississippi, traversing from north to south almost the whole interior, with innumerable rivers on every side of those mountains, some of vast extent, many of which take their sources near to each other, give the great outline. The details are to be seen on the valuable maps of our country.

It appears by the light already before the public that it is practicable and easy to connect by canals the whole coast from its southern to its northern extremity in one continued inland navigation, and to connect in like manner in many parts the Western lakes and rivers with each other. It is equally practicable and easy to facilitate the intercourse between the Atlantic and the Western country by improving the navigation of many of the rivers which have their sources near to each other in the mountains on each side, and by good roads across the mountains between the highest navigable points of those rivers. In addition to the example of the Cumberland road, already noticed, another of this kind is now in train from the head waters of the river James to those of the Kanawha; and in like manner may the Savannah be connected with the Tennessee. In some instances it is understood that the Eastern and Western waters may be connected together directly by canals. One great work of this kind is now in its progress and far advanced in the State of New York, and there is good reason to believe that two others may be formed, one at each extremity of the high mountains above mentioned, connecting in the one instance the waters of the St. Lawrence with Lake Champlain, and in the other some of the most important of the Western rivers with those emptying into the Gulf of Mexico, the advantage of which will be seen at the first glance by an enlightened observer.

Great improvements may also be made by good roads in proper directions through the interior of the country. As these roads would be laid out on principle on a full view of the country, its mountains, rivers, etc., it would be useless, if I had the knowledge, to go into detail respecting them. Much has been done by some of the States, but yet much remains to be done with a view to the Union.

Under the colonial governments improvements of this kind were not thought of. There was, it is believed, not one canal and little communication from colony to colony. It was their policy to encourage the intercourse between each colony and the parent country only. The roads which were attended to were those which led from the interior of each colony to its principal towns on the navigable waters. By those routes the produce of the country was carried to the coast, and shipped thence to the mercantile houses in London, Liverpool, Glasgow, or other towns to which the trade was carried on. It is believed that there was but one connected route from North to South at the commencement of the Revolution, and that a very imperfect one. The existence and principle of our Union point out the necessity of a very different policy.

The advantages which would be derived from such improvements are incalculable. The facility which would thereby be afforded to the transportation of the whole of the rich productions of our country to market would alone more than amply compensate for all the labor and expense attending them. Great, however, as is that advantage, it is one only of many and by no means the most important. Every power of the General Government and of the State governments connected with the strength and resources of the country would be made more efficient for the purposes intended by them. In war they would facilitate the transportation of men, ordnance, and provisions, and munitions of war of every kind to every part of our extensive coast and interior on which an attack might be made or threatened. Those who have any knowledge of the occurrences of the late war must know the good effect which would result in the event of another war from the command of an interior navigation alone along the coast for all the purposes of war as well as of commerce between the different parts of our Union. The impediments to all military operations which proceeded from the want of such a navigation and the reliance which was placed, notwithstanding those impediments, on such a commerce can not be forgotten. In every other line their good effect would be most sensibly felt. Intelligence by means of the Post-Office Department would be more easily, extensively, and rapidly diffused. Parts the most remote from each other would be brought more closely together. Distant lands would be made more valuable, and the industry of our fellow-citizens on every portion of our soil be better rewarded.

It is natural in so great a variety of climate that there should be a corresponding difference in the produce of the soil; that one part should raise what the other might want. It is equally natural that the pursuits of industry should vary in like manner; that labor should be cheaper and manufactures succeed better in one part than in another; that were the climate the most severe and the soil less productive, navigation, the fisheries, and commerce should be most relied on. Hence the motive for an exchange for mutual accommodation and active intercourse between them. Each part would thus find for the surplus of its labor, in whatever article it consisted, an extensive market at home, which would be the most profitable because free from duty.

There is another view in which these improvements are of still more vital importance. The effect which they would have on the bond of union itself affords an inducement for them more powerful than any which have been urged or than all of them united. The only danger to which our system is exposed arises from its expansion over a vast territory. Our Union is not held together by standing armies or by any ties other than the positive interests and powerful attractions of its parts toward each other. Ambitious men may hereafter grow up among us who may promise to themselves advancement from a change, and by practicing upon the sectional interests, feelings, and prejudices endeavor under various pretexts to promote it. The history of the world is replete with examples of this kind—of military commanders and demagogues becoming usurpers and tyrants, and of their fellow-citizens becoming their instruments and slaves. I have little fear of this danger, knowing well how strong the bond which holds us together is and who the people are who are thus held together; but still, it is proper to look at and to provide against it, and it is not within the compass of human wisdom to make a more effectual provision than would be made by the proposed improvements. With their aid and the intercourse which would grow out of them the parts would soon become so compacted and bound together that nothing could break it.

The expansion of our Union over a vast territory can not operate unfavorably to the States individually. On the contrary, it is believed that the greater the expansion within practicable limits—and it is not easy to say what are not so—the greater the advantage which the States individually will derive from it. With governments separate, vigorous, and efficient for all local purposes, their distance from each other can have no injurious effect upon their respective interests. It has already been shown that in some important circumstances, especially with the aid of these improvements, they must derive great advantage from that cause alone—that is, from their distance from each other. In every other way the expansion of our system must operate favorably for every State in proportion as it operates favorably for the Union. It is in that sense only that it can become a question with the States, or, rather, with the people who compose them. As States they can be affected by it only by their relation to each other through the General Government and by its effect on the operations of that Government. Manifest it is that to any extent to which the General Government can sustain and execute its functions with complete effect will the States—that is, the people who compose them—be benefited. It is only when the expansion shall be carried beyond the faculties of the General Government so as to enfeeble its operations to the injury of the whole that any of the parts can be injured. The tendency in that stage will be to dismemberment and not to consolidation. This danger should, therefore, be looked at with profound attention as one of a very serious character. I will remark here that as the operations of the National Government are of a general nature, the States having complete power for internal and local purposes, the expansion may be carried to very great extent and with perfect safety. It must be obvious to all that the further the expansion is carried, provided it be not beyond the just limit, the greater will be the freedom of action to both Governments and the more perfect their security, and in all other respects the better the effect will be to the whole American people. Extent of territory, whether it be great or small, gives to a nation many of its characteristics. It marks the extent of its resources, of its population, of its physical force. It marks, in short, the difference between a great and a small power.

To what extent it may be proper to expand our system of government is a question which does not press for a decision at this time. At the end of the Revolutionary war, in 1783, we had, as we contended and believed, a right to the free navigation of the Mississippi, but it was not until after the expiration of twelve years, in 1795, that that right was acknowledged and enjoyed. Further difficulties occurred in the bustling of a contentious world when, at the expiration of eight years more, the United States, sustaining the strength and energy of their character, acquired the Province of Louisiana, with the free navigation of the river from its source to the ocean and a liberal boundary on the western side. To this Florida has since been added, so that we now possess all the territory in which the original States had any interest, or in which the existing States can be said, either in a national or local point of view, to be in any way interested. A range of States on the western side of the Mississippi, which already is provided for, puts us essentially at ease. Whether it will be wise to go further will turn on other considerations than those which have dictated the course heretofore pursued. At whatever point we may stop, whether it be at a single range of States beyond the Mississippi or by taking a greater scope, the advantage of such improvements is deemed of the highest importance. It is so on the present scale. The further we go the greater will be the necessity for them.

It can not be doubted that improvements for great national purposes would be better made by the National Government than by the governments of the several States. Our experience prior to the adoption of the Constitution demonstrated that in the exercise by the individual States of most of the powers granted to the United States a contracted rivalry of interest and misapplied jealousy of each other had an important influence on all their measures to the great injury of the whole. This was particularly exemplified by the regulations which they severally made of their commerce with foreign nations and with each other. It was this utter incapacity in the State governments, proceeding from these and other causes, to act as a nation and to perform all the duties which the nation owed to itself under any system which left the General Government dependent on the States, which produced the transfer of these powers to the United States by the establishment of the present Constitution. The reasoning which was applicable to the grant of any of the powers now vested in Congress is likewise so, at least to a certain extent, to that in question. It is natural that the States individually in making improvements should look to their particular and local interests. The members composing their respective legislatures represent the people of each State only, and might not feel themselves at liberty to look to objects in these respects beyond that limit. If the resources of the Union were to be brought into operation under the direction of the State assemblies, or in concert with them, it may be apprehended that every measure would become the object of negotiation, of bargain and barter, much to the disadvantage of the system, as well as discredit to both governments. But Congress would look to the whole and make improvements to promote the welfare of the whole. It is the peculiar felicity of the proposed amendment that while it will enable the United States to accomplish every national object, the improvements made with that view will eminently promote the welfare of the individual States, who may also add such others as their own particular interests may require.

The situation of the Cumberland road requires the particular and early attention of Congress. Being formed over very lofty mountains and in many instances over deep and wide streams, across which valuable bridges have been erected, which are sustained by stone walls, as are many other parts of the road, all these works are subject to decay, have decayed, and will decay rapidly unless timely and effectual measures are adopted to prevent it.

The declivities from the mountains and all the heights must suffer from the frequent and heavy falls of water and its descent to the valleys, as also from the deep congelations during our severe winters. Other injuries have also been experienced on this road, such as the displacing of the capping of the walls and other works, committed by worthless people either from a desire to render the road impassable or to have the transportation in another direction, or from a spirit of wantonness to create employment for idlers. These considerations show that an active and strict police ought to be established over the whole road, with power to make repairs when necessary, to establish turnpikes and tolls as the means of raising money to make them, and to prosecute and punish those who commit waste and other injuries.

Should the United States be willing to abandon this road to the States through which it passes, would they take charge of it, each of that portion within its limits, and keep it in repair? It is not to be presumed that they would, since the advantages attending it are exclusively national, by connecting, as it does, the Atlantic with the Western States, and in a line with the seat of the National

Government. The most expensive parts of this road lie within Pennsylvania and Virginia, very near the confines of each State and in a route not essentially connected with the commerce of either.

If it is thought proper to vest this power in the United States, the only mode in which it can be done is by an amendment of the Constitution. The States individually can not transfer the power to the United States, nor can the United States receive it. The Constitution forms an equal and the sole relation between the General Government and the several States, and it recognizes no change in it which shall not in like manner apply to all. If it is once admitted that the General Government may form compacts with individual States not common to the others, and which the others might even disapprove, into what pernicious consequences might it not lead? Such compacts are utterly repugnant to the principles of the Constitution and of the most dangerous tendency. The States through which this road passes have given their sanction only to the route and to the acquisition of the soil by the United States, a right very different from that of jurisdiction, which can not be granted without an amendment to the Constitution, and which need not be granted for the purposes of this system except in the limited manner heretofore stated. On full consideration, therefore, of the whole subject I am of opinion that such an amendment ought to be recommended to the several States for their adoption.

I have now essentially executed that part of the task which I imposed on myself of examining the right of Congress to adopt and execute a system of internal improvement, and, I presume, have shown that it does not exist. It is, I think, equally manifest that such a power vested in Congress and wisely executed would have the happiest effect on all the great interests of our Union. It is, however, my opinion that the power should be confined to great national works only, since if it were unlimited it would be liable to abuse and might be productive of evil. For all minor improvements the resources of the States individually would be fully adequate, and by the States such improvements might be made with greater advantage than by the Union, as they would understand better such as their more immediate and local interests required.

In the view above presented I have thought it proper to trace the origin of our institutions, and particularly of the State and National Governments, for although they have a common origin in the people, yet, as the point at issue turned on what were the powers granted to the one government and what were those which remained to the other, I was persuaded that an analysis which should mark distinctly the source of power in both governments, with its progress in each, would afford the best means for obtaining a sound result. In our political career there are, obviously, three great epochs. The colonial state forms the first; the Revolutionary movement from its commencement to the adoption of the Articles of Confederation the second, and the intervening space from that event to the present day the third. The first may be considered the infant state. It was the school of morality, of political science and just principles. The equality of rights enjoyed by the people of every colony under their original charters forms the basis of every existing institution, and it was owing to the creation by those charters of distinct communities that the power, when wrested from the Crown, passed directly and exclusively to the people of each colony. The Revolutionary struggle gave activity to those principles, and its success secured to them a permanent existence in the governments of our Union, State and National. The third epoch comprises the administration under the Articles of Confederation, with the adoption of the Constitution and administration under it. On the first and last of these epochs it is not necessary to enlarge for any purpose connected with the object of this inquiry. To the second, in which we were transferred by a heroic exertion from the first to the third stage, and whose events give the true character to every institution, some further attention is due. In tracing in greater detail the prominent acts of a movement to which we owe so much I shall perform an office which, if not useful, will be gratifying to my own feelings, and I hope not unacceptable to my readers.

Of the Revolutionary movement itself sentiments too respectful, too exalted, can not be entertained. It is impossible for any citizen having a just idea of the dangers which we had to encounter to read the record of our early proceedings and to see the firmness with which they were met and the wisdom and patriotism which were displayed in every stage without being deeply affected by it. An attack on Massachusetts was considered an attack on every colony, and the people of each moved in her defense as in their own cause. The meeting of the General Congress in Philadelphia on the 6th of September, 1774, appears to have been the result of a spontaneous impulse in every quarter at the same time. The first public act proposing it, according to the Journals of the First Congress, was passed by the house of representatives of Connecticut on the 3d of June of that year; but it is presumed that the first suggestion came from Massachusetts, the colony most oppressed, and in whose favor the general sympathy was much excited. The exposition which that Congress made of grievances, in the petition to the King, in the address to the people of Great Britain, and in that to the people of the several colonies, evinced a knowledge so profound of the English constitution and of the general principles of free government and of liberty, of our rights founded on that constitution and on the charters of the several colonies, and of the numerous and egregious violations which had been committed of them, as must have convinced all impartial minds that the talent on this side of the Atlantic was at least equal to that on the other. The spirit in which those papers were drawn, which was known to be in strict accord with the public sentiment, proved that, although the whole people cherished a connection with the parent country and were desirous of preserving it on just principles, they nevertheless stood embodied at the parting line, ready to separate forever if a redress of grievances, the alternative offered, was not promptly rendered. That alternative was rejected, and in consequence war and dismemberment followed.

The powers granted to the delegates of each colony who composed the First Congress looked primarily to the support of rights and to a redress of grievances, and, in consequence, to the restoration of harmony, which was ardently desired. They justified, however, any extremity in case of necessity. They were ample for such purposes, and were executed in every circumstance with the utmost fidelity. It was not until after the meeting of the Second Congress, which took place on the 10th May, 1775, when full proof was laid before it of the commencement of hostilities in the preceding month by a deliberate attack of the British troops on the militia and inhabitants of Lexington and Concord, in Massachusetts, that war might be said to be decided on, and measures were taken to support it. The progress even then was slow and reluctant, as will be seen by their second petition to the King and their second address to the people of Great Britain, which were prepared and forwarded after that event. The arrival, however, of large bodies of troops and the pressure of war in every direction soon dispelled all hope of accommodation.

On the 15th of June, 1775, a commander in chief of the forces raised and to be raised for the defense of American liberty was appointed by the unanimous vote of Congress, and his conduct in the discharge of the duties of that high trust, which he held through the whole of the war, has given an example to the world for talents as a military commander; for integrity, fortitude, and firmness under the severest trials; for respect to the civil authority and devotion to the rights and liberties of his country, of which neither Rome nor Greece have exhibited the equal. I saw him in my earliest youth, in the retreat through Jersey, at the head of a small band, or rather in its rear, for he was always next the enemy, and his countenance and manner made an impression on me which time can never efface. A lieutenant then in the Third Virginia Regiment, I happened to be on the rear guard at Newark, and I counted the force under his immediate command by platoons as it passed me, which amounted to less than 3,000 men. A department so firm, so dignified, so exalted, but yet so modest and composed, I have never seen in any other person.

On the 6th July, 1775, Congress published a declaration of the causes which compelled them to take up arms, and immediately afterwards took measures for augmenting the army and raising a navy; for organizing the militia and providing cannon and small arms and military stores of every kind; for raising a revenue and pushing the war offensively with all the means in their power. Nothing escaped the attention of that enlightened body. The people of Canada were invited to join the Union, and a force sent into the province to favor the Revolutionary party, which, however, was not capable of affording any essential aid. The people of Ireland were addressed in terms manifesting due respect for the sufferings, the talents, and patriotism of that portion of the British Empire, and a suitable acknowledgment was made to the assembly of Jamaica for the approbation it had expressed of our cause and the part it had taken in support of it with the British Government.

On the 2d of June, 1775, the convention of Massachusetts, by a letter signed by their president, of May the 10th, stated to Congress that they labored under difficulties for the want of a regular form of government, and requested to be favored with explicit advice respecting the taking up and exercising the powers of civil government, and declaring their readiness to submit to such a general plan as the Congress might direct for the colonies, or that they would make it their great study to establish such a form of government there as should not only promote their own advantage, but the union and interest of all America. To this application an answer was given on the 9th, by which it was recommended to the convention "to write letters to the inhabitants of the several places entitled to representation in assembly, requesting them to choose such representatives, and that the assembly, when chosen, should elect councilors, and that said assembly or council should exercise the powers of government until a governor of His Majesty's appointment will consent to govern the colony according to its charter."

On the 18th October of the same year the delegates from New Hampshire laid before Congress an instruction from their convention "to use their utmost endeavors to obtain the advice and direction of Congress with respect to a method for administering justice and regulating their civil police." To this a reply was given on the 3d November, by which it was recommended to the convention "to call a full and free representation of the people, and that the representatives, if they thought it necessary, should establish such a form of government as in their judgment would best promote the happiness of the people and most effectually secure peace and good order in the Province during the continuance of the present dispute between Great Britain and the colonies."

On the 4th November it was resolved by Congress "that if the convention of South Carolina shall find it necessary to establish a form of government in that colony it be recommended to that convention to call a full and free representation of the people; and the said representatives, if they think it necessary, shall establish such a form of government as in their judgment will best promote the happiness of the people and most effectually secure peace and good order in the colony during the continuance of the present dispute between Great Britain and the colonies."

On the 4th December following a resolution passed recommending the same measure, and precisely in the same words, to the convention of Virginia.

On the 10th May, 1776, it was recommended to the respective assemblies and conventions of the united colonies, where no government sufficient to the exigencies of their affairs had been established, "to adopt such government as should, in the opinion of the representatives of the people, best conduce to the happiness and safety of their constituents in particular and America in general."

On the 7th June resolutions respecting independence were moved and seconded, which were referred to a committee of the whole on the 8th and 10th, on which latter day it was resolved to postpone a decision on the first resolution or main question until the 1st July, but that no time might be lost in case the Congress agree thereto that a committee be appointed to prepare a declaration to the effect of that resolution.

On the 11th June, 1776, Congress appointed a committee to prepare and digest a plan of confederation for the colonies. On the 12th July the committee reported a draft of articles, which were severally afterwards debated and amended until the 15th November, 1777, when they were adopted. These articles were then proposed to the legislatures of the several States, with a request that if approved by them they would authorize their delegates to ratify the same in Congress, and, which being done, to become conclusive. It was not until the 21st of March, 1781, as already observed, that they were ratified by the last State and carried into effect.

On the 4th July, 1776, independence was declared by an act which arrested the attention of the civilized world and will bear the test of time. For force and condensation of matter, strength of reason, sublimity of sentiment and expression, it is believed that no document of equal merit exists. It looked to everything, and with a reach, perspicuity, and energy of mind which seemed to be master of everything.

Thus it appears, in addition to the very important charge of managing the war, that Congress had under consideration at the same time the Declaration of Independence, the adoption of a confederation for the States, and the propriety of instituting State governments, with the nature of those governments, respecting which it had been consulted by the conventions of several of the colonies. So great a trust was never reposed before in a body thus constituted, and I am authorized to add, looking to the great result, that never were duties more ably or faithfully performed.

The distinguishing characteristic of this movement is that although the connection which had existed between the people of the several colonies before their dismemberment from the parent country was not only not dissolved but increased by that event, even before the adoption of the Articles of Confederation, yet the preservation and augmentation of that tie were the result of a new creation, and proceeded altogether from the people of each colony, into whose hands the whole power passed exclusively when wrested from the Crown. To the same cause the greater change which has since occurred by the adoption of the Constitution is to be traced.

The establishment of our institutions forms the most important epoch that history hath recorded. They extend unexampled felicity to the whole body of our fellow-citizens, and are the admiration of other nations. To preserve and hand them down in their utmost purity to the remotest ages will require the existence and practice of virtues and talents equal to those which were displayed in acquiring them. It is ardently hoped and confidently believed that these will not be wanting.

PART X

The Monroe Doctrine

INTRODUCTION

THE MONROE DOCTRINE was a statement that the systems of despotism of the European powers could not be applied to the Western Hemisphere. Monroe was not a doctrinaire person; above all he was a man of practical affairs, but also of firm principles. There is no evidence that Monroe thought he was proclaiming a "doctrine"—only that he was laying down principles of foreign policy in response to a very specific problem. That is why his statements, which today we call "The Monroe Doctrine" are embedded almost incidentally in two places in his Seventh Annual Message to Congress of December 2, 1823, a message which like contemporary presidential statements on "The State of the Union" is filled with domestic concerns and financial issues.

Yet the "Principles of 1823" rightfully acquired the status of a founding document of the United States. The original artifact is a manuscript perfectly engrossed by a document clerk and signed by the president in his own hand. The recipient of that document, the U.S. Senate, bound it in fine purple leather stamped with gold, and kept it proudly in the Senate Library (a little-known institution separate from, and not to be confused with, the Library of Congress). With the construction of the National Archives building in Washington in 1935, the Senate deposited the document for safekeeping in one of the Archive's vaults, where only the occasional scholar, wearing white gloves, can peruse its venerable lines.

Those lines acquired such power as an image of American conduct because they were the mature deliberation of a statesman who had spent some 48 years in public life preparing to formulate them. He was a man who still carried a British rifle ball in his shoulder from the days when he was put to the ultimate test of patriotism in the War of 1776. He was a man whose first public controversies on behalf of the nation centered on the proposed treaty with Spain in 1784. He was the patron of republican principles who, nevertheless, took hardheaded views of the insurgent mobs of Paris in 1796. He was the diplomat who had actually had a personal interview with George III, had a private dinner with Napoleon Bonaparte, been in attendance at the Emperor's coronation in Notre Dame cathedral, was presented formally to Charles IV of Spain. Moreover, he knew all of their ministers, all of their stratagems, all of their wiles. He was a man of infinite negotiations, skilled in the intricacies of international finance. As Secretary of State and Secretary of War during the War of 1812, he had brutal confrontations with invading European armies, and organized the defenses of the nation as it stood on the verge of collapse. There was nothing that he did not know about the world and its ways.

Yet he had further strengths. In formulating the Principles of 1823, he sought out the advice of two former presidents, Jefferson and Madison, not to speak of the man he chose as his Secretary of State, John Quincy Adams, son of a president, and about to be president himself. Was there ever such a parley of titans?

Monroe had long looked forward with hope towards the revolutions in Latin America. Thus when, as Secretary of State, he sent Joel Barlow as Minister to France in 1811, his instructions to Barlow included the following: "A revolution in the Spanish provinces, south of the United States, is making rapid progress. The provinces of Venezuela have declared themselves an independent and announced the event to this Government. The same step, it is said, will soon be taken at Buenos Ayres [sic] and in other quarters. The Provinces of Venezuela have proposed to the President the recognition of their independence and reception of a minister from them; and altho' such recognition in form has not been made yet a very friendly and conciliatory answer has been given to them. You will not fail to attend to this object which is through to be equally due to the just claims of our Southern Brethren, to which the United States cannot be indifferent and to the best interests of this country." This was the first intimation of the Monroe Doctrine.

As president, one of his first actions was to take up with his cabinet the question of diplomatic recognition of the new governments of "our southern brethren." It was a delicate matter, since he was negotiating with Spain for the cession of the Floridas and the drawing of the western boundary of Louisiana. Spain viewed U.S. recognition of the independence of the Spanish colonies as a grievance, since she hoped to reassert control over them. Always cautious, Monroe sent a team of commissioners to South America to find out the facts on the ground. Once the commissioners reported back, and once the Transcontinental Treaty with Spain had been signed, Monroe laid the groundwork for diplomatic recognition. In an 1819 memo to Secretary of State John Quincy Adams proposing that a commercial agent be sent to South America, Monroe wrote: "As the [Spanish] Colonies are our neighbors, and we shall of necessity have much intercourse with them, especially if they become independent, which may be presumed, and at no distant period, it is highly important that our relations be of a very amicable nature."

On March 5, 1822, a year after Spain finally ratified the treaty, Monroe sent a message to Congress judging that the time was ripe for diplomatic recognition of the Latin American countries. He told them: "The revolutionary movement in the Spanish Provinces in this hemisphere attracted the attention and excited the sympathy of our fellow citizens from its commencement." Only one member of Congress, Robert Gannet of Virginia, voted against the proposal. On March 29, Monroe sent Gannet a letter chiding him for being the lone holdout. Gannet obligingly rose in the House the next day to explain that he had no objection to the principle of recognition, but was only questioning the timing— and he now acquiesced in the judgment of the House.

Europe meanwhile was once again in turmoil. The defeat of Napoleon in 1814 let loose revolutions in Greece, Italy, and Spain. In 1822, the Holy Alliance— Austria, Russia, and Prussia) meeting in congress at Verona, agreed to back France, now led by Louis XVIII, to invade Spain. The great powers seemed to be united to put down the revolutions, and even to get the colonies back again.

Great Britain feared such a combine. On August 19, 1823, George Canning, the British Foreign Minister, called in the U.S. minister to London, Richard Rush, to make a startling suggestion: Would the U.S. government be pleased to join with His Majesty's government in a declaration that both countries would resist any effort by the European powers to restore the colonies to Spain?

Only ten years previously the two countries had been at war, and the U.S. capital burned. But now old adversaries had common interests. Astonished, Rush could reply only that the answers to those questions exceeded his instructions. Diplomatic communications with the United States were still at the mercy of the winds and tides. In the summer of 1823, Monroe had withdrawn from Washington to his new estate in Loudoun County, Oak Hill. John Quincy Adams had fled to the cooler clime of New England. Rush wrote several dispatches enclosing his correspondence with Canning. But the President and the Secretary of State did not see first the Rush inquiries until October 9, and a few days later Monroe went to Oak Hill and wrote two extraordinary letters which, with their replies, still remain in the National Archives with their crabbed handwriting and scratched-out mistakes.

The letters were to his old friends and neighbors living at Monticello and Montpelier. "Shall we entangle ourselves, at all, in European politics and wars?" Monroe asked. And if it is generally a sound maxim that we should not, is this not a case, he wrote, where the maxim "ought to be departed from?" Was this not an opportunity to join with Britain to take a stand "either in favor of despotism or of liberty?" Besides, Monroe added, if the European powers succeeded in an attack on the Spanish colonies, "they would extend it to us."

It was at this point, on October 24, that Jefferson responded that the question "is the most momentous which has been ever offered to my contemplation since that of independence made us a nation." And then he added, with prophetic insight, "This sets our compass and points the course which we are to steer through the ocean of time opening on us."

Madison's reply of October 30 reflected his realism: he stated his opinion that Great Britain was ready to go ahead anyway. "But this consideration ought not to divert us from what is just and proper in itself. Our co-operation is due to ourselves and to the world."

Monroe nonetheless felt a deepening concern. More August correspondence had just arrived from Rush indicating that Canning no longer seemed interested in the proposal, since he had not gotten a reply. Besides, the British navy seemed to be making it less likely that the Holy Alliance would menace South America. Despite this, Monroe decided to move ahead alone, indeed, he felt it was better to move alone. Furthermore he decided that he should make a public declaration in his forthcoming message to Congress, rather than in a private diplomatic note. The President returned from Oak Hill on November 5th full of enthusiasm. On November 15th, John Quincy Adams recorded his dour outlook on the matter in his Memoirs:

I received a note from Mr. D. Brent [Chief Clerk of the State Department] saying that the President wished to see me at the office at noon. I went, and found him there. He asked for the correspondence relating to the intercourse with the British American Colonies, with a view to the particular notice which he intends to take of it in the message; which I thought should have been only in genteel terms. He also showed me two letters which he had received—one from Mr. Jefferson, 23rd October, and one from Mr. Madison, of 30th October, giving their opinions on the proposals of Mr. Canning. . . . Mr. Jefferson thinks them more important than anything that has happened since our Revolution. He is for acceding to the proposals, with a view to pledging Great Britain against the Holy allies;

though he thinks the Island of Cuba would be a valuable and important acquisition to our Union. Mr. Madison's opinions are less decisively pronounced, and he thinks, as I do, that this movement on the part of Great Britain is impelled more by her interest than by a principle of general liberty. Monroe's draft was presented to the cabinet on November 21, and on December 2 it was sent to Congress.

What we call the Monroe Doctrine today was not stated in abstract principles. Rather it was presented very concretely in the midst of a wide range of issues. For example, with regard to the settlement of Russian and British claims on the Northwest Pacific coast, Monroe stated: "The occasion has been judged proper for asserting a principle. . . that the American continents, by the free and independent condition which they have assumed and maintain, are henceforth not to be considered as subject for future colonization by any European power. . . ." Although both Russia and Great Britain had agreed to the specific settlement in the Oregon question, doubtless neither had any idea that they were agreeing to a general principle.

But at a later point in the message to Congress, Monroe went even further, attacking the very foundations of the Holy Alliance. It was not just the particular geopolitical concerns of the moment that animated his objections. He attacked the system, the very system of despotism:

The political system of the allied powers is essentially different from that of America. . . . We . . . declare that we should consider any attempt on their part to extend the system to any portions of this Hemisphere as dangerous to our peace and safety. With the existing Colonies and dependencies of any European power, we have not interfered, and shall not interfere. But with the governments who have declared their independence, and maintained it, and whose independence we have acknowledged, we could not view any interposition for the purpose of oppressing them, or controlling in any other manner their destiny, by any European power, in any other light than as the manifestation of an unfriendly disposition towards the United States.

These words were received with calculated indifference by the European powers. What was the United States to make such a statement? How large was its navy? How rich was its treasury? What standing armies did it have to repulse the will of the Alliance? The attributes of power were pitifully small. On the other hand, only Great Britain had the resources to put the Americans in their place, and Great Britain already had experienced what their own traders said would happen if there was any interference with their U.S. trade—the United States, after all, was Britain's single large largest customer. The United States had no power to enforce these principles, but, once stated, their truth became manifest to so many that they became self-enforcing.

As the years went by, the principles of 1823, known as the Monroe Doctrine, and they became part of the unwritten constitution—the part that the written Constitution delegated to the President for the conduct foreign affairs. They constituted an American doctrine, as interpreted by the American President. Nor did other nations always agree with such an interpretation. But they provided the vitality of our independence, and they can continue to provide vitality in an age when the growing networks of economic and political interchange seek to dissolve the essence of nationhood.

TO JOEL BARLOW.
November 27, 1811.

SIR,—A Revolution in the Spanish Provinces, South of the United States, is making a rapid progress. The Province of Venezuela have declared themselves independent and announced the event to this Government. The same step, it is said, will soon be taken at Buenos Ayres and in other quarters. The Provinces of Venezuela have proposed to the President the recognition of their independence and reception of a minister from them; and altho' such recognition in form has not been made yet a very friendly and conciliatory answer has been given to them. They have also been informed that the Ministers of the United States in Europe, will be instructed to avail themselves of suitable opportunities to promote their recognition by other powers. You will not fail to attend to this object which is thought to be equally due to the just claims of our Southern Brethren, to which the United States cannot be indifferent and to the best interest of this Country. . . .

"SKETCH OF INSTRUCTIONS FOR AGENT FOR SOUTH AMERICA— NOTES FOR DEPARTMENT OF STATE."
WASHINGTON, March 24, 1819.

In pursuing the policy which this government has long since adopted, and to which it has heretofore steadily adhered, in the dispute between Spain and the Colonies, care must be taken not only to observe toward the parties a perfect impartiality, but to satisfy them that it is maintained. This is at all times an important duty, but certain considerations make it at this time peculiarly so.

The late Act of Congress for the suppression of piracy will, it is presumed, be found, in its execution, to apply more to the Colonies than to Spain. Few of the vessels which have been employed as privateers under the authority of any of the colonies were built there, as there is much reason to believe. It is understood that the greater part of them were built in the United States, and expressly for the service for which they were afterwards engaged. It is said that most of the privateers which cruise along the coast under the flag of the Colonies, & commit outrages on the commerce of all nations, are of this description, and that they are manned for the most part from other countries, and not from the Colonies. It is presumable that the late Act will be found to operate principally on these vessels, affecting in consequence in like degree the interest, character, and sensibility of those whose commissions they bear.

As the Colonies are our neighbours, and we shall of necessity have much intercourse with them, especially if they become independent, which may be presumed, and at no distant period, it is highly important that our relation be of a very amicable nature. From the nature of things it will be either of that character, or an opposite one. It can hardly be presumed that it will be such as exists between other nations, neither of one or the other, but indifferent. The character assumed must depend essentially on ourselves, and particularly on the impression that may be made at the present time. With this view it will be proper to explain to their governments the friendly part which we have heretofore acted towards them, and are now pursuing, and to which it is intended steadily to adhere, with the good effect which has already attended, and which may hereafter be expected from it, provided they view it in a just light, & act in a manner to derive from it all the advantage which it may afford.

The policy heretofore pursued in this contest has been explained by Acts of Congress; by the correspondence between the Secretary of State & the Minister of Spain; by the mission to Buenos Ayres, & the messages to Congress respecting it; and by the communications of our Ministers to the governments of Great Britain, France, & Russia. It was also made known by Lord Castlereagh to the allied powers in the congress lately assembled at Aix la Chapelle, with the addition of the important feature, that it was contemplated to recognize Buenos Ayres at an early period, if not in the course of the last winter. This fact therefore has doubly been communicated to the government of Spain by the Ministers of some of the powers assembled there attached to her interest. No injury can therefore be incurred by making it known to the Colonial governments.

The best service which it was in our power to render the Colonies, keeping our ports open, & extending to them all the advantages that are enjoyed by Spain, was, by the attitude assumed, and by our communications with other powers, to promote on their part likewise a strict neutrality in the war, so as to leave its fortune to be decided altogether by the parties themselves. If this was done the result could not be doubted. The exhausted state of Spain, in consequence of the long and expensive wars in which she has been engaged, the distance of the Colonies from the parent country, their great superiority in numbers, & in other respects, gave them advantages which, if they managed their affairs with tolerable prudence, could not fail to ensure their complete success. Equally certain was it that the best mode of promoting this object was to take no part in the contest ourselves, or any measure of so marked a character as to induce them to change their attitude in it. Had we recognized them there is much reason to believe that we should have given offence to every other power, and excited in them a disposition to counteract its probable effect. The least injury which could have attended such a measure would have been to increase the indisposition of other powers to recognize the Colonies, & to delay that event on their part. Had the United States recognized the independence of the Colonies, and had Spain made the recognition a cause of war, other and greater evils might have followed. The allies might have been drawn into it, equally against the United States and the Colonies, the ill consequences of which need not be enumerated.

By the course heretofore pursued by the United States they have given to the colonies all the advantages of a recognition, without any of its evils. The mission to Buenos Ayres was particularly calculated to produce that effect, and actually did produce it. Our weight was thrown into the scale of the colonies in a way to be felt by the parties and by other powers. It was so considered by all Europe, as well as by the United States, and the Colonies. It might fairly be inferred from that measure, by the allies, that if they took part with Spain, the United States would take part with the Colonies, although they were under no positive obligation to do it, and that presumption doubtless formed a motive with them not to engage in the war with Spain so long as the U. States abstained from taking part with the Colonies, even by the recognition of their independence.

All the allied powers, except Great Britain, wish the restitution of the Colonies to the crown of Spain unconditionally, and she wishes it on the condition of their being allowed a free trade, with some improvements in their colonial governments. The proposition made by the British government to the Allies was to this effect. When the sentiments of the United States in favor of the independence of the Colonies, with their intention to recognize it at some earlier period, were made known to the Congress at Aix la Chapelle we were assured, by unquestionable authority, that all the allies, especially France and Russia, expressed great disapprobation of the proposed recognition, and that the Minister of Great Britain, the power most favorable to the Colonies, declared that he should consider it as rash. It is understood that some agreement was entered into on this subject, the nature and tendency of which we have not been able to ascertain. While we retain our present attitude it may be presumed that we shall preserve the same weight in their councils. There appears to be no compromitment of the allied forces in favor of Spain, and it is hoped that if we take no decisive step in favor of the Colonies to excite the sensibility, or affect the interest of the allies, that they will abstain from any in favor of Spain. Our present relation with the allies is of the most friendly character. We have been long in free communication with them in favor of the Colonies, pushing their cause to the utmost extent that circumstances would permit. Our object is to promote a recognition of their independence by the allies at the earliest day at which it may be obtained, and we are satisfied that the best mode of accomplishing it is by moving in concert with the allies, postponing the recognition on our part until it can be obtained from them, or until it shall be manifest that it will at least do them no harm.

The recognition by the United States would render to the Colonies very little service, if any, in our own ports. It could be useful only by promoting a like measure in their favor by other powers. If it did not produce that effect, and it certainly would not, great mischief would be the consequence, as our present amicable relation with the allies on that very important subject would be destroyed, jealousies of our views & unkind feelings be excited, & a new impulse & greater force be given to the claims of Spain on them. It will be proper to state distinctly to the colonial governments that instructions have been given to our Ministers in Great Britain, France, & Russia, to propose to those governments the immediate recognition of the Colonies, in concert with the U. States, to which no answer has yet been received.

It is important that a just view of our friendly disposition & conduct towards the Colonies be fully impressed on their councils, & for that purpose a detail of the material facts above alluded to be communicated to them. A knowledge of the services which we have already rendered them, and of our intention to adhere to the same course of policy in their favor, cannot fail to produce the desired effect, in securing their support of it. We wish no return but their good opinion, and good wishes, & such coöperation as may be best calculated to promote their own success and welfare.

In the contemplated communication it will be proper to explain again the considerations which induced the suppression of the establishment at Amelia Island, shewing distinctly the tendency of that establishment by its piratical practices to wound the interest, and excite the indignation of every European power against the Colonies, the consequence of which would have been to unite them on the side of Spain against the Colonies, commencing with expeditions against the pirates, which might have terminated in attacks upon those by whom they were commissioned. Indications of this kind were seen in communications which were received at that time from the Ministers of Great Britain & France, who complained of the seizures of British & French vessels by privateers bearing the commissions of the Colonies, some of which were equipped from Amelia Island. By the latter minister it was proposed by the order of his government to establish a cordon of frigates along our coast, and in the gulf of Mexico, to protect the commerce of France against these piracies. By the suppression of that establishment these dangers were averted.

Of late these piratical practices have assumed a more extensive range. Their effect has been very seriously felt on the commerce of our country, & on that of other powers, particularly Portugal. A detailed sketch of these piracies, as known to the Department, in relation to other powers, as well as to the U. States, should likewise be communicated to the Colonial governments, to induce them to take decisive measures to suppress them. With regard to ourselves there is other serious cause of complaint. It is well known that blank commissions have been sent to this country, to be issued within its jurisdiction, & that our laws for supporting our neutrality have been eluded and violated in many other ways, to the great injury of our citizens, as well as of our national character. The conduct of several of the agents of the Colonies has been in these respects in the highest degree reprehensible, particularly of Mr. Aguirre, Mr. Thompson, Mr. Clemente and Mr. Guall. Mr. Thompson is dead, and Mr. Guall has left the country, whose offence consisted in granting the commission to Genl. M^c.Gregor. Mr. Aguirre & Mr. Clemente, in addition to other acts already noticed, have insulted the government, and in many instances in the most offensive manner. This government would fail in what it owes to the rights & interests of the United States, as well as to itself, if it did not make these acts a weighty & special cause of complaint.

If these piracies are continued it is impossible that they should not produce the worst effect on the interest of the Colonies. The allied powers, as already stated, are not friendly to them, and Spain has resolved to push the war with the utmost vigour against them. If many more prizes are taken from any of the allies it may reasonably be expected that they will send a naval force along the southern coast to put an end to privateering, & be led from that step to others of greater hostility to the Colonies.

Satisfied that these piratical practices did essential injury to the cause of the Colonies, and indulging a just sensibility to the sufferings of our fellow citizens, as well as to the character of the nation, Congress thought it proper, at the last session, to pass an Act for their suppression. A copy of this Act should be communicated to the Colonial governments.

If the Colonial governments will recall all the commissions which were not issued by the proper authorities, & in a proper manner, all piracy will be at an end. They will cease to injure their friends, and to aid the cause of their enemies. They will repair the wound already inflicted on their own character. There will, in that case, be nothing for this government to perform under the late Act. We expect also that they will immediately recall Mr. Aguirre & Mr. Clementes, who have given so much cause of complaint to this government, and that they will employ such others as will pay due respect to the laws & public authorities. A copy of the laws for the maintenance of a fair neutrality should be communicated to them, & the laws be likewise fully explained.

If any privateers have been regularly equipped & commissioned, on receiving a list of them from the colonial governments, they will not be molested in the performance of their lawful duties. To the giving such a list there can, it is presumed, be no objection. It will therefore be requested.

Bound to execute the law, & to protect our commerce from piracy, & being unwilling that any unfounded suspicion should be entertained of our views towards them, or that any odium should be cast on the Colonial governments which we can possibly avoid, this communication will be made to them, in the hope that they may suppress the practice themselves, or at least afford such coöperation in the suppression of it as they may be able. This government feels great repugnance at making an attack on any vessels bearing the commissions of the Colonial governments if it can be avoided, & in any event without a previous communication to them, & deriving all the sanction & aid which they can afford.

The government has a just claim to the confidence of the Colonial governments, and expects it, and a conduct founded on it. A different course will not only be improper in itself, but must prove injurious to the Colonies, as well as to ourselves. More dangers await them than they are perhaps aware of, or than are yet distinctly known to us. We judge of them only by the well known temper of other powers, and the presumption that the present calm, so unusual & inconsistent with the fixed habits of European governments, if not with the principles on which they are founded, will be temporary. It is not probable that a suspicious and illiberal conduct will divert us from a course adopted under the influence of strong motives, & on great consideration, but it is certain that less effect may be expected from it, even in respect to the Colonies themselves, than if their governments reciprocated the friendly policy which we have pursued towards them.

SOUTH AMERICAN AFFAIRS.
March 8, 1822.

To the Senate and House of Representatives of the United States:
In transmitting to the House of Representatives the documents called for by the resolution of that House of the 30th. January, I consider it my duty to invite the attention of Congress to a very important subject, and to commu-

nicate the sentiments of the Executive on it, that, should Congress entertain similar sentiments, there may be such coöperation between the two departments of the Government as their respective rights and duties may require.

The revolutionary movement in the Spanish Provinces in this hemisphere attracted the attention and excited the sympathy of our fellow citizens from its commencement. This feeling was natural and honorable to them, from causes which need not be communicated to you. It has been gratifying to all to see the general acquiescence which has been manifested in the policy which the constituted authorities have deemed it proper to pursue in regard to this contest. As soon as the movement assumed such a steady and consistent form as to make the success of the Provinces probable, the rights to which they were entitled by the law of nations as equal parties to a civil war were extended to them. Each party was permitted to enter our ports with its public and private ships and to take from them every article which was the subject of commerce with other nations. Our citizens, also, have carried on commerce with both parties, and the Government has protected it with each in articles not contraband of war. Through the whole of this contest the United States have remained neutral, and have fulfilled with the utmost impartiality all the obligations incident to that character.

This contest has now reached such a stage and been attended with such decisive success on the part of the provinces that it merits the most profound consideration whether their right to the rank of independent nations, with all the advantages incident to it in their intercourse with the United States is not complete. Buenos Ayres assumed that rank by a formal declaration in 1816, and has enjoyed it since 1810 free from invasion by the parent country. The Provinces composing the Republic of Columbia after having separately declared their independence, were united by a fundamental law of the 17th. of December 1819. A strong Spanish force occupied at that time certain parts of the territory within their limits and waged a destructive war. That force has since been repeatedly defeated, and the whole of it either made prisoners or destroyed or expelled from the country, with the exception of an inconsiderable force only, which is blockaded in two fortresses. The Provinces on the Pacific have likewise been very successful. Chili declared independence in 1818, and has since enjoyed it undisturbed; and of late, by the assistance of Chili and Buenos Ayres, the revolution has extended to Peru. Of the movement in Mexico our information is less authentic, but it is, nevertheless, distinctly understood that the new Government has declared its independence and that there is now no opposition to it there nor a force to make any. For the last three years the Government of Spain has not sent a single corps of troops to any part of that country, nor is there any reason to believe it will send any in future. Thus it is manifest that all those Provinces are not only in the full enjoyment of their independence, but, considering the state of the war and other circumstances, that there is not the most remote prospect of their being deprived of it.

When the result of such a contest is manifestly settled, the new governments have a claim to recognition by other powers which ought not to be resisted. Civil wars too often excite feelings which the parties cannot control. The opinion entertained by other powers as to the result may assuage those feelings and promote an accommodation between them useful and honorable to both. The delay which has been observed in making a decision on this important subject will, it is presumed, have afforded an unequivocal proof to Spain, as it must have done to other powers, of the high respect entertained by the United States for her rights and of their determination not to interfere with them. The Provinces belonging to this hemisphere are our neighbors, and have successively, as each portion of the country acquired its independence, pressed their recognition by an appeal to facts not to be contested, and which they thought gave them a just title to it. To motives of interest this Government has invariably disclaimed all pretension, having resolved to take no part in the controversy or other measure in regard to it which should not merit the sanction of the civilized world. To other claims a just sensibility has been always felt and frankly acknowledged, but they in themselves could never become an adequate cause of action. It was incumbent on this Government to look to every important fact and circumstance on which a sound opinion could be formed, which has been done. When we regard then, the great length of time which this war has been prosecuted, the complete success which has attended it in favor of the Provinces, the present condition of the parties, and the utter inability of Spain to produce any change in it, we are compelled to conclude that its fate is settled, and that the Provinces which have declared their independence and are in the enjoyment of it ought to be recognized.

Of the views of the Spanish Government on this subject no particular information has been recently received. It may be presumed that the successful progress of the revolution through such a long series of years, gaining strength and extending annually in every direction, and embracing by the late important events, with little exception, all the dominions of Spain south of the United States on this Continent, placing thereby the complete sovereignty over the whole in the hands of the people, will reconcile the parent country to an accommodation with them on the basis of their unqualified independence. Nor has any authentic information been recently received of other powers respecting it. A sincere desire has been cherished to act in concert with them in the proposed recognition, of which several were some time past duly apprised; but it was understood that they were not prepared for it. The immense space between those powers, even those which border on the Atlantic, and these Provinces makes the movement an affair of less interest and excitement to them than to us. It is probable, therefore that they have been less attentive to its progress than we have been. It may be presumed, however, that the late events will dispell all doubt of the result.

In proposing this measure it is not contemplated to change thereby in the slightest manner our friendly relations with either of the parties, but to observe in all respects, as heretofore, should the war be continued, the most perfect neutrality between them. Of this friendly disposition an assurance will be given to the Government of Spain to whom it is presumed it will be, as it ought to be, satisfactory. The measure is proposed under a thorough conviction that it is in strict accord with the law of nations; that it is just and right as to the parties and that the United States owe it to their station and character in the world, as well as to their essential interests, to adopt it. Should Congress concur in the view herein presented, they will doubtless see the propriety of making the necessary appropriation for carrying it into effect.[1]

MEMORANDUM

"Note for a reply from Mr. Adams to a letter from Mr. Russell—It will be proper to state to Mr. Russell, in reply to his letter, that the President having stated in his message, that almost the whole of the country south of the U.S. had declared its independence, and ought to be recognized, it would be proper to make such an appropriation as would enable him to give effect to such recognition, in a manner regarding those considerations which may claim attention, relating particularly to the number of missions, their grade and the time of appointment of each, as in the exercise of his constitutional functions, he should find most consistent with the honor & interest of the U.S. The sense of Congress as to the boldness & extent of measures to be taken will have its due weight with him. In executing this policy attention will be due to the opinion & wishes of each of the powers to be recognized, as to the grade of the mission as it will be to every other circumstance which may be gratifying and useful to them, without injury to ourselves." [HAMILTON.]

1. "My situation, as you well know, renders it impossible for me to write you often or regularly. At this time it was my intention to have written you fully on the subject of a message sent in yesterday which you will see in the Intelligences' but I have been so much interrupted all the morning that I have but one moment to refer you to it, and assure you of the sincere regard with which I am your friend."—To Madison, March 9th. [HAMILTON.]

TO THOMAS JEFFERSON.
WASHINGTON, March 14, 1822.

DEAR SIR,—I have had the pleasure to receive your letter of the 6th., & to forward that to D^r. Morse inclosed in it, in the manner directed. I have read with great interest & satisfaction, the very harmonious view, which you have taken, of the many & very serious objections to the association of which he may be said to be the author. I concur with you thoroughly in every sentiment which you have express'd on the subject, & I hope you will excuse a liberty which I have taken, to retain a copy of it, & that you will also permit me to show it to the members of the administration & some other friends here. I have shown it to M^r. Hay, who expresses a strong desire that it could be made publick, as he thinks that it would produce a very happy effect, in checking combinations of the kind. M^r. Gouverneur who copied it, is the only other person who has seen it, or who will see it, without your permission.

You have I doubt not read the message respecting the independent governments to the South of the U. States. There was *danger* in standing *still* or moving *forward,* of a nature, in both instances, which will readily occur to you. I thought that it was the wisest policy, to risk that, which was incident to the latter course, as it comported more with the liberal & magnanimous spirit of our own country than the other. I hope that you will concur in the opinion that the time has arriv'd, beyond which it ought not to have been longer delayed.

TO ROBERT S. GARNETT.
WASHINGTON, March 29, 1822.

DEAR SIR,—Your vote of yesterday against the recognition of our Southern neighbors has given many of your friends, and among them myself, much concern, partly as it affects the public, it being the only vote against it, but more especially, the great unanimity accomplishing every public object, as it respects yourself. Permit me to make some remarks on the subject for your own consideration. The question being carried, it is important, as relates to the character of the measure and the public feeling, that it be unanimous. The report of it to the world will produce a very strong effect everywhere, particularly with Spain, & the provinces; with the former, by announcing that if she resents it that we shall be united in meeting her resentment; with the latter, by showing the deep interest which the whole American people take in their welfare. For you to stand alone against that sentiment will deprive your country of that advantage, and without the possibility of any indemnity for it. The incident, in my opinion, affords you an excellent opportunity of conciliating the public opinion, as well as of Congress towards you, which may be done by stating in your place that you had thought, on great reflection, that the measure was hazardous, but seeing that your country had taken its step you were resolved to go with it, & therefore changed your vote. Forgive the liberty I have taken in making this suggestion, & be assured that it proceeds only from a friendly motive, being with sincere regard yrs.

In going the length you have done you have shown your firmness and independence. It now remains for you to show your moderation & conciliation.

April 1st, Mr. Garnett made the following declaration to be entered on the Journal of the House of Representatives: "I Robert S. Garnett, a member from Virginia, make the following declaration: That I voted against the recognition of the independence of the late American provinces of Spain, because, considering it a question of policy, not of principle, I believed that no immediate advantage could grow out of it to either country, whilst many considerations, affecting the interests of both, rendered it at this time inexpedient. I am not opposed to the independence of the late provinces; on the contrary, in common with the rest of my countrymen, I heartily rejoice in its accomplishment, and in the prospects of freedom and happiness which it opens to them." [HAMILTON.]

TO GENERAL DEARBORN.
WASHINGTON, May 3, 1822.

MR. RUSH TO MR. ADAMS: No. 323. LONDON, August 19, 1823. (Rec'd 9th October) SIR,—When my interview with Mr. Canning on Saturday was about to close, I transiently asked him whether, notwithstanding the last news from Spain, we might still hope that the Spaniards would get the better of all their difficulties. I had allusion to the defection of Baltasteros, in Andalusia, an event seeming to threaten with new dangers the Constitutional cause. His reply was general, imparting nothing more than his opinion of the increased difficulties and dangers with which, undoubtedly, this event was calculated to surround the Spanish cause.

Pursuing the topick of Spanish affairs, I remarked that should France ultimately effect her purposes in Spain, there was at least the consolation left, that Great Britain would not allow her to go farther and lay her hands upon the Spanish Colonies, bringing them too under her grasp. I here had in my mind the sentiments promulgated upon this subject in Mr. Canning's note to the British Ambassador at Paris of the 31st of March, during the negociations that preceded the invasion of Spain. It will be recollected that the British government say in this note, that time and the course of events appeared to have substantially decided the question of the separation of these colonies from the mother country, although their formal recognition as independent States by Great Britain might be hastened or retarded by external circumstances, as well as by the internal condition of those new States themselves; and that as his Britannic Majesty disclaimed all intention of appropriating to himself the smallest portion of the late Spanish possessions in America, he was also satisfied that no attempt would be made by France to bring any of them under *her* dominion, either by conquest, or by cession from Spain.

By this we are to understand, in terms sufficiently distinct, that Great Britain would not be passive under such an attempt by France, and Mr. Canning, on my having referred to this note, asked me what I thought my government would say to going hand in hand with this, in the same sentiment; not as he added that any concert in action under it could become necessary between the two countries, but that the simple fact of our being known to hold the same sentiment would, he had no doubt, by its moral effect, put down the intention on the part of France, admitting that she should ever entertain it. This belief was founded he said upon the large share of the maritime power of the world which Great Britain and the United States shared between them, and the consequent influence which the knowledge that they held a common opinion upon a question on which such large maritime interests, present and future, hung, could not fail to produce upon the rest of the world.

I replied, that in what manner my government would look upon such a suggestion, I was unable to say, but that I would communicate it in the same informal manner in which he threw it out. I said, however, that I did not think I should do so with full advantage, unless he would at the same time enlighten me as to the precise situation in which His Majesty's government stood at this moment in relation to those new States, and especially on the material point of their own independence.

He replied that Great Britain certainly never again intended to lend her instrumentality or aid, whether by mediation or otherwise, towards making up the dispute between Spain and her colonies; but that if this result could still be brought about, she would not interfere to *prevent* it. Upon my intimating that all idea of Spain ever recovering her authority over the colonies had long since gone by, he explained by saying that he did not mean to controvert that opinion, for he too believed that the day had arrived when all America might be considered as lost to Europe, so far as the tie of political dependence was concerned. All that he meant was, that if Spain and the colonies should still be able to bring the dispute, not yet totally extinct between them, to a close upon terms satisfactory to both sides, and which should at the same time secure to Spain commercial or other advantages not extended to other nations, Great Britain would not object to a compromise in this spirit of preference to Spain. All that she would ask would be, to stand upon as favored a footing as any other nation after Spain. Upon my again alluding to the improbability of the dispute ever settling down even upon this basis, he said that it was not his intention to maintain such a position, and that he had expressed himself as above rather for the purpose of indicating the feeling which this cabinet still had towards Spain in relation to the controversy, than of predicting results.

Wishing, however, to be still more specifically informed, I asked whether Great Britain was at this moment taking any step, or contemplating any, which had reference to the recognition of these states, this being the point in which we felt the chief interest.

He replied that she had taken none whatever, as yet, but was upon the eve of taking one, not final, but preparatory, and which would still leave her at large to recognize or not according to the position of events at a future period. The measure in question was, to send out one or more individuals under authority from this government to South America, not strictly diplomatic, but clothed with powers in the nature of a commission of inquiry, and which in short he described as analogous to those exercised by our commissioners in 1817; and that upon the result of this commission much might depend as to the ulterior conduct of Great Britain. I asked whether I was to understand that it would comprehend all the new states, or which of them; to which he replied that, for the present, it would be limited to Mexico.

Reverting to his first idea he again said, that he hoped that France would not, should even events in the Peninsula be favorable to her, extend her views to South America for the purpose of reducing the colonies, nominally perhaps for Spain, but in effect to subserve ends of her own; but that in case she should meditate such a policy, he was satisfied that the knowledge of the United States being opposed to it as well as Great Britain could not fail to have its influence in checking her steps. In this way he thought good might be done by prevention, and peaceful prospects all 'round increased. As to the form in which such knowledge might be made to reach France, and even the other powers of Europe, he said in conclusion that that might probably be arranged in a manner that would be free from objection.

I again told him that I would convey his suggestions to you for the information of the President, and impart to him whatever reply I might recieve. My own inference rather is, that his proposition was a fortuitous one; yet he entered into it I thought with some interest, and appeared to receive with a corresponding satisfaction the assurance I gave him that it should be made known to the President. I did not feel myself at liberty to express any opinion unfavourable to it, and was as careful to give none in its favour.

MR. CANNING TO MR. RUSH: (Private & Confidential.) Foreign Office, Aug 20, 1823.—MY DEAR SIR,—Before leaving Town, I am desirous of bringing before you in a more distinct, but still in an unofficial and confidential, shape, the Question which we shortly discussed, the last time that I had the pleasure of seeing you.

Is not the moment come when our Governments might understand each other as to the Spanish American Colonies? And if we can arrive at such an understanding, would it not be expedient for ourselves, and beneficial for all the world, that the principles of it should be clearly settled and plainly avowed?

For ourselves we have no disguise.

1. We conceive the recovery of the Colonies by Spain to be hopeless.

2. We conceive the question of the Recognition of them, as Independent States, to be one of time and circumstances.

3. We are, however, by no means disposed to throw any impediment in the way of an arrangement between them and the mother country by amicable negotiation.

4. We aim not at the possession of any portion of them ourselves.

5. We could not see any portion of them transferred to any other Power with indifference.

If these opinions and feelings are, as I firmly believe them to be, common to your government with ours, why should we hesitate mutually to confide them to each other; and to declare them in the face of the world?

If there be any European Power which cherishes other projects, which looks to a forcible enterprize for reducing the colonies to subjugation, on the behalf or in the name of Spain; or which meditates the acquisition of any part of them to itself, by cession or by conquest; such a declaration on the part of your government and ours would be at once the most effectual and the least offensive mode of intimating our joint disapprobation of such projects.

It would at the same time put an end to all the jealousies of Spain with respect to her remaining colonies—and to the agitation which prevails in those colonies, an agitation which it would be but humane to allay; being determined (as we are) not to profit by encouraging it.

Do you conceive that under the power which you have recently received, you are authorized to enter into negotiation, and to sign any Convention upon this subject? Do you conceive, if that be not within your competence, you could exchange with me ministerial notes upon it?

Nothing could be more gratifying to me than to join with you in such a work, and, I am persuaded, there has seldom, in the history of the world, occurred an opportunity, when so small an effort, of two friendly Governments, might produce so unequivocal a good and prevent such extensive calamities.

I shall be absent from London but three weeks at the utmost; but never so far distant, but that I can receive and reply to any communication, within three or four days.

MR. RUSH TO MR. CANNING: LONDON, August 23, 1823, MY DEAR SIR,— Your unofficial and confidential note of the 20th. instant reached me yesterday, and has commanded from me all the reflection due to the interest of its subject, and to the friendly spirit of confidence upon which it is so emphatically founded.

The government of the United States having, in the most formal manner, acknowledged the independence of the late Spanish provinces in America, desires nothing more anxiously than to see this independence maintained with stability, and under auspices that may promise prosperity and happiness to these new states themselves, as well as advantage to the rest of the world. As conducing to these great ends, my government has always desired, and still desires, to see them received into the family of nations by the powers of Europe, and especially, I may add, by Great Britain.

My government is also under a sincere conviction, that the epoch has arrived when the interests of humanity and justice, as well as all other interests, would be essentially subserved by the general recognition of these states.

Making these remarks, I believe I may confidently say, that the sentiments unfolded in your note are fully those which belong also to my government.

It conceives the recovery of the colonies by Spain, to be hopeless.

It would throw no impediment in the way of an arrangement between them and the mother country, by amicable negotiation—supposing an arrangement of this nature to be possible.

It does not aim at the possession of any portion of those communities, for or on behalf of the United States.

It would regard as highly unjust, and fruitful of disastrous consequences, any attempt on the part of any European power to take possession of them by conquest, or by cession; or on any ground or pretext whatever.

But, in what manner my government might deem it expedient to avow these principles and feelings, or express its disapprobation of such projects as the last, are points which none of my instructions, or the power which I have recently received, embrace; and they involve I am forced to add considerations of too much delicacy for me to act upon them in advance.

It will yield me particular pleasure to be the organ of promptly causing to be brought under the notice of the President, the opinions and views of which you have made me the depository upon this subject, and I am of nothing more sure than that he will fully appreciate their intrinsick interest, and not less the frank and friendly feelings towards the United States in which they have been conceived and communicated to me on your part.

Nor, do I take too much upon myself, when I anticipate the peculiar satisfaction the President will also derive from the intimation which you have not scrupled to afford me, as to the just and liberal determinations of His Majesty's government, in regard to the colonies which still remain to Spain.

With a full reciprocation of the personal cordiality which your note also breathes, and begging you to accept the assurances of my great respect, I have the honor &c.

MR. RUSH TO MR. ADAMS: N°. 325. LONDON, August 23, 1823. (Rec'd 9th October). SIR,—I yesterday received from Mr. Canning a note headed "private and confidential" setting before me in a more distinct form the proposition respecting South American affairs, which he communicated to me in conversation, on the 16th, as already reported in my number 323. Of his note I lose no time in transmitting a copy for your information, as well as a copy of my answer to it written and sent this day.

In shaping the answer on my own judgment alone, I feel that I have had a task of some embarrassment to perform, and shall be happy if it receives the President's approbation.

I believe that this government has the subject of Mr. Canning's proposition much at heart, and certainly his note bears, upon the face of it, a character of cordiality towards the government of the United States which cannot escape notice.

I have therefore thought it proper to impart to my note a like character, and to meet the points laid down in his, as far as I could, consistently with other and paramount considerations.

These I conceived to be chiefly twofold; first, the danger of pledging my government to any measure or course of policy which might in any degree, now or hereafter, implicate it in the federated system of Europe; and, secondly, I have felt myself alike without warrant to take a step which might prove exceptionable in the eyes of France, with whom our pacifick and friendly relations remain

I presume undisturbed, whatever may be our speculative abhorrence of her attack upon the liberties of Spain.

In framing my answer I had also to consider what was due to Spain herself, and I hope that I have not overlooked what was due to the colonies.

The whole subject is open to views on which my mind has deliberated anxiously.

If the matter of my answer shall be thought to bear properly upon motives and considerations which belong most materially to the occasion, it will be a source of great satisfaction to me.

The tone of earnestness in Mr. Canning's note and the force of some of his expressions naturally start the inference that the British Cabinet cannot be without its serious apprehensions that ambitious enterprizes are meditated against the independence of the South American States, whether by France alone, I cannot say, on any authentick grounds.

MR. CANNING TO MR. RUSH: Private & Confidential. LIVERPOOL, Aug. 23^d. 1823. MY DEAR SIR,—Since I wrote to you on the 20th, an additional motive has occurred for wishing that we might be able to come to some understanding on the part of our respective Governments on the subject of my letter; to come to it soon, and to be at liberty to announce it to the world.

It is this. I have received notice, but not such a notice as imposes upon me the necessity of an immediate answer or proceeding—that so soon as the military objects in Spain are achieved (of which the French expect, how justly I know not, a very speedy achievement) a proposal will be made for a Congress or some less formal concert and consultation, specially upon the affairs of Spanish America.

I need not point out to you all the complications to which this proposal, however dealt with by us, my lead.

Pray receive this communication in the same confidence with the former & believe with great truth &c.

MR. RUSH TO MR. CANNING: LONDON, August 27, 1823. MY DEAR SIR,—Your favor of the 23d. dated at Liverpool, got to hand yesterday, and I perceive in its contents new motives for attaching importance to the subject to which it relates.

In the note which I had the honor to address to you on the 23^d. two principal ideas have place.

1. That the government of the United States earnestly desires to see maintained permanently, the independence of the late Spanish provinces in America.

2. That it would view with uneasiness any attempt on the part of the powers of Europe to intrench upon that independence.

I will add, in the present note, that my government would view with like uneasiness any interference whatever by the powers of Europe in the affairs of these new states, unsolicited by the latter and against their will. It would regard the convening of a congress, for example, at this period of time, to deliberate upon their affairs, as a measure uncalled for, and indicative of a policy highly unfriendly to the tranquility of the world. It could never look with insensibility upon such an exercise of European jurisdiction over communities now of right exempt from it, and entitled to regulate their own concerns unmolested from abroad. In speaking thus, I am entirely confident that I do nothing more than strictly interpret the opinions of my government, and of the whole people of the United States. It is only as to the mode in which the former might choose to give expression to its strong disapprobation of such enterprizes, that my instructions at this moment, as I think, fail me.

If you suppose any of the sentiments of this, or my preceding, note, susceptible of being moulded by me into a form promising to achieve the object proposed in your note of the 20th., or make any useful approximation to it, I shall be most happy to take into consideration whatever suggestions you may favor me with, towards this end, either immediately in writing, or in the more unreserved intercourse of conversation when you return to town, being in this respect altogether at your disposal.

I will, for the present, only add that could His Majesty's government see fit to consider the time *now* arrived for a full acknowledgment of the independence of the South American States by Great Britain, it is my unequivocal belief, entertained not on light grounds, that it would accelerate the steps of my government in a course of policy intimated as being common to this government, for the welfare of those states. It would also naturally place *me* in a new position in my further conferences with you, upon this interesting subject.

MR. RUSH TO MR. ADAMS: No. 326. LONDON, August 28, 1823. (Rec'd 9th October.) SIR,—Since my last despatch, I have received a second confidential note from Mr. Canning, dated at Liverpool, the 23rd., a copy of which and of my answer, dated yesterday, are enclosed. The subject of our correspondence being, as appears to me, of deep interest, I think proper to apprize you of it from step to step, without waiting for the further developments to which it may possibly lead. I hence hope that this communication will be in time to accompany my last, in the packet ship that will leave Liverpool on the first of September.

Mr. Canning having now distinctly informed me, that he has received notice of measures being in projection by the powers of Europe relative to the affairs of Spanish America, as soon as the French succeed in their military movements in Spain,—which it would seem they expect soon to do,—I cannot avoid seeing this subject under the complications to which Mr. Canning alludes.

My first object will be, to urge upon this government the obvious expediency of an immediate and unreserved recognition of the independence of the South American states.

It will be seen by my note to Mr. Canning of yesterday, that I have made a beginning in this work, and, should the opportunity be afforded me, it is my intention to follow it up zealously.

Should I be asked by Mr. Canning, whether, *if the recognition be made by Great Britain without more delay,* I am, on my part, prepared to make a declaration in the name of my government that it will not remain inactive under an attack upon the independence of those states by the Holy Alliance, the present determination of my judgment is, that I will make this declaration explicitly, and avow it before the world.

I am not unaware of the responsibility which I should, by such a measure, assume upon myself. My reasons for assuming it, I have not, at present, the leisure to recount with the requisite fulness. The leading ones would be, in brief, as follow.

1. I may thereby aid in achieving an immediate and positive good to those rising states in our hemisphere; for such I should conceive their recognition at this juncture by Great Britain, in itself to be.

2. Such recognition, co-operating with the declaration which this government has already in effect made, that it will not look quietly on if Spanish America is attacked, and followed up by a similar (though not joint) declaration from me that neither will the United States, would prove at least a probable means of warding off the attack. The minister of foreign affairs of this government, it appears, is under a strong persuasion that it would forestall it, and this without the recognition by England being, as yet, a part of his care.

3. Should the issue of things be different, and events notwithstanding arise, threatening the peace of the United States, or otherwise seriously to commit them, under such a declaration from me, it would still remain with the wisdom of my government to disavow my conduct, as I should manifestly have acted without its previous warrant, though hoping for its subsequent sanction. I would

take to myself all the reproach, consoled if not justified under the desire that had animated me to render benefits of great magnitude to the cause of South American independence and freedom at a point of time, which, if lost, was not to be regained; and believing that at all events, I should have rendered some benefits to it, in being instrumental towards accelerating the recognition by Great Britain.

My conduct might be disavowed in any issue of the transaction, and I should still not be left without a hope, that the President would see in it proofs of good intention, mixed with a zeal for the advancement of great political interests, not appearing, at the moment, to be indifferent ultimately to the welfare of the United States themselves.

The result of my reasoning in a word then, is, that I find myself placed in a situation in which, by deciding and acting promptly, I may do much publick good, whilst public mischiefs may be arrested by the controuling hand of my government, should my conduct be likely to draw any down.

Mr. Canning to Mr. Rush: Private & Confidential. Storrs, West-moreland, Aug. 31, 1823. My Dear Sir,—I have to acknowledge the receipt of your answer to both my letters; & whatever may be the practical result of our confidential communication, it is an unmixed satisfaction to me that the spirit in which it began on my part, has been met so cordially on yours.

To a practical result so eminently beneficial I see no obstacle; except in your want of specific powers, & in the delay which may intervene before you can procure them; & during which events may get before us.

Had you felt yourself authorized to entertain any formal proposition, and to decide upon it, without reference home, I would immediately have taken measures for assembling my Colleagues in London, upon my return, in order to be enabled to submit to you as the *act* of my government, all that I have stated to you as my own *sentiments* & theirs. But with such a delay in prospect, I think I should hardly be justified in proposing to bind ourselves to anything positively & unconditionally; and think on the other hand that a proposition *qualified* either in respect to the contingency of your concurrence in it, or with reference to possible change of circumstances, would want the decision & frankness which I should wish to mark our proceeding.

Not that I anticipate any change of circumstances, which could vary the views opened to you in my first letter:—nor that, after what you have written to me in return, I apprehend any essential dissimilarity of views on the part of your government.

But *we* must not place ourselves in a position, in which, if called upon from other quarters for an opinion, we cannot give a clear and definite account not only of what we think and feel, but of what we have done or are doing, upon the matter in question. To be able to say in answer to such an appeal, that the United States & Great Britain concur in thinking so and so—would be well. To anticipate any such appeal by a voluntary declaration to the same effect—would be still better. But to have to say that we are in communication with the United States but have no conclusive understanding with them, would be inconvenient—our free agency would thus be fettered with respect to other Powers; while our agreement with you would be yet unascertained.

What appears to me, therefore, the most advisable is that you should see in my unofficial communication enough hope of good to warrant you in requiring Powers & Instructions from your Government on this point, in addition to the others upon which you have recently been instructed & empowered; treating that communication *not* as a proposition made to you, but as the evidence of the nature of a proposition which it would have been my desire to make to you, if I had found you provided with authority to entertain it.

MR. RUSH TO MR. ADAMS: No. 330. LONDON September 8, 1823. (Rec'd 5 November.) SIR,—I yesterday received another confidential note from Mr. Canning, dated the thirty-first of August, a copy of which I have the honor to enclose herewith for the President's information.

From this note it would appear, that Mr. Canning is not prepared to pledge this government to an immediate recognition of the independence of the South American States. I shall renew to him a proposition to this effect when we meet; but should he continue to draw back from it, I shall on my part not act upon the overtures contained in his first note, not feeling myself at liberty to accede to them in the name of my government, but upon the basis of an equivalent. This equivalent as I now view the subject could be nothing less than the immediate and full acknowledgment of those states, or some of them, by Great Britain.

I shall send this despatch by this evening's mail to Liverpool, and have reason to hope that it will go in a ship that sails on the eighth, whereby there will have been not a moment's delay in putting you in possession of all the correspondence that has passed between Mr. Canning and me, or that now seems likely to pass, upon this delicate subject. I cannot help thinking, however, that its apparent urgency may, after all, be lessened by the turn which we may yet witness in affairs, military and political, in Spain.

TO THOMAS JEFFERSON.
OAKHILL, October 17th, 1823

DEAR SIR

I transmit to you two despatches, which were receiv'd from Mr. Rush, while I was lately in Washington, which involve interests of the highest importance. They contain two letters from Mr. Canning, suggesting designs of the holy alliance, against the Independance of S°. America, & proposing a co-operation, between G. Britain & the UStates, in support of it, against the members of that alliance. The project aims, in the first instance, at a mere expression of opinion, somewhat in the abstract, but which, it is expected by Mr. Canning, will have a great political effect, by defeating the combination. By Mr. Rush's answers, which are also enclosed, you will see the light in which he views the subject, & the extent to which he may have gone. Many important considerations are involved in this proposition. 1st Shall we entangle ourselves, at all, in European politicks, & wars, on the side of any power, against others, presuming that a concert, by agreement, of the kind proposed, may lead to that result? 2d If a case can exist in which a sound maxim may, & ought to be departed from, is not the present instance, precisely that case? 3d Has not the epoch arriv'd when G. Britain must take her stand, either on the side of the monarchs of Europe, or of the UStates, & in consequence, either in favor of Despotism or of liberty & may it not be presum'd that, aware of that necessity, her government has seiz'd on the present occurrence, as that, which it deems, the most suitable, to announce & mark the commenc'ment of that career.

My own impression is that we ought to meet the proposal of the British govt. & to make it known, that we would view an interference on the part of the European powers, and especially an attack on the Colonies, by them, as an attack on ourselves, presuming that, if they succeeded with them, they would extend it to us. I am sensible however of the extent & difficulty of the question, & shall be happy to have yours, & Mr. Madison's opinions on it. I do not wish to trouble either of you with small objects, but the present one is vital, involving the high interests, for which we have so long & so faithfully, & harmoniously, contended together. Be so kind as to enclose to him the despatches, with an intimation of the motive.

MR. RUSH TO THE PRESIDENT. (Private) LONDON, October 23, 1823—The Spanish American topick has been dropped by Mr. Canning in a most extraordinary manner. Not another word has he said to me on it since the 26th. of last month, at the interview at Gloucester Lodge, which I have described in my despatches to the department, and he has now gone out of town to spend the remainder of this, and part of the next month. I shall not renew the topick, and should he, which I do not expect, I shall decline going into it again, saying that I must now wait until I hear from my government. Of European affairs since the fall of Cadiz, I know nothing and shall probably hear nothing from this Government, unless it may propose to itself the accomplishment of any fresh objects through my means. With the diplomatic corps I am at present in as little communication. To not one of them (I mean of the European Corps) have I said a word of Mr. Canning's late advances to me respecting South America.

THOMAS JEFFERSON TO JAMES MONROE: MONTICELLO, Oct. 24, '23. DEAR SIR,—The question presented by the letters you have sent me, is the most momentous which has been ever offered to my contemplation since that of Independence. That made us a nation. This sets our compass and points the course which we are to steer thro' the ocean of time opening on us, and never could we embark on it under circumstances more auspicious. Our first and fundamental maxim should be never to entangle ourselves in the broils of Europe, our second never to suffer Europe to intermeddle with Cis-Atlantic affairs. America, North and South has a state set of interests distinct from those of Europe, and peculiarly her own. She should therefore have a system of her own, separate and apart from that of Europe. While the last is laboring to become the domicile of despotism our endeavor should surely be to make our hemisphere that of freedom. One nation, most of all, could disturb us in this pursuit; she now offers to lead, aid, and accompany us in it. By acceding to her proposition, we detach her from the band of despots, bring her mighty weight into the scale of free government and emancipate a continent at one stroke which might otherwise linger long in doubt and difficulty. Great Britain is the nation which can do us the most harm of any one, or all, on earth; and with her on our side we need not fear the whole world. With her then we should the most sedulously cherish a cordial friendship; and nothing would tend more to knit our affections than to be fighting once more, side by side, in the same cause. Not that I would purchase even her amity at the price of taking part in her wars. But the war in which the present proposition might engage us, should that be its consequence, is not her war, but ours. It's object is to introduce and establish the American system, of keeping out of our land all foreign powers, of never permitting those of Europe to intermeddle with the affairs of our nations. It is to maintain our own principle, not to depart from it, and if, to facilitate this, we can effect a division in the body of the European powers, and draw over to our side it's most powerful member, surely we should do it. But I am clearly of Mr. Canning's opinion that it will prevent, instead of provoking war. With Great Britain withdrawn from their scale and shifted into that of our two continents, all Europe combined would not undertake such a war. For how would they propose to get at either enemy without superior fleets? Nor is the occasion to be slighted which this proposition offers of declaring our Protest against the atrocious violations of the rights of nations, by the interference of any one in the internal affairs of another so flagitiously begun by Buonaparte, and now continued by the equally lawless alliance, calling itself Holy.

But we have first to ask ourselves a question. Do we wish to acquire to our own confederacy any one or more of the Spanish provinces? I candidly confess that I have ever looked on Cuba as the most interesting addition which could ever be made to our system of states. The controul which, with Florida point, this island would give us over the Gulph of Mexico, and the countries, and the isthmus bordering on it, as well as all those whose waters flow into it, would fill up the measure of our political well-being—yet, as I am sensible that this can never be obtained, even with her own consent, but by war; and it's independence, which is our second interest, (and especially it's independance of England) can be secured without it, I have no hesitation in abandoning my first wish to future chances, and accepting it's independance with peace, and the friendship of England, rather than it's association at the expence of war & her enmity.

I could honestly therefore join in the declaration proposed that we aim not at the acquisition of any of those possessions, that we will not stand in the way of any amicable arrangement between them and the mother country, but that we will oppose, with all our means, the forcible interposition of any other power, as auxiliary, stipendiary, or under any other form or pretext, and most especially their transfer to any power by conquest, cession, or acquisition in any other way.

I should think it therefore advisable that the Executive should encourage the British Government to a continuance in the dispositions expressed in these letters, by an assurance of his concurrence with them as far as his authority goes, and that as it may lead to war, the declaration of which requires an act of Congress, the case shall be laid before them for consideration at their first meeting, and under the reasonable aspect in which it is seen by himself.

I have been so long weaned from political subjects, and have so long ceased to take any interest in them, that I am sensible I am not qualified to offer opinions on them worthy of any attention, but the question now proposed involves consequences so lasting, and effects so decisive of our future destinies, as to rekindle all the interest I have heretofore felt on such occasions, and induce me to the hazard of opinions, which will prove only my wish to contribute still my mite towards anything which may be useful to our country. And praying you to accept it at only what it is worth, I add the assurance of my constant and affectionate friendship and respect.

THOMAS JEFFERSON TO JAMES MADISON: I forward you two most important letters sent to me by the President and add his letter to me by which you will perceive his primâ facie views. This you will be so good as to return to me, and forward the others to him. I have received Trumbull's print of the Dectn of Independence, & turning to his letter am able to inform you more certainly than I could by memory that the print costs 20. D. & the frame & glass 12. D. say 32. D. in all. To answer your question, Pythagoras has the reputation of having first taught the true position of the sun in the center of our system & the revolution of the planets around it. His doctrine, after a long eclipse, was restored by Copernicus, and hence it is called either the Pythagorean or Copernican system. Health and affectionate salutations to Mrs Madison and yourself.

MONTICELLO, Oct. 24, '23.

JAMES MADISON TO JAMES MONROE: MONTPELIER, Oc^t. 30, 1823. DEAR SIR,—I have rec^d from M^r. Jefferson your letter to him, with the correspondence between M^r. Canning & M^r. Rush, sent for his and my perusal, and our opinions on the subject of it.

From the disclosures of M^r. Canning it appears as was otherwise to be inferred, that the success of France ag^st Spain would be followed by attempts of the Holy Alliance to reduce the revolutionized colonies of the latter to their former dependence.

The professions we have made to these neighbours, our sympathy with their Liberties & Independence, the deep interests we have in the most friendly relations with them, and the consequences threatened by a command of their resources by the great powers confederated ag^st the Rights & Reforms of which we have given so conspicuous & persuasive an example, all unite in calling for our efforts to defeat the meditated crusade. It is particularly fortunate that the policy of G Britain tho' guided by calculations different from ours, has presented a co-operation for an object the same with ours. With that co-operation we have nothing to fear from the rest of Europe; and with it the best reliance on success to our just & laudable views. There ought not to be any backwardness therefore, I think, in meeting her in the way she has proposed; keeping in view of course the spirit & forms of the Constitution in every step taken in the road to war which must be the last step, if those short of war should be without avail.

It cannot be doubted that M^r. Canning's proposal tho' made with the air of *consultation* as well as concert, was founded on a predetermination to take the course marked out whatever might be the reception given here to his invitation. But this consideration ought not to divert us from what is just and proper in itself. Our co-operation is due to ourselves & to the world: and whilst it must ensure success in the event of an appeal to force, it doubles the chance of success without that appeal. It is not improbable that G B would like best to have the sole merit of being the Champion of her new friends notwithstanding the greater difficulty to be encountered, but for the dilemma in which she would be placed. She must in that case either leave us as neutrals to extend our commerce & navigation at the expence of hers, or make us Enemies by renewing her paper blockades, and other arbitrary proceedings on the Ocean. It may be hoped that such a dilemma will not be without a permanent tendency to check her proneness to unnecessary wars.

Why the British Cabinet should have scrupled to arrest the calamity it now apprehends, by applying to the threats of France agst Spain the 'small effort' which it scruples not to employ on behalf of Spanish America, is best known to itself. It is difficult to find any other explanation than that *interest* in the one case has more weight in her casuistry than principle had in the other.

Will it not be honorable to our country & possibly not altogether in vain to invite the British Gov^t to extend the avowed disapprobation of the project agst the Spanish Colonies, to the enterprize of France agst Spain herself; and even to join in some declaratory act in behalf of the Greeks? On the supposition that no form could be given to the act clearing it of a pledge to follow it up by war, we ought to compare the good to be done, with the little injury to be apprehended to the U.S. shielded as their interests would be by the power & the fleets of G. Britain united with their own. These are questions however wch may require more information than I possess, and more reflection than I can now give them.

What is the extent of M^r. Canning's disclaimer to 'the remaining possessions of Spain in America'? Does it exclude future views of acquiring Porto Rico &c. as well as Cuba? It leaves G B free as I understand it, in relation to Spanish possessions in other Quarters of the Globe.

I return the correspondence of M^r. R. & M^r. C. with assurances of the highest respect & sincerest regard.

JAMES MADISON TO THOMAS JEFFERSON:

MONTPELLIER, Nov. 1, 1823. D^r. SIR,—I return the letter of the President. The correspondence from abroad has gone back to him as you desired. I have expressed to him my concurrence in the policy of meeting the advances of the B. Gov^t. having an eye to the forms of our Constitution in every step in the road to war. With the British power & navy combined with our own we have nothing to fear from the rest of the nations and in the great struggle of the Epoch between liberty and despotism, we owe it to ourselves to sustain the former in this hemisphere at least. I have even suggested an invitation to the B. Gov^t. to join in applying this 'small effort for so much good' to the French invasion of Spain, & to make Greece an object of some such favorable attention. Why Mr Canning & his colleagues did not sooner interpose agst the calamity wh^{ch} could not have escaped foresight cannot be otherwise explained but by the different aspect of the question when it related to liberty in Spain, and to the extension of British Commerce to her former colonies.

Health & every other blessing.

FROM THE *MEMOIRS* OF JOHN QUINCY ADAMS.

The President returned from Oakhill on November 5th. Under date of the 15th. Mr. Adams records: [HAMILTON.]

I received a note from Mr. D. Brent (Chief Clerk, State Department) saying that the President wished to see me at the office at noon. I went, and found him there. He asked for the correspondence relating to the intercourse with the British American Colonies, with a view to the particular notice which he intends to take of it in the message; which I thought should have been only in general terms. He also showed me two letters which he had received—one from Mr. Jefferson, 23rd October, and one from Mr. Madison, of 30th October, giving their opinions on the proposals of Mr. Canning. The President had sent them the two dispatches from R. Rush, of 23rd and 28th August, enclosing the correspondence between Canning and him, and requested their opinions on the proposals. Mr. Jefferson thinks them more important than anything that has happened since our Revolution. He is for acceding to the proposals, with a view to pledging Great Britain against the Holy Allies; though he thinks the Island of Cuba would be a valuable and important acquisition to our Union. Mr. Madison's opinions are less decisively pronounced, and he thinks, as I do, that this movement on the part of Great Britain is impelled more by her interest than by a principle of general liberty."

SEVENTH ANNUAL MESSAGE.

WASHINGTON, *December 2, 1823.*

NOTE: The two passages commonly considered the "Monroe Doctrine" traditionally have been printed in italics although Monroe gave them no emphasis. [Ed.].

Fellow-Citizens of the Senate and House of Representatives:

Many important subjects will claim your attention during the present session, of which I shall endeavor to give, in aid of your deliberations, a just idea in this communication. I undertake this duty with diffidence, from the vast extent of the interests on which I have to treat and of their great importance to every portion of our Union. I enter on it with zeal from a thorough conviction that there never was a period since the establishment of our Revolution when, regarding the condition of the civilized world and its bearing on us, there was greater necessity for devotion in the public servants to their respective duties, or for virtue, patriotism, and union in our constituents.

Meeting in you a new Congress, I deem it proper to present this view of public affairs in greater detail than might otherwise be necessary. I do it, however, with peculiar satisfaction, from a knowledge that in this respect I shall comply more fully with the sound principles of our Government. The people being with us exclusively the sovereign, it is indispensable that full information be laid before them on all important subjects, to enable them to exercise that high power with complete effect. If kept in the dark, they must be incompetent to it. We are all liable to error, and those who are engaged in the management of public affairs are more subject to excitement and to be led astray by their particular interests and passions than the great body of our constituents, who, living at home in the pursuit of their ordinary avocations, are calm but deeply interested spectators of events and of the conduct of those who are parties to them. To the people every department of the Government and every individual in each are responsible, and the more full their information the better they can judge of the wisdom of the policy pursued and of the conduct of each in regard to it. From their dispassionate judgment much aid may always be obtained, while their approbation will form the greatest incentive and most gratifying reward for virtuous actions, and the dread of their censure the best security against the abuse of their confidence. Their interests in all vital questions are the same, and the bond, by sentiment as well as by interest, will be proportionably strengthened as they are better informed of the real state of public affairs, especially in difficult conjunctures. It is by such knowledge that local prejudices and jealousies are surmounted, and that a national policy, extending its fostering care and protection to all the great interests of our Union, is formed and steadily adhered to.

A precise knowledge of our relations with foreign powers as respects our negotiations and transactions with each is thought to be particularly necessary. Equally necessary is it that we should form a just estimate of our resources, revenue, and progress in every kind of improvement connected with the national prosperity and public defense. It is by rendering justice to other nations that we may expect it from them. It is by our ability to resent injuries and redress wrongs that we may avoid them.

The commissioners under the fifth article of the treaty of Ghent, having disagreed in their opinions respecting that portion of the boundary between the Territories of the United States and of Great Britain the establishment of which had been submitted to them, have made their respective reports in compliance with that article, that the same might be referred to the decision of a friendly power. It being manifest, however, that it would be difficult, if not impossible, for any power to perform that office without great delay and much inconvenience to itself, a proposal has been made by this Government, and acceded to by that of Great Britain, to endeavor to establish that boundary by amicable negotiation. It appearing from long experience that no satisfactory arrangement could be formed of the commercial intercourse between the United States and the British colonies in this hemisphere by legislative acts while each party pursued its own course without agreement or concert with the other, a proposal has been made to the British Government to regulate this commerce by treaty, as it has been to arrange in like manner the just claim of the citizens of the United States inhabiting the States and Territories bordering on the lakes and rivers which empty into the St. Lawrence to the navigation of that river to the ocean. For these and other objects of high importance to the interests of both parties a negotiation has been opened with the British Government which it is hoped will have a satisfactory result.

The commissioners under the sixth and seventh articles of the treaty of Ghent having successfully closed their labors in relation to the sixth, have proceeded to the discharge of those relating to the seventh. Their progress in the extensive survey required for the performance of their duties justifies the presumption that it will be completed in the ensuing year.

The negotiation which had been long depending with the French Government on several important subjects, and particularly for a just indemnity for losses sustained in the late wars by the citizens of the United States under unjustifiable seizures and confiscations of their property, has not as yet had the desired effect. As this claim rests on the same principle with others which have been admitted by the French Government, it is not perceived on what just ground it can be rejected. A minister will be immediately appointed to proceed to France and resume the negotiation on this and other subjects which may arise between the two nations.

At the proposal of the Russian Imperial Government, made through the minister of the Emperor residing here, a full power and instructions have been transmitted to the minister of the United States at St. Petersburg to arrange by amicable negotiation the respective rights and interests of the two nations on the northwest coast of this continent. A similar proposal had been made by His Imperial Majesty to the Government of Great Britain, which has likewise been acceded to. The Government of the United States has been desirous by this friendly proceeding of manifesting the great value which they have invariably attached to the friendship of the Emperor and their solicitude to cultivate the best understanding with his Government. In the discussions to which this interest has given rise and in the arrangements by which they may terminate the occasion has been judged proper for asserting, as a principle in which the rights and interests of the United States are involved, that the American continents, by the free and independent condition which they have assumed and maintain, are henceforth not to be considered as subjects for future colonization by any European powers.

Since the close of the last session of Congress the commissioners and arbitrators for ascertaining and determining the amount of indemnification which may be due to citizens of the United States under the decision of His Imperial Majesty the Emperor of Russia, in conformity to the convention concluded at St. Petersburg on the 12th of July, 1822, have assembled in this city, and organized themselves as a board for the performance of the duties assigned to them by that treaty. The commission constituted under the eleventh article of the treaty of the 22d of February, 1819, between the United States and Spain is also in session here, and as the term of three years limited by the treaty for the execution of the trust will expire before the period of the next regular meeting of Congress, the attention of the Legislature will be drawn to the measures which may be necessary to accomplish the objects for which the commission was instituted.

In compliance with a resolution of the House of Representatives adopted at their last session, instructions have been given to all the ministers of the United States accredited to the powers of Europe and America to propose the proscription of the African slave trade by classing it under the denomination, and inflicting on its perpetrators the punishment, of piracy. Should this proposal be acceded to, it is not doubted that this odious and criminal practice will be promptly and entirely suppressed. It is earnestly hoped that it will be acceded to, from the firm belief that it is the most effectual expedient that can be adopted for the purpose.

At the commencement of the recent war between France and Spain it was declared by the French Government that it would grant no commissions to privateers, and that neither the commerce of Spain herself nor of neutral nations should be molested by the naval force of France, except in the breach of a lawful blockade. This declaration, which appears to have been faithfully carried into effect, concurring with principles proclaimed and cherished by the United States from the first establishment of their independence, suggested the hope that the time had arrived when the proposal for adopting it as a permanent and invariable rule in all future maritime wars might meet the favorable consideration of the great European powers. Instructions have accordingly been given to our ministers with France, Russia, and Great Britain to make those proposals to their respective Governments, and when the friends of humanity reflect on the essential amelioration to the condition of the human race which would result from the abolition of private war on the sea and on the great facility by which it might be accomplished, requiring only the consent of a few sovereigns, an earnest hope is indulged that these overtures will meet with an attention animated by the spirit in which they were made, and that they will ultimately be successful.

The ministers who were appointed to the Republics of Colombia and Buenos Ayres during the last session of Congress proceeded shortly afterwards to their destinations. Of their arrival there official intelligence has not yet been received. The minister appointed to the Republic of Chile will sail in a few days. An early appointment will also be made to Mexico. A minister has been received from Columbia, and the other Governments have been informed that ministers, or diplomatic agents of inferior grade, would be received from each, accordingly as they might prefer the one or the other.

The minister appointed to Spain proceeded soon after his appointment for Cadiz, the residence of the Sovereign to whom he was accredited. In approaching that port the frigate which conveyed him was warned off by the commander of the French squadron by which it was blockaded and not permitted to enter, although apprised by the captain of the frigate of the public character of the person whom he had on board, the landing of whom was the sole object of his proposed entry. This act, being considered an infringement of the rights of ambassadors and of nations, will form a just cause of complaint to the Government of France against the officer by whom it was committed.

The actual condition of the public finances more than realizes the favorable anticipations that were entertained of it at the opening of the last session of Congress. On the 1st of January there was a balance in the Treasury of $4,237,427.55. From that time to the 30th September the receipts amounted to upward of $16,100,000, and the expenditures to $11,400,000. During the fourth quarter of the year it is estimated that the receipts will at least equal the expenditures, and that there will remain in the Treasury on the 1st day of January next a surplus of nearly $9,000,000.

On the 1st of January, 1825, a large amount of the war debt and a part of the Revolutionary debt become redeemable. Additional portions of the former will continue to become redeemable annually until the year 1835. It is believed, however, that if the United States remain at peace the whole of that debt may be redeemed by the ordinary revenue of those years during that period under the provision of the act of March 3, 1817, creating the sinking fund, and in that case the only part of the debt that will remain after the year 1835 will be the $7,000,000 of 5 per cent stock subscribed to the Bank of the United States, and the 3 per cent Revolutionary debt, amounting to $13,296,099.06, both of which are redeemable at the pleasure of the Government.

The state of the Army in its organization and discipline has been gradually improving for several years, and has now attained a high degree of perfection. The military disbursements have been regularly made and the accounts regularly and promptly rendered for settlement. The supplies of various descriptions have been of good quality, and regularly issued at all of the posts. A system of economy and accountability has been introduced into every branch of the service which admits of little additional improvement. This desirable state has been attained by the act reorganizing the staff of the Army, passed on the 14th of April, 1818.

The moneys appropriated for fortifications have been regularly and economically applied, and all the works advanced as rapidly as the amount appropriated would admit. Three important works will be completed in the course of this year—that is, Fort Washington, Fort Delaware, and the fort at the Rigolets, in Louisiana.

The Board of Engineers and the Topographical Corps have been in constant and active service in surveying the coast and projecting the works necessary for its defense.

The Military Academy has attained a degree of perfection in its discipline and instruction equal, as is believed, to any institution of its kind in any country.

The money appropriated for the use of the Ordnance Department has been regularly and economically applied. The fabrication of arms at the national armories and by contract with the Department has been gradually improving in quality and cheapness. It is believed that their quality is now such as to admit of but little improvement.

The completion of the fortifications renders it necessary that there should be a suitable appropriation for the purpose of fabricating the cannon and carriages necessary for those works.

Under the appropriation of $5,000 for exploring the Western waters for the location of a site for a Western armory, a commission was constituted, consisting of Colonel McRee, Colonel Lee, and Captain Talcott, who have been engaged in exploring the country. They have not yet reported the result of their labors, but it is believed that they will be prepared to do it at an early part of the session of Congress.

During the month of June last General Ashley and his party, who were trading under a license from the Government, were attacked by the Ricarees while peaceably trading with the Indians at their request. Several of the party were killed and wounded and their property taken or destroyed.

Colonel Leavenworth, who commanded Fort Atkinson, at the Council Bluffs, the most western post, apprehending that the hostile spirit of the Ricarees would extend to other tribes in that quarter, and that thereby the lives of the traders on the Missouri and the peace of the frontier would be endangered, took immediate measures to check the evil.

With a detachment of the regiment stationed at the Bluffs he successfully attacked the Ricaree village, and it is hoped that such an impression has been made on them as well as on the other tribes on the Missouri as will prevent a recurrence of future hostility.

The report of the Secretary of War, which is herewith transmitted, will exhibit in greater detail the condition of the Department in its various branches, and the progress which has been made in its administration during the three first quarters of the year.

I transmit a return of the militia of the several States according to the last reports which have been made by the proper officers in each to the Department of War. By reference to this return it will be seen that it is not complete, although great exertions have been made to make it so. As the defense and even the liberties of the country must depend in times of imminent danger on the militia, it is of the highest importance that it be well organized, armed, and disciplined throughout the Union. The report of the Secretary of War shews the progress made during the three first quarters of the present year by the application of the fund appropriated for arming the militia. Much difficulty is found in distributing the arms according to the act of Congress providing for it from the failure of the proper departments in many of the States to make regular returns. The act of May 12, 1820, provides that the system of tactics and regulations of the various corps of the Regular Army shall be extended to the militia. This act has been very imperfectly executed from the want of uniformity in the organization of the militia, proceeding from the defects of the system itself, and especially in its application to that main arm of the public defense. It is thought that this important subject in all its branches merits the attention of Congress.

The report of the Secretary of the Navy, which is now communicated, furnishes an account of the administration of that Department for the three first quarters of the present year, with the progress made in augmenting the Navy, and the manner in which the vessels in commission have been employed.

The usual force has been maintained in the Mediterranean Sea, the Pacific Ocean, and along the Atlantic coast, and has afforded the necessary protection to our commerce in those seas.

In the West Indies and the Gulf of Mexico our naval force has been augmented by the addition of several small vessels provided for by the "act authorizing an additional naval force for the suppression of piracy," passed by Congress at their last session. That armament has been eminently successful in the accomplishment of its object. The piracies by which our commerce in the neighborhood of the island of Cuba had been afflicted have been repressed and the confidence of our merchants in a great measure restored.

The patriotic zeal and enterprise of Commodore Porter, to whom the command of the expedition was confided, has been fully seconded by the officers and men under his command. And in reflecting with high satisfaction on the honorable manner in which they have sustained the reputation of their country and its Navy, the sentiment is alloyed only by a concern that in the fulfilment of that arduous service the diseases incident to the season and to the climate in which it was discharged have deprived the nation of many useful lives, and among them of several officers of great promise.

In the month of August a very malignant fever made its appearance at Thompson's Island, which threatened the destruction of our station there. Many perished, and the commanding officer was severely attacked. Uncertain as to his fate and knowing that most of the medical officers had been rendered incapable of discharging their duties, it was thought expedient to send to that post an officer of rank and experience, with several skillful surgeons, to ascertain the origin of the fever and the probability of its recurrence there in future seasons; to furnish every assistance to those who were suffering, and, if practicable, to avoid the necessity of abandoning so important a station. Commodore Rodgers, with a promptitude which did him honor, cheerfully accepted that trust, and has discharged it in the manner anticipated from his skill and patriotism. Before his arrival Commodore Porter, with the greater part of the squadron, had removed from the island and returned to the United States in consequence of the prevailing sickness. Much useful information has, however, been obtained as to the state of the island and great relief afforded to those who had been necessarily left there.

Although our expedition, co-operating with an invigorated administration of the government of the island of Cuba, and with the corresponding active exertions of a British naval force in the same seas, have almost entirely destroyed the unlicensed piracies from that island, the success of our exertions has not been equally effectual to suppress the same crime, under other pretenses and colors, in the neighboring island of Porto Rico. They have been committed there under the abusive issue of Spanish commissions. At an early period of the present year remonstrances were made to the governor of that island, by an agent who was sent for the purpose, against those outrages on the peaceful commerce of the United States, of which many had occurred. That officer, professing his own want of authority to make satisfaction for our just complaints, answered only by a reference of them to the Government of Spain. The minister of the United States to that court was specially instructed to urge the necessity of the immediate and effectual interposition of that Government, directing restitution and indemnity for wrongs already committed and interdicting the repetition of them. The minister, as has been seen, was debarred access to the Spanish Government, and in the meantime several new cases of flagrant outrage have occurred, and citizens of the United States in the island of Porto Rico have suffered, and others been threatened with assassination for asserting their unquestionable rights even before the lawful tribunals of the country.

The usual orders have been given to all our public ships to seize American vessels engaged in the slave trade and bring them in for adjudication, and I have the gratification to state that not one so employed has been discovered, and there is good reason to believe that our flag is now seldom, if at all, disgraced by that traffic.

It is a source of great satisfaction that we are always enabled to recur to the conduct of our Navy with pride and commendation. As a means of national defense it enjoys the public confidence, and is steadily assuming additional importance. It is submitted whether a more efficient and equally economical organization of it might not in several respects be effected. It is supposed that higher grades than now exist by law would be useful. They would afford well-merited rewards to those who have long and faithfully served their country, present the best incentives to good conduct, and the best means of insuring a proper discipline; destroy the inequality in that respect between military and naval services, and relieve our officers from many inconveniences and mortifications which occur when our vessels meet those of other nations, ours being the only service in which such grades do not exist.

A report of the Postmaster-General, which accompanies this communication, will shew the present state of the Post-Office Department and its general operations for some years past.

There is established by law 88,600 miles of post-roads, on which the mail is now transported 85,700 miles, and contracts have been made for its transportation on all the established routes, with one or two exceptions. There are 5,240 post-offices in the Union, and as many postmasters. The gross amount of postage which accrued from the 1st July, 1822, to the 1st July, 1823, was $1,114,345.12. During the same period the expenditures of the Post-Office Department amounted to $1,169,885.51, and consisted of the following items, viz.: Compensation to postmasters, $353,995.98; incidental expenses, $30,866.37; transportation of the mail, $784,600.08; payments into the Treasury, $423.08. On the 1st of July last there was due to the Department from postmasters $135,245.28; from *late* postmasters and contractors, $256,749.31; making a total amount of balances due to the Department of $391,994.59. These balances embrace all delinquencies of postmasters and contractors which have taken place since the organization of the Department. There was due by the Department to contractors on the 1st of July last $26,548.64.

The transportation of the mail within five years past has been greatly extended, and the expenditures of the Department proportionably increased. Although the postage which has accrued within the last three years has fallen short of the expenditures $262,821.46, it appears that collections have been made from the outstanding balances to meet the principal part of the current demands.

It is estimated that not more than $250,000 of the above balances can be collected, and that a considerable part of this sum can only be realized by a resort to legal process. Some improvement in the receipts for postage is expected. A prompt attention to the collection of moneys received by postmasters, it is believed, will enable the department to continue its operations without aid from the Treasury, unless the expenditures shall be increased by the establishment of new mail routes.

A revision of some parts of the post-office law may be necessary; and it is submitted whether it would not be proper to provide for the appointment of postmasters, where the compensation exceeds a certain amount, by nomination to the Senate, as other officers of the General Government are appointed.

Having communicated my views to Congress at the commencement of the last session respecting the encouragement which ought to be given to our manufactures and the principle on which it should be founded, I have only to add that those views remain unchanged, and that the present state of those countries with which we have the most immediate political relations and greatest commercial intercourse tends to confirm them. Under this impression I recommend a review of the tariff for the purpose of affording such additional protection to those articles which we are prepared to manufacture, or which are more immediately connected with the defense and independence of the country.

The actual state of the public accounts furnishes additional evidence of the efficiency of the present system of accountability in relation to the public expenditure. Of the moneys drawn from the Treasury since the 4th March, 1817, the sum remaining unaccounted for on the 30th of September last is more than a million and a half of dollars less than on the 30th of September preceding; and during the same period a reduction of nearly a million of dollars has been made in the amount of the unsettled accounts for moneys advanced previously to the 4th of March, 1817. It will be obvious that in proportion as the mass of accounts of the latter description is diminished by settlement the difficulty of settling the residue is increased from the consideration that in many instances it can be obtained only by legal process. For more precise details on this subject I refer to a report from the First Comptroller of the Treasury.

The sum which was appropriated at the last session for the repairs of the Cumberland road has been applied with good effect to that object. A final report has not yet been received from the agent who was appointed to superintend it. As soon as it is received it shall be communicated to Congress.

Many patriotic and enlightened citizens who have made the subject an object of particular investigation have suggested an improvement of still greater importance. They are of opinion that the waters of the Chesapeake and Ohio may be connected together by one continued canal, and at an expense far short of the value and importance of the object to be obtained. If this could be accomplished it is impossible to calculate the beneficial consequences which would result from it. A great portion of the produce of the very fertile country through which it would pass would find a market through that channel. Troops might be moved with great facility in war, with cannon and every kind of munition, and in either direction. Connecting the Atlantic with the Western country in a line passing through the seat of the National Government, it would contribute essentially to strengthen the bond of union itself. Believing as I do that Congress possess the right to appropriate money for such a national object (the jurisdiction remaining to the States through which the canal would pass), I submit it to your consideration whether it may not be advisable to authorize by an adequate appropriation the employment of a suitable number of the officers of the Corps of Engineers to examine the unexplored ground during the next season and to report their opinion thereon. It will likewise be proper to extend their examination to the several routes through which the waters of the Ohio may be connected by canals with those of Lake Erie.

As the Cumberland road will require annual repairs, and Congress have not thought it expedient to recommend to the States an amendment to the Constitution for the purpose of vesting in the United States a power to adopt and execute a system of internal improvement, it is also submitted to your consideration whether it may not be expedient to authorize the Executive to enter into an arrangement with the several States through which the road passes to establish tolls, each within its limits, for the purpose of defraying the expense of future repairs and of providing also by suitable penalties for its protection against future injuries.

The act of Congress of the 7th of May, 1822, appropriated the sum of $22,700 for the purpose of erecting two piers as a shelter for vessels from ice near Cape Henlopen, Delaware Bay. To effect the object of the act the officers of the Board of Engineers, with Commodore Bainbridge, were directed to prepare plans and estimates of piers sufficient to answer the purpose intended by the act. It appears by their report, which accompanies the documents from the War Department, that the appropriation is not adequate to the purpose intended; and as the piers would be of great service both to the navigation of the Delaware Bay and the protection of vessels on the adjacent parts of the coast, I submit for the consideration of Congress whether additional and sufficient appropriation should not be made.

The Board of Engineers were also directed to examine and survey the entrance of the harbor of the port of Presquille, in Pennsylvania, in order to make an estimate of the expense of removing the obstructions to the entrance, with a plan of the best mode of effecting the same, under the appropriation for that purpose by act of Congress passed 3d of March last. The report of the Board accompanies the papers from the War Department, and is submitted for the consideration of Congress.

A strong hope has been long entertained, founded on the heroic struggle of the Greeks, that they would succeed in their contest and resume their equal station among the nations of the earth. It is believed that the whole civilized world take a deep interest in their welfare. Although no power has declared in their favor, yet none, according to our information, has taken part against them. Their cause and their name have protected them from dangers which might ere this have overwhelmed any other people. The ordinary calculations of interest and of acquisition with a view to aggrandizement, which mingles so much in the transactions of nations, seem to have had no effect in regard to them. From the facts which have come to our knowledge there is good cause to believe that their enemy has lost forever all dominion over them; that Greece will become again an independent nation. That she may obtain that rank is the object of our most ardent wishes.

It was stated at the commencement of the last session that a great effort was then making in Spain and Portugal to improve the condition of the people of those countries, and that it appeared to be conducted with extraordinary moderation. It need scarcely be remarked that the result has been so far very different from what was then anticipated. Of events in that quarter of the globe, with which we have so much intercourse and from which we derive our origin, we have always been anxious and interested spectators. The citizens of the United States cherish sentiments the most friendly in favor of the liberty and happiness of their fellow-men on that side of the Atlantic. In the wars of the European powers in matters relating to themselves we have never taken any part, nor does it comport with our policy so to do. It is only when our rights are invaded or seriously menacea that we resent injuries or make preparation for our defense. With the movements in this hemisphere we are of necessity more immediately connected, and by causes which must be obvious to all enlightened and impartial observers. The political system of the allied powers is essentially different in this respect from that of America. This difference proceeds from that which exists in their respective Governments; and to the defense of our own, which has been achieved by the loss of so much blood and treasure, and matured by the wisdom of their most enlightened citizens, and under which we have enjoyed unexampled felicity, this whole nation is devoted. We owe it, therefore, to candor and to the amicable relations existing between the United States and those powers to declare that we should consider any attempt on their part to extend their system to any portion of this hemisphere as dangerous to our peace and safety. With the existing colonies or dependencies of any European power we have not interfered and shall not interfere. But with the Governments who have declared their independence and maintained it, and whose independence we have, on great consideration and on just principles, acknowledged, we could not view any interposition for the purpose of oppressing them, or controlling in any other manner their destiny, by any European power in any other light than as the manifestation of an unfriendly disposition toward the United States. In the war between those new Governments and Spain we declared our neutrality at the time of their recognition, and to this we have adhered, and shall continue to adhere, provided no change shall occur which, in the judgment of the competent authorities of this Government, shall make a corresponding change on the part of the United States indispensable to their security.

The late events in Spain and Portugal shew that Europe is still unsettled. Of this important fact no stronger proof can be adduced than that the allied powers should have thought it proper, on any principle satisfactory to themselves, to have interposed by force in the internal concerns of Spain. To what extent such interposition may be carried, on the same principle, is a question in which all independent powers whose governments differ from theirs are interested, even those most remote, and surely none more so than the United States. Our policy in regard to Europe, which was adopted at an early stage of the wars which have so long agitated that quarter of the globe, nevertheless remains the same, which is, not to interfere in the internal concerns of any of its powers; to consider the government de facto as the legitimate government for us; to cultivate friendly relations with it, and to preserve those relations by a frank, firm, and manly policy, meeting in all instances the just claims of every power, submitting to injuries from none. But in regard to those continents circumstances are eminently and conspicuously different. It is impossible that the allied powers should extend their political system to any portion of either continent without endangering our peace and happiness; nor can anyone believe that our southern brethren, if left to themselves, would adopt it of their own accord. It is equally impossible, therefore, that we should behold such interposition in any form with indifference. If we look to the comparative strength and resources of Spain and those new Governments, and their distance from each other, it must be obvious that she can never subdue them. It is still the true policy of the United States to leave the parties to themselves, in the hope that other powers will pursue the same course.

If we compare the present condition of our Union with its actual state at the close of our Revolution, the history of the world furnishes no example of a progress in improvement in all the important circumstances which constitute the happiness of a nation which bears any resemblance to it. At the first epoch our population did not exceed 3,000,000. By the last census it amounted to about 10,000,000, and, what is more extraordinary, it is almost altogether native, for the immigration from other countries has been inconsiderable. At the first epoch half the territory within our acknowledged limits was uninhabited and a wilderness. Since then new territory has been acquired of vast extent, comprising within it many rivers, particularly the Mississippi, the navigation of which to the ocean was of the highest importance to the original States. Over this territory our population has expanded in every direction, and new States have been established almost equal in number to those which formed the first bond of our Union. This expansion of our population and accession of new States to our Union have had the happiest effect on all its highest interests. That it has eminently augmented our resources and added to our strength and respectability as a power is admitted by all. But it is not in these important circumstances only that this happy effect is felt. It is manifest that by enlarging the basis of our system and increasing the number of States the system itself has been greatly strengthened in both its branches. Consolidation and disunion have thereby been rendered equally impracticable. Each Government, confiding in its own strength, has less to apprehend from the other, and in consequence each, enjoying a greater freedom of action, is rendered more efficient for all the purposes for which it was instituted. It is unnecessary to treat here of the vast improvement made in the system itself by the adoption of this Constitution and of its happy effect in elevating the character and in protecting the rights of the nation as well as of individuals. To what, then, do we owe these blessings? It is known to all that we derive them from the excellence of our institutions. Ought we not, then, to adopt every measure which may be necessary to perpetuate them?

TO THOMAS JEFFERSON.
WASHINGTON, Decr. 4, 1823.

DEAR SIR,—I now forward to you a copy of the message, more legible than that which was sent by the last mail. I have concurr'd thoroughly with the sentiments express'd in your late letter, as I am persuaded you will find, by the message, as to the part we ought to act, toward the Allied powers, in regard to S^o. America. I consider the cause of that country as essentially our own. That the crisis is fully as menacing, as has been supposed, is confirm'd, by recent communications, from another quarter, with which I will make you acquainted in my next. The most unpleasant circumstance, in that communication is, that M^r. Canning's zeal, has much abated of late. Whether this proceeds from the unwillingness of his gov^t., to recognize the new gov^{ts}. or from offers made to it, by the Allied powers, to seduce it, into their scale, we know not. We shall nevertheless be on our guard against any contingency.

TO THOMAS JEFFERSON.
WASHINGTON, Dec^r.—1823.

DEAR SIR,—Shortly after the receipt of yours of the 24th. of October, & while the subject treated in it was under consideration, the Russian Minister drew the attention of the gov^t to the same subject, tho' in a very different sense from that in which it had been done by M^r. Canning. Baron Tuyll, announced in an official letter, and it was understood by order of the Emperor, that having heard that the republic of Colombia had appointed a Minister to Russia, he wished it to be distinctly understood that he would not receive him, nor would he receive any minister from any of the new gov^{ts}. de facto, of which the new world had been recently the theatre. On another occasion, he observed, that the Emperor had seen with great satisfaction, the declaration of this gov^t., when these new gov^{ts}. were recognized that it was the intention of the U States, to remain neutral. He gave this intimation, for the purpose of expressing the wish of his Master, that we would persevere in the same policy. He communicated soon afterwards, an extract of a letter from his gov^t., in which the conduct of the Allied powers, in regard to Naples, Spain, & Portugal, was reviewed, and that policy explain'd, distinctly avowing their determination, to crush all revolutionary mov'ments, & thereby to preserve order in the civilized world. The terms "civilized world" were probably intended to be applied to Europe only, but admitted an application to this hemisphere also. These communications were receiv'd as proofs of candour, & a friendly disposition to the U States, but were nevertheless answer'd, in a manner equally explicit, frank, & direct, to each point. In regard to neutrality it was observ'd, when that sentiment was declar'd, that the other powers of Europe had not taken side with Spain—that they were then neutral—if they should change their policy, the state of things on which our neutrality was declar'd, being alter'd, we would not be bound by that declaration, but might change our policy also. Informal notes, or rather a process verbal, of what pass'd in conference, to such effect, were exchang'd between M^r. Adams & the Russian Minister, with an understanding however that they should be held confidential.

When the character of these communications, of that from M^r. Canning, & that from the Russian minister, is consider'd, & the time when made, it leaves little doubt that some project against the new gov^{ts}., is contemplated. In what form is uncertain. It is hoped that the sentiments express'd in the message, will give a check to it. We certainly meet, in full extent, the proposition of M^r. Canning, & in the mode to give it the greatest effect. If his gov^t. makes a similar decl^n. the project will, it may be presumed, be abandoned. By taking the step here, it is done in a manner more conciliatory with, & respectful to Russia, & the other powers, than if taken in England, and as it is thought with more credit to our gov^t. Had we mov'd in the first instance in England, separated as she is in part, from those powers, our union with her, being masked, might have produc'd irritation, with them. We know that Russia dreads a connection between the U States & G. Britain, or harmony in policy moving on our own ground, the apprehension that unless she retreats, that effect may be produc'd, may be a motive with her for retreating. Had we mov'd in England, it is probable, that it would have been inferr'd that we acted under her influence, & at her instigation, & thus have lost credit as well with our Southern neighbours, as with the Allied powers.

There is some danger that the British gov^t., when it sees the part we have taken, may endeavour to throw the whole burden on us, and profit, in case of such interposition of the allied powers, of her neutrality, at our expense, but I think that this would be impossible after what has pass'd on the subject; besides it does not follow, from what has been said, that we should be bound to engage in the war, in such event. Of this intimations may be given, should it be necessary. A messenger will depart for Eng^ld. with despatches for Mr. Rush in a few days, who will go on to S^t. Petersbg. with others to Mr. Middleton. And considering the crisis, it has occurr'd, that a special mission, of the first consideration from the country, directed to Eng^ld. in the first instance, with power, to attend, any Congress, that may be conven'd, on the affrs. of S°. Am: or Mexico, might have the happiest effect. You shall hear from me further on this subject.

FROM MADISON TO MONROE: [December 1823] "Yours of the 20th was duly received. The external affairs of our country are I perceive assuming a character more & more delicate and important. The ground on which the Russian communications were met was certainly well chosen. It is evident that an alienation is going on between G. Britain & the ruling powers on the Continent & that the former is turning her views to such a connection with this side of the Atlantic as may replace her loss of political weight & commercial prospects on the other. This revolution was indicated by the coaxing speech of Canning at the Liverpool dinner; and is fully displayed by his project for introducing the United States to a Congress on the Continent. Whilst the English Gov^t. very naturally endeavors to make us useful to her national objects, it is incumbent on us to turn, as far as we fairly can, the friendly consultations with her, to ours; which besides being national, embrace the good of mankind everywhere. It seems particularly our duty not to let that nation usurp a meritorious lead in any measures due to our South American neighbors; one obstacle to which was aptly furnished by Mr. Rush in his proposal to Mr. Canning that their independence should be forthwith acknowledged. Nor ought we to be less careful in guarding against an appearance in the eyes of Europe, at which the self-love of G. Britain may aim, of our being a satellite of her primary greatness. This last consideration will of course be felt in the management of the invitation which Mr. Canning is inviting for us in the expected Congress. A participation in it would not be likely to make converts to our principles; whilst our admission under the wing of England would take from our consequence what it would add to hers. Such an invitation nevertheless will be a mark of respect not without a value & this will be more enhanced by a polite refusal, than by an acceptance; not to mention that the acceptance would be a step leading into a wilderness of politics & a Den of Conspirators.

"Whether any of these hasty ideas ought to be changed by a further acquaintance with existing circumstances, or under the influence of others now in embryo only, you can better judge than myself.

"If there be no error in the account of the French reception given to the notification of the British Ambassador at Paris, it would almost justify a suspicion of some original understanding that if the British Government would not interfere against the French invasion of Spain, the French would not thwart the policy of G. B. with regard to South America. Or, must we suppose that France with the Great Powers at her back is ready to defy the united strength of Great Britain & America? She would not surely flatter herself with the hope of reconciling them to the scheme of fixing anew the Spanish Yoke on those who have thrown it off. Events may soon unravel these and other mysteries."

HENRY CLAY AS SECRETARY OF STATE TO JOEL R. POINSETT (Commissioned Envoy Extraordinary and Minister Plenipotentiary to Mexico, March 8, 1825), in his Instructions dated March 26, 1825: "You will bring to the notice of the Mexican government the Message of the President of the United States to their Congress, on the 2nd December 1823, asserting certain important principles of intercontinental law in the relations of Europe and America. The first principle asserted in that message is that the American continents are not henceforth to be considered as subjects for future colonization by any European powers. In the maintenance of that principle all the independent governments of America have an interest, but that of the United States has probably the least. Whatever foundation may have existed three centuries ago, or even at a later period, when all this continent was under European subjection, for the establishment of a rule, founded on priority of discovery and occupation, for apportioning among the powers of Europe parts of this Continent, none can be now admitted as applicable to its present condition. There is no disposition to disturb the colonial possessions, as they may now exist, of any of the European powers, but it is against the establishment of new European colonies upon this Continent that the principle is directed. The countries in which any such new establishments might be attempted are now open to the enterprise and commerce of all Americans; and the justice, or propriety, cannot be recognized of arbitrarily limiting and circumscribing that enterprise and commerce by the act of voluntarily planting a new

Colony, without the consent of America, under the auspices of foreign powers belonging to another, and a distant continent. Europe would be indignant at any American attempt to plant a colony on any part of her shores; and her justice must perceive, in the rule contended for, only perfect reciprocity.

"The other principle asserted in the Message is that, whilst we do not desire to interfere in Europe, with the political system of the allied powers, we should regard as dangerous to our peace and safety any attempt on their part to extend their system to any portion of this Hemisphere. The political systems of the two Continents are essentially different. Each has an exclusive right to judge for itself what is best suited to its own condition, and most likely to promote its happiness, but neither has a right to enforce upon the other the establishment of its peculiar system. This principle was declared in the face of the world at a moment when there was reason to apprehend that the allied powers were entertaining designs inimical to the freedom, if not the independence, of the new governments. There is ground for believing that the declaration of it had considerable effect in preventing the maturity, if not in producing the abandonment, of all such designs. Both principles were laid down after much and anxious deliberation on the part of the late Administration. The President, who then formed a part of it, continues entirely to coincide in both. And you will urge upon the government of Mexico the utility and expediency of asserting the same principles on all proper occasions."

DANIEL WEBSTER, Speech on "The Panama Mission" delivered in the House of Representatives of the United States on the 14th of April, 1826.

"I must now ask the indulgence of the committee to an important point in the discussion, I mean the declaration of the President in 1823. Not only as a member of the House, but as a citizen of the country, I have an anxious desire that this part of our public history should stand in its proper light. The country has, in my judgment, a very high honor connected with that occurrence, which we may maintain, or which we may sacrifice. I look upon it as a part of its treasures of reputation, and, for one, I intend to guard it. Sir, let us recur to the important political events which led to that declaration, or accompanied it. In the fall of 1822, the Allied Sovereigns held their congress at Verona. The great subject of consideration was the condition of Spain, that country being then under the government of the Cortes. The question was, whether Ferdinand should be reinstated in all his authority, by the intervention of foreign force. Russia, Prussia, France and Austria were inclined to that measure; England dissented and protested; but the course was agreed on, and France, with the consent of those other Continental powers, took the conduct of the operation into her own hands. In the spring of

1823, a French army was sent into Spain. Its success was complete. The popular government was overthrown, and Ferdinand re-established in all his power. This invasion, Sir, was determined on, and undertaken, precisely on the doctrines which the allied monarchs had proclaimed the year before, at Laybach; that is, that they had a right to interfere in the concerns of another State, and reform its government, in order to prevent the effects of its bad example; this bad example, be it remembered, always being the example of free government. Now, Sir, acting on this principle of supposed dangerous example, and having put down the example of the Cortes in Spain, it was natural to inquire with what eyes they would look on the colonies of Spain, that were following still worse examples. Would King Ferdinand and his allies be content with what had been done in Spain itself, or would he solicit their aid, and was it likely they would grant it, to subdue his rebellious American provinces?

"Sir, it was in this posture of affairs, on an occasion which has already been alluded to, that I ventured to say, early in the session of December, 1823, that these allied monarchs might possibly turn their attention to America; that America came within their avowed doctrine, and that her examples might very possibly attract their notice. The doctrines of Laybach were not limited to any continent. Spain had colonies in America, and, having reformed Spain herself to the true standard, it was not impossible that they might see fit to complete the work by reconciling, in their way, the colonies to the mother country. Now, sir, it did so happen, that, as soon as the Spanish King was completely reestablished, he invited the co-operation of his Allies in regard to South America. In the same month of December, of 1823, a formal invitation was addressed by Spain to the courts of St. Petersburg, Vienna, Berlin, and Paris, proposing to establish a conference at Paris, in order that the plenipotentiaries there assembled might aid Spain, in adjusting the affairs of her revolted provinces. These affairs were proposed to be adjusted in such manner as should retain the sovereignty of Spain over them; and though the co-operation of the Allies by force of arms was not directly solicited, such was evidently the object aimed at. The King of Spain, in making this request to the members of the Holy Alliance, argued as it has been seen he might argue. He quoted their own doctrines of Laybach; he pointed out the pernicious example of America; and he reminded them that their success in Spain itself had paved the way for successful operations against the spirit of liberty on this side of the Atlantic.

"The proposed meeting, however, did not take place. England had already taken a decided course; for as early as October, Mr. Canning, in a conference with the French minister in London, informed him distinctly and expressly, that

England would consider any foreign interference, by force or by menace, in the dispute between Spain and the colonies, as a motive for recognizing the latter without delay. It is probable this determination by the English government was known here at the commencement of the session of Congress; and it was under these circumstances, it was in this crisis, that Mr. Monroe's declaration was made. It was not then ascertained whether a meeting of the Allies would or would not take place, to concert with Spain the means of reestablishing her power; but it was plain enough they would be pressed by Spain to aid her operations; and it was plain, also, that they had no particular liking to what was taking place on this side of the Atlantic, nor any great disinclination to interfere. This was the posture of affairs, and, Sir, I concur entirely in the sentiment expressed in the resolution of a gentleman from Pennsylvania, that this declaration of Mr. Monroe was wise, seasonable, and patriotic.

"It has been said, in the course of this debate, to have been a loose and vague declaration. It was, I believe, sufficiently studied. I have understood, from good authority, that it was considered, weighed, and distinctly, and decidedly approved, by every one of the President's advisers at that time. Our government could not adopt on that occasion precisely the course which England had taken. England threatened the immediate recognition of the provinces, if the Allies should take part with Spain against them. We had already recognized them. It remained, therefore, only for our government to say how we should consider a combination of the Allied Powers, to effect objects in America, as affecting ourselves, and the message was intended to say what it does say, that we should regard such combination as dangerous to us. Sir, I agree with those who maintain the proposition, and I contend against those who deny it, that the message did mean something; that it meant much; and I maintain, against both, that the declaration effected much good, answered the end designed by it, did great honor to the foresight and the spirit of the government, and that it cannot now be taken back, retracted, or annulled, without disgrace. It met, Sir, with the entire concurrence and the hearty approbation of the country. The tone which it uttered found a corresponding response in the breasts of the free people of the United States. That people saw, and they rejoiced to see, that, on a fit occasion, our weight had been thrown into the right scale, and that, without departing from our duty, we had done something useful, and something effectual, for the cause of civil liberty. One general glow of exaltation, one universal feeling of the gratified love of liberty, one conscious and proud perception of the consideration which the country possessed, and of the respect and honor which belonged to it, pervaded all bosoms. Possibly the public enthusiasm went too far; it certainly did go far. But, Sir, the sentiment which this declaration inspired was not confined to ourselves. Its force was felt everywhere, by all those who could understand its object and foresee its effect. In that very House of Commons of which the gentleman from South Carolina has spoken with such commendation, how was it received? Not only, Sir, with approbation, but, I may say, with no little enthusiasm. While the leading minister expressed his entire concurrence in the sentiments and opinions of the American President, his distinguished competitor in that popular body, less restrained by official decorum, and more at liberty to give utterance to all the feeling of the occasion, declared that no event ever created greater joy, exultation, and gratitude among all the free men in Europe; that he felt pride in being connected by blood and language with the people of the United States; that the policy disclosed by the message became a great, a free, and an independent nation; and that he hoped his own country would be prevented by no mean pride, or paltry jealousy, from following so noble and glorious an example.

"It is doubtless true, as I took occasion to observe the other day, that this declaration must be considered as founded on our rights, and to spring mainly from a regard to their preservation. It did not commit us, at all events, to take up arms on any indication of hostile feeling by the powers of Europe towards South America. If, for example, all the States of Europe had refused to trade with South America until her States should return to their former allegiance, that would have furnished no cause of interference to us. Or if an armament had been furnished by the Allies to act against provinces the most remote from us, as Chili and Buenos Ayres, the distance of the scene of action diminishing our apprehension of danger, and diminishing also our means of effectual interposition, might still have left us to content ourselves with remonstrance. But a very different case would have arisen, if an army, equipped and maintained by these powers, had been landed on the shores of the Gulf of Mexico, and commenced the war in our own immediate neighborhood.

"Such an event might justly be regarded as dangerous to ourselves, and, on that ground, call for decided and immediate interference by us. The sentiments and policy announced by the declaration, thus understood, were, therefore, in strict conformity to our duties and our interest.

"Sir, I look on the Message of December, 1823, as forming a bright page in our history. I will help neither to erase it, nor tear it out; nor shall it be, by any act of mine, blurred or blotted. It did honor to the sagacity of the government, and I will not diminish that honor. It elevated the hopes, and gratified the patriotism, of the people. Over those hopes I will not bring a mildew; nor will I put that gratified patriotism to shame."

PART XI

The Final Months

INTRODUCTION

MONROE RETIRED to Oak Hill in 1824. But if he had hoped to look forward to a period of golden contentment, he was mistaken. What he found instead was the crushing burden of debt that he had undertaken for the service of his country. In the old days, Virginia gentlemen had expected to have a decent income from their property, and a spectacular one if the property were well managed. Neither was true in Monroe's case.

Although he frequently expressed his interest in living upon his estates to manage them carefully, or paying careful attention to the practice of law, his income was never sufficient to meet his obligations. What with wars, embargoes, financial panics, bank failures, and the general unavailability of sound currency, the dream of a financial competency eluded him. Moreover, during his frequent absences in public service—to Congress, to the General Assembly, to the Senate, to the governorship, to his extended time abroad—he had to depend upon incompetent overseers who could not manage the planting or the property. In his first mission abroad he was gone three years; in his second, five years, both times leaving on a few day's notice without properly preparing his own affairs.

Then as now, travelling abroad was expensive. The legislative representatives of a simple society did not understand the problems faced by an ambassador—the cost of decent transportation by ship; the high prices for food in France where scarcity reigned and no conveyance was available; the hyperinflation; the need to entertain members of the National Assembly; sums that had to be advanced to Americans in distress; the three or four clerks that had to be hired and fed to take care of the business papers of diplomacy. Nor was it better in England, where the smoke of London was making Mrs. Monroe ill, and she had to be moved to the country, and where to appear at court one had to wear very expensive court costumes of little use anywhere else. Monroe willingly expended his capital for these purposes because he thought it was for the good of the country.

When Monroe returned, he was under strong political attack. Congress refused to reimburse him for his expenses. In vain did he invite full Congressional scrutiny, itemize every penny with receipts and affidavits. He pointed out that he was sent not to one country, but three, and had been paid salary and transportation only for one. The controversy dragged on through Congress after Congress. Yet during the War of 1812, with the U.S. Treasury empty, and the armies of Jackson in need of funds, he pledged his private credit to raise the funds for the war—and never even recovered the interest he had paid to make that possible.

His Kentucky lands were put up first, but no buyer could be found. Then came the tract near Monticello which was sold in distress while he was away for a fraction of its value, and finally became the campus of the University of Virginia. Then it was time for Ashlawn-Highland, and the wait for a reasonable offer in the depressed real estate market, with the bank holding the mortgage simply taking over the property in 1827. In the last months of his life, his beloved Elizabeth gone, his health broken, even Oak Hill was put on the market, without a buyer. Just weeks before he died, Congress did come to his aid with a sum of about half what was actually owed for his expenses on behalf of the country. But it was too late. On a visit to his daughter in New York City, he took to his bed and died without seeing Oak Hill again.

In 1824 and 1825 he was preoccupied with gathering the evidence for the sums that were owed to him. He wrote to both Jefferson and Madison in December 1824 requesting specific information to back up his claims. He wrote to Congress in January 1825 requesting a Congressional investigation of his accounts, confident that all would be approved. He writes again and again to Jefferson and Madison, to General Dearborn, to Judge Brooke. In 1826, in the midst of his own distress, he is shocked to hear that Jefferson must sell Monticello. In 1827, after making a trip to transfer the deed to his Kentucky lands to the bank in a foreclosure, he fell from his horse, and was in bed for many weeks.

In the midst of this, another controversy developed. Did he or did he not order Jackson to invade Florida? It was a question all mixed up with Jackson's political ambitions for the presidential campaign, so there could be no objective discussion on the matter. Partisans from both sides lept into the fray. Monroe is forced to write to eyewitnesses of the events, such as John Quincy Adams, to get their statements of exoneration. John C. Calhoun criticises him. He is forced to write to his accusers time and time again to get the matter straight. It is a sad correspondence. He even has to write to Joseph Bonaparte, the exiled brother of the Emperor, affirming that he, Monroe, received no compensation from the Louisiana Purchase.

Sometime in 1831, an undated letter to the Governor of Virginia stated: "My reduced and weak state of health, having rendered it impossible for me to perform any publick duties, imposes on me the necessity of resigning my appointment as a visitor to the University of Virginia." On March 11, he writes to John Quincy Adams: "My very low state of health has rendered it impossible for me to give an earlier answer to your letter." On March 18, He writes to Dr. Charles Everett from New York: "My own health continues to be very infirm & weak. Little change has taken place in it since I came here. I have in consequence, yielded to the wishes of my daughters to remain with them, & the connection generally; to accomplish which object, with any degree of comfort, I am compelled to sell my estate in Loudoun, which is advertised, in the gazettes of Washington & Richmond for sale on the second Wednesday of June next. . . . I am free from pain, but my cough annoys me much, both night and day." On April 11, he wrote his last letter to Madison:

> My ill state of health continuing, consisting of a cough, which annoys me by night and by day. . . . In such a state I could not reside on my farm. The solitude would be very distressing, and its cares very buthensome. . . . The accounting officers have made no decision in my claims, & have given me much trouble. . . . I have told them that I would make out no account adapted to the act, which fell far short of making me a just reparation, and that I had rather lose the whole sum than give to it any sanction. . . . It is very distressing to me to sell my property in Loudoun, for besides parting with all I have in the State, I indulged a hope, if I could retain it, that I might be able occasionally to visit, and meet my friends, or many of them there. But ill health & advanced years prescribe a course which we must pursue. I deeply regret that there is no prospect of our ever meeting again, since so long have we been connected and in the most friendly intercourse, in public & private life, that a final separation is among the most distressing incidents which could occur.

On June 19, Monroe dictated his last public statement, a denunciation of a certain John Rhea, the man who insinuated that Monroe had told him indirectly to suggest to Jackson the invasion of Florida. "It is utterly unfounded & untrue that I ever authorized John Rhea to write any letter whatsoever to Genl. Jackson, authorizing or encouraging him to disobey, or deviate from the orders which had been communicated to him from the Department of War." It was his final act of vindication.

GEORGE WASHINGTON DIED ON DECEMBER 14, 1799.
JOHN ADAMS AND THOMAS JEFFERSON EACH DIED ON JULY 4, 1826.
JAMES MONROE DIED ON JULY 4, 1831.
JAMES MADISON DIED ON JUNE 28, 1836, SIX DAYS SHORT OF THE 60TH
ANNIVERSARY OF THE REPUBLIC.

TO THOMAS JEFFERSON.
WASHINGTON, Decr. 11, 1824.

DEAR SIR,—I sent you the other day a copy of the message as first printed, & with errors in it. I now enclose a copy which is I presume correct. I send also a copy of the documents relating to the negotiations with the British gov^t. for the suppression of the slave trade.

In the settlements of the accounts of both my missions to Europe, that commencing in 1794 under Genl. Washington, and that of 1803 under you, I have thought that injustice was done me. A more serious injury has been attempted in the two last sessions of Congress, in an apparently organized form, it being in that of a committee in each Session. The period of my retirement approaching, I intend to invite the attention of Congress to both subjects, that I may place both in the light in which they ought to stand, and to protect myself in the latter from malignant aspersions after my departure. It would be gratifying to me to be permitted by you to show to the Committee to whom the subject will probably be referred the first paragraph of your letter of the 13th of January, 1803, announcing to me my appointment, or such parts of it as you may think proper. No copy would be given, and the sole object, in addition to the evidence it affords of your good opinion, would be to shew the haste with which I hurried from home, & from the country, leaving my private concerns, in consequence, unsettled. I need not add of you and Mr. Madison, in the settlement of the acc^t. for the latter mission, I have no complaint, as will be distinctly stated.

At this time I am much pressed or should say something on the subject of internal improv'ment, explanatory of the principles on which I have acted, tho' I can add but little to what is stated in a former message to Congress on the subject. Should I say anything hereafter it will be explanatory only, and to which I shall wish no reply. I hope that your health is perfectly restored.

TO JAMES MADISON.
WASHINGTON, Decr. 13, 1824.

DEAR SIR,—I send you herewith a more correct copy of the message than that which I lately forwarded, & to which I add a copy of the documents relating to the negotiations with the British gov^t. for the suppression of the slave trade.

You may recollect that one of the items in my acc^t. for compensation in my last mission to Europe, the 8th, involving the expenses incurred in England after my return from Spain, by various causes, and particularly the special mission in which I was associated with Mr. Pinkney, was suspended by your order for further consideration when the acc^t. was settled. In that state it has remain'd since. I came into the Dep^t. of State soon afterwards, and in consequence deemed it improper ever to mention the subject while you remain'd in office, or to touch it after your retirement. There are other items in that acc^t. the settlement of which I have always thought required revision. For example I was not allowed an outfit, in the mission to France, when I left the country, nor till after my return years afterwards. In my absence my tract of land above Charlottesville, of 950 acres, was sold, to pay neighborhood debts, which, if the outfit had been allowed me, might have been avoided. On a revision of the subject you, on your own responsibility, kindly allowed me the outfit. All other ministers were allowed outfits. Interest on the delay appears to be a fair claim, & from that time. There are other items in that mission which may merit notice. In the settlement of the acc^t. for the first mission I was very seriously injured, as I think may be shewn. It is my intention to bring the subject before Congress, with a view to give the explanations necessary before my retirement, & to leave them to be recurr'd to, at another Session, when decided on. I have another, & much stronger motive for inviting the attention of Congress to a concern relating to myself. An attempt has been made to injure me in another form, with which, as it has been treated on in Congress, you are, I presume, somewhat acquainted. I cannot withdraw and leave this unnoticed. I intend to bring both subjects under consideration, with a view to do myself justice, and to protect myself, after I am gone, from malignant aspersion. The attempt referr'd to was made in the last two Sessions, by a committee in each, or rather under the sanction of such an appointment, & who pursued the object with great industry & system, as well as malignity.

The reception of General La Fayette by Congress has corresponded with that given him by the people throughout the Union, and will, I doubt not, have a very happy effect in Europe, as well as in the U States.

TO CONGRESS, REQUESTING AN INVESTIGATION OF HIS ACCOUNTS.
WASHINGTON, January 5, 1825.

To the Senate and House of Representatives of the United States:

As the term of my service in this high trust will expire at the end of the present session of Congress, I think it proper to invite your attention to an object very interesting to me, and which in the movement of our Government is deemed on principle equally interesting to the public. I have been long in the service of my country and in its most difficult conjunctures, as well abroad as at home, in the course of which I have had, a control over the public moneys to a vast amount. If in the course of my service it shall appear on the most severe scrutiny, which I invite, that the public have sustained any loss by any act of mine, or of others for which I ought to be held responsible, I am willing to bear it. If, on the other hand, it shall appear on a view of the law and of precedents in other cases that justice has been withheld from me in any instance, as I have believed it to be in many, and greatly to my injury, it is submitted whether it ought not to be rendered. It is my wish that all matters of account and claim between my country and myself be settled with that strict regard to justice which is observed in settlements between individuals in private life. It would be gratifying to me, and it appears to be just, that the subject should be now examined in both respects with a view to a decision hereafter. No bill would, it is presumed, be presented for my signature which would operate either for or against me, and I would certainly sanction none in my favor. While here I can furnish testimony, applicable to any case, in both views, which a full investigation may require, and the committee to whom the subject may be referred, by reporting facts now with a view to a decision after my retirement, will allow time for further information and due consideration of all matters relating thereto. Settlements with a person in this trust, which could not be made with the accounting officers of the Government, should always be made by Congress and before the public. The cause of the delay in presenting these claims will be explained to the committee to whom the subject may be referred. It will, I presume, be made apparent that it was inevitable; that from the peculiar circumstances attending each case Congress alone could decide on it, and that from considerations of delicacy it would have been highly improper for me to have sought it from Congress at an earlier period than that which is now proposed—the expiration of my term in this high trust.

Other considerations appear to me to operate with great force in favor of the measure which I now propose. A citizen who has long served his country in its highest trusts has a right, if he has served with fidelity, to enjoy undisturbed tranquillity and peace in his retirement. This he can not expect to do unless his conduct in all pecuniary concerns shall be placed by severe scrutiny on a basis not to be shaken. This, therefore, forms a strong motive with me for the inquiry which I now invite. The public may also derive considerable advantage from the precedent in the future movement of the Government. It being known that such scrutiny was made in my case, it may form a new and strong barrier against the abuse of the public confidence in future.

TO JUDGE MARSHALL.
WASHINGTON, March 10, 1825.

DEAR SIR,—I have received with great interest your letter of the 7th. with the Vol: of your history of our Colonial state, which I shall retain as a testimonial of your regard.

The favorable opinion which you have expressed of my conduct, in discharge of the arduous duties of the very important office from which I have just retired, affords me the highest gratification. We began our career together in early youth, and the whole course of my public conduct has been under your observation. Your approbation therefore of my administration of the affairs of our country deserves to be held, & will be held by me in the highest estimation. For your own welfare & happiness be assured of my best wishes.

TO GENERAL JACKSON.
OAKHILL, LOUDON, July 3, 1825.

DEAR SIR,—Although you are entitled to a copy of the report of the Committee on my message to Congress at the last Session on my private concerns, with the documents connected with it, yet, as it is possible that you may not have received it, I take the liberty to send you one here. I am very anxious that the subject should be well understood in all its parts, and especially by those for whose good opinion I entertain the highest respect. The first part will of course be examined by reference to the rule which was established and observed in regard to others. It fell to my lot to suffer under the decision of one party when the contest was at the highest between them, and of the other when the sentiment in favor of economy had its greatest force. There never was a time that I could expect, or ask an important decision on the subject, until that of which I avail'd myself. I wish, as I have stated, nothing but justice, and shall never touch the subject again, if every claim is rejected. The second part is that respecting which I have most feeling. After 42 years of public service, in the most trying & difficult conjunctures of our country, & in stations, in most instances, of the highest responsibility, to be exposed to such an attack as that which these papers shew, was undoubtedly the most mortifying incident of my whole life. Had I been disposed to take advantage of my country a thousand opportunities had before presented themselves, in which I might have made an immense profit, & escaped detection. These opportunities existed abroad, as well as at home, & especially in the late war, when I was compelled, at the most difficult period, to take the affairs of the Treasury, as well as of the Departments of War & State, under my care. I speak of facts which are known, & cannot be disputed. Did I look to myself at that time at the expense of the public, or at any other time? To have become the object of a malignant & systematic persecution in the two preceding Sessions, under circumstances which I could not notice sooner than I did, excited equally my mortification & indignation. Was I compelled to use my furniture, and if I was, to what purpose did I apply the money receiv'd for it? and how does the business now stand? Is not everything in the hands & under control of the government, and was it not so from the beginning? Were the letters written at the time the transaction occur'd, and with honest intentions, and a generous confidence in the government, or since, after this scrutiny was set on foot, and for the purposes of fraud & deception? By those visits of our maritime & inland frontiers, and the establishment I was forced to keep up in the house whenever absent, while there were so many workmen employ'd about it, I am satisfied that I expended a sum which would have relieved me from all my difficulties had I so employed it. But pecuniary concerns I never regarded, and indeed I now feel that I have regarded too little the just claims of my family. It is to character that I look, and in doing that I only seek justice. In sending you these documents I have been led, in the spirit which has hitherto existed between us, to enter more into this subject than I usually do. You will excuse me for it.

I hope that you and Mrs. Jackson arrived in good health at home, and that you both still enjoy it. Mrs. Monroe left me some weeks since for N. York, on a visit to our youngest daughter, where she now is, but we expect her back soon, that is, in a month. Her health has been much improved by the journey. We hope that as you return to Congress you and your Lady will come by, & stay some days with us. It will afford us great pleasure. Mr. & Mrs. Hay are with us, who desire their best respects to you both.

With great respect & sincere regard I am, dear Sir, yours.

TO JUDGE McLEAN.
OAK HILL, August 7, 1825.

DEAR SIR,—I had the pleasure to receive your letter of the 2nd inst. some days since, and was much gratified to hear that Major Lee was willing, and had decided to recur to all the necessary documents, to enable him to render justice, in the interesting occurences which took place between Genl. Jackson and me, during my service in the Administration. Strict justice is all that I desire, and which may be rendered, without detracting in the slightest degree from his merit.

To accomplish this all that will be necessary will be to give to well authenticated facts their due weight. To misrepresent them, which might be innocently done if not known, and the proof not seen, would not be right, nor for the interest of either party. That this proof has not been published heretofore, considering the call for it, has proceeded from causes which may be readily conceived. They certainly indicate no unkind feeling to Genl. Jackson, nor any ardent desire, knowing the ground on which I stood, to rescue my own fame from misconception, and misrepresentation. To make you thoroughly acquainted with what has passed between Major Lee & me, on this subject, I send you a copy of two letters to him; the first of which was written at New York, and the second on my return here, which you will be so kind as to return me at your leisure.

Knowing the jealousy with which every movement is watched, at this time, by the contending parties on each side, great care must be taken in making Major Lee acquainted with the facts and documents, a knowledge of which it is his desire to obtain, as to the manner by which it shall be done. If he comes here very improper inferences might, and probably would be drawn from it. It will, I am persuaded, be most advisable for me to deposit with some very confidential friend, in this city, all these papers; and for him to show them to him at moments of leisure. Will it be convenient for you to render me this service? Mr. G. Graham will, I am satisfied, aid you in it, should any aid be necessary.

Very sincerely your friend.

P.S. With respect to my claims, the sentiment which you express, in regard to my further agency concerning them, has my entire concurrence. My land and slaves have all been sold in Albemarle, as has been the tract of 20,000 acres in Clay county, Kentucky, in satisfaction of debts contracted in the public service, and large balances are still due. But I have no thought of taking any steps which might degrade the character of my country, arising from the trusts with which I have been honored, or be inconsistent with the well vouched incidents of my past life.

TO H. U. ADDINGTON
September 7 (?) 1825

Henry Unwin Addington, Secretary of Legation, acted as British Chargé d'Affaires ad interim from August 9, 1823, the date of Sir Stratford Canning's departure, to August 20, 1825. [HAMILTON.]

I have just had the pleasure, on my return from Albemarle, to receive your letter of the 7th instant, which I hasten to answer in the hope that you will receive it before you leave the country.

The very kind and friendly sentiments which you have expressed in favor of my public conduct have excited in a high degree my sensibility. The impression is the stronger because I know that they are sincere. It has been my fortune, in a long course of public service, to have been thrown into different countries, & to have resided many years in yours in the discharge of important duties. I left it with sentiments and feelings the most favorable to many with whom I had official relation, & many others in private life—Sentiments and feelings which I have never ceas'd to entertain. May I ask the kindness of you to intimate this on my part to your uncle L^d. Sidmouth, to Lord Holland, & to Mr. Canning. Should you be in Washington, and have time to pass a few days with me, it will afford me great satisfaction. Wher'ever you may be, I beg you to be assured that your conduct and character in the discharge of your duties have commanded my high respect, & that you will carry with you my best wishes for your future welfare.

TO THOMAS JEFFERSON.
Jany. 15, 1826.

DEAR SIR,—The communication which you made to me when last at your house, of the correspondence between you & M^r. Giles, in reference to a communication made to you by Mr. Adams, pending the embargo, of certain combinations which menac'd the Union, & produc'd its repeal, has engaged my attention since, as far as the urgent business in which I have been engag'd would permit. I have reflected more on it, since, that business was concluded, and now on the road, take the liberty to drop you a few lines on it.

My opinion is that M^r. Giles in himself, may write what he pleases, & do no harm. My fear is, that if your name is connected, with that very important occurrence, by any act of your own, and especially, by a correspondence with him, that it will become the cause of great inquietude to you, and do a public injury. It will in the first instance connect you, with whatever he may do hereafter, that is with his writings, and his whole career, for it may, & probably will be inferr'd, that you would not have sanction'd that publication by a disclosure of all the facts connected with it, without approving the use to be made of it.

Whether the communication made to you, by M^r. Adams, was of a confidential nature, is a point, which you have no doubt, fully weighed, & on which I shall, in its relation to Mr. Adams, say nothing. In other views, however, the disclosure is important, to yourself, as well as to the public. The disclosure by you, of a fact, which forc'd the gov^t., from its ground, to save the Union, is of the most serious import. The fact was never known before, and would not be believ'd, if not vouched by you. What the effect may be, on the State of the Union, at this time, I know not, for I have not had time, to trace it, in all its bearings, in the present divisions, with which it is agitated, and which, altho' very much of a personal nature, may under certain excit'ments lead to great results. I suggest for your consideration.

I Write you this in haste, and in profound confidence, and from the motives stated, a regard for the public welfare, and for your happiness, being very sincerely, etc.

The object of this is to bring the subject under your consideration, in the light suggested, that you may, if in your power, controul it, should you deem it proper.

TO GENERAL DEARBORN.
OAK HILL, Jany. 30, 1826.

DEAR SIR,—I have just had the pleasure to receive yours of the 27th. by which I learn, that the committee have called on the Secry. of State for information whether, my detention in Engld. 2 years and 4 months, after my, return from Spain was voluntary or not. On this point, there can be no question, because it was stated, in the observations which I presented to the Dept. in 1810, when my acct. was settled, and not controverted. Had it not been admitted, the item wod. I presume, have been decided on then. But there are many documents in the Dept. of State which are conclusive on the subject. A letter to the Secry. of State, of Octr. 18, 1805.—to Ld. Mulgrave of the 10th same month, to the Secry. of State of Novr. 11th. of Jany. 28th. 1806 & Sepr 13th and also my letter from Richmond, Feby 28th. 1808, after my return.—I have written to Mr. Gouverneur, in the expectation that he will be with you, by the time this reaches you, or in a day or two afterward, and given him a memo. of these letters, and have also enclosed to him a paper, in a letter, endorsed as heretofore, to Mr. Graham, open, for his and your inspection, which contains a review of every item of my claims, with a view to repell such objections to them as have come to my knowledge, without noticing the quarter from whence they come. In this paper, I have dwelt particularly on the claim to interest, on the outfit which was withheld, on my last mission to Fe. & interest in the aggregate, from the time it was allowed to the present time, and also on the 8th item, in the acct. presented in 1810, for extra expenses, incurred in Engld. on my return from Spain. The paper is concise, but still it sheds new lights on the subject.

I have added two separate sheets, or rather parts of sheets, on the subject of the documents, sent down long since, to Mr. Gouverneur, and which I presume, you have seen, in the hands of Mr. Graham, relating to the cause, or rather suspicion, which induc'd my recall from the first mission, and also to the house. If it is deem'd proper to present the other parts of the paper, these may be included with it, or not, as may be judged expedient. I wish you to read the paper, including those two sheets, immediately, so as to decide, with Mr. Gouverneur, if arriv'd, or as soon as he does, & Mr. Graham, whether any or the whole shall be presented to the committee. The paper is written with care, and in a manner to throw light on the claims, and in the latter parts, to wound the feelings of no one, while it may, as I presume, promote the general object. I speak of Genl. W. as I have always felt and thought, when under no excitement, and in a way rather to heal wounds than to open them.

My impression has been, that as the question of character is involved, in the whole proceeding, the more my conduct is sifted into and explain'd, in every instance in which it has been at any time attacked, the better. But this I leave to you & the other friends, including Mr. Taliafero, of the House, of which I beg you to apprize him, for his family in all its branches & himself, have always been among my best friends.

In the course of political events, taking the whole range of our aff^{rs}. into view, from an early period, I have stood, on many points of policy, essentially on my own & distinct ground. If it has been a sound basis, the more the development suggested is made, the better the effect will be. If I am properly sustaind, my views of policy will have more weight, and with that view, the more every thing connected with character, is brought fully before the public, the greater support will be given to them.

If Mr. Gouverneur does not come, in a day or two after you receive this, I wish whatever it is deemed proper to communicate to the committee, to be communicated to it. I wish you therefore, to read the paper in Mr. Graham's possession, with him immediately. Mr. Clay should be apprized of the references to letters in his Dep^t. on the subject referr'd to him, as should Mr. Ingham immediately.

I Write you in great haste, am
dear sir, your friend.

TO THOMAS JEFFERSON.
OAKHILL, Feby. 13, 1826.

DEAR SIR,—It was my intention, as it was my desire, to have communicated to the Committee no part of your letter of the 13th. of Jany. 1803., Announcing my appointment, to France & Spain, and on that principle I acted, at the last Session. From this however, I have been induced to depart reluctantly, by intimations which have been recently given me, by some friends in Washington, that no evidence being shewn, of any particular solicitude, on your part, for my acceptance of that Mission, & prompt departure in execution of its duties, the fact might, and probably would be, denied, in the house, where by an essential ground on which a part of my claims rest would be shaken. I therefore copied the first paragraph of that letter, in the form prescrib'd, by that of the last writer, & gave it to M^r. Gouverneur, when here last week, to be deliver'd to the Chairman of the committee, which I presume he has done. Independant of any effect, which it may have on my claim, the evidence which it affords, of your favorable opinion of my previous services, & friendly feelings towards me, will always be a source of great gratification to me.

Altho my inheritance in Westmoreland county, was small, yet by the sale of it, and the judicious investment of the amount receiv'd from it, in western lands, in early life, and the application thereof, in fortunate purchases elsewhere, & particularly in Albemarle, where I expected & wished to have pass'd the remainder of my days, I had laid the foundation with some small professional aid, of independence, which had I remained at home a few years longer, would, I have no doubt, have been completed. By my public employments, and especially those abroad, this hope, has been defeated, and such is actually my situation, that I do not think that the grant of my claims will nearly relieve me, by which I mean, will leave me enough to exist in tolerable comfort with my family. My debts abroad were great, and my plantations in Albemarle & here, have added considerably to them every year, so that with accumulated loans and interest, compound added to simple, they have become immense. This is a true, tho' a melancholy picture of the actual state of my affairs. I have been led to give it, by the obligation I have felt, to explain to you my motive, for communicating to the committee, the extract from your letter, above notic'd.

With great respect, etc.

Feby 14th.

P.S.—I have this moment receiv'd a paper from Richmond, which gives an account of your application to the legislature, for the grant of a lottery for the sale of your estate, to relieve you from embarrassment. I cannot express the concern which this view of your affairs has given me, altho' I can readily conceive the causes which have led to it. They are such as the State, and indeed the whole Union, must feel. I will write to you again on the subject.

TO THOMAS JEFFERSON.
OAK HILL, Feby. 23, 1826.

DEAR SIR,—I mention'd in a letter which I lately wrote to you, that I had seen in a paper from Richmond, a notice of an application which you had made to the legislature, for permission to sell a large portion of your estate, by lottery, for the payment of your debts, and that I should write you again on the subject. Since then I have been much indisposed, with the influenza, from which, I have not yet intirely recover'd. I have been much concern'd to find, that your devotion to the public service, for so great a length of time & at so difficult an epoch, should have had so distressing an effect, on your large private fortune, and my regret is the greater, from the interest I take, in what relates to your family as well as to yourself. It is a concern, in which I am satisfied, the people will take a deep interest, and that the legislature will grant to you, who have such very high claims on your country, what it seldom refuses to any one, cannot be doubted. As soon as I saw that notice, I communicated it to my friends in New York, and particularly to M^r. Gouverneur, with a request, that they would promote the object, and which they will do. I shall do the same to others in other quarters. My motive in this, is, to assure you that if in any way, I may be useful to you, it will be very gratifying to me, to be apprized of it.

TO JUDGE BROOKE(?)
OAK HILL, March 15th, 1826.

DEAR SIR,—I have perused several times with great attention, the sketch of the report given to you by Mr. Ingham, intended to be made by the committee on my claims, and now communicate such ideas as occur to me on the subject.

The report is drawn with delicacy and with care, and indicates on the part of Mr. Ingham, the most friendly feeling towards me personally, as it does his very favorable opinion of my services, and the disinterested principles by which I have been govern'd in rendering them. On the principles adopted by the committee, & in conformity with which, he has been bound to make the report, I shall make some remarks, commencing with the items in the order in which they stand.

The first item in the first mission is admitted, being a claim to compensation for the 3 months & 20 days, after my recall, during which I could not leave the country.

2^d. item for contingent expenses, during that mission. The average of the allowances made to our ministers is adopted. Was any minister ever placd in similar circumstances before? Did any minister before ever employ 3 or 4 assistant secretaries, for the whole term of his service, hire a house for them, with furniture, one or more servants, & entertain them in his family at a considerable increased expense? Was the emergency such as to require it? This cannot be doubted. The crisis between the two countries, as stated in the sketch, declares it, & with great truth & force. My predecessor was not listened to, nor appealed to by his fellow citizens, who ran to me for aid, as soon as I was rec^d. by the convention. I spard no expense, in measures deemd necessary to aid them. There are hundreds living who can prove it, in addition to those whose documents are adduced. Mr. Wm. Lee, in the city, if calld on, can give very detailed & ample testimony to that effect. From delicacy, I presume, he will not come forward unless called on.

3^d item, interest, on outfit, to France, Spain, &c. in second mission, which was withheld. This is refus'd by the project of the report, & by the committee.

It is shown, by Mr. Madison's letter to me, of the 2^d of March, 1803, included in the documents communicated in the President's message, of 23^d. of Jany last, that $9.000 were advancd to me "for my expenses to Paris, including those of a journey from home to Washington, & thence to New York, & in travelling between the places, at which I might be requir'd to attend." This sum was advancd, in lieu of the outfit & would have remaind applicable to the purposes specified, until the termination of the mission, had not the President given a new direction to my services, & to the claims arising under them. Had I gone to Spain immediately after the conclusion of the Louisiana treaty, as I intended, & for which I requested a passport of Mr. Talleyrand, and returnd to the U States from Spain, after the negotiation there sh^d. have been concluded, the acct. for the 9000 dolls. thus advancd would not have been settled until after my return. All that could be claim'd of me was, on my appointment to Engl^d. that the balance of those $9,000, after allowing me every fair discount, including the outfit to Engl^d. which was not, & could not be disputed, should be applied to the current purposes of my new mission. My expenses to Paris, &c. cost me, according to my memoranda, $2.300 including the sum paid for my passage in a vessel in which it was engagd but in which we did not sail. $546. for contingent expenses at Paris, & $4500. were then due me for six months salary, & adding the outfit to Engl^d. would make the sum of $16,346. I had receivd up to that time, including the $9.000 advancd me in the UStates, $18.195. so that at that period, on the principle adopted on my first appointment, giving me credit for the outfit to England, which became due by the change made by the adm^n. itself, the gov^t. was in advance to me, the sum only of $1,849.

Take a like view at the end of a year from my first appointment, and I think it will appear that the gov^t. was then in advance to me on the principles stated, $340. only. My expenses were met by loans, for it is certain that my mission to Engl^d. threw me under the necessity of making those, from which I was not relieved by the subsequent mission to Spain, as it likewise is, that my expenses, after my return to Engl^d., during my detention there for the term of two years and four months, augmented my debts to an amount from which I fear that I shall never recover.

You will observe that in my mission to Engl^d., expecting the order of the gov^t in a few months, to return thro' France to Spain, I was at the same expense, through the whole interval, after my arrival there, in July, 1803, until Octr. 1804, a period of 14 or 15 months, as if I had been sent on a special mission, and the same case existed after my return from Spain, during my detention in Engl^d. for the 2 years & 4 months.

It has been intimated to me, that some gentlemen thought, that the $9000. were advanced to me, as an outfit for Engl^d. but this is most certainly an error, for I did not know that I should be appointed to Engl^d. until I rec^d. my commission. I knew that it was the desire of the adm^n. to give me extensive & important trusts, in the then emergencies of the country, but that it would be thus directed, was not known to, or sought by me. Besides, do not the well authenticated facts before the committee prove the contrary. If that advance was made as an outfit for Engl^d., what allowance was to be made to me for the missions to France & Spain? How was I to get to France or Spain or accommodate my little aff^{rs}. at home? on a salary alone, admitted by all to be very inadequate for current expenses, after you have taken your station.

On every view that I have been able to take of the subject, after due consideration of the objections made to my claim, I do not think that the advance alluded to ought to be placd on the ground of an outfit, or that the interest for withholding such allowance, until it was allowed, at the time of the settlement, ought to be refused to me.

What the equitable considerations, adverted to by the committee, are, I cannot conceive. If it ought to have been allowed, when the appointment was conferrd on me, an injury was done me, by not allowing it. The manner of my appointment, without consulting me, & hurrying me from home, left me no alternative, as to the acceptance, and in its consequences subjected me to the sacrifice of an estate above Charlottesville, on which the university has been placd, which now sells from $50 to $500 the acre. I abandoned also a profession

in which I had succeeded while at the bar, and had the best prospect of succeeding on my return to it. These are equitable considerations which operate
strongly in my favor, and which more than overbalance those on the other side.

As to the Crossing am^t. which the gov^t. was in advance to me, at any time,
beyond what was due to me, is that of sufficient weight to justify the claim of
interest against me, as an offset against mine, supported as it is by such powerful considerations, a claim never set up, in any instance, by the gov^t.?

I send you a memo. prepard in haste, illustrative of the view I have of this
item, and the objections to it, in the commencement of these remarks on it.
I send also a statement of the acc^t. communicated to me by Mr. Duvall in 1810.

Item 4th., demurrage. This is allowed. I send the receipt, which you will be
so kind as to deliver to Mr. Ingham.

5th., contingencies in Engl^d.—I am satisfied that mine exceeded Mr. Kings.
He was stationary. I was minister to three powers, & in constant correspondence, on the subject of each, with the gov^t. & our ministers in every country.
Mr. King was there in a more tranquil period also. The average is undoubtedly
more justifiable, in this instance than in that of the first mission, but I do not
think that it is in this.

6th. item, detention in Engl^d. after return from Spain, &c. The claim is
allowed.

But the interest on this item, and on the others, on which it is allowed, is to
commence on the settlement of the last acc^t. or rather of the acc^t. for the last
mission in 1810. Surely the acc^t. of the two missions are unconnected with each
other, & if the claim is just, with respect to either, the indemnity ought to reach
the period at which each injury was rec^d. I stated, in my observations delivered
to the committee at the last session, that I left this acct. to Mr. Dawson, to be
settled by him, in the best manner he could, & the inference is clear, that if my
pay was stopped on the 6th. of Octr. instead of the 1st of Jany. when I obtain
my audience of leave, in obedience to my instructions, that a proposition to
allow it to the 20th of April, would not have been listend to. It is now for
Congress to go back on those transactions, and to adjust them with a liberal
spirit, and it is my candid opinion that the more that spirit is manifested, by the
body as well as by individuals, the more it will redound to their credit. However,
this is for them to determined, and not for me to advise.

I cannot perceive on what ground the non-paym^t. of my claims can be attributable to me. Had I not been brought into the adm^n., I never would have asked
the allowance of them by any adm^n. as I stated in my observations to the Com.
last session. The divisions among ourselves, my subsequent mission, &c. renderd

any application on my part, improper, even to Congress, at an earlier period & for great part of the time impossible.

Respecting the correspondence with the gov^t. and its permission to me, to come home, immediately after my return to Engl^d. from Spain, I should presume that the fact of my having stated it, in the observations which I presented to the dep^t. in 1810, in reference to that item, & the suspension of a decision on it, for farther consideration was an admission of the fact and a proof of it. But many letters of mine to the dep^t. & my letter to L^d. Mulgrave likewise show it. What passed between us was, in all matters of a personal nature, in private correspondence, & the fact is, that I had permission to return when I pleased, and staid only, because very urgent emergencies requird it, & the gov^t. desird it. I had no residence which could be called a permanent one; on my first arrival in Engl^d. I resided in Winpole street, in a house for which I gave 500 guineas a year; on my return, I took a house for some time in Great Cumberland place, and after Mr. Pinkney's arrival, in Portland place, but always at that price or more, as I took the houses for short terms. All these facts can be proved, if proof sho^d. be deemd necessary. It is known to every one, who know me there, of whom there are many, that I took houses suited to the station, and being immersed in business of the highest importance, with that, as well as other governments, and presuming that thus attention was in some measure drawn to me, disregarded any expense which was necessary to give weight to the office I held.

It does not appear that the publication of Mr. Jefferson's letter of Jany 13. 1803, announcing my appointment & hurrying me from home, is contemplated by the com.—I am satisfied that its bearing on my claims in that mission, would be sensibly felt in my favor. I think also, on equitable considerations, that the publication of Mr. Ringgold's deposition, as to my agency in obtaining loans in the late war, would have a good effect; I merely mention these circumstances, for yours & Mr. Ingham's consideration.

Very sincerely your friend,

P.S. I send you some extracts of private letters between Mr. Jefferson & me, relating to my return to the U States, on my return from Spain, which you may show to Mr. Ingham. The copy of that to L^d. Mulgrave you may give to him, or rather a copy of it.

As the $9000. would have balanced the acc^t. had it been advancd me as an outfit when appointed, I sho^d. not have falln in debt, when the acc^t. was settled. The refusing me the interest on it, for the time it was withheld, on the principle that I was in debt to the gov^t. is palpably unjust. To bring me in debt, by withholding a just claim, & so make that debt thus forcd on me, a motive for refusing me the interest for the time it was withheld, is incompatable with the principle on which the acc^t. was settled. A knowledge that that money was my own, and not [to] be accounted for, wo^d. have been worth to me more than the interest.

TO THOMAS JEFFERSON.
OAK HILL, April 9th, 1826.

DEAR SIR,—The committee to whom the business was committed, have recently made a report on my claims, a copy of which, I have requested a friend at Washington, to procure & forward to you. I regret to find, that it has not met my expectation, either in regard to some of the items, or the period at which, interest shall commence. If for example, money was withheld, which ought to have been allowed me, on the first mission, the interest should I presume, commence from the date at which it was due. I can conceive no reason, why its commencement, should be postponed, until the settlement of the account, for the second mission 12. years, or more, afterwards. I did never ask, an indemnity for injuries done me, in the first mission, of you, or M^r. Madison, nor could I do it, with honor. To touch the subject, after I came into the adm^n, was utterly impossible. There never was a period, at which, I could bring it into view, until that of which I avail'd myself. Nor should I have done it, even then, had I alone been interested in it. In addition to the just claims of my family, there are creditors, and friends, who are pledg'd for me, for whom I was bound, to procure every amt: that I thought justly due to me. No more did I ask, & that I have expected. For the money which I advanc'd to Thomas Paine, and for the loans, which I extra: officially made in the late war, I asked nothing. Had I not been minister in Paris, that afflicted veteran, in our service, could not have applied to me for aid; and had not very extraordinary emergencies occurr'd in the late war, I should neither have been in the dep^t. of war, or had any thing to do with loans. You will pardon me for touching on those subjects, and attribute it, to its true cause, the freedom with which I write you in confidence on such as have been, and are interesting to me. I have another motive, which is indeed that, which induces me more particularly to write you this. The Committee requir'd evidence of your permission to me, to come home, in a few weeks, after my return to London from Spain, which I had affirm'd to be the fact. From all your letters to me, I understood, that after the mission to France had terminated, I might come when I pleased, and that the epoch alluded to, was particularly fixed on. I looked over our correspondence in haste, & extracted from it, the few paragraphs, which bore more on it, than any others, & sent them forthwith to the

Committee, understanding that despatch was necessary. As they contain nothing, but what relates to that subject, and are in the same sentiment, with the extract, the communication of which, you sanction'd, I trust that you will approve it. It is my intention to visit Albemarle, in a few weeks, when I hope to find your health much improved. I am etc.

TO JAMES MADISON.
ALBEMARLE, June 16, 1826.

DEAR SIR,—I have failed in the sale of my lands in this country,: or any part thereof, and in consequence, being informed that there were several persons desirous of purchasing, tho' not willing to give the price I asked, I have advertized both tracts for sale, to the highest bidder, on the 18th & 20th of the next month. My hope is to produce thereby a combination among them, and a result satisfactory to my creditors, and useful to my family. Among my debts is one due to the bank of Virg^a., for the arrangement of which I am compelled to proceed immediately to Richmond, whither I sho^d. have set out this morning, had I not been prevented by the rain, which is heavy, & promises to continue. I shall hasten thence home, and, after assigning the money lately voted to me to banks & individuals to whom it is due, return, by your house, to this place, if the state of my health, which is yet good, will permit it. I did hope to have arranged my affairs here to my satisfaction, & to have passed a day with you on my return, but you will see, by the view presented, that it is not in my power. I shall, I trust, have more leisure at the time specified.

TO JAMES MADISON.
OAK HILL, Jany. 22, 1827.

DEAR SIR,—Since my last the fever has left me, and the cold diminished, so that I hope in a few days to be able to leave my chamber, & be restored to good health.

Your remark is perfectly just, as to the impropriety of our giving opinions, on the subject submitted to us by Mr. Causten, for public use, or any use whatever. We did our duty, each of us, in regard to those claims, in the stations we have held, and our conduct, as well as that of our predecessors, will come into view in the investigation of them, & of the subject generally, &, in consequence, it seems due to ourselves, as well as to them, to say nothing on its merits.

I hear with great regret that the conduct of the hotel keepers has been so exceptionable. The course you have taken appears to me very proper. I am satisfied that the dependant state in which they were placed, on the students, has had a strong tendency to involve them in that dilemma.

I offered to the bank my mountain land, 940 acres, at the price given me by Mr. Goodwyn, & the land adjoining at $10. the acre, and to add 300 acres thereto. They declined it, evincing a disinclination to release any portion of the tract from the mortgage, until the whole balance of the debt was paid, which it appears, with interest, amounts to $25,000. They stated that if I would take a price which they could give, and the land conveyed should sell for more than the debt, they would restore the surplus to me. I then offered to sell the whole to them on that condition, in a letter lately forwarded. The subject is now under consideration & I hope will soon be decided, by the acceptance of the proposal. I am still too weak to enter into other subjects. Best regards to your family.

TO JUDGE HUGH L. WHITE.
OAKHILL, Jany. 26th 1827.

DEAR SIR,—I should not address this letter to you if I had not the most perfect confidence in your integrity and candour, and also in your judgment and prudence. In times of great excitement to which our system is exposed, the excess of which is one of its greatest dangers, it is natural for a person like me, who has retired after long and laborious service, to cherish tranquility, & not to risk it, when it can be avoided with honor, and especially in a communication with one who does not hold in my estimation the confidence w^h. I repose in you. My object is to do justice to myself, in an instance in which it appears that I have been injur'd, & by a full & friendly communication with you, who, I fear, have been under some misapprehension on the subject. The instance to which I allude is the charge of neglect in not making, while acting in the Dep^t. of War, the necessary provision for the defense of N. Orleans, when menaced with invasion in the late war, by forwarding to the scene of action the troops, arms, and other munitions of war which the emergency called for. The charge to which I allude will be seen in the *Telegraph* of the City of the 5th. of Octr. last, taken from a Tennessee paper, and a remark made by you on the 8th. of this month, at a dinner given in honor of General Jackson, for his very gallant & meritorious conduct in defense of that city, "that he supplied the implements of war, which his gov^t. had not placed within his reach," is the circumstance which has made the impression on my mind, of the misapprehension in yours, above suggested. The mere statement of the fact, that the gov^t. had not placed the arms within his reach, without explanation, implies neglect, but taken in connection with the publication from Tennessee, and apparently on the authority of General Jackson, the inference is the more natural. I do not believe such was your intention, nor do I that General Jackson has ever express'd, or entertain'd that sentiment. It seems nevertheless proper that I should give this explanation to you.

I think that I can satisfy you that nothing was omitted on my part, that was necessary for the defense of that city, which the resources of the Union, at that critical juncture, enabled me to perform; that I anticipated this danger of invasion, and provided for it, at an early period, by ordering, in aid of the troops then under the command of General Jackson, & others in the neighborhood subject to his order, large reinforcements from Tennessee, Kentucky & Georgia, with arms, & every other proper equipment. That the subject may be better understood I will communicate to you the substance of the letters to the Governor of each of those States, and also of those to the General, with their respective dates.

The first letter to the Governor of Tennessee bears date on the 25th. of Sepr., by which he was advised of the menaced invasion, and requested to send immediately to General Jackson, by such routes as he should prescribe, 5000 troops, in addition to those which had before been detailed, and to arm and equip those troops, in the best manner possible, according to the resources of the State. On the 3rd. of Octr. he was informed that the Govr. of Kentucky had been requested to detach to Genl. Jackson 2500 men, provided the circumstances of the State would permit it large draughts having been made on it for the defense of the No.western frontiers. Of the ability of the State to furnish the troops called for the Govr. of Kentucky was desir'd to give information to the Govr. of Tennessee, and, in case the call could be complied with, the requisition on Tennessee could be proportionably reduced. Octr. 10th. Instructed, on advice recd. from our Ministers at Ghent that 12 or 15000 men had sailed from Ireland, to send the whole force down. On the 3d. of Novr. he was advised that 5000 stand of arms had been order'd from Pittsburg, with ammunition, tents, and camp equipage, to the commanding officer at Baton Rouge, for the use of the militia of Tennessee & Kentucky, but he was nevertheless still urged to have all the troops sent from his State, armed and equipped before they left it, as that supply would be very limited, even as a deposit in reserve, at that point. On the 4th. the information given, as to the order of arms, &c. from Pittsburg, was repeated, as was the warning respecting the menaced invasion. A notice was taken, in this, of the $100.000 which had been previously sent to him to support the operations under Genl. Jackson, with instructions to whom to transfer the money. On the 30th. of Jany. 1815, the victory which had been obtained over the British forces, near N. Orleans, on the 8th., by Genl. Jackson, was acknowledged in appropriate terms, & 2500 additional troops ordered to his aid, and an assurance given that $150,000, in Treasury notes, would be forwarded to him in a few days, on which he was authorized to negotiate loans from the banks. On the 13th. of Feby the brilliant success at N. Orleans was again noticed, with the invasion of the Island of Orleans, as a motive to dispense with the late call for an additional force from Tennessee. On the 14th., in a circular addressed to the Govrs. of all the States, the arrival of a treaty of peace was announced, with an intimation that, as its conditions were honorable, it would probably be ratified.

The Governor of Kentucky, was requested, by a letter of Octr. 3d., to detach from that State 2500 men to Genl. Jackson, in lieu of a like number from Tennessee, provided the State could furnish them, of which he was desired to apprize the Govr. of Tennessee, who had instructions correspondent with either event. On the 10th. he was advised of the menaced invasion, & urged to hasten the 2500 men down the river, subject to the orders of General Jackson; he was informed also that the additional 5000 ordered from Tennessee would not be diminished, but would be hastened to the scene of action. On the 25th. this request was rejected, as likewise that they should be armed & equipped, with an intimation that, if the State could not supply the arms and equipments, they might be obtained from the deposit at Newport. On November 3d. he was advised of the 5000 stand of arms which had been ordered from Pittsburg, with tents, blankets, &c., but still urged to furnish all the arms that he might be able. On Jany 30th. a corresponding one was written to him with that addressed to the Govr. of Tennessee of the same date, speaking in the highest terms of approbation & commendation of the victory obtained at N. Orleans, and requesting, as the enemy's force was very strong, and their movements uncertain, that an additional number of 4000 militia of the State be hurried down the river, armed with rifles, or muskets. He was also informed that transportation would be prepared for the troops by the time they should be collected, & $150.000, in Treasury notes, were transmitted to him, to pay for expenses already incurred, by the transportation of the troops before sent. On the 10th. of Feby information respecting the remittance was repeated, and that transportation for the troops would be provided by the Govt., Col: James Morrison having been employed by the Dept. to have boats built at Pittsburg, & in Kentucky. By a letter to Col: Morrison of the same date it appears, that orders to that effect had been given to him, and also to employ steamboats. Feby. 13. a letter was written to him to the same effect with that to the Govr. of Tennessee of the same date. 14th. the circular already mentioned, addressed to the Govrs. of all the

States, announcing the arrival of the treaty of peace, & that it would probably be ratified, was forwarded to him.

On the 25th. of Sept. a letter was addressed to the governor of Georgia, apprizing him of the menaced invasion of Louisiana, and of the intention of the British govt., by means of the enlarged force at its command in consequence of its successes on the continent of Europe, to occupy the whole country from Cape Florida to the Provinces of Spain west-ward of the Mississippi. To repel this invasion, in aid of the other troops ordered out for the purpose, he was requested to organize, arm & equip 2500 men, & to hold them in readiness to join Genl. Jackson when called for by him. October 10. advice of the menaced invasion on good authority repeated, with instructions to put those troops in motion in a direction for and subject to the order of Genl. Jackson, with whom he was also instructed to communicate on the subject. Decr. 10. the same request was repeated in a very urgent manner. Feby. 13th he was informed that 10.000 stand of arms had been ordered to Genl. Pinckney for the troops employed in the defense of that section, of which he was authorized to take 1500. On the 14th the circular above mentioned, announcing the treaty of peace, was forwarded to him.

To Genl. Jackson the following letters were written. Sept. 5th. In this the propriety of repairing to N. Orleans was suggested. An anonymous letter was enclosed in it, the author of which was stated to be known, and entitled to credit on the information contained in it. It is probable the intimation was given Sept. 27. He was assured that there was great cause to believe that the invasion menaced would take effect, in the expectation that while so strong a pressure was made from Canada, & in this quarter, whereby the force of the country, & attention of the govt. would be much engaged, a favorable opportunity would be afforded them to take possession of the lower parts of Louisiana, & of all the country along the Mobile. The troops then under his command were adverted to. The regular troops in the district; the militia already detached from Louisiana; the Mississippi territory, & Tennessee, with authority to employ all the warriors from the Choctaw, Chickesaw and Creek nations. He was informed that 5000 additional troops were ordered from Tennessee, and 2500 to be held in readiness, subject to his order, in Georgia; and also that $100.000 had been transmitted to the Govr. of Tennessee, for the support of the operations under him, for any portion of which he was authorized to draw. October 10th. he was advised that our Ministers at Ghent had apprized the gov^t. that a British force of 12. or 15.000 men had sailed from Ireland, early in Sept., for N. Orleans and the Mobile, to take possession of the city and country.—Advised again of the additional force, ordered from Tennessee, of 5000, and from Kentucky 2500, & from Georgia 2500, subject to his order. Octr. 21st. acknowledges his letter of the 9th. ult^o. communicating his correspondence with the Govr. of Pensacola.— Informs him of the desire of the President that he take no steps which should involve the gov^t. in a contest with Spain.—That a Minister had been appointed to Spain, & that it was deemed more advisable that a representation of the insolent and unjustifiable conduct of the govt. of Pensacola should be made to his gov^t., than that the General should resent it by an attack on Pensacola. The spirit & tone of the correspondence are approved. Information repeated of the force ordered to his aid. Decr. 4th. his letters of 26th & 31st of Octr. acknowledged by Mr. Ringgold, & the satisfaction of the President expressed, at the information communicated in them, that the remittance in Treasury notes had enabled him to supply the wants of his army. Decr. 7th. refers to the letter of Octr. 21st., with the expression of a hope that he had rec^d. it in due time to prevent an attack on Pensacola; ordered to withdraw the troops if he had made the attack, & urged to repair to N. Orleans. Decr. 10th. the same request repeated, and new reasons assigned. Feby. 5th. acknowledges the receipt of his letters of the 9th & 13th ulto., giving an account of his victory, in terms of high commendation of his conduct in the action.—Instructs him to return the thanks of the President to the troops.— Informs him of the efforts which had been made to supply him with the arms & munitions of war of every kind, of which latter a statement is forwarded, with instruction to investigate the conduct of those to whom committed, & should it appear that any one had been guilty of criminal neglect, to inflict on them the punishment which the laws would authorize. He is advised also that 5000 additional troops were ordered from Kentucky, & 2500 from Tennessee, & that Genl. Gaines was ordered to join, and act under him. Feby. 13th. sends him the act of Congress authorizing the acceptance of State troops, & the raising of volunteers, with an instruction to raise two regts. of the latter from the militia then under his command, & to appoint the officers, under an assurance that his appointments wo^d. be confirmed by the President. 16th. the circular, to the generals commanding military districts, announcing the receipt & ratification of the treaty of peace.

  All these letters are of record in the Dept. of War. As the epoch of that war was one, and especially that period of it, of the highest importance that our country had ever known, & my service in it was fraught with the greatest responsibility, & otherwise attended with the most interesting circumstances, I took copies of my own letters, when I left the Dept., which I now have with me. They form a folio vol: of 394 pages. Whether they were all received, by the persons to whom addressed throughout the Union, I do not know. If they were answered, the answers are, of course, in the Dept. of War. The usual precautions were, I well know, taken for forwarding them, and in most instances, as I presume, thro' the Dept of the General Post Office. The copying of letters, and forwarding of them is the duty, in all the Depts., of the clerks. That I was attentive to those forwarded to Genl. Jackson is evident from the note, which it is stated in the Tennessee paper, I wrote on the back of that which was intended to announce to him the peace. If the circular forwarded to the other generals was mislaid in his instance, and other papers inserted, it was the fault of the clerk, & not mine. I had no suspicion of such oversight, or neglect, admitting that it did occur, or should have corrected it.

With respect to the transportation of the men, arms, &c. down the river, every possible exertion was made, & precaution taken, to insure despatch & safety, that could be divined. My orders to that effect were issued to those under me, & in what related to arms, to the officer at the head of the ordnance dept., who, I always believed, has performed his duty faithfully. It will be observed that the governors were all requested to arm & equip their men in the best manner possible, & that those forwarded were intended to guard against deficiencies, & to form, with the surplus, a deposit, for that purpose. With the agent at Pittsburg I was unacquainted, nor do I now know who he was. Coming, as I did, suddenly into the Dept., all that I could do, especially at a distance, and in relation to subalterns, was to avail myself of the service of those in office.

At the time I entered the Dept. of War our Union was invaded, or threatened with serious invasion, from Detroit, along the lakes Erie & Ontario, along the St. Lawrence, & Lake Champlain, & from Maine to the Mississippi, thro' the whole extent of the coast. The city had just before been taken, & the public buildings destroyed. Strong naval and land forces were in the bay, & the city was menaced with a new attack. The British govt. relieved from the war on the continent of Europe, had it in its power to send its whole force here, & we had abundant cause to believe that it would do so. In this state of affairs my duties were very extensive & arduous, especially when it is recollected that I was also charged with the Dept. of State, and was compelled, by the then state of the Treasury, to make loans of money to a great event, to support the operations of our arms. I had a chain of expresses established from the city, thro' Baltimore, to Philadelphia; another to the mouth of the Potomac, & a third to Richmond. It is well known that, for the first month at least, I never went to bed; that I had a couch in a room in my house on which I occasionally reposed, but from which, even in the night, I was called every two hours, when the expresses arrived, to receive the intelligence which they brought, & to act on it. I well know that I neglected no part of the Union, and am satisfied, had I been charged with making a provision for the defense of N. Orleans alone, that I could not have done more for it.

There is, in my opinion, no feature in my public conduct more marked than my exertions in favor of the free navigation of the Mississippi, & of the western country. This fact rests on authentic documents, some of which were published in Novr. last by me, & others adverted to in that publication. My exertions in 1786 raised against me powerful enemies, the ill effect of which has been often felt since. To be assailed from that quarter, and from Tennessee, has excited in me the most painful sensations. That injustice has been done me the communication which I now make will, I am persuaded, fully demonstrated to you.

TO JUDGE HUGH L. WHITE.
Oak Hill, Feby. 9, 1827.

Dear Sir,—I have had the pleasure to receive your letter of the 29th. ult°., and am gratified by the frankness with which you have explained, in reply to mine of the 26th., the motives which governed you in the remarks which you made, on the 8th., which bore on the conduct of the gov^t., & particularly of the Dept. of War, in reference to the provision made by it for the defense of N. Orleans in the campaign of 1814. 15. I shall, in the same spirit, give you further explanations on that subject, & for the purpose of promoting the cause of justice, which I am satisfied you likewise have in view.

I was aware, when I wrote to you that letter, that you were a friend of General Jackson, and that you had long held that relation, reciprocally, with each other. It was the knowledge of that fact, in addition to the motives stated in that letter, which induced me to make that communication to you. I would not have made it to anyone not his friend, and probably should not have noticed, at the present period, the attack made on me in the *Telegraph,* had not your remarks induced the idea of misapprehension on your part which I wished to remove, brought to my view a particular friend of his, one too in whom I could repose the confidence stated in that letter. It is proper to add that I should pursue the same course should an attack like that in the *Telegraph* be made on me by the friends of Mr. Adams, by communicating on the subject with some friend of his, and not with those opposed to him. I take no part in the question depending between the candidates, and am restrained from it by feeling, as well as principle. I left office with very friendly feelings to both, which I wish to preserve, and if placed in a different relation with either it will be by the acts of others, and not at my instance.

By referring to the publication in the *Telegraph,* the n°. containing which I now enclose to you, I did not mean to convey the idea that you had written, or ever seen it. That you had written it never occurred to me. The estimation in which I hold your character places you above it. That you might have seen it, as others had done, I thought probable, but on that point your intimation is perfectly satisfactory. By that publication I am charged, on the authority of Genl. Adair, and in concurrence with sentiments ascribed by him to Genl. Jackson, with the most culpable neglect, in failing to make the necessary provision for the defense of New Orleans at the period adverted to. As you will have this paper before you I need not repeat the other instances of gross misconduct asserted, and insinuations made in it to my prejudice. By stating, in your address to the citizens who were assembled in Washington, on the 8th of Jany. last, that Genl. Jackson had supplied the implements of war, which the govt. had not placed within his reach, and had created, as well as concentrated his army, I was apprehensive that it would be inferred by the public generally, especially as it had been so recently asserted, and apparently on such high authority, that you intended to impute to the gov^t., & of course to the Dept. of War, a failure to perform all its duties in regard to the defense of N. Orleans, & of that important section of the Union at that great crisis. By the general imputation of failure, as to the supply of implements of war, it is implied there were no arms, or munitions of war of any kind, in the city, and, by not explaining the measures which had been taken for forwarding the arms from Pittsburg, & the cause of the failure, it might be inferred that you meant to sanction the allegations against me in that respect; and, by the statement that he had created, as well as concentrated his army, it seemed to be implied that he had called out the force, & directed the routes which the several detachments should take; and, in fact, that the government had adopted no decisive measure on its part. My impression was different. It was that you were not acquainted with all the circumstances of the case, & had formed an opinion which, had they been known to you, would not have existed. I am satisfied that the motive which governed you in making those remarks is that which you state: that you took your impression from what had been publicly reported & written, & for the sole purpose of doing justice to General Jackson, without intending to impute to the govt., or Dept. of War, neglect, or misconduct, in performing what you thought due to him. On this part of the subject it is proper to observe that I never read a biographical sketch of General Jackson, and therefore cannot say whether the authors of such sketches have taken a full view of the whole subject, so as to do justice to the govt., as well as to him, in those occurrences. I had not leisure for it, & being also well acquainted with the conduct of all the parties concerned, I wanted no information from any writer respecting the part which he had acted in them. I apprehended no injury from that quarter, and was anxious that due commendation should be bestowed on him, for his very gallant & meritorious conduct in defense of that city. I knew that illiberal abuse had been bestowed on me from other quarters, but, knowing the ground on which I stood, I disregarded it. If all the facts were not known to the authors of such works it would have been impossible for them to have done justice to the conduct of the govt., in the measures taken by it for the defense of that city. This remark is equally applicable to yourself. It is an unquestionable truth that all the facts have never been before the public: that the whole correspondence of the Dept. of War with the Governors of Kentucky, Tennessee, Georgia and others; the orders given for the prompt march of troops, and the supply of those troops with arms, and other munitions of war, were never published. I infer therefore, from the view taken by you, that these facts were unknown to those writers as well as to you. I am sensible that I have been too inattentive to this object, & have suffered great injury by it, since improper impressions have thereby been made on correct and honorable minds who have sought only the truth.

The letters to the Governors of Tennessee, Kentucky & Georgia, of which I sent you a note in mine of Jany. 26th., prove that, on intelligence received from our Ministers at Ghent, and from other quarters, the force was called out, & ordered to march directly to the scene of action, unless advice should be received from General Jackson, before they did march, that their service was unnecessary. Of these Genl. Jackson was advised, and authorized to direct the routes which the troops should take. He, the commander, being on the coast, would best know the point at which the enemy might be expected. Whether he received the letters addressed to him in time to give any direction on that point, regarding his situation & the difficulty of communicating with him thro' the Indian country, I have no document to show, but that due precaution was taken for their safe delivery I am confident. I observe that in the letter to Governor Blount, of the 25th, of Sept., which announced the intelligence which had been received of the menaced invasion, and called out the large force from that State to meet it, he was requested to transmit a copy of it immediately to Genl. Jackson, & that in the letter to Genl. Jackson of Decr. 10th, which was sent by Dr. Cozzens, it is noted that a previous one had been forwarded to him by Major Fanning, a copy of which was then enclosed, & that copies of other letters which had already been sent should be forwarded by the route of Tennessee. As to the fact stated in the *Telegraph,* relating to the contents of the packet which was intended to announce to him the peace, I was as much surprised to hear the report of them as he could have been, if true, to have received such a packet. By the letter book, which I have here, it appears that a circular announcing that event was written to all the commanding generals, of which it was concluded by me that one had been sent to him. For the neglect, admitting it to have occurred, I could not have been to blame, for a reason given to you in my letter of the 26th. ulto. It is proper to add another, which alone would be sufficient. So extensive and heavy had been my duties, from the moment that I entered into the Dept. of War until the peace, that I had become exhausted by them, and just before that event occurred was prostrated by an indisposition which had nearly taken me off, and from which I did not entirely recover until long after the peace.

I transmit to you a report, which was made to me on the of 4th. Feby. 1815, by the officer at the head of the Ordnance Dept., of the orders given by me for the transportation of arms, & other munitions of war, from Pittsburg, & elsewhere in that quarter, in 1814, for the troops employed under Genl. Jackson for the defense of N. Orleans. By this you will see that, in obedience to an instruction which I gave in person to the officer then at the head of the Dept., an order was issued by him, to the officer acting under him at Pittsburg, to forward down with despatch to Baton Rouge 5000 stands of arms with accountrements, equipments & ammunition, to the general, or officer commanding the U States troops in that quarter. It is stated in this order that the service was urgent, and that his active attention was required, and further, that if, according to any information he might have received, it should appear that more cannon would be necessary, he should forward such as he could spare, having due regard also, as I presume, to the demand on the lakes, & north western frontier. This order bears date on the 2d. of November, 1814, and to it an answer was given from Captain Woolly, of the 8th, that he had then ready to deliver 4000 stands of arms, with flints, and cartridges, for transportation to Baton Rouge, & that they would leave Pittsburg on the 7th. & 8th., & reach their destination in 20 days. The other 1000 were to be forwarded from Franklinton, & with equal despatch. Repeated calls having been made for information on Captn. Woolly, relative to the despatch used in the transportation of the arms, a letter was rec^d. from him, of the 14th. of Decr., in which he states that they had left Pittsburg on the 11th. & 15th. of Novr., & he had no doubt had then arrived at Baton Rouge. By this report you will see, that pressing orders were given to the officers relied on, in other cases, for forwarding these arms down the river with great despatch, and that the utmost solicitude was afterwards shewn, and the proper inquiries made, as to the result, the reports to which were calculated to inspire a confidence that they had been duly executed. By this report you will also see a statement of the number of arms, cannon, muskets & munitions of war of every kind which were reported to the Dept. on the 1st. of Octr. 1814, with the condition in which they were, to be then deposited in N. Orleans. This resource justified a fair and reasonable presumption that, with the other precautions taken, there would be no deficiency in these respects, should the enemy make the menaced attack.

It is proper to remark that, advice being given to the gov^{rs}. of Kentucky & Tennessee of the supply of arms ordered from Pittsburg for their militia, the controul over those arms was essentially given to them, & it doubtless was expected, if they could not arm their men, which they were urged to do, that they would have procured those intended for them, and pointed out to them, before they marched, or if they suffered them to depart unarmed, having the arms from Pittsburg in view, it would have been in confidence that the troops would have sought for and obtained them in their passage down the river. The governors of those States were patriotic men. Governor Shelby was a patriot, & gallant soldier of the Revolution. They undoubtedly had a right to take them, find them where they might. No agent would have refused to deliver them up to the troops for whom intended, nor could he hide himself, with such a charge, from the pursuit of those entitled to it. I mention this to shew that, in ordering the arms down for the Kentucky & Tennessee militia, & apprizing the governors of it, full confidence was entertained that they would have been obtained, for the troops of those States, should they want them.

My object in writing to you has been, as heretofore stated, to remove erroneous impressions, by making you acquainted with all the facts belonging to the case. With that view I would most willingly shew you all the letters contained in the little book which I have here. I have been able to copy a few only, which I now forward to you. By these you will see that the best disposition has existed in the govt. to do full justice to General Jackson for his very important services, in availing himself, & turning to the best account, all the materials which he could command, & by his gallant defense of N. Orleans. The letter addressed to him on receiving the intelligence of his victory on the 8th. of Jany. is a full proof of this fact. My object is to shew that I was not unmindful of, or inattentive to my duty at that great crisis, and such is my confidence in his honor, that I am satisfied he would disdain to accept a credit at the expense of others, & more especially by fixing on them a reproach which they did not deserve. Indeed I have always understood that he has expressed a very different sentiment of my conduct on that occasion, and particularly at Lynchburg, where it is said that he did justice to the exertion I made to call out the troops, & hurry them down to N. Orleans, by means of which he was enabled to make the gallant defense by which the city was saved.

With great respect & esteem, I am, dear sir, your obedient servant—

P.S. I will thank you to return to me the copy of the report of the officers at the head of the ordnance, after perusing it, as I have no other, & likewise the *Telegraph.*

TO U.S. REPRESENTATIVE THOMAS NEWTON.
OAK HILL, Feby. 26, 1827.

DEAR SIR,—Since the receipt of your letter I have been so intensely occupied, with my arrangement with the bank of the U. States, by which the whole, of my tract of land in Albemarle, at the mountain, which has been my home since 1789; till mortgagd to it, just before I left office, is transferred to that bank in discharge of the balance which I owed it of $25,000, that I have not been able to answer it. As to young Quarrier, my respect for his youthful merit, & sincere regard for his aged father, will induce me to do, whatever I can with delicacy & propriety, in his favor. But you know, that on leaving office, I was bound, to adopt some general rule, applicable even to those, to whom I was most attached, or I should be overwhelm'd, with applications from every quarter. My letter to the bank, by which the arrangement is concluded goes down, by this mail, so that I can only promise you, to write you by the next, in regard to our young friend.

It would afford me the highest satisfaction, to see you, & I hope if you cannot come up, on the adjournment of Congress, that you will find some early opportunity to pay us a visit—

OAK HILL, April 2^d, 1827.

TO JAMES MADISON.
OAK HILL, Octr. 3, 1827.

DEAR SIR,—I have yours of the 22^d. ult°., communicating the purport of a letter to you, from H. Lee, at Nashville, of Augt. 24. with an extract from him, of a letter to him from Genl. Armstrong, respecting his provisional order to Genl. Jackson, of July 18, 1814, to take possession of Pensacola on certain conditions, as to the presumed cause of the delay in the transmission of that letter,

and the circumstances under which it was received by the General. You think
it probable that I have been written to also, on the subject, and wish me to communicate to you any knowledge that I may have respecting it. I do not recollect ever to have heard before of such an order; if it was recorded in the letter
book in the Dept., & I ever made it, I have forgotten it; as I likewise have if you
mentioned it to me when, by your instruction, after I entered the Dept., I wrote
to the General a prohibitory order, bearing date on the 21 of Oct^r., in reply to
one from him of the 9th. of Sepr. 1814, intimating such a project. With respect
to the deposit of the letter on the table of the then Secretary of State, it follows,
from what I have already remarked that I have no recollection of it, and I have
no hesitation to add, that I do not believe the assertion, if actually made, to be
true. I have no communication on the subject, nor do I expect any. I informed
you, when we were last together, of a communication which had passed
between Judge White of Tennessee & me last winter, respecting an attack made
on me in a Tennessee paper, charging me with neglect of duty, in not furnishing the necessary supplies, in troops, arms, &c, for the defense of New Orleans
in 1814, 15, and the countenance which he gave to that charge in his speech,
on the 8th of Jany. in the city. This subject seems to be in part connected with
that referred to in your letter. In any event it will be interesting, & may be useful to you, to see the communication which I made to him on that subject, and
with that view I send you a copy of my two letters to him. After perusing them
I will thank you to return them to me, as I wish to retain copies, & I have none
other. At the time that this correspondence took place I had no knowledge
of that between General Jackson & Judge Southard. Mine was therefore altogether distinct from, and unconnected with theirs. When apprised of the latter by Judge Southard, I urged him not to publish it, since the effect would be to
involve me in the controversy, and to make me a party likewise in that which
is now depending, of a different character & which I assured him could not fail
to injure him & his friends, since the motive assigned for it would be a desire to
make use of me for their purpose, rather than to vindicate my character—What
part they will take I know not, but presume they will pursue that which I have
suggested. I send you a letter from Mr. Ringgold, which I have just rec^d., communicating to me, at the instance of Genl. Jessup his knowledge of the actual
deposit of arms at N. Orleans, at the time of the invasion, of every kind, with
munitions of war, & the reason why they were not taken advantage of by the
General, at that interesting juncture. I had an official report, essentially to the
same effect, from the ordnance dep^t., in Feby. 1815, but I shall nevertheless
obtain the document offer'd by Genl. Jessup, since they will corroborate each

other. Return me this letter, with the others enclosed. Affectionate regards to you all.

If the acting President or Secretary of State had delayed the letter in its transmission to Genl. Jackson, I should have supposed they would have destroyed it. I can conceive no motive why they should keep it back, & send it to him afterwards, in the state in which he rec^d. it. It does not appear at what time he rec^d. mine. Much delay occurrd in the rec^t. of several of my letters to him, in consequence of his movement to Pensacola, & in the Indian country, as I have reason to believe—whether a letter from you, at this time, in his favor, regarding his actual state in the opposite scale, may not be misconstrued to his prejudice. You will pardon this suggestion, to which I am impelled by the most sincere regard for both of you.

TO WILLIAM WIRT.
OAK HILL, Oct. 24, 1828.

DEAR SIR,—I was much gratified, by the receipt of your letter of the 14th. a few days past, to hear of your return from a journey to the Falls of Niagara, and other parts of the Eastern country, in good health, and that your daughter Catharine's health had been improved by it. We hope that it will soon be completely restored. Would not a visit here, at this season, be useful to her? Be assured that it will always afford my whole family a very sincere pleasure to see you and yours, whenever you can do us that favor.

In Mr. Gouverneur's appointment I take great interest, but I well know that you, and several other friends, will do all in your power to promote it. I am now satisfied, also, that the President entertains a very friendly feeling for me, and will with pleasure confer it on him, should it comport with his views of propriety and policy.

I hear with great satisfaction, that Mr. Trist is appointed a clerk in the Dept. of State, with a salary of $1400. per annum. Mrs. Randolph and family will move, and take her residence with him. Her small income, added to his, will give them a comfortable support, in some retired situation on the heights of Georgetown, as I presume, where, at a distance from her former residence, which could excite only painful sensations, she may enjoy some consolation. I have felt much for them, and am much gratified by this appointment.

On all subjects, public & private, I should be happy to have an opportunity of communicating with you, as we have always done, with the most intimate confidence in each other. Whether the present Administration ought to withdraw, in the event that Mr. Adams should not be reelected, is a question of great delicacy, as to the numbers, & of interest, by way of example, as to principle. They hold their offices, as others do, as servants of the public, not his. Their appointments do not cease with his. They are responsible, each, for the faithful performance of their duties. He likewise is responsible for them. In this respect there is a difference between our govt. and that of G. Britain; in the latter the Minister alone is responsible. The office of the Chief being hereditary, he is beyond the reach of impeachment. With us, both may be impeached, the Chief and Minister. They are also his counsellors. In some views, therefore, they may be considered as holding an independent ground, that is, as depending on their good conduct in office, and not on the change of the incumbent. In others, the opposite argument appears to have force. Where a difference of principle is involved, it would seem as if a change would be necessary; but where such difference does not exist the danger is, by connecting the members with the fortune of the incumbent, of making them the mere appendages & creatures of the individual, which may have, in certain views, in the progress of affairs, an unfavorable effect on our system. Whenever things get to that state, that manners are approved, or disapproved, by parties contending for power, to promote the success of their favorite, principle is lost sight of, and the people cease to be the sovereign, or rather to exercise the sovereign power in a manner to preserve it. They become instruments, whereby the basis of the system will be shaken. Still as the heads of the Dept. are her Counsellors, and wield important branches of the Govt., I do not see how they can remain in office without her sanction, or wait after his election till apprised of his decision by himself. This view is much less applicable, in every instance and circumstance, to your case than to theirs. Your duties are different. He has less connection with, and less responsibility for the performance of them. Your standing is likewise such, nothing unfriendly having occurred between you, that I should think he would wish to retain you.

Oct. 31. I had written the preceding on the date attached to it, with intention to finish and send it by mail of the next day, but being called to Middleburg, with Mrs. Monroe, to meet two magistrates, to attest a deed for the conveyance of land in Kentucky, on account of the debt contracted for the house in Paris, I was thrown from my horse, on my return, and greatly injured. The fever has left me, but my leg, which was badly wounded, still confines me to my bed, and will for some time. I can only assure you, that should you remove to N. York, where I have no doubt you will soon establish yourself, I would give you all the aid, among personal friends, in my power.

TO DR. CHARLES EVERETT.

OAK HILL, Novr. 24, 1828—

DEAR SIR,—Since the last accident of a fall from my horse, as I returned alone from Middleburg village, I have been confined to my room, & great part of the time to my bed, by a fever, & a wound which I received in my leg. The shock was very severe to my whole frame. I lay motionless on the ground for about twenty minutes, doubting whether my leg was not broken. The fever has now left me, & the wound is nearly healed, so that I hope soon to be restored to health.

I have not been able to write sooner, or I should have written to you, & other friends, before, to acknowledge my sense of the great kindness you have shown me, by the address you have signed & published in favor of my services, & claims on my country, thro' the whole of my past life. There is not one fact stated but what is true, & supported by unquestionable documents.

I beg you to remember me kindly to Mr. Rogers, who gave me a strong proof of his friendship, when I was in Spain, by taking charge of my property in Albemarle, at the request of Mr. Jones, on the sale of my land above Charlottes, & for which he neither asked, or would receive one cent. I feel under great obligations to all of you for this, & other proofs of friendship.

Should you leave home this winter cannot you come here, & stay some time with us? The whole family will be happy to see you.

TO JAMES MADISON.

OAK HILL, March 20, 1829.

DEAR SIR,—I am just recovering from a very severe attack of cold & fever, by which I have been confined to my room, & until a few days past to my bed, nearly three weeks. The fever has left me, but I am very weak, & able to sit up a portion of the day only. This is the second, since we parted, under which I have suffered. The first proceeding from a fall from my horse, who fell with me, &, in rising, gave me a severe wound in my leg. I lay ab^t. 20 minutes incapable of motion, & believing my leg to be broken. On rising I was discovered by a neighbour, Mr. Lucket, who took me to his house, & as soon as I could bear the fatigue, brought me home in his carriage. From those injuries; & the fever attending them, I had recovered sometime before that by which I am still confined. Mrs. Monroe is also now suffering under a similar indisposition, which has been less severe, & from which she is recovering in some degree. We hope that you & Mrs. Madison have been blessed with good health.

I have heard of the attacks which have been made on you by Mr. Giles, but have not been able to read them. They will do you no injury. Our system is in operation on its principles, unaided, in the councils, by the props which supported it in the revolution, and by revolutionary characters since. A complete remedy to a political disease is seldom found until something like a crisis occurs, and this is promoted by the abuse of those who have rendered the most important services, and whose characters will bear the test of enquiry. I think the period not distant when a very different view will be taken of this, and many other subjects now in agitation.

I understand that you have been nominated as a candidate for the approaching convention, & have declined serving. A like nomination has been made of me, as I am informed, and I think that I shall follow your example. The whole family unite in best regards to you & Mrs. Madison.

TO S. M. EDWARDS.
Oak Hill, April 6, 1829.

Dear Sir,—I have received your letter of the 2nd. instant, intimating your desire, and that of others of my fellow citizens of the district, to elect me to the convention which is to be held for the amendment of our constitution, and requesting to be informed whether I would be willing to undertake the trust, should they confer it on me. I feel, with great sensibility this proof of the high confidence of those of my fellow citizens who have expressed this sentiment in my favor, because I see in it the approbation of my conduct, in the service of my country, on the difficult conjuncture thro' which we have passed. Many considerations admonish me, at this period, impaired as my health has been of late, to cherish retirement; among which is a fear that it would not be in my power to render the service which might be expected from me, and which might be performed by others in the district. These have doubtless been weighed by my fellow citizens alluded to, and who are willing to make a generous allowance for such defects as time, & labor in other stations, may have produced. It is a cause of consoling reflection to me, to recollect that I never declined any service, however arduous, to which my fellow citizens invited me.

Should the trust be conferred on me, I shall, most certainly, pay great attention to the very important points specified in your letter. Having devoted my best faculties, with ardent zeal, thro' life, to the establishment and support of our free system of government, I can never be indifferent to any of the great principles on which it rests. The support, however, of these principles must depend on the union of the State, as it likewise must on contentment among the people, and harmony in its councils. If either part thinks itself oppressed it will be discontented & unhappy. The affection of each part should be promoted, on equal and just principles; towards the others. Our system of government is new, and we find little cause for consolation in the example, and fate, of other republics, all of which have failed. Much light will be thrown on the subject, in every branch, by the discussion which will be given to it, by the very able men who will be placed in that body. Should I be elected to it, it will be my object to adopt such amendments as will correspond with the great principles to which you allude, maintain equal liberty among our fellow citizens, inspire confidence, promote affection, and bind the State, in all its parts, more closely together.

TO JAMES MADISON.
OAK HILL, June 25, 1829.

DEAR SIR,—We heard with great regret of your serious indisposition, but were relieved from anxiety by a letter, sometime since, from Mr. R. Taliaferro, which assured us that you had nearly recovered to perfect health. I have been much afflicted by repeated attacks since we parted, & by a recent one, which is the third, but am now so far restored as to entertain a hope that I shall be able to attend the meeting of the Visitors at the University, which I understand will be on the 10th. of next month. Our gd. daughter, Hortensia Hay, is engaged to be married to Mr. Rogers, of Baltimore, & the union will be formed on the 5th. I propose, if my health permits, to set out on the 7th., in the hope of reaching your house on the 8th. or 9th., & on the 8th. if possible, to proceed with you, as heretofore, to the University. Be so kind as to drop me a line, to inform me whether the meeting takes effect at the time suggested.

TO JAMES MADISON.
OAK HILL, Sept. 10, 1829.

DEAR SIR,—I am anxious to know the state of your health, & whether it is such as will enable you to attend the convention. I most earnestly hope that you will be able to attend it, for, if I go, I shall be much gratified to meet you there, and, whether I do, or not, I am satisfied that your presence, altho' you might take no part in the discussion, would have a very useful effect. My health, since we parted, has been very weak, and often affected with slight bilious attacks, which, altho' removed with prompt remedies, have, nevertheless, kept me in the state in which you saw me. At this time it is rather better than it has been, and the prospect is favorable of my being able to attend, but this will depend on there being no future impediment. Mrs. Monroe intended to accompany me, but this is now rendered impossible, since her state at best will only be such as to justify my leaving her, under the care of our daughter, Mrs. Hay. We hope that Mrs. Madison enjoys good health, to whom present the best regards of our whole family. Very sincerely I am, dear sir, your friend—

Still I would risk nothing.

TO JOSEPH BONAPARTE.
RICHMOND, Decr. 21, 1829.

SIR,—When your letter of the 10th Inst. reached me I was confined to my bed by sickness, and tho' I hope I am now convalescent, I am still so confined. I use the earliest opportunity that returning health affords me to acknowledge the receipt of, and to give a concise answer to it.

The representation contained in the *notice sur La Cession de La Louisiane* (a copy of which was enclosed in your letter), that, on the negotiation of the treaty by which that province was ceded to the United States, I gave to you & Mr. Tallyrand each a million, & to Labouri 300.000, is false and utterly destitute of foundation. For the services you, or any other person, may have rendered in that negotiation not one cent was directly, or indirectly, advanced to you, or to Mr. Talleyrand, or to any other person whatever.

I have given this brief answer at this time, for the circumstances under which it is written prevent me from giving any other. When I recover my health I will write to you more fully on the subject.

I have the honor to be, with high consideration & esteem, your most obt. & hble. sert.

TO DR. CHARLES EVERETT.
OAK HILL, May 18, 1830.

DEAR SIR,—Since my return home I have been free from fever, and other complaint, except that of weakness. I have in some degree recovered, but am far from being restored to my former state. I take exercise on horseback daily, when the weather permits, but I ride a few miles only. My cough continues, without pain. I hope when the weather becomes settled, and I may pursue a regular system of exercise, that my health will be restored.

Mrs. Hay, my daughter, is now with hers near Baltimore, who expects soon to be confined. She has been with her husband sometime in the city, whither he went to consult Dr. Hunt, who is acquainted with his constitution on a complaint with which he has been afflicted for more than two months, & still continues. It was thought to be the rheumatism, his pain in his body & limbs being excruciating, but it is now thought to be bilious. He is uncertain when he will be able to reach home. My daughter will return to, & bring him if able to come, here, as soon as she can leave hers. Mrs. Monroe's health has rather improved. Our accounts from Mr. Gouverneur & our daughter in N. York are favorable.

It would give us great pleasure to see you here, if convenient to you to make us a visit. I fear it will be utterly out of my power to attend at the university at the next meeting of the visitors. Unless a great change in my health takes place it will be impossible, and that can hardly be expected, in so short a time, at my period of life. This increases my desire to see you here, as indeed I should be happy to see some other friends with whom you are intimately acquainted.

The report in favor of my claims has not yet been taken up, and there is cause to apprehend that it will not be reached, in regular order, during the session, & in which event that it will not be acted on before the adjournment. I have experienced many difficulties thro' life, and have met them as I trust I ought to do. I shall make the same effort in future, let what may happen, though under circumstances not so favorable to success.

I am engaged in works, as you know, which give me an interesting occupation, and amusement. If you could come over I would communicate what I have executed to you, & be glad to have your sentiments respecting them. I mention this in confidence. Present my best regards to Mr. Rogers.

TO JOHN C. CALHOUN.
OAKHILL, May 19, 1830.

DEAR SIR,—I have received your letter of the 17th and hasten to answer it. I well remember that when I received the letter from Genl. Jackson, to which you allude, of the 5th of Jany. 1818, I was sick in bed, and could not read it. You were either present, or came in immediately afterwards, and I handed it to you for perusal. After reading it you replaced it, with a remark that it required my attention, or would require an answer, but without any notice of its contents. Mr. Crawford came in soon afterwards, and I handed it also to him, for perusal. He read it, and returned it, in like manner, without making any comment on its contents, further than that it related to the Seminole war, or something to that effect. I never shewed it to any other person, and I am not certain whether it was he, or you, who observed that it related to the Seminole war. Having made all the arrangements respecting that war, and being sometime confined by indisposition, the letter was laid aside, and forgotten by me, and I never read it until after the conclusion of the war, and then I did it on an intimation from you that it required my attention. You ask whether that letter was before the Cabinet, in the deliberation on the despatches received from the General communicating the result of that war, or alluded to by any member of the administration. My impression decidedly is that it was not before the cabinet, nor do I recollect, or think that it was alluded to in the deliberation on the subject. Had it been I could not, I presume, have forgotten it. I received the dispatches referred to here, & had made up my mind before I left home as to the part I ought to take in reference to its management, especially if I should be supported, in the opinion formed, by the Administration. That support was afforded, and I pursued the course which my judgment dictated, with a view to the honor and interest of my country, and the honor of the General who commanded. With sincerest regard I am, dear Sir, yours—

TO JOHN C. CALHOUN.
May 21, 1830.

DEAR SIR,—Your visit here was so short, and the subject to which you attracted my attention so interesting, that I could not do justice to it, in some views, at the time, nor can I, I fear, even at present. The facts stated in my answer to your letter, according to my recollection are strictly correct, in every circumstance. The material circumstances are, was the letter in question [From General Jackson, of January 5, 1818, HAMILTON] alluded to in the Cabinet consultation, & if alluded to, was it brought before the Cabinet? My opinion is as stated,—that it was neither alluded to, nor brought before the Cabinet. You could not allude to it, as I presume, because it would be to invalidate, if it had any effect, the ground you had already taken, that the attack on the Spanish posts was a breach of order. I could not have alluded to it, because I was ignorant of its contents. Whether brought before the Cabinet, or alluded to in the deliberation, are questions which touch the character, in the first instance of myself, in the next of yourself, I mean if brought before the public. Who are impartial witnesses in such a case? Undoubtedly Mr. Adams, Mr. Wirt and Mr. Crowninshield. Their recollection and opinion are, therefore, of the highest importance. But will the subject be brought before the public, and by whom? A publication by anyone involves an attack on General Jackson, provided the letter was an important one. He will not bring it forward, nor will any friend of his, as I presume. My impression is, in regard to yourself, that I would not bring the subject forward, nor notice it in any form, before the public, unless it were brought forward before them first by others, and then on the defensive only. In that state, the more candid, full, & independent, the better the effect. In the present state, I would meet the communication, from the General, in a friendly manner—give him all the explanation necessary, as to the whole proceeding, your opinion of his breach of orders, the time you read his letter to me, I being then sick in bed, the hint you afterwards gave me, & the motive for it.—

Any step which might be considered as an attack on him, at the present time, might have an ill effect on the individual, and likewise on public concerns. The period is eminently delicate & interesting for our country, & its system of gov^t., and therefore great caution, in every political movement, or which may have that bearing, especially by those in high public trusts, is peculiarly proper. I write you in great confidence, & under impressions which you will duly appreciate.

The propriety of measures will be judged of by a strict analysis of their merit, or demerit, and a correct opinion, I doubt not, will be formed.

P.S. I sho^d. have no objection sho^d. you deem it proper to your shewing to the General your late letter to me and my answer.—You will, I presume, shew it to Mr. Wirt, to whom I wrote a short one by last mail, as you may this.

TO JOHN C. CALHOUN.
Oak Hill, May 26, 1830.

Dear Sir,—I have this moment received your letter of yesterday, and altho' I give it a prompt answer, to meet your views, yet my mind is made up, as to the course it is incumbent on me to pursue. The letter from Genl. Jackson to me was private, & from its nature, confidential. Had I been in health & read it, I would never have shewn it to any one, however great my friendship for, or confidence in him might be. Our appeal to Mr. Wirt, in whose honor & friendship we have the utmost confidence, has been produced by causes which I need not mention to you. His declaration that, according to his recollection and belief, the letter was not before the Cabinet, & that he had never heard of it before his late communication with you, concurrent with our view, confirms me in that sentiment. We will therefore consider the communication to him as confidential. I deem it improper for me to go beyond it, or extend the communication to any other person. In taking this course I am not led by a want of confidence in Mr. Adams and Mr. Crowninshield, but by a sentiment of delicacy in regard to myself. If the case related to me only, I sho^d. promptly give them that proof of my confidence. But it relates to another, and under circumstances which will make any disclosure, no matter to whom, bear more forcibly on me than any other person. This sentiment gains force from the reference which you & Mr. Wirt have kindly made to me, by declining to take any step, with others, which might by any possibility, subject me to compromitment.

TO JAMES MADISON.
July 2, 1830.

DEAR SIR,—Being very anxious to join, & proceed with you to the University, to perform our duties there, I have delayed answering your letter of May the 18, in the hope that my health would be so far restored as to enable me to do it. In this I am disappointed. I am still too weak to sustain such an exertion. I am, and have been since my return, free from fever, and I take exercise on horseback in the morning, daily, and think that I gradually recover strength, but it is in a very limited degree. Through the heat of the day I am forced to repose on a bed, incapable of any effort, without exposing myself to injury. Under these circumstances it would be improper for me to make the attempt. Other obstacles present themselves; Mrs. Monroe could not accompany me; her weak state forbids it, and I could not leave her here alone. Our daughter, Mrs. Hay, is still with her husband in Washington, whose fate is equally uncertain as when I last wrote to you. Various experiments have been made on different views of his malady, all of which have failed, and the medicine he has taken, in each instance, has tended only to weaken him. His physicians advise that he come home, if he can bear the journey, which they doubt. In this state it would be distressing to me to leave home, even if my strength was equal to it.

I have not heard from Mr. Sparks, nor is it necessary, in reference to the publication of Reneval's statement of which you furnished a copy. He is at liberty to publish it without any communication with me. I have one also from Mr. Vaughan, who was the confidential agent of Ld. Shelburne, which differs in certain respects from the other. Ought not this likewise to be published? He intimated to me a year ago that he intended to make some alterations in it, but I have not since heard from him. Perhaps a communication between Mr. Sparks and him might be useful. Of this however you will judge, & of which, if you think such communication proper & necessary, you will be so kind as suggest it to him. Ought I to say anything to Mr. Vaughan, or to Mr. Sparks on the subject?

I send you a small addition to the report I drew for an Executive govt. for the University. It is a respect due to the institution at West Point, & its management, & was casually omitted. I feel no personal solicitude respecting the decision on that report. Being called on to draw one, I have done so, and am perfectly willing that it be placed among the papers of the institution without further acting on it.

It is a cause of great regret that I cannot be with you, at your house & the University, as I should have been much gratified to meet other friends there. Be so kind as present our best regards to Mrs. Madison.

TO J. M. COWPERTHWAITE.

The chair with which you have presented me today, on the part of the chairmakers of this city, I accept with the most grateful emotion. The accommodation which it afforded me while I remained on the Platform was sensibly felt, but the sentiment produced by your attention, and the motives which led to it, roused feelings of a different character. That you should recollect the humble service which I rendered, in early youth, in our revolutionary struggle, and have taken so kind and generous a view of my conduct, in all the important trusts with which I have been honoured by my country, has made a lasting impression.

The revolution of France undoubtedly took its origin from that of the U. States. Her citizens fought and bled in our service. They caught the spirit of liberty here, & carried it home with them. We can never look back to that era, without fixing our eyes on an illustrious individual, who has been equally distinguished for his service, in support of that great cause, in both hemispheres.

That you sho^d. have manufactured this chair in the [two words illegible] is a proof of your talent in the art, which affords me great pleasure. I beg you to assure the chairmakers of the city, that I shall preserve it, as a testimonial of their approbation to whom I shall always attach an high value.

I have no doubt that the late glorious triumph in favor of liberty [will] promote the general interest of the civilized world.

TO JOHN QUINCY ADAMS.
Jany. 25, 1831.

I had the pleasure to receive your very kind and interesting letter of the 10th. sometime since, and sho^d. have answered it before had I not been prevented by my weak state of health, and great depression by the inclemency of the season. Of your sympathy with me under the heavy afflictions with which I have been lately visited, I was well aware, & feel sensibly the kind manner in which you have expressed it.

The present revolution in France opens a new epoch to that country & to the world, the consequences attending which cannot now be estimated with any degree of certainty. The first revolution was marked, especially in its early stages, with a violence & cruelty, which laid the foundation for its overthrow. In this sentiment I concur with you, as I do that the present one has occurred under much more favorable circumstances. They have stopped at a point to which the people of that country may be competent, as I trust they are. The sanction promptly given to it by Engl^d. will I think afford it support both at home and abroad. It admits the revolutionary principle, but confines it to limited monarchy, by which she intended, as I presume, to support the existing state in France, and by means thereof her own gov^t. and likewise to put an end to the holy alliance. If France & Engl^d. adhere to this policy, and are able to sustain it, the example may extend its influence to other people, to Spain & Italy, & even to the north. Its effect on Belgium is involved in too much darkness at present to admit any rational conjecture respecting it. It is equally difficult to calculate what effect on Engl^d., as to Ireland or in her interior, as to reform; altho' the new ministry may be friendly to it, as I think it is. I think that the change will operate in our favor with both France and Engl^d. The part Genl. La Fayette takes in it will be felt in every quarter, and will give great support to the system.

My papers relating to the occurrence to which you allude are in London. I have, however, I think, a distinct recollection of all the material circumstances attending its important features, and if there be any point on which you wish immediate information, and will state it, I will communicate it to you. If you sho^d. afterwards desire copies of any of them, I will furnish—[remainder of draft missing, HAMILTON].

TO JOHN C. CALHOUN.
January 27, 1831
[DRAFT]

I have received your letter   of enquiring what were the motives which induced you to ask of me whether Genl. Jackson's letter of the 7th. of Jany. 1814, had been mentioned in the Cabinet, by either of the members, & whether, in consequence, I had found it among my papers, & read it to the Cabinet. I well remember that, in making this enquiry, you communicated to me Mr. Crawford's letter to Mr. Forsyth, and Genl. Jackson's to you, with which he transmitted it to you. In Mr. Crawford's letter he stated that you had mentioned in the Cabinet the letter of the Genl. referred to, and that I had, in consequence, taken it from among my documents, brought it in, and read it to the Cabinet. This therefore submitted the question, in both views, before me, in the most impressive manner, and resting on facts respecting which I entertained no doubt, I was particularly guarded in my answer to your enquiry. I was sorry that Mr. Crawford's view differed from mine, but the incident, in its origin, & all its consequences, being one of high importance to my country, & to myself, there was no portion of it which would not have made a deep impression on my mind. As I had never read the letter, being sick in bed when I recd. it, had the incidents in question occurred I was satisfied that I could not have forgotten them. But as Mr. Crawford entertained a different sentiment, & I knew nothing of the other members who were present, I owed it to myself, as well as to him & them, to express myself with delicacy & caution. The information which you afterwards gave me of Mr. Wirt's opinion, on consulting him, gave me the more confidence in what I had before said.

Had I read the Genl.'s letter when I recd. it, I shod. never have shewn it to anyone, as I have heretofore observed. Coming from the commanding general I concluded that it must relate either to men or money, & therefore handed it to the heads of each department, as he entered, but as neither suggested anything of the kind, the subject being disposed of, the letter was deposited with other papers, & forgotten when I arose from my sick bed.

In your communication with me you appeared to indulge no unfriendly feeling to anyone, but to seek my unreserved and candid sentiment on the subject of your enquiry.

TO JUDGE SOUTHARD.
February 8, 1831.

I have yours of the 1st. asking my sanction to a communication to Mr. Calhoun, at his request, of what was said by Mr. Crawford, in the Cabinet, when the conduct of Com: Porter, for his attack on Foxardo, was under consideration, at a special meeting, which I called to obtain its advice, as to the measure which shod. be adopted in consequence thereof. You well know, as did the whole administration, and likewise Com: Rodgers & Chauncey, the part which I acted in every instance towards Com: Porter, & how he requited me for it. I never noticed his conduct, however, by entering into any discussion with him, & I have still the same object in view. I do not perceive, however, on what principle, publick or private, regarding the state in which the controversy to which I allude is, that I can withhold my sanction, as the act of a private individual. If the Chief Magistrate has any power of restraint while in office, it must cease after his retirement. The parties in question are at variance, in which I take no part, and will not be seen further than in inevitable. In this instance, as my sanction is a private & personal act between ourselves, I wish you not to mention my name, but to act as if coming from yourself. The relation the Com: bears to me is an additional motive for this caution.

TO A COMMITTEE
[OF TAMMANY HALL].
1831—

I have received your invitation to attend the meeting, to be held this evening, at Tammany Hall, of the mechanicks, workmen & other citizens of N. York, to celebrate the late glorious revolution, in France, in favor of liberty, with the sensibility which so generous a mark of your confidence was calculated to excite.

An effort in favor of liberty, by the people of any country, has always commanded my high respect, and its failure excited my deep regret. This remark applies with peculiar force to France, from whom we derived great aid in our own struggle. Having witnessed, for several years, in my mission to that country, the exertions of that people in support of that great cause, in which they displayed a gallantry & patriotism, which repulsed the surrounding nations, & astonished the civilized world, I could not otherwise than be deeply affected by its failure. I have rejoiced to find that that most afflicting disaster did not extinguish, nor even diminish the spirit, as has been proved by the recent most glorious event. The moderation and humanity which they have displayed shew that they have derived useful admonition from the errors of their former struggle. The prudence also with which they have adopted the counsel of enlightened & virtuous men, to whom they have committed the direction of affairs, affords an additional strong ground on which to confide in their success.

Having seen, in our revolutionary struggle, the most satisfactory proof of the virtue, talent & gallantry of our fellow citizen, Genl. La Fayette, & known him afterwards, & been intimately connected with his affairs, in my missions to France, in which his devotion to liberty, and every previous impression in his favor, was confirmed, I have seen with delight his call to the station which he now holds, because I find in it a generous reward of his merit, & likewise great support to the cause in which France is engaged.

It is my intention to attend your meeting if my health will permit it, and I certainly shall do it, delicate as it is, if no unfavorable change occurs.

TO THE GOVERNOR OF VIRGINIA.
1831

My reduced and weak state of health, having rendered it impossible for me to perform any publick duties, imposes on me the necessity of resigning my appointment as visitor to the University of Virginia, which I now do in this communication to you. I adopt this measure with great regret, as I take a deep interest in the success of the institution, which, as well from my affectionate regard for my native state, as the support which the institution gives, by spreading intelligence among our fellow citizens, to our free system of govt., will never cease. With my best respects to your family, & the members of the council, I am yr. very obt. servant.

TO JOHN QUINCY ADAMS.
New York, Feby. 14, 1831.

Dear Sir,—I received in regular time your letter of the 29th ulto., and regret that my weak state of health, and the pressure of my private concerns, have prevented my giving you an earlier answer.

Your remarks on the state of England are highly interesting, and shew the difficulties which her govt. must experience in making any reform in the parliament, or even in preventing convulsions, which may, at no distant period, shake the whole system. Her affairs have reached a stage, under expedients to unite forces which, if suffered to advance, in a regular course, menaces an overthrow, and in which a change in any of the prominent features menaces a like result. I do not see how the British govt. can get rid of the debts, and of the corn laws without a convulsion—and with the immense mass of poor collected around the manufacturing establishments, the coal pits & elsewhere, added to the laboring class, who are all poor, if the govt. be essentially thrown into their hands the same fate may be apprehended. A conflict with Ireland, which seems to approach, merits the same view, so that I do not see how Great Britain can long sustain her present rank in Europe, or preserve internal tranquility.

To the independence of Belgium I see no evidence of opposition, either from France or Great Britain. The sentiment of France, as may be inferred from a declaration of our friend, Genl. La Fayette, seems to favor it, & the unsettled state of Engl^d. affords proof that she will not embark in war to prevent it. The first impression which the decision of Engl^d., in favor of the present revolution in France, made on my mind was that she intended to connect herself with that country by a new bond; that she intended to offer her support to France for the acquisition of Belgium, in return for that of France to maintain her authority over Ireland. But this impression has been removed by what has already transpired. Engl^d. appears to stand by herself, connected, as yet, with France only by the declaration in favor of her present revolution, & by the effect it may have on the Holy Alliance, & the general system of Europe in regard to gov^t. France, by what has transpired, in relation to Belgium & Poland, seems to mingle more, & to assume a more imposing attitude, in the affairs of the other powers. Into what this may lead, & what may be the progress of her revolution & gov^t. must now be mere matter of conjecture. I consider her situation more favorable.

The disorder and imbecility of other gov^ts., especially those with whom we have most intercourse, must give some security to our own, provided we sustain the attitude, on land and sea, which we have done since the late war. If we complete our fortifications, & have a force to occupy & keep them in order, and sustain our navy at the point contemplated, exhibiting squadrons in the several seas which they have hitherto visited, I have no doubt we shall command their respect, especially if our gov^t. pursues a pacific policy.

My correspondence with Genl. Jackson, relative to his conduct in the Seminole war; with Mr. Calhoun, as to what passed in the Cabinet respecting it, except a recent communication incidental to the matter, is at Oak Hill. You shall see, and have copies when I have access to it, if you wish them. I think that you are already well acquainted with the subject in all its parts, unless it be the correspondence with Genl. Jackson; but if there is any point on which you wish information, and intimate it, I will immediately communicate it as far as I may be able.

The danger is, if the right of suffrage is extended to the whole population, without any qualification, as to property, that as the difference of interest begins to operate, as it will soon do, that the mass of poor, which will be by far the most numerous, will elect persons who will be instruments in the hands of leaders who will overthrow the govt., &, by convulsive movements, restore the despotism.

You have stated the difficulties which Engl^d. has to encounter to sustain her present state. France has a better prospect of maintaining her present system than any of the gov^ts. of Europe, less trammelled.

That the present ministry entered with a determination to make a reform, if in their power, I am confident. I am confirmed in this sentiment by my knowledge of those entertained by several of the members, particularly Grey, Holland, Landsdowne & Mr. Brougham.

TO JOHN C. CALHOUN.
February, 1831.

DEAR SIR,—I have yours of the 4th. and readily perceive the cause of my mistake of the object of your enquiry in that of the 27th. ulto. I was, I presume, led into it by reference, in the interrogation in your letter, to what occurred in London only, no mention having been made there of the proceedings in the Cabinet.

I have a very imperfect recollection of the conduct of the several members in the consultation in the Cabinet, respecting the conduct of Genl. Jackson in the Seminole war. I recd. his despatches in Loudon, and my mind was made up on a variety of considerations, founded on my previous service abroad & at home, as to the course which policy dictated, before I left Loudon, and which, after due deliberation was adopted. My object was to reconcile the members to that policy, by giving the necessary explanations; and I pursued it, until it was accomplished. I did not even remember, until you reminded me of it in Loudon, that you had advised his arrest for disobedience of orders, nor was I aware, until advised of it by Mr. Adams, as he passed thro' town this winter, that he was of opinion that the conduct of the Spanish authorities justified the General in his attack on the Spanish posts, & would justify the govt. in taking the responsibility on itself, and likewise that a very animated discussion took place between you & him, concerning the opinions which you respectively advanced. I mention this in strict confidence. The defect of my memory alone, is a strong argument against my statement of anything relative to the conduct of the individual members, further than what relates to the letter of Genl. Jackson, which stands on its own peculiar ground, and asserts what was not done, and to which, had it been done, being a party, as was asserted, I cod. not have forgotten. Other considerations are equally conclusive. The difference of opinion & animated discussion, between you & Mr. Adams, was warm, in the deliberations on that subject, and as Mr. Adams thinks it probable that he may be called forth, that fact will of course be stated by him in that event. It is better that that warmth should be ascribed to mere difference of opinion between independent men, as to a measure, than to any particular hostility to the Genl., & which it might be if any sentiment shod. be expressed respecting it in the present stage. By disproving everything relating to the letter, on which Mr. Crawford's remarks are principally founded, his inferences in other respects will be shaken, & as I presume, be deemed erroneous. To this view you may give proper tone, in the candid & independent avowal which you will make, of the sentiments you entertained, & of the part which you acted, in the deliberations on that interesting subject, without appearing to vindicate yourself against any charge whatever. You had just entered the Cabinet & had had no variance with the General, and were, I presume, slightly acquainted with him. I need not add that I communicate these sentiments with the best view to you as well as to myself.

TO JOHN QUINCY ADAMS.
March 11, 1831.

DEAR SIR,—My very low state of health has rendered it impossible for me to give an earlier answer to your letter of the 15th ulto. My memory is very defective, as to what occurred in the Cabinet, in the deliberations on the result of the Seminole war. I will, however, communicate to you all the information that I may be able, without the aid of my papers, which are at Oak Hill.

My opinion remains unchanged, that the letter of Genl. Jackson, of Jany. 6, 1818, was not read in the Cabinet, nor mentioned, nor do I think, had it been known to Mr. Crawford that it had not been answered, that it would have justified the inferrence, he has drawn from it, that Genl. Jackson might have considered it as a sanction to his proposition. He especially requested in it an informal sanction from Genl. Rhea & without which, in the spirit of his letter, none could be inferred. Besides what is the fair import of the letter? He does not ask an official authority from me. He asks only my consent as an Individual, and evidently with an intention not to compromit me, even in that character. The letter therefore, had it been answered, & the sanction been given, was an affair of confidence between him & me, never to be disclosed. On what principle it can be relied on as an authority to attack the posts, & to make me responsible for it, I cannot conceive. If it was his intention, had I given the sanction, to take the responsibility on himself, and his letter admitted only this construction, the obligation was much stronger when none was given, & his instructions forbade the attack. The statement given was strictly true that the letter was not read, nor mentioned in the Cabinet, and, according to my memory, I never read it, or thought of it, till after the meeting of Congress, and then on the suggestion of Mr. Calhoun, that the existence of such a letter was known to, and spoken of, by Genl. Lacocke, who made the attack on Genl. Jackson in the Senate. In stating to Genl. Jackson, that I had never recurred to that letter, until after the arrival of Mr. Hambly, I meant not until after the affair was terminated, to convey the idea that it had not weight in my decision on the subject. That was the only point involved between us at that period, & to which that statement could alone refer. I never met Mr. Crawford & Mr. Calhoun by themselves on the subject, nor do I recollect that I had any conversation with Mr. Crawford on it after the decision of the Cabinet, tho' in this latter instance I may be mistaken.

I concur with you in the sentiment that no motion was made, either by Mr. Calhoun, or Mr. Crawford, for the arrest or trial of Genl. Jackson, and that the whole discussion turned on the question whether all his proceedings sh^d. be approved, or the capture of the Spanish ports disavowed. Of the marked nature of the discussion to which you recur I have no recollection, nor have I of the notes drawn by you and Mr. Wirt for publication, or of the modifications which I gave to that which was published. The view which you have presented is very satisfactory to me. Sho^d. I have any of the papers relating to it, you shall have copies, or the originals if you prefer them.

With the origin of Genl. Jackson's variance with Mr. Crawford, & of that between the latter & Mr. Calhoun, I am ignorant. I knew at an early period that much hostility existed between the two former, and that the two latter had no friendly communication with each other. I never inquired into the cause in either instance, but knowing the fact, had it [in] view, with respect to the two latter, in our Cabinet consultations. The publications already made have given almost all the material documents, relating to the conduct of Genl. Jackson in the Seminole war, and have furnished much light as to the origin and causes of the differences of the respective parties, and also of the merits of the controversy on each side. Any that I have, when I return to Loudon, you shall possess, & in the interim, any information relating to any occurrence, not sufficiently exhibited, that I possess, you shall command.

TO DR. CHARLES EVERETT.
NEW YORK, MARCH 28th, 1831.

DEAR SIR,—I have heard with much regret that you have been indisposed, but hope that you have completely renewed your health. My own health continues to be very infirm & weak. Little change has taken place in it since I came here. I have, in consequence, yielded to the wishes of my daughters to remain with them, & the connection generally; to accomplish which object, with any degree of comfort, I am compelled to sell my estate in Loudon, which is advertised, in the gazettes of Washington & Richmond, for sale on the second

Wednesday of June next, & for which full power is given to Mr. Gouverneur & Captain James Monroe. I regret much to be forced to part with that estate, as I should meet there occasionally, if my health permitted, my friends from different parts of the State, and have other strong reasons to be attached to it. It is my intention, if I shall be able, to visit it the latter end of next month, when I shall be happy to see you. I beg you to explain the above to Mr. Rogers, & other friends in the neighborhood.

I am free from pain, but my cough annoys me much, both night and day. I take no medicine but to moderate it, such as syrup of horehound, horehound candy, &c. My physician, Dr. Bibby, thinks that I am too much reduced to take any medicine which should operate on the liver, & that, when the season permits, exercise, and the Saratoga waters will relieve me. This was also the opinion of the physicians in Loudon and Washington. It would afford me great pleasure to have your opinion, & that of my friend Dr. Carter, who know my constitution, and were so kind to me at Richmond. After the severe service to which I have been exposed thro' life, and the heavy pressure on me since my retirement, I have, I fear, little cause to hope for a perfect recovery at my advanced years.

TO JAMES MADISON.
[*Last letter, Ed.*]
NEW YORK, April 11, 1831.

DEAR SIR,—I have intended for some time to write and explain to you the arrangement I have made for my future residence, and respecting my private affairs, with a view to my comfort, so far as I may expect it, but it has been painful to me to execute it. My ill state of health continuing, consisting of a cough, which annoys me by night and by day into considerable expectoration, considering my advanced years, although my lungs are not affected, renders the restoration of my health very uncertain, or indeed any favorable change in it. In such a state I could not reside on my farm. The solitude would be very distressing, and its cares very burthensome. It is the wish of both my daughters, and of the whole connection, that I should remain here & receive their good offices, which I have decided to do. I do not wish to burthen them. It is my intention to rent a house near Mr. Gouverneur, and to live within my own resources, so far as I may be able. I could make no establishment of any kind without the sale of my property in Loudon, which I have advertised for the 8th of June, and given the necessary power to Mr. Gouverneur & my nephew

James. If my health will permit I will visit it in the interim, to arrange affairs there for that event, and my removal here. The accounting officers have made no decision in my claims, & have given me much trouble. I have told them that I would make out no account adapted to the act, which fell far short of making me a just reparation, and that I had rather lose the whole sum than give to it any sanction, be the consequences what they may. I never recovered from the losses of the first mission, to which those of the second added considerably.

It is very distressing to me to sell my property in Loudon, for, besides parting with all I have in the State, I indulged a hope, if I could retain it, that I might be able occasionally to visit it, and meet my friends, or many of them there. But ill health & advanced years prescribe a course which we must pursue. I deeply regret that there is no prospect of our ever meeting again, since so long have we been connected, and in the most friendly intercourse, in public & private life, that a final separation is among the most distressing incidents which could occur. I shall resign my seat as a visitor at the Board in due time to enable the Executive to fill the vacancy that my successor may attend the next meeting. I beg you to assure Mrs. Madison that I never can forget the friendly relation which has existed between her and my family. We often remind us of incidents of the most interesting character. My daughter, Mrs. Hay, will live with me, who with the whole family here unite in affectionate regards to both of you.

MADISON'S FAREWELL TO MONROE
MONTPELIER, *April* 21, 1831.

DEAR SIR,—I have duly received yours of [April 11]. I considered the advertisement of your estate in Loudoun as an omen that your friends in Virginia were to lose you. It is impossible to gainsay the motives to which you yielded in making New York your residence, though I fear you will find its climate unsuited to your period of life and the state of your health. I just observe, and with much pleasure, that the sum voted by Congress, however short of just calculations, escapes the loppings to which it was exposed from the accounting process at Washington, and that you are so far relieved from the vexations involved in it. The result will, I hope, spare you at least the sacrifice of an untimely sale of your valuable property; and I would fain flatter myself that, with an encouraging improvement of your health, you might be brought to reconsider the arrangement which fixes you elsewhere. The effect of this, in closing the prospect of our ever meeting again, afflicts me deeply; certainly not less so than it can you.

The pain I feel at the idea, associated as it is with a recollection of the long, close, and uninterrupted friendship which united us, amounts to a pang which I cannot well express, and which makes me seek for an alleviation in the possibility that you may be brought back to us in the wonted degree of intercourse. This is a happiness my feelings covet, notwithstanding the short period I could expect to enjoy it; being now, though in comfortable health, a decade beyond the canonical three-score and ten, an epoch which you have but just passed.

As you propose to make a visit to Loudoun previous to the notified sale, if the state of your health permits, why not, with the like permission, extend the trip to this quarter? The journey, at the rate of your own choice, might cooperate in the reestablishment of your health, whilst it would be a peculiar gratification to your friends, and, perhaps, enable you to join your colleagues at the university once more at least. It is much to be desired that you should continue, as long as possible, a member of the Board, and I hope you will not send in your resignation in case you find your cough and weakness giving way to the influence of the season and the innate strength of your constitution. I will not despair of your being able to keep up your connection with Virginia by retaining Oak Hill and making it not less than an occasional residence. Whatever may be the turn of things, be assured of the unchangeable interest felt by Mrs. Madison, as well as myself, in your welfare, and in that of all who are dearest to you.

In explanation of my microscopic writing, I must remark that the older I grow the more my stiffening fingers make smaller letters, as my feet take shorter steps, the progress in both cases being, at the same time, more fatiguing as well as more slow."

[DENUNCIATION OF THE INSINUATIONS OF JOHN RHEA.]

A letter of John Rhea of Tennessee is shown to me this nineteenth day of June, 1831, for the first time, nor have I previously had any intimation of the receipt of such a letter, or of its contents. It was received by Mr. Gouverneur, as I am told by him, and after having been read, kept from me, for reasons which he will explain, until this time. Had it been communicated to me before, I should have made, as I now do, the following declaration & reply thereto, which I wish to be filed with the said letter, as my reply to its contents.

Ist. It is utterly unfounded & untrue that I ever authorized John Rhea to write any letter whatever to Genl. Jackson, authorizing or encouraging him to disobey, or deviate from the orders which had been communicated to him from the Department of War.

2^d. That it is utterly unfounded & untrue that I ever desired the said John Rhea to request Genl. Jackson to destroy any letter written by him, the said John Rhea to Genl. Jackson, nor did I at any time wish or desire that any letter, document, or memorandum, in the possession of Genl. Jackson, or of any other person, relating to my official conduct, in respect of the Seminole war, or any other public matter, should be destroyed.

A note applicable to this subject will be found among my papers at Oak Hill in Virginia, to which, as well as to my whole correspondence with General Jackson, as well as others, I refer, for the truth of this statement.

JAMES MONROE.

This statement was signed by James Monroe and declared to be true in the presence of us—on this 19th day of June 1831.

M. GELSTON,
EDW^D. M. GREENWAY.

At the height of General Jackson's quarrel with Calhoun, which turned in part on the Seminole affair, John Rhea—better known to the public men of the day as "Johnny Rhea," a member of Congress for many years from Tennessee, "a man never of much reputation, who is remembered in history only as one of Andrew Jackson's constant parasites"—wrote to Monroe hoping to elicit from him something that would implicate him as having approved Jackson's course.

At the time of the delivery of Rhea's letter, Monroe's situation was such as to render it highly desirable to keep him free from all excitement and anxiety. He had been gradually declining for some time past and his family had no hope that he would be restored to health. For some weeks he had been confined to his bed. Mr. Gouverneur, Monroe's son-in-law, acting as his secretary and in charge of his papers, received and opened Rhea's letter. In his astonishment and perplexity Gouverneur sought counsel of friends in whose judgment and regard for his venerable and illustrious father-in-law he had great confidence. He sent the Rhea letter to William Wirt, remarking, "It is a singular production and seems to have some singular object in view. The lapse of time since the subject of it became a matter of discussion and the most extraordinary statement of the burning of a letter of the most vital consequence to the possessor strike me with singular effect. All the statements respecting conversations with Mr. Monroe I know from his own lips to be false and unfounded. It is really important that Mr. M. should be made acquainted with its contents. I know it would create considerable excitement in his mind and might have an injurious effect. Again, Would I be justified in assuming the responsibility of keeping it from him?"

Mr. Wirt agreed with Mr. Gouverneur in his estimate of Rhea's letter and urged that Monroe's solemn statement be procured. "The design is obvious," he replied to Mr. Gouverneur. "It has grown out of the Calhoun correspondence and the object is to prop up the falling character of A. J. at the expense of that of our venerable and most excellent friend. The letter I have no doubt is designed for publication—it will be published with a statement that Mr. M. has not dared to contradict it—and it will probably be supported by the certificates or affidavits of A. J. and J. R. The reputation of Mr. M. is deeply and vitally concerned in this affair and if he were my own father and at the last gasp, I should feel it my duty to show it to him at every hazard, and receive his explanation or contradiction. If I were in his place I should consider myself ill treated to have such a charge concealed from me in the hour of death. That such would be his sentiment too I have no doubt for I have known him for thirty-five years and have never seen the day when he did not value his character above his life, and surely it is of far more consequence now both to himself, his country and his friends than the small remnant of days that may belong to him. His denial of the statement made in the awful moment of approaching dissolution would outweigh with the virtuous and enlightened of the community a hundred such witnesses and posterity will acquit him of the vile duplicity which this letter imputes."

Mr. Gouverneur followed Wirt's advice and accordingly on the 19th. of June Monroe made his deposition. His name is signed legibly and firmly with only a slight tremulous indication of his enfeebled state. On the ensuing 4th. of July James Monroe was dead and with his death the controversy subsided. No exigency ever arose for the production of Monroe's deposition. Whether the affair was dropped because this triangular quarrel between Jackson, Calhoun, and Crawford had ended in a permanent rupture of relations or because the public would bear no more of it, or possibly because the administration had learned from some source that there was a statement made in extremis which might be forthcoming, history does not record. But it may now be positively affirmed that Monroe's most intimate friends were informed confidentially of this deposition and that one of them at least—John Quincy Adams—has left on record an opinion as to the "depth of depravity in this transaction" expressed in language sufficiently clear and explicit. (Diary, August 30, 1831.)
[HAMILTON.]

PART XII

The People, the Sovereigns

INTRODUCTION

ONROE WAS NOT A speculative thinker or a constructor of abstract
systems. The endless flow of writing that he poured from his mind was
almost all keyed to some particular event or action—a vivid report
of what was taking place in a given situation, or a logical analysis of a legal or
political problem. But this does not mean that he was a pragmatist without principles, or an activist carried on the crest of events. On the contrary, he was
guided by constant principles to which he returned no matter what pressures
were placed upon him.

These principles were sorely tried by the struggles of his varied career as legislator, diplomat and president. His experience of the world was broader than
most of his contemporaries, sufficing to give him a long-range vision of the
national interest. Nor was he only buffeted by narrow-minded men; even his
closest friends, such as Jefferson and Madison, sometimes did not understand
that the politics of Monroe was above politics. And if his presidency was "The
Era of Good Feeling," it was because of a lofty vision that sought to bring the
whole nation together under a unifying myth.

We catch glimpses of that vision in his earliest letters, in his reportage of the
French Revolution, in his relations with Lafayette, in his dream (largely realized) of transcontinental expansion, in his rising stature as the defender of the
nation in the War of 1812, in the presidency itself, and in the principles of the
Monroe Doctrine. Not until he retired to his beloved Oak Hill did this practical man of affairs have the leisure to begin a systematic statement of his political philosophy.

The work which he began, *The People, the Sovereigns*, was never completed.
It was first published in 1867 by Samuel L. Gouverneur who, from among the
family papers, gathered together the several parts which Monroe had written.
"Not one word had been added to the original text, neither has one been erased

from the manuscript copy," Gouverneur wrote. Indeed, he stated, the ascription of sovereignty to the people was "the true exposition of the Monroe Doctrine."

Monroe's plan was "to go to first principles," and then make an comparative study historically of those principles in Athens, Laecedemon [Sparta], Carthage, Rome, and "if my health permits," Great Britain. Athens and Laecedemon received extensive analysis, but as his health declined (and that of his wife) Carthage was dispatched in a few pages, whereas Rome and Great Britain never made an appearance. Yet the reader has a feeling that the proposed treatment of Rome and Great Britain, however interesting it might have been, was no irreparable loss. Monroe's talent was not in historical scholarship, despite his deep reading. Far more stimulating is his analysis of the principles of free government, and the underlying currents of the American and French revolutions, of which he had first-hand knowledge.

The opening chapter, accordingly, is the most profound. Monroe seeks to solve the question of why "other republics have failed," whereas the United States, at the time he wrote, had already endured fifty years and outlived the rest. "If we have been thus blessed, it must follow that the example of other republics cannot touch ours, and that we have just cause to calculate on a destiny altogether different from that which befell other people, even those who were most free. We shall have gained an eminence, which no other nation ever reached, and from which, if we fall, the fault will be in ourselves, and we shall thereby give the most discouraging example to mankind that the world ever witnessed," he says.

Monroe's central thesis is that "There are two great principles in government, in direct opposition to each other, on one or other of which singly and exclusively, or on a compound of both, all governments have been and must be founded. One supposed the sovereignty to be in the people and in them only. The other that it is in an individual or a few, and that the people have no participation in it, but are the subject matter on which it operates. If in the people, according to our view, it is called a Democracy; if in an individual, a Despotism; and if in a few, Aristocracy." But Monroe was too great a lover of liberty to be a simple-minded democrat. After examining Aristotle's categories of government, he proclaims that "names count for nothing; that principle is everything."

The great principle he expounds is that, in a free society, sovereignty rests in the people, not in the government or in a despot. Yet he who had stood in the streets of Paris and watched the mobs assault the National Assembly, did not believe that direct popular rule was sustainable. He ridicules Rousseau's idea of plebiscitary democracy in *The Social Contract*, and holds that while Locke's *Two Treatises on Government* was useful to England at the time it was written, "there is little in it. . . which can be considered applicable to us."

Monroe recognized that despotism could reside in the popular will if popular sovereignty were applied without mediating structures. "Man should be looked at in his true character; his virtues and defects should be duly estimated, and the organization be such as to call into activity and give full force to the former, and to suppress the latter." That organization was this: The sovereignty of the people and government should be separated. He believed that if government had to go to the people to obtain particular authority, then government could not become a despot. By establishing a separation between the people as sovereigns and the government, which held only powers delegated from the people, Monroe believed that the state could function in an orderly manner. "The government which is the instrument, and inferior, operates on those who hold the sovereignty, and in consequence, on the superior," says Monroe; "but it operates on the people individually, and not collectively, and as citizens, not as subjects. The government is the agent which executes the compact between the citizens."

That is why his criticism of the French Revolution was based on its failure to separate the sovereignty of the people from the work of the National Convention. "That body formed the government, because by its act, the public actions were sanctioned; but it was rather as the organ and the instrument of the popular feeling and will under the excitement which prevailed, than a calm and deliberative assembly, acting according to its own judgment. The people might be said, and especially until the fall of Robespierre, to rule, en masse, and under the greatest possible disadvantages. The government was in effect united with the sovereignty in the people, and all power, legislative, executive, and judicial, concentrated in them. . . . [A]t its head was a leader who yielded to the worst passions which could animate the breast of an ambition competitor for power."

The corrective to this tendency is that the government itself should be divided into three bodies—legislative, executive, and judicial. "Unite the government with the sovereignty, although it be in the people, and every species of abuse, with the certain overthrow of both will follow. Concentrate all the power in one body, although it be representative, and the result, if not so prompt, will nevertheless, be equally fatal," he says.

Monroe, with a lifetime of experience in legislative bodies, perceived the legislature to be the most dangerous threat to liberty. "If the members of the legislature lose sight of the nation, and look to their sections only, the system is in the utmost danger. . . . A national policy must be cherished and prevail. If the people possess virtue, intelligence, and are devoted to self-government, this danger can never assume a serious form."

Yet he was fully aware that "the people" did not always possess virtue, intelligence, and a devotion to self-government. In commenting on the Athenian democracy's practice of choosing its leaders from among all citizens by lot, rather than by election, Monroe says: "Every citizen of the state is not competent to the discharge of the duties of its highest offices, or of any office whatever. Many are unfit for other reasons than the mere want of suitable qualifications. To commit to the unlettered, ignorant, and vicious, trusts whose duties require the highest talents and greatest virtue, would be to sacrifice the interests of the community, to abandon all respect for principle or character."

Nevertheless, he was confident that "a government founded on the sovereignty of the people with the wise organization and distribution of its powers, is practicable over very extensive dominions and very populous communities." He was concerned to avoid controversies between the rich and the poor, between the virtuous and the selfish. "All this is necessary," he says, "is that the inhabitants generally be intelligent, that they possess some property, to be independent and moral, and that they organize a government by representation into three branches, a legislative, executive and judiciary, under a wise arrangement, and vest in each the powers competent to its objects."

Even though *The People, The Sovereigns* was never completed, it still remains the summing up of Monroe's life's work, the most relevant analysis of the principles which guided his years of service.

CHAPTER I

A COMPARATIVE ELEMENTARY VIEW
OF GOVERNMENT AND OF SOCIETY

HAVING served my country, from very early life, in its most important trusts, abroad and at home, my mind has been turned in the discharge of my public duties to the principles of the system itself, in the success of which I have taken, and always shall take, a deep interest. I have witnessed our difficulties, and have seen with delight the virtue and talent by which they were surmounted. In looking to our future progress, some important questions occur to which great attention is due. Are we not still menaced with dangers? Of what nature are they and to what cause or causes imputable? To these objects my mind has also been drawn with great interest; and having now leisure, it is my intention to express my sentiments freely on them, in the hope that I may thereby render some service, and under the conviction that in those instances in which I may err I shall do no harm.

It has been often affirmed that our Revolution forms the most important epoch in the history of mankind, and in this sentiment I fully concur. But whence does it derive its importance? The sentiment is founded in a belief that it has introduced a system of new governments better calculated to secure to the people the blessings of liberty, and under circumstances more favorable to success, than any which the world ever knew before. If such be the fact, the truth of the affirmation must be conceded, for surely no event can be so important, as the establishment of a new system of government, which by its intrinsic merit, and the force of example, promises to promote so essentially the happiness of mankind.

Other republics have failed. Their career, though brilliant, was marked by contentions which frequently convulsed and finally overthrew them. To what causes were those contentions imputable? Was it that the governments respectively were so defective that their failure was inevitable? Or were the societies, of which those republics were composed, incapable of such governments? To one or other of those causes, or to a combination of them, their fate must have been imputable. Do like causes exist here? If they do, it follows that we are exposed in a certain degree at least to a like fate. These are fair objects of inquiry, and I propose to inquire into them.

To present in a clear and distinct light the difference between the governments and people of the United States, and those of other countries, ancient and modern, and to show that certain causes which produced disastrous effects in them do not exist in most instances, and are inapplicable in all, to ours, is an inquiry of great extent, if pursued in all its parts. It involves all the great principles of free government, with a comparative view of their respective merits, and likewise of the society, regarding the state in which it may be, over which such government is established. The subject, nevertheless, admits of great condensation, without impairing its necessary illustration. The questions to be solved are, have we so far avoided the errors and corrected the defects of other free governments, as to have attained a degree of perfection which was unknown to them? Are our societies in a state better adapted to the support of such governments, than those of any other people ever were, over whom such governments were established? If we have been thus blessed, it must follow that the example of other republics cannot touch ours, and that we have just cause to calculate on a destiny altogether different from that which befell other people, even those who were most free. We shall have gained an eminence, which no other nation ever reached, and from which, if we fall, the fault will be in ourselves, and we shall thereby give the most discouraging example to mankind that the world ever witnessed.

To do justice to the subject, we must not only go to first principles, but trace all the causes which bear on them to their source. If a people be free and their government be defective, why do they not amend it? As the injury arising from the defects of the government must be felt in its operation, and the defects be in consequence, apparent, it is strange having the power exclusively in their hands, if they do not amend them. And if the people participate only in the government, by the occupation of any strong and independent ground in the system, it cannot but excite surprise, having numbers and force on their side, if they should be driven from it; if instead of improving their position, they should lose it altogether. However defective, therefore, the government of the ancient republics may have been, it is obvious that their overthrow could not have been imputable to those defects only; that it may be traced in part at least, to a higher source, to the people themselves. No people blessed with liberty could be deprived of it, if they were not made dupes and the instruments of their own destruction. If they possessed the necessary intelligence and virtue, acted together, and made a common cause in defense of their rights, the artifices of unprincipled and designing men, however deep and well-contrived they might be, would be sure to fail.

It follows then, that the subject on which I have to treat, merits attention in two views; the first, as to the different kinds of government which have existed in different communities in different ages; the second, as to the condition of the society, in the several communities, over which such governments respectively were established. In both branches there are many grades or classes. Government is divisible, from one which is compatible with, and secures to the people under it perfect liberty, to that which subjects them to abject slavery; and society, from a state of entire barbarism, ignorance and depravity, to that of great improvement, intelligence and purity. No proposition according to my judgment, admits of a more satisfactory demonstration, than that in the formation of government, the condition of the society on which it is to operate is to be regarded: that the government which suits one state will not suit another, and that the most improved state of society is that which is best suited to the most free government, if it is not the only one that admits of it. In treating then of government, we must treat of man, for it is for him that the government is formed, and for whom it is indispensable, from the aggregation of a few individuals to that of the most stupendous masses. What then is man? Naturalists give him the highest grade among created beings, and our religion makes his soul immortal. Still he is in a great measure the creature of circumstances. His natural endowments, his passions and principles, are always the same, but these are essentially controlled by moral causes; by the state in which he is, and in consequence in which the society is, of which he is a member. The two branches are therefore intimately connected with, and in the view suggested, inseparable from each other. I will commence with that of government, it being the power which acts on the people, and on which under whatever form, or on whatever principle founded, their happiness must depend. As everything which may be said on this branch must be guided by principle, I will bring to view those, which it is presumed are too well established, to be controverted by any one.

Our system is two-fold, State and National. Each is independent of the other, and sovereign to the extent, and within the limit of specified powers. The preservation of each is necessary to that of the other. Two dangers menace it; disunion and consolidation. Either would be ruinous. It was by the Union that we achieved our independence and liberties, and by it alone can they be maintained. It must therefore be preserved. Consolidation would lead to monarchy and to despotism, which would be equally fatal. That danger must be averted. Both governments rest on the same basis, the sovereignty of the people. Other nations have given us examples of both, of national as well as state, with each of which a comparison of our institutions may be useful, and with which I propose to make it. As however the powers of the National Government originated with the people of each state, and passed from them in the extent to which granted, in their character, as separate and distinct communities, the people of each state form the basis of the system. Consolidation, so far as it has gone, is a diminution of state power, but still the basis in other respects remains unchanged. In looking to either branch, we must look to the source from whence the power emanated, as that is the great feature in our system, in both branches, with the modification given to it in each, which has placed us on more advantageous grounds than was ever held by any other people. In executing this work, therefore, the view which I shall take of the principles of government, and of the state of society, will be equally applicable to both, as well to form a just estimate of the merits of our system, as a fair comparison between it and those of other countries, in both branches.

The view which I shall present in this paper will be elementary, founded on the lights derived from history, and my own observations and reflections, or what I have read and seen through life. In this form and in this stage it is presumed that an illustration may be given, and principles be established, applicable to the whole subject in all its parts, which will be more perspicuous, be better understood, and likewise lessen the labor, than if delayed, until I reach the republics with whose governments and people the comparison will be made.

There are two great principles in government, in direct opposition to each other, on one or other of which, singly and exclusively, or on a compound of both, all governments have been and must be founded. One supposes the sovereignty to be in the people, and in them only. The other that it is in an individual or a few, and that the people have no participation in it, but are the subject matter on which it operates. A third class is compounded of those two principles, partaking in a greater or less degree of the one or the other, and with two or more orders. If in the people, according to our view, it is called a Democracy; if in an individual, a Despotism; and if in a few, Aristocracy. If the government be founded, partly, on each principle, with distinct orders and an hereditary chief at its head, invested with the executive power, we should call it Monarchy. If there be no hereditary chief, and the executive power be vested in an officer elected by the people, we should call it a Republic. This is a generic term, applicable alike to all governments, in which the people hold the sovereignty exclusively, or participate in it, and which are of a mixed character, in which there is no hereditary chief. The ancient authors who have written on the subject of government have made many distinctions which do not accord with the view herein presented. They all had just ideas of the great distinction between liberty and slavery, and of the cause which produced the one or the other state; but in the classification of governments, they seem to have been guided more by the comparative wealth of the parties, and merit or demerit of those who held the office, and exercised its powers, and by the manner in which they were exercised, than as a just regard to principle. Aristotle, one of the most profound writers of that epoch, if not the most profound, on the subject of government, made four species of Democracy;[1] four of Aristocracy;[2] and five of Monarchy;[3] whereas, I can conceive regarding principle, but one of the two first classes, let the government be organized, and its powers be distributed as they may; and but two of the latter, limited and unlimited. He likewise made four species of Oligarchy, which he blended so much with the different grades or classes of Aristocracy, that it is hardly possible to distinguish the one from the other. The basis of both was the rule of a few, but that seems to have been more on the contingencies above stated, than of hereditary right in the parties; Book the 4th, chap. 5. The cause to which this vague classification is attributable may, I presume, be easily explained; and in the prosecution of this work, I may endeavor to explain it. I shall simply remark here, that names count for nothing: that principle is everything, and that the great distinction is between a government in which the people rule, and one, in which they are ruled by a power which is absolute. Governments of the latter kind, whatever be their modification, can furnish no example applicable to us. A despot, if a good and wise man, may govern with integrity, humanity and wisdom. A weak and depraved one can do nothing well. The difference reflects honor or disgrace on the individual. It may give to the one exalted fame, for personal merit, and to the other infamy, for his vices and his follies. Such governments, whether the power be in an individual, or a few, turn on different principles from our own, and are subject to consequences corresponding with their principles. The same remark is applicable, in a certain extent, to mixed governments, such as are compounded of the two principles. Where distinct orders exist, an arrangement, by which the people form one, must always have been an affair of compromise, and on their part, of compulsion. Numbers and power being on their side, they could never have consented, voluntarily, to elevate any class above themselves. Compromises in such cases must have been the result of conflicts, in which each party obtained all that it could, and the preponderance was given to either, according to its good or bad fortune. In the formation of such a government, principle can never have been the ruling object, nor can its example, either in its career or fate, be considered as applicable to us. It may easily be shown that

1. Aristotle on Politics: Book 4, chap. 4.
2. *Ibid.* Book 4, chap. 7.
3. *Ibid.* Book 3, chap. 10, 11.

many of the causes which convulsed governments of this mixed character, and finally overthrew them, do not exist here. It is only from governments of the first class, such as were founded on the sovereignty of the people, that incidents which had any influence on their fortune can be cited as strictly applicable to us; nor indeed can they be so considered, unless they were formed in all respects, precisely like our own: and there was likewise a concurrence in every other circumstance to which those incidents were imputable. It is not sufficient that the principle be sound. The government must be sound also, in the organization of its powers, or it will inevitably fail.

It will nevertheless be proper to recur to the three classes of government, to those which are founded on each of the opposite principles, and likewise to those which are mixed, or compounded of both. It is impossible to treat of governments in their most perfect form, or of mixed governments in any form, so as to take a comparative view of their respective merits, without looking at them likewise in their worst state. They all furnish instruction, though it be in different ways, and for opposite purposes. Those in which the sovereignty is vested in an individual, or a few, show an abyss, into which if we fall we are lost. The tendency that way should be guarded against, and to do which it will be useful to see all the avenues which lead to it. Those of a mixed character, which recognize distinct orders, in which opposite and conflicting principles are brought into operation, furnish instruction peculiar to themselves, each class according to its modification. This is the class which stands in competition with our own, and to which of course particular attention is due. Whether a government composed of discordant materials can, under any circumstances, and from any cause whatever, preserve equal harmony in its movement, and promote as effectually the happiness of the people, as one which is homogeneous in all its parts, is the point in contest between them. The organization of those mixed, with the power which each order holds in them, respectively; where deposited, and how exercised, must be looked into. Some of them were better than others. The slightest shade of difference must have been sensibly felt. These differences must, therefore, be shown, and be tested, by the consequences attending them in each.

I have so far treated of the principles on which all governments must be founded, in the outline only. There are incidents to those principles, which form distinctions between the governments founded on each, which it is proper to notice here. These incidents are inseparable from those principles, and may be considered constituent parts thereof. It is necessary, therefore, to trace them in their consequences, to enable us to form a correct idea of the governments founded on each principle, and by means thereof, a fair comparison of their respective merits. The subject must be thoroughly analyzed in all its parts. The government to be compared, and those with which it is to be compared, must be placed respectively in a clear and distinct light, with all their features, with the differences between them, in every, the most minute circumstance, or the comparison cannot lead to a satisfactory result. (There are differences in governments of the same class, as well as in the classes themselves). These differences must also be noticed, since they enter essentially into the character of each government, and form important distinctions between our own and all others that have ever existed.

The terms Sovereignty and Government have generally been considered as synonymous. Most writers on the subject have used them in that sense. To us, however, they convey very different ideas, as they must to all who analyze the subject on principle. The powers may be separated and placed in distinct hands, and it is the faculty of making that separation, which is enjoyed by one class of governments alone, which secures to it many of the advantages which it holds over all others. This separation may take place in the class in which the sovereign power is vested in the people. It cannot in that in which it is vested in an individual, or a few, nor can it in that which is mixed, or compounded of the two principles. This view admits of a clear and simple illustration.

The sovereign power, wherever vested, is the highest in the state, and must always remain so. If vested in an individual or a few, there is no other order in the state. The same may be said of those governments which are founded on the opposite principle. If the people possess the sovereignty, the king and nobility are no more. A king without power is an absurdity. Dethroned kings generally leave the country, as do their descendants. Whatever the sovereign power may perform at one time, it may modify or revoke at another. There is no check in the government to prevent it. In those instances in which it is vested in an individual or a few, the government and the sovereignty are the same. They are both held by the same person or persons. The sovereign constitutes the government, and it is impossible to separate it from him without a revolution. Create a body in such a government with competent authority to make laws, treaties, etc., without reference to the party from whom it was derived, and the government is changed. Such agents must be the instruments of those who appoint them, and their acts be obligatory only after they are seen and approved by their masters, or the government is no more.

In mixed governments in which there are two or more orders, each participating in the sovereignty, the principle is the same. Neither can the king or nobility in such governments create a power, with competent authority, to rule distinct with themselves. In these governments the sovereignty is divided between the orders, and each must take care of its own rights, which the privileged orders cannot do if their powers should be transferred from them. The government is divided between the orders in like manner, each holding the station belonging to it, and performing its appropriate duties. They therefore constitute the government. It follows as a necessary consequence, that the sovereign power and the government even in governments of this class are the same, and that they cannot be separated from each other. It is only in governments in which the people possess the sovereignty that the two powers can be placed in distinct bodies; nor can they in them otherwise than by the institution of a government by compact, to which all the people are parties, and in which those who fill its various departments and offices are made their representatives and servants. In those instances the sovereignty is distinct from the government, because the people who hold the one are distinct from their representatives who hold and perform the duties of the other. One is the power which creates; the other is the subject which is created. One is always the same; the other may be modified at the will of those who made it. Thus the Constitution becomes the paramount law, and every act of the government, and of every department in it, repugnant thereto, void.

It is proper to notice another distinction, not less important, between governments founded on this principle and all others, even those which approach nearest to it. It is only in these governments that defects, which are pointed out by the light of experience, and are sensibly felt, can be amended voluntarily, and with strict regard to principle. When the sovereignty is vested in an individual, or a few, no change can be made without a struggle, nor can any amelioration of the condition of the people be sought otherwise than by petition, nor be granted otherwise than by favor. The sovereign cannot negotiate for a transfer of his powers to another body. The admission of the right in the people to negotiate, would be to admit an equality between the parties, which is incompatible with the principles of the government, and would be sure to subvert it. A change can be wrought only by compulsion, and the necessity of it must be apparent before it will be yielded to. The power must, in fact, be in the hands of those who seek the change, and he or they who hold it be reduced to nothing, before any change can be made. The government will then take such form as those who possess the power may choose to give it; and its late proprietors will likewise experience the fate which the people or their leaders may dictate. The same view is applicable to mixed governments, at least to a certain extent. The power held by the privileged orders, as has already been remarked, was never granted to them by the people as equal parties. It took its origin in a different source, and assumed its shape in any and every stage, as acted on by other causes. To bring the rights of the parties respectively into negotiation, for the purpose of extending the powers of the people, would place them in that respect, essentially in the same relation with each other as in the instances adverted to, and would in all probability have the same result. I speak here of the people moving in a body, under an organization formed specially for the purpose.

In governments of this mixed character, in which the sovereignty and government are united, changes may be made in the same mode by which those orders were established. Such governments always originated with the privileged orders, generally with the prince; never with the people; and were the result of compromises arising from the exertions of the people in favor of their liberties. Changes thus produced, rest on the same ground with the government itself, and will be equally obligatory, while the system is acquiesced in. They must, however, be viewed in the light of the first arrangement, as compulsive on the people, and not as affecting the principles herein laid down.

In governments founded on the sovereignty of the people, in which the two powers are separated from each other, there is a reciprocal action of the government on the people, and of the people on the government, which is unceasing. The people prescribe the rule by compact by which they shall be governed, and in so doing they prescribe the functions and duties of the governing power, which acts on themselves individually and equally. They prescribe also, in the same instrument, the manner in which their own power in the capacity of sovereign shall be exercised. Each party has its duties to perform, on the faithful performance of which the success of the system depends. Precision, therefore, is equally important in both instances. The government must be competent to its objects, and enjoy a freedom of action in the discharge of its duties, within the sphere prescribed, and on the principles of the compact. Misconduct and delinquency in those who administer it should be punishable and be punished, in the mode provided for by the system and executed under it. As the power proceeds from the people, it must be made subservient to their purposes, and this cannot be accomplished, unless those who exercise it feel their responsibility to their constituents in every measure which they adopt, and look to the people and not to themselves. The whole system, therefore, in all its operations, must turn on their suffrages. They must elect those who immediately take their place, and on whom the success of the government essentially depends, and provide for the discharge of their duties. They must elect all who they can elect, and provide for the appointment of all others, by vesting the power in officers who will be responsible to them for their conduct therein in the same manner as for other acts of their official duty. The precise extent to which the election by the people should be carried should be marked with great circumspection and precision. If carried too far, the principles of free government will be violated and the government be overthrown. If carried in any instance beyond the checks of their representatives in the legislative branch, guards should be provided to avert the danger incident to, and inseparable from it, for the more they are drawn beyond that limit the greater will be the danger. The election to that branch should be made as frequent as would be necessary to preserve in full force the powers of the people, but not more so. If too often, the people are always in action and the government loses its force. If too seldom, the people lose their power, which the government gains at their expense and against principle. In making the election, enlarged views should prevail. The community as well as the district should be looked to by every elector.

In the arrangement of the departments of the government, and distribution of their powers, great care should be taken. It must be divided into three branches: legislative, executive and judicial, and each endowed with appropriate powers and made independent of the other. Liberty cannot exist if adequate provision be not made for this great object. The other instances in which the people may exercise their sovereign power relate to the compact itself. If defects are seen in it, they have a right to amend it, and to correct them according to their best judgment, and at pleasure. The regular mode of proceeding is by convention, and which should be invariable in the institution of the government. If in the case of amendments, the agency of the government is admitted in any form, it must be in the mode prescribed by the existing Constitution, and in which it will act merely as the instrument of the people in their character as the sovereign power of the state.

The separation, however, of the sovereignty from the government, when the people possess the sovereignty, depends altogether on their will. They may be united in their hands, in like manner as in the other classes. This is done when the whole people act together and exercise the powers of the government themselves, en masse. This union in their hands, although it differs in certain respects from a like union in those of an individual, or a few, nevertheless produces consequences which are not less important and injurious. It may be shown by an attentive view of the subject, that many of the objections which apply on principle to despotism itself, in its worst form, are equally applicable to this union of the two powers in the people; and that in practice, by the abuses to which it is exposed, and which are inseparable from it, it is often more oppressive.

When it is known that the government of an individual, in which the people have no participation, is despotic, it might be inferred that that which passed to the opposite extreme, in which the whole power was vested in, and exercised by, the people collectively, was the most free and the best that human wisdom could devise. If men were angels, that result would follow, but in that case, there would be no necessity for any government. It is the knowledge that all men have weaknesses, and that many have vices, that makes government necessary; and in adopting one, it is the interest of all that it should be formed in such manner as to protect the rights and promote the happiness of the whole community. The great object is to promote the celestial cause of liberty and humanity; and the perfection of government must consist in its being formed in such a manner as to accomplish this object, by depriving the vicious of the power to do harm, and enlisting not the virtuous only, but all who are not abandoned and outlawed, in support of the government thus instituted. If all enjoy equal rights, merit is rewarded, and punishment inflicted on those only who have committed crimes; the number of discontented and disorderly will be inconsiderable; the great mass will cling to and cherish the government which is strictly their own.

The advocates for governments which recognize distinct orders contend that liberty cannot exist unless the people are held together by a common interest, which must be by restricting them to a limited share in the government, and committing the other portions to distinct hereditary orders. They say that each branch must have a separate interest, and that the power held by the people, and in consequence their liberties, must be exposed to great and unceasing danger, otherwise they will divide into parties, fall under the control of leaders, and become their tools and instruments, to the ruin of the cause. They admit that the portion of power held by the people should be in the legislature; but contend that even in that branch there should be an hereditary check; that the executive should be hereditary, and that the judiciary should be placed beyond their control. In favor of this doctrine they urge that if the sovereignty be vested in the people, under any modification which can be given to the government, there will be but one interest, and in consequence, that the three powers will be concentrated in the ruling authority of the community, which will be the predominating party, and the leader of that party by whom every enormity will be committed and the government be overthrown. They urge particularly, that the chief executive officer should hold his station by hereditary right, and that the people should have no agency in the election or appointment, since, if they have, as there will be many candidates, and each have his partisans, who will embark with great zeal in his support, they will become by excitement, personal interest, and other causes, so identified with their favorite, that the person elected will be opposed on the one side, and supported by the other, without regard to principle or policy.

It will be easy to show that this view is not only erroneous, but that the very facts, which are relied on in support of it prove directly the reverse. The view is founded on the fate of the ancient republics, all of which failed, and on the comparative duration of those which were democratical, with those which recognized distinct orders, the latter of which were more permanent. Why did the democratical governments fail, and why was their existence so transitory? It was because the government was united with the sovereignty in the people, and all the powers, in consequence, concentrated in one body. Why were those of distinct orders more permanent? It was because the powers of the government were separated from each other. In the one class, their concentration was inevitable. It was formed by the government itself, and owing to the then state of the science, and other causes which will be explained hereafter, irremediable. In the other, they were separated by a cause equally powerful, the existence of hereditary orders, and in consequence, likewise, by the government itself. Each order took a portion of the power from the people, and in the degree confined them to one branch only, the legislative, that which they could best execute. If then the separation of the powers of the government by hereditary orders, under all the disadvantages incident to that class; of distinct rights, with the degradation of the body of the people and discordant interest, could secure to those governments a longer existence, does it not furnish ample proof that if separated under more favorable circumstances, the government would be permanent? Will it be contended, that the people cannot be kept together by any other interest than fear? That the enemy must be in the field, in sight, and they be menaced by the bayonet, otherwise, they will divide into parties, yield to their passions, and destroy themselves? If the concentration of the powers of the government, with the sovereignty in the people, subverted the ancient Democracies, as it certainly did, and that fatal cause be removed, and every other precaution which experience has suggested be adopted, how can the system be overthrown? Where are the dangers which menace it? Liberty has its charms and its blessings, in the one case, as well as in the other. The interest of the whole people to unite in its preservation is the same. Can it be believed if they would contend for liberty under the greatest disadvantages; expose their lives, and millions of them perish in the contest, that, when it was placed secure in their own hands, under the wisest organization, that human wisdom, aided by experience, could devise, they would by their vices and their follies break down those strong barriers, and destroy it?

Every danger, however, to which a government founded on the sovereignty of the people is exposed, should be looked at, and guarded against, by all the precautions which human wisdom, aided by experience, can suggest. Man should be viewed in his true character; his virtues and defects should be duly estimated, and the organization be such as to call into activity and give full force to the former, and to suppress the latter.

These two great principles must, therefore, be considered fundamental and invariable, in regard to government, in which the people hold the sovereignty— first, that the government be separated from the sovereignty; the second, that it be divided into three separate branches, legislative, executive and judicial, and that each be endowed with its appropriate powers, and be made independent of the others. It is by a faithful observance of these principles, and a wise execution of them, that tyranny may be prevented; the government be made efficient for all its purposes; and the power of the people be preserved over it, in all its operations. Unite the government with the sovereignty, although it be in the people, and every species of abuse, with the certain overthrow of both, will follow. Concentrate all power in one body, although it be representative, and the result, if not so prompt, will, nevertheless, be equally fatal.

The duties of a government designate the powers necessary to execute them, and the nature of these powers points out the departments in which they ought to be vested with the organizations and number of persons best qualified to execute them. The organization of every free government must be adapted to the duties it has to perform; and the government will be most free in which the organization is most perfect, and the best security provided for the strict observance of the rules prescribed. The prominent duties of a government consist in the enactment of laws, in pronouncing judgment on those laws, and in the execution of them. There are other duties of the highest importance which require the unceasing attention of the government, such as the appointment to office under the government, the intercourse and transactions with foreign powers, in peace and war; the supervision and control of the administration in all its departments, civil and military, in every situation in which the country can be placed. Those of the first two classes belong to the legislature and judiciary. The others fall within the scope of the executive, for it is by it alone, under certain guards, which will have a good effect, that they can be executed with advantage.

The legislature forms the basis of the system. It is the branch to which it belongs to give the best prop to the government, and the greatest support to the liberties of the people, or which by its failure in these respects becomes the principal cause of their overthrow. Its duties connect it, in all its measures, immediately with the whole population of the state, and with the whole territory. The objects of legislation, in the protection of the rights of persons and property, in the imposition of burdens, to promote the welfare and sustain the character of the state in its foreign and domestic concerns, require enlarged views, as well as an upright and legal policy. The legislature of every free state should be divided into two branches, and the number placed in each be regulated by principle, so as to enable it most effectually to accomplish the object intended by it. One should be more numerous than the other, to carry the representation more completely home to the body of the people. The other should be so formed as to be able, by a more calm deliberation, to correct any error arising from a hasty decision of the popular branch. To both there is an obvious limit. I am satisfied that an assembly consisting of four or five hundred members, in its most popular branch, would be sufficiently numerous for the wise management of the affairs of any community, however great its population or extensive its territory; and that the augmentation of it beyond that number could not fail to produce an ill effect. It follows, that the greater the augmentation the worse the effect, by weakening the responsibility of the representative and impairing the power of the people until the government be subverted. The other branch should consist of a sufficient number to inspire confidence, but comparatively of a few, and be composed of persons more advanced in years and of greater experience. The duties of the other branches being altogether different, the number placed in each must correspond therewith. As the judiciary is restricted to an exposition of the constitution and the laws, in cases brought before it, it is manifest that the corps should consist of a few members only. Extend it beyond that number, and it becomes a multitude, incapable of calm deliberation and pronouncing a wise decision. A still greater limitation is necessary for the executive, and for a like reason, a due regard to its duties. It is equally the dictate of reason and experience, according to my judgment, that it be committed to one.

The reasons in favor of committing the executive department to an individual appear to be conclusive. Increase the number to five, or even to three, and the corps will be less efficient in the discharge of its duties, and less responsible to the people. If there be more than one, experience shows that there will be a rivalship between them, and intrigues carried on by each, with the members of the legislature, and through them, with the people, which will produce the worst effect. The same practice will be extended to the departments under the government, which will weaken the administration. The responsibility will also be impaired, because as the numbers would make parties in their favor, through-out the nation, the people would take sides with their respective favorites, and thus the necessary inquiries into misconduct would be checked, and punishment for it often prevented. The members would likewise be elected from different parts of the community, on the representative principle, whereby that tendency would be much promoted, as each section would take an interest in favor of the member sent from that quarter. By committing the power to a single individ-ual, these evils may be averted, and as is believed, without any increased danger to the country. Standing alone, his decision would in all cases be conclusive, and the ministers under him be compelled promptly to obey his orders. There would, therefore, be more energy in the government. His responsibility would also be increased, since the sectional feeling, even in his own quarter, would be dimin-ished, and there would be none elsewhere. By standing alone also, the suspicion of his abuse of power would be much increased, and in consequence his con-duct more closely watched, whereby it might be prevented, and if committed, be more easily detected and punished.

As to the mode of securing complete responsibility in this officer to the people, and the faithful discharge of his duties, none can be devised so effectual as by committing the right of impeachment to the popular branch of the legis-lature, and of trial to the other. The legislature is by far the most numerous; the election of its members is more frequent; they come from every part of the country, and are absent from their constituents a short term only. It is the branch which stands nearest to the people, and is more immediately identified with them; their duties are also of a nature corresponding more with those which the people could perform, if they exercised the government themselves en masse. It is that branch, a misconduct in any of whose members should be punishable by the loss of confidence and non-election only. In every view, therefore, it is the branch on which the people must depend, principally, for their safety, and to which they must commit all those powers in regard to the supervision of the conduct of those in the other departments which they cannot execute, as the sovereign power, directly themselves. To suffer the punishment for misconduct in the chief executive magistrate to rest on the loss of confidence, and non-election by the people only, would neither suit the nature of the office, nor a vio-lation of many of its important powers. The force of the country being in his hands; the intercourse with foreign powers; the supervision and control of the administration, in all its departments, in peace and war; with the appointment to office, and the patronage incident to it; misconduct in many ways might endanger the system, and would evince a perfidy, which would require the severest punishment. Even neglect or idleness, distinctly proved, to the public injury, should not escape notice or censure. The legislature is the only branch within the pale of the system which can exercise this power with effect. Being present, and a party in the government, and in some views, a rival one, the deposit of the power with it will in itself form a great check on misconduct in the other. In this mode, the machine will be kept in motion by its own powers, and on a proper balance. If the power should be taken from the legislature, and vested elsewhere, a new feature would be introduced into the government which would weaken it in all its parts, and might disorganize it. It could not be committed, with propriety, to the judiciary, for that would connect it with the political movement, and the parties which may occasionally be formed by it, which would be incompatible with its duties. A new branch could not be instituted for the purpose, without making the system more complicated, and exposing it to a like danger. The right of impeachment and of trial by the legislature is the main spring of the great machine of government. It is the pivot on which it turns. If preserved in full vigor, and exercised with perfect integrity, every branch will perform its duty, and the people be left to the performance of theirs, in the most simple form, and with complete effect, as the sovereign power of the state. It is not believed that this right could be abused by the legislature. An attack on the executive would draw the public attention to it, and if unfounded, rather benefit, than injure the individual. The whole proceeding would be before the public, in the case of trial, and if innocent, the sympathies of the people would be excited in his favor.

It is indispensable that the three branches be made independent of, and a check on each other. By vesting in the legislature the right to impeach and try the chief executive officer and the members of the judiciary for misconduct, this object will be fully accomplished, as to that branch. Even without this resource, the legislature is less exposed to encroachments from the other branches, than they from it. If the executive should transcend its powers, by acts not authorized by the Constitution or a law, the breach would be so palpable, that it would be immediately discovered, and the incumbent be called to account and punished for it. For the judiciary to make encroachments on either of the branches seems to be impossible, the nature of its powers and duties being so different and obvious. The object most difficult to be provided for, is to arm these two branches with the means of preventing encroachment on them by the legislature; and none occur, which it is thought are so competent, and free from objection, as to invest the executive with the right to negative acts of the legislature, and the judiciary with that to declare a law, which it should deem unconstitutional, void. By vesting these branches with these powers no injury could result, and much benefit might, in many ways. If the right in the executive to negative acts be qualified, as it might be, it would bring the subject again before the legislature, with new light thrown on it, and secure to it a more deliberate consideration. The division between the two branches would draw the attention of the people to the subject, and should the act pass, and be exposed to the objections made to it by the executive, the judiciary, if repugnant to the Constitution, might declare it void; or if consistent with the Constitution, and the power in itself be objectionable, the people might correct the evil, by an amendment of the Constitution. If objectionable on other ground, the people might furnish a remedy, by the declaration of their sentiments respecting it, which might be done in different ways, and with effect. Instances might occur in the progress of affairs, of a political nature, in which the better opportunity enjoyed by the executive to acquire full information, might enable it to negative a bill with advantage to the country. The exercise of the proposed power by the judiciary, could never involve the question of conflicting rights between it and the legislature, in the character of encroachment on those of the latter. In exercising that power, the judiciary could be viewed only as a tribunal of the people, invested with it, to prevent encroachments, tending to subvert the Constitution, and with it, their rights and liberties.

The legislature and the executive are the branches from which the greatest danger to free government may be apprehended. The union of the government with the sovereignty, and the concentration of all power in one body, is that to which such governments are exposed by the former, and usurpation by the latter. Against usurpation and the monopoly of all power by the legislature, a sufficient guard is provided by the power vested in the executive and judiciary. The danger arises from other causes—the possibility of a tendency to the opposite extreme. If the members of the legislature lose sight of the nation, and look to their sections only, the system is in the utmost danger. Combinations will be formed in support of local interests by means whereof those of a general character will be sacrificed, to the injury of every part, including those who commenced the opposition. At the head of each combination will be found a leader, who will push its cause to an extreme, for his own advancement, at the expense of the public good. A national policy must be cherished and prevail. If the people possess virtue, intelligence, and are devoted to self-government, this danger can never assume a serious form.

In governments in which the sovereignty is vested in the people, and the government is separated from it, a very extraordinary effect is produced. The government which is the instrument, and inferior, operates on those who hold the sovereignty, and in consequence, on the superior. But it operates on the people individually, and not collectively, and as citizens, not as subjects. The government is the agent which executes the compact between the citizens. In governments in which the sovereignty is in an individual, he stands above the law, and cannot be affected by it. His will forms the law by which all others are governed. The government is his instrument, and for others, not for him. In mixed governments, in which there is an hereditary chief holding a portion of the sovereign power, he likewise is above the law, and is not amenable to it. He can do no wrong.

When the government is thus separated from the sovereignty, the people can exercise the sovereign power in the two modes above specified only. One by the election, in the mode and in the extent prescribed by the Constitution; the other by the election of representatives, to serve them in convention for special purposes. In each instance the object is different. In the one, it is to give effect to the government and preserve it, in its course, according to the compact. In the other, it is to act on the government itself, by amendment or otherwise. The people cannot go beyond that limit, in either instance, without taking the government into their own hands, and overthrowing the existing one. If they act directly on those in office, to punish them, for example, for offenses, whether it be by popular movement, or in convention, the government is at an end. To make the government competent to its objects, its powers must be commensurate, under proper guards, with those of the sovereignty, and to preserve the sovereignty in the people, the means of restraining each department within the limits prescribed to it by the Constitution; of enforcing a faithful execution of the duties enjoined on it, and punishing a violation of them by those in office, must be vested in, and be performed by the government itself. The whole system, as heretofore observed, must turn on the suffrage of the people, and the government so formed, that those in office may find that they can obtain nothing independent of the people, nor from them, nor even escape punishment, otherwise than by a faithful discharge of their duties. If the government be thus formed, it cannot fail to accomplish all the objects intended by it; to fulfill its own duties, and to give complete effect to the sovereignty of the people, within the mild and lenient scale specified. The spirit of the government itself will always produce the happiest effect. Men selected by their fellow-citizens for their virtue and talents will not forget the obligations thereby imposed on them. High and honorable sentiments will prevail and be felt in every department and trust under it; and be infused among the great body of the people.

It has been my object in this sketch of the organization and endowment of governments in which the people hold exclusively the sovereignty, to give an outline only, but so far as I have been able, a distinct one. As I shall have to treat of the subject, when I proceed to make the proposed comparison between our government and those which have been mentioned, and must then do it in detail, I will postpone any further remarks on it, until I reach that stage.

When the character of each of these three classes of government is duly considered, it cannot fail to excite surprise, that more than one, that of the people, in its best form, should ever have existed; that the government of an individual, or a few, should ever have been established. Nor can it fail to excite surprise, that a government should have been formed by compromise between the opposite principles, for if the one be radically wrong, how is it possible that anything should be taken from it to improve that which is radically right? How does the fact correspond with this view? What has been the condition of our globe, as to the governments which have existed in its various parts, from the earliest record of time? First of Asia? Was any free government ever heard of in that quarter? Extend the inquiry to Africa, and what the reply? Carthage exhibits the only example, and that for a short period. I come next to Europe, the third quarter, and what has been its fate? The Republics of Greece and Rome arrest our attention with deep interest. They adorned the ancient world, but have long since passed away. They live only in history, through which medium, compared with other governments, they are the objects of our highest respect and admiration. View Europe in modern times, and what the result? Of the attempts which have been made in different countries to establish governments of the kind in question, and of their fate, I shall only remark here, that they have all failed.

Of democratic governments, by representation in its best form, we have no example in ancient or modern times prior to our revolution. The government of the people, wherever it has existed, has been of the people collectively, or en masse, in its worst form, and in consequence its existence has been transitory. Mixed governments have been more durable, but their reign has been short, compared with that in which the people have had no participation; in which they have been slaves. Despotism has been the prevailing government in all ages throughout the globe, including even that portion of time during which the Republic of Rome held an extensive sway, for her government in the conquered provinces which composed more than four-fifths of her territory was likewise perfectly despotic. The tendency has been invariably to despotism, and in it all the ancient republics terminated: To what cause has it been owing that the best government has heretofore never been established anywhere? That so large a portion of mankind have abandoned their rights, and sunk down voluntarily, or at least, without any manifestation of a desire to prevent it, under the dominion of an individual? Many causes have undoubtedly combined to produce this result. I will point out those which appear to me to have had most weight. To do this, we must go to the origin of society, for to it we must trace that of all government. They commence together. Society cannot exist without government, and the nature of the government must depend on the state of the society.

In entering on this, the second branch of the subject, I might pursue the course of naturalists, and examine man, as a class of animals, from the highest northern to the highest southern habitable regions; from the Arctic to the Antarctic circle, in every latitude, climate and country, in both hemispheres, and note all those circumstances, proceeding from either cause, which are presumed to have any influence on his intellect and on the manners and state of society in each community. All naturalists agree in one sentiment, that whatever differences there may now be found between men in intellect, size, form, color or otherwise, there was but one race;[4] that they had a common origin. This analysis, therefore, however correctly it might be formed, would furnish us no consolation; nothing to exalt our ideas of the human race; and in regard to the object which I have in view, leave me essentially in the state in which I now am. The decision does not turn on the point, whether a Laplander, a Samoide, a Tartar, a Mogul, an Arabian, Chinese, Turk or Persian is capable of self-government. It is admitted that the capacity for it depends on the state of society, and as those societies never had such government among them, or made an attempt to establish one, or showed any disposition to do so, it may fairly be conceded, that, be the cause what it may, they are incapable of such government. The scale, therefore, within which the inquiry must be confined, is a very limited one. Among the ancients it includes the Republics of Greece, Carthage and Rome; and among the moderns, the Government of Great Britain furnishes the most striking example.

Such is the nature of man, of the best class of the human race, that so soon as a society is formed, a government must be established over it. Such are his wants his passions, his principles, and his faculties, and such the elevation and depression of which he is susceptible, that without such government there can be no order or safety in society. So well known is this fact, that if two men were to meet in a wilderness, beyond the reach of law, and the protection of any gov-

---

4. Buffon.

ernment, who were strangers to each other, whether rude and savage, or civilized, they would each, instinctively, be apprehensive of danger, having no security for his safety but in his own strength, and doubtful of the character and views of the other. If they should remain together, and find from experience, that their apprehension was unfounded, confidence would grow up between them, and a friendly co-operation in their pursuits ensue. If these two should meet others, the apprehension would revive on their part, and be reciprocated, nor would it be removed on either side without like experience. Even while the number should be limited to a few persons, and their pursuits be equally limited, to that of game for example, a leader of the band would be necessary to preserve order within it, and to take the command in case they should meet other collections of a like kind, the encounter with which might be either hostile, or otherwise, according to circumstances.

Governments being then necessary for every society, however small the number of which it may consist, and in whatever state it may be, the question is, how does it originate? Whence does it derive its authority? These propositions must be examined and decided on principle, and with reference to man and to society in the lights which we are taught by reason and experience to view them.

The origin of government has been traced by different writers to four sources; divine right, paternal authority, election and force. I trace it to two only, election and force, and believe that it has originated, sometimes in the one and sometimes in the other, according to the state of the society at the time, and the number of which it was composed. I think that this proposition admits of a clear and satisfactory demonstration. Before, however, I attempt it, it will be useful to take a brief notice of the other sources, especially as it is to them, that the advocates for despotism and hereditary right have traced it. By confining the attention then to these two sources, the subject will be simplified, and it may then be more easily shown to which source, and to what cause or causes, it is imputable in any and every instance.

Divine and paternal right appear to me to rest upon the same basis, although they have not been so understood by the writers who have traced government to these sources. If divine, the claimant or pretender must prove his title by some miracle, or other incontestable evidence, or it must commence with the parent, and beginning with him be subject to all the views applicable to that title. They must either accord, or be in opposition to each other. No advocate of either places them in opposition, and if they accord, it must be by meaning the same thing, under different names. So absurd are both pretensions, that I should not even notice them, if they had not gained such weight, in one of the communities, of whose government I propose to treat, and at a marked epoch, as to form an important feature, in the works of two distinguished and able writers, on the subject of government, and if I did not wish also, in this elementary sketch, to simplify the subject by getting rid of all such absurd doctrines. Those writers have refuted them, more by reference to sacred history, in reply to the author by whom they were advanced, than as evinced by his faculties, his passions, and career through all ages to the will of the Creator, as marked on the character of man. I shall confine my remarks to the latter, and be very concise in the view I take within that limit.

In tracing regal power to the paternal source, we trace it to a single pair, from whom the whole community must have descended, for otherwise the origin could not have been paternal. If this be the source of power, it must have commenced with the human race, and admitting the authenticity of the Mosaic account, with our first parents, and to preserve the succession, have descended in the right line, to the oldest son, from generation to generation, to the present day. If the right ever existed, it must have commenced at that epoch, and still exist, without limitation as to time, generation, population, or its dispersion over the earth. A limitation of the right, in either of those respects, would be subversive of it. To what term confine it? Through how many generations should it pass? To what number of persons, or extent of territory, carry it? How dispose of it after those conditions should have been fulfilled? The mere admission that such limitations were prescribed, would be to admit that the right never existed; and if not limited, it would follow, that one man would now be the sovereign or lord of all the inhabitants of our globe, than which nothing can be more absurd.

The objection is equally strong to this source of power, rejecting the Mosaic account of our origin, in a single pair, had there been a hundred or a thousand pair, and each been placed at a distance from the others, in different parts of the earth, to form by their descendants, different communities, to give a like origin to the governments established everywhere. The right must have descended, in like manner, to their lineal successors, and their governments extended over the other branches of their offspring, from generation to generation, and still exist, wherever they might be. The only difference in the two modes would consist in the number of sovereigns first created, and still existing, for there could be no more. In all other circumstances, the cases would respond with each other, and the objections applicable to the one, would be equally so to the other, and equally strong. For the government to be paternal, the origin must be in a single pair, descend in the right line, comprise within it the whole offspring in every branch, and through all time.

If it was the intention of the Creator that the government of this globe should rest on paternal authority, it must have been, either by confining it to the descendants of a single pair, and to subject the whole human race to one ruler, or to have created as many pairs as he intended that there should be monarchs, and to have dispersed them, at the time of their creation, over the earth. And to give effect to this plan, either all inter-mixture of the one with the other must have been prohibited, or the earth have been divided by special limits between the several pairs and their descendants, so that there might be no dispute respecting the title. In either case it would follow, that the human race was not created for the benefit and common happiness of the whole, but of one only, in case there was but one pair, and of a few, if more than one. It would follow also, that it was not intended that the first parents should be monarchs, since they would have no subjects except their immediate offspring, and a few of their descendants, but were created as instruments for the aggrandizement of their lineal descendants, some hundreds of years afterwards, when the societies should have increased, and governments become indispensable.

How does this doctrine correspond with Divine authority, as marked by the character of man, or by any other indications by which it may be traced? Cain murdered his brother Abel. Would the commission of that crime have deprived him of the succession? By what authority could this have been done? Could Adam have disinherited him? There existed then no tribunal to decide the question, and had there been such the existence of the power, either in Adam, or such tribunal, would have been subversive of the right. Supposing the government to have descended to Cain, what a strange spectacle would thus have been exhibited, that of a murderer of his own, and then, only brother, inheriting the government, and transmitting it to his descendants? How inconsistent with the character, as well as the history of that epoch? Adam inflicted no punishment on Cain, nor did he claim the right to do it. The punishment which he suffered was inflicted, according to the Mosaic account, by divine authority. A curse was pronounced against him, and a mark set on him, whereby he was degraded below, and separated from the rest of the human race. These facts are not calculated to prove that it was intended by the Divine Author of our existence that Adam should be a monarch, or that the right of governing the human race, or any portion of it, should descend to his oldest son.

Do any of the sovereigns of the present day trace their title to Adam, or to any other first parent, or would they be willing to rest it on that ground? We know that they would not, and if they did, that it would fail, since the commencement of all the existing dynasties may be traced to other sources; to causes, such as operated at the moment of their elevation, and varied in different countries. Does any community of Europe, or elsewhere, trace its origin to a single pair, unless it be to our first parents, and which is common to the human race? We know that except in their instance, and at the creation of mankind, societies have never commenced in that form, and that such have been the revolutions in every part of the globe, that no existing race or community can trace its connection in a direct line with Adam, Noah, or others of that early epoch. In the infant state of every society individuals seek each other for safety and comfort. Those who are born together, no matter from whence their parents came, live together, and thus increase and multiply, until the means of subsistence become scanty. A portion then withdraws to some other quarter where those means can be procured, and thus new societies have been formed, and the human race spread over the earth, through all its habitable regions.

Paternal authority has its rights and duties, and is common to every class of animals. It is derived from nature, and has its extents and limits. It is seen in the lion, the tiger, the fish and the bird, as well as in man. It is *parental,* common to the *mother* as well as to the *father,* and binding for a certain term only. As soon as the infant attains maturity, it ceases. It does not extend in any form to the second race, because their parents intervene, and occupy the ground in regard to them which was held by the first over their offspring. If the whole population of any tribe consisted of the descendants of one male and female, all would be equally free in succession, after attaining maturity. No one individual among them would have a right to govern the other. If the parental authority extended in the right line, for example, to the male descendants of one ancestor, it would extend on the same principle, to those of every other, and thus there would be formed by it as many governments within the same limits, and over the same territory, as there were parties to the first association, or rather, there would be no government at all.

From every view that can be taken of the subject, reasoning on principle, the doctrine of divine or paternal right, as the foundation of a claim, in any one, to the sovereign power of the state, or to any power in it, is utterly absurd. It belonged to the dark ages, and was characteristic of the superstition and idolatry which prevailed in them. All men are by nature equally free. Their Creator made them so, and the inequalities which have grown up among them, and the governments which have been established over them, founded on other principles, have proceeded from other causes, by which their natural rights have been subverted. We must trace government, then, to other sources, and in doing this, view things as they are, and not indulge in superstitious, visionary and fanciful speculations.

The remaining sources from which the power may be derived are election and force, and it is from one or other of these, that it always has been, and always will be, derived, for there is none other. The nature of the government, and the manner of its origin, whether attributable to the one or the other cause, must depend on the state of the society at the time it originated, and of which there are two in direct opposition to each other; the one unlettered, rude and savage, the other civilized; and the distance between them, from the most rude to the point to which civilization may be carried, is immense. In the first state, man approaches nearly to the brute creation. He lives, like other animals, on the natural fruits of the earth, and being carnivorous, kills and feeds on them. In the second, he is capable of a very high degree of elevation. Agriculture, commerce, navigation and the arts engage his attention and give him support. A vast range of science is opened to and explained by him. His mind embraces objects, and receives an expansion, unknown to the other state. Government is indispensable in every stage, and becomes more imperiously so in the progress from the one to the other, from the rude to the civilized, according to the degree to which civilization is carried.

I will examine the institution of government in both these states, with the incidents attending it, in each. When formed in a rude state, the remarks which are applicable to one community are in a general view equally so to all. In such a state there is little variety between different communities in reference to the object in question. All unlettered and savage societies resemble each other, and the causes which produce government in each, and the manner of its creation and its form are likewise similar. When formed in a state of civilization, difference may take place between them regarding the advance therein made, and other causes incident thereto, which will produce a corresponding effect. In this state they must be formed, either by a change of the existing government (there having been one from the origin of the society), or by the formation of a new and distinct society, by emigration of a portion of the numbers thereof to a new position, and the institution of a new government over them at that position. As all original societies with whose origin we have any knowledge, both of the ancient and modern world, commenced in the rude state in which state governments were formed over them, and as all the changes in those governments arose from the changes in those societies by their progress from the one to the other state, I will begin with the rude state, and describe according to my best judgment, the government of which it is susceptible, and of necessity adopts. I will then proceed to notice the progress of such societies in civilization, with their capacity to institute a new government better adapted to the state in which they may be, and to maintain such government of these societies, which are formed by migration from civilized communities, and of the governments of which they are capable, I shall take a distinct view in the proper place.

When we speak of man in a state of nature, we contemplate him as rude, unlettered, and unrestrained. In this state he is free and at liberty to do what he pleases. In that state few are seen. Man is by nature a sociable being, and pursuing the impulse derived from nature, clings to his fellowman. As soon as such numbers are collected, no matter from whence they come, or how thrown together, as to merit the name, a society is formed, and over it such government as they are capable of forming. In this state the government must be of the most simple form, and with very limited powers; it must be that of an individual, or of a few, rather than of laws; and its powers must be confined to the causes which produced it, and principally to the protection of the virtuous against the vicious, of the weak against the strong. When the government is formed as it were, by nature, unaided by science or experience of any kind, it would be impossible for the parties to look profoundly into principles, or to devise the means of preserving them. The provisions of such governments can extend to nothing which those who form them do not understand. All societies in this state must stand on the same ground. It may be shown that this influence is not only justified by experience and reason, but is confirmed by the authority of the most enlightened authors who have treated of the subject.

We have examples in our neighborhood of governments instituted by a people in the rude state, the aborigines of the country, which correspond with those above described. In many instances the power in those tribes is committed to an individual, and in others to a few, who are called elders, and who exercise it in the spirit and extent above stated. Unlettered, they have no written laws, and holding their lands in common, and living principally on game, those which they have are confined to a few objects, such as nature dictates, and are traditional. The cabins which they inhabit, the fruits of their industry, raised on the lands contiguous thereto, and the game which they kill, are their own; and their laws in relation to property extend no further. In respect to wrongs, the code is equally simple. No man is allowed to kill another, because murder is a crime which revolts the feeling of the whole community, and in an exemplary punishment for which they all agree. No reasoning or refinement is necessary to prove it. As these people are free and high-minded, the governments instituted by them may be considered as fair specimens of all governments which have been or may be instituted by a people in a like state.

The progress of these tribes in civilization has been slow, and is yet inconsiderable, even with those most advanced. It is believed that the establishment of schools among them for the education of the youth of both sexes, is the most practicable mode that can be adopted for their civilization; and that by the continuance of such schools, through several successive generations, the object might be accomplished. It is by acting on the infant state only, that civilization can be introduced among them. The aged are beyond its reach. This object it is presumed, might be aided by the institution of a government for them, to be committed in part to our citizens, and in part to their people, by means whereof they might be instructed, gradually, in the science of government, and trained to the exercise of its powers on a more enlarged scale, and on just principles. This, it is presumed, by the influence which we enjoy over all the tribes near us, might be done, with their consent. Whether they will ever be civilized without some such effort on our part is uncertain. Many tribes known to the first emigrants have become extinct, and there is good cause to apprehend, if they remain in their present savage state, that all of them will be. Whether it is our interest to civilize them, or we are bound by the obligations of humanity to do it, are questions which merit the most serious consideration. In their present state they are utterly incompetent to the discharge of the duties of a well organized, free, representative government. Establish such an one over them, and leave the execution of its duties to themselves, and it will soon fail. This remark is applicable to all people in the same state.

If we trace the origin of government to election in this early stage, it must be understood that the persons collected together finding a government necessary, consented that its powers should be exercised by such a person or persons, rather than that the election was made in any regular form, or by the limitation of power, or of the term of service, in the sense in which it is now practiced. If we trace it to force, it may be inferred that crimes being committed or apprehended, and the safety of the society requiring that provision should be made against them by the punishment of the offenders,[5] resistance being made by the worst class, a contest ensued, which terminated in favor of the best, whereby the power was placed in the hands of one or more, who took the lead on the right side. By this view of the origin of power or government over society in such a state, election and force mean essentially the same thing. None would be

5. Diodorus Siculus, Vol. 1. page 19.

instituted, if the necessity was not imperative, and in such a state none could be instituted in any regular form, or other than of the most imperfect kind.

Governments thus instituted, however defective in form, or great the power committed to those placed in them, must be free in their origin. The natives being in all other respects equally rude, unlettered, and without property by accumulation, so as to form distinctions between them, as is done in the progress of civilization, the ruler, if there be one, is rather the instrument of the society, than that the members of it are his slaves. They hunt together, prince and subject, if the distinction is admissible; live alike in cabins; and feed on the same fare. Those in power are generally persons of advanced age, and chosen for their good qualities and merit. If one, he is called father, and respected as such; and to this source, it is presumed that the doctrine of paternal power is to be traced. When crimes are committed which require punishment, and the cries of the injured and their connections are heard, the eyes of all are fixed on him, and in consequence he takes the seat of justice, which is that of distinction, and performs the duties of the station. The decision which he pronounces accords with that of all the good members of the society, who constitute always the great majority, and is supported by them. From that seat he then retires to the same simple state of equality with the other members which he held before.

It is in the progress of societies that the relation between the parties changes. The persons thus chosen, generally hold their power through life, and often transmit it to their descendants. The election having had no limitation as to time, and the necessity for the office increasing with the population, to dismiss the aged incumbent and put another in his place, especially if he had given satisfaction, would be an act of injustice which all would disapprove. The possession of the power by the first incumbent for many years, if he had discharged its duties with fidelity, would naturally excite in his favor, and in that of his family, the feeling of the whole community, or at least, of the best portion of it, and hence on his demise, his oldest son would be a fair competitor for the vacant station. Should he succeed, the claim to hereditary right would grow up, which would be sure to beget opposition to it. From this period the ranks in society would be divided. A struggle would commence between those who were friends of self-government and of liberty, and those who preferred a government founded on opposite principles. Sometimes one party might prevail, and sometimes the other. The success of either would take all power with it. If the hereditary claimant succeeded (there having been no division of power into legislative, executive and judicial), the whole would centre in him. If the people succeeded, the whole would vest in them collectively, or en masse. In this state there could be no improvement of the government by the institution of the representative system, or by the delegation of power in any form. The state of the science would not permit it, and besides, the people would always be in a state of alarm, and on the watch, afraid of every one and of every thing. The struggle would thus go on, and under circumstances the most unfavorable to the cause of liberty.

The progress of societies in the rude unlettered state has a strong tendency to augment the power of the chief, and to lessen that of the people. As the population increases, the pursuits of the members become more diversified. Some take to agriculture, others to navigation, commerce, and the arts, while many still hunt the game. The duties of the chief become proportionally more extended and various. The people are also put at a greater distance from him, and each party is less acquainted with the other. His agency would in consequence, in the cases in which he might be called on to act, proceed more directly from himself, and thus he would gradually imbibe the doctrine, especially a chief of the second race, that the power belonged to him, and not to them. If contests should take place, and the people succeed, the effect would only be to transfer the government from one chief to another. Their incompetency to govern themselves, en masse, would be increased with the increase of population, the diversity of their pursuits, and more dispersed situation. The same causes would call for a more efficient government, which they would be equally incompetent to organize, even should the power be in their hands, in any well-digested form, such as should preserve order in society, and secure to themselves the enjoyment of their liberties. With the pursuits of industry a corresponding change would likewise take place in the habits and manners of the people. The two great classes of rich and poor would grow up in each society, which would move in separate bodies, and in opposition to each other. As the latter would form the great majority, it would follow, should the government fall into the hands of the people, that that class would have the complete control. Hence the rich, dreading its consequences, would be apt to incline to the side of the chief or prince.

In such a state of society it would be hardly possible, even should the prince be entirely put aside, for the other parties to institute any regular government for themselves. The state of the science then existing in the world would, in all probability, still render such an institution impractical, for the wisest heads among them. For an unlettered community, divided into parties different in their circumstances, and in a state of variance and hostility with each other, to accomplish it would be altogether impossible. Should a government be instituted for them by any virtuous and enlightened member of the community to whom they might appeal, organize it as he might, its fate might easily be anticipated. If he should vest the power in the hands of the rich only, it would soon be overset. If in the hands of the people, en masse, under any modification which he might give to it, it might sustain itself longer, but could not be permanent.

The period now adverted to is a very marked one in the history of societies and of man. It is one in which the rude state is essentially abandoned, and considerable progress made in civilization, and in the arts of civilized life. The mass in each society is devoted to liberty, but unable to maintain it. Distinct interests have arisen, by which separate classes have been formed in each community, which are often at variance with each other. While tyrants rule in some, the rich have gained the ascendency in others, and the numerous class of poor retain it in others. Under such circumstances changes would be frequent. Tyrants would occasionally be deposed, and again recover their power. Contests between the rich and the poor would be unceasing, and whenever the latter wrested the government completely from the hands of the former, the power would be sure to pass to leaders who would be apt to quarrel with, and to cut each other off, and thus it would be lost. In this state of civil discord compromises would be apt to take place between the contending parties, which although not formed by regular compact, would have like effect by the acquiescence of the parties. Sometimes the arrangement would come from the prince, who, seeking to retain his power, and knowing that it could not be done unless he tranquilized the state by admitting both the other classes to a participation in the government, he would make an arrangement to that effect. Sometimes it might be the result of conflicts which the exhausted parties could not renew. Such an arrangement could never proceed from the people by accord, as equal parties. In this manner distinct orders would be introduced into the government.

In such a society, in which each extreme, the government of an individual and of the people, under any modification which they could form, being found to be impracticable, and the rich having acquired a force not to be disregarded, it would be natural that experiments should be made of governments of this mixed class, through the whole range between perfect democracy and despotism, that the power of the people should prevail in one, that of the prince in another, and of the aristocracy in others. Although these governments of the mixed character would originate in strife, and take the form which casual events might give them; and although the principle of discord is deeply engrafted in them, and unceasingly felt in their operation, yet they have been more durable than any of the ancient democracies. The tendency however of all governments of this mixed character has been to despotism. When the power of the prince is sustained, if wars ensue with neighboring nations, conquests are made, and new conquests are made, and new dominions acquired, such result becomes almost inevitable. The people remaining in the same unlettered state, reduced to subordination and submission, their minds are broken. The government of the conquered territories is by provinces, and each province by creatures of the crown. The people can have no general meeting, nor in any other mode, in their unlettered state, act in concert. The pursuits of industry, in the great mass, tie them to the soil. If any change in favor of liberty is made, it must proceed from a new state of things, and from other causes. The society must be raised from the depressed and degraded state into which it has fallen; knowledge must be diffused among the people, commencing with a few, and extending by degrees to the whole community, and this can be done only by making those pursuits of industry which contribute to the depression instrumental to their elevation. Property must be acquired by agriculture, commerce and the arts, and knowledge with it. The success of a few will excite emulation with others, and inspire the whole community with hope. By degrees the society may thus be raised to the grade to which it is entitled by nature, and acting with moderation and wisdom, may maintain it.

This view of societies, in their origin and progress, may be considered as applicable to all the ancient republics. It may fairly be inferred, therefore, if the view be correct, that the cause of the people never had a fair experiment in those republics, either from the state of society, or under a government by which such experiment could be made. The governments which they were able to institute, or which the science then permitted, failing, the power passed over directly to the opposite extreme. Fortunate were they when they could escape abject slavery, even for a time, under those of a mixed character. How far it might have been practicable for the people who composed those republics to have improved their system, and to have preserved their liberties, had they been left to the operation of internal causes only, is uncertain. It is known that while the issue was depending, they were all overwhelmed by the warlike spirit, the gigantic growth, and overweening ambition of Rome.

I have so far treated of governments established over societies, in the rude and unlettered state, and of the incidents to such governments, while the mass of the people remained in that state. I will now notice such as may be instituted by societies, in a state of civilization, and which may be done either by old and populous communities, or by emigration of a portion of the inhabitants of such communities to a new position, and the establishment of a new government over them, at such position. I will commence with the effort by an old and populous community, to institute a new government over it, and proceed afterwards to take a view of such government as may be established by emigrants from such community.

In contemplating the institution of a government by an old and populous community, the change of the existing government, and the adoption of another more favorable to liberty, is that which I have in view. We will suppose that the society had passed through a process something like that which has been described; that it had its origin in the rude state, at which period the people were equal and free, but had submitted to such a government as they were, in that state, competent to; that they had had, in their progress, struggles for liberty, and experienced changes of various kinds, until, by the increase of population, and other causes adverted to, they had finally been reduced under despotism. We will suppose also, that they had remained for centuries in that state, until by the extension of commerce, improvement in agriculture, and in the arts and sciences, a new era had arrived; that the mass of the people had become more intelligent; that many among them had acquired great wealth and consideration by their manners, talents and services, which had exalted them by the just standard of merit above any in the privileged orders. A change in this state, by the overthrow of the existing despotism, and the establishment of a free government, could be accomplished only by a revolution and by force. Are a people thus circumstanced competent to such a change? Are they capable of surmounting the difficulties which they would have to encounter in the effort, and to maintain the government should they succeed, after its establishment? These questions involve considerations of high importance to the whole human race. They bear, however, in the first instance, more especially on Europe.

That a government founded on the sovereignty of the people with a wise organization and distribution of its powers, is practicable over very extensive dominions and very populous communities, is certain, provided the state of society throws no impediment in its way. What that state must be, to give effect to such a government, has already been fully explained. All that is necessary is that the inhabitants generally be intelligent, that they possess some property, be independent and moral, and that they organize a government by representation into three branches, a legislative, executive and judiciary, under a wise arrangement, and vest in each the powers competent to its objects. If such a people were possessed of the sovereignty, and were left free under such a government to the operation of internal causes only, having the whole force in their hands, if united and competent, how is it possible that they should fail? It happens, however, that all the most distinguished communities of modern Europe, those which are most advanced in civilization and improvement of every kind, are placed under governments of the monarchic character, many of which are despotic. The institution of free governments in those countries could not be wrought without a struggle. Those in power would not voluntarily submit, nor could the government be maintained afterwards, without encountering serious difficulties, arising from foreign, as well as internal causes. I think proper to remark here, that the people of many of the countries of Europe adverted to, occupy, according to my judgment, much more advantageous ground than was held by those of any of the ancient republics. The class called the people is more intelligent, more independent in its circumstances, and respectable in its character. Skilled in the arts, and intelligent in other respects, as many of the inhabitants of the ancient republics were, still there was a limit within which their knowledge was confined, and beyond which the light of modern times has passed. Science in all its branches has been more extensively explored, and more generally spread among the people. The discovery of the compass has opened all parts of the habitable globe to the enterprising and curious. Commerce has taken a much more extensive range, by means whereof those engaged in it have in successive ages acquired a degree of wealth which has placed them, with their merit in other respects, in elevated stations in every community. The discovery of the art of printing has had an effect still more extensive and important. It has diffused knowledge among the mass of the people, and thereby rendered them better acquainted with their rights, and more able to support them. The different classes of society have been brought into greater intercourse and harmony with each other. The spirit of equality is more sensibly felt, and there are in all those countries many of their most enlightened citizens, in the highest ranks in society, who are devoted to free principles. The light of ages has been shed on the subject of government, and improvements made, especially by representation, which were unknown to the ancient world. Such has been the effect produced by the causes, that it is obvious that several of these governments which are held by monarchs have changed their policy, if not their principles, by accommodating their measures to the popular opinion and feeling. What further changes may be made in any of them time will develop. Nothing that has occurred can be considered as decisive against them, or ought to be discouraging, provided that those who take the lead, act with moderation and humanity. Violence and cruelty will be sure to defeat any attempt that may be made.

Two instances have occurred in modern Europe, of efforts made by the people of old and populous communities to wrest the government from the privileged orders, and to establish one founded on equal rights. The first took place in England during the reign of the family of Stuart, and commenced in that of Charles the First. The second in France, and commenced near the end of the century. As it is my intention if in my power to extend the comparison of our governments with that of England, and in making which it will be necessary to notice that effort in some detail, as an example of the governments and of the state of society of this epoch, I shall postpone what I have to say on it until I reach that stage. Of the second, of recent date, I was present and an attentive observer of its most difficult conjunctions. As this epoch forms one of the most interesting events of the modern world, some attention is thought to be due to it in this sketch.

I arrived in Paris on the 2nd of August, 1794, a few days after the fall and execution of Robespierre, and I saw the revolutionary government in operation in its subsequent stages; under the convention; under the directory and the two councils; under the consuls; and I was present when it finally terminated under the Emperor. I was anxious to trace to their sources the causes which produced the very extraordinary occurrences which marked that great struggle. I was a friend of the French Revolution, not as an enemy of the Bourbons, for as a citizen of the United States, I was always grateful to them for their services in our Revolution, and lamented the extremity to which the cause had been pushed by their execution. I was the friend of that Revolution as the friend of liberty, in which avowed character I was sent to France as the representative of my government and country. I was therefore an interested spectator as to the cause to which I wished success, but respecting those on the theatre, who acted in its support, and whose merit I could judge only by the view which I took of their conduct, I was altogether impartial.

It was a movement instructive to mankind in regard to the dangers incident to an effort, by an old and populous community, which had been long ruled by despotism, to subvert that government and establish a free one. The movement was in truth revolutionary, and under circumstances which put all the passions in motion under the strongest excitement, without any balance in the system, especially in the early stages, which could give it a proper direction. It was impossible that such an effort should be made without encountering the most serious difficulties arising from internal as well as foreign causes. A monarchy so long established and deeply rooted, could not be overthrown without the concurrence of a large majority of the people, and the collection of such a force as would crush all opposition. Nor could its overthrow fail to leave in full activity the most conflicting elements of which a society can be composed. If civil war in its most formidable shape did not ensue; discontent, which would pervade all the adherents of the former government would still exist and show itself in a variety of ways in the progress of the revolution. Foreign wars would be inevitable, for as the governments of all the other great powers were monarchical, it would be natural for those at their head to conclude that if the monarchy of France should be overthrown, a like fate would befall them. Some time would also elapse before a regular government could be established, and in the interim, the popular movement would control everything. All these difficulties occurred, under circumstances which called into activity, and put to the severest trial, all the faculties and resources, mental and physical, of the nation. The whole people moved, as it were, in a body, and gave proofs of a devotion to liberty, of patriotism and gallantry in the field, which were never surpassed by any other nation. It is not my intention to enter into the details of this great struggle. I shall simply make those comments on it, founded on occurrences which passed under my own view; and others that are well authenticated, which belong to the subject on which I treat.

Each government formed an epoch peculiar to itself, and characteristic of the crisis which had occurred. Extraordinary agitation marked its early stages, of which the government under the Convention gave the most signal proofs. That body formed the government, because, by its acts, the public actions were sanctioned; but it was rather as the organ and the instrument of the popular feeling and will under the excitement which prevailed, than a calm and deliberative assembly, acting according to its own judgment. The people might be said, and especially until the fall of Robespierre, to rule, en masse, and under the greatest possible disadvantages. The government was in effect united with the sovereignty in the people, and all power, legislative, executive, and judicial, concentrated in them. The popular sentiment was ascertained, not from a meeting of the whole people of France in one body, for that was impossible, but from movements in different quarters: Paris, Marseilles, Bordeaux, Lyons, and elsewhere, under local excitements, and without deliberation. Of this sentiment, thus proclaimed, the Convention was the instrument, and at its head was a leader who yielded to the worst passions which could animate the breast of an ambitious competitor for power. Two parties were formed in it, at an early period, one of which was called the Mountain, and the other the Plain. The former was distinguished for its violence and cruelty, the latter for its moderation and humanity. Both were friends to liberty and the Revolution, but they differed as to the means of accomplishing it; and it was that difference, combined with other causes, which gave to each the character it held. Jacobin societies were established from the commencement of the Revolution, through

France, at the head of which stood that in Paris, and by which the impulse was given to the others. In the early stages those societies promoted with just views the success of the Revolution, but they afterwards became instrumental to the greatest enormities. Between the Mountain party and this society in Paris the most perfect harmony and concert existed, and which extended in consequence to all the other societies. Robespierre became the leader of the Mountain party, and likewise of the Jacobin society in Paris, and by him, or by his instrumentality, the distinguished members of the party of the Plain, and other illustrious friends of the Revolution, were cut off. The extent to which those enormities were carried, by cutting off innocent persons who took no part in the contest, women as well as men, sapped the foundation of the Revolution, and will always be viewed with horror. This atrocious individual was at length overwhelmed, and led to the guillotine, by which he suffered the fate he merited.

On my arrival at Paris at this awful moment, I beheld a state of affairs of which I had before seen no example, nor anything which in the slightest degree resembled it. Our Revolution exhibited a very different spectacle. The movement of the people with us, in every stage, was tranquil, and their confidence in their representatives unlimited. No animosity or rivalry was seen among them. If any had previously existed, it ceased at that great crisis. We had no distinct hereditary order in the community; no hierarchy. We had but one order, that of the people; nor had we any citizen among us who did not rest on his merits and the opinion entertained of it by his fellow-citizens at large. The whole body, therefore, clung together on the purest principles, and the most simple and perfect form. But on the theatre then before me, all the conflicting elements to which I have referred were in full activity, the effect of which was visible on every object which presented itself to view. The adherents of the monarchical government were anxious to overthrow the existing one, and active in promoting that result. The nobility, who had remained behind, were generally of that class, all of whom were degraded, and most of whom had suffered by the Revolution. The hierarchy formed a corps equally numerous and active. Their lands had been wrested from them and sold, or were at market. All these classes acted in concert, but being overwhelmed, moved as it were under the mask. The people contributed their part to this disorderly and frightful spectacle. The Convention was, for the moment, comparatively calm, as was the city, but the tranquillity was of a character to show that the passions which had produced the late storm were rather smothered than extinguished. Other explosions were dreaded, and confidence, even among those who had been most active on each side, seemed to be, in a great measure, withdrawn. The Mountain party still held the majority in the committee which were charged with the executive government, and that party was not entirely crushed in the Convention.

My own situation was the most difficult and painful that I had ever experienced. Our treaty of commerce of 1778 had been set side, and many of our vessels seized and condemned, with their cargoes, in violation of it. Some hundreds of our citizens were then in Paris, and the seaports of France, many of them imprisoned, and all of them treated more like the subjects of their enemies, than the citizens of a friendly and allied power. An hostile attitude was assumed toward our government and country, and war seriously menaced. Of this disposition I felt, personally, the most mortifying effect, my recognition being delayed and likely to be refused. I saw distinctly that no impression could be made on the Committee of Public Safety, and was fearful if I should acquiesce in the delay of my recognition, the ill will toward us which pervaded that body would be extended generally to the Convention, and throughout the nation. On full consideration I was satisfied that the injuries already received would not be redressed, nor greater averted, without making an appeal as it were to the real government, the people, through the nominal one, the Convention, and by means thereof to bring the cause fairly before the nation. I knew their object was liberty, and that they had caught the spirit in our struggle, by the part they had taken in it, many of whom had carried it home, and infused it into the great body of the people. Our eyes are naturally turned to an illustrious individual who lately visited us, who fought and bled in our cause, and whose services in its support can never be too highly appreciated or liberally rewarded. I knew that there stood at the head of our government one, who by his devotion to that cause, and the services he had rendered to it, was entitled to, and held in the highest veneration by the French people; and was persuaded, if I brought before them convincing proofs of his good wishes for their success, supported by that of the other branches of our government, that the hostile spirit which had been manifested towards us by the French Government, would be subdued, and my recognition immediately follow. It was on this principle that I addressed the convention, and with the desired effect, having been received by that body itself on the next day. That such should have been the state of affairs, as to compel me to resort to such an expedient, is in itself a sufficient proof of the disorder in which the Government of France then was, and of the difference between it and all settled governments, whatever be their form.

From this period the power was transferred to the party of the Plain, who held it the residue of the term of the government by the convention. The conduct of this party corresponded with its well-known principles. It looked to the cause, and pushed it forward with zeal and perseverance, and as I thought with perfect integrity. It sustained also its character for moderation and humanity, for I saw in its progress, in the trial of some of the leading members of the Mountain party who had survived, and were denounced before it, a disposition rather to forgive, than avenge the injuries it had received from that party. Several attacks were made on the convention during the rule of this party, by popular movements in Paris, particularly by those of Germinal, Prarial, and Vendemiare, which were met with firmness, and repulsed by the force arrayed on its side. These movements were either excited by foreign powers or by members of the Mountain party. Among the important objects which now engaged the attention of the convention, was the formation of a constitution, in which it succeeded by the institution of the government of the Directory, and the two Councils, to which the power was transferred on the 31st of October, 1795. The proceedings under this government assumed a different character from that which had been acquired by those under the convention. They were more tranquil and orderly, and the government itself, in all its departments, more operative and efficient. The people confined themselves more within the limit of their appropriate duties, as the sovereign power of the state, and left the government more free to perform those which belonged to it, as their representative and responsible organ. The government of the Consuls was a step toward monarchy, in which it terminated in the imperial form.

In the progress of this Revolution I beheld, with great interest and satisfaction, the wonderful effect which it had, from year to year, by the agency of the people in the government on their intelligence and capacity for self-government. I noticed this in my first mission, during my residence in Paris, from 1794 till 1797; and I was more sensibly struck with it on my return to France in 1803. It was by the patriotic zeal and devotion to liberty of the whole French people, that the most gallant exploits were performed that the modern world had witnessed: that all the surrounding nations had been repulsed, and many subdued, so that in truth the Revolution was accomplished when the last change took effect. Satisfied I am, had those who had gained great popularity, by the eminent services which they had rendered, looked to the cause a few years longer, and not to themselves, the Republic might have been saved. The people had much improved in their capacity for self-government, yet their emancipation from the opposite extreme had been too sudden, and the interval too short for them to have become, in all respects, competent to it. They were devoted to the Revolution, and were grateful to those who had signalized themselves in its support, especially by gallant exploits in the field, and by victories over the powerful armies which assailed them. The names of those commanders became identified with the cause, and in their elevation without making the proper discrimination, they looked to its support, rather than to its overthrow, and thus their best propensities, as well as their frailties, were practiced on and made instrumental to that result. In making this remark, I indulge no feeling of personal hostility to Napoleon Bonaparte, in whose favor the change was wrought, and who was the principal actor in it. No one thought more highly than I did of his gallantry in the field, and of his talents as the commander of his army, and personally I had no cause of complaint against him, for in my second mission to France, when he was at the head of the Consular Government, I was treated by him with kindness and attention. I look only to the change, and to the causes which produced it.

An enlightened and virtuous people, who are blessed with liberty, should look with profound attention to every occurrence which furnishes proof of the dangers to which that cause is exposed. The effort was made by a great nation, distinguished for its improvement in civilization and in all the arts of civilized life; advanced to the utmost height in every branch of science that the human intellect has attained, and respected for every useful as well as polished acquirement throughout the civilized world. Having witnessed personally that effort, in the extent that I have stated, I have thought that a brief notice in this place of its progress and fate might have a good effect, and have, therefore, given it.

I will now proceed to notice such societies as may be formed by emigration of a portion of the inhabitants from civilized communities into another country, with the establishment of new governments over them in such country. I shall note some prominent distinctions between governments established by societies in this and the other state, to show the eminent advantages which the latter have over the former, as well in the capacity to institute free governments, as to preserve them.

Of this class, that is by emigration, there may be two of different character. The emigrants may take possession of a new territory, and institute an independent government of their own, such as they prefer, or they may emigrate under the protection and authority of the parent country. Of the first kind, the state of improvement to which the science has been carried is the natural limit of any human institution. Prudent men will be more disposed to adopt institutions under which they have lived, if of the free class, than to make experiments of untried projects, which are suggested by conjecture and fancy only. Governments thus instituted corresponding in their form with those of the parent countries, and the state of society being the same, would be apt to experience a like

fate. If the government of the colony is formed by the parent country by charter, its fate will depend on a variety of circumstances, and particularly on the
interest which the parent country takes in the emigration, and the connection
which it intends to preserve with the colony; on the spirit in which the emigration is made and the causes which produced it; and on the character of the
emigrants. If the institution is made in its great features popular, and the power
of that branch of the government falls into the hands of enlightened and virtuous emigrants, the control of the colony, during its infant state by the parent
country, will form a nursery of the best kind for free principles. Civilized men
will take possession of the woods, and the freedom of the hunting state be preserved, without the barbarism incident to that state. The widely separated parties of extreme wealth and poverty will not be known among them. The
pressure from the parent country, however slight, will unite them at home, and
thus form but one class among them, the whole of which will be united, when
the emergency requires it, against oppression and in favor of liberty. The intelligence and correct principles of the parents will descend to their offspring, and
thus the society will grow up from its infant state to maturity, instructed in the
knowledge, and trained to the support of popular rights and dismemberment,
find them in the best state to preserve them. An enlightened community, perfectly free, having the whole power in their hands, with no opposing interest to
contend with, may organize the best government that human wisdom can
devise, and be sure to preserve it.

CHAPTER II

A COMPARATIVE HISTORICAL VIEW OF THE GOVERNMENT OF THE UNITED STATES AND THE REPUBLICS OF ATHENS, LACEDEMON AND CARTHAGE

THE elementary view above presented of government in its principles, and the incidents to those principles in the different classes of government, and of society in the different states of which it is susceptible, and of its capacity for self-government, regarding the state in which it may be, will aid me in the prosecution of the work in which I am engaged. There is no part of the subject in either branch to which this view will not apply, or in which it is not supported, as is believed, by the well attested history of the human race in all ages, throughout the globe.

The comparison which I propose to make of our government with those of other countries, will be confined, as has already been observed, to those of Greece, Carthage and Rome, among the ancients, and if my health permits of Great Britain among the modern. With those of Greece, I shall confine it to those of Athens and Lacedemon. The first of these was a simple democracy, organized and exercised in the manner known to the ancients. The second was a mixed government with distinct orders. In regard to the first, the principle being the same with that on which our governments are founded, the example of a single government will be sufficient. In the view taken of it the defects of all governments of that class applicable to our own system, must proceed from other causes than the principle; and in treating of the defects of our government, those of all others of the same class may be noticed. When the principle is different, several examples may be necessary, and with that view I shall extend the comparison to the other governments mentioned, which differed from each other in the number of orders and division of power between them. In examining the Government of Athens, I shall have in view that which was instituted by Solon, it being admitted by all to have been the best they ever had, and in effect the best of that class that was known to the ancients. Considering the society and the government connected and identified with each other, as I do, and having an influence each on the other, I shall commence with the origin of both, and trace them, with the great events which marked their career, to the adoption of that institution, and during its existence. In examining the Government of Lacedemon, I shall have in view the Constitution of Lycurgus, and pursue the same course in tracing the origin of the society and government of that people with their progress, that I propose to do with those of Athens. I shall likewise endeavor to do equal justice to those of Carthage and Rome, noting their best epochs, with the causes of their decline and fall.

In regard to the modern world, the government of Great Britain furnishes the most interesting example. In treating of it, the distinctions between it and governments of a like kind among the ancients, and likewise between the societies of those two great and distant epochs, may be noticed.

In a development of the organization and endowment of the Democratical Government of Athens, and of its defects, with the proper remedies for them, a wide range will be opened for the practical illustration of the great principles of the science. There was nothing sound in that government but the principle on which it was founded. A full development therefore of its defects, with the remedies for them, will in those respects, if well executed, leave nothing untouched in relation to governments of that class, and include much which is applicable to the other. It will be found that the principles which apply to the organization and endowment of a government founded on the sovereignty of the people, will embrace all the considerations that are applicable to this class, and many that are equally so to the other; will apply to those which recognize distinct orders, and to all governments in which the people participate, or that have any pretension to liberty. In governments in which the people possess, exclusively, the sovereignty, the people must be protected against themselves, otherwise, such is the nature of man, that oppression, with the overthrow of the government, will be inevitable. The rule of a single body, and of a single man, must be prevented. Contests for power between individuals, if they cannot be controlled, must terminate there, and guards must be provided for the purpose adequate to the end. The door must be closed against ambition, and against selfish views of every kind which, by being yielded to, may operate to the injury of the cause. A fair compensation should be allowed for service, and honorable distinction for exalted merit; but such should be the organization and endowment, as to make the government by the operation of selfish as well as more lofty motives in those in office the instrument of its own preservation, rather than of its subversion. The guards which are deemed necessary for the accomplishment of these objects, have been noticed in the preceding part of this sketch. In the view which I propose to take of the defects of the Athenian Government I shall treat the subject more in detail.

In governments which recognize distinct orders, be the state of society what it may, the people must likewise form the basis of the system. The legislative power must be essentially in their hands, and it must be well organized, or they will soon have none. Place it in an hereditary branch, and there can be no liberty. Give to a prince a larger portion than is prescribed by principle, and strictly executive, and he will soon absorb the whole, or be overthrown. The same remark is applicable to the aristocratic branch, or that of the nobles. Its powers must be limited, and the possibility of encroachment by it on the other branches be prevented, or a like result will follow. The nearer therefore such governments approach to well established principles, both in the organization and endowment of their branches, the more tranquil will their movement be, and the longer their duration. A defect in those respects will operate differently in the different classes, arising from the difference of principle in the government, and of interest in the parties, but an irregular and disorderly movement, with the final overthrow of the government, will be certain in both. I shall endeavor, therefore, in treating of the Government of Athens, to illustrate and establish those principles, and in a manner to admit their application, so far as it may be practicable to both classes of government, with a view to abridge what I should otherwise have to say, when I treat of the governments of the other class, and on the presumption that the illustration thus given will throw light on the subject generally as I advance in the execution of the work.

The same view is applicable to governments which recognize distinct orders with opposite interests contending against each other. The hold which each order has in such governments, the people on their part, and the other order or orders, when there be more than one in theirs, with its nature and extent, the manner in which it has been exerted and the effect produced by it will claim a like attention. The power which the people or either of the other orders held in any given instance, when contending with another, having an opposite interest, would, it is presumed, be exerted in like manner, and produce the same effect in every other instance that it had on that, the circumstances being in all respects equal. When a principle is established as to either class, it will be conclusive as to all like cases of that class, and of the other, so far as it is strictly applicable. The same view will be taken, and of course pursued, in regard to the societies of the several communities, of whose governments I shall treat. Where the state is the same, corresponding effects, under like causes, may be expected in every instance. I shall say nothing more of any government or people than is indispensable to the object I have in view. In this mode I shall abridge essentially the work, as I shall the labor, which I should otherwise be forced to bestow on it.

When a principle is supported by the example of a single government, and that example is strictly applicable in all its circumstances to other governments and people of which I shall treat, I shall make the application without a further illustration of the principle. Principles in government, where the circumstances are in all respects similar, as to order, distribution of its powers, and the state of society, are as invariable and eternal, as in any other science, mathematics, or any branch of experimental philosophy.

In taking a view of the origin and progress of the Athenian and Lacedemonian Governments and communities, for the purposes contemplated, I must look in a certain extent to those of all Greece. Those Republics formed, from the earliest period of which we have any knowledge, two of the principal states of Greece. They took a distinguished part in all the concerns of that people internally, as they likewise did in those which bore on foreign nations. The misfortunes of Greece, as well as her glory, were in an eminent degree attributable to them. Their progress, therefore, was connected with that of the other states, as was their fate, for they were all involved in one common ruin. This view is necessary in making the proposed comparison with the state governments, but in extending it to that of the general government it is indispensable.

Of the confederated system, other people, and particularly those of Greece, have also given us examples, of which, so far as they may merit attention, I shall take notice at the proper time. All such bonds rest on the elements of which they are composed, and in consequence of which the states and people, thus held together, are composed. It is necessary, therefore, to form a just idea, in the first instance, of those elements in all their parts.

There are different modes by which the object I have in view may be accomplished. One by a preliminary digest of a government, in its principle, organization and endowment, which I should consider the most perfect, and to test all the governments above enumerated, including our own, by that standard. Another to make the comparison with the democratical government of Athens, separately, showing its defects, with the remedies for them, and then to show that we have avoided those defects, and attained by our organization and endowment the utmost degree of perfection of which any government is susceptible. This being done, to compare our governments with those of a mixed character, with a view to decide the relative merit of the two classes. A third is, to make the analysis of all the governments above enumerated, in the manner stated, and to give a sketch of the career and fate of each in succession; and then to make the comparison between our governments and each of the others in all the points which they respectively involve, commencing with that of Athens. To the first it might be objected, that the sketch which would be given of the most perfect government would be theoretical only, and that the references which might be made to other governments might be regarded as forced constructions, for the purpose of supporting such theoretical dogma. To this it may be added, that the elementary view above presented goes as far in the establishment of the standard suggested, as we can go, without the aid of example, supported by the career and fortune of the governments referred to. If this view be correct, the organization and endowment of a government corresponding with it are so obvious that they will occur to all who are conversant with the subject. To the second it might be objected, that the view presented would be equally limited and unsatisfactory. The example of the Athenian Government, which had failed, however great and numerous its defects, and well-established by reason and arguments, and supported by its career and fate, might not be deemed sufficient to prove that that was the best class, or that we had attained by the organization and endowments of our governments that standard of perfection to which we aspire. To do justice to the subject, and make a fair comparison between our governments, which are founded on the sovereignty of the people, and those which recognize distinct orders, we must place each class on the best ground on which it can stand, and give to it, also, by the most incontrovertible evidence, all the support which can be adduced in its favor.

On full consideration, I am satisfied that the third mode ought to be preferred. It secures all the advantages which may be derived from either of the others, with many peculiar to itself, and is at the same time free from the objections applicable to each. The comparison must be practical, founded on the experience of each government, and extend to principle, as well as the organization and endowment of each, and likewise to the state of society in each community; and this can be better done by having the whole subject before us at the same time than its detached parts. The ancient republics formed a system peculiar to themselves. Their governments varied from each other, not in principle alone, but in many other important circumstances; still there were analogies between them, even when the principle was different, which were peculiar to that epoch. Our governments differ from them all; from the Athenian, not in principle, but in other circumstances of vital importance. The Government of Athens was founded on the sovereignty of the people, but the power was exercised in a manner to defeat its purposes. The accord in principle was in fact, as will be shown, nominal only, for such were the organization and endowment of that government that it could not fail to be oppressive. The other governments enumerated were of a mixed character, founded partly on one principle, and partly on the other. Their defects, so far as the sovereignty of the people was recognized in them, being of a like character with those of Athens, would of course produce, in what related to the power of the people, a corresponding effect in those governments with that which they produced in the Government of

Athens. It follows, therefore, that by keeping them together, and taking a minute view of each, and a combined view of the whole, the defects of each, and of the ancient system generally, may be more distinctly shown, than by detaching them from each other. The connection is such even between those which are simple, or founded exclusively on the sovereignty of the people, and those which are mixed or compounded of the two principles, that the illustration of either cannot fail to throw light on the others. The British Government, although it varies essentially from the ancient republics in the modes in which the power of the people is exercised in it, yet as it recognizes distinct orders, all the objections which apply to them on that ground, apply with equal force to it. It must therefore be placed in that class, noticing with impartiality and candor the distinctions to be taken between them. I shall therefore proceed, in the execution of this work, in the manner stated, commencing with the Government of Athens, proceeding next to that of Lacedemon, and afterwards to the others, in the order in which I have placed them.

The view which will thus be presented of the governments of the ancient republics and that of Great Britain, and likewise of the state of society in each community, will be practical. The cause of the failure of each of those republics may be distinctly seen. There is no material fact relative to the government of either as to its principle, its organization, or the endowment of its branches, with the effect produced thereby, or as to the society of each, involving its capacity for self-government, but what may be clearly proved. The same remark is clearly applicable to the British Government from its origin to the present time. In this mode it is presumed that a correct standard, tested by experience, may be formed of the best government in principle, organization, and endowment, which human wisdom can devise; of that which is most free, and best calculated to preserve liberty; and to maintain order, as it may likewise be of the state of society necessary to give effect to such government. With this standard our system may be compared, and a correct judgment be thereby formed, whether it has attained the utmost degree of perfection of which government is susceptible, or is defective in any branch, and if in any, in what particular circumstance, and what the proper remedy is for such defect. The latter is a great object of the present inquiry. All the moral as well as the physical sciences admit of demonstration, but none with greater certainty than that of government. When the cause and effect are distinctly seen, as may be done in that science by the examples which history furnishes, no mistake can be made by those who are unprejudiced and seek the truth. The demonstration may be considered as complete. In this mode I shall pursue this inquiry, and with that sole object in view.

There are three great epochs in the history of the human race, or rather of that portion of it, whose manners and institutions form the object of this inquiry. The first commenced with the origin of the ancient republics, and terminated with them. The second commenced with the governments which were erected on the ruins of the Roman Empire, and comprises their career to the present time. The third was formed by the discovery of this hemisphere, and the revolution into which it led, with the governments which have been founded on its principles in these states. Each of these epochs is marked by characteristics which are peculiar to itself. Government in each took its origin under the influence of special causes applicable to the epoch. In the first the race of man was limited. The collections were small, and each band or tribe adopted the government which suited it best, or submitted to that which the exigency required and nature dictated. The changes which occurred in the progress of those societies, especially in the early stages, were attributable more to internal than to external causes. These primeval institutions were cherished and maintained by each society, so far as it was able, until they were all subdued and reduced under one which happened to be the most powerful. In the second epoch the earth had become crowded with inhabitants, and that republic which had risen to the greatest height, which had conquered all the others, and a great part of the other known regions of the globe, was now destined to experience the ill fortune which it had inflicted on other states. This nation, which owed its elevation and grandeur to free principles, had abandoned those principles, and by the indulgence of every species of debauchery and vice, sunk down under despotism into a state of the most miserable decrepitude and imbecility. At this period many barbarous nations, incensed at the usurpation and tyranny which had been exercised over them, distant from each other, and without concert, fell on different parts of that vast empire, and overcame it. These nations established in the parts which they respectively conquered, such governments as they thought best calculated to preserve their conquests, and to keep the people whom they had subdued in subjection. These governments were essentially military, a chief at the head of each, with inferior and subaltern officers under him, of different grades, the same, as is presumed, in the first instance, leader and others, who had commanded the invading force and made the conquests. Under such circumstances it would be long before the conquerors and the conquered could be completely incorporated and become one people; and hence the order which was established in the commencement would be preserved. In this manner the governments of modern Europe originated, the strong features of which are still marked on all of them, and especially those most free. The third epoch commenced in a form different from either of the others. The parties to it were of the same European race, but they commenced their career by emigration to the new world. The state of civilization and improvement to which the emigrants had arrived, the causes which produced the emigration, and the spirit with which it was made, with the institutions under which they settled, placed them in their origin on more favorable ground than was ever held by any other people. It is to the governments which have been instituted by the descendants of these emigrants, that we owe the felicity which we now enjoy, and that the present epoch owes its importance.

The writers on the subject of government, ancient and modern, composed their works under the influence of the examples before them, and of the state of society existing at the time. Their works are characteristic of the epochs at which they lived. In the first there were two dangers, that of despotism, and the government of the multitude, both of which were equally menacing, and both of which they viewed with equal horror. In that age society was comparatively in its infant state, and in the governments that were mixed, the orders were not distinctly marked by any well-digested principle. In guarding against one extreme, they were apt to run into the other. It was owing to these causes, that we find the definition given of the several classes of government at that epoch, so vague and indeterminate, so little accordant with principle. In reasoning on man, under the influence of the different classes of government, with the modifications then known, and on all abstract subjects connected with his principles and passions their works are profound, but they are nevertheless confined within that scale. The same remark is applicable to those who lived in the second epoch, which was threatened with a single danger only, that of despotism. It was natural that those writers who lived under governments which extended to the people a portion of liberty only, and which were menaced with despotism, should look to that danger alone, and exert all their faculties to prevent it. It could not be expected that they would look to the abuses and dangers of a system which they put in contrast with that which they dreaded and wished to avoid.

When we are informed that Aristotle had collected the constitutions of one hundred and fifty-eight people, from which he digested his work called Politics or the Science of Government, we are enabled to form a tolerably correct idea of the number of inhabitants and extent of territory of each state, and likewise of the causes to which the form of those governments was attributable. We see at once that each community must have consisted of the inhabitants of a village, and that its territory could not have extended much beyond it. He treated of free governments, or of such as were so considered by him, and in consequence, of those in which the people held either the entire sovereignty, or a portion of it. His object was, in making this collection, to show the good features and defects of each, and to give his opinion in favor of that which appeared to him the best, with a view to promote the liberty and happiness of mankind. There were then few free governments beyond the limits of Greece. The Carthagenian was one, and of which he spoke in very favorable terms. Of the Government of Rome he said nothing, which proves that the collection consisted almost altogether of the Governments of Greece. That work was lost. His essay on the Science of Government has been preserved. If one-tenth of the number of constitutions said to have been collected by him consisted of those of Grecian states, it would follow that they were of the character above mentioned.

Among the writers of the second epoch, Locke and Sydney of England, and Montesquieu and Rousseau of France, hold a very distinguished rank. The essays of the two former correspond with the remark already made. They lived at a very unsettled period, and looked at one danger only. Those of the two latter are more elementary and general, more in accord and spirit with those of the first epoch, arising as is presumed from the government under which they lived, and the fear of giving offense to those in power. The works of all these writers are very able, and exalt the fame of the authors. They nevertheless do not point out either the advantages or the special dangers of our system, for they did not contemplate it. I may take further notice of them hereafter. My object is to look at the dangers as well as the advantages of our system, and to point out its dangers, so far as I may be able, with the means of averting them. With us there is at present no existing disease. We are on the contrary blessed with perfect health. Our object is to preserve that state, and prevent a disease. It is, therefore, our duty to look to the dangers which threaten liberty, from any and every direction, and to guard against them.

Considering government and society as identified, each depending on the other, it has been my object in this elementary sketch, after fixing the principles of government with their incidents and a brief outline of the best organization and endowment that can be adopted for free governments of every kind, to present the most correct view of both branches of the subject that I have been able, as they have existed in the two preceding epochs. There are two sources from which the most correct information may be obtained of the best organization and endowment of free governments that can be adopted, authentic history and scientific essays on the subject of government itself, compared in both instances by enlightened men. From history we derive a knowledge of wants, from the origin of the communities of which the authors respectively treat, to the period at which their narrative terminates. The state of society and of government, with the changes which occur in each, in the progress of such communities, fall within the scope of this class of writers, but rather as descriptive of the actual state in every stage, than a profound analysis of the subject, in either of its branches, so as to meet the precise objects of this inquiry. It is more the duty of an historian to narrate the transactions of a government in its internal concerns, and those with foreign nations, than to analyze with vigor its parts, and to compare its merits with the governments of other people. It belongs to a writer on government to take a more comprehensive and minute view of the subject on principle, its organization, endowment, and every other circumstance connected with it. If the essay be of that character, and the writer be blessed with great talents, nothing that belongs to it, which was then known, would escape his attention. If he does not treat of the state of society, especially if a writer of the second epoch, it must be because the condition of the people was such that the share in the government for which he contended in their favor, was so limited, as to preclude all discussion on the subject, without an acknowledgment that they were incompetent to the discharge of any of the duties of any regular free government whatever.

I have stated that there are three great epochs in the history of the human race, and that each was marked by characters as to government and society peculiar to itself. I have stated also, that the third, to which we belong, has placed us on different and more advantageous ground, in both respects, and as to the means of supporting free government, than was ever held by any other people. To prove this beyond all doubt, it is necessary to place the governments and societies of each epoch in their true character, and to show the difference between them in every material circumstance. In the view which has already been presented, I have derived all the aid from both the sources alluded to, as to the first two, that I have been able. There is not a fact stated, which is not supported by the best authorities in each, and where they apply, in both. As however the writers on the subject of government draw more distinctly the line between governments of different classes, and in consequence between those of the different epochs, and likewise between the epochs themselves, I have thought that a summary but correct view of the contents of the works of the most distinguished writers of the two preceding epochs, would give a more satisfactory confirmation of the government and state of society in each, and thus enable me to show the difference between ours and both, than could otherwise have been done, and have therefore drawn it. The authors of whose works I shall give such sketch, are considered the ablest that have written on the subject of government. They are so regarded in our schools of instruction, in our literary institutions, and by scientific men generally in the United States and in all free countries. As they do not embrace our system, they could not show its advantages over those which preceded it. On the contrary, the writers of the second epoch, whose works are most read and relied on, have preferred and recommended governments of a different kind. Had our governments been before them in successful experiment, as they have been since their institution, they would, I have no doubt, have recommended them in preference to all others. Having their own, or rather those for which they contended, for there was then nothing settled, and the ancient system only before them, it may fairly be inferred that they concluded that the alternative was between those two; and preferring their own, for their own country, and for obvious reasons, have declared that sentiment in the matter stated. In the study of the science of government, especially by our youth, it is proper that their attention should be drawn to this feature in those works, with the probable cause of it. It is improper that they should adopt an opinion unfavorable to our system, on the sentiment expressed by those writers, which it may fairly be presumed, had they been acquainted with it, they would not have entertained. I have therefore found in this circumstance an additional motive for giving a sketch of their contents.

Among the writers of the first epoch, Aristotle is the most distinguished. Plato composed a work on the subject of government. He drew two projects, but they are so theoretical and objectionable in every view; so little applicable to us, and even to the age in which they were written, that they need not be noticed. Plutarch, in his Lives of Distinguished Men, gives sketches of the governments which were formed in the progress of different communities, from their earliest ages to this time, by the princes or chiefs at the head of each, voluntarily, or by persons to whom the power was committed by the contending parties, which are instructive in that view, as well as for the purposes of general history. Diogenes Laertius may be placed in the same class, but in a very limited degree. Polybius was an author of great talents. His works are principally historical, great part of which have been lost, but in some of the extracts which have been preserved we find essays on government which are very interesting. He lived at the times of Scipio Africanus, and although a Greek, resided at Rome, at a period when the character of the Roman Government was fully unfolded, and by whose example he was enabled to present some features distinct from those which are to be found in Aristotle. His work, however, is strictly characteristic of that epoch. Considering the work of Aristotle as the most comprehensive, systematic, and truly descriptive of the governments of that epoch; of the state of the science, and of the manners of the people, I shall take from it the sketches which I deem material for the object which I have in view.

The work of this author, to which I allude, is called, as has been observed, his Essay on Politics or the Science of Government.

He commences this work in the elementary form, which was adopted by Plato in his two projects, with the origin of society, and in the smallest number of which it can consist. Man and wife form the first stage,[6] father and children the second,[7] master and slave the third.[8] In the first the power is marital; in the second paternal; but in both limited. In the third it is absolute. He asserts that in each it is founded in nature. He then traces the origin of a city with equal minuteness. Into these details I shall not enter, because the opinion with us is too well formed in each instance to require it, and because, likewise, whether his doctrine be well founded or otherwise, no light can be derived from that incipient stage, either as to the organization or the endowment of a government which is necessary to protect liberty and maintain order over the very populous communities of the present day. I think proper to notice only that feature in it which relates to slavery, as it was known to and practiced in the ancient republics. As slavery exists in many of the states of our Union, and involves political considerations of very high importance to those states, and in consequence to the whole Union, I may, in the prosecution of this work, deem it proper to notice it, and it is on that presumption that I make the exception.

It has already been observed that Aristotle made four species of Democracy, four of Aristocracy, four of Oligarchy, and five of Monarchy. It is proper to add that he made a fifth class of government, which he called a Republic, and separated it by certain shades of difference from the others. Of his definition of each species of these several classes of government, I will endeavor to convey a just idea, beginning with Democracy.

The first species of this class, he says, consists of a government in which there is an equality between the rich and the poor, so that neither governs.[9]

The second, where the qualification for office in point of revenue is very moderate, and that all who have it are eligible.[10]

The third, where every citizen is eligible to office, under the condition that the law, and not the multitude, shall govern.[11]

---

6. Diogenes Laertius, Vol. I. Book III. chap. iv.
7. Ibid. Book I. chap. iii.
8. Ibid. chap. iv. p. 188.
9. Aristotle, Book IV. ch. iv. Vol. I. page 270.
10. Ibid. page 271.
11. Ibid.

The fourth, is that in which the multitude is the sovereign, and not the law; where the decrees of the multitude at every meeting give the rule, and there is no fixed government or permanent law.[12]

The first species of Aristocracy, he says, is a government which is founded on absolute and not relative virtue, and vested in persons of property. This government, he observes, is the only one in which the virtue of a man of wealth is strictly that of a good citizen. Virtue, in every other instance, he adds, is relative to the kind of government.[13]

His second species is founded on a combination of riches, virtue and liberty.

His third consists of a government which is founded on virtue and liberty without regard to wealth.

The fourth comprehends all the shades of the republic inclining to oligarchy.

His first species of oligarchy is a government which excludes the majority of citizens from office by making the qualification of property so high that few can attain it, but which leaves the door open to all who do.[14]

The second, when the revenue required is small, but the appointment to office committed to the magistrates, and in consequence, to those already in office.

The third, when the sons succeed to the offices held by their fathers.

The fourth, when the magistrate is supreme director, without law.[15]

His first species of monarchy consists of a government in which the power of the chief is limited to the perpetual command of the armies, and which may be either elective or hereditary.[16]

The second approaches to tyranny, and is that which is adopted by a certain class of barbarians. It is nevertheless legal, although its forms are tyrannical, because it is adopted by the consent of the people, is supported by law, and accords with their manners. Of this class he gives the governments and people of Asia as examples. Legitimate monarchy, he says, is that in which submission is voluntary and tyrannical when it is forced. In the one instance the guard, who protects the sovereign, is composed of his subjects, in the others, of foreigners.

His third species is that which was known in the remote ages of Greece, and called Asymnetia. It was tyrannical in its powers, but constituted by the suffrage of the people, and to meet extraordinary emergencies. In some cities it was for life; in others it terminated with the cause which produced it.

12. Ibid.
13. Aristotle, Book IV. ch. 7, gives his idea of the second species of aristocracy, page 280.
14. Aristotle, vol. I. Book 4, ch. 5. page 174.
15. Ibid. page 274.
16. Aristotle, Vol. I. Book III. ch. 10, page 227.

The fourth was that of the Jewish ages. It was formed by law and accorded with the manners and will of the people. The chiefs of that age were the benefactors of the people; they led them to victory, instructed them in the arts, and united them in society. Gratitude made them kings, and the consent of the people transmitted the throne to their descendants. They had the supreme direction of every concern relative to war; were chiefs of religion, and judges of the people. By degrees, in the progress of time, some of these relinquished a portion of their power; others were deprived of it by the people.[17]

The fifth species was that of absolute power in an individual, or of despotism.[18]

On a view of these several classes of government, and of the different species of each, the shades of difference between the classes themselves and between the species of each class, and in some instances, between the species of one class and those of another, are so slight, and little regulated by principle, that it is scarcely possible to discriminate between them, or to form a correct idea of his meaning.

Of the first class, that of Democracy, there is less difficulty in comprehending his meaning in each instance than in either of the others. The sovereignty, being admitted to be in the people and the government united with it, and exercised by them en masse, there is no distinction between the several species, as to principle, and little as to the organization. He graduates the several species from that which he considers the best, to the worst, making the condition of the citizens in point of property the basis in each species. The first contemplates such an equality in that respect, that neither the rich nor poor will govern; that such distinct and conflicting classes will not exist; that the whole society will have a common interest. The second forms a slight restraint on the poorer class, by excluding from office those in the most wretched state only, the government being still vested in the whole body of the citizens, and wielded by a majority. The third rejects the distinction by property, and requires simply, that the law shall govern, by which is understood some fixed rule applicable to the whole community, which should be executed with uniformity by the proper tribunals. The fourth places the government exclusively in the hands of the multitude, in which state, he says, that the law is nothing, and their decrees everything. On this last species he descants at large. He represents it as forming a state of anarchy, the most oppressive that can be conceived. The people, he says, are the sovereign, not individually, but in a body; a monarch with a thousand heads.

---

17. The four species of monarchy are found in Book III. chap. 10.
18. Book III. chap. 11.

Of Aristocracy, it is more difficult to comprehend his meaning, either as to the principle on which the government is founded or the different species of which it is composed. His first species consists of a government composed of persons of wealth, and of absolute, not relative, virtue. He does not state how they become possessed of it, whether by hereditary right or election, nor the extent of its powers, nor duration in office, if by election. He supposes these men to be as pure as angels, and to look to no object but the public good, and with consummate wisdom. By relative virtue, it is presumed that he meant governments of the other species and of the other classes, in which those who fill them are ruled by the principles and passions incident to man. It is evident that this species contemplates a government which is altogether theoretical and imaginary, not founded in nature or fact. It cannot therefore be reasoned on, as the principle of any class, or any species of either. Virtue, whether it be of an individual, or of several, can be ascertained by the conduct of the party only. It is not hereditary. A virtuous father often has a vicious son. If dependent on good conduct, there must be some tribunal to judge of it, and the result must depend on the judgment of such tribunal. To reason on a government we must know the principle on which it is founded; how those in office came there, and by what title they hold it, and likewise how it is formed and endowed. As he has not given the necessary information on these points, we cannot view it in any other light than that stated. The same remarks are essentially applicable to his second and third species, the first of which he founds on riches, virtue and liberty; the other on virtue and liberty only. Of wealth as a basis, a distinct idea may be formed, and by liberty, it is understood that he meant the rights of the whole people. If virtue is a visionary basis in one instance, it must be in all others. In founding his fourth species on all the shades of the republic with an inclination of Oligarchy, we must ascertain his meaning by the definition which he gives of those classes, which as to the republic is vague, and as to Oligarchy, explicit in one feature only: that it is a government of the few, and of the rich, in opposition to that of the multitude, and the poor.

The view which he presents of the several species of Oligarchy, confirms the remark which has just been made respecting it. He makes the rich and the few the basis of the class. The qualification for office in the first species is raised so high, that few can attain it. The sum required in the second is diminished, and may be in the third, but as the right is given to those in power in the one to appoint their successors, and as the sons succeeded their fathers in the offices held by them, in the other, the same result might follow. His fourth and last species, consisted of a government in which there was no law other than the will of the magistrate.

From a view of every species of these two classes, of Aristocracy and Oligarchy, it may fairly be inferred, that he did not consider either as hereditary, as holding the government in its own right, and the people as its slaves. If such was the fact, the declaration of it would fix the grade and character of the government, and there could be but one species. In making the shades of difference between the several species of each class he shows that there was nothing settled in either, and that in the contentions for power between ancient families and the body of the people, between the rich and the poor, some of those governments in which the former had gained the ascendancy were better than others. In every instance in which the right of the class depended on the qualification by property, or on any contingency, it may be presumed that the decision rested with the opposite class, the people, and, in consequence, that the government, if not elective, was not strictly hereditary.

The same difficulty occurs in discriminating between his different species of Monarchy. The power in the first was confined to the command of the armies, and might be elective or hereditary. In this species, the chief had no share in the government. His second, although absolute, he deemed legal, being adopted by the consent of the people, and accordant with their manners. He illustrates his idea of this species by the example of the government and people of Asia. By the term legal, it is presumed that he meant that they were made so, by the voluntary submission of the people; that he did not mean to convey the idea, that such governments were free, or any idea respecting the principles of government, or the character of the people themselves. Voluntary submission to such a government is a proof only that the people were competent to none other; that they were fitted only to be slaves. His third species was that which existed in the earliest ages of Greece. It was elective, and in some instances for life; in others for special emergencies with which it terminated. This government, he says, was legal, although tyrannical, because it was the only one to which the people of that age were competent. The same remark is applicable to this species as to the preceding one, with this difference, that it was in all instances elective, and the people in consequence not slaves; the species being attributable to the early and rude age in which it was known. His fourth species applied to the Jewish ages, and had its origin in like manner with those of the third, in the good will and choice of the people. At this period the population of the states had increased, and the manners of the people undergone some change. The call for a more stable and efficient government became, in consequence, proportionally more urgent, while the science had not experienced a corresponding improvement. His fifth species is that of Absolute Monarchy, and which he delineates at great length, reviewing the different species, and explaining the distinctions between them. On the examples which he gives of this class. I shall remark only, that it cannot fail to excite surprise that he should place in it governments that were elective, as those of the first, third and fourth species were, and more especially those in which the term of service of the incumbent might be, for a very short period, a year or less, dependent on the emergency which gave birth to it. The surprise must be equally great to find that he considered the despotism of Asia legal, and for the sole reason, that the people were incompetent to any other.

The view above presented, taken from the work of Aristotle, gives in my estimation, a just representation of the origin of the governments and of the changes which took place in them; of the causes which produced those changes; of the state of society, and likewise of the science of government, during the first epoch. All the governments originated then in monarchy, and were of a limited character, called for by the exigencies of the society, and not claimed by any right in the incumbents. The people were free, and their rulers their instruments, rather than their masters. The descendants of those first advanced to power set up higher claims, which in the progress of time, produced contentions and changes in the government of every state. Of nobility, as a distinct hereditary order, entitled to a share in the sovereignty by hereditary right, no clear and satisfactory evidence is seen. That such a class existed, and often participated in the governments is certain, and that it might be hereditary in some, probable. This class, in every state, seems to have taken its origin in the families of the princes of the early ages who were rich, and whose wealth descended to their posterity, of which the Heraclidae, Pelopidae, etc., furnish examples. When the government by princes was overthrown, the power of the nobility, which was an appendage to it, experienced essentially the same fate. They were however rich, and the mass of the people being poor, and government indispensable, and the people in the states most free having never enjoyed the right to originate any proposition, or any other right than to decide on those which were presented to them from the other branches, and having no talent to institute a free government on sound principles, they remained in the same degraded state which they had held in all preceding ages. The communities were small, and neither extreme, either of liberty or slavery, could be tolerated, or was practicable; for when the power was wrested from the princes by the people they could not exercise it en masse, the only form then known to them, and hence every possible variety was assumed. Aristotle, in the collection which he made of the constitutions of one hundred and fifty-eight people, described what he saw, or of which examples were given, and within which scope he confined his digest. His organization of the different powers of government, with the revolutions to which they were respectively subject, and the means of averting them, extends to every class of free government, and to every species of each class then known. To these causes it is to be attributed that the shades of difference, in point of principle, between the several classes of government are so slight, and in the modification of the several species of each class, in some instances, scarcely perceptible. His work, however, according to the limit within which he moved, does honor to his fame, and will, in many views, and in all ages, be instructive and useful. He gave by full illustration, the example only of the Governments of Lacedemon, Crete, Carthage, and Athens, which he thought the best of their kind.

I will now proceed to take a like view of the works of the writers of the second epoch, among which those of Locke, Sydney, Montesquieu and Rousseau are particularly entitled to attention. A long space had intervened between the writers of those two epochs, which was, especially after the overthrow of the Roman Empire, an interval of barbarism and darkness. In both epochs the contest was for liberty on the part of the people. In the first, it was between the two extremes, the multitude and individuals. What were the rights of kings, what of the nobility, what of the people, were the great questions in both, and the distinction between the classes, especially the two latter, did not apply so much in the first to hereditary right in the nobility, as between the rich and the poor. The governments which were founded on the ruins of the Roman Empire were in their origin comparatively free, but they soon terminated, especially with the principal powers, in despotism. From that state Europe began to emerge when those authors appeared. The old system, with all its changes, was before them, and to it the new had added nothing, by any example it afforded, to the improvement of the science itself. The modern governments were more simple. The territory of each community was of vast extent, as was its population, compared with those of Greece, and the classes in society were more completely separated from each other. The approach to despotism was rapid, and its continuance of long duration, because in countries of such extent the power of the people was soon lost, and in their unlettered and ignorant state they had no means of recovering it. The power of the nobility was too feeble to form any check on the career of the prince. The rights of that corps, however, were more distinct than in any of the ancient governments. Wherever it existed, whether it held the government exclusively in its hands, or belonged to absolute monarchy, it was hereditary. In the latter governments it was a mere appendage to the prince, having no rights in opposition to his, but it supported his power in contests with the people, because in so doing, it supported its own, holding immense possessions, and the people, in a state of vassalage, under them. The people of England were the first who put seriously to issue the great principles on which free government turned; and these authors may be considered, and especially those of that country, the first who took the lead in their illustration and support.

The works of the two first mentioned writers were composed at a period very interesting to this country, as it likewise was to that of their own. It was one of great commotion, produced by a context for power between the friends of liberty on the one side, and of despotism on the other. The English nation had then reached a stage when in the progress of society, some fixed and permanent form to its government had become indispensable, and which must terminate in a complete revolution in favor of the one or other party, or in a compromise between them. To produce either result, great contention violence and civil war were inevitable. These conflicts were connected with the emigration and settlement of our ancestors in these states, and with the great events which have since followed in them. The works of these writers, therefore, are interesting to us in two views. They are so in reference to the nature of the governments which then existed throughout Europe, and of the state of society, and of the science at the time. They are so likewise, from the influence which that state and the convulsions which followed in their own country had on the emigration of a portion of its inhabitants to this territory, and on the career and fortune of their descendants. The general characteristics of this epoch have been described. All the ancient republics had been overthrown, and a new state of affairs introduced and established throughout Europe. Different forms of government were established, and the whole system changed.

Locke's work occupies about 150 pages, folio, and is divided into two books, the first of which contains an examination and refutation of a work of Sir Robert Filmer, which was written in favor of the divine right of kings. The second forms a regular essay on civil government. In the first, he states the doctrine of Filmer, in full extent, with his argument in support of it, and refutes it by scriptural authority and sound reasoning. In the second he traces the origin of government to its true source the consent of the people and the equal rights of all. He speaks of the different classes of government, Democracy, Monarchy and Oligarchy, omitting that of Aristocracy, but which, it is presumed, he comprised in Oligarchy. He treats also of mixed governments.

Mr. Locke contemplates, as other writers do, two distinct ages in society; the one, the early and rude age; the other, the more advanced and civilized state. In the first, he admits that government originates, generally, in an individual, and may be paternal, but contends, that in every period of that age it is elective and free. In both ages, he considers the people as the source of power, and having an inalienable right to give to the government what form they please. If they tolerate a bad one, it is either because they are incompetent to any other, or are prevented from making a change by other causes.[19] In all that he advances in favor of the rights of the people, his view is unquestionably correct, and is supported with great ability; but it is confined to the epoch specified, and to the governments which characterized it. The Feudal system, which had been founded by the nations who had overthrown the Roman Empire, and established themselves on its ruins, precluded, especially among the principal powers, all idea of self-government.

In treating of the organization of a government, and the manner in which the people must exercise their power, in case of abuse, we see distinctly that he had the British Constitution in view. He considers the legislature as the supreme power of the state, comprising the House of Commons, the House of Peers, and the king. That it comprehends the three branches is inferred from the fact, that each has a participation in its powers; the king by a negative on the laws, and likewise by a distinction which he makes between an executive magistrate who has that power, and one who has not. The former he places on elevated ground above the laws; the latter he considers subject to be changed and displaced at pleasure.[20] In this he concurs with Blackstone, who says that the Parliament is omnipotent. It is only in governments which recognize distinct orders, of the class called free, that the legislative power can be viewed in that light. In those of that class, the government is united with the sovereignty, and in consequence there can be no check on them within the limit of the constitution. There can be more, except by popular movements and the overthrow of the government itself. In supporting the power of the legislature, he supports that of the people against that of the kings, because it is in the legislature that the people exercise their power in the government; and in asserting that the people have the right to rise en masse and overthrow the government, in the case of abuse, he supports the doctrine, that all power originates in the people, whatever be the form of the government, or great the power of the kings.

In his definitions of the powers of government, we see no nice discrimination of those which should be vested in the executive and judiciary. In treating of prerogative, we find that he allows to the executive the power to regulate

19. Book II. chap. 8, section 105.
20. Ibid. chap. 13, sections 151–2; again, chap. 17, section 23.

the number of members in every country or borough entitled to representation, as the population may increase or diminish; and likewise to establish new corporations, and fix the number of representatives to each.[21] In this he transcends our idea of the power which should be held by that branch, even under our free representative government. We think that it should be vested in the legislature only. The objection to the exercise of it by an hereditary prince is much stronger, since by the abuse of the power, which should always be guarded against, he might multiply the dependents on him and thereby increase his influence. He says nothing in favor of the independence of the judiciary. On the contrary, by giving to it no power over an unconstitutional law, the legislature being supreme, he makes it subservient to that branch, and in consequence, to the ruling power in the state.

Mr. Locke's work was written with great ability, and was certainly very interesting and useful to his country, and as may be presumed, to Europe, at the time it was written. He touches no subject which he does not thoroughly analyze, nor advance any doctrine which he does not fully illustrate and ably support. But whoever examines it with attention, will find that there is little in it other than the support which he gives to the general cause of liberty, which can be considered applicable to us. His refutation of the work of Filmer, in favor of the divine right of kings, may certainly be viewed in this light. No one here has a claim to that station, or ever had, nor does any one entertain that sentiment. This remark is equally applicable to his argument in favor of the right of the people to change their government at pleasure, and to punish those who violate the laws, or are otherwise guilty of misconduct. There is no difference of sentiment on these points with us. All our governments are founded on that principle, and have been in practical and successful operation since the Declaration of our Independence. Mr. Locke's work may, therefore, be viewed in the light in which I have placed it; as characteristic of the epoch at which it was written; as exhibiting a true picture of the nature of the governments, the state of society, and of the science at the time. He does not look at the dangers to which our system is exposed, nor suggest the means of averting them. It is proper to add, that if it was difficult, and almost impossible to sustain the mixed form of which the British Government was composed, the preservation of one founded on the sovereignty of the people could not have been even thought of by those most friendly to liberty. This remark is justified by Mr. Locke himself, for it is manifest from the whole work, that such was his opinion, and may fairly be inferred, that he thought a mixed

21. Book II. chap. 13, section 158.

government, such as that of Great Britain, resting on its true principles, the best that could be established.

The principles which were cherished by this very able writer and virtuous man, rendered him obnoxious to the Court, and of which he felt the ill effect. He was a fellow of Christ Church College in the University of Oxford, and from which he was expelled, by the special order of the king, Charles the Second.

The view which has been taken of the work of Locke is equally applicable to that of Sydney, in reference to the objects of this inquiry. It was written to refute the doctrine of Filmer, in favor of the divine right of kings, and of which he never loss sight in any part of his essay, which comprises two volumes, octavo, of about 400 pages each. It furnishes a complete refutation of that doctrine, and likewise demonstrates, that the power of princes, however great or long its continuance, is derived from the consent of the people, and sustained afterwards when it assumes an oppressive character, by their inability to remove it. It is, however, not confined to these objects. He enters with great ability into a comparison of the merits of governments in which the people hold a portion of the sovereignty, and are free, with those which are absolute, and in which they are slaves. In the one, he gives examples of every great and noble quality that can adorn the human race and exalt the character of the community; in the other, of those only which show the degradation and decrepitude of man; of nothing but what is calculated to excite our mortification and disgust. His work displays a profound knowledge of ancient and modern history, and may be considered, in the view stated, as one of the most able ever written in favor of free government against despotism. There is scarcely an individual, of those most distinguished in any of the ancient republics, or of modern times, down to his own period, to whose talents and virtues he does not pay the respect to which they are entitled. But beyond this limit I do not perceive that his work extends. In several passages, he avows explicitly his preference of a government composed of three (3) orders, a king, lords and commons, to one founded exclusively on the sovereignty of people.[22] In this, however, it may be inferred that he had in view those only of the latter class, in which the people exercised their power en masse. None, like our own, ever existed before; and of course he could contemplate none of which history had furnished no example.

Sydney looked to the dangers which menaced liberty in his own country, and as Locke did to the means of preserving it, on the principles of the British Constitution, to which he thought the people competent, if roused to make the

---

22. Vol. I. chap. i. section 10: chap. ii. section 16.

necessary exertion. Tyranny had existed; civil war had ensued; a king had been overthrown and beheaded; a commonwealth had been established; but under circumstances which proved that liberty was not secure even under it; the family of Stuart had been restored, and with increased danger to the great cause to which he was devoted. It could not be expected, under these circumstances, that Sydney would look beyond his own country, or to other objects, than such as were connected with the existing crisis. In defense of those, he exerted his best efforts and displayed great talents, and to that great cause he fell a victim.

When it is considered that such men as Locke and Sydney found it necessary and were compelled to devote their talents and labors to the refutation of so absurd a doctrine as that of the divine right of kings, most of whom then reigning, or of their families, had been placed by casual events at the head of their respective governments, what an impression must it make on all reflecting minds, of the state of society at the epoch at which they lived? If such were the prejudices, superstition and darkness of the age, to make it difficult to convince the people that they had any rights, and were not born slaves, how idle must it have been to have drawn their attention to the organization and distribution of power, in self-government, with its various modifications, and to the dangers to which a failure, in any of those respects, would expose it.

The works of Montesquieu and Rousseau merit a like commendation with that which has been bestowed on those of Locke and Sydney. They were written in another country, under a government in a different state, and, in consequence, in a different spirit. The work of Montesquieu is called the Spirit of Laws, and it corresponds with the title; but as the laws must depend on, and be adapted to the nature and principle of the government under which they are formed, it became necessary to give a distinct idea of each class in all its most important features. This he has executed with great ability, and in support of which, he brings into view all the ancient governments, and likewise the modern down to his own time. There is no subject which falls within the scope of legislation, under any species of government, and in every part of the globe, which escapes his attention, and on which he does not make very interesting remarks. His work, therefore, may be considered, as embracing, according to his view, the circle of the science, with the examples in support of it, which history had then afforded. In the range which he has taken, it is obvious that there are many subjects on which he treats, to which no attention is necessary on my part. Whatever he says of despotic governments, and of the laws that are adapted to them, is of this character. The same remark is applicable to mixed governments, and indeed to every class; for if self-government is sound in principle, and merits the opinion entertained of it, under the improvement it has received with us, those who execute it will adopt the laws correspondent therewith, and necessary to its support. My object relates to that point, and in referring to the works of different writers. I do it to show that they apply to governments differently circumstanced, and that so far as liberty is an object, and cherished by them, there is not only nothing discouraging in their works to our system, but everything in its support.

Montesquieu occupied different ground from that which had been held by Locke or Sydney. He was not a party to any existing conflict, and saw the improvement which had been given to the British Government by that, for their services in promoting which both had suffered, and one fallen a victim. He had with them all the advantages which could be derived from the examples of the ancient republics, and the science of the ancient world, and likewise of the modern, aided by the improvement in the government referred to, and by their works in support of that great cause. His work is very favorable to liberty, and has given much support to it, but living under a despotic government caution was necessary on his part. It was, therefore, of a nature so elementary, extended to so many objects unconnected with it, and was written in a spirit of such moderation, that it could not be considered an attack on his own government.

In his view of the ancient republics, and of governments generally, he rejects the classification which had been given of them by Aristotle, as he likewise does the number of species which he ascribes to each class. He notices his first species of Monarchy, which he considers visionary, being founded on the good or ill-conduct of the incumbent, and not on principle.[23] His view is more simple than that of the ancient authors, arising from the character of the Feudal system; but it does not extend to the precise objects of this inquiry, and in some points which involve general principles, is not free from objection. This, however, may fairly be attributed to the state of the science at the time, and to the nature and form of the government to which, in comparison with all others, he gave the preference.

In treating of Democracy he contemplated that only which was known to the ancients, in which the people exercised their power, en masse, and the government was united with the sovereignty. Whatever he says of this class of government, is under this impression, and can, in consequence, refer only to the defects of that state, and not to the improvements of the present day by representation.[24] Such a government would be impracticable, as will be shown, even for a small state. For a large one it could not have been thought of.

23. Book XI. chap. ix.
24. Book II. chap. i.

In the view which he took of the Constitution of England, and his remarks on it, it is obvious that he considered it the most that perfect human wisdom could devise. That it was the best then known I readily admit; but that it is inferior to our own, is, according to my judgment, certain. As I propose to treat of this government, and to make a comparison between it and those of the United States hereafter, it is unnecessary, and it would be improper to enter into the subject here.

He observes that the constitution may be free, and the citizen not: that the citizen may be free, and the constitution not.[25] From this it may be inferred, that he meant that liberty does not depend altogether on the government, and his illustration of the idea does not preclude the inference. It must now be obvious, that the liberty of the citizen depends solely on the government, and that if the government be founded on just principles, and be in the hands of a virtuous and intelligent people, he cannot fail to enjoy liberty. Such a people will always see that such laws are made, and are so executed, as in a manner to secure to every citizen the enjoyment of that blessing. It is also equally obvious, that if the government be absolute, the people must be slaves. A virtuous and humane prince might not molest them, but as their security and peace would depend on his will they could have no rights of their own. Objections occur to other passages in this work, but it does not fail within the limit of this inquiry to enter into the subject in that view. Many of these have been shown by Mr. De Tracy, a French writer of talents, in a work which will, I doubt not, be read with great attention and satisfaction by those who peruse that on which it is a commentary. On a view of the whole work it certainly merits the commendation which has been bestowed on it.

The work of Rousseau, to which attention is next due, is entitled the Social Compact. It traces government to the people, and maintains with great force that none is legitimate, which is not founded on their consent. The manner in which the compact is formed, when regularly entered into, its extent and the obligation which it imposes on the people who are parties to it, are treated with ability, and the work, taken in all its parts, is consistent with itself, and an able essay. It is obvious that he was thoroughly acquainted with ancient and modern history, and with the works of the writers of both epochs on the subject of government.

He explicitly avows his opinion that the government should be vested in and be exercised by the people collectively, in a general assembly, and in consequence

25. Book XII. chap. i.

be united with the sovereignty. He maintains the doctrine that the sovereignty cannot be represented.[26] Every law which the people do not pass themselves he considers void. The people of England, he says, think that they are free, but they deceive themselves. They are free only while engaged in the election of members to Parliament, and as soon as that act is performed, they are slaves.[27] He asserts that the idea of representation is modern, and derived from the Feudal system, by which the human race are degraded, and the name of man dishonored. He adds that in the ancient republics the people had no representatives: that even the term was unknown to them.[28]

His whole work is founded on this principle, and the organization which he gives to the government, and the distribution of its powers, correspond with it. The legislative power is vested in a general assembly of the people, without the aid of any other branch, to digest measures for their consideration or to form a check on their decision. He contemplates an executive distinct from the legislature, but as forming in effect no part of the government, its members being merely commissaries or agents under it. Respecting the judiciary, he makes no comment, nor does he propose any plan for the performance of that portion of the public duties, in questions arising either between the citizens themselves or between the government and the citizens. The legislature, according to his view, held the sovereignty of the state. When the people were assembled, the government in all its functions was suspended.[29] The magistrates became members of that body with no other rights or authority than belonged to every other citizen. Every power was concentrated in a general assembly of the people. He made some nice distinctions between those powers which that assembly would exercise, calling one portion, such as were of a general nature, and applied to the whole community, acts of sovereignty; and such as related to special objects, or to individuals, the acts of magistrates, giving thus to the same body, and to the same man, in the discharge of their ordinary duties, a different character.[30] He was aware that such a government could apply only to a state of very limited extent and population; to a village, and little more; and that it would be exposed to imminent danger, both internal and external. For these evils he suggests a remedy, by extraneous and temporary provisions, such as the Tribunate of Rome, or the Ephori of Sparta, and in great emergencies of a dictatorship. The plan of this

26. Book III. chap. xv. Vol. II. page 185.
27. *Ibid.* page 186.
28. *Ibid.*
29. Book III. chap. xiv. Vol. II. page 161.
30. Chap. xvii.

writer was evidently founded on that of the ancient republics, with some modifications which experience, aided by his reflections, had suggested. It is obvious that he considered the alternative to be between the government of the people en masse and that in which they were to hold a very limited portion of power only, to form what was called the tiers etats or third estate; and that he preferred the former. Having been born in Geneva, a small state, it may be inferred that he took his impressions in part from that circumstance; and in many respects his plan accords with that of Athens, one of those with which I propose to compare our system. As therefore all the remarks which I shall make on that government will apply to this sketch, it will be unnecessary to make further comments on it.

I might, with propriety, notice the works of other writers, and particularly of Machiavel and De Lolme; the first of whom composed an essay on the first decade of Livy, and the other on the Constitution of England, both of which display talent. But as they relate to the two preceding epochs, and not to the third, it is deemed unnecessary to enter on them. When I reach the subjects on which they treat I may advert to them. The works of the writers to which I have referred are sufficient for my object. They give a clear and distinct idea of the state of society, of the governments, and of the science in the first two epochs, which was my motive for referring to them. They confirm the opinion advanced, that the contest on the part of the people in the first was for the whole power to be exercised by them en masse; and in the second, that it was to prevent their entire exclusion from the government in any and every form whatever; to rescue themselves from abject slavery.

In reference to the second epoch, and to Great Britain, whose people took the lead among the great powers in support of human rights, I think proper to insert here a comment from the posthumous works of an enlightened patriot and great statesman, Mr. Fox, which confirms the view taken of the character of that epoch, and of the dangers incident to it. The struggle to which I allude was that during which the works of Locke and Sydney were composed, and which commenced in the reign of Charles the First, of the family of Stuart, and in which all hope of success depended on the part which the House of Commons might act in it. In adverting to that crisis, he states the following propositions, which all people should constantly have in view who may be engaged in such a struggle, or who may be blessed with free governments of the best kind. Under the excitement of party feeling, those who take the lead on each side have it much in their power to abuse the confidence of the people, especially if the controversy be carried to great extent, and of which they seldom fail to take advantage, and for the worst purposes. He asks, "In what manner will that house conduct itself? will it be content with its regular share of legislative power, and with the influence which it cannot fail to possess, whenever it exerts itself upon the other branches of the legislative and executive power? or will it boldly (perhaps rashly) pretend to a power commensurate with the natural rights of the representatives of the people? If it should, will it not be obliged to support its claims by military force? And how long will such a force be under its control? How long before it follows the usual course of all armies, and ranges itself under a single master? If such a master should arise, will he establish an hereditary or an elective government? If the first, what will be gained by a change of dynasty? If the second, will not the military power, as it chose the first king or protector (the name is of no importance), choose in effect all his successors? Or will he fail, and shall we have a restoration, usually the most dangerous and worst of all revolutions?" These interrogatories contemplate the great epochs of such a struggle, with the means by which the people, in case they succeed and overthrow their antagonist, may be made in each and every stage, by the abuse of their confidence, by those who take the lead on their side, the instruments of their own destruction. They afford a very strong proof of the enlightened mind of a practical statesman who watched with care the dangers to which the great cause to which he was devoted was exposed. They apply particularly to the state in which the people of England then were; but the example to which they refer must be instructive to all people, under every species of free government. The work of this writer was not finished, which is much to be regretted, since had it been completed it cannot be doubted that it would have shed much light on every branch of the subject to which it might have extended.

The people of England held their station in the House of Commons, and they were the only people of any great power in Europe who enjoyed that advantage at that period. That hold enabled them to prostrate every order in the state, because they moved with vast force and with great energy to the accomplishment of that result. In suffering their leader to take essentially the station of the chief whom they had deposed and beheaded, they furnish a strong proof that they were incompetent to the support of a government which belonged exclusively to themselves. If any doubt existed on that point, the restoration to the throne of a member of the same family soon after the decrease of that leader would remove it. It is proper to add that Mr. Fox, in speaking in terms of high commendation of the works of Locke and Sydney, gives a further confirmation of the difference between that and the preceding epoch, by observing that they had never conceived the wild project of assimilating the Government of England to that of Athens, of Sparta, or of Rome.

The third epoch is that, as has been observed, which is marked by the emigration of our ancestors to this territory, by the Revolution which followed, and the governments which have been erected on its basis, in all of which the sovereignty is vested in the people, but the government separated from it and committed to representative bodies. This epoch is, therefore, altogether different from the others. The governments being different, the dangers which menace them are likewise so. Happily they are in all respects of inferior magnitude. Such dangers however do, and will exist, which ought to be understood and guarded against. The principles and passions of men are always the same, and lead to the same result, varying only according to the circumstances in which they are placed. Self-interest is the ruling passion, whether under free or despotic governments. Highly improved and generous minds will move on a scale correspondent therewith, but a large portion of mankind will look to themselves, and turn every incident of which they may take advantage to their own account. It is against these propensities that we have to guard. The principle of the government will go far to infuse a correct spirit into the body of the people, and will have great influence on those who are appointed to high and honorable trusts, provided the people perform, with judgment, their essential duties. A failure, and even a relaxation on their part, may produce the worst consequences. If they make judicious selections for office, reward those who have merit, and punish those who commit offenses: if they act for themselves, are intelligent, impartial and firm, and do not become the instruments of others, the whole movement cannot fail to be mild, harmonious and successful.

In what relates to the ancient world, we read with peculiar interest the history of the ancient republics, and particularly of those specified. Indeed there is nothing beyond that limit, relating to that epoch, in which we take a serious interest. The career of despotic governments viewed internally exhibits a gloomy spectacle; and externally, even where talents are displayed, by their respective chiefs, being generally of a military character, and employed in the subjugation and oppression of other people, although it may excite a species of admiration, it cannot give pleasure. The people are held by such governments in a state of degradation and oppression, deprived of opportunities of displaying those noble and generous qualities which do honor to the human race. Their conduct is watched in every circumstance, and reported by a vigilant and active police. High qualities are dreaded. But in republics, even in those in which the people enjoy a portion of the sovereignty only, a different state of things exists, and a different spectacle is exhibited. The society moves itself. The springs of action are within it. Great virtues and talents, wherever found, exalt the possessors, and increase the energy and stability of the government. Notwithstanding all the disadvantages to which the ancient republics were subject, we find in them a greater display of all the higher qualities of talent and virtue, more to gratify our feelings, to command our admiration and applause, than in the history of every other people from the earliest record of time. Their rise and progress form a great epoch in the history of the world. Under their protection the arts and sciences flourished, and the human mind acquired an expansion never known before. With their overthrow universal darkness overspread the earth, and held it in ignorance and barbarism for ages. From that degraded state we may date the commencement of its emancipation in several of the countries of Europe, with that of the sixteenth century, which was further marked with the discovery of this hemisphere. That great event paved the way to our Revolution, which laid the foundation of a system of government under circumstances more favorable to success than were ever enjoyed by any of the ancient republics, and with the light derived from their example, with the best means of correcting their errors and avoiding their fate.

The discovery of this hemisphere was made in a spirit of philosophic calculation and speculation, and on the part of those who first embarked in it of adventure; but the emigrants who soon followed, and who laid the foundation of the communities which have since grown up in these states, were persons of enlarged views and elevated character. Although of different political parties and of different religious sects in the parent country, yet they all flew from persecution, in pursuit of liberty, and they inculcated that sentiment on their descendants. In the convulsions to which the British Government was then subject, and the transition of power from one order to another, the cause of emigration, in the masses who came over, was different, but the moral effect soon became uniform. It is known that two of the regicides, if not more, were buried in the Eastern States, and that Cromwell himself was at one time prepared to fly. And incidents occur, even at this late day, to show that many of distinction of the opposite party found then an asylum in the Middle and Southern States. The immediate emigrants, therefore, felt this difference sensibly, but in the new relation which was formed between them and between the colonies and the parent country, that feeling subsided, and was unknown to their descendants. The charters under which they emigrated, which formed a compact between the people and the crown, nursed the infant state and reared it to maturity under the influence of free principles. Distinct orders were precluded. All the emigrants and their descendants were placed on a footing of equality. Had those of the highest rank in England visited any of the colonies without commissions authorized by their charters they would have held the grade only of private individuals. Had the king himself come over, he could have taken the place only in the colony in which he landed, of his governor. Thus successive generations grew up in each colony in the same principles, and bearing the same common relation to the crown, the only extraneous power which was recognized. As its pressure was felt, and other pretensions were advanced, the whole people were gradually drawn together by the powerful bond of interest and affections, so that when the revolutionary struggle commenced, they moved in a body as a single community.

The elevation of mind which was brought over by those emigrants was never lost; but by the operation of the causes stated was infused into the mass of each community. There never was a period when an appeal was made to the talents and virtue of the inhabitants of the colonies, notwithstanding the difficulties they had to encounter, in making their establishments in the new world, that indicated the least inferiority between them and those of the old. Their conduct in the war of 1756 extorted that confession in their favor from the government of the parent country, and the display which was made in both respects in the war of the Revolution commanded the applause, not only of the first men there, but of the whole civilized world. In these very important circumstances, therefore, the good people of these states enjoyed advantages, which there is good reason to believe were peculiar to themselves: advantages which could not fail to have the happiest effect in enabling to form, as well as to sustain, the governments which have been instituted.

In forming our governments the question of city and country, of the rich and the poor, could never have come into view. By the charters to the colonies vast territories were granted, and a great proportion thereof in each was settled before the commencement of the contest. As the population had increased and moved westward, each colony was laid off into counties, from which representatives were sent, to a general assembly in each. The power of the colony was in the hands of this assembly, and in consequence, of the country, the cities having their equal share in it, which was scarcely felt as such in any colony. The poor as a class, organized against the rich, was unknown, and still is. The aged and infirm, who are indigent, are provided for in every county, in every state, with houses, food, clothes, and medical aid, at the expense of the other citizens of the county. The claim is founded on motives of charity, which there is no necessity either to withhold or to carry beyond its just limits. The great mass of our population, consisting of persons who were neither very poor nor very rich, a discrimination, in any form, to protect the one against the other could not have been thought of. The sovereignty being in the people, the door might be left open with perfect safety, to every citizen, to every office, and without distinction as to the right of suffrage, other than such as marked him as an inhabitant of the county or township, with such small interest there as should enable him to act as a free agent.

The good people of these states have, therefore, been placed in a situation to make a fair experiment of the great problem, whether the people, as a people, are competent to self-government. All the circumstances with which they are blessed, more favorable to such a result than were ever enjoyed by any other people, impose on them, in like degree, the greater obligation to succeed. Satisfied I am that success is not only practicable, but certain, if equal virtue and talents are displayed in future with those which have brought us to the present age.

To do justice to the subject, it will be proper in regard to our system to extend the inquiry in like manner to its origin, and to the great events which have so far marked its career. From such a view, a fair comparison may be made of our governments, state and national, with those referred to, and a correct estimate be formed of the merits and defects of our own in both its branches. A like comparison may be made of the state of society on each side, and a fair conclusion be drawn of the competency of our people to self-government. We have had divisions which have disturbed the harmony, and at certain epochs, excited great inquietude as to the future. To what causes were these imputable? An impartial and candid statement of facts can injure no one individually, and may be useful to our country. Passions have long since subsided, and such is the state of the public mind, and even of those who felt and acted under the greatest excitement, that they can now look back with moderation and calmness on the past, and profit by the instruction it affords. Having been an active party in many of the most interesting scenes, I am aware that I may have taken impressions in some instances that were unfounded. Should this be the case, the view which I may present will be open to correction: and if, in any instance, I be in error, I wish to be corrected. My great object is the success of our system in both its branches, because I well know that on it the happiness of the whole nation depends. In pursuit of this object I have no feeling of resentment to any one to gratify; and am far from wishing to detract from the fame, or wound the feelings of those with whom I differed, many of whom had, in council and in the field, deserved well of their country.

ATHENS

It is impossible to proceed in the comparison of our governments with those of Greece, either State or National, without being forcibly struck with the difference between them in all those circumstances which are most important. There is not one, either in the extent of territory, the number of inhabitants, the state of society, the manner of instituting the government, its organization, or the distribution of its powers, in which there is the least similitude. Athens, comprising Attica, contained a territory not larger than several of the counties in some of our states. Lacedemon was not more extensive than the smallest state in our Union, and all Greece was smaller than Scotland or Portugal. The difference in the other circumstances enumerated was equally great, and still more important. These differences must be taken into view and have their due weight in the prosecution of this work.

The Government of Athens, of which I propose to treat, is that which was instituted by Solon nearly five hundred years before the Christian era. In that government many ancient regulations were incorporated, some of which had been adopted about one thousand years before, and had formed a part of the existing government in all its subsequent changes. In adopting those regulations, Solon must have done it, either because he believed them to be correct, or was satisfied that the community was so wedded to them by habit and prejudice, that it would tolerate no government of which they should not form a part. When the nature of those institutions is considered, it might fairly be inferred that the latter was the cause. The fact, however, was established by himself, he having declared that he had formed for the people of Athens, not the government which he deemed the best, but the best which he thought they were capable of sustaining. By this it appears, that in the formation of the government he considered the condition of the people, their state of civilization, their weaknesses and vices, with their intelligence and virtues. To judge correctly of the considerations which induced their adoption in the first instance, and their preservation afterwards, we must go back to the epoch at which they were adopted, and view the condition of the people at that period and in every subsequent stage. A slight knowledge of mankind will show that the condition of the people at any advanced period could not have been formed at the moment, but must have been the result of many causes operating on the community from its commencement.

Historians carry the origin of this people back to a very remote period. They nevertheless all agree in fixing on one beyond which nothing occurred that merits attention. In regard to Athens the reign of Cecrops forms that period, which, according to the most authentic chronology, occurred more than sixteen hundred years before the birth of Christ and about two thousand three hundred and fifty after the creation of the world. Cecrops emigrated from Egypt and settled in Attica, taking with him many of his countrymen, whom he incorporated into the same community with the natives, placing himself, by common consent, at their head. Before that period it is stated by the best informed historians that the inhabitants of Attica were barbarians; that they dwelt in caves, and fed on the rude productions of the earth and on game. The inhabitants of Egypt were more advanced in civilization, and in the arts and usages of civilized life, than those of Greece. Such improvements as existed in Egypt Cecrops transplanted with him into his newly adopted country. The motive for union between the parties was strong. The one sought an asylum, the other instruction.

All that region known by the name of ancient Greece was at that epoch in the same state, and the greater part of it, not the whole, owed the commencement of its improvement to the same cause, the arrival and establishment among them of colonies from Egypt, Phoenicia, and the East. Four other colonies are particularly mentioned by historians, one of which was led by Inachus, likewise from Egypt, who settled in Argos; another by Pelops, from Asia, who settled in the Peloponnesus; a third from Phoenicia, by Cadmus, who settled in Boetia; a fourth by Danaus, likewise from Egypt, who settled in Argos. The first preceded Cecrops about three hundred years. The other three followed shortly after him. The leaders of those colonies had each the same fortune which had attended Cecrops, of being placed at the head of the community in which they respectively settled, and for the same reason the superior intelligence which they possessed, and the desire of the people to avail themselves of it.

Thucydides, the author of the "Peloponnesian War," which occurred rather more than one hundred and fifty years after the institution of the Government of Solon, considers the history of Greece as involving no event of real importance, either of a military or political nature, prior to that war. His opinion is the more interesting, because the war with Persia and the invasions by Darius and Xerxes had preceded the Peloponnesian war, the latter a few years only, and had in fact led to it. It justifies the inference which has been drawn from a passage in his work, that he thought that Herodotus had greatly exaggerated the force which had been brought against Greece in those invasions; as it does the opinion entertained of the feeble and effeminate character of the troops and people of Persia, compared with those of Europe. Thucydides states that the war with Troy was the first enterprise in which the Greeks united, and that they were drawn into that war more by the power and influence of Agamemnon,

King of Argos, and leader of the expedition, than by any general feeling or policy of their own. That war united them in the expedition, but their union terminated with it, and the absence of the chiefs from their respective dominions had so far impaired their power at home that the efforts they were compelled to make to regain it on their return exhibited scenes of internal commotion and civil war for a long time afterward, in many of the states, of the most frightful character. There was then no regular bond of union between the states, nor were the people known, until a remote subsequent period, by the common name of Greeks. Homer, who composed his poems long after the Trojan war, called those of each state by the name appropriate thereto, Danians, Argives, Acheens, etc. There can be no doubt that that expedition owes its renown more to the splendid genius of Homer, and the poetic license of which he availed himself, than to the talents which were displayed, or to the exploits that were performed in it. The people were uncivilized before the war, and they remained equally so a long time after its conclusion.

The enlightened and faithful historian referred to, confirms the elementary view heretofore presented, founded on the principles, the passions, and the qualities of man, of the origin of societies and of governments over them, in the rude state, and of the incidents to such societies and governments in their progress from that state to a state of civilization. He describes them as unlettered and uncivilized; the states, he says, were small, and their governments for a long time monarchical and hereditary, but with limited authority. The first step to improvement was the Trojan war, and simply by embarking them on the sea, and making them better acquainted with navigation. Piracy ensued, and was long deemed an honorable occupation in all the maritime states, and in some even down to his own time. Tyrannies then grew up, and civil wars were the consequence. His sketch is concise, but it may fairly be concluded from the facts which he states, that the limitation affirmed by him to have existed to the power of the prince in the early stages, proceeded from the manner in which the office originated, and the inability of the people in their rude state to form any other kind of government, or to limit its powers in any precise form or on any just principles. It may also be inferred with equal certainty that the changes which afterwards occurred in those governments, with the contentions and civil wars which attended them, proceeded from the change which had taken place in the pursuits, the names and condition of the people, and which required a more extended legislation and greater vigor in the administration, at a period when the science of government had not experienced a degree of improvement adequate to the object.

A general view of the state of Greece at this early epoch is all that is deemed necessary. I will give a more detailed one of that of Athens, whose government is now the particular object of attention.

The regulations which were adopted by Cecrops corresponded with the barbarous state in which the people of Athens then were, and with the knowledge which he had acquired in Egypt, the country of his nativity. This coast was infested by pirates, and the frontiers by banditti from the neighboring state of Boetia. To protect the people from these invasions, he drew them together into cities, of which twelve were founded; Athens being the principal one. He transplanted the fruits of Egypt into Attica, and trained the inhabitants to agriculture, by showing them the manner, as well as the blessings resulting from it. I give these details, in which all historians agree, merely to show the rude state in which the people then were.

His political institutions, as might naturally be expected, were few. He divided the people into tribes, of which he formed four, and regulated marriages by law. In each of the villages he instituted a species of corporation, with power to administer justice for the inhabitants thereof, and he likewise gave it a council for civil purposes. The power of these bodies approached nearly to a state of independence, and formed in a great measure so many separate republics. Some writers ascribe to him the institution of the Court or Senate of the Areopagus, while others trace it to his son. It certainly owed its origin to that epoch, and whether to the father or the son, in reference to the object in view, is altogether immaterial. This tribunal was charged with criminal offenses, and was preserved through every change which afterwards occurred in the government of Athens, until the time of Solon, who adopted it in his constitution with increased powers.

From the reign of Cecrops to the Constitution of Solon about one thousand years intervened. The reigns of Theseus and Codrus form the most interesting epochs in the history of that people and of their government through that long interval. From Cecrops to Theseus nearly three centuries elapsed, and from the latter to Codrus rather a longer term. The government from the first to the last of these princes continued to be hereditary, during which seventeen had reigned. When Theseus mounted the throne, the power of the prince was unsettled, passing occasionally from one extreme to the other. The progress in science and civilization had been inconsiderable, while in other respects the condition and morals of the people had grown worse. Agriculture, commerce and the arts had been introduced among them, the effect of which was sensibly felt in many ways by every class of society. A portion of the people had become very rich, and another portion very poor. A distinction of ranks had grown up among them, founded on the ascendancy and control which the rich had acquired over the poor, and which was promoted by the nature of the government itself. The spirit of equality and independence which characterized the rude age was broken. With the poor, when not extinguished or smothered by the degradation to which they were subjected, it was seen only in convulsions and insurrections. And with the rich, pretensions of a different character, equally inconsistent with the principles of rational liberty were set up and acted on. The authority of the twelve villages which had been founded by Cecrops had augmented to a great height. They often quarreled with and sometimes made war on each other. The power of the prince alone could control them, and that was often opposed and shaken. Under these circumstances, the tendency was at one time to anarchy, and at another to despotism.

Such was the state of Athens when Theseus succeeded his father Egeas as its sovereign. Of his previous career it is unnecessary to treat here. He lived in an age which was distinguished by the chivalric spirit and personal achievements of individuals, among whom he had acquired great distinction, and it is conceded that he sought consideration and fame in his new and exalted station, more by useful services and concessions to his fellow men, his subjects, than by the augmentation of his power at their expense. He made many regulations, the great object of which was to improve the condition of the people by giving them a greater participation in the government. He abolished the authority of the several villages, and drew the whole power into Athens, which he made the metropolis of the state. He vested the legislative power in an assembly of the people, whom he divided into three classes; notables, agriculturalists and artisans, taking from the first the principal magistrates, and committing to them the charge of religious duties, with the interpretation of the laws. He retained to himself, in the character of chief hereditary magistrate, the command of the military force only, with the supervision and execution of the laws. With this arrangement the poor were highly gratified, and the rich, although they were dissatisfied, acquiesced.

The interval between Theseus and Codrus, rather more than three centuries, was marked by no signal event. The government remained essentially in the state in which it was placed by Theseus, although frequent dissensions had taken place between the opposite classes. The death of Codrus formed an interesting epoch. The cause and the manner afford proofs equally of his devotion to his country, of his superstition, and of that of the age. The Athenians were engaged in a war with the Dorians, who inhabited the Peloponnesus, and it being reported that the oracle had declared that the party whose king should be slain would succeed, Codrus voluntarily exposed himself in disguise, and was killed. The Dorians immediately retired, and abandoned the war. On this event the Athenians abolished royalty, on the principle that no human being ought to succeed Codrus. As a substitute to royalty they instituted the office of Archon, which they made hereditary in the family of Codrus, commencing with his son Medon, whom they placed by the side of the throne under the obligation to render an account of his administration to the people. This office passed in regular succession to the descendants of Medon, about three hundred and fifty years, when it was made elective at the expiration of every ten years. About seventy years afterwards another more important change was made in it by increasing the number to nine, and making the election annual.

Two other incidents occurred in the Government of Athens prior to the adoption of the Constitution of Solon, which it is proper to notice. The first was formed by the legislation of Draco, which occurred about sixty years after the change last mentioned; the second by that of Epeminides, which followed after that of Draco about twenty-seven years. The laws of the first were remarkable only for their extreme severity and the indiscriminate character of the punishment, no distinction being made between great and small offenses. Every crime was punished with death. His code was legislative only. It did not touch the government. The laws of the second were confined to religious duties, which he regulated to the satisfaction of the people. He was a pious man from Crete. This last agency preceded the Constitution of Solon a few years only.

So great had become the disorder in Athens at this period that the state was menaced with ruin. The divisions between the contending factions had risen to such a height that they were ready to tear each other to pieces. It might reasonably have been expected, after the village authorities were abolished, and the whole people called into one assembly by Theseus, and the legislative power vested in them, that they would have controlled the state and regulated its government and laws as they thought fit: and afterwards, when royalty was abolished, and an Archon substituted for a king, and more especially when the number was increased to nine, and their election made annual, it would seem to follow as a necessary consequence that all impediment to their power was removed. Such too would have been the result if the people of Athens had been competent to self-government. The fact, however, was that they were incompetent, and in consequence those changes operated, comparatively, little in their favor. It does not appear that the people had a right to originate, in any stage in those assemblies, any law or other act whatever. It may be inferred that the power was either in the prince or the notables; and if in the prince, that it passed, after the abolition of royalty, to the Archons, and as all offices were secured to the rich, that it always belonged to that class. Hence it would follow that the power of the king was thrown exclusively into their hands by that change, whereby a complete ascendancy was given to them in the government over the poor. All writers agree, ancient and modern, in representing the condition of the poor, at that epoch, as deplorable. So great had become the ascendancy of the rich that creditors sold their debtors as slaves and compelled parents to sell their children.[31] There were three classes in the state in different circumstances and with different views.[32] Those of the mountains who were poor, sought democracy; those of the plain, who were rich, aristocracy; and those of the coast, who held the middle ground between the two extremes, a mixed government. The poor demanded the abolition of debts and the equal division of lands, which the rich opposed with the utmost violence. They were at the edge of war and no prospect of accommodation by arrangement between themselves. In this state an appeal was made to Solon, and a power granted to him, by common consent, to institute a government for them.

It is proper to remark that in giving a sketch of the government of the ancient republics, it is impossible to do it with that precision which may be observed in describing the Government of the United States or of any of the individual States. In the latter, in both instances, the departments of the government, legislative, executive, and judicial, are so distinctly separated from each other, and the powers of each so well defined, that they may be delineated with the greatest accuracy. Each of those governments is an object, well proportioned in all its parts, standing fully before you. Whereas, in the former, powers different in their nature, and properly belonging to separate and independent branches, are so involved and mixed together, vested in and exercised by the same body, that it is difficult to ascertain what was the precise extent or limit of the powers of any branch, or the true features and character of the government in those very important circumstances. This difficulty is seriously felt in giving a sketch of the Constitution of Solon. The great outline may be taken from the works of Aristotle and Plutarch, and particularly the latter. But other writers have given details, which, under certain circumstances, affect the powers of each branch, whence I have not been able to decide whether they formed a part of the preceding government, originated with him, or were introduced by some of the changes that were afterward made in it. Much light has been shed on the sub-

31. Plutarch, Vol. II. page 29. Life of Solon.
32. Ibid, page 28.

ject by Mr. Berthelemy, the very able author of the work entitled "Anacharsis," but yet he has not entirely removed the difficulty. My object is to present the Constitution in its best form, and to found my remarks on it in that state, and in doing this to render full justice to Solon: to withhold from him nothing to which he was justly entitled; to ascribe to him nothing which was not strictly his own.

Solon did not enter on the discharge of the duties of the high trust committed to him, by commencing with its primary object, the institution of the government. His attention was drawn in the first instance to those of a different character. He met the complaints of the contending parties by a compromise, by which he afforded to each such accommodation as he thought would secure the peace of the state. He refused to make a division of lands, but abolished the debts of individuals.[33] He prohibited also the sale of any citizen for the payment of debts. He repealed some of the laws of Draco and modified others. These facts are mentioned as evidence of the nature of the power which was vested in Solon, whereby that of making laws and instituting a government were confounded together. He was called Legislator, which shows that no nice distinction was then taken between a constitution and a law.

The government which he instituted consisted of an Assembly of the People and a Senate; of a corps of tribunals or Courts of Justice; of a corps of Archons or Magistrates, and of the Senate of Areopagus. These were the only bodies whose powers gave a character to the government. By a strict examination of the organization and endowment of each, we shall be enabled to form a correct judgment of its merits.

The Assembly of the People consisted of the whole body of the people,[34] every citizen above the age of twenty having a right to a seat in it, and no qualification of property being necessary. This assembly had the power, under the restraint which will be noticed, to declare war, to make peace, to receive ambassadors, make treaties of alliance, adopt and repeal laws, establish imposts, appoint all the principal officers of the state, to reward merit, and in short perform all the great acts of the government. Six thousand votes were necessary to the passage of its most important acts, and it was a fundamental principle that that number should be present to constitute an assembly. These powers, however, were not absolute. This assembly could originate no proposition whatever: it could decide on none nor act on any but those which were submitted to it by the senate.

---

33. Plutarch, Vol. II. page 36. Life of Solon. Gilliss, Vol. II. page 108.
34. Aristotle on the Science of Government, Vol. I. Book 2d, ch. 10. Plutarch, Life of Solon, page 88.

The senate consisted of four hundred members, who were appointed in the following manner: The Republic of Athens comprised within its limits a territory of little more than thirty miles square. The whole population of the state was divided into four tribes, each of which sent annually one hundred members to that body. Rather more than eighty years afterward, on the expulsion of the Pisistratides, the number of the tribes was increased to ten by Clisthenes, and the senate to five hundred, each tribe numbering fifty. They were drawn by lot.[35] This body could adopt no act by its own authority. It formed a complete check on the Assembly of the People since the latter could take up none which had not been discussed, approved, and submitted to it by the senate.[36]

As every important measure depended on the sanction of the General Assembly of the People, frequent meetings were indispensable. It was provided therefore by the Constitution, that it should meet for the discharge of its ordinary duties four times in every thirty-five or thirty-six days, the precise day of meeting being adapted to the organization and arrangements of the senate. To each meeting special duties were assigned by a distribution between them of the subjects on which the assembly had a right to act. In the first they confirmed or rejected the magistrates who were to enter into office, examined the condition of the garrisons, heard denunciations, and published an account of the confiscations which had been decreed by the tribunals. In the second they heard the discourses of every citizen who thought proper to address them on public affairs. In the third they received ambassadors who had been presented to the senate. In the fourth they attended to concerns of a pious nature, such as holy feasts and sacrifices.

Extraordinary assemblies were convened whenever a public emergency required it. On these occasions, and especially when the state was menaced with invasion, it was expected that the whole body of the people would attend.

On the first meeting of the senate, after every new election, it was divided into ten classes, each of which in succession took the lead in public affairs for an equal term, the priority being decided by lot. This class was entertained at the public expense at a place called Prytaneum, and was from that circumstance called the Prytanus. It was subdivided into five others, the members of each of which were called Presidents. Special duties were assigned to each in succession. The one in service presided in the senate one day and performed the usual duties of that station. He also held the seal of the republic, the keys of the capitol and of the treasury for that day.

35. Anacharsis, Vol. 11. page 274.
36. Plutarch: Life of Solon, page 42.

The nine other classes of the senate had also each at its head a President, who was changed at every meeting of the class, and the successor drawn by lot by the chief of the Prytanus. These presidents carried occasionally the decrees of the senate to the assembly of the people, and the chief among them took their votes. On other occasions the chief of the Prytanus, or one of his assistants, performed that office. The Prytanus conveyed the senate and prepared subjects for its deliberation. As the senate represented the tribes, the Prytanus represented in turn the senate. It was the duty of that class to watch over the dangers to the republic and to warn the senate of any menacing circumstance. The chiefs of the senate presided in the assembly of the people, and when important subjects were agitated, the whole body attended.

These assemblies had not the power in themselves to repeal an ancient law or to pass a new one. Very extraordinary restraints were imposed on them, and forms were prescribed for the exercise of the power vested in them in every instance. The right to submit propositions to the consideration of the senate was not confined to the members of that body. Any citizen might propose to it the repeal of an ancient law if he presented at the same time a substitute for it. If the senate approved the proposition it was communicated to the assembly of the people, and to that meeting which was charged with the examination of the existing laws, which met on the eleventh day of the first month in each year. If it should appear to this assembly that the law ought to be repealed, the Prytanus sent the project to the assembly, which met nineteen days afterwards, and in the meantime published it for the consideration of the people. Five orators were then appointed to attend the assembly to defend before it the law which was attacked. Even this assembly could not decide the question. It appointed Commissioners or Legislators, sometimes one thousand and one, who were united with the Court of Keliastes, the nature of which will hereafter be explained, and who thus united formed a tribunal before which those who attacked and those who defended the law appeared and performed their respective duties. This tribunal might repeal the old law without referring it back to the assembly of the people. They then examined the substitute proposed, and if they approved it, might either confirm it themselves or submit it to the General Assembly of the People.

Such were the powers of the General Assembly of the People and of the Senate with the organization of each body and mode of communication between them. Attention is now due to the other bodies which formed a part of this government, and in the first instance to that of the tribunals or courts of justice which on a well-digested principle is the next in order.

Of these tribunals there were ten, most of which consisted of five hundred judges, and some of a greater number. The judges of these courts were drawn by lot annually by the Archons from the body of the people. No qualification of property was required for either Court. Four of them had jurisdiction of the crime of murder under the classification of accidental, self-defense, etc. No regular time was fixed for the meeting of these courts. The Archons had the power to convene them when in their judgment the duties of the department required it. As the judicial assemblies, for such with great propriety they might be called, were taken from the body of the people and formed a large portion of the same persons who constituted the general assemblies of the people, it was necessary that their meetings should not interfere with each other, and to prevent which interference power was given to the Archons to fix the time of their meeting.

Of these ten tribunals that of the Keliastes was the most distinguished. It consisted usually of five hundred judges, but on great occasions by the reunion of the other tribunals by order of the Archons the number amounted to six thousand. These judges took the oath to be governed in their decisions by the laws and decrees of the senate and people—to be impartial—to accept no present, and to support the government in its then form.

The delays and expenses of attending trials before these courts induced many to submit their cases to arbitration, and for which, the necessity being anticipated, provision was made by the constitution.

The corps of Archons consisted of nine members, who were elected annually by the people, who assembled on the last four days of each year for the purpose. Any citizen who had borne arms in defense of his country, who had the requisite qualification in property, and who enjoyed a fair reputation by the test of a strict examination in the form prescribed, might be elected to this office. It was the duty of these officers to preserve order in the city and to receive in the first instance public denunciations and the complaints of the oppressed. The first three formed each a special tribunal, in which two assessors chosen by the person himself assisted. The six others called Thermothetes formed a single tribunal only. To these tribunals different causes were assigned. The first was charged with the concerns of widows and orphans. The second with the protection of religious ceremonies from violation. The third with the supervision of foreigners in the city. The last consisting of the six other members fixed the days on which the Superior Courts should hold their sessions, and formed a police for the preservation of order in the city. The Archons who formed Courts carried to the proper tribunals the causes of which they had respectively cognizance, and presided in the trial.

The people elected at the same time with the Archons the generals of the army, infantry and cavalry; those who were charged with the receipt and safe-keeping of the public money; with the supply of the city; with the repair of the public roads; and with other duties of less importance. A chamber of accounts, composed of ten officers, was also chosen every year, and to whom the Archons, the members of the senate, the commanders of the gallies, ambassadors, ministers of the altars, and all others employed in the administration were bound to render an account of the sums which they had received, and of the disbursement thereof.

For the senate and these officers a qualification of property was required in those who held them, and with that view he divided the citizens into four classes, the first of which consisted of those who owned property worth annually five hundred measures of grain or oil; the second three hundred; the third two hundred; the fourth of all others whose property was of less value than the sum last mentioned, which latter were excluded from every office.

The senate of Areopagus was likewise incorporated into this government by Solon. The office was for life. The Archons after their term of service had expired, who could prove that they had discharged the duties of that trust with integrity, became members of that body. They were censors over the public morals; had charge of almost every crime: homicide, arson, poisoning, theft, debauchery, and likewise of innovations in the government and religion.

Such was the government of Athens as instituted by Solon according to the view which I have taken of it from the works of the most enlightened authors, ancient and modern. It will, I am persuaded, be found that no material feature has been omitted or misrepresented. Such likewise was the state of society in which that people were when that government was instituted. On this subject, therefore, in both views I shall make the remarks in execution of the work I have undertaken, which appear to me to be proper.

It will I think be easy to show that this government was altogether an impracticable one; that no government thus organized and endowed could manage the concerns of a state, however small it might be, and that disorder, convulsion, and its overthrow were inevitable. It will be equally easy to show that although the government was strictly democratical, the whole arrangement was in many important circumstances as inconsistent with principle as it was with policy. As this government has been referred to by all writers on the subject of government through the whole intermediate space since its adoption, comprising upwards of two thousand four hundred years, as furnishing the best model of this class, it will be proper to state fully the objections which occur to it. Its fate has been urged as a proof that no government founded on the sovereignty of the people can be sustained. It will be seen on the contrary that so numerous and vital were its defects, that no inference whatever unfavorable to our system can with propriety be drawn from it. I shall nevertheless be as concise as possible, for so glaring and obvious were its defects, that the mere development which has been given of its parts might be sufficient for my fellow-citizens aided as they are by the light of our experience.

In forming a just estimate of the merits of this government we must first decide to what class it belonged. That being fixed, the organization and distribution of its powers will next claim attention.

That the sovereignty was in the people cannot, it is presumed, be controverted. That there was but one order in the government, that of the people. The whole power was vested in them. The senate had no pretension to any right distinct from the people. The members were elected annually, and by lot. The Archons had none, nor had the Areopagus. The first were elected annually, and the second derived their appointment from election, the Archons becoming such after their term of service had expired. The qualification in property required for the senators and other officers did not affect the case, because any citizen who acquired it was eligible, and such changes from the one to the other state in every community are unceasing. The poor acquire property and become rich, and the rich lose it.

To the latter objects, the organization and endowments of the government, my attention will now be directed. By a like view of the above sketch it will be seen that the government was united with the sovereignty. All the great powers of the government were vested in a General Assembly of the People consisting of the whole male population of the state, or otherwise so concentrated in and exercised by them as to produce the same result. The mere enumeration which has been given of the powers vested in that Assembly shows that all those which were legislative and executive belonged to it; and from a view of the organization of the courts of justice and manner of electing the judges, it is equally manifest that although the people who composed them met at other times and at another place, they were members of and formed a large portion of that Assembly, and as may be inferred, sometimes the whole; and in consequence that the judicial power was as much vested in it as if it had been done in express terms. A check was formed by the senate on the exercise of these powers, but it was of a nature to affect only the manner of exercising them, and not the deposit or right of the Assembly to the powers themselves.

As these two features, the exercise of the government by the whole male population of the state, and the union by means thereof of the government with the sovereignty, gave the character to and essentially formed the government, I shall state the objections which occur to each in the first instance, and then proceed with a like view to the other branches. As I consider the defects in these two circumstances radical, it will become an object of inquiry in the analysis of the other branches, whether they were so formed as to mitigate in any degree the evils incident to those defects or to give them greater force. That they produced the latter effect is according to my judgment certain.

When we hear that the General Assembly of the People consisted of the whole male population of the state, and that the attendance of six thousand persons was requisite to form a meeting, the conviction is prompt that the government was altogether impracticable. The number alone would have that effect. We have all seen collections of this kind, and know from experience how incapable they are of discharging the duties of any branch of a government, and how much more so they would be to discharge those of every branch in all its concerns, foreign and domestic. It would be impossible to preserve order in such an assembly in the discussion of the subjects brought before it, without subjecting it to a kind of military discipline, which would be incompatible with its rights. And if order could be preserved all the members could not hear the debate nor understand the merits of the subject under consideration. If all spoke during the meeting, or a large proportion of them, the session would be endless. No rule could be enforced without a vote of the majority, and to ascertain that in a single instance much time would be consumed. On certain occasions and for special objects numerous assemblies of the people have a very useful effect. When serious dangers menace the republic, or great emergencies of any kind occur, it is natural and proper for the people to meet together and declare their sentiments respecting them. From such declaration the government may derive advantage, because it shows the support which may be calculated on if the course designated be pursued. But even on such occasions the debate must be managed by a few, or the proceeding would be marked with clamor, disorder and violence.

Other objections occur to the practicability of a government vested in such numerous assemblies, which are equally decisive. The people at large cannot spare the time, however limited the territory, which a proper discharge of its duties will require. Their private concerns in the various occupations in which they are engaged, with the care of their families, forbid it unless an adequate compensation is allowed for the service. Whence could this be drawn? The revenue of a state is derived from the profits of labor, and if there be no labor there can be no profits. If a trifling compensation be allowed, none but the poor would accept it, and those in the most wretched state, and thus the government would be thrown into the hands of those least competent to it, the consequence of which would be fatal.

I consider this feature alone, the number of which the General Assembly was composed, as decisive against this constitution. No government consisting of such a number can be practicable. Its failure, had there been no other objection to it was inevitable, and the only cause for surprise is that it was not instantaneous.

The objections which apply on principle to the union of the government with the sovereignty are equally strong. When the government is united with the sovereignty there can be no checks whatever on the government. All its acts being those of the sovereign power as well as of the government are conclusive. It is the sovereign power alone that can form such check, and when it is vested in those who hold the government and exercise its powers all check is gone. The party who acts in the government and exercises its powers is responsible to no one for his conduct. There is no superior to call him to account. Each individual holds an equal portion of the sovereignty, as well as of the government, and if he votes with the majority and carries the measure proposed, he has both the constitution and the law on his side be its character what it may. If in the minority and he is dissatisfied, and shows it, the worst consequences may ensue.

When these two powers are united in the people there can be no regular division of power into three branches distinct and independent of each other. The whole will be in one body, that is, in the General Assembly of the People, who will control every measure of every department. Thus all the powers of government, legislative, executive and judicial, will be concentrated in the same body, a concentration which all political writers agree is despotic, and which experience has shown is not less so when united in the people, by the abuses inseparable from it than in one individual, and for a reason which must strike the common sense of all mankind, that in the latter instance the individual when his acts are oppressive will have the whole people against him; whereas in the other the majority will stand together and support each other. If a diversity of interests exist, from whatever cause proceeding, the majority will look to its own, and make laws subservient to it. If differences had occurred and much acrimony been excited, as often happens and from a variety of causes, the oppression of the minority would be certain. Every citizen of the state is not competent to the discharge of the duties of its highest offices, or of any office whatever. Many are unfit for other reasons than the mere want of suitable qualifications.

To commit to the unlettered, ignorant, and vicious, trusts whose duties require the highest talents and greatest virtue, would be to sacrifice the interests of the community, to abandon all respect for principle or character. Unite the sovereignty with the government, and deprive the latter of all check in an Assembly whose power would be absolute and uncontrolled, and the overthrow of the government would be inevitable. It has already been shown that such large masses were by their number alone incompetent to the duties of any branch of a government, even that which required the greatest number. When these other objections are duly considered, what must be the conclusion? It must be obvious that such an assembly could not act or think for itself; that the majority would yield to a leader who by subserving their purposes had acquired their confidence, and who at a favorable moment would make use of them for the accomplishment of his own purposes.

Such are the objections which occur to these two features in this government; the number of persons of which the General Assembly was composed, and the union of the government with the sovereignty. I will now state those which apply to the other branches, and first to the Senate.

The Senate had the right, as had been shown, to originate every proposition on which the General Assembly could act. Its powers were therefore commensurate in that respect with those of that Assembly. To form a just estimate of the competency of this body to fulfil the purposes intended by it, we must take into view not only the nature and extent of its powers with its organization, but the relation which it bore to the other branch, the General Assembly of the People. The one consisted of the whole male population of the state in whom the sovereignty was vested; the other of four hundred, who were elected by the tribes by lot. This arrangement, according to every idea which we have formed of the organization of Democratical Government was utterly repugnant to principle. The powers of the Senate comprised every interest within the scope of the legislative and executive departments. Examine its competency in reference to the duties of either, and how will it bear the test? When the legislature of such a government is formed into two branches, the right to originate all laws and other measures within the limit of its powers is invariably committed to the most popular one, and if restraint is imposed on either, it is always on the less numerous. The reason for it is much stronger when that branch is composed of the people themselves. To institute a government on that principle and in that form, and to enjoin on the people to whom the sovereignty belonged, silence, until they heard from another body, would be to announce to them that they were incompetent to the duties assigned to them, and were called there merely as instruments in the hands of such body. From such an arrangement discontent and disorder would be sure to ensue. It might be expected that at every meeting the people would break through such restraint and take the power into their own hands, or that in some other manner the government would be dissolved.

The number of which the Senate consisted was too great for any of the duties assigned to it. It was too great for the popular branch of the legislature of such a state. I may add that it was sufficient for that branch of the legislature of any state, however great its population or extent of territory may be. How utterly incompetent then must it have been for the management of the duties assigned to it, and especially those of an executive nature.

By dividing the Senate into ten classes each of equal number, and giving to each in succession during its term of service thirty-five or thirty-six days, the right to propose subjects for the deliberation of the body, and to take the lead in its affairs in all other concerns, the object undoubtedly was to give greater activity and efficiency to the whole body in the discharge of all its duties. The arrangement, however, could not fail to defeat the object. By permitting the class in service called the Prytanean Corps, to serve for thirty-five or thirty-six days only, and to be succeeded by a like number for a like term, and so on by the others until the whole number had had their turn, and the year expired, would render it impossible for any of them to acquire the knowledge necessary for the discharge of any of the duties. That a provision should have been made by the constitution for a division of the Senate into classes, with the assignment of duties to each class, seems strange. If extensive powers are given to any branch or department of a government of whatever nature they may be, the more that branch is left at liberty to devise the means of carrying them into effect, and the more complete its control over those by whom the duty must be performed, in the selection of proper agents, and supervision of their conduct, especially if of its own members, the better will be the prospect of success, and the greater the responsibility of both parties in the case of failure, to the proper head. By the arrangement made these advantages were lost, for by making the class consist of the precise number which each tribe sent to the Senate, and as may be presumed, of the very members thereof, it would seem as if the government of that body was more a government of the tribes, each in succession, than of a Senate of the Republic, the ill effect of which may easily be conceived.

The mode of proceeding in the passage of laws is a feature in this government of a singular character. The forms to be observed were so complicated, and the bodies to whom the bills or projects were to be submitted, so numerous and different from the ordinary course of legislation, as were the persons who had the right to present such projects, that it seems difficult to form any just estimate of the real objects of the legislator. That which I have formed from a view of the whole subject is, that he intended for the term specified to shut the door against all change of every kind. By giving to any and every citizen the right to present to the Senate a proposition for the adoption or repeal of a law, every citizen was for that great purpose placed on the same footing with the members of that house, and in consequence the obligation on the members and on the body generally, to supervise the police of the state in the operation of the laws, as to their merit or defect was diminished if not entirely annulled. By opening the door thus wide to improvement, it might be inferred at first view that great encouragement and facility had been given to it. But the effect could not well fail to be otherwise. It is a maxim which we often hear repeated in the common concerns of life, that what is the business of every one is that of no one: a maxim which I think is founded in reason, and particularly applicable to the present case. The subsequent process was calculated to produce the same effect, as neither the Assembly of the People, or Senate, in their character as such, were by the ordinary rules and principles applicable to legislative bodies responsible for the final decision, either by the adoption or rejection of the project, they could feel in that capacity little solicitude respecting it. The trial to which the author of the project was subjected, and the punishment which might be inflicted on him if the decision should be adverse to its policy; could not fail to damp the zeal of all parties, as to any change so far, at least, as to take the responsibility on themselves, let the state of affairs be what it might.

If we ask the motive for those restraints, the following occurs: the sovereignty being the people, and they constituting also the government, and having in consequence the right to alter the constitution as well as the laws, it was deemed indispensable to preserve the constitution, to oppose almost insurmountable obstacles to the passage of laws. It is obvious that Solon had no confidence in the capacity of the General Assembly of the People to perform the duties assigned to it, and that he also thought if he did not restrain it from making any change whatever, that the constitution which he had formed would be of short duration. He preferred the Democratical principle; but in instituting the government on that principle, although he did it in the most popular form that could be devised, by vesting all the great powers of the government in the people and making them act in the discharge of those powers collectively, he subjected them in the mode prescribed to such restraints as made them passive rather than active agents in it. It was doubtless for this reason, that the right to originate propositions was inhibited to the Assembly of the People, and vested in the Senate, and for the same reason that it was vested in a company or class of that body, rather than in the body at large.

The judiciary is the branch which claims attention next in the order stated, and which it will be found merits the remarks already made respecting it. It had a species of organization, but not such as to make it an independent corps distinct from the General Assembly of the People. It formed a portion of that Assembly, and often as may be fairly concluded a great majority, if not the whole. It consisted of ten courts composed, each generally of five hundred judges who were chosen by lot from the body of the people, and some of them, particularly that of the the the Keliastes, on important occasions of six thousand. The concentration, therefore, of the judicial with the legislative and executive powers in the General Assembly of the People was complete. The objections which apply to the organization in other respects are equally decisive. The sentiment is universal that justice cannot be rendered unless those who administer it possess a thorough knowledge of the law as it is; that such knowledge can be acquired only by long study and practice in the discharge of professional duties. Numerous assemblies can never form wise and safe judicial tribunals. They can neither possess the requisite knowledge of the law, nor be capable of that calm deliberation which is so necessary to a proper discharge of the duties of the trust. Strong appeals will be made in every important case and at every meeting by skillful orators, to their feelings under the influence of which their decision will often be rendered without regard to principle, and in direct opposition to judgments previously rendered in similar cases. Experience has shown that even for the most extensive and populous communities the courts of justice should consist of a few members only, who should be selected from the whole society for their talents and virtues, and particularly those which qualify them for the office. They should likewise hold office during good behaviour, or at least so long as they were able to discharge the duties. When courts are thus organized and composed of such men they are entitled to, and command the confidence of the nation. Their decisions stand together and form a consistent and compact system which all approve. The judges are detached from and unconnected with local and political circles. They have no points to carry, nor motive in the sense in which it is generally understood to court popular favor. They represent the nation of whom they take nothing but its good opinion, founded on the rectitude and wisdom of their decisions.

By the powers vested in the corps of Archons, it appears that they were altogether of a character judicial and ministerial. This corps had long formed, as has been shown, a part of the existing government of that people. It had been substituted for monarchy and was connected with the idea of liberty, and preserved as may fairly be inferred, more in accommodation with the prejudices of the people than for any other cause. When so many courts of justice were instituted, it cannot but excite surprise that he should have taken from them any portion of the judicial power and committed it to this corps. The other power vested in it might likewise have been otherwise easily disposed of. It is obvious that by preserving the corps, he made the government more complicated and difficult of action.

The same remarks are applicable to the Senate or Court of Areopagus. This court had been instituted in the early age of the republic, at which period it formed a species of council to the King and of court for the community. All the power given to it was so much taken from the king, and a step in the degree towards popular government. This corps was therefore cherished by the people in every stage, and the more so because being composed of their most enlightened and best citizens of advanced age it merited their confidence. Solon found it necessary to preserve it, and in so doing to invest it with such powers as would make it instrumental, according to his view of the subject, to the general purposes of his constitution. It had held from its origin judicial powers. By committing to it those of that nature he made no change in principle, although he made the government more complicated. A censorship over the public morals seemed to fall within that scope, as judges generally have that kind of power. In what manner the charge given to it over innovations in government and religion was to be exercised does not appear. The court could not, as is presumed, declare a law to be void as unconstitutional, because so numerous and great were the obstacles to the passage of any law, that such a proposition would have been useless. I consider the power as monitory only in both instances. He retained the corps for the same reason that he did the Archons. To have abolished it would have shocked the public feeling, and in retaining it he was compelled to carve out for it a sphere of action in the discharge of the duties whereof if it rendered no important service, it might do little harm.

From this view of the government of Athens I think it may fairly be concluded, by the numbers of which it was composed in every department, had there been no other objection to it, that it was an impracticable one. I think also the conclusion equally obvious that the organization and endowment of its parts being repugnant to principle, were in themselves by the abuses inseparable from them sufficient to overthrow it. These causes united could not fail at an early day to produce that result. The best commentary, however, on that government is its career and fate, of which I will now give a short sketch.

It was the intention of Solon that it should be binding on the people one hundred years without any change, on the presumption, as is inferred, that if it remained in force that term the power would be permanently established in the people; and in case it should appear that any modification of it suited them better, they would acquire in the interval sufficient knowledge of the science of government to enable them to amend it without exposing themselves to any danger. All the public officers and the people bound themselves by an oath to support it as soon as it was reported. The Constitution and laws were then inscribed on rolls of wood and posted in the citadel and other public places for the inspection of the people. Immediately after the publication he was beset by persons of every class who were dissatisfied, to make amendments of it, some in one form and some in another, until, to rid himself of the annoyance, he resolved to leave the country and to remain abroad ten years, which purpose he executed. Before his departure he obtained an oath from the whole community to preserve it during his absence. On his return at the expiration of that term he found that the factions had revived with great violence, and that affairs had relapsed nearly into the same state in which they were before his government was adopted. An incident occurred soon after his return and in his presence which showed that his government had no adhesive quality or efficiency: that it was a cobweb. Pisistratus, a descendant of one of their ancient kings, a man of fortune, had to serve his own purposes become a leader of the poor, who formed the most numerous class. He fomented the discontent between the factions and exposed himself by his violence to the hatred of the rich. Seizing a favorable occasion he inflicted his body with wounds and rushed into the streets covered with blood, declaring that his enemies, who were the enemies of the people, had made an attempt on his life, and calling on them to defend him as the best means of defending themselves. The Assembly of the People and Senate were immediately convened and a guard granted to him, of which he soon afterwards availed himself, to take possession of the citadel and usurp the government. In this emergency Solon sustained his character for integrity and devotion to the rights of the people. He opposed the usurpation and exposed the fraud by which it was attempted, but without effect. The people were deceived and made the instrument of their own depression by an ambitious and unprincipled intriguer.[37]

Pisistratus lived thirty-three years after his usurpation, of which he reigned seventeen. Twice he was deposed and as often recovered the power of which

37. Herodotus, Vol. I. page 57.

he died possessed, transmitting it to his sons, Hippias and Hiprachus. The latter was killed by Harmodius and Aristogiton in revenge for a personal injury. Hippias maintained his authority a few years but was at length overthrown, principally by the exertions of Clisthenes, chief of the Alemaeonides, with the aid of Lacedemon. The usurpation of Pisistratus was of a peculiar character. It marked the rude state of the people and their incapacity for self-government, as it likewise did the dexterity with which the usurper availed himself of the good qualities as well as the weaknesses to accomplish the object of his unprincipled ambition. He did not assume the title of king, nor admit that he had subverted the constitution of Solon. He assumed only the title of magistrate or perpetual chief of the state, under which he exercised his usurped powers to what extent he pleased. He left to the government of Solon all its forms, but deprived it of all its force. He preserved the General Assembly of the People and Senate, and maintained the laws in their ordinary operation, by means whereof he secured to his own government the character of Democracy, while he ruled every department with absolute sway. His sons followed his example, but not with the same success. Hippias when expelled found a refuge in Persia, where he joined the army of Darius and was slain in the battle of Marathon fighting against his country.

The power wrested from Hippias passed over to Clisthenes, the leader of the party by whom he was overthrown. It was natural and accorded with principle that it should have returned to the people, but they were not competent to the exercise of it. He is represented to have been governed by patriotic motives and to have been a friend of liberty. He restored the constitution of Solon with some changes which do not appear to have touched the principle of the government. He increased the number of the tribes to ten, and of the Senate to five hundred, and of the officers who formed the board of accounts in like degree.

From the overthrow and expulsion of Hippias, to the subjugation of Greece by the armies of Rome under the Consul Mummius, about three hundred and sixty-four years intervened. The improvement of the people in civilization in that interval was considerable, and grew out of causes natural and obvious. Their progress in agriculture, navigation, commerce and the arts, called for an augmented population and furnished the means of supporting it. The variety of pursuit by giving birth to new ideas expanded the human mind. It was in this interval that the States of Greece acquired their greatest renown, and it is of course that portion of their history which has procured for them, in the highest degree, the respect and admiration of all succeeding ages. No one hears mention of the battles of Marathon, Salamis, or Platea; of the voluntary sacrifice of the illustrious band who perished at the Straits of Thermopylae in defense of their country; or of the abandonment of the city of Athens by the whole people when invaded by the overwhelming force of Persia, without experiencing sensations of enthusiastic delight. Characters were then formed in many of the states whose names have been handed down and will never be forgotten, which do honor to the human race. But it is not in this view that the subject on which I treat now claims my attention. How were the people of Athens governed during this interval? Did they maintain the constitution of Solon and administer it strictly according to its principles, or was that constitution set aside and some other substituted for it? If changes occurred, to what cause or causes were they imputable? These are the immediate objects of inquiry, and to which I shall confine myself with the utmost rigor. When it is proved, as it is by the concurrent testimony of all historians that this constitution was overthrown immediately after its adoption by the people who adopted it, and who were bound by an oath to support it, that this was done in the presence of its author, who exerted all his faculties to maintain it, there is little reason to presume that it could be maintained afterwards. Much might fairly be ascribed from the manner in which that event was accomplished, to the rude and unlettered state in which the people then were; but it is nevertheless true that the government was an impracticable one: that it was as ill adapted to the civilized as to the rude state, and the great cause for surprise is that as their improvement in civilization and knowledge of every kind was great, they did not in their progress, when they had the power in their hands, amend their government in such a manner as to give it a practical and efficient form. From an attentive view of the state of Athens and of Greece through the whole of that interval which is now the object of attention, it would be obvious that many causes united to produce that effect. I will notice the two principal only. The first relates to the epoch in which that government was instituted. The second to the state of Greece generally in the relation which was preserved between that people as a power and other nations, and likewise between the states themselves.

It has been shown that when the government belonged exclusively to the people they exercised its great powers collectively or en masse, and that when it was decided between different orders, of which they formed one, they always exercised their portion in the same manner. Such was then the state of society and of the science growing out of it that to part from the power, and place it in other hands, of representatives for example, would have been regarded by them as the abandonment of it. The contest which took place between the people and the prince in the several states after the societies had increased and the claim to hereditary right was set up, always involved the question whether the people should exercise the power in that mode or be governed absolutely by him, and it was the impracticability of the government when they got possession of it that soon overthrew it. An amendment, therefore, by committing their power to representatives was, it is presumed, not even thought of. They nevertheless still retained their attachment and devotion to liberty, of which they gave unceasing and very strong proofs.

The other cause alluded to formed likewise a very serious obstacle. Almost the whole of this interval was employed in wars, foreign and internal or civil. The first commenced with Persia shortly after the expulsion of the Pisistratide, and lasted with some intermissions fifty-one years. The Peloponnesian war followed soon afterward and consumed almost an equal term. This war commenced between Athens and Lacedemon, but all the other states soon became parties to it as allies on the one or the other side. It was produced by the war with Persia and by the rivalship and jealously which were excited in that war between those two states. To this war the ruin of Greece may in a great measure be ascribed, since it formed a relation between the states which had a very injurious influence on their respective governments, and also on the bond by which they were then held together. Other wars ensued, among which that between Sparta and Messenia was the most durable and destructive. That between Athens and Syracuse was the next, which shook the foundation of the Athenian state. The war between Sparta and Thebes followed, the fortune of which raised the latter from a very inferior to a very distinguished rank among the states of Greece. Other wars occurred between the states which did great injury to the local as well as the general interest, of which that between Martena and Tigra, to which almost all the states became parties, had the most pernicious effect. Such continual warfare could not fail to check their growth, to prevent all improvement in their local governments, and to weaken and almost annihilate the federal bond.

Under such circumstances it was easy for a power, even of inferior population, whose force should be united and directed against them with energy and talent to overwhelm them. Macedon presented such a power with a leader who was capable and eager to profit by these divisions between the states and to raise himself at their expense. Until then Macedon had been little known. She had made no impression on the affairs of Greece, and been dependent on some of the states, Sparta and Athens, at different intervals for protection. Her rise was owing altogether to the talent of Philip, who under various pretexts made war first on one state and then on the others, until finally he succeeded in reducing all under his dominion. From this period the affairs of Greece became connected with those of Macedon, and incidentially with the fortune of her rulers in their enterprises in Asia. Philip did not treat Greece in all respects as a conquered territory. He left each state in the enjoyment of its own government, and added but little from the dominions of either to his own. He became a member of the Amphyctionic Council, placed himself at its head and controlled its measures. His great object was a war with Persia, to which he was tempted by her wealth and a confidence in success arising from the repeated defeat of her vast armies in the recent invasions of Greece, by the comparatively small force of the Grecian states. Under his influence the Amphyctionic Council declared war against Persia, and committed the management of it to him in the character of commander-in-chief of the forces employed in the expedition.

His sudden death by assassination suspended this war, but his son Alexander who succeeded him, and who with equal if not superior talents adopted his policy, soon renewed the war and prosecuted it with great ardor and unexampled success. The death of Philip excited a hope in the Grecian states that they might extricate themselves from the Macedonian yoke, but that was transitory. In one year it was fixed more firmly on them by Alexander than it had been by his father. Of his conquests in Asia and of the disorders and revolutions produced by his death, by the contests between his lieutenants for portions of the conquered dominions to which they respectively set up their pretensions, I shall not treat. Little change was wrought thereby in the affairs of Greece. New efforts were made by several of the states to recover their liberties, which were attended with various success. The revival of the Ochaien League with its efforts in defense of that cause forms an interesting epoch in the latter stage of those republics. In Athens the Democracy was occasionally subverted and restored, but no change in the form ever attempted. Such was the train of events which occurred in the interval specified, and such the state of Athens at its termination, which was marked by the subjugation of Greece and her rendition to a Roman province.

These causes are, it is presumed, sufficient to show why the people of Athens never improved the constitution of Solon at any time during their existence as an independent state. The question still remains to be solved, how were they governed when that constitution was declared to be in force? Did the people govern themselves in the only mode which can be regarded as self-government, or were they mere instruments in the hands of individuals in whom they reposed their confidence? That the latter was the fact must be evident to all who examine their history with impartiality and candor. Their confidence was at one time placed in one individual, and at other times in others, who shaped the course pursued and ruled them absolutely while it lasted. The people stood collected in the General Assembly with their eyes fixed on the tribune, from which the orators addressed them, with their minds made up whose counsel to adopt and whose to reject, before they heard the proposition of either. Miltiades, Themistocles, and Aristides, ruled them through a great part of the Persian war; Cimon, Alcibiades, Nicias and Phocion had their turn. Pericles ruled in the Peloponnesian war, and others succeeded on other occasions. No instance can be given in which the people took affairs into their own hands, digested propositions adapted to existing exigencies, debated and amended them as they thought fit, and acted as a government. The constitution forbade it, and had it been otherwise, it would have been impracticable under the existing organization. The individuals who ruled did it altogether by personal influence. It was not by virtue of any office which they held of Senator, Areopagate, Archon and any other. In these offices no such power was vested incompetent to the discharge of its duties, and in consequence while they preserved the form and in truth held the power in their own hands, transferred the actual exercise of it to leaders whose instrument they were.

Confidence is due to exalted talents and merit, and respect to the individual to the extent of that claim; but so soon as the influence of any one citizen becomes a power which undermines and destroys the independence of the people, whether it be wielded by himself or a party, the effect is for the time despotic. Pisistratus usurped the government and exercised its powers in his own right. In the accomplishment of that object the people were his instruments. They were so, because they considered him their friend and the friend of liberty. They thought themselves free, and that in supporting him they defended their own cause. They were deceived. The principle in his case was different from that which existed in the latter instances, but the effect in regard to the agency of the people in the government was essentially the same. The power of the individual while he enjoyed their confidence was absolute, and the loss of it was marked by convulsion. They treated him as a tyrant, and punished him by banishment or death. It was the same with Miltiades, Themistocles, Alcibiades, Aristides and others, that it was with Pisistratus and his son, Hippias. Their most illustrious men either died in prison under fines which they could not pay, or were banished, and perished in foreign countries. The whole body of the people must have the knowledge necessary to make them competent to self-government, and the government must be wisely organized and endowed or it cannot be free or durable.

How happened it then that Solon should have instituted such a government? Data exist to afford the answer. The basis on which his constitution rested, and which could not be changed, furnishes it. It was not his object to take the power from the people and reduce them to slavery, nor could he have done it if he had been so disposed; and if they held any it could only be in a General Assembly of the whole people, the form in which they had held it from the time of Theseus, upwards of eight hundred years. To take it from them in that form would have been viewed in that light. The principle of election and of representation to certain offices and in certain stations was well understood and practiced in several of the Grecian republics, but it was never carried beyond a certain limit. It never touched the great powers, or what might be called the share which the people held in the sovereignty of the state. He was forced, therefore, to preserve that feature in the government. How then accommodate the differences which existed in the community between the rich and the poor, or as may be understood, the class of notables which had been instituted by Theseus, without prostrating the latter? How make an efficient government in any form whatever? If the power of the General Assembly which consisted of a vast majority of the poor was not checked, the accommodation would not have stopped with the abolition of debts. The lands would also have been sold and in all other respects the notables have been prostrated or the government have been overset. How form that check? The Archons could not be made, by any power which might be given to them, a balance against the Assembly of the People. The first of that corps had been instituted to get rid of a king, and the number was afterwards increased on the same principle to abolish all regal power. An attempt to restore the power in that form would have been absurd. Nor could the Court of Areopagus have been made instrumental to such a purpose. It had always been composed of aged men who had filled other offices and retired into that corps as it were from the contentious scene of public life. To vest it in the notables as an hereditary branch would have been impossible, as it would have been sure to have brought on the convulsions and civil war which it was sought to avoid. There seemed, therefore, to be no other resource than to institute a body, which by its numbers, mode of election and weight of character, might stand well with and command the confidence of the General Assembly, and by the qualification required for the members in property and the power vested in that body, forming in like extent a restraint on the General Assembly, should secure the rich from ruin and obtain likewise their confidence. It was on this principle and with this view, as I presume, that the Senate was instituted.

Had the Senators been elected by the whole people in any other mode, by the General Assembly for example, or by a vote of every citizen for every member, the Senate would have been in effect a Committee of the General Assembly, and would have been essentially under its control. By making the members eligible by the tribes, he detached the body in some measure from the General Assembly, and by requiring a certain portion of property as a qualification for the office he gave some security to the rich, while by leaving the door open to all who might acquire it, the objection which would have applied to hereditary rank was precluded, and some hope was presented to the poor. And by giving to the Senate the exclusive power to originate every proposition on which the General Assembly could act he gave an additional protection to the rich. Give to the General Assembly the power to originate measures and no resistance could have been made to it. The rich would have been overwhelmed at once. Confine its agency to propositions which the Senate should submit to it, and that consequence would be avoided. The rich would never propose any act which would operate against themselves. The Senate therefore seemed to be as well adapted to all these objects as any corps which he could have instituted could be. But the government was impracticable in every part, as has been shown by a fair analysis of the organization and endowment of each, when tested by the nature and qualities of man, and likewise by the career and fate of the government itself. For the defects of the system we must look to the age in which it was instituted and to the state of society and of the science in that age. That nothing better could have then been done, the devotion of the people to the government and their observance of its injunctions, so far as they understood and were able to execute them under all their difficulties afford the best proof.

The General Assembly could be preserved only by investing it with the powers committed to it; but in the execution of those powers that it should not act from its own impulse but be the instrument of some other party. To accomplish this it was necessary that it should take that position of its own accord and not by compulsion; that it should believe that it was the ruling party while it was ruled; that it did everything when it did nothing. This was seen in the instance of Pisistratus, and likewise in the others that have been noticed, for although the principle was different the effect was the same. The tendency in all governments, even those which are representative, in which the bodies are too numerous, and in which those who compose them act as the multitude connecting in the degree the sovereignty with the government, is to precipitate their overthrow and termination in one, that is, in despotism. When the sovereignty is held by a prince in the early and rude state of society, and the people in the progress of civilization and increase of population contend for their rights, compromises are natural and are generally entered into. Whatever the people obtain is so much gained, and they are often satisfied with small gains. In the early stages the power of the prince is not despotic. There is always a class of nobles around him who share a portion of the power, and the spirit of equality pervades the whole society, prince, nobles and people. The effort is therefore to improve the condition of the people, and in doing this the hold which the two hereditary branches have acquired though diminished is not always destroyed. But when the people possess the whole power, and a change is made, it is generally by a transition to the opposite extreme. Possessing the whole power and not being able to retain it they lose the whole. There is no resting-place; no point at which to stop; no party with whom to negotiate: and they will never voluntarily degrade themselves by creating a class of nobles with a prince over them, and retain a portion of the power only in the government. Changes in this state generally grow out of contests between rival parties and rival chiefs. Civil wars ensue, in the result of which the leader of the successful party is placed at the head of the government with unlimited power. Our object is to preserve the sovereignty in the people and to give them that agency in the government which will be best adapted to that end, and in those instances in which the agency of a few or of one will be most effectual, to avail ourselves of it, but in a manner which will make them or him perform their duties with fidelity as representatives and servants, without the possibility of their wresting the power from us and becoming our masters.

From the view above presented it is obvious that the Government of Athens had not a single feature in it except the principle on which it was founded, which was free from serious objection; and that its defects were so numerous and vital as to make its overthrow certain and immediate. There was no regular division of power in it; of legislative, executive and judicial, separated from each other. The whole was an amalgamation.

For these evils no remedy can be found but by the separation of the sovereignty from the government, retaining the forms in the people, and committing the latter to representatives to be by them elected or otherwise appointed, deriving their authority from them, and placed in offices or departments organized and endowed by a compact or constitution to which the whole people are parties, and by which their duties in their capacity of the sovereign power and of their representatives in the departments to which they may be called, shall be specially and distinctly defined. If the two powers be thus separated and the government be organized on just principles, divided into the three departments specified with the proper number, and proper powers be vested in each, with a line strictly drawn between them, and each be made independent of the others, and armed with the means of securing that independence by checking encroachments of either on the other, it is impossible that the government should fail, provided the people be competent to self-government and perform their duty. When the sovereign power is separated from the government by a compact to which the whole people are parties, and by which the rights and interests of all are placed on the same footing, all are equally interested in the faithful execution of its conditions according to their true intent and meaning, by a fair and just construction, and are equally bound to enjoin it on those who represent them. In this case the people may form a complete check on the government, and if they be intelligent and virtuous, keep it in its true course. The path for every department will be traced and seen by those in each, in any and every emergency as well as by their constituents. The people who are calm spectators at a distance of the measures pursued and of the conduct of those in office will be guided by principle, and expect a faithful observance of it by those who represent them. Upright and honorable men will always pursue that course, and even those who are less scrupulous, knowing that their conduct is watched will be afraid to go wrong.

LACEDEMON

I will now proceed to examine the Government of Lacedemon. The constitution instituted by Lycurgus is that of which I shall treat. It was instituted eight hundred and forty-five years before the Christian era and two hundred and fifty-one before that of Athens. It will be found that this government was in many of its features peculiar: that no such government ever existed either in the ancient or modern world. It affords in all its parts the strongest exemplification of the epoch in which it was formed.

In tracing the origin of the Athenian state with its progress for the purposes of this inquiry, it was necessary to take a concise view of that of all Greece. The view thus presented is equally applicable to Lacedemon. The early or rude ages of all the states are similar. So far as any incidents occurred in the progress of those two communities of a different character, I shall endeavor to notice and give them the weight to which they are entitled.

Their government had a like origin in princes; a form which was common to the Grecian States, and incident to the rude age in which they commenced. A difference occurred in that of Lacedemon, which distinguished it in that respect from every other state. The first prince died, leaving two sons who inherited the office of the father with equal rights, and which descended to the eldest son of each branch through successive generations for many ages.

It has been already observed that Danaus from Egypt, and Pelops from Phrygia, emigrated to the Peloponnesus at a very early age, while the people were in a rude state, and that they were each placed at the head of the section in which they settled. These princes had respectively a long train of descendants who had great power in that Peninsula. The Heraclidae were the offspring of Danaus, so called from Hercules, one of his descendants, the Pelopidae of Pelops. These two houses contended for the supremacy in the Peloponnesus, in which struggle the Pelopidae succeeded, and the Heraclidae were banished from it. This occurred some time before the Trojan war, in which Agamemnon of the house of the Pelopidae took the lead as commander of the confederate force employed in it. The long absence of the chiefs engaged in that war had so far impaired their authority in their respective dominions, that many of them were compelled on their return, to engage in new wars, to reinstate themselves. Agamemnon was betrayed by his wife, and cut off immediately after his return. The Heraclidae, aware of these disorders, and of the favorable opportunity which it presented, made several attempts to regain their power, in which they failed; but at length they succeeded. In the latter they were aided by the Dorians and Etolians.

Temenus, Cresphontes, and Aristodemus, three brothers in the fifth degree from Hercules, led the invading force. Almost the whole of the Peninsula was conquered. In the division of the portion claimed by the Heraclidae, Argos was allotted to Temenus, Messinia to Cresphontes, and Laconia to the two twin brothers, Euryelpenes and Procles, the infant sons of Aristodemus, who died pending the struggle. The other conquered provinces were divided between the Dorians and Etolians, who had assisted in making the conquest.

The Heraclidae were thus restored to their possessions in the Peloponnesus about eighty years after the taking of Troy, and one thousand three hundred and five before the Christian era. Two kings were thus placed at that early period in the government of Lacedemon, and in that state Lycurgus found it when he instituted his constitution, four hundred and sixty-eight years afterwards. What were at that period the other modifications of the Lacedemonian government does not distinctly appear in any work that I have seen, ancient or modern. It may be inferred from the remarks of some writers that there existed a class of nobles with limited powers. The power of the kings is said to have been absolute whenever they could agree, but that differences between them were frequent, and sometimes serious; and that these differences laid the foundation of the power held either by the nobles or people. In general it is understood from the view which has been presented by different writers, that the progress of affairs in Lacedemon was similar in other respects to that which occurred in the other states. There were frequent contentions through the whole interval, between the different orders for power, and it may be presumed had not the difference between the two kings, mitigated in the exercise of that which belonged to them, and thereby given a popular cast to the government, that it would have experienced the fate which befell monarchy in all the other states, and been overthrown at the same time. All writers agree that these contentions had risen to a great height at the period when Lycurgus was called on, apparently by the general voice, to institute the government of which I shall give a sketch.

The attention was drawn to him by causes which marked the epoch at which the constitution was formed, as well as the confidence reposed in his virtue and talents. He was the son of Eunomus, and brother of Polydaetes, one of the reigning kings and a descendant of Hercules in the eleventh degree. His brother dying without offspring, he was supposed to be entitled to the crown, and actually did succeed to it for a short term; but it appearing that the deceased king had left his wife pregnant, he disclaimed any right to it, in case the offspring should be male. The widow offered to destroy the infant if he would marry her. He amused her with hope until a son was born, whom he acknowledged, and in whose favor he immediately abdicated. This proof of disinterested virtue elevated his character in the state; but the disappointment and mortification to which the widow was thereby subjected excited her deep resentment, and exposed him to danger. She soon raised factions against him, in consequence whereof he left the state and traveled into Crete, and thence to Asia, studying the laws and governments of different countries, and comparing them with each other as to their relative success in promoting the happiness of people. In his absence Lacedemon was convulsed by factions and the state menaced with dangers, for which no remedy could be found within it. They all united in pressing his return, and in giving him a power to make such reforms as would avert the impending ruin. I shall present this constitution as instituted by him, and notice the changes afterwards made in it while in force. He compiled with the invitation and reported the constitution which was established before the Christian era, of which I will now give a sketch, with the changes.

The government of Lacedemon consisted of two kings, of a Council of twenty-eight members, and of an Assembly of the People. The crown was hereditary in both branches, descending to the oldest son of each, and if no son to the brother, or other nearest connection of that branch; but in no event to the other house. Their rights were joint and equal, not divided between them. The senators who composed the Council were elected for life by the people. The election was made in full assembly. The kings presided in the senate. The measures carried there were communicated to the people in General Assembly, who were bound either to accept or reject them without amendment.

When the two kings concurred in any proposition there was no opposition to it. Neither could leave the state in time of peace, nor could both do so in time of war; unless there were two armies in the field, in which case each took the command of one. They were placed at the head of religion, and had the command of the armies, might sign truces, and receive and dismiss ambassadors while in the field. In peace they were regarded only as the first citizens of the state. They mixed in society with the other citizens on a footing of equality, and were received with respect but without parade.

The Senate being the Supreme Council of the state, war and peace, alliances, and all the other high concerns, were treated of in the first instance in it. No person under the age of sixty could be elected to it. In addition to the high political powers already noticed, others of a judicial character belonged to that body. When a king was accused of having betrayed the state, or having violated the laws, the Senate with the other king and five Ephori, after that corps was instituted, formed the tribunal by which he was tried.

Of the Assembly of the People there existed two distinct species. One regulated affairs which were peculiar to the inhabitants of Sparta. The other those which were common to them, and to the inhabitants of the different villages of Laconia. The kings, senators, and different classes of magistrates assisted in both.

When the succession to the throne was regulated, magistrates were chosen or dismissed. The Assembly was composed of Spartans only. This Assembly was convened in the ordinary course of affairs every month at full moon, and at other times when circumstances required it.

The other Assembly was convened when war, peace, or alliances were treated of. It was composed of Spartans, and likewise of deputies from the villages of Laconia, and often of those from their allies, and of nations who came to solicit aid from Lacedemon. In these Assemblies their mutual pretensions and complaints, the infractions of treaties by other people, the means of conciliation, the projects of campaigns, and the contributions they had to furnish, were brought forward and discussed.

Other provisions were introduced into this government of a very peculiar character, which although they do not constitute essentially a part of the organization, or of the endowment of either branch, or touch directly the question of hereditary or popular right, yet as they formed a part of the compact between the people and the kings, and the people themselves, and had great influence on the fortune of the government, it is equally proper to notice. These provisions were the basis on which the system rested, and were in fact a part of the constitution itself. I shall notice the most important only. They mark distinctly the state of society at the age of which I treat.

He made an equal division of all the land among the citizens of the state. He divided Laconia into thirty thousand parts or lots, and distributed them among the people of the country. He divided Sparta into nine thousand, which he distributed in like manner among the people of that section. The proprietors of these lots could neither sell nor divide. They descended to the oldest son of each citizen, and were rather the property of the state than of the individual. He banished gold and silver and substituted iron as the currency, and of such weight and little value that it required a cart and two oxen to carry a piece worth comparatively a few dollars. He expelled the fine arts by prescribing the kind of furniture which should be used, and giving every other possible discouragement to them. He established public repasts, and made all the citizens mess together on the same food, which was regulated by law, of the simplest kind, and dressed in like manner. Each table consisted of fifteen persons, and each person furnished monthly an equal portion of the provisions requisite, which was calculated with great precision. The kings attended these tables, and partook of the public repasts with the citizens without other distinction than the allowance of a double portion to each. From these tables they were obligated to return to their houses in the dark. It was ordained that the laws should not be written, but preserved in the memory alone; and science of every kind was discountenanced except that of war and the exercises connected with it. Marriages, births, and the education of children were specially provided for. Girls were taught to perform manly exercises, to throw the quoit and the javelin, to run the race, and wrestle in public naked. The same instruction was given to boys. The infant as soon as born was inspected by persons appointed for that purpose and taken in charge of the government. If well formed and robust, vigorous nourishment was provided for him, and a lot of land assigned to him. If deformed, delicate and weak, he was thrown into a bog and destroyed. He discouraged all intercourse between the citizens of Sparta and those of other nations by a visit of either to the country of the other, especially in that class whose example could have any effect, from a fear that the morals of the Spartans might thereby be corrupted. His object was to keep them as much as possible at home under the daily influence of the institutions which he had established, and to exclude all extraneous usages which might tend to produce a change.

Such was the government of Lacedemon, as instituted by Lycurgus, and in which state it remained about one hundred and thirty years, in the course of which time the people being dissatisfied with the restraint imposed on them, either to accept or reject the propositions which were sent to them by the senate, without amendment, gradually assumed the right of making such alterations as they thought fit. This abuse, as it was called, was corrected in the reign of Potedorus and Theoporapus, by whom the constitution was restored to its original state. The discontent which that measure produced among the people may easily be conceived. To reconcile them to it, the corps called the Ephori was instituted as a substitute in defense of their rights, and by which a very important change was introduced into the system. I shall make the remarks which appear to me to be proper on this constitution, as originally formed by its author, and then notice the effect which was produced by this change.

The most celebrated writers of antiquity represent this government as one of the best, if not the best, which was instituted at that epoch. Aristotle, Polybius, and Plutarch have explicitly avowed that sentiment, and some modern writers of great merit seem to acquiesce in it. I will examine it on principle, giving full force to every provision in it which could have had any influence on its fortune. I will then test it by its career, since that is the best criterion by which a just estimate can be formed of its merit. With this view, it will be proper to inquire in the first instance to what class did it belong? Did it recognize distinct orders in such extent as to belong strictly to that class, and to move on that principle?

The character of a government must depend on the source from whence it derives its powers. All governments which emanate directly from the people, whether the term of service of those who fill its branches be long or short, are popular or democratical, provided when the term expires the vacancy is supplied by election. The length of the term will vitiate the government, but cannot be said to change the principle although it be for life. It is not the name or title given to any incumbent in any branch which fixes the character of the government. An officer may be called king, and the office may be hereditary in his family, and yet if he has no power, or the power vested in him be very limited, and especially if the people have a control over his conduct, the government cannot be considered as strictly monarchical. For the government to be placed in that class, the person having the title must hold a portion of the sovereignty, otherwise it will be nominal only. This may be done in various forms and in different degrees in different governments, but still in the degree that the control of the great affairs of the state, and especially the power which is generally considered as executive, is taken from him and vested in the people and the office made ministerial, will the principle and character of the government be changed, and an approach be made to democracy.

The power of the kings was very limited. They were chiefs of religion, and commanded the armies in time of war. In the internal government of the state they had no effective power whatever. They were members of and presided in the senate, but their votes were counted like those of other members, and they had in its measures when they disagreed no other weight than what arose from the respect which was due to their talents and merit. They did not receive ambassadors from nor appoint them to foreign powers, nor instruct them when appointed, nor make treaties, nor appoint officers, nor had they any other powers than those above enumerated.

The government of Lacedemon resembled that of Athens in its most important features. The sovereign power was essentially in the people, in the one government as well as in the other, and all the great powers of the government were vested in and exercised by the people collectively in a General Assembly in both. The government was united with the sovereignty, and in consequence the same concentration of legislative, executive and judicial powers existed in the General Assembly of the one state as in that of the other. The material difference between the two governments consisted in the power held by the two kings, in that of

Lacedemon and in the hereditary quality of that power; and likewise in the number of members of which their senates respectively were composed, and in their term of service. How far these differences may be considered as forming a difference between the two governments on principle, and introducing distinct orders into that of Lacedemon, and were calculated to produce a difference in their fate, are objects of inquiry which merit attention.

The senators of Lacedemon held their offices for life; those of Athens for one year only. In both states they were elected by the people. The length of service, as has been remarked, will weaken the tone and spirit of the government, but cannot change the principle; nor will it entirely change the principle of action in those who hold the office, for as their offspring will be in the hands of the people the dread of the revenge which might fall on them, would deter the incumbents from committing acts to incur their resentment. The hereditary right of the kings as members of and to preside in the senate, and to command the armies in war, are the only powers over which the people had not a direct control, by the election of those in whom vested; and is, therefore, the only feature in the government of Lacedemon which takes it out of the democratic class.

If a democratical government be so badly formed as to be impracticable, and the people avail themselves of a resource founded on the opposite principle, to sustain it, of very limited extent, and with effect, it can furnish no proof other than the excellence of the democratical principle. It can furnish none of the excellence of that of the opposite character, nor of the comparative merit of democratical government in its best form, with those which are mixed.

When a principle opposite to that on which the government is founded has no hold on the government, and is merely an outward prop or stay on which it rests, under difficulties which admit of obvious remedies, we cannot reason on it as a conflicting power, nor can it afford any proof of the defect of one principle or merit of the other. A drowning man it is said will catch at a straw. He will certainly take the hand of his enemy to save his life. If the opposite principle has such strong hold on the government as to be able to check its progress in case of division, and to endanger its existence in that of conflict, then the question of distinct orders, and the comparative merit of the two classes will come fairly under consideration. But if the hold is trifling, and the hereditary right essentially at the mercy of the governing power, then the person in whom vested must be in constant dread of destruction; and, in consequence, be the mere creature of such power, administering to its aid in such manner as it pleases.

From this view it appears to me that the government of Lacedemon could not be considered as one which moved on the principle of distinct orders, or which derived its support from that source. The senate did not rest on that ground, nor could it resist the Assembly of the People in case of conflict, nor could the kings afford them any aid, for it was only as members of the senate that they had any share in the government. In time of war commanders of the troops were necessary, and they held that station by hereditary right, but it was distinct from and subordinate to the government and under its control. By what means then was the government supported for the term that it existed? We must look for these to other causes, and not to that to be derived from a balance between distinct orders, or the principle on which such government is founded.

The government of Athens was found to be an impracticable one, and it was made so by the union of the government with the sovereignty in the people, and the exercise of all the great powers of the government by the people collectively. All the objections then which apply to the Athenian government in those respects are equally applicable to the Lacedemonian. How happens it then that the government of Lacedemon was more permanently tranquil in its movement than that of Athens? Many causes contributed to that result, but the career and fate of the Athenian government alone afford all the demonstration on this point which can be desired by the most skeptical. Where the defects are the same, the remedy which saved the one government would save the other. To sustain the government of Athens, some expedient which should take the exercise of its powers out of the hands of the people collectively, and commit it by their consent to another party and make them the deluded instruments was indispensable. That expedient soon presented itself, and of which they availed themselves. It has been shown that about ten years after the government of Solon was instituted, the people suffered the power to be taken from them by Pisistratus, and actually aided him in the usurpation, and supported him in the exercise of it with occasional interruptions during his life, and as they thought in defense of their rights and of the constitution, though in direct violation of both. They were afterwards ruled by Miltiades, Themistocles, Aristides, Pericles, and others, by their own consent. The people in General Assembly never ruled themselves by any arrangement of their own. Physicians administer drugs to cure diseases. The remedy is not pleasant, and a strong dose would often kill the patient. A moderate one affords relief.

If the defects of the government of Athens compelled the people of that state to resort to an expedient in actual subversion of the constitution, while the power remained in their hands ostensibly only, how much more natural was it for those of Lacedemon to avail themselves of a resource provided by the constitution itself, which should preserve the constitution and with it the powers to the exercise of which they were competent. The Senate of Lacedemon could not be an object of jealousy with the people, and consisting of fewer members than the Prytanean Corps which formed only one-tenth of that of Athens, was more capable of digesting and preparing measures to be proposed to the General Assembly of the People, and of executing all its other duties. Nor could the kings be an object of dread. Those people had always been subject to the rule of kings, and they enjoyed under the constitution of Lycurgus more freedom than they had ever experienced before. As senators, they certainly could not, and when called to the command of armies in time of war their hereditary quality in that station would give support to the General Assembly of the People in two important circumstances. By exciting a jealousy of their power and views it would unite the people more closely together: and by holding it in their own right the necessity to fill it by election, whereby contests between popular leaders for the command, the tendency of which always is in such a state of society and under a government so formed to divide the people into violent parties, and convulse, if not overthrow it, would be prevented.

The division of the regal power between two kings could not have failed to contribute much to reconcile the General Assembly of the People to the portion which they enjoyed, and to their agency in its concerns. The history of that state shows that it had an important influence on its fate at a very early period and in every subsequent stage. The constitution of Lycurgus was adopted, as has already been stated, about two hundred and fifty years before that of Solon, when the people of Greece generally, and especially those of the Peloponnesus had made but a slight progress in civilization. The tyrannies which had grown up in all the states, the offspring of the governments which had been formed in their most early and rude state, were overthrown except in Lacedemon. The preservation of monarchy in that state was owing to that cause, the division of the royal power between two kings, descendants of Hercules, but of different branches of that house. The rivalry and jealousy which existed between them and which descended to their successors weakened their power, and gave to the government a milder tone. Each to sustain himself and undermine his competitor courted popular favor, and thus the government was thrown more immediately on the people. The motive for a change was, therefore, less urgent in Lacedemon than in the other states, and to that cause it is presumed, it was owing that monarchy was not overthrown there at the same time that it was in the other states. It may fairly be inferred, therefore; that it continued to have a like effect after that constitution was adopted, and in the mode suggested.

There were other causes which must have contributed to secure to the Lacedemonian government a more tranquil movement and a longer existence than befell that of Athens. By the equal division of lands among the citizens, the opposite and conflicting classes of the rich and the poor could not exist among them. By messing together at public tables at common charge, they formed a species of company in which the interest of one was that of the whole. All domestic concerns of the most interesting nature became those of the public. By the education of their children by the state, every individual was made a public man, and by the substitution of iron for gold and silver as a currency, by the suppression of commerce and the discouragement of all intercourse with foreign nations by the more intelligent class of society on each side, the people were attached to and preserved in the rude state in which they then were, especially as all the great powers of the government were in principle in their hands and ostensibly so in practice.

There was another cause of a character equally marked which must have had a like effect. It appears from the history of Lacedemon, that the large crowds which were collected in the general assembly at every meeting became impatient, as those of Athens likewise did of the restraint imposed on them, to accept or reject without amendment the propositions which were sent to them by the senate, and that they often broke through it, and made such amendments as they thought fit. In this course the government moved on about one hundred and thirty years, the senate and the kings yielding to the pressure. At length they took alarm from a conviction that if those encroachments were not checked, and the constitution restored to its original state, their power would be annihilated. They made an effort to that effect, and succeeded in it; but to reconcile the people to it, they proposed an amendment to the constitution by the institution of the Ephori, which was adopted and which gave a new character to the government. This amendment was adopted at the particular suggestion of Theopompus, one of the then reigning kings, and as he avowed to preserve the power which he then held.

It cannot be doubted that the institution of this corps diminished considerably the cares and duties of the General Assembly of the People, and produced in other respects a very important effect on the fortune of the government. The members of the corps being elected by the people possessed the confidence of the General Assembly, and standing between that Assembly and the senate and kings, the natural tendency of its action was to take all the powers from the General Assembly which it could not discharge with advantage, and in the exercise of them to encroach on those of the senate and kings. The members of the corps would seek popularity with their constituents, which might be gained by exciting suspicions of the views of the other branches and by an unceasing pressure on them. In pursuit of this object some might not be over scrupulous as to the means, while others would be modest and honest, and perform their duty with perfect integrity. Zeal in the representative in defending the rights and promoting the interest of his constituents is correct and honorable, but the cause may be abused. It requires great knowledge of constitutional principles, and of the policy which a due regard to the public interest dictates, to fix the precise limit to which that zeal should be carried, and great firmness of nerve and loftiness of sentiment in moments of great public excitement to stem in any degree the current, and to stop at that point on the responsibility of the individual. Some will expose themselves to that hazard. Others will go with the current regardless of the consequences, be they what they may. I speak of man as he is and has always been.

The direct tendency of the powers vested in this corps would be to enable it by the exercise of them, should selfish motives be yielded to, to acquire in the progress of affairs all those of every other branch. Being elected annually by the people and considered as the defenders of their rights, it would take from the General Assembly by its consent all the powers which it could not discharge with advantage, which would leave it a very limited sphere of action. The opinion of that Assembly would be sought and be pursued by the corps, but the latter would constitute the efficient government, with the support of the former, which would be the instrument. The General Assembly being thus relieved by a corps of its own creation, from a dependence on the kings and senate for a performance of any of the duties to which it was incompetent, would not only cease to repose on the latter for any of those aids, but yield to and cherish the jealousy which the hereditary right of the one and long service of the other would naturally inspire. The Ephori would in consequence soon acquire the control of the kings and in a great measure of the senate, and thus have the whole government in its hands. Had the corps consisted of one member only, and he been vested with the right to command an army, or had that right been vested in the president of the corps, he would soon have usurped the government, making use of the people as his instruments; but there being five, and their powers being exclusively civil, all that they could accomplish would be to supplant by means thereof the plan of the General Assembly of the People, and impair the authority of the kings and senate.

The career of the Lacedemonian government corresponded after this corps was instituted with the view thus presented. It is attested by the highest authorities that by degrees it absorbed all the great powers of the government: that it had a censorship over the public morals, supervised the conduct of the magistrates and suspended them from office at pleasure; raised troops, gave orders to their commanders, interrupted them in victory, controlled their operations and recalled them from service, two of their body attending them in the field as spies on their conduct; that it received ambassadors from foreign powers, convened the General Assembly, scrutinized the conduct of the kings, summoned them before them to answer charges alleged against them; seized their persons, brought them to trial, and sometimes imposed fines on them by their own authority. Many of these powers belonged to the General Assembly of t he People, and were exercised as may fairly be presumed, with their sanction and by their desire; the others were derived from encroachment on the senate and kings. By exercising them they supplied the defects of the one, and broke down the feeble barrier which the constitution had erected in defense of the others.

Whether the government could have sustained itself without the institution of the Ephori for the term it did, is a question of very serious, and I may add, of very doubtful import. How far the other regulations would have had that effect without the aid of that corps, must be matter of conjecture. Many writers of great distinction applaud in the highest degree the equal division of lands among the citizens, with the establishment of public repasts, and the education of children by the state. Polybius thinks that these regulations with a view to the liberty of the people and the safety of the state from foreign invasion, indicate a divine inspiration;[38] and other writers concur in that sentiment. I have no doubt, regarding the period at which that constitution was instituted, and the rude state of society at the time, that they had great effect in sustaining the government at that epoch, and in every subsequent stage while the society remained in that state. But still it is uncertain whether of themselves they would have been adequate to the object. My impression is that they would not. Under those regulations, with the aid of the kings and senate, in the manner, on the principle, and for the reasons stated, the government moved on in tolerable tranquility, one hundred and thirty years. In that interval, however, the General Assembly of the People manifested the discontent which was shown by the General Assembly of Athens, and which at the period adverted to had risen to such a height as to alarm the kings and senate and excite their opposition; the result of which was the institution of this corps at the insistence of one of the kings for

38. Polybius, Vol. III. extract iii. chap. i.

their safety. Had it not been instituted, it may fairly be presumed that the contentions which had commenced on that point would have been extended to others, and overthrown the government at a much earlier period. As soon as the friendly relation between the parties was broken, all ties between them would have ceased, and full force have been given to the defects of the system under aggravated circumstances. The institution of this corps restored tranquility to the state, and its powers in the commencement being rather of a negative than of a positive character, gaining on each side, and enlarging the sphere of action by the force of circumstances, it was thereby enabled to prevent any direct explosion, and to keep the machine in motion for a much longer term than it otherwise could have done.

This government in its organization, in the endowment of its branches, and in all its provisions and regulations was adapted to the rude state of society and none other. To that state the government was peculiarly suited, and to preserve it in that state the regulations specified were eminently well calculated. If the people were admitted into the government in that early age, whether it was in complete sovereignty, or in participation, it could only be en masse, or collectively, and if they preserved the power for any term especially, it could be only by availing themselves of extra or artificial aids, repugnant to the principle of the government, and adverse to their improvement in civilization. The defects of their power could not be cured by any provision consistent with it; and if such provision was carried beyond a very limited scope it would involve controversies which would be sure to subvert the government. No arrangement had ever been made to put the government in operation on the principle of distinct orders, in a manner to preserve a balance between them. It is thus that we account for the harmonious co-operation between the General Assembly of the People and the kings and senate. All the other provisions tended to keep the people in the rude state, and to support the government in its then form. The equal division of lands among the citizens, public repasts in which all messed together, kings, senators and laborers; the education of children by the state; the suppression of commerce; exclusion of foreigners; all had that tendency, as they had to keep affairs in their then state. Improve the society, civilize it, and the whole fabric would fall to pieces.

Had the government of Lacedemon rested on the same ground with that of Athens, on a General Assembly of the People and a numerous senate, and been left to itself without other aids, it would in my opinion have blown up at once as that of Athens did. If an edifice falls when certain props which rest against it are removed, the proof is complete that it was sustained by those props. Such too was the fate of the government of Lacedemon. By wars and other causes the state of the country was gradually changed. An intercourse took place with foreign nations. The door was opened to commerce. Iron was laid aside and gold and silver restored as the currency. The people became more civilized, and, in consequence, all those internal regulations which were adapted to the barbarous state were abandoned. The props which had sustained the government were removed and it fell of course.

CARTHAGE

The government of Carthage is that next in order, according to the plan originally laid down, which claims attention. This people inhabited Africa, another quarter of the globe, and they afford the only example ever known in that quarter of a government which might be called free. The ruins of their city are still visible on the Mediterranean, near Tunis, and are often visited by travelers. No vestige or remnant of liberty is seen there. A perfect despotism prevails, and with it an ignorance and barbarism which exhibit man in the most degraded state.

In treating of a republican government in Africa we are led to inquire by what race of people it was instituted, what their origin, and the intermediate stages in their history which led to that result. No other portion of the people in that quarter could have instituted such a government, and had one been instituted for them it must have failed immediately by their utter inability to preserve it. The aborigines of Carthage were not Africans. The founders of the city emigrated from Tyre, in Phoenicia, a province of Syria. Their origin is traced to a far more remote source. The Phoenicians emigrated from Saboa, a part of Arabia, which borders on the eastern side of the Red Sea. The history of the Phoenicians and of the Saboans of whom they were a colony, the state of civilization which they had attained, with the causes which produced it, their emigration from Saboa to Syria, and of a portion of their population thence along the Mediterranean to Carthage, with the different stages in this progress, is intimately connected with the history of the eastern world. It is nevertheless certain, that taken in its greatest extent, including the rise and fall of empires in that quarter, with the state of science, commerce, and the arts, so far as it is known, it sheds little light on the subject on which I treat. It is generally admitted that Egypt and Asia are the countries which were first settled, since in going back to the earliest records of time and comparing them with other countries, with Greece for example, we find the population there much greater than with them, and improvements in civilization and the arts generally more advanced. Emigrants from Egypt and Asia to Greece introduced commerce, agriculture, alphabetical writing, and some knowledge of the arts among the people. But what was the state of that epoch on each side? The Greeks were altogether rude and uncivilized. The Egyptians and Asiatics, the Phoenicians particularly, somewhat advanced beyond them. The improvement of the Greeks, though gradual and slow was great, while that of the eastern nations has remained in the state in which it then was.

The origin of Asia, and of Egypt, the only part of Africa which merits attention in the view under consideration, compared with that of Greece and the

European states generally is little known, and what we do know of it is derived almost altogether from Greek and Roman authors. The accounts which those writers give of those people represent them at the most distant ages known, essentially in the state in which they now are, as very populous communities; despotism with great wealth and splendor at the head; slavery with ignorance, poverty, and wretchedness among the people. The opposite classes in society were separated at a vast distance from each other, and which could have been produced only by the great age of those communities, and other causes which tend in the progress of time to promote inequality among the people. When communities reach that state, improvement in their governments in favor of the rights of the people, with corresponding checks on the power of the crown becomes extremely difficult, and must be attended with convulsion. If the people have not acquired an improvement in intelligence and other circumstances to render them capable of discharging the duties and sustaining the station thus obtained, these efforts must fail, or terminate in the case of change, in the transfer only of the power from the existing circumstances to some leader, and thus form the commencement of a new dynasty over them. In this state Asia and Africa, with the exception of Phoenicia in the former, and of Carthage in the Phoenician colony in the latter, have been always known to modern times, according to the best accounts which have been transmitted to us.

The government of Carthage resembled that of Athens in the two most important features. The sovereignty was in the people, and the government united with the sovereignty; but in many of its modifications it essentially varied from it. It consisted of a General Assembly of the People; of a Senate; and of two magistrates, who were called Suffetes, the Senators were elected by the people, as were the Suffetes. The number of members of which the Senate was composed is unknown. Their term of service was for life. The Suffetes were elected annually.

The people in General Assembly had the power to elect the magistrates, to regulate the finances, to make peace and war, and to form alliances in the mode prescribed by the constitution.

Every individual born of parents, both of whom were citizens, was a citizen. The revenue, to be eligible to office, was prescribed. Every citizen was an elector.

From the Senate two corps of councils were formed, one consisting of one hundred and four members, and the other of five. Those of the first held their offices for life. Those of the second for a term only: the precise length of which is unknown.

The Suffetes had a right to convene the Senate, to propose to it subjects for deliberation, and to take the votes of the members. They presided in the tribunals and were agents-general of the republic. They likewise sometimes commanded the armies. On retiring from that office they became Pretors, in which character they had a right to propose new laws, and to call to account those who were charged with the administration of the public finances.

The powers of the Senate were very extensive. Its decrees had the form of laws when the vote was unanimous. In case of a division the proposition was sent to the Assembly of the People. The vote of a single member in opposition produced that result. When the proposition was submitted to the people, they were not compelled to adopt or reject it as presented, but had a right to dispose of it as they thought fit.

The Council of One Hundred and Four was called the Council of Ancients, and charged with the superintendence of the constituted authorities, and particularly of the conduct of the generals and admirals of the republic. It was considered the guardian of the constitution. The Council of Five had likewise extensive powers. They appointed their colleagues when vacancies occurred, and likewise the members of the Council of One Hundred and Four, into which body they returned, when their term of services had expired.

Such was the government of Carthage, according to the best information that I have been able to obtain from the works of Aristotle, Polybius, Livy, and Diodorus Siculus, among the ancients, and such modern writers as I have had access to. Aristotle bestowed on it a very high commendation. It had existed when he wrote about five hundred years, during which, he observes, that the state had never been disturbed by sedition, nor had the liberties of the people been menaced by a tyrant. He considered it as one of the most perfect constitutions that had been known. For this tranquility very satisfactory causes may be assigned. The example of the government of Athens and Lacedemon furnishes them.

The great causes to which the overthrow of the Athenian government was imputable, were the union of the government with the sovereignty, and the exercise of the powers of the government by the people collectively. It was the inability of the people to perform the duties of a government in that manner, which enabled Pisistratus to wrest it from them and to exercise its powers in his own right, and which made them after his overthrow mere instruments in the hands of popular leaders. It was the same cause which induced the people of Lacedemon to acquiesce in the power of the Senate and kings, by whom many of those duties were performed, the discharge of which by them collectively would have overthrown it. In the government of Carthage the arrangement was the same on principle that it was in the Athenian; the government was united with the sovereignty in the people, to be exercised by them collectively, or en masse, but such was the arrangement, that they could scarcely ever be called on to act in that form. Whenever the vote of the Senate was unanimous, the question was decided. A reference to the people became unnecessary, and such was the organization of the Senate, that while it was calculated to inspire confidence in the people, it remedied in a considerable degree the defects of a body thus constituted. The great number of which it was composed enabled it to form a kind of substitute for the General Assembly of the People, and thus to prevent their discontent. Incapable of discharging the duties themselves, they would readily yield their place to so large a portion of their mass whom they had elected. And the defects inseparable from so numerous a body as the Senate in the discharge of the powers vested in it, were mitigated by the duties which were performed by the Council of One Hundred and Four, which was composed of members of the Senate, and likewise by the Council of Five, who were taken from the One Hundred and Four. All writers agree that the powers vested in these two councils were great, and which cannot be doubted, as it may fairly be inferred that every measure, legislative as well as executive, originated with that of the Five, and after being prepared were submitted by them to the whole body of the Senate. In this mode it seems as if the best provisions which such an organization admitted of, were adopted to remedy the great defects of the system.

The great difference between the government of Carthage, and that of Athens, consisted in the following circumstances. By the constitution of Athens no measure could be adopted without the sanction of the General Assembly of the People, and for this purpose they were convened regularly every month, and frequently several times in a month. By the constitution of Carthage no proposition of any kind was submitted to the people when the vote of the Senate was unanimous. The whole business of the state was managed in that event by the Senate, and the councils formed by its members, and by the Suffetes. This principle being established, it may be presumed that appeals were seldom made to the people, and were avoided, except in cases of great emergency, in accord with the wishes of both bodies, the General Assembly and the Senate. The incompetency of the people to perform the duties of a government, in General Assembly, would reconcile them to the performance of them by the other bodies, especially as they would be taken from the pursuits of industry, received no compensation for the service, and those who did perform them took their appointments from their suffrage. It is equally presumable that the Senate would harmonize in such a policy, and be glad both from personal and public considerations to be freed from the embarrassment that would attend frequent meetings of the whole people, and the control by them in General Assembly of all the measures of the state. To avoid such embarrassment it would be natural in the transaction of the business that an understanding should be formed among the members, even before the discussion of any proposition, what the sentiment of the majority respecting it would be; and that the minority would accommodate with it. It does not appear that regular meetings on fixed days in each month were provided for, and special duties assigned to each, as was done by the constitution of Athens, and would be necessary if the government was to be managed by the people, or depended uniformly on their sanction. The appeal to them being contingent, even in the most important cases, makes this view the more presumable.

What then sustained the government for such a length of time, and with such tranquility and contentment among the people? What produced a like effect with the government and people of Lacedemon when the Senate consisted comparatively of a few members, and the kings were hereditary? The great causes were essentially the same in each instances. The people were attached to liberty, and being incompetent to its preservation by the discharge of the duties of the government themselves, collectively, and incapable of instituting any other, they acquiesced in the performance of a large portion of those duties by other powers, retaining in their own hands with the sovereignty those only to which they were more competent. The division of land among the citizens with public repasts in Lacedemon, it may be presumed, contributed much to reconcile the people of that state to the commission of the power to so small a Senate, and likewise to the hereditary quality of the kings. How long could such a system be preserved, and what were the causes which would be sure to overthrow it? In tracing these I shall not advert to casual events to which all governments and people are subject, and which produce great changes in the communities in which they occur. While the morals and intelligence of the people remain unchanged, and no pressure is made from abroad which menaces to overwhelm them, their acquiescence with the government in its existing state would probably continue. If the morals of the people should become corrupted they would be incapable of sustaining the station they held in the government, and sink under a tyrant. Or if any cause occured which should induce the people to take a more active part in the administration; to assume powers to which they were incompetent; such as were exercised by the people of Athens, and which produced the overthrow of their government, a like fate would befall the government of Carthage.

This might happen while the morals of the people remain unchanged, and their attachment to liberty equally great. Instances might occur in which those who managed the affairs of the state excite the distrust and even the indignation of the people. Wars, for example, might be undertaken imprudently, which might by ill-success menace their independence. If the people had borne the existing government as the only means of preserving their liberties, the bond between them and those who wielded it, would be slight. It must have been of a nature compulsory rather than confidential. Under such circumstances it would be incumbent on a virtuous people, attached to liberty, to exert all their faculties to preserve it. Convulsions might ensue, which might be productive of the most fatal consequences.

FINIS

INDEX

Index

NOTE ON EDITORS

James P. Lucier is Senior Fellow of the James Monroe Memorial Foundation, and a member of the Board of Regents of the James Monroe Museum and Library in Fredericksburg, Virginia. He is also Chairman of the Advisory Commission of the Thomas Balch Library, an eighty-year-old archival center of local history and genealogy in Leesburg, Virginia, near Monroe's Loudoun County estate of Oak Hill. A staff member of the U.S. Senate for twenty-five years, and a former staff director of the U.S. Senate Committee on Foreign Relations, Lucier acquired a practical knowledge of diplomacy, legislative action, and separation-of-powers doctrine that led him to appreciate Monroe's career as warrior, diplomat, Senator, Secretary of State and President. Lucier is currently Senior Editor of the national newsweekly, *Insight on the News* and holds a Ph.D. from the University of Michigan.

Conservative Leadership Series editor Christopher B. Briggs holds degrees from Bowdoin College and The Catholic University of America. The assistant editor of *Humanitas,* a journal of the humanities published in Washington, D.C., he writes and edits from northern Virginia.